THE CAMBRIDGE HANDBOOK OF
EU SUSTAINABLE FINANCE

This essential reference work explores the role of finance in delivering sustainability within and outside the European Union. With sustainability affecting core elements of company, banking and capital markets law, this handbook investigates the latest regulatory strategies for protecting the environment, delivering a fairer society and improving governance. Each chapter is written by a leading scholar who provides a solid theoretical approach to the topic while focussing on recent developments. Looking beyond the European Union, the book also covers relevant developments in the United States, the United Kingdom and other major jurisdictions. Thorough and comprehensive, this volume is a crucial resource for scholars, policymakers and practitioners who aim for a greener world, a more equitable society and better-managed corporations.

Kern Alexander holds the Professorial Chair in International Financial Law and Corporate Governance at the Faculty of Law, University of Zurich. He is the author of many research articles and books, including *Principles of Banking Regulation* (2019) and *Global Governance of Financial Systems* (2006). His report *Stability and Sustainability in Banking Reform: Are Environmental Risks Missing in Basel III?* (2014) was the first study of the interrelationship between banking regulation, environmental sustainability and climate change.

Matteo Gargantini is Assistant Professor (tenure track) of Business Law at the University of Genoa. Previously, he worked at the University of Utrecht and at the Max Planck Institute Luxembourg for Procedural Law. Before joining academia, Matteo served at CONSOB, the Italian financial markets authority. He is an academic member of the Consultative Working Group for Corporate Finance of the Issuers Standing Committee at the European Securities and Markets Authority (ESMA). He is a regular lecturer at the LLM programme of Luigi Bocconi University and at the Frankfurt School of Finance and Management.

Michele Siri is Professor of Corporate Law and Financial Regulation at the University of Genoa and Director of EUSFIL, the Jean Monnet Centre of Excellence on European Union Sustainable Finance and Law. He has held a Jean Monnet Chair on the EU regulation of financial and insurance markets. Since 2018, he has been a member of the Joint Board of Appeal of the European Supervisory Authorities, which he has been appointed to chair in 2021. He is a regular lecturer at the LLM programme of Luigi Bocconi University and at the Frankfurt School of Finance and Management. He is an academic member of the Advisory Committee of the Italian Financial Markets Authority.

The Cambridge Handbook of
EU Sustainable Finance

REGULATION, SUPERVISION AND GOVERNANCE

Edited by

KERN ALEXANDER

University of Zurich

MATTEO GARGANTINI

University of Genoa

MICHELE SIRI

University of Genoa

CAMBRIDGE
UNIVERSITY PRESS

CAMBRIDGE
UNIVERSITY PRESS

Shaftesbury Road, Cambridge CB2 8EA, United Kingdom

One Liberty Plaza, 20th Floor, New York, NY 10006, USA

477 Williamstown Road, Port Melbourne, VIC 3207, Australia

314–321, 3rd Floor, Plot 3, Splendor Forum, Jasola District Centre, New Delhi – 110025, India

103 Penang Road, #05–06/07, Visioncrest Commercial, Singapore 238467

Cambridge University Press is part of Cambridge University Press & Assessment, a department of the University of Cambridge.

We share the University's mission to contribute to society through the pursuit of education, learning and research at the highest international levels of excellence.

www.cambridge.org
Information on this title: www.cambridge.org/9781009483940

DOI: 10.1017/9781009483971

First published 2025

A catalogue record for this publication is available from the British Library

Library of Congress Cataloging-in-Publication Data
NAMES: Alexander, Kern, 1968– editor. | Gargantini, Matteo, 1978– editor. | Siri, Michele, editor.
TITLE: The Cambridge handbook of EU sustainable finance : regulation, supervision, and governance / edited by Kern Alexander, University of Zurich; Matteo Gargantini, University of Genoa; Michele Siri, University of Genoa.
OTHER TITLES: Cambridge handbook of European Union sustainable finance
DESCRIPTION: Cambridge, United Kingdom ; New York, NY : Cambridge University Press, 2025. | Series: Cambridge law handbooks | Includes bibliographical references and index.
IDENTIFIERS: LCCN 2023052968 (print) | LCCN 2023052969 (ebook) | ISBN 9781009483940 (hardback) | ISBN 9781009483971 (ebook)
SUBJECTS: LCSH: Finance – Law and legislation – European Union countries. | Financial services industry – Law and legislation – European Union countries. | Financial institutions – Law and legislation – European Union countries. | Sustainable development – Law and legislation – European Union countries. | Finance – Government policy – European Union countries. | Finance – Law and legislation.
CLASSIFICATION: LCC KJE2188 .C35 2025 (print) | LCC KJE2188 (ebook) | DDC 364.24/082–dc23/eng/20231120
LC record available at https://lccn.loc.gov/2023052968
LC ebook record available at https://lccn.loc.gov/2023052969

ISBN 978-1-009-48394-0 Hardback

Contents

Figures

Tables

Contributors

Kern Alexander University of Zurich

Filippo Annunziata Bocconi University

Katrien Antonio KU Leuven

Gaia Balp Bocconi University

Roberto Barontini Sant'Anna School of Advanced Studies, Pisa

Jens-Hinrich Binder Universität Tübingen

Tomasz Braun Łazarski University

Iris Chiu University College London

Veerle Colaert KU Leuven

Simona Cosma University of Bologna

Aline Darbellay University of Geneva

Nathan de Arriba-Sellier Erasmus University Rotterdam

Jan De Spiegeleer KU Leuven

Guido Ferrarini University of Genoa

Claudio Frigeni Catholic University of Milan

Matteo Gargantini University of Genoa

Christos V. Gortsos National and Kapodistrian University of Athens

Seraina Grünewald University of Nijmegen

Geneviève Helleringer University of Oxford

Jennifer Hill Monash University

Iwa Kuchciak University of Lodz

Eugenia Macchiavello University of Genoa

Monika Marcinkowska University of Lodz

Sebastian Mock Vienna University of Economics and Business

Lorenzo Nobile University of Salento

Marleen Och KU Leuven

Iris Palm-Steyerberg University of Nijmegen

Christina Parajon Skinner The Wharton School of the University of Pennsylvania

David Ramos Muñoz Universidad Carlos III de Madrid

Paolo Saguato George Mason University

Pierre Schammo University of Durham

Giulia Schneider Catholic University of Milan

Wim Schoutens KU Leuven

Paola Schwizer University of Parma

Antonella Sciarrone Alibrandi Catholic University of Milan

Michele Siri University of Genoa

Beate Sjåfjell University of Oslo

Giovanni Strampelli Bocconi University

Arnaud Van Caenegem KU Leuven

Arthur van den Hurk University of Nijmegen

Eva Verschueren KU Leuven

Preface

Sustainability, and sustainable finance with it, have been one of the most debated matters among the public and the academic community in recent years. A growing set of laws and supervisory policies are being adopted and implemented to drive private finance towards objectives that support environmental, social and governance (ESG) purposes. Market participants have increasingly invested in ESG-compliant assets and sold their clients sustainable products, although the actual ability of such products to foster better climate or societal conditions is sometimes difficult to ascertain. Scientific research, including in the areas of law and finance, has followed suit with an impressive body of outputs. This book is an attempt to shed light on the complex system of sustainable finance that has resulted from years of legislative frenzy, changing market practices and academic efforts.

As readers will easily realise by browsing its chapters, this book is neither an enthusiastic supporter nor a sceptical challenger of the virtues of leveraging sustainable financial products, prudential regulation or corporate purpose to promote ESG targets. Rather, the book aims to provide different perspectives in understanding the intricacies of the law and regulation of sustainable finance. We hope that readers will be able to reach their own views on the merits of the specialised topics covered in the book, ranging from financial regulation and corporate governance to capital markets law and financial technology (Fintech).

While the authors have expressed their own views on specific aspects of sustainable finance, the book, as a whole, provides an image of sustainable finance that highlights its opportunities but, at the same time, does not overlook its risks – mindful that the road to hell is paved with good intentions. As Tariq Fancy highlighted, 'sustainable finance is a confusing area of finance that often means different things to different people', and it is therefore important to dispel misunderstandings because 'we're running out of time: we can no longer afford to answer inconvenient truths with convenient fantasies'.

This book is largely centred on the legal framework of the European Union. The reason is straightforward. The bulk of the most recent legal and regulatory developments concerning sustainable finance has occurred in the EU, partially as the result of the Union's attempt to become a 'regulatory superpower' that paves the way to imitations by policymakers elsewhere and leverages the size of its financial sector to force compliance by firms wishing to sell services or securities in its jurisdiction. The United States has been less eager to foster sustainable finance through the law, and the United Kingdom is designing its own way for how to regulate and supervise green finance. However, this lower dynamism has not prevented sustainable finance from growing significantly, and many analysts expect the market will further expand in the near future. Whether the sleeping beauty will awaken or not, the role of the United States as a leading international financial market – and of the United Kingdom with it – obviously remains crucial in sustainable finance, and the book duly accounts for it in many chapters.

The fast-developing landscape in the European Union is grounded on the understanding that public budgets and other regulatory strategies will not suffice to preserve the planet and humankind from major adverse climate events and social disruption. Of course, the opposite is also true. While sustainable finance and its regulatory framework can help support ESG purposes, one cannot rely on responsible investing and investor preferences alone to reduce the negative externalities of economic activities. Therefore, those with a true interest in sustainable economic growth should consider sustainable finance; and the lessons this book can hopefully give, as part of a much broader picture, should involve external constraints such as properly designed carbon taxes and other regulatory mechanisms. Hence, this book depicts a part of a larger picture but nonetheless a crucial part.

The volume and its chapters greatly benefitted from two workshops where the authors presented and discussed their drafts, one in September 2021 and the other in September 2022. We thank the Genoa Centre for Law and Finance at the University of Genoa, the Research Network for Sustainable Finance at the University of Zurich and the Utrecht Centre for Regulation and Enforcement in Europe (RENFORCE) for their organisational support.

No endeavour of any book can be completed without the precious support of colleagues and friends. Our first acknowledgement goes to the book's authors, whose commitment and enthusiasm motivated us to persist in the project. Our special gratitude goes to Guido Ferrarini, who is among the pioneers of sustainable company law and provided the initial inspiration for this book. We are also grateful to Matt Gallaway, Rebecca Jackaman, Jadyn Fauconier-Herry, Richard Walshe, Sunantha Ramamoorthy, Balaji Devadoss and all the editorial team at Cambridge University Press for their invaluable help. We also thank Sara Addamo and Martina Mantovani for their editorial support.

The book was prepared as a research project of the Jean Monnet Centre of Excellence on European Union Sustainable Finance and Law (EUSFiL) at the University of Genoa. The EUSFiL Centre has been funded with support from the European Commission (ref. Project: 620519-EPP-1-2020-1-IT-EPPJMO-CoE). This publication reflects the views of the authors alone, and the Commission cannot be held responsible for any use which may be made of the information contained therein.

The book is up to date as of 30 April 2023. Developments that occurred after that date may be taken into account occasionally.

Acknowledgements

Ref. Project: 620519-EPP-1-2020-1-IT-EPPJMO-CoE – This project has been funded with support from the European Commission. This book reflects the views only of the authors, and the Commission cannot be held responsible for any use which may be made of the information contained therein.

EUSFiL

Co-funded by the
Erasmus+ Programme
of the European Union

PART I

Introduction

The Research Handbook on EU Sustainable Finance

Regulation, Supervision and Governance

Kern Alexander, Matteo Gargantini and Michele Siri

1.1 INTRODUCTION

Sustainable finance began to occupy a prominent place in the European Union's policy agenda following the signing of the Paris Treaty on climate change in 2016 and the adoption of the United Nation's Sustainable Development Goals (SDGs).[1] The EU policy agenda was given significant support by the creation of the High-Level Task Force on Sustainable Finance in 2016, the EU Action Plan on Sustainable Finance and the Technical Expert Group on Sustainable Finance in 2018. The European Commission followed these initiatives by adopting the EU Green Deal in 2019 consisting of an ambitious package of legislative measures to assist EU citizens and businesses in benefitting from the transition to a sustainable green economy with particular focus on companies and the financial sector. The recognition of the urgency of financing the transition to a low-carbon economy and the need for mitigation of and adaptation to environmental sustainability risks are at the heart of the EU's sustainable finance strategy, which aims to mobilise and channel capital towards green and sustainable activities, products and projects.

Likewise, the EU's policy agenda and regulatory framework reflect the need to finance the green transition and limit the potential for risks and threats that could undermine economic and financial stability through a prudential approach to climate and environmental risk management, where financial institutions are expected to commit to building a resilient and sustainable financial system.

The COVID-19 pandemic also contributed to a major push for the EU's sustainable finance agenda, as it fostered the EU's green financial capacities through the NextGeneration EU (NGEU) instrument, where around 30% of the NGEU's Recovery and Resilience Fund (RRF) will be financed through green bonds.[2] The

---

[1] See THE 17 GOALS | Sustainable Development (https://sdgs.un.org/goals). In January 2015, the UN General Assembly began the negotiations on the post-2015 development agenda that culminated in the subsequent adoption of the 2030 Agenda for Sustainable Development, which included the 17 Sustainable Development Goals, at the UN Sustainable Development Summit in September 2015.

[2] European Commission, 'NextGenerationEU Green Bonds', available at: https://bit.ly/3V6APxo.

EU has also recognised the urgency for financial institutions to integrate ESG factors into their business models and risk management strategies, with the aim of ensuring that the entire financial sector plays a key role in driving the transition to a sustainable economy, and also intends to continue exploring new ways to increase the mobilisation of private capital towards sustainable investments.[3] On the latter, a number of important new policy initiatives have been emerging, but much remains to be done to address ESG-related challenges.

As policy developments are moving quickly, they represent a major challenge for financial institutions and their regulators and supervisors to adapt to these policy changes while at the same time striving to contribute to a resilient and sustainable economy and financial system. Recent EU legislation to address climate change and broader ESG challenges have precipitated a major debate across the Atlantic and globally regarding whether financial regulation and corporate governance should integrate climate and ESG concerns into day-to-day risk management and business practices. EU legislation, such as the Taxonomy Regulation, the EU Green Bond Standard, the Sustainable Finance Disclosure Regulation (SFDR), the Corporate Sustainability Reporting Directive (CSRD), the amendments to the Benchmark Regulation (extending its application to Climate Benchmarks) and the recently approved Regulation on ESG Rating Providers are influencing legislative and regulatory developments in many countries outside the EU. Not only can this legislation serve as a model for future reforms worldwide, but the EU regimes for the recognition of equivalence (or, in some cases, for the endorsement) of activities based outside the Union will inevitably have an impact on third-country service providers wishing to enter EU financial markets.

Moreover, the multiple manifestations of the environmental and climate crisis have brought a previously unknown spectrum of financial risks to the fore. Weather events and chronic shifts in temperature, as well as changes in policies and consumer preferences brought about by the transition to a low-carbon economy, are only a few examples of potential drivers of financial risks that can spill over into the banking and financial sector and the broader economy. Indeed, financially material environmental sustainability risks are posing major challenges for financial regulatory authorities.

As market actors have increasingly acknowledged the relevance of these risks, financial regulators and supervisors in countries outside of Europe have also started to take action to address them in their daily operations and supervisory activities. Transnational *fora* like the Network for Greening the Financial System (NGFS) have played a pivotal role in facilitating the exchange of best practices among central banks and other bank regulators in the design of crucial tools for the management and supervision of financially material physical and transition risks, such as the design of climate stress tests and scenario analysis. The Climate Financial Disclosure

---

[3] For this task, the EU Commission has launched the International Platform on Sustainable Finance.

Standards (TCFD) led by the Financial Stability Board have provided a benchmark for disclosure approaches that some major corporates have taken up on a voluntary basis, while the International Organisation of Securities Commissions (IOSCO) has made progress in further developing disclosure standards for listed companies that are more standardised and comparable. And the International Sustainability Standards Board (ISSB) has begun work on how to incorporate sustainability risks into accounting valuation methodologies. The G20/OECD Principles of Corporate Governance, in their 2023 edition, address companies' sustainability and long-term resilience by focusing on environmental and social risk management.

It is of utmost importance therefore for regulators and supervisory authorities to understand as well as to engage in a constructive dialogue on environmental and social-related financial risks with corporate boards and senior management. Sharing and learning from best practices are essential steps which could contribute to the global sustainable finance agenda. Against this backdrop, ESG challenges, including climate-related financial risks, have profoundly transformed, and may transform in the not-so-distant future, business strategies, governance practices and risk management.

In light of these developments, this book was undertaken as part of the research project supported by the Jean Monnet Centre on European Union Sustainable Finance and Law (EUSFiL) at the University Genoa and the Research Network for Sustainable Finance. The EUSFiL Jean Monnet Centre and the Research Network assembled a group of academics and practitioners whose research focusses on the legal implications of the integration of sustainability in the corporate and financial sector. The group of contributors to this volume comes from across disciplines, including law, economics and finance, management and accounting. They have approached their topics from the perspective of how ESG challenges are transforming how we understand the law and regulation of corporate governance and banking and financial market activities. Indeed, the work of the authors contributes to the book's overall theme of developing a better understanding of how ESG challenges are transforming financial regulation and supervision and the governance of institutions and firms from a European and comparative perspective.

Although the main focus is on developments in the European Union, the book also provides a comparative analysis between the EU and other countries outside Europe, such as the United States. The chapters aim to provide the reader with relevant knowledge and analytical tools to better understand and critically reflect on the potential opportunities and challenges posed by the new legislative and regulatory developments in the area of ESG and sustainable finance. The book's content and analytical focus is relevant for academics, policymakers, financial regulators and supervisors, and private finance and corporate governance practitioners.

The book is divided into 5 parts and 29 chapters. Part I consists of the chapter entitled 'Taking Financing Seriously: Understanding the Financial Risks of Unsustainability', which addresses various areas of corporate law and governance in the context of ESG management and stakeholder theory. In this chapter, Beate Sjåfjell investigates the relationship between finance and sustainability through a broad analysis of the risks of unsustainability beyond the established scope of financial risks related to climate change. She analyses the problems of the mainstream approach to finance, sustainability and risks, and reviews the ongoing development of a framework to manage the financial risks of biodiversity loss. She discusses the research-based concept of sustainability and how the concept of planetary boundaries has significance in finance on three interconnected levels: first, it reminds us of the ecological limits; second, it highlights the complex interaction between planet-level environmental processes and that climate change is only one aspect of the convergence of crises; third, it emphasises the importance of using the state-of-the-art natural science in making decisions on a work-in-progress basis. She also explores a systemic approach to Anthropocene risks and analyses the financial risks of unsustainability in the categories of transition, physical and societal risks. She concludes with brief reflections on the necessity of implementing a research-based approach to risks of unsustainability in law, policy reforms and practice as well as the legal basis in the European Union for achieving these tasks.

Part II, entitled 'Ethics and Sustainability in Corporate Law, Corporate Governance and Conduct', consists of seven chapters, which examine how the new concerns on sustainability and business ethics meet traditional theories on corporate governance and corporate conduct. In Chapter 3, 'Firm Value versus Social Value: Dealing with the Trade-Offs', Guido Ferrarini examines the main trade-offs between the economic value and social value of the firm and discusses how they are solved through corporate governance mechanisms under ethical and regulatory constraints. In doing so, he analyses how enlightened shareholder value (ESV) under the influence of stakeholder theory involves trade-offs between firm value and social value. He argues that the purpose of the corporation should be redefined in terms of shared value, not just in terms of shareholder profit maximisation. He then discusses the recent criticism of ESV from the perspectives of radical shareholder value and social value primacy. He suggests that ESV is conveniently complemented by business ethics, soft law and regulation. He further explores recent scholarship on corporate governance and organisational theory and analyses the theory of corporate purpose and the organisational perspective on corporate purpose in connection with sustainability. He further develops his argument to show how business ethics, soft law and regulation constrain the maximisation of firm value by forcing enterprises to internalise some of the externalities produced in their activities. Finally, he concludes that enlightened shareholder value explains how the pursuit of stakeholder value contributes to firm value maximisation and the creation of social value. The board of directors should identify the ethical and cultural values of the firm and monitor their application at all levels. In this regard, organisational purpose should play a fundamental role in the intrinsic motivation of people in corporations.

In Chapter 4, 'The Hardening of Corporate ESG', Genevieve Helleringer and Christina Parajon Skinner discuss how major businesses worldwide have declared their commitment to the stakeholder model, and how a growing number of firms have carried their stakeholder commitments forward in the form of environmental, social and governance (ESG) initiatives. This chapter questions whether the current trend of ESG that stakeholderism is a sustainable business practice over a longer time horizon and discusses how voluntary corporate ESG commitments have hardened into more formal sources of law and regulation in the US, EU and the UK. It first explores the domestic legislative initiatives in France and Germany and their potential to inspire EU ambitions before exploring the legislative initiatives in the EU and the UK, respectively. It then explores the legislative and regulatory changes in the USA at the federal and state level and how court rulings have recognised ESG norms as instruments of transforming soft ESG commitments into hard common law precedents. Finally, it argues that the hardening of the ESG commitments into formal law may risk fossilising unworkable standards for firms and forcing misallocations of capital over time as the new ESG-related rules and regulations are bound to bump up against the existing fiduciary duties of firm managers and board directors. Moreover, the EU rules on the value chain will become binding rules extraterritorially as the European value chain requirements may leave little margin of negotiation for US suppliers.

Monika Marcinkowska addresses stakeholder engagement in Chapter 5, 'Stakeholder Engagement'. She contends that stakeholder engagement is a cornerstone for the implementation of the Sustainable Development Goals (SDGs). The SDGs framework can be defined as a pragmatic stakeholder engagement model and financial institutions play a key role in achieving the SDGs through their indirect influence on a wide range of stakeholders, including customers and partners. Stakeholder engagement is essential in the implementation of a sustainable financial strategy and the management of stakeholder engagement is crucial in terms of assessing the sustainability of the financial institution. With this backdrop, she reviews stakeholder theory by analysing the concepts of stakeholders in the context of contract theory and corporate social responsibility, and of financial firms' responsibility in the four categories of economic, legal, ethical and discretionary responsibility. Finally, she reviews the concept of relational capital, which represents the totality of the firm's relationships and links with its stakeholders based on mutual trust. She then discusses the four stages of stakeholder engagement management, including the identification of stakeholders, stakeholder analysis, stakeholder prioritisation and selection of engagement strategies, and monitoring and evaluation of stakeholder relations. She concludes that creating value for shareholders requires meeting the specific expectations of different stakeholder groups and that conscious stakeholder relationship management is required to effectively create this value. Fundamentally, stakeholder relationship management is an ongoing process and successive iterations should be carried out periodically. A company's stakeholder engagement strategies may need to be adapted as the company's environment and stakeholder expectations evolve over time.

In Chapter 6, 'Bank Governance and Sustainability', Kern Alexander discusses the importance of decision-making and agency problems in bank governance with particular focus on the role of the board of directors in addressing sustainability risks that are increasingly affecting the banking business. He discusses the centrality of the banking business and the role it can play in leading the economy in the transition to net-zero carbon emissions and other sustainability objectives. The chapter then considers traditional agency theories that underpin corporate governance and suggests that they do not offer a full explanation of the 'collective' agency problems that exist in large, complex organisations, such as banks and other financial institutions. Human agency theory offers an alternative theory that emphasises the importance of organisational culture in determining standards, norms and values that influence agent behaviour. The importance of the board is considered in ensuring an adequate risk culture to address organisational failings and in confronting new business challenges, such as climate financial risks. Although the role of bank boards and senior management is primary, regulatory intervention may be necessary to ensure that organisational practices are adequately managing agency problems regarding sustainability concerns. The UK Senior Manager's Regime is considered an intrusive approach involving regulators holding bank boards and senior management personally accountable for regulatory failings as well as designing and complying with the organisation's sustainability strategy. The chapter concludes with some recommendations for how bank governance and business practices could be improved to support society's sustainability objectives.

In Chapter 7, titled 'Risk Culture and Sustainability', Paola Schwizer, Simona Cosma and Lorenzo Nobile address the challenge of regulating risk culture in companies in order to achieve sustainability outcomes. The authors note that a risk-based cultural approach that embeds sustainability values could support the adoption of pro-environmental strategies (PES) by corporations. The chapter investigates the relationship between risk culture and drivers of environmentally sustainable behaviours that could encourage the adoption of PES by board members. It analyses a survey of 120 Italian board members to test the relationship between individual risk culture and beliefs, attitudes and norms. The authors then explore the literature on corporate culture, sustainability culture and risk culture. Corporate culture is a driving factor of sustainability performance, and the failure in cultural change can be an obstacle to sustainable development. Sustainability culture implies the importance of environmental and social objectives in addition to financial performance and has qualifying characteristics such as long-term orientation and the maximisation of stakeholder value. Risk culture refers to the corporate culture that focusses on risk-taking and risk-control activities. The goal of risk management is not only the elimination of risk but also the search for an optimal balance between risk assumption and risk prevention and mitigation. The chapter then analyses the governance of emerging risks as a key driver for sustainability using Ajzen's theory of planned behaviour (ATPB). It tries to establish whether a stronger risk culture is positively related to more favourable assumptions and implicit values, which refer to beliefs about the types of goals firm members should pursue as well as ideas regarding standards of behaviour. The authors conclude that a positive relationship between directors' level of risk culture and behavioural, normative and control beliefs exists. Thus risk culture must be shaped to incorporate sustainability-related values throughout the organisation and the management style must be adapted to the risk culture to enhance the ability to explore new market opportunities.

In Chapter 8, 'Conduct Risk as a Possible Approach for Enhancing Awareness and Management of ESG-related Risks', Antonella Sciarrone Alibrandi, Claudio Frigeni and Giulia Schneider address how severe misconduct patterns in financial firms impact market integrity and financial stability. To this end, the chapter explores the sources and features of conduct risk, which they consider a direct result of poor firm culture and the outcome of short term–oriented business models. The misconduct problems in financial firms are related to both retail conduct risk and wholesale conduct risk, and European supervisory authorities have made policy statements and guidelines on managing conduct risk. However, uncertainties persist regarding what conduct risk exactly is, and what types of risk it encompasses. In this regard, the chapter highlights that conduct risk is sometimes understood in a flexible manner, encompassing all the sources of misconduct that can lead to poor outcomes for the customers, particularly in conjunction with the violation of extra-legal parameters. In other contexts, instead, conduct risk is meant to be a subset of operational risk. Against this backdrop, this chapter discusses the role of conduct risk in the evolving ESG-related regulation initiatives and argues that the flexible and cultural-sensitive nature of conduct risk makes it an effective tool for the forecast, correction and prevention of potentially harmful misconduct directly stemming from the missed or wrongful enactment of ESG policies. Therefore, while conduct risk does not coincide with ESG risk, it may be a tool to reconsider internal risk management systems with a view to reduce the risk of inappropriate behaviour that may lead to unsustainability, thus also strengthening bank stability in a prudential perspective.

In Chapter 9, entitled 'Sustainability and Executive Compensation', Roberto Barontini and Jennifer Hill observe that executive pay has undergone several major interpretations in recent decades, while a more complex picture of the corporation has emerged as the source of negative externalities from misconduct, corporate scandals and financial crises. The chapter provides an overview of developments relating to the design and regulation of executive pay over the last few decades, including the rise of integration of sustainability and ESG targets into executive compensation packages. It also examines the reasons for this development through empirical analyses focussing on the prevalence of this trend in publicly listed companies. This involves a short history of executive compensation in three aspects: a corporate theory of executive compensation design, post-scandal regulatory responses to executive compensation from Enron to the Global Financial Crisis, and executive compensation in the ESG era. The authors then provide an empirical analysis of the prevalence of 'pay for sustainable performance' in contemporary executive compensation contracts. In doing so, the chapter examines the macro-determinants of ESG compensation and the financial and corporate governance variables that influence the ESG performance and communication of the firm. The authors conclude that the increasing integration of ESG targets in executive compensation as a result of pressure from both regulators and institutional investors could be ineffective, given the risk of agency problems and greenwashing. Therefore, it is unclear whether the trend of integrating ESG into executive compensation will continue and whether it will translate into more sustainable corporate practices in the future.

Part III, entitled 'Integrating Sustainability in Financial Markets Regulation', consists of eight chapters addressing the evolving relationship between capital markets and their traditional institutions on the one hand, and the new trends in sustainability and ESG-related preferences on the other. In Chapter 10, 'Sustainability-related Materiality in the SFDR', Nathan de Arriba-Sellier and Arnaud Van Caenegem analyse the EU Sustainable Finance Disclosure Regulation (SFDR) by proposing that we should think about the SFDR as a layered system of sustainability-related disclosures, which combine the concepts of 'single materiality' and 'double materiality'. The authors offer a new perspective on popular proposals to turn the SFDR into a labelling scheme but argue that supervisors should avoid such avenues. The chapter explains the difficulties that arise from the vaguely defined principle of 'sustainable investment' under the SFDR. The SFDR provides a framework within which financial market participants can define their own objectives and contributions. Therefore, the chapter emphasises that it is not the definition of 'sustainable investment' which is relevant, but the additional disclosure requirements that apply as soon as a financial market participant deems its financial product to be in line with the definition. The SFDR encourages robust internal assessments over blind reliance on opaque ESG rating agencies and provides financial market participants with the freedom to justify what a contribution to an environmental or social objective means. This freedom sets it apart from a labelling mechanism with a clearly defined threshold of what a contribution should entail. The chapter also analyses proposed guidelines by ESMA for regulating the names of investment funds that involve sustainable investment, and concludes that those guidelines do not create a clear labelling regime since they primarily focus on disclosure rather than providing a specific framework for classifying financial products.

In Chapter 11, 'Information Intermediaries and Sustainability: The Case of ESG Ratings and Benchmarks', Matteo Gargantini and Michele Siri analyse the important role of information intermediaries, such as ESG ratings agencies and administrators of sustainability benchmarks. The chapter compares the rationale for regulating traditional providers of ratings and benchmarks with the market failures characterising those services when they focus on sustainability. The results of the comparison vary, in part, depending on the role ESG factors play. For instance, while credit ratings often include ESG factors in their assessment with a view to determining reputational and other risks (outside-in perspective), sustainability ratings that focus on impact alone (inside-out perspective) may have a different nature. In a double materiality perspective, issues of asymmetric information and agency problems may therefore be more pervasive for sustainable ratings and benchmarks compared to their traditional peers. However, those services may also be more prone to regulatory failures, if only because knowledge problems seem to affect regulators and supervisors just like investors and other users of ratings and benchmarks. In the authors' view, the EU Regulation on Benchmarks, which already provides a general framework and specific rules for sustainability benchmarks, strikes a good balance in that it addresses the most critical features of indices while calibrating its provisions in light of the benchmark's features. On the contrary, the current lack of rules concerning ESG ratings warrants adequate policy measures. While this gap will soon be filled by an EU Regulation, the authors express some doubts on the regulatory strategy behind it.

Veerle Colaert assesses in Chapter 12, 'On the Sustainability of the MiFID II and IDD Investor Protection Frameworks', the extent of integration of sustainable finance into the market in Financial Instruments Directive II (MiFID II) and the Insurance Distribution Directive (IDD) investor protection frameworks. Sustainable finance has become a new EU priority and a substantial number of measures proposed in the Eighth Climate Action Plan that the European Commission adopted in March 2018 have led to important changes to the MiFID II and IDD investor protection frameworks. As background, she explains why retail investors do not always act upon their investment preferences and the role of the investment product distributor in remedying investors' value-action gap. She discusses the main changes to the MiFID II and IDD investor protection frameworks and the challenges of the revised legal framework by analysing the new sustainability-related definitions, the amended product suitability assessment, the amended product governance process and the amended conflicts of interest procedure. She argues that full cross-sectional consistency will not be achieved in the EU investor protection framework as only the MiFID II and IDD frameworks have been amended while rules covering other product distributors remain the same. She critically evaluates the revised investor protection rules for the suitability test, product governance and conflict of interests. She also addresses the problems of inconsistency caused by sustainable finance amendments to existing legislation. Finally, she discusses the problems of applying the definition of sustainability preferences, which refer to concepts of the Taxonomy Regulation and the Sustainable Finance Disclosure Regulation, and the lack of complete a Taxonomy covering social and governance perspectives in the amended MiFID II and IDD obligations.

In Chapter 13, on 'The EU Taxonomy Regulation and the Prevention of Greenwashing', Marleen Och examines how the EU Taxonomy Regulation provides definitions to determine whether an economic activity is environmentally sustainable and therefore suitable for sustainable investment. While the Taxonomy Regulation is a significant step forward in promoting sustainable finance, she argues that the current framework falls short of reaching the proclaimed investor protection goals due to the complexity and scope of the project as well as its interdependence with the overall sustainable finance framework. She further argues that a sufficient level of investor protection would be reached once the entire portfolio is measured against a more comprehensive Taxonomy Regulation covering all economic activities. She provides an overview of the Taxonomy Regulation by exploring the goals, scope, criteria for environmentally sustainable activities and the types of economic activities that the Taxonomy allows as substantially contributing to environmental objectives. She also discusses the link between the Taxonomy and the overall sustainable finance framework of the EU. In doing so, she analyses the capacity of the Taxonomy Regulation to protect investors, focussing on the prevention of greenwashing. After identifying ambiguities and gaps in the Taxonomy Regulation, she proposes possible solutions. She concludes with an emphasis on the need to extend the Taxonomy Regulation to provide sufficient investor protection against greenwashing by providing more precise definitions and thresholds for social and governance aspects of sustainability in addition to environmental aspects.

Chapter 14, 'Integrating Sustainable Finance into the Prospectus Regulation', Iris Chiu and Pierre Schammo address important questions about how best to regulate the green bond market and ensure that investors are meaningfully protected against greenwashing. The chapter examines whether the EU prospectus framework caters to the needs of such specialist securities (i.e., sustainable securities products) and argues that specific green bond prospectus requirements should be introduced. It discuses the rationale for mandatory prospectus disclosure in general and in relation to sustainable finance more specifically. It emphasises the important role of the European Commission, as set forth in its action plan on sustainable finance, to identify prospectus regulation, particularly for green bonds, as a field where policy action is required. It also examines the market for specialist securities and discusses current market initiatives. The chapter also discusses the attempt to address the regulatory gap in the green bond market through the EU regulation on green bonds (the 'EuGB'). The EuGB is incentive-based, but it is argued that its success will depend on the market response, considering the tendency of all investors to discount long-term social costs such as the consequences of climate change. It further argues in favour of mandatory green bond prospectus requirements as the voluntary approach is unlikely to offer a long-term solution for credible investor protection or the building up of the sustainable finance markets. It concludes that further work needs to be done for EU policymakers to engage in a proper dialogue on prospectus liability in a green bond prospectus framework.

In Chapter 15, 'Disclosure Regulation and Sustainability', Kern Alexander and Aline Darbellay analyse cross-border developments in home and host country regulation of sustainability disclosure. In doing so, they analyse disclosure obligations of environmental and social sustainability risks that apply to companies in light of the growing importance to disclose sustainability risks and the potential cross-border strategies for countries to develop international standards to support global convergence. The chapter considers the international developments justifying the rationale for sustainability-related disclosures along with a discussion of the three models of cross-border disclosure regulation: (1) the home state approach, (2) the host state approach and (3) the equivalence approach. The chapter argues that the 2022 EU Corporate Sustainability Reporting Directive (CSRD) has adopted a mix-and-match model between the host state approach and the equivalence approach. The analysis emphasises the extraterritoriality of EU sustainability disclosure regulation and compares it with the models followed by the United Kingdom, the United States and Switzerland. The different sustainability disclosure requirements between EU countries and non-EU countries suggests, therefore, that cross-border regulatory coordination is important. The chapter recommends a model of ESG disclosure for capital markets that is based on the EU policy of equivalence modified by a recognition of the compliance approaches of certain foreign jurisdictions.

In Chapter 16, 'Institutional Investors as the Primary Users of Sustainability Reporting', Gaia Balp and Giovanni Strampelli analyse one of the main pillars of the European Commission's strategy for financing the transition to a sustainable economy: harmonised sustainability reporting. The chapter argues that sustainability reporting is essential to giving substance to a company's sustainability strategy. Under various EU non-financial reporting initiatives, sustainability reporting has resulted in a shared classification system for sustainable activities, ranging from how to reduce greenwashing to how to assist institutional investors in meeting their disclosure obligations under the Sustainable Finance Disclosure Regulation. Institutional investors remain the primary users of corporate sustainability disclosures, but sustainability reporting facilitates interaction between investors and other stakeholders, such as NGOs, as a lever by which to enhance stakeholders' voice and to overcome the limited ability of broadly diversified institutions, especially passive fund managers, to actively monitor portfolio firms and reduce systematic portfolio risk. The chapter further argues that in order for EU sustainability reporting to deliver on its promises, two factors are crucial: first, the current fragmentation of non-financial reporting standards based on different frameworks and, particularly, on diverging notions of materiality, should be overcome. Second, an adequate balance between the narrative and quantitative dimensions of sustainability reporting should be struck in order not only to make sustainability disclosures meaningful for its users, but also to allow for mutually connecting and achieving coordination between financial and non-financial information.

In Chapter 17, 'The Role of Non-financial Disclosure and Liability in Sustainable Finance', Sebastian Mock assesses the role of non-financial disclosure and liability in sustainable finance. He considers the integration of corporate social responsibility in financial reporting following the enactment of the European Non-financial

Reporting Directive (2014/95/EU) and raises questions about the relationship between financial disclosure and non-financial disclosure and the influence of non-financial disclosure on sustainable finance. In doing so, he explores the history of non-financial disclosure in two parts: the international origin of non-financial disclosure and the European regulation of non-financial disclosure. He then examines whether non-financial disclosure and sustainability have a common core or address the same issues by analysing the following three aspects: the scope of application, the content of reporting and the procedure for examining sustainability information. He discusses the liability for incorrect non-financial/corporate sustainability disclosure and points out the lack of a harmonised legal regime for civil liability for incorrect non-financial and corporate sustainability disclosure in the EU and points out the problem of applying the established civil liability regime for financial disclosure to non-financial disclosure. Finally, he highlights the fundamental difference between financial reporting and non-financial reporting as the former is a number-based information instrument while the latter is a text-based information instrument. Since the existing civil liability regime for financial disclosure cannot be used for incorrect non-financial disclosure cases, it is recommended to develop an independent regime of civil liability for incorrect non-financial disclosure.

Part IV, 'Ensuring Financial Stability and Sustainability', consists of seven chapters. In Chapter 18, 'Macroprudential Policies and Climate Risks', Seraina Grünewald discusses recent efforts by companies to build capacity to manage 'climate-related financial risks' (CRFR) and to identify opportunities from the low-carbon transition. As macroprudential policy has the objective of safeguarding the stability of the financial system by increasing its resilience to shocks and preventing the build-up of vulnerabilities, this chapter discusses the potential role of macroprudential policy in addressing the risks posed by climate change and argues that CRFR falls into the system-wide and preventive approaches. The chapter explores the physical, liability and transition risks that drive the CRFR and analyses climate risks as a macroprudential concern. It highlights the market failures of data gaps and methodological challenges in capturing CRFR and argues that macroprudential policy has a role to play in green finance. It then provides an analysis of the assessment of climate risks and discusses scenario analysis and macro-stress testing as soft macroprudential instruments. It also analyses whether and how the existing macroprudential toolkit is fit to build resilience against CRFR and examines the potential use of hard macroprudential tools against climate-related shocks. It concludes the analysis by arguing that macroprudential policies may play a key role in assessing and managing CRFR and the use of hard macroprudential tools may help foster robustness and resilience of the banking system against climate-induced shocks.

In Chapter 19, 'Integrating Climate Risk in Banking Regulation', David Ramos Muñoz discusses how climate change risks are being integrated into bank regulation. He finds that Pillar 1 of the Basel bank capital framework, which focusses on the calculation of capital requirements, lacks emphasis on climate change risks and broader environmental sustainability. He argues that this gap in regulatory coverage leaves the core of banking regulation maladjusted. He argues instead that bank regulatory disclosure requirements, set forth in Pillar 3 of the Basel Framework, are the most efficient way to assimilate climate risks into banking regulation. However, the path towards more relevant and comprehensive disclosures is complex and consists of various strands. The chapter discusses the three main approaches to disclosure: (1) the Non-financial Reporting Directive (NFRD), (2) the bank-specific Basel Pillar III disclosures and (3) the efforts of authorities like the EBA or the ECB. The chapter argues that while disclosures and market discipline are helpful, bank governance and supervision must be 'acclimatised' to climate change, particularly through the Supervisory Review and Evaluation Process (SREP) found in Pillar 2 of the Basel Framework. The chapter criticises the current state of integrating climate change finance risks into banking regulation as too slow because it follows a path of minimum resistance by emphasising the role of disclosures and exit strategies before seeking a more proactive regulatory stance that emphasises governance and supervision, leaving the use of penalty/coercion-based tools as a last resort. Finally, the chapter discusses the conceptual legal and non-legal challenges faced in addressing climate change in the financial sector and recommends adjustments to risk management methodologies to assess and allocate climate risks more accurately and to fix the flaws in the existing regulatory framework.

In Chapter 20, 'Prudential Requirements Framework and Sustainability', Jens-Hinrich Binder considers the growing attempts to adjust existing micro-prudential regulation arrangements to incorporate sustainability considerations at the international and European levels. The chapter discusses whether the existing framework of prudential requirements and tools can realistically fulfil the new mandate and to what extent the existing mandate could be affected by the introduction of new objectives and technical features. The focus is given to the activation of micro-prudential regulation of banks and other financial intermediaries in the context of a broad sustainability agenda and the regulatory developments within the EU. In doing so, the chapter explores the historical evolution of micro-prudential regulation of financial intermediaries and assesses the capacity of the existing toolbox for the promotion of sustainability objectives. It then examines the relevant policy initiatives at the European level and the current legislative framework as well as the steps towards implementation. The author observes that while there has been considerable progress in developing definitions of relevant ESG risk factors and recommendations relating to methodological matters, progress has been more limited in determining the link of causation between specific ESG risks and an individual firm's profitability. He also provides a critical assessment of different approaches to sustainability regulation in the EU and analyses the different uses of established micro-prudential regulatory tools by comparing a defensive strategy and a supportive strategy. He also argues that the increasing use of stress tests as a means of exploring the resilience of regulated institutions could be helpful if the tests are institutional-ised and carried out regularly. Based on his analysis of the functional capacity of the existing micro-prudential toolbox and the limitations of data to show a link between ESG risks and individual bank performance, he concludes that a more cautious approach should be adopted by regulators in requiring banks to address ESG risks.

In Chapter 21, 'Sustainable Finance under EU Law: The Gradual Shift from Capital Markets to Banking Regulation', Christos Gortsos provides an overview of the so-called EU banking package of legislative proposals that address sustain-able finance issues and discusses the policy rationale for the Capital Requirements Regulation (CRR) and Capital Requirements Directive (CRD) by highlighting the most relevant conclusions in recent European Commission and EBA reports. The chapter shows how the regulatory influence of sustainability is shifting from capi-tal markets alone to banking regulation as well, and recollects the joint role played by the manifold Commission's initiatives on sustainable finance and capital mar-kets integration. These initiatives involve banks in various respects. First, while not directly applicable to them, the most significant legislative tools in capital markets law nonetheless play a role in shaping the regulatory context for credit institutions. Second, the reform packages of the CRD and the CRR, which the chapter describes in detail, are expanding the role of sustainability in the banking sector. The chapter describes how, in the EBA's view, 'ESG factors' and 'ESG risks' should be included in the bank regulatory and supervisory framework, and highlights the effects of the new measures on the treatment of ESG-related risks. All in all, the new framework will deeply influence the way ESG risks affect bank strategies and processes for eval-uating internal capital needs and adequate internal governance.

In Chapter 22, 'Sustainability and Fit and Proper Testing in the Boards of Banks, Insurers and Investment Companies', Iris Palm-Steyerberg discusses the central question of whether and to what extent sustainability can be integrated into fit and proper testing for bank board members and senior management. Fit and proper testing is a supervisory tool in the EU to ensure that members of the manage-ment body possess the necessary knowledge, skills and expertise to perform their function. The chapter first analyses the impact of sustainability on the roles and responsibilities of boards and individual boardroom members in financial institu-tions. Members of the management body have a decisive influence on the course of the institution and are responsible for all major decision-making processes. Therefore, the chapter argues that the management body should also take the lead in ensuring that sustainability risks and the impact of the institution on sustainable factors are adequately managed. Moreover, the chapter examines how sustainabil-ity translates into the five criteria of the fit and proper test, which consist of (1) individual expertise, (2) collective suitability, (3) sufficient time commitment, (4) independence of mind and conflicts of interest and (5) good repute/properness. EU regulators and supervisory authorities have recently included ESG aspects in the fit and proper test, specifically related to the criteria of individual expertise and collective suitability. The chapter explores the relationship between collective and individual suitability. The responsibility for sustainability can be assigned to a dedicated ESG director. However, the author argues that this does not remove the need to integrate sustainability into all relevant parts of the organisation, nor does it relieve the other board members of their responsibilities. The chapter also refers to the supervisory practices of the Dutch Central Bank in assessing individual expertise of members of the management body, which integrates this criterion into fit and proper assessments. The chapter concludes that ESG affects all five elements of the fit and proper test. It suggests that other countries may want to follow the example of the Netherlands, which are the lead supervisors in integrating ESG into fit and proper assessments.

Arthur van den Hurk, in Chapter 23, entitled 'Integration of Sustainability Risks and Sustainability Factors in Insurance Regulation', provides an analysis of how sustainability risks affect the insurance industry and the risk-based measures adopted by EU regulators to affect these risks. The chapter begins with a summary of the European Commission's action plan 'Financing Sustainable Growth', which specifies the integration of sustainability into so-called fiduciary duties in sectoral legislation following the objective of facilitating green investment. With this background, the chapter discusses the integration of sustainability risks and sustainability factors into EU insurance regulation. It defines the meanings of sustainability risks and sustainability factors in the context of insurance undertakings and then describes the quantitative and qualitative requirements of the EU Solvency II framework. In particular, the framework intends to capture all material risks that an insurance undertaking may be exposed to, regardless of the nature of the risk, and points out the importance of having a resilient system of governance. The author then discusses the fiduciary duties described in the Action Plan and points out that fundamental differences between different types of financial undertakings and their relationships with their clients and capital structures should be reflected when sustainability risks and factors are considered. He then analyses the integration of sustainability in the Solvency II framework in three parts: (1) amendments to the Solvency II Delegated Regulation, (2) reflection of sustainability risks in the ORSA and (3) the prudent person principle in Solvency II. Within the prudent person principle, four observations are highlighted: (1) Article 132(1) applies the prudent person principles to all assets of the insurer; (2) Article 132(2) distinguishes between different types of liabilities; (3) Article 132(2) suggests that the prudent person principle applies to the portfolio of assets; and (4) the investment rules apply to all assets regardless of the financial liabilities they intend to cover. Finally, climate change scenarios and climate change transition plans are discussed along with the importance of considering potential amendments of the solvency capital requirements to consider sustainability risks to address the uncertainties as to the extent of sustainability risk for insurers and whether further sustainability considerations should be included in the Solvency II review process.

In Chapter 24, 'Sustainability Enforcement through Multilevel Financial Tools', Tomasz Braun considers the diverse ranges of pro-climate policies and regulatory measures that contribute to the growing universal recognition of the need to take policy and regulatory actions to protect the environment. The chapter analyses pro-climate policies and regulatory trends that support environmental and social sustainability and explores the bottom-up approach to sustainability policy implementation, stressing the need to accept multiple tools to enforce the policies adopted at the supranational level that have a cross-border impact. He discusses the top-down financial instruments that are being used by multi-level regulatory powers such as public debt instruments and green, sustainability and social bonds and their sustainable impact on the economy. He further discusses the need for unifying sustainability enforcement measures at the global level, arguing that properly implemented multi-level enforcement of sustainability programs could promote EU integration and economic development. He then analyses the interrelations among sustainability enforcement tools and corporate practices, suggesting that all stakeholders must counter environmental wrongdoings. By exploring the use of financial instruments as effective enforcement tools in global environmental policy governance, he argues that an effective strategy should involve an informed debate that engages stakeholders to assess the effectiveness of these financial instruments. He further argues that sustainability enforcement requires a corporate ethical integrity, and concludes that the lessons on sustainability policy implementation taken from the financial industry are useful in solving problems in sustainability enforcement.

Part V, entitled 'Financial Innovation and Sustainability', contains five chapters. In Chapter 25, Filippo Annunziata discusses in 'Can Financial Regulation Truly Support the Reduction of CO_2 Emissions? The Complicated Puzzle of EU Emission Allowances' how the European system for trading carbon emissions was first set up in 2003 within the broader framework of the Kyoto Protocol and the international agreements for the reduction of CO_2 emissions. The EU Commission endorsed the position that Emissions Trading Schemes (ETS) would provide a strong contribution to the global reduction of CO_2 emissions, and an EU system for trading carbon in the EU. Allowances (EUAs) were established to implement the ETS system in the European Union, which occurred in four phases. The author discusses the literature focussing on the assumption that emission allowances trading schemes produce positive externalities. He then analyses the emission allowances within the scope of capital markets and financial legislation, particularly under MiFID I, MiFID II, MAR and REMIT. He also explores the utility of exemptions applicable to emission allowances trading in MiFID II and the consequences arising from the MiFID II approach. He then discusses the pros and cons of the inclusion of EUAs into the full scope of MiFID and argues that the structure of MiFID, with its complicated exemptions, and the interplay between MiFID and other legislative measures that affect EUAs, has resulted in a complex regulatory landscape. There is no strong evidence that the inclusion of EUAs in the scope of

MiFID may effectively impact the reduction of emissions. He concludes that the reform of secondary trading in EUAs advanced by MiFID II militates against the economic effectiveness of the EU ETS.

In Chapter 26, entitled 'Climate Risk and Financial Markets: The Case of Green Derivatives', Paolo Saguato provides a US perspective on the potential for regulating green derivatives. The chapter first discusses the increasing need for significant private and public investments to meet the goals set by the EU Green Deal, which has influenced and incentivised the development of green derivatives markets. This chapter analyses the role of derivatives markets that can contribute to the green transition, enable private markets to raise capital towards sustainable goals and help market participants to manage the market and transition risk to a sustainable economy. The author provides a primer on derivatives markets, focussing on their role and functions in the financial system, and explains how derivatives can support sustainability goals by managing physical and transition risk. He then discusses how markets have incorporated ESG considerations into derivative contracts, and provides an overview of current private initiatives in the green derivatives markets. He also examines the current public initiatives in the EU and the US that envision the role of financial markets in the transition to a greener economy. In doing so, he discusses the EU Green New Deal and related EU policy initiatives and the US Commodity Futures Trading Commission's initiatives as well as Financial Stability Oversight Council's Report on Climate-related Financial Risk. He concludes the analysis by suggesting a few critical considerations on the private–public synergies and opportunities that might result from the growth of sustainable derivatives markets. He also highlights possible risks that policymakers should consider in the process of developing green derivatives markets.

Chapter 27, 'The Skin-in-the-game Bond: A Novel Sustainable Capital Instrument', examines the structure of capital instruments in promoting the transition to a sustainable economy. The authors, Katrien Antonio, Jan De Spiegeleer, Wim Schoutens and Eva Verschueren, examine the toolkit of state-of-the-art sustainable investments, such as green, social and sustainability bonds, and how the experience with these financial instruments has raised awareness about key challenges that can undermine their evolution as credible market products. In particular, the lack of punishment if the bond's issuer fails to deliver the promised sustainable results creates moral hazard as the issuer has no (skin-in-the-game) incentive to monitor the use of the proceeds for sustainable purposes. This chapter considers how the concept of a Convertible Capital Instrument (CoCo) can reduce the moral hazard problem by providing the model for a skin-in-the-game bond that is focussed on delivering the environmental, social and governance commitments. The skin-in-the-game bond is built on the principle that both issuer and investor should have skin in the game and incur costs if sustainability promises are not delivered. The chapter explains the design of several skin-in-the-game bonds, with a focus on versions with a continuous or counting benchmark. It then outlines a custom-made valuation model inspired by the credit derivatives model for CoCo bonds, and focusses on the two illustrative examples of the ESG and nuclear skin-in-the-game bonds, respectively. The authors conclude by arguing for the implementation of a sustainable debt instrument with an embedded financial penalty related to Environmental, Social and Governance commitments, and asserts that the skin-in-the-game bond provides clear incentives for the issuer to reduce excessive risk-taking, maintain a favourable benchmark value and enhance transparency for investors.

In Chapter 28, 'Financial Innovation in the Process of Financial Inclusion', Iwa Kuchciak discusses how the rapid adoption of digital technology in finance offers a large potential to increase financial inclusion as banks and non-banks have begun to offer digital financial services for financially excluded and underserved populations. This chapter analyses the challenges, problems and opportunities arising from the processes of digitalisation of financial services from a social and economic point of view. In doing so, it explores the concepts of financial inclusion, exclusion and digital financial inclusion. It discusses the importance of financial inclusion as a potential source of benefits to the economy in two broad ways: first, access to affordable credit reduces the vulnerability of the poor; and second, access to deposit and insurance products facilitates direct funding on the financial markets. The author then discusses the legal and regulatory framework at the international level and examines national financial strategies, including the engagement of the private sector and civil society in the process of developing a national strategy. She then discusses the digitalisation of financial services focussing on the development of mobile financial services, and argues that the improvement of financial inclusion was largely driven by financial technology (Fintech) innovations. She then analyses the impact of the COVID-19 pandemic on accelerating access to digital financial services as well as the importance of financial education in building financial resilience. Finally, she explores the importance of promoting digital and financial literacy.

In Chapter 29, 'Sustainable Finance and Fintech: A Focus on Capital Raising', Eugenia Macchiavello discusses how the EU has shown interest in exploring the synergies between digital finance and sustainable development, recognising the opportunities of using digital finance to promote sustainable development. Before that, international organisations such as the United Nations Environmental Programme had developed programmes to facilitate digital finance in promoting sustainable development and providing more capital to fill the funding gap to achieve the Sustainable Development Goals (SDGs). However, sustainable digital finance also presents several risks from the perspective of financial regulation and sustainability. Thus, this chapter aims to assess the benefits, risks and legal implications of each sustainable digital finance application, focussing on capital raising for small and medium-sized enterprises (SMEs). In doing so, it discusses the opportunities, characteristics and examples of crowdfunding from the perspective of sustainability, and explores the special risks and legal challenges of green crowdfunding by examining the European Crowdfunding Service Providers Regulation. The author then discusses the sustainability of distributed-ledger technology-based (DLT) finance by examining the potential of capital raising from the DLT ecosystem. She provides examples of some of the main applications, and the main risks and regulatory issues. She also analyses the EU responses to DLT-based green financing by reviewing the Regulation on Markets in Crypto-Assets (MiCAR) and other EU legislation. She concludes that opportunities and risks of sustainable digital finance should be taken into account before supporting the widespread adoption of certain instruments in sustainable finance.

2

Taking Finance Seriously

Understanding the Financial Risks of Unsustainability

Beate Sjåfjell*

2.1 INTRODUCING THE TOPIC

Finance that does not take sustainability seriously is finance that does not take finance seriously. The financial risks of the continued lack of sustainability bring sustainability into the heart of any well-founded financial decision, whatever view one might have on the role of finance and business in society.

In Europe and with knock-on effects globally, the EU's sustainable finance initiative seeks to realise the potential of finance to contribute to necessary change in the real economy.[1] In this chapter, I investigate the relationship between finance and sustainability. This entails a broad analysis of the risks of unsustainability, which go beyond the established recognition of the financial risks of climate change. Climate change has been declared code red for humanity, and horrific wildfires, droughts and floods underline that climate change is a serious risk, which is increasingly being realised, with implications for all aspects of our economies and societies. Yet what we face is a convergence of environmental, social and economic crises, calling for a mobilisation of resources to deal with these crises across sectors.

The European Commission refers to *sustainable finance* as 'the process of taking environmental, social and governance (ESG) considerations into account when making investment decisions in the financial sector, leading to more long-term investments in sustainable economic activities and projects'.[2] I position this definition of sustainable finance within a broader research-based concept of sustainability, which forms the framework for my analysis.

Section 2.2 of this chapter gives a brief overview of the problematic aspects of the mainstream conceptualisation of financial risks of climate change, also mentioning briefly the ongoing development of a framework for financial risks of

* This chapter draws on and develops further the collaborative research of the EU-funded project Sustainable Market Actors for Responsible Trade (SMART, 2016–2022), and I am grateful to the whole SMART team and especially, in the context of this publication, Jukka Mähönen, Hanna Ahlström, Tonia Novitz, Clair Gammage and Sarah Cornell.
[1] Alexander, Gargantini and Siri, Chapter 1 in this volume.
[2] European Commission n.d.

biodiversity loss. The legislative and policy initiatives under the EU's sustainable finance initiative responding to the emerging recognition of these risks are dealt with elsewhere in this volume.[3]

Section 2.3 introduces the research-based concept of sustainability that I employ as the framework for the analysis presented later in the chapter. Section 2.4 presents my analysis of financial risks of unsustainability. I outline the physical risks of various environmental issues and the transition risks of both environmental change and social aspects of unsustainability. The transition risks encompass policy risks as well as various legal risks. The technology risk – of competitors adapting to increasing drivers for sustainability – should be completed with the broader risk connected to changing business models as the necessity of shifting from unsustainable linear business models to sustainable circular ones becomes clearer. Ultimately, the risks of unsustainability are existential ones. There are a number of scenarios that can lead to societal collapse, and in none of them are steady returns for investors likely. Section 2.5 concludes with brief reflections on the necessity of and the legal basis for implementing a research-based approach to risks of unsustainability in law and policy reforms and in practice.

2.2 THE MAINSTREAM APPROACH TO FINANCE, SUSTAINABILITY AND RISKS

The 2017 recommendations of the Financial Stability Board's Task Force on Climate-Related Financial Disclosure (TCFD report)[4] highlight the potential financial impacts of climate-related risks and opportunities that they perceive as significant, drawing on 'member expertise, stakeholder engagement, and existing climate-related disclosure regimes'.[5] The TCFD report divides climate-related risks into two major categories: (1) transition risks, that is, risks related to the transition to a lower-carbon economy, and (2) physical risks, that is, related to the physical impacts of climate change. The TCFD's transition risks encompass policy risks, liability risks, reputation risks and technology risks, while their physical risks are divided into acute and chronic risks.[6]

The TCFD report was complemented by the 2017 report from the Cicero Centre for International Climate and Environmental Research in Oslo: *Shades of Climate Risk: Categorizing Climate Risk for Investors*.[7] The increasing recognition of environmental risks, including notably climate change, is also evident from the Global Risk Report 2022.[8]

---

[3] Gargantini and Siri, Chapter 11 in this volume.
[4] TCFD 2017. This is followed up inter alia by the Basel Committee 2020. See further, e.g., Alexander, Chapter 6 in this volume.
[5] TCFD 2017, iii.
[6] Ibid., 5–6.
[7] Clapp et al. 2017.
[8] 'Respondents to the GRPS [Global Risks Perception Survey] rank "climate action failure" as the number one long-term threat to the world and the risk with potentially the most severe impacts over the next decade', World Economic Forum 2022, 8.

Although laudable for contributing to awareness-raising of the significance of climate change for business and finance, the TCFD recommendations and the Cicero report have shortcomings when analysed in the context of a research-based sustainability perspective. Even limiting the scope to climate change, important aspects are excluded in the two reports.

Firstly, although both reports discuss the acute and chronic physical risks of climate change, the financial risks in the form of risk to humans relevant to the business are explored only to a very limited extent. These include the increased risk of spread of disease and of unmanageable heatwaves.[9] The reference to impacts on humans is limited in the Cicero report to the brief mention of risks to 'health and labour productivity' and 'worker unavailability' in its tables, and an even briefer mention is made of negative impacts on the 'workforce' from acute physical risks in the TCFD recommendations.[10]

Secondly, the reports stop short of explaining the potential severity of the financial risks of climate change. The TCFD recommendations mention the danger of 'catastrophic environmental and social consequences' in the introduction,[11] and the Cicero report states that 'the potential for catastrophic change is not well understood'.[12] However, neither of the reports spell out what climate change, insufficiently mitigated, may entail in the form of global catastrophic risks or even existential risks for humanity.[13]

Thirdly, neither of the reports speaks about societal risks, including the risk of societal breakdown.[14] These are all relevant as financial risks, as shown, in particular, in Section 2.4.3.2.

In 2020, an initiative was announced to establish a Task Force for Nature-Related Financial Disclosures, which was formally launched in 2021. The aim of its ongoing work is to develop and deliver 'a risk management and disclosure framework for organisations to report and act on evolving nature-related risks, with the ultimate aim of supporting a shift in global financial flows away from nature-negative outcomes and toward nature-positive outcomes'.[15]

The final recommendations were published in September 2023.[16] It is as a starting point a positive development that biodiversity is also now to have its own

---

[9] Clapp et al. 2017, 11, states that 'We exclude some important social risks such as ecological disruption and disease that are addressed in other research' (without further references), although they do thereafter actually mention the climate change related risk of disease, for example the risk of increased 'increases vulnerability to pests and disease' in Central and South America (38), referring to the risk of disease in the coffee trees.

[10] Clapp et al. 2017, 19, 21 and 23, and TCFD 2017, 10.

[11] TCFD 2017, 1 (Background).

[12] Clapp et al. 2017 under Executive Summary.

[13] See, e.g., Baum and Handoh 2014.

[14] The societal effects of the COVID-19 pandemic are reflected in the World Risks Report's recognition of threats to social cohesion, World Economic Forum 2022, 7.

[15] TNFD, Our Mission, available at: https://tnfd.global/about/#mission.

[16] TNFD 2023.

business-focussed risk recommendations,[17] with an 'integrated approach to climate-and nature-related risks, scaling up finance for nature-based solutions'.[18] However, questions have been raised about corporate capture of the process with the Task Force for Nature-Related Financial Disclosures, highlighting the risk of continued greenwashing.[19] Also, this still leaves other aspects of unsustainability untouched. We do not have time to spend years developing, piece by piece, risk frameworks for each aspect of sustainability. Rather we must deal with these together within the framework of a research-based concept of sustainability.

2.3 A RESEARCH-BASED CONCEPT OF SUSTAINABILITY

Most of us intuitively understand that there are limits to how much we can take out of nature and how much we can dump back into nature, and still expect the planet to function as a relatively safe space for humanity, providing us with air, food, water and resources with which to maintain our societies and our commerce. The recognition of ecological limits is crucial to a research-based understanding of sustainability. The planetary boundaries framework is the result of the work of an international multi-disciplinary group of environmental scientists, who, in 2009, pooled their knowledge of different Earth system processes to inform the world about the space for sustainable action within ecological limits – planetary boundaries.[20] Their work reflects the growing scientific understanding that life and its physical environment co-evolve. This pioneering effort brought together evidence of rising and interconnected global risks in several different contexts where human activities are changing environmental processes. The planetary boundaries framework flags a set of sustainability-critical issues (Figure 2.1). It presents policymakers with a dashboard of issues arising from the collective impacts of humanity, changing the fundamental dynamics of the Earth system upon which humans rely for our lives and livelihoods.[21]

Through the planetary boundaries work it is estimated that human activity in aggregate has transgressed at least six of the currently identified nine planetary boundaries: climate change, biosphere integrity (biodiversity), biogeochemical flows (nitrogen and phosphorus), land-system integrity, novel entities (microplastics, nanomaterials and various forms of chemical pollution) and global freshwater use.[22] The other three boundaries are ocean acidification, atmospheric aerosol loading and stratospheric ozone depletion.[23]

---

[17] PwC and WWF 2020.
[18] TNFD, https://tnfd.global/recommendations-of-the-tnfd/.
[19] Greep 2022.
[20] Rockström et al. 2009; Steffen et al. 2015.
[21] Cornell, S.E. (2016), 'Planetary boundaries and business: Putting the operating into the safe operating space for humanity', draft paper on file with current author, University of Oslo.
[22] Steffen et al. 2015; Persson et al. 2022a, Richardson et al. 2023.
[23] For ocean acidification 'the trend is worsening as anthropogenic CO_2 emission continues to rise', Richardson et al. 2023.

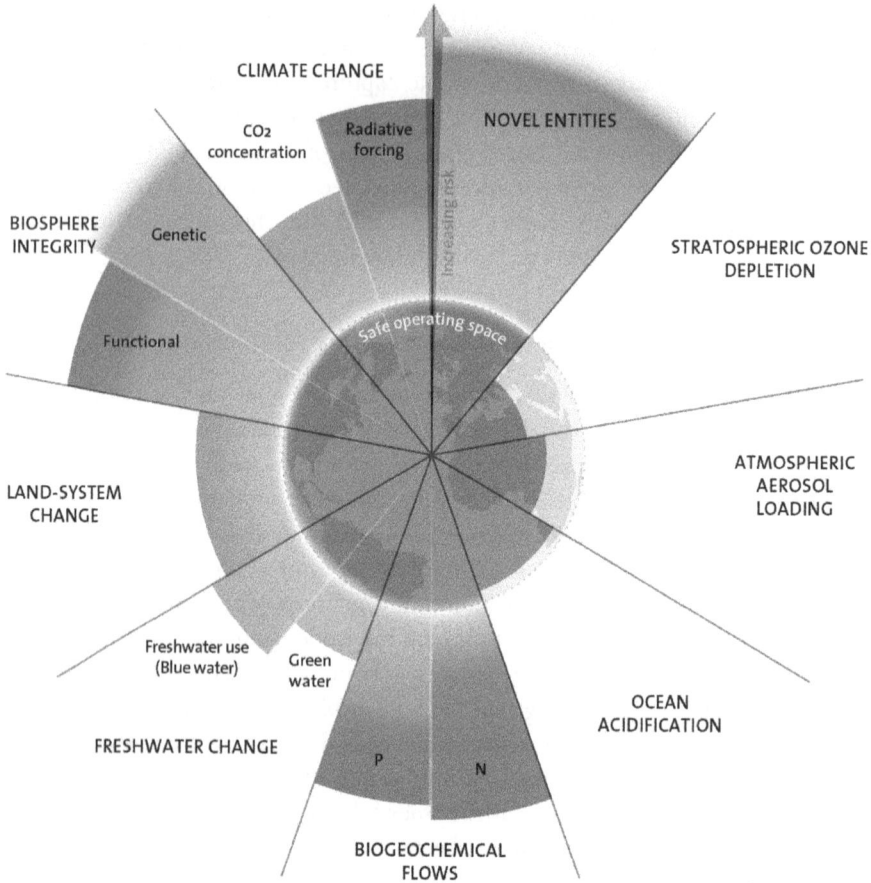

FIGURE 2.1 Planetary boundaries.
Credit: Azote and Stockholm Resilience Centre, based on analysis in Richardson et al., 2023

At least two of the transgressed planetary boundaries, climate change and bio-diversity, are what may be denoted *core boundaries*, where transgression of each of them may in itself be sufficient to bring the Earth system out of the relatively stable state of the past few millennia, which the planetary boundaries framework refers to as a 'safe operating space for humanity'.[24]

These environmental issues pose severe challenges for governance across scales due to their inherent uncertainties and complex multilevel dynamics. Responding to these challenges entails contributing to preserving, protecting and regenerating natural resources and global geophysical processes at global, regional and local levels of society and across public, private and hybrid institutions and organisations.

---

[24] Rockström et al. 2009.

The planetary boundaries framework is potentially significant on three interconnected levels for finance (as well as for business in the real economy). Firstly and
most importantly, it brings to the forefront that there are ecological limits (conversely, that merely being perceived as 'environmentally friendly' is inadequate).
Secondly, it highlights the complex interaction between planet-level environmental
processes and that, for example, climate change, however topical (and difficult to
mitigate), is only one aspect of the convergence of crises we are heading towards.
Thirdly, it continuously reminds us that state-of-the-art natural science must inform
our decisions on a work-in-progress basis, encompassing the uncertainty and complexity of the global challenges.[25]

Employing the planetary boundaries framework does not mean that sustainability
is merely about safeguarding the ecological limits of a *safe* space for humanity. It
is also about a *just* space, encompassing social, economic and governance issues.[26]
Accordingly, I employ the broadly recognised definition of sustainability as securing a safe and just space for humanity, which encompasses securing social foundations for humanity, now and for the future, while mitigating pressures on planetary
boundaries (Figure 2.2).[27]

Securing social foundations for humanity involves 'questions of justice and
inequality relating to global patterns of consumption and production, resource
allocation, benefit distribution, and so on'.[28] While the planetary boundaries
framework is based on natural science, the basis for the concept of social foundations, as launched by Kate Raworth, is the political consensus on which aspects
were important in the adoption of the United Nations Sustainable Development
Goals (SDGs).[29] As Raworth also emphasises, the minimum requirement intrinsic
to securing social foundations for humanity now and in the future is that of ensuring the realisation of basic human rights.[30] Yet the criticism against the human
rights movement may indicate that it has not done enough to mitigate the most
detrimental impacts of global business.[31] Discussing human rights in the context of
sustainability, of securing social foundations for humanity, gives rise to the question of whether protecting human rights – including socio-economic rights – is
sufficient. This further entails a recognition that those most vulnerable, including workers across value chains in slavery-like conditions,[32] and traditional and

---

[25] E.g., Ahlström and Sjåfjell 2022.
[26] Sjåfjell 2020a, which the remainder of this section draws on. See also Sjåfjell and Cornell 2024.
[27] Leach, Raworth and Rockström 2013; Sjåfjell and Cornell 2024. References to the planetary boundaries framework in EU policy documents may be found inter alia in the EU's Environment Action
Programme of 2022 (European Parliament and Council 2022) and its Circular Economy Action Plan
of 2020 (European Commission 2020).
[28] Kotzé and Kim 2019.
[29] United Nations General Assembly 2015; Raworth 2012; Leach, Raworth and Rockström 2013.
[30] Raworth 2012.
[31] E.g., Kotzé 2019, 73–5.
[32] ITUC 2016.

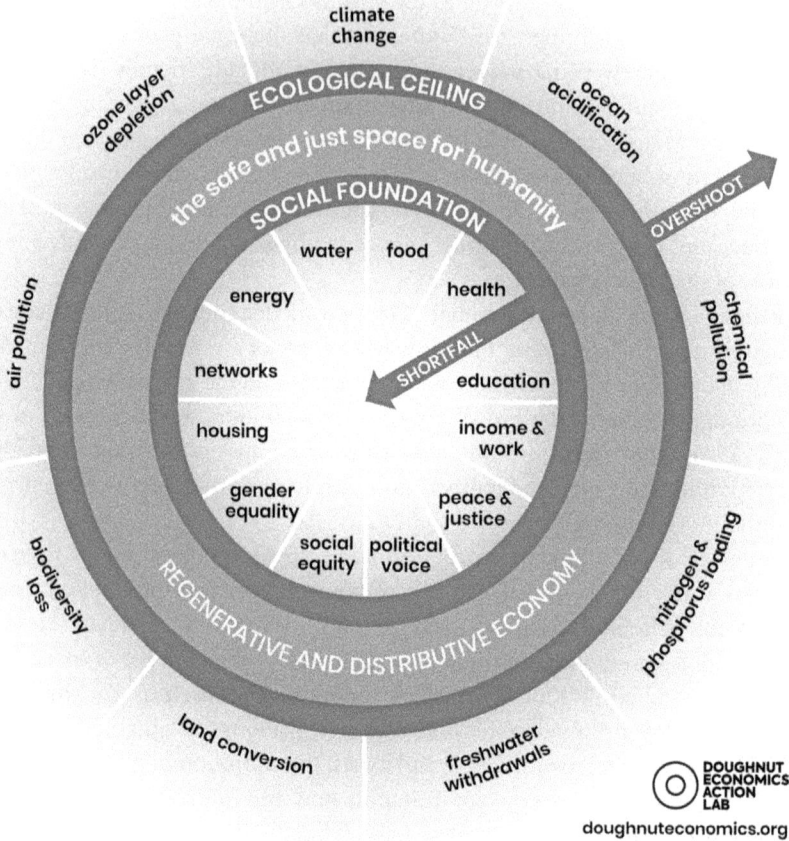

FIGURE 2.2 The safe and just space for humanity.
Source: Raworth 2017.[33]

Indigenous communities whose land and other resources are exploited, are not always encompassed in sustainability initiatives.[34]

In a similar way as the science basis for the concept of planetary boundaries must continuously evolve in light of new understanding of what is 'safe', attempts at defining and pursuing social foundations must be rigorously interrogated in light of what is 'just', which cannot be exhaustively defined by the SDGs or by a minimalistic approach to human rights. We, therefore, must look further than human rights in developing social foundations, as well as to the roots of human rights: to 'human dignity', as intrinsic to a *just* space for humanity. This is itself an area that requires more research. However, based on the work done so far, securing

---

[33] Raworth 2017.
[34] Novitz 2019a; Christensen 2019; Yu 2018.

social foundations for humanity entails attention to a range of interconnected issues. Among the pivotal aims must also be that of 'decent work', advocated in the International Labour Organization (ILO) 2008 Declaration.[35] This is reiterated and expanded on in the Global Commission Report,[36] which resists the 'commodification of labour by seeking to revitalise the voice of everyone, regardless of the types of work they do or how they are hired'.[37] This is as relevant for workers employed by large businesses as it is for small- and medium-sized entrepreneurs across the global value chains.

There are tensions inherent in global society's sustainability goals, including the risk that the most marginalised groups will not be sufficiently included in participatory processes,[38] notably excluding Indigenous Peoples[39] and other vulnerable groups. To mitigate this, it is not sufficient for experts merely to assess what is good for vulnerable people. Instead, there need to be inclusive and participatory processes (as envisaged by SDG 16) that enable vulnerable people to have access to justice and representative participation in the crafting of measures that affect their well-being.[40]

Social inequality within and across countries is a fundamental sustainability challenge.[41] The economic basis of our societies (of our welfare states) is also crucial to securing social foundations, and this pertains to the possibility of ensuring 'distributive sufficiency' as well as to the basis of good lives and to 'distributive equality'.[42] Translated into the governance of business, this encompasses issues such as fair treatment of employees as well as of workers and local communities across global value chains, with respect for international human rights and core ILO conventions as a minimum, ensuring a 'living wage' and safe working conditions. This further entails supporting democratic political processes and, at the very least not undermining these through engaging in corporate capture of regulatory processes. It also

---

[35] See ILO 2008, Articles A(i) and A(ii), and SDG 3 and SDGs targets 8.3, 8.5, 8.6 and 8.8. See further ILO 2019a, Articles II(A)(iii) and III (B), and ILO 2019b. In a Polanyian analysis, the ILO Declarations may be said to reflect 'countermovement to market dominance', that is, as a part of a 'continued attempt to navigate (and reconcile insofar as this is ever possible) conflicting market and social pressures', Novitz 2020a, 10 and 13 with further references; Novitz 2020b.

[36] ILO 2019c, which repeatedly emphasises that labour 'is not a commodity' with reference to the aim of sustainability and advocating 'sustainable work'; Novitz 2020a, 33–5.

[37] Novitz 2020a, 39.

[38] Achieving sustainability 'requires exploration of and debate about which combinations of pathways to pursue at different scales', and this process 'will need to be as open and inclusive as possible, giving voice to the knowledge, values and priorities of women and men who are marginalised, so that they are able to challenge powerful groups and interests'; Leach, Raworth and Rockström 2013, 88.

[39] That the cultural rights of Indigenous Peoples often are ignored is also a long-term criticism against sustainable development. See, e.g., Weissbrodt and Rumsey 2011; Collins 2018, 87–8; Madden and Coleman 2018.

[40] For discussion, see Novitz 2020b.

[41] World Inequality Report 2018.

[42] Moyn 2018, 13–14.

entails contributing to the economic basis of the societies in which the business interacts by not engaging in so-called aggressive tax planning and outright evasion.[43]

All this underlines that a 'safe and just' space for humanity, mitigating pressures on planetary boundaries and securing social foundations, is not something that is present now, which we (merely) need to protect. It is something that we must transition – or rather, transform – towards, with appropriate policy measures informed by a recognition of the interconnected complexities of the social-ecological systems of our Earth.

2.4 AN ANALYSIS OF THE FINANCIAL RISKS OF UNSUSTAINABILITY

2.4.1 *From Climate Risk to a Systemic Approach to Anthropocene Risks*

In sustainability science literature, the terminology 'Anthropocene'[44] is employed to describe risks, referring specifically to risks that 'emerge from human-driven processes; interact with global social–ecological connectivity; and exhibit complex, cross-scale relationships'.[45] The annual Global Risks Report from the World Economic Forum, drawing on surveys of perceptions of global risks among respondents in business, government and civil society, increasingly also takes such a broader approach, emphasising already in the 2017 report that a systemic approach is necessary.[46]

Table 2.1 exemplifies such a broader, systemic approach. It takes the TCFD categorisation as a starting point, with the two main risk categories of *Transition risks* and *Physical risks*. To these, I have added *business model change* to the transition risks and *global catastrophic risk* to the physical risks. I have also added a third main risk category: *societal risks*, including risk of unrest, risk of authoritarianism and societal breakdown risk.

As examples of other environmental *risks of unsustainability*, besides climate change, I include *biodiversity loss* and *novel entities*. Biodiversity is, like climate change, recognised as a core boundary. This means that transgressing this one boundary is regarded as sufficient to bring the Earth system out of the relatively stable state it has been in for the last 12,000 years.[47] Novel entities, including nanomaterials, microplastics and various forms of chemical pollution, are closely connected to climate change and biodiversity loss while presenting specific challenges.[48] Engaging with the 'intractable problem' of quantifying a single-dimensional boundary for

---

[43] Sjåfjell 2020a.
[44] The Anthropocene refers to 'the concept that the Earth has moved into a novel geological epoch characterized by human domination of the planetary system'; see Malhi 2017.
[45] Keys et al. 2019; Crona, Folke and Galaz 2021.
[46] World Economic Forum 2017. See also Whiteman and Williams 2019.
[47] Steffen et al. 2015.
[48] Villarrubia-Gómez, Cornell and Fabres 2018; Persson et al. 2022a.

TABLE 2.1 *Risks of unsustainability*

Risk categories		Categories of unsustainability					
		Planetary boundaries – example categories of unsustainability			Social foundations – example categories of unsustainability		
		Climate change	Biodiversity loss	Novel entities	Human rights violation	Lack of decent work	Tax evasion
Transition risks	Policy risk	●	●	●	●	●	●
	Liability risk	●	●	●	●	●	●
	Reputation risk	●	●	●	●	●	●
	Market risk	●	●	●	●	●	●
	Technology risk	●	●	●	●	●	N/A
	Business model change risk	●	●	●	●	●	●
Physical risks	Acute risks	●	●	●	●	●	○
	Chronic risks	●	●	●	●	●	○
	Global catastrophic risks	●	●	●	N/A	N/A	○
Societal risks	*Risk of unrest*	●	●	●	●	●	○
	Risk of authoritarianism	●	●	●	●	●	○
	Societal breakdown risk	●	●	●	●	●	○

Source: Slightly revised version of the table first presented in Sjåfjell 2020b.
Note: The black circles indicate that environmental degradation or social harm (in the unsustainability categories in vertical columns) entails direct risks within the various risk categories (categories in horizontal rows). The grey circles indicate indirect financial risk, while N/A explains that the category of unsustainability (horizontal columns) is not assumed to involve the specific risk category (vertical rows). Italics indicate new categories, while the ellipses highlight the seven categories from the dominant climate risk approach, introduced in Section 2.2.

the 'multitude and diversity of novel entities', Persson and colleagues characterise novel entities as a 'multidimensional dynamic boundary', evaluating several
control variables that indicate that the planetary boundary has been crossed. They
demonstrate how novel entities have resulted in 'many globally observed biologi-
cal, chemical, and geophysical changes that move the planet away from Holocene
conditions'.[49] The discussion concerning novel entities serves well to illustrate a
larger point with planetary boundaries – they are not intended as firm boundaries
within which governments and businesses can discuss how to budget and divide a
remaining quantity; they are meant to indicate zones of increasing danger with all
the uncertainty that speaking about the complex interactions between Earth system
processes in an unprecedented territory entails. Applying a strong precautionary
principle is therefore crucial.[50]

Further, I include risks of unsustainability concerning the lacking achievement
of *social foundations for humanity*. As examples of the undermining of the social
foundation, I include in Table 2.1 *human rights violations, lack of decent work* and
tax evasion. As illustrated in Table 2.1, all of these bring with them financial risks.
In what follows, I describe these risks and what they entail for finance and business
more broadly, with the explicit caveat that these are examples of the need for a
broader systemic approach.

2.4.2 *Transition Risks*

The category of transition risks refers to financial risks both for financial institutions
and for businesses in the real economy[51] that are not taking part in the transition
to sustainability, which we have begun to see the contours of, or not transitioning
quickly enough. The risks are caused by action or expected action from other actors
or institutions: policymakers, victims of environmental harm or human rights violations, investors or other financiers or competitors.

2.4.2.1 Policy Risks

Policy risks concern the 'risk' of changes in policy, which will impact different sectors and individual corporations to varying degrees. Anticipating and adapting to
changes in the regulatory environment through policymaking is clearly also a part
of the financial risk management of the corporation. Policy risks are a component

---

[49] Persson et al. 2022b.
[50] The conceptual framework for planetary boundaries itself also originally spoke of the need for a
strongly precautionary approach, by 'setting the discrete boundary value at the lower and more con-
servative bound of the uncertainty range'; Rockström et al. 2009.
[51] The TCFD concentrates on financial risks, that is, risks from an investor or financier perspective,
while the risks of unsustainability that we discuss here are equally business risks – risks that affect
the viability of the business itself. Business and financial risks are naturally closely linked, albeit not
always overlapping. I will not go further into this distinction here for reasons of space.

of traditional risk management for EU businesses, within Europe and for global-ised business activities. Typically, traditional policy risks may concern the risk of nationalisation[52] or regulatory change, perceived as market-related risks including contractual risks and enhanced definitions of net loss, business interruption, licence cancellation coverage and contingency risks[53] as well as the political risks of a proj-ect.[54] Political risks are often defined as the possibility of 'government actions which deny or restrict the right of an investor/owner (i) to use or benefit from his/her assets; or (ii) which reduce the value of the firm'.[55]

The context of climate change broadens the perception of policy risks beyond the traditional risks just outlined and opens up the possibility – the risk – of policymak-ers in Europe heavily taxing, limiting or forbidding activities that directly or indi-rectly generate greenhouse gas emissions. Such action is increasingly called for and may be necessary and more likely now than ever before. In our broader context of sustainability, the policy risk also concerns policies with other environmental aims besides climate change mitigation and with social aims. Finally, they include the possibility of European policymakers legislating to internalise the environmental, social and economic costs of globalised business within European business entities with influence over global value chains.[56]

Businesses taking what may be seen as a more cynical approach of betting against relevant policy changes could be making a correct judgement call in that respect, although the increasing societal pressure and other drivers for sustain-ability may be changing this picture. Businesses assuming a low political risk will need to see this in connection with other aspects of the financial risks of unsus-tainability, including other transition risks as well as the physical and societal risks. These risks will tend to increase if policy risks are low, that is, if policymakers do not regulate efficiently to support the transition to sustainability and to mitigate the impacts of unsustainability.

On the aggregate level of business lobbying, a more active approach to policy risk – promoting policies that will support the transition to sustainability – may accordingly be the best financial risk management.[57] Such an active approach may also be beneficial in the sense that this may give the corporate decision-makers a

---

[52] Nationalisation is perceived to be one of the primary risks for companies doing business in foreign countries due to the potential of having significant assets seized without compensation. This risk is magnified in countries with unstable political leadership and stagnant or contracting economies; Kenton 2018.

[53] James 2001.

[54] Peinhardt and Allee 2016.

[55] Gordon 2008.

[56] As we have seen in the EU over the last couple of years, with the proposals for the Corporate Sustainability Reporting Directive of 2021, finally adopted in November 2022, and the Corporate Sustainability Due Diligence Directive of 2022, for which a political consensus was achieved in December 2023.

[57] The support for changes in EU law may be seen in this light; Saastamoinen 2019.

higher degree of certainty about upcoming changes in laws and policies. Conversely, when corporations work against necessary policies, such as the petroleum industry working against climate change mitigation measures,[58] and as we have seen in Europe in the context of the EU's Sustainable Corporate Governance Agenda,[59] the financial risk in the form of, for example, liability risks rises.

2.4.2.2 Liability Risks

The international increase in lawsuits against corporations, including parent corporations, for environmental or social harm allegedly caused by their subsidiaries, and against lead corporations for negative environmental or social impacts in their global value chains, shows that the liability risk of unsustainability is materialising.[60] While many cases are rejected for procedural reasons, and many are lost, some are likely to be won, and the sheer multitude of cases makes them a driver for change in themselves. They underline the financial risk of ignoring sustainability.

Liability risks take several forms. One form is investors suing either corporations or board members directly for loss of profit arising from failure to anticipate and adapt to climate change or other environmental degradation. This includes lawsuits alleging that corporate decision-makers failed to adequately factor in the risk of policy changes and regulation by governments reacting to climate change.[61] Liability risks also take the form of lawsuits brought against the corporation or the board members directly for damage caused to people or communities by the corporation's contribution to climate change or other environmental degradation. This further applies to harm caused by the corporation through violation of human rights or complicity in corruption – the social and broader governance dimensions of sustainability.[62] Who has the standing to sue, and the likelihood of a lawsuit's success, will vary with the procedural rules across jurisdictions. Such lawsuits entail a varying degree of financial risk for the corporation. The risks arise from the lawsuit itself – the costs associated with lawyers' fees, time spent, possible damages that have to be paid and negative reputational impacts – which may lead to lower profits if there are negative reactions from potential customers, contractual parties and investors.[63]

The financial risk of carrying on with mainstream governance models through corporate groups or global value chains is also illustrated through these cases.

[58] See, e.g., Cushman 2017; Tansey 2018.
[59] Burns 2022.
[60] European Coalition for Corporate Justice 2021; Mayer 2022; Deutsch and Jessop 2022; Taylor 2020; Taylor 2021.
[61] Bowman and Wiseman 2020.
[62] For a list of cases, see Business and Human Rights Resource Centre (n.d.). See also Zerk 2014.
[63] Although the reputational effect has been called into doubt, with cases showing very few consequences in terms of consumer or investor reaction to, for example, environmental wrongdoings; Karpoff, Lott and Wehrly 2005.

The Anthropocene entails new social and environmental realities for all of humanity, including business. Failing to recognise the significance to a business of these new constraints increases the likelihood that a company will be involved in contributing to transgressing planetary boundaries or undermining social foundations in a manner that gives rise to liability for the company. Already the courts in a number of countries are being asked to treat such breaches as causes of action in civil (tort) claims or, in some cases, as criminal violations.[64] While corporate law may start from the supposition that a parent corporation is not responsible for its subsidiaries' actions, and even less so a lead company for that of its global value chains, modern financial risk management will increasingly need to take a broader approach including the full impacts throughout the global value chains. The overwhelming support initially expressed by business for mandatory environmental and human rights due diligence in the study by Smit and colleagues for the European Commission reflects the desire for a level playing field for business and legal certainty for corporate decision-makers.[65]

2.4.2.3 Reputation Risk and Market Risk

If a business is involved or perceived to be involved in unsustainable behaviour, there may be a *reputation risk* in the form of customers or clients choosing not to purchase products or services from the business, employees and job seekers looking for work elsewhere, and contractual parties, private and public, not wishing to renew or sign up with the business. With social norms and expectations gradually changing,[66] there is an indication of a shift in consumer preferences,[67] as well as in the preferences of job seekers.[68] This leads to an increasing reputational risk for businesses involved in unsustainable activities. Media also plays an important role here in revealing unsustainable business activities, as illustrated, for example, through the Panama Papers.[69]

The related *market risk* concerns changes in demand and preferences for goods and services. This can be due to a changing physical environment, such as less demand for winter sports gear and clothes or changes in demand for agricultural goods. This can also be due to increased interest in and emphasis on the sustainability impacts, for example, preference for more environmentally friendly goods with good working conditions, or goods of higher quality that are repairable and long-lasting, rather than single-use products. Changes in procurement

---

[64] Taylor 2020.
[65] Smit et al. 2020a. See also Smit et al. 2020b.
[66] Sjåfjell and Taylor 2019.
[67] Wilson 2018. However, limitations of relying on 'consumer power' are well-established; Maitre-Ekern and Dalhammer 2019; Kirchherr et al. 2017.
[68] Alonso-Almeida and Llach 2019.
[69] Carvajal et al. 2017; Acosta 2023.

regimes, such as through the EU's increased emphasis on sustainable public procurement,[70] may increase the market risk for businesses not transitioning or not transitioning quickly enough.

Similarly, changes in the financial markets involve a market risk of only getting financing at a higher premium or not all, as institutional investors and banks increasingly wish to shift to sustainable investment and lending objectives.[71] The drive to divest from coal and increasingly also from oil and gas is a case in point here,[72] while it also illustrates the limitations of relying on a well-informed market to correct the extreme unsustainabilities of our time.

The assumption that reputation and market risks will be drivers for sustainability informs policymakers' adoption of various forms of sustainability reporting regimes, as it does voluntary initiatives for similar reporting. However, together with the *liability risk*, these risks also function as a disincentive for relevant and honest reporting, especially in a regime where there is a lack of stringency and of assurance. This entails the danger that honest and sustainability-oriented businesses suffer reputational risk associated with being open about challenges in their transition to sustainability, compared to competitors who choose to greenwash (or SDG-wash).

This underlines the importance of stringent reporting regimes with assurance and enforcement, providing a level playing field.[73] Similarly, the same considerations indicate the necessity for credible and coherent trade and investment conditionality alongside effective mechanisms for their enforcement.[74]

The EU's sustainable finance initiative and its quick turn-out of legislative instruments[75] have changed the regulatory framework to a great extent and have the potential to increase the market risk for unsustainable business. However, there is also here a need to secure a level playing field, so that the financial market risk is channelled in a sustainability-promoting manner.[76]

2.4.2.4 Technology Risk and Business Model Change Risk

Further related to the above is the *technology risk*. The risk of 'stranded assets' – assets that no longer have value – to any corporation involved in exploiting fossil fuels is the obvious example here. The shift from fossil fuels to renewables presents a great financial risk to corporations planning to profit in the long run from

---

[70] Martin-Ortega, Outhwaite and Rook 2015. See also Andhov et al. 2020.
[71] E.g., Riding and Mooney 2020; International Institute for Sustainable Development 2020.
[72] Nauman 2019.
[73] Where the current developments are making only incremental steps in that direction; Mähönen 2020; Monciardini, Mähönen and Tsagas 2020.
[74] Gammage and Novitz 2019.
[75] With which a number of the chapters in this volume engage, see Part III of this volume.
[76] Ahlström and Sjåfjell 2022.

oil, gas or coal.[77] However, this risk is also borne by corporations indirectly relying on these resources, such as manufacturers of fossil-fuelled cars.

The technology risk is not limited to climate change. For example, with the emerging recognition of the impact of increasing biodiversity loss, businesses continuing with products based on exploiting biodiversity resources that are becoming scarce may find themselves outcompeted by products developed in new ways.

The broad shift from unsustainable linear business models to the sustainable circular model involves financial risk for corporations not anticipating and adapting to this shift.[78] The idea of *technology change* is insufficient to capture this risk – *business model change* (or even *systems change*) is more appropriate and therefore included as a category here.

2.4.3 *Physical Risks and Societal Risks*

Physical risks and *societal risks*, two broad risk categories, distinguish themselves from the transition risks category above in that they affect businesses also seeking to transition to sustainability. The severity of the risks depends on the speed with which global society transitions to sustainability, and will, of course, have local variations. This emphasises the importance for businesses to work together to mitigate the physical and societal risks as far as possible. This could take form of lobbying for and not against necessary legislative and policy reforms. It could take the form of transitioning in their businesses and whole sectors towards sustainability, without waiting for policy reforms. Of course, this is not only relevant for businesses. It also places the onus on the government at national levels and on the European Union to mitigate physical and social risks to citizens.

2.4.3.1 Physical Risks

The *physical risks* of climate change are those that a changing climate entails, such as sudden and gradual changes to our natural environment, including warmer, wetter and wilder weather, floods and landslides, sea level rise, droughts and heat stress. Ignoring these predictions may lead businesses to make financially risky investments, for example, in property that it will not be possible to develop, or to fail to put in place necessary measures, for example, the fortification of factories against the changing physical environment.

A similar picture may be drawn for other environmental issues, including loss of biodiversity, and novel entities such as various forms of pollution, as well as ocean

---

[77] Semieniuk et al. 2022.

[78] A linear business model takes responsibility for, e.g., a product only until it is sold, and typically does not encompass the supply chain of the product and all its components. Conversely, a circular business model takes responsibility for a product from cradle to cradle, encompassing each stage from design to recycling/ upcycling or management of the waste. See e.g., Bjørnbet and Vildåsen 2021; Maitre-Ekern 2021.

acidification, deforestation and other land-system change, and pressure on fresh water. These are complex, interconnected processes, with environmental degradation of one type also increasing the associated risk with others.

Environmental degradation may bring physical risks to humans, too, in the form of an increase in diseases[79] and changes in which diseases occur where, through insufficient food or water and through an unmanageable increase in temperature, suddenly or over time. This translates into financial risks for businesses through employees or other workers not being able to work or come to work, and it may similarly affect the customers or suppliers of a business.[80]

Human rights violations and lack of decent work may similarly bring physical risks for the workforce, undermining their ability or willingness to carry out the work. Such risks can also undermine the future potential of workers, for example, child labour can lead to harms which stunt their capabilities in the labour market, but also in other aspects of their lives.[81] It may also undercut the ability of other businesses, which do not engage in such exploitative conduct, to compete fairly in markets for goods and service, making physical risk a business norm.

Tax evasion, or other forms of undermining the economic basis for well-functioning societies,[82] may negatively impact the relevant societies' ability to protect their population against physical risks due to environmental degradation, human rights violations and lack of decent work, thereby causing the physical risks to materialise or to be strengthened. Similarly, a lack of economic resources in a country undermines its possibility of putting into place relevant measures to adapt to environmental change.

The physical risks of unsustainability may have direct financial consequences for corporations in various sectors, and decision-makers lacking awareness or knowledge about these issues may increase the financial risk for the corporation through the decisions it makes or fails to make.

There are (at least) two levels on which the physical risk of environmental degradation and undermining of the social foundation represent a financial risk for businesses. The first is on the level of the individual corporation, which needs to anticipate and adapt to physical changes in the natural environment and, for example, increases in the risk of disease as far as possible. This may involve changes in insurance levels, investments, relocating factories or the corporation's business model.

The second is on the aggregate level of the sector, in a country, a region or globally. In addition to anticipating and adapting to physical risks, a corporation or an aggregate of corporations may more actively mitigate environmental degradation, exploitation

---

[79] The impact of COVID-19 may be seen as a materialisation of this risk, see e.g., Ringsmuth et al. 2022; Jones et al. 2013.

[80] Galaz et al. 2016.

[81] Otto, Walker and Ziegler 2017; Manley 2019.

[82] Hickel 2017; Hickel 2020.

of people and undermining of the societal bases for welfare, to ensure the continued viability of the corporation's business. To take just one example linked to biodiversity loss, an agricultural sector dependent on bees, wasps and other pollinators may collectively work to reduce the use of pesticides and mitigate other threats to pollinators. Not doing so, while continuing with the same line of business, involves the financial risk of reduced crops. Anticipating and adapting to unavoidable change, and contributing to the transition to sustainability to mitigate negative changes, are therefore intrinsic aspects of risk management in the core financial sense.

Of course, the involvement of the individual business in unsustainable behaviour leading to physical risks increases the liability risks, reputation and market risks, as well as the risk of being outcompeted by sustainable businesses through the materialisation of the technology risk and the business model change risk.

Ultimately, the physical risks go beyond what can be managed through anticipation and adaption. This is reflected through changes in insurance premiums for certain areas, 'with some insurers simply withdrawing from the market'.[83] Unmitigated environmental degradation and continued overshoot of planetary boundaries bring with them global catastrophic risks,[84] defined as the risk of a scenario which takes 'the lives of a significant portion of the human population, and may leave survivors at enhanced risk by undermining global resilience systems'.[85] The financial risks to most, if not all, businesses in global catastrophe scenarios are existential.[86] This is closely linked to the 'societal collapse' risk below.

2.4.3.2 Societal Risks

Societal risks include the risk of social unrest caused by social inequality, human rights violations and the corporate undermining of the economic basis of our welfare systems.

Tax evasion is intrinsically linked to an undermining of the economic bases of our societies, the increasing inequality between and within countries and the rise of populism and the risk of societal instability that this entails. Some of the most disturbing trends in major industrialised countries reflect such a lack of social stability, and corporations and associated financial markets have a role in this.[87]

Social precarity and vulnerability have led to a significant increase in the disparity of income levels between the wealthy and the poor, and between capital,

---

[83] Cullen, Mähönen and Nilsen 2020, section 3.3. See also World Economic Forum 2020, 32: 'More common extreme weather events could make insurance unaffordable or simply unavailable for individuals and businesses: globally, the "catastrophe protection gap" – what should be insured but is not – reached US$280 billion in 2018'.

[84] Discussed also in section 3.3 of Cullen, Mähönen and Nilsen 2020.

[85] Avin et al. 2018.

[86] See also World Economic Forum 2020.

[87] See further Sjåfjell and Bruner 2019.

managers and those dependent on working for a living.[88] The International Monetary Fund (IMF) reports recommend the re-regulation of labour markets, for example, through worker voice in the form of trade union representation.[89] The motivation is not only the protection of workers' human rights or decent work, but that growing inequalities of income also affect consumer potential and, ironically, undermine capitalism as a whole. This appears also to be reflected in concern expressed by the World Bank and OECD Reports on *The Changing World of Work* and *New Forms of Work* (respectively).[90] Within this context, the emphasis on sustainability is creating added momentum to enhance the scope of representation and voice of all those at work (or in the world of work), rather than those who merely meet the current threshold requirements of protection in a standard employment relationship.[91]

Moreover, social precarity and vulnerability do not only have implications for the work force and the consumer base in global capitalism, but also for the quality of democratic engagement.[92] Precarity limits the scope to find energy for political activity and campaigning, which are becoming again a preserve of the elite. As capital gains in wealth, many employers become ever more influential in political life.

Powerful vested interests can hijack political advertising, not just through conventional media (as was the case with the Rupert Murdoch press in the 1980s and 1990s, which had to be wooed by political leaders), but through less tangible forms of communication, which can involve attempts at intervention in the democratic process (the Google and Facebook scandals).[93] This may also be linked to the attempt to blame others even more vulnerable for conditions of scarcity, prompting resort to forms of nationalism and even neo-fascism.[94]

Businesses involved in undermining the economic basis of societies, in human rights violations, exploitation of workers or manipulating the public discourse and democratic processes, may find that these bring a spectrum of societal risks. These may range from societal unrest, via paving the way for increased authoritarianism, to societal collapse. Societal unrest may take the form of rioting and lack of safety for workers, customers and creditors, with negative impacts on the business. An increase in authoritarianism can materialise through sudden regime changes with an increased risk of nationalisation or instability in the country that make it difficult to continue with business as planned.[95]

---

[88] Piketty 2014.

[89] Jaumotte and Buitron 2015, discussed in Novitz 2020c, on which this subsection draws.

[90] World Bank 2019; OECD 2019.

[91] Countouris 2019; Novitz 2019b.

[92] Jaumotte and Buitron 2015, 27 observe that: 'Inequality could also hurt society by allowing top earners to manipulate the economic and political system.'

[93] Kreiss and McGregor 2018; Cadwalladr and Graham-Harrison 2018.

[94] See Polanyi 2001, 245 and 256; Inglehart and Norris 2017; see also Norris and Inglehart 2019.

[95] See also political risks in Section 2.4.2.1.

There are a number of scenarios that can lead to global catastrophic risks, including climate change and other environmental degradation.[96] If we do not manage to reposition our economies and societies in a way that secures a safe and just operating space for humanity now and for the future, there is a risk of societal collapse, which may be caused by a combination of the factors discussed here.

All these risks are relevant for the business involved in wrongdoings, although they may be more directly at risk from social unrest, which targets those perceived to have been involved in wrongdoings. The financial risks of unsustainability are also relevant for other businesses in the same country or region. In the case of societal collapse, practically all businesses are affected. This strengthens the argument for companies to recognise these financial risks and work together, for example in a sector, to alleviate them. Finally, it underlines the importance of responsible business behaviour and the significance of business supporting appropriate policy reforms.

2.5 CONCLUDING REFLECTIONS

Global catastrophic risk and the risk of societal collapse underline that we cannot settle for a mainstream 'business case' approach. Recognising the financial risks of unsustainability does not mean that it is sufficient only to internalise environmental, social and broader governance issues to the extent that a clear cause-and-effect line can be drawn from ignoring an issue to the financial risk it entails for the corporation. Nor is risk disclosure the end goal. It is increasingly clear that a fundamental transformation is needed in business. Understanding the risks of unsustainability should give a basis for such a transformation, showing the direction and extent of changes that are necessary for business models, strategy and governance. Indeed, identifying the financial risk is not intended as a boundary of what issues are relevant to corporate sustainability. The point is to challenge the dichotomy of profits versus sustainability and show that, however little a business may care about 'ethics' and 'corporate social responsibility', (un)sustainability will sooner or later, in one way or another, affect most businesses. This is the grand challenge facing our economies, including business, and, more broadly, our societies.[97]

There is a strong legal basis in EU law to undertake the necessary regulatory changes to ensure that the risks associated with the continued extreme unsustainabilities of our time are successfully mitigated. The unprecedented speed of the follow-up of the EU's sustainable finance initiative of 2018, with the first legislative instruments adopted already in 2019 and 2020, shows that decisive, game-changing regulatory action is possible. The sustainable finance initiative is very

---

[96] Ibid.
[97] Crona, Folke and Galaz 2021.

much informed by the recognition of the financial risks of climate change in the form developed and promoted by the Task Force for Climate-related Financial Disclosure. What is needed now is further developments within a framework of a research-based concept of sustainability. This is not merely a *possibility* in the EU, considering the EU Treaty Law's overarching objectives, its environmental and social horizontal integration and policy coherence rules and the EU's high-level policy commitment to sustainability. Rather, contributing to the fundamental transformation to sustainable human societies grounded in a research- and evidence-based understanding of sustainability, with prevention and precaution as guiding principles, is the *duty* of the EU institutions according to the EU Treaties.[98]

REFERENCES

Acosta, C. M. (2023), 'Where are the key Panama Papers figures, seven years later?' *International Consortium of Investigative Journalists*, 3 April, available at: https://bit.ly/4aKwrKb.

Ahlström, H. and Sjåfjell, B. (2022), 'Complexity and uncertainty in sustainable finance: An analysis of the EU taxonomy' in Cadman, T. and Sarker, T. (eds.), *De Gruyter Handbook of Sustainable Development and Finance* (Berlin: De Gruyter), 15–40.

Alonso-Almeida, M. D. M. and Llach, J. (2019), 'Socially responsible companies: Are they the best workplace for millennials? A cross-national analysis' 26 *Corporate Social Responsibility and Environmental Management*, 238–4.

Andhov, M., Caranta, R., Stoffel, T. et al. (2020), *Sustainability through Public Procurement: The Way Forward – Reform Proposals*, SMART Report, available at https://ssrn.com/abstract=3559393.

Avin, S., Wintle, B. C., Weitzdörfer, J. et al. (2018), 'Classifying global catastrophic risks' 102 *Futures*, 20–26.

Basel Committee on Banking Supervision (2020), 'Basel Committee meets to review vulnerabilities and emerging risks, advance supervisory initiatives and promote Basel III implementation', 27 February, available at: www.bis.org/press/p200227.htm.

Baum, S. D. and Handoh, I. C. (2014), 'Integrating the planetary boundaries and global catastrophic risk paradigms' 107 *Ecological Economics*, 13–21.

Bjørnbet, M. M. and Vildåsen, S. S. (2021), 'Life cycle assessment to ensure sustainability of circular business models in manufacturing' 13 *Sustainability*, 11014.

Bowman, M. and Wiseman, D. (2020), 'Finance actors and climate-related disclosure regulation: Logic, limits, and emerging accountability' in Holley, C., Phelan, L. and Shearing, C. (eds.), *Criminology and Climate* (London: Routledge), 153–78.

Burns, A. (2022), 'Commission bends to lobby on Sustainable Corporate Governance', *Finance Watch*, 23 February, available at: https://bit.ly/3wglZLV.

Business and Human Rights Resource Centre (n.d.), 'Legal case map', available at: www.business-humanrights.org/en/corporate-legal-accountability.

Cadwalladr, C. and Graham-Harrison, E. (2018), 'Revealed: 50 million Facebook profiles harvested for Cambridge Analytica in major data breach', *The Guardian*, 17 March.

Carvajal, R., Cabra, M., Ortiz, Á., and Blat, F. (2017), 'Explore the Panama Papers Key Figures', *International Consortium of Investigative Journalists' website*, 31 January.

---

[98] Solana 2019; Nowag 2016; Sjåfjell 2019; Sjåfjell 2021.

Christensen, G. (2019), 'What does it mean to be sustainable? Regulating the relationship between corporations and Indigenous peoples' in Sjåfjell, B. and Bruner, C. M. (eds.), *Cambridge Handbook of Corporate Law, Corporate Governance and Sustainability* (Cambridge: Cambridge University Press), 416–30.

Clapp, C. et al. (2017), *Shades of Climate Risk: Categorizing Climate Risk for Investors, Report 2017:01 CICERO Center for International Climate and Environmental Research*, available at: http://hdl.handle.net/11250/2430660.

Collins, L. M. (2018), 'Sustainable Development Goals and human rights: Challenges and opportunities' in French, D. and Kotzé, L. J. (eds.), *Sustainable Development Goals: Law, Theory and Implementation* (Cheltenham: Edward Elgar), 66–90.

Countouris, N. (2019), *Defining and Regulating Work Relations for the Future of Work* (Geneva: International Labour Office).

Crona, B., Folke, C., and Galaz, V. (2021), 'The Anthropocene reality of financial risk' 4 *One Earth*, 618–28.

Cullen, J., Mähönen J., and Nilsen, H. R. (2020), 'Financing the transition to sustainability: SMART reform proposals', University of Oslo Faculty of Law Research Paper No. 2020-10, 6 May, Nordic & European Company Law Working Paper No. 20-09, available at: http://dx.doi.org/10.2139/ssrn.3594433.

Cushman, J. H. (2017), 'Harvard study finds Exxon misled public about climate change', *Inside Climate News*, 22 August, available at: https://bit.ly/3SW7GF7.

Deutsch, A. and Jessop, S. (2022), 'Activists behind Shell climate verdict target 30 multinationals', Reuters, 13 January, available at: https://reut.rs/3OFe4hq.

European Coalition for Corporate Justice (2021), 'Suing Goliath: An analysis of civil cases against EU companies for overseas human rights and environmental abuses', ECCJ, 28 September, available at: https://corporatejustice.org/publications/suing-goliath/.

European Commission (2020), 'Communication from The Commission to The European Parliament, The Council, The European Economic and Social Committee and The Committee of The Regions A New Circular Economy Action Plan For a cleaner and more competitive Europe', COM/2020/98 final, available at: https://bit.ly/456ECiE.

European Commission (n.d.), 'Overview of Sustainable Finance', available at: https://bit.ly/49w6UnV.

European Parliament and Council (2022), 'Decision (EU) 2022/591 of the European Parliament and of the Council of 6 April 2022 on a General Union Environment Action Programme to 2030', available at: https://bit.ly/3KsQfXK.

Galaz, V., Österblom, H., Bodin, Ö., and Crona B. (2016), 'Global networks and global change-induced tipping points' 16 *International Environmental Agreements: Politics, Law and Economics*, 189–221.

Gammage, C. and Novitz, T. (2019), 'Trade, investment and corporate sustainability' in Sjåfjell, B. and Bruner, C. M. (eds.), *The Cambridge Handbook of Corporate Law, Corporate Governance, and Sustainability* (Cambridge: Cambridge University Press), 15–28.

Gordon, K. (2008), 'Investment guarantees and political risk insurance: Institutions, incentives and development' *OECD Investment Policy Perspectives*, 92.

Greep, H. (2022), 'Latest draft shows that TNFD's reputation "as the next frontier in corporate greenwashing on nature" remains solidly intact', *BankTrack*, 7 November, available at: https://bit.ly/3X8rWpE.

Hickel, J. (2017), *The Divide: A Brief Guide to Global Inequality and Its Solutions* (London: Penguin Random House).

Hickel, J. (2020), 'The sustainable development index: Measuring the ecological efficiency of human development in the Anthropocene' 167 *Ecological Economics*, 106331. https://doi.org/10.1016/j.ecolecon.2019.05.011.

ILO (International Labour Organization) (2008), 'ILO Declaration on Social Justice for a Fair Globalization', 10 June, available at https://bit.ly/3Rabj9c.

ILO (International Labour Organization) (2019a), 'ILO Centenary Declaration for the Future of Work 2019', 21 June, available at https://bit.ly/3X2HFXi.

ILO (International Labour Organization) (2019b), 'Violence and Harassment Convention, 2019 (No. 190)', 21 June, available at https://bit.ly/3R8jC5q.

ILO (International Labour Organization) (2019c), 'International Labour Organization Global Commission on the Future of Work: Work for a brighter future', 22 January, available at https://bit.ly/3X6AxZQ.

Inglehart, R. and Norris, P. (2017), 'Trump and the populist authoritarian parties: The silent revolution in reverse' 15(2) *Perspectives on Politics*, 443.

International Institute for Sustainable Development (2020), 'Sustainable investing: Shaping the future of finance', February, available at: https://bit.ly/3HUuuit.

ITUC (International Trade Union Confederation) (2016), 'New ITUC report exposes hidden workforce of 116 million in global supply chains of fifty companies', 18 January, available at: www.ituc-csi.org/new-ituc-report-exposes-hidden.

James, D. (2001), 'Cooperation, competition, and the "science of pricing" in the political risk insurance marketplace' in Moran, T. H. and West, G. T. (eds.), *International Political Risk Management: Exploring New Frontiers* (Washington, DC: The World Bank), 170–79.

Jaumotte, F. and Buitron, C. (2015), 'IMF staff discussion note: Inequality and labor market institutions', 1 July, available at: www.imf.org/external/pubs/ft/sdn/2015/sdn1514.pdf.

Jones, B. A., Grace, D., Kock, R. et al. (2013), 'Zoonosis emergence linked to agricultural intensification and environmental change' 110 *Proceedings of the National Academy of Sciences of the United States of America*, 8399–404.

Karpoff, J., Lott, J. R. and Wehrly, E. W. (2005), 'The reputational penalties for environmental violations: Empirical evidence' 48 *Journal of Law and Economics*, 653–75.

Kenton, W. (2018), 'Nationalization', 30 March, available at: www.investopedia.com/terms/n/nationalization.asp.

Keys, P. W., Galaz, V., Dyer, M. et al. (2019), 'Anthropocene risk' 2 *Nature Sustainability*, 667–73.

Kirchherr, J., Hekkert, M., Bour, R. et al. (2017), 'Breaking the barriers to the circular economy', *Whitepaper*, October, available at https://bit.ly/3V8o4iL.

Kotzé L. J. (2019), 'The Anthropocene, Earth system vulnerability and socio-ecological injustice in an age of human rights' 10 *Journal of Human Rights and the Environment*, 62–85.

Kotzé, L. J. and Kim, R. E. (2019), 'Earth system law: The juridical dimensions of earth system governance' 1 *Earth System Governance*, 7–8.

Kreiss, D. and McGregor, S. C. (2018), 'Technology firms shape political communication: The work of Microsoft, Facebook, Twitter, and Google with campaigns during the 2016 US presidential cycle' 35 *Political Communication*, 155–77.

Leach, M., Raworth, K., and Rockström, J. (2013), 'Between social and planetary boundaries: Navigating pathways in the safe and just space for humanity' in *World Social Science Report 2013* (Paris: UNESCO Publishing), 84–90.

Madden, R. and Coleman, C. (2018), 'Visibility of indigenous peoples in sustainable development indicators', Working paper presented at 16th Conference of the International Association of Official Statisticians (IAOS), September, OECD Headquarters, Paris, 19–21, available at: https://bit.ly/3OMigft.

Mähönen, J. (2020), 'Comprehensive approach to relevant and reliable reporting in Europe: A dream impossible?' 12 *Sustainability*, 5277.

Maitre-Ekern, E. (2021), 'Re-thinking producer responsibility for a sustainable circular economy from extended producer responsibility to pre-market producer responsibility' 286 *Journal of Cleaner Production*, 125454.

Maitre-Ekern, E. and Dalhammar, C. (2019), 'Towards a hierarchy of consumption behaviour in the circular economy' 26(3) *Maastricht Journal of European and Comparative Law*, 394–420.

Malhi, Y. (2017), 'The concept of the Anthropocene' 42 *Annual Review of Environment and Resources*, 77–104.

Manley, R. (2019), 'Trade law and the capability approach' 53(6) *Journal of World Trade*, 1041–62.

Martin-Ortega, O., Outhwaite, O. and Rook, W. (2015), 'Buying power and human rights in the supply chain: Legal options for socially responsible public procurement of electronic goods' 19 *The International Journal of Human Rights*, 341–68.

Mayer, B. (2022), 'The duty of care of fossil-fuel producers for climate change mitigation: Milieudefensie v. Royal Dutch Shell District Court of The Hague (The Netherlands)' 11 *Transnational Environmental Law*, 407–18.

Monciardini, D., Mähönen, J. T. and Tsagas, G. (2020), 'Rethinking non-financial reporting: A blueprint for structural regulatory changes' 10 *Accounting, Economics, and Law: A Convivium*, vol. 10(2), 1–43.

Moyn, S. (2018), *Not Enough: Human Rights in An Unequal World* (Cambridge, MA: Harvard University Press).

Nauman, B. (2019), 'Sharp rise in number of investors dumping fossil fuel stocks', *Financial Times*, 9 September, available at: https://on.ft.com/3HUuBdT.

Norris, P. and Inglehart, R. (2019), *Cultural Backlash: Trump, Brexit, and Authoritarian Populism* (Cambridge, UK: Cambridge University Press).

Novitz, T. (2019a), 'Supply chains and temporary migrant labour: The relevance of trade and sustainability frameworks' in Ashiagbor D. (ed.), *Re-imagining Labour Law for Development: Informal Work in the Global North and South* (Oxford: Hart Publishing), 191–211.

Novitz, T. (2019b), 'Tripartism as sustainable governance' in Politakis, G., Kohiyama, T. and Lieby, T. (eds.), *ILO100 – Law for Social Justice* (Geneva: International Labour Office), 337–54, available at: https://bit.ly/3HZe2xl.

Novitz, T. (2020a), 'Past and future work at the International Labour Organization: Labour as a fictitious commodity, countermovement and sustainability' 17 *International Organizations Law Review*, 10–40.

Novitz, T. (2020b), 'Engagement with sustainability at the International Labour Organization and implications for worker voice' 159(4) *International Labour Review*, 463–82.

Novitz, T. (2020c), 'The perils of collective begging: The case for reforming collective labour law globally and locally too' 44(2) *New Zealand Journal of Employment Relations*, 3–19.

Nowag, J. (2016), *Environmental Integration in Competition and Free-Movement Laws* (Oxford: Oxford University Press).

OECD (2019), *Policy Responses to New Forms of Work* (Paris: OECD Publishing), 21 March to 24 April, available at: https://bit.ly/3I4Q1EV.

Otto, H.-U., Walker, M., and Ziegler, H. (eds.) (2017), *Capability-promoting Policies: Enhancing Individual and Social Development* (Bristol: Policy Press).

Peinhardt, C. and Allee, T. (2016), 'Political risk insurance as dispute resolution' 7 *Journal of International Dispute Settlement*, 205–24.

Persson, L., Carney Almroth, B. M., Collins, C. D. et al. (2022a), 'Outside the safe operating space of the planetary boundary for novel entities' 56(3) *Environmental Science & Technology*, 1510–21.

Persson, L., Carney Almroth, B. M., Collins, C. D. et al. (2022b), 'Response to comment on "Outside the safe operating space of the planetary boundary for novel entities"' 56 *Environmental Science & Technology*, 6788–9.

Piketty, T. (2014), *Capital in the Twenty-First Century* (Cambridge, MA: Harvard University Press).

Polanyi, K. (2001), *The Great Transformation: The Political and Economic Origins of Our Time. 2nd paperback edition* (Boston: Beacon Press).

PwC (PricewaterhouseCoopers) and WWF (2020), 'Nature is too big to fail. Biodiversity: The next frontier in financial risk management', January, available at: https://pwc .to/3OH4M4M.

Raworth, K. (2012), *A Safe and Just Space for Humanity: Can We Live within the Doughnut?* Oxfam Discussion Paper. (Oxford: Oxfam GB).

Raworth, K. (2017), *Doughnut Economics: Seven Ways to Think Like a 21st-century Economist* (White River Junction, VT: Chelsea Green Publishing).

Richardson, K., Steffen, W., Lucht, W. et al. (2023), 'Earth beyond six of nine planetary boundaries' 9 *Science Advances*, eadh2458.

Riding, S. and Mooney, A. (2020), 'Investors blast EU's omission of oil from ESG disclosures', *Financial Times*, 3 May, available at: https://on.ft.com/3HVJGvA.

Ringsmuth, A. K., Otto, I. M., van den Hurk, B. et al. (2022), 'Lessons from COVID-19 for managing transboundary climate risks and building resilience' 35 *Climate Risk Management*, 100395.

Rockström, J., Steffen, W., Noone, K. et al. (2009), 'Planetary boundaries: Exploring the safe operating space for humanity' 14 *Ecology and Society*, 1–33.

Saastamoinen, S. (2019), 'Sustainable corporate governance in the wake of the climate crisis', 24th European Corporate Governance Conference, 12 December, Helsinki, available at: https://bit.ly/3OGbGXX.

Semieniuk, G., Holden, P. B., Mercure, J.-F. et al. (2022), 'Stranded fossil-fuel assets translate to major losses for investors in advanced economies' 12 *Nature Climate Change*, 532–38.

Sjåfjell, B. (2019), 'The environmental integration principle: A necessary step towards policy coherence for sustainability' in Ippolito, F., Bartoloni, M. E., and Condinanzi, M. (eds.), *The EU and the Proliferation of Integration Principles under the Lisbon Treaty* (Abingdon: Routledge), 105–122.

Sjåfjell, B. (2020a), 'How company law has failed human rights – And what to do about it' 5 *Business and Human Rights Journal*, 179–99.

Sjåfjell, B. (2020b), 'The financial risks of unsustainability: A research agenda', University of Oslo Faculty of Law Research Paper No. 2020-18, 29 June, Nordic & European Company Law Working Paper No. 21-05. https://ssrn.com/abstract=3637969.

Sjåfjell, B. (2021), 'Reforming EU company law to secure the future of European business' 18 *European Company and Financial Law Review*, 190–217.

Sjåfjell, B. and Bruner, C. M. (2019), 'Corporations and sustainability' in Sjåfjell, B. and Bruner, C. M. (eds.), *Cambridge Handbook of Corporate Law, Corporate Governance and Sustainability* (Cambridge, UK: Cambridge University Press), 3–12.

Sjåfjell, B. and Taylor, M. B. (2019), 'Clash of norms: Shareholder primacy vs. sustainable corporate purpose' 13 *International and Comparative Corporate Law Journal*, 40–66.

Sjåfjell, B. and Cornell, S. E. (2024), 'What the actual ....? Tensions in the science-business-policy interface for global sustainability'. Manuscript under review in the journal European Law Open. On file with current author.

Smit, L., Bright, C., McCorquodale, R. et al. (2020a), *Study on Due Diligence Requirements through the Supply Chain: Final Report*. Luxembourg: Publications Office of the European Union, January. https://data.europa.eu/doi/10.2838/39830.

Smit, L., Bright, C., Pietropaoli, I., Hughes-Jennett, J., and Hood, P. (2020b), 'Business views on mandatory human rights due diligence regulation: A comparative analysis of two recent studies' 5 *Business and Human Rights Journal*, 261–9.

Solana, J. (2019), 'The power of the Eurosystem to promote environmental protection' 30 *European Business Law Review*, 547–75.

Steffen, W., Richardson, K., Rockström, J. et al. (2015), 'Planetary boundaries: Guiding human development on a changing planet' 347 *Science* 1259855.

Tansey, R. (ed.) (2018), *Corporate Capture in Europe – When Big Business Dominates Policy-making and Threatens Our Right*, Alliance for Lobbying Transparency and Ethics Regulation in the EU (ALTER-EU).

TCFD (Task Force on Climate-Related Financial Disclosures) (2017), *Final Report: Recommendations of the Task Force on Climate-Related Financial Disclosures*, June, available at: www.fsb-tcfd.org/publications/final-recommendations-report.

TNFD (Taskforce on Nature-Related Financial Disclosures) (2023) *Recommendations of the Taskforce on Nature-Related Financial Disclosures*. Available at https://bit.ly/3Xa1Xy2.

Taylor, M. B. (2020), 'Litigating Sustainability – Towards a Taxonomy of Counter-Corporate Litigation', 3 February, University of Oslo Faculty of Law Research Paper No. 2020-08. https://ssrn.com/abstract=3627580. http://dx.doi.org/10.2139/ssrn.3627580.

Taylor, M. B. (2021), 'Counter corporate litigation: Remedy, regulation, and repression in the struggle for a just transition' 13 *Sustainability*, 1074.

United Nations General Assembly (2015), 'Transforming our world: The 2030 Agenda for Sustainable Development', General Assembly Resolution A/RES70/1.

Villarrubia-Gómez, P., Cornell, S. E., and Fabres, J. (2018), 'Marine plastic pollution as a planetary boundary threat – The drifting piece in the sustainability puzzle' 96 *Marine Policy*, 213–20.

Weissbrodt, D. and Rumsey, M. (eds.) (2011), *Vulnerable and Marginalised Groups and Human Rights* (Cheltenham: Edward Elgar).

Whiteman, G. and Williams, A. (2019), 'Systemic planetary risks: Implications for organization studies' in Gephart Jr., R., Miller, C. C. and Helgesson, K. S. (eds.), *The Routledge Companion to Risk, Crisis and Emergency Management* (London: Routledge), 213–27.

Wilson, J. (2018), 'Consumer preferences continue to shift toward sustainability, market research shows', *TriplePundit*, 13 November, available at: https://bit.ly/49dRULx.

World Bank (2019), *World Development Report 2019: The Changing Nature of Work*, 24 April, available at: https://openknowledge.worldbank.org/handle/10986/30435.

World Economic Forum (2017), *Global Risk Report 2017*, available at: www.weforum.org/reports/the-global-risks-report-2017/.

World Economic Forum (2020), *Global Risk Report 2020*, available at: www.weforum.org/reports/the-global-risks-report-2020/.

World Economic Forum (2022), *Global Risks Report 2022*, available at: www.weforum.org/reports/global-risks-report-2022/.

World Inequality Report (2018), available at: https://wir2018.wid.world/.

Yu, C.-Y. (2018), 'An application of sustainable development in indigenous people's revival: The history of an indigenous tribe's struggle in Taiwan' 10 *Sustainability*, 3259.

Zerk, J. (2014), *Towards a Fairer and More Effective System of Domestic Law Remedies*, UN High Commissioner for Human Rights, Corporate Liability for Gross Human Rights Abuses, available at: https://bit.ly/3wglvFC.

PART II

Ethics and Sustainability in Corporate Law,
Corporate Governance and Conduct

3

Firm Value versus Social Value

Dealing with the Trade-Offs

Guido Ferrarini

3.1 INTRODUCTION

In this chapter, I analyze the trade-offs between maximizing the firm's economic value and generating social value in business activities. I refer to firm value rather than shareholder value to underline the need to take stakeholder interests into account when pursuing economic value maximization. Social value concerns stakeholder interests in general (including future generations) and the objectives relating to environmental and social sustainability covered by the ESG concept.[1] Firms can either increase social value directly – for instance by taking care of local communities or promoting the welfare of employees – or indirectly (typically by reducing carbon emissions). They can do it autonomously or under regulatory constraint. On one side, firms create long-term value by taking stakeholder interests into account through corporate purpose and corporate governance. On the other side, soft law and regulation enhance social value by constraining firm value maximization to reduce negative externalities to the environment and society ('people and planet').

In a previous paper, I connected corporate purpose with sustainability from a general perspective, redefining the former in ways which allow for environmental and social externalities to be considered in business decision making.[2] In this chapter, I deepen my analysis with reference to the main trade-offs between economic value and social value of the firm and consider how they are solved through corporate governance mechanisms under ethical and regulatory constraints. In Section 3.2, I examine how such trade-offs are dealt with from a finance perspective by analyzing the 'enlightenment' of shareholder value under the influence of stakeholder theory. In Section 3.3, I consider the criticisms recently made of enlightened shareholder value (ESV) from different perspectives. While rejecting similar criticisms, I suggest that ESV is conveniently complemented by business ethics, soft law and regulation.

---

[1] On the ESG concept, see Pollman 2022.
[2] Ferrarini 2021, 85, where I argued that corporate purpose is a multifarious concept which can be understood from different perspectives.

In Section 3.4, I focus on scholarly developments that emphasize the role of corporate governance and organizational theory in developing corporate purpose and sustainability. In Section 3.5, I examine how business ethics, soft law and regulation constrain firm value maximization and contribute to dealing with negative externalities. In Section 3.6, I draw some general conclusions on the impact of ESV, business ethics and regulation on corporate purpose.

3.2 SHAREHOLDER VALUE MAXIMIZATION AND STAKEHOLDERS

Enlightened Shareholder (or Stakeholder) Value (ESV) is the dominant approach to analyze the trade-offs between firm value and social value from a finance perspective. It was proposed by Michael Jensen at the beginning of this century as a merger of shareholder value theory and stakeholder theory[3] and is often used also by legal scholars in the analysis of director duties[4]. To introduce this approach, I briefly consider the parable of shareholder value and the rise of CSR practices and stakeholder theory as original motivators for ESV. I then examine the 'shared value' approach, which is one of ESV derivatives, often used in corporate sustainability discussions. In the next section, I consider some of the main criticisms of ESV and propose a revision of the same, emphasizing the role of business ethics and regulation.

3.2.1 *The Parable of Shareholder Value*

Milton Friedman is often considered to be the father of shareholder value and therefore also responsible, from a theoretical perspective, for its negative consequences in the two financial crises of this century[5]. His famous 1970 paper in the New York Times Magazine is widely quoted as the foundation of shareholder value theory[6]. However, this reading is not entirely correct[7], as such theory was developed later by finance scholars and consultants[8], while its diffusion in practice mainly occurred in the last two decades of the last century.[9]

Friedman referred to the corporate practices of his time, but his emphasis on corporate profits reflected a criticism of those practices and anticipated the advent of shareholder value theory. As B. Holmstrom and S. Kaplan later explained: 'Before 1980, corporate managements tended to think of themselves as representing not the shareholders, but rather "the corporation." In this view, the goal of the firm was not to maximize shareholder wealth, but to ensure the growth (or at least the stability) of

---

[3] Jensen 2002, 235 (quote from *Business Ethics Quarterly*).
[4] Davies 2020, 48.
[5] See Cheffins 2020.
[6] Friedman 1970, 32.
[7] See Cheffins 2020.
[8] See the classic work by Rappaport 1998.
[9] See Davis 2009, 50 ff.

the enterprise by "balancing" the claims of all important corporate "stakeholders" – employees, suppliers, and local communities, as well as shareholders.'[10] The external governance mechanisms available to dissatisfied shareholders, such as proxy fights and hostile takeovers, were seldom used. Corporate boards tended to be dominated by management, making board oversight weak, while internal incentives from management ownership of stock and options were also modest.[11]

Partly in response to the neglect of shareholders, the 1980s saw the emergence of the corporate raider and hostile takeovers.[12] In the 1990s, the pattern of corporate governance activity changed again, as hostile takeovers and leverage declined substantially. However, other corporate governance mechanisms began to play a larger role, particularly executive stock options and the greater involvement of boards of directors and shareholders:[13] 'With the implicit assent of institutional investors, boards substantially increased the use of stock option plans that allowed managers to share in the value created by restructuring their own companies. Shareholder value thus became an ally rather than a threat.'[14]

After the two financial crises at the beginning of this century, there were repeated practical and scholarly efforts to reconcile shareholder value with 'good' corporate governance.[15] Indeed, shareholder value showed its limits and its dark side, with flawed corporate governance and excessive executive compensation being indicated amongst the main causes of both crises.[16] Also, short-termism was considered to be one of the main causes of the failures of non-financial companies (in the 2001 crisis) and financial institutions (in the 2008 crisis).[17]

3.2.2 *The Rise of Corporate Social Responsibility and Stakeholder Theory*

In his 1970 paper, Friedman argued for the rejection of corporate social responsibility as a 'fundamentally subversive doctrine'.[18] He contended that the executives are agents of the stockholders and cannot spend the company's money for social purposes. However, CSR practices are considered today as predominantly aligned

---

[10] Holmstrom and Kaplan 2003, 10.
[11] Ibid. For example, in 1980 only 20 per cent of the compensation of U.S. CEOs was tied to stock market performance. Long-term performance plans were widely used, but they were typically based on accounting measures like sales growth and earnings per share that tied managerial incentives less directly, and sometimes not at all, to shareholder value.
[12] Ibid., arguing that 'nearly half of all major U.S. corporations received a takeover offer in the 1980s – and many companies that were not taken over responded to hostile pressure with internal restructurings that made themselves less attractive targets.'
[13] Ibid., 11.
[14] Ibid.
[15] See Lund and Pollman 2021, 2563.
[16] Coffee 2005, 198; Ferrarini and Giudici 2006, 159.
[17] Blinder 2013.
[18] Friedman 1970, 32.

with the company's interest, for they promote the reputation of the firm as an entity which regularly complies with ethical standards and satisfy the expectations of those shareholders who follow responsible investment practices.[19] In addition, the coverage of CSR has been expanded to include a range of topics which did not belong to it at its origin,[20] such as environmental sustainability, employees' welfare and supply chain monitoring.[21] Thirdly, CSR is increasingly integrated with business strategy and positively affects corporate purpose that extends to social goals in addition to the pursuit of corporate profit.[22].

Also, stakeholder theory has been developed in the last forty years to counter the dominant theory of the corporation which is shareholder-centric.[23] As originally outlined by E. Freeman,[24] this theory tried to explain how business could be understood against the backdrop of the environmental turbulence which was already in motion. Freeman assumed that the 'current approaches to understanding the business environment fail to take account of a wide range of groups who can affect or are affected by the corporation, its "stakeholders".'[25] Moreover, stakeholder theorists argue that, contrary to what traditionally assumed in economic theory, the questions of values and ethics must be considered and dealt together with economic reality.[26] They criticize the separation of business decisions from ethical decisions and suggest integrating the two types of decisions and recognizing the managers' moral responsibility for them.

---

[19] See Smith and Lenssen 2009, 2, who argue: 'The *business case* at the level of the firm is becoming increasingly clear as more companies come to understand that, aside from any moral obligation, it is in their economic interest to address environmental, social and governance issues and in a manner that is integrated with strategy and operations.'

[20] See Crane, Matten and Spence 2008, 3 ff., where current definitions of CSR and analysis of its core characteristics.

[21] As argued by academic experts of the field: '... CSR encompasses issues such as sustainability (meeting the needs of the present without compromising the ability of future generations to meet their needs), stakeholder management and corporate governance, as well as corporate philanthropy, although the latter is increasingly seen as a peripheral consideration'; Smith and Lenssen 2009, 2, also noting that the case for business to engage in ESG issues is based on the realization that a new global social contract between business, government and society is needed.

[22] See Pettigrew 2009, 12. Nonetheless, some finance studies argue that CSR is often a manifestation of agency problems within the firm and therefore problematic. See Benabou and Tirole 2010, 1, and the other works cited by Ferrell, Liang and Renneboog 2016, 585. Agency problems are manifested, for example, by corporate managers engaging in CSR that either benefits themselves rather than shareholders or reduces their engagement on core responsibilities within the firm. See Krueger 2015, 304. According to the 'agency view', CSR is generally not in the interest of shareholders. However, under another view socially responsible firms often implement value-maximizing practices, while well-governed firms are more likely to follow CSR standards. The empirical studies testing these two theories have offered mixed results. See Ferrell, Liang and Renneboog 2016, 586.

[23] See Freeman, Harrison, Wicks et al. 2010, 4.

[24] Freeman 1984.

[25] Ibid., 1.

[26] Freeman, Harrison, Wicks et al. 2010, 4.

Stakeholder theory therefore was directed to solve the problem of the 'ethics of capitalism' and show how business can be managed 'to take full account of its effects on and responsibilities towards stakeholders'.[27] Indeed, such theory was developed and discussed within the normative business ethics literature and there are many reasons to see stakeholder theory 'as having a central place in business ethics (and vice versa)', also considering that 'values, a sense of purpose that goes beyond profitability, and concern for the well-being of stakeholders were critical to the origins of stakeholder theory'.[28] Also CSR scholars have used stakeholder theory to better specify and operationalize their concepts.[29] In fact, the stakeholder approach to strategic management requires abandoning the idea that shareholder value maximization is the exclusive purpose of the corporation and accepting that specific stakeholder interests should be considered in defining it.[30]

3.2.3 *Enlightened Shareholder Value*

In his seminal paper on value maximization and stakeholder theory, M. Jensen tried to reconcile the theoretical strands examined in the preceding two paragraphs by arguing that it is logically impossible to maximize in more than one dimension at the same time.[31] Consequently, a firm should specify the trade-offs amongst the various dimensions and then identify an 'objective function' that explicitly incorporates the positive and negative effects of decisions on the firm. In essence, a firm must have a single objective that tells the directors and managers what is better and what is worse. Jensen submitted that:

> 200 years' worth of work in economics and finance indicate that social welfare is maximized when all firms in an economy maximize total firm value. The intuition behind this criterion is simply that (social) value is created when a firm produces an output or set of outputs that are valued by its customers at more than the value of the inputs it consumes (as valued by their suppliers) in such production. Firm value is simply the long-term market value of this stream of benefits.[32]

Maximizing the total market value of the firm – that is, the sum of the market values of equity, debt and any other contingent claim on the firm – will resolve the trade-off problem amongst multiple constituencies.[33] To the extent that

---

[27] Ibid., 9.
[28] Ibid., 196.
[29] Ibid., 242, with reference to Wood 1991, 691.
[30] Freeman, Harrison, Wicks et al. 2010, 242.
[31] See Jensen 2002, who argued: 'telling a manager to maximize current profits, market share, future growth in profits, and anything else one pleases will leave that manager with no way to make a reasoned decision. In effect, it leaves the manager with no objective' (238).
[32] Ibid., 239, where it is also specified: 'When monopolies or externalities exist, the value-maximizing criterion does not maximize social welfare.'
[33] Ibid.

stakeholder theory argues that firms should pay attention to all their constituencies, it is completely consistent with value maximization, which also requires managers to pay attention to all constituencies, such as customers, employees, suppliers of capital, communities and so on. The objective function must specify how to make the trade-offs between the often-conflicting demands of these constituencies. In the words of Jensen, value maximization offers an answer to these trade-offs: 'Spend an additional dollar on any constituency to the extent that the long-term value added to the firm from such expenditure is a dollar or more.'[34]

Traditional stakeholder theory, in contrast, contains no conceptual specification of how to make the trade-offs amongst stakeholders, leaving boards of directors and executives without a principled criterion for problem solving. However, according to Jensen, the conflict between value maximization and stakeholder theory can be solved by melding together what he calls 'enlightened value maximization' and 'enlightened stakeholder theory'.[35] Value maximizing tells the participants in an organization how their success in achieving a vision or in implementing a strategy will be assessed. However, it does not say anything about how to create a superior vision or strategy and about how to find or establish initiatives or ventures that create value. It only tells how success in the activity will be measured. Therefore, employees and managers must be given a 'structure' that will help them to resist the temptation to maximize the short-term financial performance of the organization, which is a way to destroy value.

Enlightened stakeholder theory plays an important role by leading corporate managers and directors to think more generally and creatively about how the organization treats all constituencies of the firm; not only financial markets, but stakeholders in general.[36] Value cannot be created in the absence of good relations with customers, employees, investors, suppliers, regulators, communities and so on. Moreover, the value criterion can be used for choosing among those competing interests, because no constituency can be given full satisfaction if the firm is to flourish and survive.[37] However, as critically noted by Edmans, when decisions are instrumental 'they'll be made only on the basis of outcomes that can be quantified with some degree of accuracy. But most important outcomes can't be quantified.'[38]

---

[34] Ibid.

[35] Ibid., 245.

[36] Ibid.

[37] Ibid., 246, where it is also stated that Enlightened stakeholder theory includes the processes and audits to measure and evaluate the firm's management of its relations with all important constituencies, while specifying that the objective function of the firm is to maximize total long-term firm market value. In fact, changes in total long-term market value of the firm are the scorecard by which success is measured. The reference to long-term market value is justified by the fact that markets may not know the full implications of a firm's policies until they show up in cash flows over time. Markets will recognize the real value of the firm's decisions as they become evidenced in market share, employee loyalty and finally cash flows and risk.

[38] Edmans 2020, 45.

This is particularly true for intangible assets like stakeholder capital: 'The returns to intangibles aren't only *uncertain*, but also *distant* – even if they do arise, they will be far into the future.'[39]

3.2.4 *Shared Value*

Shared value is an interesting specification of ESV which seems particularly relevant to the discussion on sustainable governance. In a highly influential paper of 2011, Porter and Kramer essentially propose to merge the two concepts of shareholder value and societal value into one of 'shared value'.[40] The latter concept refers to creating economic value in a way that also creates value for society by addressing its needs and challenges. The two authors argue that in the old view of capitalism, business contributed to society by generating a surplus, which supports employment, wages, purchases, investments and taxes. The firm is a self-contained entity and social issues fall outside its proper scope, as argued by Milton Friedman in his critique of CSR.[41] Today, a growing number of companies make important efforts to create shared value by 'reconceiving the intersection between society and corporate performance'.[42]

The purpose of the corporation should therefore be redefined in terms of shared value, not just profit. The new concept includes the policies and operating practices that enhance the competitiveness of a company while simultaneously advancing the economic and social conditions in the communities in which it operates.[43] The underlying premise is that both economic and social progress must be addressed through value principles, i.e., by looking at benefits relative to costs. Value creating has long been recognized in business, where profit is revenues earned from customers minus the costs incurred.[44] However, societal issues have rarely been approached from a value perspective.

Rebecca Henderson similarly argues that a new conception of capitalism can be grounded on 'shared value'. In fact, the evidence supports 'a business case for creating shared value or for treating people well and reducing environmental damage'.[45] She considers particularly three cases of large companies which have shown how business and therefore capitalism can be rethought. The first is Unilever's switching to the distribution of 100 per cent sustainably grown tea under the Lipton brand, which took place after the beginning of this century and was motivated by risk management and marketing considerations. One reason was that ensuring the supply of

---

[39] Ibid., 46.
[40] Porter and Kramer 2011, 3.
[41] Ibid., 6.
[42] Ibid., 4.
[43] Ibid., 6.
[44] Ibid.
[45] Henderson 2020, 49.

tea would reduce the firm's exposure to risk, given that the prevailing practices of growing tea – such as deforestation and large-scale application of insecticides, pesticides and fertilizers – were putting the entire viability of the supply chain at risk.[46] Another argument also concerned risk exposure on the supply chain, with particular regard to the grim working conditions on conventional tea plantations: tea workers were often paid less than $1 a day and many suffered from inadequate housing and sanitation.[47] The third argument stated that embracing sustainability would increase consumer demand for Unilever's teas. Indeed, most consumers are not willing to pay more for sustainable products, which are seen by most of them as something 'nice to have' rather than a 'must have'.[48] However, 'if they find a product that they like – one that ticks all the right boxes in terms of quality, price, and functionality – then many of them will switch to the more sustainable product'.[49] As a result of this and other initiatives, 'in June 2019, Unilever announced that its "sustainable living" brands were growing 69 percent faster that the rest of the business and generating 75 percent of the company's growth'.[50]

The second case referred to by Henderson is that of Walmart, the gigantic retail company, which over thirty years reinvented its business, developing skills in logistics, purchasing and distribution that led to it becoming one of the largest companies in the world.[51] After being increasingly under fire for anti-union activities, gender discrimination, employment of illegal immigrants, child labour etc., Walmart decided to take a strong stance on corporate responsibility.[52] As a result of its sustainability programmes, the company found to its surprise that saving energy was making it gain a great amount of money: 'By 2017 Walmart had met its goal of doubling the transportation fleet's efficiency and was saving more than a billion dollars a year in transportation costs – around 4 percent of net income.'[53] While at Unilever building a sustainable business model meant identifying fundamental shifts in consumer behaviour, Walmart's success came from focussing on the everyday operational details of its business from the profoundly different perspective of sustainability: 'In its way, Walmart's commitment was just as transformative as Lipton's.'[54]

The third business case concerns renewable energy and in particular CLP, one of the largest investor-owned utilities in Asia. CLP announced in 2004 that 5 per cent of its power would come by 2010 from renewables and in 2007 reiterated that 20

---

[46] Ibid., 52.
[47] Ibid., 53.
[48] Ibid., 54.
[49] Ibid., 59.
[50] Ibid.
[51] Ibid., 60.
[52] Ibid., 62.
[53] Ibid., 64.
[54] Ibid., 64–65.

per cent of its generating capacity would be carbon-free by 2020.[55] In 2013 the CEO of CLP explained the company's strategy by saying: 'We see carbon as a long-term threat to any business. In 2050, if you are a carbon-intensive business, you are in big trouble; chances are you won't be in business by then.'[56] Henderson comments that 'the flip side of risk is opportunity … moving to carbon-free energy ahead of the competition was potentially an exceedingly attractive business opportunity'.[57] Subsequent events have proven this assumption to be correct, as alternative energies like solar and wind are already in some places cheaper than coal.

Henderson concludes the case studies just summarized by noting that there is enormous opportunity to create shared value.[58] By addressing environmental and social problems firms can build successful new businesses (CLP), reduce their costs (Walmart) and ensure long-term sustainability of their supply chains while increasing demand for their products (Unilever).[59]

3.3 CRITIQUE OF ENLIGHTENED SHAREHOLDER VALUE

ESV has been criticized from two different perspectives. Some scholars argue that ESV is nothing but traditional shareholder value, while others emphasize the role of social value in corporate governance, criticize ESV as too narrow and propose an approach grounded on social value primacy. After considering both types of criticism, I suggest a third view under which ESV is complemented by business ethics and regulation.

3.3.1 *Radical Shareholder Value*

Lucian Bebchuk and Roberto Tallarita warn against the growing acceptance of stakeholderism.[60] Their opposition to this rising trend in corporate governance is unconditional. Stakeholderism should not be expected to benefit stakeholders; on the contrary, it would impose substantial costs on them and society, as well as on shareholders.[61] The two authors argue that corporate leaders have strong incentives to enhance shareholder value, but little incentive to treat stakeholder interest as an end. Corporations will pursue stakeholder interests only to the extent that it is

---

[55] Ibid., 65.
[56] Ibid., 69.
[57] Ibid.
[58] Ibid., 82.
[59] Ibid.
[60] Bebchuk and Tallarita 2020, 93; Bebchuk, Kastiel and Tallarita 2022. In a similar direction, see Gatti and Ondersma 2020, 2, focussing, however, on stakeholderism's incapacity to redress inequality. The authors aim to demonstrate that a stakeholder approach can do nothing to ameliorate inequality concerns and suggest a multidisciplinary framework to evaluate policies inside and outside corporate governance.
[61] Bebchuk and Tallarita 2020, 96.

beneficial to shareholders. In addition, stakeholderism makes corporate leaders less accountable by insulating them from shareholder pressures, as the support of corporate leaders for stakeholderism is motivated, at least in part, by a desire to obtain insulation from hedge fund activists and institutional investors.[62]

Bebchuk, Kastiel, and Tallarita distinguish between two types of stakeholderism: the 'enlightened shareholder value' (ESV) approach and the 'pluralistic approach'.[63] They define the former as 'instrumental stakeholderism' but suggest that it is not different to shareholder value *tout court*. In their opinion, whenever treating stakeholders well is useful for long-term shareholder value maximization, such treatment would be called for under either ESV or shareholder value.[64] They ask what the reason could be for switching to ESV and offer some possible explanations. One is that referring to stakeholder effects has 'informational and educational value' for the board and management of corporations.[65] However, they argue that there is no evidence that corporate leaders have systematically underestimated the stakeholders' effects on shareholder value maximization, finding therefore no reason for educating the same. Another reason is that ESV provides 'moral support and practical coverage for directors who wish to offer some benefit to stakeholders at the expense of shareholders'.[66] They object nonetheless that also under 'old-fashioned' shareholder value directors would be able to justify a stakeholder-friendly decision on the basis that it would contribute to long-term value maximization. A further reason is that the move to ESV would improve the way in which corporations are perceived by outsiders and therefore produce positive reputational effects.[67] Nevertheless, they argue that such a move could have significant adverse effects by reducing demand for meaningful legal and regulatory reforms that could effectively protect stakeholders.

I submit that their objections are important but not decisive. Firstly, the fact that directors and managers already consider stakeholder interests that are instrumental to long-term shareholder value maximization does not deprive ESV of educational value. In fact, reiterating the benefits of similar behaviour is not costly and may be beneficial in some cases. Secondly, the fact that not only ESV, but also 'old-fashioned' shareholder value allow directors and managers to act in the interest of selected stakeholders when their actions are in the long-term interest of shareholders is insufficient to discard ESV, which is different to shareholder value exactly for its emphasis on the long-term, enlightened view of the corporation. Thirdly, there are no doubt reputational advantages from the corporations' acting in the interest of selected stakeholders, but this should not necessarily lead legislators to exclude or limit stakeholder protection, especially when the incentives for

[62] Ibid., 100–101.
[63] Bebchuk, Kastiel and Tallarita 2022.
[64] Ibid., 3 ff.
[65] Ibid., 22 ff.
[66] Ibid., 28.
[67] Ibid., 25 ff.

corporations to further the interest of given stakeholders at the expense of share-holders' short-term interest are low.

Bebchuk, Kastiel, and Tallarita describe the second version of stakeholderism as one treating 'stakeholder welfare as an end in itself rather than a mere means'. It is a 'pluralistic approach' because it requires directors to weigh and balance a plurality of autonomous ends. They see several conceptual problems arising in this respect. The first is to identify the stakeholder groups whose interests should be considered. The term 'stakeholders' usually refers to individuals who are affected by corporate decisions; however, 'for many companies, the set of individuals who are directly or indirectly affected by the activities of the corporation is very large indeed'.[68] Deciding which stakeholders should be especially considered is difficult, and the criteria for taking this type of determinations are often impossible to establish *ex ante*. As a result, much discretion is left to directors, who are therefore free to choose which interests should be prioritised and for what reasons. Moreover, the two authors note that 'potential trade-offs between shareholders and stakeholders are ubiquitous', and that the criteria for solving them are often left unexplored by stakeholderists.[69]

This critique of stakeholderism has solid grounds, given the risk that the interests of stakeholders will unduly prevail over those of shareholders even on a long-term view, if the decision criteria are not specified *ex ante* and the corporate decision makers want to advantage selected stakeholders. However, managerial actions can be justified on a sound basis even when they cannot be justified on economic grounds.[70] As argued below, ethical norms may be applicable to managerial choices which protect given stakeholders, such as employees or local communities. These norms are known in advance, for they are either stated in the companies' codes of conduct or included in the international soft law which applies to multinational corporations. Their application can be monitored also by external observers and assessed with reference to the relevant standards. The discretion of boards and managers is limited as a result and the risk that shareholders' interests are neglected is consequently reduced. Moreover, only shareholders are entitled to appoint directors and are therefore able to prevent directors' and managers' repeated deviations from their interests. This should work as a disincentive for disproportionate protection of stakeholders' interests by the corporation.

3.3.2 *Social Value Primacy*

A different view of the trade-offs between firm value and social value is expressed by Alex Edmans in *Grow the Pie*.[71] The pie represents the value that an enterprise

---

[68] Ibid., 18.
[69] Ibid., 20.
[70] See, in general on this topic, Sandel 2012, 47 ff.
[71] See Edmans 2020.

creates for society. The different members of society capture different slices of the pie, depending on what strategy management chooses to adopt. They are investors on one side and stakeholders (customers, employees, suppliers, environment, government and communities) on the other. Investors enjoy profits, but the pie includes more than profits. It includes the value that an enterprise gives to its employees, 'their pay, but also training, advancement opportunities, job security, and the ability to pursue a vocation and make a profound impact on the world'.[72]

The pie also includes the value that customers enjoy over and above the price they pay ('surplus'). Moreover, it includes the value accruing to suppliers through a stable source of revenue.[73] Furthermore, the pie includes the value provided to the environment, by reducing resource consumption and carbon emissions. In addition, it includes the value enjoyed by communities, as an enterprise provides employment opportunities, contributes to schools, donates its knowledge or products to local initiatives, etc. Lastly, the pie includes the value given to the government through tax revenues. On the whole, stakeholders enjoy value, while investors enjoy profits which are a form of value.

Edmans defines the traditional approach to his topic as 'pie-splitting mentality'. Such approach views the pie as being fixed in size, so that the only way to increase one member's share of the pie is to split it differently. Since the pie is fixed, at least in the short term, the only way to maximize profits is by taking from stakeholders.[74] Pie-splitting can be done almost immediately at zero cost. Enterprises can take surplus from customers either by 'price-gouging' or by pushing products that customers don't need or don't understand.[75] They can also exploit employees – e.g., by paying workers below the minimum wage – or squeeze suppliers by paying them as late as possible.[76]

The new approach suggested by Edmans – which he dubs 'pie-growing mentality' – sees the pie as expandable 'to create value for society ... Profits, then, are no longer the end goal, but instead arise as a by-product of creating value (...).'[77] Investors do not need to take from stakeholders, and stakeholders don't need to defend themselves from investors. Edmans uses the term *Pieconomics* to capture 'an approach to business that seeks to create profits only through creating value for society'.[78] His views differ from traditional CSR, which in his opinion typically refers to activities such as charitable contributions. *Pieconomics* rather ensures that the

---

[72] Ibid., 19.

[73] Ibid., arguing that 'what matters is not only how much money suppliers receive, but how promptly they're paid'.

[74] Ibid., 20.

[75] Ibid., 23, noting that from 1990 until the mid-2010s, UK banks sold payment protection insurance to customers who took out mortgages, loans and credit cards. This insurance had the potential to create value by repaying customers' debts if they lost their jobs or became ill, but it was mis-sold.

[76] Ibid.

[77] Ibid., 26.

[78] Ibid.

primary mission of the core business is to serve society. Being a responsible business isn't about splitting the pie differently (e.g., sacrificing profits to reduce carbon emissions), but about growing the pie by innovating and being excellent at its own business. Indeed, enterprises often fail to serve society not by giving too much to leaders or investors, but by failing to grow the pie by sticking to the status quo.[79]

Pieconomics has many similarities with ESV. Both highlight the criticality of companies investing in their stakeholders. Both argue that investor value and stakeholder value are highly correlated in the long run. Both stress the importance of profits. However, ESV assumes that an enterprise's ultimate goal is to increase long-term profits, while Pieconomics claims that an enterprise should create value for society and profits will increase as a by-product. Profits are an outcome, not a goal.[80] Moreover, Pieconomics takes externalities into account, while ESV considers only profits. As stated in the previous paragraph, most actions creating social value will increase long-run profits, but a few will not. Pieconomics claims that corporate leaders should go beyond their legal responsibility to shareholders and care about externalities. Investors care about externalities not only due to being stakeholders themselves, but also for altruistic reasons. As argued by Hart and Zingales, shareholder welfare includes not only shareholder value, but also externalities.[81] Indeed, these externalities are becoming increasingly important to investors who largely invest under Socially Responsible Investing (SRI) strategies, which choose stocks on social rather than purely financial criteria.[82] Even many mainstream investors, who are not classified as 'socially responsible', take externalities very seriously.[83]

3.3.3 *Our Approach*

ESV has been widely adopted in policy discussions and in corporate practice, possibly with variations like those suggested by the 'shared value' approach. However,

---

[79] Ibid., 27.

[80] Edmans 2020 concedes that ESV is better than Pieconomics under two angles. Firstly, ESV is 'concrete', having a single, clear objective: to increase long-term profit. Pieconomics has multiple objectives and therefore does not offer a clear-cut way to take decisions: ibid., 43. Secondly, ESV is 'focused'. A company practising ESV will only take an action if it boosts its profits. It won't spend millions on reducing emissions if they're already below the level that would lead to a fine, whereas a pie-growing enterprise might do so, simply to help the environment and such actions may reduce profits. Edmans argues, nonetheless, that the pie-growing mentality is preferable because it is 'intrinsic' rather than 'instrumental'. Under ESV, a company should only create value for stakeholders if this increases profits in the long term. In other words, for ESV an enterprise should be instrumentally motivated to create profits, whereas for Pieconomics it should be intrinsically motivated to create social value.

[81] Hart and Zingales 2017, 247.

[82] Ibid., 53.

[83] Ibid., arguing that 'Across all investors, 2,372, representing $86.3 trillion of assets, had signed the UN Principles for Responsible Investment – a commitment to incorporate environmental, social and governance (ESG) issues into investment decisions – by March 2019. That's substantially higher than the 63 investors and $6.5 trillion of assets when the principles were founded in 2006.'

ESV needs reviewing today in the light of the current discussion on stakeholder capitalism. Indeed, stakeholder protection should not be seen exclusively as instrumental to long-term value maximization – as narrowly suggested by ESV – but also as an outcome of the compliance with legal rules and ethical standards, which apply to different types of firms and aim to internalize externalities that either directly or indirectly derive from their activities. In a rising number of situations firms internalize externalities not only because it is profitable in the long run or at least suitable to reduce their risk exposures, but also to comply with the regulatory and ethical standards that protect relevant stakeholders, as I argue below under Section 3.5.[84]

Business ethics and regulation complement ESV leading to outcomes similar to those suggested by Pieconomics. As argued by Edmans, 'enlightened shareholder value believes an enterprise should be *instrumentally* motivated to create profits, whereas Pieconomics believes it should be *intrinsically* motivated to create social value'.[85] In our approach, the motivation of the managers to internalize externalities often derives from business ethics and soft law (mainly incorporating ethical standards) and/or regulation. The fact that corporate managers instrumentally motivated to create profits internalize externalities confirms that ESV and business ethics/regulation are complementary. Indeed, managers pursue profits whether we define them as a primary or secondary goal of the firm, while reference to social values is a powerful motivator of people in the firm, as we shall see in Section 4.2.

3.4 ROLE OF CORPORATE GOVERNANCE

Recent scholarship has further developed the social instances expressed by traditional CSR and stakeholder theory in works leveraging corporate governance and organizational theory, as I show in this section.

3.4.1 *Corporate Governance as Governance of Purpose*

Colin Mayer's *Prosperity* reformulates stakeholder theory from a corporate governance perspective by emphasizing the role that the latter can play in redefining corporate purpose.[86] His 'enlightened corporations' balance and integrate the six

---

[84] Interestingly, these regulatory and ethical constraints on firm behaviour do not necessarily determine a reduction in firm value. Some empirical studies on the relationship between CSR and economic performance rather prove the opposite. Ferrell, Liang and Renneboog 2016, 585 find that well-governed firms that suffer less from agency concerns engage more in CSR and have higher CSR ratings. They also find that a positive relation exists between CSR and value, suggesting at least that CSR is not inconsistent with shareholder value maximization. Their general argument is interesting for present purposes: 'Corporate social responsibility need not to be inevitably induced by agency problems but can be consistent with a core value of capitalism, generating more returns to investors, through enhancing firm value and shareholder wealth'.

[85] Ibid., 44.

[86] Mayer 2018; more recently Mayer 2022.

components of capital that ground business activities: human, intellectual, material, natural, social and financial capital.[87] Mayer believes that it is wrong to protect shareholders by emphasizing their rights and powers and viewing the corporation as their instrument. However, it would be wrong to transfer control of the corporation to stakeholders such as creditors, customers or employees, for this would make it difficult to raise capital. Mayer rather suggests enhancing the separation of management control from ownership of the firm and focussing on the fiduciary responsibility of directors to the members of the corporation.[88] This is what Hansmann and Kraakman define as the 'trustee model' of stakeholder governance, distinguishing it from the 'representative model'.[89] Both models address the problem of protecting non-shareholder interests in the corporation. However, under the representative model qualified non-shareholder constituencies appoint their own directors, who together elaborate policies that maximize the joint welfare of all stakeholders, subject to the bargaining between different groups in the boardroom. Under the trustee model the board of directors and the senior managers act on behalf of the enterprise by co-ordinating the contributions and returns of all its stakeholders.

In Mayer's proposed model, directors balance the interests of shareholders with those of creditors, employees, customers and communities, in pursuit of the long-term prosperity of the corporation. In fact, an excessive focus either on shareholders' returns or on stakeholder interests would jeopardize the delicate balance between present members and future generations.[90] He assigns to the board the role of defining and implementing corporate purpose and of monitoring the firm's commitment to it. In his theory, corporate purpose should be defined by contract and fiduciary duties should be based on the corporate purpose so defined. This would originate trust in the corporation by its members. The solution proposed is clearly grounded on private law, as Mayer argues that regulation has been a failure because the interests of regulators are opposed to those of shareholders. Company law should be reformed to replace regulation, which would require redefining corporate purpose and avoiding its identification with the pursuit of profit.

Mayer describes corporate governance as 'governance of purpose', while defining purpose as 'the reason for a company's existence'.[91] However, 'corporate governance is not and should not be about enhancing shareholder value'.[92] The correct focus of corporate governance should be about how all aspects of ownership, boards and

---

[87] Ibid.

[88] Ibid.

[89] See Hansmann and Kraakman 2001, 439.

[90] A similar argument was advanced by Blair and Stout 1999, 247, who focussed attention on the mediating role of the boards of directors. See also Blair 2015, 257.

[91] Mayer 2018, 109. He also argues that companies exist to do things, not simply to make profits: 'The purpose of companies is to produce solutions to problems of people and planet and in the process to produce profits, but profits are not per se the purpose of companies'.

[92] Ibid., 113.

remuneration promote corporate purpose and the success of companies. A company's customers should comprise all its consumers, communities and citizens. In this way, corporate governance enhances economic growth, entrepreneurship, innovation and value creation. It may also lead to increased shareholder value; but in an inversion of the traditional ranking, 'purpose is primary and shareholder value derivative'.[93] This last statement reflects the widespread and well-known criticism of the shareholder value philosophy. However, similar criticism is usually addressed to managerial excesses in the pursuit of corporate profits, particularly short-term profits, rather than to the practice of long-term value maximization, which also considers stakeholders' interests.

If we take the suggested 'inversion' literally – purpose is primary and shareholder value derivative – Mayer's theory appears to be a radical version of stakeholder theory. Under the prevailing theory, stakeholders' interests are satisfied subject to long-term shareholder value maximization, whereas Mayer subordinates shareholder value maximization to the realization of corporate purpose. Therefore, shareholder wealth is not necessarily maximized when corporate purpose, as announced in the corporate charter, is fulfilled. Indeed, there might be cases in which the activities required by the commitment to corporate purpose are pursued by the managers even in the absence of a foreseeable long-term value maximization.

While sharing Mayer's view on the importance of corporate governance to corporate purpose, I believe that regulation should have a greater say in disciplining corporations than Mayer suggests. We cannot expect firms to fully internalize the social costs of their externalities in areas like, for instance, climate change or corruption. Similarly, we cannot rely on corporate governance and shareholders as the main instruments to preserve the integrity of corporations. We need regulation and to some extent criminal law to obtain compliance with the legal principles protecting the environment and the social conditions within the firms. No doubt, corporate governance and ownership (including institutional investors and controlling shareholders) can contribute to effective compliance and are therefore good complements to regulation, but we should not expect them to become substitutes for it. Environmental and social issues are, for many aspects, like the stability and systemic issues generated by financial institutions, which are widely dealt with under financial regulation.

3.4.2 *Organizational Purpose as Key to Change*

An organizational perspective on corporate purpose is offered by Rebecca Henderson in *Re-imagining Capitalism*, where she argues that, in addition to shared value, organizational purpose is key to change.[94] The reasons for it are grounded on organizational

---

[93] Ibid., 114.
[94] Henderson 2020, 83.

psychology, as purpose 'aligns everyone in the organization around a common mission'; 'it gives everyone a reason to work toward the goals of the organization as a whole'; 'it unleashes ... creativity, trust and sheer excitement'.[95] Henderson acknowledges the importance of 'extrinsic' motivation – such as that deriving from money, status and power – but argues that 'intrinsic' motivation is often more powerful.[96] 'Shared purpose' makes people in the organization feel that their work has 'meaning', 'creates a strong sense of identity' and enhances 'positive emotions'.[97]

This is the language of behavioural science and motivational theory. We know that human motivation has at least three drivers: autonomy, mastery and purpose.[98] As argued by Daniel Pink, 'autonomous people working toward mastery perform at very high levels. But those who do so in the service of some greater objective can achieve even more. The most motivated people ... hitch their desires to a cause larger than themselves.'[99] If we translate these concepts into the language of business, we recognize that 'the profit motive, potent though it is, can be an insufficient impetus for both individuals and organizations'.[100] To sum up, the organizational perspective followed by Henderson is grounded on motivational theory, while corporate purpose plays the role of a powerful motivator. However, her approach does not exclude the ethical perspective that we follow in this chapter. Rather, business ethics contributes to defining corporate purpose together with organizational psychology but does not eliminate profit from its scope given the need to remunerate financial capital.

3.4.3 *Sustainability and Duty of Loyalty*

Mayer's 'governance of purpose' reflects one of the main tenets of comparative corporate governance, which is the role of the board of directors in setting corporate purpose together with the company's mission and values.[101] This is recognized

---

[95] Ibid., 92.

[96] Ibid.

[97] Ibid., 93.

[98] See Pink 2009, 85 ff.

[99] Ibid., 133. Mihaly Csikszentmihaly, the great psychologist, similarly remarked: 'In the lives of many people it is possible to find a unifying purpose that justifies the things they do day in, day out – a goal that like a magnetic field attracts their psychic energy, a goal upon which all lesser goals depend'. See Csikszentmihalyi 1990, 218.

[100] Pink 2009, 134. See also Hamel 2007, 76. He refers to Whole Food Market, a company with a game-changing business model and the following corporate purpose: 'to reverse the industrialization of the world's food supply and give people better things to eat' (ibid., 77). Its CEO 'sees profits as a means to the end of realizing Whole Foods' social goals'. In 2005 he wrote: 'We want to improve the health and well-being of everyone on the planet through higher quality food and better nutrition'; but also specified: 'We can't fulfil this mission unless we are very profitable.'

[101] See Gelter and Helleringer 2015, arguing that since corporate law does not provide a clear and enforceable objective, the interest of the corporation, however defined, becomes primarily the outcome of board deliberations (at 1114).

by national corporate governance codes and goes together with the deliberation of corporate strategies which is also one of the core competences of the board.[102] Henderson's 'organizational purpose' similarly focusses on corporate governance and organization as a powerful transmission chain of mission and values to the whole company, in addition to underlying the motivational aspects of corporate purpose.

Environmental and social sustainability are generally included in the formulation of corporate purpose and further described in related documents approved by the board of directors, such as the statement on non-financial disclosure. Sustainability is considered from two different angles under the concept of double materiality.[103] One underlines the impact of externalities on the firm ('outside-in'), which can be damaged either by climate change and other environmental events or by social problems affecting its reputation, like those regarding its employees (e.g., gender discrimination) and clients (e.g., confidentiality breaches in services offered by social networks).[104] The other angle ('inside-out') regards externalities that are caused by the firm to the outside world. They can also damage the firm; however, this does not necessarily internalize them.

In principle, corporate actions that reduce or eliminate negative externalities to the environment and society should be performed only if they respond to the interest of the company and its shareholders. Under the ESV model, which is accepted in several jurisdictions,[105] such a requirement is complied with whenever the corporate actions maximize the long-term value of the company while benefitting specific stakeholders. Under the shared value approach, the relevant actions produce economic value for the firm and societal value at the same time, in ways that allow the total pie to be distributed in greater amounts to shareholders and stakeholders.

However, actions that may have a negative impact on the firm's long-term value are also justified from the duty of loyalty perspective if they respond to ethical norms, such as those recognized by the standards issued by international organizations. Indeed, the company should not only maximize its long-term economic value, but also behave as a good corporate citizen and comply with the legal and moral

---

[102] Principle 1 of the UK Corporate Governance Code (2018) states: '1. A successful company is led by an effective and entrepreneurial board, whose role is to promote the long-term sustainable success of the company, generating value for shareholders and contributing to wider society. 2. The board should establish the company's purpose, values and strategy, and satisfy itself that these and its culture are aligned. All directors must act with integrity, lead by example and promote the desired culture (...).'

[103] The concept of 'double-materiality' was first formally proposed by the European Commission, Guidelines on Non-financial Reporting: Supplement on Reporting Climate-related Information, published in June 2019. It encourages a company to judge materiality from two perspectives: (1) 'the extent necessary for an understanding of the company's development, performance and position' and 'in the broad sense of affecting the value of the company'; (2) environmental and social impact of the company's activities on a broad range of stakeholders. See GRI 2021.

[104] See Gadinis and Miazad 2020, 1410.

[105] See for references Ferrarini 2021, 108 ff.

standards of the international community. Similarly, the board's deliberations, which are recommended by CSR best practices, should be considered as being in the company's interest and therefore in compliance with the duty of loyalty even if their net impact on firm value is negative.[106] Indeed, the roles of the board and of management should not be reduced to dry numerical analyses of the impact of pro-stakeholder actions on the long-term value of the company, considering also that the long-term impact of those actions may be difficult to measure. Moral considerations should rather be pondered and acted upon even when they may result in a negative impact on firm value, especially if they improve corporate reputation or enhance the firm's resilience in the long term.

The primacy of social value over shareholder value proposed by Edmans and Mayer leads to similar consequences, but risks undermining the corporation as a capitalist institution which only survives by being profitable. In my proposed view, the need for long-term value maximization still characterizes the business corporation, with the important specification, however, that the latter should act as a good corporate citizen, i.e., in compliance with CSR best practices and the ethical requirements regarding corporations in general and their specific business activities.[107] In addition, my proposal emphasizes the role of regulation in minimizing the negative externalities caused by the corporation, a task which is increasingly relevant in the current quest to protect people and planet from business and its negative impacts.

3.5 ROLE OF ETHICS AND REGULATION

We should therefore deepen our understanding of ethics and regulation in complementing corporate purpose to enhance both firm value and social value. Corporations are managed by human beings who have their own ethical standards. However, corporations generally clarify the ethical standards that they expect their managers to comply with and formalize the same in corporate documents such as codes of ethics and codes of conduct. In addition, they enforce such standards by monitoring their employees' compliance with them and sanctioning their breaches. Moreover, firms' ethical standards are usually reflected in the corporate culture, which further specifies them and eases their adoption by employees. Indeed, corporate culture establishes the conditions for compliance with ethical standards, furthering mutual respect for employees who abide by those standards and shame for those who violate them.[108]

In addition, the ethical standards regarding business activities and their stakeholders are often crystallized in international soft law documents and/or regulation. In

---

[106] See notes 22 and 83 above.
[107] On the concept of corporate citizenship, see Crew and Matten 2016, 69.
[108] See Ferrarini and Zhu 2019, 381.

this section, I show how maximizing firms' value is often conditional upon ethical and/or regulatory constraints that force enterprises to internalize some of the externalities produced in their activities. Firstly, I consider the standards issued by international organizations and adopted by firms voluntarily; secondly, I examine the standards endorsed by regulation, with special reference to corporate due diligence, which was traditionally subject to international soft law and may now become hard law in the EU.

3.5.1 *Soft Law for Multinationals*

Many actions are performed by firms, particularly the large ones, in compliance with standards of conduct that have been issued by international organizations and subscribed by individual firms for the protection of their stakeholders, such as the UN Global Compact, the OECD Guidelines for Multinational Enterprises and the International Labour Organization standards. These documents are not binding per se, but their principles are often reflected in the applicable national laws and for the rest may be followed voluntarily by corporations, especially when their managers have officially committed to respect high standards of conduct.

Notwithstanding the non-binding nature of similar standards and their limited enforcement, large companies' policies and practices increasingly comply with them and respond to investors' growing attention to the ESG performance of investee companies, including the formal adoption of due diligence in line with international standards. In the sustainable investment strategies usually followed by institutional investors, the 'norm-based screening' – which screens issuers against minimum standards of business practice based on international frameworks – is one of the most commonly used for portfolio selection.[109] Moreover, common voluntary standards have been developed, targeting investor stewardship obligations (such as the ICGN Global Stewardship principles and the EFAMA Stewardship Code)[110] or sustainable investment (such as the Principles for Responsible Investing),[111] which put further pressure on investors with regard to the sustainability-related initiatives and policies of investee companies.

The voluntary application of international standards is also motivated by reputational concerns and by the personal conviction of the managers about the morality of the actions in question. Therefore, as in the case of regulation, the calculus of instrumentalism promoted by ESV and similar theories may be 'indirect' or even absent, as the protection of stakeholders simply derives from the compliance with the relevant standards. In other words, the managers do not necessarily compare the shareholders' interests with those of given stakeholders, nor ask to what extent

---

[109] See https://bit.ly/49BGK2S. See also Eurosif 2018.
[110] Alvaro, Maugeri and Strampelli 2019, 19.
[111] Kim and Yoon 2020.

protecting the latter will enhance the long-term value of the firm, given that their action is required per se under the international standards. Of course, to the extent that discretion is left to the managers under the individual standard – particularly if the latter is broadly formulated and there are no implementing provisions – the managers will also consider the impact of their actions on the long-term value of the firm. But they might primarily decide on moral grounds, filling their discretion in a way that they deem consistent with the content and spirit of the standard to apply.

Reputational concerns will also be at play, especially in situations where either consumers or investors monitor the firm's compliance with the relevant standards. The increasing importance of sustainability multiplies this type of situations, given that not all aspects of sustainable growth are specifically dealt with by regulation. Moreover, the urgency of the problems involved requires the active cooperation of corporations, which increasingly follow (or at least declare to follow) the international guidelines and standards both in environmental and social matters. Sustainability can therefore be seen as a game changer, to the extent that not only regulation, but also conduct guidelines and ethical standards operate as constraints on the behaviour of enterprises and their pursuit of profits.[112]

3.5.2 *Main International Standards*

The UN Guiding Principles on Business and Human Rights [UN Guiding Principles] deserve special mention.[113] They provide standards for both states and business enterprises to prevent, address and remedy human rights abuses committed in business operations. The UN Guiding Principles include 14 principles specifically addressing the responsibilities of business enterprises in relation to the respect of human rights and provide a set of operational recommendations ranging from the issuance of a specific policy on human rights to the performance of a human rights due diligence and the provision of remedies to the adverse impacts the company has caused or has contributed to generating with its actions. The Human Rights Council formally endorsed the Principles in 2011 and to date at least 377 large companies adopted a formal statement explicitly referring to human rights in compliance with Principle 16 of the UN Guiding Principles on Business and Human Rights.[114] Unlike the UN Guiding Principles, the UN Global Compact is an initiative that global corporations can commit to by respecting 10 key principles of business behaviour in human rights, labour, the environment and corruption.[115] Currently, the UN Global Compact counts more than 12,000 signatories in over 160 countries covering all business sectors.[116]

---

[112] See Ferrarini 2021.
[113] The Principles are available at: https://bit.ly/3SDxxQR.
[114] See https://bit.ly/3uBttIV.
[115] See www.unglobalcompact.org/what-is-gc/mission/principles.
[116] See www.unglobalcompact.org/what-is-gc/participants.

The UN Guiding Principles deal with the corporate responsibility to respect
human rights. Amongst the 'foundational principles', Principle 11 states that business enterprises should respect human rights, while Principle 12 specifies that their
responsibility refers to internationally recognized human rights. Under Principle
13, business enterprises are required to '(a) avoid causing or contributing to adverse
human rights impacts through their own activities, and address such impacts when
they occur; (b) seek to prevent or mitigate adverse human rights impacts that are
directly linked to their operations, products or services by their business relationships, even if they have not contributed to those impacts.' Principle 15 further specifies that:

> business enterprises should have in place policies and processes appropriate to
> their size and circumstances, including: (a) a policy commitment to meet their
> responsibility to respect human rights; (b) a human rights due diligence process
> to identify, prevent, mitigate and account for how they address their impacts on
> human rights; (c) processes to enable the remediation of any adverse human rights
> impacts they cause or to which they contribute.

Amongst the 'operational principles', Principle 16 deals with the 'policy commitment' of business enterprises,[117] while Principle 17 provides for 'human rights
due diligence', which is directed to 'identify, prevent, mitigate and account for
how [business enterprises] address their adverse human rights impacts'. Human
rights due diligence should cover 'adverse human rights impacts that the business
enterprise may cause or contribute to through its own activities, or which may be
directly linked to its operations, products or services by its business relationships.'
Interestingly, the commentary to this Principle states: 'Human rights due diligence
can be included within broader enterprise risk-management systems, provided that
it goes beyond simply identifying and managing material risks to the company itself,
to include risks to rights-holders.'

The OECD Guidelines for Multinational Enterprises, firstly adopted in 1976,
are also important.[118] They consist of a set of voluntary standards and principles
for responsible business conduct addressed to multinational enterprises operating
in or from the adhering countries. Specifically, the latest version of the OECD
Guidelines was adopted in 2011 by the 42 OECD and non-OECD governments
adhering to the OECD Declaration on International Investment and Multinational

---

[117] 'As the basis for embedding their responsibility to respect human rights, business enterprises should
express their commitment to meet this responsibility through a statement of policy that: (a) is approved
at the most senior level of the business enterprise; (b) is informed by relevant internal and/or external
expertise; (c) stipulates the enterprise's human rights expectations of personnel, business partners
and other parties directly linked to its operations, products or services; (d) is publicly available and
communicated internally and externally to all personnel, business partners and other relevant parties;
(e) is reflected in operational policies and procedures necessary to embed it throughout the business
enterprise.'

[118] They are available at http://mneguidelines.oecd.org/guidelines/.

Enterprises, and today 49 governments have established a National Contact Point with the duty of ensuring the effectiveness of the OECD Guidelines by undertaking promotional activities, handling enquiries and providing a grievance mechanism to resolve cases with regard to the non-observance of the recommendations. The OECD Guidelines cover a diverse range of topics related to business behaviour, from company disclosure and reporting on financial, social and environmental material information to respect for employees, human rights, the environment, consumers' interest and the fight against bribery and other illicit conducts, as well as the promotion of science and technology development, fair competition and tax compliance. To complement the standards of behaviour established by the OECD Guidelines, in 2018 the OECD Due Diligence Guidance for Responsible Business Conduct was adopted,[119] with the aim of providing practical support to business enterprises on the implementation of the OECD Guidelines. Moreover, the OECD has developed sector-specific due diligence guidance and good practice documents for the minerals,[120] agriculture,[121] garment and footwear supply chains,[122] and for the extractive sector.[123]

The OECD Guidelines for Multinational Enterprises rely extensively on the UN Guiding Principles on Business and Human Rights but have a broader scope also including employment and industrial relations, environment, combating bribery, bribe solicitation and extortion, consumer interests, science and technology, competition and taxation. In Chapter 2 on General Policies, they state:

> Enterprises should: 11. Avoid causing or contributing to adverse impacts on matters covered by the Guidelines, through their own activities, and address such impacts when they occur. 12. Seek to prevent or mitigate an adverse impact where they have not contributed to that impact, when the impact is nevertheless directly linked to their operations, products or services by a business relationship.

These two paragraphs reflect the 'protect, respect and remedy framework' of the UN Guiding Principles, extending it beyond human rights to areas such as the environment and employment relations. In a similar vein, para. 14 states that:

> due diligence is understood as the process through which enterprises can identify, prevent, mitigate and account for how they address their actual and potential adverse impacts as an integral part of business decision-making and risk management systems. Due diligence can be included within broader enterprise risk management systems, provided that it goes beyond simply identifying and managing material risks to the enterprise itself, to include the risks of adverse impacts related to matters covered by the Guidelines. Potential impacts are to

[119] OECD 2018.
[120] OECD 2016a.
[121] OECD 2022.
[122] OECD 2017.
[123] OECD 2016b.

be addressed through prevention or mitigation, while actual impacts are to be addressed through remediation.

The Tripartite Declaration of Principles concerning Multinational Enterprises and Social Policy (MNE Declaration),[124] which was approved by the International Labour Office (ILO) in 1977 and later amended (the last time in 2017) similarly refers to the UN Guiding Principles on Business and Human Rights, extending, however, their reach to the fundamental rights set out in the ILO Declaration on Fundamental Principles and Rights at Work.

3.5.3 *Regulation and Externalities*

The role of regulation in constraining shareholder wealth maximization is eas-ily understood. Environmental protection, to take an obvious example, largely depends on government regulation, which is binding on firms and influences their actions.[125] No doubt, firms comply with regulation not only for ethical and reputa-tional reasons, but also to avoid the administrative and criminal sanctions which would derive from violations of the relevant rules and would negatively affect their economic value. Stakeholder protection in similar cases cannot be seen as directly instrumental to firm value maximization, for it is primarily required by regulation. Moreover, regulation takes care of negative externalities, forcing firms to internalize them beyond what firms would spontaneously do given the costs of internalization.

However, a new type of sustainability regulation is emerging in the EU, based on the Commission's 2021 proposal for a Directive on corporate sustainability due diligence.[126] The new Directive will transform soft law principles, such as those included in the UN guidelines on business and human rights, in hard law rules that member states will adopt to implement the directive. Such rules will give rise to human rights and environmental due diligence obligations that companies will

---

[124] The MNE Declaration is available at: www.ilo.org/empent/areas/mne-declaration/lang–en/index .htm.

[125] For a thoughtful introduction, see Young 2016.

[126] See the Proposal for a Directive of the European Parliament and of the Council on Corporate Sustainability Due Diligence and amending Directive (EU) 2019/1937, Brussels, 23.2.2022 COM (2022) 71 final. On the origins of this proposal, see Pietrancosta 2022. When this chapter was at proof stage, the European Parliament, on 24 April 2024, formally adopted the Corporate Sustainability Due Diligence Directive (CSDDD or CS3D): see EP press release at https://bit.ly/4bMxJFS. The directive now also needs to be formally endorsed by the Council and published in the EU Official Journal. Member states will have two years to transpose the new rules into their national laws. The Parliament did not make any further changes to the text of the Directive that was endorsed by the Council on 15 March, which included some significant concessions especially on the scope of application: see Linklaters, EU Parliament gives final approval for CSDDD, at https://bit .ly/45banHF. The European Parliament legislative resolution of 24 April 2024 on the CSDDD is available at https://bit.ly/4eiD4qe.

have to comply with under the vigilance of supervisory authorities.[127] A new area of public regulation will therefore be established, which does not, however, specify in detail what firms should do or avoid doing to minimize corporate externalities.[128]

Indeed, the proposed Directive defines the due diligence obligations with reference to the adverse human rights impacts and to the adverse environmental impacts which arise from their own operations or those of their subsidiaries, and from their value chains.[129] Such adverse impacts are identified with reference to the environmental and human rights international conventions listed in the two Annexes to the Directive.[130] Moreover, companies should comply with their due diligence obligations by adopting 'appropriate measures', which must be 'commensurate with the degree of severity and the likelihood of the adverse impact, and reasonably available to the company, taking into account the circumstances of the specific case, including the characteristics of the economic sector and of the specific business relationships and the company's influence thereof, and the need to ensure prioritisation of action'.[131]

Non-compliance with such obligations will expose the companies concerned to public sanctions and civil liability for damages potentially caused to third parties.[132] As a result, negative externalities will be internalized by companies which face the costs of their prevention and mitigation, in addition to restoring the damages for which they are liable under national law towards third parties. The same companies will be accountable for the negative externalities caused by the firms operating within their value chain, which could be either direct or indirect contractors or partners involved in the business activities of the corporations directly bound by the corporate due diligence obligations.[133]

---

[127] These obligations are defined by Article 4 (1) of the proposed Directive as including the following actions: integrating due diligence into corporate policies; identifying actual or potential adverse impacts; preventing and mitigating potential adverse impacts; establishing and maintaining a complaints procedure; monitoring the effectiveness of their due diligence policy; publicly communicating on due diligence.

[128] See Ferrarini 2022.

[129] See Article 6 (1) concerning the obligation to identify actual and potential adverse impacts.

[130] Article 3 (b) defines an 'adverse environmental impact' as 'resulting from the violation of one of the prohibitions and obligations pursuant to the international environmental conventions listed in the Annex, Part II'. Article 3 (c) defines an 'adverse human rights impact' as 'resulting from the violation of one of the rights or prohibitions listed in the Annex, Part I Sec. 1, as enshrined in the international conventions listed in the Annex, Part I Sec. 2'. These definitions have been modified in the text approved by the European Parliament: see note 126 above.

[131] See Article 3(q) of the proposed Directive.

[132] See Articles 20 on sanctions applicable for infringements of national provisions adopted pursuant to the Directive which shall be effective, proportionate and dissuasive; and Article 22 on civil liability for the non-compliance with the obligations laid down in the Directive, including the liability for damages caused by an adverse impact arising as a result of the activities of an indirect partner with whom it has an established business relationship (see Article 22(2)). Both Articles have been deeply modified in the final text of the CSDDD as approved by the European Parliament: see note 126 above.

[133] See Pacces 2022.

3.6 CONCLUSIONS

In this chapter, I tried to show how firms generate social value while increasing their long-term economic value. ESV explains how taking care of core stakeholders contributes to firm value maximization and therefore to the creation of social value. Moreover, pursuing social value often generates more value to shareholders thanks to organizational and technological innovation. Indeed, firms are incentivized to improve their business models and/or processes to enhance their environmental and social sustainability, while increasing their long-term profitability. Managers are also incentivized to create social value through their business activities, for this will be reflected in the amount of their variable remuneration which is linked to financial performance and increasingly also to ESG parameters.

In addition, managers have non-pecuniary incentives to promote their firms' sustainability to the extent that the relevant behaviour reflects ethical standards which are part of their corporate culture. In similar situations, social value may be generated even if it translates into sheer costs for the enterprise. Indeed, some scholars suggest that shareholder welfare includes not only shareholder value but also externalities to which investors attach increasing importance. The opposite view that only instrumental stakeholderism should apply to firm management appears therefore too narrow, for situations exist where non-economic values are also relevant to the firm. The relevance of ethics in general is underlined by CSR and stakeholder theory. Moreover, today's management studies emphasize the importance of corporate governance and organizational theory in the promotion of social value. The board of directors should identify the ethical and cultural values of the firm and monitor their application at all levels. Moreover, organizational purpose should play a fundamental role for the 'intrinsic' motivation of people in the corporations.

The soft law on corporate due diligence further contributes to the design of corporate purpose and to the motivation of managers and employees. Once corporate due diligence is recognized by European law with the approval of the proposed Directive, specific obligations will arise for companies which will impact their governance, including risk management, and could become a source of civil liability in cases of breach. As a result, the corporate purpose orientation to sustainability will be reinforced to the extent that corporate internalization of environmental and human rights externalities becomes mandatory.

REFERENCES

Alvaro, S., Maugeri, M., and Strampelli, G. (2019), 'Institutional investors, corporate governance and stewardship codes: Problems and perspectives' *CONSOB Legal Research Papers* (Quaderni Giuridici), 19.

Bebchuk, L. and Tallarita, R. (2020), 'The illusory promise of stakeholder governance', 107 *Cornell Law Review*, 93.

Bebchuk, L., Kastiel, K., and Tallarita, R. (2022), 'Does enlightened shareholder value add value?', 77 *The Business Lawyer*, 731.

Benabou, R. and Tirole, J. (2010), 'Individual and corporate social responsibility', 77 *Econometrica*, 1.

Blair, M. (2015), 'Boards of directors and corporate performance under a team production model', in Hill, J. and Randall, T. (eds.), *Research Handbook on Shareholder Power* (Cheltenham: Edward Elgar), 249.

Blair, M. and Stout, L. (1999), 'A team production theory of corporate law', 85 *Vanderbilt Law Review*, 247.

Blinder A. (2013), *After the Music Stopped: The Financial Crisis, the Response, and the Work Ahead* (London: Penguin).

Cheffins, B. (2020), 'Stop blaming Milton Friedman!', March, University of Cambridge Faculty of Law Legal Studies Research Paper Series, Paper N. 9/2020, available at: https://papers.ssrn.com/sol3/papers.cfm?abstract_id=3552950.

Coffee, J. (2005), 'A theory of corporate scandals: Why the USA and Europe differ', 21 *Oxford Review of Economic Policy*, 2, 198.

Crane, A., Matten, D., and Spence, L. (2008), 'Corporate social responsibility in a global context', in Crane, A., Matten, D., and Spence, L. (eds.), *Corporate Social Responsibility: Readings and Cases in a Global Context* (London: Routledge), 3.

Crew, A. and Matten, D. (2016), *Business Ethics*, 4th ed. (Oxford: Oxford University Press).

Csikszentmihalyi, M. (1990), *Flow: The Psychology of Optimal Experience* (New York: HarperCollins).

Davies, P. (2020), *Introduction to Company Law*, 3rd ed. (Oxford: Oxford University Press).

Davis, G. (2009), *Managed by the Markets, How Finance Reshaped America* (Oxford: Oxford University Press).

Edmans, A. (2020), *Grow the Pie: How Great Companies Deliver Both Purpose and Profit* (Cambridge, UK: Cambridge University Press).

Eurosif (2018), '2018 SRI Study for an overview of trends related to SRI strategies in Europe', available at: https://bit.ly/48hryqI.

Ferrarini G. (2021), 'Redefining corporate purpose: Sustainability as a game changer', in Busch, D., Ferrarini, G., and Grünewald, S. (eds.), *Sustainable Finance in Europe* (London: Palgrave Macmillan), 85–150.

Ferrarini, G. (2022), 'Corporate sustainability due diligence and the shifting balance between soft law and hard law in the EU', 22 April, ECGI Blog, available at: https://bit.ly/4bAiHmX.

Ferrarini, G. and Giudici, P. (2006), 'Financial scandals and the role of private enforcement: The Parmalat case', in Armour J. and McCahery J. (eds.), *After Enron* (Oxford: Hart Publisher), 159.

Ferrarini, G. and Zhu, S. (2019), 'Culture of financial institutions', in Busch, D., Ferrarini, G. and van Solingen G. (eds.), *Governance of Financial Institutions* (Oxford: Oxford University Press), 381.

Ferrell, A., Liang, H., and Renneboog, L. (2016), 'Socially responsible firms', 122 *Journal of Financial Economics*, 585.

Freeman R. E. (1984), *Strategic Management: A Stakeholder Approach* (Indiana University: Pitman).

Freeman, R. E., Harrison, J., Wicks, A., Parmar, B., and De Colle, S. (2010), *Stakeholder Theory: The State of the Art* (Cambridge, UK: Cambridge University Press).

Friedman M. (1970), 'The social responsibility of business is to increase its profits', *The New York Times Sunday Magazine*, 13 September, 32.

Gadinis, S. and Miazad, A. (2020), 'Corporate law and social risk', 73 *Vanderbilt Law Review*, 1401.

Gatti, M. and Ondersma, C. (2020), 'Can a broader corporate purpose redress inequality? The stakeholder approach chimera', 46 *The Journal of Corporation Law*, 2.

Gelter, M. and Helleringer, G. (2015), 'Lift not the Painted Veil! To whom are directors' duties really owned?', 3 *University of Illinois Law Review*, 1070.

GRI (Global Reporting Initiative) (2021), 'The double-materiality concept. Application and Issues', invited contribution by Adams C. et al., available at: https://bit.ly/3SY5blE.

Hamel G. (2007), *The Future of Management* (Boston, MA: Harvard Business School Press).

Hansmann, H. and Kraakman, R. (2001), 'The end of history for corporate law', 89 *Georgetown Law Journal*, 439.

Hart, O. and Zingales, L. (2017), 'Companies should maximize shareholder welfare not market value', 2 *Journal of Law, Finance, and Accounting*, 247.

Henderson R. (2020), *Reimagining Capitalism: How Business Can Save the World* (London: Penguin Business).

Holmstrom, B. and Kaplan, S. (2003), 'The state of U.S. corporate governance: What's right and what's wrong?', 15 *Journal of Applied Corporate Finance* 3, 10.

Jensen, M. (2002), 'Value maximization, stakeholder theory, and the corporate objective function', 22 *Journal of Applied Corporate Finance*, 32, and 12 *Business Ethics Quarterly*, 235.

Kim, S. and Yoon, A. (2020), 'Analyzing active managers' commitment to ESG: Evidence from United Nations Principles for Responsible Investment', 17 March, available at: https://ssrn.com/abstract=3555984 or http://dx.doi.org/10.2139/ssrn.3555984.

Krueger, P. (2015), 'Corporate goodness and shareholder wealth', 115 *Journal of Financial Economics*, 304.

Lund, D. and Pollman, E. (2021), 'The corporate governance machine', 121 *Columbia Law Review*, 2563.

Mayer, C. (2018), *Prosperity: Better Business Makes the Greater Good* (Oxford: Oxford University Press).

Mayer, C. (2022), 'The research background to the final report of the Future of the Corporation programme on Policy & Practice for Purposeful Business', 10(s5), *Journal of the British Academy*, 1, available at: https://bit.ly/49y67md.

OECD (2016a), *OECD Due Diligence Guidance for Responsible Supply Chains of Minerals from Conflict-Affected and High-Risk Areas*, 3rd ed. (Paris: OECD Publishing), available at: http://dx.doi.org/10.1787/9789264252479-en.

OECD (2016b), *Recommendation of the Council on the Due Diligence Guidance for Meaningful Stakeholder Engagement in the Extractive Sector* (Paris: OECD Publishing).

OECD (2017), *OECD Due Diligence Guidance for Responsible Supply Chains in the Garment and Footwear Sector* (Paris: OECD Publishing).

OECD (2018), *OECD Due Diligence Guidance for Responsible Business Conduct* (Paris: OECD Publishing).

OECD (2022), 'Recommendation of the Council on the OECD-FAO Guidance for Responsible Agricultural Supply Chains', OECD/LEGAL/0428, available at: https://legalinstruments.oecd.org/public/doc/342/342.en.pdf.

Pacces, A. (2022), 'Supply Chain Liability in the Corporate Sustainability Due Diligence Directive Proposal', 12 April, ECGI Blog, available at: https://bit.ly/4bArZiT.

Pettigrew, A. (2009), 'Corporate responsibility in strategy', in Smith, N. and Lenssen, G. (eds.), *Mainstreaming Corporate Responsibility* (Hoboken, NJ: Polity), 12.

Pietrancosta, A. (2022), 'Codification in company law of general CSR requirements: Pioneering recent French reforms and EU perspectives', ECGI – Law Working Paper No. 639/2022, available at: https://papers.ssrn.com/sol3/papers.cfm?abstract_id=4083398.

Pink, D. H. (2009), *Drive: The Surprising Truth about What Motivates Us* (Edinburgh: Canongate).

Pollman, E. (2022), 'The making and meaning of ESG', ECGI Working Paper N° 659/2022, available at: https://papers.ssrn.com/sol3/papers.cfm?abstract_id=4219857.

Porter, M. and Kramer, M. (2011), 'Creating shared value: How to reinvent capitalism – and unleash a wave of innovation and growth', January–February *Harvard Business Review*, 3.

Rappaport, A. (1998), *Creating Shareholder Value* (New York: Free Press).

Sandel, M. (2012), *What Money Can't Buy: The Moral Limits of Markets* (New York: Penguin).

Smith, N. and Lenssen, G. (2009), 'Mainstreaming corporate responsibility: An introduction', in Smith N. and Lenssen G. (eds.), *Mainstreaming Corporate Responsibility* (Hoboken, NJ: Polity), 2.

Wood, D. (1991), 'Corporate social performance revisited', 16 *Academy of Management Review*, 691.

Young O. (2016), *On Environmental Governance: Sustainability, Efficiency, and Equity* (London: Routledge).

4

The Hardening of Corporate ESG

Geneviève Helleringer and Christina Parajon Skinner

4.1 INTRODUCTION

Although the purpose of the corporation has been debated since at least the 1930s,[1] that debate has reignited in the past several years. Much academic writing in the past two to three years has impressed the importance of a broad "purpose" to the corporation – an ethos or *"raison d'être,"* and business objective, that pursues a wide range of interests that go beyond the pecuniary interests of shareholders.[2]

The debate may be long-standing and well-developed, but the wellspring of corporate initiative which has transpired in the past few years is quite new. Whereas stakeholder capitalism was previously the province (mainly) of academics, international organizations, and special interest groups,[3] in recent years major businesses worldwide have publicly declared their commitment to this so-called stakeholder model.

Consider a few of the most prominent examples. In 2019, the "who's who" of US business leaders embraced stakeholder norms in a statement of corporate governance principles, penned by the influential Business Roundtable.[4] In it, nearly 200 executives of America's leading businesses – ranging from Amazon to Xerox – pledged to "deliver value" to customers, employees, suppliers, communities, and shareholders for "the future success of our companies, our communities and

---

[1] See e.g., Bearle and Means 1932.
[2] See e.g., Fisch and Solomon 2021, 1309–1311; Lund and Pollman 2021, 2565; Mayer 2016, 57–58; see also d'Abrera 2019, 21–22; Puchniak 2022, 2–4.
[3] Business and Human Rights Resource Centre 2011, 13–16; see also Choudhury and Petrin 2022.
[4] Business Roundtable 2022. The initiative received a skeptical assessment from some commentators, stressing that the main effect could be to insulate corporate leaders from shareholder oversight and deflect pressures for stakeholder-protecting regulation. Stakeholder governance that relies on the discretion of corporate leaders would not represent an effective way to address growing concerns about the effects corporations have on stakeholders. See, for example, Bebchuck and Tallarita 2022, 1046.

our country."[5] This declaration of principle echoed international proclamations like the UN International Bill of Human Rights, the ILO Declaration on Fundamental Principles and Rights at Work, the UNGPs, and the [OECD] Due Diligence Guidance for Responsible Supply Chain of Minerals from Conflict-Affected and High-Risk Areas.

By 2022, so many US companies had adopted similar corporate purpose statements or stances that the American Law Institute, in its first tentative draft of its new Restatement on the Law of Corporate Governance, included a foundational statement on Corporate Purpose – namely, that even in common law jurisdictions where companies are legally bound to serve the interests of shareholders primarily, a corporation may nonetheless consider "the interests of the corporation's employees," foster "business relationships with suppliers, customers and others," consider the "impact of the corporation's operations on the community and the environment," and take into account any other "ethical considerations related to the responsible conduct of business." In short, over the past few years, a broad swath of US businesses have expressed their belief that they should consider nearly any range of factors relevant to the economy and to society in deciding which projects to pursue and how.

Many firms have carried these stakeholder commitments forward by operationalizing them in the form of initiatives to pursue "environmental, social, and governance" ("ESG") goals – particularly in connection with environmental goals. In the USA, large banks have committed to net zero by 2050, and corporate giants like Google and Walmart have also made environmental pledges.[6] Many companies also gave managerial content to such visions by translating incorporating them in their internal organization and management systems, including through compliance systems training, checklists, and executive compensation reforms.[7]

Reflecting a comparable drive from UK companies, more than 1,000 companies, including the supermarket chain Iceland, the drinks producer Innocent, and the vegetarian food maker Quorn, back the Better Business Act (BBA) campaign initiated in April 2021 in order to call for an overhaul of the UK Companies Act. A suggested redrafting of Section 172 would force directors to put other stakeholders and shareholders on equal footing.[8] More specifically, the amendment would empower directors to exercise their judgement in weighing up and advancing the interests of all stakeholders and require all businesses to benefit wider stakeholders beyond shareholders as well as to deliver strategic or impact reports on how their businesses go beyond shareholder value to also benefit people and the planet.

---

[5] Ibid.
[6] See e.g., Outka 2019, 662, 671.
[7] In other words, companies tend to frame for compliance scheme purposes ESG standards in stricter terms than legal requirements, by contrast to their formerly observed washed-out managerial translation of imprecision and ambiguous legal norms in labor law and other domains, see Edelman 2016, 24–41. See also Walker 2022, 324–327.
[8] Better Business Act 2021.

The UK Institute of Directors, with 20,000 corporate directors among its members, supports the BBA, and some FTSE 100 companies' directors declared personal support for the initiative, though no FTSE 100 company has committed to support the campaign so far. Individual companies, such as the UK's largest retailer Tesco,[9] loudly announced their commitments to ESG and to helping communities in particular, and started reporting extensively on the matter, stressing how markets and consumers needed such a level of transparency to make the right decisions. Other UK companies like Schröder and Moody's, as well as European ones like the French Total, Schneider, Michelin and the German Allianz, have engaged in a well documented and advertised effort to reduce carbon emissions outside of any mandatory legal framework.[10]

Many of the institutional investors have also made strides toward ESG – an impactful move since as capital allocators institutional investors have a particularly high degree of influence over corporate behavior.[11] The optional UK 2020 Stewardship Code, and its strong uptake,[12] illustrate the progressive institutionalization of the focus on ESG displayed by asset owners, managers, proxy advisors, and other service providers. Signatories of the code are required, under the supervision of the UK Financial Reporting Council, to report annually with the expectation they will apply the principles and explain how they do so, including how their "purpose, investment beliefs, strategy and culture enable stewardship that creates long-term value for clients and beneficiaries leading to sustainable benefits for the economy, the environment and society" (principle 1) and how they are ready to "participate in collaborative engagement to influence issuers" (principle 10), or "when necessary, escalate stewardship activities to influence issuers" (principle 11).

Proxy advisors have also played an influential role in pressing asset managers in this direction. Some claim that investors in investment funds are still interested in the bottom line, but not to the exclusion of other considerations. They now "expect companies to be good corporate citizens, with a view to their environmental and social impacts and a focus on their impacts on stakeholders".[13] Whether this is an empirically accurate statement remains a heavily debated question.

Indeed, a cottage industry of ESG investment funds has developed in the past few years, employing a range of strategies to channel capital to ESG-friendly companies or projects or to have an impact on affecting changes at portfolio companies. BlackRock CEO Larry Fink, a well-known ESG champion, has emphasized his

[9] Tesco plc 2022.
[10] Science Based Targets 2022.
[11] See de Silanes, McCahery and Pudschedl 2022, 25–27.
[12] The list of signatories includes all of the world's major asset managers: (BlackRock, Vanguard, UBS, Fidelity, State Street Global Advisors, Morgan Stanley etc.). It also includes some major UK institutional investors – Tesco Pension Investment Limited, Church of England Pensions Board etc. See Financial Reporting Council 2022.
[13] Glass Lewis 2021, 8. See also US Department of Labor 2022.

view that, "[a]s stewards of our clients' capital, we ask businesses to demonstrate how they're going to deliver on their responsibility to shareholders, including through sound environmental, social, and governance practices and policies."[14]

Fink was one voice among many asset managers in the stampede toward ESG. The asset management industry has taken stands supporting ESG collectively and quite determinedly. The 4,978 global signatories of the UN Principles for Responsible Investment (all asset managers) agreed to take "actions for incorporation of ESG issues into investment practice," including, among other things, incorporating ESG issues into investment analysis and decision-making and incorporating ESG issues into ownership policies and practices, among other things. In Europe alone, sixty asset management institutions, representing around EUR 8.5 trillion in assets, signed an open letter to the European Union encouraging regulators to promote "high quality ESG standards."[15]

As a consequence of the asset managers' various initiatives, public statements, and management engagement, issuers have become more engaged with ESG. Even if the majority of shareholders in most jurisdictions have in practice little incentive or insight into how to propose items for a vote impacting the general management, a company may be aware of the questions the activist institutions (who are voting shares on the shareholders' behalf) are eager to see discussed and voted upon and may, accordingly, adjust their behavior in advance. In seeming illustration of this dynamic, several US companies have recently adopted climate transition strategies and "say on climate" votes, in a preemptive style similar to what has been observed for a few years in Europe. This trend could gain further momentum given the recent SEC staff guidance on shareholder proposals limiting the ability of public companies to exclude social issue-related shareholder proposals from proxy statements.[16]

Large banks have likewise committed to ESG goals in connection with their lending and risk-management practices. Among banks' ESG initiatives, climate change receives particularly heavy attention. In the USA, all major systemically important banks have committed to net zero by 2050 and have taken other measures to green their lending models.[17] Financial institutions in Europe have done the same.[18]

Indeed, the movement to direct capital allocators – banks and asset managers – to push companies toward environmental goals has been a concerted goal of the international community, and especially the U.N. Erstwhile Bank of England Governor Mark Carney, now UN Special Envoy for Climate, has been particularly engaged on this dimension. In April 2021, Carney launched the Glasgow Financial Alliance for Net Zero (GFANZ) in collaboration with the COP26 Private Finance Hub.

[14] Fink 2022.
[15] Ibid.
[16] Securities and Exchange Commission 2021.
[17] Light and Skinner 2022, 1896–1897.
[18] See William and Hodgson 2022; see also So 2022.

GFANZ aims to create a sector-wide coalition to accelerate the transition to a net-zero global economy by bringing together existing and new net-zero finance initiatives. GFANZ currently has "over 450 member firms from across the global financial sector representing more than \$130 trillion under management and advice."[19] Overall, Carney's claim is that "... every professional financial decision [should] take ... climate change into account," worldwide.[20]

Corporate commitment to the ethical and legal treatment of customers, employees, and communities is important, both morally and economically. There is in fact broad consensus – and Milton Friedman would agree – that corporations cannot be profitable over the longer term without adherence to these values.[21] But in this chapter we question the extent to which the current generation of ESG-stakeholderism – particularly that practiced by capital-allocating banks and funds – is in fact a sustainable business practice, capable of maintaining its current pace over a longer-term horizon.

More specifically, in this chapter, we highlight the legal and reputational risk that has been catalyzed by firms' voluntary rush into the amorphous commitments surrounding ESG.[22] We discuss how voluntary corporate ESG commitments have, over a short period of time, hardened into more formal sources of law and regulation, with examples from the USA, EU, and UK.[23] In conclusion, we suggest some adverse consequences of this trend, which we give a more complete treatment of in separate work.

4.2 FROM SOFT LAW ESG COMMITMENTS TO HARD LAW RULES: EUROPEAN UNION AND UNITED KINGDOM

In a relatively short period of time, legislators, regulators, courts, and corporations hardened the soft law norms and commitments concerning ESG into binding sources of law – statute, regulation, case law, and contractual commitments. We illustrate that this path toward the formalization of ESG commitments has been taken in the USA, EU, and UK. The analysis not only sheds light on this quickening trend, but also, from a comparative perspective, draws attention to the degree to which the pace of this lawmaking has varied in the EU, the UK, and the USA.[24]

---

[19] From the GFANZ website, available at: www.gfanzero.com/about/. GFANZ Principals Group Members include representatives from NatWest and Santander.

[20] Carney 2020, 5.

[21] Edmans 2022, 5.

[22] Pollman 2022, 4.

[23] See also Berger-Walliser and Scott 2018, 170.

[24] Which in turn have impacted the general EU framework, see e.g., Steinbach, who explores changes to European Monetary Union architecture and discusses the institutional and legal implications of the novel role of climate in the coordination of EMU policies. It addresses the relationship between Treaty mandate and policy leeway, specifically the way in which the ECB extends its focus on price stability to account for climate considerations and the fiscal legal framework relies on flexibility to

This section first focuses on the domestic legislative initiatives in France and Germany (A), the two leading EU economies since the departure of the UK, and explores their potential to inspire EU ambitions in an unreserved manner. The development of the EU value chain legislation exemplifies this post-Brexit dynamic, which also extends to the regulation of investment advice and of investment funds and to a standardized taxonomy of sustainable activity (B). Even in the UK, new legal requirements have started to record the growing commitment voiced by corporations towards corporate purpose and climate change measures (C).

4.2.1 *EU Member States: Germany and France*

German capitalism has long been noted for its support to stakeholders, and employees in particular, via the *Mitbestimmung* mode of governance, as well as for its long-standing concern for the environment.[25] While the structure of the shareholding has evolved for larger companies towards more dispersion,[26] and possibly more power in the hands of managers who are not connected to the founders, the traditional corporate culture can be seen in managers' commitment to corporate role within communities, and responsibility towards employees.[27] It is largely this paternalistic corporate ethos that is reflected in the 2021 German statute requiring companies to ensure the protection of human rights along the value chain.[28]

Companies themselves share some of the paternalistic traits just described and publicly display growing concern for communities. For example, France also adopted provisions comparable to Germany in 2017,[29] i.e., a duty of vigilance requiring large companies to identify risks to and prevent serious breaches of human rights and fundamental freedoms, the health and safety of individuals, and the environment, resulting from the company's activities and those of the companies it controls, as well as from the activities of subcontractors or suppliers with whom the company has an established business relationship, when such risky activities are related to that relationship.[30] This duty of vigilance is conducted through the implementation of a corporate "vigilance plan" drafted in consultation with stakeholders and civil

---

incentivize climate investment. It also tracks the emergence of climate stability as an EMU concept, adding to existing concepts of price, fiscal and financial stability (available at: https://bit.ly/3wnFWk9).

[25] Clift 2021, 218–221; Roe 2003, 71–82.
[26] Ringe 2015, 493–538.
[27] See empirical data gathered by Licht and Adams 2020.
[28] Gesetz über die unternehmerischen Sorgfaltspflichten in Lieferketten (Law On Corporate Duties of Care in Supply Chains), Bundesgesetzblatt (German Federal Law Gazette), Part I, 22 July 2021, 2959.
[29] Loi n° 2017-399 du 27 mars 2017 relative au devoir de vigilance des sociétés mères et des entreprises donneuses d'ordre (Statute on the Duty of Vigilance of Parent Companies and Ordering Companies), *Journal officiel de la République française* (Official Journal of the French Republic) n° 0074 du 28 mars 2017.
[30] Loi (Statute) No. 2017-399 of 27 March 2017 regarding the Duty of Vigilance of Parent Companies and Ordering Companies.

society, and must be made publicly available by the company. Failure to comply with obligations imposes liability damages on the company.[31]

In the early 2010s, prominent corporate leaders like the CEO of the CSR-oriented Michelin, Jean-Dominique Senard, and the CEO of Danone (a firm historically committed to the dual model of pursuing both social and economic values), Emmanuel Faber, voiced their attachment to stakeholders,[32] and their concern that foreign investors were progressively imposing a short-term financial culture on French companies. This corporate voice found institutional support in a 2018 official report based on 200 interviews with representatives of business circles, banks, investors, unions, think-tanks, and government, *The Company and Collective Interest*, by Nicole Notat and Jean-Dominique Senard. The report endorsed the view that the purpose of companies is not only to make profit but to carry out social and environmental missions,[33] and called for a legislative reform.

Such reform largely aligned on the content of the report,[34] and followed with the 2019 loi PACTE.[35] The statute added a new paragraph to article 1833 of the French Civil Code stating that "the company is managed in its corporate interest, taking into consideration the social and environmental stakes linked to its business."[36]

Furthermore, the French Association of Private Companies (AFEP), which gathers about 115 of the largest corporations, representing about 15 percent of French GDP and employing 2 million people,[37] and the leading network of entrepreneurs in France (MEDEF), where 95 percent of members are small and medium companies, have together developed governance standards to help listed companies improve their operations and management. The AFEP-MEDEF Corporate Governance Code, largely adhered to by French listed companies, was amended in 2018 to state that "the Board of Directors performs the tasks conferred by the law and acts at all times in the corporate interest. It endeavors to promote long-term value creation by the company by considering the social and environmental aspects of its activities."[38]

Finally, the PACTE Law amended the Civil Code to allow company bylaws to define a company's "fundamental reason for being" (*raison d'être*). These various provisions deliver clearer grounds for directors and senior management to consider ESG issues as material to a corporation's operations, knowing that there has been no history of sanctions on company directors for failing to maximize shareholder

---

[31] Law No. 2017-399 of 27 March 2017 regarding the Duty of Care of Parent Companies and Ordering Companies.

[32] It might be noted that French business law, and insolvency law in particular, have often provided for the welfare of employees as their actual central goal. See Roe 2003.

[33] Available at: https://bit.ly/3T3icdQ.

[34] Poracchia 2019, 40.

[35] Loi (Statute) No. 2019-486 of 22 May 2019 regarding the Growth and Transformation of companies.

[36] See Lucas 2018, 477; Conac 2018, 558; Pietrancosta 2019, 55.

[37] Available at: https://afep.com/en/afep/.

[38] Article 1.1 of Code AFEP-MEDEF.

value in France.[39] To date, 55 percent of CAC 40 companies have stated a *raison d'être*. Although these are often factual and linked to the company's core activities[40] Directors and managers can be held liable towards a company regarding any violation of *raison d'être*. On the same ground, contracts entered by the company may be voidable.[41]

4.2.2 *European Union*

In the post-Brexit EU, the German and French models set the EU agenda in a more definite manner. Following the momentum set by their domestic companies' social and environmental commitment, both Germany and France have given strong legislative support to ESG. It is therefore not surprising that the EU has displayed a forceful approach as well. The EU has even demonstrated that it was ready to give the system the type of shock that would force institutional gatekeepers leaning towards shareholder value to change gear.[42]

The 2019 EU "Green Deal" promised to improve the well-being and health of citizens and future generations by providing fresh air, clean water, healthy soil, and biodiversity; renovated, energy-efficient buildings; healthy and affordable food; more public transport; cleaner energy and cutting-edge clean technological innovation; longer-lasting products that can be repaired, recycled, and re-used; future-proof jobs and skills training for the transition; and globally competitive and resilient industry.[43] To honor these promises, legal requirements have been widely resorted to, including with a recent and ambitious draft regulation of the value chain.[44] Enacted regulation focuses mainly on companies' disclosure requirements, contemplated as a nudge for companies towards ESG, as well as pushing investors towards ESG investment.[45]

---

[39] Pietrancosta 2022.
[40] See Les entreprises du CAC 40 à l'âge de la raison d'être, Comfluence, March 2020; Comité de suivi et d'évaluation de la loi PACTE. Premier rapport. Annexes, Sept. 2020, 76; Second rapport, September 2021, Annexes, 213.
[41] Pietrancosta 2022, 65; see also Cass. com. 20-9-2017 No. 15-29.098 and 15-29.144: BRDA 20/17 inf. 7. regarding liability for the purpose pursued by companies when fundraising.
[42] On the shareholderism culture of proxy-advisors, stock exchanges, rating agencies, institutional investors, etc., see Lund and Pollman 2021 *passim*. While the article focuses on the USA, these actors are increasingly global and so is their culture. On the role of a political momentum to break through, see ibid. [Part IV – E].
[43] European Commission, Communication from The Commission to The European Parliament, The European Council, The Council, The European Economic and Social Committee and The Committee of The Regions, The European Green Deal, December 112019, com/2019/640 final.
[44] European Commission, Proposal for a Directive of the European Parliament and of the Council on Corporate Sustainability Due Diligence and Amending Directive (EU) 2019/1937, Brussels, 23 February 2022, Com(2022) 71 Final, 2022/0051 (Cod).
[45] See generally Colaert (2022), arguing that the EU's sustainable finance policy is an intermediate means to nudge companies to apply higher environmental, social, and governance standards than legally required, pending stricter environmental, social, and governance regulation.

4.2.2.1 Companies' Sustainability Reporting Legislation

Despite new EU sustainability reporting legislation, companies' reports are stated to "often omit information that investors and other stakeholders think is important."[46]

The EU Corporate Sustainability Reporting Directive (adopted as part of the Sustainable Finance Package of 21 April 2021) requires all large companies to publish regular reports on their environmental and social impact activities as from January 2024 for the 2023 financial year. The directive extends the scope and reporting requirements of the already existing Non-Financial Reporting Directive (NFRD), which has mandated large public interest entities to report on their sustainability performance since 2018. In particular, the new directive introduces standardization in the disclosure and an auditing requirement. Also, it extends to a wider swath of companies, including foreign companies with activities in the EU.[47]

On 25 June 2020 the European Commission (EC) issued a request for technical advice, mandating EFRAG to undertake preparatory work for the elaboration of European sustainability reporting standards (ESRS) in a revised Non-Financial Reporting Directive (NFRD). The CSRD proposal now states that the ESRS will be adopted by the European Commission as delegated acts to the CSRD.[48]

In the latest step, the Project Task Force on European Sustainability Reporting Standards (PTF-ESRS), the task force within EFRAG responsible for developing the ESRS, has submitted the interim drafts to public consultation until 2022 Fall. The main point to retain is that the ESRS are intended to build on and be compatible with the standards issued by the ISSB, in a much-needed effort to reduce the amount of paperwork required for companies to comply with both sets of standards.

A key aspect of the standards is that they adopt a double materiality approach to sustainability reports, i.e., corporate sustainability reports should not only reflect the risks sustainability poses to firms' activities (and their financial bottom lines), but also how these firms' activities impact the environment and society.[49] The Taxonomy Regulation[50] was designed as a classification system and metric for

---

[46] See Q&AQ on Corporate Sustainability Reporting Directive Proposal, available at: https://bit .ly/3OJajb6.

[47] Tröger and Steuer 2021.

[48] See the full chronology and available interim drafts of the European sustainability reporting standards here: https://bit.ly/49EcDIb.

[49] See for this: https://bit.ly/49BFEEu. "The change from non-financial to sustainability reporting implies that a different understanding is needed of both the purposes of company reporting on sustainability matters and the aims of carrying out such reporting. This change was driven by the need and desire to appropriately interpret the principle of materiality set forth in the NFI Directive. However, the recent redefinition in the shift within the EU Commission's proposals presents considerable challenges–and costs–in practice."

[50] Regulation (EU) 2020/852 of the European Parliament and of the Council of 18 June 2020 on the establishment of a framework to facilitate sustainable investment, and amending Regulation (EU) 2019/2088.

sustainable reporting. Through its implementing and delegated acts, it expanded into a benchmark to measure progress towards sustainability in the EU. By making clear which economic activities contribute most to meeting the EU's environmental objectives, it is expected to guide – or nudge – investors towards "green" investments (on the model of energy consumption labelling and its color gradient) and also pressure on economic actors to "green up."

As currently developed, the EU Taxonomy is expected to include six environmental objectives: climate change mitigation, climate change adaptation, sustainable use and protection of water and marine resources, transition to a circular economy, pollution prevention and control, and protection and restoration of biodiversity and ecosystems. Companies are required to make disclosures for each of the activities they engage in, which might be numerous given the detailed classification (e.g., plastic transformation, steel transformation, electronics manufacturing, etc.). To be classified as "taxonomy aligned," an economic activity must satisfy three conditions. First, it should make a substantial contribution to one of the six environmental objectives. Second, it should do no harm to the other five objectives. Third, it should meet minimum safeguards regarding business, labor, and human rights.

Taxonomy Delegated Acts set the indicators, which consist of the Technical Screening Criteria (TSC) performance thresholds:[51] they are drafted by a Technical Expert Group, now known as the Platform on Sustainable Finance. The Delegated Act supplementing Article 8[52] of the Taxonomy Regulation was published in December 2021 to specify the content, methodology, and presentation of information to be disclosed by financial and non-financial firms concerning the proportion of environmentally sustainable economic activities in their business, investments, or lending activities. In February 2022, the Commission also approved the Complementary Delegated Act[53] to incorporate Nuclear and Gas in the TSC, introducing specific disclosure requirements for companies in these sectors.

While Article 8(1) of the Taxonomy Regulation requires large firms to disclose how their activities are associated with environmentally sustainable economic activities, Article 8(2) specifies two performance indicators (KPIs) related to turnover, capital expenditure (CapEx), and operational expenditure (OpEx) that non-financial firms are required to disclose. These disclosure requirements complement the Non-Financial Reporting Directive (NFRD)[54] by providing a common reference point. The technical work on additional environmental objectives is ongoing in the EU Platform on Sustainable Finance.[55]

---

[51] The Climate Delegated Act came into force in December 2021, available at: https://bit.ly/4305gch.
[52] Available at: https://bit.ly/49i3TYJ.
[53] Available at: https://bit.ly/49jXnQW.
[54] Available at: https://bit.ly/42JQ1Uw.
[55] Available at: https://bit.ly/49gtMbp.

In summary, the EU's green finance taxonomy aims to hold firms accountable for greenwashing by establishing criteria for activities and financial instruments that claim to be environmentally sustainable or to contribute to a social objective. However, the taxonomy appears rather bureaucratic: its requirement to fill in multiple online forms, its activity-based linear architecture, and its operation that does not fully ensure that the standards are developed in a rigorous manner or are sheltered from political considerations. It is possible that innovation may suffer due to standards that are quite general and binary in their application ("green" or "not green").

4.2.2.2 Nudge towards ESG Investments

The Sustainable Finance Disclosure Regulation (SFDR) adopted in Spring 2019 imposes disclosure requirements on financial market participants since 10 March 2021.[56] It enacts sustainability disclosure obligations[57] for manufacturers of financial products and financial advisors toward end-investors, in relation to the integration of sustainability risks by financial market participants (i.e., asset managers, institutional investors, insurance companies, pension funds, etc., all entities offering financial products where they manage clients' money) and financial advisors in all investment processes and for financial products that pursue the objective of sustainable investment.[58]

In other words, the SFDR requires most of the asset managers, investment-product providers, and financial advisors who operate in the EU[59] to disclose how they take into account sustainability in their investment decisions and advice and how they address the adverse impact of their advice or products on sustainability,[60] whether they focus on sustainability or not. Sustainability has therefore become the default: absence of compliance with this baseline has to be explained.

Investment Advice Regulation[61] and Insurer Regulation[62] provide additional illustrations of the European Commission's purposeful effort to encourage sustainability-driven

---

[56] Regulation (EU) 2019/2088 of the European Parliament and of the Council of 27 November 2019 on sustainability-related disclosures in the financial services sector, Official Journal of the European Union no. L 317 of December 12 2019, 1.

[57] Available at: https://bit.ly/3UFssKA.

[58] Regulatory technical standards (RTS) jointly developed by the three European Supervisory Authorities the European Banking Authority (EBA), the European Insurance and Occupational Pensions Authority (EIOPA) and the European Securities and Markets Authority (ESMA) and the Commission provide assistance as to the content, methodologies and presentation of the relevant information to be disclosed.

[59] The scope is broad, see SFDR, art. 2.

[60] SFDR, art. 4 and 7.

[61] Commission Delegated Regulation (EU) of 21.4.2021 amending Delegated Regulation (EU) 2017/565 as regards the integration of sustainability factors, risks and preferences into certain organisational requirements and operating conditions for investment firms, C/2021/2616 final.

[62] Ibid.

investments driven by sustainability. It has arranged to incorporate "sustainability risks into […] organisational requirements"[63] and to "integrate […] client's preferences in terms of sustainability as a top up to the suitability assessment."[64] Under the prior regime set out by the revised Markets for Financial Instrument Directive (MIFID II),[65] investment advisors had to "act honestly, fairly and professionally, in accordance with the best interests of its clients"[66] and "to obtain the necessary information regarding the client's […] knowledge and experience in the [considered] investment field (…) and investment objectives, including risk tolerance."[67] Advisors had, to enquire about their clients' needs and assess their best interest. Under the new regime, advisors' role has changed: they need to check their clients' sustainability preference and make investment recommendations on this basis.[68]

As explained in the accompanying note, the asset managers' role even encompasses some "nudging"[69] in favor of ESG investing as advisors are required to "explain to the clients (…) that the elements demonstrating the consideration of principal adverse impacts on sustainability factors might be relevant for various environmental, social, employee or governance matters."[70] They may not recommend to their clients financial instruments "that promote environmental or social characteristics without a proportion of sustainable investments or without a proportion of investments in taxonomy-compliant activities"[71] and ought to explain in their report how the recommendation meets, inter alia, "the client's sustainability preferences."[72]

4.2.3 United Kingdom

The UK 2006 Companies Act Section 172 provides for an approach often described as "enlightened," whereby ESG interests are to be considered, but subordinate

---

[63] Ibid., at 2.

[64] Ibid., at 1.

[65] Directive 2014/65/EU of the European Parliament and of the Council of 15 May 2014 on markets in financial instruments and amending Directive 2002/92/EC and Directive 2011/61/EU, Official Journal of the European Union no. L 173 of 12 June 2014, p. 349 (MiFiD II).

[66] Ibid., art. 24(1).

[67] Ibid., art. 25(2).

[68] Commission Delegated Regulation (EU) of 21.4.2021 amending Delegated Regulation (EU) 2017/565 as regards the integration of sustainability factors, risks and preferences into certain organisational requirements and operating conditions for investment firms, C/2021/2616 final, article 1.

[69] The proposal fails short of imposing sustainable product as a default that would leave investors the option of option out. The mechanism which encourages slow thinking on the basis of raised awareness may therefore more adequately be described as 'nudge plus', to use a term coined in John (2019).

[70] Commission Delegated Regulation (EU) of 21.4.2021 amending Delegated Regulation (EU) 2017/565 as regards the integration of sustainability factors, risks and preferences into certain organisational requirements and operating conditions for investment firms, C/2021/2616 final, Explanatory Memorandum, at 2.

[71] Ibid., Explanatory Memorandum, at 5.

[72] Ibid.

to ensuring the financial welfare of the shareholders. It has been increasingly supplemented in practice by the UK Corporate Governance Code.

The UK Corporate Governance Code (CGC) was amended in 2018 to place "greater emphasis on relationships between companies, shareholders and stakeholders,"[73] thereby following the growing emphasis put by companies themselves, in the wake of the 2007–08 Global Financial Crisis and an ongoing public debate,[74] on their purpose and their role towards stakeholders. Section 1 of the Code, which previously entitled "Leadership," was renamed "Board Leadership and Company Purpose," endorsing the centrality of defining companies' role in society. On this note, the 2018 Code further laid out that the board should "establish the company's purpose" and satisfy itself that "these and its culture are aligned."

In addition, Principle D of UK Corporate Governance Code stresses "in order to meet its responsibilities to shareholders and stakeholders, the board should ensure effective engagement with, and encourage participation from, these parties." Hence, with these amendments, the increasing interest expressed by companies in defining their corporate mission and their obligation towards towards communities, the environment, and employees was turned into a requirement for large listed companies, pursuant to the Listing Rules and their obligation to annually report and account for how they have applied the CGC on a "comply or explain basis."

More recently, after the COP27 was held in Glasgow in 2021 and pushed the issue of climate change further up in general media in the UK and in the corporate agenda, The Companies (Strategic Report) (Climate-related Financial Disclosure) Regulations 2022 were adopted. Inspired by the recommendations of the Task Force on Climate-Related Financial Disclosures (TCFD), a body created by the Financial Stability Board (FSB), this regulation requires UK companies to disclose material information pertaining to all four TCFD core categories relating to climate: governance, strategy, risk management, and metrics and targets.[75]

4.3 FROM SOFT LAW ESG COMMITMENTS TO HARD LAW RULES: UNITED STATES

4.3.1 *Legislation*

In contrast to the initiatives in the EU and UK lawmakers in the USA have not, for the most part, statutorily mandated ESG in companies or with regard to their supply chain. On the federal level, there are few major pieces of corporate legislation, including the Securities Act of 1933, Securities and Exchange Act of 1934, the Investment Advisors Act of 1940, and the Investment Company Act

---

[73] Available at: https://bit.ly/3T2CAM1.
[74] Available at: https://bit.ly/3T4gbyf.
[75] See for a summary for the regulation: https://bit.ly/3T4tsH4.

of 1940, the Sarbanes–Oxley Act 2002, and the Dodd–Frank Act 2010. Only in one instance has Congress, so far, amended any of this legislation to explicitly drive forward ESG.[76]

The lack of ESG-specific legislation on the federal level is not surprising. In most cases of federal law, statutes are drafted broadly and fleshed out at the agency level through regulation. So one would expect that any federal rules addressing ESG would be found in agency-made regulation. Corporate legislation, meanwhile, mostly follows from state law – so not the federal government. Accordingly, we turn our attention to the ways in which state law and federal regulation have formalized requirements surrounding companies' ESG practices or investments.

On the state level, each state's corporate code specifies available corporate forms and powers and duties of directors and managers, and sets parameters around stock issuance, voting, mergers, asset sales, and so on.[77] And because most US corporations incorporate in the state of Delaware, there is tremendous weight and attention on the Delaware General Corporation Law (DGCL). But neither the DGCL nor the relevant federal law has directly taken up ESG.

Among the fifty states, there has been at most some peripheral, but not direct, ESG legislation authorizing a more stakeholder-oriented view in some jurisdictions. Some states have adopted "constituency" statutes that authorize, but don't require, companies to take stakeholder interests in view thereby departing from the default shareholder primacy lodestar of the corporate fiduciary duty. These statutes, first adopted in the 1980s as a tool of fending off hostile takeovers, now exist in over thirty states.

For these states, like Pennsylvania, the statute explicitly rejects "shareholder primacy" and instead gives the board of directors the ability to consider all relevant interests and makes clear that, when those interests conflict, the board need not put shareholder interests first. Of course, constituency statutes only enable – not compel – stakeholder models by which the corporation pursue ESG goals with corporate resources. But certainly, such a regime would put the thumb on the scales of management to act accordingly. However, because Delaware has not adopted a constituency statute, the majority of US corporations do not exist under such a regime – at least insofar as state law is concerned.

4.3.2 *Regulations*

Federal financial regulators – and the SEC in particular – have been much keener to take on ESG. The SEC makes rules (i.e., regulation) for US investment funds and other public companies. This agency has certainly accelerated its ESG rule-making activity in 2021 and 2022.

---

[76] Securities and Exchange Commission 2012.
[77] Delaware Code Annals 2022, Title 8, §§102, 104, and 131–136.

In March 2022, the SEC issued a proposed rule for climate-related disclosures which would apply to all public companies. In broad strokes, the rule would require a broad swath of information relating to a company's climate-related risks – including scope 1, 2, and 3 emissions. The rule also requires governance disclosures regarding the oversight and governance of climate-related risks by the registrant's board and management.[78] As of the writing of this chapter, the comment period remains open on this rule and the subject of intense debate, with thousands of public comment letter files with the SEC responding to the rule's proposals.

Notably, the disclosure framework set out in the rule was modelled on private initiative, namely, the voluntary taskforce on climate-related financial disclosures (TCFD) and drew inspiration from the Greenhouse Gas Protocol, a partnership between the World Resources Institute and the World Business Council for Sustainable Development. It is thus a case in point of voluntary initiative among firms hardening into (proposed) law in the form of US regulation.

The SEC has also taken rulemaking action with regard to ESG and investment funds specifically. In May 2022, the SEC proposed amendments to the so-called "Names Rule" that applies to 1940 Act funds (i.e., mutual funds) and some other private investment funds as well. The Investment Company Act prohibits a fund from using words or titles in the name of its fund that could be misleading. In 2001, the SEC formally adopted the Names Rule that requires any fund using a name that implies a particular kind of strategy to invest at least 80 percent of its assets consistent with that implied strategy.[79]

This recent proposal would require any fund engaging in ESG investing "to provide additional information about the funds' implementation of ESG factors in the fund's principal investment strategies. The proposed amendments are designed to provide investors clear and comparable information about how a fund considers ESG factors."[80]

More specifically, the rule would require information in the prospectus about what ESG factors a fund considers and what strategies they use – for instance, whether the fund tracks an index, uses screens, or employs proxy voting strategies to meet ESG-related objectives. It would also require funds to disclose the details about what criteria the asset managers use to achieve their intended investment goals. Finally, it would require some ESG funds to disclose certain metrics that are relevant; for example, a climate-focused fund may have to disclose certain

---

[78] The Enhancement and Standardization of Climate-Related Disclosures for Investors, 87 Fed. Reg. 21,334 (9 May 2022) (to be codified at 17 C.F.R. pts 210, 229, 232, 239, and 249); for a synopsis of the rule, see Diamond and Gez 2022.

[79] Investment Company Act 2002, 17 C.F.R. §270.35d-1.

[80] Enhanced Disclosures by Certain Investment Advisers and Investment Companies about Environmental, Social, and Governance Investment Practices, S7-17-22 (25 May 2022) (to be codified at 17 C.F.R. pts. 200, 230, 232, 239, 249, 274, and 279).

greenhouse gas metrics in portfolios and an impact fund would disclose metrics about their annual progress toward ESG goals.

Overall, the SEC's stated goal with the Names Act amendments is to induce "consistent and comparable disclosures about asset managers' ESG strategies," so that investors (and the SEC) can "understand what data underlies funds' claims" and thus equips investors to "choose the right investments for them."[81]

The SEC has also started to follow through on firms' ESG commitments through enforcement, largely aiming to punish firms for greenwashing. While banks and funds may have initially hoped to win regulatory favor – and investment – with bold ESG commitments, regulators are now holding these institutions' feet to the fire.

Several such high-profile enforcement probes unfolded in the late Spring of 2022. The asset management arm of Deutsche Bank, for example, is not only under investigation by the US Department of Justice for potentially misleading investors, it was also the subject of a police raid in its home country (Germany) in connection with these same greenwashing allegations.[82] BNY Mellon's investment advisory arm settled with the SEC for $1.5 million upon a finding that the firm had failed to disclose that some of its investment did not pass through ESG screening, despite suggesting as much to shareholders.[83] Goldman Sachs was the third in this string of hard-hitting SEC actions. Its asset management arm is under SEC investigation for potentially similar overbroad claims in connection with its ESG or similarly worded funds.[84]

The pattern of voluntary commitments hardening into formal law has also unfolded among the self-regulatory organizations, the US stock exchange Nasdaq in particular. As a "self-regulatory organization," Nasdaq can create rules for its membership which automatically harden into formal law to the extent that the SEC approves the exchange's rules as effective equivalents to regulation for those companies listed or wishing to list on the exchange. In 2021, Nasdaq proposed to amend its listing standards to require listed companies to publicly disclose board-level diversity statistics and to have, or explain why they do not have, a minimum of two diverse board members under Nasdaq Rule 5605(f).[85]

The SEC approved the rule. According to SEC Chair Gary Gensler, "[t]hese rules will allow investors to gain a better understanding of Nasdaq-listed companies' approach to board diversity, while ensuring that those companies have the flexibility to make decisions that best serve their shareholders."[86] Though Gensler may have couched this in terms of corporate choice, in fact, the listing

---

[81] Gensler 2022.
[82] Walker 2022.
[83] *In re BNY Mellon* (SEC Admin. Proceeding 2022); Seal 2022.
[84] Michaels 2022.
[85] Securities and Exchange Commission 2022.
[86] Gensler 2021.

rule has shown the SEC to have reached quite far in formalizing the goal of gender, ethnic, and sexual orientation diversity through these new Nasdaq listing rules.

4.4 ESG JUDICIAL PRECEDENT

Courts increasingly enforce – or appear primed to enforce – soft ESG norms, thereby transforming these corporate commitments into hard common law precedent that is binding on future parties in the relevant jurisdiction. Even where not binding, these court rulings have the potential to, at the very least, become persuasive precedents for judges to refer to and follow in future ESG disputes.

4.4.1 *Europe*

Courts have used tort law to hold corporations accountable to various ESG standards, as illustrated[87] by the recent judgment of the Dutch Hague District Court in Den Haag against Royal Dutch Shell plc.[88] A Dutch environmental organization, Milieudefensie, sued Shell in tort law, claiming that Shell had an "obligation ensuing from the unwritten standard of care pursuant to Book 6 Section 162 Dutch Civil Code to contribute to the prevention of dangerous climate change through the corporate policy it determines for the Shell group."[89] In its claim, Milieudefensie referenced various soft law norms that Shell had repeatedly and publicly endorsed, including the UN Guiding Principles on Business and Human Rights, the UN Global Compact, and the OECD Guidelines for Multinational Enterprises.[90] In its judgment, the court endorsed the rationale and relied on the UN Guiding Principles to interpret Shell's standard of care,[91] and recognize more generally "a responsibility of business enterprises to respect human rights, applying to all enterprises regardless of their size, sector, operational context, ownership and structure."[92]

Judiciary decisions in the field of contractual litigation may also be expected. Apple may yet provide us with a telling illustration of the mechanism whereby supply chain policy can harden soft ESG commitment into binding requirements, because they become enforceable in court. Apple's Statement on Business and Supply Chains provides that suppliers have "to operate in accordance with the

---

[87] See Collyns 2022.

[88] *Vereniging Milieudefensie, in Amsterdam, and others, versus Royal Dutch Shell plc in The Hague*, The Hague District Court, Judgment of 26 May 2021, case number C/09/571932/HA ZA 19-379 (English version), available at: https://bit.ly/49kOqqF.

[89] Judgment of The Hague District Court, at 3.2.

[90] Ibid.

[91] Judgment of The Hague District Court, at 4.4.11.

[92] Ibid., at 4.4.16.

Apple Code and Standards", which "draw upon internationally recognized rights and standards, including the UN International Bill of Human Rights (...)."[93]

When courts refer to soft law principles in order to construe positive law requirements, these soft law principles acquire a new status: they will in the future directly bind companies through the conduit of the duty of care. A similar mechanism will probably develop regarding the construction of the fiduciary duty of care.[94]

4.4.2 *United States*

In the USA, the judicial landscape has been more muted. Given the recency of SEC activity on ESG, enforcement actions have yet to trickle down to federal courts. As of late 2022, there have been no notable ESG liability cases in state court.

But that could change soon. Delaware law seems primed to adopt new theories of director and officer liability that empower plaintiffs in suits alleging failure to implement or oversee ESG systems well. In particular, under the well-known Caremark standard, officers and directors of a company can be held liable for a breach of their fiduciary duty of loyalty for oversight failures, in extreme cases. Since that eponymous standard was developed in 1996, Caremark has evolved to prescribe robust, effective compliance systems, adequate to managing relevant risk.

For most of its history, however, the Caremark – mighty on its face – was relatively toothless in application. Directors would need to "utterly fail" to implement any systems or controls or have "consciously failed" to oversee the relevant systems once installed.[95] Accordingly, absent egregious failures of oversight verging on gross negligence, courts would not fault directors for lapses or errors based on Caremark. For this reason, it was remarked again and again in the case law that the claim that corporate fiduciaries have breached their duties to stockholders by failing to monitor corporate affairs is "possibly the most difficult theory in corporation law upon which a plaintiff might hope to win a judgment."[96]

A flurry of cases in 2019 and 2020 suggest that the Delaware courts might become more open to Caremark claims alleging oversight failures where environmental or social values are concerned. In particular, the court allowed various claims involved public health and safety, environmental degradation, and sexual harassment.[97] Importantly, in one case involving the systems failures in

---

[93] Apple, 2021 Statement on Efforts to Combat Human Trafficking and Slavery in our Business and Supply Chains (18 March 2022), available at https://apple.co/49krGHt. See also Blair, Williams and Lin 2008.

[94] See Kuntz 2024.

[95] *Stone v. Ritter*, 911 A.3d 362, 370 (Del. 2006, p. 370).

[96] *In re Boeing Company Derivative Litigation* (Del. Ch. 2021, p. *1).

[97] See e.g., *Miller v. State of Delaware Department of Public Safety* WL 1312286 (Del. Ch. 2011); *see In re Boeing Company Derivative Litigation*, 2021 WL 4059934, at *1 (Del. Ch. 2021, p. *1); see *Jones v. Navient* WL 2063308 (Del. Sup. Ct. 2022); see *T.V. Spano Building Corp. v. Wilson* (Del. Sup. Ct. 1990);

connection with the Boeing 737 Max airline accident, the court put special emphasis on the directors' duty to oversee systems that are "essential and mission critical" for the firm.[98] The Delaware courts used this "mission critical" language subsequently, in ESG-flavored cases.[99] And indeed some prominent Delaware corporate jurists have expressed the view that a "board's oversight responsibilities also require it to establish and monitor programs relating to matters such as … ESG."[100]

This trend in the Delaware courts' views on this ESG subset of Caremark claims may have thus created a large opening for plaintiffs to claim oversight failure for ESG risk-management systems, especially if the company itself had at one point or another referred to its ESG programs as "mission critical" to its new firm culture.[101]

4.5 CONCLUSION

This chapter has provided a side-by-side look at the parallel paths the USA, UK, and EU have taken in transmuting voluntary corporate commitments into hard law – statute, regulation, and judicial precedent. While some may view this as a positive development in holding firms to account for their ESG commitments, we view this development with caution. For one, as ESG corporate commitments – once soft law – increasingly harden into formal, hard law, some financial institutions have become increasingly uncomfortable with and uncertain about what, exactly, they have committed their organizations (and, ultimately, their shareholders) to.[102] Blackrock's U-turn-like behavior is a case in point. Although Larry Fink was for some years, not necessary, a vocal ESG booster, by the fall of 2022 he has had to

---

see *Teamsters Local 443 Health Services & Insurance Plan v. Chou* WL 5028065 (Del. Ch. 2020); see *In re Clovis Oncology, Inc. Derivative Litigation* (Del. Ch. 2019).

[98] *In re Boeing Company Derivative Litigation* (Del. Ch. 2021, p. 26).

[99] See *In re Boeing Company Derivative Litigation* (Del. Ch. 2021, p. 26); see *Teamsters Local 443 Health Services & Insurance Plan v. Chou* (Del. Ch. 2020, p. 17–18); see *In re Clovis Oncology, Inc. Derivative Litigation* (Del. Ch. 2019, p. 12).

[100] Holland and Veasey 2021, 27.

[101] But see Bainbridge 2022, 655, arguing that extending Caremark liability to ESG oversight would "threaten […] the board-centric model of corporate governance that lies at the heart of Delaware's dominance of the market for corporate charters."

[102] In one more recent exchange between Jamie Dimon and the US House of Representatives Financial Services Committee, in September 2022, the JP Morgan Chief Executive said, "I'm close to taking us out of these global green commitments – I'm not going to allow third parties to create legal liabilities for us and our shareholders. It is immortal and irresponsible." Mr. Dimon's remarks are indicative of a general attitude shift and recognition that a full-throttled embrace of ESG is neither practicable nor socially optimal. Growing skepticism towards GFANZ has been voiced, stressing that there should be greater focus on improving PRBs and that an abrupt change to the operational model of banks will significantly affect their costs. See e.g., Griffiths 2021. Although we do not address this implication fully here, the GFANZ also now raises concern for banks' potential antitrust liability. See Jessop 2022.

backpaddle his firm's ESG narrative in light of growing energy insecurity and high inflation globally.[103]

Because the notion of ESG is shape-shifting – and imbued with politics and social values – it is whimsical and thus impossible for firms to plan around. Consequently, the hardening of these commitments into formal law may risk fossilizing unworkable standards for firms and, in the case of financial firms, forcing inefficient misallocations of capital over time.

Moreover, increasing the state's role in defining corporate purpose will no doubt disrupt traditional commitments to shareholder primacy, which is likely to impede capital formation in society. As we have demonstrated, these legal *qua* political interventions are, especially in the EU, disruptive enough to potentially force institutional actors – such as rating agencies and institutional investors and advisors – to abandon (or loosen) their commitments to a corporate culture that has traditionally been shareholder-oriented.[104] The new ESG-related rules and regulations discussed in this chapter are bound to bump up against preexisting fiduciary duties of firm managers and directors to shareholders. It is not clear who will be the net winner from such dismantling of capitalism's deep roots.

And ultimately the crowding in of law and regulation into the ESG space may well crowd *out* the private sector innovation that could ultimately be more likely to correct genuine environmental, social, or governance imbalance.

This concern about the stifling of private sector ESG innovation appears all the more serious in light of the extent to which ESG laws and rules also interfere with private contract. Typically, to comply with new value chain requirements, European companies must now pass on the human rights and environmental constraints they have to abide by onto their suppliers. And because companies supply chains are transnational, these EU rules about value chain will likely become binding extraterritorially. US suppliers might find themselves constrained by the European value chain requirement via this contractual mechanism, with little margin of freedom to refuse or negotiate their content if they wish to engage in commercial relationships.

Moreover, global firms that operate in Europe are required to comply with EU regulations for their EU entities. Consider that BlackRock already publishes its SFDR statements on its website.[105] It is even conceivable that a "Brussels effect"[106]

---

[103] Reuters 2022 referring to testimony provided to UK lawmakers that Blackrock would not divest from new oil and gas production and that "BlackRock is developing tools that help our investors and clients assess how the transition is likely to unfold and to support clients' navigation of the transition and – for those who choose – to accelerate it." The firm said, "BlackRock's role in the transition is as a fiduciary to our clients – it is not to engineer a specific decarbonization outcome in the real economy".

[104] See Lund and Pollman 2021, 2565 providing an account of the "complex governance system in the United States composed of law, institutions, and culture that orients corporate decision making toward shareholders".

[105] See BlackRock 2021a; BlackRock 2021b.

[106] See e.g., Bradford 2020.

will be at play here, too: in combination with the Taxonomy Regulation,[107] which spells out what the EU considers sustainable, the SFDR may instigate a comprehensive standard for ESG risk management and accountability in the investment sector globally. Naturally, this will drive incentives of US firms (especially asset managers) to push the US regulators (i.e., the SEC) to adopt mirror regulation to ease their burden of transnational compliance.

Overall, we offer this chapter's discussion to shed critical light on the magnitude of the transatlantic trend toward hardening ESG commitments into formal law and leave for further work a fuller discussion of the normative consequences of doing so.

REFERENCES

Bainbridge, S. M. (2022), 'Don't compound the Caremark mistake by extending it to ESG oversight', *Business Lawyer*, 77(3), 655.

Bebchuk, L. A. and Tallarita, R. (2022), 'Will corporations deliver value to all stakeholders?', *Vanderbilt Law Review*, 75(4), 1046.

Berger-Walliser, G. and Scott, I. (2018), 'Redefining corporate social responsibility in an era of globalization and regulatory hardening', *American Business Law Journal*, 55(1), 170.

Berle, A. A. and Means, G. C. (1932), *The Modern Corporation & Private Property*, 1st ed. (New York: Macmillan).

Blackrock (2021a), 'Sustainable financial disclosure regulation: EU entity level sustainability risk disclosure'. *Blackrock*, available at: https://bit.ly/3VCJ4Ts.

Blackrock (2021b), 'Sustainable financial disclosure regulation: EU entity level principal adverse impacts statement'. *Blackrock*, available at: https://tinyurl.com/2tma7db2.

Blair, M., Williams, C. and Lin, L. W. (2008), 'The new role for assurance services in global commerce', *Journal of Corporation Law*, 22, 325–360.

Bradford, A. (2020), *The Brussels Effect: How the European Union Rules the World*, 1st ed. (Oxford: Oxford University Press).

Business and Human Rights Resource Centre (2011), 'Guiding Principles on Business and Human Rights', HR/PUB/11/04, available at: https://digitallibrary.un.org/record/720245?ln=en.

Business Roundtable (2022), 'Statement on the Purpose of a Corporation', available at: https://purpose.businessroundtable.org/.

Carney, M. (2020), 'Building a Private Finance System for Net Zero. Priorities for Private Finance for Cop 26', available at: https://bit.ly/3wmbkiO.

Choudhury, B. and Petrin, M. (2022), 'Revisions to the G20/OECD principles of corporate governance – sustainability in name only', *Oxford Business Law Blog*, available at: https://bit.ly/45gkw5P.

Clift, B. (2021), *Comparative Political Economy*, 2nd ed. (London: Palgrave McMillan).

Colaert, V. (2022), 'The changing nature of financial regulation: Sustainable finance as a new EU policy objective', *Common Market Law Review*, 1, 59.

Collyns, D. (2022), 'German judges visit Peru glacial lake in unprecedented climate crisis lawsuit', *The Guardian*.

[107] Regulation (EU) 2020/852 of 18 June 2020 on the establishment of a framework to facilitate sustainable investment, and amending Regulation (EU) 2019/2088, OJ 2020 No. L198, 22 June 22 2020, 13.

Conac, P. H. (2018) 'La société et l'intérêt collectif: la France seule au monde?', Dossier "La réécriture des articles 1833 et 1835 du Code civil: révolution ou constat?", *Revue des Sociétés*, 558.

D'Abrera, B. (2019), 'Get work, go broke', *IPA Review*, 71(2), 21–22.

de Silanes, F. L., McCahery, J. A. and Pudschedl, P. C. (2022), 'Institutional investors and ESG preferences', *ECGI Working Paper Series in Law*, No. 631/2022, 25–27.

Diamond, C. J. and Gez, M. (2022), 'SEC Proposes Long-Awaited Climate Change Disclosure Rules', *White & Case*.

Edelman, L. B. (2016), *Working Law: Courts, Corporations, and Symbolic Civil Rights*, 1st ed. (Chicago: University of Chicago Press).

Edmans, A. (2022), 'The end of ESG', *ESGI Finance Working Paper*, No. 847/2022, 5.

Financial Reporting Council (2022), 'UK Stewardship Code signatory list at 10/03/2022', available at: https://bit.ly/3KJiem1.

Fink, L. (2022), 'Larry Fink's 2022 Letter to CEOs: The Power of Capitalism', *Blackrock*, available at: https://bit.ly/3yYKjDt.

Fisch, J. E. and Solomon, S. D. (2021), 'Should corporations have a purpose?', *Texas Law Review*, 99(7), 1309–1311.

Gensler, G. (2021), 'Statement on the Commission's approval of NASDAQ's proposal for disclosure about board diversity and proposal for board recruiting services', *Security and Exchange Commission*, available at: https://bit.ly/3RomWJL.

Gensler, G. (2022), 'Statement on ESG Disclosures Proposal, U.S. Securities and Exchange Commission', *Securities and Exchange Commission*, available at: https://bit.ly/3Vlz8w2.

Glass Lewis (2021), *Proxy Season Review 2021*. Glass Lewis, available at: https://bit.ly/3RlgRxM.

Griffiths, P. D. R. (2021), 'Global banks' new decarbonisation initiative at COP26 is a step backwards', *Business Standard*, available at: https://bit.ly/3XnEXMl.

Holland, R. J. and Veasey, E. N. (2021), 'Caremark at the quarter-century watershed: modern-day compliance realities frame corporate directors' duty of good faith oversights, providing new dynamics for respecting Chancellor Allen's 1996 Caremark landmark', *Business Lawyer*, 76(1), 27.

Jessop, S. (2022), 'Carney defends dropping U.N. climate initiative over antitrust concerns', *Reuters*, available at: https://reut.rs/4aWmF7O.

John, P. (2019), *Nudge, Nudge, Think, Think: Experimenting with Ways to Change Citizen Behaviour*, 2nd ed. (Manchester, UK: Manchester University Press).

Kuntz, T. (2024), 'The inclusion of ESG aims in corporate fiduciary law and the shrinking business judgement rule', in T. Kuntz (ed.), *Research Handbook on Environmental, Social, and Corporate Governance* (Cheltenham: Edward Elgar).

Licht, A. N. and Adams, R. B. (2020), 'Shareholders and stakeholders around the world: The role of values, culture, and law in directors' decisions', LawFin Working Paper, No. 13, Goethe University, Center for Advanced Studies on the Foundations of Law and Finance (LawFin), Frankfurt a. M., available at: https://doi.org/10.2139/ssrn.3766934.

Light, S. E. and Skinner, C. P. (2022), 'Banks and climate governance', *Columbia Law Review*, 121(6), 1896–1987.

Lucas, F. X. (2018), 'L'inopportune réforme du Code civil par la loi PACTE', *Bulletin Joly Sociétés*, 9, 477.

Lund, D. S. and Pollman, E. (2021), 'The corporate government machine', *Columbia Law Review*, 121(8), 2565.

Mayer, C. (2016), 'Reinventing the corporation', *The British Academy*, 4, 57–58.

Michaels, D. (2022), 'SEC is investigating Goldman Sachs over ESG Funds', *Wall Street Journal*, available at: https://on.wsj.com/4cc3AQ8.

Outka, U. (2019), '100 percent renewable: Company pledges and state energy law', *Utah Law Review*, 3, 661–708.

Pietrancosta, A. (2019), '"Intérêt social" and "raison d'être": Thoughts about two core provisions of the business growth and transformation action plan (PACTE) act that amend corporate law', *Annales des Mines – Réalités industrielles*, 4, 55.

Pietrancosta, A. (2022), 'Codification in Company Law of General CSR Requirements: Pioneering Recent French Reforms and EU Perspectives', (July 20, 2022), European Corporate Governance Institute – Law Working Paper No. 639/2022, available at https://ssrn.com/abstract=4083398 or http://dx.doi.org/10.2139/ssrn.4083398.

Pollman, E. (2022), 'The making and meaning of ESG', *ESGI Working Paper Series in Law*, No. 659/202, 4.

Poracchia, D. (2019), 'De l'intérêt social à la raison d'être des sociétés', *Bulletin Joly Sociétés*, 2019, n° 06, 40.

Puchniak, D. W. (2022), 'No need for Asia to be woke: contextualizing Anglo-America's "discovery" of corporate purpose', *ECGI Working Paper Series in Law*, No. 646/2022, 2–4.

Reuters (2022), 'Blackrock tells UK "no" to halting investment in coal, oil and gas', *Reuters*, available at: https://reut.rs/3RnyKfh.

Ringe, W. G. (2015), 'Changing law and ownership patterns in Germany: Corporate governance and the erosion of Deutschland AG', *The American Journal of Comparative Law*, 63(2).

Roe, M.J. (2003), *Political Determinants of Corporate Governance. Political Context, Corporate Impact* (Oxford: OUP).

Science Based Targets (2022), 'Case studies', *Science Based Targets*, available at: https://bit.ly/3XiokOV.

Seal, D. (2022), 'SEC fines BNY Mellon over ESG claims', *Wall Street Journal*, available at: https://on.wsj.com/4aW61Fs.

Securities and Exchange Commission (2012), 'Fact sheet: Disclosing the use of conflict minerals', available at: https://bit.ly/3Vk4FOZ.

Securities and Exchange Commission (2021), 'Shareholders proposals', Staff Legal Bulletin No. 14L (CF), available at: https://bit.ly/3VzuE6u.

Securities and Exchange Commission (2022), 'Self-regulatory organizations; financial industry regulatory authority, inc.; notice of filing of amendment no. 1 and order instituting proceedings to determine whether to approve or disapprove the proposed rule change, as modified by amendment no. 1, to amend the codes of arbitration procedure to modify the current process relating to the expungement of customer dispute information', Release No. 34-96298, available at: www.sec.gov/files/rules/sro/finra/2022/34-96298.pdf.

So, R. (2022), 'Banks undermine own net zero targets', *Sustainable Views*, available at: https://bit.ly/3XkaEWQ.

Tesco plc (2022), Sustainability. *Tesco*, available at: www.tescoplc.com/sustainability.

Tröger, T and Steuer, S (2021), 'The Role of Disclosure in Green Finance' (August 10, 2021), European Corporate Governance Institute – Law Working Paper No. 604/2021, SAFE Working Paper No. 320, LawFin Working Paper No. 24, available at https://ssrn.com/abstract=3908617 or http://dx.doi.org/10.2139/ssrn.3908617.

U.S. Department of Labor (2022), 'US Department of Labor announces final rule to remove barriers to considering environmental, social, governance factors in plan investments', U.S. Department of Labor, available at: www.dol.gov/newsroom/releases/ebsa/ebsa20221122.

Walker, D. I. (2022), 'The economic (in)significance of executive pay ESG incentives', *Stanford Journal of Law, Business & Finance*, 27(2), 324–327.

Walker, O. (2022), 'German police raid DWS and Deutsche Bank over greenwashing allegations', *Financial Times*, available at: https://on.ft.com/3z5ZpH9.

William, A. and Hodgson, C. (2022), 'Investors at top US banks refuse to back climate proposals', *Financial Times*, available at: https://on.ft.com/4ccJy8b.

5

Stakeholder Engagement

Monika Marcinkowska

5.1 INTRODUCTION

The financial system is a key component of the economy. A financial institution – like every enterprise – is part of society, the environment, and economic activity,[1] and the essence of its activity is to mediate between market participants with different needs and roles. A financial institution's objectives are a result of the expectations of its stakeholders.

UNEP FI's 'Principles for Responsible Banking' include one concerning stakeholders. The signatories declare that they 'will proactively and responsibly consult, engage and partner with relevant stakeholders to achieve society's goals'.[2] The reason for this is that achieving Sustainable Development Goals (SDGs) requires partnerships and encouraging stakeholders to engage in sustainable activities is vital.[3]

Stakeholder engagement (especially multi-stakeholder partnerships) is a cornerstone for the implementation of SDGs.[4] The SDGs framework can be defined as a pragmatic stakeholder engagement model.[5]

Financial institutions are key to achieving these goals – particularly through their indirect impact, that is, the influence on a wide range of stakeholders (their customers, suppliers and partners). Influencing through the stakeholders of financial institutions accelerates the impact on the Sustainable Development Goals. As UNEP FI further explains, 'by partnering with relevant stakeholders (notably peers, investors, clients, customers, regulators, employees, policy-makers, suppliers, scientists, academia, civil society, trade unions and communities), banks can significantly increase the impact of their actions and support action at the scale of change that is required'.[6] Thus, stakeholder engagement is essential in the implementation of a

---

[1] Anbarasan and Sushil 2018.
[2] UNEP FI 2021, 3.
[3] Chang and Chuang 2021.
[4] Cf. Maher and Buhmann 2019; Eweje, Sajjad, Nath and Kobayashi 2021.
[5] Singh and Rahman 2022.
[6] UNEP FI 2021, 27.

sustainable finance strategy – this ensures that all relevant issues raised by stakeholders are addressed, while also ensuring that the institution reduces challenges (negative stakeholder impacts).

The management of stakeholder engagement (including the very selection of the specific groups with which the financial institution will have a relationship) is crucial in terms of assessing the sustainability of the institution. This is because it is done through the lens of the life cycle concept,[7] so it is particularly important who the institution's suppliers and partners are, as well as its customers and how they use its products. Such a holistic view is particularly relevant in the case of financial institutions, which are a key element of sustainable finance (they have an indirect impact on the achievement of the Sustainable Development Goals by channelling funds to entities and projects directly addressing in them).

5.2 STAKEHOLDER THEORY

5.2.1 *Stakeholders*

The analysis of the actors who may have an interest in the activities of a business leads to the consideration of the concept of interest groups, also known as *stakeholders*. The stakeholders of a firm are the entities that are or can be influenced by the enterprise and that exert or can exert influence on the enterprise. Thus, generalising, we can say that they are all elements of the firm's environment that are actually or potentially affected by its operation. Stakeholders can exert pressure on an organisation because it is not self-sufficient – it depends on its environment (gains resources, information, social legitimacy, etc.) through exchange relationships with external actors.[8]

The objectives of any entity's activities are a product of the expectations set by its stakeholders and the circumstances in which these objectives are formulated and are to be realised. Which expectations of which stakeholders are taken into account depends on the internal conditions of the entity's activities (in particular its values, vision, and mission) and an assessment of the potential opportunities for certain interest groups to exert influence and enforce their claims. The hierarchy of expectations deemed legitimate and possible to fulfill and, consequently, the hierarchy of objectives of the entity's activities, results from the determination and strength

---

[7]   The life cycle approach looks at the whole value chain, i.e., from the product design and the supply of raw materials, through the manufacturing and distribution phases, and the purchase, usage, and disposal of the product. With this view, it is possible to assess what costs a product generates throughout its life cycle and what benefits it brings along the value chain (Cf. UNEP 2011). Life cycle management is a concept that facilitates a sustainable approach to the management of a firm that wants to reduce its environmental and socio-economic burden, while maximising economic and social values (cf. Sonnemann et al. 2015, 7).

[8]   Kolk and Pinkse 2006.

of the stakeholders formulating these expectations. A kind of feedback loop can be observed here: with its actions and attitudes, the firm influences its environment and stakeholders and can shape their changes. This, in turn, can translate into new (redefined) objectives for the company in the future.

Freeman – one of the leading popularisers of the stakeholder concept – states that the term 'stakeholders' was first used in 1963 in a Stanford Research Institute paper (in the sense of generalising the only group to whom owners should be accountable).[9] However, Harrison points to an earlier paper – Silbert's published in 1952.[10] Bebchuk et al. point out that the stakeholderism debate has been taking place since the 1930s, citing the classic exchange on the subject in between Adolf Berle and Merrick Dodd.[11] More recently, the concept of stakeholders has been extended to the theory of stakeholder capitalism.[12] This concept takes a macro-level view, considering people (society) and the planet at the centre. The concept is closely linked to the idea of sustainable development.

The stakeholder theory is not a single, unified idea. The concept of 'groups' that have an 'interest' and interact with the enterprise in various ways, making its activities possible, has various facets. The key here is the difference between two approaches: legitimacy and power dependency. The first justification of the importance of stakeholders can be considered from the point of view of contracts, exchanges, legal title, moral rights, the status of risks taken; the second points to the dominance of the enterprise or the dominance of the stakeholders, or interdependence.[13]

The concept of stakeholders is linked to contract theory and the idea of corporate social responsibility. Contract theory views the enterprise as a bundle of contracts: the individual parties to the contracts (agents) provide the enterprise with specific contributions (capital, products, services, skills, cash, etc.) in return for receiving specific entitlements (benefits – e.g., dividends, wages, cash, products, services, interest, taxes, etc.).[14] The idea of corporate social responsibility emphasises the need for the entity to have a balanced impact on the economic (key stakeholders are: owners, customers, suppliers, contractors, and local and national communities), social (employees, customers, communities) and environmental (customers, employees, local communities) spheres. The key issues addressed in each area are:[15]

- in the economic area: financial result and generated corporate value, product value, jobs, ethical trading standards, advertising standards;

---

[9] Freeman 2010, 31.
[10] Freeman et al. 2010, 31.
[11] Bebchuk, Kastiel and Tallarita 2021.
[12] See Schwab 2021.
[13] Andriof and Waddock 2002, 32.
[14] Alchian and Demsetz 1972.
[15] Andriof and Waddock 2002, 26.

- in the social area: human resources policy (equal rights, human rights, employee development, and education) and commitment to external social issues (social exclusion, community regeneration, education, culture, employee volunteering);
- in the environmental sphere: stable, sustainable growth, product life cycle, energy consumption, emissions, waste control.

It is common to divide interest groups into internal and external, and many may belong to several groups at the same time. Internal interest groups may arise, for example, in particular departments, geographical locations, at different levels in the hierarchy, etc. External interest groups include capital providers, customers, suppliers, owners, trade unions, state agencies.[16] Traditionally, owners and investors are considered to be the primary interest group, followed by other actors with a strong influence on the operation of the enterprise (and often in a stronger position vis-à-vis it and thus able to make asymmetrically high demands). These include, for example, the state and its agencies (e.g., tax offices) and capital providers (banks in particular). In the broadest classification of interest groups influencing the activities of a company, a distinction is made between primary and secondary social and non-social *stakeholders* (the latter group includes e.g., the environment, other species, future generations, environmental organisations).[17]

Given the nature of the relationship between the firm and its stakeholders, stakeholder groups can be divided into:[18]

- *consubstantial stakeholders* – stakeholders who are key to the existence of the firm (without whom it could not exist) and who contribute to the firm's existence through their work, knowledge, competencies, experience; these usually include: shareholders and owners, employees and management;
- *contractual stakeholders* – stakeholders who are bound to the entity by some kind of formal contract; this group includes: customers, suppliers, subcontractors, capital providers;
- *contextual stakeholders* – stakeholders who play a key role in gaining the organisation's credibility and acceptance of its activities; this group includes the public, local communities, all social and state institutions (e.g., supervisory institutions, public administration), opinion formers, etc.

Regardless of views on stakeholder theory and views on the extent of a company's responsibility towards stakeholders, it should be noted that every entity shapes its relations with stakeholders to a certain extent. Depending on the vision and mission adopted, this may be a very narrow group of stakeholders (for example limited to owners, customers, and creditors) or a very broad one, including a range of stakeholders to some extent.

---

[16] Johnson and Scholes 1993, 171.
[17] Cf. Wheeler and Sillanpää 1997, 5; Hund and Engel-Cox 2002, 219.
[18] Rodriguez, Ricart and Sanchez 2002.

From the perspective of sustainability and just transition the most important is engagement with the following key stakeholder groups:[19]

- employees – they build the human capital of the firm, enhance workforce capability and provide the right skills to continue delivering long-term value for the future;
- communities – they are important for social acceptance of, and support for, business operations;
- governments and authorities – they are key collaborators to ensure a successful transition and assisting business meet regulatory requirements;
- investors – they are key enablers in financing a successful transition and assisting business to meet the expectations of shareholders;
- suppliers and customers – they are key to business securing reliable supply and customer demand.

5.2.2 *Financial Firms' Responsibility*

To determine which stakeholder expectations will be considered legitimate, it is necessary to define financial firms' responsibility.[20] Social responsibilities and expectations of actors may vary, they are not a fixed category, they are subject to change with social and economic changes. Both the obligations themselves and the importance and priority assigned to them may change. In general, however, four categories of possible duties (responsibilities) of any entity can be identified:[21]

- economic responsibility – is the first and foremost duty of a business that is set up to achieve economic objectives; it must provide products or services that meet customer needs and generate a profit; other business roles are based on this fundamental premise;
- legal accountability – stems from the assumption that the company will act in accordance with applicable laws and regulations; the entity is expected to fulfill its economic tasks within the framework of the applicable regulations;
- ethical responsibility – expectations are placed on companies beyond compliance with the law; ethical obligations are poorly defined and therefore difficult to implement; they derive from the norms and values recognised in a given society;

---

[19] Cf. Deloitte 2022, 12.
[20] Stakeholder theory is utilised to operationalise the question of to whom businesses have a responsibility (see Edles-Zandén 2005). Liability issues (claims, contracts, duties, obligations) are emphasised in the legal approach, while the management approach emphasises relationships, attention, care, influence, respect. Legitimacy of those claims may be normative (legal approach) or derivative (managerial approach), cf. Fassin 2009.
[21] Caroll 1979.

- discretionary (volitional) responsibility[22] – responsibilities for which society has no clearly defined expectations – are left to the individual judgments and choices of the firm; these are purely voluntary roles and stem from the company's desire to be seen as socially responsible.

A company's obligations towards different stakeholder groups may be reflected to varying degrees in the different components of responsibility. For example, the duties towards owners fall mainly into the area of economic responsibility, but also a legal and ethical responsibility. A firm's duties towards its employees relate to its legal and ethical responsibilities, but also to its economic and discretionary responsibilities. The duties towards the state are mainly legal responsibilities, but also economic (generating income and consequently paying taxes) and ethical and – indirectly – discretionary. Obligations to customers primarily involve legal and ethical responsibilities, relating to the economic sphere, and may also be discretionary.

A firm's responsibility is related to the way it conducts its business and the extent to which it respects fundamental values in its relations with stakeholders – honesty, fairness, and integrity. One can speak, for example, of common decency in the treatment of stakeholders.[23] The discussion on corporate responsibility, therefore, refers to the social expectations formulated toward the enterprise and its moral obligations. The dimensions and limits of the duties and obligations that a company accepts and imposes on itself determine the responsibilities it recognises (legitimate expectations) and will translate into the accepted objectives of its functioning.

The evolving approach of law and corporate governance standards is worth highlighting here. The 2015 G20/OECD Principles of Corporate Governance emphasised that 'The corporate governance framework should recognise the rights of stakeholders established by law or through mutual agreements and encourage active cooperation between corporations and stakeholders in creating wealth, jobs, and the sustainability of financially sound enterprises.'[24] Today, increased board accountability is emphasised in many jurisdictions. The 2022 G20/OECD Principles of Corporate Governance review notes that there are two extremes in assessing who is effectively the recipient of directors' duty of loyalty:

> At one end of the spectrum, company law may fully adhere to the 'shareholder primacy' view, obliging directors to consider only shareholders' financial interests while complying with the applicable law and ethical standards. This still requires attention to stakeholders' interests, but only to the extent that those interests may be relevant for the creation of long-term shareholder value. At the other end of the spectrum, directors need to balance shareholders' financial interests with the best interests of stakeholders, and, in addition, to fulfill a number of public interests.[25]

---

[22] In a later article, the author calls the last group of responsibilities philanthropic: Caroll 1991.

[23] Sternberg 2000, 82.

[24] OECD 2015.

[25] OECD 2022. The 2023 version of this document includes a new chapter on "Sustainability and resilience", which incorporates the previous chapter on "The Role of Stakeholders in Corporate Governance" (OECD 2023).

The issue of accountability to stakeholders (and not just shareholders) is linked to the broader issue of sustainability. With the growing importance of ESG factors, there is increasing pressure for a 'sustainable governance' approach.[26] Also, new legislative initiatives in the European Union are promoting this approach, establishing a corporate sustainability due diligence duty.[27]

5.2.3 *Relational Capital*

Contemporary stakeholder theory is based on the premise that a company's relationships with its stakeholders are a valuable resource that managers must manage.[28] They can create relational capital, co-creating the firm's intellectual capital. Intellectual capital is seen as a source of value creation for the firm through the use of intangible resources.

There are many definitions and classifications of the component categories of intellectual capital, the one included here is just a sample compromise of many approaches.[29] When analysing intellectual capital, two of its main components are generally considered: human capital and structural capital (which includes organisational and relationship capital).[30] This study assumes that relationship capital is the third, equal component of intellectual capital, while structural capital also takes into account intellectual property[31] (which some authors attribute to relational capital) – see Figure 5.1.

It is now possible to define *relational capital* as an element of its intellectual capital, created through the company's relationships with its stakeholders, using human and social capital, also requiring the involvement of the firm's financial and structural capital. It is therefore the *totality of the firm's relationships and links with its stakeholders, based on mutual trust.*[32] This is of special importance in the case of financial firms, as they are referred to as public trust institutions. *Sustainable relationships (and thus creating relational capital) of a financial firm require mutual honesty and responsibility.* Ultimately, the market advantage will be gained by the company that is able to build a better, more sustainable network of relationships with its stakeholders; it will be the basis for creating value for that entity. Stakeholders can have different contributions to a firm business model: they

---

[26] See Sjåfjell and Bruner (eds.) 2019; Gutterman 2020.

[27] See European Commission 2022; Directive 2024/1760 of the European Parliament and of the Council of 13 June 2024 on corporate sustainability due diligence and amending Directive (EU) 2019/1937 and Regulation (EU) 2023/2859, OJ 2024 No. L1760, 5 July 2024.

[28] Post, Preston and Sachs 2002a.

[29] Some authors mention – instead of the types of capital discussed – other divisions of value drivers, e.g., Sveiby 1997 introduced the division of capitals into visible (book value) and invisible (intangible), while in this group he distinguishes: external structure (brands, relations with customers and suppliers, etc.), internal structure (organisation, management, legal structure, research and development, information systems, etc.), and individual competences (education, knowledge, experience, etc.).

[30] See e.g., Edvinsson and Malone 1997 and Roos, Roos, Dragonetti and Edvinsson 1997.

[31] A similar approach is presented by Dzinkowski 2000.

[32] Marcinkowska 2013, 152.

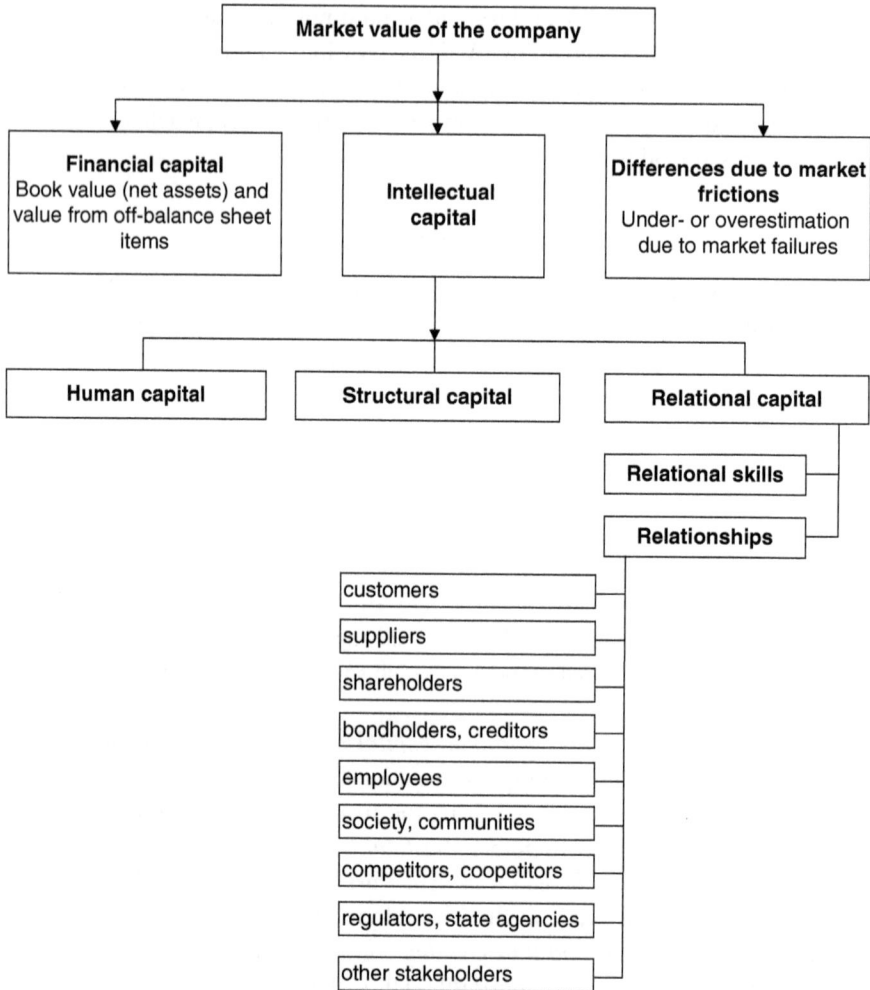

FIGURE 5.1 Relational capital in a market value tree of a company
Source: Adapted from Marcinkowska 2013, 130.

can be engaged in value intention, value proposition, value creation, value delivery, and value capture.[33]

When discussing the issue of enterprise *value*, it is worth mentioning the concepts of *shareholder value* (or *stockholder value*) and *stakeholder value*.[34] In the first case, the company has a single purpose for functioning: to generate profits and thus shareholder value; the other objectives do not count. According to the second concept, a bundle of objectives is adopted: both economic and social; the management

---

[33] Attanasio, Preghenella, De Toni and Battistella 2022.
[34] Kirsten 2000, 24.

of the company here takes ethical aspects into account. This approach is based on a vision of a specific social arrangement and takes into account the cooperation of stakeholders. In the long term, economic and social objectives are not only not in conflict but are integrally linked.[35] In practice, therefore, there has been a significant convergence of the two concepts. Indeed, it should be emphasised that it is not possible to create shareholder value without ensuring a certain value for other stakeholders (customers, employees, local communities, etc.).[36] On the other hand, it is possible to distribute the emphasis differently – to focus more on shareholder value (in this perspective, the owners' interest is seen as more important than the expectations of other stakeholders) or to accept the primacy of stakeholder value (in this perspective, the owners' interest is not overarching).[37]

The basis for defining a stakeholder relationship strategy is to answer three questions: what is the purpose of the relationship (why the organisation is engaging), who the stakeholders are (who needs to be involved in the engagement), and what the scope of the relationship is to be (what issues to engage on).[38] Sources of business relationships can be: expected benefits, mutual exchange, minimisation of transaction costs, shared values, and coercive measures.[39]

5.3 STAKEHOLDER ENGAGEMENT MANAGEMENT

5.3.1 *Introduction*

Stakeholder engagement management consists of four stages:

(1) stakeholder identification;
(2) analysis and segmentation (categorisation) of stakeholders;
(3) prioritisation of stakeholders and selection of an engagement strategy;
(4) monitoring and evaluation of engagement.

These stages should be repeated, as the outcome of the evaluation of the relationship may necessitate a change in the engagement strategy and, in the course of the company's activities, the stakeholders themselves, their expectations, and the

---

[35] Porter and Kramer 2002.
[36] Stout (2012) even states that a single 'shareholder value' is a fiction, as different shareholders may have different values. She also suggests that instead of value maximisation objective a company should pursue several objectives and 'try to do decently well (or at least sufficiently well) at each' ('satisficing approach').
[37] It can be seen that looking at both perspectives is reflected in the double materiality concept. According to it, companies reporting on sustainability issues should disclose information that is both financially relevant (i.e., affects the company's financial value) and impacts on people (society) and the environment; see EFRAG 2022.
[38] AccountAbility 2015, 16.
[39] Wheeler and Davies 2008, 231.

Monika Marcinkowska

▶ **IDENTIFICATION OF STAKEHOLDERS**	who, number type of contractual form dimension of firm's responsibility dependencies
ANALYSIS OF STAKEHOLDERS	goals, expectations, contributions power, legitimacy, predictability interest in relationship, attitude chances and risks (threats) for the firm
STRATEGY OF ENGAGEMENT CHOICE	prioritisation of stakeholders and their needs choice of the level of engagement and methods of influence
RELATIONS WITH STAKEHOLDERS	stakeholders involvement: inactive, reactive, proactive, interactive
INTERACTIONS WITH STAKEHOLDERS	communication with stakeholders: gathering information from stakeholders, one-way (stakeholders-firm or firm-stakeholders) or two-way communication
EVALUATION OF RELATIONS WITH STAKEHOLDERS	measurement of outcomes (firm's perspective) measurement of outcomes (stakeholders' perspective) evaluation of form's and stakeholders' goals achievement
REACTIONS IN CASE OF PROBLEMS	acceptability management dialog defensive measures learning process
CONTINUATION OR CHANGE OF STRATEGY	repetition of steps improving relationships

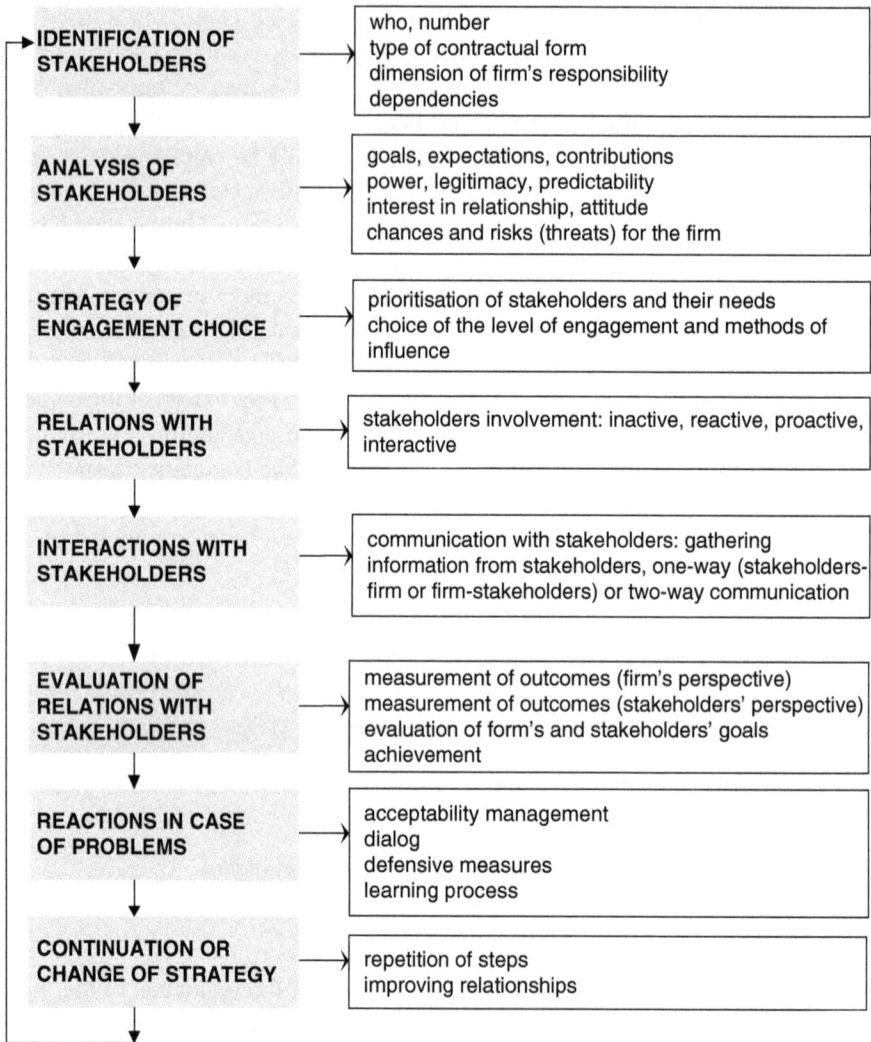

FIGURE 5.2 Stakeholder relationship management
Source: Based on Schuster (ed.) 2000, 5; Freeman, Harrison and Wicks 2007, 104; Svendsen 1998, 67.

entity's operating environment may change, which may also necessitate a change in the strategies adopted.

Figure 5.2 summarises the stakeholder relationship management process.

5.3.2 *Identification of Stakeholders*

The first step in managing a company's stakeholder relationships is stakeholder identification. A company must identify who the current, potential, and desired

MACROENVIRONMENT
- distant external stakeholders

SOCIAL
CULTURAL
RELIGIOUS
EDUCATIONAL
DEMOGRAPHIC
ENV.

MACROEVONOMIC ENV.

FINANCIAL SYSTEM
STRUCTURE

Financial markets

MICROENVIRONMENT
- closer external stakeholders

Information/data providers

. *Society (local, national, international)*
. *Public opinion*
. *Social pressure groups*
. *Educational institutions*
. *Research institutes, think-tanks*
. *NGOs*
. *Media*
. *Opinion leaders*
. *Potential customers*
. *Future generations*

Owners:
- strategic
- minority
- investors

Customers

Competitors:
- from the sector
- outside the sector
  . near-banks
  . nonbanks

Safety net
- microprudential supervisor
- macroprudential supervisor
- central bank
- deposit guarantee
- resolution inst.
- consumer protection inst.
- external audotors

Supervisory board

BANK

Internal stakeholders:

Managers Employees

Rating agencies

Industry organisations

INTERNATIONAL, GLOBAL ENV.

POLITICAL ENV.

Creditors:
- lenders
- bondholders

Cooperators Strategic partners

Suppliers:
- of services (eg. consultants, outsourcers)
- of hardware and technology

*The state
Government
State agencies
Political parties
Lobbying groups*

*Natural environment
Ecological pressure groups*

Innovators

*Regulators
Courts
Arbitration
Financial ombudsman*

NATURAL ENV.

TECHNOLOGICAL ENV.

REGULATORY
& LEGAL ENV.

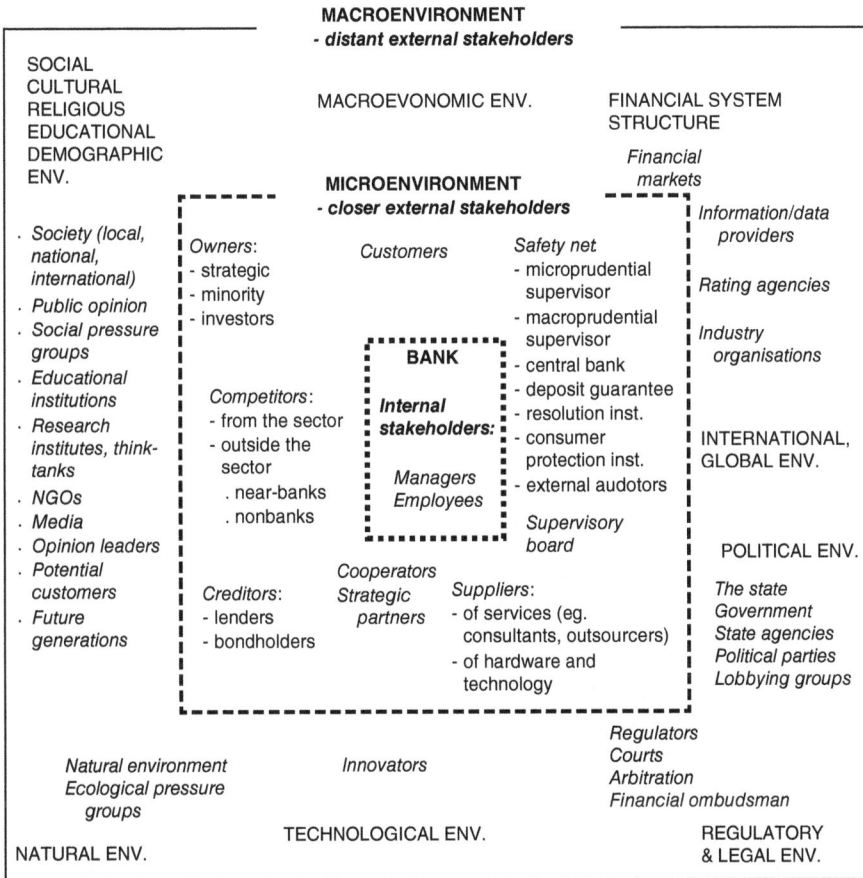

FIGURE 5.3 Example: bank's environment and stakeholders
Legend:
ITEM (CAPS) – element of bank's environment
Item (*italics*) – bank's stakeholder
Source: Adapted from Marcinkowska 2012, 168.

interest groups are, i.e., determine which interest groups influence the company and which ones are influenced by its actions. It is worth noting that some of the firm's stakeholders are 'imposed' elements of the environment – the same entities that will always appear on any company's list of interest groups (e.g., certain state institutions, the public), and some are entities that are 'voluntary' stakeholders – the decision to enter into a relationship is not imposed on the company, but stems from both parties (on the initiative of the entity or the stakeholder in question).

Figure 5.3 shows an exemplary identification of a bank's environment elements (micro and macro) and its key stakeholder groups (internal and external – near and far).

The identification of stakeholders should be done individually by each entity, taking into account the environment in which it operates and the mission it wishes to fulfill. While some interest groups will be common to all entities (e.g., regulators), some will be identified as similar, though not identical (customers, competitors, media), and some groups will be specific to a particular entity. When identifying stakeholders, one should not be guided solely by intuition and one's own conviction about the importance of the different actors in the environment. A broader survey should be carried out here, which will allow a comparison of actual and potential stakeholders.

In practice, it is possible that the actual identified stakeholders of the firm are different from the desired stakeholders. Depending on the results of the further stages of analysis and the firm's vision and mission, as well as its resources and opportunities for strategic reorientation, the firm must decide whether and to what extent it intends to adapt to its environment and to what extent it can make choices of target stakeholders. In doing so, it is important to be aware that the firm has to compete with other players in the market for certain general 'voluntary' stakeholder groups (e.g., customers, investors, employees, suppliers, co-operators). These can be entities from the same or related industry (as, for example, in the case of customers) and entities completely different (as, for example, in the case of investors – buyers of securities in the capital market). An analysis of the expectations and contributions of these stakeholders (as well as the subsequent stages of their characterisation) will be particularly important for deciding on the relevance and feasibility of a firm's engagement with a particular group.

5.3.3 *Stakeholder Analysis*

As a next step, it is necessary to carry out an analysis of these groups, to examine the general characteristics of the stakeholders in terms of shaping the relationship with them. In particular, a firm should determine their type, number, the relationships between them, and, above all, their values, needs, and expectations, as well as the legitimacy of these expectations. In addition, it is necessary to identify the most important issues (economic, political, social, technological, etc.) that will affect stakeholders in the next few years and assess how these issues affect the stakeholders themselves and the company.[40] These aspects will allow anticipating how the expectations of the interest groups may change and, consequently, how the objectives of the enterprise may evolve.

One of the dimensions of stakeholder analyses can be looked at from the point of view of contractual forms (type of relationship); two dimensions are considered here: whether the relationships are compatible in terms of ideas and relevant issues, and whether they are necessary or contingent. Combining these two dimensions, the following configurations can be classified:[41]

---

[40] Freeman 2010, 92.
[41] Cf. Friedman and Miles 2006, 103.

- compatible and necessary – explicit/implicit recognised relationships (share-holders, top management, partners);
- incompatible but necessary – explicit/implicit recognised relationships (trade unions, low-level workers, government and its agencies, customers, creditors);
- compatible and contingent – implicit unrecognised relationships (general public, companies connected through common trade associations/initiatives);
- incompatible and contingent – no contracts.

The strategic stakeholder analysis should answer three groups of questions:[42]

- In terms of interest group analysis: who are the stakeholders,[43] what impact does each group have (taking into account political, economic, and social aspects),[44] and how do stakeholders perceive this impact?
- As part of the values analysis: what are the most important organisational values, what are the values of key executives, what are the values of key stakeholders?
- In the area of social issues: what are the most important issues affecting society in the next 10 years (economic, political, social, technological, etc.), how do these issues affect the entity and its stakeholders?

Additionally, a company should identify and assess the stakeholders' engagement risks.[45]

Already at this stage, it is possible to see what is the power of mutual influence and therefore what kind of engagement level should be in place.[46] Those stakeholders who have a high or formal influence on organisation and at the same time are highly dependent on an organisation may be a strategic opportunity or threat and therefore a company must invest in the engagement process. In the case of stakeholders who have a high or formal influence on organisation but where there is no direct impact of the firm on them, the relationship will be looser (they should be kept involved

---

[42] Freeman 2010, 92.

[43] A gradual extension of the analysis according to the range of stakeholder impacts is suggested; e.g., three spheres are distinguished: resource-based (e.g., investors, employees, customers and consumers/users), industry structures (e.g., unions, strategic alliances, suppliers, regulatory authorities), socio-political (local communities, government and state authorities, private organisations). For more on this, see Post, Preston and Sachs 2002b, 55.

[44] For example, it is suggested here to draw up a matrix of individual stakeholder issues, in which the importance of the issue to a particular stakeholder (e.g., no importance, minor importance, fundamental importance) should be marked (according to a selected scale). See Freeman, Harrison and Wicks 2007, 107.

[45] AccountAbility 2015, 26, suggest a list of potential stakeholders risks (unwillingness to engage, participation fatigue, creating expectations of change that the firm is unwilling or unable to fulfill, lack of balance between weak and strong stakeholders, disruptive stakeholders, uninformed stakeholders, disempowered stakeholders, technical barriers of engagement processes, conflict between participating stakeholders) and organisational risks (damage to reputation, waste of time and resources, loss of control of issues, not meeting firm's expectations, strong criticism, creation of conflict of interest, internal disagreement on way forward, non-compliance with legal and internal policies and standards).

[46] See Deloitte 2014.

and informed). Stakeholders highly dependent on an organisation, but having no or low influence on it, should be treated fairly to keep them satisfied insofar as balance of costs and benefits allow. Other stakeholders will have low priority.

The identification and initial stakeholder analysis should lead to the development of a map or a matrix of the organisation's stakeholder groups, taking into account the importance of the different actors and the possible links between them (formal and informal[47]).[48] It is also important to identify who influences individual stakeholders (who shapes their opinions);[49] these actors should be taken into account by the firm in developing its stakeholder communication strategy.

As part of the detailed analysis of interest groups, the main focus of the assessment should be:[50]

- stakeholder power – its sources can be:
  - for internal interest groups: position in the hierarchy, influence over others, control of resources, knowledge and skills, control of the working environment;
  - for external interest groups: dependence on resources, involvement in internal processes, knowledge and skills, internal links;
- the predictability of their reactions and actions; and
- a demonstrated interest in the affairs of the firm.

Such an analysis should be multidimensional; for example, an analysis of the power of interest groups should be carried out together with an analysis of their predictability (if, for example, an interest group has a high power of influence but its behaviour is predictable, then it is less threatening to the enterprise than the same group with low predictability – it represents a big unknown: it can be either a significant threat or a significant opportunity). To these considerations must be added the aspect of the interest of pressure groups: a different attitude of the entity will be required by those players who show a high interest in its operation, and a different one by those whose interest is negligible. It is also important to confront these analyses with the objectives of the various interest groups and to identify potential conflicts. With regard to each identified group of interests, its expectations from the firm (the needs it expects to realise in its relationship with the firm) should be identified, but, on the other hand, also the contributions it can make to the relationship with the firm (the needs and expectations of the company that can be fulfilled by the stakeholders).

---

[47] Formal relationships tend to be well known, whereas informal relationships can be subtle, very common, and can often be more significant, see Akermann and Eden 2011.

[48] Stakeholder-company linkages are usually presented as dyadic. Meanwhile, the dependencies that exist between stakeholders should also be taken into account. If the network of these ties is strong, it may change the position of stakeholders and affect their relationship with the enterprise differently; see Rowley 1997.

[49] Examples of such analyses are presented in Suntook and Murphy 2008.

[50] Johnson and Scholes 1993, 175 et seq.

Table 5.1 shows examples of the needs and expectations of firm's stakeholders (stakeholders' satisfaction factors) and the needs and expectations of a firm in relation to its key stakeholders groups (stakeholders contributions). Here, too, it is imperative that the firm carries out a genuine, in-depth study of stakeholder expectations, rather than ascribing to them characteristics that are generally, standardly ascribed

TABLE 5.1 *Stakeholder satisfaction and contribution factors*

Stakeholder satisfaction (stakeholder needs and expectations)	Stakeholders	Stakeholder contributions (needs and expectations of the organisation)
Profit Security Integrity, honest information Supporting group objectives Stable development of the entity Impact on the entity's objectives, strategy, and activities	Investors, owners	Capital Support Trust Risk mitigation Recognition and status in the market
Profit Security Integrity, information Impact on the entity's activities	Creditors	Capital Trust Risk mitigation Support
Product/serviced quality Safe, reliable products/services, protection from harm Low prices Convenience Integrity, responsibility, fair treatment Honest information Innovation, modernity	Customers	Profits, value Loyalty Trust, reputation Integrity, responsibility Information, safety Cooperation and development
High salaries Protection Safety, stability Integrity Opportunity for development, satisfaction with achievements	Employees	Work, productivity Qualifications Development, innovation, improvement Honesty, loyalty, trust Relationships Human capital
Remuneration and other benefits Status, prestige Ability to realise one's own aspirations Satisfaction with achievements Security	Management	Caring for the welfare of the firm Knowledge and experience Commitment Integrity Reputation

(continued)

Monika Marcinkowska

TABLE 5.1 *(continued)*

Stakeholder satisfaction (stakeholder needs and expectations)	Stakeholders	Stakeholder contributions (needs and expectations of the organisation)
Profits Willingness to cooperate Loyalty Trust Integrity, timely payments Predictability	Suppliers	Low prices of products/services Convenience Quality Certainty, predictability Flexibility Integrity
Profits, value Loyalty Trust Integrity Joint development	Strategic partners	Profits, value Strategic resources and skills Loyalty, honesty Trust Joint development
Security Integrity, professional ethics Common standards of conduct Willingness to enter into alliances Fair competition, promoting open markets	Competitors	Security Integrity, professional ethics Common standards of conduct Willingness to enter into alliances Fair competition, promoting open markets
Compliance with regulations Integrity Security Tax revenue Stable development of the entity Promoting economic development Coherence of actions with national economic and social policy	State	Fair regulations, principles, good practices Clarity Certainty, predictability Integrity and compliance with standards Freedom to conduct business Protection against unauthorised activities
Compliance with regulations Integrity Security Workplaces Charitable activities, sponsorship Support for education, culture, etc. State and regional development Caring for the ecosystem	Communities	Principles Clarity Integrity Reputation Trust Support, integration
Caring for the ecosystem Integrity Security	Environmentalists	Reputation Support for environmental initiatives
Reliable information Fair communication	Analysts and media	Reliable information Fair analysis and communication

Source: Based on Nelly, Adams and Kennerley 2002; Post, Preston and Sachs 2002, 67; Marcinkowska 2013, 187; Weiss 2022, 206.

to a particular stakeholder group. This is because the results of this analysis are the foundation for the decisions taken in the next stages of stakeholders engagement management. Assigning needs and expectations to someone that are inconsistent with the actual state of affairs may hinder the realisation of the actual objectives of the group in question – either causing dissatisfaction on the part of the group due to the failure to realise certain expectations, or giving rise to excessive costs resulting from meeting expectations in excess. This phase of analysis therefore has a significant impact on the effectiveness of the stakeholder relations process.

The relevance of individual stakeholders to the firm is one of the key issues considered when establishing the stakeholder hierarchy. For each stakeholder group, the level of its importance on particular issues of relevance to the firm (e.g., financial performance, market position, new product development, reliability of reporting, etc.) should be determined.[51] This 'materiality matrix' usually forms the basics for the prioritisation of stakeholders (or issues raised by stakeholders).

In addition, the question of the stakeholders' interest in the company matters, and their willingness to influence its functioning should be taken into account.[52] Central to prioritising stakeholders and determining how to manage relationships with them is the question of the stakeholders' interest in the company and potential relationships with it, as well as attitudes towards the entity itself. A distinction can be made between opponents (active and passive), neutral stakeholders (fence-sitters), and supporters (active and passive).[53] Furthermore, a firm should assess potential benefits from relationships and potential threats to the organisation each stakeholder group may cause. The level of the potential threat and the stakeholder's potential for cooperation with organisation will be the basis for the diagnosis (distinguishing the type of organisational stakeholders) and suggest the strategy for each group identified.[54]

On this basis, it is even suggested to revise the definition of stakeholders: the potential list of actors can be divided into three distinct categories:[55]

(1) genuine stakeholders – internal stakeholders and those who have a real stake in the company's operations (*stakeholders*);
(2) pressure groups that influence the company (*stakewatchers*);
(3) regulators, who exercise external control and impose regulations on the entity (*stakekeepers*).

---

[51] Freeman, Harrison and Wicks 2007, 107.
[52] Savage, Nix, Whitehead and Blair 1991.
[53] Cf. Straker 2014.
[54] For example, a firm should collaborate with stakeholders that may cause high threat but are cooperative and defend from those whose potential for cooperation is low. In case of stakeholders with low potential threat, a firm should involve supportive stakeholders and only monitor those with low potential for cooperation. See Savage, Nix, Whitehead and Blair 1991.
[55] Fassin 2009.

An important issue in stakeholder analysis is to consider the strength and legitimacy of stakeholders and the 'urgency' of their expectations. This allows seven stakeholder groups to be identified, with:[56]

- 'invisible' stakeholders – of minor importance, due to the fact that only one of the three attributes is assigned to them: dormant stakeholders – only power, discretionary stakeholders – only legitimacy, demanding stakeholders – only urgency;
- 'expectant' stakeholders – of medium importance – they have two of each of the characteristics analysed: dominant stakeholders – power and legitimacy, dependent stakeholders – legitimacy and urgency, dangerous stakeholders – power and urgency;
- the decisive stakeholders – of greatest importance – they take into account all aspects considered;
- other identified groups are not stakeholders (they are irrelevant).

Research shows that these three characteristics actually influence companies' decisions to include the expectations of a given stakeholder group in a bundle of objectives.[57] Such an analysis is important because, as already highlighted, the expectations of different stakeholder groups may diverge, leading to conflict in the selection of objectives to be pursued. In cases where some expectations are mutually exclusive (cannot be fulfilled simultaneously), compromise choices have to be made.[58] These are made precisely with an assessment of the urgency of the reported needs and the strength and legitimacy of the stakeholders.

As mentioned, the selection of stakeholders with whom the entity will have a relationship is particularly important in terms of assessing sustainability from a life cycle perspective. Hence, it is common practice to set preconditions for the selection of suppliers, partners, customers, as well as the entities in whose assets the firm will invest. Both negative screening (exclusion of entities e.g., performing a certain type of activity or having certain characteristics) and positive screening (openness to entities meeting certain criteria) can be applied here.

5.3.4 *Stakeholder Prioritisation and Engagement Strategies*

The results of stakeholder analyses should lead to the prioritisation of the company's stakeholders groups (and the identification of potentially effective tools for influencing them) and the definition of the firm's strategy towards them. This decision primarily concerns the desired scope and level of stakeholder engagement. It is not

---

[56] Mitchell, Agle and Wood 1997.

[57] At the same time, it was proven that of these three characteristics, urgency of need was the most important, followed by stakeholder power and legitimacy was the last. See Agle, Mitchell and Sonnenfeld 1999.

[58] Johnson and Scholes 1993, 171.

possible to take into account all stakeholders and all their expectations. Firstly, there are conflicts of interest between different stakeholders groups (or even different stakeholders in the same group, for example, strategic and minority shareholders, different segments of customers, etc.), moreover, some stakeholders' expectations usually conflict with the firm's interests, but above all with the interests of other stakeholders groups.[59] Secondly, the company does not have sufficient resources to meet all the needs raised. It is, therefore, necessary to make a selection – a balancing of stakeholders' interests; this is a process of assessing, weighing, and selecting the competing claims of those who have a stake in the organisation's activities. Ultimately, the decision must include some sort of solution to the conflicting needs and expectations of the stakeholders.[60]

In practice, therefore, there is an undemocratic stakeholder prioritisation and selection process by management.[61] Research indicates that management's decisions about which stakeholder needs will be taken into account by an entity are influenced by general societal expectations that are typical of a particular culture – country, region, etc. (this happens through influence on state regulations and corporate business practices).[62] Managers' decisions are also influenced by their personal value systems and the roles they play.[63]

Decisions taken at this stage are crucial to the entire stakeholder relations management process. This is because the firm indicates which stakeholder claims it considers legitimate and what is the hierarchy of its aspirations. The stakeholder selection and prioritisation process is also supported to some extent by a relationship effectiveness analysis: the firm considers the expectations of the stakeholders on the one hand, but also their contributions to the relationship with the company on the other. A holistic view of the entity's relationship requires taking into account the links between these expectations and contributions, but also a combined view of all the needs and expectations raised – of the firm and towards the firm. This is because what some stakeholders can contribute can become a valuable resource for the organisation to fulfill the needs of other stakeholders. It is important to emphasise that stakeholder management is not one-sided: it does not just mean meeting the expectations of the stakeholders, but of course also of the entity itself.

For financial institutions, this step is particularly important, especially in the context of ESG strategies, including ESG risk management in particular, as these

---

[59] For example, customers expect low prices of company's products or services, while a company (and its owners) needs to gain profits on sales, investors want returns and high growth, and the economy (and thus the state) needs stable growth in the long term. In some cases there are even conflicting interests within the same group of interests: for example, the state requires banks to be safe and stable (to limit their risk), but at the same time it needs banks to grant loans to ensure the development of the economy (and thus to be exposed to risk).

[60] Reynolds, Schultz and Hekman 2006.

[61] Unerman and Bennett 2004, Mitchell, Agle and Wood 1997.

[62] Boesso and Kumar 2009.

[63] Adams, Licht and Sagiv 2011.

relationships will affect the institution's risks – financial or operational and reputational. As the relationships with the entities financed by the firm (borrowers and entities in which the company invests) affect the risk of its portfolio, their selection and the support given to them in the transition process (management directed towards meeting specific sustainability objectives) are important tools for ESG risk management. In this case, a company will only engage with a stakeholder if it is aligned with the institution's portfolio trajectory or its transition plan is compatible with this trajectory. However, if these conditions are not met, the firm will not engage in such a relationship (and, in the case of an existing one, will seek, for example, to reduce exposure, change the client's rating or terminate the relationship with the client).[64]

After selecting the key stakeholders and those of their reported needs that the firm intends to address, and taking into account its expectations that may be materialised through the relationship with these stakeholders, a decision should be made on the desired degree of involvement of each stakeholder in the operation of the firm.

The process of 'stakeholder engagement' refers to practices undertaken by an organisation to involve relevant stakeholders for a clear purpose to achieve agreed outcomes.[65] Of course, this does not necessarily (and should not even) mean that all areas of a firm's operations will incorporate stakeholder engagement. The level of such engagement need not be identical in all selected areas.

Hemphill distinguishes four phases of the stakeholder engagement continuum:[66]

- inactive engagement – unilateral decision-making, ignoring stakeholder issues;
- reactive engagement – management engages in relationships defensively, only when forced to do so;
- proactive engagement – management seeks to anticipate stakeholder interests;
- interactive engagement – the company has an ongoing relationship with its stakeholders, based on mutual respect, openness, and trust.

The approach towards specific stakeholders groups can be linked with the dimension of responsibility for the firm towards this group. In the case of legal responsibilities, the external regulations impose certain requirements (rules-based approach). When ethical responsibilities are involved, the relations are voluntary and based on self-regulation, driven by values, best practices, and ethics.[67]

---

[64] ECB cites the example of a client engagement process, in which engagement begins after a dedicated committee has assessed whether the client is willing and able to meet the institution's requirements, and in the event of a positive assessment, engagement objectives, and deadlines are set. The client is informed of these, as well as the consequences of not meeting them. Once the customer has taken the agreed action (periodically monitored by the bank), the committee assesses the results against the objectives and expectations set. On this basis, decisions are taken on further engagement. Cf. ECB 2022, 95.
[65] AccountAbility 2015, 5.
[66] Hemphill 2006.
[67] Weiss 2021, 214.

By grading the levels of stakeholder involvement and the level of influence in detail, a kind of 'governance ladder' can be defined with the following levels identified (intentions of engagement are indicated in brackets):[68]

- non-participation – autocratic nature, stakeholders have knowledge about decisions:
  (1) manipulation ('misleading' stakeholders; attempting to change stakeholder expectations);
  (2) therapy ('cure' stakeholders of their ignorance and preconceived beliefs);
  (3) informing (educating stakeholders);
- degrees of tokenism – responsive nature, stakeholders are being heard before a decision:
  (4) explaining (educating stakeholders);
  (5) placation (appease stakeholders – they can hear and be heard, but have no assurance of being heeded by the organisation);
  (6) consultation (organisation has the right to decide, stakeholders can advise);
  (7) negotiation (stakeholders provide conditional support, if conditions are not met- support is removed; the organisation determines the extent of conformity);
- degrees of involvement – responsive or proactive nature, stakeholders have an influence on decisions:
  (8) involvement (stakeholders provide conditional support, if conditions are not met- support is removed; the organisation determines the extent of conformity);
  (9) collaboration (some decision-making power afforded to stakeholders over specific projects);
- degrees of stakeholder power – responsive or proactive nature, stakeholders are forming or agreeing to decisions:
  (10) partnership (joint decision-making power over specific projects);
  (11) delegated power (minority representation of stakeholders in decision-making process);
  (12) stakeholder control (majority representation of stakeholders in decision-making process).

Ongoing communication is essential in the process of managing relations with interest groups – especially in the analysis stage of the relationship. Three groups of such pre-engagement activities can be distinguished, along with the tools that can be used:[69]

- analysing stakeholders' views (complaints, correspondence, media, websites, protests, other advocacy efforts);

[68] Friedman and Miles 2006, 162.
[69] AccountAbility 2015, 21.

- tracking information (media, Internet, social network, third-party reports);
- creating awareness (bulletins, newsletters and brochures, websites, social media, press releases, advertising and other displays, speeches and conference presentations, road shows, lobbying).

The final sphere of management in this area is preparation for conflict resolution and dealing with problems. With a well-conducted analysis of interest groups and honest communication with them, a company should be able to prepare contingency plans for unforeseen problems and implement them effectively for the benefit of itself and its stakeholders.[70]

Certain stages of building collaborative relationships with stakeholders can be distinguished: the first is laying the groundwork (including choosing such a strategic direction, redefining the company's mission, vision and values, and communicating corporate commitment). The next stage is reorienting the organisation – here, gaps and deficiencies need to be identified, systems and structures need to be assessed and necessary changes need to be made. The next stage is strategy formulation. An essential stage for the optimal implementation of a collaborative relationship is the building of trust (e.g., through the exchange of information, communication, identification of common goals, identification of areas of conflict, and provision of resources). The final stages are the evaluation and iteration of those steps that require improvements and enhancements.[71]

Stakeholder relationship management is a continuous, holistic activity – identifying stakeholders, maintaining relationships with them, and improving those relationships are ongoing simultaneously every day.[72]

In order to build mutually beneficial, long-term relationships, commitment and trust are necessary. Commitment here can be seen as the belief of the exchange partner that the relationship is important enough to justify putting maximum effort into maintaining it. It is, therefore, an ongoing desire to maintain a relationship that is considered important and meaningful.[73] Each party's decision to engage in the relationship (and the degree of that engagement) is influenced by: trust in the other party, perceived benefits and costs of the relationship and the costs of ending it, shared values, and communication. The consequences of such trust-based commitment are acceptance of the other party's actions, cooperation, reduced willingness to break the relationship, and reduced uncertainty; 'constructive conflicts' are also mentioned, i.e., such conflicts (disagreements) that, when resolved in a friendly and partnership manner, allow compromise solutions to be found.[74]

---

[70] Schuster 2000, 4.
[71] Svendsen 1998, 67.
[72] Smudde and Courtright 2011.
[73] Morgan and Hunt 1994.
[74] Ibid.

Among the basic strategies for building stakeholder value are:[75]

- change-the-rule strategies – formal rules change through regulators, change the decision forum, change the kinds of decisions made;
- offensive strategies – changing beliefs about the company, doing something different, trying to change stakeholders' objectives, adopting stakeholder positions, linking the programme to others that stakeholders views more favourably;
- defensive strategies – reinforcing current beliefs about the company, maintaining existing programmes, linking issues to others that stakeholders perceive more favourably;
- holding programmes (stabilisation) – not making any changes and monitoring existing programmes, reinforcing current beliefs about the company.

It is important to bear in mind that a firm's strategies toward its stakeholders may change over time. Each business, depending on the life cycle phase it is in, may assess the importance of its stakeholders differently and allocate resources differently to different stakeholders, depending on their perceived impact on the success of the business.[76]

Depending on the stakeholder relations strategy adopted (the level of stakeholder consideration), the firm may use different methods to engage and communicate with them. The example engagement tools on different levels of communication include:[77]

- the low level of engagement is connected with none or only one-way communication:
  - remaining passive (no communication) – letters, media, websites, stakeholder concern expressed through protest;
  - monitoring (one-way communication: stakeholder to organisation) – media and Internet tracking, second-hand reports from other stakeholders possibly via targeted interviews;
  - advocating (one-way communication: organisation to stakeholder) – pressure on regulatory bodies, lobbying efforts, other advocacy efforts through social media);
- the medium level of engagement is connected with the limited communication:
  - informing (one-way communication: organisation to stakeholder, no invitation to reply) – bulletins and letters, brochures, reports, websites, speeches, conference and public presentations;
  - transacting (limited two-way engagement: setting and monitoring performance according to terms of contract) – public–private partnerships, Private Finance Initiatives, grant-making, cause-related marketing;

---

[75] Freeman, Harrison and Wicks 2007, 117.
[76] Jawahar and McLaughlin 2001.
[77] AccountAbility 2015, 21–22.

- consulting (limited two-way engagement: organisation asks questions, stake-
    holders answer) – surveys, focus groups, meetings with selected stakeholders,
    public meetings, workshops;
- negotiating (limited two-way engagement: discuss a specific issue or range of
    issues with the objective of reaching consensus) – collective bargaining with
    workers through their trade unions;
- the high level of engagement is connected with the diverse communication:
  - involvement (two-way or multi-way engagement: learning on all sides but
      stakeholders and organisation act independently) – multi-stakeholder forums,
      advisory panels, consensus building processes, participatory decision-making
      processes, focus groups, online engagement tools;
  - collaboration (two-way or multi-way engagement: joint learning, decision-
      making and actions) – joint projects, joint ventures, partnerships, multi-
      stakeholder initiatives, online collaborative platforms;
  - empowerment (new forms of accountability; decisions delegated to stake-
      holders; stakeholders play a role in shaping organisational agendas) –
      integration of stakeholders into governance, strategy, and operations of the
      organisation.

5.3.5 *Monitoring and Evaluation of Stakeholder Relations*

A very important step in stakeholder engagement management is the evaluation of
the effects of the relationship. This requires a modification of the methods used to
measure and assess the performance of companies, in order to capture the effects
of the above-mentioned contracts and stakeholder engagement (the focus is thus
shifted from owners to broader stakeholder groups), and in many cases to include
non-financial effects. Social accounting and stakeholder auditing tools will be useful in this regard.

'Social accounting' is a broad term, encompassing many forms and tools. In its
broadest sense, it can mean all forms of data and reports that go beyond economics and therefore includes initiatives such as: social responsibility accounting, corporate citizenship accounting, social audits, corporate social reporting, employee
and employment reporting including health and safety, stakeholder dialogue/
engagement reporting, environmental accounting and reporting, triple-bottom-line
reporting. Social accounting refers to the process of creating and communicating
information to stakeholders about the performance of entities, in all relevant aspects
(in particular economic, environmental, ethical, and social).[78] It can be argued
that social accounting is 'the universe of all possible accounting and reporting'.[79]
From the point of view of management objectives, social accounting generates

---

[78] Freeman 1998, 499–519.
[79] Gray 2002.

information about stakeholders and the effects of the relationship with them. In practice, therefore, the firm prepares reports that make it possible to analyse stakeholders (as outlined in this chapter) and assess its achievements in the context of their needs, expectations but also contributions made. On a broader level, stakeholder audits can be conducted, assessing not only the effects (against expectations and plans) but also the entire relationship process.[80] To generalise, we can say that *social accounting* refers to the process of generating and communicating information to stakeholders about the performance of actors, in all relevant aspects (in particular economic, environmental, ethical, and social).

It is therefore possible to assess the extent to which the objectives of stakeholders and the firm are being met and, ultimately, to evaluate the effectiveness of the relationship with individual stakeholders. This information should be the basis for evaluating the strategies implemented and their possible redefinition or adjustment. Example tools are presented below.

One of the models used for measuring stakeholder satisfaction (mainly customers and employees) and managing stakeholder relations emphasises the need for a holistic, process approach, taking into account measurement, management, and monitoring – TRI*M™.[81] On the basis of the data obtained, it is possible to prepare adequate action strategies – managing relations with a given stakeholder group. The tool is also used to measure the entity's reputation among the relevant stakeholders and to assess quality and comparisons with competitors. The methodology used allows for the calculation of an index (a synthetic indicator that allows comparisons over time and with competitors) and a matrix, analysing the individual characteristics considered important by stakeholders in terms of their impact on overall satisfaction. The results allow the segmentation of stakeholders in terms of their satisfaction and loyalty.

A similar tool, but with a broader (for all stakeholders) scope, useful for managing stakeholder relations is a *Stakeholder Engagement Gap Analysis*. This tool provides a holistic view of stakeholder relations, comparing the expected (resulting from the adopted strategy) level of a given outcome with the actual state of affairs at a given point in time or period. The dimensions of outputs can be defined by the firm. Originally the author suggested: representativeness, transparency, accessibility, responsiveness, and accountability (economic and social).[82] Results (desired and actual) can be presented in a spider chart, for better visualisation of gaps.

The Accountability Scorecard (ASC) is based on the premise of the participation of various interest groups and their influence on the functioning of the company.[83]

---

[80] Svendsen 1998, 165.
[81] See e.g., Scharioth and Hubner 2004, Huber, Scharioth and Pallas 2004, Huber and Pallas 2006, Huber and O'Gorman 2008.
[82] Franklin 2020, 141.
[83] Nickols 2012.

The Accountability Scorecard refers to the concept of stakeholders and serves to assess the performance of a firm. It focusses on assessing the extent to which a company integrates and responds to the needs and demands of its stakeholders. It seeks a balance, not between financial and non-financial metrics, but between the organisation's relationship with its key interest groups. The scorecard facilitates the balancing of stakeholder needs and requirements. Indeed, it emphasises that the long-term success of any organisation depends on its continuing ability to convert its *outputs* into new *inputs*, i.e., the exchange of products, services, salaries, dividends, and debt service costs for materials, equipment from suppliers, labour from employees, and money from customers, investors, and creditors. In other words, long-term success ensures the ability of an organisation and its stakeholders to continuously balance, integrate, and satisfy legitimate needs and expectations without constantly or repeatedly sacrificing one for the other.

The primary purpose of the scorecard is to answer two questions:

– 'How do we manage to provide stakeholders with what they need?'; and
– 'How do we deal with getting what we want from stakeholders?'

Thus, for each group of interests, it is necessary to identify, on the one hand, their fulfilled needs and expectations ('inducement' directed to them by the firm) and, on the other hand, the contributions received from them ('contributions' made by the stakeholders). Adequate metrics need to be defined for each aspect; comparing them makes it possible to assess the level of balance between the contributions received by the company and the incentives provided, for all the stakeholder groups identified.

A more advanced concept is the *Performance Prism*. It includes an analysis of stakeholder and firm satisfaction with the relationship, the identification of a relationship strategy, and an assessment of the required capabilities and processes needed to implement this strategy. The authors build the equilateral prisms for each stakeholders groups. The sides of the prism are the strategies adopted for the group in question (at the level of the company, its internal units, and possibly its products or brands), the capabilities available (people, practices, technology, infrastructure), and the processes (product creation, demand creation, product distribution and service, etc.). The basis of the prism is stakeholder satisfaction, on the one hand, and stakeholder contributions, on the other; here, the company must define specific measures to analyse and evaluate these dimensions and the effects of shaping the relationship with the stakeholder group in question.[84]

As in any performance measurement system, it is crucial to select indicators, i.e., those measures that allow an evaluation of the important issues in a given area. It is therefore necessary that the indicators reflect well the previously diagnosed factors

---

[84] Nelly, Adams and Kennerley 2002, xi, 161, 180.

of stakeholder satisfaction and contribution,[85] with the measurement addressing those aspects on which it can take some action and which it can influence.[86]

5.4 CONCLUSIONS

Nowadays, the broader responsibilities of companies and the duties of directors – not just to owners but to a wider group of stakeholders, and not solely economic – are highlighted. Indeed, creating value for shareholders requires meeting the specific expectations of different stakeholder groups. In order to effectively create this value, conscious stakeholder relationship management is required. It requires, first of all, identifying the company's stakeholders and then conducting a thorough analysis of them. In particular, it is necessary to identify their needs and expectations (and assess their alignment with the company's values) and possible contributions, as well as the potential risks associated with them. For the selection of an adequate relationship strategy, it is also necessary to establish stakeholders' power, legitimacy, and urgency of needs. Of course, the question of the scale of stakeholders' interest in being involved in the relationship with the company and their willingness to influence it is also important. On the basis of this analysis, the company should determine the levels and methods of engagement for each stakeholder group and then, as part of the operationalisation of the strategy, how to communicate with them. The choice of strategy depends to a large extent on the values held by the company (its internal stakeholders, especially management), and cultural considerations are also important. In order to evaluate the relationship, it is necessary to continuously monitor inputs and outputs, i.e., stakeholder satisfaction on the one hand and stakeholder contributions on the other. Stakeholder relationship management is an ongoing process, with successive iterations to be carried out periodically. As the company's environment, its stakeholders and their expectations change, the company's capabilities and potentially its values evolve over time, engagement strategies may need to be adapted and changes may also result from an evaluation of the company's performance to date.

REFERENCES

AccountAbility (2015), 'AA1000 Stakeholder Engagement Standard 2015', available at: https://bit.ly/3ONNsLA [accessed 23 February 2022].

Adams, R. B., Licht, A. N. and Sagiv, L. (2011), 'Shareholders and stakeholders: How do directors decide?' 32 *Strategic Management Journal*, 12, 1331–1355.

---

[85] Examples were listed in Table 5.1.

[86] Guidance on the design of performance measurement systems and the selection of metrics is provided, for example: Eckerson 2006, Rasmussen, Chen and Bansal 2009, Spitzer 2007, Alexander 2007.

Agle, B. R., Mitchell, R. K. and Sonnenfeld, J. A. (1999), 'Who matters to CEOs? An investigation of stakeholder attributes and salience, corporate performance, and CEO value' 42 *Academy of Management Journal*, 5, 507–525.

Akermann, F. and Eden, C. (2011), 'Strategic management of stakeholders: Theory and practice' 44 *Long Range Planning*, 3, 179–196.

Alchian, A. A. and Demsetz, H. (1972), 'Production, information costs, and economic organization' 62 *American Economic Review*, 5, 777–795.

Alexander, J. (2007), *Performance Dashboards and Analysis for Value Creation* (Hoboken: John Wiley & Sons).

Anbarasan, P. and Sushil (2018), 'Stakeholder engagement in sustainable enterprise: Evolving a conceptual framework and a case study of ITC' 27 *Business Strategy and the Environment*, 3, 282–299.

Andriof, J. and Waddock, S. (2002), 'Unfolding stakeholder engagement', in Andriof, J., Waddock, S., Husted, B. and Rahma, S.S. (eds.), *Unfolding Stakeholder Thinking* (Sheffield: Greenleaf Publishing), 19–42.

Attanasio, G., Preghenella, N., De Toni, A. F. and Battistella, C. (2022), 'Stakeholder engagement in business models for sustainability: The stakeholder value flow model for sustainable development' 31 *Business Strategy and the Environment*, 3, 860–874.

Bebchuk, L. A., Kastiel, K. and Tallarita, R. (2021), 'For whom corporate leaders bargain' 94 *Southern California Law Review*, 6, 1497–1560.

Boesso, G. and Kumar, K. (2009), 'Stakeholder prioritization and reporting: Evidence from Italy and the US' 33 *Accounting Forum*, 2, 162–175.

Caroll, A. B. (1979), 'A three-dimensional conceptual model of corporate performance' 4 *Academy of Management Review* 4, 497–505.

Caroll, A. B. (1991), 'The pyramid of corporate social responsibility: Toward the moral management of organisational stakeholders' 34 *Business Horizons*, 4, 39–48.

Chang, H.-H. and Chuang, W.-J. (2021), 'Encourage stakeholder engagement in sustainable development: Drivers of consumers themselves benefits and society welfares' 28 *Corporate Social Responsibility and Environmental Management*, 2, 748–762.

Deloitte (2014), 'Stakeholder engagement', available at: https://bit.ly/49kZV1e [accessed 20 June 2022].

Deloitte (2022), 'The Chair's guide to realizing value from a just transition', available at: https://bit.ly/49wmO1K [accessed 9 October 2022].

Dzinkowski, R. (2000), 'The measurement and management of intellectual capital: An introduction' 78 *Management Accounting*, 2, 32–36.

Eckerson, W. W. (2006), *Performance Dashboards. Measuring, Monitoring, and Managing Your Business* (Hoboken: John Wiley & Sons).

Edles-Zandén, N. (2005), 'Sorting out the mess. A review of definitions of ethical issues in business', GRI-rapport No 2005(4), Gothenburg Research Institute, University of Gothenburg.

Edvinsson, L. and Malone, M.S. (1997), *Intellectual Capital. Realizing Your Company's True Value by Finding Its Hidden Brainpower* (New York: HarperCollins).

ECB (European Central Bank) (2022), 'Good practices for climate-related and environmental risk management', available at: https://bit.ly/4bEHXsj [accessed 3 November 2022].

EFRAG (2022), 'Draft European sustainability reporting Guidelines 1. Double materiality conceptual guidelines for standard-setting', available at: https://bit.ly/4bKPvKe [accessed 20 March 2022].

European Commission (2022), 'Corporate sustainability due diligence. Fostering sustainability in corporate governance and management systems', available at: https://bit.ly/49gZGo3 [accessed 20 September 2022].

Eweje, G., Sajjad, A., Nath, S. D. and Kobayashi, K. (2021), 'Multi-stakeholder partnerships: A catalyst to achieve sustainable development goals' 39 *Marketing Intelligence & Planning*, 2, 186–212.

Fassin, Y. (2009), 'The stakeholder model refined' 84 *Journal of Business Ethics*, 1, 113–135.

Franklin, A. L. (2020), *Stakeholder Engagement* (Cham: Springer).

Freeman, M. (1998), 'Social accounting', in Siegel, G. and Ramanauskas-Marconi, H. (eds.), *Behavioural Accounting* (Cincinnati: South-West Educational Publishing), 499–519.

Freeman, R. E. (2010), *Strategic Management. A Stakeholder Approach* (Cambridge, UK: Cambridge University Press).

Freeman, R. E., Harrison, J. S. and Wicks, A. C. (2007), *Managing for Stakeholders. Survival, Reputation, and Success* (New Haven & London: Yale University Press).

Freeman, R. E., Harrison, J. S., Wicks, A. C., Parmar, B. L. and de Colle, S. (2010), *Stakeholder Theory. The State of the Art* (Cambridge, UK: Cambridge University Press).

Friedman, A. L. and Miles, S. (2006), *Stakeholders. Theory and Practice* (Oxford: Oxford University Press).

Gray, R. (2002), 'The social accounting project and "Accounting, Organizations and Society": Privileging engagement, imaginings, new accountings and pragmatism over critique?' 27 *Accounting, Organisations and Society*, 7, 687–708.

Gutterman, A. S. (2020), *Sustainability and Corporate Governance: A Guide to Law and Practice* (New York: Routledge).

Hemphill, T. A. (2006), 'Corporate internal investigations: balancing firm social reputation with board fiduciary responsibility' 6 *Corporate Governance*, 5, 635–642.

Huber, M. and O'Gorman, S. (eds.) (2008), *From Customer Retention to a Holistic Stakeholder Management System: Living a Vision* (Berlin – Heidelberg: Springer).

Huber, M. and Pallas, M. (2006), *Customising Stakeholder Management Strategies. Concepts for Long-term Business Success* (Berlin – Heidelberg: Springer).

Huber, M., Scharioth, J. and Pallas, M. (2004), *Putting Stakeholder Management into Practice* (Berlin – Heidelberg: Springer).

Hund, G. E. and Engel-Cox, J. A. (2002), 'Two-way responsibility: the role of industry and its stakeholders in working towards sustainable development', in Andriof, J., Waddock, S., Histed, B. and Sutherland Ragman, S. (eds.), *Unfolding Stakeholder Thinking* (Sheffield: Greenleaf Publishing), 217–231.

Jawahar, I. M. and McLaughlin, G. L., (2001), 'Toward a descriptive stakeholder theory: An organisational life cycle approach' 26 *Academy of Management Review*, 3, 397–414.

Johnson, G. and Scholes, K. (1993), *Exploring Corporate Strategy* 3rd ed. (New York: Prentice Hall).

Kirsten, D. W. (2000), *Das bankspezifische Shareholder-Value-Konzept* (Wiesbaden: Deutscher Universitäts-Verlag).

Kolk, A. and Pinkse, J. (2006), 'Stakeholder mismanagement and corporate social responsibility crises' 4 *European Management Journal*, 1, 57–72.

Maher, R. and Buhmann, K. (2019), 'Meaningful stakeholder engagement: Bottom-up initiatives within global governance frameworks' 107 *Geoforum*, 231–234.

Marcinkowska, M. (2012), 'Wymogi stawiane bankom przez ich otoczenie' [Requirements placed on banks by their environment] 105 *Studia Ekonomiczne. Zeszyty Naukowe Wydziałowe Uniwersytetu Ekonomicznego w Katowicach*, 165–172.

Marcinkowska, M. (2013), *Kapitał relacyjny banku* [*Bank's relational capital*], vol 1 (Łódź: Wydawnictwo Uniwersytetu Łódzkiego).

Mitchell, R. K., Agle, B. and Wood, D. (1997), 'Toward a theory of stakeholder identification and salience: Defining the principle of who and what really counts' 22, *Academy of Management Review*, 4, 853–886.

Morgan, R. M. and Hunt, S. D. (1994), 'The commitment-trust theory of relationship marketing' 58 *Journal of Marketing*, 3, 20–38.

Nelly, A., Adams, C. and Kennerley, M. (2002), *The Performance Prism. The Scorecard for Measuring and Managing Business Success* (London: FT Prentice Hall).

Nickols, F. (2012), 'The accountability scorecard: A stakeholder-based approach to "Keeping Score"', available at: www.nickols.us/scorecard.htm [accessed 20 September 2022].

OECD (2015), 'G20/OECD principles of corporate governance', available at: https://bit .ly/4bKKPU0 [accessed 20 September 2022].

OECD (2022), *OECD Secretary-General's Second Report to G20 Finance Ministers and Central Bank Governors on the Review of the G20/OECD Principles of Corporate Governance*, available at: https://bit.ly/3UQkRJn [accessed 20 September 2022].

OECD (2023), 'G20/OECD principles of corporate governance', available at: www.oecd-ilibrary.org/governance/g20-oecd-principles-of-corporate-governance-2023_ed750b30-en [accessed on 26 October 2023].

Porter, M. E. and Kramer, M. R. (2002), 'The competitive advantage of corporate philan-thropy' 12 *Harvard Business Review*, 5–16.

Post, E., Preston, L. E. and Sachs, S. (2002a), 'Managing the extended enterprise: The new stakeholder view' 45 *California Management Review*, 1, 6–28.

Post, J. E., Preston, L. E. and Sachs, S. (2002b), *Redefining the Corporation. Stakeholder Management and Organisational Wealth* (Stanford: Stanford Business Books).

Rasmussen, N., Chen, C. Y. and Bansal, M. (2009), *Business Dashboards* (Hoboken: John Wiley & Sons).

Reynolds, S. J., Schultz, F. C. and Hekman, D. R. (2006), 'Stakeholder theory and manage-rial decision-making: Constraints and implications of balancing stakeholder interests' 64 *Journal of Business Ethics*, 3, 285–301.

Rodriguez, M. A., Ricart, J. A. and Sanchez, P. (2002), 'Sustainable development and the sustainability of competitive advantage: A dynamic and sustainable view of the Firm' 11 *Creativity and Innovation Management*, 3, 135–146.

Roos, J., Roos, G., Dragonetti, N. C. and Edvinsson, L. (1997), *Intellectual Capital. Navigating the New Business Landscape* (London: Macmillan Press).

Rowley, T. J. (1997), 'Moving beyond dyadic ties: A network theory of stakeholder influences' 22 *Academy of Management Review*, 4, 887–910.

Savage, G. T., Nix, T. W., Whitehead, C. J. and Blair, J. D. (1991), 'Strategies for assessing and managing organizational stakeholders' 5 *Academy of Management Executive*, 2, 61–75.

Scharioth, J. and Hubner, M. (eds.) (2004), *Achieving Excellence in Stakeholder Management* (Berlin – Heidelberg: Springer).

Schuster, L. (2000), 'The shareholder value and stakeholder discussion: An international over-view', in L. Schuster (ed.), *Shareholder Value Management in Banks* (London: Macmillan Press), 3–12.

Schwab, K. (2021), *Stakeholder Capitalism. A Global Economy that Works for Progress, People and Planet* (Hoboken: Wiley).

Singh, A. P. and Rahman, Z. (2022), 'Stakeholder engagement and corporate performances: Empirical evidence from an emerging economy' 19 *Corporate Ownership & Control*, 4, 141–152.

Sjåfjell, B. and Bruner C. M. (eds.) (2019), *The Cambridge Handbook of Corporate Law, Corporate Governance and Sustainability* (Cambridge, UK: Cambridge University Press).

Smudde, P. M. and Courtright, J. L. (2011), 'A holistic approach to stakeholder management: A rhetorical foundation' 37 *Public Relations Review*, 2, 137–144.

Sonnemann, G., Gemechu, E. D., Remmen, A., Frydendal, J. and Jensen, A. A. (2015), 'Life cycle management: Implementing sustainability in business practice', in Sonnemann, G. and Margni, M. (eds.), *Life Cycle Management* (Dordrecht: Springer), 7–22.

Spitzer, D. C. (2007), *Transforming Performance Measurement* (New York: AMACOM).

Sternberg, E. (2000), *Just Business. Business Ethics in Action*, 2nd ed. (Oxford: Oxford University Press).

Stout, L. A. (2012), *The Shareholder Value Myth. How Putting Shareholders First Harms Investors, Corporations, and the Public* (San Francisco: Berrett-Koehler Publishers).

Straker, D. (2014), *Changing Minds: In Detail. How to Change What People Think, Feel, Believe and Do*, 3rd ed. (Abergavenny: Changing Works), available at: https://bit .ly/3wmredo [accessed 3 August 2012].

Suntook, F. and Murphy, J. A. (2008), *The Stakeholder Balance Sheet. Profiting from Really Understanding Your Market* (Chichester: John Wiley & Sons).

Sveiby, K. E. (1997), *The New Organizational Wealth: Managing and Measuring Knowledge-Based Assets* (San Francisco: Berrett-Koehler Publishers).

Svendsen, A. (1998), *The Stakeholder Strategy: Profiting from Collaborative Business Relationships* (San Francisco: Berrett-Koehler Publishers).

UNEP (United Nations Environment Program) (2011), 'Global outlook on SCP policies: Taking action together', available at: https://wedocs.unep.org/20.500.11822/25922 [accessed 20 September 2022].

UNEP FI (United Nations Environment Program Finance Initiative) (2021), 'Principles for responsible banking: Guidance document', available at: https://bit.ly/3wmwg9q [accessed 29 September 2022].

Unerman, J. and Bennett, M. (2004), 'Increased stakeholder dialogue and the internet: towards greater corporate accountability or reinforcing capitalist hegemony?' 29 *Accounting, Organisations and Society*, 7, 685–707.

Weiss J. W. (2021), *Business Ethics: A Stakeholder and Issues Management Approach*, 7th ed. (Oakland: Berrett-Koehler).

Wheeler, D. and Davies, R. (2008), 'Gaining goodwill: Developing stakeholder approaches to corporate governance', in A. J. Zajheim, D. E. Palmer and M. L. Stoll, *Stakeholder Theory. Essential Readings in Ethical Leadership and Management* (New York: Prometheus Books), 222–234.

Wheeler, D. and Sillanpää, M. (1997), *The Stakeholder Corporation. A blueprint for Maximizing Stakeholder Value* (London: Pitman Publishing).

6

Bank Governance and Sustainability

Kern Alexander

6.1 INTRODUCTION

The chapter considers the importance of bank corporate governance in developing and supporting a more sustainable economy. Sustainable finance has become an important concern for policymakers in their efforts to combat climate change and achieve other sustainability objectives. Although it is a relatively new concept, it has, nonetheless, quickly been embraced as mainstream by many governments, regulators and financial markets. Most of the literature accepts the 17 United Nations Sustainable Development Goals[1] as an appropriate reference point for the policy objectives, but sustainability has many aspects. This chapter has an environmental focus, as environmental challenges are already generating significant risks for the financial sector. However, many of the arguments apply equally to other social sustainability challenges as well.

The main relevance to banks as businesses is that they depend in large part on sustained economic growth to create new assets. Sustained growth is also the objective of most governments and central banks, but the new sustainability agenda sets the horizon for growth objectives at decades rather than the short-term business or credit cycle. Taking a long-term approach to business development represents a challenge for any firm, especially banks, that needs to demonstrate ongoing returns to investors.

As banking is central to the economy, this chapter will discuss how bank governance can address sustainable finance challenges. Section 6.2 discusses the banking business and the role it can play in addressing sustainability risks and challenges and supporting the transition to a more sustainable economy. Section 6.3 considers traditional agency theories that underpin corporate governance and suggests that they do not offer a full explanation of the 'collective' agency problems that exist in large complex organisations, such as banks and other financial institutions. Human agency theory offers an alternative theory that emphasises the importance

---

[1] United Nations 2015.

of organisational culture in determining standards, norms and values that influence agent behaviour. Section 6.4 suggests that bank boards should consider the importance of 'risk culture' in addressing organisational failings and confronting new business challenges, such as climate change and other sustainability concerns. Although bank boards have the primary responsibility in setting the tone at the top of the organisation, regulatory intervention may be necessary to ensure that bank governance practices are adequately managing agency problems regarding sustainability concerns. Section 6.5 discusses how bank regulators can interact with bank management and boards to address sustainability challenges. It discusses the UK Senior Managers Regime as being one way that regulators can hold senior management responsible for management failings to meet regulatory expectations in the area of sustainability. Section 6.6 concludes with some recommendations for how bank governance and business practices could be improved to support society's sustainability objectives.

6.2 BANKING AND SUSTAINABILITY

Banks are often referred to as 'special'. This is, in part, because they create money via deposits on their own balance sheets when they lend. That means they can use leverage to create credit in a way that non-deposit financial institutions and other companies cannot. The business model of a bank involves providing services for deposit taking (including term savings), credit creation, risk management (e.g., through derivatives) and payments. But the liquidity mismatch between taking sight deposits and term credit creation makes it ideal for some types of finance and not others. This is an important issue in considering how bank finance can support sustainable development goals. Commercial banks are particularly good at assessing credit risk, especially for large numbers of smaller borrowers. Hence banks dominate in providing retail mortgages and credit for small and medium enterprises.[2] Investment banks, or the affiliates of deposit-taking banks, play a complementary role by, for example, arranging/syndicating very large corporate loans or helping companies to issue bonds or equities, or facilitating government debt markets.

Given their strengths, banks (and shadow banks, including those referred to above) have a central function in originating many other types of credit as well, including longer-term infrastructure lending. But the funding sources of banks – deposits and relatively short-term debt – mean they are not ideal as 'holders to maturity' of long-term assets. Having originated long-term loans, a bank would ideally transfer at least the lower-risk credits to be funded by marketable debt securities, or otherwise sell such loans to be held by other financial institutions. Where such

---

[2] Non-bank specialist lenders, in contrast, without cheap funding from a deposit base, typically compete by taking on niche credit risks (e.g., large mortgages, borrowers with irregular incomes, auto finance).

a process is possible, it can free up a bank's balance sheet to originate more long-term credit. In contrast, if banks were to provide a lot of large-scale, long-term loans and hold on to those assets to maturity, it could quickly use up their balance sheets and limit their contribution to sustainability. The 'originate and distribute' model for banks, and shadow banks, is a helpful process for long-term investments which could free up a bank's balance sheet for more sustainable lending.

Life insurance companies, pension funds, asset managers and other similar savings institutions are better matched holders of long-term assets than the banks. Indeed, the very purpose of such firms is to provide future incomes and/or lump sums based on a saver's life cycle or other longer-term considerations, and so the sustainability of their long-term investments is a prerequisite for successfully meeting those liabilities. Perhaps the most effective bank business strategy involves the use of simple and transparent securitisation and other credit risk transfer methods to pass long-term assets to longer-term investors such as pension funds and insurance companies. Such low-risk, long-term investors typically prefer bonds or other fixed-income instruments rather than equity, as bonds provide the income stream and risk profile that would match the investing firms' liabilities. Suitable market securities could include collateralised loan obligations or other asset-backed securities. On the other hand, the start-up phase of a new build project is typically not an ideal investment for investors that require an income stream, although they may take a limited equity position via a structured investment.

Banks deserve special attention because, in many economies, they are the dominant providers of credit. That includes providing initial development finance for new projects that can enable the economy to grow and to become more resilient to sustainability challenges. But, of course, they also provide finance for existing, unsustainable activities, which generates financial risk for themselves and systemic risks for the economy as a whole. European policymakers have already made clear that they consider banking to be important for supporting the transition to a more sustainable economy.[3] Regulators have also focused on regulating bank governance following the great financial crisis of 2007–8 primarily to control bank risk taking. In light of the Paris Climate Change Treaty and the growing recognition by policymakers and regulators of the economic risks associated with climate change and other sustainability challenges, bank corporate governance has become a key focus for oversight to ensure that bank business practices are resilient to sustainability risks and can facilitate the transition to a more sustainable economy with net-zero carbon emissions.

A few banks are public utilities, but most are not and, like other commercial firms, banks would not normally see it as their role to provide credit based on political or social factors. But bank behaviour has positive and negative externalities for society as a whole, just as individual behaviour does. One bank's loan to an unsustainable

[3]   See European Commission 2018b.

activity may be profitable for the bank – at least for a while – but such lending by banks collectively could seriously damage the economy over the longer term. So how can society influence banks to take account of these and other externalities and to direct more credit and investment towards sustainable economic activity and not just towards assets that generate only short-term rewards?

6.3 AGENCY PROBLEMS IN BANK GOVERNANCE

Agency problems take on a more complex dimension in the context of environmental sustainability challenges. This section generally discusses the main theories of the principal–agent problem in corporate governance, including human agency theory, and the metaphor of the tragedy of the commons and how it has been adapted in the sustainability debate to be the 'tragedy of the horizons'. It suggests that human agency theory is the most appropriate theoretical model to explain agency problems within large banks and other complex financial institutions and is most adaptable for addressing the economic risks associated with climate change and other environmental sustainability challenges.

6.3.1 *Agency Theory and Its Discontents*

Broadly speaking, the concept of agency can be understood in many areas of social interaction. Indeed, every time individuals or entities enter into relationships, even casually, potential agency problems exist. Within this broad sense, agency relationships may often lead to exploitative and socially costly behaviour. Traditional agency theory in the corporate governance and finance literature has analysed how asymmetric information provides firm owners with inferior information to monitor managers, who have the opportunity to engage in unobserved and costly behaviour.[4] The idea that managers have an information advantage and that this gives them the opportunity to take self-interested actions at the expense of the firm's owners represents the typical principal–agent problem.[5] Contract theorists attempt to overcome the asymmetric information problem by designing a 'complete contract' that aligns the interests or incentives of the firm's agents with those of the firm's owners.[6] For example, such incentive arrangements may take the form of tying a portion of a manager's compensation to the company's performance in the stock market through the use of stock options. A contract that does not align the interests of the firm's agents with those of the firm's owners can lead to suboptimal firm performance and

---

[4] See Shleifer and Vishny 1997, 737–783.

[5] See Jensen and Meckling 1994 and Jensen and Meckling 1976, focusing their analysis on the divergent interests of stockholders and managers in public corporations. Jensen postulates that because 'people are, in the end, self-interested they will have conflicts of interest over at least some issues any time they attempt to engage in cooperative endeavors' (Jensen 1998, 47–48).

[6] Hart 1995, 32–33, 73–83.

diminished firm value, as agents will have an incentive to shirk their responsibilities and appropriate the firm's assets.

Another form of the agency problem arises in what Arrow classified as *hidden action* and *hidden information*.[7] According to Arrow, if the agents' actions are not observable, it is impossible to design a contract based on these actions, and, similarly, if the agent's decision-making is based on information that is only available to the agent, the principal cannot then infer the agent's actions based on available information. Arrow's theory of hidden action and hidden information reveals the limitations of using contract design to address agency problems, as perfect alignment of interests is very difficult (if not impossible) to achieve because the unobservable actions of the agent cannot be perfectly inferred based on observable information. For example, the agent's amount of effort or level of output cannot provide an adequate measure of performance because other random factors may contribute to the level of output independent of the agent's effort.

The agency problems that arise from hidden action and hidden information manifest themselves in the form of moral hazard (involving hidden action) and adverse selection (involving hidden information). Although it was first introduced into the insurance literature, moral hazard encompasses situations in which the incentives of the principal (the firm owner or creditor) diverge from the incentives of the agents (employee or person using property that belongs to others). Based on the assumption that a rational agent can be expected to maximise its own utility, and where its economic self-interest conflicts with that of the principal, the principal will incur costs.

Agent moral hazard can also lead to a 'tragedy of the commons' where there is a collectivisation of losses for actions that cannot be monitored or controlled by the principals or other actors.[8] Indeed, the 'tragedy of the commons' metaphor was adapted by Carney (2015) to be the 'tragedy of the horizons' to show the moral hazard that arises from the over-use and degradation of today's natural resources by rational, utility-maximising individuals, rather than taking collective action today to conserve and limit degradation of natural resources for the benefit of future generations. This collectivisation of losses – considered either through the tragedy of the commons or the tragedy of the horizons – reflects the problems associated with negative externalities and social costs.

The collectivisation of losses that can arise from the tragedy of the commons can also occur within the organisational structure of large organisations or financial institutions in which the behaviour of many individual agents across the organisation can lead to a collective form of moral hazard, an incentive problem at the collective action level.[9] This would involve individual managers having inadequate incentives

---

[7] Arrow 1965.
[8] See Cole and Ostrom 2011, 45.
[9] Dow 2000, 15.

to monitor and solve problems because organisational norms and institutional structures are such that they constrain or limit behaviour that may 'rock the boat'. Also, organisational incentives might be structured in a unilinear or univocal way, running directly from firm owners to managers, which does not take account of the firm's organisational norms and institutional structure that can influence decision-making and strategy and which may lead to a collective form of moral hazard across the organisation. Similarly, the very personality traits that fulfil traditional corporate governance objectives, such as shareholder wealth maximisation, can result in disadvantaging the interests of other principals such as bondholders or other creditors or stakeholders such as customers and employees.[10]

In addition, the sociological perspective of agency provides another lens through which to view agency problems. Indeed, the traditional sociological theory of agency considers the thoughts and actions taken by people that express their individual power.[11] Emirbayer and Mische underline how the concept of agency is somewhat vague due to its application in a variety of contexts.[12] In an attempt to analytically disaggregate agency into its several component elements and to show the multiple ways through which the dimensions of agency interact with diverse forms of structure, they expand the concept of agency into 'human agency', which is defined as 'the temporally constructed engagement by actors of different structural environments – the temporal–relational contexts of action – which, through the interplay of habit, imagination and judgment, both reproduces and transforms those structures in interactive response to the problems posed by changing historical situations'.[13]

Other sociologists, such as Bandura, have articulated human agency theory by identifying three different ways through which it is exercised: (a) personal, (b) proxy and (c) collective[14]. Personal agency, also known as 'direct personal agency', is exercised on an individual basis. Significantly, personal agency assumes that individuals have direct control and influence over people and things. However, such control and influence cannot be direct in all contexts. Hence, the lack of direct control and influence is the basis to consider the concept of proxy agency. Where people do not have full control over the facts that relate to and affect their lives, they exercise proxy agency. Exercising proxy agency means 'relying on the efforts

---

[10] See Mahmendier and Geoffrey 2009, Khurana 2002 and Tversky and Daniel 1974.
[11] Emirbayer and Mische 1998.
[12] Ibid. Emirbayer and Mische 1998 argue that 'the concept of agency has become a source of increasing strain and confusion in social thought. Variants of action theory, normative theory, and political–institutional analysis have defended, attacked, buried, and resuscitated the concept in often contradictory and overlapping ways. At the centre of the debate, the term agency itself has maintained an elusive, albeit resonant, vagueness; it has all too seldom inspired systematic analysis, despite the long list of terms with which it has been associated: self-hood, motivation, will, purposiveness, intentionality, choice, initiative, freedom, and creativity'. Ibid., Emirbayer and Mische 1998, 962 et seq.
[13] Emirbayer and Mische 1998, 970.
[14] Bandura 1997.

of intermediaries"[15] who have resources and tools to guarantee the results others aim at achieving. Moreover, Bandura stresses that 'people do not live their lives in individual autonomy. Indeed, many of the outcomes they seek are achievable only through interdependent efforts'.[16] This is known as 'collective agency', which refers to effects produced by collective initiatives of people who share the same objectives or beliefs and therefore act as a group: 'A group's attainments are the product not only of shared knowledge and skills of its different members, but also of the interactive, coordinative, and synergistic dynamics of their transactions.' The 'interactive, coordinative, and synergistic' dimension of the group's behaviour are not necessarily driven by the economic incentives that compensation arrangements – or the opportunity to appropriate that the principal's property affords – may induce but rather are influenced by the collective initiatives of the group within the organisation whose objectives are conditioned by social norms and cultural practices, and their actions to achieve their objectives are channelled by the institutional mechanisms through which the group can interact and coordinate its actions to achieve its objectives.

6.3.2 *Collective Agency Problems and Human Agency Theory*

As commercial banking organisations are complex organisations, they can only achieve their economic objective of maximising shareholder returns through the collective efforts of many individuals – individuals who in theory share the same objectives and beliefs and who can coordinate their activities effectively. However, the size and the complex structure of large, systemically important banks gives rise to a wide range of potential agency problems that involve several major stakeholder groups, including but not limited to shareholders, creditors, depositors and other customers, employees, management and supervisory bodies. Agency problems can arise because decision-making is directly or indirectly delegated from one stakeholder group to another in situations where stakeholder groups have different objectives and preferences, and where complete information that would allow stakeholders to control decisions made on their behalf is not readily available. The most studied agency problems in the case of banks involve (a) depositors and shareholders and (b) supervisors and shareholders, and these problems have underpinned major design features of regulatory structures (e.g., deposit insurance and capital adequacy) that attempt to align the incentives of principal and agent and to limit the incentive of both principals and agents to excessive risks at society's expense.[17] However, incentive conflicts between different groups of stakeholders, such as employees, suppliers and other societal groups, based on different understandings of ethics and norms of behaviour by a variety of stakeholder groups, can also undermine the firm's pursuit

---

[15] Bandura 1999.
[16] Ibid.
[17] Alexander, Dhumale and Eatwell 2006, 242–244.

of its strategic objectives. These collective agency problems have become the focus of a growing literature on organisational and risk culture.

Human agency theory provides a conceptual framework through which to analyse collective agency problems within complex organisations, such as banks.[18] It holds that – as is the case in other complex organisations – bank workers do not pursue their objectives in a vacuum, based on the design of a contract. Instead, they are subject to societal norms and institutional values that constitute its organisational or risk culture, which influence how they coordinate their activities to achieve both their own individual objectives and the collective objectives of the institution. Successful institutional outcomes are the product of a particular organisational or risk culture that drives an effective coordination model. This type of collective agency outcome – driven by the collective pursuits of individuals throughout an organisation – is influenced substantially by the norms, standards and ethical values fostered by the institution's leaders in the pursuit of the formal objective of shareholder wealth maximisation (or other strategic objectives).

6.4 GOVERNANCE AND ORGANISATIONAL CULTURE

6.4.1 *The Board and Stewardship*

Most large banks in developed countries and many in developing countries approach environmental sustainability risks from a corporate and social responsibility perspective.[19] Often banks have established board-level committees, such as risk committees, which generally take a short-term approach to financial risks (i.e., credit risk at the transaction level or at the counterparty level) arising from climate and other environmental sustainability challenges. Some banks instruct risk committees to report to the board on climate risks and to monitor environmental sustainability risks through the risk function. However, the unique features of environmental sustainability risks require a strategic approach which is developing in parallel at different banks.

International good practices on corporate governance are comprehensive enough to address environmental sustainability challenges. Typically, boards have ultimate responsibility for the bank's business strategy and financial soundness, corporate culture, governance structure and practices, and risk management and compliance obligations.[20] Accordingly, bank boards are thus being called upon to understand and assess the financial risks caused by environmental and social sustainability

---

[18] Indeed, the traditional sociological theory of agency considers the thoughts and actions taken by people that express their individual power. See Emirbayer and Mische 1998.

[19] See Bank of England 2018.

[20] Basel Core Principle 14, EC, 1. BCP 1 and 5 and Basel Committee on Banking Supervision (BCBS), Guidelines on Corporate Governance Principles for Banks.

challenges with a forward-looking approach that integrates them into bank risk management frameworks. Boards are also expected to factor these risks into the design of the bank business models, strategy, and objectives, and to conduct effective oversight of the financial risks associated with climate change[21].

International policymakers are considering the role of bank and financial institution governance as a medium-term policy response to support enhanced financial sustainability business practices[22]. Indeed, bank governance mechanisms have proved necessary to reduce the incentives for bank management to take on excessive short-term financial risks more generally, as well as those financial risks linked to environmentally unsustainable activity. Therefore, an effective prudential regulatory framework is necessary to oversee bank risk governance and this should also address environmental sustainability risks. The main elements for designing bank governance frameworks that promote environmental sustainability are intrinsic to good corporate governance on two levels. First, good corporate governance calls on the use of ethical judgment of what is acceptable and what is not. Second, corporate governance has an important role in overseeing and ensuring effective risk management for the bank and ensuring sustainable returns for owners and shareholders. Recent studies suggest that there is a strong correlation between good bank corporate governance and effective environmental and social risk management[23].

Bank governance is also affected by stewardship codes and both formal and informal concepts of fiduciary duty. There have been legal opinions[24] issued in both Australia for all firms and the UK for pension funds[25] which conclude that boards, and others with fiduciary duties, must consider whether climate-related risks are financially material and that failing to do so is a failure of fiduciary duty which could pave the way for legal challenge.

The concept of stewardship has also been informed by the efforts of institutional investors to harmonise a global understanding of fiduciary duty. For example, the corporate governance codes of most G20 countries require the board of directors of joint stock companies to assess the financial and nonfinancial risks that relate to environmental risks, as well as social, ethical, operational and other risks, and to establish tolerable levels of risk in these areas.[26] And the EU has adopted legislation further clarifying governance requirements in the area of disclosure to ensure that sustainability is explicit, not just implicit, in the requirements and capabilities of boards.

---

[21] See BCBS 2022. See also European Central Bank 2020 and European Banking Authority 2021. Similar supervisory statements are in various regulatory instruments of a different legal nature adopted by supervisors in EU member states, such as France and Germany, as well as Australia and Hong Kong, Singapore, Vietnam and the United Kingdom.

[22] See European Commission 2018b.

[23] See Center for Sustainability Studies, Federação Brasileira de Bancos (Febraban) 2014, 34–35.

[24] Hutley and Hartford Davies 2016, 3 et seq.

[25] Bryant and Rickards 2016.

[26] See Alexander 2016, reviewing the corporate governance practices of G20 countries regarding sustainability risks.

The EU Corporate Sustainability Reporting Directive (CSRD) that took effect in 2022 aims to harmonise ESG reporting for all EU-based companies and all non-EU companies doing business in Europe.[27] The CSRD is expected to play a role in improving bank governance by requiring disclosure to investors of most of the institution's environmentally and socially unsustainable activities, including the activities of suppliers and certain counterparties in foreign jurisdictions. Institutional investors are already beginning to ask banks about their efforts to mainstream sustainability challenges into their business models and their strategies to mobilise capital for sustainable economic activity. Most countries do not yet require banks to incorporate environmental sustainability risks into the bank's risk governance and management strategy, but some countries have begun to do so. Both China and Brazil regulate bank corporate governance regarding environmental risks. China adopted 'Green Credit Guidelines' in 2012 that require banks to adopt green governance strategies. Brazil has incorporated green governance into its Basel III pillar 2 supervisory review assessments. Specifically, Brazil has adopted the principle of proportionality for individual banks to decide – based on the bank's particular risk exposures – to what extent environmental sustainability risks should be incorporated into the bank's governance and risk strategy.

Indeed, environmental sustainability poses a major challenge for banks in assessing how such risks will affect the banking business. Risk management practices are probably the key mechanism through which firms protect themselves from these risks. Because of that, oversight of risk management (also known as 'risk governance') by supervisors is a natural way to ensure that best practice prevails.

6.4.2 *Organisational and Risk Culture*

It is generally accepted that the culture within banking institutions during the period prior to the crisis of 2007–2009 emphasised (excessive) risk taking to pursue short-term profits at the expense of longer-term firm performance and sustainable shareholder value. Moreover, the risk culture within institutions was driven by compensation arrangements that relied heavily on variable pay determined by short-term performance metrics. A focus on short-term revenue and profits can place a firm's long-term viability at risk and disadvantage customers. The rational response of all staff as individuals to such short-term incentives is to focus on meeting short-term goals[28].

[27] Directive 2022/2464/EU of the European Parliament and of the Council of 14 December 2022 amending Regulation No. 537/2014/EU, Directive 2004/109/EC, Directive 2006/43/EC and Directive 2013/34/EU, as regards corporate sustainability reporting, OJ L 322, 16.12.2022 (hereinafter referred to as 'CSRD 2022').

[28] See Alvesson and Robertson 2016, discussing some of the pressures and cultural responses in investment banks.

One of the lessons of the crisis, therefore, was that regulators should play a greater role in judging how culture drives firm behaviour, and especially risk taking, and how this impacts society as a whole.[29] Although risk culture has no single definition[30], it is viewed as a subset of broader company organisational culture and thus defined as: 'the norms and traditions of behaviour of individuals and of groups within an organisation that determine the way in which they identify, understand, discuss, and act on the risks the organisation confronts and the risks it takes'[31]. Significantly, firms converge on defining risk culture as everyone's responsibility – from management to employees. In other words, they understand it as a system of values and behavioural norms that helps foster risk management processes and ensure an adequate level of risk control. In this context, risk culture is seen as an effective tool for reducing a firm's excessive risk taking[32].

But a firm's culture is not just fostered internally. Importantly, regulators and policymakers provide incentives for how practitioners define risk culture. In 2009, the Basel Committee on Banking Supervision (BCBS) encouraged regulators to strengthen risk management within banks and highlighted the importance of risk culture (as a 'critical focus') in bank business strategies[33]. This was then transposed into some of the main EU post-crisis banking legislation to 'promote a sound risk culture at all levels of credit institutions and investment firms'.[34] In this respect, in 2013 the Group of 30 (G30) declared that: 'boards should identify and deal seriously with risky culture, ensure their compensation system supports the desired culture, discuss culture at the board level and with supervisors, and periodically use a variety of formal and informal techniques to monitor risk culture'. The BCBS defined risk culture as 'a bank's norms, attitudes and behaviours related to risk awareness, risk taking and risk management and controls that shape decisions on risks' (BCBS 2014).

Risk culture influences the decisions on risk that management and employees take during day-to-day activities. Accordingly, it is the board's task to set a 'tone at the top' that promotes an effective risk culture. Supervisors are not called on to run banks, but they should liaise with the board, its risk and audit committees, to verify whether or not the institution has adequate risk governance mechanisms and effective risk culture (BCBS 2014). Furthermore, the Financial Stability Board (FSB) set out clear guidance to help regulators and supervisors assess risk culture in financial institutions. In its 2014 'Guidance on supervisory interaction with financial

---

[29] The former chief executive of the British Financial Services Authority, Hector Sants observed that: '[T]he end goal should be that firms understand their own culture and the potential risks posed by the wrong culture', Sants 2010.

[30] Ashby et al. 2014.

[31] IIF 2009.

[32] EY 2014.

[33] BCBS 2009.

[34] European Commission 2013.

institutions on risk culture', the FSB stated that: 'a sound risk culture bolsters effective risk management, promotes sound risk taking, and ensures that emerging risks or risk-taking activities beyond the institution's risk appetite are recognised, assessed, escalated and addressed in a timely manner.'[35]

6.5 A BEHAVIOURAL APPROACH TO BANKING REGULATION

Part of the answer to the challenge of changing bank governance so that sustainability challenges are adequately addressed is to design laws and regulations that aim to change the behaviour of bank management and boards so that they design business models that do more to internalise the externalities that arise from unsustainable economic activities. Regulations may accomplish this goal directly through the use of sanctions to deter undesirable conduct, or indirectly by changing attitudes about the regulated behaviour in question. Bilz and Nadler (2014) argue that the approach of changing attitudes is more efficient than by threatening to impose sanctions, particularly if the regulation changes attitudes about the underlying ethical or morality of the behaviour. Outside of public sector regulation, banks play an important self-regulatory function by deciding themselves whom and what business activities to finance. For instance, banks can reject financing socially or environmentally harmful activities or impose conditions on the provision of credit for companies to alter their practices to enhance sustainability performance. Within the organisational structure of banks, there are various sub-units, such as the Business Line, Risk Management, Legal, Compliance and Audit, that respond to their own regulatory signals and have compliance tools that may enable or obstruct the pursuit of a sustainable business strategy.

As banks also provide a crucial function in society to finance the transition to a sustainable economy, it is suggested that systemic behavioural change is needed in the banking sector and that a reconceptualisation of the tasks and duties of bank boards and the overall strategy and organisational culture by management is necessary to bring about fundamental behavioural change. Regulatory tools can play an important role in guiding bank behaviour to a more sustainable business model, but fundamental behavioural change must come from within the financial institution itself with a focus on the attitudes and ethical standards of bank management and employees. Sustainability concerns therefore should be at the heart of bank governance and risk management practices and wider business models. That would drive the development of more lending to, and investment in, sustainable sectors of the economy.

Bank regulators have an important role to play in overseeing the organisational and risk culture of banks and other financial institutions in order to ensure that

---

[35] Financial Stability Board 2014. Supervisors are recommended to conduct periodic reviews of an institution's culture, issue findings and review the extent to which culture is the underlying cause of the identified problems.

their business strategies are aligned with the objective of creating a more sustainable economy. At the core of Banking Supervision is the objective that banks ensure that they remain safe and sound[36]. To that end, bank supervisors pay close attention to environmental risks (e.g., climate risks) because they can threaten the financial health and stability of an institution and the broader financial system.

6.5.1 *UK Regulatory Approach to Risk Culture and Sustainability*

The question arises whether bank regulatory authorities should manage and seek to influence corporate governance frameworks as a key instrument to influence banks in developing a strategic response to climate and other environmental challenges.[37] The UK regulatory approach is unusual in comparison to other jurisdictions for its focus on imposing responsibility on senior management and the boards of all regulated financial institutions for putting in place a strategy to adequately manage these risks. The strategic objective of the UK regulators – the Prudential Regulation Authority (PRA) and the Financial Conduct Authority (FCA) – is to 'protect and enhance confidence in the UK financial system'. For the FCA, this primary objective is complemented by three operational objectives: (1) securing an appropriate degree of protection for consumers; (2) protecting and enhancing the integrity of the UK financial system; and (3) promoting efficiency and choice in the market for certain types of services. The UK Parliament recognised that to achieve its strategic objective, the FCA should aim to promote fair, efficient and transparent financial services markets that work well for the users of these markets, including not only the banks but also bank customers, consumers and investors. This would better reflect the Treasury's intended purpose in the legislation, which is that the FCA should ensure that business across financial services and markets is conducted in a way that advances the interests of all users and participants.

The main regulatory change applicable to risk culture was driven by the Financial Services (Banking Reform) Act 2013. That authorised the UK Treasury to adopt a Senior Managers Regime (SMR). Originally designed slightly differently for banks and insurance companies, the regime has been simplified, made consistent across banks, insurers and other financial institutions in 2019 which are authorised by either the PRA or the FCA.

One of the aims of the SMR is to ensure that there is a senior manager accountable for key conduct and prudential risks.[38] The SMR draws up lists of necessary roles and responsibilities (proportionately for smaller firms), which a firm must publicly allocate to its most senior managers. The precise mapping of responsibilities to roles is for the firm to decide, but they must be clear, must seek regulatory

---

[36] DNB 2017.
[37] World Economic Forum 2020.
[38] Alexander and Fisher 2019, 37.

pre-approval and the firm must publish its map. The nominated senior managers are then responsible for ensuring that the particular responsibilities allocated to them are fulfilled by the firm or else they will be held individually accountable. The list of responsibilities includes climate change and risk culture. In October 2018, the PRA proposed extending this to make it explicit that sustainability risks are included. It issued a consultation paper with the specific proposal that:

> The PRA expects firms to have clear roles and responsibilities for the board and its relevant sub-committees in managing the financial risks from climate change. In particular, the board and the highest level of executive management should identify and allocate responsibility for identifying and managing financial risks from climate change to the relevant existing Senior Management Function(s) (SMF(s)) most appropriate within the firm's organisational structure and risk profile, and ensure that these responsibilities are included in the SMF(s)'s Statement of Responsibilities.[39]

The UK Senior Managers Regime is the first example in a developed country to hold senior managers and designated board members of regulated financial firms civilly liable for any breaches in regulations regarding sustainability risks.

6.5.2 *The Role of Regulation*

In the past few years, regulators have started to identify the material financial risks that the potential for stranded assets and, in particular, market volatility related to climate risk represent. However, such risks are still seen by many as being long-term and therefore beyond the scope of risk management processes. They are, though, not just long-term:

- Climate events can be precipitous – there is a significant financial stability risk arising from London flooding for example, which could happen at any time.
- Technical developments are on the brink of potentially causing huge and sudden disruptions to sectors such as energy, transport (e.g., electric vehicles) and construction. That could result in very significant risks to banks exposed to those sectors crystallising within, say, the next 3–5 years.
- On top of that, government policies globally are starting to implement the Paris 2015 agreement, which could result in a lot of unanticipated policy and regulatory risks emerging.

Given these challenges, bank risk managers need to ensure that they are not blindsided by the sudden materialisation of sustainability risks. Such risks are not all so-called 'black swans'. A lot of sustainability risks are predictable in nature – just not in timing or scale. As the regulators turn up the volume and tighten the rules, banks

---

[39] Prudential Regulation Authority 2018, 12.

need to understand the systemic risks to financial services that come with tackling sustainability if they are to avoid being continually caught out by new regulations.

There is an ongoing debate about whether capital requirements should be adjusted to reflect sustainability risks. Alexander and Fisher[40] look at this question and conclude that changing mandatory capital weights under pillar 1 minimum capital charges (of the Basel III regulations) is not the right approach. Rather, using pillar 2 of the banking supervisory approach – supervisors intervening to ensure appropriate risk management is taking place, subject to discretionary capital charges – is almost certainly the more effective method of regulatory intervention.

Capital requirements need to remain risk-based to support sustainable lending. There are normal risks associated with sustainable activities, and that degree of risk is already covered by the current Basel capital calculations. If there were to be a change in capital weights, it is the newly appreciated, *increased* risk from unsustainable activities that needs to be reflected – but that would be extremely difficult to incorporate in pillar 1 capital charges. The Bank of England and other regulators seem to agree with the pillar 2 approach[41].

6.6 BANK CULTURE AND SUSTAINABILITY – WHERE SHOULD THE FOCUS BE?

As financial regulators start to treat sustainability as a mainstream financial risk, so banks in both developed and developing countries are doing more to address the economic and financial risks associated with sustainability challenges by incorporating, or mainstreaming, sustainability factors and guidelines into their risk management models and business strategies. And bank boards are also responding by beginning to incorporate sustainability into the overall organisational cultural ethos.

Nevertheless, market structures must evolve to meet environmental sustainability needs and banks face steep challenges in managing the risks associated with that transition. Potentially, these could include price volatility and increased credit risk in assets and sectors considered environmentally unsustainable. Where such transition risks are material, they may pose systemic risks to the banking sector – and this is the source of increasing regulatory attention. To adequately address these risks, bank risk culture should fully incorporate sustainability criteria and values into risk management, remuneration incentives and strategic business objectives. Where there are institutional or market barriers, policy intervention may be necessary.

Despite progress in these areas, this chapter argues that inculcating sustainability values into mainstream bank business practices demands a more concerted focus on bank risk culture. In particular, that means a longer-term, and wider, appreciation

---

[40] Alexander and Fisher 2018.
[41] Bank of England, PRA 2018.

of risks to the firm, not just of the narrow risks to a particular transaction or portfolio. Bank risk culture should address the following factors that relate to environmental sustainability:

6.6.1 *Taking Account of the Importance of Reputation*

As the financial crisis and countless other episodes have shown (e.g., the collapse of Credit Suisse in 2023), reputation is essential for any successful business to be sustained: lose it and one's business model can follow very quickly. Pressure to maintain a good reputation can be exerted by investors – bank debt or equity holders – or by clients. However, in the past, the way in which banks offered very substantial remuneration for short-term performance could lead to staff ignoring long-term reputational risks to their firms – and that needs permanent change.

Sustainability is quickly becoming a reputational issue, thanks to pressure from governments and the public alike. As appreciation of sustainability issues rises, what was defensible at one point in time can become indefensible. We have seen this in Australia, for example, in relation to financing a new coal project.[42] Public attitudes can also change rapidly: for example, the introduction in 2015 of a minimal charge on single-use plastic shopping bags led to a rapid collapse in their use in the UK. Then, during 2018, Western Europe experienced a sudden consumer/retailer shift away from single-use plastics on account of concerns about pollution of the oceans, a movement which has since gone global.[43] Obviously, any company specialising in such products has had their business model severely challenged.

6.6.2 *Taking Account of Longer-Term and Broader Risks*

In the past, banks viewed sustainability risks as a social/political/ethical issue to be managed by their corporate social responsibility departments. This has led to some good work being done, at the margin, but has not been transformative. The cultural change required is two-fold: first, large banks in particular need to appreciate that sustainability risks are existential and systemic. If economic growth is not sustainable, then banks' business models are likely to come under pressure and quite possibly collapse. That means that the risk culture needs to be much longer-term and to be focused on broader macroeconomic factors. For example, banks must examine not just the short-term risks of an individual loan, but the future risks underlying the whole portfolio and their potential impact on the banking sector.

Second, the sustainability agenda should be recognised as a great business opportunity as well as a financial risk. Picking up on sustainability trends could be highly profitable by going with the grain of economic transformation and political

[42] Robertson 2017.
[43] Buranyi 2018.

direction. Both changes could be classed as internalising risks that have hitherto been regarded as externalities.

6.6.3 *The Demand for Credit*

Banks are intermediaries and in a narrow sense cannot lend if no one wants to borrow. But the demand for credit is not wholly exogenous. Like most goods and services, demand can be influenced through identifying an unmet need, designing new products and advertising. Banks who can do this successfully will win market share. This is, of course, a normal approach to building profits – as well as an opportunity for mis-selling (e.g., financial product mis-selling scandals in UK and other EU states) which can cause severe reputational damage.

6.7 SUMMARY AND CONCLUSION

This chapter analyses bank governance in the context sustainability risks and related business challenges. Climate change and other environmental sustainability challenges pose systemic financial risks for the banking sector and broader finial system. This is why it is important for bank boards and management to address environmental sustainability challenges and related financial risks. It suggests that a fundamental transformation is necessary to realign bank corporate governance with the objectives of a sustainable economy. This requires a change in the attitudes and ethical standards of bank management regarding both their regulatory and legal duties *and* cultural norms, standards, incentives and values within the institutions. Changing attitudes, norms and incentives are vital for banks and other financial institutions to support adequately the economy's transition to a sustainable path, while maintaining the value of their individual franchises. Environmental sustainability challenges that require banks to be resilient against the financial risks associated with environmental change *and* to reorient credit and capital to more sustainable economic sectors has brought banks and other financial institutions to the fore in the sustainable finance debate.

The chapter also discusses the various agency theories and suggests that human agency theory can provide a model for bank boards and senior management to design more effective governance approaches to address sustainability risks. An important aspect of this is influencing the development of a risk culture that takes account of sustainability risks and challenges to the banking business. The post-crisis regulatory environment has brought bank culture to the fore of improving bank governance and risk management practices, particularly regarding sustainable finance. The scope of regulation in shaping and developing risk culture with the specific aim of a more sustainable outcome remains uncertain. However, the direction of travel in many countries is clear, as the proposed inclusion of responsibility for managing a firm's risks from climate change in the UK Senior Managers Regime makes clear.

The UK approach of holding senior managers and board members individually liable for regulatory, governance and risk management failings may not be an appropriate legal sanction for many jurisdictions. But the overall objective, which most countries would embrace, is to make senior management and the board accountable for directing the bank's business to be more resilient to sustainability risks and to support the economy's transition to a more sustainable economic footing.

The chapter addresses some of the major challenges that banks face in incorporating sustainability criteria into their governance and risk management practices. Banking regulation reform and other financial sector initiatives, whose impetus was provided by the financial crisis of 2007/2008, are beginning to supervise closely the governance and business practices of banks in addressing sustainability challenges and the associated financial risks. This change of regulatory focus does not only bear down on how they manage and control financial sector risks, but increasingly includes the risks associated with an environmentally unsustainable economy. The chapter sheds light on some areas where banks can adjust their governance practices and risk culture so that the banking business can be more directly aligned with the goals and values of a sustainable economy.

The financial system therefore has an important role to play in delivering a more sustainable economy and banks have a special part within that. But there needs to be raised awareness: improving organisational and risk culture is crucial if banks are to both manage their own financial risks and realise business opportunities while supporting the development of the sustainable economy that is an existential necessity for their business model.

REFERENCES

Alexander, K. (2016), 'Greening Banking Policy', Input paper in support of the G20 Green Finance Study Group 'Greening Banking Policy', September 2016, (Geneva: United Nations Environmental Programme), available at: https://tinyurl.com/5n7f5jwt [accessed 16 June 2024].

Alexander, K. and Fisher, P. (2018), 'Banking Regulation and Sustainability', SSRN Working Paper, 1–17, available at: http://papers.ssrn.com/sol3/papers.cfm?abstract_id=3299351 [accessed 16 June 2024].

Alexander, K. and Fisher, P. (2019) 'What happens when nobody is watching: Regulation, bank risk culture and environmental sustainability', in Taaffe, O. (ed.), *Banking on Change: The Development and Future of Financial Services* (Chichester: Wiley), 27–42.

Alexander, K., Dhumale, R. and Eatwell, J. (2006), *Global Governance of Financial Systems: The International Regulation of Systemic Risk* (Oxford: Oxford University Press).

Alvesson, M. and Robertson, M. (2016), 'Money matters: Teflonic identity manoeuvring in the investment banking sector', *Organization Studies*, 37(1), 7–34.

Arrow, K. (1965), *Aspects of the Theory of Risk-Bearing* (Chicago, IL: Aldine-Atherton).

Ashby, S., Palermo, T. and Power, M. (2014), 'Risk culture: Definitions, change practices and challenge for chief risk officers', in Jackson, P. (ed.), *Risk Culture Effective Risk Governance* (London: Risk Books), 25–46.

Bandura, A. (1997), *Self-efficacy: The Exercise of Control* (New York: W H Freeman).

Bandura, A. (1999), 'Social cognitive theory of personality', in L. A. Pervin and O. P. John (eds.), *Handbook of Personality* (New York and London: The Guildford Press).

Bank of England (2018), 'Transition in Thinking: The Impact of Climate Change on the UK Banking Sector', available at: https://tinyurl.com/5n8en63z [accessed 16 June 2024].

Bank of England, Prudential Regulatory Authority (PRA) (2014), 'The Use of PRA Powers to Address Serious Failings in the Culture of Firms', available at: https://tinyurl.com/ykm4abp9 [accessed 16 June 2024].

BCBS (Basel Committee on Banking Supervision) (2009), 'Enhancements to the Basel II Framework', available at: www.bis.org/publ/bcbs157.htm [accessed 19 April 2017].

BCBS (Basel Committee on Banking Supervision) (2014), 'Consultative Document: Corporate Governance Principles for Banks', available at: www.bis.org/publ/bcbs294.pdf [accessed 10 January 2019].

BCBS (Basel Committee on BankingSupervision) (2022), 'Principles of Supervisory Review for Climate Change Risks', available at: www.bis.org/bfcbs/publ/d532.htm [accessed 16 June 2024].

Bilz, K. and Nadler, J. (2014), 'Law, moral attitudes, and behavioral change', in E. Zamir and D. Teichman (eds.), *The Oxford Handbook of Behavioral Economics and the Law* (Oxford: Oxford University Press), 241–267.

Bryant, Q. C. and Rickards, J. (2016) *The Legal Duties of Pension Fund Trustees in Relation to Climate Change, Abridged Joint Opinion* (London: ClientEarth).

Buranyi, S. (2018), 'The plastic backlash: What's behind our sudden rage – And will it make a difference?', *The Guardian*, 13 November, available at: https://tinyurl.com/2fjyzkku [accessed 16 June 2024].

Carney, M. (2015), 'Breaking the tragedy of the horizon – Climate change and financial stability', speech to Lloyd's of London, September, available at: https://bit.ly/4bFW54t [accessed 17 June 2024].

Center for Sustainability Studies, Federação Brasileira de Bancos (Febraban) (Sept. 2014), 'The Brazilian Financial System and the Green Economy: Alignment with Sustainable Development', (United Nations Environment Programme, Geneva), available at: https://tinyurl.com/mpja7h3 [accessed 17 June 2024].

Cole, D. H. and Ostrom, E. (2011) 'The variety of property systems and rights in natural resources', in D. H. Cole and E. Ostrom (eds.), *Property in Land and Other Resources* (Cambridge, MA: Lincoln Institute of Land Policy), 37–66.

DNB (De Nederlandsche Bank) (2017) *2016 Annual Report*, available at: www.dnb.nl/media/vxumoetl/2016-anual-report.pdf [accessed 16 June 2024].

Dow, J. (2000), *What Is Systemic Risk? Moral Hazard, Initial Shocks, and Propagation*. Institute for Monetary and Economic Studies, Bank of Japan.

Emirbayer, M. and Mische, A. (1998), 'What is agency', *The American Journal of Sociology*, 103(4), 962–1023.

European Banking Authority (2021), *Report on the Management of ESG Risks*, available at: https://tinyurl.com/yd75h3cw [accessed 17 June 2024].

European Central Bank (2020), *Final Guidance on Climate-related and Environmental Risks*, available at: https://tinyurl.com/bdhtjc3b [accessed 16 June 2024].

European Commission (2013), Directive 2013/36/EU of the European Parliament and of the Council of 26 June 2013 on access to the activity of credit institutions and the prudential supervision of credit institutions and investment firms, amending Directive 2002/87/EC and repealing Directives 2006/48/EC and 2006/49/EC, OJEU L 176/338, Recital 54.

European Commission (2018), *High-Level Expert Group on Sustainable Finance* (Final Report), available at https://tinyurl.com/36rv2kv3 [accessed 24 January 2019].

EY (2014), *Shifting Focus: Risk Culture at the Forefront of Banking*, available at: https://go.ey .com/3I6Gqhe [accessed 19 January 2019].

Financial Stability Board (2014), 'Guidance on Supervisory Interaction with Financial Institutions on Risk Culture: A Framework for Assessing Risk Culture', available at: www .fsb.org/wp-content/uploads/140407.pdf?page_moved=1 [accessed 10 January 2019].

G30 (2013), 'A New Paradigm: Financial Institution Boards and Supervisors', available at: https://bit.ly/3T3zHe3 [accessed 19 June 2022].

Hart, O. (1995), *Firms, Contracts, and Financial Structure* (New York: Oxford University Press, USA).

Hutley, S. C. and Hartford Davies, S. (2016), 'Climate Change and Directors' Duties', Memorandum of Opinion published by The Centre for Policy Development and the Future Business Council via Minter Ellison, Solicitors, Melbourne. https://tinyurl .com/4tyww2wm [accessed 16 June 2024].

Institute of International Finance (IIF) (2009), *Reform in the Financial Services Industry: Strengthening Practices for a More Stable System* (Washington, DC: IIF).

Jensen, M. C. (1998), *Foundations of Organizational Strategy* (Cambridge, MA: Harvard University Press).

Jensen, M. C. and Meckling, W. H. (1976), 'Theory of the firm: Managerial behavior, agency costs, and ownership structure', *Journal of Financial Economics*, 3(4), 305–360.

Jensen, M. C. and Meckling, W. H. (1994), 'The nature of man', *Journal of Applied Corporate Finance*, 7(2), 4–19.

Khurana, R. (2002), 'Market triads: A theoretical and empirical analysis of market intermediation', *Journal for The Theory of Social Behaviour*, 32(2), 239–262.

Mahmendier, U. and Geoffrey, T. (2009), 'Superstar CEOs', *The Quarterly Journal of Economics*, 124(4), 1593–1638.

Prudential Regulation Authority (2018), 'Enhancing Banks' and Insurers' Approaches to Managing the Financial Risks from Climate Change', consultation paper 23/18, available at: https://bit.ly/3OQSmap [accessed 24 January 2019].

Robertson, J. (2017), 'Big Four banks distance themselves from Adani Coalmine as Westpac rules out loan', *The Guardian*, 28 April, available at: https://tinyurl.com/3kw3dv5u [accessed 16 June 2024].

Sants H. W. H. (2010), 'Do regulators have a role to play in judging culture and ethics?' Speech at the Chartered Institute of Securities and Investments Conference, available at: https://bit.ly/3ONX5K4 [accessed 17 June 2024].

Shleifer, A. and Vishny, R. (1997), 'A survey of corporate governance', *Journal of Finance*, 2, 737–783.

Tversky, A. and Daniel, K. (1974), 'Judgment under uncertainty: Heuristics and biases', *Science, New Series*, 185(4157), 1124–1131.

United Nations (2015), 'About the Sustainable Development Goals', available at: https://bit .ly/3T3bcgZ [accessed 25 January 2019].

World Economic Forum (2020), *Measuring Stakeholder Capitalism, Towards Common Metrics and Consistent Reporting of Sustainable Value Creation*, September, Pilar: Principles of Governance.

7

Risk Culture and Sustainability

Paola Schwizer, Simona Cosma and Lorenzo Nobile

7.1 THE KEY ROLE OF CORPORATE GOVERNANCE AND RISK CULTURE IN DRIVING ENVIRONMENTAL SUSTAINABILITY

Sustainable development and orientation towards sustainable production and consumption models are objectives to which the European and international community attaches great importance. In the European context, time priority has been given to environmental sustainability or the green transition. The road is traced by the European Green Deal, a plan with which all 27 Member States have made a commitment to make the EU the first continent with net-zero CO_2 emissions by 2050.

Although the target desired by the stakeholders and set by the regulator is clear to companies, and the pressure exerted by them in this sense is strong,[1] the necessary change in business models collide with uncertainties about impacts, risks and performances, which may translate into greenwashing and behaviours that are not aligned with the statements made.[2]

The Action Plan recognizes that, despite the efforts made by several European companies, pressures from capital markets lead company directors and executives to fail to consider long-term sustainability risks and opportunities and be overly focussed on short-term financial performance. In other words, board directors, who are primarily responsible for defining the strategies that should incorporate sustainability objectives and promote cultural change toward sustainability, seem to be more focussed on maximizing short-term profits than on the investments needed to ensure long-term sustainability due to pressures by investors with a short-term horizon.[3]

The certainties regarding the onerousness of the necessary investments and the uncertainties regarding the expected benefits, in terms of time and amount,

---

[1] Zhang and Zhu 2019.
[2] Ferrón-Vílchez et al. 2021.
[3] European Commission 2020.

combined with consolidated values, beliefs and behaviours may hinder decisive actions towards a paradigm change and the adoption of sustainability-driven behaviours. This chapter focusses on environmental sustainability and a better understanding of the various levers with which one can act to direct behaviours towards new environmental goals. Environmental sustainability generally addresses how the needs of the present can be met without compromising the ability of future generations to meet their own needs, with an emphasis on the protection of natural resources and the environment.[4] In this chapter, we try to respond to scholars' recent calls to better address the ways in which organizations and their individuals can contribute to sustainable development.[5]

There is still little research about the types of internal factors that drive corporate sustainability within organizations. However, previous studies agree on the fundamental role of a culture of sustainability, that is, shared beliefs, values and behaviours about the importance of pursuing environmental and social objectives in addition to financial performance. Similarly, there is a high consensus on the role of leaders in the process of spreading a culture that effectively sees sustainability objectives as important criteria for allocating resources in addition to traditional risk and return assessments.

One way to encourage change, undermining doubts and uncertainties about the convenience and opportunity of adopting pro-environmental strategies (PES) and behaviours, could be the belief and awareness that the risks of "unsustainability", i.e., the risks of a failure to change in the adoption of PES, are severe and exceed the costs of change and, furthermore, that the expected benefits in terms of revenues in the medium/long term are high. In this sense, a risk-based cultural approach or a stronger risk culture, which embeds sustainability values, could support the dissemination of a cultural model oriented towards sustainability goals and the adoption of pro-environmental behaviour.

Risk culture is characterized by a long-term orientation and an approach to risk that does not aim at its elimination but at its active management, in the awareness that taking a risk in a conscious and informed way is a source of profitability.[6] In the context of capital allocation, the optimization of the risk/return trade-off or, for pure risks, the comparison between potential losses and risk management strategies (e.g., hedging) costs guide decision making. A stronger risk culture implies a better ability to evaluate the costs and opportunities of an action or strategy, not only in the short term but above all in the medium/long term, and to assess the consequent risks and opportunities and the ability to assume and manage them. Risk-adjusted profitability measures, stress tests, scenario analysis and risk exposure assessment methodologies are the basis of effective strategic planning, in particular in financial companies

[4]   Keeble 1987.
[5]   Golden-Biddle and Dutton 2012; Walsh et al. 2003.
[6]   Pan et al. 2017.

where the regulators impose such practices. For example, financial institutions are required to take a forward-looking view in their risk management, strategic planning, capital planning and liquidity planning as part of their internal capital adequacy assessment process (ICAAP) required by Directive 2013/36/EU and one of the tools that institutions can use to facilitate this forward-looking perspective in risk management is stress testing.[7]

Risk culture, environmental sustainability culture and pro-environmental behaviour are issues that have been investigated in academic research separately and any interconnections between them have never been investigated. In this chapter, we intend to explore the relationship between risk culture and attitudes and beliefs that could encourage the adoption of PES by board members. Inspired by Ajzen's theory of planned behaviour (ATPB), we will investigate the relationship between risk culture and drivers of environmentally sustainable behaviours. These drivers, according to ATPB, refer to what is convenient to do in order to achieve expected findings (behavioural beliefs), what should be done as required by regulators and induced by stakeholders' pressure (normative beliefs) and the conviction of possessing skills, resources and opportunities to perform a certain behaviour (control beliefs). According to ATPB, behavioural beliefs, normative beliefs and control beliefs represent, in turn, predictors of an individual's attitudes, subjective norms and perceived control beliefs, respectively. All these variables affect the intention to perform a behaviour and, in this case, to adopt pro-environmental strategies.

The choice to investigate these relationships by observing the behaviour of board members is due to several reasons:

1) According to the upper echelons theory,[8] individual attributes of organizations' decision-makers are important determinants of companies' behaviours and actions.[9] The adoption of pro-environmental strategies, therefore, passes through the values, beliefs and attitudes of decision-makers.[10]
2) The studies carried out to date on the drivers of environmental sustainability are mainly focussed on analysing the performance and characteristics of companies and less focussed on the individual behaviour of their leaders and, specifically, of board directors.
3) Tone from the top is one of the four characterizing and determining elements of risk culture. Therefore, observing the topic from the point of view of board directors members appears to be consistent with an assessment of the same.[11]

---

[7] Stress testing means assessing the impact of certain developments, including macro- or microeconomic scenarios, on the overall capital position of an institution by means of projecting the institution's capital resources and requirements, highlighting the institution's vulnerabilities and assessing its capacity to absorb losses and the impact on its solvency position.
[8] Hambrick and Mason 1984.
[9] Hutzschenreuter and Kleindienst 2006.
[10] Goodpaster 1983; Smith et al. 2010.
[11] FSB 2014.

4) To date, to the best of our knowledge, the values and beliefs of directors have not been investigated due to the difficulty in interviewing this target. Our study aims to fill this gap by investigating directors' individual risk cultures and beliefs, which may predict stronger attitudes and behaviours toward pro-environmental strategies.

The research analyses data obtained from a survey of 120 Italian board members, using a partial least square methodology to test the relationship between individual risk culture and beliefs, attitudes and norms. The choice to focus on a single country comes from the consideration that attitudes and beliefs toward pro-environmental actions, which are components of the environmental sustainability culture, could be affected by various external factors and, specifically, national cultures.[12] Hence, focussing on directors who operate in the same country, in which the external context is homogeneous (with a prevailing religion, regulation on environmental protection, pressure and sensitivity of stakeholders), is necessary to avoid a possible bias driven by the heterogeneity at the national level, and to focus on the differences in individual attributes. Local policymakers are putting considerable effort into promoting pro-environmental behaviour and fostering sustainable development. The Italian government has also allocated funding to environmental protection and provides incentives to companies in the form of subsidies and tax exemptions and reductions. The ability of companies to collaborate with governments in pursuing sustainability goals is critical, and consequently, the study of the conditions that could favour the development of a sustainability culture is of utmost importance.

Our findings add to previous work on the role of risk culture and provide a new theoretical perspective to guide green policy and changes aimed at increasing environmental sustainability.

7.2 THE SPECIAL "CULTURE" OF EMERGING RISKS AND SUSTAINABILITY

7.2.1 *Corporate Culture*

In literature, there are several definitions of "corporate culture". O'Reilly and Chatman[13] define corporate culture as "a system of shared values that define what is important, and norms that define appropriate attitudes and behaviours for organizational members". Schein[14] defined it as consisting of practices, values, symbols and assumptions that the members of a firm share about appropriate behaviour. Schein[15] argues that organizational culture, at its root, is composed of individuals

---

[12] Cicatiello et al. 2020; Uzzell 2000.
[13] O'Reilly and Chatman 1996, 160.
[14] Schein 1990.
[15] Schein 2010.

whose responses derive from assumptions and beliefs shared in an organization. Organizational culture is a manifestation of formal processes, systems and interactions (ability of leaders to manage processes and people, policy mechanisms to regulate employee behaviour, reward systems) and informal (values, implicit behavioural norms, role models, organizational rituals, beliefs, language etc.).[16] According to Shein,[17] an ethical culture exhibits two distinct languages. One is defined by espoused values, and the other by values in action.

Formal values are those embraced by the organization to influence behaviour and define goals (an organization's mission, vision and value statements, as well as codes of conduct and ethics). On the other hand, practised values are generally unwritten and behavioural in nature, are actively practised within the organization, and can have a negative or positive impact on organizational goal outcomes. In the case of a misalignment between declared and practised values, the latter generally prevails. As the misalignment gap increases, organizational dysfunctions increase and operational effectiveness decreases.[18] Alignment and consistency between the formal and informal components of the culture are essential in order to avoid ineffectiveness and unwanted behaviours. In this, personal moral development and the display of authenticity by leaders are essential.[19]

Research shows that corporate culture influences firms' behaviour and performance.[20] The culture of the principal influences the managerial "moral hazard" in the principal-agent framework,[21] and if managers and employees face choices that cannot be properly regulated ex-ante, corporate culture may be crucial to explain their decisions, contributions and, ultimately, corporate performance,[22] according to the incomplete contract theory framework.[23] Culture originates from top management and is passed on by example throughout the organization. The personal behaviour of business leaders defines acceptable and desirable behaviour and conveys the values of an organization.

7.2.2 *Sustainability Culture*

Great consensus in literature has the thesis that beyond any technical, managerial solution, the real change in the direction of sustainability requires a change in human values, attitudes and beliefs of people or a cultural change.[24] However,

[16] Dion and Dion 1996; Nelson 2004.
[17] Shein et al. 2004.
[18] Ardichvili et al. 2009.
[19] Ibid.
[20] Wilkins and Ouchi 1983; Schein 1990; Van den Steen 2010.
[21] Gorton 2015.
[22] Guiso et al. 2015.
[23] Grossman and Hart 1986.
[24] Lozano et al. 2013a; Marshall et al. 2015; López-Torres 2019; Schneider et al. 1996; Hart and Milstein 1999; Jabbour and de Sousa Jabbour 2016.

there is still a lack of clarity in the existing literature on which attributes qualify the sustainability-oriented corporate culture.

Corporate culture (CC) is considered a driving factor of sustainability performance[25]; on the other hand, a failure in culture change, including the values and beliefs,[26] can be an obstacle to sustainable development.[27]

A culture of sustainability implies that environmental and social objectives, in addition to financial performance, are important. In the literature, it emerges that a culture oriented towards sustainability has qualifying characteristics. Shared qualifying elements are the long-term orientation and the maximization of stakeholder value. Leaders have responsibilities and obligations toward several groups of stakeholders with specific interests.[28] This heterogeneity generates difficulty in reconciling interests and instances. Stakeholder management, through increased dialogue with stakeholders, becomes the key to balancing the needs of stakeholders. A further qualifying element, closely connected to the first, lies in the long-term orientation. A "sustainable" culture has long-term strategic objectives for long-term survival and value creation and does not aim only at short-term gains. Business leaders are called upon to evolve and design strategies that promote both long-term growth and progressive innovation.

Although the interests of stakeholders may conflict with the interests of shareholders to whom business leaders must guarantee profits in the short term, meeting the needs of other stakeholders, such as employees, through investment in training, or customers through good customer service, directly creates value for shareholders.[29]

Specifically, Islam et al.[30] state that companies with a strong culture of "economic" sustainability aim to achieve resource efficiency without degrading environmental and social aspects, instructional communication, and goal setting in light of environmental demand,[31] emphasizing the branding of green initiatives to push green products and increase revenues, adopting the culture of quality management systems, including ISO 14001[32] to reduce waste and emissions.

According to Islam et al.,[33] a culture oriented towards the "social" aspect supports the adoption of the following actions and policies:

- employee engagement in participative decision making and interpersonal communication[34];

---

[25] Linnenluecke and Griffiths 2010; Tseng 2017; Jabbour and de Sousa Jabbour 2016; Lozano et al. 2013b.
[26] Linnenluecke and Griffiths 2010.
[27] Lozano 2015; Acquaye et al. 2017.
[28] Freeman 1994.
[29] Freeman and Ambady 2010; Porter and Kramer 2011.
[30] Islam et al. 2019.
[31] Linnenluecke and Griffiths 2010.
[32] Govindan et al. 2015; Rao and Holt 2005.
[33] Islam et al. 2019.
[34] Linnenluecke and Griffiths 2010.

- greater corporate responsibility for workforce development, equal opportunity, work-life balance, workplace diversity, and social justice[35];
- a social policy reflected in missions, values, beliefs and business processes[36];
- a mission that includes a statement of caring for society[37];
- incorporating sustainability criteria in recruitment process[38];
- continuous empowerment of staffs through training and reward system[39];
- regular training to share sustainable development information and build capacity as well as integrating sustainable development goals into a performance measurement system[40];
- employee welfare solutions, including long-term employment growth and stability as well as pension, bonus and health care plans for employees;
- financial benefits to help employees focus on a non-financial aspect of the business[41];
- the ability to attract and retain talent in order to have satisfied employees who contribute to the development of innovation[42];
- minimizing the use of the toxic chemicals in the operation process, replacing humans with robots in dangerous workplaces and providing in-house medical facilities as some of the health and safety.[43]

Moreover, developing a sense of belonging and interaction with the community/company helps to avoid harmful actions. Therefore, a social sustainable company should have values such as a shared commitment to health and safety concerns for employees, customers and community.[44]

A culture oriented toward "environmental" sustainability is qualified by dynamism and flexibility. According to Islam et al.,[45] it fosters:

- the ability to adapt and change mission, values, goals, strategies and human resources levels;
- non-rigid decision making and informal and non-hierarchical coordination and control mechanisms[46];
- a clear mission statement with a declaration that environmental protection is important[47] in order to clarify priorities and corporate identity and guide the behaviour of the employees;

[35] Benn et al. 2014.
[36] Eccles et al. 2012.
[37] Dermol 2012.
[38] Jabbour and de Sousa Jabbour 2016.
[39] Galpin et al. 2015.
[40] Dessler 1999; Tseng 2017; Galpin et al. 2015.
[41] Eccles et al. 2014.
[42] Tseng 2017.
[43] Lozano and Huisingh 2011.
[44] Domahidi et al. 2014; Galpin et al. 2015.
[45] Islam et al. 2019.
[46] Galpin et al. 2015.
[47] Jacopin and Fontrodona 2009.

 – values and shared commitment to protect the environment to influence the decision-making process and the thinking process
 – the ability to publicly communicate sustainable development and make their practices transparent.[48]

Sustainable development initiatives should be integrated into firms' strategies so that it can help articulate the mission, values and goals into practices[49]; environmental impacts across the value chain should be evaluated; and objectives should be clearly defined in order to mitigate the environmental impact and should be used to evaluate employee performance. Ethical leadership is essential for guiding and shepherding people towards achieving sustainable development objectives[50] as well as environmental training, staff empowerment, teamwork and transfer of environmental knowledge from managers to their staff.[51]

New European Union requirements for sustainability reporting converted voluntary efforts into legally mandated ones. The obligation of non-financial disclosure in this sense accelerates the leadership's decision on the level of commitment to the sustainability road, which, in turn, will be determined by the personal values of leadership, stakeholder pressure, business culture and other factors.[52] A gap exists in both the empirical and practitioner literature regarding the development and assessment of the organizational factors that foster a culture of sustainability. Moreover, no clear model exists with the expressed purpose of helping leaders create such a culture.

7.2.3 *Risk Culture*

Risk management in any company is necessary to allow the achievement of the set objectives and requires continuous interactions and comparisons with policies, strategy and governance. Although the ultimate responsibility for risk governance is of the board of directors, good management of the same requires that all people be risk managers within their specific responsibilities.[53]

The culture of risk is a topic that has recently been frequently recalled by European regulators.[54] For risk culture, we refer to an expression of corporate culture that focusses on risk-taking and risk-control activities.

Sheedy and Griffin,[55] according to Ehrhart et al.,[56] define risk culture as the perceptions that employees share of the relative importance given to risk management, risk-related practices and behaviours that are expected, valued and supported.

---

[48] Eccles et al. 2012.
[49] Galpin et al. 2015.
[50] Lozano 2015.
[51] Wilkinson et al. 2001; Huang et al. 2001.
[52] Cosma et al. 2021b.
[53] Schrøder 2006.
[54] Carretta et al. 2017a.
[55] Sheedy and Griffin 2018.
[56] Ehrhart et al. 2014.

If the concept is borrowed from the financial sector, whose core business is risk management/transformation, the culture of risk is the set of "norms, attitudes, and behaviors related to risk awareness, risk-taking, and risk management, and controls that shape decisions on risks".[57]

Risk culture does not imply a defensive attitude towards risk, which, by definition, could also involve gains and opportunities, but an active attitude aimed at limiting losses and increasing profits through knowledge of the mechanisms, dynamics and factors that can generate risks and making use of available forecasting systems and techniques. So, the goal of risk management is not only its elimination or reduction but the search for a correct balance between risk assumption and risk prevention and mitigation. Effective risk management requires that skills, attitudes and awareness are not the exclusive property of the responsible functions but be disseminated at all levels. In other words, effective risk management requires the spread of the risk culture across the organization.

ISO 31000, a standard intended for those who create and protect value in organizations while managing risks, refers to the integration of risk management into an organization's culture, stating that the risk management process should be an integral part of the management, embedded in culture and practices, and adapted to the organization's business processes.[58] In the same document, some aspects of effective risk management clearly emerge that concern the importance of not forgetting mistakes, experiences and, therefore, the past, compliance with supervisory rules, fairness and respect for all interested parties, awareness of responsibility for the actions taken and the consequences, transparency and long-term orientation to time. A good risk culture means that staff have a clear understanding of the boundaries of acceptable risk-taking and are committed to ensuring that those boundaries are respected.

A risk cultural framework that is largely accepted is proposed by FSB.[59] Essential elements of the risk culture are: (i) tone from the top, that is, the board members and senior managers are responsible for promoting risk culture and including it in the bank's strategy; (ii) accountability, i.e., the banks must develop a policy of ownership of risk in which employees are held accountable for their actions and are aware of the consequences for not adhering to the desired behaviours toward risk; (iii) effective communication and challenge, i.e., top managers must encourage alternative views and pay attention to risk managers' suggestions to make informed risk decisions; and (iv) incentives or banks need a risk-linked rewarding system based on monetary and non-monetary incentives.

In other words, the framework recalls the responsibilities of everyone, but in particular of the company leaders, in building the conditions and mechanisms so that everyone can make informed and risk-aware decisions, evaluating the risks

---

[57] BCBS 2015, 2.
[58] ISO 31000 2021.
[59] FSB 2014.

consequent to each action taken in the context of their activity in terms of costs and benefits. Risk culture is not static: it is a continuous process, which repeats itself and is renewed, therefore it requires organizations to be not rigid but flexible. Every day, external change generates new challenges and risks, as well as changes in legislation, which require different responses from an organizational point of view. Regulation has undoubtedly been a major driver of risk culture change programmes.

Previous studies on risk culture refer to business organizations and countries (collective approach) or to ordinary people (individualistic approach). Several scholars have investigated risk culture referring to countries.[60] Others have examined risk culture referring to business organizations because legislation and competitive pressure have exacerbated the intersectoral differences and the divergences between managers' risk aversion. Agarwal et al.,[61] Carretta et al.[62] and Ring et al.[63] focussed on the financial sector, Bui et al.[64] and Mechelli et al.[65] investigated non-financial entities and Agarwal and Kallapur[66] the insurance sector.

Broad consensus emerges on the fact that risk culture is a dynamic concept because it reflects the risk attitudes of corporate leaders and is subject to evolution through generations.[67] Although it may refer to business organizations or countries, behind the concept of risk culture there are always ordinary people and their conduct towards risk and uncertainty.

A transversal reading of the studies on risk culture highlights the following qualifying elements of risk culture:

- long-term vision promoted by business leaders through talent research and development and succession planning;
- a clear understanding by all of the risk appetite (RAF) and corporate strategy;
- ability to learn from mistakes made in the past and not to feed a culture of fear of error in order not to generate immobility;
- assumption of risks according to the rules of the RAS (risk appetite statement) and support in the management of situations in which limits are exceeded[68];
- mechanisms for sharing information on emerging risks and making the various members of the organization responsible in the event that the actions are not in line with the values promoted, regardless of the financial result achieved;
- possibility to report problems or new opportunities regarding products or practices (e.g., whistleblowing);

---

[60] Reuter et al. 2019; Cornia 2015; Hasegawa 2017.
[61] Agarwal et al. 2019.
[62] Carretta et al. 2017a.
[63] Ring et al. 2016.
[64] Bui et al. 2018.
[65] Mechelli et al. 2017.
[66] Agarwal and Kallapur 2018.
[67] Pan et al. 2017.
[68] Dickson 2015.

- ability to encourage and respect new points of view;
- incentives (such as remuneration policies) that support correct behaviour in line with the values of the company;
- training programmes aimed at the organization chart to allow the possibility of developing shared risk management skills;
- the ability of the organization to change and modify itself;
- communication consistent with the declared values, strategy and risk management by executives and management;
- implementation of platforms through which staff can share knowledge of risky events, bad news and problems to discuss in order to learn new lessons;
- openness and transparency towards the supervisory authorities;
- recruitment, insertion and exit processes that emphasize corporate values and risk management objectives.

From a regulatory point of view, the development of a risk culture that takes into account sustainability risks, and in particular climate and environmental risks, is fundamental to directing the organization towards sustainability objectives.[69]

With reference to the financial sector, supervisors identify sustainability risks with risks of non-change, attributing the inability of banks with a poor corporate culture to comply with principles such as equal pay or equal representation as well as workforce diversity to become the subject of complaints and be affected by legal action, market pressure and/or reputational damage. Corporate cultures which respect equality, inclusiveness, fair labour standards and support for communities are signs of good governance. On the other hand, negative conditions for employees, unfair treatment of customers or low interest in contributing to the company can lead to additional governance risks.

In the scope of the relationship between risk culture and the development of sustainability culture, supervisors recall the fundamental role of the involvement of the management body in the creation of a risk culture and in the definition of risk appetite, and the implementation of a solid internal control framework, which are considered key aspects for an effective implementation of ESG policies and ESG risk management processes.

7.3 TONE FROM THE TOP: THE GOVERNANCE OF EMERGING RISKS AS A KEY DRIVER FOR SUSTAINABILITY

The upper echelons theory indicates that leaders' values, knowledge and experience determine the thinking process and decision-making process and thus affect corporate behaviour.[70] Previous studies have shown that demographic characteristics

---

[69] EBA 2021.
[70] Lee et al. 2018.

significantly affect their ethics, moral values and ethical behaviours.[71] Several research contributions have identified education, gender and local-global conditions as key cultural factors in predicting environmental intent and behaviour.[72]

Despite the numerous critical arguments that have contested Ajzen's theory of planned behaviour (ATPB) (e.g., Sniehotta et al.),[73] this remains one of the most utilized models explaining how behavioural intentions are formed. The relative influence of these factors depends on the particular issue under study and the sample,[74] but the ATPB model is robust and effective.[75] In the theory of planned behaviour, a person is more likely to perform a behaviour as behavioural intention increases, and a person's intention to perform a behaviour increases as behavioural beliefs, subjective norms and perceived behavioural control become more favourable. Attitude toward the behaviour refers to the degree to which a person has a favourable or unfavourable evaluation or appraisal of the behaviour in question. Subjective norms refer to the perceived social pressure to perform or not to perform the behaviour. Perceived behavioural control refers to the perceived ease or difficulty in performing the behaviour, and it is assumed to reflect past experience as well as anticipated impediments and obstacles. As a general rule, the more favourable the attitude and subjective norm with respect to a behaviour, and the greater the perceived behavioural control, the stronger should be an individual's intention to perform the behaviour under consideration.

In turn, attitudes toward a behaviour arise from a person's beliefs about the consequences resulting from their behaviour and the person's affective response to those consequences. Subjective norms are a function of a person's perception of important referents' evaluation of behaviour and the person's motivation to conform to those evaluations. The perceived behavioural control reflects aspects of the person, such as the level of self-efficacy, and aspects of the behaviour, such as the necessity of obtaining the cooperation of others to accomplish it.

In this study, we use the Ajzen model to try to establish whether a stronger risk culture is positively related to more favourable assumptions and implicit values, which refer to beliefs about the types of goals firm members should pursue, as well as ideas regarding standards of behaviour.

7.3.1 *Risk Culture at the Board Level and PES Drivers*

Behavioural beliefs are the result of evaluations regarding the business case of the adoption of environmental behaviours. The fear that an increase in

[71] Cacioppe et al. 2008; Davidson and Freudenburg 1996.
[72] Milfont 2012; Zelezny et al. 2000.
[73] Sniehotta et al. 2014.
[74] Sánchez-Medina et al. 2014.
[75] Armitage and Conner 2001; Chao 2012.

pro-environmental strategies will lead to an increase in costs and a decrease in the competitiveness of companies is an obstacle to engagement in environmental sustainability.[76] In fact, previous studies theorize that a harmonious relationship between companies and the environment generates a long-term competitive advantage:[77] the company's actions to prevent pollution, produce cleanly, recycle waste, innovate production can generate a sustainable competitive advantage by ensuring a long-term sustainable dominance of companies.[78] Additionally, Hart[79] claims in his theory of natural resource-based view (NRBV) that to consolidate their future position, firms must have a pollution prevention strategy as well as an environmental consideration during a product design and development process. Ethical beliefs, norms and culture and pro-environment behaviours of enterprises are the valuable, rare, inimitable, non-substitutable key resources and may represent sources of competitive advantage.[80] Behaviours different from those indicated may involve risks of penalties and reputational damage, especially if such behaviour is reported in the media. Stakeholders are increasingly sensitive to these issues, and therefore behaviours in violation of environmental laws or harmful to the environment could undermine trust and relationships with stakeholders, compromising medium/long-term results. From another point of view, pro-environment strategies could be a source of opportunities[81] allowing the company to increase the rate of use of resources, to obtain cost savings deriving from efficiency gains (think of the internal policies of reuse and recycling or innovation of systems that allow energy savings), to support its customers in cost savings, to obtain more financing or financing at lower costs, to establish positive and collaborative relationships with stakeholders, earning their trust,[82] to promote corporate reputation and be more efficient and competitive,[83] to obtain higher levels of employee performance and commitment, to outperform over the long term, both in terms of stock market and accounting performance,[84] and to increase market share by establishing niches and new markets due to the environmental and social credentials.[85]

Having a risk culture, characterized by a better ability to evaluate the opportunities and expected benefits net of the resulting risks, could allow board members to develop more favourable behavioural beliefs.

---

[76] Garcés-Ayerbe et al. 2016; Hart and Ahuja 1996.
[77] Hart 1995; Menguc and Ozanne 2005.
[78] McWilliams and Siegel 2011.
[79] Hart 1995.
[80] Barney 1991; Sugita and Takahashi 2015.
[81] Chen 2011.
[82] Sharma and Vredenburg 1998; Aragón-Correa and Sharma 2003; Russo and Fouts 1997.
[83] Chan et al. 2012; Reyes-Rodríguez et al. 2016.
[84] Eccles et al. 2012.
[85] Hespenheide et al. 2010.

Normative beliefs are affected by the stakeholders' pressure. Literature highlights that the pressure of stakeholders has got a great influence on the adoption of environmental strategies.[86] In the case of external stakeholders, the strongest direct effect on environmental strategies was observed by regulators, whereas in the case of internal stakeholders, the strongest effect was exerted by top management and shareholders.[87] Henriques and Sadorsky,[88] Buysse and Verbeke,[89] Sarkis et al.,[90] Darnall et al.[91] and Murillo-Luna et al.[92] demonstrated a direct and positive effect of stakeholder pressure on pro-environmental strategies. This is consistent with Porter's hypothesis, which states that only strict environmental regulations stimulate enterprises to implement PES.[93] However, many researchers have different views on the relationship between PES and regulatory pressure.

Risk culture means a better ability to assess compliance and reputational risk, the value of positive relationships with stakeholders and the ability to adapt in a timely manner to the new regulation. Hence, a sounder risk culture could favour stronger normative beliefs.

Finally, a stronger risk culture means a better ability to govern uncertainty, better knowledge of risks and regulation and better assessment and management skills and, consequently, greater self-confidence and greater self-efficacy that affect control beliefs.

In light of the previous considerations, we assume that:

H1a: There is a positive relationship between directors' behavioural beliefs regarding PES and their attitude to engage in pro-environmental behaviours.

H1b: There is a positive relationship between directors' normative beliefs regarding PES and their subjective norm to engage in pro-environmental behaviours.

H1c: There is a positive relationship between directors' control beliefs regarding PES and their perceived behavioural control to engage in pro-environmental behaviours.

H2a: There is a positive relationship between directors' risk culture and their behavioural beliefs regarding PES.

H2b: There is a positive relationship between directors' risk culture and their normative beliefs regarding PES.

H2c: There is a positive relationship between directors' risk culture and their control beliefs regarding PES.

---

[86] Buysse and Verbeke 2003; Delmas and Toffel 2004; Rueda-Manzanares et al. 2008.
[87] Seroka-Stolka and Fijorek 2020.
[88] Henriques and Sadorsky 1999.
[89] Buysse and Verbeke 2003.
[90] Sarkis et al. 2010.
[91] Darnall et al. 2010.
[92] Murillo-Luna et al. 2011.
[93] Porter and Linde 2000.

7.4 RESEARCH DESIGN

The research consists of three main steps. First, we developed the questionnaire to collect empirical data in order to examine all drivers of behaviours of board members. Second, we used different procedures to address potential concerns on standard methods and source biases: exploratory factor analysis (EFA), reliability, convergent validity and discriminant validity, and confirmatory factor analysis (CFA) of the construct. Finally, we performed a partial least square (PLS) path modelling technique to test our hypotheses. The risk culture of board members was captured through two proxies: control and risk committee (CRC) membership and the financial sector.

In Figure 7.1, we graphically show the conceptual model adopted. The model does not evaluate the effects of attitude, subjective norm and perceived behavioural control on intention to perform, but we put in the graph intention to engage in PES and pro-environmental behaviour to show the complete ATPB model.

7.4.1 *Sample*

The data used in this study were collected through a questionnaire submitted to a group of Italian board members. The questionnaire was developed by a "reflection group on leadership and sustainable success" within Nedcommunity, the Italian association of non-executive and independent directors, and was pre-tested on five directors, and members of Nedcommunity. The questionnaire was administered electronically by e-mail between May and July 2020. The questionnaire was uploaded onto a web platform and sent as a link via e-mail, including detailed instructions for its completion. Reminder e-mails were sent every 15 days. All participants were assured that their answers were anonymous, they could withdraw at any time and there were no right or wrong responses, and they were told to answer questions as honestly as possible. The completed questionnaires contained no missing values (i.e., all responses were mandatory).

In developing the questionnaire, multi-items were used to measure the constructs of the ATPB via seven-point Likert scales. All the scales employed in the survey were original scales developed for the study except for the attitude.[94] The study involved a sample of about 600 Italian board members, with a total response rate of 20 per cent (120 responses out of 600). The sample composition is summarized in Table 7.1. Of the 120 respondents, 40 per cent were male and 60 per cent female. In terms of age, 45 per cent were under 55 and 54 per cent were over 60. Regarding governance variables, 72 per cent of the respondents were non-executive and independent directors.

---

[94] Dibrell et al. 2011; Cosma et al. 2021a.

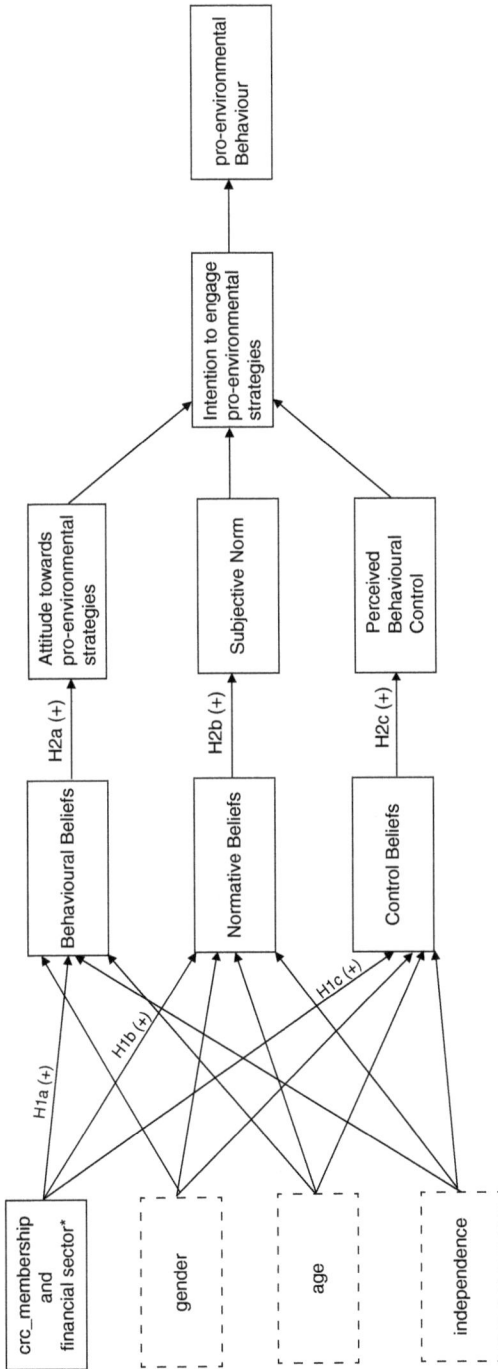

FIGURE 7.1 A conceptual model

*For the financial sector, the hypothesis are the same

TABLE 7.1 *Sample profile of the respondents*

Variable	Category	Frequency	%
1. Gender	Female	72	60.00
	Male	48	40.00
2. Age	39–55	66	45.00
	>55	54	55.00
3. Education	University degree	76	63.33
	Master post-university degree	28	23.33
	PhD	16	13.33
5. Role	Independent directors	74	72
	Other	46	38
6. Committee membership	Committee Risk & Control Joint	40	33.33
	Other	80	66.67
7. Industry	Financial	42	35.00
	Non-financial	78	65.00
8. Listing	Listed	70	58.33
	Not-listed	50	41.67
9. Firm size	+500	72	60.00
	−500	48	40.00

Note: n = 120

7.4.2 *Questionnaire Development and Constructs*

7.4.2.1 Drivers of Intention to Perform a Behaviour

Attitude (ATT). Environmental attitudes were measured by a five-item scale derived from the earlier works of Klassen (2001) and then used by Dibrell et al.,[95] Pagell and Gobeli,[96] Roxas and Coetzer[97] and Cosma et al.[98] This scale was preferred to alternatives, because it refers to strategic policies relating to the natural environment. Items measure the attitudinal propensity of the company's director to allocate firm resources to business and natural environmental initiatives aimed at protecting the natural environment.[99] An initial confirmatory factor analysis (CFA) model was built on the five items, which were extracted from the exploratory factor analysis (EFA). Subsequently, the five items of the initial construct have been reduced to four and were found to meet the benchmark model fit criteria. The results of the confirmatory factor analysis using maximum likelihood estimation are illustrated in Table 7.2. The construct shows appropriate statistical properties.[100]

[95] Dibrell et al. 2011.
[96] Pagell and Gobeli 2009.
[97] Roxas and Coetzer 2012.
[98] Cosma et al. 2021a.
[99] Dibrell et al. 2011.
[100] Chin 1998; Hulland 1999.

TABLE 7.2 *Confirmatory factor analysis*

	Dependent variable	Cronbach's α	AVE	Factor loadings
	Values (*Likert* 1 = *not at all important,…,* *7 = absolutely essential*)	0.758	0.502	
	Businesses need to spend more on environmental protection.			0.867
	In the future, environmental protection should be considered part of the "final result" of the enterprise			0.827
ATT	Business leaders should be spearheading environmental protection efforts.			0.906
	We must protect the environment even if it means that jobs in our community will be lost			0.614

CFA: (χ^2 = 237.11, *df* = 6, *p value* >0.05, CFI = 0.999, GFI = 0.998, SRMR = 0.011, RMSEA = 0.000 IFN = 0.998)

	Dependent variable	Cronbach's α	AVE	Factor loadings
	Values (*Likert* 1 = *not at all important,…,* *7 = absolutely essential*)	0.848	0.587	
	Public opinion/community approves			0.823
NS	Investors approve			0.744
	Non-governmental organizations (NGOs) approve			0.635
	Regulators and supervisors approve			0.750

CFA: (χ^2 = 203.23, *df* = 2, *p value* >0.05, CFI = 0.994, GFI = 0.986, SRMR = 0.022, RMSEA = 0.072 IFN = 0.984)

	Dependent variable	Cronbach's α	AVE	Factor loadings
	Values (*Likert* 1 = *not at all important,…,* *7 = absolutely essential*)	0.855	0.542	
	Availability of skills, abilities and specialized figures			0.617
PBC	Awareness of the potential benefits			0.724
	Easy access to reliable data			0.788
	Sharing by management			0.665
	Ease in changing the mindset of management			0.770

CFA: (χ^2 = 146.644, *df* = 10, *p value* >0.05, CFI = 0.988, GFI = 0.959, SRMR = 0.045, RMSEA = 0.072 IFN = 0.073)

	Dependent variable	Cronbach's α	AVE	Factor loadings
	Values (*Likert* 1 = *not at all important,…,* *7 = absolutely essential*)	0.765	0.655	
INT	I purpose to commit to promoting the adoption of environmental strategies			0.810
	I plan to commit to promoting the adoption of environmental strategies			0.810

The model was tested for reliability, convergent validity and discriminant validity. Convergent validity is indicated by the AVE statistic.[101] As shown in Table 7.2, the values obtained for Cronbach's α (>0.7) and the average variance extracted from the dependent variables (AVE>0.5) confirm, respectively, internal consistency reliability and convergent validity[102] of the variables included in the survey. Due to the sensitivity of Cronbach's α to the number of measures in a construct, composite reliabilities (0.7<CR>0.9)[103] of the variables have also been included in Table 7.2, which corroborates the reliability of the survey items. Additionally, the discriminant validity of the variables was recognized by the AVE of each pair of dependent variables being greater than their squared (see Table 7.2).

Subjective norm (NS). An initial confirmatory factor analysis (CFA) model was built on the 12 items, which were extracted from the exploratory factor analysis (EFA). Subsequently, the 12 items of the initial construct have been reduced to four and were found to meet the benchmark model fit criteria. The construct shows appropriate statistical properties, with loadings well above the 0.50 threshold, a composite reliability of 0.8 and an AVE of 0.58[104] (see Table 7.2). The statistics in Table 7.2 also indicate adequate discriminant validity.[105] Moreover, the results of the confirmatory factor analysis using maximum likelihood estimation are illustrated in Table 7.2. The construct shows appropriate statistical properties.[106]

Perceived behavioural control (PBC). An initial confirmatory factor analysis (CFA) model was built on the 12 items, which were extracted from the exploratory factor analysis (EFA). Subsequently, the 12 items of the initial construct have been reduced to five and were found to meet the benchmark model fit criteria. The statistical properties of the construct are adequate, with loadings above the 0.50 threshold, composite reliability of 0.85 and AVE of 0.54[107] (see Table 7.2). The discriminant validity of the construct is also appropriate[108] (see Table 7.2). Finally, the results of the confirmatory factor analysis using maximum likelihood estimation are illustrated in Table 7.2. The construct shows appropriate statistical properties.[109]

7.4.2.2 Behavioural, Normative and Control Beliefs

In the questionnaire, a 7-level Likert-type scale was used to assess behavioural beliefs, normative beliefs and control beliefs. We preferred a 7-point Likert scale,

---

[101] Chin 1998; Chin 2010.
[102] Fornell and Larcker 1981.
[103] Nunnally and Bernstein 1994.
[104] Chin 1998; Hulland 1999.
[105] Chin 1998.
[106] Chin 1998; Hulland 1999.
[107] Ibid.
[108] Chin 1998.
[109] Chin 1998; Hulland 1999.

rather than a 5-point one, as the first is more sensitive than stairs with a lower number of levels,[110] more suitable for questionnaires sent by e-mail,[111] as well as more useful in the presence of questions that include preferences that present a bipolar scale of the same, i.e., from negative (totally disagree) to positive (totally in agreement).

Behavioural beliefs (composite). Following Thoradeniya et al.,[112] the measure of behavioural beliefs consists of 12 items of behavioural outcomes. For example, a possible outcome of pro-environmental strategies is an improvement in the reputation of the company. Respondents were asked to rate their agreement with this outcome and the desirability of such an outcome. Following Ajzen,[113] behavioural belief (i.e., BB) was measured as the sum of the cross-products of the beliefs about anticipated consequences/outcomes of pro-environmental strategies (B_i) and outcome evaluation for each behavioural belief item (E_i):

$$BB = \sum B_i \ x \ E_i$$

Normative beliefs (composite). Following Thoradeniya et al.,[114] the social pressure that directors may experience when deciding whether to engage in pro-environmental strategies is a multiplicative function of how she/he thinks stakeholders (i.e., referents) would approve or disapprove of the behaviour and how willing she/he is to comply with each of the stakeholders' wishes. Twelve stakeholder groups relevant to pro-environmental strategies were identified. Normative belief (NB) was measured by the sum of the cross-products of the beliefs about identity and expectations of stakeholders towards engaging in pro-environmental strategies (N_i) and motivation to comply with those stakeholders for each normative belief item (M_i):

$$NB = \sum N_i \ x \ M_i$$

Control belief (composite). Following Thoradeniya et al.,[115] 12 factors facilitating or impeding pro-environmental strategies were identified. Control belief (CB) was measured as the sum of the cross-products of beliefs about the presence of factors that may facilitate or impede pro-environmental strategies (C_i) and perceived power of the factor for each control belief item (P_i):

$$CB = \sum C_i \ x \ P_i$$

Control variables. Three control variables were included. They were: a dummy variable for a female director (gender), a dummy variable for a younger director (age) and a dummy variable for an independent director (independent). These control variables were selected because prior research showed that females, younger

[110] Jaeschke et al. 1990; Diefenbach et al. 1993.
[111] Finstad 2010.
[112] Thoradeniya et al. 2015.
[113] Ajzen 1991.
[114] Thoradeniya et al. 2015.
[115] Ibid.

and independent directors exhibit more concern about the environment[116] and we wanted to isolate the effect of risk culture.

Next, we computed the descriptive statistics (i.e., mean and standard deviation) for all the constructs involved in our conceptual model (Figure 7.1), along with their bivariate correlations (see Table 7.3).

The correlation and descriptive statistics of the constructs presented in Table 7.3 show that, on average, participants had a relatively high level of behavioural beliefs (mean of 416, theoretical maximum of 588), normative beliefs (mean 138, theoretical maximum of 441) and control beliefs (mean 185, theoretical maximum of 637). The mean for attitude (towards pro-environmental strategies), perceived behaviour control and subjective norm show small absolute differences, but these are not statistically significant (means of 5.11, 6.22 and 5.75, respectively, theoretical maximums of 7). The ratings for subjective norm and perceived behavioural control appear to correlate to the slightly higher values of behavioural beliefs and normative beliefs.

7.4.3 *Model and Results*

The partial least square (PLS) path modelling technique was used to analyse the data. The PLS-R (Partial Least Squares Regression) technique was developed to avoid the effect of multicolinearity (among other factors) in the estimation of regression parameters. In turn, the PLS-R model seeks to predict dependent variables. In practice, this objective represents an attempt to maximize the explained variance of the said variables (variance of Y explained by the correlation existing between X and Y). Therefore, PLS Regression may be more appropriate for predictive purposes.[117]

The structural model tests the relationship among the latent variables. The estimated path coefficients of the structural model, as well as their statistical significance, are shown in Figure 7.2a. Based on the ATPB, we predicted that attitude, subjective norm and perceived behavioural control would depend, respectively, on the underlying behavioural beliefs, normative beliefs and control beliefs that a person holds about a particular behaviour (H1a, H1b and H1c hypothesis). We assume that directors that are a member of the risk and control committee and directors that serve in financial companies could be considered directors with a stronger risk culture than others. The PLS analysis provides strong support for hypotheses H1a, H1b and H1c ($p < 0.001$), with standardized path coefficients of 0.011, 0.043 and 0.029, respectively. H2a, H2b and H2c posit a positive relationship between directors' level of risk culture (that is proxied by crc_membership) and their behavioural beliefs, normative beliefs and control beliefs regarding pro-environmental strategies. The directors' level of risk culture shows a significant positive association with normative, behavioural beliefs and control beliefs. The corollary of this finding is

---

[116] Forte 2004; Diamantopoulos et al. 2003; Post et al. 2011; De Villiers et al. 2011; Cosma et al. 2021a.
[117] Chin et al. 2003.

TABLE 7.3 *Descriptive statistics and correlation coefficients*

		Mean	St. dev.	1	2	3	4	5	6	7	8	9	10	11
1	Gender	0.60	0.49	1										
2	Age	0.55	0.50	0.28**	1									
3	sector	0.35	0.48	0.03	0.102	1								
4	Ned	0.62	0.49	0.41**	0.045	0.00	1							
5	Cr	0.33	0.47	−0.07	−0.071	−0.29**	0.12	1						
6	Bb	416	99.18	−0.02	−0.109	−0.04	0.06	0.00	1					
7	Nb	138	30.59	0.09	0.201*	−0.15	0.11	−0.07	0.55**	1				
8	Cb	185.6	48.03	−0.26**	−0.045	−0.02	−0.04	−0.02	0.68**	0.45**	1			
9	Att	5.11	0.73	−0.01	0.03	0.08	0.03	−0.00	0.39**	0.23*	0.39**	1		
10	Sn	6.22	0.84	0.19*	0.28**	−0.14	0.18	0.06	0.54**	0.75**	0.37**	0.32**	1	
11	Pbc	5.75	0.95	−0.17	−0.044	−0.22*	−0.10	0.00	0.45**	0.31**	0.62**	0.15	0.35**	1

Note: ** $p < 0.01$; * $p < 0.05$

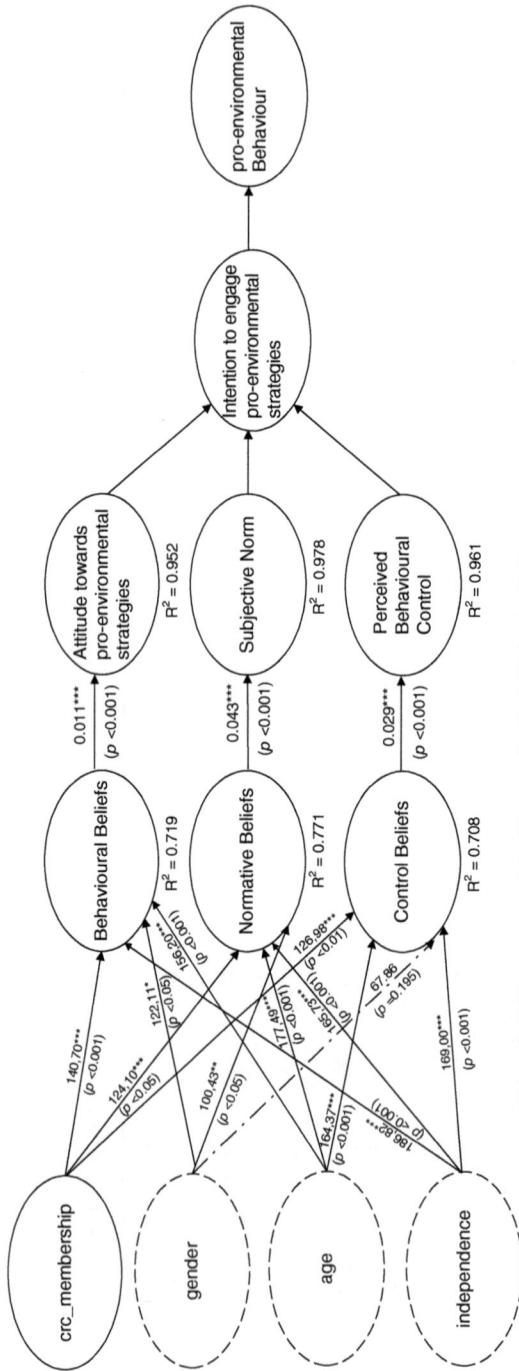

FIGURE 7.2 Proxies of risk culture: (a) risk and control committee membership as a proxy of risk culture; (b) financial sector served as a proxy of risk culture

Notes: Solid lines represent significant paths. *p<0.05 (one-tail); **p<0.01 (one-tail); ***p<0.001 (one-tail). Dashes circles are the control variables

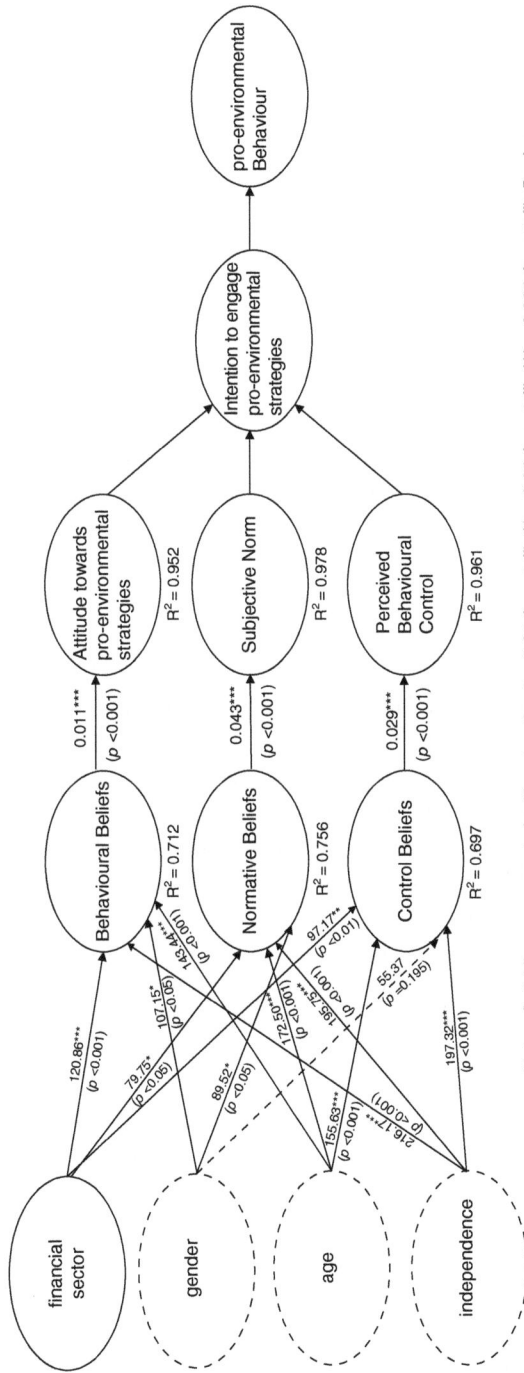

FIGURE 7.2 (cont.)

Notes: Solid lines represent significant paths. *p<0.05 (one-tail); **p<0.01 (one-tail); ***p<0.001 (one-tail). Dashes circles are the control variables

177

that directors' level of risk culture indirectly influences their intention to engage in pro-environmental strategies behaviour via normative beliefs and subjective norms.

Hypotheses H2a, H2b and H2c are also tested by using the sector on which board members serve (Figure 7.2b) as a proxy for a higher level of risk culture. We posit a positive relationship between "financial" directors (the second external variable) and their behavioural beliefs, normative beliefs and control beliefs regarding pro-environmental strategies. The analysis provides strong support for H2a, H2b and H2c ($p < 0.001$, $p < 0.05$ and $p < 0.01$, respectively). This finding indicates that a director that serves on the board of a financial company indirectly influences their intention to engage in pro-environmental strategies behaviour via behavioural, normative and control beliefs.

Finally, the study controlled for the effect of gender, age and independence (Figure 7.2a and 7.2b). The model estimates that all three control variables have a positive association with behavioural and normative beliefs. However, unlike the other two control variables, in both cases (crc_membership and financial sector) female gender did show a not significant association with control belief.

7.5 CONCLUSIONS AND IMPLICATIONS

In this chapter, we provided a better understanding of the various drivers of environmental sustainability at the board level. Following Ajzen and his theory of planned behaviour, we explored the relationship between risk culture and attitudes and beliefs, which could encourage the adoption of pro-environmental strategies by board members. We defined some main features of the attitudes and beliefs of a sustainability-oriented corporate and risk culture, separately considering a culture oriented towards "economic", "social" and "environmental" sustainability.

Following the ATPB, we showed that attitude, subjective norm and perceived behavioural control depend, respectively, on the underlying behavioural beliefs, normative beliefs and control beliefs that directors hold about pro-environmental strategies. We also found a positive relationship between directors' level of risk culture and behavioural, normative and control beliefs. Therefore, indirectly, we find that a greater risk culture positively affects the intention to engage in pro-environmental strategies.

So, a conclusion to be drawn, which confirms the existing literature and managerial argument that culture is the main driver of organizational and individual behaviours, is that corporate and risk culture must be shaped in order to incorporate values and beliefs linked to sustainability and that this sustainability-driven culture must be managed, widespread and developed over time throughout the organization. In this view, ESG culture also acts as an internal control mechanism, complementing existing tools, such as risk and performance measures. In this respect, it also affects compliance and conduct risk, driving transparent and sound relationships with stakeholders. Management style must be adapted to this new culture and has to foster, through leadership by example and consistent HR policies, a long-term view, an appropriate treating of errors and mistakes as sources of experience and potential innovation, continuous training, creativity and diversity.[118] Furthermore, a risk culture, which embeds appropriate sustainability risk and goals, can act as a driver for innovation in business and enhance the ability to explore new market opportunities.

As risk culture is an important object of attention for regulators and supervisors, along with the awareness that weaknesses in risk culture were at the base of the global financial crisis and misconduct of many financial institutions,[119] we expect banking and financial authorities to consider, as an element of value, the embeddedness of sustainability issues in their monitoring on banks' risk culture. This should allow to check for substantial compliance with sustainability policies, and avoid the risk that non-financial reports, as well as top management speeches, proclaim a stakeholder-oriented mission and governance model without following up in day-to-day practices and behaviours.

REFERENCES

Acquaye, A., Feng, K., Oppon, E. et al. (2017), 'Measuring the environmental sustainability performance of global supply chains: A multi-regional input-output analysis for carbon, sulphur oxide and water footprints', *Journal of Environmental Management*, 187, 571–585.

Agarwal, A., Poelchau, M. H., Kenkmann, T., Rae, A. and Ebert, M. (2019), 'Impact experiment on gneiss: The effects of foliation on cratering process', *Journal of Geophysical Research: Solid Earth*, 124(12), 13532–13546.

Agarwal, R. and Kallapur, S. (2018), 'Cognitive risk culture and advanced roles of actors in risk governance: A case study', *The Journal of Risk Finance*, 19(4), 327–324.

Ajzen, I. (1991), 'The theory of planned behavior', *Organizational Behavior and Human Decision Processes*, 50(2), 179–211.

Aragón-Correa, J. A. and Sharma, S. (2003), 'A contingent resource-based view of proactive corporate environmental strategy', *Academy of Management Review*, 28(1), 71–88.

Ardichvili, A., Mitchell, J. A. and Jondle, D. (2009), 'Characteristics of ethical business cultures', *Journal of Business Ethics*, 85(4), 445–451.

Armitage, C. J. and Conner, M. (2001), 'Efficacy of the theory of planned behaviour: A meta-analytic review', *British Journal of Social Psychology*, 40(4), 471–499.

Barney, J. (1991), 'Firm resources and sustained competitive advantage', *Journal of Management*, 17(1), 99–120.

Basel Committee on Banking Supervision (BCBS) (2015), 'Guidelines – Corporate governance principles for banks', July, available at: www.bis.org/bcbs/publ/d328.pdf.

Benn, S., Edwards, M. and Williams, T. (2014), *Organizational Change for Corporate Sustainability* (London: Routledge).

Bui, D. G., Fang, Y. and Lin, C. Y. (2018), 'The influence of risk culture on firm returns in times of crisis', *International Review of Economics & Finance*, 57, 291–306.

---

[118] Carretta et al. 2020.
[119] Carretta et al. 2017b.

Buysse, K. and Verbeke, A. (2003), 'Proactive environmental strategies: A stakeholder management perspective', *Strategic Management Journal*, 24(5), 453–470.

Cacioppe, R., Forster, N. and Fox, M. (2008), 'A survey of managers' perceptions of corporate ethics and social responsibility and actions that may affect companies' success', *Journal of Business Ethics*, 82(3), 681–700.

Carretta, A. and Schwizer, P. (2017a), 'Risk culture', in Carretta, A., Fiordelisi, F. and Schwizer, P. (eds.), *Risk Culture in Banking* (London: Palgrave Macmillan), 11–30.

Carretta, A. and Schwizer, P. (2017b), 'Risk culture in the regulation and supervision framework', in Carretta, A., Fiordelisi, F. and Schwizer, P. (eds.), *Risk Culture in Banking* (London: Palgrave Macmillan), 73–96.

Carretta, A., Schwizer, P. and Fattobene, L. (2020), 'Errors and failures in European banking: A cultural perspective', in Vanderheiden, E. and Mayer, C.-H. (eds.), *Mistakes, Errors and Failures across Cultures* (Berlin: Springer), 259–280.

Chan, R. Y., He, H., Chan, H. K. and Wang, W. Y. (2012), 'Environmental orientation and corporate performance: The mediation mechanism of green supply chain management and moderating effect of competitive intensity', *Industrial Marketing Management*, 41(4), 621–630.

Chao, Y. L. (2012), 'Predicting people's environmental behaviour: Theory of planned behaviour and model of responsible environmental behaviour', *Environmental Education Research*, 18(4), 437–461.

Chen, Y. S. (2011), 'Green organizational identity: Sources and consequence', *Management Decision*, 49(3), 384–404.

Chin, W. W. (1998), 'The partial least squares approach to structural equation modeling', *Modern Methods for Business Research*, 295(2), 295–336.

Chin, W. W. (2010), 'How to write up and report PLS analyses', in Esposito Vinzi, V., Chin, W. W., Henseler, J. and Wang, H. (eds.), *Handbook of Partial Least Squares* (Berlin, Heidelberg: Springer), 655–690.

Chin, W. W., Marcolin, B. L. and Newsted, P. R. (2003), 'A partial least squares latent variable modeling approach for measuring interaction effects: Results from a Monte Carlo simulation study and an electronic-mail emotion/adoption study', *Information Systems Research*, 14(2), 189–217.

Cicatiello, L., Ercolano, S., Gaeta, G. L. and Pinto, M. (2020), 'Willingness to pay for environmental protection and the importance of pollutant industries in the regional economy. Evidence from Italy', *Ecological Economics*, 177, 106774.

Cornia, A. (2015), 'In search of an Italian risk culture: Prevalent approaches towards disasters among experts, survivors and people at risk of natural and industrial hazards', *International Journal of Risk Assessment and Management*, 18(2), 125–139.

Cosma, S., Leopizzi, R., Nobile, L. and Schwizer, P. (2021a), 'Revising the Non-Financial Reporting Directive and the role of board of directors: A lost opportunity?', *Journal of Applied Accounting Research*, 23(1), 207–226.

Cosma, S., Schwizer, P., Nobile, L. and Leopizzi, R. (2021b), 'Environmental attitude in the board. Who are the "green directors"? Evidences from Italy', *Business Strategy and the Environment*, 30(7), 3360–3375.

Darnall, N., Henriques, I. and Sadorsky, P. (2010), 'Adopting proactive environmental strategy: The influence of stakeholders and firm size', *Journal of Management Studies*, 47(6), 1072–1094.

Davidson, D. J. and Freudenburg, W. R. (1996), 'Gender and environmental risk concerns: A review and analysis of available research', *Environment and Behavior*, 28(3), 302–339.

De Villiers, C., Naiker, V. and Van Staden, C. J. (2011), 'The effect of board characteristics on firm environmental performance', *Journal of Management*, 37(6), 1636–1663.

Delmas, M. and Toffel, M. W. (2004), 'Stakeholders and environmental management practices: An institutional framework', *Business Strategy and the Environment*, 13(4), 209–222.

Dermol, V. (2012), 'Relationship between mission statement and company performance', *Analele Ştiinţifice ale Universităţii 'Alexandru Ioan Cuza' din Iaşi. Ştiinţe economice*, 59(1), 325–341.

Dessler, G. (1999), 'How to earn your employees' commitment', *Academy of Management Perspectives*, 13(2), 58–67.

Diamantopoulos, A., Schlegelmilch, B. B., Sinkovics, R. R. and Bohlen, G. M. (2003), 'Can socio-demographics still play a role in profiling green consumers? A review of the evidence and an empirical investigation', *Journal of Business Research*, 56(6), 465–480.

Dibrell, C., Craig, J. B. and Hansen, E. N. (2011), 'How managerial attitudes toward the natural environment affect market orientation and innovation', *Journal of Business Research*, 64(4), 401–407.

Dickson, J. (2015), 'The Relevance of the Supervision of Behavior and Culture to the SSM', Amsterdam, NED, *Looking Forward: Effective Supervision of Behavior and Culture at Financial Institutions*, Conference in the Tropenmuseum, De Nederlandsche Bank, Amsterdam, September 24.

Diefenbach, M. A., Weinstein, N. D. and O'reilly, J. (1993), 'Scales for assessing perceptions of health hazard susceptibility', *Health Education Research*, 8(2), 181–192.

Dion, K. K. and Dion, K. L. (1996), 'Cultural perspectives on romantic love', *Personal Relationships*, 3(1), 5–17.

Domahidi, E., Festl, R. and Quandt, T. (2014), 'To dwell among gamers: Investigating the relationship between social online game use and gaming-related friendships', *Computers in Human Behavior*, 35, 107–115.

EBA (2021), *EBA Report on Management and Supervision of ESG Risks for Credit Institutions and Investment Firms*, Eba/Rep/2021/18, available at: https://bit.ly/3wwLzfF.

Eccles, R. G., Ioannou, I. and Serafeim, G. (2012), *The Impact of a Corporate Culture of Sustainability on Corporate Behavior and Performance*, Vol. 17950 (Cambridge, MA: National Bureau of Economic Research).

Eccles, R. G., Ioannou, I. and Serafeim, G. (2014), 'The impact of corporate sustainability on organizational processes and performance', *Management Science*, 60(11), 2835–2857.

Ehrhart, M. G., Schneider, B. and Macey, W. H. (2014), *Organizational Climate and Culture: An Introduction to Theory, Research, and Practice* (New York: Routledge).

European Commission (2020), *Study on Directors' Duties and Sustainable Corporate Governance: Final Report*, available at: https://data.europa.eu/doi/10.2838/472901.

Ferrón-Vílchez, V., Valero-Gil, J. and Suárez-Perales, I. (2021), 'How does greenwashing influence managers' decision-making? An experimental approach under stakeholder view', *Corporate Social Responsibility and Environmental Management*, 28(2), 860–880.

Finstad, K. (2010), 'Response interpolation and scale sensitivity: Evidence against 5-point scales', *Journal of Usability Studies*, 5(3), 104–110.

Fornell, C. and Larcker, D. F. (1981), 'Structural equation models with unobservable variables and measurement error: Algebra and statistics', *Journal of Marketing Research*, 18(3), 382–388.

Forte, A. (2004), 'Antecedents of managers moral reasoning', *Journal of Business Ethics*, 51(4), 315–347.

Freeman, R. E. (1994), 'The politics of stakeholder theory: Some future directions', *Business Ethics Quarterly*, 4(4), 409–421.

Freeman, J. B. and Ambady, N. (2010), 'MouseTracker: Software for studying real-time mental processing using a computer mouse-tracking method', *Behavior Research Methods*, 42(1), 226–241.

FSB (Financial Security Board) (2014), *Guidance on Supervisory Interaction with Financial Institutions on Risk Culture. A Framework for Assessing Risk Culture*, available at: www.fsb.org/wp-content/uploads/140407.pdf.

Galpin, T., Whitttington, J. L. and Bell, G. (2015), 'Is your sustainability strategy sustainable? Creating a culture of sustainability', *Corporate Governance*, 15(1), 1–17.

Garcés-Ayerbe, C., Scarpellini, S., Valero-Gil, J. and Rivera-Torres, P. (2016), 'Proactive environmental strategy development: From laggard to eco-innovative firms', *Journal of Organizational Change Management*, 29(7), 1118–1134.

Golden-Biddle, K. and Dutton, J. E. (eds.) (2012), *Using a Positive Lens to Explore Social Change and Organizations: Building a Theoretical and Research Foundation* (London: Routledge).

Goodpaster, K. E. (1983), 'The concept of corporate responsibility', *Journal of Business Ethics*, 2(1), 1–22.

Gorton, G. (2015), 'Stress for success: A review of Timothy Geithner's financial crisis memoir', *Journal of Economic Literature*, 53(4), 975–995.

Govindan, K., Soleimani, H. and Kannan, D. (2015), 'Reverse logistics and closed-loop supply chain: A comprehensive review to explore the future', *European Journal of Operational Research*, 240(3), 603–626.

Grossman, S. J. and Hart, O. D. (1986), 'The costs and benefits of ownership: A theory of vertical and lateral integration', *Journal of Political Economy*, 94(4), 691–719.

Guiso, L., Sapienza, P. and Zingales, L. (2015), 'The value of corporate culture', *Journal of Financial Economics*, 117(1), 60–76.

Hambrick, D. C. and Mason, P. A. (1984), 'Upper echelons: The organization as a reflection of its top managers', *Academy of Management Review*, 9(2), 193–206.

Hart, S. L. (1995), 'A natural-resource-based view of the firm', *Academy of Management Review*, 20(4), 986–1014.

Hart, S. L. and Ahuja, G. (1996), 'Does it pay to be green? An empirical examination of the relationship between emission reduction and firm performance', *Business Strategy and the Environment*, 5(1), 30–37.

Hart, S. L. and Milstein, M. B. (1999), 'Global sustainability and the creative destruction of industries', *MIT Sloan Management Review*, 41(1), 23.

Hasegawa, K. (2017), *Risk Culture, Risk Framing, and Nuclear Energy Dispute in Japan before and after the Fukushima Nuclear Accident* (London: Routledge), 9–27.

Henriques, I. and Sadorsky, P. (1999), 'The relationship between environmental commitment and managerial perceptions of stakeholder importance', *Academy of Management Journal*, 42(1), 87–99.

Hespenheide, E., Pavlovsky, K. and McElroy, M. (2010), 'Accounting for sustainability performance: Organizations that manage and measure sustainability effectively could see benefits to their brand and shareholder engagement and retention as well as to their financial bottom line', *Financial Executive*, 26(2), 52–57.

Huang, J. C., Newell, S. and Pan, S. L. (2001), 'The process of global knowledge integration: A case study of a multinational investment bank's Y2K program', *European Journal of Information Systems*, 10(3), 161–174.

Hulland, J. (1999), 'Use of partial least squares (PLS) in strategic management research: A review of four recent studies', *Strategic Management Journal*, 20(2), 195–204.

Hutzschenreuter, T. and Kleindienst, I. (2006), 'Strategy-process research: What have we learned and what is still to be explored', *Journal of Management*, 32(5), 673–720.

Islam, M. S., Tseng, M. L. and Karia, N. (2019), 'Assessment of corporate culture in sustainability performance using a hierarchical framework and interdependence relations', *Journal of Cleaner Production*, 217, 676–690.

Jabbour, C. J. C. and de Sousa Jabbour, A. B. L. (2016), 'Green human resource management and green supply chain management: Linking two emerging agendas', *Journal of Cleaner Production*, 112, 1824–1833.

Jacopin, T. and Fontrodona, J. (2009), 'Questioning the corporate responsibility (CR) department alignment with the business model of the company', *Corporate Governance: The International Journal of Business in Society*, 9(4).

Jaeschke, R., Singer, J. and Guyatt, G. H. (1990), 'A comparison of seven-point and visual analogue scales: Data from a randomized trial', *Controlled Clinical Trials*, 11(1), 43–51.

Keeble, B. R. (1987), 'The Brundtland Commission: Environment and development to the year 2000', *Medicine and War*, 3(4), 207–210.

Klassen, R. D. (2001), 'Plant-level environmental management orientation: The influence of management views and plant characteristics', *Production and Operations Management*, 10(3), 257–275.

Lee, W. S., Sun, K. A. and Moon, J. (2018), 'Application of upper echelon theory for corporate social responsibility dimensions: Evidence from the restaurant industry', *Journal of Quality Assurance in Hospitality & Tourism*, 19(3), 387–414.

Linnenluecke, M. K. and Griffiths, A. (2010), 'Corporate sustainability and organizational culture', *Journal of World Business*, 45(4), 357–366.

López-Torres Hidalgo, J. (2019), 'Effectiveness of physical exercise in the treatment of depression in older adults as an alternative to antidepressant drugs in primary care', *BMC Psychiatry*, 19(1), 1–7.

Lozano, R. and Huisingh, D. (2011), 'Inter-linking issues and dimensions in sustainability reporting', *Journal of Cleaner Production*, 19(2–3), 99–107.

Lozano, R., Lozano, F. J., Mulder, K., Huisingh, D. and Waas, T. (2013a), 'Advancing higher education for sustainable development: International insights and critical reflections', *Journal of Cleaner Production*, 48, 3–9.

Lozano, R., Lukman, R., Lozano, F. J., Huisingh, D. and Lambrechts, W. (2013b), 'Declarations for sustainability in higher education: Becoming better leaders, through addressing the university system', *Journal of Cleaner Production*, 48, 10–19.

Lozano, R. (2015), 'A holistic perspective on corporate sustainability drivers', *Corporate Social Responsibility and Environmental Management*, 22(1), 32–44.

Marshall, D., McCarthy, L., McGrath, P. and Claudy, M. (2015), 'Going above and beyond: How sustainability culture and entrepreneurial orientation drive social sustainability supply chain practice adoption', *Supply Chain Management: An International Journal*, 20(4), 434–454.

McWilliams, A. and Siegel, D. S. (2011), 'Creating and capturing value: Strategic corporate social responsibility, resource-based theory, and sustainable competitive advantage', *Journal of Management*, 37(5), 1480–1495.

Mechelli, A., Cimini, R. and Mazzocchetti, F. (2017), 'The usefulness of the business model disclosure for investors' judgements in financial entities. A European study' [Utilidad de la divulgación del modelo de negocio para los criterios de inversores en entidades financieras. Un estudio europeo], *Revista de Contabilidad – Spanish Accounting Review*, 20(1), 1–12.

Menguc, B. and Ozanne, L. K. (2005), 'Challenges of the "green imperative": A natural resource-based approach to the environmental orientation–business performance relationship', *Journal of Business research*, 58(4), 430–438.

Milfont, T. L. (2012), 'The interplay between knowledge, perceived efficacy, and concern about global warming and climate change: A one-year longitudinal study', *Risk Analysis: An International Journal*, 32(6), 1003–1020.

Murillo-Luna, J. L., Garcés-Ayerbe, C. and Rivera-Torres, P. (2011), 'Barriers to the adoption of proactive environmental strategies', *Journal of Cleaner Production*, 19(13), 1417–1425.

Nelson, R. R. (2004), 'Evolutionary theories of cultural change: An empirical perspective', Papers on Economics and Evolution 2004–22, Philipps University Marburg, Department of Geography.

Nunnally, J. C. and Bernstein, I. (1994). *Psychometric Theory*, 3rd ed. (New York: McGraw-Hill).

O'Reilly, C. A. and Chatman, J. A. (1996), 'Culture as social control: Corporations, cults, and commitment', in Staw, B. M. and Cummings, L. L. (eds.), *Research in Organizational Behavior: An Annual Series of Analytical Essays and Critical Reviews*, Vol. 18 (Greenwich, CT: JAI Press), 157–200.

O 'Reilly, C. A., & Chatman, J. A. (1996). Culture as social control: Corporations, cults, and commitment. In Staw, B. M. and Cummings, L. L. (eds.), *Research in Organizational Behavior: An Annual Series of Analytical Essays and Critical Reviews*, Vol. 18 (Elsevier Science/JAI Press), 157–200.

Pagell, M. and Gobeli, D. (2009), 'How plant managers' experiences and attitudes toward sustainability relate to operational performance', *Production and Operations Management*, 18(3), 278–299.

Pan, Y., Siegel, S. and Wang, T. Y. (2017), 'Corporate risk culture', *Journal of Financial and Quantitative Analysis*, 52(6), 2327–2367.

Porter, M. and Kramer, M. R. (2011), 'Creare valore condiviso', *Harvard Business Review Italia*, 1(2), 68–84.

Porter, M. and Linde, C. (2000), 'Green and competitive: Ending the stalemate', *The Dynamics of the Eco-Efficient Economy*, 33, 120–134.

Posner, R. A. (2010), *How Judges Think* (Cambridge, MA: Harvard University Press).

Post, C., Rahman, N. and Rubow, E. (2011), 'Green governance: Boards of directors' composition and environmental corporate social responsibility', *Business & Society*, 50(1), 189–223.

Rao, P. and Holt, D. (2005), 'Do green supply chains lead to competitiveness and economic performance?', *International Journal of Operations & Production Management*, 25(9), 898–916.

Reuter, C., Kaufhold, M. A., Schmid, S., Spielhofer, T. and Hahne, A. S. (2019), 'The impact of risk cultures: Citizens' perception of social media use in emergencies across Europe', *Technological Forecasting and Social Change*, 148(1), 1–17.

Reyes-Rodríguez, J. F., Ulhøi, J. P. and Madsen, H. (2016), 'Corporate environmental sustainability in Danish SMEs: A longitudinal study of motivators, initiatives, and strategic effects', *Corporate Social Responsibility and Environmental Management*, 23(4), 193–212.

Ring, P. J., Bryce, C., McKinney, R. and Webb, R. (2016), 'Taking notice of risk culture – The regulator's approach', *Journal of Risk Research*, 19(3), 364–387.

Roxas, B. and Coetzer, A. (2012), 'Institutional environment, managerial attitudes and environmental sustainability orientation of small firms', *Journal of Business Ethics*, 111(4), 461–476.

Rueda-Manzanares, A., Aragón-Correa, J. A. and Sharma, S. (2008), 'The influence of stake-holders on the environmental strategy of service firms: The moderating effects of complexity, uncertainty and munificence', *British Journal of management*, 19(2), 185–203.

Russo, M. V. and Fouts, P. A. (1997), 'A resource-based perspective on corporate environmental performance and profitability', *Academy of Management Journal*, 40(3), 534–559.

Sánchez-Medina, L., González-Badillo, J. J., Pérez, C. E. and Pallarés, J. G. (2014), 'Velocity-and power-load relationships of the bench pull vs. bench press exercises', *International Journal of Sports Medicine*, 35(03), 209–216.

Sarkis, J., Gonzalez-Torre, P. and Adenso-Diaz, B. (2010), 'Stakeholder pressure and the adoption of environmental practices: The mediating effect of training', *Journal of Operations Management*, 28(2), 163–176.

Schein, E. H. (1990), 'Organizational culture', *American Psychological Association*, 45(2), 109.

Schein, E. H. (2010), *Organizational Culture and Leadership*, Vol. 2 (San Francisco: Jossey-Bass John, Wiley & Sons).

Schneider, B., Brief, A. P. and Guzzo, R. A. (1996), 'Creating a climate and culture for sustainable organizational change', *Organizational Dynamics*, 24(4), 7–19.

Schrøder, P. W. (2006), 'Impediments to effective risk management', in Andersen T. J. (ed.), *Perspectives on Strategic Risk Management* (Copenhagen: Copenhagen Business School), 65–87.

Seroka-Stolka, O. and Fijorek, K. (2020), 'Enhancing corporate sustainable development: Proactive environmental strategy, stakeholder pressure and the moderating effect of firm size', *Business Strategy and the Environment*, 29(6), 2338–2354.

Sharma, S. and Vredenburg, H. (1998), 'Proactive corporate environmental strategy and the development of competitively valuable organizational capabilities', *Strategic Management Journal*, 19(8), 729–753.

Sheedy, E. and Griffin, B. (2018), 'Risk governance, structures, culture, and behavior: A view from the inside', *Corporate Governance: An International Review*, 26(1), 4–22.

Shein, N. L., Chuda, H., Arakawa, T., Mizuno, K. and Soyano, K. (2004), 'Ovarian development and final oocyte maturation in cultured sevenband grouper Epinephelus septemfasciatus', *Fisheries Science*, 70(3), 360–365.

Smith, S. K., Trevena, L., Simpson, J. M. et al. (2010), 'A decision aid to support informed choices about bowel cancer screening among adults with low education: Randomised controlled trial', *BMJ*, 341.

Sniehotta, F. F., Presseau, J. and Araújo-Soares, V. (2014), 'Time to retire the theory of planned behaviour', *Health Psychology Review*, 8(1), 1–7.

Sugita, M. and Takahashi, T. (2015), 'Influence of corporate culture on environmental management performance: An empirical study of Japanese firms', *Corporate Social Responsibility and Environmental Management*, 22(3), 182–192.

Thoradeniya, P., Lee, J., Tan, R. and Ferreira, A. (2015), 'Sustainability reporting and the theory of planned behaviour', *Accounting, Auditing & Accountability Journal*, 28(7), 1099–1137.

Tseng, S. M. (2017), 'Investigating the moderating effects of organizational culture and leadership style on IT-adoption and knowledge-sharing intention', *Journal of Enterprise Information Management* 30(4): 583–604.

Uzzell, D. L. (2000), 'The psycho-spatial dimension of global environmental problems', *Journal of Environmental Psychology*, 20(4), 307–318.

Van den Steen, E. (2010), 'On the origin of shared beliefs (and corporate culture)', *The RAND Journal of Economics*, 41(4), 617–648.

Walsh, J. P., Weber, K. and Margolis, J. D. (2003), 'Social issues and management: Our lost cause found', *Journal of Management*, 29(6), 859–881.

Wilkins, A. L. and Ouchi, W. G. (1983), 'Efficient cultures: Exploring the relationship between culture and organizational performance', *Administrative Science Quarterly*, 28(3), 468–481.

Wilkinson, A., Hill, M. and Gollan, P. (2001), 'The sustainability debate', *International Journal of Operations & Production Management*, 21(12), 1492–1502.

Zelezny, L. C., Chua, P. P. and Aldrich, C. (2000), 'Elaborating on gender differences in environmentalism', *Journal of Social Issues*, 56(3), 443–458.

Zhang, F. and Zhu, L. (2019), 'Enhancing corporate sustainable development: Stakeholder pressures, organizational learning, and green innovation', *Business Strategy and the Environment*, 28(6), 1012–1026.

8

Conduct Risk as a Possible Approach for Enhancing Awareness and Management of ESG-Related Risks

Antonella Sciarrone Alibrandi, Claudio Frigeni and Giulia Schneider[*]

8.1 THE RELEVANCE OF THE CATEGORY OF CONDUCT RISK IN THE CONTEMPORARY FINANCIAL SECTOR

Attention, rooted in the aftermath of the financial crises, on financial firms' misconducts has lately been consolidating at the regulatory[1] and policy level[2]. The growing importance given to the category of conduct risk by regulators and supervisory authorities[3] reflects the acknowledgment that severe patterns of misconduct have an impact that goes well beyond the (itself not negligible) violation of consumers' interests, and ultimately touches upon the more systemic chords of market integrity and financial stability[4], from both a micro- and a macro-prudential perspective[5].

Misconducts undermine the firm-client relationship, harm financial institutions' reputation and affect consumers' trust and confidence. This leads, in turn, to financial losses resulting from missed opportunities to sell products, litigation and regulatory sanctions that impose either direct payment obligations or behavioural commitments onto financial firms[6].

From here, the path to the production of systemic impacts on the stability and well-functioning of markets is relatively short. Misconduct of one firm may trigger a "downsize effect" on other market players, potentially undermining trust in a whole sector. This "downsize effect" can also easily turn into a "withdraw effect", caused by competitors' disincentive to engage in the sector, with related anticompetitive market distortions[7].

---

[*] Although this chapter is the result of joint work, Sections 8.4–8.6 should be attributed to Giulia Schneider.
[1] See lately EBA 2022a, para. 276; 291; 293–297 and EBA-ESMA 2022, para. 11; 51; 253; 255–256. Also in the insurance sector, conduct risk has been given recent consideration in EIOPA 2019a.
[2] See G20 2022; FSB 2018 and ESRB 2015.
[3] In particular, FCA 2020. See also EBA 2022a, para. 293–297.
[4] Moloney 2018, 251.
[5] Stressing the prudential relevance of conduct risk, Cherednychenko 2021, 159.
[6] For an analysis of the implications of conduct risk, see Sciarrone Alibrandi and Frigeni 2019, 468.
[7] ESRB 2015, 5.

As far as the drivers of conduct risk are concerned, these have been traditionally identified in the market failures arising from information gaps between financial firms and their clients; the biases grounding consumers' irrational behaviour with respect to their market choices; and ultimately the conflicts of interests characterizing the relations with clients[8].

More recently, further sources of misconduct have been spotted. Technological development and the novel complexity of the digital infrastructures appear to open new chances of misconduct, with respect to, for example, the adequate choice and governance of implemented technologies – such as the eventually missed enactment of interoperability techniques causing the overall malfunctioning of employed systems[9] – or the difficulties in retaining control over transactions occurring through automated means[10]. Also, the pandemic has contributed to the origination of additional determinants of misconduct, given by new smart working arrangements and the increase of employees' emotional distresses[11].

The cited drivers point towards a deeper feature of conduct risk, namely its strict relation to poor firm culture, occurring in the case of a solely short-term profit-oriented business model[12], lacking specific principles or values centred on the benefits of consumers and of the market as a whole[13]. Poor firm culture can be thus considered as being the overarching driver of conduct risk[14].

A first direct response to the increasingly pressing concerns regarding the tackling and promotion of financial businesses' good conduct is given by the development of a body of norms known as conduct of business (COB) rules[15], directly rooted in businesses' fiduciary duties. In Europe, a direct example of this specific type of regulation is given by some provisions of the MiFID II Directive, generally requiring financial intermediaries to "act honestly, fairly, and professionally in accordance with the best interests of (their) clients"[16]. The best interest duty serves as a fundamental guiding benchmark in the implementation of

---

[8] Sciarrone Alibrandi and Frigeni 2019, 472.
[9] Stressing the importance of the interoperability of IT systems Joint ESAs 2022, para. 53.
[10] For a deeper reflection see De Pascalis 2019, 947.
[11] FCA 2020, 3.
[12] See G30 2018.
[13] FSB 2014.
[14] This is well expressed by 5 Conduct Questions of the FCA, which have the declared aim of supporting the ongoing effort of wholesale banks to improve conduct risk management and, with that, conduct risk culture. In light of this goal, the report stresses that although a significant improvement in awareness and engagement with conduct risk has been made by the larger wholesale banks, what is still largely missing is a deeper understanding of conduct risk and the development of tools relevant to the identification and monitoring of conduct risk. Among the main determinants of effective conduct risk management, the FCA identifies (i) remuneration and performance assessments; (ii) culture and leadership; and (iii) clarity on the firms' purpose and values. FCA 2020, 27. Also G30 2018 and Federal Reserve Bank of New York 2017.
[15] Cherednychenko 2021, 153.
[16] Directive 2014/65/EU, art. 24

other more specific provisions regarding the structuring and issuing of financial instruments[17].

Overall, the conduct of business rules appear to broadly consider the case of misconduct from the twofold perspective[18] of the conduct of financial institutions entering into transactions with or on behalf of their clients (so-called retail conduct risk), and of the conduct of financial institutions acting as the principal or the counterparty in capital market transactions (so-called wholesale conduct risk[19]). If the first standpoint majorly addresses consumer protection concerns, the second one clearly addresses market integrity stances. In both cases, however, the overarching objective of this category of rules lies primarily outside the financial institution and may be considered as that of reducing the risk of poor conduct vis-à-vis either end clients or the broader market dynamics.

More recently, the objective of mitigating misconduct in the financial sector has been given growing consideration within the prudential sphere, where a trend of introducing conduct risk into existing risk management frameworks has emerged. In accordance with this newly unfolding conception, conduct risk shall be considered an autonomous category within the risk management framework[20].

Against the backdrop of the illustrated developments, nonetheless, great uncertainties still persist regarding what conduct risk exactly is, and what type of risk it encompasses or relates to. Existing policy statements focusing on conduct risk are, for example, not consistent in clarifying the actual link between conduct risk and other types of risks, such as operational risk, legal risk or strategic and reputational risk. The question thus arises whether conduct risk is to be considered as an autonomous category or whether it is rather to be considered as a subset of already existing categories[21].

Far from being of merely theoretical significance, this preliminary inquiry is functional to the identification of the functions the category of conduct risk may have with respect to the wider risk management framework: the development of governance strategies regarding conduct risk, without having first ascertained what this notion refers to, may give rise to mere window-dressing efforts[22].

From a further perspective, only a clear understanding of conduct risk(s) offers a secure starting point for assessing the viability and the effectiveness of the considered

---

[17] See, for example, the rules related to suitability or appropriateness assessments under art. 24(2)(3), conflict of interest under art. 23 and recital 56, inducements under art. 24(8)(9), remuneration practices under art. 24(10) and best execution under art. 27, Directive 2014/65/EU. For the literature, see Siri and Zhu 2019, 9–16.

[18] This twofold perspective from which conduct risk has to be assessed is well stressed in the literature: Tuch 2015, 537; MacNeil 2015.

[19] The distinction between retail conduct risk and wholesale conduct risk can be found in FCA 2013.

[20] EBA 2022a, para. 293–297 and EBA-ESMA 2022, para. 253; 255–256. Similarly, in the insurance sector, see EIOPA 2022, 7–8, where specific reference is made to the supervisory activities exercised in respect to conduct risk as an autonomous risk category.

[21] De Pascalis 2019, 947.

[22] FSB 2018. See also G20 2022, 5.

category in the evolving state of EU financial regulation, and in particular with respect to evolving risk management policies, under the sustainable finance package of measures.

Against this backdrop, this study enquires about the role of conduct risk with respect to the currently evolving ESG-related regulation wave[23]. More precisely, it questions the relevance of conduct risk as an additional determinant of banks' effective intermediation in the ESG value chain, in addition to normatively set non-financial reporting, governance and due diligence duties.

The suitability of a conduct risk-based approach to the identification and management of ESG risks is first of all grounded in the conceptualization of ESG regulations as (sustainable) conduct of business rules centred on the management of ESG risk. This systemic reading of ESG-related rules explains and at the same time supports the main assumption underlying this study, namely that, while setting norms of conduct for the management of sustainability risks, the emerging framework engenders new risks of unsustainable conduct.

As will be demonstrated, these risks of unsustainability are further sharpened, from a regulatory perspective, by the fact that the sustainable finance framework is still under construction and raises complex interpretative questions. At a deeper level, however, and beyond the regulatory superstructure, unsustainability risks are further driven by the absence of effective ESG-related risk culture, affecting financial institutions' sound adherence to the emerging sustainable finance framework.

In light of the new misconduct scenarios entailed in the European financial reform project, the analysis argues that the flexible and cultural-sensitive nature of conduct risk makes it an effective tool for the forecast, correction and even prevention of potentially harmful misconducts directly stemming from either the missed or wrongful enactment of ESG policies. Ultimately, the employment of conduct risk in the field of ESG is useful to re-conceptualise the bank's internal risk management of inappropriate behaviour, also from a prudential perspective.

8.2 THE DEFINITION OF "CONDUCT RISK" AND ITS FUNCTION: BRIDGING CONDUCT RISK AND ESG RISKS

The definition of the outright borders of conduct risk is not an easy task. At the policy level, two major conceptions of conduct risk can be identified[24]. A first market- and third-party-oriented conception is promoted by the UK FCA[25], whose understanding of conduct risk is based on a flexible and dynamic approach encompassing very different conduct risk profiles. Following this interpretation, the essence of conduct risk is to be found in the causal effect stemming from a firm's poor conduct

[23] The link between conduct risk and ESG risks has been recently highlighted by EBA 2022b.
[24] De Pascalis 2019, 947.
[25] The FCA has been the first agency to refer to conduct risk, see FCA 2013.

and resulting in poor outcomes for customers. Ultimately, the FCA refrains from providing an all-encompassing definition of conduct risk and advances the opportunity for a firm-specific understanding

A broad and flexible notion of conduct risk is also upheld at the international level: here, the Financial Stability Board has defined misconduct as "conduct that falls short of expected standards, including legal, professional and ethical standards"[26]. The same FSB acknowledges that this definition potentially captures under the umbrella of misconduct many different conducts. From this perspective, thus, conduct risk may relate differently to legal, strategic or reputational risks, grounded in the generation of market-relevant harm, that is a, harm of either legal or merely economic nature to third parties, acting outside the firms' sphere.

Along these lines, according to a strand of the literature, conduct risk should be distinguished from legal risk and be referred to the harmful consequences of the violation of extra-legal parameters regarding a firm's ethical and strategical precepts of good governance[27].

The focus on the internal impacts of financial institutions' misconduct, especially with respect to capital requirements, is conversely promoted at the European level. Here, conduct risk is considered as a subset of operational risk by both the European Systemic Risk Board[28] and the European Banking Authority[29]. In the 2022 Guidelines on common procedures and methodologies for the supervisory review and evaluation process SREP and supervisory stress testing, the EBA requires national authorities to consider conduct risk for the purposes of the evaluation of capital requirements. Conduct risk is also included among the risks measured in the context of stress tests[30].

In accordance with this conception, conduct risk – as resulting from poorly designed distribution channels, conflicts of interest in the conduct of business, product mis-selling, in both retail and wholesale markets, and unfair processing of customer complaints – amounts to additional costly capital requirements for banks[31]. Indicators for the identification of conduct risk and thus for the assessment of related capital requirements are primarily given by the number and degree of sanctions issued by relevant authorities or complaints addressed to the banks and their "peers"

---

[26] FSB 2017.
[27] English et al. 2018.
[28] ESRB 2015, 4.
[29] EBA 2022a, para. 276.
[30] EBA 2022a, para. 293–297, clarifies the relevance of conduct risks in the wider risk management framework. Specifically related to conduct risk in investment firms, see EBA-ESMA 2022, para. 255–256.
[31] The new EBA SREP guidelines for banks and investment firms introduce also new elements, as the "manipulation of benchmark interest rates, foreign exchange rates or any other financial instruments or indices to enhance the institution's profits"; "barriers to switching financial products during their lifetime and/or to switching financial service providers"; and "automatic renewals of products or exit penalties"; EBA 2022a, para. 293. For investment firms, EBA-ESMA 2022, para. 256, which refers, amongst others, also to "closure or suspension of a fund".

for misconduct practices[32]. The requirement to shield prospective losses arising from misconduct with capital charges should incentivize firms to behave fairly, especially with respect to customers, so as to minimize the needed capital coverage.

Overall, the European prudential-based formulation of conduct risk has both a micro- and a macro-prudential bearing: from a micro-prudential perspective, the measurement of conduct risk becomes a new benchmark of the capital coverage and thus of the stability benchmark of a single entity; on the macro-prudential side, misconduct undermines trust in the financial system as such, and the ensuing widespread imposition of sanctions for misconduct, in turn, impacts on the capitalization of the whole system.

Following this approach, national authorities, such as the Bank of Italy, have also adopted the definition of conduct risk as an operational risk[33].

Although providing a more circumscribed definition of the considered risk and a more effective way to measure it in relation to capital requirements, this second option of identifying conduct risk with operational risk also comes along with significant practical flaws. The same notion of operational risk is surrounded by significant uncertainties: the Basel Committee on Banking Supervision defines it as the "risk of loss resulting from inadequate or failed internal processes, people and systems or from external events"[34]. According to the Basel Committee, operational risk relates to legal risk but not to strategic and reputational risk[35]. Conversely, the CRD-IV package under Reg. EU 575/2013 does not expressly exclude strategic and reputational risks from the scope of operational risk but expressly refers to legal risks, with that leaving open significant interpretative uncertainties[36]. Completing the spectrum of definitions of operational risk, a minor strand of the scholarship stresses the importance of linking operational risk to the spheres of strategic and operational risk. These perspectives are deemed useful for capturing the systemic implications of operational risk.

In the maze of these definitional varieties, it can be noted that both the recalled interpretations of conduct risk – the one promoted by the UK FCA and the one defined at European level – suggest the primary function of conduct risk as a tool for the anticipation and early mitigation, if not outright prevention, of firms' misconducts that ultimately harm the primary goals of financial regulation, namely investor protection, market integrity and financial stability. From this general standpoint, conduct risk is meant to supplement the efficacy of the evolving hard law framework through a value and interest-oriented approach[37]. This approach

---

[32] EBA 2022a, para. 296 lett. b.

[33] Circular 285 of 17 December 2013 of the Bank of Italy (41st revision of 20 December 2022).

[34] BCBS 2001.

[35] BCBS 2006.

[36] Art. 4(52), Regulation 575/2013/EU. Studies on operational risk bring to our attention the complexity of this risk and the fact that, on its own, it encompasses a wide variety of other types of risks in addition to legal risk: liquidity risk. See Moosa 2006, 97 and Moosa 2008, 83.

[37] This is directly expressed at EBA 2022a, para. 297.

relies on heightening the standards of awareness of risk-taking through the joint fostering of a robust culture of voluntary compliance with the law and of enacted risk culture.

Risk culture serves the primary function of filling normative gaps through the values that stem the unfolding of misconduct in those behavioural (misconduct) spaces that are not strictly covered by regulatory dictates and that occur in between legal rules and principles. Framed in these terms, conduct risk cannot be detected and cured through the application of legal precepts, but rather with cultural and behavioural education[38].

Hence, the attention given over the last years to conduct risk is a direct consequence of a failed risk culture within institutional entities: conduct risk should orient subjects' behaviours in those areas where the law – either hard or soft law – does not provide clear indications. Moreover, the widespread recourse to standards instead of rules[39] in the law-making practice instigates an open-ended array of potentially lawful – or unlawful – conducts[40]: indeed, a standard does not *ex ante* define expected conduct, and the area of acceptable conduct required from a financial intermediary is to be defined through the value- and social-oriented substantiation of general clauses, ultimately given by the same entity's general cultural orientations, also beyond mere risk culture.

The category of conduct risk is expected to intervene in the behavioural spaces left open by a standard-centred legal system, and thus to detect the discrepancy between the expected and actual risk culture so as to safeguard long-term financial stability and to restore trust in the financial system[41].

Hence, this general predictive and corrective function of conduct risk renders it particularly suited to prevent strategic and reputational risks as well.

The relevance of the cultural determinant of conduct risk[42] raises the question regarding the possible significance of the considered category with respect to the prevention or mitigation of ESG risks, now at the forefront of the European regulatory agenda.

The sustainability wave that is hitting European financial markets is expressly driven by the need for cultural renewal with respect to financial matters. This is

---

[38] This because conduct risk helps in detecting misconducts which may be subsequently qualified as unfair by regulators.

[39] For a conceptualization of the rules/standards debate see Kaplov 1992, 557.

[40] The link between financial regulation and conduct risk is well stressed by Cherednychenko 2021, 151.

[41] Omarova 2018, 805. Stressing the importance of risk culture in respect of sustainability objectives, see also Chapters 6 and 7 in this volume.

[42] In its 2018 survey, Thomson Reuters investigated how firms around the world (including G-SIFIs) are managing the challenges presented by the regulatory focus on culture and conduct risk. Firms were asked, *inter alia*, whether they recognized any correlation between culture and conduct risk, resulting in 44 per cent of them not only considering culture and conduct risk to be intrinsically linked, but also regarding culture as a predominant aspect in managing conduct risk. See English et al. 2018. Reflecting on this see also Manes 2019, 985. See also the remarks by Angelini 2021.

well reflected in the policy statements enshrined in the Sustainable Finance Action Plan[43]. The new approach to financial affairs underlying the sustainable finance reform project is at the roots of the relevance given to ESG risks by ongoing regulatory reforms in the field.

As will be shown in the following paragraphs, while targeting the minimization of ESG risks, the emerging ESG-related framework opens many – some still rather unexplored – risks of unsustainability related to the behavioural and cultural factors co-determining, in addition to the newly introduced normative requirements, the implementation of the sustainable finance project.

Presently enacted ESG regulations do indeed set reporting, organizational and governance objectives, which assume a cultural adherence to sustainability goals by financial entities. However, by setting rules of sustainable conduct upon the players acting within the financial market, the current sustainable finance framework does not, at present, tackle the ineffective or merely formal application of ESG-related commands, directly given by the lack of incorporation of ESG-related risk culture into financial entities' conducts.

Due to its functional relation to risk culture, the category of conduct risk may be relevant for filling some of the unsustainability loops undermining the construction of a sustainable European financial market.

8.3 ESG REGULATIONS AS RULES OF SUSTAINABLE CONDUCT

Rooted in the more general objectives of the European Green Deal[44], the 2018 Action Plan on Financing Sustainable Growth[45] has set the political foundations of the transition to sustainable European financial markets. This shift has been consolidating with the more recent (and operative) Strategy for Financing the Transition to a Sustainable Economy[46].

The declared policy objectives have so far been substantiated at European normative level along the two major regulatory trajectories of non-financial disclosure and of the sustainable governance of financial entities.

On the disclosure side, the Regulation on sustainability-related disclosures in the financial services sector[47], which entered into force on 10 March 2021, has imposed specific obligations on financial market participants to communicate their sustainability-related policies to the market. The first parameters around which financial entities' disclosure strategies are structured are provided by the Taxonomy Regulation[48], which is centred upon environmental factors and needs

---

[43] European Commission COM/2018/097 final.
[44] European Commission COM//640 final.
[45] European Commission COM/2018/097 final.
[46] European Commission COM/2021/390 final.
[47] Regulation 2019/2088/EU.
[48] Regulation (EU) 2020/852.

to be integrated by delegated acts of the European Commission[49]. The directive regarding corporate sustainability reporting[50] enriches the set of disclosure obligations of "large" financial institutions, amending existing non-financial disclosure requirements through the introduction of more detailed reporting standards, the need to audit reported information and certification and digital logging requirements regarding rendered information[51].

On the governance side, the set reporting requirements are strictly related to new organizational and governance requirements specifically related to the management of ESG risks. In this respect, the SFRD, by requiring the disclosure of the adoption of remuneration policies that are consistent with the integration of sustainability risks, implicitly hints at remuneration policies as a first governance tool relevant to the management of sustainability risks[52]. The delegated acts issued by the European Commission in August 2021 establish additional governance requirements for the management of sustainability risks, in terms of the institution of adequate internal controls for the monitoring of ESG risks[53]; of conflicts of interest-related policies[54], product governance policies[55] and suitability assessments[56]. These are sensitive to the integration of sustainability risks into financial institutions' processes.

---

[49] To date, the Delegated acts are the Complementary Climate Delegated Act (Commission Delegated Regulation 2022/1214/EU); the Disclosures Delegated Act (Commission Delegated Regulation 2021/2178/EU); the Climate Delegated Act (Commission Delegated Regulation 2021/2139/EU).

[50] Directive 2022/2464/EU.

[51] For a critical assessment, see Bodellini and Singh 2021, 163.

[52] Art. 5, Regulation /2088/EU.

[53] "It is necessary to clarify that processes, systems and internal controls of AIFMs reflect sustainability risks, and that technical capacity and knowledge are necessary to analyze those risks." So recital 3, Commission delegated regulation 2021/1255/EU regarding the sustainability risks and sustainability factors to be taken into account by Alternative Investment Fund Managers. Similarly, recital 3, Commission delegated directive 2021/1270/EU regarding the sustainability risks and sustainability factors to be taken into account for Undertakings for Collective Investment in Transferable Securities (UCITS); recital 3, Commission delegated regulation 2021/1253/EU regarding the integration of sustainability factors, risks and preferences into certain organizational requirements and operating conditions for investment firms.

[54] See Commission delegated regulation 2021/1253/EU, at recital 4 where it is stated that investment firms should, when identifying the types of conflicts of interest the existence of which may damage the interests of a client or potential client, including those types of conflicts of interest that stem from the integration of the client's sustainability preferences. See also recital 5 of Commission delegated regulation 2021/1255/EU.

[55] Commission delegated directive 2021/1269/EU regarding the integration of sustainability factors into the product governance obligations.

[56] Commission delegated regulation 2021/1253/EU, at recital 5 affirming that "investment firms that provide investment advice and portfolio management should be able to recommend suitable financial instruments to their clients and potential clients and should therefore be able to ask questions to identify a client's individual sustainability preferences. In accordance with an investment firm's obligation to act in the best interest of its clients, recommendations to clients and potential clients should reflect both the financial objectives and any sustainability preferences expressed by those clients. It is, therefore, necessary to clarify that investment firms should have in place appropriate arrangements to ensure that the inclusion of sustainability factors in the advisory process and portfolio management

Ultimately, the Directive on corporate sustainability due diligence[57] requires companies, including financial entities[58], to identify and mitigate adverse impacts on human rights and the environment[59].

Against the backdrop of the recalled evolutions, it seems the proactive protection of ESG factors is emerging as a regulatory objective reshaping financial institutions' reporting, organizational and governance arrangements[60].

All these three areas of regulatory intervention – and in particular the governance layer, which structures governance first, and then resulting reporting patterns – rely on behavioural commitments for sound management of ESG risks.

Hence, the ultimate corollary of ongoing reforms is that ESG risks become a new benchmark in financial entities' decision-making processes: sustainability risks now have to be integrated in investment decisions as well as in investment or insurance advice[61], in product governance policies and more generally into due diligence processes[62]. The introduction of this new decision-making criterion not only informs the new procedures and organizational settings that are being specified at both regulatory and self-regulatory levels but will orient the very core function of financial business strategy-making that is entrusted to the board, and, in turn, the downstream conduct of established lines of defence.

As a result, sustainability and long-term objectives grounding the emerging body of laws in the field of sustainable finance embody a new foundational norm of conduct for financial entities. Framed in these terms, ESG-related regulations can be considered as a "next generation" of business-of-conduct rules, which amplify the range of interests to be considered by corporate action, including – but also transcending – customers' interests.

Well beyond mere stances of ecological transition, the emerging rules of sustainable finance bear in our reading a greater systemic relevance: that of being a direct concretization of the fairness standard at the core of the notion of conduct risk in the spheres of financial entities' environmental, social and governance choices. In this vein, the integration of ESG risks within the general financial normative framework and thus in the financial decision-making chain can be regarded as the latest expression of the effort to reframe the ethical and conduct-based layers of financial decision-making processes.

---

does not lead to misselling practices or to the misrepresentation of financial instruments or strategies as fulfilling sustainability preferences where they do not".

[57] Directive 2024/1760/EU.

[58] The Directive nonetheless establishes some exceptions and derogations specifically regarding the financial sector. See, amongst others, the definition of the 'chain of activities' for financial undertakings illustrated under recital 26 Directive 2024/1760/EU.

[59] See arts. 8 to 11 Directive 2024/1760/EU.

[60] See Colaert 2022, 1669.

[61] Art. 6(2) lett a., Regulation 2019/2088/EU.

[62] Recital 20, Regulation 2019/2088/EU.

8.4 "UNSUSTAINABILITY" AS AN IMPORTANT NEW DRIVER OF CONDUCT RISK

The regulatory and cultural drivers of good financial conduct are currently being moulded by the emerging European paradigm of sustainable finance.

In light of the suggested conceptualization of ESG regulations as rules for sustainable financial conduct, ESG regulations appear indeed to lay the grounds for a composite conduct matrix for financial entities, which is only partly structured by the strict regulatory layer and is largely shaped by the cultural driver of the ongoing transition.

On the one hand, indeed, as the conduct of business rules, the newly proposed norms introduce into the financial marketplace behavioural incentives to heighten ESG standards in order to exploit the new opportunities given by "green" financing channels. From this standpoint, thus, the emerging framework of sustainable finance ultimately aims at nudging companies towards sustainable business behaviour and thus to respect higher environmental, social and governance standards[63].

However, this nudging effect from sustainable finance norms to sustainable finance incentives is at present undermined by the flaws currently characterizing ESG-related regulations. These flaws are majorly given by the structural incompleteness of a framework that is still under construction within the sustainable finance policy site[64]: many announced measures, such as the ones regarding ESG benchmarks are still awaited; and many of the enacted regulations, such as the Taxonomy Regulation and the SFRD, defer the organizational and governance underpinnings to various delegated acts.

Moreover, the vagueness of many provisions[65] raises new interpretative challenges, in particular related to the ultimate duties of financial entities' directors with respect to the positive protection of ESG factors as well as the applicability of the business judgment rule to the definition of relevant ESG-related strategies. Overall, the incompleteness and complexity of the present framework undermine the homogeneity and certainty of enacted regulatory requirements.

Against this backdrop, it appears that the same regulatory framework, as currently shaped, offers new significant gaps facilitating financial entities' choice to remain inactive or turn to abuses in the management of ESG risks.

Shifting from the regulatory to the cultural dimension, sustainable business conduct targeted by ESG regulations is, in accordance with the traced conduct matrix, not only driven by regulatory compliance but needs to leverage deeper cultural endeavours. Indeed, the sustainable finance framework is only capable of activating

---

[63] Colaert 2022, 1674.

[64] See also the recent observations by Enriques 2021, 319.

[65] This was the main critique advanced against the first draft of the corporate sustainability due diligence directive published by the European Parliament in its resolution in March 2021. See Davies et al. 2021.

a virtuous cycle of sustainable conduct incentives if the adherence to set norms is supported by a consistent cultural background. This means that only a cultural and behavioural change in the governance of sustainability factors may lead to a full accomplishment of the normative dictates. In turn, only if supported by culturally sound organization and governance arrangements can ESG regulations be considered an effective tool for addressing financial entities' good conduct specifically related to sustainability.

Conversely, a formal (or better said, empty) obedience to set normative standards does not trigger the envisaged market changes and thus appears to ultimately run contrary to the very objectives underlying the integration of sustainable business of conduct rules into the broader financial rulebook.

Under these premises, the growing normative weight given to ESG risks in the shaping of financial institutions' reporting, organizational and governance settings requires a deeper reflection regarding how these risks are to be identified and measured.

From a first perspective, indeed, the traced regulatory evolutions suggest a consolidating trend towards the inclusion of ESG risks within the area of legal risks, intended as a risk of violating a (legal) "rule".

However, the still-uncertain contours – despite the recent efforts made by the European legislator – of the legal tools, namely non-financial disclosure and sustainable governance arrangements, established for the control of ESG-related risks, render the mere compliance perspective incapable of tackling the complexity of sustainability risks. As the EIOPA has stressed, these risks also entail a significant strategic as well as a reputational determinant[66]. This means that the management of sustainability risks is widely shaped by the behavioural and cultural orientations underlying financial firms' organizational and governance options[67].

Framed in these terms, it appears that the scope of sustainability risk is amplified by the risks of unsustainable conduct in the management of the rule-based constructed ESG risks.

Given both the regulatory and cultural formants of sustainable conduct detected above, the risks of unsustainability may be related by the missed implementation of ESG-related legal obligations – as the missed enactment of reporting obligations or the missed institution of internal controls and governance checkpoints – or by wrong or ineffective implementation of these same legal requirements. This second type of sustainability misconduct may be the result of a weak sustainability risk culture upholding abuses or at least the exploitation of regulatory gaps.

---

[66] EIOPA 2019b. See also Blackrock 2021, 36: "environmental and social materiality was mentioned by many respondents as being partly covered by reputational risk, as the impact of their banking activity on the environment is often subject to public scrutiny and, hence, associated with reputational considerations".

[67] Colaert 2022, 1669; Omarova 2018, 818.

A mere tick-boxing perspective is capable of capturing only the first category of unsustainability risks: a formalistic reading of set sustainability reporting obligations, for example, detects only whether a financial entity has published or not a non-financial statement in accordance with the normatively established criteria, but not whether the rendered information, although compliant with formal requirements is truthful and soundly generated by the relevant governance underpinnings.

The example suggests how the existence of specific ESG regulations and the link of these with the different behavioural levels of good sustainable conduct give rise to new sources of misconduct related to the missed adherence of a financial firm to ESG-based parameters set at both compliance *and* behavioural levels. It also shows the ineffectiveness of the tools currently enshrined in the sustainable finance regulations to oversee the new behavioural spaces and thus the new sustainability-related conduct risks opened up by the new sustainable conduct rules.

Conversely, a systemic reading of the risks of "unsustainable" compliance or "unsustainable" behaviour vis-à-vis the emerging ESG-related framework shows how the call for a transition to a sustainable finance paradigm is sensitively reshaping both the regulatory ("environmental") and the behavioural ("structures and behaviours") factors that drive conduct risk.

The enlargement, from a substantial perspective, of the scope of conduct risks triggered by the ongoing regulatory reforms suggests, at the same time, the enlargement of its procedural significance within the evolving European "sustainable-based" financial system, offering new perspectives of employment of the considered category in respect to the identification and measuring of ESG risks: the preventive and corrective function of conduct risk may thus provide further guidance for financial intermediaries in the challenging governance of ESG risks (as here majorly qualified as conduct risks), exactly considered beyond the (still relatively weak) legal perspective and evaluated through a different behavioural and cultural frame, which the category of conduct risk is genetically set to measure[68].

Exactly because of the delicate balance between regulatory and behavioural factors in the construction of a sustainable European financial system, the category of conduct emerges as a relevant "good" governance tool of ESG-related factors, both in the internal dimension of the development by banks of their sustainable governance and related reporting policies and in the external dynamics of the assessment and fruition by banks of sustainability information rendered by third parties along the new sustainable financial value chain.

Before exploring the uncharted relationship between conduct risk, ESG risks and "unsustainability", it is worth looking deeper into the different emerging risks of "unsustainability", in the light of a possible taxonomy of these.

---

[68] Stressing these aspects from a prudential perspective, EBA 2022b, 21.

8.5 MAPPING THE NEW RISKS OF UNSUSTAINABILITY

The risks of misconduct in the management of ESG risks in the financial sector are to be found along the whole financial ESG value chain and are respectively related to (i) the identification of ESG risks; (ii) the measurement and quantification of ESG risks; (iii) the implementation of ESG-related reporting and governance requirements.

8.5.1 *The Identification of ESG Risks*

The risks of misconduct in the identification of ESG risks are rooted in the still unsettled definition of sustainability risks currently provided at the European level[69].

Since the issuing of the Sustainable Finance Action Plan in 2018, both stakeholders and regulators have struggled to agree on a conceptual as well as practical framework regarding ESG risks. In the ESMA's technical advice to the European Commission on integrating sustainability risks and factors in MiFID II[70], the lack of a common definition of the actual meaning of the environmental, social and governance factors has emerged as a serious concern, impairing the effective uptake of sustainability-related policies.

The environmental factor has attracted greater attention by regulators as reflected, at the international level, by the Paris Agreement and at EU level, first by the policy declarations enshrined in the EU Green Deal[71], and then in the EU Taxonomy and related delegated acts[72], as well as by the ECB Guide on Climate and Environmental Risk[73]. Only lately, the Platform on Sustainable Finance established by the European Commission has published a first Social Taxonomy, clarifying the social dimension of the ESG acronym[74], foreshadowing a legislative intervention in the field. To the contrary, the last fragment of the acronym, related to governance matters, is still underdeveloped.

A first general outline of the substantial meaning of each ESG factor has been provided by the European Commission in a Study on the *Integration of ESG Factors into the EU Banking Prudential Framework and into Banks' Business Strategies and Investment Policies*[75]. Environmental factors are here related to the sphere of climate change, as given by physical weather events and transition to low-carbon economy; and to the dimension of natural resources and pollution, as given by water management, biodiversity and land use.

---

[69] Siri and Zhu 2019, 5–6.
[70] See ESMA 2019a and ESMA 2019b.
[71] European Commission COM/2019/640 final.
[72] See supra note 49.
[73] See ECB 2020.
[74] Platform on Sustainable Finance 2022.
[75] Blackrock 2021, 29.

Social factors are conversely associated to internal stakeholder management, as resulting from the protection of workers' rights and the establishment of diversity and inclusion policies; as well as to external stakeholder management, sensitive to human rights and customer rights.

Finally, governance factors are linked both to board quality, in terms of board effectiveness and independence, and to corporate behaviour as defined by ownership control and business ethics. Along these lines, the EBA has generally referred the governance factor to the compliance with corporate governance codes as well as to the governance of environmental and social factors[76]. In this last respect, the new framework laid down by the proposed corporate sustainability due diligence directive, to the extent that it is applicable to the financial sector, provides first normative grounds for substantiating the environmental and social-related dimension of the governance factor.

These evolutions in the definitions of the various components of the ESG trinomial are, however, not backed up by indications on how to identify in the practice these factors. Although the Taxonomy Regulation and the proposal for a directive on corporate sustainability due diligence have started to set procedural safeguards for the identification of set standards, no consensus has been reached yet regarding the need to develop a single ESG indicator or a distinct indicator for each of the E-S-G components.

In 2019, in response to the ESMA consultation on sustainability risks, the majority of stakeholders declared to assess clients' ESG preferences in accordance with a single indicator or in accordance with a mixed approach[77].

In the absence of clearer indications by legislators, firms are following different frameworks and standards for the definition of ESG parameters[78]. The 2015 UN Sustainable Development Goals are one of the standards that are mostly followed especially by financial firms[79] as well as the Principles on Responsible Banking (PRB)[80].

With specific regard to the banking sector, the study conducted by Blackrock for the European Commission[81] shows how the definition of ESG risks by banks is often based on a combination of statements, standards and external guidance from international organizations, civil society organizations and supervisors. Overall, it appears that banks, in line with regulatory developments, are giving greater relevance to the environmental pillar, compared to the S and G pillars[82].

---

[76] See EBA 2021, 34.
[77] It is also recalled by Siri and Zhu 2019, 10.
[78] EBA 2021, para. 29.
[79] Blackrock 2021, 191.
[80] See PRB 2019.
[81] Blackrock 2021, 28.
[82] Blackrock 2021, 31.

This is also related to the fact that the changes made to the Benchmark Regulation in 2019 have introduced only two benchmarks, both environmentally related: the EU Climate Transition Benchmarks and the EU-Paris aligned benchmarks[83]. This is to be considered an important step forward for the purposes of the identification and qualification of environmental risks.

Conversely, the missed introduction of benchmarks related to the social and governance factors should be traced back to the physiological pace of regulatory developments, which have until now moved slower in respect to the consideration of these other two factors[84]. However, the uncertainty currently related to the means of identification, especially of the social and governance factors may engender the risk of a missed consideration by financial entities of *all* the relevant factors forming, concretely, the firm-specific sustainability risks. This risk of misconduct in the identification of the sustainability factors to be concretely measured and governed is even greater in light of the absence, to date, of a framework regarding ESG ratings[85], which may eventually incentivize undertakings to adopt a more comprehensive approach to sustainability factors.[86]

Ultimately, the present state of the art of ESG-related regulations leaves open significant interpretative and operational gaps in the identification of ESG risks that, in the absence of further interventions, only the cultural lever can close in a manner that is consistent with the ultimate objectives of the sustainable finance reform as well as with emerging investors' and society's expectations more in general. Conduct risk appears to be an effective tool for focussing on the risks stemming from unfair behaviour at the early stage of defining which ESG risks an institution shall deal with, signalling the existence of a cultural gap in this regard, both vis-à-vis the minimal shared culture and the specific declared culture of a financial entity.

8.5.2 *The Measurement and Quantification of ESG Risks*

While the first reference to ESG factors can be found in Directive EU 2014/95 on the disclosure of non-financial and diversity information, which considers "environmental matters, social and employee matters, respect of human rights, anti-corruption issues"[87] and diversity on company boards (in terms of age, gender,

---

[83] Reg. 2089/2019/UE. See also EU Technical Expert Group on Sustainable Finance 2019.
[84] See European Commission 2022b. See also ESMA 2022 and also European Commission 2022a.
[85] An ESG rating framework has been announced in the Commission's Strategy for a Sustainable Finance. European Commission COM(2021) 390 final.
[86] This positive effect of ESG ratings on the identification patterns of ESG risks by financial entities largely depends, of course, on how a concrete regulation in this matter will address ESG ratings. If the ESG rating frameworks consider majorly environmental factors, the risk for financial entities missing the greater sustainability picture will remain and consolidate.
[87] Recital 6 Directive 2014/95/EU.

educational and professional background)[88], a normative definition of sustainability risks has come along only with the SFDR, which defines these as an "environmental, social or governance event or condition that, if it occurs, could cause an actual or a potential material negative impact on the value of the investment"[89]. This definition entails some first indications regarding the measurement of ESG risks: only those sustainability risks that are likely to have an actual or potential impact on the value of investments are to be considered by financial entities in their risk management framework. The notion of double materiality under Directive 2022/2464/EU confirms and strengthens this approach.

The policy choice of anchoring ESG risks to a materiality impact has been opposed by the EIOPA, which has found this limitation to materiality short-sighted with respect to the complex nature of ESG risks[90].

As has been observed in the literature, the declared materiality dimension of ESG risks has not been accompanied by the definition of correspondent indicators of sustainability-related materiality indicators, this leaving economic operators "in the dark"[91]. As a result, banks are currently performing assessments of ESG-related risk factors, especially with respect to climate change, through pilot exercises based on portfolio risk measurement and scenario analysis, for the purposes of quantifying impacts on exposures[92]. The main concern related to the development of ESG materiality indicators is that ESG materiality is to be captured in the long-term perspective, differently from traditional financial materiality that is traditionally short-term focussed[93].

ESG risks are difficult to quantify in the long term: this is why, while environmental risks are often measured in their materiality impact, because these risks have become over time easier to quantify, no such measuring operation is conducted at present in respect of social and governance risks, which are mostly perceived as strategic and reputational risks[94].

Hence, also, with respect to the moment of the measuring of ESG risks, the existence of a solid risk culture becomes essential. Conduct risk may spot eventual

---

[88] Ibid. recital 18 and 20.

[89] Art. 2(22) Reg. 2019/2088/UE. See also the similar definition given by EBA defining ESG factors as "ESG factors are environmental, social or governance matters that may have a positive or negative impact on the financial performance or solvency of an entity, sovereign or individual"; EBA 2021, 6.

[90] See EIOPA 2019b.

[91] Zetsche and Anker-Sørensen 2022, 47. See, however, the 'Final Report on draft Regulatory Technical Standards, with regard to the content, methodologies and presentation of disclosures pursuant to Article 2a(3), Article 4(6) and (7), Article 8(3), Article 9(5), Article 10(2) and Article 11(4) of Regulation (EU) 2019/2088', EBA-EIOPA-ESMA 2021.

[92] Blackrock 2021, 36, further stresses that according to respondents, "financial materiality should be prioritized for the time being, as discussions on sustainability may often be abstract and high-level, and hence, lack the financial relevance aspect that is needed to bring the topic to the attention of financial institutions".

[93] Blackrock 2021, 36.

[94] Blackrock 2021, 8.

gaps in this respect, and be used as a tool to monitor – well before the closing of existing legislative gaps – if and to which degree eventual gaps in the risk culture are addressed.

8.5.3 *The Implementation of ESG-Related Reporting and Governance Requirements*

A further category of unsustainability risk is related to the risk of misconduct in the application of the requirements posed by enacted ESG-related regulations. These unsustainability risks may affect both the reporting and the governance require-ments introduced by the sustainable finance framework.

The imposed pivot of financial institutions' reporting and governance substruc-tures towards the appraisal of ESG risks surely constitutes a novel source of legal risk for financial entities, in case these do not establish sustainability-centred reporting and governance safeguards. However, a different question regards *how* these same safeguards are designed and enacted, when a financial institution moves its steps towards compliance with these requirements.

In this respect, an area of misconduct risk appears to emerge in relation to those reporting and governance structures that formally comply with set governance requirements, but substantively do not meet their underlying (sustainability) objec-tives. Many examples can be given of practices of "ESG-washing" of reporting and governance requirements in the field of sustainability. These washing practices arise specifically in the case of "apparent" management of ESG factors, which renders the enacted reporting and governance structures unsustainable.

On the side of reporting requirements, the recently published regulatory tech-nical standards[95] to the SFDR aim to ensure the quality and comparability of the sustainability information to be rendered, specifying the methodology and con-tent of financial reporting statements. On its side, the new corporate sustainability reporting directive has engaged in the effort of standardizing sustainability reporting through digital logs and certification requirements[96]. It also lays down a framework for the auditing of sustainability reports[97].

Although clearly aiming at a more sophisticated structuring of sustainability reports and thus at raising their trustworthiness, the newly enacted and proposed measures are incapable of tproviding for the risk that financial entities provide a distorted picture of their sustainability policies[98]. These risks may be related to both reputational and, strictly related to these, by commercial drivers.

---

[95] Commission Delegated Regulation 2022/1288/EU (6 April 2022).

[96] Art. 29d Directive 2022/2464/EU.

[97] The Directive 2022/2464/EU indeed amends the Audit Directive (Directive 2014/56/EU), the Audit Regulation (Regulation 537/2014/EU) and the Accounting Directive (Directive 2013/34/EU).

[98] Fletcher and Oliver 2022, 17.

In this last regard, the persisting uncertainty regarding the reporting standards[99] may favour practices of exploitation of end-investors preferences for sustainable investments (where present), ultimately distorting their investment decisions[100].

The existence of a comply or explain mechanism under art. 6 SFDR does not appear to be an effective remedy to these concerns: to the contrary, it may lead financial entities to prefer a falsified "comply" solution, rather than the more burdensome "explain" option.

Outside of the box of the strict sustainability reports, the risks of fictional claims may be further enhanced by the existence of other, less regulated information venues, such as websites or managers' statements, which provide, as the practice has shown, further alleys for the dissemination of inflated sustainability information[101].

The previously mentioned shortcomings of reporting obligations confirm the fact that the achievement of sound sustainability financial disclosure policies needs the backup of effective governance underpinnings[102].

As has been recalled above, ESG regulations, and specifically the Commission's delegated acts, have established new governance obligations, demanding the internalization of ESG risks into financial entities' internal control structures[103], due diligence processes and monitoring systems[104].

However, just as in respect of reporting obligations, sustainable governance obligations also may be distorted or bound to purposes that are different from the outright management of ESG risks.

As the EBA has interestingly suggested, the governance factor may be undermined by poor conduct[105]. Since (good) governance, at the general level, also involves the governance of environmental and social factors with specific regard to their risk drivers, the risk of poor conduct at the governance level could concern a wrong or negligent governance of the physical, transition and technology[106] risks determining environmental factors[107]; or the failed alignment with changes in policy and market sentiment driving, in accordance with the EBA, social risks[108]. In the absence of specific legal obligations in this sense, this type of unsustainability risk

---

[99] The complexity of RTS may sharpen instead of reducing the uncertainty surrounding non-financial reporting standards; This is documented by some studies that aimed to test the effectiveness of the draft RTS onto investors. Cicirko, Kawiński and Petelczyc 2020.

[100] This risk is also acknowledged by recital 77 Regulation 2019/2088/EU.

[101] Decision of the Tribunal of Gorizia in Italy, issuing an injunction against the publication of misleading sustainability information on the undertaking's website. With respect to managers' statements, see the recent cases of Deutsche Bank; DWS and HSBC. See Walker and Miller 2022; Morris 2022.

[102] Fish 2019, 923.

[103] See references supra notes 53–56.

[104] See European Commission, arts. 5; 7 and 8, COM/2022/71 final.

[105] EBA 2021, para. 48.

[106] EBA 2021, para. 63.

[107] EBA 2021, para. 47–74.

[108] EBA 2021, para. 75–83.

is evidently to be ascribed to the sphere of financial institutions' strategic choices, which are ultimately grounded in entities' choices of conduct – for example, the choice to consider or to not consider the physical and transition risks or the social implications of a given operation.

On a different note, sustainable governance obligations are increasingly pointing towards the need to involve stakeholders in the definition of undertakings' sustainability strategies[109], it appears that the same tool of the dialogue with stakeholders may be misused along the lines of an outright "stakeholder washout". If enacted, stakeholder consultations may not be sustained by adequate strategies for the dialogue with stakeholders, enabling the managers to acquire a more solid understanding of the relevant matters for long-term value creation. The dialogue with stakeholders risks being an ineffective tool if not supported by adequate governance tools for the identification of the relevant interested or affected third parties and for the monitoring of the subsequent integration within corporate actions of the indications rendered by stakeholders.

A further governance layer providing fertile grounds for the blossoming of unsustainability risks relates to product governance policies and investment decisions. Also, in this respect, the Commission's delegated acts have requested financial entities to consider investors' preferences for the purposes of product governance policies, suitability assessments and the identification of conflicts of interests[110]. These requirements evidently entail an important evaluative – thus behavioural – component, for they rely on the ability (and willingness) of financial entities to assess the sustainability preferences of clients and investors. Where present[111], these preferences may be falsely interpreted by financial businesses for the purposes of extending the supply of non-green products. Conversely, in the scenario in which clients or investors do not have developed sustainability preferences yet, new areas of misconduct arise with respect to the missed development by financial entities of adequate testing and awareness-raising procedures regarding these preferences.

A distorted evaluation of clients' ESG preferences may ultimately result in the offering of unsuited green products, especially in the absence of uniform ESG labels[112].

An ultimate corollary of the traced picture is that the identified risks of unsustainability may not be correctly evaluated by banks in their borrowing practices. The acknowledgement of these risks may potentially also be bypassed in the case of the advocated inclusion within credit processes of the assessment regarding how

---

[109] So, for example, the Italian Corporate Governance Code and also the Directive 2024/1760/EU at art. 13.

[110] See supra references in notes 53–56.

[111] Doubting this, Colaert 2022, 1669.

[112] JRC 2021.

environmental and social factors are managed by counterparties[113], further fuelling the circle of unsustainable conduct in the moment of fruition by credit institutions of ESG-related information rendered by borrowers.

Overall, the identified unsustainability risks at the governance level again point to the need to develop stronger accountability safeguards for a sustainable corporate governance model that may well go beyond non-financial disclosure obligations[114]. On the grounds of the cultural and behavioural driver of the detected risks, conduct risk may be a relevant tool, first of all, for uncovering these unsustainability risks and to address them, through the orientation of financial entities' governance choices and the strengthening of supervisory policies.

8.6 THE ALMOST UNEXPLORED RELATIONSHIP BETWEEN CONDUCT RISK, ESG RISKS AND "UNSUSTAINABILITY"

As the analysis has shown, the category of conduct risk has been prioritized by regulators and policymakers as a tool for enhancing financial entities' responsiveness towards socially harmful consequences of conduct that falls below certain expected standards (legal or ethical)[115]. The move of ESG risks at the top of the regulatory agenda can be inscribed in the same policy trajectory. This "evolutive" perspective shows how conducting risk entails an anticipatory function not only with respect to newly emerging behavioural risks, but also with respect to newly emerging interests that may acquire legal relevance as a result of subsequent legislative interventions or through evolutive interpretation of standards[116].

Under these premises, the alignment of conduct risks and ESG risks is supported by the objectives as well as the object of these two categories.

As far as the objectives are concerned, it has been shown above how the very rationale of conduct risk lies in the finalization of financial entities' conduct towards the ultimate goals of investor protection, market integrity and financial stability underlying financial regulation, in particular in respect of those frameworks' loopholes that risk to undermine the effectiveness of the financial system vis-à-vis these goals[117]. In the same vein, some studies have shown how the sustainable finance regulations, as currently shaped, do not introduce sustainability as an autonomous objective of financial regulation but rather a as new tool for more effectively pursuing the traditional goals of financial regulation, as reinterpreted in accordance with a long-term

---

[113] Blackrock 2021, 33, noting that some respondents emphasized that the assessment regarding borrowers' governance practices and management quality "should be further expanded to capture, among other elements, how E&S risks are managed by the counterparties, for instance through the set-up of adequate governance structures and control mechanisms for climate risk management".
[114] Manes 2019, 985.
[115] Omarova 2018, 814.
[116] EBA 2022a, para. 297.
[117] Cherednychenko 2021, 158.

and value-inflected approach[118]. As a result, both of the risk categories considered, namely conduct risk and ESG risks, entail the primary function of intervening upon the best practices surrounding the application of the hardcore rules of the financial sector and the achievement of their original goals. Both risk categories ultimately entail a methodological prescription addressed towards financial actors, rooted in need for a cultural and behavioural shift towards more responsible economic choices. Both tools thus point to a value-oriented risk culture transcending formal normative commitments.

Moreover, the categories at stake share a similar object. If the focus of conduct risk, as reflected by the latest policy declarations, is to be largely determined on the basis of investor protection concerns and, even more generally, of good governance concerns minimizing the risks of both external and internal harms for financial entities, the social and governance factors substantiating sustainability risks cover pretty much the same behavioural terrain. These factors are, it is true, up to now so broadly – and uncertainly – defined that they appear to be capable of covering most of the potential areas of entities' misconduct.

Far from being of merely theoretical significance, the systemic conceptualization of ESG risks as a specific normative evolution of conduct risks highlighting the relevance of the social and governance factors, which, at least until now, are lagging behind the environmental-centred regulatory discourse regarding sustainable finance. The conduct-based reading of ESG risks reveals how the concretization of the social and governance factors, if effectively addressed at a cultural level and beyond formal regulatory requirements, may be an opportunity to address some of the recurrent trends of misconduct in the financial sector.

However, notwithstanding these common elements, in order to identify the role of conduct risk in the sustainable financial environment and its function in respect of the governance of ESG risks, it is important to acknowledge the respective specificities of the two analysed categories.

Indeed, on closer inspection, conduct risk and ESG risks differ in their scope and means: while conduct risk is a category to be differently declined and identified at the individual entity level[119] and maintains an extra-regulatory relevance precisely because of its corrective and (normative) gap-closing function, ESG risks as set by the sustainable finance agenda are supposed to intervene upon the broader systemic dynamics of financial markets through the channels of direct normative interventions.

The integration of conduct risk within financial institutions' risk management framework is meant to provide concrete measures of the single financial business's risk culture, signalling necessary intervention against the attitudes at the roots of harmful misconduct. On the contrary, although ESG risks will also have to be

---

[118] Colaert 2022, 1669.
[119] See Omarova 2018, 825.

implemented at a firm-specific level, the introduced measures aim to proceduralize and standardize the management of ESG risks across the financial industry, as reflected by the recalled sustainable reporting and governance obligations as well as by the expected regulations regarding ESG labels and benchmarks. Instead of the bottom-up approach of conduct risk, the sustainable finance policy leverages traditional top-down regulatory means as primary triggers of new sustainability-related risk culture and as a basis for the generation of further soft law incentives.

The reform related to the introduction of ESG risks in the financial sector is ultimately intended to shape business conduct by changing the regulatory baselines and, thus, the norms that (are supposed to) orient the culture of financial businesses.

As a spillover effect, the sustainability-related risk culture incentivized through the emerging regulatory framework should minimize conduct risks: first of all, because, in consistency with the conceptualization of ESG risks proposed here, a sound implementation of ESG-related conduct of business rules per se addresses those conduct risks from which the whole sustainable finance framework derives; and secondly, because a solid ESG-related risk culture should also be functional to avert those behavioural risks arising directly from the normatively defined sustainability commands.

Specifically in respect of these last behavioural risks, which we have appointed here as risks of unsustainability, the category of conduct risk acquires a new and essential relevance within the project of building a European sustainable financial marketplace. Indeed, exactly because ESG-related regulations are, to a great extent, business of conduct rules, which are still highly uncertain and undefined in their actual scope and lines of enforcement, these come along with a wide range of unsustainability risks that have been described in the previous paragraph. Just like traditional conduct risks, these unsustainability risks derive from a formalistic implementation of structurally incomplete ESG-related rules without effectively addressing the underlying interests and goals.

The many gaps that are left open by the evolving sustainable finance framework thus offer a fertile terrain for the application of the category of conduct risk as a means to detect early the unsustainability risks entailed in the financial regulation reform project as well as the widely acknowledged risks of greenwashing, and prevent these from becoming a systemic threat to market integrity and financial stability in the changing regulatory landscape.

Seemingly, the ability of conduct risk as a tool to spot poor risk culture appears to hold its greatest promise in relation to a wave of regulatory reforms, such as the current sustainable finance ones, that are grounded specifically in the ambition of promoting a cultural change, supposedly by means of a new sustainable "market sentiment"[120].

---

[120] Colaert 2022, 1669.

Framed in these terms, the link between conduct risk and ESG risks becomes even deeper: the use of conduct risk as a means of measuring ESG-related risk culture becomes essential to ensure that financial institutions developing sustainable strategies, for example with respect to the offering of green products, and also have a consistent underlying culture. Conduct risk as applied with respect to ESG-related norms thus serves the overarching objective of ensuring that the ongoing regulatory interventions are accompanied by a proper turn in financial institutions' culture. In this respect, it should be considered a primary pillar of the construction of a sustainable financial system, offering new governance and also supervisory scenarios.

More concretely, the practical relevance of conduct risk with respect to the management of ESG risks is to be found at the prudential level. In line with the European conception of conduct risk as an operational risk[121], the integration of ESG-related conduct risks into the broader conduct risk frame would ensure capital coverage for the losses potentially deriving from the distorted implementation of sustainable finance regulation and complete the path towards a comprehensive integration of ESG risks into the EU prudential framework[122]. In this vein, the actual occurrence of conduct risk events could serve as a proxy for the measurement of the actual level of culture and, in this perspective, conduct risk events in the ESG area could serve as a proxy for ESG culture (and perhaps also be relevant in the assessment of governance risks).

At the operational level, thus, the recalibration of firm-specific indicators of conduct risks vis-à-vis the behavioural standards underlying evolving sustainable financial regulations would render conduct risk-sensitive to the measuring of sustainability-related risks in the changing normative and cultural financial landscape.

The link between conduct risks indicators and capital charges would thus offer quantitative evidence regarding what educational interventions are still needed to effectively match financial institutions' ESG-related practices with sustainable finance objectives. The exploitation of conduct risk's prudential measuring functions would, in turn, be relevant for raising awareness regarding the risks of unsustainable conduct and thus make financial entities' risk culture suitable for the effective implementation of the (still holey) sustainable finance regulations.

REFERENCES

Angelini, P. (2021), 'La cultura del rischio', speech held at the Università Cattolica del Sacro Cuore, Milan, 15 October, available at: https://bit.ly/4bOaGuo.

BCBS (2006), 'International Convergence on Capital Measurement and Capital Standards – A Revised Framework', available at: www.bis.org/publ/bcbs128.htm.

BCBS (2001), 'Sound Practices for the Management and Supervision of Operational Risk Operational Risk', available at: www.bis.org/publ/bcbs86.pdf.

---

[121] See above para. 2.
[122] See lately EBA 2022c.

Blackrock (2021), 'Study on the "Development of Tools and Mechanisms for the Integration of ESG Factors into the EU Banking Prudential Framework and into Banks' Business Strategies and Investment Policies"', May, available at: https://bit.ly/4c3UPrT.

Bodellini, M. and Singh, D. (2021), '*Sustainability and finance: Utopian oxymoron or achievable companionship?*' 10 *Law and Economics Yearly Review* 1, 163–188.

Cherednychenko, O. O. (2021), 'Two sides of the same coin: EU financial regulation and private law' 22 *European Business Organization Law Review*, 147–172.

Cicirko, M., Kawiński, M. and Petelczyc, J. (2020), *Consumer Testing of Pre-contractual and Periodic ESG Financial Product Information*. Warsaw School of Economics.

Colaert, V. (2022), 'The changing nature of financial regulation: Sustainable finance as a new EU policy objective' 59 *Common Market Law Review* 6, 1669–1710.

Davies, P. et al. (2021), 'Commentary: The European Parliament's Draft Directive on Corporate Due Diligence and Corporate Accountability' ECGI, 19 April.

De Pascalis, F. (2019), 'Conduct risk: Meaning, interpretation and dissension' 30 *European Business Law Review* 6, 947–964.

EBA (European Banking Authority) (2021), *Report on Management and Supervision on ESG Risks for Credit Institutions and Investment Firms*, EBA/REP/2021/18, 23 June, available at: https://bit.ly/4c4hvaI.

EBA (European Banking Authority) (2022a), *Guidelines on Common Procedures and Methodologies for the Supervisory Review and Evaluation Process (SREP) and Supervisory Stress Testing under Directive 2013/36/EU*, EBA/GL/2022/03, available at: https://bit.ly/3x2HTmL.

EBA (European Banking Authority) (2022b), *Report on Incorporating ESG Risks in the Supervision of Investment Firms. Report Complementing EBA/REP/2021/18*, EBA/REP/2022/26, 24 October, available at: https://bit.ly/3Rclf2c.

EBA (European Banking Authority) (2022c), *Discussion Paper on the Role of Environmental Risks in the Prudential Framework*, EBA/DP/2022/02, 2 May, available at: https://bit.ly/3Vg1isi.

EBA-EIOPA-ESMA (European Banking Authority/European Insurance and Occupational Pensions Authority/European Securities and Markets Authority) (2021), *Final Report on Draft Regulatory Technical Standards, with Regard to the Content, Methodologies and Presentation of Disclosures Pursuant to Article 2a(3), Article 4(6) and (7), Article 8(3), Article 9(5), Article 10(2) and Article 11(4) of Regulation (EU) 2019/2088*, JC 2021 03, 2 February, available at: https://bit.ly/4aX93ZT.

EBA-ESMA (European Banking Authority/European Insurance and Occupational Pensions Authority) (2022), *Joint EBA and ESMA Guidelines on Common Procedures and Methodologies for the Supervisory Review and Evaluation Process (SREP) under Directive (EU) 2019/2034*, EBA/GL/2022/09, ESMA35-36-2621, 21 July 2022, available at: https://bit.ly/4aVZk6a.

EIOPA (European Insurance and Occupational Pensions Authority) (2019a), 'Framework for Assessing Conduct Risk Through the Product Lifecycle', available at: https://bit.ly/4aPJiuD.

EIOPA (European Insurance and Occupational Pensions Authority) (2019b), 'Technical Advice on the integration of sustainability risks and factors in the delegated acts under Solvency II and IDD', EIOPA-BoS-19/172, 30 April, available at: https://bit.ly/3yJx9di.

EIOPA (European Insurance and Occupational Pensions Authority) (2022), *Report on EIOPA Supervisory Activities in 2021*, available at: https://bit.ly/4aPJiuD.

English, S., Hammond, S., Kovas, A. and Parry, H. (2018), *Culture and Conduct Risk 2018: Benchmarking Five Years of Implementation*. Thompson Reuters.

Enriques, L. (2021), 'The European Parliament Draft Directive on Corporate Due Diligence and Accountability: Stakeholder-oriented governance on steroids', 2/3 *Rivista delle Società*, 319–324.

ESMA (European Securities and Markets Authority) (2019a), 'ESMA's technical advice to the European Commission on integrating sustainability risks and factors in MiFID II', 30 April.

ESMA (European Securities and Markets Authority) (2019b), 'ESMA's technical advice to the European Commission on integrating sustainability risks and factors in the UCITS Directive and AIFMD', 30 April.

ESMA (European Securities and Markets Authority) (2022), 'Call for evidence on market characteristics for ESG Rating Providers in the EU', 3 February – 11 March, available at: https://bit.ly/4e5djtr.

ESRB (2015), *Report on Misconduct Risk in the Banking Sector*, available at: https://bit.ly/4aN5Dc9.

EU Technical Expert Group on Sustainable Finance (2019), *Taxonomy Technical Report*, June, available at: https://bit.ly/3OZW7dO.

European Central Bank (2020), 'Guide on climate-related and environmental risks', available at: https://bit.ly/3RfCgZc.

European Commission (2018), 'Action Plan: Financing Sustainable Growth', COM/2018/097 final, July.

European Commission (2019), 'The European Green Deal', COM/2019/640 final, 11 December.

European Commission (2021), 'Strategy for Financing the Transition to a Sustainable Economy', COM/2021/390 final, 6 July.

European Commission (2022a), 'Consultation on the functioning of the ESG ratings market in the European Union and on the consideration of ESG factors in credit ratings', 4 April – 6 June.

European Commission (2022b), 'Study on feasibility, minimum standards and transparency requirements of an EU ESG benchmark Label', April.

FCA (Financial Conduct Authority) (2013), 'Risk Outlook 2013', available at: https://bit.ly/3KuFWm2.

FCA (Financial Conduct Authority) (2020), '"Messages from the Engine Room" 5 Conduct Questions', Industry Feedback for 2019/20, Wholesale Banking Supervision, September.

Federal Reserve Bank of New York (2017), 'Misconduct, Culture and Supervision', available at: https://nyfed.org/3XabxRy.

FSB (Financial Stability Board) (2014), 'Guidance on Supervisory interaction with Financial Institutions on Risk Culture – A Framework for Assessing Risk Culture', available at: https://bit.ly/3X9i5jh.

FSB (Financial Stability Board) (2017), 'Stocktake of Efforts to Strengthen Governance Frameworks to Mitigate Conduct Risk', available at: https://bit.ly/3Vx2hpB.

FSB (Financial Stability Board) (2018), 'Strengthening Governance Framework to Mitigate Misconduct Risk: A Toolkit for Firms and Supervisors', available at: www.fsb.org/2017/05/stocktake-of-efforts-to-strengthen-governance-frameworks-to-mitigate-misconduct-risks/.

Fish, J. E. (2019), 'Making sustainability disclosure sustainable' 107 *The Georgetown Law Journal*, 923–966.

Fletcher, L. and Oliver, J. (2022), 'Green funds risk a red flag' *Financial Times*, 21 February.

G20 (2022), 'High Level Principles on Financial Consumer Protection', available at: https://bit.ly/3RgjnFn.

G30 (2018), 'Banking Conduct and Culture – A Permanent Mindset Change', available at: https://owy.mn/4bOldps.

Joint ESAs (2022), *Final Report on Digital Finance*.

JRC (2021), *Development of EU Ecolabel Criteria for Retail Financial Products – Technical Report 4.0: Draft Proposal for the Product Scope and Criteria*, March, available at: https://bit.ly/3KxJtjr.

Kaplov, L. (1992), 'Rules vs. standards, an economic analysis' 42 *Duke Law Journal* 3, 559–629.

MacNeil, I. (2015), 'Rethinking Conduct Regulation', University of Glasgow Working Paper.

Manes, P. (2019), 'Assessing conduct risk: A new challenge for sustainable corporate governance' 30 *European Business Law Review* 6, 985–1014.

Moloney, N. (2018), 'EU financial market governance and the retail investor: Reflections at an inflection point' 37 *Yearbook of European Law* 251–304.

Moosa, I. A. (2006), 'Misconceptions about operational risk' 4 *Journal of Operational Risk* 1, 97–104.

Moosa, I. A. (2008), *Quantification of Operational Risk under Basel II: The Good, Bad and Ugly* (London: Palgrave Macmillan).

Morris, S. (2022), 'HSBC Faces Greenwashing Accusations from UK Advertising Watchdog' *Financial Times*, 29 April.

Omarova, S. T. (2018), 'Ethical finance as a systemic challenge: Risk, culture, and structure' 27 *Cornell Journal of Law and Public Policy* 3, 799–839.

Platform on Sustainable Finance (2022), *Final Report by Subgroup 4: Social Taxonomy*, 28 February.

Sciarrone Alibrandi, A. and Frigeni, C. (2019), 'Managing conduct risk: From rules to culture', in D. Bush, G. Ferrarini and G. Van Solinge (eds.), *Governance of Financial Institutions* (Oxford: Oxford University Press), 468–488.

Siri, M. and Zhu, S. (2019), 'Will the EU Commission Successfully Integrate Sustainability Risks and Factors in the Investor Protection Regime? A Research Agenda' *Sustainability*, 8 November.

Tuch, A. F. (2015), 'Conduct of business regulation', in N. Moloney, E. Ferran and J. Payne (eds.), *Oxford Handbook of Financial Regulation* (Oxford: Oxford University Press), 537–568.

UNEPF (2019), Principles on Responsible Banking (PRB), available at: www.unepfi.org/banking/more-about-the-principles/.

Walker, O. and Miller, J. (2022), 'German police raid DWS and Deutsche Bank over Greenwashing Allegations' *Financial Times*, 31 May.

Zetsche, D. A. and Anker-Sørensen, L. (2022), 'Regulating sustainable finance in the dark' 23 *European Business Organization Review*, 47–85.

9

Sustainability and Executive Compensation

*Roberto Barontini and Jennifer Hill**

9.1 INTRODUCTION

The history of corporate law has been characterised as a 'clash between the different visions of corporatism',[1] exemplifying the tension between a public and private image of the corporation.[2] Corporate law and governance have shifted between these two ends of the spectrum across time and jurisdictions.

This tension also underlies developments in executive compensation. In recent decades, executive pay has undergone several major reinterpretations, which have affected both its design and regulation. Corporate theory, together with 'problem framing',[3] have played an important role in these reinterpretations.[4]

Developments in executive pay from the early 1990s onwards were firmly based on a private theory of the corporation. According to this theory, the central problem in business law was that of financial underperformance by corporations. In recent times, a more complex picture of the corporation has emerged – one in which the corporation straddles both private and public law.[5] A series of scandals and crises highlighted a second major problem in corporate law, namely the danger that corporate conduct can create negative externalities and harm to society.[6] Recognition of this second problem has prompted an increased focus on issues relating to sustainability and ESG, including in the area of executive compensation.[7]

[*] We would like to thank Eusfil Workshop participants and, in particular, Guido Ferrarini, for helpful suggestions. We also thank Monash University, which provided funding for this project under a Network of Excellence grant on the topic, 'Enhancing Corporate Accountability'. Thanks also go to Mitheran Selvendran and Emma Ward for excellent research assistance.
[1] Bratton and Wachter 2008, 124.
[2] See generally Allen 1992.
[3] 'Problem framing' is a key feature of transnational legal ordering. See generally Bowley and Hill 2024a.
[4] See generally ibid.
[5] Hill 2021.
[6] Ibid.
[7] Ibid.

This chapter provides a broad overview of developments relating to the design and regulation of executive pay over the last few decades, including the recent rise of integration of sustainability and ESG targets in executive compensation packages. The chapter examines some of the reasons for this development and provides empirical evidence relating to prevalence of this trend in public listed companies today.

9.2 A SHORT HISTORY OF EXECUTIVE COMPENSATION: THEN AND NOW

9.2.1 *Corporate Theory and Executive Compensation Design: From Corporate Governance Problem to Corporate Governance Solution*

Show me the incentive and I will show you the outcome.

Charlie Munger, Berkshire Hathaway[8]

Just over 30 years ago, Jensen and Murphy adopted a law and economics lens to redirect debate concerning executive compensation in their watershed article, 'CEO incentives – it's not how much you pay, but how'.[9] The article transformed executive pay, which had traditionally been treated as a corporate law problem related to breach of fiduciary duty,[10] into a corporate governance solution.

The article served as a prelude to the era of performance-based compensation,[11] which was designed to address agency problems involving corporate underperformance.[12] According to this model, performance-based pay operated as a self-executing mechanism to align managerial interests with those of the company's shareholders.[13] Performance-based pay also functioned as a legitimising device, offering the promise of enhanced pay for superior corporate performance and reduced pay for sub-standard performance.[14] Under this 'just deserts' approach,[15] the quantum of pay was irrelevant, provided that it enhanced shareholder wealth.[16]

The 1990s, which has been described as the 'decade of corporate governance',[17] was also a decade of soaring executive pay in United States, particularly for the largest firms.[18] The widespread adoption of performance-based pay, coupled with huge

---

[8] See Lean CX 2020.
[9] Jensen and Murphy 1990.
[10] Yablon 1999, 279–80.
[11] Ibid.
[12] Jensen and Murphy 1990.
[13] See Ellis 1998, 402.
[14] Jensen and Murphy 1990; Frydman and Saks 2010.
[15] See Hill 2012a.
[16] See Loewenstein 1996, 206–7; Ferrarini, Moloney and Ungureanu 2010, 80.
[17] Conoley 1999, quoted in Cheffins 2015, 733.
[18] See, e.g., Bebchuk and Grinstein 2005; Conyon et al. 2013, Figure 1.1, 18; Edmans, Gabaix and Jenter 2017, 388–95.

option grants, contributed to this trend.[19] So, too, did a notable reform during this period, §162(m) of the US tax code.[20] Although this legislative provision was conceived as a control on excessive compensation,[21] by the time it became law in the mid-1990s, a subtle wording change subverted that original policy goal and led to a disproportionately large component of variable pay compared to fixed pay in US executive compensation packages,[22] thereby accelerating the trend toward dramatically higher pay.[23]

It has been said that Europe was 'quick to catch up' with performance-based pay, and compensation packages of executive directors of EU listed companies soon followed the US trend of adopting performance targets, in combination with large cash bonuses and stock option awards.[24] Yet, in spite of many convergent trends at an international level,[25] executive compensation is an area where corporate culture plays an important role.[26] Cultural differences are evident in relation to matters, such as design of executive contracts,[27] tolerance for high levels of pay and income inequality[28] and attitudes to disclosure of compensation.[29] Pay levels for CEOs in the United States, for example, have traditionally been far higher than in the United Kingdom and Europe,[30] although the gap between US and UK executive pay narrowed in recent decades.[31]

Capital market structure is also relevant in relation to executive pay. The capital market structure in many EU listed companies is quite different to that of US public corporations. Unlike the dispersed ownership system, with high levels of institutional investor ownership, that is common in the United States, many companies in continental Europe exhibit concentrated ownership structures, due to

---

[19] See, e.g., Yablon 1999, 293–4; Perry and Zenner 2000, 145; Conyon et al. 2013, 18. See generally Edmans, Gabaix and Jenter 2017, 398–404 (discussing changes in the structure of executive pay, including the escalation (in the 1980s–1990s) and the decline (from 2000 on) of outsized option grants in favour of restricted stock grants). However, outsized option grants are by no means a thing of the past. In 2018, Tesla CEO, Elon Musk, received a performance-based stock option grant potentially worth US$55 billion. See Chase and The Associated Press 2022.

[20] Internal Revenue Code (I.R.C.) of 1995 § 162(m).

[21] The original iteration of the provision would have disallowed corporate tax deductions for any compensation exceeding US$1 million on the basis that such pay was 'unreasonable'. See generally Conyon et al. 2013, 24.

[22] See, e.g., Miske 2004; Conway 2008, 396; Murphy and Jensen 2018.

[23] See Loewenstein 1996, 219–20; Murphy and Jensen 2018. See also Winter 2012 (arguing, from a behavioural economics perspective, that performance-based pay is inherently flawed and exacerbates, rather than alleviates, agency problems).

[24] Winter 2012, 199.

[25] Ferrarini and Moloney 2005.

[26] Levitt 2005.

[27] See, e.g., Hill, Masulis and Thomas 2011.

[28] Conyon and Murphy 2000, F646–7.

[29] Ferrarini and Moloney 2005.

[30] See, e.g., Thomas 2004; BIS 2010, 27; Ferrarini, Moloney and Ungureanu 2010, 79; Edmans, Gabaix and Jenter 2017, 421–4.

[31] BIS 2010, 25–7.

family control and other forms of blockholding.[32] These factors potentially alter the nature of the agency problems[33] that US-style performance-based pay was designed to solve.[34] For example, in a dispersed capital market context, the central problem regarding executive pay is a principal-agent conflict, whereas in jurisdictions such as continental Europe where concentrated ownership is prevalent, the main problem is one of 'principal-principal conflicts' between majority and minority shareholders.[35] Although concentrated ownership can mitigate some free-riding and monitoring problems relating to executive pay, it can also generate different problems, such as appropriation of private benefits and tunnelling.[36]

Since the introduction of performance-based pay, academic debate has raged as to whether this form of compensation was efficient and determined at arm's length by disinterested directors (the optimal contracting theory) or skewed due to a power imbalance between managers and shareholders (the managerial power model).[37]

9.2.2 *Executive Compensation: From Enron to the Global Financial Crisis*

The levels of compensation that we are talking about here would certainly seem to be a powerful incentive for anyone to do anything.

Stephen Meagher[38]

A string of international corporate scandals and collapses in the early 2000s increased debate about the design of performance-based pay. Scandals, such as Enron and WorldCom in the United States, and Parmalat, Vivendi and Royal Ahold in Europe, highlighted the fact that performance-based pay could create perverse incentives to engage in misconduct, including earnings management.[39]

In spite of the existence of similar structural defects in the executive pay packages of the relevant companies, the regulatory responses of jurisdictions differed significantly, largely due to variances in problem framing. For US legislators, the primary explanation for the collapse of Enron and WorldCom was lack of auditor

---

[32] See, e.g., Faccio and Lang 2002; Barontini and Caprio 2006; OECD 2021, 24–6.

[33] See Cheng, Lin and Wei 2015 (discussing the complex agency problems that can arise in the context of concentrated ownership of Chinese family firms).

[34] Ferrarini and Moloney 2005, 306. Cf. Ferrarini, Moloney and Ungureanu 2010, 78, 82–3 (noting that performance-based pay structures can still perform a role in aligning managerial interests with those of minority shareholders in blockholding companies). In spite of the focus of corporate governance literature, including that relating to executive pay, on the United States and the United Kingdom, in fact, ownership concentration is at a company level is increasing around the world. OECD 2021, 12.

[35] See Barontini and Bozzi 2011.

[36] Sánchez-Marín et al. 2022, 2820.

[37] See generally Bebchuk and Grinstein 2005; Core, Guay and Thomas 2005; Thomas and Wells 2011; Hill and Thomas 2012, 1–3; Edmans, Gabaix and Jenter 2017.

[38] See Eichenwald 2002, quoting comments by Stephen Meagher, a former federal white-collar crime prosecutor, in relation to executive pay at Enron.

[39] See Gordon 2002; Coffee 2004; Ferrarini, Moloney and Ungureanu 2009.

independence, rather than misaligned incentives in executive pay.[40] The Sarbanes–Oxley Act of 2002 ('Sarbanes–Oxley Act'), accordingly, paid minimal attention to the regulation of executive compensation,[41] or to strengthening shareholder rights in relation to executive compensation.[42]

The post-scandal regulatory responses to executive pay and shareholder rights in the United Kingdom and continental Europe were more robust than in the United States.[43] In 2002, the United Kingdom became the first jurisdiction to require an annual non-binding shareholder vote on executive pay ('Say on Pay'),[44] in response to public outrage about so-called 'fat cats'[45] and government concern about 'rewards for failure'.[46] The European Commission ('EC'), as part of the 2003 Company Law Action Plan, adopted two important Recommendations – the 2004 Recommendation on Directors' Remuneration[47] and the 2005 Recommendation on the Role of Non-executive Directors[48] – which have been described as 'the heart of the EU's remuneration regime'.[49] The 2004 Recommendation, for example, contained enhanced disclosure rules for remuneration policy and for individual directors' remuneration packages, as well as providing shareholders with a (binding or non-binding) vote on remuneration policy.[50] Unlike the approach taken in the US Sarbanes–Oxley Act, the UK and EU reforms sought to align shareholder and management interests by elevating the role of shareholders and strengthening their rights in the context of executive pay.[51]

Executive pay again became a regulatory flashpoint in the 2007–2009 global financial crisis ('GFC'). Regulatory responses to the crisis reflected the view that flawed executive compensation structures played a direct role in the crisis by creating perverse incentives that encouraged short-termism and excessive risk-taking,[52] although some commentators disputed this assessment.[53]

At a supranational level, transnational networks, such as the Group of Twenty (G20), stressed the need for greater global coordination to monitor

---

[40] See Coffee 2004.
[41] See Sarbanes–Oxley Act of 2002, Pub. L. 107–204, 116 Stat. 745, § 304 and § 402.
[42] See Chandler and Strine 2003, 999 (describing the failure to confer stronger rights on shareholders as potentially the 'forgotten element' of the Sarbanes–Oxley Act).
[43] See generally Ferrarini, Moloney and Ungureanu 2009.
[44] Directors' Remuneration Report Regulations 2002 (now found in Companies Act 2006, s. 439). See generally Ferri and Maber 2013; Gordon 2009.
[45] See, e.g., Jackson 1998; The Economist 2003.
[46] See, e.g., Trade and Industry Committee 2002.
[47] Official Journal of the European Union 2004.
[48] Official Journal of the European Union 2005.
[49] Ferrarini, Moloney and Ungureanu 2009, 26. See generally Ferrarini, Moloney and Ungureanu 2010.
[50] Ferrarini, Moloney and Ungureanu 2009, 26.
[51] Ibid., 28.
[52] See, e.g., Crotty 2009, 565; Avgouleas 2009, 42–5; Bebchuk and Spamann 2010, 255–68.
[53] See, e.g., Fahlenbrach and Stulz 2011; Ferrarini and Ungureanu 2011.

systemic financial risks[54] and implementation of financial market reforms, including those relating to executive compensation.[55] The Financial Stability Board ('FSB') sought to achieve cross-border regulatory harmonisation by formulating *Principles for Sound Compensation Practices*[56] to provide a blueprint for national prudential standards relating to remuneration in financial institutions.

In the United States, Timothy Geithner, former US Secretary of the Treasury, stated that perverse incentives for short-term gain in compensation contracts had 'overwhelmed the checks and balances meant to mitigate against the risk of excess leverage'.[57] Although US reforms were originally restricted to companies receiving government bail-out funding, they subsequently expanded to cover executive pay and shareholder empowerment more generally.[58] The Dodd–Frank Wall Street Reform and Consumer Protection Act of 2010 ('Dodd–Frank Act')[59] adopted a range of statutory provisions concerning executive pay, including the first US 'Say on Pay' requirement;[60] disclosure re pay disparity within firms[61] and compensation claw-back policies.[62]

Developments in the United Kingdom and Europe during this period emphasised the connection between executive pay and excessive financial risk,[63] as well as the potential threat this risk posed to economic stability. The influential 2009 UK Walker Review[64] explicitly linked effective risk management with the policy goals of societal benefit and sustainability, stating:

> [i]f banks are to be able to contribute to the nation's economic recovery and well-being, it is of critical importance that remuneration practices be reconstructed to provide incentives in support of sustainable performance.[65]

UK and European post-crisis executive compensation reforms focussed strongly on the issue of risk management.[66] In 2010, for example, the UK Financial Services Authority ('FSA') published revisions to its remuneration code ('Revised Remuneration Code').[67] The revisions were designed to take account of developments, such as the Walker Review, and the need to comply with the European Parliament's Capital Requirements Directive ('CRD III')[68] on compensation

---

[54] See Hill 2012b, 225–6.
[55] Ibid., 263–4.
[56] See FSF 2009. The FSB was originally named the Financial Stability Forum (FSF).
[57] See Braithwaite 2009.
[58] See generally Hill 2012a, 224–6.
[59] Dodd–Frank Wall Street Reform and Consumer Protection Act of 2010, Pub. L. 111–203, 124 Stat. 1376.
[60] Dodd–Frank Act § 951.
[61] Dodd–Frank Act § 953(b).
[62] Dodd–Frank Act § 954.
[63] See, e.g., FSA 2009, 79–81.
[64] Walker 2009, Chapter 7.
[65] Ibid., [7.1].
[66] See generally Ferrarini and Ungureanu 2010, 207–10.
[67] FSA 2010.
[68] See Official Journal of the European Union ('CRDIII') 2010. CRDIII implemented the FSB's *Principles for Sound Compensation Practices*. Ibid. at (1).

structure and performance measures,[69] as well as guidelines of the Committee of European Banking Supervisors ('CEBS').[70] The Revised Remuneration Code stated that its key objectives were to promote market confidence and financial stability by reducing incentives for excessive risk-taking[71] and by ensuring consistency between compensation policies/practices and effective risk management.[72] The EU reforms were considerably more detailed and rule-based than those adopted in the United States.[73]

The GFC highlighted the 'interconnectedness' of markets and the potential for international regulatory coordination to address concerns about negative externalities and moral hazard, particularly in the banking sector.[74] The crisis led to a new risk-based approach to the design of performance incentives in executive pay and increased emphasis on long-term value creation and sustainability.[75] Regulatory responses to the crisis were also underpinned by a re-evaluation of the concept of interest alignment, and the need to align the interests of management not merely with those of shareholders, but also with the interests of society as a whole.[76]

These developments provided the basis for further refinement of incentives in the ESG era.

9.2.3 *Executive Compensation in the ESG Era*

9.2.3.1 Introduction

Virtue itself turns vice, being misapplied.

William Shakespeare[77]

The US and European scandals at the turn of the twenty-first century, together with the global financial crisis, demonstrated that 'major financial crises have a habit of changing the executive pay debate'.[78] More recent examples, such as the Wells Fargo fraudulent accounts scandal[79] and the Volkswagen emissions scandal,[80] reinforced concerns that flawed remuneration practices can create perverse incentives for

---

[69] See generally Cleary Gottlieb 2010. CRDIII was introduced by Directive 2010/76/EU (Official Journal of the European Union ('CRDIII') 2010) and was subsequently repealed and replaced by Directive 2013/36/EU (Official Journal of the European Union 2013). See EBA 2016, 7; EBA 2021, 5–6.

[70] CEBS 2010. See also Ferrarini and Ungureanu 2010, 198, 215–16.

[71] See FSA 2010, [1.16].

[72] Ibid. at [1.17].

[73] Cleary Gottlieb 2010, 7.

[74] See, e.g., Ferrarini and Ungureanu 2010, 198, 214–6.

[75] Ibid., 202; Hill 2012a, 231–2.

[76] Hill 2012a, 233–4.

[77] *Romeo and Juliet*, Act 2, Scene 3.

[78] Ferrarini, Moloney and Ungureanu 2010, 74.

[79] See, e.g., Wattles et al. 2018.

[80] See generally Armour 2016a; Armour 2016b.

corporate misconduct and negative externalities.[81] They also showed that an exclusive focus on financial success can 'dull the senses' of institutions, boards of directors and managers to other kinds of risk.[82]

Today, the world is facing a new, and unprecedented, set of risks concerning the environment, particularly in relation to climate change. These risks are now treated as key financial risks for corporations.[83] BlackRock, for example, has estimated that climate change poses a US\$ 8.2 billion risk to its portfolio.[84] Controversial proposed corporate climate risk disclosure rules by the US Securities and Exchange Commission are premised on the view that enhanced disclosure is justified precisely because climate risk is a financial risk.[85]

Heightened recognition of these new risks has led to another U-turn in the design and regulation of executive pay, with growing integration of sustainability and ESG targets in compensation packages. Executive pay is again being presented as a corporate governance solution, but to a different set of problems. The new approach focusses attention on corporate commitment to ESG values.[86] Developments concerning integration of sustainability and ESG considerations into executive pay focus attention, not merely on profit maximisation, but on broader questions about *how* profits were achieved and whether profits were made by creating negative externalities and causing societal harm.

Executive compensation is arguably entering a new era of 'pay for sustainable performance'. A key issue is: what are the main drivers of this development?

9.2.3.2 What Is Driving the Shift to 'Pay for Sustainable Performance'?

Sustainability is here to stay, or we may not be.

Niall FitzGerald, Unilever[87]

There are several drivers of the movement toward pay for sustainable performance, which involves recognition that performance can no longer be measured 'in purely financial terms'[88] and that ESG factors are an integral part of a company's

---

[81] Some scholarship has suggested that stock-based executive remuneration can create systematic perverse incentives for senior managers to underinvest in compliance programs. See Armour, Gordon and Min 2020.

[82] See APRA 2018, 3.

[83] See, e.g., Summerhayes 2017; Price 2018.

[84] Jaeger 2021.

[85] See SEC 2022 (stating that 'investors representing literally tens of trillions of dollars support climate-related disclosures because they recognize that climate risks can pose significant financial risks to companies'). Cf. Pierce 2022.

[86] See, however, Maas 2018, 574 (stating that the concept of corporate social performance has been present in accounting and management literature for nearly half a century).

[87] Changing the Present, 'Quotes about agriculture', available at: https://bit.ly/48tmQXd.

[88] See HBR Editors 2014. See also HBR Editors 2019 (noting that that its ranking since 2015 of the best-performing CEOs in the world has related, not only to financial performance, but also to ESG ratings).

long-term value.[89] Firms adopt ESG-linked pay for various reasons, some of which are market-based and some of which are due to regulatory requirements.[90] These pressures form part of a complex 'global stewardship ecosystem'[91] that has, in recent years, helped ESG go 'mainstream'.[92]

International organisations associated with the United Nations ('UN') have played a particularly important norm-creating role in this area. For example, the UN-sponsored Global Compact,[93] which describes itself as 'the world's largest corporate sustainability initiative',[94] has undertaken various important projects involving sustainability, ESG and responsible investment.[95] Another prominent UN-affiliated organisation in this area is the Principles for Responsible Investment ('PRI'),[96] whose current strategic plan seeks, *inter alia*, to 'champion climate action'.[97] In 2016, the PRI released an influential paper, specifically tying ESG goals to executive pay.[98] The paper, which described the integration of ESG issues and executive pay as being 'in its infancy',[99] called on investors to play a larger role in achieving a 'holistic approach towards sustainable performance'[100] in relation to executive pay. The International Corporate Governance Network ('ICGN') has also highlighted the need for such an approach in the wake of the Covid-19 health crisis.[101]

Sustainable investment has increased dramatically in recent years.[102] So too has institutional investor engagement with companies on ESG matters,[103] and this now constitutes one of the most potent pressure points relating to ESG and

---

[89] See, e.g., Edmans 2022.

[90] See, e.g., PricewaterhouseCoopers, London Business School & Leadership Institute 2022, 3–6.

[91] See Bowley and Hill 2024b.

[92] See Edmans 2022, 2 (noting 'ESG's evolution from a niche subfield into a mainstream practice').

[93] In 1999, then-Secretary General, Kofi Annan, proposed that the UN and business leaders establish a 'global compact of shared values and principles'. See UN 1999. The Global Compact was officially launched in 2000. See UN 2000.

[94] See www.unglobalcompact.org/what-is-gc.

[95] Indeed, it appears that the Global Compact was the first to use the 'environmental, social and governance' term and its 'ESG' acronym. See Pargendler 2021, 1796; The Global Compact 2004. The 'Who Cares Wins' scheme was a joint initiative of the UN Global Compact and the Swiss Federal Department of Foreign Affairs.

[96] The PRI was launched by the Global Compact in 2006. See PRI, 'About the PRI', available at: www .unpri.org/pri/about-the-pri. The PRI is an investor initiative, which operates in partnership with the United Nations Environment Programme Finance Initiative ('UNEP Finance Initiative') and the UN Global Compact. See generally Bowley and Hill 2024b.

[97] PRI 2017, 9, 11.

[98] PRI 2016.

[99] Ibid., 4, 14.

[100] Ibid., 14.

[101] See ICGN 2020, 2. See also PricewaterhouseCoopers, London Business School & Leadership Institute 2022, 10 (noting the acceleration of ESG due to the Covid-19 crisis).

[102] See Sullivan and Bujno 2021 (noting that sustainable investing increased 43% between 2018 and 2021).

[103] See generally Bowley and Hill 2024a.

sustainable business practices.[104] This development is also reflected in international Shareholder Stewardship Codes, a growing number of which now explicitly refer to investors' ESG stewardship responsibilities,[105] with the 2020 UK Stewardship Code leading the way.[106]

Much of this pressure arises from institutional investors' concerns about the systemic financial risks,[107] particularly those associated with climate change, as exemplified by the 2020 activist campaign at ExxonMobil.[108] Such concerns are amplified for large, widely diversified institutional investors. This has led such investors to tackle negative externalities affecting their entire portfolio and they are increasingly willing to announce their commitment to ESG stewardship publicly in relation to matters such as emissions reductions.[109] The so-called 'Say on Climate' initiative for shareholders (which mirrors shareholders' 'Say on Pay' vote)[110] is another indication of this trend.[111] Numerous companies in Europe, the United States and the Asia-Pacific region have now adopted a 'Say on Climate' vote following shareholder pressure.[112]

Including ESG metrics in compensation packages is another way in which boards can signal their commitment to sustainability goals to investors and the market generally.[113] According to Hart and Zingales, the burgeoning ESG engagement by institutional investors represents a paradigm shift from 'shareholder value maximisation' to 'shareholder welfare maximisation'.[114]

ICGN has stressed that, although investors were traditionally more focussed on the link between pay and performance, in the era of Covid-19, they must also be attuned to issues related to the quantum of executive pay, inequality and fairness, and the connection to employee health and safety.[115] ICGN also supports the integration into executive pay of sustainability-performance factors, such as climate risk, which corporate executives 'can be held accountable for and directly influence'.[116]

---

[104] Indeed, shareholder interest in ESG matters is by no means limited to institutional investors. Millennial and Gen Z investors are equally focused on ESG. See PricewaterhouseCoopers, London Business School & Leadership Institute 2022, 3, 13; Bowley, Hill and Kourabas 2024.

[105] See generally Bowley and Hill 2024a.

[106] See FRC 2020, 2, 15 (Principle 7 requires signatories to report any ESG initiatives). See also Katelouzou and Klettner 2022.

[107] PricewaterhouseCoopers, London Business School & Leadership Institute 2022, 6.

[108] Although the campaign was spearheaded by a small hedge fund, Engine No. 1 LLC, large institutional investors were pivotal to the ultimate success of the campaign. See Bowley and Hill 2024a.

[109] See, e.g., Condon 2020; Coffee 2021; Gordon 2022.

[110] See, for example, Official Journal of the European Union 2017, Article 9(a), 'Right to vote on the remuneration policy'. See generally Thomas and van der Elst 2015.

[111] See Bowley and Hill 2024a; Galloway 2022.

[112] See generally Bowley and Hill 2024a.

[113] Bonham and Riggs-Cragun 2022.

[114] Hart and Zingales 2022.

[115] See ICGN 2020, 1–2.

[116] Ibid., 2.

Regulatory developments provide another pressure point in the ESG/sustainability stakes, with Europe a clear leader in this regard. Two recent European regulatory developments that may potentially prompt greater use of ESG-linked executive pay are the EU Taxonomy for Sustainable Activities (the 'EU Taxonomy')[117] and the proposed Directive on Corporate Sustainability Due Diligence ('CSDD').[118]

The EU Taxonomy is designed to be a uniform classification tool, predominantly focused on the environment. Its main goal is to promote sustainability and provide consistency in Europe by defining which economic activities are regarded as sustainable.[119] It has been said that the taxonomy is effectively the EU's answer to 'what is green?' for the purposes of achieving net zero carbon by 2050.[120] The EU Taxonomy also includes disclosure measures against sustainability, as opposed to merely financial, targets.[121]

The EU Platform on Sustainable Finance ('PSF') has recently explored extending the EU Taxonomy from environmental to social issues.[122] In its Final Report on Social Taxonomy,[123] the PSF stated that linking executive pay to ESG should constitute part of the EU Taxonomy given that it is already a widespread business practice in continental European and UK companies listed on major equity indices.[124]

The proposed CSDD, which constitutes another part of the EU's sustainable corporate governance initiative, imposes sustainability due diligence ('SDD') duties and liability risks[125] on corporate entities and their directors, who are defined to include members of senior management.[126] The proposed Directive also addresses ESG-related obligations in compensation design in Art. 15(3).[127] This provision has been described as essentially 'hortatory',[128] because there is no specified liability in the CSDD for failure to comply with the provision. Nonetheless, it is another potential pressure point that it may interact with ESG-related shareholder activism.[129]

---

[117] See Official Journal of the European Union 2020; European Commission, 'EU taxonomy for sustainable activities', available at: https://bit.ly/3OTOANL; EU Technical Expert Group on Sustainable Finance 2020.

[118] European Commission 2022.

[119] For a succinct summary of the EU Taxonomy's goals and structure, see Doyle 2021. See also PRI 2021.

[120] See Worldfavor, 'What Is the EU Taxonomy?', available at: https://blog.worldfavor.com/what-is-the-eu-taxonomy.

[121] See, e.g., comments by Will Martindale, PRI 2021.

[122] See PSF 2022. For a succinct discussion of the PSF 2022 report, see, e.g., Travers Smith 2022.

[123] PSF 2022.

[124] Ibid., 62.

[125] See generally ECGI and Stockholm School of Economics 2022.

[126] European Commission 2022, Art. 3(o)(i), which defines 'director' to mean 'any member of the administrative, management or supervisory bodies of a company'.

[127] European Commission 2022, Art. 15(3) requires Member States to ensure that companies 'duly take into account the fulfilment of…[certain obligations aligned with limiting emissions in accordance with the Paris Agreement] when setting variable remuneration, if variable remuneration is linked to the contribution of a director to the company's business strategy and long-term interests and sustainability'.

[128] See Armour 2022.

[129] Ibid.

Despite the momentum building for ESG-linked executive compensation (and that momentum is considerable),[130] enthusiasm for this development is by no means universal. Common arguments against pay for sustainability include the idea that extrinsic monetary rewards may 'crowd out' genuine motivations to behave in a pro-social way;[131] that ESG is already aligned with long-term business strategy, so that there is no need to measure and reward it separately;[132] that 'ESG' is an overly broad and ambiguous a concept,[133] ill-suited to serving as an effective benchmark;[134] and that ESG-linked executive pay may constitute a new soft 'money for jam' style of target.[135]

Another common criticism is that ESG-related pay simply promises more than it can deliver. For example, evidence is 'decidedly mixed'[136] as to whether companies that adopt ESG metrics in executive compensation lead to improved outcomes and the ability to outperform competitors.[137] Some empirical studies present a positive picture of the long-term effects of ESG-linked executive pay,[138] suggesting that it can break the focus on short-term shareholder profit maximisation,[139] in favour of long-term innovation and value creation.[140] Other studies, however, suggest that any clear causal link between ESG-linked executive pay and improved corporate social performance by corporations is elusive.[141]

Other concerns relating to sustainability and executive pay include fears that institutional investor ESG pressure will not necessarily persist;[142] that corporate greenwashing is an omnipresent risk;[143] that broad or vague ESG goals in executive pay are unlikely to be effective;[144] and that widespread adoption of ESG-linked executive

[130] According to one study, 82% of senior corporate leaders around the world now have ESG targets in their pay. See PricewaterhouseCoopers, London Business School & Leadership Institute 2022, 2.

[131] See, e.g., Winter 2012; PricewaterhouseCoopers, London Business School & Centre for Corporate Governance 2021, 6, 22.

[132] See PricewaterhouseCoopers, London Business School & Centre for Corporate Governance 2021, 11, 21; Gosling and O'Connor 2021.

[133] See Pollman 2021.

[134] See, e.g., PricewaterhouseCoopers, London Business School & Centre for Corporate Governance 2021, 6, 22 (distinguishing between 'old' and 'new' ESG performance measures).

[135] Maas 2018, 576.

[136] Edmans 2021.

[137] Cf. ibid.; Gore and Blood 2020. See also Koors, Meyer and Partners LLC 2019.

[138] See, e.g., Flammer, Hong and Minor 2019 (arguing that linking environmental and social performance goals to executive pay can enhance corporate governance by directing corporate managers' attention to 'stakeholders that are less salient but financially material to the firm in the long run'). Ibid. at 1098.

[139] But see, e.g., Lund and Pollman 2021 (describing the powerful 'shareholderist orientation' of the complex set of rules and processes that constitute the US 'corporate governance machine').

[140] Flammer, Hong and Minor 2019, 1100, 1103–04.

[141] Maas 2018.

[142] For example, BlackRock has recently indicated that it is unlikely to support climate change-related proposals it considers to be too onerous on companies, given the economic and geopolitical challenges resulting from the Russian invasion of Ukraine. See Masters 2022.

[143] See, e.g., Stobbe and Zimmerman 2022. See, e.g., Edmans, Gabaix and Jenter 2017, 387 (stating that '[a]ny high-powered incentive contract creates incentives to manipulate the performance measure(s) it relies upon').

[144] Flammer, Hong and Minor 2019, 1102.

pay could increase managerial power and executive payoffs, while simultaneously decreasing shareholder oversight.[145] Also, at this point in time, ESG-linked pay tends to represent only a relatively small proportion of total compensation packages[146] and therefore may fail to override a managerial focus on other short-term goals.

In spite of these concerns about the effectiveness of ESG-linked executive pay, studies, such as that by Cohen et al.,[147] suggests that it is no longer accurate to describe the phenomenon as being 'in its infancy'.[148] It is now considered to constitute 'good governance' and a growing number of major public corporations include ESG factors, such as reductions in greenhouse gas emissions, into their executive pay packages.[149] The next section of this chapter provides empirical evidence on the recent growth in ESG-linked executive compensation. It also examines the relevance of firm financial and corporate governance features on the adoption of ESG-linked pay.

9.3 HOW PREVALENT IS 'PAY FOR SUSTAINABLE PERFORMANCE' TODAY?

To change something, build a new model that makes the existing model obsolete.

R. Buckminster Fuller[150]

How widespread are sustainable performance factors in contemporary executive compensation contracts? To investigate the frequency and the determinants of the adoption of compensation policies linked to sustainability metrics, we built a large panel of listed firms selected from the Refinitiv Asset4 database over the period 2002–2021. Starting from an unbalanced panel of 8,649 publicly traded firms, covering 58 countries and 19 industrial sectors, we selected all firms with available data on the link of executive compensation to ESG performance.

The Asset4 database includes two closely related variables on this issue: 'Sustainability Compensation Incentives' and 'Policy Executive Compensation ESG Performance'. Although according to their definitions they are expected to be closely correlated,[151] the behaviour of the variable 'Sustainability Compensation

---

[145] Bebchuk and Tallarita 2022.

[146] See Flammer, Hong and Minor 2019, 1101; PricewaterhouseCoopers, London Business School & Leadership Institute 2022, 15 (noting that average ESG weightings are currently around 10%, but that investors are pushing for an increase to 20%).

[147] Cohen et al. 2022, p. 1 and fn 1.

[148] PRI 2016.

[149] See, e.g., Flammer, Hong and Minor 2019, 1098 (noting that Alcoa, American Electric Power, Intel, Novo Nordisk and Xcel Energy now integrate CSR criteria into executive pay). See also Gadinis and Miazad 2020, 1407, 1419 (noting that companies such as Microsoft, Pepsi, Walmart, BP, Total and Chevron integrate ESG targets in executive pay). See generally, ibid., 1419–22.

[150] Cited in Breckenridge 2020.

[151] 'Sustainability Compensation Incentives' (Eikon Code = TR.AnalyticCSRCompIncentives), is defined as 'Is the senior executive's compensation linked to CSR/H&S/Sustainability targets?', while 'Policy Executive Compensation ESG Performance' (code = TR.PolicyExecComp-ESGPerformance)

Incentives' raises some concerns about its quality, regarding its consistency and dynamics.[152] We therefore decided to select 'Policy Executive Compensation ESG Performance' as our main dependent variable of interest.

We detected that quite a large number of firms show multiple changes in the compensation policy for the variable 'Policy Executive Compensation ESG Performance'. Since we are interested in evaluating the determinants of a stable adoption of ESG-linked pay, we decided to delete all the firms with multiple changes of the variable (473 firms), obtaining a final number of 1,903 adopters that were contrasted with all non-adopters included in the Asset4 database.[153]

The final sample is a panel composed of 53,602 firm-year observations, and 6,863 firms. This data set has a considerably larger size than the samples exploited in previous studies[154] and covers a relatively long period of time. This allows us to propose, to the best of our knowledge, the first global study on the determinants for ESG-linked executive compensation.

We begin our discussion with some descriptive statistics and an analysis of several 'macro-determinants' for ESG compensation. We then focus on the impact of firm financial and corporate governance characteristics on the likelihood of adopting an ESG-linked compensation policy.

9.3.1 *Macro-Determinants of ESG Compensation*

A growing number of listed firms included drivers related to sustainable performance in their executive remuneration packages. As shown in Figure 9.1a, at the beginning of the first decade only a small fraction of firms adopted a compensation policy linked to ESG issues, and this proportion further decreased in the wake of the

states if the company has the ESG compensation policy ('Does the company have an extra-financial performance-oriented compensation policy? The compensation policy includes remuneration for the CEO, executive directors, non-board executives, and other management bodies based on ESG or sustainability factors').

[152] The variable 'Sustainability Compensation Incentives' is focused on senior executives while 'Policy Executive Compensation ESG Performance' covers a broader range of managers (the CEO, executive directors, non-board executives and other management bodies), so it could be argued that the second variable should be TRUE when the former is TRUE. However, about 5% of data-points show 'Sustainability Compensation Incentives = TRUE' while 'Policy Executive Compensation ESG Performance = FALSE'. Furthermore, for 'Sustainability Compensation Incentives' this variable shows a very large volatility both at the aggregate level (the proportion of firms that adopted the policy drops from 33% in 2012 to 9% in 2016, while it remains quite stable for 'Policy Executive Compensation ESG Performance') and at firm level (on average, according to the variable 'Sustainability Compensation Incentives' firms changed their compensation policy 2.33 times, versus only 1.29 times for the variable 'Policy Executive Compensation ESG Performance').

[153] We also find 118 firms that discontinued the use of ESG compensation policies. Due to space constraints, they will not be studied in this chapter.

[154] Maas and Rosendaal 2016, analysed a cross-section of 490 listed firms in 2010; Derchi et al. 2021, selected a panel of 5,070 firm-year observations corresponding to 848 US-based firms for the period 2002–2013; Cohen et al. 2022, analysed a global panel of 22,603 firm-years observations and 4,395 firms.

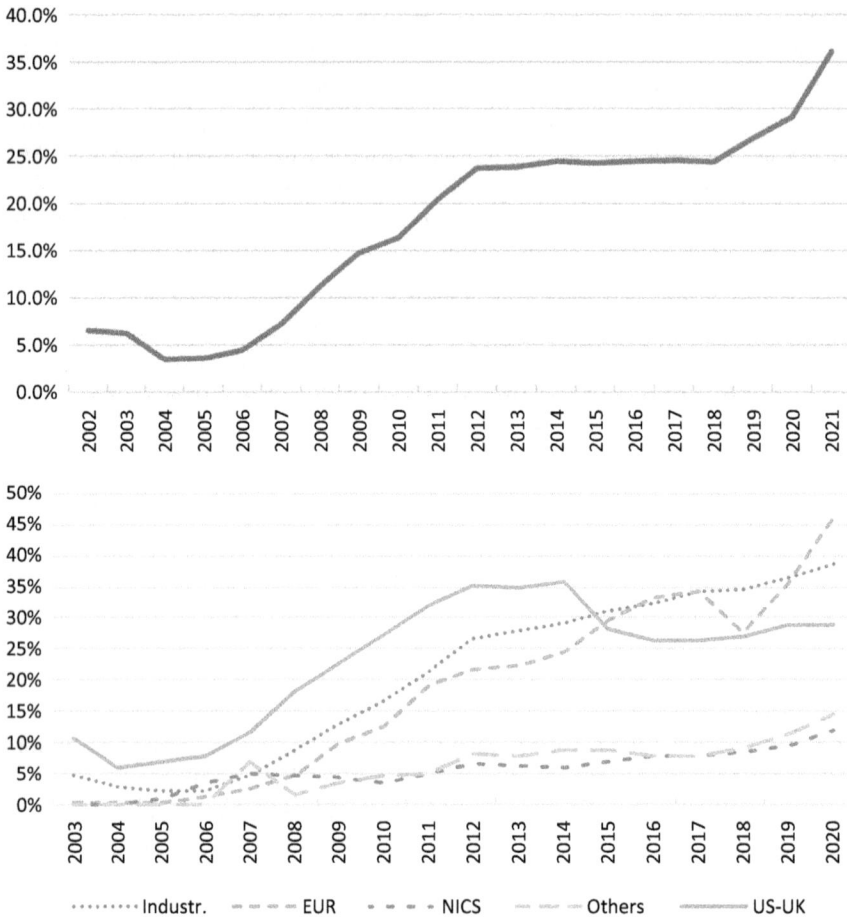

FIGURE 9.1 Dynamics of ESG-linked executive compensation: (a) global dynamics; (b) dynamics by region

early 2000s recession. Since 2006 the increase in the adoption of sustainable compensation has been impressive, from 4.4% to 36.1% in 2021.

This global picture can be better interpreted if we consider the behaviour of firms headquartered in different countries. Figure 9.1b shows that firms in the United States and United Kingdom, which are the most important stock market-oriented economies, led the other countries in the first half of the period examined. However, in the following years, although ESG-linked executive compensation continued to increase in the United Kingdom, its rate of adoption in the United States stabilized and then shrank by more than 5%.

In Western Europe and, to a lesser extent, in other industrialised countries, the positive trend has been vigorous. Following the proposal of the Green Deal,

European firms increased the adoption of some form of sustainable compensation from 35% to around 60%, filling the gap from UK firms.

Newly Industrialised Countries (NICS) and the residual group of less developed countries (Others) show very similar dynamics in the average adoption of ESG compensation. They present much lower values than more developed countries, even though a notable increase can be observed in recent years.

It is noteworthy, however, that individual countries show a significant discrepancy within each cluster; in particular, the 'Other Industrial Countries' cluster includes nations with quite limited average values (Argentina, Japan, Russian Federation, Turkey) and a few countries – Australia, South Africa and to a lesser extent, Canada – with a very high percentage of ESG-linked executive pay. Australia, with a stunning average of 53% over the whole period, is the country with the most frequent use of ESG executive compensation, a result probably influenced by the large proportion of firms operating in sectors with significant environmental impact.

The frequency in the use of ESG executive compensation could indeed be influenced by specific institutional features,[155] but it could also be related to its sectoral specialisation, since a large proportion of firms with significant environmental impact can be associated with a broader diffusion of ESG pay. As expected, Figure 9.2 shows that firms operating in industries with higher CO_2 emissions or other environmental concerns (Fossil Fuels, Mineral Resources and Utilities) had a spectacular increase in the adoption of ESG compensation policies.

In sum, this descriptive analysis confirms the significant impact of common factors related to time, country and industrial sector on employing compensation policies[156] linked to sustainability metrics. In the following analysis, which seeks to identify factors correlated to the adoption of ESG compensation, we remove the effect of these common factors by applying a battery of dummy variables in all our econometric estimates.

The first test we perform is aimed at understanding if the adoption of ESG-linked executive compensation is related to global economic conditions, highlighted by stock market returns. If the probability of adopting sustainable compensation practices should be negatively related to stock market returns, it could be argued that ESG policies are used to substitute the impact of the crisis on traditional stock-based compensation. We therefore estimated the following logit regression:

$$\text{ESG\_comp}_{i,t} = b_0 + b_1 \text{ Mkt\_ret}_{i,t} + B_2 \text{ Sector}_i + e_{i,t}$$

where ESG_comp is a variable that takes the value of 1 when the firm adopts a compensation policy linked to extra-financial performance, 0 otherwise (obviously, firms

[155] Institutional and social features like legal origin, stronger political institutions, regulations and social preferences are significant predictors of CSR adoption and performance at the firm level. See, e.g., Liang and Renneboog 2017.

[156] For a cross-country analysis of differences in the level and structure of executive compensation see Barontini et al. 2013, Conyon et al. 2013.

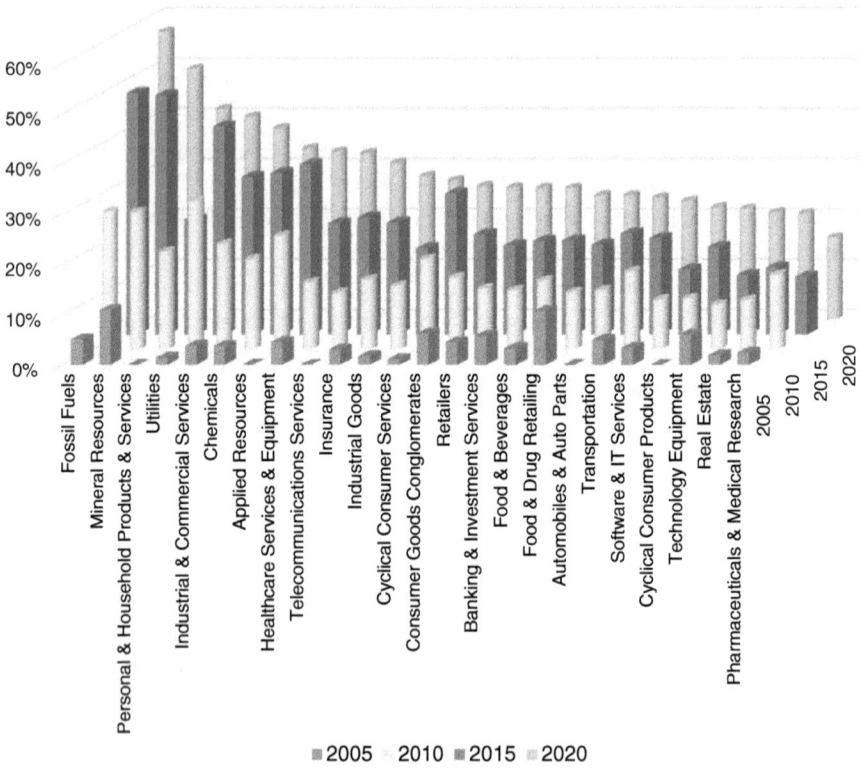

FIGURE 9.2 The adoption of ESG-linked executive compensation, by industry

that already adopted the ESG compensation policy are excluded from the sample); Mkt_ret is, alternatively, the global stock market index MSCI WORLD or MSCI indexes of the corresponding geographic areas; Sector is a battery of dummy variables that identify the business sector of each firm.[157]

Quite surprisingly, estimates for both regressions are negative and statistically significant (for the global index, $b_1 = -0.4184^{***}$; for local indexes $b_1 = -0.5291^{***}$), showing that lower stock returns are associated to a higher likelihood of the adoption of an ESG compensation policy. In this simple specification, it cannot be ruled out that a bias due to omitted variables may affect the results. However, within the agency framework, they could be consistent with the objective of ensuring the compensation affected by a low stock-based pay.

The second test is aimed at estimating the impact of institutional characteristics on ESG-linked compensation policies. We try to explain if the considerable differences among economic areas previously shown in Figure 9.1 can be at least partially

[157] We apply the four-digit business classification of Refinitiv, made up of 30 classes (the reference sector is '5010 = Fossil Fuels').

TABLE 9.1 *Government quality and the adoption of ESG compensation policies*

WGI variable	Coefficient	Std error
Democratic Freedom	+0.2772***	0.0238
Government Effectiveness	+0.0255	0.0161
Regulatory Quality	+0.1772***	0.0227
Rule of Law	+0.2448***	0.0208
Corruption Control	+0.1687***	0.0186
Political Stability	+0.0620***	0.0216

Year and sector fixed effects (always statistically significant) omitted for brevity.
* $p < 0.10$; ** $p < 0.05$; *** $p < 0.01$.

explained by the characteristics of the institutional environment at individual country level[158]. Using the Worldwide Governance Indicators (WGIs) as a proxy of government quality,[159] we estimated the following logit regressions:

$$\text{ESG\_comp}_{i,t} = b_0 + b_1\,\text{WGI}_{i,t} + B_2\,\text{Sector}_i + B_3\,\text{Year}_t + e_{i,t}$$

in which the WGI variables capture the estimates of Democratic Freedom, Government Effectiveness, Regulatory Quality, Rule of Law, Corruption Control, Political Stability, and Absence of Terrorism (Political Stability).[160] Since individual WGIs are quite highly correlated, we included each variable in the logit regressions separately, obtaining the results included in Table 9.1.

All the World Governance Indicators are positively and significantly (with the exclusion of Government Effectiveness, whose p-value is 11.3%) correlated with the adoption of ESG-linked compensation policy. Since all these indicators of governance performance are standardised – they range from approximately −2.5 (weak) to 2.5 (strong) – the larger coefficients of Democratic Freedom[161] and Rule of Law[162] signal a higher impact on the likelihood of adopting an ESG-related compensation scheme.

These results are in line with other studies, showing that the quality of country regulation or corruption control is positively related to a firm's environmental

---

[158] For a cross-country analysis on the link between the level of investor protection and CEO compensation see Bozzi, Barontini and Miroshnychenko 2017.

[159] World Bank discloses the indicators at https://info.worldbank.org/governance/wgi.

[160] In the prior literature that used these variables see Chen et al. 2014; Ding, Qu and Wu 2016; Miroshnychenko et al. 2021.

[161] Democratic Freedom corresponds to the variable Voice and Accountability and reflects perceptions of the extent to which a country's citizens are able to participate in selecting their government, as well as freedom of expression, freedom of association and a free media.

[162] Rule of Law '[r]eflects perceptions of the extent to which agents have confidence in and abide by the rules of society, and in particular the quality of contract enforcement, property rights, the police, and the courts, as well as the likelihood of crime and violence'.

practices and ESG disclosure.[163] According to institutional theory, in countries with
high government quality, firms could be induced to adopt ESG compensation to
seek legitimacy and respond to the pressures exerted by stakeholders.[164]

9.3.2 *Financial and Corporate Governance Firm Characteristics*

After the analysis of global economic and institutional effects on the adoption of
sustainable compensation policies, we focus on individual variables covering the
financial, corporate governance and ESG profile of the firm. The definition of the
variables is included in Appendix, Table 9.A1.

Since the estimation of a multiple regression, including all the control variables,
could be affected by collinearity and missing data problems, we start by exploring,
for each independent variable X, the following logit regression:

$$\text{ESG\_comp}_{i,t} = b_0 + b_1\, X_{i,t-1} + B_2\, \text{Sector}_i + B_3\, \text{Country}_i + B_4\, \text{Year}_{t-1} + e_{i,t}$$

which also includes fixed effects for sector, country and year. In all regressions,
explanatory variables X are lagged because their causal effect on the change in the
compensation policy is assumed to occur gradually.

For the sake of brevity, coefficients of the dummy variables will always be omitted.
It is worth noting, however, that they are always statistically significant, confirming
our previous discussion on 'macro-determinants' of ESG compensation. Obviously,
since the impact of county, sector and business cycle fluctuations is captured by this
set of dummy variables, the coefficients of the explanatory variables should be interpreted as a pure, differential effect within each firm's cluster.

9.3.2.1 Financial Variables

Starting with financial variables, we selected widely used proxies of firm size (computed as the log of Total Assets), profitability (Return on Investments and Return
on Assets), valuation (Market to Book Value), employee 'intensity' and growth
(Employee/Total Assets and Employees 1Year Growth), firm growth (Sales 1Year
Growth) and financial leverage (Debt/Equity ratio).

As expected, results in Table 9.2 show that Size is strongly correlated with the
adoption of ESG compensation policies. Large companies operate in a complex
net of relationships and could be more influenced by external pressures on ESG
strategies. Large firms, therefore, could be induced to implement a compensation
policy linked to sustainability drivers, with the aim of aligning manager actions to
stakeholders' preferences.

---

[163] See, e.g., Fredriksson and Svensson 2003; Cahan et al. 2016; Ioannou and Serafeim 2012; Boura,
     Tsouknidis and Lioukas 2020.
[164] Delmas and Toffel 2008.

TABLE 9.2 *Financial variables and the adoption of ESG compensation policies*

Independent variable	Coefficient	Std error
Size	+0.2632***	0.0215
Return on Investments	+1.0613***	0.2937
Return on Assets	+0.0123***	0.0034
Market To Book Value	−0.0051	0.0137
Sales 1Y Growth	−0.0015	0.0015
Employee/Total Assets	−9.1994	8.2544
Employees 1Y Growth	−0.0028	0.0021
Debt/Equity ratio	+0.0004	0.0005

Country, year and sector fixed effects (always statistically significant) omitted for brevity.
* $p < 0.10$; ** $p < 0.05$; *** $p < 0.01$.

The positive coefficients of Return on Investments and Return on Assets show that, after taking into account the average profitability captured by the sector, country and year fixed effects, relatively more profitable firms are induced to include ESG incentives in executive pay. This result could be associated with different explanations: shareholders can try to induce a long-term strategy when it is perceived as financially sustainable, given the actual positive economic returns. On the other hand, managers can take the opportunity to increase their remuneration in a less transparent way, adopting a new form of 'camouflage compensation' when good financial results lessen shareholder control.[165]

The other financial variables are not statistically significant. Indicators linked to firm growth, and therefore a long-term orientation (Market to Book Value and Sales 1Y Growth), are not correlated with the decision to adopt ESG-linked compensation policies. Quite surprisingly, the same result emerges for firms with a higher ratio between the number of employees and Total Assets or those that report an increase in the number of employees.

9.3.2.2 Corporate Governance Variables

Table 9.3 shows the results obtained for a set of Corporate Governance indicators on the adoption of ESG compensation policies, focussing on variables that capture the characteristics of the board of directors and its interaction with shareholders on compensation issues.

[165] Adding the lagged stock market returns to this regression, both Return of Investments and Return on Assets confirm the results included in Table 2, while the variable 'Local Stock Market Returns' has negative and statistically significant coefficients – respectively −1.3846 (p-value 1.39%) and −1.3566 (p-value 1.58%). This evidence, which confirms the preliminary result at macro-level, could signal the aim to substitute stock-based compensation with ESG drivers when market returns are low.

TABLE 9.3 *Corporate governance variables and the adoption of ESG compensation policies*

Independent variable	Coefficient	Std Error
Board Size	0.0345***	0.0084
Board Diversity	0.0184***	0.0021
Executives Gender Diversity %	0.0060***	0.0018
Non-Executive Board Members %	0.0118***	0.0021
Independence Board Members %	0.0101***	0.0014
Board Meeting Attendance Average	0.0137***	0.0038
Board Specific Skills	−0.0017	0.0012
Experienced Board	−0.0320***	0.0074
Chairman is Ex-CEO	−0.0344	0.0305
CEO-Chairman Duality	−0.0436	0.0295
Anti-Takeover Devices	−0.0017	0.0145
Shareholders' Approval of Stock Comp.	−0.0072	0.0316
Shareholders' Vote on Executive Pay	−0.0169	0.0305
CSR Sustainability Committee	0.3318***	0.0273

Country, year and sector fixed effects (always statistically significant) omitted for brevity.

* $p < 0.10$; ** $p < 0.05$; *** $p < 0.01$.

The variable Board Size, as expected, is strongly correlated to ESG pay. This result is however linked to the effect of firm size, and if both variables are included in the same regression, only the latter remains statistically significant. After taking into account the size of the firm, larger boards of directors do not seem to be more oriented towards the adoption of sustainable compensation.

The four variables capturing the diversity and independence of board members are all significantly correlated to the adoption of ESG compensation. The effect of gender diversity on firms' ESG profile has been recently studied in the literature, often finding a positive relationship[166] that can be driven by the environmentally-friendly attitudes and more effective environmental actions of female directors.[167] Our results confirm this picture, showing that the adoption of remuneration policies linked to sustainability drivers is more likely with a higher female representation on the board.

Similarly, the association of a high ratio of non-executive or independent board members with the adoption of ESG compensation is consistent with previous literature. A large proportion of non-executive and independent directors provides alternative views of ESG strategies compared to insiders, taking into account the perspective of external stakeholders. By monitoring executives, these directors encourage decisions aimed at maximising long-term value, also through the adoption of environmental

[166] Bear, Rahman and Post 2010; Post, Rahman and Rubow 2011; Li et al. 2017.
[167] See Liu 2018; Cosma et al. 2021. Liu 2018, in particular, finds that US firms with high board gender diversity are sued less often for environmental infringements.

and CSR practices.[168] The positive correlation between board independence and the adoption of ESG compensation is therefore consistent with this literature.

The variables Board Meeting Attendance, Board Specific Skills and Experienced Board explore the relationship between the implementation of sustainable pay and, respectively, the activity of the board and competencies of its members. As could be expected, frequent participation in board meetings signals a proactive management style that is also focussed on ESG strategy and related incentives. On the other hand, the variable Specific Skills – i.e., the percentage of board members who have either an industry-specific background or a strong financial background – is not statistically significant, while a negative impact is associated with the variable Experienced Board, which captures the average tenure of board members. Long-term relationships, probably linked to the presence of strategic blockholders, could in fact be associated with lower (both financial and ESG) variable compensation, due to the alignment of incentives determined by ownership concentration.[169]

The next five variables in Table 9.3 capture the effect of the power of top managers (or the impact of a tight shareholder control) on the probability of adoption of ESG compensation. When there is strong managerial control – e.g., when the Chair is (or has been) the CEO of the company, or when top managers are protected by multiple anti-takeover devices – a negative impact can be expected on the adoption of ESG incentives, because managers are less exposed to stakeholder pressure. By way of contrast, shareholders' approval of executive compensation plans is expected to be associated with implementation of ESG drivers within incentive pay schemes. Nevertheless, none of these variables are statistically significant.

The last independent variable in Table 9.3 captures the presence of the CSR Sustainability Committee. Previous literature detects a significant role of CSR committees in supporting the achievement of better non-financial performance.[170] As expected, our results show a positive effect of the CSR Committee on the adoption of ESG compensation, which could be a driver for a change in the firm strategy towards sustainability.

9.3.2.3 ESG Performance and Communication

In this section, we conclude our empirical analysis by showing the relationship between previous ESG performance and the adoption of ESG compensation policies. We also analyse whether companies that do not 'walk their green talk' – i.e., those

---

[168] In previous literature, independent directors have been associated to compliance with environmental standards (Johnson and Greening 1999; Post, Rahman and Rubow 2011; Mallin, Michelon and Raggi 2013) and improved CSR (Cuadrado-Ballesteros, Rodríguez-Ariza and García-Sánchez 2015).

[169] For example, Mehran 1995 and Ryan and Wiggins 2001 find that blockholder ownership is negatively related to stock option compensation.

[170] For example, Baraibar-Diez, Odriozola and Sánchez 2019 find that sustainable compensation policies affect environmental performance especially when firms have a corporate social responsibility committee.

TABLE 9.4 *ESG scores and the adoption of pay for sustainable performance*

Independent variable	Coefficient	Std error
ESG Score	0.0227***	0.0016
Environmental Score	0.0138***	0.0012
Social Score	0.0168***	0.0014
Corporate Governance Score	0.0151***	0.0013
ESG Controversies Score	−0.0060***	0.0013

Country, year and sector fixed effects (always statistically significant) omitted for brevity.
* $p < 0.10$; ** $p < 0.05$; *** $p < 0.01$.

that present a misalignment between environmental practices and green communication have a higher propensity to adopt ESG compensation.

The ESG performance is summarised thanks to the scoring methodology developed by Refinitiv on a large number of individual data-points included in Asset4. Refinitiv provides several score measures, from which we selected the ESG score and the specific Environmental, Social and Governance pillars. A Controversies Score is also available, which captures how scandals and legal disputes are published in the media. All scores have values between 0 and 100 and are calculated as percentile rankings that are weighted and combined into a single ESG score.[171]

Table 9.4 shows that the Global ESG score is statistically significant, revealing that firms adopting ESG-linked executive compensation in the previous year already had a better ESG profile compared to all non-adopters in the same year/sector/country cluster. The effect is similar for each pillar score, so it could be argued that the implementation of sustainable incentive schemes is more likely for firms with better pre-existing Environmental, Social or Governance profiles.

Somewhat surprisingly, the ESG Controversies Score is negatively related to the adoption of ESG compensation. Since a better firm profile is coded with higher values (companies with no controversies will get a score of 100), it seems that firms with significant controversies have been induced to give further incentives to the managers related to ESG characteristics.

As previously discussed, the adoption of ESG compensation has been criticised due to the possibility that it could disguise and exacerbate the agency problem of

---

[171] Starting from 186 variables, the scoring process obtains 10 category scores which represent several environmental, social and governance firm characteristics. To calculate the category scores, a percentile ranking methodology is adopted, aimed at assigning scores which are based on the performance of other firms in the same industry. The category scores are then rolled up into three pillar scores which correspond to the main ESG dimensions. To consider the importance of the ESG themes in different industries, a proprietary ESG Magnitude Matrix is implemented in the form of category weights. Similarly, the pillar scores are summed up to originate the aggregated ESG score which provides a general indication of the ESG performance of the firm. For additional information on the Refinitiv ESG methodology see: Refinitiv 2022.

TABLE 9.5 *Environmental performance, communication and the adoption of ESG compensation policies*

Independent Variable	Coefficient	Std Error
Green Performance Index	0.3903***	0.0462
Green Communication Index	0.5387***	0.0463
Discrepancy Index	0.2311***	0.0548
{ Discrepancy index	0.4947***	0.0599
{ Green Performance Index	0.5649***	0.0515

Country, year and sector fixed effects (always statistically significant) omitted for brevity.
* $p < 0.10$; ** $p < 0.05$; *** $p < 0.01$.

executive pay.[172] As regards the environmental profile, these conflicts could induce greenwashing practices, or simply a misalignment between environmental practices and green communication. In order to check if the adoption of sustainable compensation policy is correlated with this discrepancy, we used the Green Performance (GPI) and Green Communication (GCI) indices, and computed the discrepancy index (DI) as their difference.[173]

More specifically, the Green Performance Index (GPI) is computed as the average of the following green practices: pollution prevention, green supply chain management and green product. The Green Communication Index (GCI) is estimated as the average of a company's integration/vision and strategy KPIs, which proxy for the firm's commitment that has been disclosed about the development of an overarching vision and strategy. The Green Communication Index proxies the firm's capacity to competently display and communicate that financial, social and environmental dimensions are integrated in its daily decision making.

We trace firms where green communication efforts diverge from green practices implementation, computing a discrepancy index (DI) that reflects the difference between firm's green communication and operational practices. Both components have been standardised to have a mean of 0 and a standard deviation of 1, thereby ensuring their comparability in the derivation of the discrepancy index DI. Therefore, a DI lower than zero would suggest that a firm has a 'Walker' attitude since more green practices are implemented compared to environmental communications. Conversely, a DI higher than zero would suggest a 'Talker' approach, more focussed on external communication than real practices.

Results in Table 9.5 show that Green Performance is positively related to the adoption of ESG-related pay, confirming the results obtained with the

---

[172] Bebchuk and Tallarita 2022.
[173] We refer to Miroshnychenko, Barontini and Testa 2017 and Testa et al. 2018 for a detailed description of the variables used to compute the indices.

Environmental Score. Nonetheless, the effect of Green Communication is stronger, and also the coefficient of the Discrepancy Index is positive and statistically significant. In both DI and GPI regressions, misalignment is confirmed as significantly correlated with the adoption of ESG compensation schemes.

9.4 CONCLUSION

ESG issues have become much more important for us as long-term investors.

Cyrus Taraporevala, State Street Global Investors[174]

This chapter reviews theories, regulation and empirical analyses of executive compensation from a historical and international perspective, while also providing new evidence on the adoption of ESG targets in executive pay packages.

We start by examining some of the reasons underlying the rise of the performance-based compensation, which was proposed as a powerful tool aimed to align managerial interests with those of the company's shareholders within large corporations with dispersed ownership. The US trend toward higher pay quickly spread to other economic environments, such as continental Europe, where concentrated ownership, which creates conflicts between majority and minority shareholders, is prevalent. Furthermore, corporate scandals in the early 2000s and the 2007–2009 global financial crisis provoked vigorous debate about the design of performance-based pay and, in some jurisdictions, a strong regulatory response, particularly from Banking Supervisors.

More recently, increased attention to sustainability (especially for risks related to climate change) has led firms to focus on stakeholders' preferences regarding sustainability and has led to greater integration of ESG targets in executive compensation. As a result of pressure from both regulators and institutional investors, this trend has spread quickly across industrialised countries, with the goal of increasing corporate commitment to ESG values. However, the response to these pressures could ultimately be ineffective. There exists a risk, for example, that ESG-related pay might actually increase managerial power and executive payoffs, giving rise to a new form of extraction of private benefits.

The final section of our chapter looks at the prevalence today of ESG-linked executive pay. It provides new empirical evidence on the adoption of compensation policies linked to sustainability metrics, analysing a panel of 8,649 publicly traded firms, covering 58 countries and 19 industrial sectors, in the period 2002–2021. We show that a growing number of listed firms included drivers related to sustainable performance in their executive remuneration packages, with notable differences related to sector and country characteristics. In particular, using the Worldwide Governance Indicators as a proxy of institutional quality, we find that, in countries with better government features, firms are more likely to adopt ESG compensation.

---

[174] Cited in ILO 2021.

Focussing on individual financial and governance characteristics, we find a direct relationship between ESG pay and firm size, as well as with accounting returns. We do not, however, find such a relationship between ESG pay and market valuations and returns, or variables capturing firm growth. This evidence seems inconsistent with a correlation between a long-term perspective and the adoption of ESG compensation. Future research could therefore examine this issue more directly, considering the impact of ESG compensation on long-term ESG and financial performance, a topic on which the literature shows mixed results.

Moreover, many characteristics of the board of directors seem clearly related to the adoption of ESG compensation. Variables capturing the diversity and independence of board members are all statistically significant, confirming that a board which is concerned with the perspective of external stakeholders will be more supportive of adopting remuneration incentives linked to ESG practices.

Finally, we analyse the relationship between previous ESG performance and the adoption of a sustainable compensation policy. We find that firms are more likely to employ ESG-linked executive pay when they already have a significant global ESG profile, and better scores in specific Environmental, Social or Governance profiles. We also find that companies that do not appear to be 'walking their green talk', i.e., those that present a misalignment between environmental practices and green communication, have a higher propensity to adopt ESG compensation.

The evidence on the factors related to the adoption of ESG compensation therefore presents a mixed picture. There has clearly been dramatic growth in ESG-linked executive pay in recent times. However, given the risk of agency problems and greenwashing, it as yet unclear whether this trend will continue and translate into more sustainable corporate practices in the future.

APPENDIX

TABLE 9.A1 *Explanatory variables*

Variable	Description
Size	Firm's size proxied by the log of Total Assets.
Return on Investments	The ratio between EBIT (Earnings Before Interests & Taxes) and Total Assets.
Return on Assets	The ratio between operating income after taxes and Total Assets.
Market To Book Value	The ratio of Equity Market Value to Equity Book Value.
Sales 1Y Growth	1 year growth of Net sales or revenues.
Employee/Total Assets	The ratio between the number of employees and Total Assets.
Employees 1Y Growth	1 year growth of the number of employees.
Debt/Equity ratio	The ratio between Total Financial Debt and Book Equity Value.

(continued)

TABLE 9.A1 *(continued)*

Variable	Description
Board Size	The number of Board Members.
Board Diversity	Is there female representation on the board OR is there foreign culture representation on the board? (% board members)
Executive Members Gender Diversity %	Percentage of female executive members.
Non-Executive Board Members %	Percentage of non-executive board members.
Independent Board Members	Percentage of independent board members, as reported by the company.
Board Meeting Attendance Average	The average overall attendance percentage of board meetings as reported by the company.
Board Specific Skills	Percentage of board members who have either an industry specific background or a strong financial background.
Experienced Board	Average number of years each board member has been on the board.
Chairman is Ex-CEO	Has the chairman previously held the CEO position in the company?
CEO-Chairman Duality	Does the CEO simultaneously chair the board OR has the chairman of the board been the CEO of the company?
Anti-Takeover Devices	The number of anti-takeover devices in place in excess of two.
Shareholders' Approval of Stock Compensation Plan	Does the company require that shareholder approval is obtained prior to the adoption of any stock-based compensation plan? – relates to any stock-based compensation plan approval or the renewal of an existing plan by shareholders.
Shareholders' Vote on Executive Pay	Do the company's shareholders have the right to vote on executive compensation?
CSR Sustainability Committee	Does the company have a CSR committee or team?
ESG Score	Overall company score based on the self-reported information in the environmental, social and corporate governance pillars.
Environment Pillar	Weighted average relative rating of a company based on reported environmental information and the resulting three environmental category scores.
Social Pillar	Weighted average relative rating of a company based on reported social information and the resulting four social category scores.
Governance Pillar	Weighted average relative rating of a company based on reported governance information and the resulting three governance category scores.
ESG Controversies Score	Measures a company's exposure to environmental, social and governance controversies and negative events reflected in global media.
Green Performance Index	GPI, the index of Green Operational Practices, as described in Miroshnychenko, Barontini and Testa (2017).
Green Communication Index	GCI, the index of Green Communication Practices, as described in Miroshnychenko, Barontini and Testa (2017).
Discrepancy Index	The Discrepancy Index, computed as the difference between GCI and GPI.

REFERENCES

Allen, W. T. (1992), 'Our schizophrenic concept of the business corporation', 14 *Cardozo Law Review*, 261.

APRA, Australian Prudential Regulation Authority (2018), 'Prudential Inquiry into the Commonwealth Bank of Australia', 30 April, available at: https://bit.ly/42NBtDs.

Armour, J. (2016a), 'Volkswagen's emissions scandal: Lessons for corporate governance? (Part 1)', *Oxford Business Law Blog*, 17 May, available at: https://bit.ly/3wtWHuo.

Armour, J. (2016b), 'Volkswagen's emissions scandal: Lessons for corporate governance? (Part 2)', *Oxford Business Law Blog*, 18 May, available at: https://bit.ly/3wtWPcY.

Armour, J. (2022), 'Directors' duties and climate remuneration', presentation at Online Policy Workshop on European Commission Directive on Corporate Sustainability Due Diligence, 28–29 March, available at: https://bit.ly/3uAos3x.

Armour, J., Gordon, J. N. and Min, G. (2020), 'Taking compliance seriously', 37 *Yale Journal on Regulation*, 1.

Avgouleas, E. (2009), 'The Global Financial Crisis, behavioural finance and financial regulation: In search of a new orthodoxy', 9 *Journal of Corporate Law Studies*, 23.

Baraibar-Diez, E., Odriozola, M. D. and Fernández Sánchez, J. L. (2019), 'Sustainable compensation policies on environmental, social, and governance scores', 26 *Corporate Social Responsibility and Environmental Management*, 1457.

Barontini, R. and Bozzi, S. (2011), 'Board compensation and ownership structure: Empirical evidence for Italian listed companies', 15 *Journal of Management and Governance*, 59.

Barontini, R., Bozzi, S., Ferrarini, G. and Ungureanu, M. C. (2013), 'Directors' remuneration before and after the crisis: Measuring the impact of reforms in Europe' in Belcredi, M. and Ferrarini, G. (eds.), *Boards and Shareholders in European Listed Companies* (Cambridge, UK: Cambridge University Press), 251.

Barontini, R. and Caprio, L. (2006), 'The effect of family control on firm value performance: Evidence from continental Europe', 12 *European Financial Management*, 689.

Bear, S., Rahman, N. and Post, C. (2010), 'The impact of board diversity and gender composition on corporate social responsibility and firm behaviour', 97 *Journal of Business Ethics*, 207.

Bebchuk, L. A. and Grinstein Y. (2005), 'The growth of executive pay', 21 *Oxford Review of Economic Policy*, 283.

Bebchuk, L. A. and Spamann, H. (2010), 'Regulating bankers' pay', 98 *Georgetown Law Journal*, 247.

Bebchuk, L. A. and Tallarita, R. (2022), 'The perils and questionable promise of ESG-based compensation', 48 *Journal of Corporation Law*, 37–75.

BIS (Department for Business Innovation & Skills) (2010), 'A long-term focus for corporate Britain: A call for evidence', October, available at: https://bit.ly/3SSt9xF.

Bonham, J. and Riggs-Cragun, A. (2022), 'An accounting framework for ESG reporting', Working Paper, cited in Cohen, S., Kadach, I., Ormazabal, G and Reichelstein, S. (2022), 'Executive compensation tied to ESG performance: International evidence', ECGI Finance Working Paper No. 825/2022, April, available at: https://bit.ly/3wz1o73.

Boura, M., Tsouknidis, D. A. and Lioukas, S. (2020), 'The role of pro-social orientation and national context in corporate environmental disclosure', 17 *European Management Review*, 1027.

Bowley, T. and Hill J. G. (2024a), 'Stewardship codes, ESG activism and transnational ordering' in Kuntz, T. (ed.), *Research Handbook on Environmental, Social, and Corporate Governance* (Cheltenham, UK: Edward Elgar Publishing Ltd), 112.

Bowley, T. and Hill, J. G. (2024b), 'The global stewardship ecosystem', 25 *European Business Organization Law Review*, 229.

Bowley, T., Hill J. G. and Kourabas, S. (2024), 'Shareholder engagement inside and outside the shareholder meeting' in Enriques, L. and Strampelli, G. (eds.), *Board-Shareholder Dialogue: Best Practices, Legal Constraints and Policy Options* (Cambridge, UK: Cambridge University Press) (forthcoming), 368.

Bozzi, S., Barontini, R. and Miroshnychenko, I. (2017), 'Investor protection and CEO compensation in family firms', 14 *Corporate Ownership & Control*, 17.

Braithwaite, T. (2009), 'US 'Pay Tsar' to vet executive packages', *Financial Times*, 10 June.

Bratton, W. W. and Wachter, M. L. (2008), 'Shareholder primacy's corporatist origins: Adolf Berle and the modern corporation', 34 *The Journal of Corporation Law*, 99.

Breckenridge, G. (2020), 'You say you want a revolution: What blockchain can learn from one man's attempt to save the world', *Cointelegraph Magazine*, 9 June.

Cahan, S. F., De Villiers, C., Jeter, D. C., Naiker, V. and Van Staden, C. J. (2016), 'Are CSR disclosures value-relevant? Cross-country evidence', 25 *European Accounting Review*, 579.

CEBS (Committee of European Banking Supervisors) (2010), 'Guidelines on Remuneration Policies and Practices', 10 December, available at: https://bit.ly/48mc7oF.

Chandler, W. B. III and Strine, L. E. Jr (2003), 'The new federalism of the American corporate governance system: Preliminary reflections of two residents of one small state', 152 *University of Pennsylvania Law Review*, 953.

Chase, R. and The Associated Press (2022), 'Elon Musk's longtime friend defends his role designing the Tesla CEO's $55 billion pay package: "He has been as hard working a CEO as there can be"', 15 November, *Fortune*.

Cheffins, B. R. (2015), 'Corporate governance since the managerial capitalism era', 89 *Business History Review*, 717.

Chen, Q., Hou, W., Li, W., Wilson, C. and Wu, Z. (2014), 'Family control, regulatory environment, and the growth of entrepreneurial firms: International evidence', 22 *Corporate Governance: An International Review*, 132–144.

Cheng, M., Lin B. and Wei, M. (2015), 'Executive compensation in family firms: The effect of multiple family members', 32 *Journal of Corporate Finance*, 238.

Cleary Gottlieb (2010), 'Alert memo: The Revised FSA Remuneration Code', 22 December, available at: https://bit.ly/490KtRX.

Coffee, J. C. Jr (2004), 'What caused Enron?: A capsule social and economic history of the 1990s', 89 *Cornell Law Review*, 269.

Coffee, J. C. Jr (2021), 'The coming shift in shareholder activism: From 'firm-specific' to 'systematic risk' proxy campaigns (and how to enable them)', 16 *Brooklyn Journal of Corporate Financial & Commercial Law*, 45.

Cohen, S., Kadach, I., Ormazabal, G. and Reichelstein, S. (2022), 'Executive compensation tied to ESG performance: International evidence', April, ECGI Finance Working Paper No. 825/2022, available at: https://bit.ly/3wz1073.

Condon, M. (2020), 'Externalities and the common owner', 95 *Washington Law Review*, 1.

Conoley, M. (1999), 'Moves to halt another decade of excess', August 5, *Financial Times*, 10.

Conway, M. R. (2008), 'Money for nothing and the stocks for free: Taxing executive compensation', 17 *Cornell Journal of Law & Public Policy*, 383.

Conyon, M. J., Fernandez, N., Ferreira, M. A., Matos P. and Murphy, K. J. (2013), 'The executive compensation controversy: A transatlantic analysis' in Boeri, T., Lucifora, C. and Murphy, K. J. (eds.), *Executive Remuneration and Employee Performance-Related Pay* (Oxford: Oxford University Press), 16.

Conyon, M. J. and Murphy, K. J. (2000), 'The Prince and the Pauper? CEO pay in the United States and the United Kingdom', 110 *The Economic Journal*, F640.

Core, J. E., Guay, W. R. and Thomas, R. S. (2005), 'Is US CEO compensation inefficient pay without performance?', 103 *Michigan Law Review*, 1142.

Cosma, S., Schwizer, P., Nobile, L. and Leopizzi, R. (2021), 'The stakeholder engagement in the European banks: Regulation versus governance. What changes after the NF Directive?', 28 *Corporate Social Responsibility and Environmental Management*, 1091.

Crotty, J. (2009), 'Structural causes of the global financial crisis: A critical assessment of the "new financial architecture"', 33 *Cambridge Journal of Economics*, 563.

Cuadrado-Ballesteros, B., Rodríguez-Ariza, L. and García-Sánchez, I.-M. (2015), 'The role of independent directors at family firms in relation to corporate social responsibility disclosures', 24 *International Business Review*, 890.

Delmas, M. A. and Toffel, M. W. (2008), 'Organizational responses to environmental demands: Opening the black box', 29 *Strategic Management Journal*, 1027.

Derchi, G.-B., Zoni, L. and Dossi, A. (2021), 'Corporate social responsibility performance, incentives, and learning effects', 173 *Journal of Business Ethics*, 617.

Ding, S., Qu B. and Wu, Z. (2016), 'Family control, socioemotional wealth, and governance environment: The case of bribes', 136 *Journal of Business Ethics*, 639.

Directors' Remuneration Report Regulations (2002), N° 1986 (UK).

Doyle, D. H. (2021), 'A short guide to the EU's taxonomy regulation', *S&P Global*, 12 May, available at: https://bit.ly/49qn1Uh.

EBA, European Banking Authority (2016), 'Guidelines on Sound Remuneration Policies Under Articles 74(3) and 75(2) of Directive 2013/36/EU and Disclosures Under Article 450 of Regulation (EU) No 575/2013', EBA/GL/2015/22, 27 June, available at: https://bit.ly/3Iayqf1.

EBA, European Banking Authority (2021), *Final Report on Guidelines on Sound Remuneration Policies Under Directive 2013/36/EU*, EBA/GL/2021/04, 2 July, available at: https://bit.ly/49u0FBl.

ECGI and Stockholm School of Economics (2022), 'European Commission Directive on Corporate Sustainability Due Diligence', Online Policy Workshop, 28–29 March, https://bit.ly/3uAos3x.

Edmans, A. (2021), 'Is sustainable investing really a dangerous placebo?', *Medium*, 30 September, available at: https://bit.ly/3PgyQVh.

Edmans, A. (2022), 'The End of ESG', ECGI Finance Working Paper No. 847/2022, September, available at: https://papers.ssrn.com/sol3/papers.cfm?abstract_id=4221990.

Edmans, A., Gabaix, X. and Jenter, D. (2017), 'Executive compensation: A survey of theory and evidence' in Hermalin, B. and Weisbach, M. (eds.), *Handbook of the Economics of Corporate Governance*, vol. 1 (Amsterdam: North-Holland), 383.

Eichenwald, K. (2002), 'Enron's many strands: Executive compensation', *The New York Times*, 1 March.

Ellis, R. D. (1998), 'Equity derivatives, executive compensation, and agency costs', 35 *Houston Law Review*, 399.

European Commission, 'EU taxonomy for sustainable activities', available at: https://bit.ly/3OTOANL.

European Commission (2022), 'Proposal for a Directive of the European Parliament and of the Council on Corporate Sustainability Due Diligence and amending Directive (EU) 2019/1937', 23 February, available at: https://bit.ly/4bPQmsM.

EU Technical Expert Group on Sustainable Finance (2020), *Taxonomy: Final Report of the Technical Expert Group on Sustainable Finance*, March, available at: https://bit.ly/49p9GM2.

Faccio, M. and Lang, L. H. P. (2002), 'The ultimate ownership of Western European corporations', 65 *Journal of Financial Economics*, 365.

Fahlenbrach, R. and Stulz, R. M. (2011), 'Bank CEO incentives and the credit crisis', 99 *Journal of Financial Economics*, 11.

Ferrarini, G. and Moloney, N. (2005), 'Executive remuneration in the EU: The context for reform', 21 *Oxford Review of Economic Policy*, 304.

Ferrarini, G., Moloney, N. and Ungureanu, M. C. (2009), 'Understanding Directors' Pay in Europe: A Comparative and Empirical Analysis', ECGI Working Paper N° 126/2009, August, available at: https://papers.ssrn.com/sol3/papers.cfm?abstract_id=1418463.

Ferrarini, G., Moloney, N. and Ungureanu, M. C. (2010), 'Executive remuneration in crisis: A critical assessment of reforms in Europe', 10 *Journal of Corporate Law Studies*, 73.

Ferrarini, G. and Ungureanu, M. C. (2010), 'Executive pay at ailing banks and beyond: A European perspective', 5 *Capital Markets Law Journal*, 197.

Ferrarini, G. and Ungureanu, M. C. (2011), 'Economics, politics and the international principles for sound compensation practices: An analysis of executive pay at European banks', 64 *Vanderbilt Law Review*, 429.

Ferri, F. and Maber, D. A. (2013), 'Say on pay votes and CEO compensation: Evidence from the UK', 17 *Review of Finance*, 527.

Flammer, C., Hong, B. and Minor D. (2019), 'Corporate governance and the rise of integrating corporate social responsibility criteria in executive compensation: Effectiveness and implications for firm outcomes', 40 *Strategic Management Journal*, 1097.

FRC (Financial Reporting Council) (2020), *The UK Stewardship Code*, available at: https://bit.ly/3IaHsZu.

Fredriksson, P. G. and Svensson, J. (2003), 'Political instability, corruption and policy formation: The case of environmental policy', 87 *Journal of Public Economics*, 1383.

Frydman, C. and Saks, R. E. (2010), 'Executive compensation: A new view from a long-term perspective, 1936–2005', 23 *The Review of Financial Studies*, 2099.

FSA (Financial Services Authority) (2009), 'The Turner Review: A Regulatory Response to the Global Banking Crisis', March. https://webarchive.nationalarchives.gov.uk/ukgwa/20090320232953/http://www.fsa.gov.uk/pubs/other/turner_review.pdf.

FSA (Financial Services Authority) (2010), 'Revising the Remuneration Code: Feedback on CP 10/19 and Final Rules', December. www.fca.org.uk/publication/consultation/cp10_19.pdf.

FSF (Financial Stability Forum) (2009), *FSF Principles for Sound Compensation Practices*, 2 April, available at: www.fsb.org/wp-content/uploads/r_0904b.pdf.

Gadinis, S. and Miazad, A. (2020), 'Corporate law and social risk', 73 *Vanderbilt Law Review*, 1401.

Galloway, J. (2022), 'Policy insights: Say on climate', Harvard Law School Forum on Corporate Governance, 8 June. https://corpgov.law.harvard.edu/2022/06/08/policy-insights-say-on-climate/

Gordon, J. N. (2002), 'What Enron means for the management and control of the modern business corporation: Some initial reflections', 69 *The University of Chicago Law Review*, 1233.

Gordon, J. N. (2009), '"Say on pay": Cautionary notes on the U.K. experience and the case for shareholder opt-in', 46 *Harvard Journal on Legislation*, 323.

Gordon, J. N. (2022), 'Systematic stewardship', 47 *The Journal of Corporation Law*, 627.

Gore, A. and Blood, D. (2020), 'Capitalism after the coronavirus', Wall St Journal, 29 June.

Gosling, T. and O'Connor, P. (2021), 'Executive pay and ESG performance', Harvard Law School Forum on Corporate Governance, 12 April. https://corpgov.law.harvard.edu/2021/04/12/executive-pay-and-esg-performance/

Hart, O. and Zingales, L. (2022), 'The new corporate governance', ECGI Law Working Paper No. 640/2022, August, available at: https://bit.ly/3SNsM7l.

HBR Editors (2014), 'The best-performing CEOs in the world', *Harvard Business Review*, November.

HBR Editors (2019), 'The best-performing CEOs in the world, 2019', *Harvard Business Review*, November–December.

Hill, J. G. (2012a), 'Regulating executive remuneration after the global financial crisis: Common law perspectives' in Thomas, R. S. and Hill, J. G. (eds.), *Research Handbook on Executive Pay* (Cheltenham: Edward Elgar Publishing Ltd.), 219.

Hill, J. G. (2012b), 'Why did Australia fare so well in the global financial crisis?' in Ferran, E., Moloney, N., Hill, J. G. and Coffee, J. C. Jr., *The Regulatory Aftermath of the Global Financial Crisis* (Cambridge, UK: Cambridge University Press), 203.

Hill, J. G. (2021), 'Corporations, directors' duties and the public/private divide' in Laby, A. and Russell, J. H. (eds.), *Fiduciary Obligations in Business* (Cambridge, UK: Cambridge University Press), 285.

Hill, J. G., Masulis, R. W. and Thomas, R. S. (2011), 'Comparing CEO employment contract provisions: Differences between Australia and the United States', 64 *Vanderbilt Law Review*, 557.

Hill, J. and Thomas, R. S. (2012), 'Introduction' in Thomas, R. S. and Hill, J. G. (eds.), *Research Handbook on Executive Pay* (Cheltenham: Edward Elgar Publishing Ltd), 1–3.

ICGN (International Corporate Governance Network) (2020), *ICGN Viewpoint: Covid-19 and Executive Remuneration*, June, available at: https://bit.ly/48sbSkF.

ILO (International Labour Organisation) (2021), 'Investor relation: The real value of gender equality', 27 October. www.ilo.org/jakarta/whatwedo/eventsandmeetings/WCMS_833123/lang--en/index.htm

Ioannou, I. and Serafeim, G. (2012), 'What drives corporate social performance? The role of nation-level institutions', 43 *Journal of International Business Studies*, 834.

Jackson, T. (1998), 'The fat cats keep getting fatter', *Financial Times*, 1 August, 9.

Jaeger, F. (2021), 'Say no to climate change, say yes to "say on climate"', *Oxford Business Law Blog*, 13 July. https://blogs.law.ox.ac.uk/business-law-blog/blog/2021/07/say-no-climate-change-say-yes-say-climate

Jensen, M. C. and Murphy, K. J. (1990), 'CEO incentives – It's not how much you pay, but how', 68 *Harvard Business Review*, 138.

Johnson, R. A. and Greening, D. W. (1999), 'The effects of corporate governance and institutional ownership types on corporate social performance', 42 *Academy of Management Journal*, 564.

Katelouzou, D. and Klettner, A. (2022), 'Sustainable finance and stewardship: Unlocking stewardship's sustainability potential' in Katelouzou, D. and Puchniak, D. W. (eds.), *Global Shareholder Stewardship* (Cambridge, UK: Cambridge University Press), 549.

Koors, J., Meyer P. and Partners LLC (2019), 'Executive compensation and ESG', Harvard Law School Forum on Corporate Governance, 10 September, available at: https://corpgov.law.harvard.edu/2019/09/10/executive-compensation-and-esg/

Li, J., Zhao, F., Chen, S., Jiang, W., Liu, T. and Shi, S. (2017), 'Gender diversity on boards and firms' environmental policy', 26 *Business Strategy and the Environment*, 306–315.

Liang, H. and Renneboog, L. (2017), 'On the foundations of corporate social responsibility', 72 *Journal of Finance*, 853.

Lean CX (2020), 'Leadership quote – Charlie Munger on incentives and outcomes', November 24, available at: https://bit.ly/3Ib6vM8.

Levitt, A. Jr (2005), 'Corporate culture and the problem of executive compensation', 30 *The Journal of Corporation Law*, 749.

Liu, C. (2018), 'Are women greener? Corporate gender diversity and environmental violations', 52 *Journal of Corporate Finance*, 118.

Loewenstein, M. J. (1996), 'Reflections on executive compensation and a modest proposal for (further) reform', 50 *SMU Law Review*, 201.

Lund, D. S. and Pollman, E. (2021), 'The corporate governance machine', 121 *Columbia Law Review*, 2563.

Maas, K. (2018), 'Do corporate social performance targets in executive compensation contribute to corporate social performance?', 148 *Journal of Business Ethics*, 573.

Maas, K. and Rosendaal, S. (2016), 'Sustainability targets in executive remuneration: Targets, time frame, country and sector specification', 25 *Business Strategy and the Environment*, 390.

Mallin, C., Michelon, G. and Raggi, D. (2013), 'Monitoring intensity and stakeholders' orientation: How does governance affect social and environmental disclosure?', 114 *Journal of Business Ethics*, 29.

Masters, B. (2022), 'BlackRock to vote against climate resolutions', *Financial Times*, 12 May, 6.

Mehran, H. (1995), 'Executive compensation structure, ownership, and firm performance', 38 *Journal of Financial Economics*, 163.

Miroshnychenko, I., Barontini, R. and Testa, F. (2017), 'Green practices and financial performance: A global outlook', 147 *Journal of Cleaner Production*, 340.

Miroshnychenko, I., De Massis, A., Miller, D. and Barontini, R. (2021), 'Family business growth around the world', 45 *Entrepreneurship Theory and Practice*, 682–708.

Miske, R. (2004), 'Can't cap corporate greed: Unintended consequences of trying to control executive compensation through the tax code', 88 *Minnesota Law Review*, 1673.

Murphy, K. J. and Jensen, M. C. (2018), 'The politics of pay: The unintended consequences of regulating executive compensation', 3 *Journal of Law, Finance, and Accounting*, 189.

OECD, Organisation for Economic Co-operation and Development (2021), *OECD Corporate Governance Factbook 2021*, available at: https://bit.ly/3ORPqKG.

Official Journal of the European Union (2004), 'Commission Recommendation of 14 December 2004 fostering an appropriate regime for the remuneration of directors of listed companies', 2004/913/EC, L385/55, available at: https://bit.ly/3OPHHgc.

Official Journal of the European Union (2005), 'Commission Recommendation of 15 February 2005 on the role of non-executive or supervisory directors of listed companies and on the committees of the (supervisory) board', 2005/162/EC, L52/51, available at: https://bit.ly/3I86GaQ.

Official Journal of the European Union ('CRDIII') (2010), 'Directive 2010/76/EU of the European Parliament and of the Council of 24 November 2010 amending Directives 2006/48/EC and 2006/49/EC as regards capital requirements for the trading book and for re-securitisations, and for the supervisory review of remuneration policies', L 329/3, available at: https://bit.ly/3I7x199.

Official Journal of the European Union (2013), 'Directive 2013/36/EU of the European Parliament and of the Council of 26 June 2013 on access to the activity of credit institutions and the prudential supervision of credit institutions and investment firms, amending Directive 2002/87/EC and repealing Directives 2006/48/EC and 2006/49/EC', L176/338, available at: https://bit.ly/3wlN8Ns.

Official Journal of the European Union (2017), 'Directive (EU) of 2017/828 of the European Parliament and of the Council of 17 May 2017 amending Directive 2007/36/EC as regards the encouragement of long-term shareholder engagement', L132/1, available at: https://bit.ly/3UQCyID.

Official Journal of the European Union (2020), 'Regulation (EU) 2020/852 of the European Parliament and of the Council of 18 June 2020 on the establishment of a framework to facilitate sustainable investment, and amending Regulation (EU) 2019/2088', L198/13, available at: https://bit.ly/3V89uwz.

Pargendler, M. (2021), 'The rise of international corporate law', 98 *Washington University Law Review*, 1765.

Perry, T. and Zenner, M. (2000), 'CEO compensation in the 1990s: Shareholder alignment or shareholder expropriation?', 35 *Wake Forest Law Review*, 123.

Pierce, C. H. M. (2022), 'We Are Not the Securities and Environment Commission – At Least Not Yet', US Securities and Exchange Commission Statement, 21 March, available at: https://bit.ly/3T9WYLe.

Pollman, E. (2021), 'Corporate social responsibility, ESG, and compliance' in van Rooij, B. and Sokol, D. D. (eds.), *Cambridge Handbook of Compliance* (Cambridge, UK: Cambridge University Press), 662.

Post, C., Rahman, N. and Rubow, E. (2011), 'Green governance: Boards of directors' composition and environmental corporate social responsibility', 50 *Business & Society*, 189.

PRI (Principles for Responsible Investment) (2016), 'Integrating ESG issues into executive pay: A review of global utility and extractive companies', available at: www.unpri.org/download?ac=1798.

PRI (Principles for Responsible Investment) (2017), 'PRI strategic plan 2018–21: Making the blueprint a reality', October, available at: https://bit.ly/3IaHNve.

PRI (Principles for Responsible Investment) (2021), 'EU taxonomy: Final report', Video, available at: www.youtube.com/watch?v=b4HNZ2Gmxgk.

Price, J. (2018), 'Climate change', Keynote Address, Centre for Policy Development: Financing a Sustainable Economy, Sydney, 18 June. https://asic.gov.au/about-asic/news-centre/speeches/climate-change/

PricewaterhouseCoopers, London Business School & Centre for Corporate Governance (2021), 'Paying Well by Paying for Good', available at: https://pwc.to/3uLemNi.

PricewaterhouseCoopers, London Business School & Leadership Institute (2022), 'Paying for good for all', available at: https://pwc.to/3T8iYGB.

PSF, Platform on Sustainable Finance (2022), *Final Report on Social Taxonomy: Platform on Sustainable Finance*, February, available at: https://bit.ly/3T5TGZE.

Refinitiv (2002), *Environmental, Social and Governance Scores from Refinitiv*, available at: https://lseg.group/45e6FwM.

Ryan, H. E. Jr and Wiggins, R. A. III (2001), 'The influence of firm- and manager-specific characteristics on the structure of executive compensation', 7 *Journal of Corporate Finance*, 101.

Sánchez-Marín, G., Encarnación, L.-P. M., Baixauli-Soler, S., Main, B. G. M., Mínguez-Vera, A. (2022), 'Excess executive compensation and corporate governance in the United Kingdom and Spain: A comparative analysis', 43 *Managerial and Decision Economics*, 2817.

SEC, Securities and Exchange Commission (2022), 'SEC Proposes rules to enhance and standardize climate-related disclosures for investors', Press Release, 21 March, available at: www.sec.gov/news/press-release/2022-46.

Stobbe, A. and Zimmerman, H. (2022), 'Ahead of the curve: Tie executive pay to climate targets', *IPE Magazine*, June, available at: https://bit.ly/3OQAjRC.

Sullivan, K. and Bujno, M. (2021), 'Incorporating ESG measures into executive compensation plans', Harvard Law School Forum on Corporate Governance, 24 May. https://corpgov.law.harvard.edu/2021/05/24/incorporating-esg-measures-into-executive-compensation-plans/.

Summerhayes, G. (2017), 'Australia's new horizon: Climate change challenges and prudential risk', Speech, Insurance Council of Australian Annual Forum, Sydney, 17 February. www.apra.gov.au/news-and-publications/australias-new-horizon-climate-change-challenges-and-prudential-risk.

Testa, F., Miroshnychenko, I., Barontini, R. and Frey, M. (2018), 'Does it pay to be a greenwasher or a brownwasher?', 27 *Business Strategy and the Environment*, 1104.

The Economist (2003), 'Fat cats feeding', *The Economist*, 9 October.

The Global Compact (2004), 'Who cares wins: Connecting financial markets to a changing world', available at: https://bit.ly/49lGbus.

Thomas, R. S. (2004), 'Explaining the international CEO pay gap: Board capture or market driven?', 57 *Vanderbilt Law Review*, 1171.

Thomas, R. S. and Wells, H. (2011), 'Executive compensation in the courts: Board capture, optimal contracting and officers' fiduciary duties', 95 *Minnesota Law Review*, 846.

Thomas, R. S. and van der Elst, C. (2015), 'Say on pay around the world', 92 *Washington University Law Review*, 653.

Trade and Industry Committee (2002), *Rewards for Failure*, 2002-03 HC 914, available at: https://bit.ly/49u25f9.

Travers Smith (2022), *EU Platform on Sustainable Finance: Final Report on Social Taxonomy*, 4 March, available at: https://bit.ly/48moR7q.

UN (United Nations) (1999), 'Secretary-General proposes global compact on human rights, labour, environment, in address to World Economic Forum in Davos', Press Release, 1 February, available at: www.un.org/press/en/1999/19990201.sgsm6881.html.

UN (United Nations) (2000), 'Executive summary and conclusion of high-level meeting on global compact', Press Release, 27 July, available at: www.un.org/press/en/2000/20000727.sg2065.doc.html.

Walker, D. (2009), 'A review of corporate governance in UK Banks and other financial industry entities', 16 July, available at: https://bit.ly/3OOE8ag.

Wattles, J., Geier, B., Egan, M. and Wiener-Bronner, D. (2018), 'Wells Fargo's 20-month nightmare', *CNN Business*, 24 April.

Winter, J. (2012), 'Corporate governance going astray: Executive remuneration built to fail' in Thomas, R. S. and Hill, J. G. (eds.), *Research Handbook on Executive Pay* (Cheltenham: Edward Elgar Publishing Ltd), 199.

Yablon, C. M. (1999), 'Bonus questions – Executive compensation in the era of pay for performance', 75 *Notre Dame Law Review*, 271.

PART III

Integrating Sustainability in Financial Markets Regulation

10

Sustainability-Related Materiality in the SFDR

Nathan de Arriba-Sellier and Arnaud Van Caenegem

10.1 INTRODUCTION

Since its inception,[1] the Sustainable Finance Disclosure Regulation (SFDR) has been one of the most controversial and criticized pieces of EU sustainable finance regulation, notably because of its broad general principles, which led to challenges in their implementation.[2] Yet the SFDR has not compromised the success of sustainable finance.[3] Over a third of funds sold in the European Union make sustainability disclosures provided under the SFDR. Thus a sustainability profile is in 2023 assessed and disclosed for a staggering 4.6 trillion euros in assets under management, representing 55% of the European fund industry.[4] Nonetheless, the success in the wide adoption of the regulatory disclosure framework stands in sharp contrast with the legal uncertainty which has prevailed since the SFDR entered into force on 10 March 2021.[5]

Much is expected from the European Commission's delegated regulation to put the SFDR back on track to Union-wide harmonization of sustainability-related disclosures since 2023.[6] Yet, in the meantime, the European Commission and European Supervisory Authorities were repeatedly forced to provide further clarifications.[7]

---

[1]   The authors are grateful to Matteo Gargantini and Charlotte Gardes for their helpful comments.
[2]   Regulation 2019/2088 of 27 November 2019 on sustainability-related disclosures in the financial services sector, OJ 2019 No. L317, 9 December 2019. See Busch 2021; Zetsche and Anker-Sørensen 2022.
[3]   On a critic of the need for regulation, see Curtis, Fisch and Robertson 2021.
[4]   Morningstar 2023, 1.
[5]   Article 20(2) Reg. 2019/2088. Morningstar 2022a, 19 ("percentages are in any case difficult to gauge given the different interpretations made by asset managers"). Andrew 2022b ("several asset managers [downgrade] their funds over the past six months, with many still choosing to interpret the regulation differently").
[6]   Article 68 Commission Delegated Regulation 2022/1288 of 6 April 2022 supplementing Regulation (EU) 2019/2088, OJ 2022 No. L196, 25 July 2022.
[7]   Decision Commission C(2021)4858 of 6 July 2021 on the adoption of the answers to be provided to questions submitted by the European Supervisory Authorities; Decision Commission C(2022)3051 of

This endeavour is in line with the European Securities and Markets Authority's (ESMA) commitment to promote high-quality sustainability disclosures as the way to maintain investor confidence in environmental, social and governance (ESG) investments as a central element in its next five-year strategy.[8] Indeed, the European Supervisory Authorities, which are responsible for the consistent application of EU financial regulation,[9] recognized that differing interpretations of the regulatory framework could be a driver of greenwashing in a call for evidence.[10]

Recent scholarship has identified that some SFDR disclosure obligations are akin to product regulation, notably since they integrate disclosures in client documentation. Gargantini and Siri show that the SFDR does not include regulatory incentives to rely on the sustainability assessment made by external ESG rating agencies.[11] The financial sector's association Eurosif argues that some disclosure obligations are standards that share features with a product standard or labelling regime.[12] While the SFDR may go beyond the scope of a classic measure of disclosure regulation, its objective is to support transparency. Indeed, while the SFDR may be a basis for product regulation,[13] this chapter will show that the SFDR's purpose and nature is first and foremost to require disclosures from financial market participants and financial products.

Furthermore, a general theorization of the appearance of more demanding disclosure obligations in the SFDR is missing.[14] This chapter seeks to fill that gap. Throughout our discussion it will appear that some disclosure rules are more detailed in the sustainability-related information they require, are "of high quality", or, as the European Commission has called it, pursue "sustainability-related materiality".[15] Contrary to most of the provisions of the SFDR which leave asset managers free in

13 May 2022 on the adoption of the answers to be provided to questions submitted by the European Supervisory Authorities; Joint Committee of the European Supervisory Authorities 2022a; Joint Committee of the European Supervisory Authorities 2022b; ESMA 2022a; Joint Committee of the European Supervisory Authorities 2022c; Joint Committee of the European Supervisory Authorities 2022d; Notice Commission 2023/C 211/01 on the interpretation and implementation of certain legal provisions of the EU Taxonomy Regulation and links to the Sustainable Finance Disclosure Regulation, OJ 16 June 2023, C 211, 1; Decision Commission C(2023)2281 of 5 April 2023 on the answers to be provided to questions requiring the interpretation of Union law submitted on 9 September 2022 by the European Supervisory Authorities under Article 16b(5) of Regulations (EU) No 1093/2010, (EU) No 1094/2010 and (EU) No 1095/2010 of the European Parliament and of the Council, and amending Commission Decisions of 6 July 2021 and 13 May 2022.

8 ESMA 2022b, 27.
9 Article 1(5) Regulation 1095/2010 of 24 November 2010 establishing a European Supervisory Authority (European Securities and Markets Authority), amending Decision No 716/2009/EC and repealing Commission Decision 2009/77/EC, OJ L 331, 15 December 2010.
10 European Supervisory Authority 2022, 37.
11 Gargantini and Siri 2022, 13.
12 Eurosif 2022, 10.
13 See in this regard Partiti 2023.
14 For a theorization of the *purpose* of sustainable finance disclosure, see Steuer and Tröger 2022.
15 Draft Commission Delegated Regulation C(2021)2616 of 21 April 2021 amending Delegated Regulation (EU) 2017/565, 2.

substantiating sustainability of their investment strategies, we argue that the SFDR also contains a set of disclosure rules which are distinct as they appear to limit the possible ways to justify what sustainability means, similarly to a comply-or-explain mechanism. As new regulatory developments are putting emphasis on these more demanding disclosure obligations, a theory underlying these tendencies is necessary to guide the focus of national supervisory practices. Such theory will show that, in the eyes of the EU, a shift from prescribing the provision of information as a financial market participant sees fit towards an increasing focus on the demandingness of justification requirements in disclosure regulation ought not to be confused with the instalment of a label which typically explicates substantive requirements on the investment strategies or certifies voluntary disclosures.[16]

In what follows, we will first explain how communications about sustainability by financial services providers are regulated. We will then argue that the mere existence of more demanding disclosure obligations should not lead to the conclusion that the SFDR is a labelling mechanism. Making the SFDR a labelling regime could go directly against the evolution towards demandingness in disclosures and risks to be a step back from high-quality sustainability disclosures. As much as the more demanding disclosure obligations tighten the range of possibilities to justify a contribution to sustainability, the SFDR's disclosure obligations still provide sufficient leeway to determine what sustainability means. Transforming the SFDR into a labelling regime risks distracting from the mechanisms that improve the justification of achieving sustainability and could decrease the effectiveness of other initiatives, like the EU Ecolabel,[17] which would be a more suitable instrument in that regard.[18]

10.2 REGULATORY SET-UP

10.2.1 *Scope of Application*

The SFDR applies to "financial market participants", "financial products" and "financial advisers". "Financial market participants" reflect a broadly defined group of collective investment managers, including asset managers with an insurance or pension finality, and individual portfolio management.[19] Their collective investment, insurance and pension products, along with individual portfolio management, are called together "financial products".[20] "Financial advisers" are entities

---

[16] For example, Central Labelling Agency 2023.
[17] Regulation (EC) No 66/2010 of 25 November 2009 on the EU Ecolabel, OJ L 27, 30 January 2010.
[18] Even though there has been little progress in that respect, despite the first recommendations for an EU Ecolabel for financial products dating back to 2018; High-Level Expert Group on Sustainable Finance 2018, 29.
[19] Article 2(1) Reg. 2019/2088 of 27 November 2019 on sustainability-related disclosures in the financial services sector, OJ 2019 No. L317, 9 December 2019.
[20] Article 2(12) Reg. 2019/2088.

that provide investment or insurance advice in the distribution of financial products,[21] and which will process data provided by financial market participants when distributing financial products.[22]

10.2.2 *Structure of the Disclosure Obligations*

Especially for financial products, the SFDR disclosure obligations consist of layers of stringency which will prompt the structure of the discussion below. The SFDR first makes a distinction between disclosures about sustainability considerations from the perspective of safeguarding the value of the investment alone, or single materiality,[23] and the consideration of sustainability for other purposes.[24] The disclosure rules that only focus on the value of the investment will be discussed first. The consideration of sustainability for all other purposes will be discussed second. In this respect, there is a difference between voluntarily and mandatory consideration of prescribed sustainability data.[25] For financial products that must consider sustainability data, there is a difference between financial products that must evidence their contribution to sustainability by comparing it to a specialized index or a list of economic activities considered sustainable by the European Commission, and those that are free to use any other way to evidence a contribution to sustainability.[26]

10.3 BASELINE "SINGLE MATERIALITY" DISCLOSURES

10.3.1 *Website Disclosures*

In accordance with the duty of care, financial market participants seek to preserve the value of investments against any actual or potential financially material negative impact on the financial return.[27] The SFDR clarifies that this is not different if the source of the risk is an environmental, social or governance "event" (such as an acute climate-related event) or "condition" (such as biodiversity loss).[28] As a result, the regulation does not only ensure the disclosure of both physical and transition risks, but it also supports their management by recognizing that the same legal regime is applied for these risks as for other financial risks. Financial market participants

---

[21] Article 2(11) Reg. 2019/2088.

[22] Recital 8, Commission Delegated Regulation 2022/1288 of 6 April 2022 supplementing Regulation (EU) 2019/2088, OJ 2022 No. L196, 25 July 2022.

[23] Gargantini and Siri 2022, 3. On the importance of considering sustainability risks, see Condon 2019.

[24] Annex to Decision Commission C(2021)4858 of 6 July 2021 on the adoption of the answers to be provided to questions submitted by the European Supervisory Authorities, 8 ("integration per se of sustainability risks […] is not sufficient for Article 8 to apply").

[25] Article 26(2)a, 39a, 51(d)i, 59(e)i Commission Delegated Regulation 2022/1288.

[26] Article 9(1) Reg. 2019/2088.

[27] Recital 12 Reg. 2019/2088. See Colaert, Chapter 12 in this volume.

[28] Article 2(22), 3, 5 & 6 Reg. 2019/2088.

must consider these "sustainability risks" when they manage assets for investors or for individuals in the scope of the SFDR. These risks should be integrated in risk policies and remuneration policies, which must appear on the website.[29] The same applies for financial advisers. Thus the SFDR goes here beyond a pure disclosure approach but entails some due diligence on the part of financial market participants with respect to sustainability risks. Such requirements form the new baseline for financial market participants, from which they cannot derogate, regardless of their integration of sustainability considerations in their investment policies.

10.3.2 *Precontractual Disclosures*

The precontractual information of any financial product should specify the relevant sustainability risks, the way they are integrated and the likely impacts on the financial returns. This requirement applies for financial market participants and financial advisers alike. Upon justification, sustainability risks can be deemed irrelevant.[30] However, it is unclear what reasons to overlook such risks could be provided by financial market participants,[31] particularly since the ESAs clarified that irrelevance of sustainability risks is unlikely.[32] Thus, even in absence of obligations for financial market participants to take account of sustainability risks, the SFDR demands careful consideration of sustainability-related risks through disclosure regulation. Financial products for which the sustainability analysis is limited to assess sustainability from the lens of financial risks for the investments are commonly called "Article 6 products". However, this designation is misleading, as all financial products must comply with the requirements provided under Article 6 even if they go beyond the solely risk-based approach in integrating sustainability considerations. It is therefore an essential component of SFDR and a step forward in the disclosure regulation of financial products.

10.4 ADDITIONAL "DOUBLE MATERIALITY" DISCLOSURES

10.4.1 *From "Single Materiality" to "Double Materiality"*

If financial market participants consider the sustainability performance, and particularly the contribution to sustainability, of the financial products they manage beyond solely the value of their investments, they are said to adopt a "double materiality" approach.[33]

---

[29] Article 3 and 5 Reg. 2019/2088.
[30] Article 6 Reg. 2019/2088.
[31] Van Caenegem and van de Werve 2021, 150–151.
[32] Joint Committee of the European Supervisory Authorities 2022d, 17.
[33] Chiu 2022; Gargantini and Siri 2022, 3.

The double materiality approach is based in the SFDR on the concept of "sustainability factors", which are defined as "environmental, social and employee matters, respect for human rights, anti-corruption, and anti-bribery matters".[34] Employee matters, human rights and anti-corruption replace in this definition's scope the reference to governance in sustainability risks. In the same vein, the upcoming Corporate Sustainability Reporting Directive (CSRD) requires *companies* to disclose on a wider range of sustainability matters.[35]

The SFDR regulates disclosure about how investment decisions and financial advice consider the adverse impacts on these factors differently from single materiality disclosures. This is the case both for website disclosures and for the precontractual disclosures of the financial products they offer. The lack of detail of the information financial market participants must consider in disclosure statements about "single materiality" stands in sharp contrast with the template adopted by the European Commission to guide the fact-finding exercise in double materiality.[36] This template is meant to appear on the website of financial market participants as a Principal Adverse Impact Statement ("PAI Statement").[37]

10.4.2 *Difference in Scope*

Unlike the regulation of sustainability risks, which applied to all financial market participants, financial advisers and financial products, the publication of the PAI Statement as a separate section on the website is only mandatory for financial market participants with more than 500 employees on average, counted on the balance sheet dates published throughout the financial year.[38] Financial advisers as well as other financial market participants must publish a PAI Statement only if they consider adverse impacts. If they do not, they should prominently state that they do not consider any adverse impacts, explain their refusal, and indicate whether and when they intend to disclose a PAI Statement if they deem such information relevant.[39]

Since 30 December 2022, the precontractual information of financial products should indicate the choice to consider principal adverse impacts on sustainability factors. Large financial market participants and other financial market participants that opted to make a PAI Statement on the website can consider the principal adverse impacts at an individual financial product level. The details of such consideration should be included in the financial product's precontractual information.[40]

---

[34] Article 2(24) Reg. 2019/2088. See also Commission Guidelines on non-financial reporting: Supplement on reporting climate-related information, C(2019) 4490 final, 17 June 2019.

[35] Directive 2022/2464 of 14 December 2022 as regards corporate sustainability reporting, OJ 2022 No. L322, 16 December 2022.

[36] Article 4(2) Reg. 2019/2088 & Annex I to Commission Delegated Regulation 2022/1288.

[37] Article 4(1)a Reg. 2019/2088.

[38] Ibid., Article 4(3–4).

[39] Ibid., Article 4(1 & 5).

[40] Ibid., Article 7(1)a.

In the absence of a PAI Statement on the website, the precontractual disclosure documents of each financial product offered must indicate that principal adverse impacts are not considered.[41] Contrary to what a literal reading of the SFDR would suggest, the European Commission has clarified that a financial market participant without a PAI Statement on the website may still offer a product that pursues a reduction of negative externalities caused by the investments underlying that product.[42]

When information is provided about the consideration of principal adverse impacts in precontractual disclosures, there is no requirement to use the template adopted by the European Commission for website disclosures.[43] However, ESMA indicated that, in the supervision on the precontractual disclosures, it should be verified if the mandatory indicators mentioned in the template used on the website have been considered, where relevant.[44] The Commission clarified that the procedural obligation to consider principal adverse impacts also entails the description of procedures put in place to mitigate those impacts. The Commission clearly requires engagement to address these impacts, but abstains from setting out minimum criteria for such engagements.[45]

10.4.3 *Prescriptive Template of the PAI Statement*

The Principal Adverse Impact Statement (PAI Statement) is a disclosure document selecting sustainability information deemed important by regulators. The PAI Statement distinguishes three asset classes: investee companies, sovereigns and supranationals, and real estate assets. For each asset class, financial market participants must disclose information about a set of prescribed sustainability themes, which consist of environmental and social indicators, which in turn comprise different metrics.[46] The metrics are quantifiable and need to be measured as averages, assessed quarterly.[47] Next to the standardized quantifiable metrics, additional quantitative or qualitative information about the indicator can be provided.

---

[41] Ibid., Article 7(2).
[42] Annex to Decision Commission C(2022)3051 of 13 May 2022 on the adoption of the answers to be provided to questions submitted by the European Supervisory Authorities, 1 ("notwithstanding the criteria set out in Article 7(1), first subparagraph, of Regulation (EU) 2019/2088, manufacture a financial product that pursues a reduction of negative externalities caused by the investments underlying that product").
[43] Joint Committee of the European Supervisory Authorities 2022a, 2 ("the disclosure of PAI consideration at product level is set out in Article 7 SFDR and is not further specified except for fields in the templates to provide the information required by that Article").
[44] ESMA 2022a, 7.
[45] Annex to Decision Commission C(2023) 2281 of 5 April 2023 on the answers to be provided to questions submitted by the European Supervisory Authorities, 8. Joint Committee of the European Supervisory Authorities 2022c, 3.
[46] Article 6(1) Commission Delegated Regulation 2022/1288.
[47] Ibid., Article 6(3).

Data for each indicator going five years backwards must be shown in the template
in order to enable historical comparisons.[48] For example, "social and employee
matters" is a sustainability theme for investee companies featuring "board gender
diversity" among the indicators, which is quantified as the metric: average ratio of
female to male board members in investee companies, expressed as a percentage
of all board members. Next to this metric, there is a narrative section to provide
qualitative contextualization for the indicator "board gender diversity".[49]

Certain indicators are mandatory, as the European Commission deemed that those
consistently lead to principal adverse impacts. Other indicators are merely optional.[50]
Financial market participants must disclose information on nine environmental and
seven social indicators for investee companies; one environmental and one social indicator for investments in sovereigns and supranationals; and two environmental indicators for real estate assets.[51] On top of the mandatory indicators, information about at
least two additional optional indicators must be provided with one being environmental and the other social.[52] A financial market participant can also add additional indicators that it uses to identify and assess principal adverse impacts on a sustainability
factor.[53] A description of these indicators must be summarized in a two-pager.[54]

In disclosing these indicators, financial market participants should be transparent
about their data sources, identification, assessment and prioritization of indicators,
and margins of error in their assessment.[55] In principle, data that is readily available must be used. This is expected to be more widely the case as the CSRD starts
to apply.[56] Where data is not readily available, financial market participants must
employ best efforts to get information directly from the company, or by conducting
additional research, by buying data from third parties or by making reasonable
assumptions. In each of these cases, financial market participants must document
the data gathering process in the PAI Statement.[57] Such data collection requirements may be particularly burdensome for some financial market participants that
have little related experience, but should support the provision of more reliable,
consistent, and comparable sustainability information.[58]

The European Commission links the gathering of data to the financial market participants' adherence to responsible business conduct codes, internationally

---

[48] Ibid., Article 10.
[49] Ibid., Annex I.
[50] Ibid., Recital 4.
[51] See also Joint Committee of the European Supervisory Authorities 2023, 8–9 (proposing additional
      mandatory social indicators).
[52] Article 6(1)a–b Commission Delegated Regulation 2022/1288.
[53] Ibid., Article 6(1)c.
[54] Ibid., Article 5.
[55] Ibid., Article 7(1).
[56] Joint Committee of the European Supervisory Authorities 2022d, 8.
[57] Article 7(2) Commission Delegated Regulation.
[58] Esty and Karpilow 2019, 687.

recognized standards or the objectives of the Paris Agreement.[59] The measurement of adherence must be disclosed by identifying the relevant indicators, and describing methodologies capable of making forecasts about indicators, either by using forward-looking climate scenario analysis or by justifying the irrelevance of forward-looking climate scenarios.[60]

The European Commission also considered the disclosures in the PAI Statement to be evolutive in nature. Financial market participants should indicate their planned actions to reduce the impacts or the targets they set to reduce impacts.[61] This obligation entails the disclosure of climate-related targets, such as net-zero commitments. However, financial market participants are not required to justify their plans or to provide details on their targets and how they plan to meet them. Such an obligation falls short of more expansive requirements under the CSRD.[62] By contrast, there is a stronger focus on the exercise of shareholders' rights. Financial market participants should provide summaries of voluntarily adopted engagement policies to reduce the principal adverse impacts or of general shareholder engagement policies mandated by national law.[63] There is an obligation to identify the specific indicators addressed by the engagement policy in these summaries and, if no positive change has occurred with respect to an indicator after more than one year, the summary must include the ways these policies will be adapted.[64]

10.5 DISCLOSURES FOR SUSTAINABLE FINANCIAL PRODUCTS

If an investment strategy integrates sustainability for any other purpose than for risk management, additional disclosure requirements apply beyond the minimum standards set under Article 6 and that apply for all financial products.[65] Financial market participants could have financial products that promote environmental or social characteristics provided that the companies these financial products invest in follow good governance practices.[66] This legal description of "promotion of environmental or social characteristics" emerged from the political negotiations between the European Parliament and Council but has been left undefined.[67]

---

[59] Article 9(1) Commission Delegated Regulation 2022/1288.

[60] Ibid., Article 9(2).

[61] Ibid., Article 6(2).

[62] See Strampelli and Balp, Chapter 16 in this volume.

[63] Article 8(1) Commission Delegated Regulation 2022/1288.

[64] Ibid., Article 8(2).

[65] Annex to Decision Commission C(2021)4858 of 6 July 2021 on the adoption of the answers to be provided to questions submitted by the European Supervisory Authorities, 8 ("integration per se of sustainability risks [...] is not sufficient for Article 8 to apply").

[66] Article 8(1) Reg. 2019/2088.

[67] Article 5 Proposal Commission, COM(2018) 354 of 24 May 2018 for a regulation on disclosures relating to sustainable investments and sustainability risks and amending Directive (EU) 2016/2341 (for example, the phrasing in the European Commission's proposal was "has as its target sustainable

An alternative, more ambitious, classification of a financial product is one that "has sustainable investment as its objective".[68] The SFDR provides a definition of "sustainable investment", but the definition is not sufficiently specific to guarantee uniform application.[69] The definition, found in Article 2(17) SFDR has three cumulative conditions an investment must meet:

(1) the activity underlying the investment contributes to an environmental or social objective;
(2) the investment does not significantly harm an environmental or social objective; and
(3) the investee companies follow good governance practices, in particular with respect to sound management structures, employee relations, remuneration of staff and tax compliance.[70]

As it appears from the SFDR, the reasons for the distinction between financial products that promote environmental or social characteristics and those that have sustainable investment as their objective is meant to recognize that there are various degrees of ambition in the market of sustainable financial products, and that disclosure requirements should reflect that reality.[71] Still, it is up to financial market participants to consider which disclosure standard applies to their financial products under the SFDR.

10.6 SUSTAINABLE INVESTMENT

10.6.1 *Specification in the Taxonomy*

The two first conditions of "sustainable investment" cannot be fully understood without taking into account the Taxonomy Regulation, which promotes and legally defines environmentally sustainable investments by reference to the definition of environmentally sustainable economic activities.[72] The Taxonomy Regulation effectively provides for three conditions to qualify as an environmentally sustainable economic activity.[73] The economic activity must "substantially contribute"

---

investments or investments with similar characteristics", which also left the term "characteristics" undefined, but at least linked it to the defined legal term "sustainable investment", which is not the case in the SFDR).

[68] Article 9(1) Reg. 2019/2088.
[69] Klasa 2022; Partiti 2023.
[70] Article 2(17) Reg. 2019/2088. Article 14(3)(a) Commission Delegated Regulation 2022/1288.
[71] Recital 21 Reg. 2019/2088.
[72] Article 2(1) Regulation 2020/852 of 18 June 2020 on the establishment of a framework to facilitate sustainable investment, and amending Regulation (EU) 2019/2088, OJ 22 June 2020 No. L198, 22 June 2020. The Taxonomy Regulation applies beyond the mere scope of the disclosure obligations provided under the SFDR. See Och, Chapter 13 in this volume.
[73] Ibid., Article 3.

to one of six predefined environmental objectives: climate change mitigation, climate change adaptation, the sustainable use and protection of water and marine resources, the transition to a circular economy, pollution prevention and control, and the protection and restoration of biodiversity and ecosystems.[74] Furthermore, the economic activity must "significantly harm" none of these environmental objectives.[75] Science-based quantitative and qualitative "technical screening criteria" are set by the European Commission to this effect.[76] The actual EU Taxonomy is, as a result, drawn up by the European Commission via delegated acts, pursuant to the procedure set in Article 290 TFEU.[77] Next to compliance with the technical screening criteria, the activity must be performed in compliance with minimum safeguards for human rights and labour rights.[78]

The technical screening criteria for climate mitigation and adaptation objectives were the first adopted by the European Commission,[79] before it more recently completed the EU Taxonomy with the criteria for the other four objectives.[80] As the EU Taxonomy is only a so-called "green taxonomy" that identifies *environmentally* sustainable activities, it does not include all economic activities in all sectors of the economy, even though it covers the activities that are responsible for approximately 90% of the EU's greenhouse gas emissions.[81] If an economic activity is included in the delegated act, it is "taxonomy-eligible";[82] if it also meets the threshold which the Commission

---

[74] Ibid., Articles 9 to 16 Regulation.

[75] Ibid., Article 17.

[76] Ibid., Article 19.

[77] Ibid., Article 23.

[78] Ibid., Article 18.

[79] Commission Delegated Regulation 2021/2139 of 4 June 2021 supplementing Regulation (EU) 2020/852 of the European Parliament and of the Council by establishing the technical screening criteria for determining the conditions under which an economic activity qualifies as contributing substantially to climate change mitigation or climate change adaptation and for determining whether that economic activity causes no significant harm to any of the other environmental objectives, OJ 2021 No. L442, 9 December 2021. See also Commission Delegated Regulation 2023/2485 of 27 June 2023 amending Delegated Regulation (EU) 2021/2139 establishing additional technical screening criteria for determining the conditions under which certain economic activities qualify as contributing substantially to climate change mitigation or climate change adaptation and for determining whether those activities cause no significant harm to any of the other environmental objectives, OJ 2023 No. L, 2023/2485, 21 November 2023.

[80] Commission Delegated Regulation 2023/2486 of 27 June 2023 supplementing Regulation (EU) 2020/852 of the European Parliament and of the Council by establishing the technical screening criteria for determining the conditions under which an economic activity qualifies as contributing substantially to the sustainable use and protection of water and marine resources, to the transition to a circular economy, to pollution prevention and control, or to the protection and restoration of biodiversity and ecosystems and for determining whether that economic activity causes no significant harm to any of the other environmental objectives and amending Delegated Regulation (EU) 2021/2178 as regards specific public disclosures for those economic activities, OJ 2023, No L, 2023/2486, 21 November 2023.

[81] Gardes, Sourisseau and Voisin 2022, 34.

[82] Article 1(5) Commission Regulation 2021/2178 of 6 July 2021 supplementing Regulation (EU) 2020/852 of the European Parliament and of the Council by specifying the content and presentation of

established per activity to guarantee substantial contribution and no significant harm to one of the six predefined environmental objectives, it is "taxonomy-aligned".[83] At a later stage, the Commission included energy generation from fossil gas and nuclear energy generation activities as taxonomy-eligible activities,[84] a decision that has been challenged before the General Court.[85] These activities, subject to technical screening criteria, were included as "transition" activities, a category provided under Article 10(2) of the Taxonomy Regulation, which qualifies those activities for which there should be "no technologically and economically feasible low-carbon alternative" but which nonetheless support the transition to a climate-neutral economy.[86]

The Taxonomy Regulation amended the SFDR to require disclosure against the EU Taxonomy for financial products that have sustainable investment as their objective and, *"mutatis mutandis"*, for those that promote environmental or social characteristics.[87] From the Latin phrasing, the European Supervisory Authorities initially derived that the "less ambitious" category of financial products must be able to first earmark part of its portfolio as "sustainable investment" in order to use the definitions of the Taxonomy Regulation.[88] After the European Commission clarified that taxonomy-related disclosures ought not to be conditional on the earmarking of sustainable investments, it is clear that taxonomy-aligned investments are distinct from sustainable investments.[89] However, this appears to be only a transparency

---

information to be disclosed by undertakings subject to Articles 19a or 29a of Directive 2013/34/EU concerning environmentally sustainable economic activities, and specifying the methodology to comply with that disclosure obligation, OJ 2021 No. L443, 10 December 2021.

[83] Ibid., Article 1(2).

[84] Commission Regulation 2022/1214 of 9 March 2022 amending Delegated Regulation (EU) 2021/2139 as regards economic activities in certain energy sectors and Delegated Regulation (EU) 2021/2178 as regards specific public disclosures for those economic activities, OJ 2022 No. L188, 15 July 2022.

[85] Case T-625/22, *Austria* v. *Commission* (lodged on 7 October 2022).

[86] See also the regime for "enabling" activities under Article 16 Reg. 2020/852 of 18 June 2020. See Och, Chapter 13 in this volume.

[87] Articles 5 and 6 Reg. 2020/852 of 18 June 2020.

[88] See also Joint Committee of the European Supervisory Authorities (2021), 8 ("[Taxonomy-related disclosures] for Article 8 SFDR products should apply only to those investments that have sustainable investment as their objective.")

[89] Annex to Decision Commission C(2022)3051 of 13 May 2022 on the adoption of the answers to be provided to questions submitted by the European Supervisory Authorities, 11. See also Annex II to Decision Commission C(2023)2281 of 5 April 2023 on the answers to be provided to questions requiring the interpretation of Union law submitted on 9 September 2022 by the European Supervisory Authorities under Article 16b(5) of Regulations (EU) No 1093/2010, (EU) No 1094/2010 and (EU) No 1095/2010 of the European Parliament and of the Council, and amending Commission Decisions of 6 July 2021 and 13 May 2022, 4–5. Joint Committee of the European Supervisory Authorities (2022e), 4. The interpretation by the Commission leaves a somewhat awkward result. If Article 8 products had to be able to make "sustainable investment" in order not to contradict the amendments made by the Taxonomy Regulation, but later guidance clarifies that meeting the requirements of the taxonomy is no longer conditional on earmarking the portfolio as sustainable investment, one would expect that the Commission also leaves out the ability of making sustainable investment from Article 8 because it is no longer supported in its interpretation of the text of Level 1 regulations, but the Commission

requirement, and not an obligation for financial products promoting environmental or social characteristics to contain sustainable investments or taxonomy-aligned investments. Despite the Commission's interpretation, it remains hard to understand what else taxonomy-aligned investment could be, other than a subset of the broader legal notion of "sustainable investment". The Commission later specified that investments in a funding instrument of which the use of proceeds directly finance taxonomy-aligned activities are automatically sustainable investments, but that for all other types of investments in an undertaking with some degree of taxonomy alignment the Commission expects an analysis of the conditions of "sustainable investment" for the whole investment in that undertaking.[90]

Hence, not all sustainable investments have to be taxonomy-aligned, whether they are part of the portfolio of a financial product that promotes environmental or social characteristics, or of the portfolio of a financial product with a sustainable investment objective.[91] This is not surprising given that the EU Taxonomy is supposed to be a living instrument which is selective in its scope of activities covered and whose technical screening criteria evolve to support the transition.[92] Besides, it is only a "green taxonomy" and not a social taxonomy, even though limited minimum social safeguard are required for an economic activity to be aligned with the Taxonomy. Thus some activities, such as education, that are *per se* neither environmentally sustainable nor unsustainable could be considered socially sustainable investments. Therefore, the concept of "sustainable investment" is broader than the scope of taxonomy-aligned investments.

When a financial product promotes environmental or social characteristics, part of its portfolio can but does not have to meet the definition of sustainable investments. However, the European Commission cautions that when claiming carbon emissions reductions as part of an investment strategy under Article 8, it should not mislead investors into thinking that the product pursues sustainable investment when carbon emissions reductions are only a characteristic.[93]

Once an investment strategy integrates sustainability considerations beyond the mere risk perspective required by the SFDR, it no longer falls solely under the Article

---

nevertheless maintained the category of Article 8 products making sustainable investments that do not align with the Taxonomy Regulation. Annex II Reg. 2023/363 of 31 October 2022.

[90] Notice Commission 2023/C 211/01 on the interpretation and implementation of certain legal provisions of the EU Taxonomy Regulation and links to the Sustainable Finance Disclosure Regulation, OJ 16 June 2023, C 211, 5.

[91] Annex to Decision Commission C(2021)4858 of 6 July 2021 on the adoption of the answers to be provided to questions submitted by the European Supervisory Authorities, 5 ("clarify that 'sustainable investment' include investments into 'environmentally sustainable economic activities' within the meaning of that Regulation").

[92] For instance, at the time of the writing, the aviation sector is not covered by the EU Taxonomy. Yet, investing in the research and development of electricity-powered jets should be considered as an environmentally sustainable investment in the sense of SFDR.

[93] Annex to Decision Commission C(2023) 2281 of 5 April 2023 on the answers to be provided to questions submitted by the European Supervisory Authorities, 5.

6 regime.[94] The financial market participant should classify the financial product as either a financial product that promotes environmental or social characteristics, which is more commonly known as an "Article 8 product", of which it can earmark part of the portfolio as sustainable investment, including taxonomy-aligned investment. Or the financial market participant can classify the product as having sustainable investment as the objective, which are more commonly known as "Article 9 products".

10.6.2 *"Sustainable Investment" to Differentiate between Articles 8 and 9*

The difference between Articles 8 and 9, according to the European Commission, is quantitative. Thus a product complying with Article 9 SFDR should be, in principle, entirely invested in sustainable investments.[95] However, this interpretation exceeds the (admittedly confusing) letter of the SFDR, since sustainable investment merely refers to "an objective" under both Article 2(17) and Article 9. A restrictive interpretation of sustainable investment could undermine the transition to a sustainable economy, as most of the economy relies today on unsustainable bases and needs to be transitioned, including through engagement policies, rather than left stranded. Even though the SFDR's recitals specify that Article 9 is regulating those financial products that have "as an objective a positive impact on the environment and society",[96] a valid interpretation could support the exclusion of unsustainable investments without necessarily requiring the sole inclusion of sustainable investments. This view is confirmed by the Commission Delegated Regulation, which admits investments in economic activities that are not environmentally sustainable under the EU Taxonomy, even where the financial product invests in activities that contribute to an environmental objective, as long as a justification is provided by the financial market participant.[97] Such an interpretation is further supported by the introduction of the Do No Significant Harm (DNSH) principle in the SFDR, which posits that a "sustainable investment" must not significantly harm "objectives" of social and environmental sustainability.[98] This debate echoes a similar one with the EU Taxonomy: the EU Taxonomy only covers environmentally sustainable economic activities, but this does not imply that all other activities are accordingly unsustainable. Moreover, the Commission's interpretation undermines the original purpose of the SFDR, which is to support disclosures and deter greenwashing while recognizing that financial products pursuing sustainability have "various degrees of ambition".[99]

---

[94] Ibid., 8 ("integration per se of sustainability risks [...] is not sufficient for Article 8 to apply").
[95] Decision Commission C(2021)4858 of 6 July 2021 on the adoption of the answers to be provided to questions submitted by the European Supervisory Authorities, 5; Commission Delegated Regulation (EU) 2022/1288, rec. 15.
[96] Recital 21 Reg. 2019/2088.
[97] Article 19(1)(c) Commission Delegated Regulation (EU) 2022/1288.
[98] Article 2(17) Reg. 2019/2088; Article 25(1) Reg. 2020/852; Article 2a Reg. 2019/2088.
[99] Recital 21 Reg. 2019/2088.

According to the SFDR, the main difference following the classification lies in the possibility of an Article 8 product to still assign a mainstream index as reference benchmark, whereas Article 9 products should assign a sustainable index or no index at all, supposing that the investment strategy does not typically require the use of an index as benchmark.[100] Consistently with our own interpretation, the guidance of the European Supervisory Authority indeed states that "the requirement [to] explain 'how' the designated index differs from a broad market index suggests that the designated index cannot itself be a broad market index, notwithstanding the accompanying 'why' question".[101]

10.6.3 *Sustainable Investment Left Undefined*

Much scholarly debate exists on how to interpret the "classification" of sustainable financial products under the SFDR. Rightly so, as according to Morningstar, 55% of funds available for sale in the EU in 2023 are Article 8 and Article 9 funds by assets under management (37.8% in terms of number of funds).[102] Breaking down the assets under management, an overwhelming 52.5% are classified as promoting environmental and social characteristics (Article 8), while only 3.3% are classified as falling under Article 9.[103] In other words, the applicable disclosure regime under the SFDR has been (ab)used by financial market participants for the marketing of their "Article 8" and "Article 9" financial products to investors. This is the reverse logic of the SFDR, which is to first require disclosures and then ensure that the marketing communications of financial market participants and financial advisers do not contradict those disclosures.[104] However, confusion about what "sustainable investment" means has led to a wave of reclassifications, resulting in downgrades from Article 9 to Article 8 for a total of €175 billion of assets under management.[105] At that time, it was still unsettled how a company could classify as sustainable investment, even for the European Supervisory Authorities.[106] The European Commission has now clarified that financial market participants can choose between measuring sustainable investment at the level of a company or at the level of a specific activity, and that they can determine the key parameters of a "sustainable investment", but in doing so they should live up to an increased responsibility towards the investment community.[107]

---

[100] Recital 21; Articles 8(1) and (2) and 9(1) and (2) Reg. 2019/2088.
[101] Joint Committee of the European Supervisory Authorities 2022d, 18. However, the European Supervisory Authorities did not yet address the main counterargument, namely that Article 9(2) SFDR also refers to the situation "where no index has been designated as a reference benchmark"; Gargantini and Siri 2022, 18.
[102] Morningstar 2023, 4–6.
[103] Ibid.
[104] Article 13 Reg. 2019/2088.
[105] Klasa 2022; Morningstar 2023, 5.
[106] Joint Committee of the European Supervisory Authorities 2022c, 1.
[107] Annex to Decision Commission C(2023) 2281 of 5 April 2023 on the answers to be provided to questions submitted by the European Supervisory Authorities, 2–3.

While environmental sustainability may be determined by reference to the EU Taxonomy, the European Supervisory Authorities stated for socially sustainable investments that financial market participants should create their own framework adhering to the letter of the definition of "sustainable investment", which they should apply consistently.[108] This restrictive interpretation of the SFDR thus creates an imbalance, if not a loophole, in the Article 9 regime, since financial market participants have little discretion to determine environmentally sustainable investments and significant discretion to define socially sustainable investments.[109]

In other words, "sustainable investment" is a principle which is vaguely defined,[110] and provides a framework within which financial market participants can in principle define their own objectives and contributions. The Commission Delegated Regulation changes little in that. Instead, it provides for box-checking templates to indicate whether the financial product promotes environmental or social characteristics – and whether it earmarks part of its portfolio as "sustainable investment" – or "has sustainable investment" as its objective. However, the concern that the definition of "sustainable investments" is too vague[111] may be exaggerated. Stating that parts of a portfolio consist of sustainable investments should not be deemed to mean anything else than that financial market participants bring themselves within a disclosure framework that not only requires the mere provision of information, but also regulates the quality of that information in a way that could be understood as a comply-or-explain mechanism.

10.6.4 *Disclosures about Sustainable Investment*

When a financial product is classified under Article 8 SFDR, the template leniently allows financial market participants to define those characteristics, provide indicators to measure characteristics, describe the investment strategy – which requires the inclusion of binding elements in the selection of the investments to attain the characteristics – and explain in a narrative section the planned asset allocation.[112] In the words of the European Commission, "financial products that fall under Article 8 of the SFDR might integrate different strategies, even including those that, despite

---

[108] Joint Committee of the European Supervisory Authorities 2022d, 17.

[109] Still, a socially sustainable investment is defined as "an investment in an economic activity that contributes to a social objective, in particular an investment that contributes to tackling inequality or that fosters social cohesion, social integration and labour relations, or an investment in human capital or economically or socially disadvantaged communities." Article 2(17) Reg. 2019/2088.

[110] Article 2(17) Reg. 2019/2088.

[111] Eurosif 2022, 11.

[112] Annex 1 Commission Delegated Regulation 2022/1288.

claiming ESG, socially responsible investing (SRI) or sustainability orientation, might lack sustainability-related materiality".[113]

However, when an Article 8 product earmarks part of its portfolio as "sustainable investment", three additional obligations apply.

First, the product must indicate whether it pursues environmental objectives mentioned in the Taxonomy Regulation, and disclose the minimum extent to which "sustainable investments" are taxonomy-aligned following the strict rules for calculating taxonomy-alignment, including a prohibition to rely on assumptions.[114] The taxonomy-alignment is zero if data cannot be collected in the way prescribed in the delegated regulation.[115] In addition, a justification of any investments that are part of sustainable investment with an environmental objective but that are not in taxonomy-aligned economic activities must be provided. This also applies for products regulated under Article 9.[116] In other words, while financial products promoting environmental characteristics under Article 8 and those pursuing an environmental objective under Article 9 must disclose against the Taxonomy, they are not barred from investing in economic activities that do not follow the technical screening criteria of the Taxonomy or pursue other environmental objectives than those provided under the Taxonomy.[117]

Second, as part of the second condition of the definition of "sustainable investment", the DNSH principle, the mandatory indicators of the template of the PAI Statement on the website must be used, but determining how the indicators have been respected is up to the financial market participants.[118] The European Supervisory Authorities indeed only indicate that it would be a "best practice" to extract the mandatory indicators from the PAI Statement and, by using appropriate values, they should disclose how there is no significant harm to environmental or social objectives.[119] The European Commission clarified that transition plans that would avoid significant harm in the future should not be part of this assessment.[120] Thus the PAI Statement provides some legal clarity for interpreting the broad DNSH principle, which exceeds under the SFDR the scope of the synonymous principle under the Taxonomy Regulation.[121] In addition, the DNSH assessment must

---

[113] Draft Commission Delegated Regulation C(2021)2616 of 21 April 2021 amending Delegated Regulation (EU) 2017/565, 2.

[114] Article 15–17 Commission Delegated Regulation 2022/1288.

[115] Annex to Decision Commission C(2022)3051 of 13 May 2022 on the adoption of the answers to be provided to questions submitted by the European Supervisory Authorities, 10. Joint Committee of the European Supervisory Authorities 2022d, 23.

[116] Article 19(1)(c) Commission Delegated Regulation 2022/1288.

[117] Ibid., Articles 15(1)(c) and 19(1)(c).

[118] Ibid., Article 51(d)i, Article 39(a) and 59(d)i.

[119] Joint Committee of the European Supervisory Authorities 2022a, 11.

[120] Annex to Decision Commission C(2023) 2281 of 5 April 2023 on the answers to be provided to questions submitted by the European Supervisory Authorities, 3.

[121] For a critic, see Partiti 2023.

indicate whether the investments align with specified international human rights instruments.[122] It is important to note that a taxonomy-aligned investment should still meet the DNSH assessment to qualify as a sustainable investment except if the investment is a funding instrument of which the use of proceeds is directly financing taxonomy-aligned activities.[123]

Third, to satisfy the last condition of "sustainable investment", policies must be adopted to assess good governance practices.[124] This term is defined by reference to examples like sound management structures, employee relations, remuneration of staff and (remarkably) tax compliance.[125] The ESAs clarified that there are no reference metrics prescribed.[126] Interestingly, some of these examples are also defined as part of the PAI Statement. In particular, for governance with regard to tax matters an optional indicator for investment in sovereigns and supernationals refers to the EU list of non-cooperative jurisdictions for tax purposes.[127] However, no guidance has been issued regarding the relationship between the good governance assessment and the PAI indicators, even if the examples as part of the definition of "sustainable investments" overlap with the indicators of the PAI Statement. Especially if the use of the indicators is only a best practice under a DNSH assessment in which the mandatory PAI indicators are explicitly referred to, it does not seem appropriate to restrict the good governance assessment in any way to the metrics for measuring PAI indicators, in particular when it comes to optional indicators.

The type of information that an Article 8 product must provide depends on whether it earmarks part of its portfolio as "sustainable investment". The earmarking of sustainable investment within the portfolio of an Article 8 product requires the mapping of adverse impacts indicators, for which the ESA strongly encourage financial market participants to use the mandatory indicators in the Principal Adverse Impact Statement. It also increases the burden of motivating the contribution to an environmental objective if it deviates from the technical screening criteria of the European Commission.

If the financial product has sustainable investment as its objective, the entire portfolio, in principle, complies with the three cumulative criteria of "sustainable

---

[122] Articles 39b, 51 & 59 Commission Delegated Regulation 2022/1288. ("OECD Guidelines for Multinational Enterprises and the UN Guiding Principles on Business and Human Rights, including the principles and rights set out in the eight fundamental conventions identified in the Declaration of the International Labour Organization on Fundamental Principles and Rights at Work and the International Bill of Human Rights").

[123] Notice Commission 2023/C 211/01 on the interpretation and implementation of certain legal provisions of the EU Taxonomy Regulation and links to the Sustainable Finance Disclosure Regulation, OJ 16 June 2023, C 211, 5.

[124] Note that "good governance" is also a requirement of Article 8 products without sustainable investments. Annex II–III Commission Delegated Regulation 2022/1288.

[125] Article 2(17) Reg. 2019/2088.

[126] Joint Committee of the European Supervisory Authorities 2022d, 17. The ESAs provide examples of optional metrics such as UN Global Compact, OECD or ILO principles.

[127] Annex I Commission Delegated Regulation 2022/1288.

investment".[128] Similarly, if part of a portfolio falling under Article 8 classifies as "sustainable investment", a DNSH assessment must be made in which the adverse impacts indicators that are mandatory in the Principal Adverse Impact Statement need to be considered as a best practice and the contribution to a sustainability objective should be explained if it deviates from the technical screening criteria of the European Commission.[129]

Recognizing the importance of passive investing, both Articles 8 and 9 SFDR provide for specific disclosure requirements where the financial products have reference benchmarks. In general, a justification for the use of the benchmark and its sustainability-related appropriateness must be provided.[130] Unlike Article 8, Article 9 requires that if the product refers to an index, it must be a specialized one.[131] Specialized means that the index must be aligned with the sustainability objective pursued by the financial product, which should differ from a broad market index. This means that the index does more than excluding a small number of securities, and that its holdings should be materially different from a similar non-ESG index.[132] If the objective of the product is to reduce carbon emissions, the index used should be a Paris-aligned Benchmark (PAB) or an EU Climate Transition Benchmark (EU CTB), unless no such benchmark is available.[133] Although the Commission appears to have watered down this requirement by emphasizing that it does not prescribe the use of any specific type of index, the detailed explanation required to justify the efforts in meeting the environmental or social objective arguably lead to the same result as requiring the use of a specialized index, or a regulated one in case of a carbon reduction objective.[134]

While using a reference benchmark is not required by the SFDR for financial products subjected to Articles 8 and 9, the European Commission clarified that active investment strategies are also covered by this requirement to use a labelled index, which use indices to show superior performance, both financially and in terms of sustainability.[135] The application of Article 9 would be slightly different, because these

---

[128] Article 9(1) Reg. 2019/2088. Article 61(b) Commission Delegated Regulation 2022/1288; Annex to Decision Commission C(2021)4858 of 6 July 2021 on the adoption of the answers to be provided to questions submitted by the European Supervisory Authorities, 5, ("in order to meet requirements in accordance with prudential, product-related sector specific rules may next to 'sustainable investment', also include investments for certain specific purposes such as hedging or liquidity which, in order to fit the overall financial product's sustainable investment' objective, have to meet minimum environmental or social safeguards").

[129] Article 59(e)i Commission Delegated Regulation 2022/1288; Article 62(1)(b)vi Commission Delegated Regulation 2022/1288.

[130] Article 8(1) and (2) Reg. 2019/2088.

[131] Article 9(1) Reg. 2019/2088; Joint Committee of the European Supervisory Authorities 2022d, 18.

[132] ESMA 2022ab, 10.

[133] Article 9(1) and (3) Reg. 2019/2088. See Gargantini and Siri, Chapter 11 in this volume.

[134] Annex to Decision Commission C(2023) 2281 of 5 April 2023 on the answers to be provided to questions submitted by the European Supervisory Authorities, 4; Article 9(3) Reg. 2019/2088.

[135] Annex to Decision Commission C(2023) 2281 of 5 April 2023 on the answers to be provided to questions submitted by the European Supervisory Authorities, 4. Joint Committee of the European Supervisory Authorities 2022c, 2–3.

financial products are required to show how they aim to attain their sustainable invest-ment objective.[136] If their objective is to reduce carbon, they are measuring their per-formance against a regulated index. The question came up whether the text of the SFDR implies that only *tracking* of an index – that is, passive investment strategies – requires the use of a labelled index, which the Commission did not clearly answer.[137]

While the SFDR was introduced, the EU CTB and PAB benchmarks were cre-ated to support the alignment of low-carbon indexes to the objectives of the Paris Agreement.[138] Both require a decarbonization strategy of investee companies to ensure a minimal average of 7% in annual reduction of greenhouse gas intensity (expressed as ton CO_2e/EVIC[139] in millions) or of absolute greenhouse gas emis-sions (expressed as ton CO_2e) depending on the type of security and the issuer of the security.[140] Furthermore, the absolute GHG emissions or the GHG intensity of the EU CTB must be 30% lower compared to the set of all investable instruments in a given asset class or group of asset classes, taking into account both scope 1 and 2 emissions and with a phase-in of scope 3 emissions.[141] The threshold is set at 50% for the PAB.[142] In addition, the EU CTB, and to a larger extent the PAB, are subject to mandatory exclusions, especially regarding the fossil fuel sector.[143] Curiously, the European Supervisory Authorities asked the European Commission whether the requirements of the PAB and the EU CTB would be in compliance with the defini-tion of sustainable investment.[144] A negative answer would contradict the letter and spirit of the SFDR, given that financial products subjected to Article 9 are encour-aged to follow such reference benchmarks. Hence, the European Commission clar-ified that financial products that passively track an EU CTB or PAB labelled index are "deemed to have sustainable investments".[145] However, as the Commission's

[136] Article 9(2) Reg. 2019/2088.
[137] Annex to Decision Commission C(2021)4858 of 6 July 2021 on the adoption of the answers to be pro-vided to questions submitted by the European Supervisory Authorities, 5–6. Note that this guidance was also deleted by the Commission in a later Decision: Annex II to Decision Commission C(2023) 2281 of 5 April 2023 on the answers to be provided to questions submitted by the European Supervisory Authorities, 2.
[138] Regulation 2019/2089 of 27 November 2019 amending Regulation (EU) 2016/1011 as regards EU Climate Transition Benchmarks, EU Paris-aligned Benchmarks and sustainability-related disclosures for benchmarks, OJ 2019 No. L317, 9 December 2019.
[139] Article 1(d) Commission Delegated Regulation 2020/1818 of 3 December 2020 supplementing Regulation (EU) 2016/1011 of the European Parliament and of the Council as regards minimum stan-dards for EU Climate Transition Benchmarks and EU Paris-aligned Benchmarks, OJ 2020 No L406, 3 December 2020 (EVIC or "enterprise value including cash" means the sum, at fiscal year-end, of the market capitalization of ordinary shares, the market capitalization of preferred shares, and the book value of total debt and non-controlling interests, without the deduction of cash or cash equivalents).
[140] Ibid., Article 1(b–c).
[141] Ibid., Article 9.
[142] Ibid., Article 11.
[143] Ibid., Articles 10 and 12.
[144] Joint Committee of the European Supervisory Authorities 2022c, 3.
[145] Annex to Decision Commission C(2023) 2281 of 5 April 2023 on the answers to be provided to ques-tions submitted by the European Supervisory Authorities, 6.

guidance was provided as part of analysis of the first "contribution to an environmental objective" condition of the three-prong sustainable investment test, it is
likely that a DNSH and good governance assessment should still be made.[146]

Although the definition of "sustainable investment" is not entirely clarified, it
encourages robust internal assessments over blind reliance on opaque ESG rating agencies by leveraging the PAI Statement, the Taxonomy Regulation and the
Benchmark Regulation.[147] But because of its vagueness, it cannot be understood
as a labelling regime; it is not the definition of "sustainable investment" that is relevant, but the additional disclosure requirements that apply as soon as a financial
market participant deems its financial product to be in line with the definition. The
main benefit of the legal framework is to constrain the justifications why a financial
product is sustainable based on the self-classification of the portfolio as "sustainable
investment". Justifying sustainability within the framework of "sustainable investment" plays a central role in the legal framework, which is also reflected in the
predominance of "sustainable investment" in the legal definition of "sustainability preferences", in the proposal for a fund name's rule and in ESMA's guidance
on supervisory practices discussed below. Hence, contrary to what proponents of a
labelling regime aim to achieve, it is not in the nature of the SFDR to define sustainability substantively.

10.7 PROMINENCE OF SUSTAINABLE INVESTMENT IN REGULATORY DEVELOPMENTS

10.7.1 *Sustainability Preferences*

Following the recommendations of the High-Level Experts Group on Sustainable
Finance,[148] the European Commission emphasized the need for investment firms
and insurance distributors to ask investors about their sustainability preferences and
take those preferences into account as part of their fiduciary duties.[149] As is well
known, these firms and distributors must perform a suitability test before providing investment or insurance advice, or portfolio management to non-professional
investors; they must ask information about the knowledge and experience, ability to bear losses, and – traditionally financial – objectives, like risk tolerance, of
the investors.[150] On 21 April 2021, the European Commission adopted a regulatory

---

[146] Annex to Decision Commission C(2023) 2281 of 5 April 2023 on the answers to be provided to questions submitted by the European Supervisory Authorities, 6.
[147] Gargantini and Siri 2022, 1 and 13.
[148] High-Level Expert Group on Sustainable Finance 2018, 28.
[149] Communication Commission COM(2018)97 of 8 March 2018 Action Plan: Financing Sustainable
Growth, 6–7.
[150] Article 25(2) Directive 2014/65/EU of 15 May 2014 on markets in financial instruments and amending
Directive 2002/92/EC and Directive 2011/61/EU (recast), OJ 2014 No. L173, 12 June 2014. Article 30(1)

package to integrate clients' sustainability preferences as part of the suitability test.[151] For sustainability preferences, there is no explicit reference in the legal definition to the classification of financial products as Article 8 or 9 under the SFDR.

To the contrary, in the preparation of the amendments to the suitability test, the European Commission considered that part of the obligations of the SFDR lack "sustainability-related materiality". In particular, the Commission noted that disclosures of Article 8 products could cover such a wide variety of sustainable investment strategies that for some strategies sustainability would not be material.[152] This let the Commission focus the definition on principal adverse impacts, sustainable investment and taxonomy-alignment.

First, the client can choose which data she wants the financial product to gather, or in other words, she can determine the qualitative or quantitative elements that demonstrate the consideration of principal adverse impacts on sustainability factors.[153] As mentioned above, in precontractual financial product disclosures, the supervisory guidance on the consideration of principal adverse impacts does not require the use of the prescribed indicators on the template which the European Commission adopted for the PAI Statement on the website, but urges national supervisors to verify whether the indicators are considered, if relevant.

Second, the client can choose the minimum proportion of "sustainable investment" in a financial product.[154] As discussed, "sustainable investment" automatically includes a consideration of principal adverse impacts, and as a best practice, the mandatory impacts under the PAI Statement. It also means that an additional requirement exists if the product pursues an environmental objective and must justify how the objective can be achieved without investing in environmentally sustainable economic activities in compliance with the Taxonomy's technical screening criteria. The provision does not distinguish based on the requirement to justify the deviation from a specialized index or a regulated carbon reduction benchmark.

Third, the client could choose to have a percentage of taxonomy-alignment.[155]

Directive 2016/97 of 20 January 2016 on insurance distribution (recast), OJ 2016 No. L26, 2 February 2016. Article 54 Commission Regulation 2017/565 of 25 April 2016 supplementing Directive 2014/65/ EU of the European Parliament and of the Council as regards organisational requirements and operating conditions for investment firms and defined terms for the purposes of that Directive, OJ 2017 No. L87, 31 March 2017. Article 9 Delegated Regulation 2017/2359 of 21 September 2017 supplementing Directive (EU) 2016/97 of the European Parliament and of the Council with regard to information requirements and conduct of business rules applicable to the distribution of insurance-based investment products, OJ 2017 No. L341, 20 December 2017.

[151] Article 54 Commission Delegated Regulation 2017/565. See Colaert, Chapter 12 in this volume.
[152] Draft Commission Regulation C(2021)2616 of 21 April 2021 amending Delegated Regulation (EU) 2017/565, 2.
[153] Article 2(7)c Commission Delegated Regulation 2017/565.
[154] Ibid., Article 2(7)b.
[155] Ibid., Article 2(7)a.

10.7.2 *Name's Rule*

In 2022, ESMA proposed guidelines to regulate the names of investment funds in which "sustainable investment" plays an essential role.[156] This "name's rule" proposal is a response to the SFDR-related categorization of financial products by the industry, and must be read in view of other similar proposals made in the United States and the United Kingdom.[157]

First, both product categories, Article 8 and Article 9, would be subject to exclusion criteria applicable to Paris-aligned Benchmarks.[158] Second, the proposed guidelines suggest that 80% of investments should reflect the ESG-related words used in a fund's name, regardless of whether the fund is subjected to Article 8 or 9. This 80% rule is also applicable to a fund which uses the word "sustainable" in its name, but in addition, ESMA proposes to have the fund make at least 50% of its total investments in "sustainable investment".

In other words, the name's rule does not change much about the architecture of the disclosure framework as described above. It does not affect Article 9 funds, as these funds already require in principle a 100% alignment with sustainable investment, rendering an 80% rule irrelevant. If anything, the name's rule creates three new categories within Article 8 (non-ESG names, ESG names, Sustainability names), for which their common classification as Article 8 does not change. However, the name's rule is a disclosure rule too. Application of the 80% rule will in particular affect the narrative used in the disclosures related to the promotion of characteristics for funds that adopt an ESG-related name. It is a quantification of the legal concept "promoting characteristics" that nevertheless still lacks a definition and any safeguards regarding the determination and justification of sustainability.

ESMA's proposed rule is much less explicit in neglecting product categorization than the definition of "sustainability preferences", and even aims to further develop product categorization. However, it cannot be said that the meaning of "promoting characteristics" and the related disclosure requirements have fundamentally shifted into a labelling regime. To the contrary, ESMA proposed not to differentiate between Article 8 and Article 9 based on mandatory exclusions. Instead, it proposed to apply the exclusions to both categories. In the same vein, ESMA appears to clearly distinguish the Article 8 and Article 9 funds based on the 80% rule and the related naming restrictions, but it could also be argued that it blurred the line between product categories by introducing the 50% rule. It identified a quantitative distinction between

---

[156] ESMA 2022c.

[157] Ibid., 7. See also Investment Company Names, 85 FR 13221 (proposed May 25, 2022) (to be codified at 17 CFR Parts 232, 270 and 274); FCA, Sustainability Disclosure Requirements (SDR) and investment labels, CP22/20.

[158] ESMA 2022c, 10.

both product categories as a clear line when the word "sustainable" is used in the name, but, as a result, both, Article 8 funds with 50% sustainable investments and Article 9 funds will be able to be called "sustainable". In other words, the name's rule too can be read as a tool to make the earmarking of the portfolio as sustainable investments central in the disclosure regime, rather than creating a definitional distinction between Article 8 and 9 which would be a recognition of the SFDR as a labelling.[159] Awaiting the finalization of the proposal, ESMA already indicated that the term "sustainable" in a fund's name would be reserved to Article 9 products and Article 8 products with a proportion of sustainable investment.[160]

While the proposal would *de facto* introduce a name's rule, it cannot be confused with a regulatory measure. While financial market participants and national competent authorities are required to "make every effort to comply",[161] ESMA's guidelines are genuinely soft-law instruments that operate according to a "comply or explain" obligation.[162] Thus national competent authorities and financial market participants could well disapply this name's rule. However, where national competent authorities comply with ESMA's guidelines, those may be enforced against financial market participants placed under their supervision.[163]

10.7.3 *Supervisory Guidance*

In ESMA's non-binding supervisory briefing on sustainability risks and disclosures, the reference to a classification under Articles 8 and 9 was specifically addressed and deemed necessary to integrate in precontractual disclosures.[164] This seems to be the only guidance that deems it relevant under which Article disclosures are made. However, ESMA clearly states that reference to the provisions of the SFDR cannot create the impression that a labelling regime is used. Instead, ESMA urges that national supervisors should focus on claims of "sustainable investment" which should lead to scrutiny on compliance with the requirements of sustainable investment and efforts in seeking more information from financial market participants if clarifications are needed.[165]

---

[159] ESMA 2022c, 9.

[160] Ibid.

[161] Article 16(3) Regulation No 1095/2010 of 24 November 2010 establishing a European Supervisory Authority (European Securities and Markets Authority), OJ 2010 No. L331, 15 December 2010.

[162] ECJ (Grand Chamber) 15 July 2021, Case C-911/19, *Fédération Bancaire Française (FBF)* v. *Autorité de Contrôle Prudentiel et de Résolution*, ECLI:EU:C:2021:599, paras. 45 and 48.

[163] ESMA 2022c, 21.

[164] ESMA 2022a, 8–9 ("Without giving the impression of a 'label' to investors, an indication as to under which Article of SFDR (and if relevant, the TR) the UCITS/AIF discloses the relevant information should be mentioned in the fund documentation").

[165] Annex to Decision Commission C(2023) 2281 of 5 April 2023 on the answers to be provided to questions submitted by the European Supervisory Authorities, 4. Joint Committee of the European Supervisory Authorities 2022d, 16. ESMA 2022a, 13.

10.8 SUSTAINABLE INVESTMENT AS A SUPERVISORY FOCUS

Regulators could not be blunter in their rejection of turning the SFDR into a labelling regime.[166] The European Commission clarified that the main standard in the legal regime, namely that of "sustainable investment", should be interpreted as allowing the financial market participant to set out their own understanding of the key parameters.[167] This guidance fits in with the view of the SFDR as a transparency framework. Once the framework is applied, the financial product should consider principal adverse indicators as part of the DNSH requirement and disclose against the taxonomy if the financial product highlights environmental performance. In addition, financial products invested only in "sustainable investment" and which designated an index as reference benchmark are subject to the additional requirement to use a specialized index.

What should be prevented is additional criteria on Article 8 products. When Morningstar downgraded 23% of Article 8 products because it was not convinced by their adherence to sustainability, this was not done on the basis of lack of compliance with "sustainable investment", the only standard in the SFDR, but because Morningstar used its own definitions of sustainability, which goes against the inclusiveness of the disclosure framework.[168] In the same vein, Eurosif argues that regulators should recognize that the SFDR is used as a labelling instrument and better delineate the different categories.[169] Thus the European Commission went as far as to propose to consider minimum standards for what is understood as "promotion of environmental or social characteristic".[170]

Similarly, our analysis shows that the European Commission raises the bar for some disclosures by reducing the freedom of financial market participants to justify the sustainability of their investments at will.[171] We agree that the current use of product categorization is used for marketing purposes. Still, we consider that establishing minimum requirements to the categories of the SFDR should not lead to an overemphasis on product categorization. Additional criteria that are not based on the concept of sustainable investment not only go against the current trend in regulation, but could simply divert the attention away from disclosure rules that constrain the freedom of financial market participants in defining sustainability. Implementation must thus be carefully calibrated, as the SFDR rightly recognizes that financial products with "various degrees of ambition" regarding sustainability

---

[166] Draft Commission Delegated Regulation C(2021)2616 of 21 April 2021 amending Delegated Regulation (EU) 2017/565, 2.

[167] Annex to Decision Commission C(2023) 2281 of 5 April 2023 on the answers to be provided to questions submitted by the European Supervisory Authorities, 3.

[168] Andrew 2022a.

[169] Eurosif 2022, 10.

[170] Communication Commission COM(2021) 390 of 6 July 2021 Strategy for Financing the Transition to a Sustainable Economy, 7.

[171] Eurosif 2022, 10.

have been developed to date. In this view, the SFDR's primary purpose is to support market transparency, not discourage it. If the Commission or the European Supervisory Authorities wish to discipline the marketplace with labels, there are other instruments better suited than disclosure regulation.

In line with ESMA's guidance, we therefore argue in favour of increased scrutiny on "sustainable investment" and the obligations that follow from the application of "sustainable investment".[172] As the SFDR regime takes its final shape, supervision will be critical for ensuring investor protection and market transparency. In this respect, the supervisory competence lies in the hands of the national competent authorities in accordance with sectorial legislation.[173] This creates risks for further fragmentation in the application of the law.[174] It is therefore important that national supervisors strictly monitor the use of principal adverse indicators, in particular as part of the DNSH requirement of sustainable investment but also for principal adverse impact disclosures in precontractual documents.[175] In achieving streamlined disclosures, supervisors should make their practices such that financial market participants are urged to use the indicators, and likely also use the metrics of the PAI Statement on a product level. Also, the national supervisors should closely monitor the disclosures about the contribution to an environmental objective, which in principle requires the use of the Taxonomy, but allows for deviations as long as these are adequately justified. In particular, with regard to the application of sustainable investment, the freedom provided to financial market participants comes with increased responsibility towards the investment community and supervisors should play their role in ensuring financial market participants perform cautious measurement of the key parameters.[176] Moreover, they should be strict in monitoring the justification of what it means to use a materially different index than a broad market index if the financial product is an Article 9 product.[177] Supervisors should not accept Article 9 product classifications if the index used does not sufficiently differ from a broad market index. Finally, for all the attention on sustainable investment, it is important that supervisory authorities do not lose sight that most financial products are only required to consider sustainability risks, and that those cannot be left without proper scrutiny.

10.9 CONCLUSION

The first of its kind, the Sustainable Finance Disclosure Regulation was adopted in 2019 to harmonize sustainability disclosures of financial services providers and to

---

[172] ESMA 2022a, 13.
[173] Article 14 Reg. 2019/2088.
[174] Busch 2021.
[175] ESMA 2022a, 7.
[176] Annex to Decision Commission C(2023) 2281 of 5 April 2023 on the answers to be provided to questions submitted by the European Supervisory Authorities, 3.
[177] ESMA 2022a, 10.

reduce information asymmetry for investors.[178] This sweeping reform originates from the 2018 Action Plan Financing Sustainable Growth to regulate the consideration of sustainability risks and factors by asset managers and institutional investors and resulted in a highly technical disclosure framework that is still under construction.[179] While the European Union has experimented the pitfalls of being a "first mover" in regulating sustainability disclosures, the SFDR has also been greatly influential, with the International Monetary Fund taking it as an example for sustainability disclosures.[180]

In this chapter, we presented the SFDR as a layered system of sustainability-related disclosures.

We argue that supervisory authorities should focus on the more demanding disclosure rules within the disclosure framework of "sustainable investment". We show that the focus on classification under Articles 8 and 9 is not relevant for the choice of clients in sustainability preferences, is not a decisive factor in the proposed name's rule and is not a factor for which ESMA would deem increased supervisory scrutiny important. To the contrary, any further definition of what "promotion of environmental or social characteristics" means that does not refer to "sustainable investment" could divert the attention from the "sustainable investment" analysis.

The application of the Commission Delegated Regulation could mark a new era for the SFDR, as it will provide a new impetus for national supervisory authorities to enforce sustainability-related materiality, limit the excessive focus on classifications and decrease the urge to denaturalize this disclosure framework in a labelling mechanism. It means that supervisors enforce those obligations that increase the burden of proof for financial market participants in the way that is beneficiary for considering clients' sustainability preferences.

As a disclosure framework, the SFDR gives financial market participants the freedom to justify what a contribution to an environmental or social objective means. That is what sets it apart from a labelling mechanism with a clearly defined threshold for what a contribution should entail.[181] This does not mean that any explanation should be accepted. Both the SFDR and the Taxonomy Regulation provide some tools to discipline financial market participants in justifying their contribution.

Our argument gives a new perspective on popular proposals to have the disclosure framework embrace its role as labelling scheme. We consider these to be avenues supervisors should avoid because it will divert the attention from the rules that are considered high-quality sustainability disclosures to practices that do little more than embracing the status quo in sustainability disclosures.

---

[178] Recital 10 and Article 1, Reg. 2019/2088.
[179] Communication Commission COM(2018)97 of 8 March 2018 Action Plan: Financing Sustainable Growth, 8–9. See, e.g., some of the main provisions of the SFDR still in need of clarification: Joint Committee of the European Supervisory Authorities 2022c.
[180] International Monetary Fund 2022, 63.
[181] See, for example, Konstantas et al. 2021 (setting out potential criteria for an EU Ecolabel applicable to financial products, *inter alia*, based on a minimum proportion of taxonomy-aligned investment).

REFERENCES

Andrew, T. (2022a), 'Morningstar: Quarter of SFDR Article 8 funds do not meet ESG criteria', available at: https://bit.ly/3OUItss (last accessed 22 October 2022).

Andrew, T. (2022b), 'BlackRock and UBS AM to downgrade €21bn worth of Article 9 ETFs', available at: https://bit.ly/49pQJbT (last accessed 22 October 2022).

Busch, D. (2021), 'Sustainability disclosure in the EU financial sector', in Busch, D., Ferrarini, G. and Grünewald, S. (eds.), *Sustainable Finance in Europe. Corporate Governance, Financial Stability and Financial Markets* (Cham: Palgrave Macmillan), 397–443.

Central Labelling Agency (2023), 'Revised Towards Sustainability Quality Standard: Final criteria', available at: https://bit.ly/3ws57Cb (last accessed 14 March 2023).

Chiu, I. (2022), 'The EU sustainable finance agenda: Developing governance for double materiality in sustainability metrics', 23 *European Business Organization Law Review*, 87–123.

Condon, M. (2019), 'Externalities and the common owner', 95 *Washington Law Review*, 1–81.

Curtis, Q., Fisch, J. and Robertson, A. (2021), 'Do ESG funds deliver on their promises?', 120 *Michigan Law Review*, 393–450.

ESMA (2022a), 'Supervisory briefing: Sustainability risks and disclosures in the area of investment management', ESMA34-45-1427, available at: https://bit.ly/3yR4Vok.

ESMA (2022b), 'ESMA Strategy 2023–2028', ESMA22-439-1076, available at: https://bit.ly/3yN4p3j.

ESMA (2022c), 'Consultation paper on Guidelines on funds' names using ESG or sustainability-related terms', ESMA34-472-373, available at: https://bit.ly/4edhkfm.

Esty, D. and Karpilow, Q. (2019), 'Harnessing investor interest in sustainability: The next frontier in environmental information regulation', 36 *Yale Journal on Regulation*, 625–692.

European Supervisory Authority (2022), 'ESAs call for evidence on better understanding greenwashing', available at: https://bit.ly/4c4ShsS.

Eurosif (2022), 'EU sustainable Finance & SFDR: Making the framework fit for purpose', Eurosif Policy Recommendations, June, available at: https://bit.ly/3KzSA36.

Gardes, C., Sourisseau, S. and Voisin, S. (2022), 'Appliquer la Taxonomie Européenne: Le cas du financement de la décarbonation de l'industrie cimentière', 2022 *Cahiers de droit de l'entreprise*, 30–40.

Gargantini, M. and Siri, M. (2022), 'Information Intermediaries and Sustainability', ECMI European Capital Markets Institute, Working Paper no 15, November, available at: https://papers.ssrn.com/sol3/papers.cfm?abstract_id=4316820.

High-Level Expert Group on Sustainable Finance (2018), *Financing A Sustainable European Economy, Final Report*, available at: https://bit.ly/3IQc5U9.

International Monetary Fund (2022), *Global Financial Stability Report: Navigating the High-Inflation Environment*, available at: https://bit.ly/3VsoLot.

Joint Committee of the European Supervisory Authorities (2021), *Final Report on draft Regulatory Technical Standards*, JC 2021 50, available at: https://bit.ly/3Xviw83.

Joint Committee of the European Supervisory Authorities (2022a), *Clarifications on the ESAs' Draft RTS under SFDR*, JC 2022 23, available at: https://bit.ly/3x9QCUb.

Joint Committee of the European Supervisory Authorities (2022b), *Joint ESAs' Report on the Extent of Voluntary Disclosure of Principal Adverse Impact under the SFDR*, JC 2022 35, available at: https://bit.ly/3Kvm6r1.

Joint Committee of the European Supervisory Authorities (2022c), *List of Additional SFDR Queries Requiring the Interpretation of Union Law*, JC 2022, 47, available at: https://bit.ly/4c8Pr6b.

Joint Committee of the European Supervisory Authorities (2022d), *Questions and Answers (Q&A) on the SFDR Delegated Regulation*, (Commission Delegated Regulation (EU) 2022/1288), JC 2022 62, available at: https://bit.ly/4crZeoj.

Joint Committee of the European Supervisory Authorities (2022e), *Final Report on Draft Regulatory Technical Standards*, JC 2022 42, available at: https://bit.ly/3yODvYV.

Joint Committee of the European Supervisory Authorities (2023), 'Joint ESAs' Consultation Paper on the review of SFDR Delegated Regulation regarding PAI and financial product disclosures', JC 2023 09, available at: https://bit.ly/3yScvrF.

Klasa, A. (2022), 'European asset managers blame regulatory confusion for downgrade of ESG funds', *Financial Times*, available at: www.ft.com/content/d74445d5-1275-4a1e-a118-70f2750ce7c9.

Konstantas, A., Faraca, G., Dodd, N. et al. (2021), 'Development of EU Ecolabel criteria for financial products: Technical report 4.0', available at: https://bit.ly/3KxJtjr (last accessed 22 October 2022).

Morningstar (2022a), 'SFDR Article 8 and Article 9 Funds: Q3 2022 in Review', available at: https://bit.ly/3V5mH04 (last accessed 22 October 2022).

Morningstar (2022b), 'The European ESG Template (EET) Ahead of MiFID II Amendment', available at: https://bit.ly/3UT9rEy, 1–21 (last accessed 22 October 2022).

Morningstar (2023), 'SFDR Article 8 and Article 9 Funds: Q4 2022 in Review', available at: https://bit.ly/3UPu708 (last accessed 14 March 2023).

Partiti, E. (2023), 'From disclosures to classification regime and sustainability due diligence. Tackling the flaws of the Sustainable Finance Disclosure Regulation', TILEC Discussion Paper No. 2023–05.

Steuer, S. and Tröger, T. (2022), 'The role of disclosure in green finance', 8 *Journal of Financial Regulation*, 1–50.

Van Caenegem, A. and van de Werve, T. (2021), 'Regulating sustainability communications in the financial services sector: The Sustainable Finance Disclosure Regulation', in Colaert, V. (ed.), *Sustainable Finance in Europe and Belgium* (Limal: Anthemis), 145–162.

Zetsche, D. A. and Anker-Sørensen, L. (2022), 'Regulating sustainable finance in the dark', 23 *European Business Organization Law Review*, 47–85.

Information Intermediaries and Sustainability

The Case of ESG Ratings and Benchmarks

*Matteo Gargantini and Michele Siri**

11.1 SCOPE OF THE ANALYSIS: INFORMATION INTERMEDIARIES IN THE ESG WORLD

Sustainable finance has been steadily expanding over the last years. Financial products that qualify as 'sustainable' (or display equivalent labels such as 'green' or 'ESG-compliant') represent a significant portion of capital markets – according to some metrics, the value of sustainable assets under management (AUM) at the end of 2021 was equal to USD 2.74 trillion worldwide, with EU-domiciled funds having an 80% lion's share.[1] The regulatory lining of this impressive growth was an explosion of new European rules aimed at addressing a broad array of concerns that surround investors' reliance on the quality of sustainable financial products. At the time of writing, other measures are also in the pipeline to fill regulatory gaps and to update statutes that only entered into force a few years ago.

Key elements in the development of sustainable finance are sustainability ratings, benchmarks and indices as well as listing requirements that support investment decisions in this field. In turn, firms providing these services rely on external reviewers to ascertain the reliability of the data they use to release a sustainability rating or include a financial instrument in an index. All these entities are collectively referred to as 'information intermediaries' due to their role in the analysis of data and the production of derived information, often through synthetic indicators, that other financial market participants can use when determining the composition of their

[*] Although the chapter is the result of shared reflections, Sections 11.2, 11.3 and 11.5 shall be attributed to Matteo Gargantini and Sections 11.1 and 11.4 to Michele Siri. The authors wish to thank Veerle Colaert, Youcef Rahmani and the participants of the EUSFiL Conference of 9 September 2022 and of the ECMI-CEPS Annual Conference of 9 November 2022 for their comments on a previous version of this chapter. All errors remain the authors' sole responsibility. The working paper on which this chapter is based has received the Best Paper Award at the 2022 Annual Conference of the European Capital Markets Institute (ECMI) and the Centre for European Policy Studies (CEPS), whose financial support is gratefully acknowledged.
[1] Morningstar 2022.

portfolios. Due to their importance in the world of sustainable finance, information intermediaries have been – or will be – made subject to specific rules, with the ultimate purpose of fostering investors' trust in the quality of the financial products that are labelled as sustainable.

The overall impression is that a brand-new area of European law has developed that mirrors in many respects the 'old' world of financial law, and that this exercise has rapidly generated a system whose complexity is comparable to that of traditional financial law. In this chapter, we will rely on this parallel between the law of sustainable finance and traditional financial law to explore the role and the regulation of information intermediaries in supporting ESG targets in the European Union (EU). We will focus on sustainability (or ESG) rating agencies (SRAs) and benchmarks, in light of their relevance in the current market for sustainable investments. Therefore, we will use the expression 'information intermediaries' to collectively refer to these two classes of intermediaries alone. We believe, however, that the methodology we adopt can fruitfully apply to other ESG intermediaries, as well.

In particular, we will explore to what extent market failures that justify the regulation of traditional information intermediaries such as rating agencies and financial analysts can also explain (from a positive perspective) and shape (from a normative perspective) existing and prospective rules on information intermediaries in the world of sustainable finance within the EU. By the same token, we also consider whether regulatory failures form the past have been – or, respectively, should be – considered in the design of that regulatory framework. The analysis proceeds as follows: Section 11.2 provides a synthetic theoretical framework for the analysis; Section 11.3 addresses ESG ratings; Section 11.4 deals with ESG indexes and benchmarks; and Section 11.5 concludes with some policy recommendations.

11.2 INFORMATION INTERMEDIARIES IN FINANCIAL MARKETS: THE OLD, THE NEW AND THE NOT-SO-NEW

A key objective of financial regulation is to prevent market failures. These are situations where equilibria resulting from the free interactions among market forces determine suboptimal outcomes in terms of efficiency and, therefore, in terms of social welfare maximisation.[2] Among the various market failures that taint financial markets are asymmetric information and agency costs, both of which are particularly relevant to understand the role and the functioning of information intermediaries.

11.2.1 *Market Failures and Information Intermediaries*

Free interactions in the market for financial assets may lead to misallocation of resources when some investors are unable to access the same information their

---

[2] Lambert 2017, 10–13.

counterparty possesses. This dynamic leads to typical adverse selection and moral hazard problems, and exacerbates agency costs after the investment is made. The nature
of financial products as experience or credence goods makes asymmetric information
particularly intractable because investors will only have full knowledge of the quality
of their purchase long after the decision to invest – possibly as far into the future as the
maturity date. Or they may not even gain this knowledge by the maturity date, when
it proves impossible to tell whether the unsatisfactory performance of the investment
is due to mismanagement or to the vagaries of market conditions. For ESG factors,
even measuring performance can be a complex matter and lead to no clear-cut result.

    While the parties to the contract who are in possession of material information
may have strong incentives to share their superior knowledge to prove the quality
of the asset they are selling, finding ways to convey credible signals may prove difficult despite the commitment of market participants – especially in the financial
sector. Some firms developed precisely to help address the negative consequences
of asymmetric information and agency costs. Such firms do so by gathering relevant
data and by disseminating, as a specific output, derived information of a synthetic
nature that is easier for investors to handle. For this reason, such entities are normally referred to as 'information intermediaries'. Information intermediaries also
give credibility to the information they release by putting their reputation on the
line in a way that their clients (or the public at large) can trust. This kind of credibility explains why such entities are also labelled as 'reputational intermediaries'.

    Unfortunately, just like in a matryoshka-doll game, the market for informational
intermediaries' services is subject, in turn, to the same kind of market failures that
taint the market for financial products, although with a different level of intensity.
In this chapter, we will discuss the role and the functioning of two informational
(or reputational) intermediaries, namely sustainability rating agencies (SRAs) and
index providers, and will explore how regulation does (and should) approach the
market failures that impact their activities.

11.2.2 *Different Approaches to Sustainable Finance*

All markets are, with variable intensity, prone to asymmetric information or agency
problems, and the markets for traditional and sustainable finance are no exception.
However, the dynamics of these market failures are not necessarily identical in the
'old' and the 'new' world.

    In a traditional setting, material information includes all the data the investors
involved in the transaction would use as a basis for their investment decisions,[3] and particularly the factors that determine the risk/return profile of the financial product. How
different things can look when ESG factors come into play depends on the context.

---

[3] We borrow here the paradigm of the model investor in EU law (see in particular Article 7(4)
     Regulation (EU) 596/2014 on market abuse – MAR).

In a first scenario, investors may include ESG factors in their strategies because they believe that aligning with sound ESG practices will (most likely) have a positive effect on returns or reduce the risks to which the investments are exposed ('outside-in perspective').[4] Here, the new world of sustainability is, indeed, not entirely new. Factoring ESG criteria into the definition of the portfolio is not qualitatively different than factoring other relevant criteria that measure financial risks. In this context, due consideration to sustainability improves the assessment of investments by including a broader range of relevant data in the analysis. This does not mean, however, that the regulatory problems are identical to those of traditional finance. Methodologies for the definition of ratings as well as indices and benchmarks may need to be adjusted. Moreover, the specific nature of the data selected to assess the investment may trigger 'garbage in, garbage out' problems that are peculiar to ESG criteria.

In a second scenario, investors may want to look not so much (or not only) at the quality of their investments alone, but rather (or also) at the impact of those investments on ESG targets, regardless of the potential ability of these consequences to backfire on the risks or the returns of their exposure ('inside-out perspective'). This approach, which is less profit-oriented and more focussed on pure sustainability, is very different from the traditional one. This is because the information that the asymmetry refers to is focussed not so much on the issuer as such, but rather on the consequences the investment can have on environmental, social and governance matters.

To be sure, the boundaries between the two scenarios may be blurred. For instance, metrics that assess the risk of principal adverse environmental impacts of an investee company (the inside-out perspective) are crucial for evaluating the reputational and liability risks of that company.[5] To differentiate between the outside-in and the inside-out perspectives of sustainability metrics, this chapter relies on the European Commission's distinction between the two prongs of double materiality, one that looks at how non-financial factors affect the value of the company, the other at the impact of the company's activities on ESG factors.[6] It therefore looks at what ratings, indices and benchmarks measure rather than how users can include those assessments in their decision-making processes.

The following sections will flesh out how the differences between the old, the new and the not-so-new world play a role in the positive and normative analysis of the legal frameworks on information intermediaries in sustainable finance. The analysis will then proceed with some reflections on the most suitable regulatory strategies to address the market failures that affect ESG ratings and benchmarks. As we shall see, these services are often subject to more pervasive and more intense market failures compared to their traditional equivalent. However, this does not

---

[4] European Commission 2021a, 1.

[5] See Bengo et al. 2022, 814, classifying metrics of principal adverse impacts on sustainability factors as pertaining to the assessment of long-term financial risks.

[6] European Commission 2019, 6–7.

automatically lead to the conclusion that stricter regulation is required. First, market failures leading to large welfare losses may originate from simple dynamics that light-touch strategies can successfully tackle. Second, pervasive strategies may lead to heightened regulatory failures, which might more than compensate for the reduction of market failures.

11.3 SUSTAINABILITY RATINGS

An explosion of sustainability-related products has fuelled the burgeoning market for sustainable investments, and sustainability ratings have played an essential role in this development. For this reason, sustainability ratings have been in the policymakers' spotlight since the outset of the agenda for sustainable finance, even though this has led to *ad hoc* reforms only recently. Already in its 2018 Action Plan, the Commission identified the lack of a clear framework for sustainability ratings as an area of concern.[7] More recently, in its 2021 Action Plan, it anticipated that it would 'take action to improve the reliability and comparability of ESG ratings'[8] and then followed up on the commitment with a proposal for a Regulation submitted in June 2023.[9] The proposal later became a Regulation (hereinafter: the ESG Ratings Regulation), which was adopted by the European Parliament on 24 April 2024 and was not yet published on the Official Journal at the time of writing.[10]

The urge to adopt measures addressing SRAs is the result of a combination of the rapid increase in the number of products and suppliers with a generalised perception that such a development has not been met by adequate levels of transparency. This applies first and foremost to what ESG ratings are actually measuring. In line with the broad distinction we drew in Section 11.2.2, the main dividing line differentiates 'ESG risk ratings', which focus on issuers' exposure to ESG risks and assess issuers' ability to manage such risks (outside-in perspective), from 'ESG impact ratings', whose purpose is instead to measure the overall effects of issuers' operations on sustainability factors (inside-out perspective).[11]

11.3.1 *Sustainability Ratings, Credit Ratings and Investment Recommendations Compared*

While SRAs may be regulated entities for other activities they perform,[12] the preparation and dissemination of sustainability (or ESG) ratings will become only in the near future a regulated activity the performance of which requires a licence. The

---

[7] European Commission 2018, 7–8 (Action 6).
[8] European Commission 2021b, 16 (Action 4).
[9] European Commission 2023a.
[10] We will refer to European Parliament (2024).
[11] ESMA 2020, 16–17; Larcker et al. 2022.
[12] ESMA 2022a, 8.

ESG Ratings Regulation will drive this change by introducing a new entity into EU law, namely the 'ESG rating provider', subject to authorisation. In this chapter, we refer to such entities as SRAs, for the sake of brevity.

In this sub-section, we compare sustainability ratings with two activities that have been long regulated and show material similarities with ESG ratings, namely credit ratings by credit rating agencies (CRAs) and investment recommendations by financial analysts. To be sure, there are other good candidates for a comparison, including proxy advisors and external reviewers. Proxy advisors, in particular, are interesting due to the kind of analysis they perform on ESG factors (although voting recommendations and sustainability ratings are different outputs) and the strong role of self-regulation in their legal framework (Article 3j Directive 2007/36/EC on the exercise of certain rights of shareholders in listed companies – SHRD). We cannot further explore this analogy due to the limited space in this chapter. However, we believe CRAs and financial analysts seem more suitable to our purpose due to the kind of the analysis they run, the type of synthetic information they release as an output and the sophistication of their regulatory framework.

11.3.1.1 Services and Methodologies

SRAs do not qualify as CRAs as they do not assess the creditworthiness of debtors or debt instruments. First, they address equity and debt indifferently. Second, when they deal with debt, they do not measure credit risk (or the issuers' ability to pay back their debt).

The services offered by traditional CRAs consist of assessing the creditworthiness of a debtor or of a financial obligation, quantified through a system of symbols that ranks the result of the evaluation (Article 3(1)(a) Regulation (EC) 1060/2009 on credit rating agencies – CRA Regulation). As we mentioned, this exercise can hardly ignore the risks stemming from ESG factors.[13] For this reason, CRAs often stress they include ESG factors in their methodologies,[14] although with few details on the assessment criteria.[15]

To help shed light on these aspects, ESMA has adopted specific guidelines to enhance disclosure about which key driving factors, among those that determined a rating or an outlook, CRAs consider to be ESG factors and the reasons why they were material.[16] At the same time, ESMA has also stressed the importance of not considering credit ratings as an opinion on the sustainability of the rated entity and has suggested that rules mandating the inclusion of ESG factors in CRAs' methodologies be avoided.[17] However, the Commission has more recently maintained its commitment

[13] High-Level Expert Group on Sustainable Finance 2018, 76.
[14] S&P Global Ratings 2022.
[15] European Commission 2022a, 4–5; Cash 2021, 69.
[16] ESMA 2019a, 26.
[17] ESMA 2019b, 32.

to ensure that CRAs consider those factors when determining credit ratings and credit outlooks,[18] so that some more pervasive rules might come in the future.

Not only do SRAs not qualify as CRAs under EU law, but they do not typically convey their conclusions through communications that directly or indirectly propose an investment decision. Hence, SRAs are not financial analysts for the purpose of Market Abuse Regulation, either (Regulation (EU) 596/2014 – MAR). While one can imagine that robust financial analysis can hardly ignore sustainability-related risks, financial analysts do not appear to make broad use of ESG data,[19] apparently because they do not entirely trust the reliability of such information.[20]

This shows how the availability of trustworthy ESG ratings (and benchmarks, which may rely on them) is still not optimal, which is likely a symptom of market failures. This situation may connect to the more challenging task SRAs face compared to CRAs and financial analysts. The main difference lies with the higher complexity of the multivariate analyses that underlie their exercise. To begin with, significant uncertainties surround the reliability of data, which may lack the support of quality assurance mechanisms comparable to those used for credit ratings.[21] Even if one leaves aside these concerns and trusts external reviewers, many scholars criticise the robustness of ESG ratings in general, as they rely on backward-looking information and are prone to inevitable shortcuts as well as to issues in the identification of causation.[22]

To give just an idea of the arduous methodological choices underlying ESG ratings and their implications, let us briefly focus on the different perspectives that can be adopted to address the impact of certain activities on greenhouse gases.[23] Some investors may prefer to avoid investing in any activity that significantly contributes to carbon dioxide emissions, and therefore may prefer not to fund any fossil-intensive products at all (constant approach[24]). Others may instead start from the assumption that fossil-intensive industrial processes are still entrenched in the economic system and, therefore, reward firms that rely on those processes but credibly strive to improve them (dynamic approach). The methodologies of sustainability ratings SRAs can and do adopt one or the other criteria,[25] which is understandable in the light of heterogenous investor preferences. Yet ESG ratings may also diversify their criteria depending on the geographical area of the concerned issuers.[26] For instance,

---

[18] European Commission 2022b, 12, 14 (Action 3).
[19] Hinze and Sump 2019, 145.
[20] Abhayawansa 2018.
[21] European Commission and ERM 2021, 82, 89–92.
[22] Ingo 2020, 331–2.
[23] A comparison of ESG rating methodologies can be found in Larcker et al. 2022.
[24] This static assessment is also the most common among the technical screening criteria (TSC) defined in Regulation (EU) 2021/2139, which supplements Regulation (EU) 2020/852 (Taxonomy Regulation). However, not only does Regulation 2139 also include dynamic TSC, but all the TSC are subject to periodical revision to keep pace with technological development (Platform on Sustainable Finance 2021, 16).
[25] Pagano et al. 2018, 357, 359.
[26] Ibid.

they can adopt a stricter approach for developed countries and a more flexible one for developing countries – and different metrics could be adopted to adjust for the level of a particular country's development.

Other uncertainties may add on the difference between a constant and a dynamic approach based on the nature of the financial instrument. For instance, equity instruments may accommodate for dynamic criteria better than debt, if only because they allow investors to have a voice in the investees' governance.[27] However, how much greener the investment could be would depend on the asset manager's engagement policy or the institutional investors, as well as on the implementation thereof, which are both difficult to measure objectively.

Also casting doubts on ESG rating is the discretional nature of the weight of each indicator (such as the tons of carbon dioxide released into the atmosphere over a certain period) in the pertinent criterion (such as climate risk). The same applies to the aggregation of each rating criterion into its respective pillar (such as gathering environmental factors – 'E'), let alone into the overall ESG rating.[28] While quantifying the relative importance of indicators within the context of ESG risk ratings may be challenging, it becomes entirely subject to value judgement in ESG impact ratings.

Interactions with issuers are also a sensitive part of methodologies. While disclosure to ESG rating agencies of inside information remains subject to the limitations of the market abuse regime (Articles 10 and 18(1)(a) MAR),[29] the communication of other confidential information is not subject to limitations under EU law. Some ESG rating agencies, nonetheless, commit to rely only on publicly available information in their methodology.[30] This reduces the risk that ESG ratings may be subject to capture, although at the risk of reduced accuracy.

The same trade-off affects the sharing of preliminary results with issuers.[31] Once again, market practices are diverse. Some ESG rating agencies anticipate their draft assessment and collect feedback from the issuers,[32] while others make the report public and rely on issuers' initiative in case of complaints.[33] This is, of course, a sensitive practice, which may reduce the risk of mistakes but may facilitate capture when combined with issuer-pays remuneration models.[34] Frequent exchanges of information in this fashion have reportedly contributed to the inflation of credit ratings for structured

---

[27] See e.g. Recital 6 and Article 3 Regulation (EU) 2020/1818 (requiring equity EU Climate Transition Benchmarks and equity EU Paris-aligned Benchmarks to retain exposure to oil, gas, mining and transportation. On these benchmarks see Section 11.4.3).

[28] Ibid., 333–4. For a breakdown of the steps that lead from ESG indicators to ESG ratings see Neisen 2021.

[29] On the potential nature of ESG-related information as inside information see Mülbert and Sajnovits 2021, 287–8.

[30] MSCI 2023, 6, 14; lPagano et al. 2018, 357.

[31] IOSCO 2021, 33.

[32] Sustainalitics 2021, 14; IOSCO 2021, 30, 41, considers this as a best practice.

[33] MSCI 2023, 9; MSCI 2024, 14.

[34] AMF and AFM 2020, 10.

finance (securitisation) transactions that preceded the 2007–8 financial crisis.[35] For this reason, these practices are subject to ESMA's scrutiny for CRAs (Articles 17(1)(c), 18(a) and Annex VII(2)(c) and (4)(g) Regulation), and financial analysts that are banks, investment firms or independent analysts must disclose whether the recommendations they release have been disclosed to the relevant issuers and, if so, whether they have been consequently amended (Article 4(1)(a) Regulation (EU) 2016/958). This is without prejudice to the general ban preventing banks and investment firms from sharing draft reports that are labelled as investment research with the issuers, even when this is meant to verify the accuracy of factual statements, as long as the drafts include a recommendation or a target price (Article 37(2)(f) Regulation (EU) 2017/565).

The ESG Ratings Regulation requires SRAs to disclose their policy concerning the engagement with rated entities, including on-site reviews or visits (Article 22 and Annex III(2)(c) ESG Ratings Regulation), which shows that engagement does not seem to be in contrast with general principles such as the need to ensure that the SRAs act independently (Articles 14(1) and 23). Most importantly, issuers are given the right to access the dataset the SRA used to issue the rating and verify the accuracy of the data therein. Such verification can lead to highlighting any material factual errors, but cannot lead to influencing the rating methodologies or their outcome (Recital 12). To this end, SRAs will make issuers aware that they will be subject to coverage by notifying them before the first issuance of the rating (but not of any following updates) (Article 14(11a)).

Concerns about conflicts of interest also stem from the joint provision, in addition to sustainability ratings, of advice or other services that support corporates and financial market participants in the definition of their ESG risk profile.[36] Once again, the history of credit ratings shows that rating agencies may have an incentive to be more lenient towards clients that purchase additional services from them.[37] Today, CRAs are subject to organisational requirements for the identification, management and disclosure of conflicts of interest (Article 6(4) and Annex I(A)(7), (B)(I) and (E)(I) CRA Regulation).

For financial analysts, the regulatory framework relies primarily on disclosure instead, but it does so with more detailed provision. This divergence reflects two different regulatory strategies. Where supervisors are policing conflicts of interest, as is the case with CRAs, disclosure towards the public at large does not play as important a role as it does when, in the absence of a registration system, investors directly assess the kinds of conflicts they are willing to tolerate, as is the case with financial analysts.

Transparency addresses all relationships and circumstances that may reasonably be expected to impair the objectivity of financial analysists' recommendations, including interests or conflicts of interest originating from the provision of additional services to the issuers. For banks and investment firms, this information also includes the internal organisational and administrative arrangements as well as

---

[35] Phillips 2018, 61; European Commission 2016, 111.
[36] MSCI 2023, 14.
[37] ESMA 2022b, 19.

Chinese walls that have been set up for the prevention and avoidance of conflicts of interest. The same entities disclose a breakout that shows how many of their recommendations, calculated as a percentage over each class (such as 'hold', 'buy' or 'sell'), concerns issuers that have received investment or ancillary services from the analyst in the previous year (Articles 5 and 6 Regulation (EU) 2016/958). When investment recommendations come from banks or investment firms, once again the law differentiates depending on the way investment recommendations are presented to the public. If recommendations are described as 'investment research' or presented as objective or independent, the conduct of business rules require the adoption of organizational measures that ensure the independence of financial analysis from any conflicting interest of the intermediary (or other intermediary's clients) and prohibit certain trading activities that can jeopardise that independence (Article 16(3) Directive 2014/65/EU on markets in financial instruments – MiFID II – and Article 37 Regulation (EU) 2017/565). If recommendations are neither labelled as 'investment research' nor are presented as objective or independent, banks and investment firms shall prominently disclose that such recommendations have not been prepared under this regime (Article 36 Regulation (EU) 2017/565).

The ESG Ratings Regulation follows a different path compared to the rules on financial analysis and adopts instead the same approach of the CRA Regulation, as it mostly relies on structural measures and supervision, although some space is left to disclosure as well. In principle, SRAs will be prevented from providing certain services that may jeopardise their integrity of judgement (Articles 15).[38] This particularly strict requirement – which surprisingly does not formally apply, however, to the whole corporate group of the SRA – cannot be deviated from for some services, such as consultancy and credit rating services. SRAs will be enabled to perform, instead, investment and banking services, but only as long as they take measures to ensure the independent provision of ESG ratings and the prevention of conflicts of interest. Moreover, benchmark administrators may ask to be authorised to provide ESG rating services. In addition, SRAs will be subject to organizational requirements concerning potential conflicts of interest (in this case, the provision includes the whole SRA's group), with ESMA having the power to take action when the steps SRAs adopt to protect their opinions from conflicts of interests fail to deliver (Article 23).[39]

11.3.1.2 Market Structure

Although mapping ESG rating providers is not always easy,[40] the market structure of ESG ratings displays remarkable similarities to traditional credit ratings, thus raising comparable regulatory concerns. According to ESMA, the market is divided

---

[38] Other provisions address SRAs' analysts and employees (Articles 16 and 24).
[39] The measure is inspired by a similar provision in Regulation (EU) 2016/1011 (Benchmark Regulation – see below).
[40] Douglas 2017.

into two segments. The first one comprises large firms based in third countries that hold a significant market share. Small EU-based providers with no market power make up the second segment. Overall, this reveals a relatively high level of market concentration,[41] which appears to increase over time.[42] The new ESG Ratings Regulation does not seem likely to foster competition, compared to the status quo ante. First, the Regulation relies on an authorisation mechanism, which in and of itself creates a barrier to entry. Second, while common ownership is subject to restrictions, that of course does not prevent further aggregations (Article 23(3a) ESG Ratings Regulation). Third, the simplifications the ESG Ratings Regulation provides for SMEs providing ESG ratings are quite limited, if one considers that deviations from rules such as those on internal procedures and oversight functions are subject to the adoption of compliance procedures and, in any event, to a proportionality test (Article 20).

Just like in the realm of CRAs, competition is in any event a double-edged sword when it comes to regulatory concerns.[43] On the one hand, as in any other industry, low market concentration easily leads to allocative efficiency and it may reduce the systemic impact of major misjudgements. On the other hand, some market power enables incumbent firms to reduce the risk of rating shopping.

Unsurprisingly, traditional players in the market for credit ratings have also entered the market for sustainability ratings,[44] partially through the direct provision of those services (which will still be allowed only through separate companies within the same group: Article 15(1)(b) ESG Ratings Regulation) and partially by external growth via acquisitions.[45] These developments may be the result of various factors, possibly in combination. The most obvious one seems to be the synergy between the methodologies supporting credit ratings and sustainability ratings. Even if the traditional methodologies can hardly be transplanted in the sustainability segment, ESG factors became part of the risk analyses supporting credit ratings. Therefore, firms developing expertise in measuring ESG factors from an outside-in perspective will likely develop economies of scope when assessing inside-out impacts.

More uncertain is the role of reputational capital. On the one hand, brands play a role for reputation intermediaries, so that a well-established name can leverage on the trust gained in the old market to attract customers to the new one. At the same time, it appears that some rating agencies prefer to allocate ESG-related services in separate organisational units and to sell them with distinct brands. This strategy may respond to the fear that the low quality of ESG ratings may backfire, causing reputational damage to the main brand.

---

[41] Larcker et al. 2022.
[42] ESMA 2022a, 3, 19.
[43] Coffee 2006, 289; Dombalagian 2011, 70.
[44] IOSCO 2021, 7; Cash 2021, 1–2.
[45] AMF and AMF 2020, 5.

Finally, SRAs are mostly paid by investors, which reduces the risks of conflicts of interest. However, the issuer-pays model is also widely used, so that the risk of some rating shopping may exist also for sustainability-related assessments.[46]

11.3.2 *What Do ESG Ratings Measure?*

The obvious distinction between ESG risk ratings and ESG impact ratings raises some regulatory concerns from the perspective of transparency. While the bulk of the available ESG ratings are in fact risk ratings,[47] the public at large – and reportedly even professional investors – seems to believe that those ratings measure issuer ability to promote ESG factors (impact ratings).[48] As we mentioned, there may be good reasons why a company that performs well from an outside-in perspective might do so because of its positive impact on ESG factors. This is for the simple reason that a smaller environmental footprint or better care for societal and governance matters will likely reduce corporate exposure to the corresponding regulatory, reputational and liability risks. However, the reverse may not be true because there are other actions that may improve ESG risk scorings, including hedging strategies.

In this regard, an essential regulatory measure is the duty to disclose the very nature of the ESG ratings involved, as the ESG Ratings Regulation does (Article 21 and Annex III(1)(d)). This form of transparency should refer not only to the alternative between outside-in and inside-out perspectives, but also to other forms ('any other dimensions', in the wording of the Regulation) of ESG ratings – or scorings, in this case – that only measure instrumental factors, such as the availability and (possibly) the quality of non-financial disclosure documents.[49] For ratings that have a composite nature, rating agencies should also quantify the weight of each approach in their methodology.

A different question relates to the regulatory strategy that can best support the development of ESG impact ratings in a world where private incentives are mostly supporting ESG risk metrics.[50] As we shall see, in the world of sustainability benchmarks, a soft-law provision delivered good results, but a 'comply or explain' rule for ratings could further support the mechanisms by asking for a justification of the decision by SRAs not to publish any ESG impact ratings.

11.3.3 *The Quality of ESG Ratings*

But there are other concerns surrounding the methodology of ESG ratings – and particularly of ESG risk ratings, due to their larger market share. Sustainability

---

[46] IOSCO 2021, 18; ESMA 2022b, 3.
[47] European Commission 2021a, 58.
[48] Simpson 2021; ESMA SMSG 2022, 2–3; 2DII 2022.
[49] On this matter see: ESMA 2020, 16–17.
[50] Chiu 2022, 102.

metrics try to convey soft information through symbols that are typical of hard data, or at least information that can be quantified, such as the probability of default in credit ratings. This sits uneasily with the nature of sustainability as soft information, which makes it often more amenable to being assessed than to being measured.[51] But even when measurement is possible, poor construction of ESG ratings may lead to weighting issues – just like William Edwards Deming claimed that the most important things cannot be measured, in the realm of sustainability one wonders to what extent the most important things can be compared. To give just one example, greenhouse gas emissions are certainly measurable, and so is the intensity of child labour in a supply chain. A different problem, however, is the relative importance that each of the two variables should have in a synthetic ESG rating. How many CO_2 tons is one hour of child labour worth?

Therefore, it is not surprising that a growing literature has noticed low levels of correlation among ESG ratings addressing the same issuers.[52] To be sure, inconsistent outputs are not necessarily a matter of concern, the question being whether they result from the noncongruent scope of the underlying assessments (looking at different ESG factors would justify different ratings), dissimilar methodological assumptions (ESG ratings may legitimately rely on different indicators when measuring the same criteria) or different levels of robustness in the methodology or the quality of data.[53] Therefore, one should not rush to the conclusion that low correlation is a sign of poor quality, as only the third alternative would reveal a market failure.

Unfortunately, the empirical literature does not rule out – to say the least[54] – this third alternative, which leaves the question of the reliability of ESG ratings open.[55] While some qualified opinions believe that divergences among ESG ratings are more pronounced at an aggregate level and tend to disappear at the more granular stage of indicators,[56] part of the empirical literature reaches opposite conclusions.[57] This seems to show that ESG ratings may be even less consistent than a superficial analysis would imply, as different assessments of indicators could compensate each other in the aggregations that lead to the final score.[58] Rules addressing SRAs' methodologies and their disclosure will therefore be crucial to restoring trust.

---

[51] Edmans 2020.

[52] Kumar et al. 2020; Berg et al. 2022; Gibson et al. 2021; Chatterji et al. 2016; Dimson et al. 2020; Kennedy 2024.

[53] For a calibrated analysis of the pros and cons of low correlation among ESG ratings and a comparison among different methodologies see Dell'Erba and Doronzo (2023), 378–83 and 398–400.

[54] The consensus is in the sense that lack of quality provides a strong explanation for the heterogeneity of ESG ratings relating to the same issuer (Ramos Muñoz and Smolenska 2023, 8).

[55] European Commission 2021b, 120–1 and 172–3.

[56] EU Technical Expert Group on Sustainable Finance 2019, 20.

[57] Berg et al. 2022, noticing that poor methodology may explain low correlation among ESG ratings.

[58] Dimson et al. 2020, showing that divergence among SRAs assessments is not only at the 'macro' ESG level, but also at 'micro' E, S or G levels.

Once again, let us consider the legal framework for CRAs and financial analysis as a starting point. CRAs are subject to a detailed set of rules and to strict supervision over their methodology. Substantive requirements include the duty to ensure that ratings are based on a thorough analysis of all the available information and that such information is reliable and originates from reliable sources. The methodologies shall be 'rigorous, systematic, continuous and subject to validation based on historical experience, including back-testing', and they should entail a review of the ratings every year (twice a year for sovereign ratings). Methodologies should be reviewed on an annual basis and, in case of material changes, these should be subject to public consultation (Articles 8(2)–(7) and Annex I(A)(9) CRA Regulation; Articles 4–7 Regulation (EU) No 447/2012).

Transparency requirements support the substantive regime by mandating the disclosure of the methodologies, models and key assumptions underlying credit ratings, including the mathematical or correlation assumptions (Article 8(1) and Annex I(D)(2)(b), (2a) and I(E)(I)(5)). All these requirements are subject to ESMA supervision, subject to the Authority's duty not to interfere with the contents of the ratings or their methodology (Articles 22a and 23 CRA Regulation).

The regulatory regime for financial analysts also relies on substantive and information requirements but its provisions have a more open texture. Investment recommendations must clearly distinguish facts from interpretations and estimates, and have to refer to reliable sources of information (a warning is added in the case of uncertainty as to their reliability). Financial analysts shall also make public their basis of valuation and methodology, together with their underlying assumptions, or information on the proprietary models they use. A summary of these data must accompany each recommendation, together with a sensitivity analysis of the assumptions.

An overview of all the recommendations disseminated during the previous year is also made public, together with the price target and the relevant market price at the time of dissemination and the validity time period of the price target or of the recommendation (Articles 3 and 4 Regulation (EU) 2016/958). As to supervision, financial analysts are bound to substantiate their recommendations to the competent authority upon request (Article 3(3)).

Unsurprisingly, the ESG Ratings Regulation takes inspiration from its equivalent on CRAs by mandating that methodologies be rigorous, systematic, objective and capable of validation, and that the SRAs review them every year (Article 14(7) and (8)). By the same token, methodologies are made subject to mandatory disclosure, both for their main features towards the public and with more detailed requirements when the information addresses subscribers and rated entities (Articles 21 and 22, as well as Annex III, of the Commission proposal). Once again, ESMA cannot interfere with the contents of the methodologies (Article 26).

A remarkable provision in the Regulation, which did not appear in the Commission proposal, requires that sustainability ratings should in principle focus on environmental, social or governance issues separately, rather than providing a single indicator for the three factors combined. Aggregation of E, S and G ratings is allowed, by way of derogation to this principle, only when the SRA provides the weighting of the tree factors and explains the weighting method (Article 21 and Annex III(1)(f) ESG Ratings Regulation). This break-out of synthetic ESG ratings into smaller opinions (or scorings) is to be welcomed, as it reduces the concerns surrounding the subjective nature of weighting among the relevant metrics.[59]

11.3.4 *A Risk of Overreliance?*

The low level of correlation among ESG ratings has played a crucial role in the design of the ESG Ratings Regulation, because the concerns about the quality of the assessments of sustainability have not reduced the use of those ratings by investors, which is reportedly widespread.[60] Just like with traditional CRAs, overreliance is a matter for both market participants and regulators to consider (Articles 5a, 5b and 5c CRA Regulation), and its regulatory implications depend in part on whether such reliance is spontaneous or induced by the applicable rules. The following sub-sections explore to what extent the regulatory framework relies on ESG ratings, and to what extent financial market participants are induced to refer to ESG ratings, even in the absence of explicit requirements. This analysis is all the more relevant as the ESG Ratings Regulation pays scant attention to overreliance, as the next sub-sections show.

11.3.4.1 Avoiding Regulatory Licences

Regulatory failures stemming from overreliance on ratings are particularly intractable. The risk is that rules incentivising the use of sustainability ratings may lead to an implicit licence that directly or indirectly adopts ratings as a requirement to enter the market. As the credit ratings experience has demonstrated,[61] this approach can magnify the systemic consequences of misjudgements. In the world of sustainability ratings, this risk can manifest itself through overinvestments in assets that turn out to be not as sustainable as expected. In this regard, however, policymakers seem to have learned from the past and the current regulatory framework should be praised for its attention in avoiding blind recourse to ESG ratings by market participants.[62] EU provisions defining transparency obligations for financial market participants perfectly illustrate this point.

Financial market participants must disclose their policies on the integration of 'sustainability risks' in their decision-making process, be it part of an investment

---

[59] For a proposal to unbundle ESG ratings, see Gordon 2023.
[60] Deloitte 2021, reporting that 65% of investors declare as using ESG assessments at least once a week.
[61] Partnoy 1999.
[62] Steuer and Tröger 2022, 17.

or advisory activity (Articles 3 and 6 Regulation 2019/2088 on sustainability-related disclosures in the financial services sector – SFDR).[63] In this context, 'sustainability risks' refers to possible future occurrences that, if materialised, can 'cause an actual or a potential material negative impact on the value of the investment' (Article 2(22) SFDR), which is relevant from an outside-in perspective.[64] Remarkably, no reference is made to ESG or credit ratings in any of these rules. Therefore, while the inclusion of ESG or credit ratings in the financial market participants' statements is certainly not prohibited, nothing in this regime determines an implied regulatory licence in favour of sustainability rating agencies.

Even more evident is the lawmaker's care in avoiding excessive reliance on ESG ratings from an inside-out perspective. Here, disclosure is also due at entity level and product level, in this latter case through both pre-contractual and periodic information. The central legal concept for such disclosure is that of adverse impacts on sustainability factors (Article 2(24) SFRD), which market participants have to identify and prioritise in their investment policy – the requirement is mandatory for large market participants and applies on a 'comply or explain' basis otherwise (Article 4(1)(a) and (2)(a) SFDR).[65] Entity-level and product-level disclosure include reference to the 'indicators' adopted to measure principal adverse sustainability impacts (Articles 4(2)(a) and 7(1), para. 2, SFDR). This also applies to products that claim to 'promote' environmental or social characteristics (Articles 8 and 10 SFRD – 'light green products') or have sustainable investments as their objective (Articles 9 and 10 SFRD – 'dark green products').[66]

How 'green' a financial product can be is, of course, not just a matter of purpose, as in the alternative between light and dark-green. It also depends on the allocation of investments among alternative assets (Articles 5, para. 2, and 6 Regulation – Taxonomy Regulation). Quantifying this allocation may be up to discretion, however, because the exercise involves the selection of suitable metrics and criteria for their aggregation. This is another area where the SFDR defines, in combination with the Taxonomy Regulation (Regulation (EU) 202/852), standardised methodologies to ensure comparability. In so doing, the SFRD also reduces the need to resort to metrics provided by external suppliers, such as ESG rating

---

[63] For corresponding organisational duties for AIF and UCITS managers see Regulation (EU) 2021/1255 and Directive (EU) 2021/1270, respectively. On the SFRD system see Chapter 10 by de Arriba-Sellier and Van Caenegem in this book.

[64] Chiu 2022, 92.

[65] This is mandatory for large financial market participants, i.e. for firms having more than 500 employees. For smaller firms, an alternative exists to declare that no consideration is given to those adverse impacts, subject to a duty to explain why ('comply or explain' approach (Article 4(1) SFDR)).

[66] Consistency between indicators adopted for entity-level and product-level disclosure is ensured by cross-references between Articles 2a (for the 'do no significant harm' principle), 4(6) and (7) (for entity-level indicators concerning the principal adverse impacts on climate and environmental matters and, respectively, social and employee matters) as well as 7(1), para. 2, SFDR (for product-level disclosure of principal adverse impacts). See also Articles 10 and 11 for website and periodic reports on those matters.

agencies. In particular, the default key performance indicator to measure the ratio of the taxonomy-aligned investments and the total investments underlying the product is the turnover (Recitals 36 and Articles 15, 17 and 19 Regulation (EU) 2022/1288).[67] The aggregation of the data on the 'green' turnover occurs on the basis of the specific activity (Annex II Regulation (EU) 2022/1288).

The regulatory licence effect in favour of ESG ratings has also been carefully avoided for benchmarks. As we shall see,[68] benchmarks play a crucial role in orienting investors' decisions on sustainable finance, so that reliance on ratings in that context would bring back what was thrown out by the SFDR. In the framework of the European Benchmark Regulation (Regulation (EU) 2016/1011 on indices used as benchmarks – Benchmark Regulation), disclosure obligations concerning the role of ESG factors in the index are drafted in such a way that all the many references to ESG ratings are marked as 'voluntary' (Annex II Regulation (EU) 2020/1816).

One last way to reduce a regulatory-induced demand for ESG ratings is to ensure that there is no need to translate issuer information on ESG factors into different metrics under other mandatory disclosure frameworks, such as the SFDR. In this regard, ongoing regulatory efforts are aiming to ensure that common reporting standards for issuers under the Directive on corporate sustainability reporting (Directive (EU) 2022/2464 – CSRD,[69] the successor of Directive 2014/95/EU on non-financial reporting – NFRD) are aligned with the indicators financial market participants have to adopt for their investment products or advisory services.[70] This should help streamline the information flow from the raw data to disclosure provided under the SFDR without the mandatory involvement of sustainability ratings in the process.

Finally, the consequences of the low correlation among ESG ratings also reverberate on prudential regulation. This is an area where reliance on credit ratings is embedded in the law, a regulatory choice that has already raised criticisms because of the risk it creates in jeopardising bank stability.[71] Such concerns apply even more to the inclusion of sustainability factors in the definition of own funds and capital requirements.[72]

A possible expansion of this kind should inevitably rely on the availability of robust methodologies and, for the standardised approach to the definition of capital requirements, on the fact that ECAIs actually adopt them. These are matters that EBA has already considered from an outside-in perspective.[73] Policy choices on the

---

[67] Capital expenditure (CapEx) and operational expenditure (OpEx) are the available alternatives, but their adoption requires the disclosure of the reasons why they are able to reflect the features of the portfolio better than the turnover (ESAs Joint Committee 2022, 8).
[68] See Section 11.4.
[69] European Commission 2021c.
[70] ESMA 2022b, 5–6.
[71] Alexander 2014.
[72] Zetzsche and Anker-Søresen 2022, 79–80
[73] EBA 2021, 30–3, 73–4.

role assigned to ESG ratings would become critical should the regulatory framework consider focussing on the inside-out prong of double materiality through any means, including adjustments of own funds requirements based on sustainability supporting factors or capital buffers targeted on ESG-related concerns.[74] For the time being, disclosure duties on ESG risks due under Article 449a Regulation (EU) No 575/2013 (Capital Requirement Regulation – CRR) do not make express reference to ESG ratings, which shows awareness of these matters from the supervisory side.[75]

11.3.4.2 The Need for Simplification in the Investment Process

Section 11.3.4.2 tested the level of regulators' reliance on ESG ratings, and it concluded that this is relatively low. However, direct legal requirements are not the only reason why financial market participants make use of rating services. Investment and divestment decisions consist of relatively simple elements (buy or sell a certain quantity at a certain price at a certain time), but they often involve decision-making processes that factor in a very broad set of information on the potential target assets. Sustainability ratings help this process because they reduce the complexity of ESG factors to the simplicity of symbols.[76]

The importance of sustainability ratings therefore stems from the natural tendency to use synthetic indicators to simplify difficult decision-making processes.[77] This inclination is well known to EU policymakers, which require CRAs to warn users that ratings are merely the opinions of CRAs 'and should be relied upon to a limited degree' (Article 8(2) CRA Regulation). By the same token, the ESG Ratings Regulation requires SRAs to explicitly mention that their ESG ratings are their own opinion (Article 14(11)). Regardless of such warnings, there is, however, a clear interest in reducing the costs of decision-making and ratings perfectly satisfy this demand. Rational and less-rational attitudes co-mingle to magnify the effect of this reliance. On the one hand, there are obvious economies of scale and specialisation factors that make recourse to ratings an efficient way to take decisions. On the other hand, availability and representativeness heuristics may boost reliance on ratings even when their accuracy is notoriously low.[78]

The traditional concerns about the passive approach towards the use of credit ratings are all the more pertinent to ESG ratings. As we have seen, not only are the metrics on which ESG ratings rely prone to uncertainties but the aggregation of those metrics into synthetic indicators relies on subjective assumptions.[79] In spite

---

[74] Dankert et al. 2018; Neisen 2021. See Chapters 19 and 20 by Ramos Muñoz and Binder in this book.
[75] EBA 2022.
[76] Dombalagian 2011, 63–4.
[77] Steuer and Tröger 2022, 7.
[78] Avgouleas 2009.
[79] IOSCO 2021, 10.

of the detailed regulatory framework of the SFDR and the Taxonomy Regulation, many open questions remain as to its implementation by financial market partic- ipants. For instance, it is uncertain to what extent the quantification of a 'significant harm' under the SFDR, on the one hand, and the Taxonomy Regulation, on the other hand, can rely on identical quantification techniques.[80] At the same time, the disclosure of 'principal adverse impacts' and compliance with the 'do no significant harm' principle require the use of the same indicators, but the relationship between the two measures remains blurred and entails, especially for the latter requirement, broad discretion in the assessment.[81]

Some of these uncertainties are not necessarily inherent to ESG-related regula- tions and progressive clarifications may help to solve them. Others, however, seem more ingrained with the very need to handle complexity when aggregating activity- level metrics, first into investment-level or company-level and then into product-level ones. Economic 'activities' are the main target of the Taxonomy Regulation and are the reference point for the definition of 'sustainable investments' in the SFDR. However, the SFDR refers the 'do no significant harm' principle to the 'investment' and requires compliance with good governance practices by companies for an invest- ment to qualify as 'sustainable'.[82] Yet at another level of granularity, disclosure duties under the SFDR require aggregation at the product and entity level.

There are various ways to combine the building blocks of more granular metrics (such as those referring to the assets) to produce more general indicators (such as those referring to the entity). For instance, one may prefer to proceed with a strict proportionality principle that mirrors the disclosure on the alignment of the asset allocation of 'light green' and 'dark green' products with the Taxonomy Regulation.[83] Industry may follow other criteria, however. For instance, financial market partic- ipants may decide to only deem activities as 'green' when they pertain to companies that also meet, in combination with other activities, certain requirements. These could include a minimum percentage of green turnover or the absence of principal adverse impacts on ESG factors.[84]

For the reasons highlighted at the outset of this section, financial market partic- ipants, such as institutional investors and asset managers, have strong incentives to rely on information intermediaries to fill these gaps between, on the one hand, infor- mation concerning the investee activities and on the other hand, the labelling of their products (in terms of greenness) as well as the disclosure duties that accompany them.

However, financial market participants can only be satisfied that the quality of an asset with a good ESG score is consistent with their investment strategy after

---

[80] Busch 2021, 406–7; ESAs Joint Committee 2022, 11.
[81] ESAs Joint Committee 2022, 10–11.
[82] Ibid., 11.
[83] See text accompanying n. 66.
[84] Pierron and Carabia 2022.

thoroughly checking the assumptions and the methodology underlying that opinion. In this regard, disclosure of the methodology on the model of credit ratings (Article 8(1) and Annex I(E)(I)(5) CRA Regulation) will be a key requirement for sustainability rating agencies (Articles 21 and 22 ESG Rating regulation).[85] In a context where different methodologies may lead to divergent results, overreliance on ESG ratings is even more detrimental than in the traditional segment of credit ratings.

Therefore, financial institutions should endeavour to run an internal assessment of the investment and refrain from implicitly outsourcing the evaluation of ESG criteria to ratings. Once again, this would mirror the requirement that financial institutions do not 'solely or mechanistically rely on credit ratings for assessing the creditworthiness of an entity or financial instrument' under Article 5a CRA Regulation. IOSCO follows a similar approach in its recommendations, which are, however, not followed on this point by the ESG Ratings Regulation.[86] In this regard, however, a major difference between credit and ESG ratings is that ESG ratings do not seem to have as many alternatives as credit ratings have. While the latter can be complemented by market-based tools such as the price of bonds or credit default swaps, in the case of sustainability, internal assessment methodologies seem to be the only viable solution.[87] It is therefore unsurprising that users rarely perform their own verification of ESG ratings, reportedly, while more attention seems to be paid to assessing SRAs as such.[88]

One may also wonder whether low rating consistency strengthens the need for measures that support the engagement of small ESG rating agencies even beyond the limited flexibility granted to SME SRAs under Article 20 ESG Ratings Regulation (see Section 11.3.1.2). The reference is to the soft-law provision asking issuers to consider appointing an additional credit rating agency with no more than 10% of the total market share (Article 8d CRA Regulation). In the credit rating market, this measure aims to reduce the market power of large incumbents by artificially inflating the demand for ratings issued by small agencies. A similar rationale would also hold for sustainability ratings, whose market, as we have seen, is also increasingly concentrated.

For sustainability ratings, due to low correlation, different metrics would be more likely to show divergent results, thus increasing the informative value of the additional assessments, while comparable results would confirm reliability. Currently, users of ESG ratings often rely on multiple providers, sometimes to have broader coverage in terms of relevant assets but also to cross-validate ratings on the same assets.[89] Crucial in making sure that these practices prove helpful is the ability of issuers – or, in principle, financial institutions – to select the second rating agency

---

[85] Enhanced transparency on methodologies was suggested already in European Commission 2018.

[86] IOSCO 2021, 40.

[87] On the relationship between internal evaluation systems and market-based criteria see ESAs Joint Committee 2016.

[88] IOSCO 2021, 25–6.

[89] IOSCO 2021, 25; ESMA 2022b, 17–18.

based on its methodology, in a somewhat strengthened version of the equivalent rule that enables issuers to evaluate whether the second credit rating agency they engage is 'capable of rating the relevant issuance or entity'. In this context, two results delivered by comparable methodologies would be telling about the actual sustainability of the issuer corporate business.

11.4 SUSTAINABILITY INDICES AND BENCHMARKS

Most of the market failures that taint sustainability ratings also affect the market for indices that rely on ESG factors. Both services assess the underlying activities to bridge the information gap between issuers and investors through synthetic indicators. Most importantly, even in the absence of regulatory incentives to do so,[90] benchmark administrators heavily rely on ESG ratings to define their indices.[91] On top of this, many administrators of ESG benchmarks are also SRAs,[92] which is testament to how the two services often operate as communicating vessels and rely on economies of scope. The ESG Rating Regulation is cognizant of this proximity and allows SRAs to ask ESMA for an authorization to overcome the general ban on the joint provision of sustainability ratings and benchmarks (Article 15).

In spite of the strong similarities between the two activities, EU law has not followed the same approach for sustainability benchmarks and ratings. It already set foot in the market for ESG benchmarks through *ad hoc* provisions aimed at supporting the development of sustainable finance, in contrast to the more prudent approach initially taken for sustainability ratings.[93] The Commission also envisions other measures will support the adoption of sustainability benchmarks in the future.[94] To be sure, regardless of this proactive approach, sustainability benchmarks were – and are – 'benchmarks' for the purpose of the Benchmarks Regulation, while sustainability ratings do not qualify as 'credit ratings' under the CRA Directive. Therefore, sustainability benchmarks merely needed some fine-tuning in an already existing regulatory framework, while regulating sustainability ratings required some deeper reflections and an expansion of the activites subject to regulation.

11.4.1 *The Role of Sustainability Indices and Benchmarks*

Sustainability indices define a subset of the investable universe that is selected according to criteria that take ESG factors into account.[95] Strictly speaking, an index

---

[90] See text accompanying n. 101.

[91] European Commission 2022b.

[92] Pagano et al. 2018, 344.

[93] The need for sound regulation of ESG benchmarks is well known also outside the EU. For the UK, see Andrew 2022.

[94] European Commission 2022a, 7 (Action 1).

[95] European Commission and ERM 2021, 64.

is a public figure that synthesises the value of a basket of underlying assets based on a predefined methodology. When that public figure is adopted as a reference by market participants, it qualifies as a benchmark (Article 3(1)(1) and (3) Benchmarks Regulation – therefore, all benchmarks are indices, but the reverse is not true). In the case of sustainable finance, the importance of an index may lie with the figure itself but also with the composition of the underlying basket, depending on the way market participants refer to the benchmark. For instance, active asset managers may use benchmarks as a yardstick to measure their performance – and calculate their remuneration – in terms of returns, sustainability objectives or both. For passive managers, the composition of the index is key, rather than the figure that displays its performance, as it drives the selection of the target investments.[96]

The criteria that define indices and benchmarks may, for instance, exclude some financial instruments when they do not satisfy certain sustainability requirements, include only a predefined number of top-ranking securities or refer to an open number of financial instruments that meet minimum ESG rating levels.[97] To determine inclusion or exclusion from the index, ESG factors may therefore follow a discrete binary approach, but they may also take continuous values that contribute to the weighting of each component in a more calibrated assessment.[98]

The role of indices in orienting investments combined with the variety of the criteria a benchmark administrator can select explain why proper functioning of benchmarks is crucial in addressing agency problems along the investment chain. Just like ESG ratings, ESG benchmarks may trigger issues of excessive reliance. In traditional finance, blind reliance on benchmarks is an issue for actively managed collective investment schemes, but is part of the game when the passive approach to asset allocation is declared.[99] In the ESG world, complete dependence on benchmarks is seen as more problematic when financial market participants sell light- or dark-green financial products,[100] irrespective of the active or passive asset allocation strategy. In this case, enhanced disclosure duties help investors understand the consequences of indexing and therefore incentivise financial market participants to be more active in the selection of the benchmark, upstream of the alignment to such a benchmark.

In the SFDR, disclosure duties are calibrated depending on the nature of the product (Recital 19 Regulation (EU) 2022/1288). For light-green products, financial market participants shall disclose if they refer to a benchmark and, if so, 'whether and how' the benchmark is consistent with the environmental or social

---

[96] High-Level Expert Group on Sustainable Finance 2018, 53. On benchmarks as yardsticks for active managers in the field of portfolio management see Article 47(2) and (3)(c) Regulation (EU) 2017/565.

[97] For instance, certain companies cannot be part of EU Paris-aligned Benchmarks but can be part of EU Climate Transition Benchmarks at the administrators' discretion (on these labels see more extensively Section 11.4.3).

[98] Pagano et al. 2018, 341–2.

[99] See e.g. Article 7(1) Reg. (EU) No 583/2010 (for UCITS funds).

[100] On these categories of sustainable products see Section 11.3.4.1.

characteristics that such products promote (Article 8 SFDR; Article 36 Regulation (EU) 2022/1288). For dark-green products, the SFDR regime focusses instead on sustainability benchmarks (Recital 21 SFDR). Hence, disclosure is due as to whether financial market participants make reference to any such benchmark and, if so, 'how' that benchmark is aligned with the sustainability objectives of the product (Article 9 SFDR).

In spite of the unclear wording of level 1 and level 2 provisions, reference to a benchmark also seems to remain voluntary with regard to benchmarks that qualify as EU Climate Transition Benchmarks or EU Paris-aligned Benchmarks – the two labels that, as we shall see in the next sub-sections, qualify indices aiming at decarbonisation targets (Article 9(2) and (3) para. 2 SFDR and Article 49(1)(b) Regulation (EU) 2022/1288). Indeed, reference to EU Climate Transition Benchmarks or EU Paris-aligned Benchmarks seems to be required only for dark-green products that have a reduction in carbon emissions as their objective and, at the same time, designate an index as a reference benchmark, which is not mandatory (Article 9(2) SFDR).[101]

For both light- and dark-green products that have designated a reference benchmark, periodic performance reports shall compare the performance of three terms of reference: that of the financial product, that of the reference benchmark, and that of a relevant broad market index. The comparisons involving the reference benchmark should focus on the sustainability indicators that characterise the product, and compare them with the ESG factors that characterise the benchmark in light of the methodology the benchmark administrator discloses (Article 57 and 63 Regulation (EU) 2022/1288).[102]

11.4.2 *Governance of Administrators and Data Providers for Sustainability Benchmarks*

Due to the applicability of the regulatory framework in force for benchmarks, policymakers did not need to set up a brand-new system to foster sustainable indices. The framework therefore also applies to ESG benchmarks, which take on the calibrated regime that distinguishes between critical, significant and non-significant benchmarks. These labels hang on the importance of the benchmark as defined by a supervisory decision or measured in terms of assets under management (AUM) that refer to it and lack of substitutes that can avoid adverse consequences in case of cessation (Articles 20, 24 and 26 Benchmark Regulation). At the moment, no ESG benchmark qualifies as critical[103] but the systemic impact of such indices is already material and likely to increase in the future.

---

[101] See Chapter 10 by de Arriba-Sellier and Van Caenegem in this book for more extensive analysis.
[102] On the contents of such disclosure see Section 11.4.3.
[103] Regulation (EU) 2016/1368 establishing a list of critical benchmarks used in financial markets (last amended on 8 July 2021).

The tripartite taxonomy for benchmarks determines different regimes, from access to market onwards. All administrators of critical benchmarks are subject to authorisation, as well as administrators of significant benchmarks that are not supervised entities. Supervised entities that are administrators of significant benchmarks, as well as any administrator (supervised or not) of non-significant benchmarks are subject to simple registration (Article 34 Benchmark Regulation). In terms of the supervisory assessment of the application, authorisation entails stricter scrutiny than registration but does not lead as such to a stricter regime (Recital 48).[104] ESMA is the competent authority for critical benchmarks[105] and for third-country benchmarks that are recognised in the EU, while otherwise supervision remains at the national level (Article 40).

Authorisation or registration brings the administrator within the scope of the benchmark regime. While critical benchmarks are subject to the entire regulatory framework, administrators of significant and non-significant benchmarks may deviate from some specific provisions, subject to a duty to explain the reasons for doing so. For significant benchmarks, the scope of the provisions subject to the 'comply or explain' principle is narrower than that applicable to non-significant benchmarks. Moreover, for significant benchmarks the justification due in the case of deviation from the default regime shall be based on proportionality, in light of the nature or impact of the benchmark or the size of the administrator. For non-significant benchmarks the explanation can also refer to any other reasons. Finally, only for significant benchmarks can the competent authority overrule the administrator's decision and force the application of the relevant provisions, when this is appropriate (Article 25(3)).

Among the many provisions of the Benchmark Regulation that can be relevant to ESG benchmarks, some are worth recalling here due to their ability to adjust to the broad discretion that characterises certain assessments of sustainability and the high relevance of such evaluations to stakeholders in general. The most noticeable rules relate to the organisational requirements for the administrators and the governance of the input data. Administrators shall identify and prevent or manage conflicts of interests with contributors or users and shall particularly focus on areas where the determination of the benchmark involves 'judgement or discretion' from their side (Article 4(1)). When conflicts cannot be mitigated, the competent authority may mandate the creation of an independent oversight function that includes a 'balanced representation of stakeholders' (Article 4(2)).

Equally suitable to the ESG context is the regime for the governance of input data. The risks stemming from the lack of reliable inputs are a feature shared by traditional and ESG benchmarks. The very origin of the Benchmark Regulation

---

[104] Wundenberg 2022, 664.
[105] With the exception of benchmarks that qualify as critical due to a national assessment (Articles 20(1)(b) and 40 Benchmark Regulation).

is rooted in LIBOR's manipulation through misleading incoming data from participating banks concerning the estimated reference interest rates for hypothetical transactions,[106] so that part of its provisions addresses the risk of 'garbage in, garbage out' dynamics. Once again, the approach is gradual. The general rule is that input data shall always accurately and reliably represent the reality that the benchmark is supposed to measure (Article 11(1)(a)). The highest quality comes from data consisting of values from transactions that have occurred among independent parties (transaction data – Article 3(1)(15)), as this reduces the level of discretion characterising estimates on future transactions. However, when this kind of data is not available, as is normally the case with ESG indices which do not refer to transaction prices, other input data are admissible as long as they are verifiable.

The administrator of the benchmark adopts guidelines that define the types of input data and their contribution to the benchmark and that delineate the exercise of discretion as to the way those data contribute to the benchmark ('expert judgement'; Articles 3(1)(13) and 11(1)(c)). Specific control mechanisms verify the quality of the input data and the ability of contributors to provide data from reliable sources supported by their own oversight and verification procedures (Article 11(2) and (3)). Once again, the requirements are more stringent for critical benchmarks and become progressively more flexible for significant and non-significant benchmarks. For administrators of benchmarks other than the non-significant ones, the criteria for the quality assurance of data by both the administrator and the contributors are further detailed in delegated measures (Regulation (EU) 2018/1638). In the ESG world, these practices can help support trust in data, the supply chain for which may be complex and prone to material mistakes.

The Benchmark Regulation also sets forth governance and control requirements for contributors of input data that are supervised entities (such as banks, asset managers or insurance undertakings; Articles 3(1)(17) and 16). However, in the case of sustainability, more relevant are the codes of conduct that administrators prepare for each benchmark (or family of benchmarks). These codes are an example of 'regulated self-regulation'[107] and provide the backbone of the regulatory approach to the quality of data along the supply chain. They specify the requirements for contributors and the data they provide, including control systems, validation procedures and measures to ensure that all the relevant input data reach the administrator while, at the same time, suspicious input data are flagged and managed (Articles 11(1)(e) and 15 Benchmark Regulation; Regulation (EU) 2018/1639).

Securities exchanges also play a relevant role in the development of sustainability indices. Operators of regulated markets have traditionally provided indices or green labels to support investors' decisions and they are now active in the sustainability

---

[106] Ashton and Christophers 2015.
[107] Wundenberg 2022, 658–9. The alignment of the codes with the Benchmark Regulation is subject to supervision and, in the case of divergence, to enforcement (Article 15(4)).

world with new dedicated products, which they sometimes develop with the support of CRAs or SRAs.[108] To the contrary, they have made more limited use of listing requirements to support specific ESG targets,[109] possibly to avoid excessive fragmentation in their markets.[110] As a matter of fact, ESG-related requirements in the listing standards have traditionally addressed transparency,[111] a focus that has also been mirrored by the creation of common disclosure standards through the networks of regulated markets.[112] Notable exceptions are market segments for green bonds[113] or other forms of aggregation of bonds sharing sufficient sustainability levels.[114]

11.4.3 *Disclosure and Labelling of Sustainability Benchmarks*

A well-established backdrop of pre-existing rules has also facilitated the main regulatory strategy that specifically addresses ESG benchmarks, namely disclosure. All administrators – regardless of the nature of the benchmark they provide as critical, significant or non-significant – shall disclose, together with the other key elements of their methodologies, whether these reflect ESG factors (Article 13(1)(d) Benchmarks Regulation; Regulation (EU) 2020/1817). Additionally, the benchmark statement, which describes the procedures and the criteria followed to determine the benchmark with a separate indication of the elements subject to discretion,[115] shall specify whether the benchmark pursues ESG objectives and, if so, how (Article 27(2a) Benchmarks Regulation; Regulation (EU) 2020/1816). This disclosure, as we have already seen, enables financial market participants to provide, in turn, information on the performance of their financial products under the SFDR.

The most salient feature of the European regulatory strategy on sustainability indices is, however, the creation of standardised labels for benchmarks. Once again, second-degree market failures explain this strategy. As benchmarks themselves may be subject to asymmetric information, defining labels facilitates the aggregation and sharing of information concerning the quality, in terms of ESG impact, of the indices that decide to adopt those labels. The 2018 amendments to the Benchmark Regulation have added two labels characterised by the inclusion of objectives related to carbon

---

[108] For indices see e.g. Euronext, ESG Indices, available at https://live.euronext.com/en/products/ indices/esg-indices. In the literature Myklebust 2014, and, on funding platforms more in general, Wendt 2017. For labels see e.g. the Nasdaq 2023, which also relies on external reviewers.

[109] For an overview see Sustainable Stock Exchanges Initiative 2017.

[110] See, however, High-Level Expert Group on Sustainable Finance 2018, 80, recommending stock exchanges create dedicated segments for sustainable financial instruments. See also Dell'Erba and Doronozo (2023), 405–8.

[111] Chiu 2022, 99.

[112] Fornasari 2020.

[113] For a list see Climate Bonds Initiative, Green Bond Segments on Stock Exchanges, available at www .climatebonds.net/green-bond-segments-stock-exchanges.

[114] See e.g. Euronext ESG Bonds.

[115] Wundenberg 2022, 659.

emissions in the selection of the underlying assets. The two labels differentiate themselves based on the ambition of the targets, but they share many features.

Albeit with variable intensity, both types of benchmarks aim to reduce greenhouse gas emissions. Therefore, they do not rule out investments in companies that release these gases (Scope 1 emissions) or use energy that determines their release (Scope 2 emissions) or whose upstream and downstream value chains involve it (Scope 3 emissions).[116] For equity benchmarks, exposure to these companies is even mandated for an aggregate value that is at least equal to the aggregate exposure of the relevant underlying investable universe (Article 3 Regulation (EU) 2020/1818).[117] However, the allowed investments must have an intensity of greenhouse gas emissions (for Scope 1, 2, and 3 emissions[118]) that is simultaneously (i) lower than the investable universe and (ii) in line with a predefined decarbonisation trajectory of 7% on an annual basis (Article 7 Regulation (EU) 2020/1818). These two requirements guarantee the overall high sustainability of the underlying assets, both from a backward-looking and, respectively, a forward-looking perspective.

The most ambitious label, dubbed the 'EU Paris-aligned Benchmark', identifies benchmarks selecting assets that, taken together, should allow to reach the Paris Agreement target to keep the global temperature increase well below 2 °C (and possibly 1.5 °C) above pre-industrial levels (Article 3(1)(23b) Benchmark Regulation).[119] The intensity of greenhouse gas emissions connected to the underlying assets shall be at least 50% lower than that of the investable universe (Article 11 Regulation (EU) 2020/1818). The benchmark is also subject to a 'do no significant harm' principle with regard to other ESG objectives, which entails the exclusion of investments in critical companies. These are, for instance, companies producing controversial weapons or that derive a predefined percentage of their revenues from activities related to fossil fuels (Article 12 Regulation (EU) 2020/1818).

The other *ad hoc* category of benchmarks falls under the 'EU Climate Transition Benchmarks' label. In this case, the intensity of greenhouse gas emissions connected to the underlying assets shall be, less ambitiously, at least 30% lower than that of the investable universe (Article 9 Regulation (EU) 2020/1818). Just like EU Paris-aligned Benchmarks, EU Climate Transition Benchmarks are bound to exclude certain companies, but the scope of the exclusion is narrower (for instance, producers of controversial weapons are excluded but not companies that derive their revenues from fossil fuels); they shall have a policy concerning additional exclusions, however, and shall make that policy public with their methodologies (Article 10 Regulation (EU) 2020/1818). A soft-law provision has successfully encouraged the

[116] See Annex III Benchmark Regulation.
[117] For an explanation of the rationale see text accompanying n. 27.
[118] Scope 3 emission are included after the expiration of a phase-in period (Article 5 Reg. (EU) 2020/1818).
[119] See also Recital 5 Council Decision (EU) 2016/1841 on the conclusion, on behalf of the European Union, of the Paris Agreement.

creation of EU Climate Transition Benchmarks by asking administrators of significant benchmarks to 'endeavour to provide one or more' of such benchmarks by 1 January 2022 (Article 19d Benchmark Regulation).

11.5 STOCKTAKING: MARKET FAILURES AND HOW TO ADDRESS THEM

In this section, we take stock of the previous analysis and highlight some differences between market failures affecting 'traditional' finance and their equivalent in the more recent world of sustainability. This comparison will help us draw some policy recommendations, also in the light of the most recent regulatory developments.

11.5.1 *Regulatory and Market Failures in the Old and the New World – How Different Are They?*

The previous sections have shown the main features of the markets for sustainability ratings and benchmarks. The failures that impact those markets are currently addressed by the regulatory framework for benchmarks and will soon be addressed for ESG ratings as well. But how similar are the market failures that affect traditional services and the comparable new services that relate to sustainability? While asymmetric information and agency problems pervade both the old and the new world, there are some differences that are worth pointing out in the limited space of this chapter.

One element to consider in this comparison is that market mechanisms may not work in the same way as in traditional finance when one factors sustainability considerations into investment decisions and, hence, into the dynamics of price discovery.[120] This has some remarkable implications on the ability of equilibrium market prices to approximate market participants' preferences. While in a traditional setting market participants will all look, although with their own personal assessments and biases, at the risk-adjusted discounted expected value of an asset's future cash flow, attention to ESG factors (particularly from an inside-out perspective) introduces a set of other preferences, the diversity and variance of which are typically higher than those focussing on risk/return considerations. This exacerbates the negative consequences of asymmetric information because it reduces the ability of market prices to protect weak market participants, such as retail investors, by enabling them to free ride on the more sophisticated market participants that move market prices. This mechanism is one of the main drivers of investor protection, not only on secondary markets[121] but also during IPOs, where book-building mechanisms may support prices' ability to reflect information.[122]

---

[120] For a thorough analysis see Steuer and Tröger 2022, 19–23 and 29–31.
[121] Armour et al. 2016, 164.
[122] CJEU, C-910/19, Bankia, 3 June 2021, ECLI:EU:C:2021:433.

In the 'new world', market prices still perform their role as aggregators of information, at least under the paradigm of the efficient capital markets hypothesis. However, the statistical dispersion of individual investors' preferences around market prices will be higher, compared to the 'old world' where investor preferences are aggregated along a univariate variable. As the previous analysis has shown, each investor can have her own preferences as to the ESG factors to consider, and on the relative weight they should have. Therefore, redress through private litigation may be hard to obtain and quantify. First, the legal presumption that the damage suffered by any investor can be calculated on the basis of market prices, even without proving reliance on a misleading rating or benchmark – which is the basis of the fraud on the market theory (FOMT)[123] – might be harder to defend, for the simple reason that market prices may say little about sustainability.

This brings us to a second connected element that exacerbates market failures in the sustainability world, which is the weaker role that private enforcement can play in penalising misleading information or misguided assessments related to sustainability factors. At least until the regulatory framework starts to address these matters – but the ESG Ratings Regulation does not contain any provision in this regard – the already-weak role of civil liability in policing information intermediaries[124] seems to be even more problematic for sustainability-related matters. Not only may investors have to demonstrate reliance on ESG ratings or benchmarks, but even quantifying the damage for less-than-expected performance in any of the ESG factors will be challenging.[125]

Finally, asymmetric information and agency problems may also be more intense in the realm of sustainability because, at least for the time being, knowledge of ESG matters is not yet as widespread in the investment chain as the well-established expertise in traditional finance.[126] For this reason, justifying regulatory measures is easier than in the traditional world. Unfortunately, this knowledge problem also affects policymakers, not only because pooling the necessary expertise requires time and effort, just like in the investment chain, but also because anticipating and quantifying the impact of rules fostering sustainability may prove impossible.[127] The risk of regulatory failures suggests that, while regulation should play a crucial role, caution is warranted in its design.

At the same time, some systems may be devised to tackle these shortcomings through private ordering solutions. For instance, public interest litigation might play a role in enforcing misleading ESG disclosure, ratings or benchmarks.[128] Some forms of guarantees that attach claims to the violation of predefined ESG targets

---

[123] For an application to credit ratings see Picciau 2018, 391.
[124] Ibid.
[125] Lenzi 2021, 314. See also Chapter 17 by Mock in this book.
[126] Zetzsche and Anker-Søresen 2022.
[127] Ibid., 74.
[128] Macchi 2021.

may also facilitate *ex ante* quantification of damages and partially address asymmetric information issues. This technique is well known in many markets for non-financial assets where guarantees support credible commitments[129] but it normally cannot support transactions on financial instruments where investors look – as is the case in traditional financial markets – at the risk/return profile of the product they buy. Transferring the risk of negative performance to the issuer would usually contradict the very essence of the contract underlying the financial instrument. To be sure, specific covenants such as negative pledges can support commitment to pre-defined performance requirements, but criteria that go beyond these instrumental metrics may be hard to define and ascertain, considering also the nature of financial instruments as credence goods.

When performance instead relates to sustainability, nothing prevents the issuers from committing to attaining predefined ESG targets and to paying damages when the targets are missed.[130] Unfortunately, the ability of such remedies to fix the serious market failures we identify above remains dubious, as the ascertainment of these targets will be subject, in turn, to issues of asymmetric information which will make information intermediaries all the more necessary.

11.5.2 *Learning from the Past: 'The $64,000 Question' Game Show*

The previous sections have explained why regulation will play a crucial role for sustainability ratings, as it already does for sustainability benchmarks. They have also highlighted, however, that the risk of regulatory failures is quite pervasive. EU policymakers have been careful not to create a form or regulatory licence that delegates asset quality screening to SRAs or benchmarks administrators. The risk remains, however, that such dynamics will develop in certain areas, including banks' capital requirements.

Moreover, even in a context where no rules explicitly rely on ESG ratings or benchmarks, the whole regulatory framework for sustainable finance provides strong incentives to resort to ESG ratings services or to use sustainability benchmarks. Financial market participants need to address many uncertainties when assessing sustainability-related information and will always use synthetic indicators to manage the complexity of ESG metrics. While legal requirements on the definition of ESG factors, pillars and indicators can be streamlined and clarified over time, the cognitive need to simplify complexity is here to stay.

Against this backdrop, there is little doubt that targeted disclosure duties can support financial market participants and – ultimately – investors in the selection and handling of ESG ratings and benchmarks. Enhanced transparency on the crucial matters we have highlighted above, and in particular for methodologies and conflicts

---

[129] Lambert 2017, 201.
[130] See Chapter 27 by Antonio et al. in this book.

of interests, is the cheapest and least intrusive form of regulation that can help tackle asymmetric information and agency problems in the market for sustainability ratings and benchmarks. The Benchmark Regulation provides a well-established framework, and the ESG Ratings Regulation sets forth a series of disclosure duties that seem adequate to reach this target.

The remaining question is whether the uncertainties surrounding ESG ratings and their quality justify regulatory measures that go beyond mandatory disclosure, as the new ESG Ratings Regulation does. Policymakers are always facing a conundrum in these contexts. On the one hand, strengthening the standards for the provision of services can increase their quality. On the other hand, regulation comes at a cost because it can have pervasive side effects in terms of barriers to entry and of implicit regulatory backup. As to entry barriers, history tells us that the most enthusiastic supporters of the first railway regulations in the US were incumbent railway companies, and similar dynamics can of course develop elsewhere.[131] As to the implicit regulatory backup, past reforms of credit ratings that involved strengthened supervision have been criticised for underscoring the importance of CRAs, thus offsetting the efforts to reduce reliance.[132]

However, regulators are in a better position than the players of 'The $64,000 Question' game show.[133] The choice is not necessarily between doing nothing and quitting the regulatory game to avoid regulatory failures, on the one hand, or going all-in with the full menu of possible measures, on the other. Other intermediate models could help address the conundrum.

The CRA Regulation has been the main model for the ESG Ratings Regulation and, in as sense, has raised the bet on ESG ratings. The commercial practice of dubbing ESG ratings as 'ratings' may also have contributed to this choice by creating an anchoring effect that has influenced the public debate in this regard. The results of the Commission consultation on the 'Functioning of the ESG ratings market' showed a strong preference not only for transparency measures but also for more pervasive strategies and, among these, an authorisation or registration system.[134] ESMA has equally supported the adoption of a registration system for ESG ratings, based on the analogies between credit and ESG ratings.[135]

The ESG Ratings Regulation goes all-in by replicating, with a lower level of detail, the bulk of the CRA Regulation approach, including the need for an authorisation to release ESG ratings regardless of their use for regulatory purposes – an option that was preferred over a mere registration and industry-led codes of conducts, which might have also been considered in combination with a comply-or-explain duty, on the model of proxy advisors (Article 3j SHRD).[136] Taking inspiration from the CRA

---

[131] Support by the ESG industry for stricter regulation is reportedly increasing, see Kishan 2022.
[132] Manns 2013, 767.
[133] Enriques and Gargantini 2010.
[134] European Commission 2021a, 4.
[135] ESMA 2021, 3–4.
[136] European Commission 2023b, 35–42.

Regulation seems the safest solution at first sight, as it relies on the full array of the measures that already characterise the complex market for credit ratings. However, the risk exists that investors and other market participants will perceive the authorisation as a quality label which exempts them from too strict a scrutiny on the ESG ratings methodologies. Just like the metaphor above suggests, this is a bet. ESMA will certainly make ESG ratings more credible, but this dynamic will occur in a market segment where little certainty exists as to the criteria to assess the robustness of methodologies and where value judgement plays a larger role compared to credit ratings, as this chapter has shown.

In this respect, the vast array of exemptions from the ESG Ratings Regulations reduces the salience of the authorization regime and its implications. Among the many exemptions, it is worth mentioning here, for the importance it can be expected to have, the one concerning regulated financial undertakings that incorporate an ESG rating in their products or services (Article 2(2)(ba)). These entities will only be subject to disclosure requirements, but not to the other specific organisational measures. However, exceptions of this kind deliver a suboptimal result in that they lead to regulatory fragmentation insofar as the same service may be subject to different rules depending on the provider, with the ensuing risk of regulatory arbitrage.

At the same time, the Regulation may be underinclusive on the critical issue of the governance of the input data, even if it sets forth the general principle that SRAs shall adopt all necessary measures to ensure that the information they use is of sufficient quality and from reliable sources (Article 14(11)) and delegates the Commission to assess whether the scope of the Regulation should be expanded to include 'providers of data products on environmental, social and human rights, and governance factors' (Article 49(2)). As the chapter has shown, the Benchmark Regulation displays a more sophisticated framework that might have served as a useful reference point to the lawmakers.

Should reality fail to meet the expectations of the ESG Ratings Regulation, the regulatory strategy underpinning the proposal might lead to a feedback loop where the systemic effects of flawed methodologies are magnified. Remarkably, this risk occurs in a moment when market participants are increasingly developing their own proprietary models as they became cognizant of the weaknesses embedded in ESG ratings.[137] Time will tell whether the forthcoming rules on SRAs will lead to such unintended consequences.

In this regard, the decision to define an authorisation system has also another drawback – it is difficult to change in case it proves counterproductive. Viable alternative strategies that look at other models could have been explored, instead. These strategies might have taken inspiration from the regulation of financial analysts, with its lighter-touch approach that differentiates depending on the nature of the analysts as an 'expert' and its reduced barriers to entry. In combination with this, recourse

---

[137] IOSCO 2021, 27.

could also be had to self-regulation and 'comply or explain' models in the definition of methodologies and governance requirements.[138] A wise policy agenda could have started with this lighter-touch approach, to later assess its results. Should market failures persist after a reasonable time, a higher bet could have been made with a fully-fledged authorisation system along the line of credit ratings.

REFERENCES

2DII (2° Investing Initiative) (2022), 'Do we speak the same language? A market survey on the future of ESG ratings', available at: https://2degrees-investing.org/resource/survey-esg-ratings/.

Abhayawansa, S., Elijido-Ten, E., and Dumay, J. (2018), 'A practice theoretical analysis of the irrelevance of integrated reporting to mainstream sell-side analysts', 59 *Accounting and Finance*, 1615.

Alexander, K. (2014), 'The risk of ratings in bank capital regulation', 25 *European Business Law Review*, 295.

AMF and AFM (Autorité des marches financiers and the Autoriteit Financiële Markten) (2020), 'Position Paper: Call for a European Regulation for the Provision of ESG data, ratings, and related services', available at: https://bit.ly/3TdrmEK.

Andrew, T. (2022), 'Misleading benchmarks creating "trust deficit" for ESG ETFs, FCA warns', ETF Stream, available at: https://bit.ly/4cb5m3T.

Armour, J., Awrey, D., Davies, P., et al. (2016), *Principles of Financial Regulation* (Oxford: Oxford University Press).

Ashton, P. and Christophers, B. (2015), 'On arbitration, arbitrage and arbitrariness in financial markets and their governance: unpacking LIBOR and the LIBOR scandal', 44 *Economy and Society*, 188.

Avgouleas, E. (2009), 'What future for disclosure as a regulatory technique? Lessons from the global financial crisis and beyond', Working Paper, available at: https://papers.ssrn.com/sol3/papers.cfm?abstract_id=1369004.

Bengo, I., Boni, L., and Sancino, A. (2022), 'EU financial regulations and social impact measurement practices: A comprehensive framework on finance for sustainable development', 29 *Corporate Social Responsibility and Environmental Management*, 809.

Berg, F., Kölbel, J. F., and Rigobon, R. (2022), 'Aggregate confusion: The divergence of ESG ratings', 26 *Review of Finance*, 1.

Busch, D. (2021), 'Sustainability disclosure in the EU financial sector', in Busch, D. et al. (eds.), *Sustainable Finance in Europe. Corporate Governance, Financial Stability and Financial Markets* (London: Palgrave Macmillan).

Cash, D. (2021), *Sustainability Rating Agencies vs Credit Rating Agencies. The Battle to Serve the Mainstream Investor* (London: Palgrave Macmillan).

Chatterji, A. K., Durand, R., Levine, D. I., and Touboul, S. (2016), 'Do ratings of firms converge? implications for managers, investors and strategy researchers', 37 *Strategic Management Journal*, 1597.

Chiu, I. (2022), 'The EU sustainable finance agenda: Developing governance for double materiality in sustainability metrics', 23 *European Business Organization Law Review* 87.

Coffee Jr, J. C. (2006), *Gatekeepers: The Professions and Corporate Governance* (Oxford: Oxford University Press).

---

[138] For a calibrated approach see Chiu 2022, 112–17.

Dankert, J., van Doorn, L., Reinders, H. J., and Sleijpen, O. (2018), 'A green supporting factor – The right policy?', *SUERF Policy Note Issue No 43*.

Dell'Erba, M. and Doronzo, M. (2023), 'Sustainability gatekeepers: ESG ratings and data providers', 25 *University of Pennsylvania Journal of Business Law*, 355.

Deloitte (2021), 'ESG Ratings: do they add value? How to get prepared?', available at: https://bit.ly/3x8oVbc.

Dimson, E., Marsh, P., and Staunton, M. (2020), 'Divergent ESG ratings', 47 *Journal of Portfolio Management*, 75.

Dombalagian, O. (2011), 'Regulating informational intermediation', 1 *American University Business Law Review*, 58.

Douglas, E., van Holt, T., and Whelan, T. (2017), 'Responsible investing: Guide to ESG data providers and relevant trends', 8 *Journal of Environmental Investing*, 92.

EBA (European Banking Authority) (2021), *Report on Management and Supervision of ESG Risks for Credit Institutions and Investment Firms*, EBA/REP/2021/18, available at: https://bit.ly/3KBSCaV.

EBA (European Banking Authority) (2022), *Implementing Technical Standards (ITS) on Prudential Disclosures on ESG Risks in Accordance with Article 449a CRR*, EBA/ITS/2022/01, available at: https://bit.ly/4c7UZhk.

Edmans, A. (2020), *Grow the Pie: How Great Companies Deliver Both Purpose and Profit* (Cambridge, UK: Cambridge University Press).

Enriques, L. and Gargantini, M. (2010), 'Regolamentazione dei mercati finanziari, rating e regolamentazione del rating', 9 *Analisi Giuridica dell'Economia*, 475.

ESAs Joint Committee (2016), *Final Report. Good Supervisory Practices for Reducing Mechanistic Reliance on Credit Ratings*, JC 2016 71, December 20, available at: https://bit.ly/3VaIrit.

ESAs Joint Committee (2022), 'Clarifications on the ESAs' draft RTS under SFDR', JC 2022 23, June 2, available at: https://bit.ly/3x9QCUb.

ESMA SMSG (European Securities and Markets Authority Securities and Markets Stakeholder Group) (2022), 'Summary of conclusions', ESMA22-106-4146, October 7: available at: https://bit.ly/4bNOOzn.

ESMA (European Securities and Markets Authority) (2019a), *Final Report. Guidelines on Disclosure Requirements Applicable to Credit Rating*, ESMA33-9-320, July 18, available at: https://bit.ly/3VwuZXm.

ESMA (European Securities and Markets Authority) (2019b), *Technical Advice to the European Commission on Sustainability Considerations in the Credit Rating Market*, ESMA33-9-321, July 18, available at: https://bit.ly/3ySiUTC.

ESMA (European Securities and Markets Authority) (2020), *Response to Public Consultation EC Consultation on a Renewed Sustainable Finance Strategy*, ESMA30-22-821, available at: https://bit.ly/4eb14LM.

ESMA (European Securities and Markets Authority) (2021), *Letter to the Commissioner in Charge of Financial Services, Financial Stability and Capital Markets Union*, ESMA30-379-423, 28 January 2021, available at: https://bit.ly/3Vy3FIv.

ESMA (European Securities and Markets Authority) (2022a), *Outcome of ESMA Call for Evidence on Market Characteristics of ESG Rating and Data Providers in the EU*, ESMA22-328-603, June 24, available at: https://bit.ly/4ebxZQq.

ESMA (European Securities and Markets Authority) (2022b), *Response to Public Consultation. ESMA's Response to EFRAG's Consultation on the First Set of Draft ESRS*, ESMA32-334-551, August 8, available at: https://bit.ly/3RhLVi6.

EU Technical Expert Group on Sustainable Finance (2019), *Report on Benchmarks. Handbook of Climate Transition Benchmarks, Paris-Aligned Benchmark and Benchmarks ESG Disclosures*, December 20, available at: https://bit.ly/3RfQzNe.

European Commission (2016), *Study on the State of the Credit Rating Market Final Report*, MARKT/2014/257/F4/ST/OP, available at: https://bit.ly/3Vh43d7.

European Commission (2018), 'Action plan: Financing sustainable growth', COM(2018) 97 final, March 8, available at: https://bit.ly/497N6GU.

European Commission (2019), 'Communication. Guidelines on non-financial reporting: Supplement on reporting climate-related information', C(2019) 4490 final, June 17, available at: https://bit.ly/3XbBIHy.

European Commission (2021a), '2021 strategy for financing the transition to a sustainable economy', COM(2021) 390 final, July 6, available at: https://bit.ly/3VxrT5y.

European Commission (2021b), 'Proposal for a Directive as regards corporate sustainability reporting', COM(2021) 189 final, April 21, available at: https://bit.ly/3X8FMs9.

European Commission and Environmental Resources Management (ERM) (2021), 'Study on Sustainability-Related Ratings, Data and Research', Report prepared by *SustainAbility*, available at: https://bit.ly/4c7LAGD.

European Commission (2022a), 'Received contributions: Functioning of the ESG ratings market in the European Union and on the consideration of ESG factors in credit ratings', June 14, available at: https://bit.ly/4egMe6D.

European Commission (2022b), 'Summary report: Targeted consultation on the functioning of the ESG ratings market in the EU and on the consideration of ESG factors in credit ratings', August 3, available at: https://bit.ly/4egMe6D.

European Commission (2023a), Proposal for a Regulation on the transparency and integrity of Environmental, Social and Governance (ESG) rating activities (COM(2023) 314 final), June 13, available at: https://bit.ly/3XdPnxP.

European Commission (2023b), Impact Assessment Report accompanying the document Proposal for a Regulation of the European Parliament and of the Council on the transparency and integrity of Environmental, Social and Governance (ESG) rating activities (SWD(2023) 204 final), June 13, available at: https://bit.ly/4cdyasL.

European Commission and ERM (Environmental Resources Management) (2021), 'Study on sustainability-related ratings, data and research', Report prepared by *SustainAbility*, available at: https://bit.ly/4c7LAGD.

European Parliament (2024), Legislative resolution of 24 April 2024 on the proposal for a regulation of the European Parliament and of the Council on the transparency and integrity of Environmental, Social and Governance (ESG) rating activities (COM(2023)0314 – C9-0203/2023 – 2023/0177(COD)), available at: https://bit.ly/3XjuDF7.

Fornasari, F. (2020), 'Knowledge and power in measuring the sustainable corporation: stock exchanges as regulators of ESG factors disclosure', 19 *Washington University Global Studies Law Review*, 167.

Gibson, R., Krueger, P., and Steffen Schmidt, P. (2021), 'ESG Rating Disagreement and Stock Returns', ECGI Finance Working Paper N° 651, available at: https://papers.ssrn.com/sol3/papers.cfm?abstract_id=3433728.

Gordon, J. (2023), 'Unbundling Climate Change Risk from ESG', Columbia Law and Economics Working Paper No. 667, available at: https://papers.ssrn.com/sol3/papers.cfm?abstract_id=4547679.

High-Level Expert Group on Sustainable Finance (HLEGSF) (2018), *Final Report. Financing a Sustainable European Economy*, available at: https://bit.ly/3IMTNDv.

Hinze, A. and Sump, F. (2019), 'Corporate social responsibility and financial analysts: a review of the literature', 10 *Sustainability Accounting, Management and Policy Journal*, 126.

Ingo, W. (2020), 'Sense and nonsense in ESG ratings', 5 *Journal of Law, Finance and Accounting*, 307.

IOSCO (International Organization of Securities Commissions) (2021), *Environmental, Social and Governance (ESG) Ratings and Data Products Providers. Final Report* (FR09/21), available at: www.iosco.org/library/pubdocs/pdf/IOSCOPD690.pdf.

Kennedy, L. (2022), 'ESG v sustainability. Are we heading in the right direction?', available at: https://bit.ly/3XaHZmL.

Kishan, S. (2022), 'ESG insiders demand course correction to fix industry woes', *Bloomberg Europe Edition*, June 7, available at: https://bloom.bg/3XaISf5.

Kumar, R., Nathalie Wallace, N., and Funk, C. (2020), 'Into the mainstream ESG at the tipping point', *Harvard Law School Forum on Corporate Governance*, available at: https://bit.ly/3x7Ii7h.

Lambert, T. (2017), *How to Regulate. A Guide for Policymakers* (Cambridge, UK: Cambridge University Press).

Larcker, D. F., Pomorski, L., Tayan, B., and Watts, E. M. (2022), 'ESG ratings: A compass without direction', Working Paper, available at: https://papers.ssrn.com/sol3/papers.cfm?abstract_id=4179647.

Lenzi, D. (2021), 'Corporate social bonds – A legal analysis', 18 *European Company and Financial Law Review*, 291.

Macchi, C. (2021), 'The climate change dimension of business and human rights: The gradual consolidation of a concept of "climate due diligence"', 6 *Business and Human Rights Journal*, 93.

Manns, J. (2013), 'Downgrading rating agency reform', 81 *George Washington Law Review*, 749.

Morningstar (2022), 'Global sustainable fund flows: Q4 2021 in *Review. Flows and assets continue to grow at the end of a landmark year*', January 31, available at: https://bit.ly/3RmD12D.

MSCI (2023), 'ESG general FAQs for corporate issuers', available at: https://bit.ly/3Rd4CDd.

MSCI (2024), 'ESG ratings methodology', available at: www.msci.com/esg-and-climate-methodologies.

Mülbert, P. and Sajnovits, A. (2021), 'The inside information regime of the MAR and the rise of the ESG era', 18 *European Company and Financial Law Review*, 256.

Myklebust, T. (2014), 'The role of stock exchanges in shaping more sustainable company and market practices', available at: https://papers.ssrn.com/sol3/papers.cfm?abstract_id=2324743.

Nasdaq (2023), 'Nasdaq green equity designation', available at: https://bit.ly/3RmDiCH.

Neisen, M. (2021), 'ESG rating as input for a sustainability capital buffer', 15 *Journal of Risk Management in Financial Institutions*, 72.

Pagano, M., Yang, T., and Sinclair, G. (2018), 'Understanding ESG ratings and ESG indexes' in Boubaker, S. et al. (eds.), *Research Handbook of Finance and Sustainability* (Cheltenham: Edward Elgar), 357.

Partnoy, F. (1999), 'The Siskel and Ebert of financial markets: Two thumbs down for the credit rating agencies', 77 *Washington University Law Quarterly*, 619.

Phillips, G. (2018), 'Are ABS credit ratings = free speech?', 24 *Journal of Structured Finance*, 55.

Picciau, C. (2018), 'The evolution of the liability of credit rating agencies in the United States and in the European Union: regulation after the crisis', 15 *European Company and Financial Law Review*, 339.

Pierron, A. and Carabia, A. (2022), 'Sustainable investment calculations under MiFID II and SFDR remain perplexing for ESG investors', available at: https://bit.ly/3VeNaQf.

Platform on Sustainable Finance (2021), *Public Consultation. Report on Taxonomy Extension Options Linked to Environmental Objectives*, available at: https://bit.ly/3wXlYgN.

Ramos Muñoz, D. and Smolenska, A. (2023), 'The governance of ESG ratings and benchmarks (infomediaries) as gatekeepers: exit, voice and coercion', EBI Working Paper Series 149/2023, available at: https://papers.ssrn.com/sol3/papers.cfm?abstract_id=4531520.

S&P Global Ratings (2022), 'General criteria: Environmental, social, and governance principles in credit ratings', available at: https://bit.ly/4aVw2ER.

Simpson, C., Rathi, A., and Kishan, S. (2021), 'The ESG mirage', *Bloomberg Businessweek,*
available at: https://bloom.bg/45eiSS4.

Steuer S. and Tröger T. (2022), 'The role of disclosure in green finance', 8 *Journal of Financial
Regulation,* 1.

Sustainable Stock Exchanges Initiative (2017), 'How stock exchanges can grow green finance:
A voluntary action plan', available at: https://bit.ly/3Kvd1hQ.

Sustainalitics (2021), 'ESG risk ratings – Methodology abstract', January, 14, available at:
https://bit.ly/3yZMiHs.

Wendt, K. (2017), 'Social stock exchanges – Democratization of capital investing for impact',
Working Paper, available at: https://papers.ssrn.com/sol3/papers.cfm?abstract_id=3021739.

Wundenberg, M. (2022), 'Regulation of benchmarks', in Veil, R. et al. (eds.), *European
Capital Markets Law* (London: Hart, Bloomsbury Publishing).

Zetzsche, D. and Anker-Sørensen, L. (2022), 'Regulating sustainable finance in the dark', 23
European Business Organization Law Review, 47.

12

On the Sustainability of the MiFID II and IDD Investor Protection Frameworks

Veerle Colaert[†]

12.1 INTRODUCTION

Even though the sustainable finance idea dates back to at least 1992,[1] it only gained momentum in the EU in 2015, after the United Nations adopted its Sustainable Development Goals (SDG) and the EU signed the United Nations' Paris Climate Agreement.[2] In 2017 the European Commission appointed a High-Level Expert Group ('HLEG') to prepare a comprehensive blueprint for reforms.[3] Shortly after, on 8 March 2018, the European Commission adopted its eighth Climate Action Plan, entirely dedicated to sustainable finance and heavily reliant on the recommendations of the HLEG ('Action Plan').[4] It defined the following three main objectives of sustainable finance: (i) reorienting capital flows towards sustainable investment in order to achieve sustainable and inclusive growth, (ii) managing financial risks stemming from climate change, resource depletion, environmental degradation and social issues and (iii) fostering transparency and long-termism in financial and economic activity.[5] The Action Plan was the start of a re-writing of

[†] This contribution is a fully revised and updated version of Colaert 2021. The author would like to thank Matteo Gargantini, Arnaud Van Caenegem and Danny Busch for their feedback and stimulating comments on earlier drafts. She is also much indebted to Michaël Van Den Spiegel, Compliance Regulatory Expertise Officer and Head of Compliance Financial Information at Degroof Petercam, Chris Vervliet, Senior Risk Advisor at KBC Asset management, and Adina Gurau Audibert, Head of Asset Management at the French Asset Management Association (AFG), for helpful suggestions.
[1] In the context of the 1992 Rio Earth Summit the 'United Nations Environment Programme' set up a cooperation with the banking sector, resulting in the 'UNEP Statement by Banks on the Environment and Sustainable Development', later extended to become the 'UNEP Statement of Commitment by Financial Institutions on Sustainable Development'. See for a brief historic overview: https://bit.ly/43gVbaI (retrieved on 30 April 2023).
[2] United Nations, 'Paris Agreement' (2015) https://bit.ly/48Q9ggE (retrieved on 30 April 2023). See especially Art. 2(1)(c).
[3] HLEG 2018.
[4] European Commission 2018a.
[5] Ibid., 2.

the financial rulebook in the EU, to ensure that the sustainable finance objectives would be reflected in each and every aspect of EU financial regulation.

A substantial number of proposed measures intervene in the relationship between investment product distributors and investors,[6] and have led to important changes in the MiFID II and IDD investor protection frameworks. This is not surprising given the important part which financial services providers play in ensuring retail investors' access to sustainable investments.

This contribution will evaluate the revised MiFID II and IDD investor protection frameworks from three perspectives: (i) their contribution to remedying the 'value-action-gap' which leads many investors to invest in products which do not correspond with their sustainability values, and their contribution to a more sustainable economy more generally; (ii) their contribution to the creation of a level playing field between economically similar investment products; and (iii) their coherence with other sustainable finance measures. To that end, this contribution will first dwell on the behavioural problems explaining why retail investors do not always act upon their investment preferences, and on the role the investment product distributor can play to remedy those issues (Section 12.2). The next section will offer a critical overview of the most important changes to the MiFID II and IDD investor protection frameworks and discuss the main challenges of the revised legal framework (Section 12.3). A final section concludes.

12.2 ROLE OF THE INVESTMENT PRODUCT DISTRIBUTOR IN REMEDYING INVESTORS' 'VALUE-ACTION-GAP'

Multiple studies have shown a gap between investors' intentions and preferences on the one hand, and their actual behaviour on the other hand ('value-action-gap'). This gap has been attributed to a lack of notoriety and availability of ESG products and, when investors do have access to ESG products, a perception of high volatility and less profitability of ESG investments.[7] The ESG disclosure obligations on sustainability, introduced by the Corporate Sustainability Reporting Directive[8] and the Sustainable Finance Disclosure Regulation ('SFDR')[9] are an important part of the regulatory response to the lack of availability of ESG information on investment products, and should help in increasing the notoriety of ESG products. However, disclosure requirements alone may not suffice to reorient retail investor capital towards sustainable investment. Even when investors are well informed and convinced of the benefits of ESG products, limited attention at the moment of decision-making and procrastination in respect of complex decisions – such as changing an investment

---

[6]   Ibid., 6–7.
[7]   Paetzold and Busch 2014, 348–349; Pilaj 2017, 743; Eurosif 2018, 76.
[8]   Directive (EU) 2022/2464.
[9]   Regulation (EU) 2019/2088. See the contribution of de Ariba Sellier and Van Caenegem in this book.

strategy – explain why even correctly informed investors do not always act upon their preferences.[10] Pilaj makes the interesting comparison with a hypothetical supermarket, where fair-trade products are kept in storage, available only on explicit request, while most consumers do not make use of an explicit shopping list. Even consumers with a preference for fair trade will in such circumstances often end up with other products.[11] Investment product distributors can then play an important role in bridging the gap between the values of investors and their actual investment choices. They can raise knowledge and awareness of sustainable products at the very moment investors need to make a choice, thus helping to counter problems of bounded rationality and, more particularly, the limited attention problem, which has been defined as one of the main causes of the gap.[12] Distributors can not only do so by including a substantial number of ESG products in their product range and providing information, but also by including ESG factors in the definition of the target market of their products and by asking their clients about their ESG preferences before giving advice or investing on their behalf.[13] The Sustainable Finance Action Plan explicitly recognized the important role of investment product distributors in this regard, noting that '[b]y providing advice, investment firms and insurance distributors can play a central role in reorienting the financial system towards sustainability'.[14]

These ideas have only partially been integrated in the EU investor protection framework. The second version of the Markets in Financial Instruments Directive or MiFID II[15] determines the greater part of the legal framework governing the relationship between investment product distributors and their clients. However, MiFID II only covers investment services relating to the financial instruments listed in its annex and to structured deposits,[16] while services relating to other investment products are regulated in other directives and regulations. The Insurance Distribution Directive or IDD[17] introduced a 'MiFID-like' regime for 'insurance-based investment products'; the PEPP Regulation[18] regulates pan-European pension products; the Crowdfunding Regulation[19] deals with loans, transferable securities and 'admitted instruments for crowdfunding purposes'[20]

---

[10] Paetzold and Busch 2014, 348–349; Pilaj 2017, 743; Eurosif 2018, 76.

[11] Pilai 2017, 745 and 748.

[12] Pilaj 2017, 750.

[13] Pilai 2014, 749–750; Eurosif 2018, 76; European Commission 2018a, 6–7.

[14] European Commission 2018a, 6.

[15] Directive 2014/65/EU of 25 April 2014 on Markets in Financial Instruments.

[16] Annex I. A lists the investment services; Annex I. C lists the MiFID financial instruments. Art. provides that most of the MiFID II conduct of business rules also apply to investment firms and to credit institutions when selling or advising clients in relation to structured deposits.

[17] Directive 2016/97/EU of 20 January 2016 on insurance distribution (recast).

[18] Regulation (EU) 2019/1238 of 20 June 2019 on a Pan-European Personal Pension Product (PEPP).

[19] Regulation (EU) 2020/1503 of 7 October 2020 on European crowdfunding service providers for business.

[20] Defined in Art. 2(1)(n) of the Crowdfunding Regulation as shares of a private limited liability company that are not subject to restrictions that would effectively prevent them from being transferred, including restrictions to the way in which those shares are offered or advertised to the public.

offered via crowdfunding platforms;[21] and the Markets in Crypto-assets Regulation (MiCAR) deals with the offer and distribution of crypto-assets.[22] And yet only the MiFID II and IDD frameworks have been amended in view of the Sustainable Finance Action Plan. The PEPP Regulation, the Crowdfunding Regulation and the MiCAR have been adopted when the Sustainable Finance Action Plan was already in place. Nevertheless, the PEPP Regulation only mentions sustainable finance in a recital,[23] while the Crowdfunding Regulation only requires the Commission to present a report to the European Parliament and the Council, before 10 November 2023, among other things on the possibility of introducing specific measures to promote sustainable and innovative crowdfunding projects,[24] and the MiCAR does not refer to sustainable finance obligations for intermediaries providing services relating to crypto-assets.[25]

In April 2020 the European Commission launched a consultation to inform its Renewed Sustainable Finance Strategy. The 3rd and 50th questions of this consultation revealed further potential measures involving product distributors in efforts to increase retail investments in sustainable investment products: 'Question 3: When looking for investment opportunities, would you like to be systematically offered sustainable investment products as a default option by your financial adviser, provided the product suits your other needs?' and 'Question 50: Do you think that retail investors should be systematically offered sustainable investment products as one of the default options, when the provider has them available, at a comparable cost and if those products meet the suitability test?'[26] The final text of the renewed strategy, however, did not reflect those ideas.[27]

---

[21] See for a cross-sectoral comparison of the assist-your-customer-regimes applicable to those products: Busch, Colaert and Helleringer 2019, 343–376.

[22] Markets in Crypto Assets Regulation (EU) 2023/1114.

[23] Recital 8 refers to the creation of a personal pension product with a long-term retirement nature and which takes into account environmental, social and governance (ESG) factors as referred to in the United Nations supported Principles for Responsible Investment.

[24] Art. 42(2)(s) Crowdfunding Regulation.

[25] MiCAR only refers to the need for issuers of certain crypto-assets to include information on principal adverse impacts on the climate and other environment-related adverse impacts of the consensus mechanism used to issue the crypto-asset, in the white paper they should publish when offering certain crypto-assets to the public or when certain crypto-assets are admitted to trading on a trading platform for crypto-assets (see Art. 6(1)j, 19(1)h, 51(1)g) and for crypto-asset service providers to publish such information on each crypto-asset in relation to which they provide services, on their website (Art. 66(5)). No sustainability-related provisions have, for instance, been inserted in the suitability test (Art. 81(1) and (8)), while it does mention 'including risk tolerance' when referring to the investment objectives of the client. It is, however, possible that Level 3 guidelines will interpret the investment objectives as 'including sustainability preferences'. Whereas in the MiFID and IDD frameworks this has been dealt with in delegated acts (infra), the MiCAR does not foresee delegated acts, but only requires ESMA to specify the relevant article in Level 3 guidelines (Art. 81(15) MiCAR).

[26] European Commission 2020.

[27] European Commission 2021b.

12.3 CRITICAL OVERVIEW OF MAIN CHANGES TO THE MIFID II AND IDD FRAMEWORKS

12.3.1 *Introduction*

In 2018 the European Commission launched two Draft Commission Delegated Regulations on the integration of sustainability risks and factors into the MiFID II and IDD frameworks, amending MiFID Delegated Regulation (EU) 2017/565 ('MiFID Delegated Regulation') and IDD Delegated Regulation (EU) 2017/2359 respectively.[28] After consultations[29] and a technical advice by ESMA[30] and EIOPA,[31] the original draft Commission proposals were fine-tuned and additional draft proposals were issued to amend MiFID Delegated Directive 2017/593/EU ('MiFID Delegated Directive') and IDD Delegated Regulation (EU) 2017/2358.[32] After a public consultation the Commission adopted the amending regulations and directive on 21 April 2021.[33] Moreover, ESMA has revised its Suitability Guidelines in September 2022 and its Product Governance Guidelines in March 2023, amongst other things, in view of the above-mentioned changes to the MiFID II framework.[34] Also EIOPA, even though it does not provide general suitability guidelines, has issued specific Guidance on the integration of sustainability preferences in the suitability assessment under the IDD.[35]

In the explanatory memoranda to the amending Regulations and Directive, the Commission states that by explicitly including sustainability preferences into the MiFID and IDD frameworks, the legislator wishes to reinforce the new sustainable finance regulations – that is, the SFDR, Climate Transition Benchmark Regulation (EU) 2019/2089 and Taxonomy Regulation (EU) 2020/852 – and to integrate

---

[28] Draft Commission Delegated Regulation amending Regulation (EU) 2017/565 (Ref. Ares(2018)2681500, 24 May 2018); Draft Commission Delegated Regulation amending Delegated Regulation (EU) 2017/2359 (Ref. Ares(2018)2681527, 24 May 2018).

[29] ESMA 2018c; EIOPA 2018. EIOPA also did an online survey between 17 September and 3 October 2018 seeking stakeholders' views and current approaches regarding the consideration of sustainability factors.

[30] ESMA 2019.

[31] EIOPA 2019.

[32] Draft Commission Delegated Regulation amending Delegated Regulation (EU) 2017/565 (Ref. Ares(2020)2955205, 8 June 2020); Draft Commission Delegated Directive amending Delegated Directive (EU) 2017/593 (Ares(2020)2955234, 8 June 2020); Draft Commission Delegated Regulation amending Delegated Regulation (EU) 2017/2358 and Delegated Regulation (EU) 2017/2359 (Ref. Ares(2020)2955230, 8 June 2020).

[33] COM(2021)2616, published in OJ L277 on 2 August 2021 as Commission Delegated Regulation (EU) 2021/1253 amending Delegated Regulation (EU) 2017/565; COM(2021)2612, published in OJ L277 on 2 August 2021 as Commission Delegated Directive (EU) 2021/1269 amending Delegated Directive (EU) 2017/593; COM(2021)2614, published in OJ L277 of 2 August 2021 as Commission Delegated Regulation (EU) 2021/1257 amending Delegated Regulations (EU) 2017/2358 and (EU) 2017/2359.

[34] ESMA 2022c; ESMA 2023.

[35] EIOPA 2022.

sustainability considerations into the investment, advisory and disclosure processes in a consistent manner across sectors.[36] In this contribution we will, among other things, evaluate to what extent such a consistent cross-sectoral integration has indeed been achieved.

As mentioned in the introduction to this contribution, only the MiFID II and IDD frameworks have been amended, while the rules covering other product distributors (PEPPs, crowdfunding) have not. Full cross-sectoral consistency will therefore not be achieved in the EU investor protection framework. In the rest of this section we will discuss the main changes in the MiFID and IDD frameworks as well as the challenges those changes bring.[37] We will discuss successively (i) the new sustainability-related definitions, (ii) the amended suitability assessment, (iii) the amended product governance process and (iv) the amended conflicts of interest procedure.

12.3.2 *Definitions*

12.3.2.1 Sustainability Factors and Sustainability Risks

Both the amended MiFID II and IDD Delegated Acts introduce a number of sustainable finance-related definitions, making cross-references to definitions of the SFDR. Sustainability factors are defined as 'environmental, social and employee matters, respect for human rights, anti-corruption and anti-bribery matters',[38] whereas sustainability risk means 'an environmental, social or governance event or condition that, if it occurs, could cause an actual or a potential material negative impact on the value of the investment'.[39]

12.3.2.2 Sustainability Preferences

Moreover, the MiFID and IDD Delegated Regulations introduce a new definition of 'sustainability preferences'.[40] In earlier drafts all three amending acts defined the term 'sustainability preferences'. In the final text, however, the amended rules on product governance no longer use the term 'sustainability preferences', but instead

---

[36] Explanatory Memorandum to COM(2021)2616, 3; Explanatory Memorandum to COM(2021)2612, 2; and Explanatory Memorandum to COM(2021)2614, 3–4. Cross-sectoral consistency was also the ambition of ESMA when revising its suitability guidelines. See ESMA 2022a, 8, para. 10.

[37] We will not discuss the changes to the governance requirements and the risk management process, which only indirectly aim at investor protection.

[38] Art. 2(8) MiFID Delegated Regulation (EU) 2017/565; Art. 2(5) IDD Delegated Regulation (EU) 2017/2359. The definitions refer to Art. 2(24) SFDR.

[39] Art. 2(9) MiFID Delegated Regulation (EU) 2017/565. The definition refers to Art. 2(22) SFDR.

[40] Art. 2(7) MiFID Delegated Regulation (EU) 2017/565; Art. 2(4) IDD Delegated Regulation (EU) 2017/2359. The definitions are the same, except for the word 'financial instrument' in MiFID Delegated Regulation (EU) 2017/565, and 'insurance-based investment product' in the IDD Delegated Regulation (EU) 2017/2359.

refer to the undefined 'sustainability-related objectives'. It is unclear why this distinction has been made in the final stage of the legislative process.

Sustainability preferences are defined as 'a client's/customer's or potential client's/customer's choice as to whether and, if so, to what extent one or more of the following financial instruments/products shall be integrated into his or her investment':

(a) a financial instrument/insurance-based investment product for which the (potential) client/customer determines that a minimum proportion shall be invested in environmentally sustainable investments, as defined in Article 2(1) Taxonomy Regulation;[41]

(b) a financial instrument/insurance-based investment product for which the (potential) client/customer determines that a minimum proportion shall be invested in sustainable investments, as defined in Article 2(17) SFDR;[42]

(c) a financial instrument/insurance-based investment product that considers principal adverse impacts on sustainability factors, where the qualitative or quantitative elements demonstrating that consideration are determined by the (potential) client.

The definition of sustainability preferences raises a number of questions and problems, which will be discussed in the next paragraphs.

First, products of categories (a), (b) and (c) are not three distinct product groups. In fact, the category (a) product group is in principle a subset of the category (b) product group, and categories (a) and(b) are partly subsets of category (c). This is visualized and further explained in Figure 12.1.

Second, the question arises how the three product categories in the definition of sustainability preferences relate to Article 8 and Article 9 SFDR. This is visualized and explained in Figure 12.2.

Figure 12.2 shows that each of the categories (a) to (c) can be 'Article 8 products'. It is clear, however, that 'Article 8' products do not always have a minimum percentage of Taxonomy-aligned investments (a), nor a minimum percentage of sustainable investments (b), nor do they necessarily consider principle adverse impacts (c). Until the entry into force of the MiFID II and IDD amendments relating to sustainability preferences, financial institutions typically offered 'Article 8' products as (less ambitious) ESG products to their clients. The definition of sustainability preferences means that it will be up to the investment intermediary to decide for each Article 8 product whether it can be considered under one of the

---

[41] Art. 2(1) Taxonomy Regulation (EU) 2020/852 defines an environmentally sustainable investment as an investment in one or several economic activities that qualify as environmentally sustainable under the Taxonomy Regulation.

[42] Art. 2(17) SFDR defines a sustainable investment as an investment in an economic activity that contributes to an environmental objective, or to a social objective, provided that they do not significantly harm any of those objectives and that the investee companies follow good governance practices.

Products categories in the definition of sustainability preferences

Products considering PAIs (c)	Min. proportion invested in sustainable investments (b) **
	Min. proportion invested in environmentally sustainable investments (a)
	***
	***

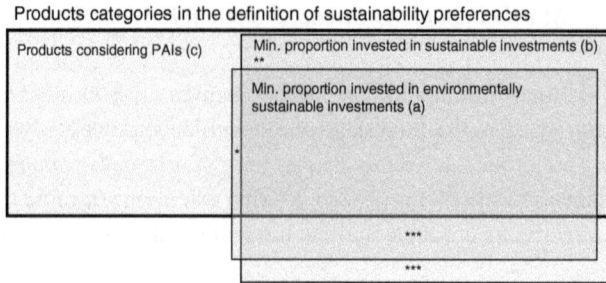

FIGURE 12.1 Definition of sustainability preferences – relationship between product categories

* An environmentally sustainable investment under the Taxonomy Regulation will in the vast majority of cases also be a sustainable investment under the SFDR, since the definition of 'sustainable investment' in Article 2(17) SFDR encompasses investments in 'an economic activity that contributes to an environmental objective'. However, Article 2(17) SFDR also requires that sustainable investments do no significant harm to any of those (environmental and social) objectives and that the investee companies follow good governance practices, whereas the Taxonomy Regulation only has a 'no significant harm' requirement in regard of environmental objectives, merely a requirement to comply with 'minimum safeguards' in regard of the social objectives listed in that directive, and no requirements in relation to good governance. It would therefore be possible in theory that certain environmentally sustainable investments are not covered by the definition of sustainable investments. The Commission, however, clarified that the SFDRs do no significant harm principle and the requirement to ensure that an investee company follows good governance practices are deemed to be fulfilled for investments in Taxonomy-aligned economic activities when they comply with the Taxonomy's minimum safeguards.[43] Products with a minimum proportion invested in environmentally sustainable investments (a) are then a subset of products with a minimum proportion invested in sustainable investments (b), and the area marked with * is, according to the interpretation of the Commission, empty.

** In practice, a large majority of sustainable investments available today are environmentally sustainable investments. Sustainable investment products that contribute to a social objective, without also contributing to environmental objectives are much less prevalent. Products of which a minimum proportion is invested in sustainable investments that are not also environmentally sustainable investments will therefore also be much less prevalent (area marked with **).

*** Sustainable investments should do no significant harm to other environmental or social objectives and therefore should consider principal adverse impacts on sustainability factors. The same is true for environmentally sustainable investments, which should do no significant harm to environmental objectives and should respect minimum safeguards in regard of social objectives. However, if the minimum proportion determined by the client in respect of (a) and (b) products is less than 100%, the DNSH principle should be complied with only for the taxonomy-aligned products or the sustainable products in the portfolio, not for the rest of the portfolio. (a) and (b) products with a proportion of less than 100% therefore do not necessarily consider PAIs for the full portfolio. (a) and (b) products are therefore no full subsets of the (c) product type.

---

43 European Commission 2023, 7. The legal authority of this document is, however, limited, in view of the following disclaimer: 'The FAQ is merely intended to assist financial and non-financial undertakings in implementing the relevant legal provisions. Only the Court of Justice of the European Union is competent to authoritatively interpret EU law. The views expressed in this Notice cannot prejudge the position that the European Commission might take before the EU and national courts.'

Products promoting E/S characteristics (art. 8 SFDR)

Products categories in the definition of sustainability preferences

Products considering PAIs (c)

Min. proportion invested in sustainable investments (b)

Min. proportion invested in environmentally sustainable investments (a)

Products with sustainability objectives (art. 9 SFDR)

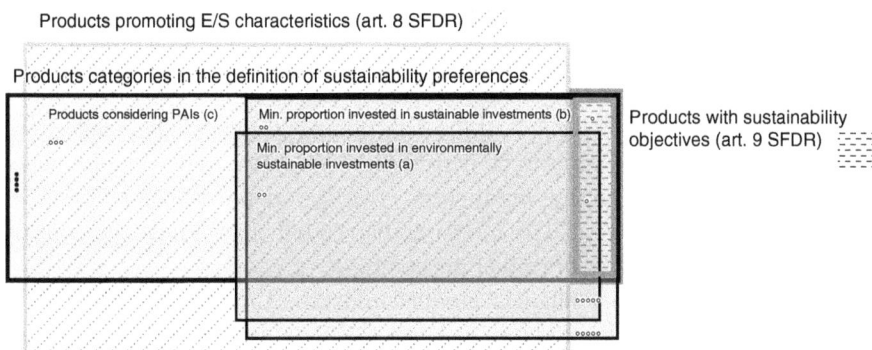

FIGURE 12.2 Relationship between product categories in the definition of sustainability preferences and 'Article 8' and 'Article 9' products

° For product categories (a) and (b) clients/customers should determine the minimum proportion that should be invested in environmentally sustainable investments (a) or in sustainable investments (b). Only if the client/customer determines a minimum proportion of 100% to be invested in environmentally sustainable investments (a), or in sustainable investments (b), will those products be considered as a financial product with sustainable investment as its objective (Article 9 SFDR).

°° Whenever clients determine a minimum proportion of less than 100% to be invested in environmentally sustainable investments (a) or in sustainable investments (b), the (a) and (b) categories in the definition of sustainability preferences will not be considered as financial products with sustainable investment as their objective (Article 9 SFDR), but as products promoting environmental or social characteristics (Article 8 SFDR). It should be noted that products with a minimum proportion of less than 100% to be invested in environmentally sustainable investments (a) will still qualify under Article 9 if the rest is invested in investments which contribute to a social objective.

°°° The vast majority of products that consider principal adverse impacts (c), other than Article 9 products, will qualify as products promoting environmental or social characteristics under Article 8 SFDR, in view of (i) the European Commission's interpretation of Article 7(1) SFDR as a requirement to *describe* both the adverse impacts and the *procedures put in place to mitigate them* and (ii) its very broad interpretation of 'promoting' (including such disclosures).[44]

¦ Nevertheless, it would in theory still be possible that products which consider principal adverse impacts invest in companies which do not follow good governance practices, in which case they would not qualify as products promoting environmental and social characteristics under Article 8 SFDR.

°°°°° Similarly (a) and (b) product types that are only partly invested in environmentally sustainable, or sustainable products, might not follow good governance practices for rest of the portfolio, meaning that they would then not qualify as products promoting environmental and social characteristics under Article 8 SFDR.

---

44 European Commission and Joint Committee 2023, 12 and 29–30.

categories of the definition of sustainability preferences and therefore be offered to clients with corresponding sustainability preferences.[45]

Third, whereas categories (a) and (b) of the definition of sustainability preferences explicitly refer to defined concepts of the Taxonomy and the SFDR, category (c) does not, even though it seems to be derived from the transparency requirements on adverse sustainability impacts in Article 7(1) SFDR. This provision was, however, not meant to define a product type and raises many questions.[46] The exact scope of product category (c) is therefore rather uncertain.

Fourth, the definitions of 'financial product' under the Taxonomy and the SFDR only refer to 'portfolio-style' products, such as UCITS funds, AIFs, insurance-based investment products or discretionary managed portfolios,[47] while the MiFID II definition of 'sustainability preferences' uses the broader term 'financial instrument'. Even though the Explanatory Memorandum[48] states that it was not the legislator's objective to limit the scope of the definition to funds, the application by analogy to all financial instruments is not straightforward. ESMA is aware of the problem, stating that 'the concept of "minimum proportion" does not apply to financial instruments for which it is not practically possible to define such minimum proportion (for instance bonds or shares etc).' According to ESMA these types of products could refer to the actual proportion instead of the minimum one.[49] Moreover, when a suitability assessment is based on the consideration of the client's portfolio as a whole (in case of portfolio management of investment advice), the suitability preferences, including the minimum proportion determined by the client, can be applied on average at the level of the portfolio, or the part/percentage of the portfolio the client wants to be invested in products with sustainability features.[50]

Fifth, the impact of the Taxonomy and the SFDR on non-EU investee companies and financial instruments is not clear at this stage. The question of what products will be available under what product category of the definition of sustainability preferences, is therefore unsure, as is the question whether a sufficient number and a sufficiently diverse range of such instruments will be available to match investor preferences (see also 12.3.3.5(e)).[51] Moreover due to a lack of reliable data, it is often simply not possible to correctly assess the (degree of) sustainability of certain products or activities (see also 12.3.3.5(c)).

---

[45] See SMSG 2022a, 12, para. 52.
[46] See for instance European Commission and Joint Committee 2023, 12, question 3.
[47] Art. 2(12) SFDR; Art. 2(3) Taxonomy Regulation (EU) 2020/852.
[48] Explanatory Memorandum COM(2021)2616, 5.
[49] ESMA 2022b, 10, footnote 13. In response to ESMA's question, the SMSG has advised ESMA on different types of products for which the reference to a minimum proportion does not apply, such as shares, bonds, structured securities, private equity funds and infrastructure funds with a fund of funds structure and RMBS (SMSG 2022b, 5, para. 25). See also ESMA's response: ESMA 2023, 26–27, paras. 42–43.
[50] ESMA 2022c, 26, para. 38 and 60, para. 81; ESMA 2023, 28, para. 48.
[51] SMSG 2022a, 1, 3, paras. 3 and 8, paras. 28–32.

In conclusion, the concept of 'sustainability preferences' is not very straightforward. It takes quite some expertise to fully comprehend the distinction between the different product categories and the way in which they relate to each other. For investors, the fact that the three categories to a large extent overlap, may, moreover be quite confusing. Therefore, firms may find it extremely difficult to fulfil their obligation to explain all those concepts to clients in a clear and understandable manner (see 12.3.3.2).

12.3.3 *Suitability Assessment*

12.3.3.1 Background

When providing portfolio management, investment advice or insurance advice, investment intermediaries have to assess whether their investment services, financial instruments or insurance-based investment products are 'suitable' for a particular client. For that purpose, they have to obtain information regarding the client's knowledge and experience, financial situation and investment objectives.[52]

The HLEG report recommended to 'require investment advisers to ask about, and then respond to, retail investors' preferences about the sustainable impact of their investments as a routine component of financial advice'.[53] In March 2018 the Commission held a consultation on the integration of ESG considerations into the suitability assessment. The consultation showed that information regarding the investment objectives of the client generally related to financial objectives, while non-financial objectives of the client, such as sustainability preferences, were usually not addressed. Only a minority of the clients proactively raised such preferences themselves. The Commission saw the following reasons for this: (i) insufficient transparency of the available information on sustainability-related financial instruments, (ii) high risk of 'greenwashing' in existing documentation and (iii) a lack of education.[54] The Commission concluded that investment intermediaries consistently did not appropriately consider sustainability factors in the suitability process. Nonetheless, respondents also indicated that the overall interest of their clients for sustainable products was growing, as was evident from the increase in information requests linked to ESG issues. In response to the question of what regulatory action should be taken in this respect, respondents were split among the options of (i) not integrating sustainability in the suitability test, using non-binding guidance only and (ii) clearly requiring it in legislation.[55] The Commission, however, decided 'to

---

[52] Art. 25(2) MiFID II *juncto* Art. 54 MiFID Delegated Regulation (EU) 2017/565; Art. 30(1) IDD *juncto* Art. 9 IDD Delegated Regulation (EU) 2017/2359.

[53] HLEG 2018, 28.

[54] Explanatory Memorandum COM(2021)2616, 1; Explanatory Memorandum COM(2021)2614, 1–2.

[55] European Commission 2018b, 129.

amend the MiFID II and IDD Delegated Acts in Q2 2018 to ensure that sustainability preferences are taken into account in the suitability assessment'.[56]

In the meanwhile, ESMA already updated in May 2018 its Guidelines on the MiFID II suitability assessment, providing that 'it would be a good practice for firms to consider non-financial elements when gathering information on the client's investment objectives, and [...] collect information on the client's preferences on environmental, social and governance factors'.[57] In 2021 both the Delegated MiFID II and Delegated IDD Regulations have been amended in order to explicitly transpose such good practice into binding legal provisions. ESMA has, moreover, updated its MiFID II Suitability Guidelines and EIOPA has issued specific Guidance on the integration of sustainability preferences in the suitability assessment under IDD to clarify and interpret the new provisions.[58]

12.3.3.2 Providing Information to Clients

Investment intermediaries should enable (potential) clients/customers to understand the different degrees of sustainability-related ambition of investment products and to take informed investment decisions in terms of sustainability. To that end, they should explain the distinction between on the one hand the different types of products in the definition of 'sustainability preferences' and on the other hand products without those specific features that should not be eligible for recommendation to customers/clients with individual sustainability preferences.[59] During the consultation process preceding ESMA's revised Suitability Guidelines, many respondents, and also the SMSG, requested guidance on how to explain to clients the concept of sustainability preferences and the distinction between the different elements of the definition, without using technical language. Some respondents asked for examples; others requested standard information material to explain in plain language some of the key concepts.[60] Nevertheless, in its final guidelines, ESMA merely confirmed that firms should help clients understand the concept of 'sustainability preferences' and the choices to be made in this context. ESMA clarified that firms should explain the terms and the distinction between the different elements of the definition, and also between these products and products without such sustainability features. Moreover, firms should also explain terms and concepts used when referring to environmental, social and governance aspects. ESMA did not go into detail on how investment firms should do this, apart from stressing that they should explain these distinctions and concepts in a clear manner, avoiding

---

[56] European Commission 2018a, 7.
[57] ESMA 2018b, 38, para. 28.
[58] See footnotes 36 and 37.
[59] Recital 6 Commission Delegated Regulation (EU) 2021/1253; Recital 12 Commission Delegated Regulation (EU) 2021/1257.
[60] ESMA 2022c, Annex III. Feedback Statement, 17–18; SMSG 2022a, 11, para. 42.

technical language, explaining terms and concepts used when referring to ESG aspects.[61] Remarkably, EIOPA did give further guidance on this, maintaining that insurance intermediaries/undertakings could use, for example, the explanatory notes included in the margins of the compulsory SFDR templates to explain such notions. EIOPA further clarified that those explanations can be provided in 'layers', for instance in the introduction to a questionnaire on sustainability preferences, and that the explanations should be given prior to addressing the questions on sustainability preferences as part of the collection of information on the investment objectives.[62] It is regrettable that ESMA and EIOPA clearly did not consult on this matter in order to come forward with one and the same approach.

In our view the requirement to explain to investors/customers the terms and the distinctions between the different elements of the definition of sustainability preferences is an almost impossible task. It is, moreover, misguided and unnecessary. While it is indeed useful for clients/customers to have a high-level understanding of what the term 'sustainability preferences' means, it is first and foremost important for them to be able to express their sustainability preferences in a nuanced manner. Rather than overwhelming clients with concepts that are difficult to grasp and distinguish from each other even for professionals in the sector (see 12.3.2.2 and following), investment intermediaries should allow their clients/customers to nuance their preferences by asking additional questions, in layman terms, which should enable the intermediary to qualify the client/customer's sustainability preferences in terms of the different elements of the definition, without burdening the client with that complex terminology.

12.3.3.3 Obtaining Client/Customer Information

The updated MiFID II and IDD provisions explicitly require that when investment intermediaries obtain information on the investment objectives of their clients/customers, this should include information on any sustainability preferences they have.[63] In its first assessment, ESMA acknowledged that, as is the case for the assessment of other criteria relevant for the suitability assessment, firms could develop different methodological approaches to comply with the amended provision. In a simplified approach the client could, for instance, be asked which percentage of their portfolio they wish to invest in E, S and/or G investments. In a more advanced portfolio approach the investment firm could determine and assess the 'ESG profile' of the client's portfolio on the basis of the client's preferences for E, S and/or G investments.[64] In the final guidelines, ESMA still discusses the portfolio approach separately, but

---

[61] ESMA 2022c, 42–43, para. 16.
[62] EIOPA 2022, 8–9, with reference to Commission Delegated Regulation (EU) 2022/1288 supplementing Regulation (EU) 2019/2088.
[63] Amended Art. 54(2)(a) and 54(5) MiFID Delegated Regulation (EU) 2017/565; amended Art. 9(2)(a) IDD Delegated Regulation (EU) 2017/2359.
[64] ESMA 2019, 23, para. 12.

makes very clear that granularity of information on sustainability preferences is key in all circumstances (at least granular questioning is key – for the situation where the client does not want or is not able to give granular information, see below).

Both ESMA and EIOPA clarify that the information on clients' sustainability preferences should include all aspects mentioned in the definition of 'sustainability preferences' and should be sufficiently granular to match the client's sustainability preferences with the sustainability-related features of products on offer.[65] Both ESMA and EIOPA confirm that, obviously, investment intermediaries should adopt a neutral and unbiased approach throughout the process, so as to not influence clients' answers.[66] ESMA and EIOPA differ substantially on how this information should be obtained, however., and EIOPA has added a clear flowchart in its guidance, which the ESMA guidelines lack.[67]

ESMA's guidelines suggest flexibility in the approach that firms can take, indicating one approach that firms 'could' choose. The Securities and Markets Stakeholder Group explicitly appreciated this flexibility for market participants in the face of the many uncertainties.[68] In ESMA's suggested approach, firms could, in a first step, collect information on the sustainability preferences of the client referring to one or more of the product categories expressed in points (a) to (c) of the definition; this could be assessed through closed-ended yes/no-questions. In a second step they could collect information on whether the client's sustainability preferences with regard to categories (b) and (c) have a focus on either environmental, social or governance sustainability factors, or a combination of them, or whether the client does not have such a focus. As a third step, where the client expresses preferences in terms of the 'minimum proportion' referred to in categories (a) and (b), firms could collect this information not by reference to an exact percentage but to minimum percentages. These percentages should be presented in a neutral way and be sufficiently granular. Firms could, for example, assist the client to identify the minimum proportion by approximating it by standardized minimum proportions, such as 'minimum 20%', 'minimum 25%' etc. Fourth, in case the client wishes to include a financial instrument that considers principle adverse indicators, the collected information should cover the qualitative and quantitative elements mentioned in category (c). Firms could test clients' preferences and appetite for principal adverse impacts (PAI) integration with regard to the families of PAI indicators as a whole, based on a focus of the client on environmental, social or governance aspects, using the categories presented in the SFDR RTS[69] (instead of an approach based on each PAI indicator) such as emissions, energy performance, water & waste, etc. A qualitative evaluation

[65] ESMA 2022c 45–46, guideline 2, para. 26; EIOPA 2022, 10–11.
[66] ESMA 2022c, 46, guideline 2, para. 26; EIOPA 2022, 10.
[67] EIOPA 2022, 11–12.
[68] SMSG 2022a, 6, para. 19.
[69] Commission Delegated Regulation (EU) 2022/1288.

could then be initiated for each category that is important or key for the client, based on the approaches in which products consider PAI (e.g. exclusion strategies, controversies policies, voting and engagement policies). In case the client wishes to include a financial instrument that considers PAI, firms could also ask the client if there are specific economic activities that, on the basis of relevant PAIs, it wishes to exclude from its investments (for example, specific economic activities that are considered as significantly harmful under the EU Taxonomy framework and/or that are opposed to the environmental and ethical views held by the client and that are linked to certain principal adverse impacts on sustainability factors).[70]

EIOPA is firmer in its guidance on what information insurers and insurance intermediaries 'need to obtain'. They should first request whether the customer has sustainability preferences (yes/no). If so, the information to be obtained should include all aspects of the customer's sustainability preferences, such as (i) whether the customer has sustainability preferences with regard to sustainable investments or PAI as defined in categories (b) or (c) or a combination of them; and (ii) if the customer has a preference with regard to category (b), whether with regard to aspects defined in category (a).[71] For categories (b) and (c) information could for example be obtained on whether the customer's sustainability preferences have a focus on either environmental or social criteria or a combination, or whether the customer does not have such a preference.[72] In addition, information on employee matters, respect for human rights, anti-corruption and anti-bribery matters could be obtained (with yes/no questions). With respect to environmental criteria, information could be obtained on whether the customer has a preference for investments aligned with the EU Taxonomy under category a) or not. As of January 2023 insurers and intermediaries could explain to their customers that there are two key performance indicators used to calculate the proportion of investments that are aligned with the EU Taxonomy. They could ask the customer whether the extent to which their investment should be aligned with the Taxonomy should be based on all the investments of the IBIP (KPI 1) or only on the assets that are not government bonds (KPI 2).[73] As a second step, they should consider for products of categories (a) and (b) what would be the minimum proportion; and for products of category (c) which principal adverse impacts should be considered, including quantitative or qualitative criteria demonstrating that consideration. If the (c)-category product is a multi-option product (MOP), EIOPA requires that information should be obtained on whether all underlying options should consider PAI of investment decisions on sustainability factors, or only a proportion.[74] Insurers and insurance intermediaries

---

[70] ESMA 2022c, 46–47, para. 27.
[71] EIOPA 2022, 11.
[72] Ibid., 12 and 14.
[73] Ibid., 13–14.
[74] Ibid., 10.

could assist the customer in identifying the minimum proportion by approximating the minimum proportion by standardized minimum proportions, such as 'minimum 10%, minimum 20%, etc'.[75] The information collected should cover the PAI and qualitative/quantitative elements mentioned in category (c). Customer's preferences and appetite for integrating PAI could, for example, be tested with regard to the families of PAI indicators as a whole, based on a possible focus of the customer on environmental, social or governance aspects.

ESMA furthermore clarifies that, when providing portfolio management or investment advice with a portfolio approach, firms should collect information on the client's sustainability preferences with the same granularity. Moreover, firms should also ask the client which part or percentage of the portfolio (if any) the client wants to be invested in products meeting the client's sustainability preferences. Where firms work with model portfolios that combine some or all of the criteria, they should nevertheless allow for a granular assessment of the client's preferences and should ensure not to use questionnaires that push the client into a certain combination of criteria that would not meet the client's sustainability preferences.[76] EIOPA has not provided guidance on this, which seems logic since insurance intermediaries/insurers typically advise on individual IBIPs and not on 'portfolios of IBIPs'.

It is also possible that clients do not wish to be granular in their sustainability preferences. ESMA requires that firms have in place policies and instructions for their client-facing staff for situations where clients confirm to have sustainability preferences, but do not specify a preference with regard to any of the specific aspects mentioned in categories (a) to (c) or with regard to minimum proportions. The firm could then, for example, consider any of the aspects of categories (a) to (c). Firms should explain this and inform the client about the sustainability features of the investment product(s) recommended or invested in on behalf of the client. Moreover, they should document in the suitability report the client's choice not to further specify their sustainability preferences. ESMA adds that similar arrangements should be in place when firms provide robo-advice services.[77]

The EIOPA guidance on the other hand does not refer to policies and instructions for client-facing staff. EIOPA confirms that the insurer or insurance intermediary can in such circumstances still recommend an IBIP that has sustainability features matching the customer's preferences as best [*sic*] as possible, taking into account the sustainability preferences as expressed by the customer in general terms. EIOPA moreover clarifies that the suitability statement should in that case record (i) a description of the customer's sustainability preferences, even if in broad or general terms; (ii) the fact that even though the customer has sustainability preferences, (s)he has not specified a preference with regard to any aspect(s); and (iii) if a

---

[75] Ibid., 15.
[76] ESMA 2022c, 47, para. 29.
[77] Ibid., 47, para. 28.

personal recommendation of an IBIP is made based on the customer's sustainability preferences, the reasons underlying that personal recommendation.[78]

Finally, the question arose what an investment firm should do in case an investor does not want to provide information on sustainability preferences or simply neglects the investment firm's request to fill out an additional questionnaire. An investment intermediary should, in principle, not recommend investment services or financial instruments to the client/customer if it does not obtain the information required under the suitability test.[79] Both ESMA and EIOPA have, however, clarified that when a client/customer does not answer the question whether it has sustainability preferences, or answers 'no', the firm may consider this client as 'sustainability-neutral' and recommend products both with and without sustainability-related features.[80] In other words, products with sustainability-related features can be suitable for clients without sustainability preferences, but products without sustainability-related features are not suit.able for clients with sustainability preferences. That is, unless the new 'safe haven' would be applied (see 12.3.3.5(e)).[81]

The MiFID Delegated Regulation has been explicitly amended to clarify that clients' objectives include their sustainability preferences. However, an equally important question is whether – and to what extent – all investors fully understand the sustainable finance products on offer, the risks involved and their risk and reward profile. In order to properly perform the suitability test, investment firms should, in our view, not only question sustainability preferences, but also whether, and to what extent, the investor actually understands the concept of sustainable investment and the characteristics and consequences (risks, link with performance, etc.) of the sustainable products on offer. Additional questions on knowledge of and experience with sustainable products might therefore be necessary. Neither the MiFID Delegated Regulation nor ESMA's revised Suitability Guidelines explicitly require this,[82] but it seems inevitable in the light of the general pre-existing obligation to test the knowledge and experience of the client.

12.3.3.4 Staff's Understanding of Financial Products

A second amendment of the MiFID Delegated Regulation, is the requirement for investment firms to have *adequate policies and procedures* to ensure that they understand the nature, features (including costs) and risks of the investment services and

---

[78] EIOPA 2022, 27.
[79] Article 54(8) MiFID Delegated Regulation; Art. 9(5) IDD Delegated Regulation (EU) 2017/2359.
[80] ESMA 2022c, 61, para. 85; EIOPA 2022, 16.
[81] Art. 54(10) MiFID Delegated Regulation (EU) 2017/565; Art. 9(10) IDD Delegated Regulation (EU) 2017/2359.
[82] ESMA only states, in general, and without reference to sustainability preferences, that it is particularly important that firms consider the level of complexity of products, and this should be matched with how much client information the firm should obtain, in particular in regard of clients' knowledge and experience (ESMA 2022c, 58, para. 72).

financial instruments selected for their clients, which should from now on also include any sustainability factors.[83] The IDD framework has not been amended on this point. However, the more general provision of Article 10(1) and (2) IDD requires insurance distributors and employees of insurers to possess appropriate knowledge and ability to complete their tasks and perform their duties adequately and to comply with continuing professional training and development requirements. EIOPA has clarified that this also means that employees of insurers and insurance intermediaries selling IBIPs need to have basic knowledge and competences to know how to assess the customer's sustainability preferences. Moreover, if they sell IBIPs that promote environmental or social characteristics or that have a sustainable investment objective, they should have a more detailed knowledge and competence, in accordance with the nature of the products they provide advice on.[84]

12.3.3.5 Matching Clients with Products

(A) DIFFERENT ACCENTS BY ESMA AND EIOPA. In order to allow an adequate matching process of products and clients' sustainability preferences, both ESMA and EIOPA provide guidance. Their guidance is quite different though. ESMA stresses that firms should adopt robust and objective procedures, methodologies and tools that allow them to appropriately consider the different characteristics, including sustainability factors of each investment product they may recommend or invest in on behalf of clients. ESMA explicitly states that this should include taking into consideration the firm's analysis conducted for purposes of product governance obligations.[85] EIOPA, on the other hand, deems it key for insurance intermediaries to use the sustainability information which has to be disclosed prior to the conclusion of the contract (on the basis of the SFDR and Solvency II), as well as the information which is disclosed via the insurer's website, to assess whether a product matches the sustainability preferences of the customer.[86] EIOPA clarifies that for all IBIPs, including those with a long recommended holding period where the asset allocation may change over time, the features of the product disclosed by the insurer prior to the conclusion of the contract represent sufficient information.[87] EIOPA furthermore stresses that when a customer has indicated a preference for a combination of points (a), (b) and (c), the recommended product should match the specific combination expressed by the customer.[88] EIOPA also provides a figure showing how the SFDR disclosures are to be used to assess whether an IBIP matches the customer's preferences, and describes in detail how insurers and insurance

[83] Amended Art. 54(9) MiFID Delegated Regulation (EU) 2017/565.
[84] EIOPA 2022, 29, key principle 7.
[85] ESMA 2022c, 58, para. 72.
[86] EIOPA 2022, 19, key principle 4.
[87] Ibid.
[88] Ibid., 20.

intermediaries should assess whether an IBIP matches the customer's sustainability preferences as regards points (a), (b) and (c).[89]

(B) RANKING AND GROUPING OF PRODUCTS. When considering the sustainability factors of products in view of the subsequent matching with the client's sustainability preferences, investment intermediaries could rank and group the financial products they offer in terms of: (i) the proportion invested in economic activities that qualify as environmentally sustainable; (ii) the proportion of sustainable investments; (iii) the consideration of PAIs and other environmental, social and governance sustainability features. Both ESMA and EIOPA stress that such grouping of financial instruments cannot replace the collection of information from clients[90] ESMA again adds that such grouping should be consistent with the firm's analysis conducted for the purposes of product governance obligations.[91] EIOPA on the other hand zooms in on how to assess whether a multi-option product (MOP) matches the customer's sustainability preferences.[92]

(C) LACK OF DATA. In order to be able to correctly use sustainable products in discretionarily managed portfolios or to advise clients on them, investment intermediaries should collect relevant and sufficient granular information on the sustainability factors of the products they distribute. While this data collection might be easier for large, international players, it can be quite burdensome for smaller, local firms. Moreover, the information on certain investment products (e.g. small cap companies, non-EU companies or products) may simply not be available. The Securities and Markets Stakeholder Group has repeatedly addressed this problem of limited data availability, as a result of which it will often not be possible to rank and group products as suggested by the ESAs. EIOPA has explicitly recognized the problem, pointing out that part of the regulatory framework is not yet finalized, and that the application date of the new IDD provisions (the same is true for the new MiFID provisions) preceded the application dates of the Corporate Sustainability Reporting Directive and of the Delegated Regulation supplementing the SFDR. EIOPA concludes that insurers and insurance intermediaries need to responsibly disclose on sustainability, based on the data currently available, and make best efforts to ensure good data quality.[93]

A separate issue is 'greenbleaching'[94] (also referred to as 'grey-washing'), where investment funds invest in sustainable investment products without making any

---

[89] Ibid., 20–22.
[90] ESMA 2022c, 58–59, para. 73; EIOPA 2022, 22.
[91] ESMA 2022c, 58–59, para. 73.
[92] EIOPA 2022, 22–23.
[93] Ibid., 4.
[94] SMSG 2022a, 3, paras. 1–3, 11, paras. 42–43 and 12, paras. 50–51.

sustainability claims, to avoid disclosure obligations. This makes data collection on sustainability factors of products even more difficult.

(D) AVOIDING MIS-SELLING. Recital 5 of Regulation (EU) 2021/1253 amending MiFID II Delegated Regulation (EU) 2017/565[95] provides the following:

> [I]nvestment firms should have in place appropriate arrangements to ensure that the inclusion of sustainability factors in the advisory process and portfolio management does not lead to mis-selling practices or to the misrepresentation of instruments or strategies as fulfilling sustainability preferences where they do not. In order to avoid such practices or misrepresentations, investment firms should first assess the investor's investment objectives, time horizon and individual circumstances, before asking their clients for their potential sustainability preferences.

Even though the corresponding amending IDD Delegated Regulation does not feature a similar recital, both ESMA and EIOPA have confirmed in their respective guidance that sustainability preferences should only be addressed once suitability has been assessed in accordance with the criteria of knowledge and experience, financial situation and other objectives. Once the range of suitable products has been identified following this assessment, in a second step the product or investment strategy should be identified that fulfils the customer's/client's sustainability preferences. EIOPA also visualized this process in a figure.[96]

In our opinion, this approach is not underpinned by the Level 1 and Level 2 suitability provisions. The amended MiFID II and IDD Delegated Regulations explicitly consider sustainability preferences as *part of* the assessment of the client's investment objectives ('investment objectives, including sustainability preferences').[97] This is indeed the only approach compliant with the Level 1 text. In our view, the inclusion of sustainability preferences into the 'investment objectives' test means that a transaction can only be considered suitable if it complies both with the financial objectives and the sustainability preferences of the client. The result of the suitability test should not differ on the basis of what assessment comes first. In its feedback statement, ESMA implicitly confirms this, as 'the guidelines do not state that firms cannot use one unique questionnaire to collect information from clients (as long as questions on "sustainability preferences" are not given precedence over questions on the client's investment objective(s))'. ESMA also clarified that it has merely wished to draft the guidelines in line with the principle the Commission set out in the Explanatory Memorandum.[98]

---

[95] See for the legal history of this recital: Colaert 2021, 458–459.

[96] ESMA 2022c, 60, para. 81; EIOPA 2022, 25.

[97] Art. 54(2)(a) and 54(5) of MiFID II Delegated Regulation (EU) 2017/565; Art. 9(2)a of IDD Delegated Regulation (EU) 2017/2359.

[98] The Commission deemed 'a differentiation between investment objectives on the one hand and sustainability preferences on the other hand important to avoid mis-selling' and clarified that

(E) AVOIDING GREENWASHING. The final texts of the amending Regulations have put an increased emphasis on a specific form of mis-selling related to greenwashing.[99] The recitals define 'greenwashing' as 'the practice of gaining an unfair competitive advantage by recommending a financial instrument as environmentally friendly or sustainable, when in fact that financial instrument does not meet basic environmental or other sustainability-related standards', and confirm the obvious: in order to prevent mis-selling and greenwashing, financial institutions should not recommend or decide to trade financial products as meeting individual sustainability preferences where those financial products do not meet those preferences. Financial institutions should furthermore explain to their (potential) clients the reasons for not doing so, and keep records of those reasons.[100]

In view of the limited range of sustainable products and the very diverse sustainability preferences investors may have,[101] the amended rules provide for a 'safe haven'. The recitals of the amending Regulations clarify that financial products that are not eligible for individual sustainability preferences can still be recommended, but not as meeting individual sustainability preferences. To that end, a client/customer should have the possibility to adapt their sustainability preferences when the product offer of the intermediary does not include financial products meeting the client's/customer's sustainability preferences as well as the other aspects of the investor profile.[102] The MiFID II and IDD prohibitions to recommend a product or to decide to trade for a client if none of the services or products are suitable have been amended accordingly. An investment intermediary should in principle still not recommend or decide to trade when a financial product does not meet the client's/customer's sustainability preferences. The intermediary should explain to the client or potential clients the reasons for not doing so and keep records of those reasons. When no financial product meets the sustainability preferences of the (potential) client/customer, however, and they decide to adapt their sustainability preferences, the financial institution shall keep records of their decision, including the reasons for their decision.[103] EIOPA deems it important that, if no products match the sustainability

---

'[s]ustainability factors should not take precedence over a client's personal investment objective'. The Commission concluded that the sustainability preferences should therefore only be addressed within the suitability process 'once the client's investment objective has been identified'. See Explanatory Memorandum COM(2021)2616, 3; Explanatory Memorandum COM(2021)2614, 3; ESMA 2022c, Annex III. Feedback Statement, 28–29, paras. 48–49.

[99] Explanatory Memorandum COM(2021)2616, 2; Explanatory Memorandum COM(2021)2614, 2.

[100] Recital 7 Commission Delegated Regulation (EU) 2021/1253; Recital 13 Commission Delegated Regulation (EU) 2021/1257.

[101] In its advice to ESMA in respect of the Suitability Guidelines, the Securities and Markets Stakeholder Group expressed its concern that there will be, for a considerable period, a serious mismatch between the expectations of investors and the availability of products. See SMSG 2022a, 8, para. 28.

[102] Recital 8 Commission Delegated Regulation (EU) 2021/1253; Recital 14 Commission Delegated Regulation (EU) 2021/1257.

[103] Amended Art. 54(10) MiFID Delegated Regulation (EU) 2017/565; Amended Art. 9(6) IDD Delegated Regulation (EU) 2017/2359.

preferences of the customer, the insurer or insurance intermediary informs the customer that (s)he can adapt their sustainability preferences.[104] ESMA has stressed that such adaptation of investor profile only refers to the sustainability preferences, and that with regard to the other criteria of the suitability assessment, the product should meet the client profile and should otherwise not be recommended. The firm's explanation regarding the reason to adapt the client's preferences as well as the client's decision should be documented in the suitability report.[105] Moreover, for ESMA an adaptation of the sustainability preferences should only refer to the investment advice in question and not to the client's profile in general, unless the firm provides portfolio management or investment advice with a portfolio approach, in which case an adaptation of sustainability preferences after the initial suitability assessment should trigger a reassessment of the entire portfolio.[106] ESMA stresses that only after the client has expressed their intention to adapt their preferences the firm can disclose to the client information about its offering of products with sustainability features.[107] EIOPA formulates it a bit differently, stating that when a customer decides to adapt their sustainability preferences, the insurer or intermediary can disclose to the customer information about the products closest to the sustainability preference expressed by the customer that are available in the market and/or by the insurer or insurance intermediary providing advice. In that case, the insurer or insurance intermediary should clearly inform the customer, at the same time as the product information is provided, whether such information is based only on the products he/she makes available or represents information the products available on the market.[108] Finally, EIOPA also devotes a separate key principle to record keeping where a customer adapts its sustainability preferences.[109]

The possibility to adapt sustainability preferences where no product of the investment intermediary meets the sustainability preferences of the client/customer is an important deviation from the previously established principle that if the firm has no products on offer that fit the investor's profile, it should refrain from providing advice or portfolio management for that investor. Even though the new possibility to adapt sustainability preferences may seem to be a solution to the problem that insufficient ESG-related information on products would overly diminish choice for clients with ESG preferences, it is not without risks. In particular, ESMA's interpretation, that only after the client has expressed its intention to adapt its preferences can firms disclose to the client information about *their* offering of products with sustainability features, may have perverse effects. It may result in investment firms not making sufficient efforts to build up a large and diverse ESG product range and/or to obtain ESG information

---

[104] EIOPA 2022, 26.
[105] ESMA 2022c, 60, para. 82.
[106] ESMA 2022c, 62, para. 83–84.
[107] Ibid., 62, para. 83.
[108] EIOPA 2022, 26–27.
[109] Ibid., 28.

on the products in their product range. EIOPA requires insurance intermediaries to clearly inform the customer, on whether the information provided is based only on the products offered by the intermediary or represents on the products available on the market. The latter requirement at least raises customers' awareness that they might find products matching their preferences via other intermediaries.

(F) SWITCHING SUSTAINABLE PRODUCTS FOR NON-SUSTAINABLE PRODUCTS. Even though the rules on switching have not been amended in view of the integration of sustainability preferences into the MiFID II and IDD framework, the pre-existing rules need re-interpretation in this regard. Switching has always been a delicate issue, since investment intermediaries might be induced to advise a client to switch one product for another, merely to be able to charge transaction costs, whereas the added value of the new product compared to the previous one may be very limited or non-existent for the client. The MiFID II and IDD suitability frameworks therefore provide that switching is only allowed under strict conditions (mainly a cost-benefit-analysis). The question arises how to apply those provisions taking into account sustainability preferences. Should it be possible to switch an ESG product with a non-ESG product and vice versa? For clients without sustainability preferences, this should be no problem, as long as the general criteria for switching are fulfilled.[110] For clients with sustainability preferences, a switch from a product fulfilling the investor's preferences to a product that does not should, in principle, not be possible. If, however, the former product is, for some reason, not interesting anymore or not fulfilling other aspects of the suitability test anymore, and the client/ customer wants to adapt their preferences, the situation may be different (subject to the rules on adaptation of preferences discussed above). For clients with sustainability preferences, a switch from a non-ESG product to an ESG product in line with the client's/customer's preferences should in principle not be a problem. This can even be considered a 'non-monetary factor' in the cost-benefit analysis required for the switch, in view of 'a change in the investor's circumstances and needs'.[111]

(G) EQUIVALENCE CHECK. A related question concerns the MiFID II suitability requirement to check whether an equivalent product (less complex or less expensive) exists that could suit the investor.[112] In our view, an ESG product could be considered as equivalent to a non-ESG product for clients without sustainability preferences, if those products have 'similar target markets and similar risk-return profiles', except for the ESG profile of the products.[113] For clients with sustainability preferences,

---

[110] In accordance with Art. 54(11) MiFID Delegated Regulation (EU) 2017/565 and Art. 9(7) IDD Delegated Regulation (EU) 2017/2359. See also ESMA 2022c, 65–66, para. 96 and following.
[111] ESMA 2022c, 65–66, para. 96.
[112] Article 54(9) MiFID Delegated Regulation; ESMA 2022c, 64, guideline 9, para. 91 and following. IDD does not feature a similar provision.
[113] This wording is used by ESMA 2022c, 64, para. 92.

however, this will obviously not be the case, since their 'needs' are clearly defined in terms of sustainability preferences. For them, products can only be considered equivalent if they both meet the clients' specific suitability preferences and their other needs and circumstances).

12.3.3.6 Suitability Report/Statement

Finally, the requirement to provide retail investors with a suitability report has been amended to ensure that the outline of the advice and the explanation of how the recommendation is suitable for the retail client/customer also explain how they meet the investor's sustainability preferences.[114] Already before the sustainability amendments were introduced, the wording of the IDD Delegated Regulation differed substantially from the corresponding provision of the MiFID II Delegated Regulation, using the term 'suitability statement' instead of 'suitability report'; 'customer' instead of 'retail client', 'his financial situation' instead of 'his capacity to sustain losses', etc. It is not surprising, then, that the additional reporting on 'sustainability preferences' has also been framed differently. The MiFID II Delegated Regulation introduces sustainability preferences as a separate point to report on, whereas the IDD Delegated Regulation has inserted sustainability preferences as part of the statement on investment objectives. It is difficult to assess whether this new difference in wording also means that a different emphasis should be given to sustainability preferences in the MiFID II suitability report and the IDD suitability statement. This legal insecurity is in any event regrettable, since this question could have been easily avoided by using the same wording in both regulatory frameworks.

As discussed above, the suitability report/statement should include specific extra information in case the client/customer wants to adapt its sustainability preferences when none of the products offered by the investment intermediary matches the client's/customer's preferences (see 12.3.3.5(e)).

12.3.3.7 Transitional Measures: Periodic Assessment

Investment intermediaries need to update the investor profile of existing clients/customers in view of their sustainability preferences. During the consultation period preceding ESMA's guidelines, many respondents asked for the Commission to postpone the implementation of the MiFID II Delegated Regulation until 2 August 2023 or for ESMA to foresee a 12-month transition period for implementation of the final guidelines in the supervisory practice. ESMA considered that it was not competent to postpone the date of application of the L2 requirements, but set the date of application of the guidelines to six months after the publication of the translation of the

[114] Amended Art. 54OK(12) MiFID Delegated Regulation (EU) 2017/565; amended Art. 14(1) IDD Delegated Regulation (EU) 2017/2359.

guidelines. ESMA stressed, however, that firms are still required to fully comply with the legal requirements of the L2 text as from 2 August 2022.[115] Since guidelines can only interpret rules, postponing their entry into force should in principle not make much difference if the rules they interpret already apply. It may, however, induce national supervisory authorities to be more lenient in enforcing the new rules until the date of application of the revised guidelines.

EIOPA's guidance was adopted before the entry into force of the new IDD L2 provisions on 2 August 2022 and does not address transitional measures. EIOPA clarifies that the objective of its guidance is to promote better understanding of the new rules and facilitate a correct implementation by presenting the new requirements in a more user-friendly language and presentation. This seems to imply that the guidance has entered into force together with the L2 text. EIOPA did announce, however, that it may revisit work on a stronger convergence tool after some experience has been gathered by insurers and insurance intermediaries and NCAs in applying the new legislative framework.[116]

In reality, however, ESMA and EIOPA have ensured a transition period in their interpretation of the rules on periodic assessments, allowing investment intermediaries to apply the new rules only gradually. ESMA's guidelines provide that for ongoing relationships, client information on sustainability preferences should be updated at the latest through the next regular update of client information following the entry-into-application of Commission Delegated Regulation 2021/1253 (2 August 2022). However, clients should be provided with the opportunity to have their profile updated immediately if they wish so. ESMA also clarifies that if the client does not request an immediate update of their profile, the client will be considered 'sustainability-neutral' and can be recommended products both with and without sustainability-related features, until the next regular update.[117] EIOPA's guidance features a similar interpretation, but does not deal with the situation where a client would explicitly request an update of its preferences at an earlier date.[118] However, an investment intermediary should always update the client profile on the explicit request of a client. Denying this would clearly infringe the investment intermediary's duty of care.

12.3.3.8 Evaluation

The integration of sustainability preferences into the MiFID II and IDD suitability test will definitely raise investor awareness of the possibility to invest in sustainable investment products. It will ensure that (at least advised) investors do not miss out on ESG products because of limited attention for this segment in their decision-making process.

---

[115] ESMA 2022c, Annex III – Feedback Statement, 14.
[116] EIOPA 2022, 5.
[117] ESMA 2022c, 54–55, para. 57.
[118] EIOPA 2022, 17, Key Principle 3.

Sustainability questions in suitability questionnaires may even awaken preferences that the investor was previously unaware of. Such influence of the suitability process on investor preferences can be considered part of awareness-raising in line with the sustainable finance goal, as long as the client/customer does not feel any implicit moral pressure to express sustainability preferences (s)he does not actually have.

However, the amended provisions are far from perfect. In the above analysis, we have pointed to several shortcomings and challenges. First, because of the needlessly complex definition of sustainability preferences and coherence issues between the Taxonomy and the SFDR (see 12.3.2.2), it seems an almost impossible task to comply with the requirement to enable (potential) clients/customers to understand the different degrees of sustainability and to explain the distinction between the different product types in the definition. We have argued that this requirement is in fact misguided and unnecessary. Second, due to a lack of data, the range of sustainable products may be (too) limited to adequately match products with investors (see 12.3.2.2 and 12.3.3.5(c)). Third, the possibility for clients to adapt their sustainability preferences if none of the products offered by the investment intermediary matches those preferences, may create perverse incentives for those intermediaries (see 12.3.3.5(e)). Finally, many uncertainties remain, which we have attempted to clarify (see for instance 12.3.3.3, 12.3.3.5(f) and (g)).

Of a different nature is the problem that the MiFID II and IDD regulatory frameworks are not fully aligned. We have argued before that regulating financial products that are from a functional perspective very similar in two different legal frameworks, unavoidably results in inexplainable differences, that are – at best – inefficient, but may also cause uncertainty, confusion and investor detriment.[119] The analysis of the integration of sustainable finance into the MiFID II and IDD suitability requirements has confirmed this finding. Apart from some minor differences (regarding the understanding of products by staff and regarding the suitability report/statement for instance), the Level 1 and 2 texts are very much aligned. The Level 3 guidance of the MiFID II and IDD provisions is, however, quite different, both in format and content. In terms of format, ESMA has integrated its guidance on sustainability preferences in its updated Suitability Guidelines, whereas EIOPA had never issued suitability guidelines, and published specific guidance on the integration of sustainability preferences in the suitability assessment. Whereas ESMA works with 'general guidelines' which are further developed in 'supporting guidelines', EIOPA puts emphasis on 'key principles', in bold and in a box, followed by further explanations of each principle under the question 'How to do it'. What EIOPA considers 'key principles', however, does not at all correspond with ESMA's 'general guidelines', since ESMA's guidance on sustainability is integrated in the supporting guidelines of pre-existing general guidelines on suitability. The emphasis on the importance of sustainability preferences is therefore totally different in both sets of guidance. EIOPA furthermore uses many schemes

---

[119] Colaert, Busch and Incalza 2019, 454–455 and 457–458.

and visualizations to facilitate comprehension, which ESMA does not. In terms of content, there seems to have been some consultation between both ESAs, as the basic principles seem to correspond well. However, the details differ quite a lot. Sometimes one authority is silent on a certain point, whereas the other authority develops it in some detail (e.g. ESMA did not give guidance on how to explain to clients the concept of sustainability preferences, whereas EIOPA did give some guidance (12.3.3.2); ESMA and EIOPA developed different details in regard of the possibility to adapt sustainability preferences (12.3.3.5(e)). Sometimes the detailed guidance is different (for instance the guidance on how to match clients with products (12.3.3.5(a)) – or at least differently formulated, making it difficult to assess whether those differences are meaningful or not (for instance the guidance on how to obtain investor information (12.3.4.3). Since the Level 2 requirements are formulated in substantially the same terms, one should assume that ESMA, EIOPA and NCAs should interpret and apply those rules in the same way. It would have been much preferable therefore if ESMA and EIOPA would have issued joint guidelines on this topic, differentiating between investment firms and insurers/insurance intermediaries only when necessary.

Finally, more far-reaching policy options are conceivable in regard of the role of the suitability test in sustainable finance. The European Commission had, for instance, consulted on the idea to offer sustainable investment products to retail clients by default.[120] Respondents generally agreed that retail investors should be systematically offered (also) sustainable investment products when they are available and meet the suitability test. However, the offering of sustainable investment products as a default option was found to be more contentious.[121] If investors would be informed of this default option, and would have the possibility to opt out if they wanted to invest in other products,[122] such a measure would not strongly affect the decision-making autonomy of investors. It would be a typical example of 'nudging', resulting in capital flows being reoriented towards sustainable investments on a larger scale. The Commission has, however, not reiterated such possibilities in its Renewed Sustainable Finance Strategy, so that chances seem remote that such options would be introduced in the foreseeable future.[123]

12.3.4 *Product Governance*

12.3.4.1 Background

MiFID II and IDD have introduced a new 'product governance' regime on top of the suitability and appropriateness requirements, in order to further reduce the risk of

---

[120] European Commission 2020, 8.
[121] European Commission 2021a, 13 and 17.
[122] Pilaj 2017, 750.
[123] See European Commission 2021b.

mis-selling.[124] Product governance rules require that MiFID and IDD product manufacturers (i) design products in such a manner that they meet the needs of an identified target market of end clients, (ii) tailor their distribution strategy to this target
market and (iii) take reasonable steps to ensure that the products are distributed to this
target market. MiFID product distributors in turn need to also identify a target market
for the products they distribute, because the product manufacturer was not subject to
MiFID II, and/or because they can refine the target market according to their knowledge of their client base.[125] No similar obligation exists for insurance distributors, who
can rely on the target market defined by the product manufacturer. MiFID and IDD
product distributors are in principle not allowed to sell products to clients outside the
target market,[126] and must provide the product manufacturer with feedback.[127]

As part of the Commission's ambition to reorient capital flows towards sustainable
investment, the sustainability factors and preferences have also been integrated into
the product governance requirements. In its 2018 Guidelines on product governance,
ESMA already provided that firms should specify which investment objectives and
client needs a product has been designed to meet, such as 'green investment', 'ethical
investment', etc.[128] In 2020 EIOPA published its 'approach to the supervision of product
oversight and governance', which, however, did not refer to ESG considerations.[129] In

---

[124] See for an elaborate overview of the MiFID product governance regime: Colaert 2020, 977–1000;
Busch 2017, 123–137.

[125] If the MiFID product manufacturer is the same institution as the product distributor, only one target
market needs to be defined (see last section of Art. 10(2) MiFID Delegated Directive (EU) 2017/593).

[126] Subject to a number of exceptions. See Colaert 2020, 983.

[127] Art. 16(3) and 24(2) MiFID II and Art. 9–10 MiFID Delegated Directive (EU) 2017/593; Art. 25 IDD
and Art. 4–11 IDD Delegated Regulation 2017/2358.

[128] ESMA 2018a, 7, para. 18. In the draft guidelines, the 'clients' needs' were even a category, separate
from 'clients' objectives'. 'Objectives' then referred to the investment objectives of target clients, i.e.
the wider financial goals or overall strategy, such as 'liquidity supply', 'retirement provision', or the
expected investment horizon. Those objectives could be 'fine-tuned' by specific clients' needs that
would narrow or broaden the scope of the objectives, and could vary from specific to more generic
such as: age, country of tax residence, special product features like 'currency protection', 'green
investment', 'ethical investment', etc. See ESMA 2016, 23–24. The final 2018 Product Governance
Guidelines, however, featured one general category 'objectives and needs'.

[129] EIOPA 2020, 13. In this document, EIOPA briefly refers to two different aspects of 'sustainability' (see
p. 13). EIOPA states that manufacturers' product governance process should not only test whether
products are 'sustainable', but also whether manufacturers assess the value of the product for the target market, and whether it is fairly priced. EIOPA specifies that products need to be 'sustainable' also
from a pricing perspective. In its first use, the term 'sustainable' seems to refer to the idea, developed
in the same section of the statement, that the identified needs, objectives and characteristics of the
product might change over the lifetime of the insurance product. In its second use, EIOPA refers to
the idea that product governance should also ensure that customers acquire 'value for money' and pay
a fair price for their product. EIOPA has developed this idea in more detail afterwards, in EIOPA 2021.
In this statement, EIOPA no longer refers to 'value for money' in terms of sustainability. Since it is
indeed, at best, only very remotely related to the sustainable finance movement, we will not consider
'value for money' as an element of sustainable finance for purposes of this paper.
    As another showcase of cross-sectoral inconsistency, the 'value for money' concept – that has become
key for EIOPA – is almost entirely absent in ESMA's approach to product governance. In its guidelines,

early 2018 the Commission engaged in an impact assessment based on targeted interviews with 23 medium-sized to large asset managers and institutional investors that had already integrated ESG factors in their investment decision process and/or have Socially Responsible Investment (SRI) products. Respondents considered ESG factors in their product selection, but with different periodicity (i.e. always or only when the product was specifically dedicated to ESG strategies).[130]

In 2021 the MiFID II and IDD Level 2 texts have been amended to integrate sustainability into the product governance requirements.[131] After consultation,[132] ESMA also published revised Product Governance Guidelines on 27 March 2023, reflecting those amendments next to certain other evolutions.[133] EIOPA has not taken any initiative yet to update its Product Governance Statement.

12.3.4.2 Scope of Target Market Obligations Relating to Sustainability

The amended legal frameworks have an important limitation: sustainability factors should only be considered in the product approval process and in the other product governance and oversight arrangements for products intended to be distributed to investors seeking products with a sustainability-related profile.[134] The Commission indeed explicitly confirmed that the possibility to identify a target market for clients without sustainability-related objectives should be maintained.[135] In such cases no information about the sustainability of the product needs to be included in the target market description, except for the statement that it is targeted to investors without sustainability preferences.

In our opinion, the limited scope of the product governance amendments is regrettable. Since product governance works as a first filter against mis-selling, sufficient target market information on all products is essential. It would have been preferable, therefore, if, similarly to the risk profile of a product, the ESG profile of *each* product would need to be defined with a high granularity. The current more limited scope may lead to undesirable outcomes, such as 'greenbleaching' (see 12.3.3.5(c)) by product manufacturers or distributors. A manufacturer could classify a product as 'targeted to clients without sustainability preferences' because he is unable or unwilling to collect the relevant sustainability information, even if, in reality, it would match on of the product types conceived in the definition of sustainability

---

ESMA only refers to it once, in Annex IV with good practices in respect of the product review process ('removing certain products from the product offer because the outcomes of the product review revealed that they do no longer offer value for money, for example due to falling interest rates').

[130] European Commission 2018b, 129.
[131] See footnote 35.
[132] ESMA 2022b.
[133] See n 36.
[134] Recital 5 Commission Delegated Regulation (EU) 2021/1257; Recital 5 Commission Delegated Directive (EU) 2021/1269.
[135] Explanatory Memorandum COM(2021)2612, 3.

preferences. If distributors, in such situations, would want to distribute the instrument to sustainability-oriented investors, they would need to deviate from the target market defined by the manufacturer and comply with the corresponding reporting and motivation requirements. They may find this excessively burdensome or may not have sufficient information to establish the sustainability profile of the product, and therefore stick to the 'bleached' target market established by the manufacturer. As a result the product range of sustainable products would be smaller than needed.

12.3.4.3 Obligations for Manufacturers

Article 9(9) MiFID Delegated Directive provides that MiFID product *manufacturers* have to identify at a sufficiently granular level the potential target market for each financial instrument and specify the type(s) of clients with whom the needs, characteristics and objectives of the financial instrument is compatible. This provision has been clarified, stating that the needs, characteristics and objectives of clients include 'any sustainability-related objectives'. Similarly, the amended Article 5(1) IDD Delegated Regulation provides that the target market should be determined at a sufficiently granular level, taking into account the characteristics, risk profile, complexity and nature of the insurance product 'as well as its sustainability factors'.[136] It is quite remarkable that the MiFID target market is defined in terms of the target *client* and their sustainability-*related objectives*, whereas the IDD target market is defined in terms of the insurance *product* and its sustainability *factors*. This different approach is regrettable because of the legal uncertainty it may create. In practice, however, this different wording will probably not lead to a different approach to defining the target market for MiFID financial instruments and IDD insurance products.

To ensure a sufficient level of granularity of the target market description, ESMA indicates that when firms identify sustainability-related objectives, they may specify, where relevant, the following aspects, in line with the definition of 'sustainability preferences': (i) the minimum proportion of the product that is invested in environmentally sustainable investments, (ii) the minimum proportion of the product that is invested in sustainable investments; (iii) which principle adverse impacts on sustainability factors are considered by the product, including quantitative or qualitative criteria demonstrating that consideration; and (iv) whether, where relevant, the product has a focus on either environmental, social or governance criteria, or a combination of them.[137] The Securities and Markets Stakeholder Group had warned that target markets should be sufficiently, but not overly granular, arguing that if target markets are defined in too much detail this may put the continued existence of an open architecture at risk, favour the largest players, and make an efficient feedback

---

[136] Amended Art. 5(1) IDD Delegated Regulation 2017/2358.
[137] ESMA 2023, 58–59, para. 20.

loop between distributor and manufacturer more difficult.[138] ESMA has clarified that the rules may be applied in a proportionate manner, which means that for simpler, more common products, the target market could be identified with less detail, while for more complex products it should be identified with more detail.[139] ESMA originally intended to add in its revised Product Governance Guidelines a new case study about an Impact Investment Fund,[140] but unfortunately did not do so in the end.

As part of the product approval process investment firms should assess whether the risk/reward profile of the product is compatible with the target market and whether the design of the product is driven by characteristics that benefit the client rather than by a business model that relies on poor client outcomes to be profitable. A requirement to check whether the financial instrument's sustainability factors are consistent with the target market has been added.[141] The IDD Delegated Regulation already provided that the product approval process should ensure that the design of insurance products meets, among other things, the objectives, interests and characteristics of customers. It now clarifies that this should include their sustainability-related objectives.[142]

Assessing and describing the sustainability of a product requires a well-developed taxonomy of environmental, social and governance standards. However, the Taxonomy Regulation is currently insufficiently developed, especially in respect of the S and G. Financial market participants have therefore joined forces and come up with a 'European ESG Template', to be read in conjunction with the- pre-existing 'European MiFID Template' that was already broadly used in the market to standardize target market descriptions.[143] The 'European ESG Template' allows different ways of describing the sustainability of the product, including a differentiation of the sustainability of a product in terms of relevant environmental, social and governance factors, in terms of adherence to the PRI/PRB-rules[144], labels, product 'categories' under the SFDR, as well as in terms of the MiFID definition of sustainability preferences. In this way the industry has provided for some standardization in this field. However, the template still allows for very diverse manners to describe the sustainability of the product, so that the client-product matching process by the distributor in the subsequent suitability process, may not always be straightforward on the basis of this target market information.

---

[138] SMSG 2022b, 1, 2, 3, 7, 8.
[139] ESMA 2023, Annex IV. Feedback on the consultation paper, 15–16.
[140] Ibid., 18–19.
[141] Amended Art. 9(11) MiFID Delegated Directive (EU) 2017/593.
[142] Amended Art. 4(3)(a)(i) IDD Delegated Regulation 2017/2358.
[143] See for the different target market templates: www.findatex.eu/ (retrieved on 31 April 2023). FinDaTex (Financial Data Exchange Templates) is a joint structure established by representatives of the European financial services sector in order to coordinate, organize and carry out standardization work to facilitate the exchange of data between stakeholders. One of its major achievements was the creation of a 'European MiFID Template' for the definition of the target market under MiFID II. It should be noted, however, that the templates also cater for IDD requirements.
[144] UN Principles for Responsible Investment/Banking. See www.unpri.org/ and www.unepfi.org/banking/bankingprinciples/ (retrieved on 30 April 2023).

12.3.4.4 Obligations for Distributors

As regards the obligations for *distributors*, the MiFID Delegated Directive provides that the products and services they wish to offer or recommend should be consistent with the needs, characteristics and objectives, including any sustainability-related objectives, of an identified target market.[145] Similarly, product distribution arrangements under IDD should ensure that the objectives, interests and characteristics of customers are duly taken into account, including any sustainability-related objectives.[146] In practice both provisions are, however, applied quite differently. In its Product Governance Guidelines, ESMA clarified that distributors should use the same list of categories used by manufacturers as a basis for defining an 'actual target market' for their products. However, they should define the target market on a more concrete level and should take into account the type of clients they provide investment services to, the nature of the products and the type of investment services they provide and the level of detail of information gathered from clients.[147] The IDD framework, however, does not explicitly require product distributors to define an actual target market.

12.3.4.5 Obligations for Manufacturers and Distributors

(A) NEGATIVE TARGET MARKET. Firms may determine a so-called 'negative' target market, that is, a group of customers for whose needs, characteristics and objectives the product is generally not compatible. Those provisions do not apply, however, in respect of sustainability factors: a product which considers sustainability factors cannot be excluded for investors without sustainability-related objectives.[148] ESMA clarifies that this means that the sustainability-related objectives of products only contribute to identifying a 'positive' target market in terms of clients (groups of clients) with compatible sustainability preferences. The same products could still be distributed to clients falling outside that 'positive' sustainability-related target market, provided that the product features of the other target market categories are compatible with the client.[149]

(B) 'CLUSTERING APPROACH'. One of the concerns in respect of the product governance requirements, is that for certain products, manufacturers or

---

[145] Amended Art. 10(2) MiFID Delegated Directive (EU) 2017/593.
[146] Amended Art. 10(2)(c) IDD Delegated Regulation (EU) 2017/2358.
[147] ESMA 2023, 63, para. 42.
[148] Amended Art. 9(9) MiFID Delegated Directive (EU) 2017/593; Amended Art. 5(2) IDD Delegated Regulation 2017/2358. Art. 10(2) MiFID Delegated Directive (EU) 2017/593 provides a similar requirement for product distributors. See also Recital 7 Directive 2021/1269 amending MiFID Delegated Directive (EU) 2017/593.
[149] ESMA 2023, 72, para. 81.

distributors will find defining a target market overly burdensome. Therefore, ESMA proposes to allow a 'clustering approach', meaning that manufacturers and distributors may decide to adopt a common target market approach for products with sufficiently comparable product features.[150] This will only be possible if those products also target the same clients in terms of specific sustainability-related objectives.

However, in order to allow an easier clustering-process, firms may be inclined to 'greenbleach' products which would be suitable for clients with specific sustainability-related objectives, in order to allow clustering with products that do not have such features (or have different features). ESMA requires that, also when using a clustering approach, the target market must be identified at a sufficiently granular level to avoid the inclusion of any groups of investors for whose needs, characteristics and objectives the products are not compatible.[151] However, in case of 'greenbleaching', the opposite problem arises: certain products which could be compatible with the sustainability preferences of certain investors, will be excluded for them, if the target market mentions that the product is targeted to investors without sustainability preferences.

(c) PRODUCT REVIEW. When reviewing products, both MiFID product manufacturers and distributors and IDD product manufacturers should consider whether the product remains consistent with the needs, characteristics and objectives, including any sustainability-related objectives, of the identified target market.[152] Distributors are, moreover, subject to information obligations to the product manufacturer. Whereas this obligation is formulated in a general manner in the MiFID Delegated Directive,[153] the IDD Delegated Regulation specifically refers to the situation where the insurance distributor 'becomes aware that an insurance product is not in line with the interests, objectives and characteristics of the customer belonging to the target market'. The latter obligation has been amended to explicitly include 'sustainability-related objectives' in the provision.[154]

12.3.4.6 Evaluation

It is definitely a big step forward that target markets will have to be defined also in view of the sustainability factors of the product/sustainability preference of

---

[150] Ibid., 29, paras. 27 and 35, para. 47.

[151] Ibid., 31, para. 30.

[152] Amended Art. 9(14) and Art. 10(5) MiFID Delegated Directive (EU) 2017/593; amended Art. 7(1) IDD Delegated Regulation (EU) 2017/2358. Since insurance distributors are not required to define a target market, there are no product review obligations for distributors either. Art. 10(6) IDD Delegated Regulation (EU) 2017/2358 does provide for a requirement for insurance distributors to regularly review their product distribution arrangements.

[153] Art. 10(9) MiFID Delegated Directive (EU) 2017/593.

[154] Amended Art. 11 IDD Delegated Regulation (EU) 2017/2358.

investors. However, this is only required if the product targets investors with sustainability preferences. Product manufacturers who do not want to comply with the extra requirements for sustainable products, may prefer to categorize their product as not targeting such investors, even if the product has some sustainability factors (so-called 'greenbleaching'). Also the opportunity to 'cluster' target market descriptions – important to reduce the cost of the product governance requirements – may induce firms to greenbleach, so that products' different ESG profiles would not stand in the way of clustering.

To allow for an easy product-client matching process in the suitability phase, target markets should use standardized wording. The standardization work by the industry, for instance with the European MiFID Template and European ESG template, is an important step in this respect.

Even though the MiFID and IDD product governance rules introduce substantially the same regime, the specific provisions were already quite different and much less aligned than the respective suitability frameworks. The integration of sustainability preferences/factors into the regulatory frameworks, has created further divergences that do not seem warranted in view of the differences between the relevant products. Even if the MiFID and IDD provisions may ultimately be applied in the same way – partly because the industry has developed one template for both financial instruments and insurance-based investment services – those differences are regrettable and create unnecessary uncertainty.

12.3.5 *Conflicts of Interest*

Conflicts of interest are one of the most prominent problems leading to mis-selling and investor detriment. The MiFID and IDD regime to contain conflicts of interest is based on organizational requirements in three steps: (i) identification of potential sources of conflicts of interest, (ii) management of conflicts of interest and (iii) disclosure if the investment firm or insurance intermediary cannot ensure that a conflict of interest will not damage clients' interests.[155] ESG considerations may give a new pretext to engage in mis-selling practices. It is therefore not surprising that the EU legislator has sought to refine the MiFID and IDD rules on conflicts of interest in the face of sustainable finance.

The sustainability amendments to the MiFID II and IDD conflicts of interest regimes focus on the first step, 'identification'. Article 33 of the MiFID Delegated Regulation lists five minimum criteria to be taken into account when identifying conflicts of interest which may damage the interests of a client, 'including his or her sustainability preferences'. Interesting is, however, (the legal history of) Recital 5 of Amending Regulation (EU) 2021/1253. In the consultation preceding its technical

---

[155] Art. 16(3) and 23 MiFID II and Art. 27 and 28 IDD.

advice to the Commission, ESMA clarified that firms would need to have in place appropriate arrangements to ensure that the inclusion of ESG considerations in the advisory process and portfolio management would not lead to mis-selling practices or misrepresentation and would not damage the interests of the clients. ESMA gave some examples of how clients' interests could be damaged under ESG pretext: selling own products or more costly products, recommending unnecessary transactions to or carrying them out for clients ('churning'), or misrepresenting products or strategies as fulfilling ESG preferences when they do not.[156] Even though the Securities and Markets Stakeholder Group (SMSG) advised to include those examples in Recital 5,[157] and ESMA confirmed in its final advice to the Commission that this would indeed be useful,[158] the examples have not made it to the final version of the Recital. This is regrettable, since they would be helpful to investment firms in complying with the conflicts of interests regime.

Also for insurance intermediaries IDD now clarifies that the 'interests of the customer' include their sustainability preferences.[159] In its technical advice, EIOPA had suggested to include in what would become Recital 10 of Commission Delegated Regulation (EU) 2021/1257 a number of non-exhaustive examples of ESG considerations when identifying conflicts of interest, including remuneration and incentive structures for external asset managers and proxy advisers as well as remuneration and incentives schemes to promote the distribution of ESG products or to achieve specific sustainability targets of the insurance undertaking which are different from the ESG preferences of the target market.[160] The final recital, however, does not mention those examples.

The amendments to the similar MiFID and IDD conflicts of interest regimes are very much in line with each other. It is clear that the EU legislator wants the same conflicts of interests regime to apply to IBIPs and other retail investment products. Having to amend and interpret two different legal frameworks, with two different competent authorities, is clearly not the most efficient way to achieve this.

12.4 CONCLUSION

In this contribution we have evaluated the revised MiFID II and IDD investor protection frameworks from three perspectives: (i) their contribution to remedying the 'value-action-gap' which leads many investors to invest in products which do not correspond with their sustainability values, and their contribution to a more sustainable

---

[156] ESMA 2018c, 10, para. 13.
[157] SMSG 2019, 9, para. 7.
[158] ESMA 2019, 14, para. 26 and at 16, with a proposal to introduce a new Recital 59*bis*.
[159] Amended Art. 3(1) IDD Delegated Regulation (EU) 2017/2359; Recital 10 of Commission Delegated Regulation (EU) 2021/1257.
[160] EIOPA 2019, 33, with a proposal to introduce a new Recital 3(*bis*) in IDD Delegated Regulation (EU) 2017/2359.

economy more generally; (ii) their contribution to the creation of a level playing field between economically similar investment products; and (iii) their coherence with other sustainable finance measures.

12.4.1 *Contribution to a More Sustainable Economy*

The new obligatory questions on ESG preferences in the suitability assessment will undoubtedly help in closing the 'value-action-gap' between investors' intentions and behaviour. They raise awareness of the options for investors to contribute to a more sustainable economy through their investment decisions and will ensure that (at least advised) investors do not miss out on ESG products because of limited attention for this segment. However, the definition of 'sustainability preferences' is needlessly complex. The obligation under the suitability test to explain to investors the terms of and the distinctions in the definition of sustainability preferences therefore seems an almost impossible task. It is, in our view, moreover misguided and unnecessary. Rather than overwhelming investors with concepts that are difficult to grasp, investment intermediaries should ask them questions in layman terms. On the basis of their answers, it is up to the intermediary to qualify their sustainability preferences in terms of the different elements of the definition, without burdening the investor with complex upfront information. Moreover, we found that stronger measures are thinkable to boost sustainable finance, such as presenting sustainable investment products as default option to retail investors, provided that the product also suits the other needs and objectives of the investor. Such measures would, however, also give a paternalistic edge to the suitability assessment, and could lead to 'stranded assets'.

The amended product governance requirements, which provide that target markets need to describe the sustainability factors of the product in view of potential sustainability preference of investors, are also an important step forward to avoid mis-selling and to allow for an efficient application of the suitability test. However, we regret that this requirement only applies if the product targets investors with sustainability preferences. To escape the extra target market obligations for sustainable products, product manufacturers may prefer to categorize their product as not targeting investors with sustainability preferences, even if the product does have sustainability factors (so-called 'greenbleaching'). Similarly, the possibility to 'cluster' target market descriptions – and thus reduce the cost of the product governance requirements – may induce firms to greenbleach, so that products' different ESG profiles would not prevent such clustering. It would have been preferable if, just as for the risk profile of a product, the regulator required that the ESG profile of each and every product be defined with a high degree of granularity. In this way 'greenbleaching' for convenience purposes would be avoided, and product distributors would more easily find ESG information on the products they offer.

In regard of the amended MiFID II and IDD conflicts of interest regimes, we have expressed regret that the examples provided by ESMA and EIOPA did not make it to the recitals of the amending Regulations in order to provide further guidance to market participants.

12.4.2 *No Cross-Sectoral Playing Field*

In the explanatory memoranda of the Regulations and Directive amending the MiFID II and IDD frameworks, the Commission expressed its intention to integrate sustainability considerations into the investment, advisory and disclosure processes *in a consistent manner across sectors*. Despite these good intentions, reality proves very different. The notion 'investment products' is very broad, including not only financial instruments, but also insurance-based investment products, pension products, crowdfunding products and crypto-assets. However, only the MiFID II and IDD frameworks have been amended to integrate sustainable finance into the EU investor protection regimes. Neither the Crowdfunding Regulation nor the Markets in Crypto-assets Regulation integrate sustainable finance in their investor protection regimes. The delay in integrating sustainable finance into those regulations, compared to the measures already taken in the MiFID and IDD frameworks, makes the uneven playing field which already existed between products, even worse.[161]

But even within the amended MiFID and IDD frameworks sustainability considerations have not been integrated in a consistent manner across sectors. On the contrary, sustainable finance amendments have created new differences between both regulatory frameworks, which the Commission does not justify, and which do not seem justified on the basis of differences between financial instruments and structured deposits on the one hand and insurance-based investment products on the other. This contribution has provided a number of striking examples. In most cases, the legal effect of both frameworks will still be more or less the same – even though further research on the implementation in practice of both regimes should confirm this. Nevertheless, the differences create legal uncertainty and make the practical implementation process of both regimes different, which is inefficient. It stresses the difficulty of creating a level playing field between economically very similar products in separate legal frameworks. Even if the legislator succeeds in drafting

---

[161] It has been argued before that retail investors – the Crowdfunding Regulation calls them 'non-sophisticated investors' – should be protected in the same way irrespective of the distribution channel (see for instance Busch, Colaert and Helleringer 2019, 363 and 373–374. The Crowdfunding Regulation clearly does not follow that idea, creating an uneven playing field by providing different rules governing the distribution of investment products, depending on the distribution channel. The Commission has justified this different approach on the basis of the consideration that the costs and therefore the compliance burden in respect of crowdfunding should not be too high. However, if one agrees that crowdfunding is, in the end, just another distribution channel through which investors get access to investment products, this is not a convincing argument (see Busch, Colaert and Helleringer 2019, 363).

relatively similar Level 1, texts – as is the case for the MiFID and IDD suitability regimes, it is almost impossible to keep this up at levels 2 and 3, and even more difficult when levels 1, 2 or 3 are amended at a later stage.[162] The different Level 3 guidance on suitability provided respectively by ESMA and EIOPA serves as further proof of this statement – and is particularly worrying. We have argued before that it would make more sense to include insurance-based investment products in the MiFID framework.[163] The current need to adapt both regimes in accordance with the Sustainable Finance Action Plan underlines the inefficiency of maintaining two separate regimes for economically similar products.

12.4.3 *Uneasy Fit with Taxonomy and SFDR*

Crucial in the amended MiFID II and IDD frameworks is the new definition of 'sustainability preferences'. The definition refers to three product categories, which explicitly and implicitly refer to concepts of the Taxonomy Regulation and the SFDR and are not easy to disentangle. It takes quite some expertise to delineate and comprehend what those categories exactly cover and how they relate to the products subject to Article 8 and Article 9 SFDR. Many difficult interpretation questions remain. The fact that these categories to a large extent overlap, does not help. As mentioned above, it makes the obligation under the suitability test to explain to investors the terms and the definition of sustainability preferences, an almost impossible task.

The amended MiFID and IDD obligations are, moreover, shaped by systematic references to sustainability risks and factors, which are defined in terms of environmental, social and employee matters, events or conditions. A key question which remains unsolved, however, is how these three elements (E, S and G) are to be understood. So far, the Taxonomy Regulation only determines when an investment or activity can be considered as environmentally sustainable. However, to comply with the revised MiFID and IDD investor protection frameworks, financial service providers also need to determine when an investment can be considered as sustainable from a social or governance perspective. They therefore typically use sustainability ratings or national sustainability labels to assess the sustainability of products and companies. However, those labels and ratings differ in content and quality and are, so far, unregulated. Moreover, separate data on the three elements (E, S and G) is often not available, further complicating the implementation of the amended MiFID II and IDD frameworks.[164] The resulting situation is far from ideal: it increases the cost of compliance, causes uncertainty and leads to different

---

[162] Colaert 2015, 1603–1605.
[163] Ibid., 1605; in respect of the know-your-customer requirements, see also: Busch, Colaert and Helleringer 2019, 363.
[164] ESMA 2019, 17; see e.g. Dutch Banking Association 2018.

implementations by different financial institutions. This results in a lack of compa-rability and transparency of products and services – two basic conditions to achieve adequate investor protection, and indeed explicit objectives of the EU's sustainable finance policy.

REFERENCES

Busch, D. (2017), 'Product governance and product intervention under MiFID II/MiFIR' in Busch, D. and Ferrarini, G. (eds.), *Regulation of the EU Financial Markets: MiFID II and MiFIR* (Oxford: Oxford University Press) 123–137.

Busch, D., Colaert, V. and Helleringer, G. (2019), 'An "assist-your-customer obligation" for the financial sector?' in Colaert, V., Busch, D. and Incalza, T. (eds.), *European Financial Regulation: Levelling the Cross-sectoral Playing Field* (London: Bloomsbury Hart) 343–376.

Colaert, V. (2015), 'European banking, securities and insurance law: Cutting through sectoral lines?' 52 *Common Market Law Review* 1579–1616.

Colaert, V. (2020), 'Product governance: Paternalism outsourced to financial institutions?' 6 *European Business Law Review* 977–1000.

Colaert, V. (2021), 'Integrating sustainable finance into the MiFID II and IDD investor pro-tection frameworks' in Busch, D., Ferrarini, G. and Grünewald, S. (eds.), *Sustainable Finance in Europe* (London: Palgrave Macmillan) 458–459.

Colaert, V., Busch, D. and Incalza, T. (2019), 'Summary and conclusions' in Colaert, V., Busch, D. and Incalza, T. (eds.), *European Financial Regulation: Levelling the Cross-sectoral Playing Field* (London: Bloomsbury Hart) 453–459.

Dutch Banking Association (2018), 'NVB Response to Commission Proposals on Financing Sustainable Growth – MiFID II Suitability Requirements' (21 June), https://bit.ly/3wSZcGh (retrieved on 31 April 2023).

EIOPA (European Insurance and Occupational Pensions Authority) (2018), 'Consultation Paper on Technical Advice on the Integration of Sustainability Risks and Factors in the Delegated Acts under Solvency II and IDD' (EIOPA-BOS-18/483, 26 November).

EIOPA (European Insurance and Occupational Pensions Authority) (2019), 'Technical Advice on the Integration of Sustainability Risks and Factors in the Delegated Acts under Solvency II and IDD' (EIOPA-BoS-19/172, 30 April).

EIOPA (European Insurance and Occupational Pensions Authority) (2020), 'EIOPA's approach to the supervision of product oversight and governance' (8 October), https://bit.ly/49PoZuf (retrieved 31 April 2023).

EIOPA (European Insurance and Occupational Pensions Authority) (2021), 'Supervisory Statement on assessment of value for money of unit-linked insurance products under prod-uct oversight and governance', (EIOPA(2021)0045739, 30 November).

EIOPA (European Insurance and Occupational Pensions Authority) (2022), 'Guidance on the integration of sustainability preferences in the suitability assessment under the Insurance Distribution Directive (IDD)' (EIOPA-BOS-22-391, 20 July).

ESMA (European Securities and Markets Authority) (2016), 'Consultation Paper – Draft guidelines on MiFID II product governance requirements' (ESMA/2016/1436, 5 October).

ESMA (European Securities and Markets Authority) (2018a), 'Guidelines on MiFID II Product Governance Requirements' (ESMA35-43-620, 5 February).

ESMA (European Securities and Markets Authority) (2018b), *Final Report: Guidelines on Certain Aspects of the MiFID II Suitability Requirements* (ESMA35-43-869, 28 May).

ESMA (European Securities and Markets Authority) (2018c), *Consultation Paper: On Integrating Sustainability Risks and Factors in MiFID II* (ESMA35-43-1210, 19 December).

ESMA (European Securities and Markets Authority) (2019), *Technical Advice to the European Commission on Integrating Sustainability Risks and Factors in MiFID II* (ESMA35-43-1737, 30 April).

ESMA (European Securities and Markets Authority) (2022a), *Consultation Paper – Guidelines on Certain Aspects of the MiFID II Suitability Requirements* (ESMA35-43-2998, 27 January).

ESMA (European Securities and Markets Authority) (2022b), *Consultation Paper – Review of the Guidelines on MiFID II Product Governance Requirements* (ESMA 35-43-3114, 8 July).

ESMA (European Securities and Markets Authority) (2022c), *Final Report – Guidelines on Certain Aspects of the MiFID II Suitability Requirements* (ESMA35-43-3172, 23 September).

ESMA (European Securities and Markets Authority) (2023), *Final Report – Guidelines on MiFID II Product Governance Requirements* (ESMA35-43-3448, 27 March).

European Commission (2018a), 'Communication–Action Plan: Financing Sustainable Growth' (COM(2018)97 final, 8 March 2018).

European Commission (2018b), 'Impact Assessment' accompanying the Proposals for a Taxonomy Regulation, Disclosure Regulation and Benchmark Regulation (SWD(2018) 264 final, 24 May 2018) (European Commission 2018b).

European Commission (2020), 'Consultation Document – Consultation on the Renewed Sustainable Finance Strategy' (8 April 2020), https://bit.ly/3x5iAzO (retrieved on 31 April 2023).

European Commission (2021a), *Summary Report of the Stakeholder Consultation on the Renewed Sustainable Finance Strategy* (10 February 2021), https://bit.ly/48WX9hU (retrieved on 31 April 2023).

European Commission (2021b), 'Strategy for Financing the Transition to a Sustainable Economy' (COM/2021/390 final, 6 July 2021) (retrieved on 31 April 2023).

European Commission (2023), 'Commission Notice on the interpretation and implementation of certain legal provisions of the EU taxonomy Regulation and links to the Sustainable Finance Disclosure Regulation' (C(2023)3719 final, 12 July 2023).

European Commission and Joint Committee of the European Supervisory Authorities (2023), Consolidated Q&A on the SFDR (JC 2023/18, 17 May 2023).

Eurosif (2023), 'European SRI Study 2018', https://bit.ly/49ozVay, 76 (retrieved on 30 April 2023).

HLEG (High-Level Expert Group on Sustainable Finance) (2018), *Final Report*. https://bit.ly/48zyVtK (retrieved on 30 April 2023).

Paetzold, F. and Busch, T. (2014), 'Unleashing the powerful few: Sustainable investing behaviour of wealthy private investors' 27 *Organization & Environment* 347–367.

Pilaj, H. (2017), 'The choice architecture of sustainable and responsible investment: Nudging investors toward ethical decision-making' 140 *Journal of Business Ethics* 743–753.

SMSG (Securities and Markets Stakeholder Group) (2019), 'Advice to ESMA–ESMA Consultation Papers on Integrating Sustainability Risks and Factors in MIFID, the UCITS Directive and AIFMD' (ESMA22-106-1683, 6 March).

SMSG (Securities and Markets Stakeholder Group) (2022a), 'Advice to ESMA – Consultation Paper on Guidelines on certain aspects of the MiFID II suitability requirements' (ESMA22-106-4032, 3 May 2022).

SMSG (Securities and Markets Stakeholder Group) (2022b), 'SMSG Advice in respect of the ESMA Consultation Paper on the Review of the Guidelines on MiFID II product governance requirements' (ESMA22-106-4247, 26 October 2022).

13

The EU Taxonomy Regulation and the Prevention of Greenwashing

Marleen Och

13.1 INTRODUCTION

The European Commission has significantly increased its ambitions in regulating sustainable finance with its 2018 Action Plan for financing sustainable growth.[1] One of the centrepieces of the Action Plan is the Taxonomy Regulation[2], which provides definitions to determine whether an economic activity is environmentally sustainable and therefore suitable for a sustainable investment. As a reaction to countless green financial products that have emerged in the financial industry in recent years, the Taxonomy Regulation aims to protect investors from false or misleading claims about the "greenness" of an investment ("greenwashing") by establishing common and science-based definitions, thereby creating a unified framework for environmentally sustainable economic activities within the EU. Despite the many promises it holds, the Taxonomy is far from uncontested. While some argue that it goes too far and places an undue burden on companies and financial market participants having to comply with it,[3] others fear it oversimplifies a complex issue[4] or that it only regulates a small niche green market rather than making sustainable finance mainstream.[5]

Whether going too far or not far enough, the Taxonomy in any case shifts a large part of the burden to prevent greenwashing away from the markets and onto the legislator. It is therefore important to evaluate to what extent the Taxonomy actually protects investors from such greenwashing practices and where it may fall

---

[1] European Commission 2018.

[2] Regulation (EU) 2020/852 on the establishment of a framework to facilitate sustainable investment, and amending Regulation (EU) 2019/2088 (Taxonomy Regulation). The other main legislative proposals that emerged from the identified actions are related to low-carbon benchmarks, Regulation (EU) 2019/2089 amending Regulation (EU) 2016/1011 as regards EU Climate Transition Benchmarks, EU Paris-aligned Benchmarks and sustainability-related disclosures for benchmarks (Climate Benchmarks Regulation) as well as the enhanced disclosure of sustainability aspects by financial market participants, Regulation (EU) 2019/2088 on sustainability-related disclosures in the financial services sector (Sustainable Finance Disclosure Regulation/SFDR).

[3] Schwartzkopff 2021; Schoenmaker and Schramade 2019; OECD 2020.

[4] Zachmann 2022.

[5] An overview of various feedback can be found at European Commission 2020a.

short. The largest pitfall this chapter identifies stems from the binary approach
the Taxonomy chooses, which only categorizes activities as either aligned or non-
aligned. The current share of Taxonomy-aligned economic activities is rather
small.[6] Apart from some front-runner green funds, only smaller shares of portfolios will initially be Taxonomy-aligned, leaving a significant share of the portfolio
undefined when it comes to its level of "greenness". This creates the possibility for
financial products to appear green and partially Taxonomy-aligned, while mainly
including environmentally unfriendly businesses. I therefore argue that a sufficient
level of investor protection is only reached once the entire portfolio is measured
against a more comprehensive Taxonomy Regulation, which covers all economic
activities and provides a scale ranging from environmentally harmful to environmentally friendly activities. This would help investors to make informed choices
on the actual "greenness" of their investment and mitigate the need to widen the
scope of the Taxonomy's definition, as currently debated,[7] thereby risking that the
Taxonomy becomes watered down, which in turn could lead to more greenwashing.

Further problems I address revolve around the specific activities covered or not
covered and the influence of lobbyism on this selection, the availability of necessary
data and its reporting, the risks related to green investments, as well as the inclusion
of social and governance aspects. While the Taxonomy Regulation is a significant
step in advancing sustainable finance, I conclude that it still contains shortcomings
and that a sufficient level of investor protection can only be reached once a number
of changes will have been made, including the extension of the Taxonomy.

This chapter is divided in two parts, with the first outlining the Taxonomy and its
functions, and the second analysing its capability to protect investors, particularly
from greenwashing.[8]

13.2 FRAMEWORK OF THE TAXONOMY REGULATION

The Taxonomy Regulation sets out four general criteria an economic activity must
adhere to in order to be considered environmentally sustainable. It also identifies
and provides a framework for six potential environmental objectives and different types of economic activities contributing to those objectives. The use of the
Taxonomy is mandatory for several groups of addressees, including Member States,
financial market participants and certain companies. In addition, the Taxonomy
provides certain rules on disclosure and modifies a number of obligations in the
Sustainable Finance Disclosure Regulation (SFDR).[9]

---

[6] TEG 2019, 92; Adelphi and ISS ESG 2020.
[7] Platform on Sustainable Finance 2021a.
[8] I have previously described and analysed the Taxonomy Regulation in Och 2020. This chapter partially builds on thoughts expressed in the Working Paper and develops them further.
[9] Regulation (EU) 2019/2088 on sustainability-related disclosures in the financial services sector
(Sustainable Finance Disclosure Regulation/SFDR).

13.2.1 *Goals*

In order to meet the climate targets the EU has set itself,[10] a reform of the financial system in light of those goals is necessary. The European financial sector manages over €100 trillion in assets and can therefore contribute significantly to reach the EU's climate goals by shifting assets towards environmentally friendly companies and activities.[11] In order to identify such activities, a unified EU-wide classification system with standard definitions was deemed necessary and has been introduced through the Taxonomy.[12] To prevent divergences within the internal market, these detailed and science-based standards must be applied by all Member States that wish to further regulate sustainable finance as well as by financial market participants, when working with sustainable financial products.[13] Such comparability across Member States is supposed to strengthen the trust in cross-border investments and build a base for other EU legislation in the field of sustainable finance, regarding disclosure, labelling and prudential rules. It could further serve as an example for other legislators aiming to regulate this field outside the European Union.[14] At the same time, unnecessary administrative burden should be avoided by focussing on practical and easily applicable technical screening criteria.[15] This unified approach should support the uptake of sustainable finance in the financial sector in Europe, while easing the task for investors to assess the environmental impact of an investment, in order to make sustainable finance "mainstream".[16]

The Taxonomy specifically sets out a number of investor protection goals. The guidance the Taxonomy provides is intended to help inform investors about which investments are environmentally sustainable.[17] In particular, it aims to "enhance investor confidence and awareness of the environmental impact of those financial products" and address problems of greenwashing, which is defined as "the practice of gaining an unfair competitive advantage by marketing a financial product as environmentally friendly, when in fact basic environmental standards have not been met."[18] Through a unified underlying system, the comparability

---

[10] The current EU Climate Law sets the long-term goal of climate neutrality by 2050, in addition to an emission reduction of at least 55% by 2030. The political agreement is awaiting formal adoption. European Commission 2020b.

[11] European Commission 2019a, 2.

[12] European Commission 2018, 4. While sustainable finance usually includes all three ESG criteria (environmental, social and governance), priority was given to the environmental aspect. There are, however, plans to extend this and develop it as a full Taxonomy for social and governance criteria at a later stage, see Article 26 Taxonomy Regulation.

[13] Article 1 Taxonomy Regulation.

[14] European Commission 2018, 4.

[15] Recital 47 Taxonomy Regulation.

[16] Recital 10 Taxonomy Regulation.

[17] Recital 6 Taxonomy Regulation.

[18] Recital 11 Taxonomy Regulation.

of different products within the internal market is facilitated for investors, given that comparing products without (or with differing) environmental explanations is disproportionally burdensome for investors and may discourage them from investing in environmentally sustainable financial products.[19] To further improve the guidance for investors, financial products should include how and to what extent the Taxonomy has been used. Investors can then see the proportion of their investment that is Taxonomy-aligned, as well as the environmental objectives supported and whether enabling or transitional activities are included.[20] The overall aim of the Taxonomy is therefore to make sure investors can access easily understandable and comparable sustainable financial products, thus strengthening their trust in those products and protecting them from greenwashing practices. By establishing those definitions and setting up the technical thresholds they are based on, the legislator reduces the risk of false or misleading green claims. In light of recent greenwashing scandals[21], such as that revolving around the fund manager DWS, this is certainly an important goal. It does, however, shift part of the responsibility, namely to identify the correct thresholds and categories, on the legislator. If the definitions, framework or disclosed data are not sound, investors can still be misled on the greenness of their investment, with the difference that now they had put their trust in EU legislation.

13.2.2 Scope

The Taxonomy Regulation itself includes three groups of mandatory users in its scope: (1) the EU and its Member States, (2) financial market participants offering financial products and (3) certain large companies (undertakings subject to the obligations to publish a (consolidated) non-financial statement).[22] For the EU or Member States, the Taxonomy applies to any legislative or other measures they might want to adopt, for example regarding labels or green bonds. These standards, mostly concerning requirements for financial market participants, need to be aligned with the Taxonomy. Member States cannot provide deviating definitions for environmental activities or objectives, but they can keep already existing labelling schemes in place or develop new ones, provided such new schemes comply or are made compliant with the Taxonomy Regulation.[23] The Taxonomy is therefore a common framework that ensures that the definitions and requirements underlying financial products are the same, while still allowing the specifics to be filled in by initiatives coming from Member States or

---

[19] Recital 13 Taxonomy Regulation.
[20] Recital 18 Taxonomy Regulation.
[21] Klasa et al. 2022.
[22] Article 1(2) Taxonomy Regulation.
[23] Article 4 and recitals 11 and 14 Taxonomy Regulation.

the industry itself. Financial market participants[24] themselves need to apply the Taxonomy at the product level by disclosing what proportion of an investment, fund or portfolio[25] is Taxonomy-aligned. The details are further regulated by the SFDR. Besides Member States and financial market participants, certain companies also fall within the scope of the Taxonomy Regulation. The companies covered are those which are subject to the requirement to publish non-financial statements.[26] They must apply the Taxonomy at the entity level, disclosing which of their activities are following environmental objectives and which policies they implement in relation to environmental protection.[27] This disclosure covers the proportion of their turnover, their capital expenditure and their operating expenditure related to assets which qualify under the Taxonomy Regulation.[28] The disclosed information is necessary in order for financial market participants to likewise disclose the alignment of their products under the SFDR. Since not only large companies are included in those investment products, voluntary disclosure is likewise encouraged for SMEs.

[24] In its definition of financial market participants, the Taxonomy Regulation refers to the SFDR. According to Article 2(1) SFDR, financial market participants are the following: (a) an insurance undertaking which makes available an insurance-based investment product (IBIP); (b) an investment firm which provides portfolio management; (c) an institution for occupational retirement provision (IORP); (d) a manufacturer of a pension product; (e) an alternative investment fund manager (AIFM); (f) a pan-European personal pension product (PEPP) provider; (g) a manager of a qualifying venture capital fund registered in accordance with Article 14 of Regulation (EU) No 345/2013; (h) a manager of a qualifying social entrepreneurship fund registered in accordance with Article 15 of Regulation (EU) No 346/2013; (i) a management company of an undertaking for collective investment in transferable securities (UCITS management company); or (j) a credit institution which provides portfolio management.

[25] In its definition of financial products, the Taxonomy Regulation refers to the Disclosure Regulation. Financial products according to Article 2(12) of the Disclosure Regulation (fn. 4) are: a portfolio managed in accordance with point (6) of the Article; (b) an alternative investment fund (AIF); (c) an IBIP; (d) a pension product; (e) a pension scheme; (f) a UCITS; or (g) a PEPP. Portfolio management as a financial product is specified as "managing portfolios in accordance with mandates given by clients on a discretionary client-by-client basis where such portfolios include one or more financial instruments" in Article 4(8) of Directive 2014/65/EU of 15 May 2014 on markets in financial instruments and amending Directive 2002/92/EC and Directive 2011/61/EU (MiFID II). For difficulties related to this classification, see EBA, ESMA, EIOPA 2020, 12.

[26] These requirements were established in Article 19a and 29a Directive 2014/95/EU amending Directive 2013/34/EU as regards disclosure of non-financial and diversity information by certain large undertakings and groups' of the amended Non-Financial Reporting Directive (NFRD). The NFDR has been replaced by Directive (EU) 2022/2464 as regards corporate sustainability reporting, 'Corporate Sustainability Reporting Directive' (CSRD), which entered into force on 5 January 2023 and applies as of the 2024 financial year. Until then the NFDR remains in force.

[27] Article 19a and 29a Non-Financial Reporting Directive.

[28] Article 8 Taxonomy Regulation and the "Article 8 Delegated Acts", see: Commission Delegated Regulation (EU) 2021/2178 of 6 July 2021 supplementing Regulation (EU) 2020/852 of the European Parliament and of the Council by specifying the content and presentation of information to be disclosed by undertakings subject to Articles 19a or 29a of Directive 2013/34/EU concerning environmentally sustainable economic activities, and specifying the methodology to comply with that disclosure obligation.

While the Taxonomy Regulation mainly targets the above-listed mandatory users, its relevance is not confined to them. As the core of a wider framework on sustainable finance, the Taxonomy Regulation will find its way into other legislation that applies to a broader scope of financial market actors.[29] Not explicitly covered by the Taxonomy Regulation are retail banking products (such as mortgages or loans), securitizations, venture capital or private equity. While institutions offering such products do not fall under the scope of mandatory users, they can still use the Taxonomy Regulation on a voluntary basis.[30] Credit institutions may use it when offering green loans or green project financing, for example. Especially large international banking groups, which cover a variety of activities, may benefit from aligning all their activities under the same framework, as suggested in the Renewed Sustainable Finance strategy's pillar "Improving the inclusiveness of sustainable finance".[31] The Taxonomy Regulation will likely be utilized as a baseline for many other policies, as recently seen with the use of the DNSH criterion for the "Next Generation EU" Recovery plan[32] or with the proposed EU Green Bond Standards, requiring that the fund must be fully allocated to Taxonomy-aligned projects.[33] The framework established by the Taxonomy Regulation may also play a role in banking supervision. Following its Renewed Sustainable Finance strategy, the Commission in coordination with the ESAs, ESRB and ECB is continuously analysing whether and how prudential tools can address financial stability risks caused by climate change.[34] While the Taxonomy Regulation does not explicitly follow a cross-sectoral approach, its role is first and foremost to identify environmentally sustainable economic activities. These definitions are of relevance for the wider financial law framework and allow for a direct or indirect application by the entire financial industry.

13.2.3 *Criteria for Environmentally Sustainable Activities*

The cornerstone of the Taxonomy Regulation consists of the four criteria[35] an activity has to fulfil to be considered environmentally sustainable: (1) the activity has to contribute substantially to one or more of six environmental objectives[36] while at the same time (2) it cannot significantly harm ("DNSH") any of the other environmental objectives.[37] The activity (3) must be carried out in compliance

---

[29] Gortsos 2020, 34. The "Next Generation EU" Recovery plan, for example, utilizes the DNSH threshold. See Article 4a in European Commission 2021a.

[30] TEG 2019, 60.

[31] European Commission 2021b, 15.

[32] See Article 4a in European Commission 2021a.

[33] European Commission 2021c.

[34] European Commission 2021b, 14. ECB 2020; EBA 2019; EBA 2022.

[35] Article 3 Taxonomy Regulation.

[36] Article 9 Taxonomy Regulation.

[37] Article 17 Taxonomy Regulation.

with minimum international social and labour standards[38] and (4) must comply with the technical screening criteria related to each of the environmental objectives. Those four criteria are discussed in more detail below.

To be Taxonomy-compliant, an activity first has to contribute substantially to the achievement of at least one of six environmental objectives. Those environmental objectives are climate change mitigation, climate change adaptation, sustainable use and protection of water and marine resources, transition to a circular economy, pollution prevention and control, and protection and restoration of biodiversity and ecosystems. Special attention has been dedicated to the first two criteria, while the technical standards for the other four are still mainly under development. For each of these objectives, the Taxonomy Regulation further outlines when the threshold of a substantial contribution is met. The criteria differ according to the environmental objectives in question, as there is no uniform definition of "substantial" that can apply to every activity. The thresholds are defined depending on the objective, industry and activity, in the Delegated Acts.[39]

A substantial contribution to climate change mitigation is made when the activity either removes greenhouse gases, for example by strengthening carbon sinks such as forests, or reduces the emission of greenhouse gases. These reduction targets are aligned with the EU's Green Deal and emission targets for 2030 and 2050.[40] For the sector of electricity generation, an overarching, technology-agnostic emissions threshold of 100g CO_2e/kWh is applied.[41] In order to reach net-zero emissions by 2050, the threshold will be reduced every 5 years. For an activity in the energy generation sector to substantially contribute to the goal of climate mitigation, it must currently meet the threshold of 100g CO_2e/kWh and if the activity goes on beyond 2050, it must technologically be capable of reaching net-zero emissions.[42] Such clear and quantitative thresholds can, however, only be applied with regard to some of the environmental objectives. For others, a more nuanced approach is necessary to establish the threshold for substantial contribution. The environmental objective of climate change adaptation aims at climate change–related risk reduction or adverse impact reduction through the economic activity in question, while not increasing the risk for other people, nature and assets. To

---

[38] Article 18 Taxonomy Regulation.

[39] The first set of Delegated Acts on climate change mitigation and adaptation were adopted in 2021, with the remaining ones scheduled for 2022. The technical screening criteria will have to be updated and thresholds tightened over time. See European Commission, Commission Delegated Regulation (EU) 2021/2139 of 4 June 2021 supplementing Regulation (EU) 2020/852 of the European Parliament and of the Council by establishing the technical screening criteria for determining the conditions under which an economic activity qualifies as contributing substantially to climate change mitigation or climate change adaptation and for determining whether that economic activity causes no significant harm to any of the other environmental objectives", further on referred to as "Climate Delegated Act".

[40] European Commission 2022, 1.

[41] Ibid., 4.

[42] Ibid., 4; TEG 2019, 232.

be more climate-resilient, an activity must substantially reduce either the adverse impact itself or all material physical climate risks, to the extent possible and on a best effort basis. To do so, monitoring and assessment of climate projections and industry-related sensitivities must be carried out.[43] The Delegated Acts specifying the requirements for the remaining four criteria are still under development.[44]

Second, an activity only complies with the Taxonomy Regulation if it does not significantly harm any of the other environmental objectives.[45] This requirement is further specified for each of the six environmental objectives.[46] Even if an activity substantially contributes to several environmental objectives, it is not eligible under the Taxonomy Regulation if it causes significant harm to another one. The objective of climate change mitigation, for example, is significantly harmed by an activity when it leads to significant greenhouse gas emissions. For the energy sector, this threshold is currently set at 270g CO_2e/kWh.[47] These thresholds have to establish a balance in order to ensure that very harmful activities are not included under the Taxonomy Regulation, while at the same time avoiding a situation where environmental activities which have some negative impact on another environmental objective are not disqualified too easily.

The third criterion includes a social component. The Taxonomy Regulation focusses on environmental objectives, even though sustainable finance in general also includes social and governance aspects ("ESG"). While priority was given to the environmental part, in order to qualify as sustainable under the Taxonomy Regulation the minimum requirements concerning social standards should nonetheless be ensured by complying with minimum safeguards such as international human and labour rights principles.[48] The Platform on Sustainable Finance ("Platform"), an expert group of the European Commission that assists in the further development of the Taxonomy and its Delegated Acts[49], is also working on developing a full social taxonomy.[50]

Lastly, while the Taxonomy Regulation provides the broader framework, the Delegated Acts define the detailed criteria, which must be based on scientific evidence, respect the principle of technological neutrality, build on existing market practices and EU legislation, and take into account lifecycle impacts.[51] The fact that an activity has to comply with these technical screening criteria is therefore not an

---

[43] European Commission 2022; TEG 2019, 386f.
[44] European Commission 2021d.
[45] Article 3(b) Taxonomy Regulation.
[46] Article 17 Taxonomy Regulation.
[47] European Commission 2022, Annex II, 103f.
[48] These safeguards not only include strict social and labour standards, but also further provisions such as those in the OECD Guidelines for Multinational Enterprises, the UN Guiding Principles on Business and Human Rights and the International Bill of Human Rights.
[49] Article 20 Taxonomy Regulation.
[50] Platform on Sustainable Finance 2021b.
[51] Article 19 and Article 23 Taxonomy Regulation.

additional criterion but rather specifies the other three criteria and how they can be met. Given that about 93% of direct greenhouse gas emissions in the EU are emitted by the energy, transport, buildings, industry and land use–related sectors, priority was given to these sectors in the development of the Delegated Acts.[52]

13.2.4 *Types of Economic Activities*

The Taxonomy Regulation allows for different ways an activity can substantially contribute to an environmental objective. The first category is a direct substantial contribution by the activity in question.[53] Alternatively, an activity can be Taxonomy-compliant if it does not meet the stringent criteria for a substantial contribution per se, but corresponds to the best performance available in the industry or sector in question.[54] Those transitional activities thereby broaden the coverage of the Taxonomy to provide incentives to enhance the performance in those highly emitting sectors. Lastly, the Taxonomy also covers activities that do not make a substantial contribution themselves but directly enable another activity to do so.[55] By adding these two alternatives to the direct substantial contribution, the scope of the Taxonomy Regulation was significantly broadened in the political agreement and the question of further broadening the category of transitional activities is being discussed.[56]

As just mentioned, an economic activity can be Taxonomy-compliant even if in itself it does not make a contribution to one of the environmental objectives, but instead directly enables other activities to do so.[57] While the enabling activity itself might be "neutral", it still falls under the Taxonomy Regulation, as it provides low-carbon activities with the necessary resources to enable their activity. This can include research and development, manufacturing for renewable energy technologies such as wind turbines, or additional infrastructure, such as the installation of energy-efficient boilers in buildings or the installation of train tracks.[58] In order to ensure that the scope is not broadened too much, enabling activities must not lead to lock-in of assets that undermine long-term environmental goals, considering the economic lifetime of those assets, and the activities must have a substantial positive environmental impact on the basis of lifecycle considerations.[59] The term "lock-in" in this context refers to the effect of certain high-emitting activities in persisting, even when less emitting alternatives are already available, and hampering

---

[52] TEG 2020, 13.
[53] See for example Article 10(1) Taxonomy Regulation.
[54] See for example Article 10(2) Taxonomy Regulation.
[55] Article 16 Taxonomy Regulation.
[56] European Commission 2020c, 4; Platform on Sustainable Finance 2021a.
[57] Article 16 Taxonomy Regulation.
[58] European Commission 2022, 14f.; TEG 2019, 33f.
[59] TEG 2020, 20.

these from entering the market. This happens usually when an activity requires high initial investments but then is relatively inexpensive to be used afterwards, for example the construction of a nuclear power plant. This initial effect tends to get reinforced through political, market and social factors.[60] The idea behind those safeguards is therefore to allow for deviation from direct low-carbon activities, but always with the goal of keeping activities as sustainable as possible. While for now a specific enabling activity might be the overall best option, new technological developments could quickly change this, which is why the Taxonomy Regulation wants to avoid the long-term lock-in of those assets.[61]

Transitional activities, on the other hand, are not providing a substantial contribution to, for example, climate change mitigation, nor do they enable another activity to do so.[62] However, they can still be considered Taxonomy-compliant because they are more environmentally friendly than the industry's standard. The rationale behind this is to promote the most environmentally friendly options within certain industries which are critical to the economy but urgently need to reduce their environmental impact.[63] One example is the production of cement, which is very carbon-intensive and yet essential to the building industry. If all cement production were excluded from the Taxonomy Regulation, as there is no low-carbon method yet, there would be fewer incentives for the industry to invest in the technology with the best environmental performance, which is especially crucial for highly emitting and economically important sectors. Therefore, an activity that corresponds to the best environmental performance within a highly emitting industry can be Taxonomy-compliant in order to incentivize a change in that industry.[64] In order not to widen the scope too much and thereby undermine the overall goals of the Taxonomy Regulation, the transition category does not apply to those fields where other, more environmentally friendly alternatives exist as a commercially feasible alternative.[65] Further, the activity's environmental advantages must be substantial, compared to the industry's average. The threshold for what is substantial, defined in the technical screening criteria, will be adapted and strengthened over time. Lastly, the activity must not result in a lock-in into carbon-intensive assets or processes.[66]

13.2.5 *Link to the Overall Sustainable Finance Framework*

The Taxonomy Regulation is one of several legislative acts that together form the EU's legislative framework of sustainable finance. While the main aim of the

[60] TEG 2020, 20.
[61] European Commission 2022, 17; TEG 2020, 20.
[62] Article 10(2) Taxonomy Regulation.
[63] European Commission 2022, 9ff.
[64] Platform on Sustainable Finance 2021a; TEG 2020, 20.
[65] Article 10(2) Taxonomy Regulation.
[66] Ibid.

Taxonomy Regulation is to define what makes an activity environmentally sustainable, the SFDR provides harmonized requirements concerning, *inter alia*, the mandatory disclosure of sustainability risks and adverse negative impacts of investment decisions on ESG factors for all investment products.[67] In addition, it imposes specific disclosure requirements for two types of sustainable financial products: those that have "sustainable investment" as their "objective"[68] ("Article 9 product"), and those that only "promote, among other characteristics, environmental or social characteristics"[69] ("Article 8 product"). Financial market participants that offer such sustainable products are obliged to use the Taxonomy Regulation in their assessment and to disclose to what extent they use it. When only using the Taxonomy Regulation for parts of the portfolio which are sustainable investments[70], the financial market participant must disclose this partial use to make it transparent for investors which parts have been assessed against the Taxonomy Regulation.[71]

Since the entry into force of the Taxonomy Regulation on 12 July 2020, the Commission and the Platform have adopted and published a number of Delegated Acts and, respectively, reports further developing and building on the Taxonomy.[72] In April 2021, the first Climate Delegated Acts specified the technical screening criteria for climate change mitigation and adoption. In June 2021, the Commission published the Delegated Acts relating to Article 8 of the Taxonomy Regulation, which specify the disclosure requirements for financial and non-financial companies. Following an intense political debate, the inclusion of certain types of nuclear and gas energy activities was also introduced through further Delegated Acts.[73]

Furthermore, the Commission published a Renewed Sustainable Finance strategy, which announces further developments of the Taxonomy Regulation.[74] Additional steps for the Taxonomy include complementary Delegated Acts to cover industries and sectors not yet included, such as agriculture and some energy sectors, and possible actions based on the reports by the Platform to extend the Taxonomy.[75]

13.3 INVESTOR PROTECTION AND GREENWASHING

The Taxonomy aims to unite a number of goals, namely to establish a detailed and science-based unified classification system, while at the same time making

---

[67] Article 6 and 7 Disclosure Regulation.
[68] Article 9 Disclosure Regulation.
[69] Article 8 Disclosure Regulation.
[70] Article 2(7) Disclosure Regulation.
[71] Article 5 and 6 Taxonomy Regulation.
[72] European Commission 2021d.
[73] Commission Delegated Regulation (EU) 2022/1214 of 9 March 2022 amending Delegated Regulation (EU) 2021/2139 as regards economic activities in certain energy sectors and Delegated Regulation (EU) 2021/2178 as regards specific public disclosures for those economic activities.
[74] European Commission 2021f.
[75] European Commission 2021d.

sustainable finance mainstream,[76] protecting investors from greenwashing, preventing divergence in the internal market and avoiding unnecessary administrative
burden with practical and easily applicable technical screening criteria.[77] Finding
the right balance between those goals proves to be difficult. This chapter primarily
focusses on investor protection and analyses the Taxonomy's suitability in reaching
that particular goal, while illustrating how this goal is interlinked with the others.
The next sections first discuss the problems that affect the current Taxonomy and
then propose some possible solutions to them.

13.3.1 *Potential Pitfalls*

Compared to the fragmented and largely unregulated market prior to the
Taxonomy, clear improvements can be observed. However, the current framework
falls short of reaching the proclaimed investor protection goals. This is largely due
to the complexity and scope of the project and to its interdependence with the
overall sustainable finance framework and the varying timelines. Some of these
difficulties will significantly improve over time, such as the availability and cost of
data, while others are intrinsic to the structure of the current Taxonomy and would
need to be addressed through amendments. In the following I discuss those problems and propose some solutions.

13.3.1.1 Cost and Reliability of Underlying Data

A first challenge lies in the availability of sustainability-related data.[78] This includes
the divergence among different disclosure requirements, the cost of sustainability
data, the reliance on third-party data providers and possible but unknown risks
associated with ESG investments. In particular, investors' trust in the Taxonomy is
undermined if the underlying data is not credible to them. Below I therefore elaborate more regarding the multiple challenges related to data.

Scope. The SFDR requires financial market participants to disclose specifics
about their sustainable financial products. These actors therefore need reliable
and standardized data about each investment product's underlying economic
activity in order to assess its compliance with the Taxonomy Regulation. Only
companies bound by the Corporate Sustainability Reporting Directive (CSRD)[79]
have to disclose environmental data on the necessary scale. While disclosure by
SMEs is encouraged, it is not mandatory. Further hurdles may appear for gathering data from companies not bound by EU law, as they do not have to disclose

---

[76] Recital 10 Taxonomy Regulation.
[77] Recital 47 Taxonomy Regulation.
[78] An OECD report points to a lack of reliable and too much complex inconsistent data: OECD 2020.
[79] Until 2024 the NFDR still applies, see footnote 26.

this information, and the metrics the technical screening criteria refer to are often based only on EU standards.[80] When companies only provide limited or incomplete data, this poses a challenge for financial market participants, which might be amplified depending on the nature and structure of the financial product.[81] The financial market participants will have to rely on their own data and/or third-party data providers, such as sustainability rating agencies.

ESG ratings. Once financial actors outsource their data gathering and assessment to rating agencies, the impact of those agencies increases significantly. Yet there is a lack of transparency on how these ratings get established and their comparability, and the supervision and scrutiny applied to the agencies falls short compared to their growing impact.[82]

Risk and diversification. With its sustainable finance package, the EU encourages private investors to shift their capital towards green investments.[83] This political strategy is aligned with the EU's commitments for emission reduction, which would likely not be reachable without private funding. Available data on the profitability and risks of ESG investments is still scarce, however.[84] The EU's clear goal is the transition to a green and circular economy, yet this needs to be balanced with other goals such as investor protection and financial stability.[85] Given the relatively low amount of current Taxonomy-alignment, it is not yet possible to only invest in Taxonomy-aligned activities and at the same time have a diversified portfolio.[86] This lack of reliable information on the risks and profitability of ESG investments should also be kept in mind when analysing the investor protection goals of the Taxonomy and whether to advance its application.

Cost of data. Gathering and analysing all the necessary data to prove compliance with the Taxonomy Regulation has economic implications for companies as well as financial actors, many of which criticized the Taxonomy Regulation for being too detailed, complex and data-intensive.[87] On the other hand, poor or limited ESG data disclosure and assessment can quickly lead to market confusion and greenwashing, while common guidelines and methodologies provided by the legislator can help return some of the lost trust in sustainable finance.[88] The disclosure and preceding gathering of data undoubtedly present themselves as additional costs to the companies and financial markets, but it is uncertain who will ultimately carry them. They could be entirely passed onto the end-investor, potentially making the sustainable

---

[80] European Commission 2022, Annex I and II.
[81] TEG 2019, 71f.
[82] Maijoor 2020, 6; ERM 2021. See also Gargantini and Siri, Chapter 11 in this volume.
[83] On the extent the EU is actually promoting sustainable investments through its policies, see Baer, Campiglio and Deyris 2021.
[84] Hong, Karolyi and Scheinkman 2020.
[85] Zetzsche and Anker-Sørensen 2021, 42.
[86] Eurosif 2021.
[87] European Commission 2020a.
[88] Siri and Zhu 2019, 18.

financial product less competitive and therefore less attractive as an investment.[89] This effect is magnified depending on how much the "non-sustainable" actors will disclose. It might be more cost-efficient to disclose that a company or financial product is not compliant with the Taxonomy Regulation than to undergo an in-depth assessment of all its activities. If a significant number of actors choose this path, the sustainable companies and financial actors would be the ones actually conducting costly and time-consuming assessments, though they might not get rewarded with more investments due enhanced costs for investors.[90] In view of the limited amount of economic activities that are currently Taxonomy-aligned, they could become a costly niche product rather than mainstream.[91]

13.3.1.2 Divergence in the ESG Product Market

Further incoherence problems arise due to the absence of a full ESG taxonomy. The current Taxonomy Regulation only defines environmentally sustainable activities and ensures compliance with minimum social safeguards, but does not address social or governance aspects as independent criteria. This, however, does not reflect the market of sustainable financial products, where social, governance and environmental aspects are often interlinked and "responsible investment" or "ESG" financial products are offered to investors. The Taxonomy currently only covers a small part of the overall sustainable investment market and therefore only provides very limited clarity for investors. Furthermore, the EU Green Deal specifically states that the EU aims to achieve a just climate transition, "leaving no person or place behind",[92] implying that a social component must be part of sustainable finance.

13.3.1.3 The Taxonomy as a Greenwashing Tool?

The goal of the Taxonomy is to provide unified definitions to avoid market-based divergences on what can be considered a green investment. It thereby shifts a large part of the burden of tackling greenwashing from the markets to the legislator. While the Taxonomy is meant to be based purely on scientific criteria, it cannot be denied that the whole creation process has been subject to economic and political pressure and heavy lobbying. The latest example is the inclusion of nuclear and

---

[89] Some funds may even over-charge, using the ESG-related disclosure and monitoring as a justification. Analysis of different ESG investment funds and their fees: Brakman Reiser and Tucker 2020, 1999ff. However, evidence on positive stock returns of Taxonomy-aligned funds show that these costs may still be lucrative for investors. Bassen, Kordsachia, Tan and Lopatta 2022.

[90] Certainly, other incentives to offer sustainable financial products remain, e.g. reputation, inclusion in an index for funds which are tracking Paris-alignment and EU transition benchmarks, EU Ecolabel, Green Bond qualification.

[91] Adelphi and ISS ESG 2020; TEG 2019, 92.

[92] European Commission 2019b, 16.

gas energies under the Taxonomy framework, a decision heavily opposed by many NGOs[93] and some Member States, and even criticized by the Platform itself.[94] While the legislator may have good intentions wanting to shelter investors from the greenwashing practices emerging due to financial market dynamics, political decisions of such a scale are also subject to intense outside pressure. Some consider the effect of this pressure so severe that they no longer view the Taxonomy as a tool to prevent greenwashing, but rather as a greenwashing tool itself.[95] Such a lack of credibility could dampen investors' trust in green financial products and also hurt its users, which still need to conduct costly disclosure.

Criticism further extends to the inclusion of transitional and enabling activities, which significantly broaden the scope of the Taxonomy.[96] They can also be confusing for investors in their application, as the production of an electric car may be Taxonomy-eligible, but the production of the car battery, while technically enabling the use of the electric car, may fall short of reaching the DNSH threshold due to the severe environmental impact of the mining involved. Projects of very different environmental impact, such as the creation of a renewable-energy power plant compared to a high-end, energy-efficient building, may present themselves similarly to investors in cost and Taxonomy-alignment.[97] Their output in terms of emission reduction is, however, significantly different. These examples show how many dimensions sustainability has, as many technologies bring along downsides to be weighed against the upsides or are conditional on other factors, such as the surrounding infrastructure.[98] These are difficult for investors to assess and are not sufficiently clarified by the binary approach of the Taxonomy.

But even if the Taxonomy Regulation is effective at targeting greenwashing by introducing ambitious and science-based mandatory standards, it is not fully equipped against indirect greenwashing, which could easily occur with complex financial products. Many "green" investment products will be layered and consist of several companies' activities. It would be difficult for an investor to determine the level of sustainability of an investment when parts of a financial product are declared as Taxonomy-compliant, but the rest remains undefined and could contain environmentally harmful activities.[99] A financial product could be 50% Taxonomy-compliant, while the remaining 50% could finance environmentally

---

[93] For example: Greenpeace 2021.
[94] Platform on Sustainable Finance 2022b.
[95] BEUC 2021.
[96] Hache 2020, 37f.
[97] Zachmann 2022.
[98] Ibid.
[99] The SFDR addresses this concern to some extent, as it does not only divide products into Taxonomy-aligned or not but offers a wider range of green categories in which the financial products must be placed. For a more detailed discussion see de Arriba-Sellier and Van Caenegem, Chapter 10 in this volume.

harmful activities.[100] Yet it could then be marketed as 50% Taxonomy-compliant. Companies that do not contribute to sustainable causes nonetheless have an interest to be included in these "green" products in order to benefit from additional investments. If there is no "harmful" or "red" category, investors can easily be misled, and unsustainable activities can be hidden in complex financial products. In its current composition, the Taxonomy Regulation does not prevent this type of abuse of its own structure.

13.3.2 *Possible Solutions*

13.3.2.1 CSRD: Closing the Data Gap?

A large part of the data gap will be filled over time by more and more companies disclosing their sustainability information. The more information and the higher the quality, the more investors will be able to trust the Taxonomy. The CSRD, which replaced the previously applicable Non-financial reporting Directive (NFRD), will likely speed up and strengthen this process. The scope of the CSRD is significantly wider, now covering approximately 50,000 companies, compared to about 11,700 companies covered by the NFDR. The scope of the CSRD furthermore includes a simplified reporting regime for listed SMEs, thereby mitigating the above-mentioned risk that they might get excluded from investment portfolios altogether, as financial market participants want to facilitate their own disclosure. In order to limit the burden on them, other SMEs and listed micro-enterprises are not included in the scope. They are, however, strongly encouraged to follow the simplified reporting regime on a voluntary basis, the reasoning being that disclosing ESG information will become a common practice in the following years, will be used as a basis for many other transactions, such as bank loans, and will be increasingly required by customers.[101] Furthermore, technological developments will likely make the challenges currently associated with this data management much easier. All companies complying with the CSRD, whether mandatory or voluntarily, will disclose data relevant for the Article 8 reporting under the Taxonomy Regulation. The data necessary for a consistent application of the Taxonomy will therefore be ensured through the new CSRD, as it will build on the Taxonomy categories of substantial contribution and DNSH and includes mandatory verification of the data, leading to increased trust in its credibility.[102]

---

[100] Article 6 Taxonomy Regulation requires only to disclose that the DHSH "applies only to those investments underlying the financial product that take into account the EU criteria for environmentally sustainable economic activities. The investments underlying the remaining portion of this financial product do not take into account the EU criteria for environmentally sustainable economic activities".

[101] European Commission 2021e, 10f.

[102] European Commission 2021e, 16.

The CSRD further introduces a "European single access point[103]" as a database that collects standardized data of European companies, thereby facilitating the comparability and accessibility of Taxonomy-relevant data.[104]

When it comes to the ESG rating market, clear legislation on the methodologies and mechanisms that rating agencies have to apply is necessary to ensure a stable and reliable stream of data, which underpins the Taxonomy.[105] The Commission's Renewed Sustainable Finance strategy addresses this issue under Action 4, as it intends to improve the comparability and reliability of ESG ratings.[106] Given the diverging models and practices ESG ratings are currently based on, this will likely be a challenge.[107] Research, however, suggests that the Taxonomy leads to improved comparability and reduced divergence between ESG ratings,[108] creating a positive loop effect that will likely lead to more reliable ESG ratings and therefore a more reliable Taxonomy.

Lastly, the problem related to data from international companies is not directly addressed through EU legislation, though some of the global initiatives the EU supports aim at developing globally accepted sustainability reporting standards.[109] One approach that could make the Taxonomy Regulation more workable for international portfolios would be to expand the screening criteria or offer guidelines for equivalent metrics outside of the EU. This step would ease the portfolio assessment and enhance the use of the Taxonomy Regulation on a global scale. It appears, however, that the EU is not focussing on making the Taxonomy Regulation more flexible for international use but rather to establishing it as a "gold standard", hoping that it will be picked up and followed by other countries.

While these proposals would mitigate or solve the various data-related problem, it will take several years until these provisions enter into force, provided they are agreed on at all. The question remains if they will lead to a consistent and investor-friendly framework and to what extent investors are protected in the meantime, when data is still scarce and chaotic and can easily lead to false categorization or costly products. Two studies point in a positive direction. First it was found that Taxonomy-alignment can already be measured rather well based on the data that companies disclosed prior to the adoption of the Taxonomy's Delegated Acts, implying that a lack of data may not be as big of a struggle for reliable results as assumed.[110] Second, studies suggest that the growing green

---

[103] European Commission 2021g.
[104] Article 29d CSRD.
[105] Discussion by ESMA on the potential need for regulatory changes: ESMA 2019.
[106] European Commission 2021b, 16.
[107] Berg, Koelbel and Rigobon 2022, 8f.
[108] Dumrose, Rink and Eckert 2022, 102928.
[109] In that regard, the European Financial Reporting Advisory Group (EFRAG) and the European Commission are coordinating with various global projects, see https://bit.ly/49zzz2H7, accessed 1 September 2022.
[110] For an overview, see: Sweatman and Hessenius 2020.

market and increasing disclosure will indeed lead to well-aligned frameworks and practices in the coming years and that the current data and definition chaos will eventually be overcome.[111] Once the dust stirred up by all these new policies has settled, a clearer picture should emerge.

13.3.2.2 E, S and G

A sub-group of the Platform worked on the extension of the Taxonomy Regulation to include social and governance aspects. It proposed in its report to facilitate the process by aligning such a Taxonomy with already existing standards. These include the European Pillar of Social Rights, the European Social Charter, the EU Charter on Fundamental Rights and the European Convention on Human Rights. Despite the added benefits of strengthening and supporting companies that respect and foster these rights and of allowing for more transparency among ESG investment products, there are also downsides and obstacles to consider. For many social goals it is more difficult to create measurable quantitative criteria, compared to the science-based metrics used for the environmental Taxonomy.[112] Furthermore, many of the social goals actually do not fall into the EU's competences but lie with the Member States, only allowing some broader coordination on the EU level.[113] The same holds true for governance aspects, as disclosure on board diversity regarding ethnicity, for example, can even be against national law.[114] Another important consideration is the burden any further reporting places on the companies and financial market participants which would fall under the scope of such a Taxonomy. This holds especially true as reporting on social criteria is not as established yet as those for environmental criteria.[115] The current environmental Taxonomy already ensures a minimum safeguard of social and governance aspects through its Article 18. A similar approach could be followed by an additional social Taxonomy, thereby defining a DNSH for social activities. A full social and governance Taxonomy would certainly be useful to clarify the impact of any ESG-labelled financial products and to direct more capital towards socially sustainable businesses, yet given the limit of measurable criteria and data, it seems more feasible to mainly link the social and governance aspects to existing standards rather than to create an entirely new set of criteria. In any case, clarification is needed, as the current framework leaves a gap for all sustainable investment products which cover more than just environmental criteria and leave investors without guidance in that regard.

---

[111] GFMA, BCG 2020.
[112] Platform on Sustainable Finance 2021b, 5.
[113] Ibid., 16.
[114] Ibid., 46.
[115] Ibid., 17.

13.3.2.3 Extension of the Taxonomy

Many of the above-mentioned data- and greenwashing-related challenges can be addressed by extending the scale of the Taxonomy Regulation to include all economic activities. The current structure of the Taxonomy Regulation only allows for an activity to be compliant or non-compliant but does not differentiate on the level of environmental sustainability. The two criteria in that regard are the threshold of "substantial contribution" that the activity has to meet while it cannot fall below the DNSH criterion. This shows that the Taxonomy Regulation already provides a scale with two indicators in order to categorize an economic activity. As mentioned above, for the environmental objective of climate change mitigation, the substantial contribution criterion can, for example, be met when the production of energy leads to less than 100g CO_2e/kWh and DNSH criterion is met once the production leads to more than 270g CO_2e/kWh.[116] Other criteria might be more nuanced depending on the different objectives and activities, but generally it is still possible to draw up a clear threshold.[117] Instead of just using these thresholds to qualify or disqualify each activity, the scale could be utilized to provide a more nuanced Taxonomy Regulation overall.[118] Rather than only allowing for an activity to be compliant and therefore "green" or not, the scope could be broadened to also include "yellow" activities that fall between the two thresholds as well as "red" activities, that significantly harm the objective.[119] There are many arguments to be raised for such an extension of the Taxonomy.

Given that the large majority of companies cannot comply with the Taxonomy in its current state, including further elements can incentivize and facilitate their transition, rather than just leaving them out of the framework altogether. The binary approach of Taxonomy-aligned and not Taxonomy-aligned treats companies close to the threshold of the Taxonomy as identical to those which very significantly harm the environment.[120] This not only disincentivizes companies but can lead to confusing or misleading investment products that lack the nuance that investors should be provided with. Furthermore, the implementation of such a scale should not be too burdensome. Given that the technical screening criteria

---

[116] European Commission 2022, Annex II, 103f.

[117] Ibid., Annex I and II.

[118] This idea has been explored at several stages of the legislative process and by several actors involved. The European Parliament for example introduced amendments referring to a "degree of sustainability" (European Parliament, Legislative Resolution for the Taxonomy Regulation, 28 March 2019) which the TEG addressed in its final report (TEG 2020, 51f.). While the idea was not included in the final text, it is part of the review clause, Article 26(2) Taxonomy Regulation. One of the sub-groups of the Platform has explored this option further and published a report: Platform on Sustainable Finance 2022a. See also Esposito, Mastromatteo and Molocchi 2020, 8.

[119] Environmental scales often use the terminology of different shades of green and brown. A "green", "yellow" or "red" terminology, however, similar to energy or nutrition labels, appears to be more precise in terminology, as different shades of green can easily be misinterpreted.

[120] Platform on Sustainable Finance 2021a.

will already provide these thresholds, it would require only few adaptations and alterations to extend the scope of the Taxonomy. Companies that realistically cannot reach the substantial contribution targets could only disclose against the DNSH threshold. As these thresholds are often aligned with already applicable EU legislation, the burden to prove compliance is likely to be relatively low. The same would apply for activities which are not related to any environmental objective at all. As soon as they can prove not to significantly harm, they would fall in the "yellow" category by default.

By the nature of their activity, some companies will always harm the environment and some of that harm is inevitable. Categorizing them as "red" is not supposed to slander or punish such companies or activities. In the context of sustainable finance, however, it must be acceptable to categorize activities as unsustainable[121] and advise against investing in them if investors explicitly want to support environmental causes with their investments. Furthermore, having a "red" or "significant harm" category allows investors to be cautious about the risks associated with these activities.

On the other hand, extending the Taxonomy certainly adds another layer of complexity and may be more burdensome on its users. While caution about "significantly harmful" activities seems advisable, it could also lead to the blacklisting of certain companies and create the risk of stranded assets due to this legislation.[122] Another consideration concerns the different varieties the Taxonomy could entail. While this chapter argues for three categories (green/substantial impact, yellow/ intermediate, red/significantly harmful), further "shades of green" could allow for a more precise distinction. Any activity that is currently neither red nor green ends up in a default yellow category. This group may then include both rather harmful, rather beneficial and also those activities which simply don't have a large impact on the environment. To mark those as an environmentally neutral, but certainly not harmful, activity, another category of "no significant impact" could be established, which would exist next to the different categories of the Taxonomy.[123] This category may be useful for risk diversification and to allow enough funding to reach those sectors. It does, however, add yet another layer of complexity and potential for confusion, as investors then have to determine whether a "neutral" activity is more or less suited than an intermediate one with strong transition potential towards green. Though it would enhance transparency for investors, the added benefit does not seem to outweigh the usability concerns in this case.

The same conclusion can be drawn for an additional "always significantly harmful" category, which would include such assets that cannot realistically

---

[121] Such a category of excluded investments are, for example, included in the EIB Energy Lending Policy (EIB 2020) and the Regulation (EU) 2021/523 establishing the Invest EU Programme.

[122] Platform on Sustainable Finance 2021c, 10.

[123] Ibid., 34ff.

transition out of being significantly harmful.[124] This may include energy generation out of solid fossil fuels (which is already explicitly excluded from the
Taxonomy) and other similar activities and sectors. While such a distinction
could prevent further investments towards activities which have no ecological
future, determining this explicitly seems to be an unnecessary burden without
many benefits, while at the same time opening the door for a very difficult debate
about which activities to include there on the basis of hypothetical assumptions
about the activities' potential future. Given the possible legal and political pitfalls
and the rather limited benefits, this additional category of "always significantly
harmful" does not appear strictly necessary from an investor protection perspective and may instead lead to more confusion.

The simpler extension to three categories, however, would lead to more transparency for investors and thereby mitigate the risk of greenwashing in complex
financial products. At the same time, it encourages companies to transition from
sustainably harmful towards a sustainability beneficial economic activities.

13.4 CONCLUSION

By agreeing on a unified approach and the extensive framework the Taxonomy
Regulation provides, the EU has taken a necessary step towards its goal of reorienting capital flows towards sustainable investments. Only an EU-wide standardization can sufficiently support the cross-border capital market, strengthen investors'
trust in sustainable investment products across the Union and ensure that the legislative targets are in compliance with the emissions and sustainability goals the EU
has set. However, many concerning problems remain. The Taxonomy requires a
significant amount of ESG-related disclosure from companies and financial market participants in order to function and it will take a few years until all relevant
players have adapted and complied with these requirements. In order to reach true
clarity and comparability on what a sustainable or ESG investment entails and to
prevent investors being misled in that regard, it is necessary to provide definitions
and thresholds not only for environmental, but also social and governance aspects
of sustainability. Furthermore, the Taxonomy Regulation could miss its goals of
protecting investors and preventing greenwashing if it is not applied to the extent
the legislators hope for. While the use of the Taxonomy is mandatory when offering green financial products, the availability and cost of gathering the necessary
data may discourage companies and financial market participants to offer such
products, thereby providing less options to investors. Greenwashing can still occur
in seemingly sustainable financial products, particularly on a portfolio level and in
the areas not covered by the current Taxonomy. To mitigate this potential effect,
the Taxonomy Regulation should get extended, to include a "yellow" and "red"

---

[124] Ibid., 24ff.

category, making its use mandatory for almost everyone. In light of the ambitious environmental targets the EU has set, the pressure on companies to be green in order to receive funding will continue to grow, and the temptation to greenwash will increase. Making sustainable finance mainstream must therefore go hand in hand with sufficient investor protection against greenwashing.

REFERENCES

Adelphi and ISS ESG (2020), 'European Sustainable Finance Survey', available at: https://sustainablefinancesurvey.de.

Baer, M., Campiglio, E. and Deyris, J. (2021), 'It Takes Two to Dance: Institutional Dynamics and Climate-Related Financial Policies', *Centre for Climate Change Economics and Policy Working Paper* No. 384.

Bassen, A., Kordsachia, O., Tan, W. and Lopatta, K. (2022), 'Revenue Alignment with the EU Taxonomy Regulation', Working Paper.

Berg, F., Koelbel, J. and Rigobon, R. (2022), 'Aggregate confusion: The divergence of ESG ratings', 26, 6 *Review of Finance*, 1315–1344.

BEUC (Bureau Européen des Unions de Consommateurs) (2021), 'EU green finance plans risk becoming greenwashing tool for climate-harming investments', 21 April, Press Release, available at: https://bit.ly/3TfvuTE, accessed 1 September 2022.

Brakman Reiser, D. and Tucker, A. M. (2020), 'Buyer beware: Variation and opacity in ESG and ESG index funds', 41 *Cardozo Law Review*, 1921–2019.

Dumrose, M., Rink, S. and Eckert, J. (2022), 'Disaggregating confusion? The EU Taxonomy and its relation to ESG rating', 48 *Finance Research Letters*, 102928.

EBA (European Banking Authority) (2019), 'Action Plan on Sustainable Finance', available at: https://bit.ly/3x7mJ6S.

EBA (European Banking Authority) (2022), 'Discussion paper on the role of environmental risk in the prudential framework', EBA/DP/2022/02, available at: https://bit.ly/3Kz2wdh.

EBA, ESMA, EIOPA (European Banking Authority/European Securities and Markets Authority/European Insurance and Occupational Pensions Authority) (2020), 'Joint Consultation Paper ESG Disclosure', available at: https://bit.ly/4cbDn4k.

ECB (European Central Bank) (2020), 'Guide on climate-related and environmental risks: Supervisory expectations relating to risk management and disclosure', available at: https://bit.ly/3VcY4pp.

EIB (European Investment Bank) (2020), 'Energy Lending Policy – Supporting the energy transformation', available at: https://bit.ly/4c8MCmk.

ESMA (European Securities and Markets Authority) (2019), 'Technical Advice to the European Commission on Sustainability Considerations in the credit rating market', available at: https://bit.ly/3ySiUTC.

Esposito, L., Mastromatteo, G. and Molocchi, A. (2020), 'Extending "environment-risk weighted assets": EU taxonomy and banking supervision', 1, 3 *Journal of Sustainable Finance & Investment*, 1–19.

European Commission (2018), *Action Plan: Financing Sustainable Growth*, available at: https://bit.ly/497N6GU.

European Commission (2019a), *Factsheet: Financing Sustainable Growth*, available at: https://bit.ly/45jl1fw.

European Commission (2019b), *The European Green Deal*, available at: https://bit.ly/3yTHBiD.

European Commission (2020a), *Consultation on the Renewed Sustainable Finance Strategy*, available at: https://bit.ly/3uYgoLB, accessed 1 September 2022.

European Commission (2020b), 'Amended proposal for a Regulation on establishing the framework for achieving climate neutrality and amending Regulation (EU) 2018/1999 (European Climate Law)', available at: https://bit.ly/3xbBNQX.

European Commission (2020c), 'Communication from the Commission to the European Parliament pursuant to Article 294(6) TFEU concerning the position of the Council on the adoption of the Taxonomy Regulation', available at: https://bit.ly/3KAwoGe.

European Commission (2021a), 'Proposal for a Regulation establishing a Recovery and Resilience Facility', available at: https://bit.ly/4cadIZx.

European Commission (2021b), 'Strategy for Financing the Transition to a Sustainable Economy', available at: https://bit.ly/3VxrT5y.

European Commission (2021c), 'Proposal for a Regulation on European green bonds', available at: https://bit.ly/4bPQJDl.

European Commission (2021d), 'EU Taxonomy for sustainable activities', available at: https://bit.ly/43coU4D, accessed 1 September 2022.

European Commission (2021e), 'Proposal for a Directive amending Directive 2013/34/EU, Directive 2004/109/EC, Directive 2006/43/EC and Regulation (EU) No 537/2014, as regards corporate sustainability reporting', available at: https://bit.ly/3X8FMs9.

European Commission (2021f), 'Sustainable Finance Package', available at: https://bit.ly/3v1Dm2K, accessed 1 September 2022.

European Commission (2021g), 'Proposal for a Regulation establishing a European single access point providing centralised access to publicly available information of relevance to financial services, capital markets and sustainability', available at: https://bit.ly/4c8b2M6.

European Commission (2022), 'Climate Delegated Act – Explanatory Memorandum', available at: https://bit.ly/3yUQOHp.

European Commission and Environmental Resources Management (ERM) (2021), 'Study on sustainability-related ratings, data and research', available at: https://bit.ly/3PbGksk, accessed 1 July 2022.

Eurosif (2021), *Fostering Investor Impact Placing it at the Heart of Sustainable Finance: Eurosif Report*, available at: https://bit.ly/49I1oQX, accessed 1 September 2022.

GFMA, BCG (Global Financial Markets Association/Boston Consulting Group) (2020), 'Climate Finance Markets and the Real Economy', available at: https://bit.ly/3V4ocod.

Gortsos, C. V. (2020), 'The Taxonomy Regulation: more important than just as an element of the Capital Market Union', *EBI Working Paper Series*, 16 December.

Greenpeace (2021), 'Leak: polluters gut EU green finance rules', 22 March, available at: https://bit.ly/3V7WLKf, accessed 1 September 2022.

Hache, F. (2020), *Sustainable Finance 2.0: The Securitization of Climate and Biodiversity Policies*, Green Finance Observatory Policy Report, March.

Hong, H., Karolyi, G. A. and Scheinkman, J. A. (2020), 'Climate finance', 33 *The Review of Financial Studies*, 1011.

Klasa, A., Temple-West, P., Palma, S. and Miller, J. (2022), 'ESG's legal showdown: "There's nothing to suggest DWS is a one off"', *Financial Times*, available at: https://on.ft.com/3wTuQ6r, accessed 1 September 2022.

Maijoor, S. (2020), 'Sustainable financial markets: translating changing risks and investor preferences into regulatory action', European Securities and Markets Authority, 12 February, available at: https://bit.ly/3VwhDdN.

Och, M. (2020), Sustainable Finance and the EU Taxonomy Regulation – Hype or Hope?', *Jan Ronse Institute for Company & Financial Law Working Paper* No. 2020/05, November, available at: https://papers.ssrn.com/sol3/papers.cfm?abstract_id=3738255.

OECD (Organisation for Economic Co-operation and Development) (2020), *Developing Sustainable Finance Definitions and Taxonomies, Green Finance and Investment* (Paris: OECD Publishing).

Platform on Sustainable Finance (2021a), *Transition Finance Report*, March, available at: https://bit.ly/3VeQN8D.

Platform on Sustainable Finance (2021b), *Draft Report by Subgroup 4: Social Taxonomy*, available at: https://bit.ly/3VeQN8D.

Platform on Sustainable Finance (2022a), *The Extended Environmental Taxonomy: Final Report on Taxonomy extension options supporting a sustainable transition*, March, available at: https://bit.ly/4c2P6SM.

Platform on Sustainable Finance (2022b), 'Response to the Complementary Delegated Act', 21 January, available at: https://bit.ly/3XgfrbO.

Schoenmaker, D. and Schramade, W. (2019), *Principles of Sustainable Finance* (Oxford: Oxford University Press).

Schwartzkopff, F. (2021), 'Fund Managers Face Delays as EU Greenwash Rules Hit Hurdles', *Bloomberg*, November 22, available at: https://bloom.bg/3wRqMDI.

Siri, M. and Zhu, S. (2019), 'Will the EU Commission successfully integrate sustainability risks and factors in the Investor Protection Regime? A research agenda', 11 *Sustainability*, 6292.

Sweatman, P. and Hessenius, M. (2020), 'Applying the EU Taxonomy', Lessons from the Front Line, Climate Strategy & Partners, Climate & Company.

TEG (EU Technical Expert Group on Sustainable Finance) (2019), *Financing a Sustainable European Economy. Taxonomy. Technical Report*, European Commission, Brussels, June, available at: https://bit.ly/3OZW7dO.

TEG (EU Technical Expert Group on Sustainable Finance) (2020), *Taxonomy: Final Report of the Technical Expert Group on Sustainable Finance*, March, available at: https://bit.ly/3VhbIb6.

Zachmann, G. (2022), 'Europe's sustainable taxonomy is a sideshow', *Bruegel Blog*, available at: https://bit.ly/48JVNao, accessed 1 September 2022.

Zetzsche D. A. and Anker-Sørensen, L. (2021), 'Regulating Sustainable Finance in the Dark', *EBI Working Paper Series* 2021, No. 97.

14

Integrating Sustainable Finance into the Prospectus Regulation

Iris Chiu and Pierre Schammo

14.1 INTRODUCTION

Sustainable finance is attracting significant investment market share and it is inevitable that issuers in capital markets are keen to leverage its attraction to fund their transition and innovative activities. In particular, so-called 'use-of-proceeds' green bonds (green bonds, in short) are proving to be popular instruments with issuers and investors. However, with growing interest have inevitably come questions about how best to regulate the green bond market, including how best to prevent so-called 'greenwashing' and ensure that investors are meaningfully protected. In the EU, the prospectus framework caters for what we call 'generic' business purposes. However, 'specialist' securities such as green bonds may require different mechanisms to ensure the credibility of such market-based instruments. In this chapter, we examine whether the EU prospectus framework caters for the needs of such 'specialist securities'. We are critical of current market practices and argue in favour of specific 'green bond' prospectus requirements. Moreover, we highlight some important shortcomings in the EU's regulatory approach to green bonds. We sketch the contours of what a specialist securities regulatory regime for green bonds should crucially cater for.

Before developing these points, it is worth observing that questions about the regulation of green bonds often go hand in hand with contrasting views about the value of the green bond market in the wider scheme of addressing climate change.[1] One vision is of a more absolutist type and more infused with broader policy considerations. According to this vision, growing the green bond market just for the sake of it cannot be the ultimate objective. The raison d'être of the green bond market is intrinsically linked to delivering a green, carbon-neutral economy. Accordingly, the fact that an issuer continues to be involved in carbon-intensive projects whilst

---

[1] Highlighting differences of views in relation to green bonds, see Freeburn and Ramsay 2020, 436–7. See also Bowman 2019.

seeking funding for green projects is not satisfactory.[2] This is all the more so because 'use of proceeds' green bonds typically finance the whole balance sheet of an issuer.[3] Moreover, the fact that green bonds commonly support investments that would have happened anyway – that is, even in the absence of a green bond issuance (the so-called additionality problem) – further undermines the green credentials of the green bond market. An alternative view is more market-based and relatively more concerned about growing the market. Whilst the green market has seen strong demand, it remains a comparatively small market. Accordingly, it is important not to stifle growth, notably by putting excess demands on issuers.[4] This is especially so because evidence regarding the existence of a pricing advantage for issuers issuing green bonds (the so-called 'greenium') remains mixed.[5] Supporting this view is a greater confidence in the willingness of firms issuing green bonds to work towards improving their overall 'green' performance of their own volition.[6]

For the purposes of this overview chapter, we do not take a principled view of the purpose of the green bond market. Instead, we consider that whatever vision of the green bond market one prefers, there is likely to be agreement on the basic importance of ensuring transparency and comparability through greater standard-isation (including of 'green' definitions), as well as the need to prevent greenwash-ing. However, in line with the ambition of the EU prospectus framework to better balance investor and issuer concerns,[7] we recognise the need to be sensitive to (legit-imate) cost concerns without undermining aims such as preventing greenwashing.

This chapter proceeds as follows. Section 14.2 discusses the rationale for manda-tory prospectus disclosure and in this context highlights the tensions which it can give rise to. Section 14.3 zooms in on the market for 'specialist' securities and dis-cusses current market initiatives, as well as the EU legislature's attempt to address the regulatory gap that currently exists in the green bond market. Section 14.4 draws

---

[2] See, for example, Clifford Chance 2018, 14, noting that '[c]an carbon-heavy businesses issue a green bond? Views in the market differ. For some, any engagement with sustainability is good and what mat-ters is the issuer's transition towards a low-carbon strategy. For others, it is inherently contradictory'. See also in this context Ehlers, Mojon and Packer 2020, 37, noting that 'issuers may be (and often are) heavily engaged in carbon-intensive activities elsewhere (e.g. coal power plants)'.

[3] See, for example, European Commission 2021a, 89. We focus on corporate issuers rather than public sector issuers who may use dedicated special purpose vehicle structures for the issue of green bonds.

[4] As put succinctly by one commentator, '[t]he fastest way for the green bond market to grow has always been for it to be less green'. See Bowman 2019. See also Freeburn and Ramsay 2020, 435, quoting the position of the Climate Bonds Initiative as stating that 'green bonds are about green assets not green entities'.

[5] See, for example, Cortellini and Panetta 2021, noting that among academics, 'there is no consen-sus on this phenomenon'. For a more sanguine view on the existence of a greenium, see European Commission 2021a, 96.

[6] See, for example, HSBC Global Asset Management 2020, 6. On the related argument of 'signalling', see Flammer 2021, 514, noting that 'by issuing green bonds, companies credibly signal their commit-ment toward the environment'.

[7] See Section 14.2.

on the insights of previous sections in order to argue in favour of 'green bond' prospectus regulation. Section 14.5 concludes.

14.2 PROSPECTUS REGULATION: ROLE AND TENSIONS

This section begins by considering the role of prospectus regulation, and the considerations which it gives rise to, as seen from the perspective of issuers and investors/markets. Section 14.2.1 discusses these themes in relation to EU prospectus regulation generally, after which Section 14.2.2 zooms in on sustainable finance.

14.2.1 *Prospectus Regulation in General*

Prospectus regulation is a key pillar of securities markets regulation. In the EU, many of the current requirements can be traced back to the Prospectus Directive (PD), which was adopted in 2003.[8] The PD introduced important changes to a disclosure framework that was hitherto characterised by divergences between Member States and minimum levels of harmonisation. It prescribed common 'maximum harmonisation' disclosure requirements in lieu of the minimum requirements that had hitherto applied. It introduced common definitions where previously there had been none.[9] It added common rules on exemptions and sought to reign in other practices which were viewed as detrimental to investor protection. It set conditions and requirements, but also banned certain practices altogether, such as allowing issuers to incorporate *future* documents in a prospectus.[10] Overall, the PD reflected a drive at political level to level the playing field and ensure high levels of standardisation. Much of the PD's substance survives in the Prospectus Regulation (PR),[11] which replaced the PD and which is nowadays the backbone of the EU prospectus disclosure framework.

By mandating firms to disclose information, policymakers can benefit from the principled support of a large community of scholars who see mandatory disclosure as superior to a voluntary system. Several arguments in support of a mandatory disclosure system are routinely put forward. One such argument concerns the benefits of greater standardisation. In short, the argument is that standardising disclosure by prescribing disclosure requirements improves the comparability of

---

[8] Directive 2003/71/EC of the European Parliament and of the Council of 4 November 2003 on the prospectus to be published when securities are offered to the public or admitted to trading and amending Directive 2001/34/EC, repealed.

[9] A prominent example is the adoption in the PD of a definition of public offer, which had been missing. See for details, Schammo 2011, 79–82.

[10] Ibid., 107.

[11] Regulation (EU) 2017/1129 of the European Parliament and of the Council of 14 June 2017 on the prospectus to be published when securities are offered to the public or admitted to trading on a regulated market, and repealing Directive 2003/71/EC [2017] OJ L168/12.

information, which in turn improves investors' ability to analyse and evaluate the disclosures among issuers. Besides emphasising the benefits of standardisation, the literature also tends to agree that, absent mandatory disclosure, issuers are likely to underproduce information. For example, it has long been argued that mandatory disclosure is necessary in order to deal with third-party externalities which can cause issuers to disclose too little information.[12] Specifically, third-party externalities can arise because an issuer's disclosure can benefit its competitors, suppliers or customers.[13] Fox argues that as a result the level of disclosure is likely to be below the social optimum absent a mandatory disclosure system.[14] Mandatory disclosure also benefits from support on principal-agent grounds. Specifically, the argument is that a mandatory system will help to alleviate agency issues that can arise between, say, a firm's managers (reluctant to voluntarily disclose negative news) and investors.[15] In short, the literature tends to agree that a mandatory disclosure system is preferable to a voluntary system.

That said, notwithstanding the merit of mandatory disclosure for markets and investors, disclosure can have substantial costs for issuers. Importantly, these cost considerations have gained greater prominence at EU policy level over the years, especially as the EU is trying to double-down on its efforts to promote market integration and market-based finance. For example, the adoption of a proportionate disclosure regime under the PD in 2010 was an acknowledgment at EU level that the PD imposed excessive burdens on certain issuers.[16] Similar efforts to stimulate market-based finance and the growth of underdeveloped markets can also be observed in the case of the PR, which was adopted as part of the EU's agenda on a Capital Markets Union. In contrast to the PD, the PR put more emphasis on differentiation. It introduced special prospectus formats in order to alleviate the burden of disclosure for certain types of issuers.[17] It revisited exemptions to the publication of a prospectus, and added new facilitative arrangements for issuers, for example, a shelf-registration system or improvements to incorporation by reference.[18]

Hence, whilst the EU prospectus framework continues to see investor protection as among its core objectives,[19] it is fair to say that over time, EU actors have shown

---

[12] See, for example, Easterbrook and Fischel 1984, 685.

[13] Fox 1999, Fox 2001.

[14] Fox 1999, 1346.

[15] Enriques, Hertig, Kraakman and Rock 2017, 243, 246.

[16] See Directive 2010/73/EU of the European Parliament and of the Council of 24 November 2010 amending Directives 2003/71/EC on the prospectus to be published when securities are offered to the public or admitted to trading and 2004/109/EC on the harmonisation of transparency requirements in relation to information about issuers whose securities are admitted to trading on a regulated market [2010] OJ L327/1.

[17] See, for example, PR Art. 14 (Simplified Prospectus), Art. 14a (EU Recovery Prospectus) and Art. 15 (EU Growth Prospectus).

[18] On the former, see Art. 9 on the universal registration document and, on incorporation by reference where the PR allows for a wider list of documents to be incorporated by reference, see Art. 19.

[19] PR, rec (7).

greater willingness to consider the cost implications of a mandatory disclosure system for different types of issuers. Accordingly, the prospectus disclosure framework is nowadays more cognizant of the need for differentiation and the fact that if not properly calibrated, mandatory disclosure can have detrimental effects on market growth. However, questions about where to strike the balance between the cost concerns of issuers, and the transparency and information needs of investors/markets are far from settled, especially as policymakers face new policy challenges and priorities. Among the latest of these priorities is the very real need to address climate change, notably by mobilising investment and finance. To achieve these objectives, it is widely thought that disclosure has an important contribution to make.[20] It is to this point that we are turning next.

14.2.2 *Prospectus Regulation and Sustainable Finance*

Sustainable finance – the 'process of taking due account of environmental and social considerations in investment decision-making' according to the European Commission – has gained noticeable traction in recent years.[21] Following the report of the High-Level Expert Group on sustainable finance,[22] the Commission came forward with an action plan to specify a strategy for sustainable finance in 2018.[23] In its action plan, it identified three objectives: to help channel capital flows towards sustainable investment; to help manage financial risks caused by climate change, resource depletion, environmental degradation as well as social issues; and to support transparency and long-termism in financial and economic activity,[24] with adequate disclosure being viewed as important for achieving these objectives. Also, sustainable finance has become the latest area in which the benefits and costs of prescribing disclosure requirements – and the related tensions between issuer and investor concerns – have come to the fore. At issue are new disclosure duties, but also the use of new standards or labels (e.g. in the European green bond market).

On the issuer side, many of the concerns associated with prescribing a new set of sustainability-related requirements are well known. A key concern is (perhaps unsurprising) the cost and potential liability issues that might arise as a result of introducing new legal duties.[25] Financial industry associations such as the International Capital Markets Association (ICMA), which represents the financial industry active in the international debt market, have been quick in pointing out that adding mandatory requirements might cause developing markets such as the European sustainable

---

[20] For a more critical take on the contribution that disclosure regulation can make in this context, see Steuer and Troeger 2022, 47.
[21] European Commission 2018, 2.
[22] EU High-Level Expert Group on Sustainable Finance 2018.
[23] European Commission 2018.
[24] Ibid., 2.
[25] See, for example, ICMA 2022a.

bond market to contract and lead to 'issuer flight'.[26] Many of the arguments in favour of prescribing climate- or sustainability-related disclosure requirements are also common ones. These include the benefits of greater standardisation, which, as pointed out earlier, makes it easier to compare information.[27] There is also the argument that, absent mandatory requirements, issuers will have incentives to disclose too little. The latter argument is discussed in the context of climate risk disclosure by Armour, Enriques and Wetzer, who point, *inter alia*, to third-party externalities, such as those mentioned earlier, that may affect issuers' willingness to voluntarily disclose information.[28] However, the literature also highlights wider benefits of climate disclosure. Armour, Enriques and Wetzer, for example, point to the beneficial impact on 'broader economic and societal dynamics' that climate disclosures can make and whose impact issuers might fail to take into account in case of a voluntary disclosure system.[29]

A more specific argument, which carries weight with regulators and policy-makers and that potentially offers support for mandatory requirements, is that of fighting 'greenwashing'. Greenwashing can come in different forms. It has been described variously and a single, unanimously agreed definition has yet to emerge. Generally, greenwashing can be described loosely as referring to practices which give false impressions about the environmental credentials of a firm or of a product to investors or consumers.[30] It includes intentional conduct, but has also been said to extend to unintentional behaviour.[31] The term itself dates back to the 1980s.[32] It has gained prominence in the sustainable finance context and is now routinely referenced in policy documents as a justification for greater regulatory or policy involvement. For example, in its 2022–2024 sustainable finance roadmap, ESMA identified greenwashing as a matter of concern.[33] Among other things, it noted the negative impact of greenwashing for investors and suggested that the EU disclosure

---

[26] Ibid., in relation to the proposal for a European 'green bonds' regulation.

[27] See, for example, Steuer and Troeger 2022, 33, noting that '[a]mong the traditional justifications for mandatory disclosure, the most important rationale underpinning recent regulatory initiatives in green finance … appears to be the standardization argument'.

[28] Armour, Enriques and Wetzer 2021b, 1118 highlighting the benefits of a firm's climate disclosure to its competitors. See also Ilhan, Krueger, Sautner and Starks 2021, 10.

[29] Armour, Enriques and Wetzer 2021b, 1122. See also Steuer and Troeger 2022, 35, suggesting wider benefits to society and other non-economic actors.

[30] Delmas and Cuerel Burbano 2011, 66, referring to the 'act of misleading consumers regarding the environmental practices of a company (firm-level greenwashing) or the environmental benefits of a product or service (product-level greenwashing)'. On greenwashing, see also Cherry and Sneirson 2011, 985; Park 2018a.

[31] See ESMA 2022, 8, referring to 'market practices, both intentional and unintentional, whereby the publicly disclosed sustainability profile of an issuer and the characteristics and / or objectives of a financial instrument or a financial product either by action or omission do not properly reflect the underlying sustainability risks and impacts associated to that issuer, financial instrument or financial product'.

[32] Watson 2016.

[33] ESMA 2022, 8.

framework had so far failed to adequately address greenwashing, leaving investors without adequate information to make investment decisions.[34] More generally, ESMA also pointed out that there was a risk of regulatory arbitrage in this area which could lead to investor protection challenges.[35] Accordingly, ESMA made the prevention of greenwashing one of its priorities under its sustainable finance road-map.[36] The Commission also identified greenwashing as calling for policy action and highlighted the role of disclosure in addressing greenwashing in its 2019 Green Deal.[37] In the sustainable finance space, several legislative measures can thus be associated with the drive to address greenwashing, including the EU Taxonomy Regulation and the Sustainability Finance Disclosure Regulation.[38]

Returning to prospectus regulation, the key issue is, as so often in the disclosure field, not just one of disclosing information. It is first and foremost to ensure that issuers make *meaningful* disclosures to investors and markets on issues that – to complicate matters further – involve varying degrees of uncertainty and that will require the exercise of judgement by issuers.[39] To get this right, whilst *also* being cognizant of the potential cost issues for issuers, is a tall order. Still, it is plain that in practice regulators and policymakers are adopting, or proposing to adopt, new specific frameworks and requirements aimed at promoting sustainable finance and/ or combat greenwashing. The European Commission, in its action plan on sustainable finance, thus also identified prospectus regulation as a field where policy action was required.[40] Specifically, the instruments which the Commission singled out for action were what we term here 'specialist' securities – green bonds, in particular.

14.3 'SPECIALIST' SECURITIES IN SUSTAINABLE FINANCE AND TREATMENT IN LAW AND REGULATION

Since 2007 when the European Investment Bank issued its first 'green bond', the last decade has witnessed the rise of innovations in the securities marketplace for

---

[34] Ibid., 13, in relation to the Non-Financial Reporting Directive (NFRD). ESMA also pointed out that new proposed rules might address these issues in the future (ibid).

[35] Ibid., 11.

[36] Ibid., 8. See also Ross 2022.

[37] European Commission 2019, 8, noting that '[r]eliable, comparable and verifiable information also plays an important part in enabling buyers to make more sustainable decisions and reduces the risk of "green washing"'.

[38] Regulation (EU) 2020/852 of the European Parliament and of the Council of 18 June 2020 on the establishment of a framework to facilitate sustainable investment, and amending Regulation (EU) 2019/2088 [2020] OJ L198/13; Regulation (EU) 2019/2088 of the European Parliament and of the Council of 27 November 2019 on sustainability-related disclosures in the financial services sector [2019] OJ L317/1.

[39] As far as the materiality criterion is concerned, some have pointed out with respect to climate risks that such risks are just too complex and uncertain to be dealt with on this basis. See Armour, Enriques and Wetzer 2021b, 1109. See also Hansen 2012.

[40] European Commission 2018, 5.

sustainable finance. The universe of sustainable securities products includes green bonds and its variants, social bonds, social impact bonds and sustainability-linked bonds.[41]

In this chapter, we call sustainable securities products 'specialist' securities, which have raised unique governance needs. In the EU, a 'bifurcated' approach away from general prospectus regulation (for 'generalist' securities) has emerged.[42] Prospectus regulation does not address certain investor protection and governance needs that arise in specialist securities, and voluntary market-based initiatives have arisen to partially fill the gap. However, the shortcomings of market-based initiatives have prompted EU policymakers to introduce specialist regulatory treatment for green bonds.

We first introduce the universe of specialist securities in Section 14.3.1. Next we focus in Section 14.3.2 on green bonds and discuss how market-based initiatives have (*inter alia*) filled a regulatory gap in this market. We discuss shortcomings of this approach, after which we briefly introduce one of the latest attempts to address this gap: that is, the regulation on European green bonds, in Section 14.3.3.

14.3.1 *The Universe of Specialist Securities in Sustainable Finance*

'Green' bonds are debt securities issued on the promise that proceeds of fund-raising are dedicated to 'green' projects.[43] These include objectives securing environmental protection or harm mitigation,[44] and for objectives dedicated to carbon emission reduction, 'climate' bonds may be regarded as a subset of green bonds. Green bonds are structured like traditional debt securities, offering investors a fixed income return. Financial returns for investors can come from revenues, such as the 'Green Use of Proceeds Revenue Bond',[45] or can be project-based, such as the 'Green Project Bond'.[46] Returns for investors can also come from underlying collateralised assets used to securitise a green bond, i.e. the 'Green Securitised Bond'.[47] What differentiates green bonds from generalist debt securities is that the purpose for proceeds is specially defined, and for investors, the achievement of 'green' outcomes is also important.[48] Otherwise, many features of such debt securities are not different

---

[41] Banahan 2019; Freeburn and Ramsay 2020.
[42] EU Green Bonds Regulation (EU) 2023/2631.
[43] Freeburn and Ramsay 2020.
[44] On the meaning of 'green', see the discussion in Sections 14.3.2 and 14.3.3.
[45] Trompeter 2017.
[46] Ibid.
[47] Ibid.
[48] Deschryver and de Mariz 2020. Further there is empirical research that indicates the achievement of substantive carbon emission reduction results from green bond issuers, there can be a stronger case for ensuring that green bonds meet certain outcome expectations, see Fatica and Panzica 2021.

from generalist debt,[49] in relation to the issuer's credit rating and well-recognised terms such as events of default. It is even possible that express exclusion for particular attainment of 'green outcomes' is found in the standard terms in representations and warranties.[50]

Debt securities can also be issued for social development goals, such as access to healthcare, education, reducing prisoner recidivism, etc. Social bonds are the social counterpart to green bonds.[51] Both the public and private sectors have increasingly engaged in social bond issuance.[52] Social bonds may be seen to have evolved from social impact bonds, a structure for private financing of public goods akin to a public–private partnership than a debt security structure.[53] Social impact bonds[54] are issued by public entities to achieve social outcomes set to certain performance metrics. The performance is outsourced to a third party, and investors only get a return conditional upon the performance targets being met. There have been successful issues of such bonds, although their contingency features raise investor protection concerns.[55] Depending on how performance targets are defined, it can also be questioned what real social good is achieved. The impact bond structure is particularly suitable for public entity issuances where public good is the key deliverable and there is significant uncertainty in the achievement of social outcomes.[56] The social bond may be more widely marketable due to its fixed income nature and greater resemblance to generalist debt securities. On the other hand, investors may not obtain as much assurance in terms of social outcome verification, compared to the impact bond for which such is contractually integrated.

Sustainability-linked bonds have also become popular fund-raising instruments. These are debt securities issued for general-purpose use of proceeds, but tied to certain performance targets in terms of sustainable outcomes. These sustainable outcomes are defined by the issuer, such as the conversion of existing marine fleet to alternative green fuel[57] or promoting access to medicines in emerging countries.[58] Investors receive a 'margin ratchet', that is, an increased interest rate payout if the issuer fails to deliver the sustainable outcomes. Issuers may also design the

---

[49] Chiesa and Barua 2019.
[50] Corke 2019.
[51] Lenzi 2021.
[52] 'European Commission successfully places first EU SURE bond in 2021' (27 January 2021), https://bit.ly/45j4kRq. See also Danone's social bond, 'Danone Social Bond Framework' (9 March 2018), available at: https://bit.ly/3XeKSmP.
[53] Schäfer and Höchstötter 2015.
[54] Ramsay and Tan 2018.
[55] Silber 2014.
[56] Tortorice, Bloom, Kirby and Regan 2020.
[57] 'Seaspan Announces Pricing of US $200 Million Senior Unsecured Sustainability-Linked Bond Issue' (PR Newswire, 21 Jan 2021).
[58] 'Novartis reinforces commitment to patient access, pricing a EUR 1.85 billion sustainability-linked bond' (Legal Monitor Worldwide, 17 Sep 2020).

bonds to be convertible into ordinary shares.[59] It may be queried why issuers would choose a sustainability-linked bond instead of a generalist debt security if proceeds are for general-purpose use. Issuers may seek to benefit from potentially lower cost of capital-raising, called a 'greenium', although empirical evidence points to incon-clusiveness that such a greenium is always achieved.[60] However, such bonds have also been critiqued to induce perverse incentives on the part of investors as investors would gain for the failure to achieve sustainability results.[61] It may be argued that other design structures such as the skin-in-the-game bond may mitigate investors' perverse incentives and connect to the actual achievement of an ESG outcome.[62]

The rise of specialist securities in the primary market can be attributed to the growth in investor allocations to sustainable finance. Not only are pro-social motivations at work,[63] but some empirical findings show that sustainable investments can financially deliver.[64] The EU Regulation on Sustainable Disclosure 2019[65] also introduces a man-datory baseline obligation for all institutional investors to integrate sustainability risks in portfolio management, incentivising investment management entities towards mak-ing sustainable allocations. Empirical evidence also shows that sustainable finance changes corporate behaviour, from allocation[66] to shareholder engagement.[67]

14.3.2 *Market-based Governance for Green Bonds*

Offerings of specialist securities are subject to the PR. As discussed in Section 14.2, the Regulation meets investor protection objectives by ensuring comprehensive and standardised material disclosures. However, standardised disclosure is fundamen-tally issuer-oriented in nature,[68] focussed on matters such as creditworthiness, pros-pects and reputation. Investors' expectations, whether for fixed income or equity, are based on trust *in the issuer*. Although the Regulation expects issuers to disclose use of proceeds,[69] this can be framed generally, for corporate or business purposes. The lack of regulatory governance over use of proceeds is understandable for generalist securities. But where specialist securities are offered on the promise of dedication to sustainable activities, the regulation exposes a gap in relation to protecting this aspect of investors' expectations. This gap is different from the call for the regulation

---

[59] 'Edenred successfully placed its first sustainability-linked convertible bonds for a nominal amount of approximately EUR400 million' (Thomson Reuters, 9 June 2021).
[60] Gianfrate 2019.
[61] Armour, Enriques and Wetzer 2021a.
[62] Antonio, De Spiegleer, Schoutens and Verschueren 2022.
[63] Delsen and Lehr 2019.
[64] Dorfleitner, Utz and Wimmer 2018; In, Ki and Monk 2021.
[65] Regulation (EU) 2019/2088 on sustainability-related disclosures.
[66] Fatica and Panzica 2021; de Angelis, Tankov and Zerbib 2021.
[67] Kölbel et al. 2020.
[68] Art. 6, Prospectus Regulation (EU) 2017/1129.
[69] Art. 11, Green Bonds Regulation.

to include material 'environmental, social and governance' information relevant to issuers,[70] as such information is focussed on issuer-oriented risk factors,[71] not specific to desirable activities associated with specialist securities.

Further, the PR's focus is on disclosing financially material information, assuming that the purpose of investment is attaining financial returns. This assumption feeds through to secondary market regulation providing material ongoing transparency by issuers.[72] This securities regulation set-up exposes another gap that does not address non-financial outcomes that specialist securities investors may concurrently be interested in. This gap is different from the expansion of issuers' obligation to disclose material non-financial matters,[73] as such disclosure is again issuer-oriented and need not shed light on what outcomes have been achieved by particular activities that specialist securities are supposed to fund.

Limited market-based mechanisms have arisen to address investors' expectations in relation to purpose of funding in specialist securities. The key risk for investors is that issuers are left to define for themselves, possibly in a self-serving manner, what 'green' or 'sustainable' means,[74] not necessarily meeting investors' pro-social interests. In particular, specialist securities can be offered to refinance existing projects, adding nothing new to pro-social outcomes.[75] However, what activities meaningfully contribute to the Paris climate goals,[76] protection of planetary boundaries,[77] or the UN Sustainable Development Goals,[78] are continually subject to empirical research and validation, and for-profit activities do not always directly and fully meet these goals.[79] In this challenging area of defining meaningful green or sustainable activities, the Climate Bonds Initiative (CBI) has provided a Taxonomy[80] of carbon-reduction activities so that issuers who wish to attain the CBI certification can direct their activities accordingly. Many green and social bond issuers adhere to the industry standards offered by the ICMA,[81] but these are less prescriptive on the types of projects regarded as 'green' or 'social'. ICMA's lists are non-exhaustive and indicative only, leaving issuers with room to define their purposes.

Still, market-based mechanisms arguably provide some disclosure that protects investors absent product regulation. The ICMA Principles require issuers to disclose

---

[70] For example, Stamenkova Van Rumpt 2012.

[71] Disclosure of risk factors is broadly framed, Art. 24, Commission Delegated Regulation (EU) 2019/980.

[72] Transparency Directive 2004/109/EC; Art. 17, Market Abuse Regulation (EU) No 596/2014.

[73] Art. 19a, Corporate Sustainability Reporting Directive (EU) 20142022/952464.

[74] Freeburn and Ramsay 2020 opine that objectives attached to green projects can be undertaken by even issuers with poor ESG reputations.

[75] Bongaerts and Schoenmaker 2020.

[76] Available at: https://bit.ly/3TK4AVm.

[77] Available at: https://bit.ly/3VnAiHE.

[78] Available at: https://sdgs.un.org/goals.

[79] 'Green investing "is definitely not going to work", says ex-BlackRock executive' (The Guardian, 30 March 2021).

[80] Available at: https://bit.ly/4ce6Drc.

[81] ICMA 2021a, ICMA 2021b.

processes they use for selecting suitable projects. Further, the Principles recommend, but not compel, that issuers obtain a second verifier opinion on their adherence to the ICMA principles. The principles are process-based in nature, relating to the use of proceeds (i.e. purpose of funding), process for selecting projects, application and management of proceeds and how issuers' reporting to investors would be made.

However, voluntary market-based disclosure seems limited for investor protection. Disclosure of processes such as selection of projects is a meta-level type of transparency, and it is for investors to draw any conclusions regarding how this proxies for project credibility. The selection process is usually internally based, and its quality depends on the robustness of internal or corporate governance structures. Next, gatekeeping mechanisms like second verifiers suffer from two problems limiting their infomediation credibility. One is that verification is confined to the scope of disclosure curated by the issuer. Second verifiers do not introduce additional critical opinions. Further, commentators have raised concerns about second verifiers' conflicts of interest in being paid by the issuer and perhaps having other business relationships, jeopardising opinion credibility.[82] It is noted that no second verifier opinion for green bonds issued under the ICMA principles has been negative.[83] Hence, instead of gatekeepers being a sufficient governance mechanism for investor protection, these gatekeepers may need to be regulated themselves,[84] if investors rely on them heavily.[85] Nevertheless, CBI's Approved Verifier scheme may provide market-based governance if approval criteria and processes are made transparent and robust and gain market credibility. It may also be argued that investors have other sources of information signalling such as stock exchanges which curate green or sustainable bond indices[86] or specialist social stock exchanges that list these securities.[87] The diligence undertaken by exchanges would be motivated by their business incentives[88] to attract capital flows as well as investor adoption, particularly by investment funds. Nevertheless, indices are found to differ greatly in terms of their underlying assumptions and methodologies[89] and these are not readily scrutable for investors. Although the EU has begun to regulate index providers as benchmark providers, the regulatory provisions are too procedural, relating to organisational, governance and process-based soundness rather than substantive outcomes.[90] Social stock exchanges on the other hand have not flourished.[91]

---

[82] Banahan 2019; Chiesa and Barua 2019.
[83] Banahan 2019.
[84] Ibid.
[85] Sangiorgi and Schopol 2021.
[86] Liaw 2018.
[87] Wendt 2017.
[88] Myklebust 2014.
[89] Bianchi and Drew 2012; Coeslier, Louche and Hétet 2016.
[90] Regulation (EU) 2016/1011 on financial benchmarks.
[91] Wendt 2017.

Ex ante market-based mechanisms remain limited for protecting investors' expectations with regard to specialist securities. This is arguably insufficient governance since specialist securities are marketed in a specifically labelled manner and issuers may enjoy a green/sustainability premium. *Ex post* protection for investors in private law is also limited as investors may not be able to sue for misrepresentation or mis-selling regarding their different perceptions of how funds should be used.[92] The lack of standardised definitions for green/sustainable projects is likely to impede such actions. Investor actions against verifiers would also be highly unlikely given the limited nature of process-based verification.

Next, investor protection is also needed regarding issuers' post-offer conduct not captured by generalist securities regulation. Investors are particularly concerned with how issuers continue to apply and manage proceeds towards specialist purposes, and what outcomes are achieved by their implementation. What investors may need is a form of continuing conduct governance for issuers, and continuing disclosure on specialist outcomes beyond what is covered in generalist securities regulation.

Limited market-based mechanisms address investors' expectations in relation to application of proceeds. The ICMA principles require issuers to disclose the management of proceeds; again, such disclosure is process-based. Second verifier opinions, if any, relate to pre-issuance and would not cover *ex post* matters. The CBI requires post-issuance reporting as well as verification of processes relating to proceeds management and achievement of outcomes. Under the ICMA Principles, issuers are free to determine what and how frequently they would report *ex post*. Although CBI is less self-regulatory than the ICMA Principles, both are disclosure-based approaches. It is queried if there is a need for conduct-based regulation, such as duties to use proceeds in a certain way or ring-fencing them.[93] Conduct regulation is a departure from the ethos of securities regulation, but is likely to provide a form of intermediate discipline for issuers whether by regulatory or investor enforcement.[94] Although conduct failure relating to proceeds management does not necessarily translate into non-attainment of green or sustainable outcomes, an intermediate form of discipline can steer issuers away from deviation or shirking. Voluntary market-based initiatives would not amount to conduct governance or enforcement.

On investors' expectations for accountability regarding outcomes achieved by specialist securities financing, self-regulatory *ex post* reporting under the ICMA Principles may be insufficiently credible. However, even the CBI's yearly verified reporting does not address the problem of the self-regulatory nature of performance

---

[92] Talbot 2017; Lenzi 2021.
[93] Corke 2019.
[94] Mimicking the concept of duties such as imposed under the EU Markets in Financial Instruments Directive 2014 for investment firms, or duties of care, such as discussed in Busch and van Dam 2019.

indicator selection and metrics adoption.[95] There is scope for considering the standardisation of metrics for green or sustainability outcomes measurement and reporting, in connection with an *ex ante* Taxonomy initiative.[96] This prevents issuer selectivity regarding performance metrics which may obscure other areas of anti-sociality.[97] Regulatory governance in this area provides second-party verifiers with objective yardsticks, and also regulators and investors with potential bases for exercising enforcement discipline. Left to private law, investors have little redress for failures of green or sustainable outcomes as these are usually excluded as events of default.[98] The CBI's initiative to require issuers to self-report non-attainment of outcomes leading to the loss of certification is a form of discipline, but this may not meet investors' redress needs. It is also highly questionable that investors have a case for mis-selling for lost certification, as that can be construed as an *ex post* event not affecting the point of sale. Nevertheless, it is arguable that issuers can offer the 'margin ratchet' as a market-based mechanism for investor protection or other skin-in-the-game mechanisms.[99] This is offered with sustainability-linked bonds where investors get a higher coupon payout for issuers' failure to hit outcome targets. However, this measure only addresses investors' financial incentives. Indeed, the margin ratchet works to 'pay' investors off for overlooking the non-attainment of green or sustainable outcomes, therefore marginalising and jeopardising these purposes. The margin ratchet structure can also induce perverse incentives for issuers where hitting green or sustainable targets proves more costly than raising the cost of funding.

Ultimately, secondary market exit, alongside the weaknesses of market-based governance, is insufficient for investor protection. Although secondary markets for green bonds are reasonably liquid,[100] only investors' financial needs would be met and unmet specialist needs remain unaddressed. The EU has now enacted a regulatory framework for green bonds and we examine below to what extent it meets investors' specialist needs.

14.3.3 *The EU Regulation on Green Bonds*

The European Commission proposed a distinct regulatory regime for green bonds in June 2021, which came to fruition in the form of a Regulation (the Regulation).[101] In this sub-section, we briefly discuss some key aspects of the Regulation, without intending to provide an exhaustive treatment.

---

[95] Boiral, Heras-Saizarbitoria and Brotherton 2019.
[96] Lock and Seele 2016; Mosca and Picciau 2020.
[97] Park 2018b argues that social goals' assessment need not integrate human rights performance in a self-regulatory state.
[98] Corke 2019; Freeburn and Ramsay 2020.
[99] Antonio et al. 2022.
[100] Gianfrate 2019.
[101] See n 42.

The Regulation reflects how the green bond market has developed around product standards. It provides for a European green bond standard ('EuGB standard'), which co-exists with other industry-based standards. The EuGB standard does not create a mandatory framework for all green bond issues – issues that are aligned with CBI or ICMA principles remain legally marketable in the EU. However, the Regulation signals intent towards European standardisation, as environmentally sustainable or sustainability-linked bonds are also offered voluntary templates of disclosure according to standards that are part of Commission legislation introduced subsequent to the main Regulation.

The voluntary nature of the EuGB standard signals a benchmark for aspiration, to begin with. It relies on markets to be incentivised to adopt requirements that exceed the rigours of existing market-based governance (or lack thereof). Arguably, this is likely to be attractive to investors who can exert demand side pressure[102] on issuers to 'race to the top' in choosing the EuGB standard. However, cost is likely to be unavoidable in complying with the requirements of the EuGB standard. Any 'greenium' may not be sufficient to incentivise issuers to bear such cost. The voluntary and incentivising nature of the EuGB as well as the voluntary templates more broadly for 'environmentally sustainable' and 'sustainability-linked' bonds may signal a transitional step for more formal standardisation in the future depending on the evidence regarding uptake of these voluntary regimes.

The regulatory governance of the EuGB seeks to address some key gaps in market-based governance for investors' expectations. The Regulation introduces product regulation for green bonds, as the EuGB funds objectives defined in the Taxonomy Regulation.[103] Issuers need to produce a Green Bond Factsheet which sets out concrete funding goals for the proceeds, as well as what environmental objectives are intended to be met, in alignment with the Taxonomy.[104] The Taxonomy Regulation is often described as the 'hub'[105] for sustainable finance policy as it consolidates definitively what specific environmental outcomes count as sustainable. Investors benefit from certainty in what 'green' objectives are. The Taxonomy should, however, not become an impediment to future identification of new sustainability goals. The Commission demonstrates endeavours towards developing a social taxonomy,[106] arguably indicating a future for dynamic[107] and comprehensive product regulation for specialist securities.

---

[102] See the 'law and finance' thesis explaining why certain securities markets are strong and attractive, La Porta, Lopez-De-Silanes and Shleifer 2006.
[103] Regulation (EU) 2020/852.
[104] European Commission, 'Questions and Answers' 2021.
[105] Malecki (2023).
[106] Platform on Sustainable Finance 2022, 12.
[107] Social goals are dynamic based on local contexts, Nachemson-Ekwall 2019.

The Regulation also provides conduct regulation for the use of proceeds, as issuers can only apply proceeds in full to capital, operating expenditures or fixed or financial assets for the selected Taxonomy objective. This is framed as a regulatory duty, so arguably issuers' conduct failure could attract consequences of regulatory enforcement. The Regulation, like the CBI principles, provides for extensive disclosure regulation throughout the life of the application of proceeds, exceeding ICMA's approach. The robustness of such regulation, compared to market-based governance, comes from two aspects: the direct regulation of second opinion verifiers underpinning issuers' disclosure credibility and the potential for regulatory enforcement for failed or defective disclosures. Issuers adopting the EuGB must, just as under the CBI approach, provide pre- and post-issuance verification, with the latter provided annually alongside annual reporting on the allocation of proceeds. However, issuers only report once on outcomes achieved in the lifetime of proceeds allocation, or at least when full allocation is completed. Such a manner of outcomes reporting is less demanding than under the CBI approach but may nevertheless be consistent with longer-term horizons for achieving certain environmental outcomes. Hence, reporting and verification are standardised, safeguarding investors' expectations, and seem no more onerous than the CBI's approach.

Extensive gatekeeper regulation for verifiers underpins the credibility of disclosure regulation. Verifiers are regulated not dissimilarly from credit rating agencies[108] (CRAs) in terms of organisational and governance soundness, staff competency and conflict of interest management. The Regulation is more principles-based than prescriptive, as for CRAs. ESMA is the regulator, although supervision and enforcement powers can be delegated to national authorities. ESMA's track record in supervising CRAs[109] may also be useful in signalling credibility in its new supervisory role. The verifier industry may be braced for increased cost of compliance, making verification more expensive for issuers. However, increased cost may be minimal if verifiers have been CBI-approved and have already instituted various measures, or benefit from established compliance under the regulation of CRAs.

Of particular interest for the current purposes, is how an EuGB standard framework would interact with the PR. As noted above, the Regulation provides for the publication of an EuGB Factsheet. The latter has been described as a 'sort of "green prospectus"'[110] under the Regulation. It is to be published online. However, as far as prospectus regulation is concerned, the approach is rather timid. Where

---

[108] Regulation (EC) No 1060/2009 amended 2011, 2013.

[109] High profile enforcement decisions: 'ESMA Fines Moody's €3.7 Million for Conflicts of Interest Failures' (30 March 2021), available at: https://bit.ly/4cbjWIH. Fitch was fined €1.38 m and over €5 m in 2016 and 2019.

[110] Badenhoop 2022, 61.

a prospectus is to be published, the Regulation provides that the designation 'European Green Bond' or 'EuGB' should be used in the prospectus.[111] The latter should also state, in the section on the 'use of proceeds', that the European green bonds are issued in accordance with the Regulation. Furthermore, according to the Regulation, information which is included in the green bond factsheet is deemed 'regulated information' under the PR. Hence the information *can* (but does not have to) be incorporated by reference into a prospectus. Beyond this, the Regulation offers few details on how the EuGB standard will in practice interact with the prospectus framework.[112]

To conclude, the Regulation is incentive-based but arguably provides leadership in the market, which could lead to upward international convergence.[113] Further, the inclusion of other broadly 'environmentally sustainable' and 'sustainability-linked' bonds in the Regulation signals the policy intent towards standardisation for the European market, and a backstop against perhaps less stringent standards. Although the success of the regulation depends on market response, that is, relying on investors to seek high standards in credibility and accountability, any lack of uptake can also provide a market failure justification for legalisation of standards. Normativising these standards could prevent race to the bottom which can be chiefly driven by issuers' cost concerns.[114] There is a tendency for all investors to discount long-term social cost such as the consequences of climate change, especially since they are not easily costed. Behavioural tendencies can themselves be market failures justifying a more robust, mandatory approach. In the next section, we argue that there needs to be some mandatory catering for the needs of specialist securities. Not only are investors' expectations not optimally met in this market whilst left to the current prospectus regulation regime and market-based governance, but the social motivations for sustainable finance would likely also fall short.

14.4 ENHANCING THE REGULATORY REGIME FOR SPECIALIST SECURITIES: THE NEED FOR PROSPECTUS REGULATION

Section 14.3 explored the limitations of market-based governance and of an optional labelling regime for green bonds. The aim of this section is to sum up the case for mandatory prospectus disclosure. We argue in favour of mandatory prospectus regulation given current market practices.

---

[111] Article 14.
[112] White and Case 2021. However, note one more noteworthy provision in terms of prospectus disclosure. As adopted, the Regulation provides that a summary of the CapEx plan should be included in the prospectus. For details, See Art. 14(4) of the Regulation.
[113] European Central Bank 2022.
[114] Some have called for the EuGB standard to become mandatory. See, for example, ibid. See also Badenhoop 2022, 61; Maragopoulos 2021.

There are indeed good reasons to be critical of current market practices in the green bond market – that is, to rely on existing generic prospectus disclosure requirements together with information disclosure that is made outside the prospectus framework in the so-called 'bond framework' and which typically offers (substance- or process-based) 'green bond' disclosure on the use of proceeds, the issuer's approach to the evaluation and selection of eligible projects, as well as the management of proceeds and reporting. Such an approach fails to adequately address the risk of firms providing inconsistent or potentially misleading information about the green bonds to prospective investors. The point is not just academic. Following a limited survey of green bond issues, the UK FCA noted that in practice, information which was disclosed outside the prospectus (i.e. in the bond framework) often suggested 'a stronger commitment' with regard to the use of proceeds than the prospectus disclosure.[115] However, after consulting the market, the FCA was hesitant to target these practices specifically. Instead, it decided to remind market actors of their duties under its existing rules, whilst encouraging issuers to make use of voluntary industry bond standards.[116] It is doubtful that the FCA's approach offers an effective solution. Existing rules have proved inadequate and the substance- and process-based requirements of existing industry initiatives lack 'teeth'. In particular, the fact that, in the absence of specific 'green bond' prospectus requirements, prospectuses can in practice serve to row back on the use of proceeds and other green aspects is deeply unsatisfying. This is especially so because the use of proceeds and other (substance- or process-based) green information are central to specialist green bonds. The fact that such information figures prominently in the bond framework (that is, outside the prospectus) drives the point home that the information is viewed as meaningful by issuers and investors alike. Arguably, the adoption of the EuGB standard might help to address inadequacies in the green bond market. Whether the regime goes far enough is, however, debatable.

Admittedly, proponents of the status quo might argue that the current framework offers sufficient protection to investors. Specifically, they might argue that issuers that fail to fulfil investor expectations will suffer a loss of reputational capital, and that this will act as an effective deterrent to ignore their (non-contractual) promises. However, whilst reputational risk might have some value as deterrent, history teaches us that it is an unreliable deterrent in the absence of appropriate legal mechanisms.

Hence, given (i) the principled support that mandatory disclosure has received by scholarship;[117] (ii) the relevance of substance- and process-based 'green bond' disclosure for green bond investors; and (iii) the possibility of rowing back on aspects such as the use of proceeds in prospectuses under current regulation, we are in favour of

---

[115] Financial Conduct Authority 2022, 18.
[116] Ibid. In a subsequent paper, the FCA reiterated that it was concerned about potential divergences. See Financial Conduct Authority 2023, 14.
[117] See Section 14.2 for details.

transitioning to mandatory 'green bond' prospectus requirements, based on common definitions to support the prospectus disclosure framework. Accordingly (where a prospectus needs to be published) we also support mandatory 'green bond' disclosure requirements under a mandatory EuGB framework.[118] A voluntary approach is unlikely to offer a long-term solution for credible investor protection, the building up of sustainable finance markets, or the achievement of real issuer behavioural change and substantive outcomes. In terms of defining disclosure duties, the information that is currently provided in the bond framework offers a useful starting point for considering amendments to the PR framework.[119] To mitigate issuer concerns about more stringent disclosure requirements, several 'issuer friendly' arrangements should also be explored. In particular, transitional or phase-in periods should be carefully considered.[120]

To be sure, notwithstanding the optional nature of the EuGB standard, recent developments suggest that the EU is increasingly cognizant of the need to improve prospectus disclosure as regards 'use of proceeds' green bonds. ESMA, for example, has issued a public statement on sustainable disclosure in prospectuses, which also addressed disclosure for 'use of proceeds' bonds. Whilst the statement is concerned only with existing prospectus disclosure requirements, it sets out ESMA's views on information that ought to be provided in the case of (*inter alia*) 'use of proceeds' bonds. Moreover, although the statement is addressed to competent authorities, ESMA also pointed out that its 'contents should be taken into account by issuers and advisors when drawing up prospectuses...'.[121] Even more recent are the revisions of the PR which are part of the so-called EU Listing Act and which are at the time of writing in the final stages of the legislative process. Once adopted, the Commission will be empowered to develop new prospectus disclosure schedules by way of subordinate acts. Specifically, the (draft) legislative text offers the European Commission a mandate to (*inter alia*) adopt subordinate 'green' disclosure requirements for debt securities that are advertised as including ESG factors or as having ESG objectives.[122] As regards European Green Bonds in particular, the text goes on to say that an EuGB prospectus is to include by reference 'relevant information' found in the

---

[118] In this sense, see also European Central Bank 2022, para. 3.6.3.

[119] See also in this context the suggestions on proposed disclosure duties made by ESMA as part of the Commission consultation on a renewed sustainable finance strategy. See ESMA 2020, 22. On the European Green Bond factsheet, see European Central Bank 2022, para. 3.6.3.

[120] In the context of the Commission's proposal for a EuGB standard, see European Central Bank 2022, para. 3.1.

[121] ESMA 2023.

[122] Art. 13(1) sub-para 2, point (g) of the Position of the European Parliament adopted at first reading on 24 April 2024 with a view to the adoption of Regulation (EU) 2024/... of the European Parliament and of the Council amending Regulations (EU) 2017/1129, (EU) No 596/2014 and (EU) No 600/2014 to make public capital markets in the Union more attractive for companies and to facilitate access to capital for small and medium-sized enterprises, (P9_TC1-COD(2022)0411), available at www.europarl.europa.eu/doceo/document/TA-9-2024-0350_EN.html.

EuGB factsheet.[123] What these new provisions entail for the drafting of the new prospectus disclosure schedules remains to be seen.

However, the elephant in the room is arguably not the prospectus disclosure duties as such. It is the question of investor redress in case where investors' 'green' expectations are not met. Accordingly, much of the resistance among issuers to making 'hard' green commitments in prospectuses stems from the risk of facing the 'hard' consequences of failing to meet these commitments – say, for example, in terms of facing a bond default[124] or in terms of facing prospectus liability. As far as the latter is concerned, it is a trite observation that prospectus liability is an essential aspect of a prospectus framework. It acts as a deterrent and offers redress in case of wrongdoing. Specifically, as far as green bonds are concerned, a prospectus liability regime that is properly calibrated to the particularities of 'use of proceeds' green bonds could prove to be an essential element in the toolkit for preventing greenwashing.[125]

That said, it is also worth acknowledging that depending on the nature or extent of any future green bond prospectus disclosure duties, issuers might have legitimate concerns about liability risk; concerns which are likely to be exacerbated in the absence of a significant 'green bond' pricing advantage. In the context of the recent negotiations on an EuGB standard, ICMA for example singled out as problematic some of the European Parliament's proposed amendments because of the subjective or forward-looking nature of the statements or commitments that would be required.[126] Space precludes a detailed assessment of the merit of such claims, especially since prospectus liability regimes can differ markedly between jurisdictions.[127] Hence, what is ultimately required as part of a discussion on a green bond prospectus framework is to have a proper conversation on (1) the importance

---

[123] Art. 13(1a).

[124] On avoiding defaults whilst offering investors actionable rights, see the proposals by Doran and Tanner 2019, 25.

[125] See in a US context Czerniecki and Saunders 2016 who note that in case of 'use of proceeds' bonds, economic loss might be difficult to prove where an issuer uses proceeds for non-green purposes whilst the bonds continue to deliver financially.

[126] See ICMA (2022b), 2. Forward-looking statements, whilst offering valuable insights to investors, do not convey the same objectivity and certainty that is associated with statements of facts. On the challenges of forward-looking statements, see, for example, Task Force on Climate-Related Financial Disclosures 2020, 5–6.

[127] Note that forward-looking statements can, depending on the jurisdiction, benefit from protection under statutory provisions or judicial doctrines. In the US, see, for example, the 'bespeaks caution' doctrine which can offer protection for forward-looking statements that are included in a prospectus. See for details Langevoort 1993, for example. In the UK, no special protections appear to exist for forward-looking disclosures. However, the UK government has announced, as part of the post-Brexit reform proposals to prospectus regulation, that it intends to raise the threshold that can trigger prospectus liability for certain categories of forward-looking information that are included in prospectuses. See HM Treasury 2022, [14]. Note that as part of the consultation to these reforms, The City of London Law Society and the Law Society have suggested that the definition of forward-looking information for these purposes should be construed broadly in order to also include 'climate and net zero transition plans'. See The City of London Law Society and The Law Society 2021, 5.

and relevance of prospectus liability under a green bond framework; (2) whether concerns about liability risk are justified under (differing) national liability regimes and, if necessary, (3) how best to respond to such concerns in a targeted way without undermining the objective of greenwashing. Prospectus liability is a corollary of prospectus disclosure and accordingly it is entirely natural to ask these questions in the context of policy discussions on a new regulatory framework for green bonds. However, it is here where an EU green bond strategy quickly reaches its limits. Thus, for all the discussion at EU level on a green bond framework and preventing greenwashing, very little attention has been paid to prospectus liability. Furthermore, the EU prospectus framework has traditionally had little to say about prospectus liability. Defining the substance of prospectus liability regimes remains by and large a Member State task,[128] except that the PR makes some inroads in relation to the persons to which liability attaches, besides creating a limited liability carve-out for prospectus summaries.[129]

However, it is not all bad news. The recent revisions of the PR might signal the beginning of a change of heart. Whilst the revisions have yet to be formally adopted, the latest draft states that the European Commission should examine and report on 'the issue of liability' by the end of 2025. As part of this assessment, the Commission is also asked to consider whether further harmonisation might be justified and, if relevant, propose amendments.[130] Hence, the text does not insist on amendments and is framed broadly with respect to the Commission's remit. However, it does offer an opportunity to address prospectus liability at EU level, including with respect to green bonds. We press on the European Commission to take this opportunity and address, as part of this assessment, the points which we identified above.

14.5 CONCLUSION

The aim of this chapter was to reflect on prospectus disclosure in relation to 'specialist' instruments such as green bonds. We take stock of the well-trodden rationales for mandatory disclosure but also explore increased investor needs, not only in terms of transparency, but in terms of commitment on the part of issuers where green bonds are concerned. Such expectations of commitment in terms of financing green projects and evaluating green achievements are unique to specialist securities, and there is arguably scope for the prospectus regulation, alongside the mosaic of EU regulatory initiatives in corporate social disclosure and investment regulation for sustainable finance, to do more. We reflect on the broader visions underpinning prospectus disclosure in relation to green bonds. Whilst not providing detailed proposals on prospectus disclosure duties, we highlight an essential disclosure problematic in

---

[128] See in this context, ESMA 2013.
[129] For details, see PR Art. 11.
[130] Art. 48(2a).

the green bond market that is key to disciplining 'commitment'. We are critical of current practices to disclose key 'green' information outside the prospectus framework whilst being able to row back on aspects such as the use of proceeds of green bonds in prospectuses. Accordingly, we argue in favour of mandatory 'green bond' prospectus requirements. We stress the need to have a proper conversation on the place of prospectus liability in a green bond prospectus framework. We urge EU policymakers to engage in these discussions.

REFERENCES

Antonio, K., De Spiegleer, J., Schoutens, W. and Verschueren, E. (2022), 'The skin-in-the-game bond: A novel sustainable capital instrument', available at: https://papers.ssrn.com/sol3/papers.cfm?abstract_id=3827001.

Armour, J., Enriques, L. and Wetzer, T. (2021a), 'Corporate carbon reduction pledges: Beyond greenwashing', *ECGI Blog*, 2 July, available at: https://bit.ly/3Pa9AzR 2021a.

Armour, J., Enriques, L. and Wetzer, T. (2021b), 'Mandatory corporate climate disclosures: Now, but how?', 2021 *Columbia Business Law Review*, 1085.

Badenhoop, N. (2022), 'Green bonds – An assessment of the proposed EU Green Bond Standard and its potential to prevent greenwashing', European Parliament – ECON study, April, available at: https://bit.ly/438796s.

Banahan, C. M. (2019), 'The bond villains of green investment: Why an unregulated securities market needs government to lay down the law', 43 *Vermont Law Review*, 841.

Bianchi, R. J. and Drew, M. E. (2012), 'Sustainable stock indices and long-term portfolio decisions', 2 *Journal of Sustainable Finance & Investment*, 303.

Boiral, O., Heras-Saizarbitoria, I. and Brotherton, M.-C. (2019), 'Assessing and improving the quality of sustainability reports: The auditors' perspective', 155 *Journal of Business Ethics*, 703.

Bongaerts, D. and Schoenmaker D. (2020), 'The next step in green bond financing', available at: https://ssrn.com/abstract=3389762.

Bowman, L. (2019), 'ESG: Green bonds have a chicken and egg problem', *Euromoney*, 19 June, available at: https://bit.ly/3wMQxVY.

Busch D. and van Dam C. (eds.) (2019), *A Bank's Duty of Care* (Oxford: Hart).

Cherry, M. and Sneirson, J. (2011), 'Beyond profit: Rethinking corporate social responsibility and greenwashing after the BP oil disaster', 85 *Tulane Law Review*, 983.

Chiesa M. and Barua, S. (2019), 'The surge of impact borrowing: The magnitude and determinants of green bond supply and its heterogeneity across markets', 9 *Journal of Sustainable Finance & Investment*, 138–161.

Clifford Chance (2018), 'Greening the financial system', February, available at: https://bit.ly/3Ts7gGN.

Coeslier, M., Louche, C. and Hétet, J.-F. (2016), 'On the relevance of low-carbon stock indices to tackle climate change', 6 *Journal of Sustainable Finance & Investment*, 247.

Corke, C. (2019), 'When green bonds go brown', *Mondaq Business Briefing*, 28 October, available at: https://bit.ly/3XamYsz.

Cortellini, G. and Panetta, I. (2021), 'Green bond: A systematic literature review for future research agendas', 14 *Journal of Risk and Financial Management*, 589.

Czerniecki, K. and Saunders, S. (2016), 'Green bonds: An introduction and legal considerations', *Bloomberg Law*, 12 February, available at: https://bit.ly/4a95Bvz.

de Angelis, T., Tankov, P. and Zerbib, O. D. (2021), 'Climate impact investing', available at: https://ssrn.com/abstract=3562534.

Delmas, M. and Cuerel Burbano, V. (2011), 'The drivers of greenwashing', 54 *California Management Review*, 64.

Delsen, L. and Lehr, A. (2019), 'Value matters or values matter? An analysis of heterogeneity in preferences for sustainable investments', 9 *Journal of Sustainable Finance & Investment*, 240.

Deschryver, P. and de Mariz, F. (2020), 'What future for the green bond market? How can policymakers, companies, and investors unlock the potential of the green bond market?', 13 *Journal of Risk and Financial Management*, 61.

Doran, M. and Tanner, J. (2019), 'Critical challenges facing the green bond market', *International Financial Law Review*, October/November, 22.

Dorfleitner, G., Utz, S. and Wimmer, M. (2018), 'Patience pays off – Corporate social responsibility and long-term stock returns', 8 *Journal of Sustainable Finance & Investment*, 132.

Easterbrook, F. and Fischel, D. (1984), 'Mandatory disclosure and the protection of investors', 70 *Virginia Law Review*, 669.

Ehlers, T., Mojon, B. and Packer, F. (2020), 'Green bonds and carbon emissions: Exploring the case for a rating system at the firm level', *BIS Quarterly Review*, September, 31.

Enriques, L., Hertig, G., Kraakman, R. and Rock, E. (2017), 'Corporate law and securities markets' in Kraakman, R., Armour, J., Davies, P., Enriques, L., Hansmann, H., Hertig, G., Hopt, K., Kanda, H., Pargendler, M., Ringe, W.-G. and Rock, E. (eds.), *The Anatomy of Corporate Law – A Comparative and Functional Approach* (Oxford: Oxford University Press), 243–266.

ESMA (European Securities and Markets Authority) (2013), 'Comparison of liability regimes in Member States in relation to the Prospectus Directive', ESMA/2013/619, 30 May, available at: https://bit.ly/45dt8dr.

ESMA (European Securities and Markets Authority) (2020), 'Response to public consultation – EC consultation on a renewed sustainable finance strategy', ESMA30-22-821, 15 July, available at: https://bit.ly/3VdKmTu.

ESMA (European Securities and Markets Authority) (2022), 'Sustainable finance roadmap 2022–2024', ESMA30-379-1051, 10 February, available at: https://bit.ly/45dqpAF.

ESMA (European Securities and Markets Authority) (2023), 'Public statement - sustainability disclosure in prospectuses', ESMA32-1399193447-441, 11 July, available at: https://tinyurl.com/2aacrmc3.

European Central Bank (2022), 'Opinion of the European Central Bank of 5 November 2021 on a proposal for a regulation on European green bonds', OJ C27/4, available at; https://bit.ly/3XewgDW.

European Commission (2018), 'Action plan: Financing sustainable growth', (COM(2018) 97 final), available at: https://bit.ly/497N6GU.

European Commission (2019), 'The European Green Deal', (COM(2019) 640 final), 11 December, available at: https://bit.ly/4aUdKnv.

European Commission (2021a), 'Impact Assessment Report – Proposal for a Regulation … on European Green Bonds', SWD(2021) 181 final, 6 July, available at: https://bit.ly/4ccI91u.

European Commission (2021b), 'Proposal for a regulation of the European Parliament and of the Council on European Green Bonds', COM/2021/391 final, 6 July, available at: www.ncbi.nlm.nih.gov/pmc/articles/PMC10010204/.

EU High-Level Expert Group on Sustainable Finance (2018), 'Financing a Sustainable European Economy', available at: https://bit.ly/3IvUVv4.

Fatica S. and Panzica, R. (2021), 'Green bonds as a tool against climate change?', 30 *Business Strategy and Environment*, 2688.

Financial Conduct Authority (2022), 'ESG integration in UK capital markets: Feedback to CP21/18', Feedback Statement FS22/4, June, available at: www.fca.org.uk/publication/feedback/fs22-4.pdf.

Financial Conduct Authority (2023), 'Engagement Paper 4 – Non-equity securities', May, available at: https://tinyurl.com/2xdx6fab.

Flammer, C. (2021), 'Corporate green bonds', 142 *Journal of Financial Economics*, 499.

Fox, M. (1999), 'Retaining mandatory securities disclosure: Why issuer choice is not investor empowerment', 85 *Virginia Law Review*, 1335.

Fox, M. (2001), 'The issuer choice debate', 2 *Theoretical Inquiries in Law*, 563.

Freeburn, L. and Ramsay, I. (2020), 'Green bonds: Legal and policy issues', 15 *Capital Markets Law Journal*, 418.

Gianfrate, G. (2019), 'The green advantage: Exploring the convenience of issuing green bonds', available at: https://ssrn.com/abstract=3329823.

Hansen, R. (2012), 'Climate change disclosure by SEC registrants: Revisiting the SEC's 2010 interpretive release', 6 *Brooklyn Journal of Corporate, Financial & Commercial Law*, 487.

HM Treasury (2022), 'UK prospectus regime review – Review outcome', March, available at: https://bit.ly/49ZJfME.

HSBC Global Asset Management (2020), 'Interest with principle: Green bonds – A user's guide', available at: https://bit.ly/4c56C9z.

Hansen R. (2012), 'Climate change disclosure by SEC registrants: Revisiting the SEC's 2010 interpretive release', 6 *Brooklyn Journal of Corporate, Financial & Commercial Law*, 487.

Ilhan, E., Krueger, P., Sautner, Z. and Starks, L. (2021), 'Climate risk disclosure and institutional investors', *ECGI Finance Working Paper* No. 661/2020, October.

In, S. Y., Ki, Y. P. and Monk, A. (2021), 'Is "being green" rewarded in the market?: An empirical investigation of decarbonization and stock returns', available at: https://ssrn.com/abstract=3020304.

ICMA (International Capital Market Association) (2021a), 'Green bond principles', available at: https://bit.ly/3wQhuIs.

ICMA (International Capital Market Association) (2021b), 'Social bond principles', available at: https://bit.ly/3T7voxi.

ICMA (International Capital Market Association) (2022a), 'Analysis of the amendments to the EuGB regulation proposed by the Rapporteur of the EU Parliament', 5 January, available at: https://bit.ly/3ThpeL8.

ICMA (International Capital Market Association) (2022b), 'Updated analysis of the proposals for the EuGB regulation', 22 June, available at: https://bit.ly/3wNbBeY.

Kölbel, J. F., Heeb, F., Paetzold, F. and Busch, T. (2020), 'Can sustainable investing save the world? Reviewing the mechanisms of investor impact', 33(4) *Organisation and Environment*, available at: https://doi.org/10.1177/1086026620919202.

La Porta, R., Lopez-De-Silanes, F. and Shleifer, A. (2006), 'What works in securities laws', 61 *Journal of Finance*, 1.

Langevoort D. (1993), 'Disclosures that bespeak caution', 49 *Business Lawyer*, 481.

Lenzi, D. (2021), 'Corporate social bond: A legal analysis', 18 *European Company and Financial Law Review*, 291.

Liaw, K. T. (2018), 'Asset allocation and the green bond market' in Boubaker, S., Cumming, D. and Khuong Nguyen, D. (eds.), *Research Handbook of Investing in the Triple Bottom Line* (Cheltenham: Edward Elgar), 314–332.

Lock, I. and Seele, P. (2016), 'The credibility of CSR (corporate social responsibility) Reports in Europe. Evidence from a quantitative content analysis in 11 countries', 122 *Journal of Cleaner Production*, 186.

Malecki, C. (2023), 'Taxonomy regulation and sustainable finance disclosure regulation: The European impetus', in Chiu, I. H.-Y. and Hirt, H.-C. (eds.), *Investment Management, Stewardship and Sustainability* (Oxford: Hart Publishing), 165–182.

Maragopoulos, N. (2021), 'Towards a European Green Bond: A Commission's proposal to promote sustainable finance', *EBI Working Paper*, October, available at: https://papers.ssrn.com/sol3/papers.cfm?abstract_id=3933766.

Mosca, C. and Picciau, C. (2020), 'Making non-financial information count: Accountability and materiality in sustainability reporting', available at: https://papers.ssrn.com/sol3/papers.cfm?abstract_id=3536460.

Myklebust, T. (2014), 'The role of stock exchanges in shaping more sustainable company and market practices', available at: https://papers.ssrn.com/sol3/papers.cfm?abstract_id=2324743.

Nachemson-Ekwall, S. (2019), 'A Swedish market for sustainability-related and socially labelled bonds: Institutional investors as drivers', available at: https://ssrn.com/abstract=3518685.

Park, S. K. (2018a), 'Investors as regulators: Green bonds and the governance challenges of the sustainable finance revolution', 54 *Stanford Journal of International Law*, 1.

Park, S. K. (2018b), 'Social bonds for sustainable development: A human rights perspective on impact investing', 3 *Business and Human Rights Law Journal*, 233.

Platform on Sustainable Finance (2022), 'Final Report on Social Taxonomy', February, available at: https://bit.ly/3T5TGZE.

Ramsay, I. and Tan, C. (2018), 'Social impact bonds in Australia', 29(3) *Journal of Banking and Finance Law and Practice*, 248.

Ross, V. (2022), 'Greening the financial markets: Challenges and opportunities at the current juncture', ESMA24-442-86, 9 June, available at: https://bit.ly/4bU4Yr0.

Sangiorgi, I. and Schopol, L. (2021), 'Why do institutional investors buy green bonds: Evidence from a survey of European asset managers', available at: https://ssrn.com/abstract=3814937.

Schäfer, H. and Höchstötter, D. (2015), 'Social impact bonds', available at: https://ssrn.com/abstract=2635400.

Schammo, P. (2011), *EU Prospectus Law – New Perspectives on Regulatory Competition in Securities Markets* (Cambridge, UK: Cambridge University Press).

Silber, N. I. (2014), 'Considering the allure and peril of nonprofit social impact bond arrangements', available at: https://ssrn.com/abstract=3457233.

Stamenkova Van Rumpt, J. (2012), 'Integrating CSR principles in capital markets through the prospectus directive', 9 *European Company Law*, 81.

Steuer, S. and Troeger, T. (2022), 'The role of disclosure in green finance', 8 *Journal of Financial Regulation*, 1.

Talbot, K. M. (2017), 'What does green really mean: How increased transparency and standardization can grow the green bond market', 28 *Villanova Environmental Law Journal*, 127.

Task Force on Climate-Related Financial Disclosures (2020), 'Forward-looking financial sector metrics', *Consultation*, October, available at: https://bit.ly/4a3m7x4.

The City of London Law Society and The Law Society (2021), 'City of London Law Society and Law Society response to HM Treasury: UK prospectus regime review – Consultation', 24 September, available at: https://bit.ly/4a95P5T.

Tortorice, D. E., Bloom, D. E., Kirby, P. and Regan, J. (2020), 'A theory of social impact bonds', available at: https://ssrn.com/abstract=3643195.

406   *Iris Chiu and Pierre Schammo*

Trompeter, L. (2017), 'Green greed is good: How green bonds cultivated into Wall Street's environmental paradox', 17 *Sustainable Development Law and Policy*, 4.

Watson, B. (2016), 'The troubling evolution of corporate greenwashing', *The Guardian*, 20 August, available at: https://bit.ly/3TciEW8.

Wendt, K. (2017), 'Social stock exchanges – Democratization of capital investing for impact', available at: https://ssrn.com/abstract=3021739.

White & Case (2021), 'The new EU Green Bond Regulation – Fortune green or fortress green?', 23 July, available at: https://bit.ly/4a7jNF1.

15

Disclosure Regulation and Sustainability

Kern Alexander and Aline Darbellay

15.1 INTRODUCTION

This chapter considers disclosure obligations of environmental sustainability risks that apply to companies. It analyses recent international developments by highlighting how the disclosure requirements for environmental and social governance (ESG) risks have evolved in the European Union, Switzerland, United Kingdom and United States. A shift of paradigm relating to sustainability disclosure regulation is underway. This chapter explains the disclosure requirements in light of the growing importance for companies to disclose environmental and social risks and related factors that are relevant to their operations. It also discusses potential cross-border strategies for countries to develop international standards to support global convergence. In recent years, both international standard-setters and national policymakers and regulators have established some standards and principles for sustainability-related disclosure. Despite limited progress internationally, the European Union adopted a Sustainable Finance Disclosure Regulation (SFDR)[1] in 2019 applicable to regulated financial firms and a delegated regulation in 2022 that intends to harmonise sustainability-related disclosures across Member States for financial sector firms.[2] The EU also adopted a Corporate Sustainability Reporting Directive (CSRD) in 2022 that aims to harmonise ESG reporting for all EU-based companies and all non-EU companies doing business in Europe.[3] The different sustainability disclosure requirements between EU countries and

---

[1] Regulation 2019/2088/EU of the European Parliament and of the Council of 27 November 2019 on sustainability-related disclosures in the financial services sector, OJ L 317, 9.12.2019 (hereinafter referred to as 'SFDR').

[2] Commission Delegated Regulation 2022/1288/EU of 6 April 2022 supplementing Regulation 2019/2088/EU with regard to regulatory technical standards (RTS), OJ L 196, 25.07.2022 (hereinafter referred to as 'SFDR RTS').

[3] Directive 2022/2464/EU of the European Parliament and of the Council of 14 December 2022 amending Regulation No. 537/2014/EU, Directive 2004/109/EC, Directive 2006/43/EC and Directive 2013/34/EU, as regards corporate sustainability reporting, OJ L 322, 16.12.2022 (hereinafter referred to as 'CSRD 2022').

non-EU countries suggests, therefore, that cross-border regulatory coordination is important.

The chapter addresses the question of what regulatory approach for cross-border coordination would be most beneficial for the convergence and eventual harmonisation of sustainability disclosure standards. The application of home-state rules versus the application of host-state rules is a recurring issue in financial regulation, and sustainability-related disclosure is no exception. Moreover, issues may arise such as how to avoid redundant and conflicting requirements. In considering an appropriate model, the overarching principle of investor protection should be given priority.[4] In addition, the interests of broader stakeholders should be taken into account. Given the global reach of sustainability risks, the chapter suggests that extraterritorial application of a country's regulations and laws may be necessary to promote convergence and eventual harmonisation of regulatory disclosure standards.[5]

Besides the analysis of how to resolve conflicting jurisdictional requirements for sustainability-related disclosures, the chapter will also discuss the transparency duties of corporations and more specifically the mandatory disclosure of non-financial or extra-financial information by companies. Particular focus will be given to the 2022/2464/EU CSRD,[6] which increases the non-financial disclosure obligations of European companies and non-European companies doing business in Europe, and the CSRD's predecessor legislation, namely the 2014/95/EU Non-Financial Reporting Directive (NFRD), which required the disclosure of non-financial and diversity information by certain large undertakings and groups.[7]

Section 15.2 considers the international developments justifying the rationale for sustainability-related disclosures and related economic and legal theories of corporate governance along with a discussion of the three models of cross-border disclosure regulation. The three models of disclosure regulation countries can adopt are presented with a view to assessing what rules apply to cross-border activities. These models are (i) the home state approach, (ii) the host state approach and (iii) the equivalence approach. By referencing to these three models, Section 15.3 analyses the EU CSRD legislation for corporate sustainability reporting to argue that it has adopted a mix-and-match model between the host state approach and the equivalence approach. Our analysis emphasises the extraterritoriality of EU sustainability disclosure regulation. Section 15.4 analyses the models followed by the UK, the US and Switzerland with a view to assessing the cross-border challenges posed by evolving sustainable disclosure regulation. Section 15.4 also recommends a model

---

[4] Tafara and Peterson 2007, 31, 32.
[5] Avi-Yonah 2003, 16.
[6] CSRD 2022.
[7] Directive 2014/95/EU of the European Parliament and of the Council of 22 October 2014 amending Directive 2013/34/EU as regards disclosure of non-financial and diversity information by certain large undertakings and groups, OJ L 330, 15.11.2014 (hereinafter referred to as 'NFRD 2014').

of ESG disclosure for capital markets that is based on the EU policy of equivalence modified by the selective substituted compliance approach.

15.2 INTERNATIONAL DEVELOPMENTS

15.2.1 *Evolving Perspectives on Sustainability*

Sustainability disclosure regulation relies on the definition of sustainability by the scientific community. The 1987 report of the World Commission on Environment and Development, also called the 'Brundtland Report', was one of the first documents of an international body wherein a definition of the notion of sustainable development could be found.[8] Sustainable development was defined as '[the] development that meets the needs of the present without compromising the ability of future generations to meet their own needs'.[9] This concise definition has raised awareness of the need for the current generation to act in a way that is not harmful for future generations' development.[10] Other international bodies, such as the IPCC or the United Nations Educational, Scientific and Cultural Organisation (UNESCO), have adopted this definition in official statements.[11] More precisely, a strong emphasis has been laid on climate change risks. In 2014, the IPCC made it clear that climate change is increasingly manifesting itself in more extreme weather events.[12] Since the pre-industrial era, the concentration of greenhouse gases (GHG) in the atmosphere has increased to unprecedented level.[13] Scientists tend to attribute high GHG levels to industrial development and related economic activity, resulting in significantly warmer average temperatures.[14] The seas and oceans are also facing an increase in their temperature.[15] Given human influence on this phenomenon, the scientific community has called for action to be taken.

Standard economic models have been designed on the assumption that the market can efficiently allocate resources and typically do not incorporate the

---

[8] World Commission on Environment and Development (WCED), Our Common Future (March 1987) (hereinafter referred to as 'Brundtland Report'); Richelle 2021, 147; Yohe et al. 2007, 819; Rankin 2014, 1379.

[9] Brundtland Report, 41; Lambooy 2006, 221; Scanlan 2021; Monsma and Buckley 2004, 170.

[10] Scanlan 2021, 13.

[11] See Brundtland Report, 41 or UNESCO 2011.

[12] Landrigan et al. 2017, states that the: 'Evidence of observed climate change impacts is strongest and most comprehensive for natural systems'; IPCC 2014, 6 (hereafter referred to as 'The Fifth Assessment Report').

[13] Ibid., 4: 'Anthropogenic greenhouse gas emissions have increased since the pre-industrial era, driven largely by economic and population growth, and are now higher than ever.'

[14] See Ibid., 6: 'In recent decades, changes in climate have caused impacts on natural and human systems on all continents and across the oceans'. See also de Cendra de Larragán 2017, 150; Moulin 2020; see also United Nations 2015 (hereafter referred to as 'Paris Agreement'), 1.

[15] Landrigan et al. 2017, 40.

environmental and social costs of economic activity.[16] However, asymmetric information and negative externalities[17] arising from inadequate investor understanding of the risks to which they are exposed can lead to misallocation of capital that can cause social and environmental costs.[18] In this respect, the current environmental and climate crisis can be seen as a consequence of inefficient allocation of capital caused in part by inadequate disclosure to investors of the material financial risks arising from environmental degradation.

From the corporate law perspective, the shift from shareholder primacy (i.e., shareholder wealth maximisation) to alternative concepts and practices of corporate purpose is underway.[19] We argue that disclosure is a key topic of sustainable corporate governance. Transparency has always played an essential role in ensuring good corporate governance. Traditionally, mandatory company reporting requirements focussed on the disclosure of information that was economically and financially material, but in recent years more jurisdictions have begun requiring the disclosure of a broader array of information, much of it not directly financially material in the short-term. Also, company boards, under pressure from longer-term investors such as pension funds and insurance companies, have begun to disclose more information to investors about their long-term strategies to support ESG objectives.[20] In that sense, disclosure is a core element in the assessment of the viability and long-term view of the corporation.[21]

Companies are also under pressure to disclose non-financial information related to their perceived corporate social responsibilities. Such disclosures are often made in order to enhance their reputation with investors and the public.[22] This can potentially improve financial results and have a positive impact on the company's share price.[23] Disclosure of such information can also lead to enhanced stakeholder confidence in the company.[24] Furthermore, from a competition point of view, the disclosure of non-financial information can influence competitor firms to disclose more

[16] Koopmans 1951; Cobbaut 2018, 405.
[17] See Pigou 1920, stating the classic externality problem of dirty smoke generated by a firm in its production process and the need to impose 'bounties' or 'taxes' on the polluting firm. See also Helbing 2010; Mitchell Polinsky 1979; Yandle 1999.
[18] Lee 2006; de Cendra de Larragán 2017, 149.
[19] See Helleringer and Skinner, Chapter 4 in this volume; Christensen, Hail and Leuz 2019, calling for corporations to account for their social responsibilities; George et al. 2022; Henderson and Ramanna 2015 (stating that managers are 'agents not only of their shareholders but also of the system that sustains market capitalism').
[20] Coibion and Filbiche 2021, 62; CDBS 2020, 8.
[21] Ahern 2016, 600.
[22] European Commission 2001, para. 66 (European Parliament Resolution C24/28 of 6 February 2013 on corporate social responsibility: accountable, transparent and responsible business behaviour and sustainable growth, OJ 2016 C 24/28, para. 23, 22 January 2016 (hereinafter referred to as 'European Parliament 2013 Resolution'): '[the European Parliament] stresses that corporate responsibility must not be reduced to a marketing tool […]').
[23] Gasser 2020, 46.
[24] Ibid., 46.

non-financial information as well. The lack of standards and definitions, however, regarding non-financial disclosures has led to calls for more regulation to protect investors against misleading disclosures and the lack of comparability between companies in what they disclose.[25] As a result, policymakers and regulators around the globe have responded with a variety of approaches to encourage companies to provide more relevant and comparable information for investors regarding ESG and other socially responsible reporting.

15.2.2 *The Rise of International Standards*

The Paris Climate Change Treaty of 2015 sets forth binding requirements on countries to reduce the level of carbon in their economies.[26] Under the Paris Treaty, states have committed to limiting global warming to well below 2, preferably to 1.5 degrees Celsius, compared to pre-industrial levels. The Treaty requires states to disclose carbon emissions and to report on whether they are achieving their reduction targets.

International standards on the disclosure of climate change risks have emerged with the adoption of the recommendations of the Task Force on Climate-related Financial Disclosures (TCFD) in 2017.[27] The TCFD serves as an international catalyst by contributing to enhancing corporate reporting in the realm of climate change risks. A large number of states have adapted their laws to comply with the TCFD recommendations. Annual reviews have shown progress among various states in adjusting their company reporting requirements to meet the TCFD standards.[28] Yet, annual reviews have also reported that companies should have more precise and comparable standards upon which to base their disclosures. With respect to materiality, the TCFD has recognised the insufficiency of disclosure around material financial risks.[29] A major recommendation consists of including material climate-related risks in the mainstream annual financial filings.[30] It includes a recommendation to disclose the actual and potential impacts of climate-related risks and opportunities as well as metrics and targets in the annual financial filings where such information is material.[31] In addition, the TCFD makes the recommendation that certain large companies provide such information in other reports even when the information is not deemed material in terms of short-term effect on share price because of the likelihood that these companies will be financially impacted over time.[32] In so doing,

---

[25] Ahern 2016, 626; European Parliament 2013 Resolution, para. 24.
[26] United Nations 2015.
[27] TCFD 2017.
[28] For example, TCFD 2022.
[29] TCFD 2021a.
[30] Ibid., 14.
[31] Ibid., 15.
[32] Ibid., 14.

the TCFD has recognised the importance and the evolution of the notion of materiality; however, it does not mark a significant departure from the traditional notion of financial materiality that is the basis for most company reporting requirements.[33] In so doing, it contributes to the financialisation of sustainability.[34] Further, the TCFD has determined what sustainability-related information has to be disclosed separately from an assessment of the information's materiality: initially, such information only covered disclosures relating to governance and risk management.[35] In its 2021 Annex, the TCFD recommends a wider scope of disclosure to include metrics such as Scope 1 and Scope 2 greenhouse gas (GHG) emissions independent of a materiality assessment, while recommending that Scope 3 GHG emissions remain subject to a materiality assessment.[36]

Regarding securities regulation, the International Organisation of Securities Commissions (IOSCO) has played a leading role in promoting disclosure requirements on a global scale. In 2021, the IOSCO issued a report on sustainability-related issuer disclosure, thereby aiming at promoting sustainability disclosures for the capital markets.[37] The IOSCO has positioned itself as the global standard-setter for ESG capital markets. It has attempted to place itself in a position to influence the development of disclosure requirements for sustainability information. Similarly, the International Accounting Standards Board (IASB), which promulgates the International Financial Reporting Standards (IFRS), has established the International Sustainability Standards Board (ISSB). Enhanced coordination between the IOSCO and ISSB would add more coherence and consistency between company sustainability disclosure standards and accounting reporting standards.

15.2.3 *Three Models of Cross-Border Disclosure Regulation*

With a view to regulating on a cross-border basis, national jurisdictions can adopt one or more of the three following models, thereby typically using a mix-and-match of different approaches as follows. First, the home state of the company approach, which is also referred to as the country-of-origin principle, mandates the application of the law of the country of origin of the company and restricts the application of the rules of the country of destination.[38] An example stems from the passporting mechanism prevailing among EU/EEA states. The country-of-origin approach between EU/EEA states is built on the idea of mutual recognition. Accordingly, the home country licence provides a passport that suffices for the entire Single Market,

---

[33] Darbellay and Caballero Cuevas 2023, 47.
[34] Hösli and Weber 2021.
[35] TCFD 2017, 14.
[36] TCFD 2021a, 7; TCFD 2021b.
[37] IOSCO 2021.
[38] Ralf 2006, 196.

meaning that no further authorisation is required to provide financial services in other EU/EEA Member States.[39]

At the global scale, regulators in home countries may apply their national law on an extraterritorial basis. For instance, whenever the unilateral application of the law to the entire multinational corporate group (consisting of many subsidiaries established in multiple jurisdictions) is justified, the home country would typically be the one applying its law to the entire corporate group on an extraterritorial basis.[40] In various areas of regulatory law, the public interest justifies the unilateral and extraterritorial reach of the home state's regulatory requirements.[41] In terms of sustainability disclosure regulation, it is understandable that home jurisdictions may seek an extraterritorial application of their laws. Indeed, it makes sense for home-state regulators to ensure that entities registered in their territories comply with the same sustainability disclosure requirements with respect to their conduct abroad.

Second, under the host state approach, foreign entities have to comply with host-state regulation.[42] Financial services providers may only access the market if they have registered with host-state authorities and obtained an authorisation or a license. This approach often results in an extraterritorial application of host-state law and regulation to foreign entities. For instance, the US Sarbanes–Oxley Act of 2002 had – at the time of its entry into force – unexpected extraterritorial implications for foreign issuers with securities listed on US exchanges.[43] Further, in the realm of derivatives regulation, the US Dodd–Frank Act of 2010 gives authority to the SEC and CFTC to prevent the evasion of US rules requiring the central clearing of derivatives by authorising US regulators to impose uniformity through the extraterritorial application of US law.[44] In terms of sustainability disclosure regulation, it is not surprising that host jurisdictions may consider applying their laws to the cross-border activities of foreign entities in host countries, thereby pursuing the regulatory objective of investor protection.

The extraterritorial application of laws, however, has drawbacks. If a host state applies its laws extraterritorially to foreign business entities and the latter are already subject to home-state regulation, they would be required to comply with the rules of two jurisdictions. Multiple compliance with two or more jurisdictions may impose unnecessary burdens on regulated entities or may even lead to conflicting obligations, thereby making it difficult to operate on a cross-border basis. This leads to consideration of a third approach based on an equivalence determination by the

---

[39] Alexander 2022, 17–18.
[40] Avi-Yonah 2003, 17.
[41] Ibid., 20.
[42] Host states may for instance be the countries where investors are based and/or the countries where securities are listed.
[43] Alexander et al. 2007, 3.
[44] Griffith 2014, 1329–30.

host-state regulator. A host state's decision to grant equivalence to the home country of a firm seeking market access into the host country market is based on a comparability assessment of the home country's regulatory standards, rules and laws. This can lead to exemption from certain compliance requirements for the firm whose home country's regulations and laws have been granted equivalence.

There is no uniformly accepted global approach for granting market access to foreign financial firms. A recurring issue in the EU-US financial services dialogue concerns the issues related to the extraterritorial application of local laws and the solution provided by exempting foreign entities from host-country requirements provided that they are subject to acceptable regulatory oversight in their home jurisdiction.[45]

Alternatively, some consideration might be given to the principle of reciprocity. Reciprocity would condition cross-border coordination on mutual recognition of regulations and laws by home and host countries. Nevertheless, mutual recognition has its weaknesses.[46]

As a subset of the equivalence approach, the theory of substituted compliance consists of accepting foreign legal requirements as an acceptable substitute for domestic requirements.[47] This involves avoiding the requirement to register with host-state regulators and being deemed in compliance with host-state law and regulation by complying with their home-state law and regulation.[48] Substituted compliance is the opportunity for a foreign entity to substitute compliance with its home-state regulator for compliance with host-state regulation.[49] Host-state regulators may make their determinations by taking into account several factors for determining comparability, including (i) comparable scope and objectives, (ii) comparable comprehensiveness of regulation and (iii) comparable supervisory capacity and enforcement authority.[50]

Selective substituted compliance may be designed as to give regulators the opportunity to influence substantive components of foreign regulatory systems or as to grant exemptive relief without regard to the quality of supervision in foreign jurisdictions.[51] One possibility is to perform a subjective evaluation of the quality of supervisory oversight in individual jurisdictions.[52]

For instance, the SEC did not offer a blanket exemption but merely an exemption for foreign issuers that comply with IFRS standards.[53] Further, substituted compliance consists of the primary instrument of extraterritoriality in the Dodd–Frank

---

[45] Alexander et al. 2007, 22.
[46] Yadav and Turing 2015.
[47] Jackson 2015, 178.
[48] Artamonov 2015, 209.
[49] Griffith 2014, 1334.
[50] Ibid.
[51] Jackson 2015, 182.
[52] Ibid., 179.
[53] Ibid., 177.

Act's OTC derivatives reforms.[54] Selective substituted compliance can be tailored to discourage regulatory arbitrage.[55] In fact, it promotes a regulatory diversity in the context of derivatives regulation while combating regulatory arbitrage through the exercise of extraterritorial jurisdiction.[56]

Regarding the EU equivalence approach, the EU Commission examines whether the third-country state complies with international standards that are implemented in the EU. For instance, the European Market Infrastructure Regulation (EMIR) established an equivalence regime, which provided the EU Commission with the power to declare that the legal, supervisory and enforcement arrangements of a third country are equivalent to the EMIR requirements towards derivatives transactions.[57] While making an equivalence determination, the EU Commission can request ESMA's technical advice with respect to third-country regulatory frameworks, which consists of a line-by-line analysis of the similarities and differences between the requirements as well as an objective-based approach.[58]

Further, the equivalence approach may be divided into equivalence subject to dispute resolution *versus* policy-based equivalence. If it is subject to dispute resolution, it is possible to challenge the host state's refusal to grant equivalence in court. If it is policy-based, granting equivalence is discretionary for the host state and no legal appeal is possible against the decision. The EU equivalence process has been policy-based. The challenges it can generate include the contingent nature of the Commission equivalence decision, the opacity of the equivalence process, and its limited justiciability.[59] In fact, the EU explicitly adopted the policy of equivalence in 2003 as a market access mechanism to assist in assessing the quality and acceptability of third-country regulations as part of its decision to accept or decline market access. Following the June 2016 decision of the United Kingdom to leave the EU (Brexit), the EU has used the process of granting equivalence as a political bargaining tool.[60] The political nature of the equivalence assessments has also affected other third countries such as Switzerland.[61]

In terms of sustainability disclosure regulation, since there has been a fragmentation of international standards and national rules, the equivalence approach may be useful for jurisdictions that have relatively similar regulatory requirements and processes. Equivalence decisions can lead over time to regulatory convergence.

---

[54] Artamonov 2015.

[55] Tafara and Peterson 2007, 67.

[56] Griffith 2014, 1294.

[57] Artamonov 2015, 217; Art. 13 of the Council Regulation 648/2012 of 4 July 2012 on OTC derivatives, central counterparties and trade repositories, OJ 2012 No. L201, 27 July 2012. See also Yadav and Turing 2015, 11–12.

[58] Artamonov 2015, 218.

[59] Moloney 2023, 858.

[60] Conac 2019, 77.

[61] Ibid.

15.3 EU LEGISLATIVE DEVELOPMENTS ON SUSTAINABLE DISCLOSURE REGULATION

15.3.1 *Major Developments*

The EU has been at the forefront of sustainable corporate governance, in particular by reforming disclosure regulation.[62] The desire to work towards the development of a sustainable economy was one of the political objectives set by the European Council in Lisbon at its special meeting in March 2000.[63] One year later, in 2001, the European Commission published its Green Paper, in which it highlighted the increasing trends of large companies to act and assume their corporate social responsibility (CSR), in particular by doing reporting.[64] At the same time, some international initiatives were gaining attention from major companies. These international developments – in parallel with the EU's increasing focus on CSR and environmental reporting – have had a direct impact on the legislation adopted by the EU from 2014 onwards. Moreover, one of the points to be improved was the disclosure of social and environmental information by companies. Information needed to be published to '[...] facilitate engagement with stakeholders and the identification of material sustainability risks'.[65]

A few Member States had already taken steps in this direction prior to the call of the European Parliament to take action. The French legislator had adopted important CSR instruments since 2001.[66] For instance, the Grenelle II Act adopted in 2010 imposed an extra-financial reporting obligation for large companies listed on the stock exchange.[67] The extra-financial reporting framework was, at the time, focussed on 42 reporting indicators.[68] Among other Member States, Denmark also introduced a disclosure requirement for non-financial information in 2008.[69] The legislative initiatives were adopted under the pressure from civil society and

---

[62] Conac 2022, 112.

[63] European Council, Presidency Conclusion (Lisbon, 23/24 March 2000) EUCO 10/00 (2000): 'The Union has today set itself a new strategic goal for the next decade: to become the most competitive and dynamic knowledge-based economy in the world capable of sustainable economic growth with more and better jobs and greater social cohesion.'

[64] European Commission 2001, para. 66.

[65] European Commission 2011, 11.

[66] Delbard 2008; Schweizerisches Institut für Rechtsvergleichung 2018, 27; Knudsen and Moon 2017, 85; Doucin 2017, 480–481.

[67] Art. 225 of the French Legislative Act No. 2010–788 of 12 July 2010 on national commitment for the environment, NOR: DEVX0822225L, OJ 2010 No. 610, 13 July 2010 (Loi n 2010–788 du 12 juillet 2010 portant engagement national pour l'environnement, NOR: DEVX0822225L: JO n 610, 13 Juillet 2010); see generally Szabo and Sorensen 2015.

[68] French Legislative Act on national commitment for the environment (n 66); Schweizerisches Institut für Rechtsvergleichung 2018, 27.

[69] Danish Legislative Act No. 1403 of 27 December 2008 on the amendment of the Annual Accounts Act, j.nr. 2008–0017695 (Lov n 1403 af 27 December 2008 om om ændring af årsregnskabsloven, j.nr. 2008–0017695). See also Buhmann 2013.

different stakeholders.[70] The main difference underlined by the literature between the two approaches is the level of flexibility given to firms.[71] In Denmark, the choice of the model was left at the discretion of the firms, while in France, the requirements were specified in detail by the legislator.[72]

15.3.2 *Non-Financial Reporting as a Regulatory Concept*

In 2014, the EU legislator amended the Accounting Directive by adopting the Non-Financial Reporting Directive (NFRD).[73] The European legislator defined the notion of Non-Financial Reporting (NFR) as referring to 'a non-financial statement containing information to the extent necessary for an understanding of the undertaking's development, performance, position, and impact of its activity, relating to, as a minimum, environmental, social and employee matters, respect for human rights, anti-corruption, and bribery matters'.[74] The adoption of the NFRD marked the first legislative action at the EU level for disclosing a company's non-financial activities.[75] The NFRD made it mandatory to disclose environmental and social information that is relevant to a company's economic activity.[76] However, the NFRD was only applicable to certain large undertakings and groups and not applicable to small and medium enterprises.[77]

The EU NFRD adopted a hybrid model which permitted reliance on standards derived from market practice with some new legally binding rules.[78] In terms of disclosure obligations, companies were required to make a statement containing information of a non-financial nature. Reporting requirements ranged from business models of the undertakings in question to pursued goals and policies, including due diligence processes that had been implemented.[79]

In addition, the European legislator opted for a 'comply or explain' approach, that is, a methodology that combines self-regulation and hard law. Accordingly, if they were required to provide information regarding, for instance, the policies put in place to reduce their environmental footprint, a company that decided not to publish this information had to provide a clear and reasoned explanation for not doing so.[80]

---

[70] See Doucin 2017, 481.
[71] Szabo and Sorensen 2015.
[72] Blin-Franchomme 2015.
[73] NFRD 2014.
[74] Ibid., Art. 1(1) as modifying Directive 2013/34/EU by inserting Art. 19a.
[75] Scanlan 2021, 26.
[76] NFRD 2014, preamble para. 8.
[77] Ibid., preamble para. 14. NFRD 2014 imposed a reporting obligation on large firms which exceeded an average number of 500 employees during the financial year and had a balance sheet total of € 20 million or a net turnover of € 40 million.
[78] See Wagner 2018.
[79] Art. 1(1) of the NFRD 2014, as modifying Directive 2013/34/EU by inserting art. 19a(1)(b)(c).
[80] Ibid. See discussion in Ahern 2016, 620.

Furthermore, the European legislator gave the choice to the Member States, when implementing the Directive, to allow, in exceptional cases, companies to not have to publish certain pieces of information covered by the NFR duty, if '[...] the disclosure of such information would be seriously prejudicial to the commercial position of the undertaking [...]'.[81] Altogether, the NFRD followed a minimum harmonisation approach that left the question of which model to follow to the discretion of companies.[82]

15.3.3 *The Corporate Sustainability Reporting Directive: A Paradigm Change*

In April 2021, the Commission published a proposal to amend the NFR framework. In November 2022, the Corporate Sustainability Reporting Directive (CSRD) was enacted as a part of the EU Sustainable Finance package.[83] The revised directive amends four existing pieces of legislation as follows: the Accounting Directive, the Transparency Directive, the Audit Directive, the Audit Regulation. The scope of the directive is significantly extended to apply to a larger number of European and non-European companies listed and operating in the EU-regulated markets.[84]

The CSRD marks a shift of paradigm in corporate sustainability reporting. Above all, it moves to a hard law model. Companies that have to report under the CSRD will be required to use a set of sustainability reporting standards developed by the European Financial Reporting Advisory Groupe (EFRAG).[85] The CSRD departs from the previous qualification of sustainability information as non-financial. In so doing, the EU seeks to treat sustainability reporting on an equal footing with financial reporting. The CSRD consistently requires the publication of sustainability-related information through the management report.[86] In order to guarantee the reliability of the reported information, the CSRD mandates independent auditing

---

[81] NFRD 2014; La Torre et al. 2018. For example, in Belgium, use was made of this provision: art. 3(6), para. 4; see also: Gollier 2018.

[82] NFRD 2014, preamble para. 9: '[...], undertakings which are subject to this Directive may rely on national frameworks, Union-based frameworks such as the Eco-Management and Audit Scheme (EMAS), or international [...]'. In this regard, different institutional frameworks can be referred to, such as the United Nations (UN) Global Compact, the Guiding Principles on Business and Human Rights implementing the UN 'Protect, Respect and Remedy' Framework, the OECD Guidelines for Multinational Enterprises, the International Organisation for Standardisation's ISO 26000, the ILO's Tripartite Declaration of principles concerning multinational enterprises and social policy, the Global Reporting Initiative, or other recognised international frameworks.

[83] CSRD 2022 (n 3).

[84] Ibid. Art. 1 as amending Art. 19a(1) and art. 29a(1) of Directive 2013/34/EU.

[85] EFRAG, Draft European Sustainability Reporting Standards: Due Process Note, November 2022; see also EFRAG, Draft European Sustainability Reporting Standards: Explanatory Note of How Draft ESRS Take Account of the Initiative and Legislation Listed in Article 1 (8) of the CSRD Adding Article 29(b)-5 to the Accounting Directive, November 2022.

[86] CSRD 2022 (n 3) preamble para. 79.

and certification of the reports.[87] To clarify its far-reaching approach, it explicitly adheres to the double materiality perspective.[88] Accordingly, reporting companies have to disclose both exposure of the company to ESG and companies impact on ESG. Owing to the fact that the selection of a disclosure regulation model reflects the legal approach to corporate governance, mandatory disclosure requirements relating to more sustainability-related information than before support the modern view of the corporation. Accordingly, this approach falls within the evolving concept of the company as seeking a corporate purpose. This is transforming how companies approach their decision-making processes by adopting governance mechanisms while taking into account the interest of stakeholders.

15.3.4 *Financial Sector–Specific Sustainable Disclosure Regulation under the Sustainable Finance Action Plan*

Disclosure has so far been the main regulatory tool deployed in the realm of EU sustainable finance regulation.[89] While corporate reporting as addressed by the CSRD is part of the EU Sustainable Finance Action Plan, there are also other types of information covered by the law that are more specifically related the financial sector. The cornerstones of the sustainability disclosure regulation relating to financial institutions consist of the SFDR and the Taxonomy Regulation, which are complementary to and aligned with the CSRD.[90]

The High Level Expert Group (HLEG) on Sustainable Finance appointed by the Commission in 2016 made important recommendations in its final report in January 2018.[91] The HLEG report recommended enhanced disclosure as one of the measures and governance practices that could be explored and made a proposal for a green taxonomy so that definitions of green assets are set by official public bodies and not the banks themselves.[92] In March 2018, the Commission published a Sustainable Finance Action Plan with a view to incentivising investors to make sustainable investments.[93]

The EU introduced the SFDR with a view to imposing sustainability disclosure obligations on banks and other financial institutions.[94] The SFDR requires them

---

[87] Ibid.

[88] Ibid., preamble para. 29 (stating that the double materiality perspective is often misunderstood and clarifying the fact that the directive 2013/34/EU requires to report both on the impacts of the activities of the undertaking on people and the environment, and on how sustainability matters affect the undertaking).

[89] Moloney 2023, 58.

[90] SFDR (n 1); Regulation 2020/852/EU of the European Parliament and of the Council of 18 June 2020 on the establishment of a framework to facilitate sustainable investment, and amending Regulation 2019/2088/EU, OJ L 198, 22.6.2020 (hereinafter referred to as 'Taxonomy Regulation'); CSRD 2022 (n 3).

[91] European Commission High Level Experts Group on Sustainable Finance 2018.

[92] Alexander and Fisher 2019.

[93] European Commission 2018.

[94] See Busch 2021; Hooghiemstra 2020.

to be transparent about their integration of sustainability risks into their investment policies, remuneration policies, general pre-contractual disclosures and their marketing of financial instruments. Articles 8 and 9 of the SFDR are more remarkable, as they impose additional requirements for those financial products, including investment funds, that promote sustainable characteristics or have sustainability objectives, respectively.[95] The SFDR has been completed by regulatory technical standards (RTS) adopted by the European Commission to ensure that sustainability-related disclosures in the financial services sector are sufficiently clear, concise and prominent to enable end investors to make informed decisions.[96]

In addition, the Taxonomy Regulation supports the EU objective of reorienting capital flows toward a more sustainable economy. With respect to financial institutions, it established the framework of criteria to be met in order to consider an activity or a product as environmentally sustainable. So far, the focus has been limited on environmental risk. The idea is to expand it in the future with a view to involving all ESG aspects.[97] While transparency standards have existed long before they were amended to incorporate sustainability requirements, green taxonomies have emerged in recent years as a new, unorthodox instrument of financial regulation. They are meant as dictionaries of those investments and economic activities that are environmentally sustainable, that is, that can be labelled as green. To determine those activities that are environmentally sustainable, the Taxonomy Regulation refers to six environmental objectives: climate change mitigation, climate change adaptation, the sustainable use and protection of water and marine resources, the transition to a circular economy, pollution prevention and control and the protection and restoration of biodiversity and ecosystems.[98] In this respect, the EU goes beyond other taxonomies focussing on climate change. To qualify, an economic activity should substantially contribute to one or more of these environmental objectives, not do any significantly harm to any of those objectives, be carried out in compliance with minimum human rights and labour safeguards and comply with the technical screening criteria of the actual EU Taxonomy to be adopted by the European Commission via delegated acts.

15.4 SUSTAINABLE DISCLOSURE REGULATION AND CROSS-BORDER COORDINATION

15.4.1 *UK, US and Swiss Law Approaches to Sustainable Disclosure Regulation*

This section summarises the ongoing developments relating to sustainable disclosure regulation in the UK, the US and Switzerland. The comparative analysis

[95] See further de Arriba-Sellier and Van Caenegem, Chapter 10 in this volume.
[96] SFDR RTS (n 2), preamble para. 1.
[97] Taxonomy Regulation (n 88), preamble para. 6.
[98] Ibid., Art. 9.

underlines the major differences between the approaches, thereby emphasising the need to select a model of cross-border coordination. The question arises as to whether national law should provide a legal basis for cross-border coordination with other national authorities, and also whether to create a regulatory mechanism for national authorities to coordinate and interact with international financial standard-setting bodies.

Similar to the EU SFDR, the UK's Green Finance Technical Standards Commission has also recommended that sustainability risks should be subject to mandatory disclosure requirements under the UK's post-Brexit prospectus, market abuse and *ad hoc* disclosure requirements. The Financial Conduct Authority (FCA) consulted in 2021 on how to incorporate the sustainability-related disclosures of the Sustainable Finance Disclosure Regulation into the UK listing rules.[99] The FCA issued a policy statement in late 2021 that provides an overview for the application of the climate-related financial disclosure requirements and how they can be extended to issuers of standard-listed shares and Global Depositary Receipts representing equity shares.[100]

The FCA will likely recognise the financial materiality of sustainability-related information in terms of the UK market abuse rules.[101] Given the increasing importance of sustainable finance to UK financial regulation, the FCA will define the situations in which sustainability-related information is deemed to be inside information, that is, likely to have a significant effect on the prices of an issuer's financial instruments, if such information were made public. Another question relevant to the UK market abuse regime is to what extent sustainability-related information is subject to *ad hoc* disclosure requirements. Finally, as sustainability-related information is increasingly recognised as financially material to an issuer, the FCA may well consider it to be 'specific' or 'precise' information as defined under UK criminal insider dealing law. As a result, corporate issuers have substantial criminal and civil liability exposure for failing to disclose sustainability-related information (or mis-reporting it) if the information is likely to have a significant impact on the price of the issuer's securities. With respect to corporate law, the UK 2006 Companies Act Section 172 continues to primarily focus on the interest of shareholders, nevertheless while also listing other stakeholders. In so doing, the UK moved toward the enlightened shareholder value (ESV) model.[102] This has an effect on the scope of sustainability information that has to be disclosed.

Recent US regulatory initiatives have required the disclosure of climate finance risks. For example, in March 2022, the Securities and Exchange Commission (SEC) proposed a rule that will impose transparency obligations for publicly listed

---

[99] See FCA 2021a.

[100] FCA 2021b; *d* also for enhanced climate-related disclosures by asset managers, life insurers and FCA-regulated pension providers FCA 2021c.

[101] In relation to financial materiality of sustainability-related information, see Ruth 2019.

[102] Helleringer and Skinner, Chapter 4 in this volume.

companies in the US related to their climate risk exposure.[103] Given the integrated disclosure system prevailing in the US, the SEC's proposed rules would apply to all listed companies, which not only include large systemically-important banks, but also other issuers from various sectors. The SEC proposal establishes a mandatory sustainability disclosure regime that broadly follows the framework proposed by the Task Force on Climate-Related Disclosures (TCFD). If adopted, the SEC's proposed rule will require securities issuers to disclose all climate-related financial risks likely to affect their businesses in their annual reports, including relevant information on governance and risk management processes.[104] Issuers will have to be transparent about the climate-related risks and opportunities, including in their financial statements.[105] Disclosure of scope 1 and 2 emissions will be required, while value chain emissions disclosure will only be mandatory where those scope 3 emissions are material to the business.[106] Also, the proposal only partly responds to widespread doubts about the quality, methodological underpinnings, comparability and integrity of corporate sustainability metrics, which have represented a major obstacle to having effective disclosure requirements for climate finance risks. Regarding scope 1 and 2, the SEC's proposed rules would require an attestation report by an independent third party, which will at least provide limited assurance in a first phase and then scale up to reasonable assurance after a transition period.[107] Despite the high likelihood of judicial challenges, the SEC's rule may be considered on a par with the US Supreme Court's definition of financial materiality, which centres on disclosure of information that a 'reasonable investor' would view as significant in making an investment decision.[108]

The more cautious US approach, which focusses only on disclosing climate finance risks, can be contrasted with the EU approach, which involves a series of laws and regulations requiring disclosures of most ESG risks. Therefore, the EU disclosure rules cover a broader definition of sustainability risks, by reference to three dimensions of ESG. Moreover, the US approach is essentially limited to disclosure and is not combined with corporate law reforms at the state level. Overall, while a couple of US states have adopted provisions that include some form of stakeholder

---

[103] SEC 2022.

[104] Ibid., 21336.

[105] Ibid., 21349.

[106] Ibid., 21468; see TCFD 2021a, 7.

[107] SEC's proposed rules, 21395.

[108] See, for example, Securities Act of 1933, Section 7, 15 USC § 77g and Securities Exchange Act of 1934, Sections 12, 13, and 15, 15 USC §§ 78l, 78m, and 78o (regarding SEC's authority to promulgate disclosure requirements that are necessary or appropriate in the public interest or for the protection of investors); see Susko 2018, 10989, 10990, 11000 (analysing the uncertain judicial treatment of compelled commercial disclosures and proposing a return to a balanced rational basis review so that the SEC can adopt mandatory disclosure requirements in the realm of corporate sustainability reporting); Strine 2022 (stating that the SEC's statutory authority to require climate-related financial disclosures is firmly rooted in the statutory text).

governance, most US states still rely on the more traditional shareholder-centric view of the firm.[109]

In Switzerland, the financial market authority FINMA has amended its circulars in July 2021 to include the disclosure of climate-related reporting based on TCFD recommendations.[110] The scope of FINMA's disclosure requirements is limited to regulated financial intermediaries. Corporate sustainability reporting is part of the corporate law framework. In this regard, the Swiss Code of Obligations (SCO) was amended in 2020 to include an obligation to disclose non-financial information.[111] It is worthwhile noting that these amendments were based to a great extent on the EU NFRD approach. In so doing, this gives the advantage of not imposing additional compliance burdens on Swiss companies who are also subjected to the extraterritorial reach of the EU requirements. However, the framework is already outdated at the time of entry into force of the EU CSRD. Therefore, the Swiss sustainable disclosure regulation regime may eventually lag behind. With respect to international standards, Switzerland seeks to adopt TCFD-aligned disclosure requirements. The Federal Ordinance on climate reporting makes a static reference to the 2017 TCFD recommendations and its 2021 Annex.[112] In terms of corporate governance, Swiss corporate law tends to follow the enlightened shareholder value (ESV) model. Adherence to the Business Judgment Rule has awarded some level of discretion to company boards with a view to taking into account the interest of stakeholders.

15.4.2 *The Preferred Model of Cross-Border Sustainable Disclosure Regulation*

Since the EU, the UK, the US and Switzerland diverge in the regulation of ESG disclosure, it is crucial to select a particular model of cross-border coordination. The preferred model should seek the overarching objective of investor protection while also taking into account other stakeholder interests. The features of the three main models should be analysed with these objectives in mind, thereby allowing an assessment of which of the three models of cross-border disclosure regulation are the most suitable.

First, the preferred model discourages regulatory arbitrage. The divergences between the EU, the UK, the US and Switzerland in the regulation of ESG

---

[109] Helleringer and Skinner, Chapter 4 in this volume (stating that most US corporations incorporate in the state of Delaware and that the Delaware General Corporation Law (DGCL) has not directly taken up ESG).

[110] FINMA, Amendments to Circular 2016/01 on the public disclosure of banks and 2016/02 on the public disclosure of insurance companies (May 2021).

[111] Art. 964a–c of the Federal Act of 30 March 1911 on the Amendment of the Swiss Civil Code (Part Five: The Code of Obligations), SR 220.

[112] Art. 3 para. 1 of the Federal Ordinance on Climate Disclosures (OCD) of the Swiss Federal Council, as adopted by the Federal Council in November 2022 and entering into force on 1st January 2024, SR 221.434.

disclosure result in the risk of regulatory arbitrage. Due to different rules, regulated actors may pick the jurisdiction where compliance costs are lower. It is indeed problematic if some states have lower standards. The risk exists in the three models of cross-border disclosure regulation. The only way to eliminate regulatory arbitrage would be to achieve global convergence, raising the question of how to reach a convergence of standards. The end goal should be to achieve standardisation internationally. However, the diversity of sustainability disclosure regulations will not be overcome in the near future. Nevertheless, it is argued that regulatory arbitrage may be reduced under the equivalence approach. According to selective substituted compliance, legal systems are recognised provided that they are equivalent in quality. This approach limits the incentive for national jurisdictions to lower standards to attract businesses.

Second, the best model promotes competitiveness in the realm of achieving sustainability objectives. There are two sides of the same coin. On the one hand, competition and regulation are intertwined. The diversity of laws and regulations remains a positive point as we are in a trial and error phase. On the other hand, the issue arises as to promoting competitive markets, that is, ensuring a level playing field where all market participants compete on an equal footing. This is linked with the question of regulatory arbitrage. States would like to ensure that actors do not move elsewhere.

Third, the preferred model promotes standardisation. This contributes to achieving the regulatory objective of investor protection. Indeed, users of information need comparable, relevant and reliable ESG information. The question arises as to whether substituted compliance may be promoted as a way of promoting standardisation. For instance, selective substituted compliance may be realised by looking at the implementation of international standards. While assessing the quality of foreign law regulation, it makes sense to take into account the implementation of international standards, for instance TCFD-aligned disclosure. Also, the ISSB is developing a comprehensive global framework for sustainability-related disclosure standards. Since the IOSCO has expertise in comparing regulatory regimes, a possibility may come from strengthening the role of the IOSCO in promoting cross-border regulation.[113]

Finally, the best model promotes the integration of ESG capital markets. There is a need to avoid market fragmentation. 'Host country regulations are often an excuse for financial protectionism.'[114] The equivalence approach may be used as a liberalisation tool provided that it is designed to facilitate cross-border activities.[115] Also, the objective should consist of avoiding duplicative and conflicting rules. Drawing upon the application of substituted compliance in the case of the

---

[113] Conac 2019, 79.
[114] Persaud 2010.
[115] Conac 2019, 76.

transatlantic agreement between the ESMA and the CFTC with respect to clearing derivatives, we argue that this could also be achieved in the area of ESG.

15.4.3 *The Benefits of the Equivalence Model in Light of the Extraterritorial Reach of EU Sustainable Disclosure Regulation*

One of the most groundbreaking aspects of the EU CSRD is its extraterritorial reach, which is commonly referred to as the Brussels effect. This directive is a particularly good example of a mix-and-match of different approaches, including both the host state model and the equivalence model. Concern has thus been raised about the application of the equivalence approach to the NFR framework.

The scope implies extraterritorial reach. Owing to the reference to Arts. 2 and 3 of the Directive 2013/34/EU, the approach is aligned with the regime prevailing for the disclosure of financial information. The CSRD covers both EU and non-EU issuers whose securities are listed on EU-regulated markets and the disclosure obligations apply to the entire enterprise.[116] This means that large third-country firms that have debt securities listed on EU-regulated markets will be subject to the rules regardless of the place of listing of their shares.[117] It covers large EU undertakings and third-country undertakings with substantial activity on the EU Single Market with a European subsidiary or a European branch. The fact that the presence of third-country undertakings implies the disclosure of a sustainability report by the parent company applying to the entire enterprise was debated in the legislative process. This is a question of the entity versus enterprise approach. The EU decided to require reporting at the consolidated level. If an EU subsidiary or branch is subject to the CSRD, the third-country parent company is indirectly subject to it. To this end, an intermediate solution was found. The subsidiary or branch must make its best efforts to obtain the necessary information from the third-country undertaking. If not all required information is provided by the third-country undertaking, the subsidiary or branch provides the information in its possession and indicates that the third-country undertaking did not make the required information available.[118] Due to the extraterritorial application of the CSRD, this approach corresponds to the trend of going for host country regulation, which is unfortunately a step back in terms of global integrated markets.

Nevertheless, the CSRD provides for a legal basis for the equivalence approach.[119] Accordingly, the Commission should be empowered to establish a mechanism for the determination of equivalence of sustainability reporting standards applied by third-country issuers of securities. The idea is to seek consistency with accounting

---

[116] Art. 1 of the CSRD 2022 (n 3) as amending Art. 19a(1) and art. 29a(1) of Directive 2013/34/EU.

[117] Conac 2022, 115.

[118] Art. 1 of the CSRD 2022, preamble para. 20.

[119] Ibid., preamble para. 24 and Art. 2 as amending Art. 23 para. 4 of Directive 2004/109/EC.

standards. This has the advantage of consistency but misses the fact that sustainability disclosure regulation is different from traditional disclosure requirements in the capital markets.

In particular, the CSRD has addressed the topic of the exempted subsidiary undertaking[120] as well as the exempted parent undertaking.[121] For instance, accordingly, there is a possibility of exempting a subsidiary undertaking on the basis of the sustainability reporting of the parent undertaking. The exemption should not apply to large listed undertakings. Finally, due to the concern of the competitiveness of EU markets, there is a possibility to exempt a parent undertaking established in the EU when its subsidiary in a third-country applies sustainability reporting abroad, which is a form of deference to host country regulation from the perspective of the enterprise.

In sum, the use of the concept of equivalence may help the EU export its sustainable disclosure regulation to other jurisdictions and promote the widespread adoption of international standards.[122] There is a need to strike the right balance between adopting a far-reaching sustainability disclosure regulation framework and accepting foreign rules as sufficient. Further, the standards may avoid disproportionate compliance burdens on companies by taking into account the work of global standard-setting initiatives for sustainability reporting.

15.5 CONCLUSION

This chapter shed light on recent developments in the realm of sustainable disclosure regulation. We analysed the shift of paradigm relating to sustainability reporting disclosure requirements in the context of the evolving debate over whether company boards have a duty to focus mainly on shareholder wealth maximisation and/or on broader ESG stakeholder interests. Accordingly, companies are required to disclose more information to the public, including both their exposure to ESG risks and their impacts on achieving sustainability objectives. Nevertheless, even under the shareholder primacy view of the firm, the concept of financial materiality may be expanded to encompass a broader array of information, including ESG information, that is necessary for investors to make an informed investment decision. This chapter addressed the international standards of sustainability disclosure from a cross-border perspective with a focus on EU legislative developments and how they contrast with those in Switzerland, the United Kingdom and the United States with a view to assessing the feasibility for developing a framework to support global convergence. The regulatory approach for cross-border coordination is an important regulatory consideration in light of the divergences between various jurisdictions in the regulation of ESG disclosure. Emphasis was laid on EU legislative

[120] Ibid. as amending Art. 19a(9) of Directive 2013/34/EU.
[121] Ibid. as amending Art. 29a(8) of Directive 2013/34/EU.
[122] Conac 2019, 76.

developments in the field of corporate sustainability reporting, given the fact that the EU has been at the forefront of sustainable disclosure regulation. The chapter further suggests that the extraterritorial application of the EU sustainability disclosure regulations under the CSRD will influence the emerging sustainable finance architecture. Finally, we concluded that selective substituted compliance may help address the cross-border aspects relating to ESG capital markets.

REFERENCES

Ahern, D. (2016), 'Turning up the heat: EU sustainability goals and the role of the reporting under the Non-Financial Reporting Directive', 13 *European Company and Financial Law Review*, 599–630.

Alexander, K. (2022), 'International financial regulation: Post-2010 developments covering certain financial market transactions and market access principles', *OECD Background Paper*, 17–18.

Alexander, K. and Fisher, P. G. (2019), 'Banking regulation and sustainability' in F.-J. B. Van den Boezem, C. Jansen and B. Schuijling (eds.), *Sustainability and Financial Markets* (Alphen aan den Rijn: Wolters Kluwer), 7–33.

Alexander, K., Ferran, E., Jackson, H. E., and Moloney, N. (2007), 'A report on the transatlantic financial services regulatory dialogue', Harvard John M. Olin Center for Law, Economics and Business, Discussion Paper 576.

Artamonov, A. (2015), 'Cross-border application of OTC derivatives rules: Revisiting the substituted compliance approach', 1 *Journal of Financial Regulation*, 206–225.

Avi-Yonah, R. S. (2003), 'National regulation of multinational enterprises: An essay on comity, extraterritoriality, and harmonization', 42 *Columbia Journal of Transnational Law*, 5–34.

Blin-Franchomme, M.-P. (2015), 'Le droit économique au soutien de la protection de l'environnement: les apports de la loi Grenelle 2 à la gouvernance des entreprises et des consommateurs', 5 *Revue juridique de l'environnement*, 129–176.

Buhmann, K. (2013), 'The Danish CSR reporting requirement as reflexive law: Employing CSR as a modality to promote public policy', 2 *European Business Law Review*, 187–216.

CDBS (Climate Disclosure Standards Board) (2020), 'Falling short?: Why environmental and climate-related disclosures under the EU Non-Financial Reporting Directive must improve', May, 8, available at: https://bit.ly/3KzyVAp (accessed 17 April 2024).

Busch, D. (2021), 'Sustainability disclosure in the EU financial sector', 70 European Banking Institute Working Paper Series, available at: https://papers.ssrn.com/sol3/papers.cfm?abstract_id=3650407 (accessed 22 December 2021).

Christensen, H. B., Hail, L. and Leuz C., (2019) 'Adoption of CSR and sustainability reporting standards: Economic analysis and review', 26169 NBER Working Papers, 8–10, available at: https://bit.ly/4eciuHU (accessed 17 April 2024).

Cobbaut, E. (2018), 'La loi du 3 septembre 2017 relative a la publication d'informations non financières: une mise en perspective', 3 *Revue de Droit Social*, 397–455.

Coibion, A. and Filbiche, J. (2021), 'La publication d'informations non financières et le rôle des organes sociaux des sociétés belges' in T. Tilquin (ed.), *Les instruments de droit des sociétés et de droit financier de l'économie durable* (Brussels: Larcier), 61–90.

Conac, P.-H. (2019), 'The International Organisation of Securities Commission (IOSCO), Europe, Brexit, and rethinking cross-border regulation: A call for a World Finance Organisation', 17 *European Company and Financial Law Review*, 72–98.

Conac, P.-H. (2022), 'Sustainable corporate governance in the EU: Reasonable global ambitions?', 4 *Revue Européenne du Droit*, 111–118.

Darbellay, A. and Caballero Cuevas, Y. (2023), 'The materiality of sustainability information under capital markets law', [2023] *Swiss Review of Business and Financial Market Law*, 44–59.

de Arriba-Sellier, N. and Van Caenegem, A., 'Sustainability-related materiality in the SFDR', Chapter 10 in this volume.

de Cendra de Larragán, J. (2017), 'EU climate change law and consumers', 1 *Revue européenne de droit de la consummation – REDC*, 149–176.

Delbard, O. (2008), 'CSR legislation in France and the European regulatory paradox: An analysis of EU CSR policy and sustainability reporting practice', 4 *Corporate Governance: The International Journal of Business in Society*, 397–405.

Doucin, M. (2017), 'À petits pas et à reculons, les mutations en cours de la soft law' in I. Daugareilh (ed.), *La responsabilité sociale de l'entreprise, vecteur d'un droit de la mondialisation?* (Brussels: Bruylant), 473–486.

European Commission (2001), 'The European Green Paper: Promoting a European Framework for Corporate Social responsibility', (COM 2001) 366, 18 July, available at: https://bit.ly/45eDzgQ (accessed 17 April 2024).

European Commission (2011), 'Communication for a Renewed EU Strategy 2011–14 for Corporate Social Responsibility', (COM 2011) 681 final, 25 October, available at: https://bit.ly/4bNKMqw (accessed 17 April 2024).

European Commission (2018), 'Action Plan: Financing Sustainable Growth', (COM 2018) 97 final, 8 March, available at: https://bit.ly/497N6GU (accessed 17 April 2024).

European Commission High Level Experts Group on Sustainable Finance (2018), 'Financing a Sustainable European Economy', January, available at: https://bit.ly/3IQc5U9 (accessed 17 April 2024).

Financial Conduct Authority (FCA) (2021a), 'Enhancing climate-related disclosures by standard listed companies and seeking views on ESG topics in capital markets', Consultation Paper CP21/18, June, available at: www.fca.org.uk/publication/consultation/cp21-18.pdf (accessed 17 April 2024).

FCA (Financial Conduct Authority) (2021b), 'Enhancing climate-related disclosures by standard listed companies, Policy Statement PS21/23', December, available at: www.fca.org.uk/publication/policy/ps21-23.pdf (accessed 17 April 2024).

FCA (Financial Conduct Authority) (2021c), 'Enhancing climate-related disclosures by asset managers, life insurers and FCA-regulated pension providers', Policy Statement PS21/24, December, available at: www.fca.org.uk/publication/policy/ps21-24.pdf (accessed 17 April 2024).

Gasser, A. (2020), 'La finance verte labellisée pour les épargnants : l'exemple scandinave du cygne blanc à suivre pour la création d'un écolabel européen', [2020] *Revue Internationale des Services Financiers – International Journal of Financial Services*, 40–48.

George, G., Haas, M. R., McGahan, A. M., Schillebeeckx, S. J. D. and Tracey, P. (2022), 'Purpose in the for-profit firm: A review of and framework for management research', 49 *Journal of Management*, 3–50.

Gollier, J.-M. (2018), 'Publication d'informations non financières. Commentaire de la loi du 3 septembre 2017', 11 *Journal des Tribunaux*, 241–250.

Griffith, S. J. (2014), 'Substituted compliance and systemic risk: How to make a global market in derivatives regulation', 98 *Minnesota Law Review*, 1291–1373.

Helbing, T. (2010), 'What are externalities?', 4 *Finance & Development*, 48–49.

Henderson, R. and Ramanna K. (2015), 'Do managers have a role to play in sustaining the institutions of capitalism?', 20 Center for Effective Public Management at Brookings Institution, available at: https://bit.ly/3Ttyv3I (accessed 17 April 2024).

Hooghiemstra, S. N. (2020), 'The ESG disclosure regulation – New duties for financial market participants & financial advisers', 22 March, available at: https://ssrn.com/abstract=3558868 (accessed 22 December 2021).

Hösli, A. and Weber, R. H. (2021), 'Climate change reporting and due diligence: Frontiers of corporate climate responsibility', 18 *European Company and Financial Law Review*, 948–968.

IOSCO (International Organisation of Securities Commissions) (2021), 'Report on Sustainability-related Issuer Disclosures', Final Report, June, available at: www.iosco.org/library/pubdocs/pdf/IOSCOPD678.pdf (accessed 17 April 2024).

IPCC (Intergovernmental Panel on Climate Change) (2014), *Fifth Assessment Report of the Intergovernmental Panel on Climate Change: Impacts, Adaptation, and Vulnerability – Summary for Policymakers* (Cambridge, UK: Cambridge University Press).

Jackson, H. E. (2015), 'Substituted compliance: The emergence, challenges, and evolution of a new regulatory paradigm', 1 *Journal of Financial Regulation*, 169–178.

Knudsen, J. S. and Moon, J. (eds.) (2017), *Visible Hands: Government Regulation and International Business Responsibility* (Cambridge, UK: Cambridge University Press).

Koopmans, T. C. (1951), 'Efficient allocation of resources', 4 *Econometrica*, 455–465.

La Torre, M., Sabelfeld, L., Blomkvist, M., and Larquinio, L. (2018), 'Harmonising non-financial reporting regulation in Europe: Practical forces and projections for future research', 26 *Meditari Accountancy Research*, 598–621.

Lambooy, T. (2006), 'Sustainability reporting by companies is necessary for sustainable globalisation' in E. Nieuwenhuys (ed.), *Neo-Liberal Globalism and Social Sustainable Globalisation* (Leiden: Brill), 215–235.

Landrigan, P. J., Fuller, R., Acosta, N. J. R. et al. (2017), 'The Lancet Commission on Pollution and Health', 391 *The Lancet Commissions*, 462–512.

Lee, M. (2006), 'Environmental economics: A market failure approach to the commerce clause', 2 *The Yale Law Journal*, 448–492.

Mitchell Polinsky, A. (1979), 'Controlling externalities and protecting entitlements: Property right, liability rule, and tax-subsidy approaches', 1 *The Journal of Legal Studies*, 1–48.

Moloney, N. (2023), *EU Securities and Financial Markets Regulation*, 4th ed. (Oxford: Oxford University Press).

Monsma, D. and Buckley, J. (2004), 'Non-financial corporate performance: The material edges of social and environmental disclosure', 11 *University of Baltimore Journal of Environmental Law*, 151–170.

Moulin, J.-M. (2020), 'La finance au service de quelle transition climatique?', 4 *Revue Internationale des Services Financiers – International Journal for Financial Services*, 7–75.

Persaud, A. (2010), 'The locus of financial regulation: Home versus host', 86(3) *International Affairs*, 637–646.

Pigou, A. C. (1920), *The Economics of Welfare*, vol. I (London: Macmillan and Co.).

Ralf, M. (2006), 'EU law as private international law? Reconceptualising the country-of-origin principle as vested-rights theory', 2 *Journal of Private International Law*, 195–242.

Rankin, W. J. (2014), 'Sustainability' in S. Seetharaman (ed.), *Treatise on Process Metallurgy*, vol 3a (Amsterdam: Elsevier), 1376–1424.

Richelle, J. (2021), 'Nouveau cadre réglementaire en matière d'investissements durables: impacts pour les sociétés', 2 *Revue Pratique Des Sociétés*, 147–160.

Ruth, J. (2019), 'The convergence of financial and ESG materiality: Taking sustainability mainstream', 56 *American Business Law Journal*, 642–702.

Scanlan, M. K. (2021), 'Climate risk is investment risk', 36 *Journal of Environmental Law and Litigation*, 1.

Schweizerisches Institut für Rechtsvergleichung (2018), 'Die Umsetzung der Richtlinie 2014/95/EU (CSR-Richtlinie) in verschiedenen Mitgliedstaaten der EU', E-Avis ISDC ISDC 2018-10, available at: https://bit.ly/3yTlwRg (accessed 16 May 2024).

SEC (US Securities and Exchange Commission) (2022), 'The Enhancement and Standardization of Climate-Related Disclosures for Investors', Proposed Rule, 87 FR 21334, April, available at: https://bit.ly/3RiJkUQ (accessed 17 April 2024).

Strine, L. E. (2022), 'The enhancement and standardization of climate-related disclosures for investors', Harvard Law School Forum on Corporate Governance, 28 June, available at: https://bit.ly/4c9aFS7 (accessed 17 April 2024).

Susko, R. (2018), 'The First Amendment implications of a mandatory environmental, social, and governance disclosure regime', 48 *Environmental Law Reporter*, 10989–11000.

Szabo, D. G. and Sorensen, K. E. (2015), 'New EU Directive on the Disclosure of Non-Financial Information (CSR)', 3 *European Company and Financial Law Review*, 307–340.

Tafara, E. and Peterson, R. J. (2007), 'A blueprint for cross-border access to U.S. investors: A new international framework', 48 *Harvard International Law Journal*, 31–68.

TCFD (Task Force on Climate-Related Financial Disclosures) (2017), 'Recommendations of the Task Force on Climate-related Financial Disclosures', Final Report, June, available at: https://bit.ly/3T9f8f5 (accessed 17 April 2024).

TCFD (Task Force on Climate-Related Financial Disclosures) (2021a), '2021 Annex, implementing the recommendations of the Task Force on Climate-related Financial Disclosures', 5 October, available at: https://bit.ly/48T8EXw (accessed 17 April 2024).

TCFD (Task Force on Climate-Related Financial Disclosures) (2021b), 'Guidance on metrics, targets, and transition plans', 15 October, available at: https://bit.ly/48NbH3q (accessed 17 April 2024).

TCFD (Task Force on Climate-Related Financial Disclosures) (2022), 2022 *Status Report*, 2 September, available at: https://bit.ly/3TxVXx6 (accessed 17 April 2024).

UNESCO (2011), 'Learning for the future: Competences in Education for Sustainable Development', AC13/2011/6, April, available at: https://bit.ly/4c74ey8 (accessed 17 April 2024).

United Nations (2015), 'Framework Convention on Climate Change', Adoption of the Paris Agreement, 21st Conference of the Parties, Paris, 30 November, in force 4 November 2016, FCCC/CP/2015/10/Add.1, Decision 1/CP.21, available at: https://unfccc.int/resource/docs/2015/cop21/eng/10a01.pdf (accessed 17 April 2024).

Wagner, C. Z. (2018), 'Evolving norms of corporate social responsibility: Lessons learned from the European Union Directive on Non-Financial Reporting', 19 *Transactions: The Tennessee Journal of Business Law*, 619–693.

Yadav, Y. and Turing, D. (2015), 'The Extra-Territorial Regulation of Clearinghouses', 15–24 *Vanderbilt Law and Economics Research Paper*, available at: https://ssrn.com/abstract=2659336 or http://dx.doi.org/10.2139/ssrn.2659336.

Yandle, B. (1999), 'Public choice at the intersection of environmental law and economics', 8 *European Journal of Law and Economics*, 5–27.

Yohe, G., Lasco, R. D., Ahmad, Q. K. et al. (2007), 'Perspectives on climate change and sustainability' in M. Parry, O. Canziani, J. Palutikof et al. (eds.), *Climate Change 2007: Impacts, Adaptation and Vulnerability, Contribution of Working Group II to the Fourth Assessment Report of the Intergovernmental Panel on Climate Change* (Cambridge, UK: Cambridge University Press), 811–842.

16

Institutional Investors as the Primary Users of Sustainability Reporting

Gaia Balp and Giovanni Strampelli

16.1 INTRODUCTION

Regulating non-financial information is one fundamental component of a wider legislative design aimed at favoring the transition towards a more sustainable economic model that is now being pursued (yet to a different extent) on both sides of the Atlantic. In the EU, the 2013 non-financial reporting directive (NFRD), and the amendments thereof introduced by the 2022 corporate sustainability reporting directive (CSRD), to be transposed by the Member States by 6 July 2024, are key within the context of the European 'Green Deal', by which the European Commission intends to make Europe 'a modern, resource-efficient and competitive economy', put it 'on a new path of sustainable and inclusive growth' and ultimately make it 'the first climate-neutral continent'[1]. In the United States, a hot debate was triggered by the SEC's unveiling, in March 2022, of its long-awaited Climate Disclosure Rule proposal, which would force companies to include certain climate-related disclosures in their registration statements and periodic reports, including information about climate-related risks that are reasonably likely to have a material impact on their business, results of operations, or financial condition, and certain climate-related financial statement metrics in a note to their audited financial statements[2].

As such regulatory developments clearly show, when drawing the framework for sustainability reporting it is essential to highlight that non-financial disclosures are not functional to the pursuit of moral objectives only. Quite to the contrary, sustainability reporting provides information that is indeed essential to the shareholders and investors to assess the value created by the firms they are invested in.

So much clearly emerges from the relevant definitions of the key terms. Although in this chapter the terms 'non-financial' and 'sustainability' information are used as synonyms for the sake of convenience, the European Commission explicitly

---

[1] See European Commission 2019a.
[2] See SEC 2022.

underscored that the term 'non-financial' information is misleading, and is considered inappropriate by many market participants, since it falsely suggests that such information has no financial relevance[3]. For this very reason, reference is made in the CSRD exclusively to the term 'sustainability' information.

To name but one example, the financial relevance of sustainability information was clearly shown by the events occurred at Danone SA, the first French company to include an ideal purpose in its articles of association and to adopt – following the 2019 *loi PACTE* – the form of the *entreprise à mission*[4]. As is well known, Danone became the subject of financial news after the CEO, who had promoted taking the steps mentioned, was removed from office on the spur of the initiative taken by two activist funds maintaining that the company's financial performance was poor relative to its most direct competitors[5]. According to the prevailing (and perhaps more obvious) view, the Danone case confirms that shareholders are mainly interested in profits, so that the pursuit of different objectives is supported by them only insofar as they do not impair financial returns.

Reasonably, that view grasps part of the story. However, the Danone case may very well be considered from a different perspective too. Given that the CEO was blamed for the company's underperformance relative to peers, the case suggests that sustainability endeavors are 'sustainable' only if the company is able to measure, and communicate to its shareholders and investors, the financial value created while pursuing ESG objectives[6].

Measurability of a company's ESG financial performance is all the more essential where time horizons for the deployment of corporate ESG strategies are

[3] See Recital 8 to Directive (EU) 2022/2464 of the European Parliament and of the Council of 14 December 2022 – so-called Corporate Sustainability Reporting Directive (CSRD).
[4] Adopted on 22 May 22 2019, the PACTE law for the growth and transformation of businesses (loi n. 2019-486, www.legifrance.gouv.fr/dossierlegislatif/JORFDOLE000037080861/) allows companies to better consider social and environmental issues in their strategy. More specifically, under Article 176 of such law, a corporation may publicly state that it is a 'mission corporation' (*société à mission*) when its articles of incorporation specify: (1) a purpose, within the meaning of article 1835 of the Civil Code; (2) one or more social and environmental objectives that the company has set itself to pursue in the course of its business; (3) the procedures for monitoring the execution of the mission set. In June 2020, Danone adopted the status of a *'société à mission'*, as embedded in Article 1 of its by-laws, under which '[t]he social and environmental objectives that the Company sets as its mission to pursue as part of its activities [...], integrated into its model of profitable and sustainable growth, are as follows (the 'Mission'): Impact people's health locally, with a portfolio of healthier products, with brands encouraging better nutritional choices and by promoting better dietary habits; Preserve and renew the planet's resources, by supporting regenerative agriculture, protecting the water cycle and strengthening the circular economy of packaging, across its entire ecosystem, in order to contribute to the fight against climate change; Entrust Danone's people to create new futures: building on a unique social innovation heritage, give each employee the opportunity to impact the decisions of the Company, both locally and globally; Foster inclusive growth, by ensuring equal opportunities within the Company, supporting the most vulnerable partners in its ecosystem and developing everyday products accessible to as many people as possible' (see Danone SA 2022).
[5] Abboud 2021.
[6] Editorial Board 2021.

considered. In fact, it is reasonable to hypothesize that the value created by integrating sustainability objectives into corporate strategies may emerge on an economic level in the long term, with financial and overall performance gradually aligning (where overall performance also includes benefits different from profits, such as the improvement of employee life quality or the reduction of the company's pollution load). In the short term, however, it is very likely that the pursuit of ESG objectives reduces profits, thus giving rise to shareholders' reaction, as occurred in the Danone case.

Therefore, it is clear that non-financial information and its regulation play a dual fundamental role.

First, an appropriate regulation of sustainability reporting is the prerequisite for giving substance to the debate around corporate purpose (or, according to an alternative view, around the stakeholders/shareholders divide), and for such purpose to actually affect a company's conduct. As stated by the Principles for Purposeful Business promoted by the British Academy, delivery of purpose relies, amongst other things, on the adoption of a reporting model that makes it possible to measure 'impacts and investment by companies in their workers, societies and natural assets both within and outside the firm'[7]. Similarly, according to Fisch and Davidoff Salomon, 'a corporation's identification and disclosure of tangible metrics both reinforces its commitment to the objectives identified in its purpose and renders its statement of purpose enforceable'[8]. Further, as already mentioned, it can hardly be denied that, without a disclosure framework capable of credibly revealing the value created by corporate strategies inspired by ESG objectives, such strategies would in fact not be feasible, since they would face dissent from a large part of the shareholders, many of which are still predominantly profit-oriented.

Second, an adequate non-financial disclosure system is necessary to tackle the (currently widespread) greenwashing phenomenon, consisting in the practice of some companies giving a false impression of their environmental impact or benefits by unduly claiming that they pursue certain sustainability strategies when in fact basic sustainability standards have not been met, thus causing evident distortions in the direction of investment flow[9]. More generally, the absence of a sufficiently harmonized non-financial disclosure regime is a serious roadblock to identifying a shared classification system for sustainable activities.

This makes it clear why sustainability information (to be provided also in alignment with Regulation (EU) 2020/852 – the Taxonomy Regulation) is one pillar of the Commission's Strategy for Financing the Transition to a Sustainable Economy[10]. In fact, institutional investors can meet the transparency obligations they are imposed on by Regulation (EU) 2019/2088 relating to information on sustainability in the

[7] British Academy 2019, at 8.
[8] Fisch and Davidoff Solomon 2021.
[9] European Commission 2021.
[10] European Commission 2021.

financial services sector (SFDR) only on condition that, in turn, they receive adequate information from investee companies.

16.2 THE DIFFICULT PATH TOWARDS HARMONIZATION OF NON-FINANCIAL REPORTING STANDARDS

As already mentioned, non-financial corporate information currently provided under the NFRD is not, in many cases, meaningful, since companies do not report information that users of sustainability reports consider relevant, while disclosing information that is not material. In addition, the existence of different sets of non-financial reporting standards significantly impairs the comparability of the information provided. As noted by the European Commission in the CSRD proposal, the effectiveness of the NFRD is limited by the fact that 'some companies from which users want sustainability information do not report such information, while many that do report sustainability information do not report all the information that is relevant for users. When information is reported, it is often neither sufficiently reliable, nor sufficiently comparable, between companies. The information is often difficult for users to find and is rarely available in a machine-readable digital format'.

These limitations are largely attributable to the fact that no objective and widely shared measurement system exists for many of the items to be included in sustainability reports. A company's CO_2 emissions, or the number of accidents to workers recorded by it, can be measured with some degree of reliability (in spite of the fact that there remain non-irrelevant margins of discretion regarding the criteria for classifying, for example, the severity of employee accidents). However, quantifying with a sufficient degree of objectivity the effects, also in financial terms, of the use of antibiotics by food producers included in the supply chain of a company that owns a restaurant chain is much more complex[11].

Various initiatives launched at the European and international level to foster greater harmonization of financial reporting standards are aimed at overcoming such hurdles. The most significant initiative is certainly the establishment of the International Sustainability Standards Board (ISSB) by the IFRS Foundation in November 2021[12]. The Foundation is the same organization that promotes the IAS/IFRS international accounting standards, which, as is well known, are the financial reporting standards most widely used globally. This very circumstance and the support provided to the ISSB by other standard setters (some of which integrated into it), as well as by many market participants and supervisory authorities, make it likely that the new Board could become the main player in the process of harmonization of sustainability reporting.

---

[11]   Christensen, Hail and Leuz 2019, at 5 ff.
[12]   IFRS Foundation 2021.

Given these developments, the position taken by the EU to develop its own set of mandatory non-financial reporting standards deserves specific consideration (see Recital 38 to the CSRD). To be sure, the Commission and the European Financial Reporting Advisory Group (EFRAG) have made it clear that these principles should be developed in constructive two-way cooperation with major international initiatives – in this perspective, cooperation initiated by the EFRAG with the Global Reporting Initiative (GRI) for the development of new standards is significant[13]. Recitals 37 and 43 to the CSRD also recommended that the EU principles should align as far as possible with those initiatives while taking into account the European specificities. However, such decision can still lead to the undesirable result of making the process of harmonization more complex.

In effect, the adoption of EU standards may contradictorily, and counterproductively, contribute to enhancing divergence of sustainability reporting at the international level, and impose heightened costs on reporting companies and on global investors. Above all, the IOSCO 'has strongly supported the IFRS Foundation in its work towards delivering a global baseline for *investor-oriented* sustainability-related disclosure standards focused on enterprise value creation which jurisdictions could consider incorporating or building upon as part of their mandatory reporting requirements as appropriate and consistent with their domestic legal frameworks' (emphasis is added), and – contrary to the European approach (see para. 4) – the Sustainability Accounting Standards Board (SASB) framework (now under the oversight of the ISSB, following consolidation into the IFRS Foundation) does not rely on the principle of double materiality. In such a scenario, non-negligible negative effects for European companies are predictable if sustainability reports were to be prepared based on 'domestic' standards not used at the international level, since this could easily translate into additional costs and reduced attractiveness for international investors, in particular for those who most weigh ESG factors in their investment strategies and policies.

16.3 THE USERS OF NON-FINANCIAL INFORMATION

Having thus drawn a picture of the current state of the regime for non-financial reporting, examining some key issues will allow hypothesizing possible solutions to the limitations of such framework. Specifically, it is necessary to more closely identify the users of sustainability information as well as the contents of non-financial reporting. Hence, delimiting the scope of the relevant information is needed (the notion of materiality being decisive to this end), as well as defining how sustainability information needs to be presented. To that effect, consideration is to be given, in particular, to how (in order to make non-financial information more effective and

[13] EFRAG and GRI 2021.

usable) the quantitative component of the information must integrate with the narrative dimension in sustainability reports.

Starting with the users of sustainability information, the CSRD itself clarifies that
users of non-financial information include investors and non-governmental organizations, social partners and other stakeholders, and that these categories of users
have different needs. While investors are interested in better understanding the risks
posed, and the opportunities afforded, by sustainability issues for their investments,
as well as the impacts of those investments on the people and the environment,
the other user categories are mainly interested in holding undertakings to greater
account for their impacts on the people and the environment[14].

While these statements are fully acceptable, it seems correct to assume that the
main users of sustainability reports are indeed institutional investors and asset managers (in their capacity of corporate shareholders or potential equity investors) and,
in particular, widely diversified investors, such as the major passive investors whose
investment strategies tend toward replicating certain benchmark stock indices.

Non-financial information is relevant to highly diversified investors from various perspectives. First, reliable and comparable corporate sustainability reports are
essential for stock price discovery, as market prices need to also reflect the incidence
of externalities generated by the company[15]. However, price is not crucial in the case
of passive investors, which, due to their investment strategy, are largely compelled to
buy, and hold, the securities included in the benchmark index regardless of market
prices[16]. More so, passive investors are bound to buy, as a rule, just when stock prices
rise, since the weight of the stocks in the index can vary based on the trend in prices,
so that the weight of the stock in the index increases in proportion to the increase in
the stock's market price.

Precisely because their investment decisions are largely dictated by the composition of the benchmark indices, passive funds managers cannot (or can only slightly)
change the weight in the fund of the stocks of the companies included in the index
to seize favorable investment opportunities. To increase the value of the portfolio,
they must rather act with a view to reducing systemic portfolio risk by monitoring
externalities caused by portfolio firms and, hence, by engaging with investee companies to mitigate systemic risk. Therefore, for widely diversified investors and, in
particular, for passive ones, monitoring the impact of the externalities generated by
investee companies is essential, not only to the extent that such externalities affect
the financial performance of the company that originates them, but also on account
of the negative consequences that they may have on the activities and results of the
rest of the portfolio firms[17].

[14] See Recital 9 to the CSRD.
[15] Tsagas and Villiers 2020.
[16] Strampelli 2018a.
[17] Gordon 2021; Condon 2020; Coffee 2020, 22 ff.

Second, regardless of portfolio value maximization, sustainability information is of paramount importance for ESG 'light green' funds, which promote environmental and/or social characteristics, among others – and whose incidence in the investment landscape is growing in the face of growing end-investor demand – as well as for so-called impact, or 'dark green', funds, which have as an objective a positive (and measurable) social or environmental impact alongside, or in place of, a financial return[18].

And, finally, on the regulatory level, as mentioned earlier[19], sustainability information disclosed by investee companies is the information basis institutional investors need to meet the disclosure requirements they are imposed on by the SFDR.

The central position occupied by institutional shareholders and investors, and, in particular, by passive funds in the audience of users of non-financial information does not, however, exclude that other categories of stakeholders may also have a relevant interest in such information. To better understand which types of stakeholders can actually use sustainability information to promote the pursuit of sustainability objectives by the company, it should once again be noticed that non-financial information is functional to the implementation by institutional investors and asset managers of policies aimed at reducing systematic portfolio risk.

As is well known, highly diversified investors hold stakes in a very large number of companies[20], making it impossible for the asset manager to monitor every individual company in the portfolio (or even only a substantial part of portfolio firms) and to implement engagement policies aimed, for example, at favoring a reduction in greenhouse gas emissions, or in the incidence of other types of externalities, at the individual level.

Since firm-specific engagement is not feasible except for a very limited number of portfolio companies, highly diversified investors – being also those capable of exerting more influence on investee companies due to the size of the equity investments held – apply pre-determined voting policies across portfolio firms. By adopting and disclosing voting policies that set ESG objectives common for all portfolio firms, investors disclose their preferences, thus anticipating the criteria based on which they will vote their shares regarding the issues covered in the guidelines.

Such approach, defined as systematic stewardship[21], is not, however, comprehensive, since in some cases, due to the particular nature of the business carried out by an individual portfolio company and the type of externalities it generates, or the presence of specific transactions, ignoring firm-specific analysis and initiatives is not possible. However, even the largest investors do not have resources sufficient to carry out these activities autonomously on all occasions they are necessary. One

---

[18] Cambridge Associates – Global Impact Investing Network 2015.
[19] See Section 16.1.
[20] For example, BlackRock's pooled vehicles are invested in approximately 17,000 companies.
[21] Gordon 2021.

way to overcome (at least in part) these limits is collective engagement, that is, cooperation between major investors and other institutions that focus their analytical skills on a smaller number of companies. As recent cases recorded in the United States and the United Kingdom show, including cases of ESG-driven hedge fund activism[22], collaboration may occur with non-governmental organizations (so-called NGOs) that are attentive to environmental and social issues. Among the organizations most active in promoting joint engagement initiatives are, for example, the Interfaith Center for Corporate Responsibility (ICCR), the Coalition for Environmentally Responsible Economies (Ceres) and the Network for Sustainable Financial Markets. To protect the values they are driven by, these and other similar bodies are interested in promoting campaigns aimed at pursuing sustainability objectives by certain companies, and in taking action to gather support of large institutional investors[23]. Interaction with institutional investors, in fact, allows overcoming both the hurdles that isolated engagement initiatives by NGOs have met in the past[24], and the limited ability of broadly diversified institutions to actively monitor portfolio firms.

16.4 THE CONTENT OF NON-FINANCIAL INFORMATION

Turning to the content of non-financial reports, it should be noticed that sustainability information is useful to the extent that it provides additional information to that which can be inferred from the financial reports. As obvious as it may seem, this simple fact raises issues that are hard to tackle, since the divide between financial and non-financial information is far from clear, and financial and non-financial information are not impermeable to each other. Protecting the interests of some categories of stakeholders, even if attributable to the scope of sustainability strategies, may very well affect the company's financial statements – for example, if the firm incurs costs in the course of improving employee working conditions, or to purchase less-polluting machinery.

Against this background, it is possible to identify three different types of information in the context of sustainability reports. First, as mentioned above, there is ESG information that is financial in nature, and that is included in the company's financial reports as it affects the income statement and the balance sheet.

Further, information that could be defined as having a genuine non-financial nature can be classified into two different types: on the one hand, information relating to ESG issues that are not included in the financial statements but are likely to affect the value of the firm and therefore to influence investors' decisions; on the other hand, information relating to facts and events concerning the company's

---

[22] Christie 2021, 26 ff.
[23] Gordon 2021; Standen and McGuire n.d.
[24] Sullivan 2013.

operations that affect the environment and the surrounding community but that (in theory) have no impact on the value and performance of the firm.

Which of those types of information should be included in sustainability reports depends on the reporting standards used, which diverge in outlining the scope of the relevant information. Divergence between the different sets of non-financial reporting standards depends, in particular, on what notion of materiality they adopt, which, in turn, determines the scope of the information to be included in the financial and non-financial reports of the company[25].

As is well known, one single notion of materiality applies in the field of financial disclosure, based on which – as stated, for example, by paragraph 7 of IAS 1 – information is considered material 'if omitting, misstating or obscuring it could reasonably be expected to influence decisions that the primary users of general purpose financial statements make on the basis of those financial statements, which provide financial information about a specific reporting entity'.

On the contrary, standard setters do welcome divergent notions of materiality in the field of non-financial disclosure. The SASB principles do evolve around a notion of materiality that substantially coincides with the (financial) one mentioned above. According to the exposure draft of the soon-to-be adopted SASB Conceptual framework, information is considered material (and must therefore be included in sustainability reports) if 'omitting, misstating, or obscuring it could reasonably be expected to influence investment or lending decisions that users make on the basis of their assessments of short-, medium-, and long-term financial performance and enterprise value'[26]. This concept of materiality differs from that of IAS/IFRS only in the reference to the medium and long-term performance and value of the company.

According to the approach underlying the SASB principles, sustainability information is therefore directed (just like financial information) mainly to shareholders and other investors. More so, the SASB exposure draft explicitly clarifies that the adoption of a definition of materiality substantially coinciding with that provided by the IAS/IFRS principles is dictated by the fact that information required under the SASB principles is aimed at satisfying 'the information needs of providers of capital'[27].

However, this approach is not shared by other standard setters that have based the development of non-financial reporting principles on a broader notion of materiality, the so-called double materiality. Double materiality is adopted, for example, under the GRI principles[28], which are widespread in many countries for non-financial reporting (even if the GRI principles are sometimes combined with those developed

---

[25] Guillot and Hales 2021.
[26] SASB 2020.
[27] SASB 2020.
[28] GRI 2021.

by other standard setters, such as the SASB or the IIRC, as happens in Italy)[29]. The European Commission itself coined this new definition of materiality in 2019[30], and double materiality is among the characterizing features of the CSRD amending the NFRD.

In fact, under the CSRD, companies are required to disclose 'information necessary to understand the undertaking's impacts on sustainability matters, and information necessary to understand how sustainability matters affect the undertaking's development, performance and position'[31]. Hence, the CSRD considers materiality of ESG issues in both a financial (according to an outside-in perspective), and impact (according to an inside-out perspective) dimension, requiring companies to include in their sustainability reports not only information necessary to understand 'the undertaking's development, performance and position', but also 'information necessary for an understanding of the impact of the undertaking's activities on environmental, social and employee matters, respect for human rights, anti-corruption and bribery matters'[32]. Even more so, the CSRD reiterates that mandatory EU sustainability reporting standards to be adopted by means of delegated regulations will be based on the principle of double materiality, thus confirming that double materiality is the cornerstone of the European strategy concerning sustainability reporting[33]. The EU believes that developing its own set of non-financial reporting standards is needed because '[n]o existing standard or framework satisfies the Union's needs for detailed sustainability reporting by itself'[34], also considering the need for such standard to align, amongst others, with the disclosure requirements laid down in the Taxonomy Regulation and the underlying indicators and methodologies set out in the delegated acts adopted under the SFDR.

Double materiality entails, at least theoretically, a radical change in perspective by virtue of which materiality becomes a concept that is 'socio-economic and political' in nature, and not merely a technical accounting concept. As such, double materiality is mainly aimed at promoting the understanding of the process of sustainable development and the way companies contribute to it[35].

Although clear at a theoretical level, the notion of double materiality raises significant questions when it comes to its application, since distinguishing information that affects the value and performance of the company from that relating to its environmental and social impact is far from being unproblematic. For instance, taking up an example formulated by Milton Friedman himself in his famous article that

---

[29] Assonime 2020, at 3.
[30] European Commission, 2019b 6 ff.
[31] See Articles 19(a) and 29(a).
[32] Recital 29 to the CSRD.
[33] Recital 37 to the CSRD.
[34] Recital 38 to the CSRD.
[35] GRI 2021; Carpenter, Dirsmith and Gupta 1994; Lai, Melloni and Stacchezzini 2017.

laid the theoretical foundations of the shareholder value maximization theory[36], investing in the establishment of an asylum for the local community residing near the firm's production sites has certainly a positive impact on the community, but it can also positively impact the company's business and financial situation, as it can reduce employee turnover and thus increase efficiency in the production process. Similarly, implementing policies and strategies aimed at reducing the company's polluting load to make it compatible with the ability of the local ecosystem to absorb it is certainly an environmentally friendly endeavor to the benefit of the local community and its collective interest. At the same time, such endeavor can also affect the firm's economic situation, and therefore the choices of shareholders and potential investors. In effect, absent any initiatives by the firm, local or national authorities may take some measures against the company (such as fines or an increase in tariffs for the use of certain services) that financially impact the firm, also on account of the possible reputational damage vis-à-vis the consumers which could lead to a loss of customers.

Furthermore, sustainability risks and financial risks are likely to overlap to an ever-increasing extent, as the markets and public policies evolve in response to climate change and the positive and/or negative consequences that businesses may have on climate will increasingly translate into business opportunities and/or financially significant risks. Such trend seems bound to consolidate due, in particular, to the increasing number of investors that do integrate ESG factors into their investment strategies, or value the pursuit of sustainability objectives alongside financial ones[37].

The current fragmentation in the regime for non-financial disclosures impacts the extent and nature of the sustainability information provided, which is highly dependant on the reporting standards used, which, in turn, significantly differ (to begin with, as regards the non-coinciding notion of materiality accepted). Within such scenario, it is possible to distinguish sets of standards aimed at providing information relevant, first of all, for investors[38] from those that are aimed at satisfying the information needs (also) of other categories of stakeholders[39].

The current limited degree of harmonization makes it necessary to consider the extent to which non-financial disclosure requirements provide an incentive for company directors to protect interests other than those of the shareholders too, since the scope of such incentive varies according to the standards used.

Each sustainability reporting system requires that companies disclose the externalities they generate, regardless of whether the firm is oriented towards shareholder value maximization or the protection of other categories of stakeholders. From this perspective, it could therefore be said that – regardless of the reporting

---

[36] Friedman 1970.
[37] See Section 16.3.
[38] For example, the SASB principles.
[39] For example, the GRI principles and those to be adopted by the European Commission.

standards used – the discipline of non-financial information is neutral in terms of the interests pursued by the company.

However, it can hardly be denied that the system for non-financial reporting used can actually have an impact on the company's purpose, since sustainability information due can provide an incentive for the firm subject to non-financial disclosure requirements to enhance the protection of diverse interests. The intensity of such (indirect) impact on the company's purpose depends on the number and seriousness of the externalities generated by the firm that must be included in the sustainability reports[40]. The wider the scope of the externalities, the more reasonable is it to hypothesize that non-financial disclosure requirements can incentivize the firm to take into account, and protect, the interests of the stakeholders other than the shareholders. Indeed, information referred to externalities can trigger potential consequences, at least at the reputational level[41].

From a different (but complementary) perspective, it is worth noting that, where investor-oriented reporting standards based on the traditional notion of (single) materiality apply, sustainability disclosures align with the model of enlightened shareholder value[42] – a model explicitly embraced under section 172 of the UK Companies Act (concerning directors' duty to promote the success of the company). Based on this approach, directors need to consider the interests of the stakeholders in order, ultimately, to create value for the shareholders in the long term. Significantly enough, when promoting the pursuit of long-term value creation, some major investors urge portfolio companies to adopt reporting principles (such as those issued by the SASB and the TCFD) that limit sustainability information to that necessary for understanding the company's performance and results.

On the contrary, non-financial disclosures are more consistent with the transition to a multi-stakeholder, not shareholder-centric, model where sustainability reports are drafted according to standards based on the principle of double materiality (such as the GRI standards or the soon-to-be-issued EU standards), which also require reporting on firm-generated externalities impacting the environment, the different stakeholder categories and, ultimately, the community at large.

16.5 THE FORM OF NON-FINANCIAL DISCLOSURES, AND THE NEED FOR BALANCING THE NARRATIVE AND QUANTITATIVE DIMENSIONS OF SUSTAINABILITY INFORMATION

Where the methods of presenting information to be included in sustainability reports are considered, the need to adequately balance the narrative and quantitative components of non-financial information cannot be ignored.

---

[40] CDP, CDSB, GRI, IIRC, SASB 2020.
[41] On the controversial extent of such incentive effect, see, however, European Commission 2020, 121.
[42] Lund 2021; Bruno 2015.

Given the financial interests of a large part of the users of non-financial information, sustainability reports cannot, in fact, be exhausted in narrative-only information. The growing need for institutional investors to assess how ESG factors impact firm profitability and risk and, therefore, the overall portfolio return, makes it (increasingly) necessary to measure the effect of sustainability policies implemented by investee companies. Not surprisingly, the main sets of non-financial reporting principles clearly focus on measurability. The exposure draft of the new version of the SASB Principles Framework explicitly states that sustainability disclosure is aimed at 'identifying metrics that can be used to set targets and measure performance on the environmental, social, and human capital issues most relevant to long-term enterprise value creation'[43]. Similarly, the EFRAG clarified that non-financial reporting is aimed at providing relevant, reliable and comparable information that allows users 'to understand the reporting entity's sustainability objectives, position and performance and to inform [users'] decisions relating to their engagement with the entity'[44].

The need for sustainability information to also, and necessarily, include a quantitative component is acknowledged by the current European legislation as well, and, specifically, by Article 8 of the Taxonomy Regulation. In effect, Article 8 requires that undertakings subject to an obligation to publish non-financial information disclose (a) the proportion of their turnover derived from products or services associated with economic activities that qualify as environmentally sustainable and (b) the proportion of their capital expenditure and the proportion of their operating expenditure related to assets or processes associated with economic activities that qualify as environmentally sustainable under Articles 3 and 9 of the same Regulation. Similarly, in its communication of 20 June 2019 on 'Guidelines on non-financial reporting: Supplement on reporting climate-related information', the Commission recommends that

> [C]ertain large companies report on certain climate-related key performance indicators (KPIs) that are based on the framework established by this Regulation. In particular, information on the proportion of the turnover, capital expenditure (CapEx) or operating expenditure (OpEx) of such large non-financial companies that is associated with environmentally sustainable economic activities, as well as KPIs that are tailored for large financial companies, is useful to investors who are interested in companies whose products and services contribute substantially to any one of the environmental objectives set out in this Regulation.

The relevance of the quantitative dimension of non-financial information is bound to gradually increase, at the same pace of the refinement of reporting standards and measurement techniques.

While financial information is largely backward-looking in nature, non-financial information is, largely, necessarily forward-looking, since the reference time horizon

---

[43] SASB 2020.
[44] EFRAG 2021.

of certain information may be particularly distant in time[45]. The divergence between financial and non-financial information is made clear, for example, by the request for more precise information to be provided about the different phases that lead to the achievement of sustainability objectives. The request for scenario information[46] is illustrative of the problems that may arise in this respect. As a consequence of the accrual principle regulating financial statements, projections included in scenario information do not necessarily entail the recognition of items in the financial statements[47] in the financial year considered, as they pertain to a medium and long-term time horizon.

On the other hand – and this aspect seems, in perspective, fundamental – the more sustainability information is precise, also at the quantitative level, the more relevant becomes the connection between financial and non-financial information, as the latter can indeed influence the former and hence affect the company's income and assets.

For example, if information regarding the firm's plans to reduce CO_2 gradually becomes more precise also from the quantitative standpoint, disclosure of such information in sustainability reports is likely to involve the recognition of certain items in the financial statements, thus establishing a stricter mutual connection between financial and non-financial information. Taking up the example just mentioned, it is reasonable to assume that the company should evaluate the need to either recognize provisions for the expenses it will incur for the energy requalification of its production sites, or write-down the polluting plants to be dismissed (provided that dismission is to be considered in the financial forecasts functional to the implementation of the impairment test associated)[48].

In addition to confirming the importance of the quantitative dimension of sustainability disclosure, these examples highlight the need to adopt an integrated approach to sustainability and financial disclosures, allowing for mutually connecting the relevant information, in line with Article 8 of the Taxonomy Regulation.

Still, the narrative component of sustainability reports is equally essential to achieve coordination of financial and non-financial information, as well as to increase the informative value of sustainability reports (to the benefit, also, of less sophisticated users).

First, the narrative dimension of sustainability reporting is a necessary complement to quantitative information where the latter is less reliable due to the absence of precise measurement systems (think, for example, of the information referred to employee working conditions along the firm's supply chain), or to the forward-looking nature of sustainability information, which requires that the assumptions be explained based on which information is provided.

---

[45] Think, for example, of disclosure associated with the objective of reducing CO_2 emissions by 2050.
[46] That is, of information foreshadowing various possible developments.
[47] Think, for example, of the recording of provisions for risks and charges.
[48] Thomas 2021.

Further, as already mentioned, the narrative dimension of sustainability disclosure is essential to foster the interconnection between financial and non-financial information. As clarified by the EFRAG[49] and the IIRC, the links between financial statements and non-financial reports can be either direct or indirect[50]. In the first case, sustainability information can be directly reconciled with information included in the financial statements, as is the case, for example, for the information referred to in Article 8 of the Taxonomy Regulation. On the other hand, direct reconciliation between the financial statements and sustainability reports is not possible where the financial consequences of sustainability information are not measurable, as is the case, for example, for scenario analysis or long-term forecasts that go beyond the time horizon in which estimates of future cash flows are reliable. In such cases, the narrative dimension of sustainability reporting becomes fundamental to connect non-financial information with the financial statements of the reporting entity. In fact to help illustrate how ESG strategies create value, the effects of such strategies need to be read in connection with the firm's financial performance. More broadly, the narrative component of sustainability reporting is functional to understanding how ESG strategies align with the purpose of the company, if such purpose is made explicit in the articles of association or elsewhere[51].

It obviously remains that, for those objectives to be meaningfully met, the narrative component of sustainability disclosures must be clear and concise enough to avoid the risk of information overload that could impair the usefulness of sustainability reports even for sophisticated investors, such as asset managers and ratings providers, given the large number of companies they need to monitor. Therefore, standard setters or supervisory authorities should draft guidelines aimed at establishing good practices to be used to prevent information overload and fully preserve the information value of sustainability reports[52].

16.6 CONCLUSIONS

The role that non-financial reporting can play in encouraging reporting entities to adopt sustainability strategies depends primarily on two issues that need to be addressed.

First, non-financial reports should be increasingly able to illustrate how sustainability strategies contribute to create value, and to justify their implementation also to the shareholders, given that such strategies can negatively affect the firm's financial performance in the short term. In this perspective, non-financial disclosures are also the prerequisite to substantiate the debate on the purpose of

---

[49] EFRAG 2021.
[50] IIRC 2021, 26 f.
[51] For example, on the company's website. EFRAG 2021.
[52] Strampelli 2018b.

the company and the protection, or, at least, the consideration, of stakeholders' interests. This is the case because, and as long as, non-financial information highlights the potential of sustainability projects also in terms of creating value for the shareholders, who are the main users of such information.

Second, for such evolution to be accomplished, overcoming the current fragmentation in the regime for sustainability reporting is needed. It is essential to complete the process of harmonization that has now begun and which seems to have reached a turning point with the establishment of the ISSB by the IFRS Foundation. This initiative, moreover, demonstrates the ever-closer interconnection existing between non-financial and financial reports, and the relevance of such intersection also for supporting the implementation of sustainability strategies.

In this perspective, the decision made by the European Commission to develop its own set of sustainability reporting standards is questionable, since it not only contradicts the need to overcome fragmentation, but could even penalize European companies by either limiting the comparability of their sustainability reports with those of non-European companies or, in any case, impose additional costs on EU firms. In fact, it is likely that – precisely in order to reduce the lack of comparability in sustainability information – EU companies subject to sustainability reporting based on mandatory, double materiality–principled EU standards will still need to draft non-financial reports based on reporting standards adopted at the international level as well.

REFERENCES

Abboud, L. (2021), 'Danone board ousts Emmanuel Faber as chief', *Financial Times*, 15 May.

Assonime (2020), 'Consultation 6/2020 – Reply to consultation on the revision of the non-financial reporting directive', available (in Italian only) at: https://bit.ly/3V9rFSf.

British Academy (2019), 'Principles for Purposeful Business', available at: https://bit.ly/3wML8hJ.

Bruno, S. (2015), 'The "Enlightened Shareholder Value" in UK Companies Ten Years Later: What the European Directive N. 2014/95/EC Can Do', available at: https://papers.ssrn.com/sol3/papers.cfm?abstract_id=2674706.

Cambridge Associates – Global Impact Investing Network (2015), 'Introducing the Impact Investing Benchmark', available at: https://bit.ly/4a6u9VN.

Carpenter, B. W., Dirsmith, M. W. and Gupta, P. P. (1994), 'Materiality judgments and audit firm culture: Social-behavioral and political perspectives', 19(4–5) *Accounting, Organizations and Society*, 355.

CDP, Climate Disclosure Standards Board (CDSB), Global Reporting Initiative (GRI), International Integrated Reporting Council (IIRC), and Sustainability Accounting Standards Board (SASB) (2020), 'Statement of Intent to Work Together Towards Comprehensive Corporate Reporting', available at: https://bit.ly/3wSyHkw.

Christensen, H. B., Hail, L. and Leuz, C. (2019), 'Adoption of CSR and Sustainability Reporting Standards: Economic Analysis and Review', Finance Working Paper N° 623/2019, available at: http://ssrn.com/abstract_id=3427748.

Christie, A. (2021), 'The agency costs of sustainable capitalism', 55(2) *UC Davis Law Review*, 875–954, available at: https://papers.ssrn.com/sol3/papers.cfm?abstract_id=3766478.

Coffee Jr, J. C. (2020), 'The future of disclosure: ESG, common ownership, and systematic risk', *Columbia Business Law Review*, 602, available at: https://ssrn.com/abstract=3678197.

Condon, M. (2020), 'Externalities and the common owner', 95 *Washington Law Review*, 1.

Danone SA (2022), 'By-laws', updated September 22, available at: https://bit.ly/3Pfbuzh.

Editorial Board (2021), 'Danone: a case study in the pitfalls of purpose', *Financial Times*, 18 March, available at: https://on.ft.com/4c3Tphr.

EFRAG (European Financial Reporting Advisory Group) (2021), 'Proposals for a relevant and dynamic EU sustainability reporting standard setting', available at: https://bit.ly/3wPo2Ha.

EFRAG (European Financial Reporting Advisory Group) and GRI (Global Reporting Initiative) (2021), 'Landmark Statement of Cooperation', available at: https://bit.ly/4c7k64F.

European Commission (2019a), 'The European Green Deal. Communication from the Commission to the European Parliament, the European Council, the Council, The European Economic and Social Committee and the Committee of the Regions', COM (2019) 640 final, 11 December, available at: https://bit.ly/4aUdKnv.

European Commission (2019b), 'Guidelines on Non-Financial Reporting: Supplement on Reporting Climate-related Information', available at: https://bit.ly/48Jwhlm.

European Commission (2020), 'Study on the Non-Financial Reporting Directive', available at: https://data.europa.eu/doi/10.2874/229601.

European Commission (2021), 'Strategy for Financing the Transition to a Sustainable Economy', available at: https://bit.ly/3wPnDVa.

Fisch, J. E. and Davidoff Solomon, S. (2021), 'Should corporations have a purpose?', 99 *Texas Law Review*, 1345.

Friedman, M. (1970), 'The social responsibility of business is to increase its profits', *The New York Times Magazine*.

Gordon, J. N. (2021), 'Systematic Stewardship', European Corporate Governance Institute – Law Working Paper No. 566/2021 Columbia Law and Economics Working Paper No. 640, available at: https://papers.ssrn.com/sol3/papers.cfm?abstract_id=3782814.

GRI (Global Reporting Initiative) (2021), 'The double-materiality concept. Application and issues', available at: https://bit.ly/3SY5blE.

Guillot, J. and Hales, J. (2021), 'Materiality: The Word That Launched a Thousand Debates', *Harvard Law School Forum on Corporate Governance*, available at: https://bit.ly/43biumk.

IFRS (International Financial Reporting Standards) Foundation (2021), 'IFRS Foundation announces International Sustainability Standards Board, consolidation with CDSB and VRF, and publication of prototype disclosure requirements', 3 November, available at: https://bit.ly/43bJDWd.

IIRC (International Integrated Reporting Council) (2021), 'Integrated Reporting Framework', available at: https://bit.ly/49J9Z4D.

Lai, A., Melloni, G. and Stacchezzini R. (2017), 'What does materiality mean to integrated reporting preparers? An empirical exploration', 25(4) *Meditari Accountancy Research*, 533.

Lund, D. S. (2021), 'Enlightened shareholder value, stakeholderism, and the quest for managerial accountability' in E. Pollman and R. B. Thompson (eds.), *Research Handbook on Corporate Purpose and Personhood* (Cheltenham: Edward Edgar), 91.

SASB (Sustainability Accounting Standards Board) (2020), 'Proposed Changes to Conceptual Framework and Rules of Procedure', available at: https://bit.ly/3Pb7RKn.

SEC (Securities and Exchange Commission) (2022), 'The Enhancement and Standardization of Climate-Related Disclosures for Investors', 17 CFR 210, 229, 232, 239, and 249 [Release Nos. 33-11042; 34-94478; File No. S7-10-22].

Sullivan, R. (2013), 'Financial sustainability: Why NGOs are failing to engage investors', *The Guardian*, 16 May.

Standen, M. and McGuire, N. (n.d.), 'NGOs: A growing force in governance', available at: https://bit.ly/3Texcoh.

Strampelli, G. (2018a), 'Are passive index funds active owners? Corporate governance consequences of passive investing', 55 *San Diego Law Review*, 809.

Strampelli, G. (2018b), 'The EU issuers' accounting disclosure regime and investors' information needs: The essential role of narrative reporting', 19 *European Business Organization Law Review*, 554.

Thomas, H. (2021), 'Climate change should already be in the company accounts', *Financial Times*, 6 July.

Tsagas, G. and Villiers, C. (2020), 'Why "less is more" in non-financial reporting initiatives: Concrete steps towards supporting sustainability', 10 *Accounting, Economics, and Law: A Convivium*, 29.

The Role of Non-Financial Disclosure and Liability in Sustainable Finance

Sebastian Mock

17.1 INTRODUCTION

The enactment of the European Non-financial Reporting Directive (2014/95/EU) introduced aspects of corporate social responsibility to the world of financial reporting for almost all listed corporations in the common market. Although this directive does not impose any obligation to consider aspects of corporate social responsibility for managers of listed corporations, it nevertheless creates a considerable pressure on them. The integration of corporate social responsibility into financial reporting raises especially the questions of the relation of financial disclosure to non-financial disclosure, of whether investors that rely on this information are entitled to damages and of whether the management of the issuer can be held responsible. This chapter analyses these aspects and provides an insight into the influence of non-financial disclosure on sustainable finance.

17.2 HISTORY OF NON-FINANCIAL DISCLOSURE

The origins of non-financial disclosure are somewhat hard to determine. Although the European Non-financial Reporting Directive of 2014 (2013/34/EU)[1] established a complex legal regime for non-financial disclosure, similar regulatory aspects were already addressed before by European legislators and by some national legislators.[2]

17.2.1 *International Origin of Non-Financial Disclosure*

For the first time non-financial disclosure was addressed in the United Nations Global Compact, which was announced by the Secretary General of the United

---

[1] Directive 2014/95/EU of the European Parliament and of the Council of 22 October 2014 amending Directive 2013/34/EU as regards disclosure of non-financial and diversity information by certain large undertakings and groups, OJ L 330, 15.11.2014, 1 ff.

[2] For an overview see Mock 2018, 125 (128 ff).

Nations Kofi Annan at the World Economic Forum in 1999 and later officially launched in 2000.[3] This United Nations Global Compact included nine – later ten – principles addressing various aspects of corporate social responsibility. According to this United Nations Global Compact, business enterprises could voluntarily adopt these principles and issue a report about their efforts to comply with them on a yearly basis. Although the United Nations Global Compact was a merely voluntary initiative, it can be considered as the origin of non-financial disclosure. Later, in 2011, the Human Rights Council of the United Nations[4] issued a report stating that states should encourage and require business enterprises to *communicate how they address their human rights impacts.*[5] However, this principle focused only on the impact of business enterprises on human rights and therefore did not address other aspects of corporate social responsibility. Nevertheless, it was considered to be a major step forward for non-financial disclosure since the reporting requirements were designed to be mandatory although the Human Rights Council of the United Nations had no power to implement them.[6] Besides the fact that these reporting requirements were voluntary, the interesting aspect of these initiatives was that they hardly addressed the scope of application but (probably) assumed that business entities only decided to opt for this non-financial disclosure where it actually had an impact on corporate social responsibility or specifically on human rights.

17.2.2 *(Continuous) European Regulation of Non-Financial Disclosure*

In comparison, the topic of non-financial disclosure was addressed earlier by the European legislator. Already in 1998, the European Council set up the High Level Group on Economic and Social Implications of Industrial Change, which invited all companies of more than 1,000 employees to voluntarily publish a "Managing change report", that is, an annual report on employment and working conditions. Later in 2001 the European Commission published a green paper on promoting a European framework for corporate social responsibility,[7] in which a voluntary non-financial disclosure was also preferred.[8] Also in 2001, the European Commission issued a recommendation on the recognition, measurement and disclosure of environmental issues in the annual accounts and annual reports of companies,[9] which was, however, limited to environmental aspects and did not establish a mandatory non-financial disclosure.

---

[3] See www.unglobalcompact.org for further details.
[4] United Nations, UN Guiding Principles on Business and Human Rights, UN doc A/HRC/17/31.
[5] Principle B.3. of the UN Guiding Principles on Business and Human Rights, supra note 4, states: "In meeting their duty to protect, States should:…(d) Encourage, and where appropriate require, business enterprises to communicate how they address their human rights impacts".
[6] For the non-binding effect of these reports see Karrenstein 2011, 158 ff.
[7] European Commission, Green Paper – Promoting a European framework for Corporate Social Responsibility, COM(2001) 366 final.
[8] For these early developments on the European level see Szabó and Sørensen 2015, 311.
[9] European Commission, Commission Recommendation of 30 May 2001, OJ L 156, 13.6.2001, 33 ff.

Such a mandatory non-financial disclosure was only introduced in 2003 by the Accounting Reform Directive of 2003 (2003/51/EC)[10] – amending the "old" accounting European accounting directives[11] – which introduced a reporting requirement for non-financial key performance indicators in the annual report.[12] These non-financial key performance indicators were defined in the new Art. 46 as information related to environmental and employee matters. The introduction of this new reporting requirement as part of the existing European accounting directives[13] established a path dependency between non-financial disclosure, sustainability and "classic" corporate law which was deepened further by later legislative activities and can be considered as the origin for numerous legal problems of sustainable finance which are still determining the understanding of non-financial disclosure today.[14] An interesting and hardly discussed aspect of this early non-financial reporting obligation was that it did not define a specific scope of application but just applied to all business entities within the scope of application of the "old" European accounting directives. Moreover, although this reporting requirement can be considered as an early mandatory non-financial disclosure regime it had almost no practical impact in most Member States.

The actual breakthrough of non-financial disclosure in Europe was initiated by the Non-financial Reporting Directive of 2014 (2013/34/EU),[15] which introduced a complex non-financial reporting regime. Although up to this point non-financial disclosure was not necessarily considered to be part of accounting law or of accounting in general, the European legislator decided to establish this new (complex) non-financial disclosure regime as a part of the management report (Art. 19ff. [New] Accounting Directive [2013/34/EU][16]). By implementing the corporate

---

[10] Directive 2003/51/EC of the European Parliament and of the Council of 18 June 2003 amending Directives 78/660/EEC, 83/349/EEC, 86/635/EEC and 91/674/EEC on the annual and consolidated accounts of certain types of companies, banks and other financial institutions and insurance undertakings, OJ L 178, 17.7.2003, 16 ff.

[11] These are the Fourth Council Directive 78/660/EEC of 25 July 1978 based on Article 54(3)(g) of the Treaty on the annual accounts of certain types of companies, OJ L 222, 14.8.1978, 11; the Seventh Council Directive 83/349/EEC of 13 June 1983 based on the Article 54(3)(g) of the Treaty on consolidated accounts, OJ L 193, 18.7.1983, 1; the Council Directive 86/635/EEC of 8 December 1986 on the annual accounts and consolidated accounts of banks and other financial institutions, OJ L 372, 31.12.1986, p. 1 and the Council Directive 91/674/EEC of 19 December 1991 on the annual accounts and consolidated accounts of insurance undertakings, OJ L 374, 31.12.1991, 7.

[12] The new Art. 46 of the Directive 78/660/EEC as amended by Directive 2003/51/EC stated: "The annual report shall include… non-financial key performance indicators relevant to the particular business, including information relating to environmental and employee matters".

[13] See supra note 11.

[14] See Section 17.3 for further details.

[15] Supra note 1.

[16] Directive 2013/34/EU of the European Parliament and of the Council of 26 June 2013 on the annual financial statements, consolidated financial statements and related reports of certain types of undertakings, amending Directive 2006/43/EC of the European Parliament and of the Council and repealing Council Directives 78/660/EEC and 83/349/EEC, OJ L 182, 29.6.2013, 19.

social responsibility reporting in the management report the European legislator intensified the path dependency between non-financial disclosure, sustainability and corporate law which was already established in 2003 by the amendment by the Accounting Reform Directive of 2003 (2003/51/EC).[17] However, the European legislator seemed to be a little bit undetermined in this regard since Art. 19a subs. 4 (New) Accounting Directive (2013/34/EU) provided the possibility not to include the non-financial statement in the management report but to prepare a separate report which then only had to be published together with the management report.

This non-financial reporting regime was even enlarged by the new Corporate Sustainability Reporting Directive (2022/2464/EU).[18] Here again the European Commission followed the path already taken in 2003 to consider corporate social responsibility reporting as an integral part of accounting law. In fact, the European legislator eliminated the possibility of preparing a separate corporate social responsibility report – which was optional under the Non-financial Reporting Directive of 2014 (2013/34/EU) – therefore implementing an even stronger relationship between financial and non-financial reporting. Since Art. 19b and Art. 19c of the new Corporate Sustainability Reporting Directive (2022/2464/EU)[19] empower the European Commission to adopt sustainability reporting standards as delegated acts and similar initiatives were initiated by some standard setters, a race for the development of (binding) CSR standards started which will have an enormous impact of the understanding and definition of the term "sustainability".

17.3 NON-FINANCIAL DISCLOSURE AND SUSTAINABLE FINANCE: TWO SIDES OF THE SAME COIN?

This legislative path dependency initiated by the European legislator[20] raises the question whether non-financial disclosure and sustainability have indeed a common core or address the same issues; or, to put it in other words: are non-financial disclosure and sustainability two sides of the same coin? This question becomes relevant in three different ways.

17.3.1 *Scope of Application*

First, this question applies to the scope of application for the obligation to financial and non-financial disclosure. Although at least under European law financial and non-financial disclosure have the same legislative origin, the scope of application

---

[17] See supra note 10.
[18] Directive (EU) 2022/2464 of the European Parliament and of the Council of 14 December 2022 amending Regulation (EU) No 537/2014, Directive 2004/109/EC, Directive 2006/43/EC and Directive 2013/34/EU, as regards corporate sustainability reporting, OJ L 322, 16.12.2022, 15.
[19] Ibid.
[20] See Section 17.2.2.

is not identical. Pursuant to Art. 1, 39 (New) Accounting Directive (2013/34/EU), all undertakings listed in Annex I and II of the directive must publish within a reasonable period of time the duly approved annual financial statements and the management report. However, Art. 19a (New) Accounting Directive (2013/34/EU) – as amended by the Non-financial Reporting Directive (2014/95/EU) – states that only large undertakings, which are public-interest entities exceeding on their balance sheet dates the criterion of having an average number of 500 employees during the financial year, shall include a non-financial statement in the management report. This non-financial statement must contain information to the extent necessary for an understanding of the development, performance, position and impact of the undertaking's activity relating to, as a minimum, environmental, social and employee matters, respect for human rights, anti-corruption and bribery matters. Consequently, only a small portion of undertakings within the (general) scope of application of the (New) Accounting Directive (2013/34/EU) fall within the scope of application of non-financial disclosure.

This distinction also remains under the new Corporate Sustainability Reporting Directive (2022/2464/EU),[21] although this directive will expand the scope of application to all large undertakings in general and to listed small and medium-sized undertakings. Also, under the new regime only a fraction of the undertakings within the general scope of application of the (New) Accounting Directive (2013/34/EU) will have the obligation to make non-financial disclosure since especially all non-listed small and medium-sized undertakings are outside the scope of application.

17.3.1.1 Creditor Protection as Driving Force of Financial Reporting

This distinction raised the question why the scope of application of financial and non-financial disclosure is not identical. The answer to this question is rather simple, since the purpose of financial and non-financial disclosure is different. Financial disclosure as provided by the (New) Accounting Directive (2013/34/EU) derives its scope from the problem of limited liability of certain undertakings. The mandatory disclosure of certain financial information is based on the concept that creditors and contractual partners of these undertakings are confronted with an undertaking where only the undertaking itself but not its shareholders are liable for its debts. To compensate for this limited liability the mandatory disclosure of certain financial information provides a mechanism for these creditors and contractual partners to protect themselves by deciding not to contract with these undertakings in a case where the published financial information indicates that these undertakings will not be able to fully fulfill their obligations.[22] This approach is defined in Recital No. 3 (New) Accounting Directive (2013/34/EU), which states that financial reporting

[21] See supra note 18.
[22] For the backgrounds of this concept see Lutter, Bayer and Schmidt 2018, § 23 note 1 ff; Vicari 2021, 195 ff.

is of special importance for the protection of shareholders, members and third parties; moreover, Recital No. 5 (New) Accounting Directive (2013/34/EU) states that
the scope of the directive should include certain undertakings with limited liability
such as public and private limited liability companies. However, it must be acknowledged that the protection of creditors besides the protection of shareholders and
members of the undertaking is nowadays probably of less importance than it was
during the era when the "old" accounting European accounting directives[23] were
enacted, since in the meantime many Member States have eased their national law
on the protection of creditors of business entities with limited liability, considering
creditor protection more as an issue of self-protection of creditors.[24] Nevertheless,
the Company Law Directive (2017/1132/EU)[25] is still based on the system of capital
maintenance as an instrument of creditor protection.[26]

17.3.1.2 Sustainability Risks and Investor and Consumer
Trust as Driving Force of Non-Financial Reporting

In the case of non-financial reporting, the idea of creditor protection does not apply.
In fact, the purpose of non-financial disclosure as provided by the Non-financial
Reporting Directive (2014/95/EU) and pursued by the new Corporate Sustainability
Reporting Directive (2022/2464/EU)[27] is different.[28] According to Recital No. 3 Non-
financial Reporting Directive (2014/95/EU), the purpose of non-financial disclosure
is to identify sustainability risks and to increase investor and consumer trust. This
(different) approach was further defined in Recital 8 new Corporate Sustainability
Reporting Directive (2022/2464/EU),[29] which states that the ultimate beneficiaries
of better sustainability reporting by undertakings are individual citizens and savers.
Furthermore, Recital 8 of the new Corporate Sustainability Reporting Directive
(2022/2464/EU)[30] states that two groups of beneficiaries of non-financial disclosure
exist: investors, including asset managers, who want to better understand the risks
and opportunities that sustainability issues pose to their investments and the impacts
of those investments on people, and the environment and organizations, including
non-governmental organizations and social partners, that wish to better hold undertakings to account for their impacts on people and the environment. Taking this
approach into account it would be – from a theoretical point of view – necessary to

---

[23] See supra note 11.
[24] Vicari 2021, 47 ff. with further references to the developments in the last decade.
[25] Directive (EU) 2017/1132 of the European Parliament and of the Council of 14 June 2017 relating to
      certain aspects of company law (codification), OJ L 169, 30.6.2017, 46.
[26] For this concept see, for example, Lutter, Bayer and Schmidt 2018, § 19 note 1 ff; Vicari 2021, 37 ff.
[27] See supra note 18.
[28] For the scope of the Non-financial Reporting Directive (2014/95/EU) see Lutter, Bayer and Schmidt
      2018, § 23 note 37 ff.
[29] See supra note 18.
[30] Ibid.

define the scope of application of non-financial disclosure according to the impact a business entity has on sustainability in general. Consequently, the size of the business activities of an entity, its legal form or a listing on a stock exchange would not be the determining aspects but mere indicators to define the scope of application of non-financial reporting in general.

> Example 1: *A business undertaking is a global player in the textile or food industry with business activities around the world and is not organized as an undertaking with limited liability but as a single merchant or commercial partnership.*
>
> Despite the fact that this business undertaking has an enormous impact on sustainability, this business undertaking does not fall within the scope of application of the Non-financial Reporting Directive (2014/95/EU) or the new Corporate Sustainability Reporting Directive (2022/2464/EU).[31] The mere fact that this business undertaking would change its legal form into a corporation and would seek a listing on a stock exchange would, however, establish the duty to non-financial reporting, although in both cases the impact on sustainability would not change. This is different for creditor protection since the existing legal form of the business undertaking does not trigger the scope of application. Only the change of the legal form into a corporation (with limited liability) would be the determining factor to establish the duty for financial disclosure.

17.3.1.3 Non-Financial Disclosure as Missing Piece in Half-Yearly Financial Reports and Interim Management Statements

These differences between financial and non-financial disclosure become even more obvious by taking the European regime for periodic half-yearly financial reports and interim management statements into account. Neither the (amended)[32] Transparency Directive (2004/109/EC)[33] nor the Non-financial Reporting Directive (2014/95/EU) nor the new Corporate Sustainability Reporting Directive (2022/2464/EU)[34] actually require the inclusion of non-financial information in these interim reports. In fact, half-yearly financial reports and the interim

---

[31] Ibid.

[32] Last amended by Regulation (EU) 2021/337 of the European Parliament and of the Council of 16 February 2021 amending Regulation (EU) 2017/1129 as regards the EU Recovery prospectus and targeted adjustments for financial intermediaries and Directive 2004/109/EC as regards the use of the single electronic reporting format for annual financial reports, to support the recovery from the COVID-19 crisis, OJ L 68, 26.2.2021, 1 ff.

[33] Directive 2004/109/EC of the European Parliament and of the Council of 15 December 2004 on the harmonisation of transparency requirements in relation to information about issuers whose securities are admitted to trading on a regulated market and amending Directive 2001/34/EC, OJ L 390, 31.12.2004, 38.

[34] See supra note 18.

management statements (as required by some stock exchanges) must include only financial information, although most issuers being required to publish these reports also fall within the scope of application of non-financial disclosure. Considering the scope of application of non-financial disclosure and its justification,[35] it seems doubtful that non-financial reporting is limited to an annual basis.

17.3.2 *Content*

When it comes to the actual content of financial and non-financial reporting, the differences between these two systems are obvious. In fact, non-financial information has no direct impact on profits, dividends or other information provided by balance sheets or annual/consolidated accounts in general. It constitutes only soft information, which is why they are only included in the management report and not in the balance sheet itself. This becomes evident in the title of the new Corporate Sustainability Reporting Directive (2022/2464/EU)[36]; while the original Non-financial Reporting Directive (2014/95/EU) used the term *non-financial reporting*, the new Corporate Sustainability Reporting Directive (2022/2464/EU)[37] uses the term *corporate sustainability reporting*. Pursuant to Recital No. 7, this rephrasing of the directive was done due to the fact that many organizations, initiatives and practitioners in this field refer to "sustainability" and not non-financial information. However, regarding the actual impact of these sustainability information on financial information, Recital No. 7 remains somehow vague; it only states that sustainability information does have a financial relevance. It does not become clear how sustainability information directly influences any position on balance sheet or the annual/consolidated accounts in general as stated in Annex III to IV (New) Accounting Directive (2013/34/EU). There is no doubt that especially the transformation of business entities towards a more sustainable business model often does involve large costs. However, these costs are already reflected in the balance sheet – when they incur – without being specifically indicated as being costs for this transformation process. As a consequence, sustainability information provides only information whether the business model of an undertaking has to deal with a transformation in the future or whether this transformation process was already initiated or is already completed.

> Example 2: *Corporation X has been a car producer for almost 100 years. So far its major business is the production of cars using gasoline as fuel. Due to recent legislation the corporation will stop producing this kind of car by 2030 and will only develop and produce cars running on electricity or other alternative fuels.*

[35] See Section 17.3.1.2.
[36] See supra note 18.
[37] Ibid.

In its current state the corporation would have to report in its non-financial statement especially which impact its current business model has on the environment. If the corporation starts this transformation process in order to produce only cars running on electricity or other alternative fuels it will have to bear large costs. However, these costs are not yet reflected in the annual (and consolidated) statements under the current European accounting regime since these costs have not yet been incurred. Nevertheless, the corporation has to describe this planned transformation process in the non-financial statement and the management report. Investors, shareholders, creditors and third parties can use this information to conclude that these large costs will probably prevent the corporation from distributing any dividends for the next years. Whether this is really the case will only be seen when the future annual (and consolidated) statements are actually drafted and published.

Therefore, annual (and consolidated) accounts merely represent one consistent piece of information but represent a combination of two – somehow independent – information tools. While the balance sheet and profit and loss account provide number-based information, the notes and the management report – and with it the non-financial or sustainability statement – provide text-based information. However, the non-financial or sustainability statement as introduced by the Non-financial Reporting Directive (2014/95/EU) is not the origin of this development but only a consequence of a development that already started decades ago. The original Fourth (Accounting) Council Directive (78/660/EEC) of 1978[38] contained only one article addressing the management report, which in a nutshell simply stated that the report shall give an indication of the company's likely future development (Art. 46 subs. 2 lit. c)). In contrast, the (New) Accounting Directive (2013/34/EU) contains a whole chapter for the management report providing a complex set of rules for its content. This development is also reflected in the Member States (e.g., Germany[39] and Austria), where the reporting requirements for the management report increased tremendously in the last decades, nowadays often representing more than 50% of the content of the annual/consolidated accounts.

17.3.3 *Procedure for Examining Sustainability Information*

Finally, the negative path dependency described above becomes evident by reflecting on the procedure by which annual/consolidated accounts are prepared and examined. Over the last 200 years, legislators of all major jurisdictions developed a rather complex system for the process of drafting and examining annual/consolidated accounts. In fact, large parts of the corporate governance discussion in the last

---

[38] See supra note 11.
[39] For an overview see Wöhe and Mock 2020, § 20.

decades focused on the improvement of the examination of annual/consolidated accounts.[40] When the non-financial disclosure was introduced by the Non-financial Reporting Directive (2014/95/EU) the European legislator decided to somehow use the existing mechanisms of accounting law for this new kind of reporting and yet again depend on the path dependency between financial and non-financial disclosure. Since the non-financial disclosure takes place within the management report, all existing mechanisms in this context automatically came into play. As the consequence, the Non-financial Reporting Directive (2014/95/EU) also changed Art. 33 (New) Accounting Directive (2013/34/EU), stating that the Member States shall ensure that the members of the administrative, management and supervisory bodies of an undertaking, acting within the competences assigned to them by national law, have collective responsibility for ensuring that the management report (including the non-financial statement) are drawn up and published in accordance with the requirements of the (New) Accounting Directive (2013/34/EU). However, regarding the auditing of the non-financial statement, the European legislator seemed to have some doubts, since the Non-financial Reporting Directive (2014/95/EU) also changed Art. 34 (New) Accounting Directive (2013/34/EU), stating that the non-financial statement does not need to be examined by an auditor. However, these doubts do not exist anymore since the new Corporate Sustainability Reporting Directive (2022/2464/EU)[41] will introduce a mandatory examination of the management report by an auditor. Nevertheless, the auditor will only have to express an opinion based on a limited assurance engagement as regards the compliance of the sustainability reporting with the requirements of the directive, including the compliance of the sustainability reporting with the adopted reporting standards. Moreover, the Member States may also allow an independent assurance service provider to express this opinion (Art. 34 para 3 Corporate Sustainability Reporting Directive [2022/2464/EU][42]). Although this constitutes a major shift from the legal situation under the Non-financial Reporting Directive (2014/95/EU), the European legislator still seems to have some doubts whether keeping the regular accounting procedures for the examination of financial information is the right approach for sustainable/ non-financial information. The limited approach for the auditing of the sustainability information underlines the general criticism to considering sustainability information as part of general accounting information. Alternatively, the European legislator could have followed a completely different approach in introducing non-financial reporting. Instead of considering it as part of the management report, the European legislator could have introduced a separate form of information or report which then would have to be published just like any other non-accounting report or information. However, this would have led to the fact that basically only the board

---

[40] For on overview, especially in the context of the Wirecard scandal, see Mock 2021, 520, 525 ff.
[41] See supra note 18.
[42] Ibid.

of directors/the management would have been in charge of drafting and publishing this sustainability report, which especially would have left out the supervisory board and the auditor or any other legal institution under national law being in charge of examining accounting information. Then the difficult discussion would have started of who is in charge of examining this information. This situation is not completely unknown, but is generally the case for any kind of capital market information. Neither European law nor generally the national laws of the Member States provide a regulation of who is charge of examining the publication of ad hoc or continuous public disclosure of inside information under Art. 17 Market Abuse Regulation. Although all information and especially inside information (Art. 7 MAR) is of general importance for all participants of capital markets, there is so far no discussion to introduce an examination of ad hoc announcements under Art. 17 MAR by an auditor or even a different corporate body than the board of directors/management being in charge of the publication. Interestingly enough, the situation seems to be different for sustainability information, which is hard to justify. Even by considering the fundamental importance of sustainability information for the capital markets and the public, one would hardly assume that financial information has the same importance than the profits stated in a balance sheet. Thus it is necessary to develop and adopt a different standard for examining financial and non-financial/sustainable information. The two legislative options and their impact on the role of the supervisory board and the auditor are shown in Figure 17.1.

If the European legislator would had adopted an independent and not accounting-related disclosure regime for sustainability information, it would have left other corporate bodies or the auditor out of the picture. By integrating non-financial reporting in the management report, these questions or problems never occurred and the European legislator simply adopted the existing accounting system for the purpose of sustainability reporting. That this fundamental decision created some turmoil can be seen in the new legislative approach for the examination of sustainability reporting under the new Corporate Sustainability Reporting Directive (2022/2464/EU).[43]

17.3.4 *Missing Link between Financial and Non-Financial Reporting*

To answer the initial question of this section, whether non-financial disclosure and sustainable finance are two sides of the same coin: financial and non-financial reporting are not two sides of the same coin. They are fundamentally different in their scope of application and their underlying justification for their origin. Moreover, the actual content of financial reporting and non-financial reporting is fundamentally different since financial information a is number-based information medium and sustainability information is a text-based information medium. Finally,

---

43 Ibid.

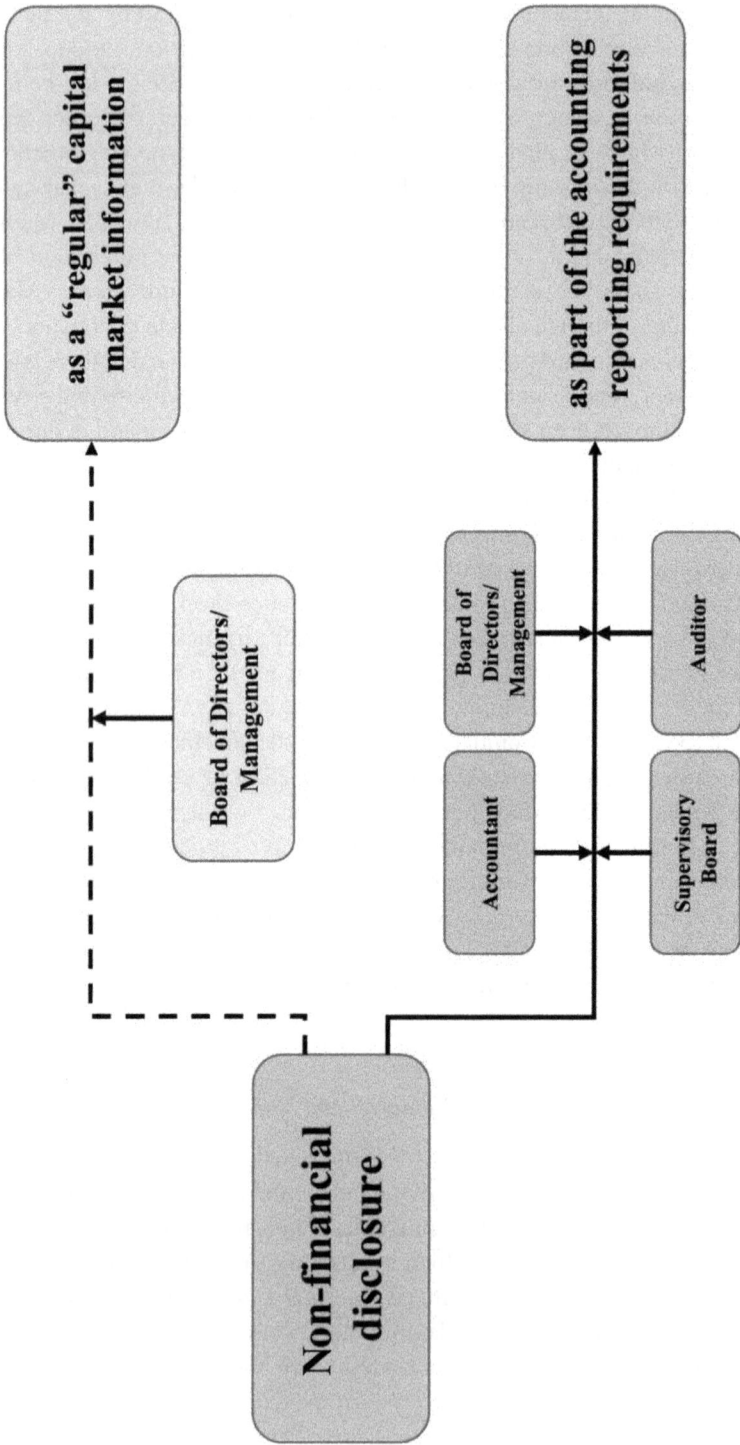

FIGURE 17.1 Legislative options and impact on supervisory board and auditor

financial information and non-financial information do not require the same governance procedure for drafting and examining. While for financial information an examination by an auditor is fundamental and unavoidable, sustainability information does not require the same extent of examination. Despite these fundamental differences the European legislator choose to integrate sustainability reporting into the management report and thereby created numerous problems, especially in the context of liability.

17.4 LIABILITY FOR INCORRECT NON-FINANCIAL/CORPORATE SUSTAINABILITY DISCLOSURE

Even though financial disclosure and non-financial disclosure are hardly connected, the existing liability regime of financial disclosure will probably have a severe impact on non-financial/corporate sustainability disclosure since this regime has already been in place for several decades and is well established. Yet again, the path dependency between financial disclosure and non-financial disclosure established by the European legislator will be the basis for a further advancement of non-financial/corporate sustainability disclosure.

17.4.1 *The Reluctant European Legislator and the Remaining Gap in National Law*

This is especially the case since the European legislator did not address the aspect of liability in the Non-financial Reporting Directive (2014/95/EU) at all. In fact, the directive itself did not even establish a separate sanction regime but only introduced additional reporting requirements in the (New) Accounting Directive (2013/34/EU). Hence the existing sanction regime of the (New) Accounting Directive (2013/34/EU) had to be applied also in the context of non-financial reporting. Here the European legislator shows some strange kind of reluctance to address civil liability. Recital 41 (New) Accounting Directive (2013/34/EU) makes this clear by stating that liability for drawing up and publishing annual financial statements and consolidated financial statements, as well as management reports and consolidated management reports, is based on national law. In this context, the (New) Accounting Directive (2013/34/EU) establishes only the requirement for the Member States to introduce appropriate liability rules, but also explicitly[44] states that the extent of liability should be determined by the Member States. This legislative reluctance of the European legislator continues with the new Corporate Sustainability Reporting Directive (2022/2464/EU),[45] which also does not establish a harmonized legal regime for civil liability for incorrect non-financial/corporate sustainability disclosure. It is therefore

---

[44] Recital 41 Sentence 3 (New) Accounting Directive (2013/34/EU).
[45] See supra note 18.

the task of the Member States to provide such a civil liability regime. Since most Member States transformed the Non-financial Reporting Directive (2014/95/EU) into national law by simply amending the financial reporting requirements – and thereby incorporated the path dependency problem of the European legislator[46] into national law –the existing civil liability regime usually applies also to non-financial/corporate sustainability disclosure. Although this seems to be logical and consistent, a closer look reveals that the application of the established civil liability regime for financial disclosure to non-financial/corporate sustainability disclosure remains problematic and creates some serious problems.

17.4.2 *The Multilayered Problem of Liability*

This is especially the case since the civil liability for financial disclosure is a multi-layered problem consisting of basically three different scenarios.

17.4.2.1 (External) Liability of the Issuer towards Investors

Firstly, the issuer itself can be held liable for an incorrect non-financial/corporate sustainability disclosure. However, such a liability is in most jurisdictions usually not subject to a specific regulation but is only derived from case law based on tort law, in which the problem of pure economic loss is often more or less bypassed or at least weakened.

17.4.2.1.1 THE PROBLEM OF CAUSATION By reflecting the usual problems in most jurisdictions to establish such a civil liability, the difficulty that is probably most common is causation and the respective burden of proof. In general capital market law, numerous concepts exist to overcome this problem, which are more or less some kind of deviation from the fraud-on-the-market theory as established in US capital market law. Nevertheless, the differences between the civil laws of the Member States remain notable in this context.[47] However, in addressing these concepts in the context of non-financial/corporate sustainability disclosure the courts of Member States might be less reluctant since non-financial/sustainability information are usually considered to have a severe impact and are generally reflected in the public to a larger extent than pure financial information, which does not address a general audience but a more specific one.

> Example 3: The so-called Dieselgate involving numerous car producers was widely covered in media all around the world. Such a level of public attention does not usually arise if a corporation has to admit that certain financial information

---

[46] See Section 17.2.2.
[47] For a larger overview see, for example, Conac and Gelter 2019 with various reports about securities litigation and enforcement.

was not correctly stated in the annual/consolidated accounts. The same applies to other scandals in recent years involving the violation of labour standards or human rights by business entities. The media reaction that is often generated causes tremendous public attention.

Nevertheless, courts might also adopt a more limited approach, arguing that the standard of proof for acquiring a financial instrument because of the non-financial/corporate sustainability disclosure of the issuer should be higher since sustainability is only one – and often not the determining – aspect for the acquisition of financial instruments. Therefore, they could argue that investors/shareholders have to meet a higher standard for providing that they acquired or sold the financial instruments because of the (incorrect) non-financial/corporate sustainability disclosure. This problem of causation might become even more complex since the (incorrect) non-financial/corporate sustainability disclosure takes place at the same time as the financial disclosure, creating a mixed information tool, making it hard to identify the impact of each piece of information. Here again the path dependency established by the European legislator precludes a necessary distinction between financial and non-financial/corporate sustainability disclosure.

> Example 4: *Corporation X publishes false non-financial statements for several years by not stating that several suppliers do not comply with some specific labour standards, although the corporation was aware of this. During the same time the corporation is extremely successful, with a certain product increasing the profits of the corporation for years.*
> Although investors could argue that they not would have bought the financial instruments issued by this corporation if correct non-financial statements had been published, it is hard to determine whether the decision of the investors was based on the (false) non-financial statements or the success of the product.

17.4.2.1.2 THE PROBLEM OF DETERMINING THE DAMAGE Apart from the problem of causation, the determination of the actual damage for the investors also remains rather unclear in the context of incorrect non-financial/corporate sustainability disclosure. For listed corporations the solution in this context is probably the same as for financial disclosure: the incorrect non-financial/corporate sustainability disclosure entitles the investor to claim restitution, meaning that he or she can hand over the respective shares in exchange for a refund of the amount invested in the corporation. However, if the investor/shareholder already sold the shares before the incorrect non-financial/corporate sustainability disclosure is discovered, he or she can claim damages in the amount of the higher price he or she could have sold the financial instruments at. This usually requires the determination of the value of the financial instruments with and without the incorrect non-financial/corporate sustainability disclosure, which in many cases might cause some serious problems.

17.4.2.1.3 INCORRECT NON-FINANCIAL/CORPORATE SUSTAINABILITY DIS-
CLOSURE AND THE VALUE OF THE ISSUER Although these two principles
can generally be applied in the context of incorrect non-financial/corporate
sustainability disclosure, it remains somewhat unclear whether a non-financial/
corporate sustainability disclosure that is simply incorrect can really cause a damage
for the investor/shareholders. It might be the case that the incorrect non-financial/
corporate sustainability disclosure has actually had no clear influence on the value
of the corporation and the financial instrument but has caused only immaterial
damage to the shareholder/investor.

> Example 5: *Corporation Y is a large retail seller of all kind of textile. Although
> the corporation had made it clear in their annual non-financial statement that
> it does not deal with suppliers being that are involved in child labour, there
> is a report in the media that one supplier is actually involved in child labour.
> However, this media report does not influence the stock exchange price of the
> shares of this corporation.*
> If the corporation can actually prove that this false non-financial statement has
> had no influence on the stock price and is widely ignored on the capital mar-
> kets, the questions arises whether investors can still claim that they suffered a
> damage entitling them to compensation.

In these cases, it remains to be seen whether the courts of the Member States
really apply the mentioned principles developed in the context of financial disclosure. This seems to be doubtful in cases where the incorrect non-financial/
corporate sustainability disclosure is not material but consists only of a smaller or
even insignificant misstatement. Some courts might even go further and generally
question whether an incorrect non-financial/corporate sustainability disclosure
can actually be the basis for a claim for damages of shareholders/investors, since
this information only relates to the impact of the business activities of the corporation on the environment and the society in general, not on the actual value
of the corporation or its financial instruments. However, this categorization of
the incorrect non-financial/corporate sustainability disclosure as no damage will
probably only be found in jurisdictions applying a rather strict interpretation of
the term *damage* requiring a real economic loss for the investor/shareholder. In
contrast, many jurisdictions apply a less strict concept for the determination of
damages, which is in some jurisdictions described as *natural damage*, requiring
only that the investor/shareholder acquired a financial instrument which he or she
simply did not want to acquire, therefore causing a wrongful composition of the
assets of the investor/shareholder. Those jurisdictions that actually follow the latter approach will probably be less reluctant to consider the acquisition of a financial instrument after an incorrect non-financial/corporate sustainability disclosure
as a damage for the investor.

17.4.2.2 (Internal) Liability of the Management/Supervisory Board Members

These problems also occur in the context of an internal liability of the members of the management or the supervisory board members. An incorrect non-financial/corporate sustainability disclosure usually does not necessarily cause a damage to the corporation. Often the loss of the corporation is limited to a loss in reputation which later might cause some material damage.

> Example 6: *Like Example 5.*
> In this case the loss of the corporation is basically limited to a loss in reputation. Even if the shareholders argue that the corporation lost some business because of these false non-financial statements, it remains doubtful that the shareholder can actually prove that such a loss of business activities is only related to the exposure of the false non-financial statements.

However, some jurisdictions also consider the pure loss of reputation as an actual damage or loss which must be compensated by the members of the management or the supervisory board members. But in these jurisdictions the determination of the exact amount to be compensated usually remains somehow unclear.

Besides the problem of determining the actual loss of the corporation because of the incorrect non-financial/corporate sustainability disclosure, the internal liability of the members of the management or the supervisory board members might face the problem of an abusive enforcement by shareholders. Nowadays most jurisdictions provide an instrument for (minority) shareholders to enforce claims on behalf of the corporation against the members of the management or the supervisory board members on behalf of the corporation.[48] These instruments often constitute derivative suits or similar concepts. If a jurisdiction provides such an instrument for shareholders and the requirements in this jurisdiction on the determination of the damage to the corporation caused by the incorrect non-financial/corporate sustainability disclosure are rather low, this instrument might be used not only to enforce claims against the corporations but also as an instrument to enforce more sustainable conduct by the corporation in business affairs. So the general or public interest of acting sustainably and not the best interest of the corporation might become the driving force in these cases. However, since some jurisdictions already provide some protection to the corporation in cases of frivolous law suits, these rules might be applicable also in cases of claims in the context of an incorrect non-financial/corporate sustainability disclosure.

17.4.2.3 Liability of the Auditor

In the context of non-financial reporting/corporate sustainability disclosure, the liability of auditors will also probably create a new chapter in this never-ending story.

---

[48] For a comparative overview see, for example, Ventoruzzo et al. 2015, 359 ff.

This is the case since the European legislator recently decided to introduce some new kind of auditing review standard for the examination of corporate sustainability reporting.[49] This new opinion, based on a limited assurance, can obviously not establish the same civil liability as the opinion expressed by the auditor in the context of financial reporting.

17.4.2.3.1 LIABILITY TOWARDS THE AUDITED COMPANY While the European legislator so far did not harmonize the liability of auditors towards the audited company, many Member States have an explicit regulation or at least some case law based on the auditing contract between the auditor and the audited corporation. However, it is doubtful that these existing regulations and case law can simply be applied in cases of incorrect non-financial/corporate sustainability disclosure. Also, the question remains what kind of damage is caused by the failure of the auditor to detect incorrect non-financial/corporate sustainability disclosure. In this context the problems might probably occur in cases relating to of the internal liability of the members of the management or the supervisory board members.[50]

17.4.2.3.2 LIABILITY TOWARDS THIRD PARTIES As regards liability towards third parties, most Member States do not provide a specific regulation but mostly rely on case law being based on general tort law.[51] Here an incorrect non-financial/corporate sustainability disclosure probably makes things even more complicated than they already are under the existing national law. Even if a jurisdiction provides a direct claim by shareholders/investors against auditors in cases of an inaccurate audit, this does not necessarily mean that this case law can simply be applied in the context of incorrect non-financial/corporate sustainability disclosure. Yet again,[52] the limited scope of review of the non-financial/corporate sustainability disclosure by the auditor as established by the new Corporate Sustainability Reporting Directive (2022/2464/EU)[53] raised the question of whether the violation of the limited standard of review can actually be the basis for a civil liability. And even if courts do consider this violation of the limited standard of review as a violation of a duty towards the investors, this does not necessarily mean that investors/shareholders can actually claim damages from the auditor. Also in this context the problem of causation and the respective burden of proof come into play as regards the problem of determining the actual damage for the investor/shareholder. Besides all other problems, the liability of an auditor towards third parties must also be considered in this context, making it less probable that an actual civil liability of auditors for an inaccurate audit of non-financial/corporate sustainability disclosure can be established.

---

[49] See Section 17.3.3.
[50] See Section 17.4.2.2.
[51] For an overview and the missing harmonization see Giudici 2012.
[52] For this limited standard of review see Section 17.3.3.
[53] See supra note 18.

17.4.2.4 Voluntary Non-Financial Disclosure

To make things even more complex and unclear, one could take the voluntary non-financial disclosure into account. Since the scope of application of non-financial/corporate sustainability disclosure is still rather limited,[54] numerous business entities outside this scope of application conduct a voluntary non-financial/corporate sustainability disclosure. In these cases, the problem of liability becomes even more significant since this disclosure is usually used as marketing or greenwashing. To deny a liability towards investors/shareholders in these cases seems to be odd and inconsistent. Nevertheless, also in these cases the same problems in establishing civil liability exist.

17.4.2.5 A New Case for Harmonization?

All these problems raise the question of whether the European legislator should opt for a harmonization of civil liability in cases of incorrect non-financial/corporate sustainability disclosure. However, it seems to be doubtful that non-financial/corporate sustainability disclosure will actually provide the basis for a harmonization of civil liability for incorrect (non-)financial disclosure. So far, the differences in the legal systems of the Member States are severe and numerous. Despite the actual importance of non-financial/corporate sustainability disclosure, it would be something of a strange development if non-financial/corporate sustainability disclosure were actually the driving force of the harmonization of civil liability in financial disclosure. If a harmonization is going to be achieved, such a harmonization should start with the civil liability for financial disclosure. However, such a harmonization might take place in criminal law since most Member States provide more or less clear criminal law sanctions in cases of a non-financial/corporate sustainability disclosure.

17.4.3 *The (Probable) Impact of Liability for Incorrect Non-Financial/Corporate Sustainability Disclosure on Sustainability in General*

Despite these existing problems in establishing civil liability in cases of non-financial/corporate sustainability disclosure, this civil liability will probably have a severe impact on the development of the legal sustainability regime in the European Union. The continuous periodic financial disclosure applies to an endless number of business entities within the European Union, providing an unlimited number of potential cases for civil liability for incorrect non-financial/corporate sustainability disclosure. Since these corporations are usually in the focus of the public, such incorrect disclosure will usually be revealed on a regular basis.

---

[54] See Section 17.3.1.

17.5 SUMMARY

European sustainable finance law is not based on an independent non-financial disclosure regime but refers to a large extent to the regime established by the CSR Reporting Directive (2013/34/EU) and the new Corporate Sustainability Reporting Directive (2022/2464/EU)[55] as its successor.

Sustainable finance is not limited to business entities that decide to issue sustainable financial instruments or that generally follow a sustainable business purpose, since the scope of application of the non-financial reporting regime established by the CSR Reporting Directive (2013/34/EU) does not distinguish between business entities with and without an impact on corporate social responsibility. Basically, all business entities within the application of the non-financial reporting regime established by the CSR Reporting Directive (2013/34/EU) and the new Corporate Sustainability Reporting Directive (2022/2464/EU)[56] can be considered as issuers of sustainable financial instruments.

The actual content of financial reporting and non-financial reporting is fundamentally different since financial information is a number-based information medium and sustainability information is a text-based information medium.

Financial information and non-financial information do not require the same corporate governance procedure for drafting and examining. While for financial information an examination by an auditor is fundamental and unavoidable, sustainability information does not require the same extent of examination. Despite these fundamental differences the European legislator choose to integrate sustainability reporting into the management report and thereby prevented the development of a unique and sustainability-shaped governance structure for non-financial/corporate sustainability disclosure.

Although financial disclosure and non-financial disclosure are based on the same principles, it is doubtful that the liability regime of financial disclosure can be used as some kind of blueprint for a civil liability regime for non-financial disclosure. Since non-financial disclosure addresses a different kind of information, the courts of the Member States will probably be reluctant to apply the existing case law for civil liability in cases of incorrect financial disclosure to non-financial disclosure.

Since the existing framework for civil liability in financial disclosure cannot be used for cases of incorrect non-financial disclosure, it is necessary to develop an independent regime of civil liability for incorrect non-financial disclosure. The existing path dependency between financial and non-financial disclosure prevents this necessary step.

---

[55] See supra note 18.
[56] Ibid.

REFERENCES

Conac, P.-H. and Gelter, M. (2019), *Global Securities Litigation and Enforcement* (Cambridge, UK: Cambridge University Press).

Giudici, P. (2012), 'Auditors' multi-layered liability regime', 13(4) *European Business Organization Law Review*, 501–555.

Karrenstein, D. (2011), *Der Menschenrechtsrat der Vereinten Nationen* (Tübingen: Mohr Siebeck).

Lutter, M., Bayer, W. and Schmidt, J. (2018), *Europäisches Unternehmens- und Kapitalmarktrecht*, 6th ed. (Berlin: De Gruyter).

Mock, S. (2018), 'Berichterstattung über Corporate Social Responsibility im Bilanzrecht' in Fleischer, H., Kalss, S. and Vogt, H.-U. (eds.), *Corporate Social Responsibility – Achtes deutsch-österreichisch-schweizerisches Symposium* (Tübingen: Mohr Siebeck), 125.

Mock, S. (2021), 'Wirecard and European company and financial law', 18(4) *European Company and Financial Law Review*, 519–554.

Szabó, D. G. and Sørensen, K. E. (2015), 'New EU Directive on the Disclosure of Non-Financial Information (CSR)', 12 *European Company and Financial Law Review*, 307–340.

Ventoruzzo, M., Conac, P.-H., Goto, G. et al. (2015), *Comparative Corporate Law* (St. Paul, MI: West Academic Publishing).

Vicari, A. (2021), *European Company Law* (Berlin: De Gruyter).

Wöhe, G. and Mock, S. (2020), *Die Handels- und Steuerbilanz – Rechnungslegungsrecht*, 7th ed. (Munich: Beck Juristischer Verlag).

PART IV

Ensuring Financial Stability and Sustainability

18

Macroprudential Policies and Climate Risks

Seraina Grünewald

18.1 INTRODUCTION

Macroprudential policies were *the* innovation of public authorities across the globe in response to the experience of the Global Financial Crisis (GFC). A key lesson of the GFC was that public concern should no longer solely focus on individual financial institutions and their idiosyncratic risk, but also include interdependencies, interconnections and joint exposures among them, leading to systemic risk.[1] A 'macroprudential overlay', complementary to the pre-existing microprudential regulation and supervision, should ensure the stability of the financial system as a whole. Basel III introduced a range of macroprudential tools, including both countercyclical and structural tools, that were transposed in the European Union (EU) through the Capital Requirements Regulation (CRR)[2] and Capital Requirements Directive (CRD).[3]

That climate change and the transition to a low-carbon economy can and will be financially material for financial institutions is widely acknowledged and has led to coining the term 'climate-related financial risks' (CRFRs). Moreover, the financial sector has a role to play in '[m]aking finance flows consistent with a pathway towards low greenhouse gas emissions and climate-resilient development'.[4] It must help support businesses and households in reducing emissions and facilitate the adjustment in the real economy and society. Over the past years, companies have started making more serious efforts to develop effective capabilities to both manage CRFRs and

---

[1] De Larosière 2009.

[2] Regulation (EU) No 575/2013 of the European Parliament and of the Council of 26 June 2013 on prudential requirements for credit institutions and investment firms and amending Regulation (EU) No 648/2012 (CRR), OJ L 176, 27.6.2013, p. 1.

[3] Directive 2013/36/EU of the European Parliament and of the Council of 26 June 2013 on access to the activity of credit institutions and the prudential supervision of credit institutions and investment firms, amending Directive 2002/87/EC and repealing Directives 2006/48/EC and 2006/49/EC (CRD), OJ L 176, 27.6.2013, p. 338.

[4] Article 2(1)(c) of the Paris Agreement, Paris, 12th December 2015, in force 4th November 2016, UNTS 3156.

identify opportunities from the low-carbon transition, conducting more sophisticated climate data analysis and setting firm-specific carbon-neutrality strategies.

Numerous initiatives are being developed to better assess and quantify the impact of CRFRs on the financial system, both internationally and at EU and national levels. Microprudential supervisors have started to include climate risks into their daily practices.[5] The Basel Committee on Banking Supervision (BCBS)[6] and the European Banking Authority (EBA)[7] are working on integrating CRFRs (and 'ESG risks' more broadly) more systematically in all three pillars of the Basel III and CRR/CRD frameworks. In addition, there is need for a complementary and distinctly macroprudential perspective on and approach to CRFRs that captures the system-wide impacts of CRFRs. Macroprudential policy has the objective of safeguarding the stability of the financial system both by increasing its resilience to shocks and by preventing the build-up of vulnerabilities to begin with. CRFRs, this chapter argues, fall squarely into its system-wide and preventive approach.

The chapter proceeds as follows. Section 18.2 discusses what CRFRs are, motivates why they are a macroprudential concern and places them within the analytical framework of macroprudential policy. Section 18.3 is devoted to the *assessment* of CRFRs. It discusses the main specificities of these risks and the methodological technique of scenario analysis that macroprudential authorities use to cope with their forward-looking nature. The *management* of CRFRs is addressed in Section 18.4. This section explores how the macroprudential toolkit could be used, adapted and/or extended to address CRFRs. Section 18.5 concludes.

18.2 CLIMATE CHANGE AS A SOURCE OF FINANCIAL INSTABILITY: CURRENT STATE OF KNOWLEDGE

The aim of this chapter is to discuss the potential role macroprudential policy can and should play in addressing the risks posed by climate change and its mitigation. But what are these risks? What do we know about them? And how do they fit into the conventional objectives and analytical framework of macroprudential policy?

18.2.1 *Materiality of Physical Risks and Transition Risks*

Going back to Marc Carney's famous speech of 2015,[8] it has become common to capture the financial risks posed by climate change as stemming from three risk

---

[5] See Ramos Munoz, Chapter 19 in this volume; Binder, Chapter 20 in this volume and Van den Hurk, Chapter 23 in this volume.

[6] Basel Committee on Banking Supervision 2023; Basel Committee on Banking Supervision 2022a; Basel Committee on Banking Supervision 2022b; see also Financial Stability Board 2022.

[7] European Banking Authority 2021; see also European Banking Authority 2024; European Banking Authority 2023; European Banking Authority 2022a; European Banking Authority 2022b.

[8] Carney 2015.

drivers. *Physical risks* refer to the financial impacts of acute extreme weather events (floods, storms, droughts) and more chronic changes in climate patterns (rising sea levels, ocean acidification). They may lead to higher direct and indirect losses for banks. *Liability risks* encompass the impacts of litigation by parties who have suffered loss or damage from climate change and seek compensation from bank counterparties or even banks directly.[9] Finally, *transition risks* are risks that may result from (sudden) changes in climate policy and consumer or investor behavior as well as technological advancements during the transition to a low-carbon economy and society. They could slow economic growth in the short term, indirectly affecting banks' profitability. More directly, transition risks can impact the probability of default of borrowers in certain economic sectors or lead to a sudden repricing of emission-intensive assets that banks are exposed to.

All three climate risk drivers may affect known financial risks of banks, including credit, market, liquidity and operational risks.[10] They transmit to banks through *direct* exposures to sovereigns, businesses and households affected, either directly or through supply-chain linkages, by physical or transition risks. Moreover, physical and transition risks may transmit to banks *indirectly* through their broader macroeconomic effects, including on inflation, labor productivity and economic output.

Because of the complexity involved, it is common to distinguish between physical and transition risks. In reality, however, both risk drivers are interconnected. If climate policy fails to mitigate climate change, transition risks will remain limited, but sovereigns, businesses and households will face higher costs from increasing physical risks. Strong climate policy action to limit greenhouse gas (GHG) emissions, on the other hand, may increase transition risks in the short term, while reducing physical risks in the long term. Policymakers, most prominently the Network for Greening the Financial System (NGFS),[11] have developed a number of hypothetical future climate scenarios that seek to capture this relationship between physical and transition risk.[12]

In whatever combination of physical and transition risks they may eventually materialize, climate science tells us that climate shocks are not only likely but have become inevitable.[13] In one way or another, all banks are exposed to climate risks. As the most recent report by the Intergovernmental Panel on Climate Change (IPCC) indicates,[14] physical risks are no longer only long-term risks. Global surface temperature has increased by 1.1 degrees Celsius already by 2020 compared to pre-industrial

---

[9] Liability risks are often broadly subsumed under transition risks.
[10] For example, Bolton et al. 2020.
[11] Network for Greening the Financial System 2023.
[12] Further on scenario analysis, see Section 18.3.
[13] This is a key difference with other financial risks, which occur with a certain probability but do not necessarily materialize. See also Monnin 2022.
[14] Intergovernmental Panel on Climate Change 2023, 4.

levels.[15] 1.1 degrees Celsius of human-induced global warming are thus already in the baseline with regard to physical risks, that is, have already occurred. The IPCC warns that the 1.5 degrees Celsius policy objective of the Paris Agreement will be reached in the near future (potentially as early as 2030) and dramatically increase the risk that climate tipping points trigger non-linear and potentially catastrophic climatic chain reactions. Accordingly, a massive adjustment is necessary in order to reduce GHG emissions to levels aligned with the goals of the Paris Agreement. This adjustment will have to occur in the next few years, not decades, rendering transition risks a near-term concern. While the low-carbon transition will inevitably lead to a repricing of emission-sensitive assets and activities, a key prudential concern is who will be exposed when this repricing takes place.

18.2.2 *Climate Risks as a Macroprudential Concern*

For these reasons, there is broad agreement that physical and transition risks should be accounted for in banks' risk management strategies and processes and warrant systematic inclusion in the (micro-)prudential framework. Despite the increasing awareness of banks, regulators and supervisors, however, several market failures continue to impede the substantial portfolio adjustments needed to manage CRFRs appropriately. The first are data gaps. While many regulatory and industry initiatives are underway, availability of data on banks' exposures to physical and transition risk remain incomplete, inconsistent and insufficient.[16] The second are methodological challenges in capturing CRFRs.[17] The high (and potentially radical) uncertainty surrounding their timing and impact, fueled by non-linear and chaotic dynamics associated with CRFRs, poses major challenges for their quantification and forward-looking projection.[18] It may also imply that banks systematically underestimate and/or underprice CRFRs, as they are incentivized to disregard CRFRs in the face of such uncertainty and in the expectation that they materialize only in a distant future.[19] And third, the systemic dimension of CRFRs is not typically captured by banks' own risk management and thus warrants an appropriate macroprudential response.[20] Reducing exposure to or hedging of CRFRs at firm level may not work in aggregate. Climate change has therefore been described as 'the ultimate systemic risk'.[21]

Banks' underestimation and/or underpricing of climate risks may lead to excessive credit provision or concentrations of exposures to climate risk-sensitive sectors

---

[15] For a real-time tracker of human-induced global warming see www.globalwarmingindex.org/.
[16] European Central Bank 2022.
[17] Grünewald 2024, 273–276; see already Grünewald 2021a, 232–236.
[18] Seminal in that regard, Bolton et al. 2020.
[19] European Systemic Risk Board 2020, 14–22; European Systemic Risk Board 2022, 49; Baranović et al. 2021.
[20] Baranović et al. 2021.
[21] Stheeman 2022.

or entities. The materialization of climate risks (or even a sudden shift in climate risk perceptions) could trigger a large-scale repricing of assets, causing losses on banks' balance sheets and potentially fire-sale dynamics with adverse effects on bank liquidity. As a result, the banking system's ability to provide financial intermediation services to the real economy may be impeded.[22]

Macroprudential policy has a natural role to play in seeking to prevent systemic risk arising from physical and transition risks. CRFRs fall squarely within the macroprudential objective of strengthening the robustness and resilience of the financial system against shocks – including shocks that are difficult to predict.[23] And yet, little clarity exists on how precisely macroprudential authorities should pursue this objective when it comes to CRFRs. In practice, using macroprudential policy to counteract CRFRs may be a tightrope exercise.

A key question is whether macroprudential policy should – beyond prudential resilience to climate risks – pursue the objective of facilitating the transition to a low-carbon economy. There are good reasons to assume that macroprudential policy has a role to play in 'greening finance'. Capital and/or buffer requirements, for example, give banks with large transition risks the capacity to withstand losses when the transition accelerates and at the same time disincentivize further investments that contribute to climate change.[24] The case is most compelling when it comes to assets that will likely become stranded in the near future due to materializing transition risks, for example investments in the coal and oil sectors. However, higher prudence towards CRFRs will not in all cases necessarily imply lower aggregate carbon emissions. Divestments from emission-intensive sectors will indeed lower the direct risk banks face from the transition. Whether they will also reduce the system-wide risks of unmitigated climate change, however, crucially depends on whether these divestments lead to an actual reduction of emissions.[25] Efforts by macroprudential policy to help 'green finance' through divestment of banks from emission-intensive activities risk being undermined if and to the extent these emission-intensive activities can continue to be financed by alternative sources outside the banking sector.

'Brown-spinning' through the migration of emission-intensive activities out of the banking sector is a serious regulatory concern[26] and implies that a well-calibrated macroprudential response to CRFRs is needed. The Bank of England, for example, pursues a macroprudential policy approach that aims to induce banks to act as stewards and steer firms through the transition, rather than to just divest emission-intensive

---

[22] Baranović et al. 2021.

[23] Grünewald 2021b.

[24] van Tilburg et al. 2022. Dafermos and Nikolaidi 2022 distinguish between weak and strong macroprudential approaches to address CRFRs depending on the extent to which the tools deployed account for the endogeneity of these risks, that is, feedback effects of the financial system on the economic transition and, hence, the aggregate level of risk.

[25] See Breeden 2022.

[26] See Oehmke 2022.

exposures on paper.[27] This would necessitate that macroprudential tools are calibrated according to forward-looking metrics that do not just reflect the status quo of firms' emissions, but take into account firms' disclosures and the credibility of their transition plans.[28] An even more granular approach would target banks' financing of projects, rather than counterparties. This would require that banks and supervisors differentiate between transition finance for firms to adapt their business models on the one hand and other lending to emission-intensive firms on the other.[29] Such approaches would avoid that financing is cut off prematurely for the 'greening' of emission-intensive firms or projects in an orderly and credible process. It would also address the concern that poorly calibrated macroprudential policy action to address CRFRs may trigger prudentially undesirable runs on emission-intensive sectors.[30]

The two objectives – reducing prudential risk for banks from climate change and creating green impact – do not necessarily always go hand in hand. While macroprudential policy may have a role to play in 'greening finance', its use to 'finance green' is more problematic.[31] An active channeling of financing into green economic activities can collide with the prudential objective of macroprudential policy, as 'green' assets are not necessarily low-risk assets. On the contrary, if the reallocation towards 'green' is too strong and/or too fast, it can give rise to 'green bubbles' and potentially destabilizing effects for the financial system. This is a risk macroprudential policymakers should keep a close eye on and warn against, if necessary.

18.2.3 *Placing Climate Risks in the Analytical Framework of Macroprudential Policy*

Physical and transition risks can and will give rise to material financial risk and have an inherent systemic dimension. They are thus clearly of macroprudential concern. However, they are also different from other, more familiar systemic risks. This sub-section thus turns to placing climate risks in the analytical framework of macroprudential policy.

Macroprudential analysis traditionally distinguishes two dimensions of systemic risk. The *time dimension* deals with how aggregate risk in the financial system

---

[27] Breeden 2022.

[28] On the need for forward-looking disclosures see ECB/ESRB Project Team on climate risk monitoring 2022, 106–109; on the use of transition plans for prudential policies see Dikau et al. 2022.

[29] Coelho and Restoy 2023, 6.

[30] See, for example, ECB/ESRB Project Team on climate risk monitoring 2022, 93; Coelho and Restoy 2023, 4–5.

[31] Coelho and Restoy 2023, 2, arguably reflect a majority view when they write: '[macroprudential measures] should not be designed with a view to pursuing broader climate change-related objectives. (…). The design and implementation of the macroprudential framework should be informed by financial stability considerations alone.'

evolves over time. The *cross-sectional dimension*, on the other hand, tackles how risk is allocated within the financial system at a certain point in time. For each dimension there is a corresponding source of system-wide stress. In the time dimension, the source of stress is the procyclicality of the financial system, which can lead to outsize financial cycles and business fluctuations. In the cross-sectional dimension, the source of stress is common exposure and interlinkages in the financial system, which may result in joint failures of financial institutions by making them vulnerable to common sources of risk. Finally, for each source of stress there is a corresponding policy principle. To address procyclicality, the principle is to build up buffers in good times, as aggregate risk grows, so that they can be drawn down in bad times, as it materializes. This is achieved through *time-varying macroprudential tools*. To address common exposures and interlinkages, the principle is to calibrate prudential requirements to each institution's contribution to systemic risk. This calibration, on the basis of *structural tools*, helps ensure that each institution pays for the externality it imposes on the system.[32]

How do climate risks fit into this systemic risk paradigm? According to current scientific knowledge, physical risks, if looked at separately, appear to be structural risks and thus concern macroprudential authorities *prima facie* in the cross-sectional dimension. They build up over a long-term horizon, as the GHG that we emit today will lead to chronic changes of climate patterns and severe acute weather events only years or even decades later. The climate processes triggered are at least partially irreversible. So physical risks will likely develop in only one direction in the foreseeable future, namely, increase. They manifest themselves as exogenous shocks that are particularly dramatic if so-called climate tipping points are crossed.

Transition risks, on the other hand, may also exhibit a time dimension, until they might eventually disappear. They are a secular trend of 10 to 40–50 years, not really a cycle in the traditional sense. However, in light of the scientific fact that CO_2 would have to be priced much higher if global warming were indeed to remain well below 2 degrees Celsius, the underlying assumption is increasingly that there is a financial imbalance or exaggeration when it comes to emission-intensive economic activities or assets. In that sense, one might think of a 'carbon cycle' as a single, very long-term cycle.[33] Along such a 'cycle' there might be shorter-term fluctuations – for example due to disappointed expectations in certain alternative energy sources. So transition risks create a sort of new 'frequency' in addition to the business and financial cycles, with which macroprudential authorities have much more experience.

Macroprudential policy must deal with a permanently changing mix of physical and transition risks, spanning the cross-sectional dimension, that is, with a view to common exposures to climate risks, and also the time dimension.[34] Both physical

[32] See Borio 2010, 3.
[33] See Grünewald 2021a, 238.
[34] See also ECB/ESRB Project Team on climate risk monitoring 2022, 3, 93, 95.

and transition risks may be amplified by classical systemic risk externalities caused by interconnectedness, contagion and second-round effects on the real economy.[35] They are complex and only beginning to be observed on a systemic level in the banking sector. How they build up and eventually materialize remains uncertain and is largely driven by climate policy measures taken (or omitted) now.

18.3 ASSESSING CLIMATE RISKS: SCENARIO ANALYSIS AND MACRO-STRESS TESTING

Section 18.2 set out what CRFRs are and discussed how these risks can be reconciled with the objective and analytical framework of macroprudential policy. This section turns to the instruments of macroprudential policy and their use to address climate risks. Macroprudential policy is primarily concerned with analyzing the evolution of risk and its propagation through the financial system. This analysis is then communicated to the markets, other authorities and the public through Financial Stability Reports or other dedicated communication channels. Much effort has been made in recent years to develop and improve climate risk analysis and communication – the 'soft' tools of macroprudential authorities. This section highlights some of the challenges associated with assessing climate risks and some of the most important outcomes of these assessments. Much less developed is the use of 'hard' macroprudential tools to improve the robustness and resilience of the banking system against climate-related shocks. These 'hard' tools are addressed in Section 18.4.

While they may feed into traditional financial risks (see Section 18.2.1), climate risks also differ from these more familiar risk types. First, they are foreseeable and uncertain at the same time. We know with certainty that climate shocks are going to materialize, but the severity and timing of these shocks as well as the precise combination of physical and transition risk remain uncertain. This uncertainty is primarily due to limitations to the scientific precision with which climate events can be forecast and to the fact that the build-up of climate risks crucially depends on policy action taken to combat climate change as well as changes in behavior of society more broadly. Secondly, there is a time gap between the level of GHG emissions and the effects these emissions have on the climate and our environment – a scientific fact to which Mark Carney famously referred as the 'tragedy of the horizons'.[36] Climate change occurs slowly over a long period of time with potentially irreversible outcomes. Action taken to mitigate climate change now will play out much later, and – conversely – inaction now will have to be compensated for in the future with a much more rapid (and potentially disorderly) transition. Accordingly, macroprudential authorities are forced to think in longer time horizons than they are

[35] Baranović et al. 2021.
[36] Carney 2015.

used to do.[37] And, third, climate change and the transition to a low-carbon economy are novel phenomena without any past record. The traditional approach of looking to the past to make extrapolations about the probability of future risk materialization is thus largely useless when it comes to CRFRs.

Recent and ongoing analytical work by macroprudential authorities seeks to incorporate these specificities of CRFRs to better understand their nature and (systemic) materiality. *Climate risk exposure mapping and measurement* attempts to understand current exposures and vulnerabilities of banks and the financial sector more broadly. First empirical evidence reveals that banks in the euro area are already significantly exposed through their lending activities to water and heat stress (amongst other physical hazards) and to high-emitting counterparties, with potential systemic implications and real economy impact.[38] Both physical and transition risks show a high concentration in specific sectors, geographies and firms. Physical risks could affect up to a third of euro area banks' credit exposure, subject to large regional differences.[39] In terms of transition risk, the emission intensity in euro area banks' loan portfolios has remained rather steady in recent years. Banks have maintained large exposures to a few climate-sensitive sectors. Their loan-weighted emission intensity of exposure to the mining, manufacturing and electricity sectors still accounts for around 60% of the total.[40] The manufacturing sector in particular is responsible for large indirect (scope 3) emissions and thus susceptible to sudden repricing due to changes in consumption behavior.[41]

When conducting climate risk exposure mapping and measurement, macroprudential policymakers need to combine climate science considerations and economic-financial variables, accounting for complex (potential) interdependencies and self-reinforcing loops within and between the climate, economic and financial systems. *Climate risk modelling* comes with an extra layer of complexity as it seeks to shed light on how these risks may further evolve under certain plausible future scenarios. Modelling frameworks need to incorporate plausible depictions of both the climate and the economy, the ways in which they interact and the ways in which policies to mitigate climate change affect both of them in the medium to long term. The level of uncertainty under which climate risk modelling takes place brings macroprudential authorities in unchartered waters. The 'epistemological break' that the authors of the Green Swan Report of 2020 called for[42] has manifested itself in practice in the form of scenario analysis. Scenario analysis breaks

---

[37] At the same time, the financial effects of climate change and the transition to a low-carbon economy are showing already in the present.

[38] See ECB/ESRB Project Team on climate risk monitoring 2022, 8–42, for the most recent upgrading of measurement techniques.

[39] ECB/ESRB Project Team on climate risk monitoring 2022, 15–19.

[40] Ibid., 11–20.

[41] See Alogoskoufis et al. 2021a, 100–114, 101–102.

[42] Bolton et al. 2020.

with the notion of forecasting the future materialization of risks. Instead, the aim is a detailed description of the transmission of physical and transition risks by asking the question: what would happen if these risks were to materialize under certain plausible scenarios?

Scenario analysis can be used in macro-stress tests to better model the interplay between physical and transition risks over longer time horizons. It involves at least three broad steps or building blocks. The first is the identification of relevant plausible climate and transition scenarios. The scenarios developed by the NGFS in collaboration with a consortium of scientists and scientific institutions have become the benchmark used by macroprudential authorities when conducting macro-stress tests.[43] They consist of seven scenarios: The orderly scenarios (Net Zero 2050, Low Demand and Below 2 Degrees Celsius) assume that climate policies are introduced sufficiently early and gradually, so that both physical and transition risks remain relatively moderate. The disorderly scenario (Delayed Transition) accounts for the possibility that transition risk is higher due to delayed policies or divergent policy action across countries and sectors. The hot house world scenarios (Nationally Determined Contributions and Current Policies) presume that global efforts to limit global warming are insufficient, leading to severe physical risk including irreversible outcomes. And, finally, the too little, too late scenario (Fragmented World) explores an outcome of high physical and transition risk due to delayed and divergent climate change mitigation action.

In a second step, macroprudential authorities must identify the channels through which physical and transition risks transmit under each scenario to the economy (that is, the corporate sector) and then spill over to the financial sector.[44] It is here where limitations to data availability (for example, regarding firm-level energy expenditures, transition plans or even project-level information) pose the greatest challenge. And third, scenario analysis involves an assessment of potential amplifiers with the real economy and within the financial system.[45]

The ECB's economy-wide climate stress test, conducted in 2021, relied on climate scenarios.[46] Complemented by further work conducted by the ECB and ESRB, it brings out two key analytical findings. The first finding relates to the sequencing with which banks and other financial institutions are shown to be affected by CRFRs. The analysis reveals that climate shocks initially impact market risk and thus primarily non-banks (investment funds), while credit risk (banks) is impacted with a lag. The second finding suggests – not surprisingly – that whether or not CRFRs materialize as systemic risks crucially depends on the

---

[43] See Network for Greening the Financial System 2023 for the latest set of scenarios.
[44] ECB/ESRB Project Team on climate risk monitoring 2022, 51–71.
[45] Ibid., 78–88.
[46] See Alogoskoufis et al. 2021b. For the results of the U.S. Federal Reserve's pilot climate scenario analysis exercise see Board of Governors of the Federal Reserve System 2024.

transition pathway. Losses of firms, banks and non-banks are larger if the transition is insufficient or ineffective.

18.4 MANAGING CLIMATE RISKS: THE MACROPRUDENTIAL TOOLKIT

As first studies and stress-testing exercises suggest that CRFRs may already constitute material financial risks for banks and other financial institutions and have systemic implications under certain plausible scenarios, the question arises of how these risks could be managed now and in the not-too-distant future. The existing macroprudential toolkit is still young and only partially tested in practice. This section turns to analyzing whether and how this toolkit is fit to build resilience against and – to some extent – counteract the build-up of CRFRs. The potential use of 'hard' macroprudential tools against climate-related shocks is much less developed than macroprudential analysis (see Section 18.3). It has only recently gained more attention following an announced review of the EU's macroprudential framework and a consultation conducted by the Commission in that regard.[47] Moreover, the Bank of England declared that it would assess whether there are 'regime gaps' in the macroprudential framework regarding CRFRs.[48]

A first question is whether there is need to introduce (a) new macroprudential tool(s) to address CRFRs specifically or whether adapting existing tools will suffice. Most respondents to the Commission's consultation indicated that they consider the introduction of dedicated macroprudential tools against CRFRs as premature. The use of existing tools should first be explored, in particular the (sectoral) systemic risk buffer and large exposure limits.[49] Only a few respondents suggested that new tools should indeed be considered, including concentration limits or charges.[50] Both suggestions will be discussed in this section.

In the existing macroprudential toolkit, four categories of macroprudential tools can be broadly distinguished: capital-based tools, borrower-based tools, liquidity-based tools and other tools (see Table 18.1). These macroprudential tools vary in their scope of application, applying either at the bank, sectoral or firm level or being activity-based. Often, their scope of application corresponds to the tools' different degrees of complexity regarding data requirements and operationalization.[51] Within the EU, most of these tools are based on the single rulebook, that is, the CRR/CRD. They can be used by national authorities and the ECB through its top-up powers.[52]

---

[47] See European Commission 2021; European Commission 2022.
[48] See Bank of England 2023, in particular paras. 49–55.
[49] European Commission 2022, 5. See on these tools further below.
[50] European Commission 2022, 5.
[51] Baranović et al. 2021.
[52] Article 5(1) and (2) of Council Regulation (EU) No 1024/2013 of 15 October 2013 conferring specific tasks on the European Central Bank concerning policies relating to the prudential supervision of credit institutions, OJ L 287, 29.10.2013, p. 63 (SSM-Regulation).

TABLE 18.1 *Overview EU macroprudential toolkit*

	CRR/CRD tools	National tools
Capital-based tools	– Countercyclical capital buffer (CCyB) – Systemic risk buffer (SyRB) – Global (G-SII) and other systemically (O-SII) important institutions buffer – Risk weights (real estate sector and intra-financial exposures) – Capital conservation buffer (CCoB) – Own funds level (incl. leverage ratio)	
Borrower-based tools		– Loan-to-value (LTV) ratio caps – Loan-to-income (LTI) ratio caps – Debt-to-income (DTI) – Debt service-to-income (DSTI) ratio caps
Liquidity-based tools	– Liquidity Coverage Ratio (LCR) – Net Stable Funding Ratio (NSFR)	– Non-stable funding levy – Loan-to-deposit (LTD) ratio caps
Other tools	– Large exposure limits – Disclosure requirements	

Source: Adapted from Constâncio et al. 2019, 22.

There are, however, some borrower-based and liquidity-based tools that remain national tools and can be used solely by national authorities for the time being.[53]

18.4.1 *Capital-Based Tools*

Previous discussions have primarily been centered on the capital-based tools.[54] These encompass a set of capital requirements, which are designed to increase the loss-absorption capacity of banks, fostering financial sector resilience. In addition,

---

[53] This chapter will not specifically address liquidity-based tools as the need for climate-specific liquidity requirements is less obvious.

[54] See, however, ECB/ESRB Project Team on climate risk monitoring 2022, 99–105, for a first comprehensive assessment of (existing and new) macroprudential tools in the context of climate risks. Most recently: ECB/ESRB Project Team on climate risk 2023, 78–98.

by altering banks' cost of capital, higher capital requirements should affect the price and volume of credit. This helps tame the financial cycle by limiting credit excesses.

Capital-based macroprudential tools or 'climate risk buffers' could increase banks' resilience to CRFRs and affect incentives and prices in the allocation of funding. They would, however, require careful calibration. Two capital-based tools – the countercyclical capital buffer (CCyB)[55] and the systemic risk buffer (SyRB)[56] – are of particular relevance when it comes to CRFRs. The CCyB is a time-varying macroprudential tool. It is designed to make banks accumulate capital buffers that strengthen the resilience of the financial system during periods of stress when losses materialize. As such, it could be used to build up buffers against the materialization of transition risks, while helping to dampen excessive credit growth in emission-intensive sectors of the economy. This makes the countercyclical capital buffer an interesting option to address CRFRs.

However, there are two difficulties associated with the use of the CCyB. The first is its calibration to transition risks. This calibration is challenging, as we cannot conclusively identify indicators for how these risks might evolve in the future. Where are we in the 'carbon cycle'? Globally, CO_2 emissions continue to rise, in Europe they have been falling since the 1980s. The price of CO_2 emission certificates has increased from €8 at the beginning of 2018 to roughly €70 per metric ton in April 2024. Can we still speak of a build-up phase or are we already at the transition to the release phase within the 'carbon cycle'? Moreover, the longer the CCyB applies without alteration, the more similar its effect becomes to a brown penalizing factor under Pillar 1, that is, it is no longer really a time-varying but rather a structural tool. The second difficulty is that the CCyB might not be precise enough to tackle CRFRs. It currently applies to all outstanding credit and cannot be limited to credit to (certain) emission-intensive sectors of the economy, for example. This lack of precision may raise questions regarding the costs and benefits of its use to tackle CRFRs.

For the time being, the SyRB seems to be the more straightforward tool.[57] It aims to address systemic risks that are not covered by capital and other buffer requirements. As a structural tool, the SyRB has a long-term focus. It can be applied to (subsets of) economic sectors, defined by the nature of the debtor, the nature of the exposure or the type of collateral, or to geographical areas.[58] Accordingly, it would be legally feasible to apply a sectoral SyRB to increase banks' resilience against (a subset of) emission-intensive exposures. It is also possible to use several SyRBs at the same time for different (subsets of) exposures. SyRBs could thus apply to both

---

[55] Articles 130 and 135–140 CRD.
[56] Articles 133 and 134 CRD.
[57] See also European Systemic Risk Board 2022, 50; Monnin 2022; ECB/ESRB Project Team on climate risk 2023, 82–92.
[58] See European Banking Authority 2020.

exposures that are strongly affected by physical risks (for example, real estate located in flood-affected areas) and exposures to firms that cause high GHG emissions. This would necessitate the complex development of criteria for identifying asset classes and/or sectors that could be exposed to CRFRs. Moreover, the application and calibration of a SyRB would ideally be coordinated closely among the Member States,[59] potentially under the auspices of the ESRB.

18.4.2 Borrower-Based Tools

Whether and how to make use of borrower-based tools to tackle CRFRs is discussed much less.[60] However, borrower-based tools are an interesting option as they apply much more directly to where the climate risks actually lie – namely with banks' borrowers. In contrast to capital-based tools, they are directed towards the contract between the bank and its borrowers and impose limits on the terms and conditions of lending related to the riskiness of loans.

The application of borrower-based tools has remained unharmonized and thus heterogeneous across the EU. To the extent available, borrower-based tools apply to residential real estate loans and households within the relevant Member State, not (yet) to commercial real estate loans and loans taken by legal persons. They consist of (a combination of) the following:

- limits on the size of the loan in relation to the value of the underlying collateral (the loan-to-value ratio – LTV);
- limits on the size of the loan in relation to the income of the borrower (the loan-to-income ratio – LTI);
- limits to the overall debt in relation to the income of the borrower (the debt-to-income-ratio – DTI); and
- limits on the debt servicing costs in relation to the income of the borrower (the debt service-to-income ratio – DSTI).

The LTV ratio aims to prevent excessive credit growth in real estate markets. It caps the percentage of the value of a property that can be financed by a mortgage, thereby ensuring an adequate cushion of collateral value for the loan. Applied to CRFRs, the LTV ratio could help reallocate mortgage credit away from high-climate-risk to low-climate-risk housing markets. CRFRs can be integrated relatively easily into the LTV ratio. The market value of the residential property should reflect physical risks (for example, due to the location of the property) and transition risks (for example, due to the energy efficiency of the property). High energy efficiency increases

[59] See also European Systemic Risk Board 2022, 50; ECB/ESRB Project Team on climate risk 2023, 87–88.
[60] The topic is discussed in central bank circles. See, for example, Bank of Lithuania 2021; Bank of Italy 2022. Most recently: ECB/ESRB Project Team on climate risk 2023, 92–98.

the value of property, so more credit, in absolute terms, can go into its financing. Low energy efficiency or a location exposed to physical hazards, on the other hand, lower the value of property and hence the absolute amount that can be financed by a mortgage.[61]

CRFRs could also be integrated into the income-related macroprudential tools, the LTI, DTI and DSTI ratios. These tools target borrowers' ability to repay and could thus be used to help prevent household over-indebtedness due to climate risk. The income projections underlying these tools could reflect potential impacts of transition risks. Rising energy prices and new regulatory energy efficiency requirements will affect borrowers' income and ability to service their debt. Accounting for CRFRs when calibrating borrower-based tools will be particularly relevant for Member States 'where climate risks are considered systemically relevant or as increasing absolute risks.'[62]

18.4.3 *Other Tools*

The other macroprudential tools include large exposure limits and disclosure requirements. Both could be instrumental in addressing CRFRs. Large exposure limits are a macroprudential tool to limit the maximum loss banks could face in the event of a sudden counterparty failure.[63] Applied to CRFRs, large exposure limits could mitigate the knock-on effect of climate-related failures of counterparties on banks.[64] By limiting excessive exposure to physical and/or transition risk through quantitative restrictions on banks' portfolios, they allow for a targeted reduction in the build-up of CRFRs. Exposure limits thus more directly restrict banks in their choice of capital allocation compared to the price-driven approach deployed with capital-based tools.[65]

A key conceptual difficulty with large exposure limits is that they apply to individual counterparties ('clients') or groups of connected counterparties, not really entire sectors.[66] To capture a broader set of emission-intensive economic activities under the large exposure limits according to the current legal framework, one would have to construct a sort of 'economic interdependence' between these activities – and that may prove to be a complex task. As the legal basis for large exposure limits varies across Member States, harmonization at EU level would be necessary.

---

[61] However, it is questionable whether the LTV ratio is actually a climate-friendly macroprudential tool. Simply put, the way it is designed is such that it converges towards 100% as the value of the property increases. An LTV ratio would therefore disproportionally affect the purchase of new, energy-efficient houses. I thank Bernd Amann for pointing this out to me.

[62] ECB/ESRB Project Team on climate risk 2023, 95.

[63] See Articles 392 and 395–403 CRR. Article 458 CRR allows for the setting of tighter large exposure limits for macroprudential purposes.

[64] See also European Systemic Risk Board 2022, 50.

[65] Baranović et al. 2021.

[66] See also ECB/ESRB Project Team on climate risk monitoring 2022, 102–103.

Because they apply to individual counterparties, large exposure limits are also costly and reporting-intense for banks to implement.[67] A simpler, but equally effective alternative might be a sectoral leverage ratio – a capital-based tool. A sectoral leverage ratio, which could apply to emission-intensive sectors, would reduce the leverage a bank may use to finance activities in these sectors. Just like large exposure limits, it would reduce the risk that banks face financial difficulties, should climate risks in these sectors materialize.[68] As the leverage ratio cannot be applied at sectoral level under the current legal framework, an amendment of the CRR would be required.[69] Moreover, a harmonized concentration threshold or concentration charges are often referred to as alternative options to target exposures to CRFRs.[70] The crossing of such threshold could trigger supervisory measures and/or capital surcharges. It would, however, have to be designed as new macroprudential tool.

Much of the regulatory action regarding CRFRs to date has revolved around disclosure requirements, including the key recommendations by the Task Force on Climate-related Financial Disclosures (TCFD)[71] and related work undertaken by the European Banking Authority (EBA). While disclosure requirements are at the core of policies to address climate risks, they also represent a key supportive macroprudential tool. The above analysis of the macroprudential toolkit demonstrates that the calibration of macroprudential tools to tackle CRFRs crucially depends on completer and more standardized climate-related disclosures across the emission spectrum.[72]

18.5 CONCLUSIONS

On 4 November 2008, the late queen Elizabeth II famously asked how the global financial meltdown could have taken so many economic experts by surprise: *Why did no one see it coming?* The response offered to her by the British Academy highlighted that there had been a systematic underestimation of the build-up of imbalances in the system as a whole: 'Individual risks may rightly have been viewed as small, but the risk to the system as a whole was vast.'[73] What followed was the establishment of macroprudential frameworks, aimed at assessing and managing systemic risks and complementing the pre-existing microprudential regulatory and supervisory regimes.

[67] Baranović et al. 2021.
[68] See Grünewald 2021a, 244.
[69] ECB/ESRB Project Team on climate risk monitoring 2022, 101, 104, however, argue against a sectoral leverage ratio as it would alter the 'general role of the leverage ratio as a non-risk based backstop'.
[70] See European Systemic Risk Board 2022, 50; Baranović et al. 2021. Most recently: ECB/ESRB Project Team on climate risk, 78–81.
[71] Task Force on Climate-Related Financial Disclosures 2017. As per October 2023, the TCFD was disbanded and the IFRS Foundation took over the monitoring of companies' climate-related disclosures.
[72] See also European Systemic Risk Board 2022, 50.
[73] British Academy 2009.

Fifteen years later, the GFC seems from a distant past. The macroprudential framework in the EU and elsewhere is still evolving, and many of its tools are subject to ongoing controversy. The COVID-19 crisis provided a first test case for the macroprudential buffers – with a mixed outcome: While the buffers proved useful, there was clearly insufficient available macroprudential 'space' when the pandemic hit in March 2020.[74] Some have argued that banks and authorities were hesitant to use the limited space that *was* available, because of fears of market stigma (due to coupon restrictions) and the uncertainty of what would happen at a later stage.

Climate change and the unprecedented and systemic change needed to limit global warming to well below 2 degrees Celsius is seen by many as a looming new threat to (global) financial stability. CRFRs in the form of different potential combinations of physical and transition risks, if not assessed and managed appropriately, could trigger 'green swan' events with potentially catastrophic outcomes.[75] However, while awareness of the materiality of CRFRs has certainly increased over the past few years, little has happened in terms of reducing systemic vulnerabilities to climate-related shocks.

This chapter argued that macroprudential policies may play a key part in assessing and managing CRFRs. It outlined how scenario analysis is yielding first insights into how climate risks may evolve over the next 30 years or so under different plausible and scientifically backed scenarios. These insights may eventually help inform the use of 'hard' macroprudential tools to foster robustness and resilience of the banking system against climate-induced shocks. The SyRB is an existing macroprudential tool that could be applied to increase banks' resilience against the materialization of CRFRs and discourage exposure to certain climate-sensitive economic sub-sectors. Macroprudential policy could also directly target concentrations in banks' exposure to emission-intensive sectors and/or regions exposed to physical hazards. This would require amendments to the large exposure tool or the introduction of an entirely new climate concentration threshold tool. Borrower-based measures could be adapted to cater for climate-related considerations. In 2021, the Commission announced a review of the macroprudential framework that includes the concern over whether that framework needs to be amended to account for CRFRs. However, concrete legislative proposals are not expected in the near future.

While this chapter has addressed CRFRs through a macroprudential lens, macroprudential policy cannot act in isolation. Many measures taken to address CRFRs will be motivated by both micro- and macroprudential concerns. Close coordination between the two policy spheres is necessary, with macroprudential policy taking a complementary role. Moreover, macroprudential policy will depend on, and interact with, a broader set of public policies aimed at limiting and adapting to climate change, including environmental and fiscal policy. It should remain

[74] See de Guindos 2021.
[75] Bolton et al. 2020.

risk-based and driven primarily by prudential concerns, while supporting the 'greening of finance' in the interest of long-term financial stability.

Climate change and its mitigation represent global challenges. It is thus inevitable to coordinate efforts in addressing systemic climate risks at the EU and global level. While much uncertainty surrounds the timing and precise manifestation of climate shocks, they will occur with absolute certainty. Are we seeing it coming this time? The jury is still out there.

REFERENCES

Alogoskoufis, S., Carbone, S., and Coussens, W. (2021a), 'Climate-related risks to financial stability', *ECB Financial Stability Review*, 1, available at: https://bit.ly/3IEWDKt (accessed 22 April 2024).

Alogoskoufis, S., Dunz, N., and Emambakhsh, T. (2021b), 'ECB economy-wide climate stress test – methodology and results', ECB Occasional Paper Series, No. 281.

Bank of England (2023), *Bank of England Report on Climate-related Risks and the Regulatory Capital Frameworks*, 13 March, available at: https://bit.ly/3wQQ9pm (accessed 22 April 2024).

Bank of Italy (2022), 'Legal conference: An EU Legal Framework for Macroprudential Supervision through Borrower-Based Measures', available at: https://bit.ly/3Iw83QO (accessed 22 April 2024).

Bank of Lithuania (2021), 'Macroprudential Policy Conference 2021 at the Bank of Lithuania on borrower-based macroprudential measures', available at: lb.lt/en/events/macroprudential-policy-conference (accessed 22 April 2024).

Baranović, I., Busies, I., Coussens, W., Grill, M., and Hempell, H. (2021), 'The challenge of capturing climate risks in the banking regulatory framework: is there a need for a macroprudential response?', *ECB Macroprudential Bulletin*, No. 15, available at https://bit.ly/4bQVQDr (accessed 24 May 2024).

Basel Committee on Banking Supervision (2022a), 'Principles for the effective management and supervision of climate-related financial risks', Bank for International Settlements, available at: bis.org/bcbs/publ/d532.pdf (accessed 22 April 2024).

Basel Committee on Banking Supervision (2022b), 'Frequently asked questions on climate-related financial risks', Bank for International Settlements, available at: bis.org/bcbs/publ/d543.pdf (accessed 22 April 2024).

Basel Committee on Banking Supervision (2023), 'Consultative document – Disclosure of climate-related financial risks', Bank for International Settlements, available at: bis.org/bcbs/publ/d560.pdf (accessed 22 April 2024).

Board of Governors of the Federal Reserve System (2024), 'Pilot climate scenario analysis exercise – Summary of participants' risk-management practices and estimates', May, available at: www.federalreserve.gov/publications/files/csa-exercise-summary-20240509.pdf (accessed 4 September 2024).

Bolton, P., Despres, M., Pereira da Silva, L.A., Samama, F., and Swartzman, R. (2020), 'The green swan – Central banking and financial stability in the age of climate change', Bank for International Settlements, available at: bis.org/publ/othp31.pdf (accessed 22 April 2024).

Borio, C. (2010), 'Implementing a macroprudential framework: Blending boldness and realism', Bank for International Settlements, available at: bis.org/repofficepubl/hkimr201007.12c.pdf (accessed 22 April 2024).

Breeden, S. (2022), 'Balancing on the net-zero tightrope, speech given at TheCityUK International Conference', available at: https://bit.ly/43gez7H (accessed 22 April 2024).

British Academy (2009), 'Letter to Her Majesty The Queen', available at: ma.imperial.ac .uk/~bino6/M3A22/queen-lse.pdf (accessed 22 April 2024).

Carney, M. (2015), 'Breaking the tragedy of the horizon – climate change and financial stability', speech at Lloyd's of London', available at: bis.org/review/r151009a.pdf (accessed 22 April 2024).

Coelho, R. and Restoy, F. (2023), 'Macroprudential policies for addressing climate-related financial risks: challenges and trade-offs', *FSI Briefs*, No. 18, 1–9.

Constâncio, V., Cabral, I., and Detken, C. (eds.) (2019), 'Macroprudential policy at the ECB: Institutional framework, strategy, analytical tools and policy', *ECB Occasional Paper Series*, No. 227, 1–86.

Dafermos, Y. and Nikolaidi, M. (2022), 'Greening capital requirements', *INSPIRE Policy Briefing Paper* 08.

De Guindos (2021), 'Macroprudential policy after the COVID-19 pandemic', Banque de France/Sciences Po Financial Stability Review Conference 2021, available at: bis.org/review/r210303d.pdf (accessed 22 April 2024).

De Larosière, J., Balcerowicz, L., and Issing, O. (2009), *Report of the High Level Group on Financial Supervision in the EU*, available at: https://bit.ly/43dKaXH (accessed 22 April 2024).

Dikau, S., Robins, N., Smolenska, A. van 't Klooster, J., and Volz, U. (2022), 'Net zero transition plans, A supervisory playbook for prudential authorities', Grantham Research Institute on Climate Change and the Environment and the Centre for Climate Change Economics and Policy, available at: https://bit.ly/3xbRszH (accessed 22 April 2024).

ECB/ESRB Project Team on climate risk (2023), *Towards Macroprudential Frameworks for Managing Climate Risk*, available at: https://bit.ly/3Kx4rz8 (accessed 22 April 2024).

ECB/ESRB Project Team on climate risk monitoring (2022), *The Macroprudential Challenge of Climate Change*, available at: https://bit.ly/43gt4bF (accessed 22 April 2024).

European Banking Authority (2020), 'Final guidelines on the appropriate subsets of sectoral exposures to which competent or designated authorities may apply a systemic risk buffer in accordance with Article 133(5)(f) of Directive 2013/36/EU' (EBA/GL/2020/13), available at: https://bit.ly/3Vjfhom (accessed 22 April 2024).

European Banking Authority (2021), *Report on Management and Supervision of ESG Risks for Credit Institutions and Investment Firms* (EBA/REP/2021/18), available at: https://bit .ly/3Kyrnhx (accessed 22 April 2024).

European Banking Authority (2022a), 'The Role of Environmental Risks in the Prudential Framework', Discussion paper, (EBA/DP/2022/02), available at: https://bit.ly/3xbRvvn (accessed 22 April 2024).

European Banking Authority (2022b), *Final Report Draft Implementing Technical Standards on Prudential Disclosures on ESG Risks in Accordance with Article 449a CRR* (EBA/ITS/2022/01), available at: https://bit.ly/45j8Z5u (accessed 22 April 2024).

European Banking Authority (2023), '*Report on the Role of Environmental and Social Risks in the Prudential Framework* (EBA/REP/2023/34), available at: https://bit.ly/4bUDTUC (accessed 22 April 2024).

European Banking Authority (2024), 'Consultation paper – Draft guidelines on the management of ESG risks' (EBA/CP/2024/02), available at: https://bit.ly/4bRGXRk (accessed 22 April 2022).

European Central Bank (2022), *Supervisory Assessment of Institutions' Climate-related and Environmental Risks Disclosures – ECB Report on Banks' Progress towards Transparent Disclosure of their Climate-related and Environmental Risk Profiles*, available at: https://bit .ly/48RokdX (accessed 22 April 2024).

European Commission (2021), 'Targeted consultation on improving the EU's macroprudential framework for the banking sector', available at: https://bit.ly/3vidC2a (accessed 22 April 2024).

European Commission (2022), 'Feedback statement of the targeted consultation on improving the EU's macroprudential framework for the banking sector', available at: https://bit.ly/48Qlaa7 (accessed 22 April 2024).

European Systemic Risk Board (2020), *Positively Green: Measuring Climate Change Risks to Financial Stability*, available at: https://bit.ly/43h1hYA (accessed 22 April 2024).

European Systemic Risk Board (2022), *Review of the EU Macroprudential Framework for the Banking Sector*, available at: https://bit.ly/48PD25g (accessed 22 April 2024).

Financial Stability Board (2022), *Supervisory and Regulatory Approaches to Climate-Related Risks: Interim Report*, available at: fsb.org/wp-content/uploads/P290422.pdf (accessed 22 April 2024).

Grünewald, S. (2021a), 'Climate change as a systemic risk in finance – Are macroprudential authorities up to the task?' in D. Busch, G. Ferrarini and S. Grünewald (eds.), *Sustainable Finance in Europe: Corporate Governance, Financial Stability and Financial Markets* (Cham: Palgrave Macmillan), 227–257.

Grünewald, S. (2021b), 'Climate-related risks: Is the macroprudential framework fit for purpose?', *Butterworths Journal of International Banking and Financial Law*, 36(11), 743–745.

Grünewald, S. (2024), 'Climate change as a systemic risk in finance – Are macroprudential authorities up to the task? in D. Busch, G. Ferrarini and S. Grünewald (eds.), *Sustainable Finance in Europe: Corporate Governance, Financial Stability and Financial Markets*, 2nd ed. (Cham: Palgrave Macmillan), 265–290.

Intergovernmental Panel on Climate Change (2023), *Climate change 2023 Synthesis Report, Summary for Policymakers*, available at: https://bit.ly/4bPbdMI (accessed 22 April 2024).

Monnin, P. (2022), 'Is the current macroprudential framework fit for climate systemic risk?', available at: https://bit.ly/3PgKdfE (accessed 22 April 2024).

Network for Greening the Financial System (2023), 'NGFS scenarios for central banks and supervisors', available at: https://bit.ly/3VeCNvx (accessed 22 April 2024).

Oehmke, M. (2022), 'Bank capital regulation and climate change', *ESRB ASC Insight*, No. 3, 1–12.

Stheeman, E. (2022), 'Why macroprudential policy needs to tackle financial stability risks from climate change', speech given at Queen's University Belfast, 3 May, available at: https://bit.ly/3veEBvx (accessed 22 April 2024).

Task Force on Climate-related Financial Disclosures (2017), *Final Report: Recommendations of the Task Force on Climate-related Financial Disclosures*, available at: https://bit.ly/3Iy3R2Z (accessed 22 April 2024).

Van Tilburg, R., Grünewald, S., Schoenmaker, D., and Boot, A. (2022), 'Climate risks are real and need to become part of bank capital regulation', *VOXEU column*, available at: https://bit.ly/3VjMd9h (accessed 22 April 2024).

19

Integrating Climate Risk in Banking Regulation

David Ramos Muñoz[*]

19.1 INTRODUCTION

Climate change is humanity's greatest challenge for the twenty-first century. Its effects can be catastrophic, wreaking havoc across the economies and financial system. If bank regulation is supposed to adopt a "prudential" approach, it should have no difficulty in accommodating these looming threats. Alas, the picture is much more complicated. Bank regulation speaks the language of "risk." For banks, this means "credit," "market," "operational," "liquidity" or "reputational" risk, which requires a "translation" effort. Legally, the complexity and protracted nature of bank regulation makes it difficult to accommodate a "new" source of risk that cuts across all categories. Practically, risk methodologies have been shaped through years of experience and have a certain inertia, which makes them resistant to change.

Breaking up the process, one realizes the enormity of the task. This chapter[1] shows where European and global authorities are succeeding, failing or not even trying. Section 19.2 discusses the current efforts at "translating" climate change into the language of risk, across international *soft law*. Section 19.3 discusses Pillar 1 measures (capital requirements), where the authorities are not yet trying to adapt the rules, and Pillar 3 (disclosure and market discipline) where reforms are serious, but ultimately

[*] This research is done within project TED2021-130293B-I00 "Climate Change and Sustainable Finance" (CCFS) funded by the Spanish AEI and the EU NextGenerationEU, doi 10.13039/501100011033; project PID2020-114549RB-I00, "Business and Markets: Digital (R)evolution, Integrity and Sustainability" funded by the State Plan for Scientific and Technical Research and Innovation 2017–2020, and Projects of the Faculty Excellence line of the Multiannual Agreement between the Community of Madrid and Uc3m (2019–2024). V PRICIT (2020–2022). Wholehearted thanks to Profs. Michele Siri, Matteo Gargantini, Kern Alexander and especially Jens-Hinrich Binder for their excellent comments, and Martina Menegat for research assistance. All errors are my own.

[1] This chapter is complementary to Chapter 20, "Prudential Requirements Framework" by Prof Jens-Hinrich Binder, in this volume. Some key legislative provisions of the Banking Package, initially proposed in 2021, were amended in 2023, during the production process for this work, and an EBA Report and a Commission Report were released in 2023 and 2024. Though mentioned, they are not fully incorporated.

insufficient. Section 19.4 discusses Pillar 2 measures (supervisory review) where reforms have momentum, but also face extraordinary challenges. Section 19.5 seeks to identify the conceptual challenges, legal and non-legal. Section 19.6 concludes.

19.2 TRANSLATING CLIMATE CHANGE INTO BANK REGULATION'S LANGUAGE: CATEGORIES OF RISKS AND GLOBAL LANDSCAPE OF NORMS

19.2.1 *Physical and Transition Risks*

Climate change must speak the language of risk to be assimilated by bank regulation. However, it can speak this language fluently. Climate risks are many and large. They include "physical risks," or the financial loss resulting from extreme weather events, gradual changes in climate, environmental degradation, pollution, water stress, biodiversity loss and deforestation,[2] and "transition risk," that is, financial losses from adjusting to a low-carbon and sustainable economy, including changes in climate policies, technology, market preferences or litigation.[3] The pathways for these risks are multiple. The Financial Stability Board (FSB) Task Force on Climate-related Financial Disclosures (TCFD) provides a classification summarized in Tables 19.1 and 19.2.

19.2.2 *Relationship between Risks and "Litigation Risk"*

Climate change risks can interact in complex and unpredictable ways. A single source, for example a flood or temperature rise, can have different impacts, for example collateral valuations, credit risk through increased probability of default (PD) and/or loss-given default (LGD), or operational risk, due to the increased probability of disruptions.[4] These can interact with increased transition costs, for example from new energy efficiency regulations, which may hurt both the bank's borrowers and the issuers of the securities in its portfolio.[5] This can increase credit risk's non-linearities.

Another, often overlooked, risk is litigation risk, which one must not simplify into the "cash" cost (i.e., fees and damages) of individual lawsuits. Litigation amplifies other risks.[6] Litigation against one project increases the risk that comparable projects become "stranded assets."[7] Litigation against high carbon-emitters may make

---

[2] ECB 2020a, 10; NGFS 2020a. This is consistent with the FSB 2017 (TCFD Recommendations).
[3] ECB 2020a, 10; NGFS 2020a; FSB 2017. Litigation is added explicitly by FSB 2017.
[4] ECB 2020a, 12.
[5] Ibid., 11.
[6] See, for example, NGFS 2021c.
[7] For example, *ClientEarth* v. *Polska Grupa Energetyczna*, 2019 (https://bit.ly/4affU1b) or *ClientEarth* v. *Enea*, in 2018 (https://bit.ly/3uZCD2l) (a court annulled the authorization of the construction of a coal-fueled plant).

TABLE 19.1 *Physical risk*

Category	Risk	Impact/Transmission channel	Financial risk
Acute	– Increased severity of extreme weather events such as cyclones and floods	– Reduced revenue from delayed/ disrupted production, health/ safety impact on workforce – Write-offs/early retirement of assets (e.g., damage to property in "high-risk" locations)	Credit risk Market risk
Chronic	– Changes in precipitation patterns; extreme variability in weather patterns – Rising mean temperatures – Rising sea levels	– Increased operating costs (e.g., inadequate water supply for hydroelectric plants or to cool nuclear/fossil fuel plants) – Increased capital costs (e.g., damage to facilities) – Reduced revenues from lower sales/output – Increased insurance premiums and potential for reduced availability of insurance on assets in "high-risk" locations	Operational risk Liquidity/ funding risk Reputational risk

Sources: FSB 2021, 75, Table A1.1., and EBA 2021d, 34, Fig. 4.

their transition more "disorderly."[8] Litigation against institutional investors may lower prices in carbon-intensive sectors.[9] Since courts tend to reason by analogy, a ruling has impact beyond the concrete asset, emitter or fund. Furthermore, lawsuits against projects may be followed by lawsuits for failure to disclose risks, or for breach of fiduciary duties.[10] Some plaintiffs are aware of these dynamics, and resort to *strategic* litigation, where cases are a form of advocacy, accompanied by PR and engagement actions.[11] Thus, "litigation risk" goes beyond legal fees, and encompasses the risk from sudden changes prompted by legal action.

19.2.3 *Global Landscape*

Notable international standards include the United Nations' Principles for Responsible Investment (UNPRI)[12] and its Environment Program Finance Initiative (UNEP FI)'s

[8] For example, the case *Milieudefensie* v. *Royal Dutch Shell*, Rechtbank Den Haag, 26 May 2021, C/09/571932 / HA ZA 19-379 (Netherlands).

[9] In *McVeigh* v. *Retail Employees Superannuation Trust* [2018] No. NSD1333/2018 (Australia), the claimant withdrew the complaint in exchange for the fund's changes in policies.

[10] In a similar sense, see Solana 2020, 344–372.

[11] Setzer and Higham 2021, 12.

[12] UN 2006.

TABLE 19.2 *Transition risk*

Category	Risk	Impact	Financial risk
Legal and policy	Higher GHG emissions pricing Enhanced emissions-reporting Products/services regulation Litigation	Increased operating costs – Asset write-off, impairment and early retirement – Higher costs or reduced demand (products and services)	Credit risk Market risk
Technology	Substitution of existing products and services with lower emissions options – Unsuccessful investment in new technologies – Costs to transition to lower emissions technology	– Asset write-offs/early retirement – Reduced demand for products/services – R&D costs in alternative technologies – Investments in tech development – Costs to adopt/deploy new practices and processes	Operational risk
Market	– Changing customer behavior – Uncertainty in market signals – Increased cost of raw materials	– Reduced demand – Higher production costs due to input prices (e.g., energy, water) and output requirements (e.g., waste treatment) – Abrupt shifts in energy costs – Decreased revenues – Re-pricing of assets (e.g., fuel reserves, land, securities)	Liquidity/funding risk
Reputation	– Shifts in consumer preferences – Stigmatization of sector – Stakeholder concerns/negative feedback	Reduced demand, delays in production, supply disruptions, difficulties attracting/retaining employees – Reduced capital availability	Reputational risk

Sources: FSB 2021, 75, Table A1.1, and EBA 2021d, 34, Fig. 4

Principles for Responsible Banking,[13] which seek to align the banks' business strategy with the objectives of the SDGs and the Paris Agreement; the Global Reporting Initiative from the Global Sustainability Standards Board (GRI-GSSB);[14] or the Equator Principles,[15] adopted by financial market institutions, which provide a common baseline and framework to identify, assess and manage environmental and social risks when financing projects.

Moving from voluntary standards for the industry to policy action was achieved through the G-20, the global policy forum for the post-Great Financial Crisis (GFC). Climate made its appearance initially linked to "funding,"[16] and after 2015, to risk. Central bankers and regulators gradually changed their mindset after Mark Carney's "tragedy of the horizon" speech.[17] The FSB received a mandate,[18] which led to the Task Force on Climate-related Financial Disclosures (TCFD).[19] The TCFD emphasized that the disclosures could be used by private-sector participants[20] but also *authorities* to assess risks "on a systemic level."[21] The TCFD Report was ambitious, focusing on "metrics and targets," "risk management," "strategy" and "governance,"[22] and recommending the use of scenario analysis.[23]

Bank regulation changed more slowly. After some early efforts, like Alexander's report,[24] the Network for the Greening of the Financial System (NGFS)[25] and its 2019 Report "A Call for Action" *officially* treated "climate risk" as "financial risk,"[26] paving the way for guides for prudential supervisors,[27] climate scenarios[28] and progress reports.[29]

These global initiatives provide the conceptual basis for national and regional efforts. The EU is one of the most active players, through its legislation, the European Banking Authority (EBA) and the European Central Bank (ECB).

---

[13] UNEP FI 2019.

[14] GSSB 2022.

[15] Equator Principles 2020.

[16] G20 Research Group 2012, paras. 70–71: G20 leaders welcomed in the Los Cabos summit declared that they would "consider ways to effectively mobilize resources taking into account the objectives, provisions and principles of the UNFCCC."

[17] Carney 2015 ("Tragedy of the horizon speech").

[18] See the "Issues for further action" part in the Communiqué of finance ministers and central banks governors of the G20 Research Group 2015.

[19] FSB 2015.

[20] Ibid.: "to develop voluntary, consistent climate-related disclosures of the sort that would be useful to lenders, insurers, investors and other stakeholders in understanding material risks."

[21] Ibid.: "disclosures by financial institutions would foster an early assessment of these risks, facilitate market discipline [...] It would also provide a source of data that can be *analysed at a systemic level, to facilitate authorities' assessments* of the materiality of any risks posed by climate change to the financial sector." (emphasis added).

[22] FSB 2017, 14.

[23] Ibid., 25.

[24] Alexander 2014.

[25] See www.ngfs.net/en.

[26] NGFS 2019.

[27] NGFS 2020a.

[28] NGFS 2020b.

[29] See, for example, NGFS 2021a.

19.2.4 *Climate Risks and Bank Regulation: The Three Pillars*

"Bank regulation" primarily refers to prudential requirements, inspired by the Basel Framework,[30] adopted by the Basel Committee on Bank Supervision (BCBS).[31]

The Basel Framework is formed by three "Pillars": Pillar 1, the most important, which covers banks' capital (and now leverage and liquidity) requirements; Pillar 2, on the Supervisory Review and Evaluation Process (SREP); and Pillar 3, on "Market Discipline," that is, mandatory disclosures. Unfortunately, as we show, climate change has not been assimilated following a comprehensive, top-to-bottom strategy, starting with Pillar 1, and proceeding to Pillars 2 and 3.

19.3 PILLAR 1 (CAPITAL REQUIREMENTS) DISAPPOINTS AND PILLAR 3 (MARKET DISCIPLINE THROUGH DISCLOSURES) PROMISES, BUT CANNOT DELIVER

19.3.1 *Underwhelming Pillar 1 (and Macroprudential) Measures*

Climate-wise, the Basel Framework's Pillar 1 is (almost) silent. The Basel Framework states that "The bank must appropriately monitor the risk of environmental liability arising in respect of the collateral, such as the presence of toxic material on a property,"[32] a statement accompanied by references to environmental factors' impact on *collateral*.[33] There are references to *economic* "climate"[34] and to "sustainable" asset values or funding structures,[35] not to actual climate and sustainability.

This blind spot for regulators is surprising. One problem is that advocates and critics of "green" prudential rules seem to equate it with a "subsidy" of green assets through more lenient regulation (see Binder's excellent critical analysis in Chapter 20 of this book). Nonetheless, the BCBS is trying to address these shortcomings step by step, first by acknowledging in its analytical reports that climate risk drivers could be captured into traditional financial risk categories: "credit," "market," "liquidity," "operational" and "insurance" risk,[36] then by seeking to clarify in its Frequently Asked Questions (FAQs) that banks could capture climate risks in its risk-weighted assets (RWA) under existing Pillar 1 standards.[37] Still, the problem is that climate change poses large, non-linear risks, including transition risk, which have not been properly assimilated. We come back to the conceptual challenges in Section 19.5.

---

[30] BCBS (version of 2019).
[31] See www.bis.org/bcbs/membership.htm.
[32] BCBS 2019, para. 36.132 (4).
[33] Ibid., para. 36.140.
[34] Ibid., para. 98.24 (Supervisory Review Process – SRP 98).
[35] Ibid., para. 20.1 (Net Stable Funding NSF 20); para. 01.38 (Bank Core Principles – BCP).
[36] BCBS 2021.
[37] BCBS 2022.

Meanwhile, the EU legislator seems reluctant to assimilate climate change in prudential rules and seems to adhere to this simplistic ("subsidization") view. The EU Capital Requirements Directive (CRD[38]) and Capital Requirements Regulation (CRR[39]), included some references only after the Commission's Sustainable Finance Action Plan,[40] and subsequent 2019 reforms of CRR and CRD.[41] Post-2019 provisions were underwhelming. CRR only included two Pillar 1 provisions. One permits a lenient application of risk calculations in exposures to Collective Investment Units (CIUs) that invest in "assets that promote sustainable development in developing countries."[42] The other, Article 501a CRR, provides for the beneficial treatment[43] of funding for entities operating or financing physical structures or facilities (or systems and networks) that provide or support essential public facilities, if they fulfil a long list of requirements, including that the assets contribute to environmental objectives, such as "(i) climate change mitigation; (ii) climate change adaptation; (iii) sustainable use and protection of water and marine resources; (iv) transition to a circular economy, waste prevention and recycling; (v) pollution prevention and control; (vi) protection of healthy ecosystems."[44] Thus, as recently as 2019 climate change only merited a regulatory subsidy for financing of specific infrastructures. The Banking Package reforms introduced new definitions in Article 4 (1) (52d) – (52i) CRR3 for "ESG risk," as well as "environmental," "physical," "transition," "social" or "governance" risk. It is a major conceptual development to include new categories of risk. What to do about them is less clear, as shown by the changes in Article 501c CRR.

Article 501c of CRR[45] after 2019 further instructed the EBA to issue a Report with an assessment on whether "*a dedicated prudential treatment* of *exposures* related to

---

[38] Directive 2013/36/EU of the European Parliament and of the Council of 26 June 2013 on access to the activity of credit institutions and the prudential supervision of credit institutions and investment firms, OJ L 176, 27 June 2013 (hereinafter: CRD).

[39] Regulation (EU) No 575/2013 of the European Parliament and of the Council of 26 June 2013 on prudential requirements for credit institutions and investment firms and amending Regulation (EU), OJ L 176, No 648/2012, 27 June 2013 (hereinafter: CRR).

[40] European Commission 2018.

[41] Directive (EU) 2019/878 of the European Parliament and of the Council of 20 May 2019 amending Directive 2013/36/EU, OJ L 150, 7 June 2019 (hereafter: Directive 2019/878); Regulation (EU) 2019/876 of the European Parliament and of the Council of 20 May 2019 amending Regulation (EU) No 575/2013, OJ L 150, 7 June 2019 (hereafter: Regulation 2019/876).

[42] Article 132a CRR provides for the use of the "look-through approach" (LTA), or the "mandate-based approach" (MBA) if the institution lacks information about a CIU's underlying exposures. If not the LTA or MBA, it must apply the "fall-back approach" (FBA), that is, a penalizing risk-weight of 1250 per cent. Article 132 CRR restricts the use of LTA or MBA under Article 132a to funds fulfilling certain conditions. Thus, Article 132(3)(2) CRR, the one that refers to assets promoting sustainable development, waives these requirements.

[43] The beneficial treatment consists in multiplying the own funds required to cover credit risk exposures by 0.75 as long as the exposure fulfils the requirements stated in Article 501a CRR.

[44] Article 501a(1)(o) CRR.

[45] Article 519a CRR was amended in 2021 with a new letter (e), requiring the Commission to report by January 2022 on developments in the securitization market, discussing "(e) how environmental sustainability criteria could be integrated into the securitisation framework, including for exposures to NPE securitisations."

assets or activities *associated substantially with environmental and/or social objectives* would be justified." (emphasis added). The Article shows the contradictions in the process. On one hand, its text may suggest that the answer is to dispense a "dedicated" (e.g., more beneficial) treatment to some "green" exposures (again, the "green supporting factor," with "subsidy" connotations), in line with Article 501's (controversial) lenient treatment of SMEs loans. On the other hand, fortunately the EBA Report should also include "criteria for the assessment of physical risks and transition risks, including the risks related to the depreciation of assets due to regulatory changes."[46] Furthermore, the Article initially required the report for 2025, which, considering that carbon emissions should be 45 per cent below current levels by 2030, was hard to justify. Then, the 2021 Banking Package reforms, which seek a better, more comprehensive assimilation of climate risks,[47] changed the deadline to 2023.[48] This shows a bit of improvisation in the process, an impression confirmed when the subsequent, amended text broke down the EBA's mandate, and, instead of one, the EBA would produce three reports, in 2023, 2024 and 2025, addressing different aspects of ESG risks in the prudential framework. The numerous changes show the difficulty of agreeing on a way forward.

The EBA published its first Discussion Paper in May 2022, and its Final report in October 2023.[49] There it emphasized some key messages. First, prudential regulation should remain risk-based, that is, prudential requirements must reflect the risk profiles of exposures. Furthermore, "to maintain a level playing field and appropriate application of these minimum requirements, the calculation should be based on objective, observable values." Also, Pillar 1 measures should bear in mind that there are already ongoing initiatives regarding Pillar 2 and 3 (see Sections 19.3.2. and 19.4). With all this in mind, in the EBA's view, environmental risks, as drivers of traditional categories of financial risk, may be already reflected in the current risk assessments; for example, through internal models, external credit ratings and valuations of collaterals and financial instruments. In those parts where the prudential framework does not reflect climate risks, this can be addressed by targeted amendments, enhancements or clarifications of existing rules, or more oversight by competent authorities (e.g., to ensure that environmental factors are duly reflected in due diligence requirements or collateral valuations). The EBA is in principle against the generality of "green" or "brown" factors. The EBA Report supports these conclusions with a comprehensive analysis of the climate sensitivity of different aspects of the prudential framework. Credit risk (the main category) could be climate-adjusted in external credit ratings or due diligence requirements,[50] and

---

[46] Article 501c (b) CRR.
[47] Including a definition of ESG risks. See new article 3 (1) (68) Commission Proposal Banking Package, 2021, cross-referenced to article 4(1)(52d) CRR.
[48] Article 501c CRR, European Commission 2021.
[49] EBA 2022b; EBA 2023.
[50] Ibid., although the paper is generally cautious on the adjustability of the Standardised Approach (which comprises external ratings, due diligence or credit mitigation techniques).

especially in the modelling of the Internal Ratings Based (IRB) approach, where the EBA insists on the need for "accuracy." The analysis is more general in the case of market risk or reputational risk.

The EBA's Report seems to try more to manage expectations and to set goals than to comprehensively address the integration of climate risk in Pillar 1 (though subsequent reports might go further). "Green" and "brown" factors are too general and interfere with Pillar 1's risk-based structure. Any support or penalization should result from the risk assessment itself. The impression that the EBA is more cautious on Pillar 1 measures than on other (Pillar 2 or 3) measures is confirmed by a look at its sustainable finance roadmap, where proposals on Pillar 1 are much more tentative, and dependent on the legislative process.[51] The problem, however, is that this places the full evidentiary burden on regulators and supervisors under conditions of deep uncertainty.

An alternative to "pure" Pillar 1 measures could be to incorporate climate risk as part of macroprudential measures, which presents other conceptual challenges.[52] Yet the legislators are reluctant to do that as well. The Banking Package 2021 accompanied the reform of the Systemic Risk Buffer (Article 133) with a recital, indicating that the buffer could be used to address climate change's *systemic* risks.[53] Even this well-intended but weak reference disappeared from the Council version, although it made a comeback in 2024, not only in a recital, but on the amendments to Article 133, which expressly acknowledges that the buffer should prevent risks "including macroprudential or systemic risks stemming from climate change."[54] The reform of the macroprudential framework follows its own cycle, which is stated in Article 513 CRR, and is independent from the Banking Package. In the Commission's Call for advice, the ECB, the European Systemic Risk Board (ESRB) and the EBA expressed favorable views about the role that the assimilation of climate change risk by macroprudential tools could play in enhancing financial stability, and the Commission's Report, in 2024 (two years after its deadline) noted the Banking Package reforms.[55] However, it is soon to tell whether the open reference in Article 133 will result in substantial changes.

By way of preliminary conclusion, even though the issue is a moving target and it evolves quickly, it appears that EU authorities are reluctant to adopt any large-scale reforms to comprehensively assimilate climate risk within Pillar 1, or macroprudential measures. Their current choice is for risk models and measurement tools to achieve that on their own, with the aid, when needed, of targeted amendments, clarifications or technical support by authorities like the EBA.

---

[51] EBA 2022d.
[52] Grünewald 2020.
[53] See Recital (36) of the Commission Proposal 2021.
[54] Directive proposal 2021/0341 (COD) Brussels, 31 October 2022 and, subsequently, 4 December 2023. Recital (36) and Article 133(1).
[55] ECB 2022b; EBA 2022c; ESRB 2022; European Commission 2024.

Whether this will lead market players to take the initiative or sit and wait is another matter. For the moment, legislators and authorities have preferred to focus on Pillar 3 and Pillar 2 measures.

19.3.2 *Climate Disclosures and the Green Asset Ratio: Pillar 3 and Beyond*

Early proponents like Carney advocated better climate disclosures, and these are still the prevalent pathway to assimilate climate into financial regulation, under the logic that "supply creates demand," that is, better disclosures will find investors willing to use them.[56] Yet the path towards "better," more relevant and comprehensive disclosures is complex and formed of different strands. First, there are the global efforts to improve climate-related disclosures *for all firms*, such as the FSB's Taskforce on Climate-Related Financial Disclosures recommendations (TCFDs[57]). These include specific recommendations for banks (and insurance companies, or asset managers[58]). These standards were assimilated by EU Law in a singular way, which, in practice, has transformed those standards. Second, there are the bank-specific Basel "Pillar III" disclosures. Here, again, EU authorities took their own path without waiting for global institutions. Third, and finally, there are the efforts by authorities like the EBA or the ECB.

First, among global efforts to improve climate disclosures, the TCFDs are the leading standard of climate disclosures for all firms, which includes numerous adjustments for banks. TCFDs are structured in four thematic areas: governance, strategy, risk management and metrics, each with its own sub-topics.

Yet the EU has assimilated the TCFDs through the Non-Financial Reporting Directive (NFRD/CSRD).[59] The NFRD is not climate-specific. Thus, climate-specific disclosures are *de facto* regulated in the European Commission Guidelines on Climate Disclosures (based on NFRD).[60] Both the NFRD and the Guidelines include categories of disclosures different from the TCFDs, namely: (i) business model, (ii) policies and due diligence processes, (iii) outcomes, (iv) principal risks and their management and (v) key performance indicators (KPIs). As Table 19.3 explains, NFRD and TCFD can match, but their approach is different, which can be confusing. We highlight in bold the TCFDs' bank specialties, since Commission Guidelines provide for bank specialties in all disclosure categories.

---

[56] Carney 2015.
[57] FSB 2017. See also FSB 2021. References will be made mostly to the FSB 2021 *Implementation*, as the more up-to-date document, which includes both the general and the supplementary guidance for banks.
[58] FSB 2021, 24–54.
[59] Directive 2014/95/EU of the European Parliament and of the Council of 22 October 2014 amending Directive 2013/34/EU as regards disclosure of non-financial and diversity information by certain large undertakings and groups, OJ L 330, 15 November 2014 (hereinafter: Directive 2014/95) replaced by Corporate Sustainability Reporting Directive (CSRD) 2022/2464.
[60] European Commission 2019.

TABLE 19.3 *TCFD recommendations and NFRD Commission Guidelines*

TCFD recommendations	Business model	NFRD – Commission Guidelines			
		Policies and due diligence	Outcomes	Principal risks and their management	Key performance indicators (KPIs)
Governance	Board's oversight of climate risks and opportunities				
	Management's role in assessing and managing risks and opportunities				
Strategy	**Risks and opportunities**				
	Impact of risks and opportunities				
	Resilience of strategy				
Risk management	Processes to identify and assess risk				
	Processes to manage risk				
	Integration in overall risk management				
Metrics and targets	**Metrics to assess climate risks and opportunities**				
	Scope 1, 2, 3 GHG emissions				
	Targets to manage risks and opportunities and performance against targets				

Source: European Commission 2019; FSB 2021.

Based on the above, companies (and **Banks**) must disclose the following:

A.   On *governance* companies should disclose (a) how frequently the board is
     informed about climate-related issues, whether it considers them in major
     decisions, and monitors climate-related goals; and (b) whether there are
     responsibilities assigned over climate-related issues at the management level,
     and what the organizational structure, information processes and monitor-
     ing of progress are.[61] TFCDs have no specialties for banks, but Commission
     Guidelines also require disclosing financial institutions' climate-related stew-
     ardship activities, for example, engagements with companies, outcomes and
     proxy voting (e.g., resolutions filed or supported).[62]

B.   On *strategy* all companies should disclose (a) climate-related *risks* and
     opportunities, time horizons and processes to assess them, while **banks**
     should also disclose significant credit exposure concentrations to carbon-
     related assets and climate-related risks,[63] and (b) climate risks' *impact* in
     business areas and financial performance,[64] for example, in lending or
     investment portfolios,[65] and climate as an input in financial decisions (or,
     in banks, lending decisions), as well as (c) business model *resilience* based
     on scenario analysis.

C.   On *risk management*, companies should disclose (a) climate-related risks' *sig-
     nificance* in relation to other risks, and assessment of their size and scope, (b)
     climate risks' management and (c) their integration in overall risk manage-
     ment, while **banks in particular** should also categorize them among credit,
     market, liquidity and operational risk.[66]

D.   On *metrics and targets*, (a) firms should disclose how performance metrics
     are incorporated in remuneration policies (if climate issues are "mate-
     rial") the internal cost of carbon (if relevant), and historical informa-
     tion, while **banks** should also include metrics on climate risk's impact
     in their lending and financial intermediation,[67] figures of carbon-related
     assets and alignment of their intermediation business with a below
     2 °C scenario. (b) All firms should disclose Scope 1 and 2 GHG emis-
     sions, and Scope 3 if appropriate, while **banks** should disclose the
     emissions for their *lending and other financial intermediary* business

---

[61]   FSB 2021, 17.
[62]   European Commission 2019, Annex I no. 2.
[63]   FSB 2021, 26. European Commission 2019, Annex I no. 2 provides further detail, including risks for
       activities, assets, exposures, collateral, etc.
[64]   FSB 2021, 26.
[65]   European Commission 2019, Annex I no. 1.
[66]   FSB 2021, 27. European Commission 2019, Annex I no. 2 provides further detail, including an assess-
       ment of climate risks' impact on regulatory capital requirements.
[67]   Metrics may relate to credit exposure, equity and debt holdings, or trading positions, broken down by
       Industry, Geography, Credit quality and Average tenor (FSB 2017, 29).

activities.[68] (c) All firms should describe their key climate-related targets, including key performance indicators (KPI).[69]

EU law assimilated the TCFDs within its own framework, as part of the NFRD's "non-financial" disclosures, which is also linked to the Taxonomy.[70] The Taxonomy Regulation adds a duty to disclose the *relative importance* of "environmentally sustainable" activities.[71] The KPIs, a fundamental element of TCFDs' "metrics and targets," are challenging for banks, because their main impact is not through a direct use of resources, but through lending and investment. The Taxonomy Regulation left the choice of KPIs for banks entirely to the Commission.[72] After a Call for Advice (CfA),[73] the Commission's Delegated Regulation[74] rejected general KPIs, like, for example, Capex in favor of the bank-specific "Green Asset Ratio."[75]

Second, on top of this very complicated picture there are the Basel "Pillar 3" disclosures. The (global) Basel Committee announced its intention to promote a common disclosure baseline for climate-related financial risks under Pillar 3,[76] but the EU has not waited for the global standard. Article 98 (8) CRR required the EBA to produce a report for Pillar 2 (supervisory review) measures (see Section 19.4) *and* Article 449a CRR[77] stated that listed banks "shall disclose information on ESG risks, including physical risks and transition risks, *as defined in the report referred to in Article 98(8).*" (emphasis added). Thus, Pillar 3 disclosures are based on the conceptual framework of the EBA's Pillar 2 Report.[78]

---

[68] FSB 2021, 29, refers to metrics such as the Partnership for Carbon Accounting Financials (PCAF Standard).

[69] European Commission 2019 includes KPIs such as asset portfolio's amount/percentage of carbon-related assets, or weighted average of carbon intensity, volume of exposures by counterparty's sector, credit exposures and collateral by geographical location, etc.

[70] Regulation (EU) 2020/852 of the European Parliament and of the Council of 18 June 2020 on the establishment of a framework to facilitate sustainable investment, and amending Regulation (EU) 2019/2088, OJ L 198, 22 June 2020 (hereinafter: Taxonomy Regulation).

[71] Article 8 of the Taxonomy Regulation.

[72] Article 8(2) Taxonomy Regulation lists the information disclosed by "non-financial undertakings", while Article 8(3) asks the Commission to determine the information for banks.

[73] European Commission 2020.

[74] Commission Delegated Regulation (EU) 2021/2178 of 6 July 2021 supplementing Regulation (EU) 2020/852 of the European Parliament and of the Council by specifying the content and presentation of information to be disclosed by undertakings subject to Articles 19a or 29a of Directive 2013/34/EU concerning environmentally sustainable economic activities, and specifying the methodology to comply with that disclosure obligation, OJ L 443, 10 December 2021 (hereinafter: Commission Regulation 2021/2178).

[75] Article 4 and Annexes V and XI (especially Annex V no 1.2.1.) of Commission Regulation 2021/2178.

[76] BIS 2021. A climate risk disclosure document was released for consultation. BCBS 2023.

[77] As amended by Regulation 2019/876.

[78] Article 98(8) CRD, as amended by Directive 2019/878.

The EBA released a draft,[79] then a final paper in 2021.[80] The paper highlights climate change as the more prominent factor, then other environmental factors, then social factors.[81] The Report instructs banks to adopt an "outside-in" perspective, that is, to measure the *impact that climate*, and other ESG factors, have *on banks* through their investments and counterparties, who themselves are *impacted by* ESG factors.[82] This narrows the scope. However, once banks start disclosing Scope 3 emissions from lending, and banks' carbon footprint is linked to their transition risk, inside-out and outside-in may not be that easy to disentangle. The Report invites banks to rely on proxies, or indicators, such as taxonomies, standards/principles, benchmarks and other frameworks for identifying ESG risks.[83]

The new drafting of Article 449a CRR after the Banking Package stresses that institutions should mandatorily disclose ESG risks, including physical risks and transition risks, on a semi-annual basis (annual for smaller institutions), and supports the EBA efforts by requiring it to develop implementing technical standards (ITS) with disclosure templates. Before Article 449a was reformed, though, the EBA already had the ITS in place[84] on Pillar 3 disclosures under (former) Article 449a CRR. Climate change is the central ESG risk, subject to quantitative and detailed information, while other ESG risks are subject to more qualitative information.[85] On climate *physical* risks, banks must disclose exposures to sectors and geographies to be negatively impacted by climate change's acute and chronic risks.[86] There is an even greater emphasis on *transition* risk. Banks must disclose exposures to high climate change contributors,[87] including details of lending to fossil fuel and other carbon-intensive corporations (likeliest to suffer policy impacts), and on the real estate portfolio's energy efficiency.[88] In line with NFRD and Commission Guidelines, the ITS also requires disclosure of financed (scope 3) greenhouse gas (GHG) emissions, the distance to a Paris-aligned scenario[89] or exposures to the world's top-20 carbon-intensive firms.[90]

---

[79] EBA 2020a.

[80] EBA 2021d.

[81] Climate change is mentioned 349 times in EBA 2021d, for 306 of "environment", 177 "social" and 170 "governance"; the "environment" section is longer, and most examples refer to climate-linked phenomena.

[82] Although the EBA formally espouses the NFRD's "double materiality", in practice it instructs banks to focus on "outside-in." The "inside-out" perspective should be considered "only to the extent that its related impacts further aggravate the impacts from the outside-in perspective", for example, if a firm's polluting credentials expose it to greater transition costs (EBA 2021d, 32).

[83] EBA 2021d, 52–59.

[84] First, the EBA released a Consultation Paper (EBA 2021b). The Final Paper was EBA 2022a.

[85] EBA 2022a, 5.

[86] Information on exposure to physical risks can be obtained from dedicated portals and databases, some examples of which are included in EBA 2022a, 20.

[87] Ibid., 15.

[88] This includes collateral distribution by energy performance certificate (EPC) label and consumption.

[89] The bank must collect company data, aggregate it to portfolio level, and compare current levels with the International Energy Agency (IEA) 2030 targets to achieve net zero by 2050, for example, a bank has exposures to the shipping industry, with a CO_2 intensity metric of 28.8 gCO_2/MJ, against the IEA target of 23.4 gCO_2/MJ, the "distance" would be $100*((28.8-23.4)/23.4) = 23$ per cent. See EBA 2022a, 18.

[90] Ibid., 19.

Notably, the ITS also emphasizes "mitigation actions," that is, the relative importance of Taxonomy-aligned investments. The EBA argued in the Commission's CfA mentioned above that non-financial companies' metrics are unsuitable for banks,[91] and suggested the Green Asset Ratio (GAR),[92] which the Commission adopted.

The GAR seeks a simplified picture of the lending ratio to Taxonomy-aligned firms, but it is not perfect. The GAR only covers banking book, not trading book exposures, excludes exposures to governments or central banks, which lack a clear taxonomy,[93] and is calculated at an EU level, given the difficulty of collecting information from non-EU counterparties.[94] Also, exposures to non-NFRD firms are considered non-green (out of the numerator, not the denominator[95]). Thus GAR disincentivizes banks from greening their trading book, government lending or lending to SMEs or to non-EU countries, which will dramatically increase their energy needs in the near future.

Third and finally, regulatory and supervisory authorities have played a crucial role in improving banks' climate disclosures not by legislating, but by *interpreting* existing legislation. The ECB Guidelines on Climate-Related and Environmental Risks,[96] despite using the non-amended versions of NFRD,[97] the EBA Guidelines on "materiality of information,"[98] and the NGFS guidance,[99] set clear, ambitious *expectations* for banks.

The ECB Guidelines do not "compartmentalize" climate change risks, but treat them as cross-cutting risks that pervade a bank's risk profile. The Guidelines expect banks to publish "meaningful information and key metrics on climate-related and environmental risks that they deem to be material,"[100] including (i) their criteria to assess the materiality of risks, (ii) their justification of a non-materiality finding and (iii) their methodologies, definitions and criteria.[101] This included (i) disclosure of Scope 3 emissions, (ii) Key Performance Indicators (KPIs) and Key Risk Indicators (KRIs) in their strategy and risk management, and their performance against those metrics and (iii) further environmental risk-related information needed to comprehensively convey their risk profile.[102] These aspects have subsequently been enshrined in legal instruments, but the ECB continues to use its own Guidelines

---

[91] Banks' main impact is through their clients' and counterparties' assets. See EBA 2021a, 4.

[92] Ibid., 4.

[93] Ibid., 5.

[94] Ibid., 5.

[95] NFR Annex V, no 1.1.2(c) of Commission Regulation (EU) 2022/1181 of 8 July 2022 amending the preamble of Annex V to Regulation (EC) No 1223/2009 of the European Parliament and of the Council on cosmetic products, OJ L 184, 11 July 2022.

[96] ECB 2020a.

[97] Directive 2014/95.

[98] EBA 2014.

[99] NGFS 2020a.

[100] ECB 2020a, Expectation 13.

[101] Ibid., Expectations 13.1, 13.2 and 13.3.

[102] Ibid., Expectations 13.5, 13.6 and 13.7.

for measurement and evaluation exercises,[103] together with the EBA[104] to "prod" banks towards better disclosures.

The ECB's Report on Climate-Related and Environmental Risk Disclosures,[105] released simultaneously with the Guidelines, was a wake-up call, as it exposed the sorry state of banks' climate disclosures. Most institutions referred to climate-related risks in their public disclosures (typically, the annual report), but not many disclosed a materiality assessment; few justified their treating the risk as "immaterial," and few disclosed metrics and targets, methodologies, etc.[106] Disclosures were similarly poor for transition risk's impact on business models, board oversight of climate-related risks, or scenario analysis and stress testing.[107]

The EBA results were not encouraging.[108] The analysis of corporate exposures[109] exposed major data gaps and classification challenges. Risk levels varied widely depending on the classification methodology.[110] There was extreme variation between banks' ability to classify their exposures as "green" (from above 65 per cent to below 2 per cent), and between banks' own "best effort" classification, and the EBA's top-down estimate based on sector-specific standardized estimates of "Taxonomy Alignment Coefficients" (TAC).[111]

The ECB's second report in 2022 acknowledged some progress, but gave a stern assessment: no bank was fully compliant with the expectations, and the insufficiency of disclosures,[112] transparency of risks and methodologies[113] and content of disclosures were worrying.[114]

19.4 PILLAR 2: CLIMATE CHANGE AND SUPERVISORY REVIEW

Disclosures and market discipline alone cannot correct the course. Banks' governance and supervision must be "acclimatized." Under Basel, this is mostly Pillar 2,

---

[103] ECB 2020b.
[104] EBA 2021c.
[105] ECB 2020b.
[106] Ibid., no. 3.1.
[107] Ibid., nos. 3.2–3.4.
[108] EBA 2021c.
[109] The exercise involved a sample of 29 volunteer banks' raw data on non-SME corporate exposures to EU countries, and focused especially on transition risk (EBA 2021c, 7).
[110] Ibid., 16–23. For example, the sector's sensitivity to transition risk yielded much higher percentages than, for example, GHG levels over the median.
[111] Ibid., 32–35. The top-down approach was based on Alessi et al. 2019.
[112] ECB 2022a, 3.
[113] "…only about one in five institutions disclose the methodologies, definitions and criteria for all of the figures, metrics and targets reported as material (ECB 2022a, 3).
[114] "Some banks publish dedicated climate-related and environmental risk reports with extensive qualitative and quantitative information, while other banks report on climate-related risks only to a marginal extent, or solely in the context of corporate sustainability, with inherent confusion between the impact of the banks' operations and that of the activities it finances" (ECB 2022a, 4).

the Supervisory Review and Evaluation Process (SREP).[115] Under the SREP: (a) banks must conduct their own Internal Capital (and Liquidity) Adequacy Assessment Process (ICAAP; ILAAP); and supervisors should (b) regularly evaluate the ICAAP/ILAAP through a SREP; and (c) have powers to require banks to operate above Pillar 1 minimum requirements; and (d) intervene before capital falls below minimum levels.

Under EU rules, banks' "internal" perspective is closely linked to the SREP's "external" one. Articles 74–96 CRD regulate the ICAAP and "internal arrangements" including governance, while 97–101 CRD regulate the SREP (and 102–104 the supervisory measures and powers). Two ideas stand out. First, this is a "relational" supervisory model, with an intense dialogue between supervisor and institution,[116] resulting in a mandatory Pillar 2 Requirement (P2R), and a non-legally binding Pillar 2 Guidance (P2G) expectation, based on the supervisory assessment of the entity's needs under stressed conditions, which does not trigger immediate action, but gives the supervisor leverage in the dialogue. Second, the supervisory review will be deeply intertwined with the bank's governance and risk management.

Globally, the NGFS's Guide for Supervisors,[117] and more recently the Basel Committee Principles,[118] seek to "acclimatize" the SREP. There are also the frameworks of individual authorities' supervisory expectations, including the Bank of England,[119] the ECB[120] or the EBA Report.[121] We discuss how climate risks are conceptualized and measured, how they should be assimilated by banks and in the SREP (supervisors) and the challenges for doing so.

19.4.1 *Climate Risk and Methodologies (Including Stress Testing)*

Climate risk is seen as a *driver* of credit, market, operational and liquidity risk.[122] To measure it, the EBA Report suggests three alternatives:

(i) To measure the **portfolio alignment** with targets like Paris's 2 °C. Tools include the Principles for Responsible Banking (PRB) or the Partnership for Carbon Accounting Financials (PCAF), which measure direct and indirect emissions.[123]

---

[115] Lamandini et al. 2022.
[116] Lamandini et al. 2022.
[117] NGFS 2020a.
[118] BCBS 2022.
[119] PRA 2019.
[120] ECB 2020a.
[121] EBA 2021d. See Section 19.3.2.
[122] NGFS 2020a, 14.
[123] They use a set of accounting principles and cover nine asset classes, for example, sovereigns to corporate and SME loan portfolios. See EBA 2021d.

(ii)   To have a **risk framework** to measure resilience against, for example, **climate risks**. This includes **climate sensitivity analysis**, a simpler exercise without fully fledged scenarios,[124] and the most popular, **scenario analysis**,[125] or **climate stress tests**, which feature fully fledged scenarios mapping out possible future developments of transition and physical variables and related changes in macro (e.g., sectoral output, GDP, unemployment) and financial variables (e.g., interest rates), and their impact in portfolio risk attributes.[126]

(iii) To assess the **exposures performance**, classifying all exposures according to their characteristics;[127] a straightforward but more limited method, as it is based on qualitative, backwards-looking and non-standardized (for some ESG factors) information.[128]

Each approach's effectiveness varies with the goal[129] and the type of risk.[130] For climate-related risks, bank supervisors are clearly betting on stress tests. Early adopters include the Dutch Central Bank,[131] the French Prudential and Resolution Authority (ACPR[132]), the ECB,[133] the Bank of England[134] or the Bank of Canada-OSFI,[135] while many more exercises are planned.[136]

"Stress tests" or scenario analyses vary: some focus on transition risks,[137] others on both physical and transition risk,[138] or even litigation risk.[139] Exercises consistent with the NGFS[140] include three scenarios: "orderly" transition, "disorderly" transition and "hot house world."[141] The exercises may differ in their macroeconomic

---

[124] It assesses portfolio risks variation when exposures' are classified as "green" or "non-green", and their vulnerability to climate-related events and policies. EBA 2021d, 67.

[125] PRA 2019 was the forerunner, and is relatively high-level, and makes few mentions to approaches or methodologies, but refers to scenario analysis in paras. 3.14 and following.

[126] EBA 2021d, 67.

[127] Ibid., 72.

[128] Ibid.

[129] The exposure method controls exposure origination, but not climate risk; portfolio alignment and, arguably, risk-based methods help guide decisions over certain sectors, or the whole portfolio. Portfolio alignment is (obviously) better for portfolio monitoring.

[130] Portfolio alignment is better for reputational risk, and the risk-based approach for financial risk.

[131] Vermeulen et al. 2018.

[132] ACPR 2021.

[133] ECB 2022b.

[134] Bank of England 2022.

[135] Bank of Canada-OSFI 2022.

[136] See NGFS 2021b.

[137] The Dutch Central Bank's exercise focused on bond and equity holdings of banks, and loan exposures, and was based on transition risk. The BoC-OSFI exercise also focused on transition risk.

[138] The ACPR, ECB and Bank of England focus on both physical and transition risk.

[139] One Bank of England scenario exercise covers litigation against insurers.

[140] ACPR, ECB, Bank of England and the BoC-OSFI expressly mention the NGFS.

[141] The three scenarios are classified in a matrix in accordance with their high/low physical *and* transition risk. The fourth scenario "too little too late" (with high physical and transition risk) was not included in the first iteration. See www.ngfs.net/ngfs-scenarios-portal/.

modelling,[142] impact assessed sectorally (typical for transition risks[143]) or geographically (physical risks), or the use of "static," "dynamic" or "hybrid" balance sheets (i.e., whether balance sheets change during the process[144]). Thus, there is no single methodology for climate stress tests, and the results are influenced by the assumptions made, a downside of operating under deep uncertainty.[145] To aid in this effort, Article 100 as amended by the Banking Package should give the ESAs Joint Committee a mandate to develop guidelines to ensure consistency, long-term considerations and common standards in stress testing the ESG risks, which "should start with climate-related factors."

19.4.2 *Assimilation by Banks*

When incorporating climate risks, first, **banks** should assess material physical and transition risk in their **business strategy and processes**,[146] by (i) monitoring the business environment and long-term resilience, extending the time horizon for strategic planning, using scenario analysis or more granular studies of exposures to geographical locations, sectors or counterparties[147]; (ii) setting strategic objectives, including KPIs[148]; and (iii) increasing engagement to gather data[149].

It is key to incorporate climate risk in **governance**, including the board and management body.[150] Some highlight the role of specific officers[151] or committees[152] and suitability (fit-and-proper) requirements.[153] Firms should assimilate climate risk in their "three lines of defense," that is, business lines,

---

[142] About half of the institutions use variations of the NiGEM macroeconomic model, others adjusted the NiGEM outputs to account for specific domestic policy targets (e.g., People's Bank of China)

[143] Integrated Assessment Models (IAMs) provide information for broad economic sectors, but can be used for more granular information. Authorities' approaches are "top-down" or "bottom-up." Some used input-output production networks models, useful to study carbon taxation propagation. Some (e.g., ECB) scaled carbon emissions down to company level in studying bank exposures risk. See NGFS 2021b, 25.

[144] Static balance sheet assumptions are easier to implement, but less realistic, especially over longer time horizons. Dynamic balance sheets are more realistic, but assume that banks will divest, and underestimate climate risks.

[145] See Section 19.5.2.

[146] BCBS 2019, Principle 1; NGFS 2020a, 38; EBA 2021d, 82–97; ECB 2020a, 16–21.

[147] NGFS 2020a, 41; EBA 2021d, 87–89; ECB 2020a, Expectations 1 and 2.

[148] For example, a maximum of exposures to certain activities or sectors, or use mitigating actions, such as seeking alignment with the Taxonomy.

[149] NGFS 2020a, 42. EBA 2021d also insists on evaluating transition actions with counterparties, clients, stakeholders, and considering developing sustainable instruments (paras. 182–189 and p. 96).

[150] BCBS 2019, Principle 2; ECB 2020a, Expectation 3; EBA 2021d, 99.

[151] NGFS 2020a, 40; PRA 2019, para 3.4.

[152] EBA 2021d, para. 214; ECB 2020a, Expectation 3.1.

[153] See, for example, NGFS 2020a, 40; EBA 2021d, para. 212.

risk function and internal audit;[154] and foment training and expertise, through policies for conflicts of interests, greenwashing and mis-selling,[155] and remuneration[156]

In the EU the latest Banking Package reinforced this message, by reforming Article 74 CRD, which now requires institutions to have "effective processes" to identify, manage, monitor risks "including environmental, social and governance risks in the short, medium and long term." Article 76 and a new Article 87a complement this, requiring institutions to have "specific plans" with targets and processes, and "strategies, policies, processes and systems," to "test their resilience" to long-term negative impacts. These provisions place "transition planning" front and center of the risk assessment by financial institutions and supervisors, and give EBA a mandate to issue guidelines for this (consultation during 2024 is ongoing). A section in the new Article 91 would incorporate ESG criteria in the suitability assessment of the management body.

The other key aspect is **risk management**, and also (for some) **capital and liquidity adequacy**. Institutions should incorporate material climate risk in their risk appetite frameworks,[157] and have policies and procedures to monitor climate risk[158] in assessing creditworthiness or developing risk-monitoring metrics.[159] Data gathering and aggregation capacities should be aligned with this.[160] The Banking Package–reformed Article 76 CRD requires management to develop concrete plans to address ESG risks, that is to say, risk assessment, transition planning and data are closely related.

Finally, climate risk should be seen as a driver of credit, market, operational and liquidity risk[161] in banks' Internal Capital (and Liquidity) Adequacy Assessment Processes (**ICAAP** and **ILAAP**) frameworks,[162] loan origination[163] or recovery planning,[164] and use stress testing to measure potential impacts.[165] The Banking Package reforms emphasize this, by including an explicit reference to ESG risks in the newly drafted Article 73 CRD.

---

[154] BCBS 2019, Principle 4: bank-client relationship (onboarding, credit application and evaluation), risk and audit functions; ECB 2020a, Expectation 5: business lines, internal units, internal control; EBA 2021d, paras. 218–222 (business lines, risk management, compliance and internal audit).

[155] EBA 2021d, para. 226 and p. 105.

[156] BCBS 2019, Principle 1, para. 13; NGFS 2020a, 40; ECB 2020a, Expectation 4.3; EBA 2021d, para. 348.

[157] BCBS 2019, Principle 6, para. 27; ECB 2020a, Expectation 4.3; EBA 2021d, paras. 237–246, and p. 123.

[158] BCBS 2019, Principles 6 and 7.

[159] EBA 2021d, para. 276, and p. 123.

[160] BCBS 2019, Principle 7; ECB 2020a, Expectation 6; EBA 2021d, paras. 249–255.

[161] BCBS 2019, Principles 8–11; ECB 2020a, Expectations 8–10, 12; EBA 2021d, paras. 258 et seq. and p. 123.

[162] BCBS 2019, Principle 5; NGFS 2020a, 42; ECB 2020a, Expectations 7 and 8; PRA 2019, para. 3.7.

[163] ECB 2020a, Expectation 8.

[164] For example, to differentiate between business lines. EBA 2021d, para. 247 and p. 123.

[165] BCBS 2019, Principle 12; ECB 2020a, Expectations 10 and 11; EBA 2021d, paras. 277–288; PRA 2019, para. 3.14.

19.4.3 *Assimilation in the SREP and Challenges*

Under Basel standards, **supervisors** should ensure that banks assimilate climate risks,[166] set expectations, engage in cross-border cooperation and information-sharing,[167] dedicate resources and capacity[168] and use scenario analysis.[169] The NGFS describes supervisors' expectations[170] and tools,[171] inspiring the ECB and the EBA. Indeed, the new Article 98(9) CRD, introduced by the Banking Package 2021, explicitly requires competent authorities to incorporate ESG risks into their SREP, including the risks under the institutions' business model, and the controls, under governance and risk management. The EBA must develop guidelines to do so, in line with its Report. Here we discuss some of the approaches and challenges.

(1) First, climate risk is key for **Business Model Analysis (BMA)**, including business environment (policy and regulatory changes) and business model viability and sustainability,[172] with special attention to large (sectoral, geographic) concentrations[173] The BMA seeks to determine "Risk Levels" (RLs), which are also used to assess capital and liquidity risks. In the ECB's SREP, for example, RLs are determined using first an automated scoring, which considers the bank's Key Risk Indicators (KRIs), and then applying "supervisory assessment," based on experience.[174]

It is unclear how climate-sensitive and non-climate-sensitive KRIs can be combined to yield aggregate RLs, or how to calculate an automated scoring. One challenge is that supervisory review time horizons are 12 months (business model viability) or 3 years (business model sustainability). Climate needs longer time horizons (10 years or more).[175] Another challenge is that supervisors' analyses of long-term impacts tend to be qualitative, but not yet quantitative.[176]

(2) Second, supervisors oversee how climate factors and risks are incorporated into the **internal governance framework**, the functioning of the management body, the corporate and risk culture, remuneration policies and practices, **risk management framework** and information systems and internal control

---

[166] BCBS 2019, Principles 13–15 stress that supervisors should ensure that banks incorporate climate-related risks as mandated by Principles 1–12.

[167] Ibid., Principle 16.

[168] Ibid., Principle 17.

[169] Ibid., Principle 18.

[170] NGFS 2020a, Recommendation 4, and pp. 38–46. Some of those expectations include indications for both entities and supervisors, for example, on stress testing (ibid., 43–44).

[171] Ibid., 47 et seq.

[172] Ibid., 49; ECB 2020a, Expectations 1.1 and 1.2.

[173] EBA 2021d, 138.

[174] ECB – Banking Supervision 2021.

[175] EBA 2021d, 138–139.

[176] Ibid.

framework.[177] Governance and risk management help to establish "Risk
Controls" (RCs), which complement RLs to assess capital and liquidity risks.
Here the assessment is mostly qualitative, which makes assimilation easier.

(3)   Finally, in the **capital and liquidity risk assessment**, climate risk may increase
      credit risk through higher probability of default (PD) or loss-given default
      (LGD), especially in large concentrations, market risk (falling prices and vol-
      atility), operational risk (reputational damage or sanctions) and liquidity risk
      (funding and asset side[178]). Supervisors can improve their measurement of
      inherent credit risk through forward-looking metrics. Sectoral concentrations
      can help measure transition risk, and geographic concentrations can help
      measure physical risk.[179] For market risk, supervisors may review the market
      risk strategy, and the presence of investment policies that consider climate
      (and ESG factors). For operational risk, supervisors can review how climate
      (and ESG) risks' reputational aspects are managed. For liquidity risk, they can
      assess whether ESG risks, asset concentrations or reputational risk may cause
      net cash outflows, impact medium-to-long-term funding stability or hinder
      market access.[180]

A major challenge is in the *aggregation* of factors. The SREP methodology is
analytical, that is, it breaks down the assessment in steps, and then adds the results
in an aggregate score. Climate may be assimilated more easily in qualitative factors
(presumably RCs) than quantitative ones (RLs). Then there is no clear roadmap to
aggregate quantitative and qualitative information, with varying degrees of precision. If the quantitative steps of the methodology cannot assimilate climate considerations, this may hinder the whole process.

Finally, the SREP is conceived to measure entity-specific risk not captured by Pillar
1 or by macroprudential measures.[181] Thus the SREP must be assessed bank-by-bank,
which hinders its usefulness to assimilate systemic risks.[182] In the EU it could also
upset the distribution of micro-and macroprudential competences between national
authorities and the ECB. Yet if, as mentioned in Section 19.3.1, the idea of using systemic risk buffers to account for (systemic) climate risk is absent, or severely diluted,
the interplay between Pillar 2 and macroprudential measures is no longer clear.

---

[177] Ibid., 142–143.
[178] NGFS 2020a, 49; ECB 2020a, Expectations 8–10.
[179] EBA 2021d, 143–146.
[180] Ibid., 146–149.
[181] Lamandini et al. 2022.
[182] Article 103 CRD originally encouraged supervisory authorities to extrapolate conclusions between
      "institutions with similar risk profiles" such as similar business models or geographical location of
      exposures, are or might be exposed to similar risks or pose similar risks to the financial system." The
      reform Proposal's Explanatory Memorandum stated that Pillar 2 measures should be constrained to a
      microprudential setting not to "undermine the effectiveness and efficiency of other macro-prudential
      instruments." See Lamandini et al. 2022.

Finally, the SREP is a credible tool because the supervisor can use supervisory powers under Article 104. The latest Banking Package includes a reform of Article 104 CRD, which would allow authorities to adopt supervisory measures to require institutions to reduce material ESG risks, including risks arising from the adjustment to national and EU (climate-related) objectives. Measures include the possibility to restrict or adjust their businesses and business models, governance and risk management. These are remarkably ample powers in theory. However, since supervisory powers are subject to constraints like legality and proportionality, the burden is on the supervisor to prove the deviation from what may be an elusive benchmark.

19.5 THE ACTUAL LEGAL AND NON-LEGAL CHALLENGES

19.5.1 *Legal Challenges: Fit, Opportunity and Suitability; Exit, Voice and Penalty*

A major legal question is whether climate change falls within the mandate of financial supervisors. Here it is useful to differentiate between various questions: whether climate change "fits" within authorities' mandate, whether the authorities should be proactive ("opportunity") and whether the authorities' tools are "suitable."[183]

Starting with "fit," some advocate that central banks and financial supervisors should make banks submit net-zero plans, or promote green investment because it is good for general welfare[184] or supportive of political institutions.[185] Skeptics question any kind of "promotional" approach towards green investments.[186]

Financial authorities' mandate must be the starting point for any exercise.[187] Yet climate change profoundly affects risk and stability, that is, their "narrow" mandate. Broader mandates, encompassing welfare, growth or sustainability, are only present in some financial authorities, as is a duty to "support" government policies.[188] A separate decarbonization mandate will not be credible if it is also feebler and fickle. Climate change fits within the authorities' primary mandate, and should be treated as such.

This also means evaluating the "opportunity" of acting early. Financial authorities should consider the side effects of their actions, yes, but the argument cuts both ways, that is, they should also consider the side effects of *inaction*, for example, a scenario of disorderly transition or "hot house" world, compounded by a cascading failure of financial institutions due to network connectivity.[189] Given that *prudential*

---

[183] Ramos Muñoz et al. 2022.
[184] Mazzucato et al. 2020.
[185] Robins et al. 2021, 9; Schoenmaker and van Tilburg 2016, 317–34; Volz 2017; Mazzucato et al. 2020; Dikau and Volz 2019. More nuanced, Smoleńska and van 't Klooster 2021 talk about "credit guidance."
[186] Demekas and Grippa 2021, 22–25.
[187] See Ramos Muñoz et al. 2022.
[188] Ibid. and authorities cited.
[189] Ramos-Muñoz et al. 2022.

authorities are supposed to anticipate risks, the case for early action is strong. The reluctance seems less "scientific" than a case of slow-changing "social norms."[190]

This brings us to objections to the "suitability" of prudential tools. Some argue that there is scant evidence for green assets' low riskiness,[191] or a "Green Supporting Factor."[192] Yet the case is different for a "Brown Factor,"[193] or a color gradation for physical and transition risk,[194] which could also account for borrowers' efforts to reduce carbon intensity or improve climate resilience. Less risk-sensitive measures, like the leverage ratio, have their counterpart in the Green Asset Ratio,[195] which could be flipped into a "Brown Asset Ratio."

Finally, if climate risk is taken seriously, it should be treated as both a micro- and macroprudential risk. In this regard, the fact that even a reference in the recitals to the fact that the systemic risk buffer may be used to tackle climate change risks was controversial enough to be initially deleted from the Council version, although it was eventually brought back (see Section 19.3.1), shows much hesitation, which is unfortunate. Climate risks need to be taken seriously by macroprudential tools as well.[196]

Another conclusion is that measures should "bite" by increasing capital requirements for firms creating the risk in the first place. Transition measures will force them to do so, and prudential rules should anticipate this added cost. Yet current approaches turn this logic upside down,[197] with Pillar 1's extremely timid adjustments, the Pillar 2 (supervisory review) adjustments being restricted to the EU and the Pillar 3 (disclosure) adjustments being the most comprehensive.

Since this path is not consistent with the seriousness of the problem, one possible explanation is that, faced with climate change's epistemological challenge, public authorities sequence the tools from "exit," "voice" and "coercion/penalty."[198]

Climate change risks' deep uncertainty and the scarcity of data are less of a problem for "exit-based" strategies: the ultimate decision (to invest/divest) is left to investors, and more transparency is always easier to advocate, as, for example, Carney did.[199] Disclosure helps to create a "language," and allows trial and error.

Yet, though that is the theory, the pervasiveness of "greenwashing" shows that the theory is incomplete, and that doubling-down on the same market forces that failed to internalize climate change may not be the best idea.

---

[190] Ibid.
[191] Giglio et al. 2020; Campiglio et al. 2018, 462–468.
[192] Demekas and Grippa 2021, 22–25.
[193] Villeroy de Galhau 2018.
[194] Demekas and Grippa 2021.
[195] See Section 19.3.2.
[196] Grünewald 2020. See Article 131(1) CRD and EBA 2020b.
[197] Smoleńska and van 't Klooster 2021.
[198] Ramos Muñoz et al. 2021.
[199] Carney 2015.

Enter "voice," which fosters change from the inside of organizations. This requires assimilating climate change into internal governance and risk management, and as a driving force of the supervisor-supervisee dialogue through the Supervisory Review and Evaluation Process (SREP). The assiduous interaction between supervisor and supervisee can enable more precise and constructive solutions than the more "binary" entry/exit dynamics.

Using "penalty" is the more explicit way to make "brown" firms absorb the cost. Yet a penalty requires legal certainty, and thus even regulatory rules, such as "brown" risk weights, place an added epistemic burden on authorities, which, as has been shown, leads them to be overly cautious.

All this suggests that, in bank prudential rules, authorities follow a path of minimum resistance. Even if the existence of climate risks is well known, authorities are wary of allocating them. They believe that, by enhancing transparency and making climate part of the conversation, such allocation will become easier. Still, even by that yardstick, bank capital rules need a comprehensive reassessment, not, as Article 501c CRR suggests, the possibility of a "dedicated prudential treatment" of ESG exposures.

19.5.2 *Beyond Legal Challenges: Complexity, Uncertainty and Social Norms*

Any critical analysis of the legal challenges needs to consider some ideas that transcend those challenges, notably the relevance of complexity, uncertainty and social norms.

(1) Financial crises may have underlying causes, but also factors that amplify the shocks. In the Great Financial Crisis (GFC) the key was leverage.[200] In a climate-induced crisis it may well be the financial system's "complexity," that is, the interplay between parts of the system, and the resulting collective behavior.[201] Complex science has helped to understand climate change, and can also help to understand its financial implications, although economic models only make limited use of it.[202]

A key aspect is the complexity resulting from finance's network connectivity,[203] as it can make climate-related shocks unpredictable and unmanageable,[204] and the transition more *disorderly*. Network dynamics can result in major structural changes at the onset of a crisis[205] *and* make early-warning

---

[200] Mishkin 2011a, 59–69; from the same author: Mishkin 2011b.
[201] Bar-Yam 2002.
[202] Dafermos et al. 2017, 191–207; Monasterolo et al. 2019, 177–82.
[203] Ramos Muñoz et al. 2022.
[204] The literature on networks and financial contagion is vast. See Allen and Gale 2000, 1–33; Freixas et al. 2000, 611–638; Babus 2009; Allen et al. 2011. For approaches that have common aspects with ours, see Acemoglu et al. 2015, 564–608; Elliott et al. 2014, 3115–3153.
[205] Georg 2013, 2216–2228.

signals had to spot.[206] Thus a major shock due to the reconfiguration of connections could be underway and yet undetected. Furthermore, if banks evaluate climate change risks in their *direct* links but not *indirect* ones, they may underestimate the risk of indirect exposures to climate risk, which creates a network externality.[207] A shock may then cause widespread contagion, hindering authorities' ability to control the situation.

(2) Climate change assimilation by bank regulation faces methodological challenges, in, for example, stress testing,[208] due to the difficulty of making assumptions about temperatures, timing or shocks, to be used in Integrated Assessment Models' (IAMs[209]) damage functions and discount rates.[210] The main factors are characterized by deep uncertainty. This links with the less obvious problem that individuals (including policymakers) are "ambiguity averse."[211] This may lead them to choose inaction, even if it is not efficient.[212]

Thus more evidence is needed on the impact of risk or ambiguity aversion in individuals' or policymakers' contribution to collective efforts to avoid large (but uncertain) damage.[213] Meanwhile, risk or ambiguity aversion supports tools, like climate stress tests, which help visualize how physical, policy and social variables may co-evolve in a complex situation, and how large damages may be even in *best case* scenarios. Even under deep uncertainty, facing the risk of error may be preferable than waiting.

(3) Ultimately, the fact is that anthropogenic climate change and risk have been known for a long time, while financial authorities have begun updating their tools only recently. If they followed a purely scientific approach, authorities should have begun updating their models when the estimates about climate change costs were known, for example after the Stern Review in 2006. Thus, their approach cannot be purely scientific. One possibility is that policy action does not depend on science, but on *social norms*, that is, the problem depends on whether the select group of regulators *and central banks* share with the general population a concern that climate change is important *for them*.[214] In

---

[206] Squartini et al. 2013.

[207] See Cabrales et al. 2017, 3086–3127. See also in 't Veld and van Lelyveld 2014; Craig and von Peter 2014.

[208] See Section 19.4.2. See, for example, Bolton et al. 2020, 25–26.

[209] These combine a climate science module (linking GHG with temperatures) with an economic module, through a damage function (linking temperature with GDP losses). See Bolton et al. 2020.

[210] Ackerman et al. 2009; Pindyck 2013; Stern 2016.

[211] Ramos Muñoz et al. 2022. Berger and Bosetti 2020, 331–355 studied a sample of participants and negotiators at the Paris UN Climate Conference (COP21).

[212] Al-Najjar and Weinstein 2009, 249–284 suggest that ambiguity aversion leads to some irrational behaviors, like an aversion to information. However, Gilboa et al. 2009, 285–296 suggest that ambiguity aversion may be an acknowledgement by decision-makers that, under subjective utility theory, more information is needed.

[213] Brañas-Garza et al. 2022.

[214] Ramos Muñoz et al. 2022.

fact, Mark Carney's "tragedy of the horizon"[215] was thinking of the tragically short time frames of monetary policy and financial stability,[216] which are not based on any mandatory rule, but on a convention among central bankers – that is, a social norm.[217]

The relevance of social norms dynamics in the interplay between climate change, economics and finance and regulation is only beginning to be explored. Some recent studies analyzed mentions to "climate change" and similar terms in top scientific journals, top economic journals, press, European Parliament questions or ECB speeches.[218] Interest in scientific journals has been high and steady for 20 years;[219] interest in the press has been growing, but volatile, and more coincident with "events" (e.g., the Paris Agreement) than with the gravity of the situation,[220] with European Parliament questions following a similar pattern.[221] The ECB offers a striking contrast between the pre-2019 era (no mentions), and 2019–2021, with constant mentions in a large proportion of speeches.[222] This cannot be explained by changes in science, the public or political bodies, but by a change in central banks' social norms. The good news is that, if social norms have changed for financial authorities, then progress may be steady and consistent.

19.6 CONCLUSIONS

Climate change is a challenge for humanity and for bank regulators, and a source of risk for banks. One cannot object to the "science" of the dire predictions; only to the "methodology" to assess and allocate risks more accurately, or the "legal" framework to do so. Currently, the "methodology" is limited, and the legal framework is flawed. The answer is not to leave climate out, but to improve them so it can be in.

Regulatory efforts have translated "climate change" into the language of credit, market, operational, liquidity or reputational "risk" (Section 19.2). Subsequently, Pillar 3 disclosures are going far to push the market to properly account for climate risk (Section 19.3). Even if such reforms are succeeding, it is ironic that regulators acknowledge climate change as a market failure, and yet primarily rely on the market to solve it. A similar paradox is present in supervisory review (Pillar 2). EU authorities' efforts to assimilate climate risks in banks' governance, risk management and supervision are genuine, but have not changed the Supervisory Review's

---

[215] See Section 19.2.
[216] Carney 2015: "The horizon for monetary policy extends out to 2–3 years. For financial stability it is a bit longer, but typically only to the outer boundaries of the credit cycle – about a decade."
[217] Bicchieri 2016.
[218] Cabrales et al. 2022.
[219] Ibid., Figure 2.
[220] Ibid., Figure 1.
[221] Ibid., Figure 3.
[222] Figure 4.

analytical approach, based on breaking down and aggregating factors, which does not fit well with climate risk (Section 19.4). Most tellingly, Pillar 1 capital requirements, the core of bank regulation, remain hopelessly maladjusted.

The overall analysis shows that the slow assimilation of climate change in bank regulation is not fully "science-driven." Nor are there "objective" doubts about the fact that climate change is a major source of financial risk. The assimilation is slow because it follows a path of minimum resistance, which first creates a "language" through disclosures (and exit strategies), less effective but less intrusive, then seeks to change the "conversation" through "voice-based" changes in governance and supervision, leaving "penalty/coercion-based" tools for the end. This enables a more gradual, more palatable change. Another explanation is that climate change has only recently permeated financial authorities' social norms. Thus authorities are slowly becoming accustomed to the idea that something that they thought "out" is actually "in" their mandate. This is only encouraging if Pillar 1 reforms follow Pillars 3 and 2, and if the first stage of slow assimilation is followed by steady progress. This remains to be seen.

REFERENCES

Acemoglu, D., Ozdaglar, A. and Tahbaz-Salehi, A. (2015), 'Systemic risk and stability in financial networks', 105 *American Economy Review*, 2, 564–608.

Ackerman, F., DeCanio, S. J., Howarth, R. B. and Sheeran, K. (2009), 'Limitations of integrated assessment models of climate change', 95 *Climate Change*, 3, 297–315.

ACPR (Autorité de contrôle prudentiel et de resolution) (2021), 'A first assessment of financial risks stemming from climate change: The main results of the 2020 climate pilot exercise', No. 122–2021, May, available at: https://bit.ly/3wRhlEy (accessed 6 October 2022).

Al-Najjar, N. and Weinstein, J. (2009), 'The ambiguity aversion literature: A critical assessment', 25 *Economics and Philosophy*, 3, 249–284.

Alessi, L., Battiston, S., Melo, A.S. and Roncoroni, A. (2019), 'The EU Sustainability Taxonomy: a Financial Impact Assessment', EUR 29970 EN, Publications Office of the European Union, Luxembourg.

Alexander, K. (2014), 'Stability and Sustainability in Banking Reform. Are Environmental Risks Missing in Basel III?', Cambridge Institute for Sustainability Leadership and United Nations Environmental Program Finance Initiative.

Allen, F. and Gale, D. (2000), 'Financial contagion', 108 *Journal of Political Economy*, 1, 1–33.

Allen, F., Babus, A. and Carletti, E. (2011), 'Financial Connections and Systemic Risk', NBER Working Paper Series No. 16177.

Babus, A. (2009), 'Network in finance' in P. Kleindorfer and J. Wind (eds.) *The Network Challenge* (Upper Saddle River, NJ: Wharton School Publishing), 367–382.

Bank of Canada and Office of the Superintendent of Financial Institutions (2022), *Using Scenario Analysis to Assess Climate Transition Risk: Final Report of the BoC-OSFI Climate Scenario Analysis Pilot*, January, available at: https://bit.ly/49LoZM8 (accessed 6 October 2022).

Bank of England (2022), 'Results of the 2021 Climate Biennial Exploratory Scenario (CBES)', 24 May, available at: https://bit.ly/3Vej8xF (accessed 6 October 2022).

Bar-Yam, Y. (2002), 'General features of complex systems', in D. Kiel (ed.) *Encyclopedia of Life Support Systems. Knowledge Management, Organizational Intelligence and Learning, and Complexity*, vol. 1 (Oxford: EOLSS Publishers), 43–96.

BCBS (Basel Committee on Banking Supervision) (2019), 'The Basel Framework', 15 December, available at: www.bis.org/basel_framework/ (accessed 4 October 2022).

BCBS (Basel Committee on Banking Supervision) (2021), 'Climate-related risk drivers and their transmission channels', April, available at: www.bis.org/bcbs/publ/d517.pdf (accessed 25 April 2024).

BCBS (Basel Committee on Banking Supervision) (2022), 'Principles for the effective management and supervision of climate-related financial risks', June, available at: www.bis.org/bcbs/publ/d532.pdf (accessed 6 October 2022).

Berger, L. and Bosetti, V. (2020), 'Are policymakers ambiguity averse?', 130 *The Economic Journal*, 626, 331–355.

Bicchieri, C. (2016), *Norms in the Wild: How to Diagnose, Measure, and Change Social Norms* (New York: Oxford University Press).

BIS (Bank of International Settlements) (2021), 'Basel Committee advances work on addressing climate-related financial risks, specifying cryptoassets prudential treatment and reviewing G-SIB assessment methodology', Press Release, 9 November, available at: www.bis.org/press/p211109.htm (accessed 4 October 2022).

Bolton, P., Després, M., Pereira da Silva, L.A., Samama, F. and Svartzman, R. (2020), 'The Green Swan: Central banking and financial stability in the age of climate change', January, Bank for International Settlements, available at: www.bis.org/publ/othp31.pdf (accessed 7 October 2022).

Brañas-Garza, P., Cabrales, A., Espinosa, M.P. and Jorrat, D. (2022), 'The effect of ambiguity in strategic environments: An experiment', Working Papers 196, Red Nacional de Investigadores en Economía (RedNIE).

Cabrales, A., Gottardi, P. and Vega-Redondo, F. (2017), 'Risk-sharing and contagion in networks', 30 *Review of Financial Studies*, 9, 3086–3127.

Cabrales, A., García, M., Ramos Muñoz, D. and Sánchez, A. (2022), 'The interactions of social norms about climate change: Science, institutions and Economics', February, available at Carlos III University repository.

Campiglio, E., Dafermos, Y., Monnin, P. et al. (2018), 'Climate change challenges for central banks and financial regulators', 8 *Nature Climate Change*, 6, 462–468.

Carney, M. (2015), 'Breaking the Tragedy of the Horizon – Climate change and financial stability', 29 September, Speech Lloyd's of London, London, available at: https://bit.ly/4bFW54t (accessed 4 October 2022).

Craig, B. and Von Peter, G. (2014), 'Interbank tiering and money center banks', 23 *Journal of Financial Intermediation*, 3, 322–347.

Dafermos, Y., Nikolaidi, M. and Galanis, G. (2017), 'A stock-flow-fund ecological macroeconomic model', 131 *Ecological Economics*, 191–207.

Demekas, D. and Grippa, P. (2021), 'Financial Regulation, Climate Change, and the Transition to a Low-Carbon Economy: A Survey of the Issues', IMF Working Paper 296/2021.

Dikau, S. and Volz, S. (2019), 'Central Bank Mandates, Sustainability Objectives, and the Promotion of Green Finance', Working Paper 222/2019, Department of Economics, SOAS University of London.

EBA (European Banking Authority) (2014), 'EBA Guidelines on materiality, proprietary and confidentiality and on disclosure frequency under Articles 432(1), 432(2) and 433 of Regulation (EU) No 575/2013', EBA/GL/2014/14, 23 December, available at: https://bit.ly/3TlUHvI (accessed 6 October 2022).

EBA (European Banking Authority) (2020a), 'EBA Discussion Paper: On management and supervision of ESG risks for credit institutions and investment firms', EBA/DP/2020/03, 30 October, available at: https://bit.ly/4a8Po9t (accessed 6 October 2022).

EBA (European Banking Authority) (2020b), *Final Report: Guidelines on the Specification and Disclosure of Systemic Importance Indicators*, EBA/GL/2020/14, 4 November, available at: https://bit.ly/3Tc9zfP (accessed 7 October 2022).

EBA (European Banking Authority) (2021a), 'Opinion of the European Banking Authority on the disclosure requirement on environmentally sustainable activities in accordance with Article 8 of the Taxonomy Regulation', EBA/Op/2021/03, 26 February, available at: https://bit.ly/3IxKeYL (accessed 6 October 2022).

EBA (European Banking Authority) (2021b), 'Consultation paper: Draft implementing standards on prudential disclosures on ESG risks in accordance with Article 449a CRR', EBA/CP/2021/06, 1 March, available at: https://bit.ly/3wRiyeW (accessed 6 October 2022).

EBA (European Banking Authority) (2021c), 'Mapping climate risk: Main findings from the EU-wide pilot exercise', EBA/Rep/2021/11, 21 May, available at: https://bit.ly/3wPoEJZ (accessed 6 October 2022).

EBA (European Banking Authority) (2021d), *EBA Report: On Management and Supervision of ESG Risks for Credit Institutions and Investment Firms*, EBA/REP/2021/18, 28 June, available at: https://bit.ly/4c4mkBM (accessed 6 October 2022).

EBA (European Banking Authority) (2022a), *Final Report: Final Draft Implementing Technical Standards on Prudential Disclosures on ESG Risks in Accordance with Article 449a CRR*, EBA/ITS/2022/01, 24 January, available at: https://bit.ly/3Tc9VDb (accessed 6 October 2022).

EBA (European Banking Authority) (2022b), 'Discussion paper: The role of environmental risks in the prudential framework', 2 May 2022, EBA/DP/2022/02, available at: https://bit.ly/48OeZU5 (accessed 10 April 2023).

EBA (European Banking Authority) (2022c), 'EBA advice on the Review of the Macroprudential Framework. Response to the Commission's Call for Advice', available at: https://bit.ly/3PhtHw7.

EBA (European Banking Authority) (2022d), 'EBA Roadmap on Sustainable Finance', December 2022, EBA/REP/2022/30. Available at: https://bit.ly/3TcUomK.

EBA (European Banking Authority) (2023), 'Final Report on the Role of Environmental and Social Risks in the Prudential Framework', October 2023, EBA/REP/2023/34 Available at: www.eba.europa.eu/publications-and-media/press-releases/eba-recommends-enhancements-pillar-1-framework-capture.

ECB (European Central Bank) (2020a), 'Guidelines on climate-related and environmental risk: Supervisory expectations relating to risk management and disclosure', November, available at: https://bit.ly/3PkXtA6 (accessed 4 October 2022).

ECB (European Central Bank) (2020b), *ECB Report on Institutions' Climate-related and Environmental Risk Disclosures*, November, available at: https://bit.ly/3Iwno3Q (accessed 6 October 2022).

ECB (European Central Bank) (2022a), *Supervisory Assessment of Institutions' Climate-related and Environmental Risks Disclosures: ECB Report on Banks' Progress towards Transparent Disclosure of Their Climate-related and Environmental Risk Profiles*, March, available at: https://bit.ly/48RokdX (accessed 6 October 2022).

ECB (European Central Bank) (2022b), 'ECB response to the European Commission's call for advice on the review of the EU macroprudential framework', March, available at: https://bit.ly/48Wkb8u.

ECB (European Central Bank) (2022c), 2022 *Climate Risk Stress Test*, July, available at: https://bit.ly/48VFarY (accessed 6 October 2022).

Elliott, M. L., Jackson, M.O. and Golub, B. (2014), 'Financial networks and contagion', 104 *American Economic Review*, 10, 3115–3153.

Equator Principles (2020), 'EP4', July (updated), available at https://bit.ly/3VeDarx (accessed 9 October 2022).

ESRB (European Systemic Risk Board) (2022), *Review of the EU Macroprudential Framework for the Banking Sector March 2022*, available at: https://bit.ly/3VaarUY.

European Central Bank – Banking Supervision (2021), 'Aggregated results of SREP 2021', available at: https://bit.ly/48LcjGQ (accessed 9 October 2022).

European Commission (2018), 'Communication from the commission to the European Parliament, the European Council, the Council, the European Central Bank, the European Economic and Social Committee and the Committee of the Regions Action Plan: Financing Sustainable Growth', COM/2018/097 final, Brussels, 8 March.

European Commission (2019), 'Communication from the Commission. Guidelines on non-financial reporting: Supplement on reporting climate-related information', 2019/C 209/01, 20 June.

European Commission (2020), 'Call for advice to the European Supervisory Authorities on key performance indicators and methodology on the disclosure of how and to what extent the activities of undertakings under the NFRD qualify as environmentally sustainable as per the EU Taxonomy', Ref. Ares (2020)4805202, 15 September.

European Commission (2021), 'Proposal for a Directive amending Directive 2013/36/EU as regards supervisory powers, sanctions, third-country branches, and environmental, social and governance risks, and amending Directive 2014/59/EU', Brussels, 27 October, COM(2021) 663 final.

European Commission (2024), Report from the Commission to the European Parliament and the Council on the macroprudential review for credit institutions, the systemic risks relating to NonBank Financial Intermediaries (NBFIs) and their interconnectedness with credit institutions, under Article 513 of Regulation (EU) No 575/2013 of the European Parliament and of the Council of 26 June 2013 on prudential requirements for credit institutions and amending Regulation (EU) No 648/2012', Brussels 24 January 2024 COM(2024) 21 final.

Freixas, X., Parigi, B., and Rochet, J. C. (2000), 'Systemic risk, interbank relations and liquidity provision by the Central Bank', 32(3, Part 2) *Journal of Money, Credit and Banking*, 611–638.

FSB (Financial Stability Board) (2015), 'FSB proposes creation of disclosure task force on climate-related risks', Press Release, 9 November, available at: https://bit.ly/48Qdoib (accessed 4 October 2022).

FSB (Financial Stability Board) (2017), *Recommendations of the Task Force on Climate-related Financial Disclosures*, Final Report, June, available at: www.fsb-tcfd.org/recommendations/ (accessed 4 October 2022).

FSB (Financial Stability Board) (2021), 'Task Force on Climate-related Financial Disclosures. Implementing the Recommendations of the Task Force on Climate-related Financial Disclosures', October, available at: www.fsb-tcfd.org/publications/ (accessed 4 October 2022).

G20 Research Group (2012), 'G20 Leader Declaration', 19 June, Los Cabos, Mexico, available at: www.g20.utoronto.ca/2012/2012-0619-loscabos.html (accessed 4 October 2022).

G20 Research Group (2015), 'G20 Finance Ministers and Central Bank Governors – Communiqué', 17 April, Washington DC, available at: www.g20.utoronto.ca/2015/150417-finance.html (accessed 4 October 2022).

Georg, C. P. (2013), 'The effect of the interbank network structure on contagion and common shocks', 37 *Journal of Banking and Finance*, 7, 2216–2228.

Giglio, S., Kelly, B. T. and Stroebel, J. (2020), 'Climate Finance', NBER Working Paper Series No. 28226/2020.

Gilboa, I., Postlewaite, A. and Schmeidler, D. (2009), 'Is it always rational to satisfy Savage's axioms?', 25 *Economics and Philosophy*, 3, 285–296.

Grünewald, S. (2020), 'Climate Change as a Systemic Risk: Are Macroprudential Authorities Up to the Task?', EBI Working Paper Series No. 62/2020.

GSSB (Global Sustainability Standard Board) (2022), 'GRI Standards: Consolidated Set of the GRI Standards', 30 June (updated), available at: https://bit.ly/4cbLrCG (accessed 9 October 2022).

in 't Veld, D. and van Lelyveld, I. (2014), 'Finding the core: Network structure in interbank markets', 49 *Journal of Banking and Finance*, 27–40.

Lamandini, M., D'Ambrosio, R. and Ramos Muñoz, D. (2022), 'Supervisory Review Evaluation Process (SREP) in the context of the exercise of supervisory powers and extraordinary measures' in B. Joosen, M. Lamandini and T. Tröger (eds.), *Capital and Liquidity Requirements for European Banks* (Oxford: Oxford University Press), 526–547.

Mazzucato, M, Ryan-Collins, J. and Voldsgaard, A. (2020), 'Central Bank's Green Mission', Project Syndicate.

Mishkin, F. (2011a), 'How Should Central Banks Respond to Asset-Price Bubbles? The 'Lean' versus 'Clean' Debate After the GFC', Reserve Bank of Australia Bulletin.

Mishkin, F. (2011b), 'Monetary Policy Lessons after the Crisis', NBER Working Paper 16755/2011, available at: www.nber.org/system/files/working_papers/w16755/w16755.pdf (accessed 7 October 2022).

Monasterolo, I., Roventini, A. and Foxon, T. (2019), 'Uncertainty of Climate Policies and Implications for Economics and Finance: An Evolutionary Economics Approach', 163 *Ecological Economics*, 177–182.

NGFS (Network for Greening the Financial System) (2019), *A Call for Action. Climate Change as a Source of Financial Risk*, First Comprehensive Report, April, available at: https://bit.ly/3PjxzfR (accessed 4 October 2022).

NGFS (Network for Greening the Financial System) (2020a), 'Guide for Supervisors: Integrating climate-related and environmental risks in prudential supervision', Technical document, May, available at: https://bit.ly/4a4dUZe (accessed 4 October 2022).

NGFS (Network for Greening the Financial System) (2020b), 'Guide to climate scenario analysis for central banks and supervisors', June, available at: https://bit.ly/3wP3oqL (accessed 4 October 2022).

NGFS (Network for Greening the Financial System) (2021a), *Progress Report on the Guide for Supervisors*, October, available at: https://bit.ly/4cnCGps (accessed 4 October 2022).

NGFS (Network for Greening the Financial System) (2021b), *Scenarios in Action: A Progress Report on Global Supervisory and Central Bank Climate Scenario Exercises*, October, available at: https://bit.ly/43h8aJO (accessed 6 October 2022).

NGFS (Network for Greening the Financial System) (2021c), 'Climate-related litigation: Raising awareness about a growing source of risk', Technical Document, November, available at: https://bit.ly/3Tg6rPZ (accessed 4 October 2022).

Pindyck, R. S. (2013), 'Climate Change Policy: What do the models tell us?', 51 *Journal of Economic Literature*, 3, 860–872.

PRA (Prudential Regulatory Authority) (2019), 'Enhancing banks' and insurers' approaches to managing the financial risks from climate change', SS3/2019, Bank of England, April, available at: https://bit.ly/49OvkcQ (accessed 6 October 2022).

Ramos Muñoz, D., Cerrato, E. and Lamandini, M. (2021), 'The EU's "green" finance. Can "exit", "voice" and "coercion" be enlisted to aid sustainability goals?', EBI Working Paper Series 90/2021.

Ramos Muñoz, D., Cabrales, A. and Sánchez, A. (2022), 'Central Banks and Climate Change. Fit, Opportunity and Suitability in the Law and Beyond', EBI Working Paper Series 119/2022.

Robins, N., Dikau, S. and Volz, U. (2021), 'Net-zero central banking: A new phase in greening the financial system', SOAS London Policy Report. London: SOAS.

Schoenmaker, D. and van Tilburg, R. (2016), 'What Role for Financial Supervisors in Addressing Environmental Risks?', 58 *Comparative Economic Studies*, 317–334.

Setzer, J. and Higham, C. (2021), 'Global trends in climate change litigation: 2021 snapshot'. London: Grantham Research Institute on Climate Change and the Environment and Centre for Climate Change Economics and Policy, London School of Economics and Political Science.

Smoleńska, A. and van 't Klooster, J. (2021), 'A risky bet: Should the EU choose a microprudential or a credit guidance approach to climate risk?', EBI Working Paper Series 104/2021.

Solana, J. (2020), 'Climate change litigation as financial risk', 2 *Green Finance*, 4, 344–372.

Squartini, T., van Lelyveld, I. and Garlaschelli, D. (2013), 'Early-warning signals of topological collapse in interbank networks', 3 *Scientific Reports*, 3357, available at: doi.org/10.1038/srep03357.

Stern, N. (2016), 'Economics: Current climate models are grossly misleading', 530 *Nature*, 407–409.

UN (United Nations) (2006), 'Principles for Responsible Investment', available at: https://bit.ly/3TcHEfO (accessed 9 October 2022).

UNEP FI (United Nations Environment Programme Finance Initiative) (2019), 'Principles for Responsible Banking', available at: www.unepfi.org/banking/more-about-the-principles/ (accessed 9 October 2022).

Vermeulen, R., Schets, E., Lohuis, M. et al. (2018), 'An energy transition risk stress test for the financial system of the Netherlands', 16 *Occasional Studies*, 7, available at: https://bit.ly/3VaPvNH (accessed 6 October 2022).

Villeroy de Galhau, F. (2018), 'Green finance – A new frontier for the 21st century', Speech at the International Climate Risk Conference for Supervisors, Amsterdam, 6 April, available at www.bis.org/review/r180419b.htm (accessed 7 October 2022).

Volz, U. (2017), 'On the role of central banks in enhancing green finance', UNEP Inquiry Working Paper 17/01.

Prudential Requirements Framework and Sustainability

Jens-Hinrich Binder*

20.1 INTRODUCTION: MICRO-PRUDENTIAL REGULATION AND SUSTAINABILITY – MAPPING THE ISSUES

Just as in other areas of financial regulation of late, the area of prudential regulation of banks – and, indeed, other financial intermediaries[1] – has embarked on a new career as the source of instruments for furthering the case of 'sustainable finance'. Given that lending activities of European banks to commercial projects associated with negative externalities continue to be substantial,[2] regulatory concerns about the role of intermediaries in the context of global efforts to promote more sustainable business practices certainly do not come as a surprise. Both at the international and the European level, attempts have been made to adjust existing 'micro-prudential' regulatory arrangements[3] with a view to incorporating sustainability considerations into regulatory objectives which hitherto focussed more or less exclusively on (different types of) financial risks. 'Micro-prudential' regulation, hitherto, had been developed so as to enhance intermediaries' resilience against financial risk through quantitative financial requirements as well as qualitative requirements relating to organisational arrangements, in order to protect clients (and client assets) and prevent spillovers from individual failures into threats for the stability of the financial system.[4] With the

* I would like to thank Kern Alexander for insightful comments, as well as Messrs Johannes Koch and Felix Rohayem for valuable research assistance. The usual disclaimer applies.

[1] As will be discussed below, the use of (micro-)prudential regulation for the promotion of sustainable business practices is a project conceptually not confined to any one financial services sub-sector, while specific practical steps, thus far, have taken place mainly in the area of banking regulation – hence this chapter's focus on that area.

[2] Cf. Smoleńska and van't Klooster 2022, 52 (reviewing the available empirical evidence).

[3] As distinct from 'macro-prudential' regulation, which has been introduced after the global financial crisis in order to address systemic risk and limit the financial system's exposure arising from factors not associated with individual firms, infrastructures, or individual markets: see generally Gortsos 2022, paras. 1.13–1.14. And see, for a discussion of the role of macroprudential regulation and supervision for the fight against climate change, Grünewald 2021.

[4] See, for further discussion, Section 20.2 below. And see, for general introductions to the traditional objectives of financial regulation, for example, Armour et al. 2016, 61–6.

integration of sustainability objectives into that framework, that is, the transformation of broader objectives into specific regulatory requirements, the existing toolbox inevitably changes its focus, provoking questions about both the consistency of the revised regulatory strategies and their technical effectiveness. Inevitably, such questions are all the more pressing to the extent that the incorporation of sustainability objectives into the existing toolbox goes beyond mere recognition of the fact of sustainability concerns, for example with regard to the financial implications of climate-related risks for the viability of banks' loan portfolios or other types of investments, or specific measures to address such risks in accordance with received strategies for the regulatory treatment of financial risks more generally.

To be sure, measures enhancing the risk sensitivity of existing requirements in order to address risks that used to be insufficiently captured are perfectly consistent with the long-term evolution of existing prudential requirements, which have been refined repeatedly in order to close existing loopholes and incentivise both bank management and investors to refrain from excessive risk-taking. However, the same cannot be said about measures intended to use existing requirements – in particular, capital charges linked to specific types of investment – to influence intermediaries' business models in order to re-engineer existing financial flows towards more sustainable uses, even where no direct causal link exists between compliance with such requirements on the one hand and individual financial performance on the other. If and to the extent that instruments designed to address institution-specific risks are remodelled in order to promote societal objectives other than financial stability, both the justification of that move and its potential impact on the functioning of the existing framework are at issue. Put simply, the question is whether the existing framework of prudential requirements and tools, given its conceptual design and functional characteristics, can realistically be expected to fulfil that new mandate – and to what extent its existing mandate could be affected by the introduction of new objectives and new technical features for their accomplishment. At the very least, the notion that micro-prudential regulations of banks and other financial intermediaries can, and should, be activated to enhance the adaptation of the financial sector towards more sustainable business patterns, in particular with regard (but not restricted) to climate-related risks, although often cited approvingly without critical reflection not just in policy papers but also in academic literature,[5] is by no means self-evident.

In recent years, relevant initiatives promoting the activation of micro-prudential financial regulation as part of a broader sustainability agenda have been presented both by international standard-setters[6] such as the Financial

---

[5] For a characteristic example, cf., for example, Smoleńska and van't Klooster 2022, 52, arguing rather programmatically that '[b]anking regulation and supervision have a key role to play in the EU's approach to climate change'.

[6] For recent surveys of international initiatives, see, for example, Demekas and Grippa 2021; see also BCBS 2020.

Stability Board (FSB),[7] the Basel Committee on Banking Supervision (BCBS),[8] the 'Network for Greening the Financial System' (NGFS), originally established by eight central banks and supervisory authorities in 2017,[9] and within the European Union, where the activation of micro-prudential regulatory requirements for the accomplishment of sustainability goals has been addressed not just by the European Commission,[10] but also, acting on a mandate in recent legislative initiatives, the European Banking Authority (EBA),[11] as well as the European Central Bank (ECB) in its capacity as supervisory authority within the Single Supervisory Mechanism (SSM) for the Eurozone.[12] In marked contrast to international standards, which have mainly focussed on the role of financial intermediaries for the combat against climate change, initiatives taken at the European level – in line with the EU's broader policies – have, in part, taken a broader perspective, addressing not just climate-related or other environmental issues, but also social and governance factors. The broader agenda notwithstanding, specific implementation measures, thus far, have remained limited in scope, and are far from reflecting a fully consistent approach.

Against this backdrop, the present chapter, focussing on regulatory developments within the EU, explores and critically analyses the activation of micro-prudential regulation of banks (and other financial intermediaries) in the context of a broader sustainability agenda. As indicated above, the very fact that prudential regulations, traditionally focussing on enhancing the financial and operational soundness of individual institutions in order to protect financial stability, have been adjusted in order to address sustainability concerns is consistent with received regulatory objectives only to the extent that relevant measures are confined to the regulatory treatment of institution-specific risks. By contrast, the use of prudential regulations for the promotion of a broader sustainability agenda is by no means self-evident. Against the backdrop of the historical evolution of micro-prudential regulation of financial intermediaries, Section 20.2 therefore assesses the capacity – and the limitations – of the (micro-)prudential instrumentarium as a toolbox for the promotion of a broader sustainability agenda. Section 20.3 then takes stock of the relevant European policy agenda and implementation efforts so far, before Section 20.4 turns to a critical assessment. Section 20.5 concludes.

---

[7] See, in particular, FSB 2017, 2020, 2021a, 2021b, 2022a and 2022b. As of November 2015, the FSB has established an industry-led 'disclosure task force on climate-related risks', in order to promote harmonised approaches to consistent disclosure frameworks for climate-related information. See FSB 2015, and see FSB 2017. Annual status reports can be downloaded via www.fsb.org.

[8] See, in particular, BCBS 2022, 2024, para. 02.18.

[9] See, in particular, NGFS 2020a, 2020b, 2022.

[10] See Section 20.3.1.

[11] See, in particular, EBA 2021.

[12] See, in particular, ECB 2021, 2022a, 2022b, 2022c.

20.2 WHY MICRO-PRUDENTIAL REGULATION? EXISTING TOOLS AND THEIR USE FOR THE PROMOTION OF SUSTAINABILITY OBJECTIVES

20.2.1 *Risk Regulation: Today's Toolbox and Its Historical Development*

In today's legal framework for financial services within the EU, substantive micro-prudential regulations include, in particular, (a) capital ('own funds') regulations (the oldest component of the regulatory toolbox), (b) restrictions on 'large exposures', that is, on the exposure to anyone particular borrower in order to avoid unsustainable losses caused by borrower's default, (c) liquidity requirements (one of the most recent additions to the toolbox, at least at the European level), (d) corporate governance regulation, including, in particular, risk management requirements, and (e) disclosure requirements, geared towards enhancing market discipline by incentivising (in particular, institutional) investors in bank equity and bank debt to exercise some degree of control over the relevant intermediaries' risk appetite. The existing legislative framework for banks and investment firms is shaped by the (revised) Capital Requirements Directive (CRD)[13] and the Capital Requirements Regulation (CRR)[14] for credit institutions, and by the Investment Firms Directive (IFD)[15] as well as the Investment Firms Regulation (IFR)[16] for investment firms (i.e., securities intermediaries not falling within the scope of the banking regime), and reflects the conceptual design of international bank regulatory standards established since the second Basel Capital Accord of 2004 ('Basel II'), which has been developed further with the existing Capital Accord ('Basel III') from 2010 onwards, established after the global financial crisis of 2007–9.[17] Within this framework, quantitative requirements on own funds form the first 'Pillar',[18] complemented

---

[13] Directive 2013/36/EU of the European Parliament and of the Council of 26 June 2013 on access to the activity of credit institutions and the prudential supervision of credit institutions and investment firms (...), OJ L 176, 338 ('CRD IV'), amended by Directive (EU) 2019/878 of the European Parliament and of the Council of 20 May 2019 amending Directive 2013/36/EU as regards exempted entities, financial holding companies, mixed financial holding companies, remuneration, supervisory measures and powers and capital conservation measures, OJ L 150, 253.

[14] Regulation (EU) No 575/2013 of the European Parliament and of the Council of 26 June 2013 on prudential requirements for credit institutions and investment firms (...), OJ L 176, 1, amended by Regulation (EU) 2019/876 of the European Parliament and of the Council of 20 May 2019 amending Regulation (EU) No 575/2013 as regards the leverage ratio, the net stable funding ratio, requirements for own funds and eligible liabilities, counterparty credit risk, market risk, exposures to central counterparties, exposures to collective investment undertakings, large exposures, reporting and disclosure requirements (...), OJ L 150, 1.

[15] Directive (EU) 2019/2034 of the European Parliament and of the Council of 27 November 2019 on the prudential supervision of investment firms (...), OJ L 314, 64.

[16] Regulation (EU) 2019/2033 of the European Parliament and of the Council of 27 November 2019 on the prudential requirements of investment firms (...), OJ L 314, 1.

[17] For introductions to the evolution of the Basel framework since the original Capital Accord of 1988, see, for example, Gortsos 2022, paras. 1.24–1.41; Theissen 2013, 31–60; and see, generally, Goodhart 2011.

[18] See, in particular, Article 12 (initial capital) CRD IV and Articles 72–80 (own funds) CRR.

with qualitative (organisational) requirements, a framework for the 'Internal Capital Adequacy Assessment Process' and a framework for the ongoing 'Supervisory Review and Evaluation Process (SREP)' of each institution's risk profile in 'Pillar 2',[19] and disclosure requirements as 'Pillar 3',[20] with powers for the supervisory authority to impose individual additional capital charges in response to findings from SREP under Pillar 2.[21]

As will be discussed in further detail below, policy initiatives towards the activation of micro-prudential regulation for the promotion of sustainable lending and investment activities, within Europe, have anticipated the imposition of Pillar 1 capital charges, while the actual implementation so far has been confined to including sustainability risks in the SREP under Pillar 2 and requiring the disclosure of relevant information under Pillar 3.[22] While this is attributable to the fact that the available empirical data on the nature and dimension of sustainability risks, which would be required in order to calibrate relevant charges, is limited,[23] it is nonetheless noteworthy. Capital charges, ever since the onset of international harmonisation of substantive prudential banking regulation, have always been *the* core instrument to address and control risk-taking by credit institutions – and would, therefore, commend themselves as the instrument of choice for addressing any type of risk, including, for that matter, climate-related (and other sustainability) risks. Already under the first Basel Capital Accord of 1988,[24] transposed into European law with three directives in 1989,[25] capital charges had been defined based on 'risk weights' attached to specific categories of counterparties.[26] The current, much more complex, regime has refined the approach developed in the second Capital Accord ('Basel II') of 2004,[27] transposed into EU law with the (recast) Banking Directive[28] and the (recast) Capital Requirements Directive of 2006,[29] which aimed at enhancing the risk sensitivity of capital charges after the first Capital Accord had taken an

---

[19]   See Articles 73–110 CRD IV.
[20]   See Articles 89 and 90c CRD IV and Articles 431–455 CRR.
[21]   See Articles 104–104c CRD IV.
[22]   See Sections 20.3.1 and 20.3.2.
[23]   See Section 20.3.3.
[24]   BCBS 1988.
[25]   That is, the Second Banking Law Directive (Second Council Directive 89/646/EEC of 15 December 1989 on the coordination of laws, regulations and administrative provisions relating to the taking up and pursuit of the business of credit institutions [...], OJ L 386, 1), the Own Funds Directive (Council Directive 89/299/EEC of 17 April 1989 on the own funds of credit institutions, OJ L 124, 16) and the Solvency Ratio Directive (Council Directive 89/647/EEC of 18 December 1989 on a solvency ratio for credit institutions, OJ L 386, 14).
[26]   See, for a detailed history of the emergence of risk-weighted capital ratios within the BCBS, Goodhart 2011, 146–88; Norton 1995, 184–98.
[27]   BCBS 2004.
[28]   Directive 2006/48/EC of the European Parliament and of the Council of 14 June 2006 relating to the taking up and pursuit of the business of credit institutions (recast), OJ L 177, 1.
[29]   Directive 2006/49/EC of the European Parliament and of the Council of 14 June 2006 on the capital adequacy of investment firms and credit institutions (recast), OJ L 177, 201.

overly simplistic approach that led to adverse incentives for bank management. In a fundamental modification of the initial approach, Basel II introduced the current three-pillar architecture of international regulatory standards, including, *inter alia*, alternatives to the traditional (now 'standardized') measurement based on banks' internal ratings of counterparties. Moreover, Basel II established, for the first time at the international level, rules for the capital treatment of operational risks. Under 'Basel III', a response to deficiencies identified with regard to the Basel II accord in the course of the global financial crisis, the Basel II framework was refined further, including with regard to the system of capital charges in Pillar 1.[30]

If it is at all possible to characterise the evolution of this framework over time in its various facets, the process arguably can be described as a series of attempts to adjust capital charges ever more closely to banks' risk profiles. Today's capital requirements reflect, and correspond to, a broad range of risks, from default risks emanating from the exposure to individual borrowers (the traditional focus of micro-prudential regulation), through market risks (that is, the implications of adverse developments in market prices) and risks associated with specific types of banking business (e.g., foreign exchange risks or settlement risks) to operational risks (which might give rise to losses because of failing technical processes or human error).[31] Conceptually, within this framework, capital charges tied to the specific business risks incurred in a bank's operations fulfil two related yet distinct functions. On the one hand, the requirement to hold a given amount of 'own funds' (i.e., equity and other instruments eligible as capital instruments for regulatory purposes)[32] seeks to ensure that each regulated intermediary holds a certain amount of own funds as a buffer against losses arising out of its assets. On the other hand, by thus requiring banks to reduce their leverage, that is, reliance on liabilities as a means for funding active business engagements, capital charges also serve as a tool to limit risk-taking initiatives, by shaping the incentive structure of bank investors and, ultimately, bank management.[33]

20.2.2 *ESG Risks and Established Concepts of Micro-Prudential Regulation*

Seen against this backdrop, the introduction of new regulatory instruments to address specific forms of environmental, social and/or governance risks to banks' profitability is, as such, fully consistent with the established regulatory arrangements. It should

---

[30] See, for a good overview, in particular Gortsos 2022, paras. 1.35–1.59 and, for an account of the adaptation in the CRD and the CRR, ibid., paras. 1.62–1.82. For an excellent, detailed description of the current system of micro-prudential capital requirements under these two legal instruments, see various chapters in Joosen, Lamandini and Tröger 2022.

[31] For a good overview of the relevant risks addressed by the current framework, see, for example, Gortsos 2022, paras. 1.17–1.22. See also, for a concise introduction to the concept of risk-weighted capital charges, Armour et al. 2016, 299–305.

[32] On regulatory requirements relating to the composition of eligible own funds, see Articles 26–31 CRR; and cf. Tröger 2022, paras. 4.13–4.34.

[33] Cf., for example, Tröger 2022, paras. 4.09–4.11.

be noted, however, that the different elements of capital charges each implicitly reflect a certain assessment of the respective risk's relevance in quantitative terms; in other words, they reflect regulatory assumptions as to the probability and dimension of losses associated with each particular category of risk.[34] Arbitrary – and, indeed, at least to some extent influenced by political considerations as to desirable levels of capitalisation – though these assumptions certainly are, the quantifiability of these aspects, from a functional perspective, certainly forms a crucial precondition for the consistency and workability of the current approach to capital regulation as a whole. In the absence of fundamental agreement as to these aspects, the historical evolution of ever more refined quantitative capital regulations since Basel I clearly would not have been conceivable. The above statement therefore needs to be qualified in a crucial respect: yes – the introduction of new instruments to address specific forms of environmental, social and/or governance risks to banks' profitability is certainly consistent with the established regulatory arrangements as a matter of principle. As far as the regulation of banks' capital is concerned, however, this is true only if and to the extent that the relevant risks are, at least in principle, quantifiable so as to facilitate a risk-sensitive calibration of corresponding capital charges. To be sure, as will be discussed in further detail with regard to the current status of legislative developments within the EU below,[35] similar restrictions do not apply with regard to other elements of the micro-prudential regulatory toolbox, in particular organisational[36] or disclosure requirements.[37] Whether and, if at all, to what extent these elements can be activated in the interest of sustainability objectives, however, certainly remains far from settled.

20.2.3 'Dual Use' beyond Risk Regulation: Capital Charges as a Means to Incentivise Sustainable Investment Strategies More Generally?

As noted before, the suitability of micro-prudential regulation for the promotion of sustainable finance policies is by no means obvious. The previous section has sought to explain why: micro-prudential regulation of financial institutions seeks to insulate against specific, identifiable and, ideally, quantifiable risks and is, at least in the case of capital regulation, calibrated *in correlation to* specific risks. If that is so, the assumption that capital charges *cannot* be used for the promotion of sustainable investment policies irrespective of the risks associated with a specific form of investment hardly needs explanation: where there are no measurable or quantifiable risks associated with certain asset classes for a given institution, it is, at first sight at least,

[34] See, for a detailed description of the relevant charges under the existing CRD and CRR, Joosen 2022, paras. 5.11–5.78.
[35] See Section 20.3.3.
[36] On the current state of organisational requirements in the CRD and CRR, see Mülbert and Sajnovits 2020.
[37] See text accompanying n. 20.

difficult to see how capital charges could be meaningfully employed (and, indeed, calibrated) to drive investment strategies either *towards* such relevant assets – or *away from* them. In the words of David Ramos Muñoz, it follows from the broader conceptual context that '[c]limate needs to speak the language of risk if it is to be assimilated by bank regulation',[38] and much the same applies to the treatment of other sustainability aspects.

Still, the very fact that capital charges, as discussed before, play an important role not just by ensuring adequate buffers against potential losses, but also by influencing the incentive structure of investors and management provokes the question of whether this latter function could not be recalibrated to gear investments according to objectives other than merely avoiding measurable risks. As has been pointed out correctly by Agnieszka Smoleńska and Jens van't Klooster by reference to Articles 501 and 501a of the CRR, the introduction of capital charges promoting broader climate-related objectives (or, indeed, other sustainability concerns) *not* related to specific default risks would not be the first example for a 'dual use' of the established framework: Article 501 CRR, introduced already by the initial version of the Regulation and modified in the CRR review in 2019,[39] provided for a so-called 'SME supporting factor', a recalibration of general requirements in order to reduce the capital charges for exposures to small and medium enterprises. Article 501a, introduced in 2019, now complements that provision with a similarly structured alleviation of capital charges for certain long-term infrastructure projects. While the SME supporting factor has been justified on the grounds that 'SMEs carry a lower systemic risk than larger corporates',[40] their beneficial treatment is clearly attributable more to the political motive to support SMEs in view of their major role in many EU Member States rather than to the need to enhance the risk sensitivity of relevant requirements.[41] Even more tellingly, the introduction of an Infrastructure Supporting Factor with Article 501a CRR has been justified only by reference to the macro-economic interest 'to encourage private and public investments' in relevant project, dropping risk considerations altogether.[42]

In view of these innovative tools, it can indeed be argued that the avenue towards the activation of (micro-prudential) capital regulation as an instrument to influence investment strategies in a broader sense has been open for some time already. In this sense, Articles 501 and 501a certainly can be interpreted as illustration that such measures can take a variety of forms, including not just capital charges to *penalise* certain types of investments, but also reductions in relation to general requirements

---

[38] Ramos Muñoz, Chapter 19 in this volume.

[39] See n. 14.

[40] Regulation (EU) 2019/876 (see n. 14), Recital 59.

[41] See ibid., emphasising that SMEs 'are one of the pillars of the Union's economy as *they play a fundamental role in creating economic growth and providing employment*' and that capital charges 'should be lower than those for large corporates *to ensure an optimal bank financing of SMEs*' (emphasis added).

[42] Cf. ibid., Recitals 60 and 61.

in order to *encourage* specific investments. Specifically, the latter variant could also be used in order to offset potential negative implications of the application of general capital requirements to the provision of financing to environmentally sustainable projects, which might otherwise be discouraged by the application of established standards if and to the extent such investments come with higher levels of risks and lower levels of profitability in the medium or short term in comparison to more traditional assets.[43]

At the same time, however, Articles 501 and 501a CRR also illustrate the potential downsides of a broader readjustment of the existing capital regime. If and to the extent that capital charges are reduced in order to influence banks' incentives in favour of investments towards specific asset classes irrespective of the risks associated with such assets, the effects are not unlikely to conflict with, if not outright contradict, the traditional objective of capital regulation, namely to enhance banks' resilience against potential losses and restrict their risk appetite accordingly. In other words: the wider the gap between profitability and riskiness on the one hand and the political desirability of investments in certain asset classes on the other hand, the more problematic the trade-off between the two objectives at stake.

20.3 THE DEVELOPMENTS SO FAR: A PIECEMEAL APPROACH

20.3.1 *Relevant Policy Initiatives at the European Level*

Within the EU, the legislative agenda promoting 'sustainable finance' has been inspired, in particular, by the findings of a 'High Level Expert Group' (HLEG) on that matter which, commissioned as early as 2016,[44] produced an Interim Report in July 2017 and a Final Report in January 2018.[45] Already in its Interim Report, the HLEG expressed support for a comprehensive activation of the existing framework for the (micro-)prudential regulation of banks as part of a broader legislative agenda, tentatively discussing the use of capital charges as instruments to induce 'sustainable' lending activities (dubbed 'green-supportive factors') and penalise 'unsustainable' ones ('brown-penalising factors'). In the words of the Interim Report:

> As the largest asset pool, banks have an essential role in the transition towards a sustainable financial system. To date, however, their potential contribution to sustainable development has not reached its full potential. Green-supportive factors or brown-penalising factors could be investigated; the appropriateness of the capital framework for project finance and specialised lending should be assessed; while Pillars II and III of prudential regulation could be strengthened with regard to sustainability.[46]

[43] Cf., for a discussion of such implications, Alexander 2014, 15–6.
[44] See, generally, https://bit.ly/3IMTNDv.
[45] See HLEG Sustainable Finance 2017 and 2018, respectively.
[46] HLEG Sustainable Finance 2017, 6.

Similar – and, indeed, similarly cautious – considerations were then presented in the HLEG's Final Report, which also promoted the use of capital regulation in order to promote sustainable investments, while warning that any attempts towards that end had to be proportionate in order to prevent undue burdens for smaller banks, and that the primary focus of capital regulations should remain on the preservation of financial stability.[47] Overall, the Report's recommendations remain rather vague, indicating a certain preference for a gradual development of sustainability-related measures in Pillar II of the Basel framework rather than the outright adoption of specific forms of 'green-supporting' and/or 'brown-penalising' factors within the existing framework for capital regulation:

> The HLEG has not sought to conduct a complete review of the bank regulatory framework and its impact on sustainability lending. It is the view of the HLEG that further development of best practice on ESG and longer-term sustainability risk assessments is still needed to ensure that sustainability is better integrated into the banking sector, while at the same time ensuring financial stability. These assessments should include a more systematic approach for banks on the impact of climate change and the transition to a lower-carbon economy. Supervisors should also ensure that banks appropriately include ESG risks in their risk management systems. This could be pursued under Pillar II of the supervisory process (…). In some cases, it might also lead to changes in an individual bank's capital requirements, provided risk management is deemed insufficient.[48]

Building on these recommendations, the relevant legislative agenda was then developed in the European Commission's Action Plan 'Financing Sustainable Growth' in March 2018, which took up the HLEG's recommendation and emphasised, again, the need to enhance funding for sustainable investments on the one hand and the need to address specific risks for intermediaries and financial stability on the other hand:

> Banks, insurance companies and pension funds are the main source of external finance for the European economy and an important channel of savings for investments. As a result, they could provide the critical mass of investments needed to close the gap for the transition to a more sustainable economy. However, banks, insurance companies and pension funds may also be exposed to risks related to unsustainable economic development (…). This calls for a better reflection of risks associated with climate and other environmental factors in prudential regulation with a careful calibration that would not jeopardise the credibility and effectiveness of the current EU prudential framework and its risk-based nature.[49]

---

[47] HLEG Sustainable Finance 2018, 67–8.
[48] Ibid., 67.
[49] European Commission 2018, 9.

In this context, the incorporation of sustainability objectives – in the form of 'green supporting factors' – and measures to enhance intermediaries' risk management in this regard into the existing legal framework for the prudential regulation of banks and insurance companies was identified as one out of altogether 10 specific policy proposals.[50] Similar considerations were then reiterated in the Commission's 2019 'Green Deal',[51] as well as the Commission's 'Strategy for Financing the Transition to a Sustainable Economy' in July 2021.[52]

20.3.2 *Where Do We Stand? The Current Legislative Framework and Steps towards Implementation*

Measured against the ambitious policy agenda summarised above, progress in legislative terms so far has been limited and rather piecemeal. In the area of banking regulation, Article 98(8) of the CRD – as reformed by Directive (EU) 2019/878[53] – introduced a mandate for the European Banking Authority ('EBA') to 'assess the potential inclusion in the review and evaluation performed by competent authorities of environmental, social and governance risks (ESG risks)' in Pillar II of the Basel framework, and to address, in this context:

at least the following:

(a) the development of a uniform definition of ESG risks, including physical risks and transition risks; the latter shall comprise the risks related to the depreciation of assets due to regulatory changes;

(b) the development of appropriate qualitative and quantitative criteria for the assessment of the impact of ESG risks on the financial stability of institutions in the short, medium and long term; such criteria shall include stress testing processes and scenario analyses to assess the impact of ESG risks under scenarios with different severities;

(c) the arrangements, processes, mechanisms and strategies to be implemented by the institutions to identify, assess and manage ESG risks;

(d) the analysis methods and tools to assess the impact of ESG risks on lending and financial intermediation activities of institutions.

In the fourth subparagraph of the same provision, EBA was also mandated to issue guidelines on the 'uniform inclusion of ESG risks in the supervisory review and evaluation process'. A similar mandate with regard to the integration of sustainability risks in the regulatory framework for investment firms has been provided by Article 35 of the IFD 2019.[54]

---

[50] Ibid. See also, for a good overview of the various proposals and subsequent actions, https://bit.ly/3IG9mge.
[51] European Commission 2019, 17.
[52] European Commission 2021b, 12–3.
[53] See n. 13.
[54] See n. 15

While no such guidelines[55] have been adopted yet, a comprehensive 'Report on Management and Supervision of ESG Risks for Credit Institutions and Investment Firms', which is based, *inter alia*, on the mandate under Article 98(8) of the CRD, has been published by EBA in 2021.[56] Moreover, draft 'Guidelines on the management of ESG risks', based on the mandate under Article 87a(5) of the CRD, were circulated for consultation in early 2024.[57]

In the CRR, Regulation (EU) 2019/876[58] introduced a total of three new provisions in order to implement the Commission's Action Plan of 2018. Among these, the adoption of new disclosure requirements pertaining to large listed banks' exposure to ESG risks in Article 449a CRR has been the most tangible step forward so far. While that provision is extremely short and does not prescribe any more detailed requirements in this regard, it should be noted that EBA, in Article 434a of the amended CRR, has been provided with a broad mandate to develop implementing technical standards ('ITS')

> specifying uniform disclosure formats, and associated instructions in accordance with which (…) disclosures (…) shall be made.

This mandate, which also covers disclosures made pursuant to Article 449a CRR, has since been exercised with a very detailed EBA Draft.[59] and resulted in the adoption of an Implementing Regulation by the European Commission in November 2022.[60] Significantly, despite the broader policy agenda covering ESG risks in general, the ITS follow

> a sequential approach, with an initial focus on climate-change-related risks, given the urgency of the topic, in line with the developments taking place at EU and at international level and taking into account the data and methodological challenges faced by institutions at this stage.[61]

The ITS build on, and are coordinated with, other elements of the legislative agenda envisaged in the Commission's Action Plan of 2018, including, in particular, the so-called Taxonomy Regulation of 2020,[62] which – along with further implementing legislation – seeks to provide the foundation of:

---

[55] Which would not be binding on supervisory authorities (or, for that matter, regulated entities), but supervisory authorities would be required to declare whether they intend to comply with the guidelines, and to give reasons if they seek to deviate from them, cf. Art. 16 of Regulation (EU) No 1093/2010 of the European Parliament and of the Council of 24 November 2010 establishing a European Supervisory Authority (European Banking Authority) (…), OJ L 331, 12.

[56] EBA 2021.

[57] EBA 2024.

[58] See n. 14.

[59] EBA 2022.

[60] Commission Implementing Regulation (EU) 2022/2453 of 30 November 2022 amending the implementing technical standards laid down in Implementing Regulation (EU) 2021/637 as regards the disclosure of environmental, social and governance risks, OJ L 324/1.

[61] Ibid., 5.

[62] Regulation (EU) 2020/852 of the European Parliament and of the Council of 18 June 2020 on the establishment of a framework to facilitate sustainable investment (…), OJ L 198, 13.

a common concept of environmentally sustainable investment when introducing requirements at national and Union level regarding financial market participants or issuers for the purpose of labelling financial products or corporate bonds that are marketed as environmentally sustainable.[63]

Moreover, the ITS have also been realigned with the (then) ongoing review of the Non-Financial Reporting Directive of 2014, which lays down rules on disclosure of non-financial and diversity information by large companies, including environmental, social and governance information.[64]

While these amendments focus on the integration of sustainability objectives into Pillars II and III of the Basel framework, only limited progress had been made – prior to the adoption of the Banking Package of 2021/2024[65] – with regard to Pillar I instruments and, in particular, the activation of bank capital regulation in the sense discussed above. To be sure, Article 501(a)(1)(o) CRR – as amended in 2019 – has introduced a reduction in the own funds requirements for credit risk in connection with exposure to providers of 'essential public services', to be made contingent, *inter alia*, on an assessment of ESG objectives with regard to the assets thus financed. Other than that, however, ESG-related risks have not yet been incorporated into the framework governing the computation of capital charges. Instead, Article 501c CRR – again, as amended in 2019 – lays down a mandate for EBA to assess:

> on the basis of available data and the findings of the Commission High-Level Expert Group on Sustainable Finance, (…) whether a dedicated prudential treatment of exposures related to assets, including securitisations, or activities associated substantially with environmental and/or social objectives would be justified.

Specifically, the assessment – due by 8 June 2025 – is required to address:

(a) methodologies for the assessment of the effective riskiness of exposures related to assets and activities associated substantially with environmental and/or social objectives compared to the riskiness of other exposure;

(b) the development of appropriate criteria for the assessment of physical risks and transition risks, including the risks related to the depreciation of assets due to regulatory changes; [and]

(c) the potential effects of a dedicated prudential treatment of exposures related to assets and activities which are associated substantially with environmental and/or social objectives on financial stability and bank lending in the Union.

This mandate has been recognised in EBA's 2021 report on the 'Management and Supervision of ESG Risks for Credit Institutions and Investment Firms'.[66]

---

[63] Ibid., Recital 14. See, for further discussion, Och, Chapter 13 in this volume. On the functional relationship between the EBA Report and the Regulation, see EBA 2021, 9 para. 8.

[64] European Commission 2021a. On the interplay between that proposal and the EBA report, see EBA 2021, 8 para. 7.

[65] See Section 20.4.3.

[66] Cf. EBA 2021, 21.

The findings developed in that document mainly focus on the first two aspects, that is: harmonised standards for the assessment of relevant risks, rather than on recommendations for the prudential treatment within Pillar I of the Basel framework. A detailed analysis of the relevance of ESG risks for the financial sector, resulting in uniform definitions of ESG factors and risks, including definitions of physical risks and transition risks as the main drivers of environmental risks, has been presented as Chapter 2 of the Report.[67] Chapter 3 then presents detailed proposals for 'Quantitative and qualitative indicators, metrics and methods to assess ESG risks'.[68] Chapter 4 follows with recommendations on the treatment of ESG risks by regulated institutions,[69] while Chapter 5, responding to the mandate in Article 98(8) CRD, discusses the treatment of such risks by supervisory authorities, in particular within the SREP.[70]

In the area of (prudential) insurance regulation and supervision, upon a request from the European Commission, the European Insurance and Occupational Pensions Authority ('EIOPA') in 2019 released a comprehensive report on 'Technical Advice on the integration of sustainability risks and factors in the delegated acts' to the relevant legislative frameworks.[71] With its Delegated Regulation (EU) 2021/1256,[72] the Commission then introduced a number of changes to corporate governance and organisational requirements for insurers with a view to incorporating sustainability risks in general risk management arrangements. A wider range of measures is anticipated in the Commission's proposal for a fundamental reform of the so-called Solvency II Directive, the main legislative act in the field.[73] Specifically, a new Article 304a of the Solvency II Directive envisages two mandates to EIOPA with regard to sustainability risks., In this context, EIOPA will be mandated to explore a dedicated prudential treatment of exposures related to assets or activities associated substantially with environmental and/or social objectives and to review regularly the scope and the calibration of parameters of the standard formula pertaining to natural catastrophe risk.

20.3.3 *What Has – and Has Not – Been Accomplished So Far*

In a number of respects, the legislative developments implemented so far clearly represent work in progress. This applies first and foremost with regard to the scope

[67] Ibid., 22–49.
[68] Ibid., 50–79.
[69] Ibid., 80–127.
[70] Ibid., 127–51.
[71] EIOPA 2019.
[72] Commission Delegated Regulation (EU) 2021/1256 of 21 April 2021 amending Delegated Regulation (EU) 2015/35 as regards the integration of sustainability risks in the governance of insurance and reinsurance undertakings, OJ L 277, 14.
[73] See European Commission 2021c. The proposals were finally accepted by the European Parliament in the first reading on 23 April 2024 (formal completion of the legislative process pending upon completion of the revision of the present chapter).

of the relevant steps: in considerable contrast to the political agenda at the European level, which, as discussed above, has been more ambitious than relevant international standards in this regard and addresses 'ESG risks' in a wide, yet vaguely defined way and has *not* focussed on climate-related risks, the measures currently in force in European law mainly address the latter. This is particularly visible in the case of EBA's interpretation of the mandates provided by Article 98(8) of the CRD and Articles 449a and 501c of the CRR, respectively. While this has been justified on the grounds of 'urgency',[74] a fundamental reason for that self-restraint clearly has been the absence of empirically sound information on the nature and relevance of the respective risks. To be sure, the 2019 EBA report has gone some way towards a common understanding both of the relevant risks and appropriate methodologies for their measurement and assessment for regulatory purposes.[75] At the same time, it is also remarkably frank with regard to the fundamental challenges to be overcome in this respect, identifying, as the most problematic ones: (a) a high level of uncertainty with regard to the 'timing and effect of policies and related regulatory interventions' as well as 'the timing and effect of physical risks', (b) the 'scarcity of relevant, comparable, reliable and user-friendly data, [which] limits the understanding of the potential impacts of ESG risks on the performance of financial assets', (c) methodological constraints with regard to the absence of historical data that could be used both for risk estimates and to the calculation of financial implications of ESG risks, (d) a time-horizon mismatch between traditional management tools and the need to account for risks whose full impact, by their very nature, is bound to materialise over a matter of decades, (e) the fact that ESG risks tend to affect financial institutions through a number of channels, ranging from direct credit risk due to exposure to individual counterparties hit by climate events to losses in market value and (f) the fact that ESG risks tend to be non-linear in nature but will materialise in 'complex chain reactions and cascade effects, which in turn could generate unpredictable environmental, geopolitical, social and economic dynamics'.[76]

This methodological backdrop clearly also explains why the general approach followed so far, for all the express political commitment to decisive and specific action, has been tentative and, almost exclusively, procedural rather than substantive in nature. As discussed above, the focus so far has been on the integration of sustainability risks in the SREP under Pillar II and disclosure requirements under Pillar III of the Basel framework for banks (and investment firms), and on specific risk management requirements for insurance companies, while the introduction of specific capital charges for either sector has been postponed to the receipt of further reports by the European supervisory agencies EBA and EIOPA. In the absence of such specific measures, any progress towards comprehensive activation of the regulatory

---

[74] For illustration, see, again, EBA 2022, 5 (quoted in text accompanying n. 29).
[75] For further discussion, see also Ramos Muñoz, Chapter 19 in this volume; Cullen 2018, 73–8.
[76] EBA 2021, 51–2.

toolbox, for the time being, has to rely on supervisory reactions to perceived deficiencies in regulated institutions' business models and risk management arrangements on the one hand, and market reactions to institution-specific information published under the new disclosure requirements on the other hand. In this regard, in particular EBA's work on risk criteria and assessment methodologies as well as the development of common disclosure standards certainly represent a substantial step forward – and should be interpreted as indication that both the regulated industry and supervisory authorities across the EU have engaged in a process of continuous adaptation and refinement of existing strategies. Within Eurozone countries, this has been reinforced by the development of harmonised approaches to the treatment of ESG risks by the ECB as single supervisory authority.[77]

All in all, the progress accomplished even prior to the adoption of the Banking Package of 2021/2024 should not be dismissed too easily. The agreement reached on the relevant risk factors is certainly an important achievement. In this context, EBA's 2021 Report, building on previous work by international standard-setters and other institutions, has made an important contribution to the development of a consistent regulatory treatment within the EU, by providing a comprehensive and, at the same time, persuasive definition of relevant 'ESG risks' ('risks of any negative financial impact on the institution stemming from the current or prospective impacts of ESG factors on its counterparties or invested assets')[78] in the first place and, in particular, the development of a complex matrix of the relevant types of risk that is consistent with applicable standards. In the terminology employed in the Report,[79] the different risks fall within a number of – partially overlapping and interconnected – categories: (a) *environmental risks*, including climate-related risks,[80] driven by either *physical risks* resulting from climate change[81] or *transition risks*, defined as 'risks of any negative financial impact on the institution stemming from the current or prospective impacts of the transition to an environmentally sustainable economy on its counterparties or invested assets',[82] (b) *social risks*, defined as 'risks of any negative financial impact on the institution stemming from the current or prospective impacts of social factors on its counterparties or invested assets'[83] and (c) governance risks, defined as 'the risks of any negative financial impact on the institution stemming from the current or prospective impacts of governance factors on its counterparties or invested assets.'[84] Likewise, the recommendations relating to methodological matters – in the words of the Report: 'quantitative and qualitative

---

[77] See, again, ECB 2021 and 2022a.
[78] EBA 2021, 33, para. 42.
[79] See, for a broader review of the available literature, for example, De Arriba-Sellier 2021, 1131–4.
[80] Ibid., 34–5.
[81] Ibid., 36–8.
[82] Ibid., 38–44.
[83] Ibid., 43–7.
[84] Ibid., 47–9.

indicators, metrics and methods to assess ESG risks' – certainly accumulate state-of-the-art information on relevant tools. At the same time, progress so far – as a direct consequence of the procedural approach followed to date – certainly has to be described as limited and interim in nature. Both the link of causation between specific risks and individual firms' profitability and the likelihood and implications of specific scenarios – and, indeed, the political responses to such scenarios – remain rather unpredictable. Particularly through the gradual implementation within the SREP, relevant knowledge will be built up by both regulated institutions and supervisory authorities only over time, and the development of dedicated Pillar I (capital) instruments for the treatment of environmental or, indeed, other ESG risks has hardly been initiated yet.

20.4 A CRITICAL ASSESSMENT: WHAT SHOULD (AND CAN) BE DONE

20.4.1 *The (Not So Clear-Cut) Case for Radical Expansion*

In the light of the foregoing, it is perhaps not too difficult to see why the current state of affairs has met with substantial criticism. Observers have noted that strategies for the treatment of ESG risks continue to vary greatly among regulated institutions, while available external ratings that could be used for the assessment of relevant risks both for risk management purposes and regulatory responses remain methodologically flawed and limited in scope.[85] Moreover, it has been noted that the legislative focus on Pillar II and Pillar III measures has resulted in rather diverse enforcement strategies and enforcement efforts across the EU, with some national authorities taking decisive action, while others have proved more lenient, resulting in a 'race to the bottom' with detrimental consequences for the attainment of sustainability objectives.[86] In order to streamline existing efforts and to fully activate the regulatory toolbox in the interest of enhancing sustainable investment, it has been suggested that relevant legislation as well as supervisory strategies could – and perhaps should – take a stricter approach, 'actively specify what types of investments are compatible with the EU's environmental objectives', and, ultimately, calibrate regulatory requirements so as to induce regulated institutions to realign their investments accordingly.[87] Instead of the current procedural approach, which relies heavily on the gradual evolution of strategies on the part of regulated institutions and supervisory agencies, such an approach could be described as substantive, in the sense that key decisions as to desirable outcomes would be taken either by legislators or, under a statutory mandate, by regulatory bodies, with comparatively 'hard' enforcement strategies relying on specific capital charges.

[85] Cf. Smoleńska and van't Klooster 2022, 61–2.
[86] Ibid., 62–3 and 68–9.
[87] See ibid., 69–74, for a detailed proposal to that effect. And see, for similar considerations, Grünewald 2021, 238–43.

Radical though they are, such proposals are certainly tempting, assuming that micro-prudential regulation effectively can play a greater role for the promotion of sustainability objectives by financial intermediaries. Measured against the findings developed above, however, some scepticism may well be justified. As discussed above, the incorporation of sustainability objectives into regulatory frameworks and corresponding mandates for supervisory authorities is consistent with traditional principles of bank regulation only as far as the protection of regulated institutions against firm-specific profitability risks is concerned.[88] Given the methodological constraints pertaining to the assessment of ESG identified, for example, in EBA's 2021 Report,[89] the scope for specific Pillar I measures consistent with that approach appears to be rather limited at the present moment in time. Again, as indicated above: if and to the extent that ESG risks – whatever their nature and origin – cannot reliably be identified and quantified in terms of their impact on individual firms' performance, a sound basis for the translation of such findings into specific regulatory tools for the micro-management of such risks, in particular through designated capital charges, does not exist.

By contrast, the activation of capital charges for the promotion of a broader sustainability agenda – in the form of 'brown-penalising' or 'green-supportive' factors, for example, tied to specific indices or the categorisation of investments prescribed by the Taxonomy Regulation – in a way that does not, or at least does not primarily, reflect assumptions about individual financial risks for regulated institutions may well be technically feasible, but potential downsides should be borne in mind. As discussed above, the 'dual use' of established micro-prudential tools in general and capital charges in particular entails the risk that potentially adverse trade-offs between conflicting objectives may remain unnoticed or, potentially worse, ignored outright. It has, in fact, been suggested that such conflicts may have to be regarded as inevitable and, indeed, tolerable, given the need for urgent action in order to combat climate change and prevent the fallout of climate-related risks not just on financial intermediaries but societies more generally.[90] This, however, takes the potential downsides in functional terms all too lightly. Encouraging investments in politically (environmentally, socially) desirable, albeit potentially risky projects may, if the underlying assumptions on the economic viability of the relevant projects prove too optimistic, well undermine individual institutions' stability and thus

---

[88] See Section 20.2.

[89] See, again, text accompanying n. 76.

[90] Cf., to that effect, Smoleńska and van't Klooster 2022, 72, expressing support for regulatory measures that 'go beyond merely specifying the risks that banks should consider in their risk management practice. Instead, they shift the focus onto how banks should adapt their lending and hence see policymakers co-determine what banks invest in. They *can* be motivated by prudential considerations, but this *need not be their exclusive focus*. [Such measures] *might well mean treating instruments favourably which are risky from a financial perspective* (think of untested green technologies). It may also involve cutting off funding for businesses which are, at least in the short term, economically viable.' (emphasis added). For a similarly positive assessment, see also Grünewald 2021, 239–43.

promote one societal objective ('sustainability', however defined) at the expense of another (financial stability). This would be all the more true, the wider the range of 'ESG risks' covered is defined, which would result in ever more complex trade-offs and potentially severe conflicts between the relevant objectives. As noted above, the relevant policy agenda at the European level extends way beyond the international initiatives to activate micro-prudential regulation in that it is not confined to climate-related environmental risks, but takes into account a wider range of social (and, indeed, governance) risks. While these have not yet made their way into specific legislative requirements (which, as noted too, remain largely focussed on climate-related risks) and supervisory practice, it is easy to see potential frictions between different elements of an increasingly politicised agenda. Consider, for example, the regulatory treatment of investments in traditional industries which may account for rather high levels of environmentally detrimental emissions but, at the same time, provide employment to sizeable shares of a given jurisdiction's workforce: while it might be absolutely desirable to close down existing facilities and terminate harmful production processes, the social implications of such decisions – for example, the loss of jobs across entire regions – might well militate for a more nuanced approach. It has been argued that it would be appropriate to leave relevant policy choices to democratically authorized regulatory decisions rather than merely the market.[91] Yet it should not be ignored that striking a proper balance between environmental and social considerations at stake will not just be difficult politically, but also difficult to calibrate technically – and, above all, difficult to reconcile with the objective to pre-serve institutions' financial soundness in order to protect systemic stability, which cannot be jeopardised without potentially highly detrimental consequences.[92] To be sure, a risk-oriented regulatory treatment of sustainability considerations, focussing on the promotion of greater awareness of institutions against specific perceivable (and measurable) risks and their implications for individual institutions' soundness may be slow and less effective in promoting a comprehensive overhaul of existing investment flows towards (environmentally) sustainable projects. But it would leave intact the fundamental profitability orientation relevant business decisions by senior management, whereas allowing for greater political control of business policies in this regard would not. At least from a financial stability point of view, there are good reasons to remain very cautious before entering and going down this path.

20.4.2 *The Way Forward: 'Defensive' vs. 'Supportive' Sustainability Regulation and the Role of Climate Stress-Testing*

In the light of the foregoing, policymakers – and, indeed, regulatory bodies exercis-ing their mandates under the existing legislative frameworks for financial regulation

---

[91] Cf. ibid., 73–4.
[92] See, for a similarly cautious assessment, Boot and Schoenmaker 2018.

within the EU – should carefully distinguish between two different uses of estab-lished micro-prudential regulatory tools for the promotion of more 'sustainable' lending: the *first* of these could be described as a 'defensive' strategy, essentially aiming at the refinement of existing tools with a view to enhancing the sensitiv-ity of existing business models and governance arrangements vis-à-vis a range of institution-specific risks whose significance for financial markets has become widely accepted, although their assessment and quantification, for reasons mentioned above, remain problematic. The *second*, alternative strategy could be described as 'supportive' regulation, aiming at a more fundamental requalification of existing tools for the promotion of 'sustainable' investment policies, more or less irrespective of profitability and financial risk implications.

As the summary of legislative developments above has demonstrated, EU finan-cial regulation – for all the Commission's commitments to a more ambitious policy agenda not restricted to environmental risks as such and irrespective of academic proposals to adopt a more aggressive stance – has so far followed the former approach, while avoiding the latter. In view of both the restricted avail-ability of empirical data that would be required for the calibration of more ambi-tious policy choices *and* the potential downsides of a politicised requalification of micro-prudential regulation, this caution should not be lamented but welcomed as realistic and, indeed, prudent. At the same time, it is undeniably the case that climate-related environmental risks will not just remain a matter of great societal concern but will, in all likelihood, also result in growing challenges to the profit-ability and, ultimately, the financial soundness of intermediaries exposed to these risks, particularly in the form of credit or, indeed, market risks. While this does not remove fundamental concerns about the viability of 'supportive' regulatory strate-gies, it certainly provokes the question of if and how 'defensive' strategies could, and should, be refined in order to address existing shortcomings and enhance their effectiveness. In this regard, it certainly seems appropriate to distinguish between different types of instruments:

Consider, first, designated capital charges (core 'Pillar I' instruments within the system of established regulatory frameworks for banks and investment firms): in all likelihood, given the absence of reliable empirical information on the finan-cial implications of sustainability risks for the profitability of financial intermediar-ies, the development of a comprehensive set of specific additional charges (or, for that matter, reductions in existing ones so as to incentivise investments in 'sustainable' projects, but 'brown-penalising' surcharges may be more consistent with the overall objective to ensure adequate levels of capital),[93] while desirable in terms of effectiveness, should be treated as a medium- to longer-term project. As argued before, without sound empirical data, it will be impossible to calibrate relevant charges – and, indeed, to avoid (or reduce) adverse repercussions for the

---

[93] Cf. Cullen 2018, 83–4; Grünewald 2021, 240–1.

effectiveness of the existing toolbox with regard to the fundamental objective of pre-serving financial stability.[94]

By comparison, Pillar II instruments, in particular the ongoing assessment of regulated institutions' risk management practices relating to ESG risks, certainly appear more flexible and, at least potentially, conducive to a gradual, iterative build-up of relevant information on the part of the regulated industry on the one hand and supervisory authorities on the other. While reliance on these instruments, at least in the absence of clear-cut sanctions, has been criticised as intransparent, vulner-able to manipulation and arbitrage and altogether less effective than outright har-monised capital charges,[95] it may still be the most viable way to overcome residual information problems and to foster a gradual move towards greater resilience against institution-specific ESG risks. To be sure, the development of harmonised criteria for the management of relevant risks, no different from progress with regard to the design and calibration of Pillar I instruments, will, at least for some time, continue to be fraught by the absence of empirical information needed for risk modelling and risk management.[96] Still, the gradual, case-by-case analysis of existing arrange-ments that is at the core of the SREP framework, arguably, should be well placed to facilitate an ongoing learning process for intermediaries and regulators alike, which could then be tapped as a source of information that could ultimately be used for the gradual expansion of regulatory responses.

Finally, with regard to the activation of disclosure requirements (Pillar III instru-ments within the regulatory framework for banks and investment firms), the case is probably even less clear than with regard to Pillar I instruments. Given the absence of reliable information on the implications of ESG risks on intermediaries' financial performance, investors' assessment of disclosed information – and, thus, the likely influence of market discipline in this regard – is impossible to predict.[97] In this respect, mandatory disclosure requirements as part of the legislative framework for the micro-prudential regulation of financial intermediaries face essentially similar difficulties to sustainability-related disclosure requirements in the promotion of sus-tainable investments in capital markets more generally.[98]

While there are, in sum, good reasons not to be overly optimistic with regard to the potential of micro-prudential regulation as an instrument to foster the reorien-tation of investments by financial intermediaries towards more 'sustainable' projects and causes, the above analysis clearly suggests that all possible means should be used for the rapid expansion of the available information base. As discussed above,

[94] See, again, also Boot and Schoenmaker 2018; Cullen 2018.
[95] See, again, Cullen 2018, 68–9.
[96] Cullen 2018, 73–8.
[97] For a similarly sceptical assessment, see also ibid., 70–3.
[98] Cf., for an excellent analysis of the theoretical foundations and empirically observable restrictions to mandatory disclosure as an instrument for the promotion of sustainable investments, Steuer and Tröger 2022, 19–46.

reliable, quasi-actuarial information on (a) the likelihood and dimension of relevant risks and (b) methods for their qualitative and quantitative assessment will be crucial for the future development of regulatory responses.

In this context, in addition to the gradual build-up of information gathered in the course of the ongoing supervision of regulated institutions, the increasing use of 'stress tests' as a means to explore regulated institutions' resilience vis-à-vis a growing range of risks could prove to be very helpful – not just in terms of addressing firm-specific risks through individual improvements to business models and/or governance arrangements, but also as a source of information that could help design more general regulatory responses. Within Europe, relevant stress tests, in line with the recommendations of international standard-setters,[99] have so far mainly (and wisely) focussed on climate-related risks rather than ESG risks more generally, and have been carried out by a number of national central banks[100] as well as, for banks in the Eurozone, the ECB.[101] To be sure, such stress tests, inevitably, also suffer from information problems and are based on stylized assumptions rather than individual, case-by-case analyses of relevant risks in loan books and investment portfolios. Yet they nonetheless should be regarded as a substantial step forward. If institutionalised and carried out on a regular basis, the results of such tests certainly could help to back up, and validate, more theoretical assumptions about the exposure of the financial system to new challenges arising from hitherto neglected risks.

20.4.3 *Next Steps: Incoming Reform Steps under the 2021/2024 Banking Package*

Notwithstanding the foregoing considerations, regulatory developments have been moving on. As part of a broader package of reform proposals released in late 2021, the European Commission has proposed a number of adjustments and additions to the CRD IV/CRR package in order to reinforce the regulatory treatment of ESG risks, which essentially follows up on the status quo discussed in Section 3.3 and takes up the recommendations published by EBA in 2021.[102] As the legislative process, upon completion of the present manuscript, has almost concluded,[103] a brief overview is appropriate: within the CRR, new statutory definitions of the terms 'environmental, social or governance (ESG) risks' and the respective components will be introduced so as to provide a basis for specific regulatory measures in this regard.[104] Moreover,

---

[99] See, in particular, NGFS 2020b.

[100] In particular, the Nederlandsche Bank and the Banque de France, see, on the former, Vermeulen et al. 2018 and, on the latter, Banque de France 2021.

[101] See ECB 2022b and 2022c.

[102] As to which, see nn. 78–84 and accompanying text.

[103] The Banking Package has been formally approved, in a revised form, by the European Parliament in first reading on 23 April 2024.

[104] See European Commission 2021d, 48, proposing new Article 4(1)(52d), (52e), (52g) and (52h) CRR, respectively.

specific disclosure requirements relating to ESG risks will be introduced.[105] Within the CRD, a series of new provisions will introduce specific requirements relating to the treatment of ESG risks in banks' risk management, Internal Capital Adequacy Assessment Processes and in the Supervisory Review Process.[106] Expertise with regard to ESG risks will also be incorporated into the reformed fit-and-proper requirements for senior management.[107] Significantly, while no specific capital charges relating to ESG risks are defined in the proposal, supervisory authorities will be given powers to apply the requirement to maintain a systemic risk buffer (Article 133 CRD IV) and the capital treatment under the SREP (Article 104 CRD IV) accordingly.[108]

In principle, these proposed amendments still can be interpreted as a consistent development of the present state of affairs: with the focus still on procedural rather than on substantive standards, the regulatory treatment will continue to be iterative and conducive to adjustments on the basis of information generated by regulated institutions in due course. Against the backdrop discussed before, this is, in principle, to be welcomed. At the same time, the concerns formulated above inevitably also apply with regard to the incoming reforms, to the extent that these merely refine the existing approaches. Moreover, the reform package also reveals a willingness to move further in the direction of specific capital charges in order to reinforce incentives for more sustainable funding and investment policies. As the problem of insufficient information base regarding the nature and dimension of relevant risks and their implications continues to exist, ambitions to that end, arguably, continue to be premature for the time being.

20.5 CONCLUSIONS

As part of a broader policy agenda promoting the reorientation of capital flows to 'sustainable' investments, policymakers and regulators world-wide have increasingly advocated the activation of traditional micro-prudential tools for the regulation of financial intermediaries as instruments to incentivise changes to existing business models and investment strategies. As discussed in this chapter, relevant measures could take a variety of forms. Under a more cautious ('defensive') approach, established tools would merely be refined in order to enhance their sensitivity to new forms of environmental, social or governance risks. Alternatively, a more progressive ('supportive') approach could seek to activate the existing toolbox in a more ambitious way, by creating new incentives in favour of specific investments or investment categories identified as politically desirable. Analysing the functional capacity of the

---

[105] Ibid., 200, introducing new Article 449a CRR.
[106] See European Commission 2021e, 12, 81–2, 85–7, 93, proposing new or reformed Articles 73, 74, 76, 87a, 97, 98 and 100 CRD IV, respectively.
[107] Ibid., 87, proposing a reformed Article 91(4) CRD IV.
[108] Ibid., 94–5 and 96–7, proposing amendments to Articles 104a and 133 CRD IV, respectively.

existing toolbox, this chapter argues that, while the latter approach would be technically feasible, a number of reasons clearly militate for self-restriction and in favour of the more cautious alternative.

REFERENCES

Alexander, K. (2014), 'Stability and sustainability in banking reform: Are environmental risks missing in Basel III?', available at: https://doi.org/10.5167/uzh-103844.

Armour, J., Awrey, D., Davies, P. et al. (2016), *Principles of Financial Regulation* (Oxford: Oxford University Press).

Banque de France (2021), 'Climate risk analysis and supervision – Analysis and synthesis no. 122: The main results of the 2020 climate pilot exercise', 5 April, available at: https://bit.ly/4cfz4Wi.

BCBS (Basel Committee on Banking Supervision) (1988), 'International convergence on capital measurement and capital standards', July, available at: www.bis.org/publ/bcbs04.pdf

BCBS (Basel Committee on Banking Supervision) (2004), *Basel II: International Convergence of Capital Measurement and Capital Standards: A Revised Framework – Comprehensive Version*, June, available at: www.bis.org/publ/bcbs128.pdf.

BCBS (Basel Committee on Banking Supervision) (2020), 'Climate-related financial risks: A survey on current initiatives', April, available at: www.bis.org/bcbs/publ/d502.pdf.

BCBS (Basel Committee on Banking Supervision) (2022), 'Principles for the effective management and supervision of climate-related financial risks', June, available at: www.bis.org/bcbs/publ/d532.pdf.

BCBS (Basel Committee on Banking Supervision) (2024), 'Core principles for effective banking supervision', April, available at: www.bis.org/bcbs/publ/d573.pdf.

Boot, A. and Schoenmaker, D. (2018), 'Climate change adds to risk for banks, but EU lending proposals will do more harm than good', 16 January, available at: https://bit.ly/3Vpiwp1.

Cullen, J. (2018), 'After "HLEG": EU banks, climate change abatement and the precautionary principle', 20 *Cambridge: Cambridge Yearbook of European Legal Studies*, 61–87.

De Arriba-Sellier, N. (2021), 'Turning gold into green: Green finance in the mandate of European financial supervision', 58 *Common Market Law Review*, 1097–140.

Demekas, D. G. and Grippa, P. (2021), 'Financial regulation, climate change, and the transition to a low-carbon economy: A survey of the issues', International Monetary Fund Working Paper WP/21/296, available at: https://bit.ly/3VtwcPF.

EBA (European Banking Authority) (2021), *EBA Report on Management and Supervision of ESG Risks for Credit Institutions and Investment Firms*, EBA/REP/2021/18, June, available at: https://bit.ly/4c4mkBM.

EBA (European Banking Authority) (2022), *Final Report – Final Draft Implementing Technical Standards on Prudential Disclosures on ESG Risks in Accordance with Article 449a CRR*, EBA/ITS/2022/01, 24 January, available at: https://bit.ly/3Tc9VDb.

EBA (European Banking Authority), 'Consultation Paper: Draft Guidelines on the management of ESG risks', EBA/CP/2024/02, January, available at www.eba.europa.eu/activities/single-rulebook/sustainable-finance/guidelines-management-esg-risks.

ECB (European Central Bank) (2021), 'The state of climate and environmental risk management in the banking sector', November, available at: https://bit.ly/43tMie3.

ECB (European Central Bank) (2022a), *Supervisory Assessment of Institutions' Climate-related and Environmental Risk Disclosures – ECB Report on Banks' Progress towards Transparent Disclosure of Their Climate-Related and Environmental Risk Profiles*, March, available at: https://bit.ly/48RokdX.

ECB (European Central Bank) (2022b), '2022 Climate risk stress test', July, available at: https://bit.ly/48VFarY.

ECB (European Central Bank) (2022c), 'Walking the talk – Banks gearing up to manage risks from climate change and environmental degradation. Results of the 2022 thematic review on climate-related and environmental risks', November, available at: https://bit.ly/3vabklZ.

EIOPA (European Insurance and Occupational Pensions Authority) (2019), 'Technical Advice on the integration of sustainability risks and factors in the delegated acts under Solvency II and IDD', 30 April, EIOPA-BoS-19/172, available at: https://bit.ly/3TmrlND.

European Commission (2018), 'Action plan financing sustainable growth', 8 March, COM(2018) 97 final.

European Commission (2019), 'Communication from the Commission to the European Parliament, the European Council, the Council, the European Economic and Social Committee and the Committee of the Regions: The European Green Deal', 11 December, COM(2019) 640 final.

European Commission (2021a), 'Proposal for a Directive of the European Parliament and of the Council amending Directive 2013/34/EU, Directive 2004/109/EC, Directive 2006/43/EC and Regulation (EU) No 537/2014, as regards corporate sustainability reporting', COM(2021) 189 final.

European Commission (2021b), 'Communication from the Commission to the European Parliament, the Council, the European Economic and Social Committee and the Committee of the Regions: Strategy for Financing the Transition to a Sustainable Economy', 6 June, COM(2021) 390 final.

European Commission (2021c), 'Proposal for a Directive of the European Parliament and of the Council amending Directive 2009/138/EC as regards proportionality, quality of supervision, reporting, long-term guarantee measures, macro-prudential tools, sustainability risks, group and cross-border supervision', 22 September, COM(2021) 581 final.

European Commission (2021d), 'Proposal for a Regulation of the European Parliament and of the Council amending Regulation (EU) No 575/2013 as regards requirements for credit risk, credit valuation adjustment risk, operational risk, market risk and the output floor', 27 October, COM(2021) 664 final.

European Commission (2021e), 'Proposal for a Directive of the European Parliament and of the Council amending Directive 2013/36/EU as regards supervisory powers, sanctions, third-country branches, and environmental, social and governance risks, and amending Directive 2014/59/EU', 27 October 2021, COM(2021) 663 final.

FSB (Financial Stability Board) (2015), 'Proposal for a disclosure task force on climate-related risks', 9 November, available at: www.fsb.org/wp-content/uploads/P070721-4.pdf.

FSB (Financial Stability Board) (2017), 'Recommendations of the Task Force on Climate-related Financial Disclosures', 29 June, available at: www.fsb.org/wp-content/uploads/P290617-5.pdf.

FSB (Financial Stability Board) (2020), 'The implications of climate change for financial stability', 23 November, available at: www.fsb.org/wp-content/uploads/P231120.pdf.

FSB (Financial Stability Board) (2021a), *Report on Promoting Climate-related Disclosures*, 7 July, available at: www.fsb.org/wp-content/uploads/P070721-4.pdf.

FSB (Financial Stability Board) (2021b), 'FSB Roadmap for Addressing Climate-related Financial Risks', 7 July, available at: www.fsb.org/wp-content/uploads/P070721-2.pdf.

FSB (Financial Stability Board) (2022a), 'Supervisory and Regulatory Approaches to Climate-related Risks', 13 October, available at: www.fsb.org/wp-content/uploads/P131022-1.pdf.

FSB (Financial Stability Board) (2022b), *Progress Report on Climate-Related Disclosures*, 13 October, available at: www.fsb.org/wp-content/uploads/P131022-2.pdf.

Goodhart, C. A. E. (2011), *The Basel Committee on Banking Supervision. A History of the early years, 1974–1997* (Cambridge, UK: Cambridge University Press).

Gortsos, C. V. (2022), 'Historical evolution of bank capital requirements in the European Union', in Joosen, B. P. M., Lamandini, M. and Tröger, T. H. (eds.), *Capital and Liquidity Requirements for European Banks* (Oxford: Oxford University Press), 3–42.

Grünewald, S. (2021), 'Climate change as a systemic risk in finance: Are macroprudential authorities up to the task?', in Busch, D., Ferrarini, G. and Grünewald, S. (eds.), *Sustainable Finance in Europe. Corporate Governance, Financial Stability and Financial Markets* (London: Palgrave Macmillan), 227–57.

HLEG (High Level Expert Group on Sustainable Finance) (2017), *Financing a Sustainable Economy, Interim Report*, 12 July, available at: https://bit.ly/3Th8T96.

HLEG (High Level Expert Group on Sustainable Finance) (2018), *Financing a Sustainable Economy, Final Report*, 31 January, available at: https://bit.ly/3IQc5U9.

Joosen, B. P. M., Lamandini, M. and Tröger, T. H. (2022), *Capital and Liquidity Requirements for European Banks* (Oxford: Oxford University Press).

Mülbert, P. O. and Sajnovits, A. (2020), *CRD IV Framework for Banks' Corporate Governance*, 2nd ed., (Oxford: Oxford University Press), 223–80.

NGFS (Network for Greening the Financial System) (2020a), 'Guide for Supervisors – Integrating climate-related and environmental risks into prudential supervision', May, available at: https://bit.ly/4a4dUZe.

NGFS (Network for Greening the Financial System) (2020b), 'Guide to climate scenario analysis for central banks and supervisors', June, available at: https://bit.ly/3wP3oqL.

NGFS (Network for Greening the Financial System) (2022), *Capturing Risk Differentials from Climate-related Risks: A Progress Report*, May, available at: https://bit.ly/4afvE3W.

Norton, J. J. (1995), *Devising International Bank Supervisory Standards* (London: Graham & Trotman/Martinus Nijhoff).

Smoleńska, A. and van't Klooster, J. (2022), 'A risky bet: Climate change and the EU's microprudential framework for banks', 8 *Journal of Financial Regulation*, 51–74.

Steuer, S. and Tröger, T. (2022), 'The role of disclosure in green finance', 8 *Journal of Financial Regulation*, 1–50.

Theissen, R. (2023), *EU Banking Supervision* (The Hague: Eleven International Publishing).

Tröger, T. H. (2022), 'Qualitative capital requirements and their relationship with MREL/TLAC', in Joosen, B. P. M., Lamandini, M. and Tröger, T. H. (eds.), *Capital and Liquidity Requirements for European Banks* (Oxford: Oxford University Press), 94–121.

Vermeulen, R., Schets, E., Lohuis, M. et al. (2018), 'An energy transition risk stress test for the financial system of the Netherlands', DNB Occasional Study 16-7, available at: https://bit.ly/3VaPvNH.

Sustainable Finance under EU Law

The Gradual Shift from Capital Markets to Banking Regulation

Christos V. Gortsos*

21.1 BRIEF OVERVIEW OF THE POLICY INITIATIVES AND THE RULES ADOPTED DURING THE PERIOD 2019–2021

21.1.1 *The 2015 Capital Markets Union (CMU) Action Plan as a Catalyst for EU Capital Markets Regulation on Sustainable Finance and Ensuing Soft Law Instruments*

(1) 'Sustainable finance' is defined as the aggregate of financing and 'related institutional and market arrangements that contribute to the achievement of strong, sustainable, balanced and inclusive growth, through supporting directly and indirectly the framework of the Sustainable Development Goals' ('SDGs').[1] These are laid down in the 2015 United Nations ('UN') global sustainable development framework ('The 2030 Agenda for Sustainable Development'), which covers sustainability's three dimensions, namely economic, social and environmental ('ESG'). An effective way for achieving this is to make available financial products which pursue environmentally sustainable objectives.[2] As part of the international financial community dealing with this issue but in some cases going even beyond the international standards,[3] the European Union ('EU') set the ambitious aim to become a major standard-setter in the field of sustainable finance.[4]

---

* The author wishes to thank the co-editors and Dimitrios Kyriazis for useful comments and suggestions; the usual disclaimer applies. The cut-off date for information included in this Chapter is 6 October 2024.
[1] G20 Sustainable Finance Study Group 2018.
[2] Gortsos 2021, 356.
[3] Noteworthy in this area is the work of the following international fora: the Task Force on Climate-related Financial Disclosures ('TCFD'), a private-sector taskforce, established by the Financial Stability Board ('FSB'), following a request made in April 2015 by the G20 Finance Ministers and Central Bank Governors (see at: www.fsb-tcfd.org); the Network for Greening the Financial System ('NGFS'), which was set up in 2017 and whose members are central banks and supervisory authorities (see at: www.ngfs.net/en); and the Basel Committee on Banking Supervision ('BCBS').
[4] As noted in Gortsos and Kyriazis 2022, *in finem*: 'The EU is leading the way in sustainable finance regulation, with more instruments in the pipeline. However, for its influence to radiate outside the

The key relevant milestones are discussed below, with a focus on identifying the gradual migration from EU capital markets regulation to EU banking regulation (meaning the EU rules governing the prudential regulation and supervision of credit institutions and the related EU crisis management framework).[5]

(2) On 18 February 2015, the (European) Commission issued a Green Paper on 'Building a Capital Markets Union'[6] ('CMU'), followed, on 30 September, by its 'Action Plan on building a capital markets union'[7] (hereinafter the '2015 CMU Action Plan'). The latter laid down a comprehensive list of actions and related measures for further integrating capital market in the EU by 2019 and a timetable of implementation, paving the way for introducing the first set of rules pertaining to sustainable finance in the EU and the transition to a sustainable economy. A series of Commission Communications (soft law instruments) ensued: *first*, its Communication of 14 September 2016 on 'Capital markets union – accelerating reform',[8] which, *inter alia*, provided for the setting up a High-Level Expert Group on Sustainable Finance (hereinafter 'HLEG') whose mandate was the development of an overarching and comprehensive EU strategy on sustainable finance, addressing climate-related and environmental risks;[9] *second*, its Communication of 8 June 2017 on the 'Mid-Term Review of the [CMU] Action Plan', which set *nine priority actions* concerning *seven issue-areas* that should constitute the basis for the foundation of the CMU by 2019[10] (priority action (6) concerned a

---

strict confines of EU-related finance projects, more major jurisdictions will need to converge around implementing a common set of standards, or at least certain key principles.' For sustainable finance as, possibly, a new EU policy objective in financial regulation, see Colaert 2022.

[5] Since the entry into force of the Lisbon Treaty, primary EU law includes a set of provisions directly related to EU environmental policy lato sensu; it is within this set of provisions that every hard and soft law initiative of the EU on sustainable finance must be developed. These include, *first*, Articles 3 and 4 of the Treaty on the Functioning of the European Union ('TFEU'), corresponding to the EU exclusive and shared competence in the field of environmental protection. *Second*, Article 11 states that 'environmental protection requirements must be integrated into the definition and implementation of the Union's policies and activities, in particular with a view to promoting sustainable development'. This horizontal clause permeates all EU (hard and soft) law and does not allow environmental protection to be ignored in any EU policy, including, evidently, sustainable finance policy. *Third*, Article 191 sets out the objectives of EU policy in the field of environmental protection, Article 192 sets out the legislative procedure to be followed for the adoption of secondary Union law rules in the field of the environment, while Article 193 confirms that these rules do not prevent Member States from maintaining and introducing enhanced protection measures. *Finally*, Article 37 of the Charter of Fundamental Rights, which guarantees the right of EU citizens to the environment and is directly related to sustainable development, is also important in shaping EU policies in the field of sustainable finance.

[6] COM/2015/63 final.

[7] COM/2015/468 final.

[8] COM/2016/601 final.

[9] On the work of the HLEG, see Alexander 2019, 366–369. On the definition of these risks, see Table 21.1 below.

[10] The consolidated set of measures is laid down in the Annex to the Communication. The Commission's Q&As on this Review are available at: http://europa.eu/rapid/press-release_MEMO-17-1528_en.htm. The most recent Action Plan on this field, amidst the pandemic crisis, is contained in the European Commission Communication 2020. The measures to support, *inter alia*, a green recovery, are contained in Section 1 (Actions 1–6). On the evolution of the CMU project, see by means of mere

concrete follow-up to the HLEG's recommendations); and *third*, its Communication of 8 March 2018 for an 'Action Plan: Financing Sustainable Growth'[11] (hereinafter the '2018 Sustainable Finance Action Plan'), which set out the foundations for a comprehensive EU sustainable finance framework, including the establishment of an 'EU taxonomy'.[12]

The Commission committed, thus, to improving disclosure and fully integrating sustainability and ESG considerations in rating methodologies and supervisory processes, as well as in the investment mandates of institutional investors, and to developing an approach for taking sustainability considerations into account in upcoming legislative reviews of financial legislation.[13]

21.1.2 *The 'Regulatory Trilogy'*

(1) Within this context, in 2019–2020, the European Parliament and the Council (hereinafter the EU 'co-legislators') adopted the following three Regulations, which constitute the 'regulatory trilogy' implementing the above initial Commission's initiatives in relation to sustainable finance:

first, on 27 November 2019, they adopted Regulation (EU) 2019/2088 'on sustainability-related disclosures in the financial services sector'[14] (the 'Sustainable Finance Disclosure Regulation', 'SFDR', which in principle applies from 10 March 2021), and Regulation (EU) 2019/2089 'amending Regulation (EU) 2016/1011[15] as regards EU Climate Transition Benchmarks, EU Paris-aligned Benchmarks and sustainability-related disclosures for benchmarks'[16] (the 'Low Carbon Benchmarks Regulation', which applies from 10 December 2019);[17] and

indication the various contributions in Busch et al. 2018; Lannoo and Thomadakis 2019, European Court of Auditors 2020, High-Level Forum on the Capital Markets Union 2020, and Gortsos 2022a.
[11] COM/2018/097 final.
[12] In the meantime, on 5 October 2016, the Council had approved the Paris Agreement by its Decision (EU) 2016/1841 of 'on the conclusion, on behalf of the European Union, of the Paris Agreement adopted under the UN Framework Convention on Climate Change' (OJ L 282, 19.10.2016, 1–3). This approval is important, *inter alia*, because, according to Article 3(5) of the Treaty on European Union ('TEU') and Article 216(2) TFEU, the EU is committed to contributing to the strict observance and the development of international law (including respect for the principles of the United Nations Charter), while international treaties concluded by the Union are binding upon its institutions and its Member States. This means that the Paris Agreement also binds the EU Commission, the Council of the EU, the EU Parliament and the European Central Bank ('ECB'). Thus, the legal ramifications are not to be taken lightly. On the fundamental tenets of the agreement, see United Nations 2016; on the legal character of the Paris Agreement, see Bodansky 2016.
[13] Gortsos 2021, 354. See further Section 21.1.4. For the interplay between corporate social responsibility and sustainable finance, see Liang and Renneboog 2020 and Winter 2024.
[14] OJ L 317, 9.12.2019, 1–16. On this legislative act, see details in Busch 2024.
[15] Regulation (EU) 2016/1011 of 8 June 2016 'on indices used as benchmarks in financial instruments and financial contracts or to measure the performance of investment funds (...)', OJ L 171, 29.6.2016, 1–65.
[16] OJ L 317, 9.12.2019, 17–27. These benchmarks are defined in Article 1(1), inserting new points (23a) and 23b) to Article 3(1) Regulation (EU) 2016/1011.
[17] On this legislative act, see Ramos Muñoz and Smoleńska (2023).

then, on 18 June 2020, they adopted Regulation (EU) 2020/852 'on the establishment of a framework to facilitate sustainable investment and amending Regulation (EU) 2019/2088'[18] (the 'Taxonomy Regulation' 'TR'), which applies from 12 July 2020.[19]

(2) These legislative acts, which are further complemented by several Commission-delegated acts, are part of EU capital markets and not of EU banking regulation. In particular, the SRFR and the TR are setting out disclosure requirements, which (only) apply to credit institutions either as undertakings subject to the obligation to publish non-financial statement or consolidated non-financial statements pursuant to the 2013 'Accounting Directive' (as in force[20]) when issuing environmentally sustainable corporate bonds, or to the extent that their operating licences cover the provision of portfolio management services (acting, hence, as 'market participants').[21] *On the other hand*, it does not *directly* apply to credit institutions' lending activity. However, the compatibility of this activity with sustainability criteria is envisaged, *inter alia*, in various acts of the ECB[22] and the European Banking Authority ('EBA'),[23] as well as in the Commission's 2021 'Sustainable Finance Strategy' Communication.[24] Indeed, the EU taxonomy classification system is gradually being embedded in various sources of EU financial law, which apply directly, *inter alia*, to credit institutions (as well as to investment firms, investment fund managers and insurance companies),[25] duly taking into account and the considerations relating to their exposure to ESG risks (as further discussed just below).

---

[18] OJ L 198, 22.6.2020, 13–43.

[19] TR, Article 27(1). On this legislative act, see Pacces 2021, Helleringer 2021 (in relation to the 'greenwashing' aspect) and in more detail Gortsos and Kyriazis 2024. On the fact that the adoption of TR has been a *novum* at international level since the EU taxonomy is not based on any international standards, *see* Zetzsche et al. 2021.

[20] Articles 19a and 29a of Directive 2013/34/EU of the co-legislators of 26 June 2013 'on the annual financial statements, consolidated financial statements and related reports of certain types of undertakings (…)' (OJ L 182, 29.6.2013, 19–76). These Articles were inserted by Directive 2014/95/EU of 22 October 2014 '(…) as regards disclosure of non-financial and diversity information by certain large undertakings and groups' (OJ L 330, 15.11.2014, 1–9, the 'Non-Financial Reporting Directive', 'NFRD'), which amended the Accounting Directive and is broadly governed by the 'comply or explain' principle; see Helleringer 2021.

[21] TR, Articles 8 and 1(2), respectively.

[22] See by means of indication ECB 2020.

[23] See further Section 21.1.4; see also EBA 2019. On the place of the EBA in the EU institutional design, see, by means of indication, Ferran 2012, Payne 2020 and Gortsos 2023, 383–485.

[24] See Section 21.1.6.

[25] See by means of mere indication Alexander and Fisher 2018 and Alexander 2019, 357–364. Related to this issue are the following two aspects, which are nevertheless not further discussed in this study. The *first* is the impact of climate-related risks on financial stability in general; on this, see by means of mere indication ECB 2021 and Grünewald 2024. The *second* refers to the link between climate-related considerations and monetary policy. Noteworthy in this respect is the ECB 'Climate Action Plan' of 8 July 2021 to include climate change considerations under its new (2021 as well) monetary policy strategy (see https://bit.ly/4cnUQHo); on the new strategy, see by means of mere indication Reichlin et al. 2021 and Zilioli 2021. Furthermore, since climate change has profound implications for price stability, a comprehensive climate-related action plan, with a concrete roadmap, was considered indispensable to further incorporate climate change considerations into its policy framework (ECB's monetary policy strategy statement, point 10), as part of this Action Plan and on the basis of a

21.1.3 *The 2019 Amendment of Two Key Sources of EU Banking Law on Prudential Banking Regulation and Supervision*

The two 2013 legislative acts governing the authorisation, prudential regulation and prudential supervision of credit institutions (and some categories of holding companies), namely the 'Capital Requirements Regulation'[26] ('CRR') and the 'Capital Requirements Directive No IV' ('CRD IV')[27] of the co-legislators of 26 June 2013, were also amended during that period, albeit under a different policy agenda. In particular, based on its Communication of 24 November 2015 'Towards the completion of the Banking Union',[28] the Commission adopted on 23 November 2016 a legislative 'banking package' with a view to reducing risks to further enhance EU credit institutions' resilience, which was completed in 2019. *Inter alia*, the CRR was amended by the so-called 'CRR II'[29] with respect to counterparty credit and market risks; exposures to central counterparties and collective investment undertakings; as well as reporting and disclosure requirements.[30] The CRD IV was amended by the so-called 'CRD V',[31] with respect to, *inter alia*, supervisory measures and powers.[32] In this respect, several rules were introduced, which laid down the basis for action by the EBA under its enhanced powers in relation to sustainable finance (as further discussed below).

21.1.4 *The 2019 Amendment of the Regulations Governing the European Supervisory Authorities (ESAs) and Key Measures Taken by Them under Their Enhanced Mandate*

(1) On the basis of the (above-mentioned[33]) 2015 CMU Action Plan, the Regulations governing the European Supervisory Authorities ('ESAs'), established by three

---

detailed 'Roadmap of climate change-related actions' annexed thereto, the ECB Governing Council announced on 4 July 2022 its decision to take further steps to include climate change considerations in the monetary policy framework (see at https://bit.ly/3TrGbCt). The measures decided upon are designed in full accordance with the Eurosystem's primary objective (i.e., to maintain price stability in the euro area); aim to better consider climate-related financial risk in its balance sheet; and, with reference to the secondary objective, support the green transition of the economy (ECB 2022). See details in Kyriazis 2022, 143–164, Wutscher 2024 and (in even more detail) Smits 2024.

[26] Regulation (EU) No 575/2013 'on prudential requirements for credit institutions and investment firms and amending Regulation (EU) No 648/2012', OJ L 176, 27/6/2013, 1–337.

[27] Directive 2013/36/EU 'on access to the activity of credit institutions and the prudential supervision of credit institutions and investment firms (…)', OJ L 176, 27/6/2013, 338–436.

[28] COM/2015/587 final.

[29] Regulation (EU) 2019/876 of 20 May 2019, OJ 150, 7.6.2019, 1–225.

[30] Gortsos 2020, 157.

[31] Directive (EU) 2019/878 of 20 May 2019, OJ 150, 7.6.2019, 253–295.

[32] These rules apply from 1 January 2021. The CRR II and the CRD V did not repeal the CRR and the CRD IV, which are still in force as amended.

[33] See Section 21.1.1(2).

Regulations of the co-legislators of 24 November 2010,[34] were also amended by virtue of their Regulation (EU) 2019/2175 of 18 December 2019.[35] This clarified and strengthened their powers, while also attributing to them new powers in targeted areas, including taking into account sustainable business models and the integration of ESG factors when acting within their scope of action and carrying out their tasks.[36]

(2) Under its enhanced mandate, the EBA published, on 26 June 2021, a Report 'On management and supervision of ESG risks for credit institutions and investment firms'.[37] This discusses how 'ESG factors' and 'ESG risks' should be included in the regulatory and supervisory framework for these institutions, focussing on their resilience to the potential financial impact of ESG risks across different time horizons, since those risks are a source of financial risk. Its main Chapters (2–5) deal, respectively, with common definitions of 'ESG factors', 'ESG risks', as well as their drivers and transmission channels;[38] quantitative and qualitative indicators, metrics, and methods to assess ESG risks; the management of ESG risks by institutions; and ESG factors and ESG risks in supervision. In accordance with a phase-in approach and with a view to further enhancing the supervisory review and evaluation process ('SREP'),[39] the Report proposes the extension of the time horizon of the supervisory assessment of the resilience of institutions' business models, applying at least a 10-year horizon to capture 'physical risks',[40] relevant public policies or broader transition trends.[41]

(3) Furthermore, on 24 January 2022, the EBA published its final draft implementing technical standards ('ITS') on Pillar 3 disclosures on ESG risks.[42] These require credit

---

[34] The EBA was established under Regulation (EU) No 1093/2010 ('EBAR'); the European Insurance and Occupational Pensions Authority ('EIOPA') under Regulation (EU) No 1094/2010; and the European Securities and Markets Authority ('ESMA') under Regulation (EU) No 1095/2010 (all of 24 November 2010, OJ L 331, 15.12.2010, 12–47, 48–84 and 84–119, respectively).

[35] OJ L 334, 27.12.2019, 1–145. Articles 1–3 and 6 of this legislative act apply from 1 January 2020, while Articles 4–5 apply from 1 January 2022 (ibid., Article 7, second sentence). For a comparative analysis of the enforcement styles of EU agencies, including the ESAs, see Joosen and Zhelyazkova 2022.

[36] ESAs Regulations, Article 1(3), as amended.

[37] EBA 2021. It was adopted, for credit institutions, pursuant to Article 98(8) CRD IV (which was inserted by the CRD V) and Article 35 of Directive (EU) 2019/2034 'on the prudential supervision of investment firms and amending (…) [the CRD IV]' (Investment Firms Directive ('IFD'), OJ L 314, 5.12.2019, 64–114) (for investments firms, since the CRD IV (and the CRR) do not anymore apply to investment firms by virtue of the IFD and of Regulation (EU) 2019/2033 'on the prudential requirements of investment firms' Investment Firms Regulation ('IFR'), OJ L 314, 5.12.2019, 1–63). This Report should be read in conjunction with the ESAs' disclosure publications under the CRR, the TR and the SFDR, which provide key metrics to support strategies and risk management.

[38] ESG factors are defined as the ESG matters that may have a positive or negative impact on the financial performance or solvency of an entity, sovereign or individual. On the other hand, ESG risks are defined as the risks of any negative financial impact on the institution stemming from the current or prospective impacts of ESG factors on its counterparties or invested assets.

[39] This is governed by Articles 97–101 CRD IV; see also Section 21.2.3.3.

[40] On the definition of physical risks, as part of the overall environmental risk, see below Section 21.2.2.

[41] This Report should be considered in conjunction with the ESAs' disclosure publications under the CRR, the TR and the SFDR, which provide key metrics to support strategies and risk management.

[42] EBA 2022a. The legal basis is Article 449a CRR, which was inserted by the CRR II. A critical (and still unresolved) aspect in this context is which of the three Pillars of the prudential framework under

institutions to make comparable disclosures showing how climate change may exacerbate other risks within their balance sheets, how they are mitigating those risks, and their ratios (including a green asset ratio ('GAR'), and a banking book taxonomy alignment ratio ('BTAR')), on their exposures financing taxonomy-aligned activities. The aim of this Pillar 3 disclosure framework is to promote transparency as a main driver of market discipline in the financial sector, reduce the asymmetry of information between credit institutions and users of information, to address uncertainties on potential risks and vulnerabilities faced by institutions and, ultimately, to ensure that stakeholders are well-informed about institutions' ESG exposures, risks and strategies, can make informed decisions and are able to exercise market discipline.[43]

21.1.5 *The 2019 Commission Communication on 'The European Green Deal' and Its Impact in Terms of New Legislative Initiatives*

(1) The Commission Communication of 11 December 2019 on 'The European Green Deal'[44] constitutes another key milestone, tabled before the final adoption of the TR and the outbreak of the pandemic crisis. On this basis, the Commission tabled, on 14 January 2020, a new Communication titled 'European Green Deal Investment Plan',[45] whose aim is to mobilise a significant amount of sustainable investments in a 10-year horizon, and then, on 6 July 2021, a proposal for a Regulation of the co-legislators on a voluntary EU Green Bond Standard ('EUGBS')[46], which was adopted on 22 November 2023.[47] This EU high-quality 'gold standard' for green bonds is expected to serve as a benchmark to other market standards and will be available to private and sovereign issuers, including those located outside of the EU, for financing sustainable investments.[48]

(2) Another major step towards implementing the Green Deal and the 2018 Sustainable Finance Action Plan was the Commission Communication of 21 April

---

the CRD IV and the CRR (namely, binding capital requirements (Pillar 1); earmarked, institution-specific capital requirements under the SREP (Pillar 2); and disclosure requirements (Pillar 3) is best suited to deal with ESG risks, or whether a combination thereof is a superior solution.

[43] EBA 2022a.

[44] COM/2019/640 final.

[45] COM/2020/21 final. On the European Green Deal, *see* Mollers 2022 (especially in relation to greenwashing) and Motani 2024.

[46] COM/2021/391 final.

[47] Regulation (EU) 2023/2631 "on European Green Bonds and optional disclosures for bonds marketed as environmentally sustainable and for sustainability-linked bonds", OJ L, 2023/2631, 30.11.2023.

[48] The establishment of such a standard for green bonds, which play an increasingly important role for raising financing in sectors such as energy production and distribution, resource-efficient housing and low-carbon transport infrastructure and, hence, in financing assets needed for the low-carbon transition, was a recommendation in the final report of the HLEG and was then included as an action in the 2018 Sustainable Finance Action Plan. On this Standard, see by means of mere indication Maragopoulos 2023 and the other contributions in Ramos Muñoz and Smoleńska (eds.) (2023). On investors' responses to corporate green bonds, see Flammer 2021, and on their pricing, see Fatica et al. 2019. On the different, but related issue of sovereign green bonds, see Giráldez and Fontana 2022. For the need for independent certification in relation to green bonds, see Ehlers and Packer 2017.

2021 'EU Taxonomy, Corporate Sustainability Reporting, Sustainability Preferences and Fiduciary Duties: Directing finance towards the European Green Deal'. Based thereon, the Commission tabled a proposal for a so-called Corporate Sustainability Reporting Directive ('CSRD'), which was adopted by the co-legislators on 14 December 2022[49] and is gradually being implemented from 2024. This legislative act amends, *inter alia*, the reporting rules of the (above-mentioned[50]) Accounting Directive as regards corporate sustainability reporting, extending its scope of application to all large companies and all companies listed on regulated markets, setting out more detailed reporting requirements and requiring that reported information will be audited.

It is noteworthy that all these legislative initiatives and acts are mainly related to EU capital markets regulation (including corporate governance[51]) albeit with an impact on credit institutions as well.

21.1.6 *A Critical Turning Point: The 2021 Sustainable Finance Strategy*

Since sustainability has been considered a main pillar of the EU's recovery from the pandemic and that the financial system can heavily contribute to meet the targets of the Green Deal, the Commission issued, on 6 July 2021, a Communication on 'Strategy for Financing the Transition to a Sustainable Economy' (hereinafter the '2021 Sustainable Finance Strategy' Communication).[52] This soft law instrument identifies four main objectives (pillars), which are necessary for the financial system – including, *explicitly for the first time*, the banking sector – to fully support the transition of the economy towards sustainability. These objectives are: financing transition; developing a more inclusive sustainable finance framework; improving the financial system's resilience and contribution to sustainability under a double materiality perspective; and fostering global ambition. These objectives are coupled by six sets of action,[53] including the improvement of the sustainable finance's inclusiveness with a view to small and medium-sized enterprises and consumers by supporting, *inter alia*, the development of 'green' loans and mortgages; as well as the monitoring of the financial system's orderly transition to sustainability and the ensuring of its integrity.

---

[49] Directive (EU) 2022/2464 of the co-legislators of 14 December 2022 '(…) as regards corporate sustainability reporting', OJ L 322, 16.12.2022, 15–80.

[50] See Section 21.1.2.

[51] On this aspect, see by means of indication de Oliveira Neves 2022, Siri and Zhu 2024 and Pacces 2024.

[52] COM/2021/390 final. On 14 July 2021, the Commission issued another Communication titled 'Fit for 55: delivering the EU's 2030 Climate Target on the way to climate neutrality', which sets out its commitment to transform the EU economy into a sustainable economy, while also dealing with the inevitable consequences of climate change.

[53] Action 1 is linked to the first pillar, Action 2 to the second, Actions 3–5 to the third and Action 6 to the fourth.

21.2 THE 2021 LEGISLATIVE 'BANKING PACKAGE' AND THE AMENDMENTS IN RELATION TO SUSTAINABILITY AND CONTRIBUTION TO THE GREEN TRANSITION

21.2.1 *General Overview of the 2021 'Banking Package'*

(1) On 27 October 2021, the Commission adopted its so-called '2021 legislative banking package',[54] which contained several legislative proposals amending the single rulebook for banking services in the EU, namely, the CRR, the CRD IV and (to a lesser extent) the Bank Recovery and Resolution Directive[55] ('BRRD'). It forms part of the constant review of EU banking legislation, which started in 2016 with the 'Risk Reduction Measures Package' that was adopted, as noted,[56] in 2019.[57] The aim of the proposed rules was to reduce risks in the financial system by ensuring that EU credit institutions become more resilient to potential future economic shocks, while contributing to the EU's recovery from the pandemic crisis and promoting sustainable financing of the economic activity. The pillars of this package were as follows:[58]

The *first pillar* referred to the implementation into EU banking law, by amendment of the CRR and the CRD IV by the so-called 'CRR III' and 'CRD VI'[59], respectively, of some recent international financial standards of the BCBS (namely, those contained in its Report of 7 December 2017 'Basel III: Finalising post-crisis reforms'[60] ('Complement to Basel III'), as in force[61]), taking into consideration the specific features of the EU banking sector.

The *second pillar* contained proposals, by amendment of the CRD IV, for strengthening prudential banking supervision to ensure EU credit institutions' sound management and better protect financial stability.[62]

The objective of the *third pillar*, on sustainability – contributing to the green transition, was to strengthen the resilience of the banking system to ESG risks as part of the Commission's new Sustainable Finance Strategy, as set out in its

---

[54] See at: https://bit.ly/3TIKKJR.
[55] Directive 2014/59/EU of the co-legislators of 15 May 2014 'establishing a framework for the recovery and resolution of credit institutions and investment firms (…)' (OJ L 173, 12.6.2014, 190–348), as in force.
[56] See Section 21.1.3.
[57] It does not, however, address issues relating to the 'unfinished' agenda for the completion of the Banking Union ('BU'), such as the establishment of a European Deposit Insurance System ('EDIS'). On this aspect, see Gortsos 2022b, 185–186 and 194–195 (with extensive further references). On the BU, see by mere indication the Commentary by Binder et al. 2022.
[58] European Commission 2021.
[59] COM/2021/663 final and COM/2021/664 final, respectively.
[60] Available at: www.bis.org/bcbs/publ/d424.htm. For a summary of its key provisions, see www.bis.org/bcbs/publ/d424_hlsummary.pdf.
[61] In June 2019, this Report was revised by the document 'Leverage ratio treatment of client cleared derivatives' (available at: www.bis.org/bcbs/publ/d467.htm).
[62] On these two pillars, see Gortsos 2022c.

(above-mentioned[63]) Communication of 6 July 2021. This aspect is discussed in more detail (under Section 21.2.2).[64]

Finally, some technical modifications to the banking resolution framework were proposed to clarify certain aspects of the prudential treatment of global systemically important institution ('G-SII') groups[65] with a multiple point of entry ('MPE') resolution strategy *and* the methodology for the indirect subscription of instruments eligible for meeting the minimum requirement for own funds and eligible liabilities ('MREL') (the so-called 'daisy chain' proposal).[66]

(2) The latter proposal was the first adopted by the co-legislators on 19 October 2022 by Regulation (EU) 2022/2036.[67] Then, on 31 May 2024, they adopted two legislative acts dealing with the aspects included in the first three pillars above: Regulation (EU) 2024/1623 "amending [the CRR] as regards requirements for credit risk, credit valuation adjustment risk, operational risk, market risk and the output floor"[68] ('CRR III'); and Directive (EU) 2024/1619 "amending [the CRD IV] as regards supervisory powers, sanctions, third-country branches, and [ESG] risks"[69] ('CRD VI').

The provisions of the CRR III will apply from 1 January 2025, except for those which already apply from 9 July 2024.[70] In relation to the provisions of the CRD VI, Member States are required to adopt and publish the legislative, regulatory and administrative provisions necessary to comply with that legislative act by 10 January 2026 and apply those measures from 11 January 2026 subject to the following qualifications:[71] in principle, the measures necessary to comply with the amendments set out in Article 1, points (9) and (13) shall apply from 11 January 2027; by way of derogation, the measures necessary to comply with the amendments set out in Article 1, point (13) as regards Articles 48k-48l shall apply from 11 January 2026,[72] and with those set out in Article 1, point (9) as regards Article 21c (5) from 11 July 2026.[73]

21.2.2 *Introductory Remarks on the Proposed Amendments in Relation to Sustainability and Contribution to the Green Transition – Definitions*

(1) The objective of the new framework amending the CRD IV and the CRR,[74] the content of which is heavily influenced by the (above-mentioned[75]) EBA 2021 Report

---

[63] See Section 21.1.6.
[64] On this aspect, see also De Arriba-Sellier 2022 and Betrosian 2021, 72–76.
[65] G-SIIs are determined in accordance with Article 131(1) CRD IV.
[66] Proposal for a Regulation of the co-legislators amending the CRR and the BRRD (COM/2021/665 final, 27.10.2021).
[67] OJ L 275, 25.10.2022, 1–10.
[68] OJ L, 2024/1623, 19.6.2024.
[69] OJ L, 2024/1619, 19.6.2024.
[70] Regulation (EU) 2024/1623, Article 2.
[71] Directive (EU) 2024/1619, Article 2.
[72] These Articles govern the newly established reporting requirements in relation to the supervision of branches established in EU Member States by third-country undertakings.
[73] This Article refers to a specific grandfathering clause in relation to the newly established rules on the direct provision of banking services in the EU by third-country undertakings.
[74] COM/2021/663 final and COM/2021/664 final, respectively.
[75] See Section 21.1.4.

'On management and supervision of ESG risks for credit institutions and investment firms', is to enhance the focus on ESG risks in the prudential framework. In that respect, and in order to promote an adequate understanding and management of these risks, competent (i.e., supervisory) authorities are required to conduct regular climate stress testing and assess ESG risks as part of the SREP, and credit institutions to systematically identify, disclose and manage them as part of their risk management.[76] As noted in the CRR III and CRD VI proposals' Explanatory Memoranda:

> Bank-based intermediation will play a crucial role in financing the transition to a more sustainable economy. At the same time, the transition to a more sustainable economy is likely to entail risks for institutions that they will need to properly manage to ensure that risks to financial stability are minimised. This is where prudential regulation is needed and where it can play a crucial role. The Strategy for Financing the Transition to a Sustainable Economy acknowledged this and highlighted the need to include a better integration of [(ESG)] risks into the EU prudential framework as the present legal requirements alone are deemed insufficient to provide incentives for a systematic and consistent management of ESG risks by institutions.[77]

(2) The CRR III introduced in Article 4(1) CRR (on definitions) new harmonised definitions of the different types of ESG-related risks, which are aligned with those proposed by EBA in its above-mentioned 2021 Report, as listed in Table 21.1 just below.

(3) The two components of environmental risk – physical and transition risks – do not constitute a separate category of financial risks. They are risk drivers translating into financial risks through various transmission channels (such as lower profitability, real estate value, household wealth or asset performance or increased compliance and/or legal cost). Reflecting their potential double materiality, they can materialise in two ways: on the 'financial materiality side', the financial performance of a counterparty (or the invested assets) can be affected by environmental factors; and 'on the environmental materiality side', the activities of a counterparty (or the invested assets) may have a negative impact on the environment, which may then become financially material for this counterparty by triggering or reinforcing a negative outside-in impact.[78]

---

[76] MOCOMILA 2022.

[77] In accordance with the considerations in recital (36) of the Proposal for a CRD VI, Article 133 CRD IV on the systemic risk buffer ('SyRB') may already be used to address various kinds of systemic risks, including climate change-related ones. Thus, competent or designated authorities considering that such risks may have serious negative consequences for the financial system and the real economy in Member States should introduce a SyRB rate for them once the introduction of such a rate is considered effective and proportionate to mitigate them. Measures taken by these authorities can be applied across certain sets or sub-sets of exposures, e.g., those subject to climate change-related physical and transition risks (ibid., Article 133(5)).

[78] See EBA 2022b, 17–19. See also Task Force on Climate-related Financial Disclosures 2007, Network for Greening the Financial System 2020, European Central Bank 2020, BCBS 2021, BCBS 2022a and BCBS 2022b.

TABLE 21.1 *Definition of risks*

Type of risk	Definition
ESG risk	the risk of losses arising from any negative financial impact on the institution stemming from the current or prospective impacts of ESG factors on its counterparties or invested assets[79]
environmental risk	the risk of losses arising from any negative financial impact on the institution stemming from the current or prospective impacts of environmental factors on the institution's counterparties or invested assets, including factors related to the transition towards the six environmental objectives set out in the TR[80] (namely: climate change mitigation; climate change adaptation; the sustainable use and protection of water and marine resources; the transition to a circular economy; pollution prevention and control; and the protection and restoration of biodiversity and ecosystems) – environmental risk includes both physical and transition risk
physical risk (as part of the overall environmental risk)	the risk of losses arising from any negative financial impact on the institution stemming from the current or prospective impacts of the physical effects of environmental factors on its counterparties or invested assets
transition risk (as part of the overall environmental risk)	the risk of losses arising from any negative financial impact on the institution stemming from the current or prospective impacts of the transition of business activities and sectors to an environmentally sustainable economy on its counterparties or invested assets
social risk	the risk of losses arising from any negative financial impact on the institution stemming from the current or prospective impacts of social factors on its counterparties or invested assets
governance risk	the risk of losses arising from any negative financial impact on the institution stemming from the current or prospective impacts of governance factors on its counterparties or invested assets

(4) Noteworthy is also a significant trade-off relationship between the two components of environmental risk. In particular, the transition to a more sustainable economy may increase the risks to credit institutions and to the overall financial stability due to the potential impact to their counterparties or invested assets. Since, *inter alia*, the continuation of unsustainable economic practices is a driver of physical risks and may exacerbate the likelihood of environmental hazards, credit institutions are also exposed to those. If (and when) transition policies are implemented, *ceteris paribus*, physical risks are expected to decrease. On the other hand,

[79] *See also* Article 3(1), (new) point (69) CRD IV with reference to Article 4(1), (new) point (52d) CRR.
[80] TR, Article 9, and recital (23).

if implementation of transition-related policies is prolonged (as no actual action is taken), the transition risk is low but physical risks will increase.[81]

21.2.3 *Amendments to the CRD IV*

21.2.3.1 New Rules Relating to Governance Issues

(1) Articles 73 and 74 CRD IV (on internal capital and on internal governance and recovery and resolution plans, respectively) are amended to the effect that they require the inclusion of an appropriate set of time horizons of ESG risks in credit institutions' strategies and processes for evaluating internal capital needs, as well as adequate internal governance. In particular, credit institutions are required to have in place 'sound, effective and comprehensive strategies, and processes to assess and maintain on an ongoing basis the amounts, types, and distribution of internal capital that they consider adequate to cover the nature and level of the risks to which they are or might be exposed in the short-, medium- and long-term time horizon, including ESG risks'.[82] They are also required to have robust governance arrangements, including, *inter alia*, 'effective processes to identify, manage, monitor, and report the risks they are or might be exposed to' in these time horizons, including (again) ESG risks.[83]

(2) Article 76 (on the treatment of risks) introduces a reference to the current and forward-looking impacts of ESG risks and a request for the management body of credit institutions to develop concrete plans to address these risks. In particular, it must be ensured that the management body *first*, approves and reviews (at least every 2 years) the strategies and policies for taking up, managing, monitoring, and mitigating the risks the institution is or might be exposed to, including, *inter alia*, those resulting from the current, short-, medium- and long-term impacts of ESG factors and *second*, develops specific plans and quantifiable targets to monitor and address the risks arising in the short-, medium- and long-term time horizon from the misalignment of the business model and strategy, with the relevant EU policy objectives or broader transition trends towards a sustainable economy in relation to ESG factors.[84]

Furthermore, Article 91 (on the suitability criteria for the management body's members) has been amended to the effect that: *first*, the management body shall possess collective knowledge, skills and experience to be able to adequately understand the credit institution's activities and the associated risks to which it is exposed in the short-, medium- and long-term, taking into account the ESG factors; and

---

[81] See the Explanatory Memorandum in the Proposals for a CRR III and a CRD VI. On the mitigation of transition risk, see (by means of mere indication) Miller and Dikau 2022.

[82] CRD IV, amendment to Article 73, first sub-paragraph.

[83] Ibid., amendment to Article 74(1), point (b).

[84] Ibid., amendment to Article 76(1) and insertion of a sub-paragraph in Article 76(2).

second, credit institutions shall devote adequate human and financial resources to the induction and training of these members, including on ESG risks and impacts.[85]

21.2.3.2 New Rules Earmarked for ESG Risks

The new Article 87a (earmarked for ESG risks) introduced a sustainability dimension in the prudential framework to ensure a better management of ESG risks and incentivise a better allocation of funding across sustainable projects. In this respect competent authorities must undertake the following:

> *first*, 'ensure that [credit] institutions have, as part of their governance arrangements, including the risk management framework required under Article 74(1), robust strategies, policies, processes and systems to identify, measure, manage and monitor ESG risks over an appropriate [set of] time horizons'; these must be 'proportionate to the scale, nature and complexity' of the ESG risks, as well as 'the business model and scope of the institution's activities, and consider short-, medium- and a long-term horizon of at least 10 years';[86]
>
> *second*, ensure that credit institutions 'test their resilience to long-term negative impacts of ESG factors, both under baseline and adverse scenarios within a given timeframe, starting with climate-related factors', and include several 'ESG scenarios reflecting potential impacts of environmental and social changes and associated public policies on the long-term business environment';[87] and
>
> *third*, assess and monitor 'developments of institutions' practices concerning their [ESG strategy]…and risk management, including the plans to be prepared in accordance with Article 76, as well as the progress made and the risks to adapt their business models to the relevant policy objectives or broader transition trends towards a sustainable economy, taking into account sustainability related product offering, transition finance policies, related loan origination policies' as well as ESG-related targets and limits.[88]

Furthermore, for the sake of ensuring the consistency of ESG risk assessments, the EBA shall issue (by 10 January 2026) Guidelines, in accordance with Article 16 EBAR, to further specify the criteria for the assessment of ESG risks (including on their identification, measurement, management and monitoring), 'as well as how credit institutions should draw concrete plans to address and internally stress test resilience and long-term negative impacts to the ESG risks.'[89]

---

[85] Ibid., new paragraphs 2b and 7 in Article 91.

[86] Ibid., new Article 87a (1)–(2).

[87] Ibid., new Article 87a (3).

[88] Ibid., new Article 87a (4). On the importance of ESG data in this respect, see Amesheva 2022.

[89] These Guidelines shall be updated on a regular basis to reflect the progress made in measuring and managing ESG factors, as well as developments of EU policy objectives on sustainability (ibid., new Article 87a (5)). For recent research on stress tests, see Konietschke et al. 2022; for 'green' stress tests, see, by means of mere indication, Reinders et al. 2020.

21.2.3.3 New Rules Relating to the Supervisory Review and Evalutation Process (SREP) and Competent Authorities' Powers

(1) To facilitate the SREP of credit institutions' exposures, governance and management of ESG risks, Article 98 has been amended to the following effect: first, the SREP shall include the assessment of their governance and risk management processes for dealing with ESG risks, as well as of their exposures to ESG risks, taking into account their business models; second, credit institutions' exposures to ESG risks shall be assessed on the basis of plans to be prepared in accordance with Article 76(2); their governance and risk management processes with regard to ESG risks shall be brought into line with the objectives set out in those plans; and third, the SREP shall include the assessment of the above credit institutions' plans, as well as of the progress made towards addressing the ESG risks arising from the process of adjustment towards climate neutrality and other relevant EU regulatory objectives in relation to ESG factors.[90]

(2) In light of the relevance of future-looking stress tests for gauging environment-related and other ESG risks in the SREP under Article 97, Article 100 has also been amended. In particular:[91]

> *First*, credit institutions and any third parties acting in a consulting capacity to them are required to 'refrain from activities that can impair a stress test (such as benchmarking, exchange of information among themselves, agreements on common behaviour or optimisation of submissions)'; in addition, all information gathering and investigatory powers necessary to detect such actions are conferred upon competent authorities.
>
> *Second*, the ESAs shall, through the Joint Committee referred to in Article 54 of their founding Regulations, develop (and publish by 10 January 2026) Guidelines 'to ensure that consistency, long-term considerations, and common standards for assessment methodologies are integrated into the stress testing of ESG risks' (this stress testing by competent authorities starting with climate-related factors), and, explore the means to integrate social and governance-related risks into stress testing.

(3) Finally, to facilitate the possibility for competent authorities to address ESG risks affecting the prudential situation of credit institutions, and to reflect the specificities of these risks, the Commission proposes to add in Article 104(1) a concrete supervisory power to address ESG risks. Hence, competent authorities are given the power to require credit institutions to reduce the risks arising from their 'misalignment with relevant policy objectives of the Union and broader transition trends relating to ESG factors over the short-, medium- and long-term, including through adjustments to their business models, governance strategies and risk management.'[92]

---

[90] CRD VI, new paragraph 9 in Article 98.
[91] *Ibid.*, new paragraphs 3 and 4, respectively, in Article 100.
[92] Ibid., new point (m) in Article 104(1).

21.2.4 *Further Amendments to the CRR*

In addition to the introduction of new definitions (as already noted[93]), two further amendments are introduced to the CRR.

First, to allow for better supervision of ESG risks, Article 430 (on reporting on prudential requirements and financial information) has been amended to the effect that credit institutions are required to report their exposure to ESG risks to their competent authorities.[94]

Second, 'to better align the timelines of any changes to the prudential rules that may be needed,' Article 501c (on the prudential treatment of exposures to environmental and/or social factors) is partly amended. In this respect, and within the mandate of that Article, the EBA, after consulting the European Systemic Risk Board ('ESRB'),[95] shall assess, on the basis of available data, the findings of the HLEG and specific criteria,[96] 'if a dedicated prudential treatment of exposures related to assets, including securitisations, or activities subject to impacts from environmental and/or social factors would be justified'. The key amendment relates to advancing the deadline for the EBA to deliver successive Reports on its findings in relation to the prudential treatment of these exposures to the European Parliament, the Council, and the Commission by specific dates (from 9 July 2024 to 31 December 2025). On the basis of these EBA Reports, the Commission shall, if appropriate, submit to the co-legislators a legislative proposal by 31 December 2026.

21.3 CONCLUDING REMARKS

Credit institutions in the EU are already subject to specific requirements deriving from the regulatory framework in force which relates to sustainable finance, pursuant to the provisions of the SFDR and the TR, which are sources of EU capital markets law.[97] They are also covered by the objectives set out in the Commission's '2021 Sustainable Finance Strategy' Communication aiming at ensuring that the financial system fully supports the transition of the economy towards sustainability.[98] However, a new, 'earmarked' EU banking regulatory framework in respect to sustainability and credit institutions' contribution to the green transition has been shaped pursuant to the CRD VI and the CRR III, which amended (respectively) the CRD IV and the CRR.[99] Taking into account that the ultimate goal is the enhancement of the focus on ESG risks in the prudential framework, the new rules set

---

[93] See Section 21.2.2(2).

[94] CRR new point (h) in Article 430(1).

[95] This Union body, without legal personality, was established by Regulation (EU) No 1092/2010 of the co-legislators of 24 November 2010 'on European Union macro-prudential oversight of the financial system and establishing a European Systemic Risk Board' (OJ L 331, 15.12.2010, 1–11), as in force.

[96] These criteria apply as amended by the CRR II.

[97] See Section 21.1.2.

[98] See Section 21.1.6.

[99] See Section 21.1.1.

out (*inter alia*) harmonised definitions of the ESG-related risks.[100] They also *first*, require credit institutions to include an appropriate set of time horizons (short-, medium- and long-term) of ESG risks in their strategies and processes for evaluating internal capital needs and adequate internal governance; *second*, impose on competent/supervisory authorities, on the one hand, specific requirements in the course of introducing a sustainability dimension in the prudential framework to ensure a better management of ESG risks, and, on the other hand, the requirement to include in the SREP the assessment of credit institutions' governance and risk management processes for dealing with ESG risks and their related exposures; and, *third*, confer upon competent authorities the power to require credit institutions to reduce the risks arising from their misalignment with relevant EU policy objectives and broader transition trends relating to ESG factors over the various time horizons.[101]

Overall, the new prudential banking regulatory/supervisory framework goes well beyond the imposition on credit institutions of (additional) disclosure requirements towards contributing to the green transition.[102] The gradual shift from capital markets to banking regulation already has significant structural implications for credit institutions, by inducing them to adjust their business models, governance strategies and risk management procedures (including in relation to their lending activities).

REFERENCES

Alexander, K. (2019), *Principles of Banking Regulation* (Cambridge, UK: Cambridge University Press).

Alexander, K. and Fisher, P. G. (2018), 'Banking regulation and sustainability', available at: https://ssrn.com/abstract=3299351.

Amesheva, I. (2022), 'The rise of ESG data: A tectonic transparency shift', in Bril, H., Kell, G., and Rasche, A. (eds.), *Sustainability, Technology, and Finance: Rethinking How Markets Integrate ESG* (London: Routledge), 251–272.

BCBS (Basel Committee on Banking Supervision) (2021), 'Climate-related risk drivers and their transmission channels', Bank for International Settlements, 14 April, available at: www.bis.org/bcbs/publ/d517.

BCBS (Basel Committee on Banking Supervision) (2022a), 'Principles for the effective management and supervision of climate-related financial risks', 15 June, available at: www.bis.org/bcbs/publ/d532.pdf.

BCBS (Basel Committee on Banking Supervision) (2022b), 'Frequently asked questions on climate-related financial risks', 8 December, available at: www.bis.org/bcbs/publ/d543.htm.

Betrosian, S. A. (2021), 'The impact of the EU Sustainable Finance framework on banking regulation', Master's thesis, Law School, National and Kapodistrian University of Athens, available at: https://pergamos.lib.uoa.gr/uoa/dl/object/2974963/file.pdf.

Binder, J.-H., Gortsos, C.V., Lackhoff, K. and Ohler, C. (eds.) (2022), *Brussels Commentary on the Banking Union* (Baden-Baden/Munich/Oxford: Nomos/C.H. Beck/Hart Publishing).

[100] See Section 21.2.2.
[101] See Section 21.2.3.
[102] See Section 21.2.4.

Bodansky, D. (2016), 'The legal character of the Paris Agreement', *Review of European, Comparative and International Environmental Law*, 25, 142–150.

Busch, D. (2024), 'Sustainability Disclosure in the Financial Sector', in Busch, D., Ferrarini, G. and Grünewald, S. (eds.), *Sustainable Finance in Europe: Corporate Governance, Financial Stability and Financial Markets* (Cham: Palgrave Macmillan), 563–602.

Busch, D., Avgouleas, E. and Ferrarini, G. (eds.) (2018), *Capital Markets Union in Europe* (Oxford: Oxford EU Financial Regulation Series, Oxford University Press).

Colaert, V. (2022), 'The Changing Nature of Financial Regulation: Sustainable Finance as a New EU Policy Objective', *Common Market Law Review*, 59, Kluwer Academic Publishers, The Netherlands, 1669–1710.

De Arriba-Sellier, N. (2022), 'Banking on Green: Sustainability in the Commission's Banking Reform', EU Law Live, Weekend edition, No 86, January 22, available at: https://eulawlive.com/weekend-edition/weekend-edition-no86.

De Oliveira Neves, R. (2022), 'The EU Taxonomy Regulation and Its Implications for Companies', in Câmara, P. and Morais, F. (eds), *The Palgrave Handbook of ESG and Corporate Governance* (Cham: Palgrave Macmillan), 249–265.

Ehlers, T. and Packer, F. (2017), 'Green bond finance and certification', *BIS Quarterly Review*, September 2017, available at: www.bis.org/publ/qtrpdf/r_qt1709h.pdf.

EBA (European Banking Authority) (2019), 'EBA Action Plan on Sustainable Finance', 6 December, available at: https://bit.ly/3TK2yEI.

EBA (European Banking Authority) (2021), 'On management and supervision of ESG risks for credit institutions and investment firms' (EBA/REP/2021/18), 26 June, available at: https://bit.ly/3vr9E7t.

EBA (European Banking Authority) (2022a), 'Final draft implementing technical standards on prudential disclosures on ESG risks in accordance with Article 449a CRR' (EBA/ITS/2022/01), 24 January, available at: https://bit.ly/3IN5CcW.

EBA (European Banking Authority) (2022b), 'Discussion paper on the role of environmental risks in the prudential framework', 2 May, available at: https://bit.ly/4aEsGXh.

ECB (European Central Bank) (2020), 'Guide on climate-related and environmental risks: Supervisory expectations relating to risk management and disclosure', 27 November, available at: https://bit.ly/3PkXtA6.

ECB (European Central Bank) (2021), 'Climate-related risk and financial stability', ECB/ESRB Project Team on climate risk monitoring, July, available at: https://bit.ly/4ammD9C.

ECB (European Central Bank) (2022), 'ECB takes further steps to incorporate climate change into its monetary policy operations', 4 July, available at: https://bit.ly/3TrGbCt.

European Commission Communication (2020), 'A Capital Markets Union for people and businesses – New action plan', 24 September (COM/2020/590 final).

European Court of Auditors (2020), *Capital Markets Union: Slow Start towards an Ambitious Goal' Special Report* 25/2020, 11 November, available at: www.eca.europa.eu/en/Pages/DocItem.aspx?did=57011.

Fatica, S., Panzica, R. and Rancan, M. (2019), 'The pricing of green bonds: Are financial institutions special?', JRC Working Papers in Economics and Finance, Issue 7, available at: https://bit.ly/3ToNURK.

Ferran, E. (2012), 'Understanding the New Institutional Architecture of EU Financial Market Supervision', in Wymeersch, E., Hopt, K. J. and Ferrarini, G. (eds.), *Financial Regulation and Supervision – A Post-Crisis Analysis* (Oxford: Oxford University Press), 111–158.

Flammer, C. (2021), 'Corporate Green Bonds', *Journal of Financial Economics*, 142(2), November, 499–516.

G20 Sustainable Finance Study Group (2018), 'Synthesis Report', July, available at: https://bit.ly/3PrTMbC.

Giráldez, J. and Fontana, S. (2022), 'Sustainability-linked bonds: The next frontier in sovereign financing', *Capital Markets Law Journal*, 17(1), 8–19.

Gortsos, C. V. (2020), *European Central Banking Law* (Cham: Palgrave Macmillan).

Gortsos, C. (2021), 'The Taxonomy Regulation: More important than just as an element of the Capital Markets Union', in Busch, D., Ferrarini, G. and Grünewald, S. (eds.), *Sustainable Finance in Europe: Corporate Governance, Financial Stability and Financial Markets* (Cham: Palgrave Macmillan), 351–395.

Gortsos, C. V. (2022a), 'The foundation of the European Capital Markets Union (CMU): From the 2015 to the 2020 CMU Action Plan and their implementation', available at: https://ssrn.com/abstract=4005259.

Gortsos, C. V. (2022b), 'The Evolution of European (EU) Banking Law under the Influence of (Public) International Banking Law: A Comprehensive Overview', e-book, 4th ed., available at: https://ssrn.com/abstract=3334493.

Gortsos, C. V. (2022c), 'The 2021 legislative 'banking package': Finalisation of the 'Basel III' reforms and supervisory enhancement in the EU, *EU LAW LIVE*', weekend edition No 94, 1–12, available at: https://eulawlive.com/weekend-edition/weekend-edition-n094.

Gortsos, C. V. (2023), *The European Banking Regulation Handbook, Volume I: Theory of Banking Regulation, International Standards, Evolution and Institutional Aspects of EU Banking Law* (Cham: Palgrave Macmillan).

Gortsos, C. V. and Kyriazis, D. (2022), 'Sustainable Finance: The EU's Legislative Trilogy and the Need for Global Convergence', available at: https://hub.uoa.gr/sustainable-finance.

Gortsos, C. V. and Kyriazis, D. (2024), 'The Taxonomy Regulation and its implementation', in Busch, D., Ferrarini, G. and Grünewald, S. (eds.), *Sustainable Finance in Europe: Corporate Governance, Financial Stability and Financial Markets* (Cham: Palgrave Macmillan), 505–561.

Grünewald, S. (2024), 'Climate change as a systemic risk in finance: Are macroprudential authorities up to the task?', in Busch, D., Ferrarini, G. and Grünewald, S. (eds.), *Sustainable Finance in Europe: Corporate Governance, Financial Stability and Financial Markets* (Cham: Palgrave Macmillan), 265–290.

Helleringer, G. (2021), 'EU vs. greenwashing: The birth pangs of transparency, comparability, cooperation and leadership', *Oxford Business Law Blog*, 5 July, available at: https://bit.ly/3VrMPLQ.

High-Level Forum on the Capital Markets Union (2020), *A New Vision for Europe's Capital Markets, Final Report*, June, available at: https://bit.ly/498BD9U.

Joosen, R. and Zhelyazkova, A. (2022), 'How do supranational regulators keep companies in line? An analysis of the enforcement styles of EU agencies', *Journal of Common Market Studies*, 60(4), 983–1000.

Konietschke, P., Ongena, S. R. G. and Ponte Marques, A. (2022), 'Stress tests and capital requirement disclosures: Do they impact banks' lending and risk-taking decisions?', Swiss Finance Institute Research Paper No. 60, July, available at: https://ssrn.com/abstract=4182633.

Kyriazis, D. (2022), *Sustainable Finance Law: Evolution and Legal Framework* (Athens: Nomiki Bibliothiki).

Lannoo, K. and Thomadakis, A. (2019), 'Rebranding Capital Markets Union: A market finance action plan', CEPS-ECMI Task Force Report, Centre for European Policy Studies, available at: https://bit.ly/493lkuQ.

Liang, H. and Renneboog, L. (2020), 'Corporate social responsibility and sustainable finance: A review of the literature', European Corporate Governance Institute – Finance Working Paper No. 701/2020, Part of the Oxford Research Encyclopedia of Economics and Finance, available at: https://ssrn.com/abstract=3698631.

Maragopoulos, N. (2023), 'Towards a European Green Bond Standard: A European Initiative to Promote Sustainable Finance', in Ramos Muñoz, D. and Smoleńska, Ag. (eds.), *Greening the Bond Market: A European Perspective* (Cham: Palgrave Macmillan), 21–50.

Miller, H. and Dikau, S. (2022), *Preventing a 'Climate Minsky Moment': Environmental Financial Risks and Prudential Exposure Limits: Exploring the Case Study of the Bank of England's Prudential Regime*, Policy Report, Grantham Research Institute on Climate Change and the Environment, London School of Economics and Political Science, March, available at: https://bit.ly/49XJDvR.

MOCOMILA (Committee on International Monetary Law) (2022), 'International Law Association Lisbon Conference', available at: https://bit.ly/493loL6.

Mollers, T. M. (2022), 'European green deal: Greenwashing and the forgotten good corporate citizen as an investor', *Columbia Journal of European Law*, 28, 203 et seq.

Motani, H. (2024), 'The European Green Deal, in Smits R. (ed.), *Sustainable Finance and Climate Change*, Elgar Financial Law and Practice (Cheltenham: Edward Elgar Publishing), 100–115.

Network for Greening the Financial System (2020), 'Guide for Supervisors – Integrating climate-related and environmental risks into prudential supervision', May, available at: https://bit.ly/4a4dUZe.

Pacces, A. M. (2021), 'Will the EU Taxonomy Regulation foster a sustainable corporate governance?', ECGI Law Working Paper No 611/2011, October, available at: https://bit.ly/4cgCOXA.

Pacces, A.M. (2024), 'The Role of EU Securities Regulation in Sustainable Corporate Governance', in Busch, D., Ferrarini, G. and Grünewald, S. (eds.), *Sustainable Finance in Europe: Corporate Governance, Financial Stability and Financial Markets* (Cham: Palgrave Macmillan), 147–183.

Payne, J. (2020), 'The institutional design of financial supervision and financial stability', in Amtenbrink, F. and Herrmann, C. (eds.), *Oxford Handbook on the EU Law of Economic and Monetary Union* (Oxford: Oxford University Press), 568–570.

Ramos Muñoz, D. and Smoleńska, Ag. (eds.) (2023), Greening the Bond Market: A European Perspective (Cham: Palgrave Macmillan).

Ramos Muñoz, D. and Smoleńska, Ag. (2023), The Governance of ESG Ratings and Benchmarks (Infomediaries) as Gatekeepers: Exit, Voice and Coercion, European Banking Institute Working Paper Series no. 149, available at: https://ssrn.com/abstract=4531520.

Reichlin, L., Adam, K., McKibbin, W. J. et al. (2021), 'The ECB strategy: The 2021 review and its future', CEPR Press, available at: https://bit.ly/3ILR6lC.

Reinders, H., Schoenmaker, D. M. Van Dijk (2020), 'A Finance Approach to Climate Stress Testing', 131 *Journal of International Money and Finance*, 1–19.

Siri, M. and Zhu, S. (2024), 'Integrating Sustainability in EU Corporate Governance Codes', in Busch, D., Ferrarini, G. and Grünewald, S. (eds.), *Sustainable Finance in Europe: Corporate Governance, Financial Stability and Financial Markets* (Cham: Palgrave Macmillan), 211–262.

Smits, R. (ed.) (2024), *Sustainable Finance and Climate Change* (Cheltenham: Edward Elgar Publishing).

Smits, R. (2024), 'The ECB's mandate in the face of climate change and biodiversity loss', in Smits R. (ed.), *Sustainable Finance and Climate Change*, (Cheltenham: Edward Elgar Publishing), 137–218.

Task Force on Climate-related Financial Disclosures (2007), 'Recommendations of the Task Force on Climate-related Financial Disclosures', 29 June, available at: https://bit.ly/43nSQuz.

United Nations (2016), 'The Paris Agreement: What is the Paris Agreement?', available at: https://bit.ly/3TK4AVm.

Winter, J. (2024), 'The role of the Board, societal responsibility and climate change', in Smits R. (ed.), *Sustainable Finance and Climate Change*, Elgar Financial Law and Practice, Chapter 4, 34-53 (Cheltenham: Edward Elgar Publishing).

Wutscher, C. (2024), 'The ECB's New Green Monetary Policy', in Busch, D., Ferrarini, G. and Grünewald, S. (eds.), *Sustainable Finance in Europe: Corporate Governance, Financial Stability and Financial Markets*, Second Edition, Chapter 11, 409–462 (Cham: Palgrave Macmillan).

Zetzsche, D.A., Bodellini, M. and Consiglio, R. (2021), *The EU Sustainable Finance Framework in Light of International Standards*, 13 December, available at: https://ssrn.com/abstract/3984511.

Zilioli, C. (2021), 'The new ECB Monetary Policy Strategy and the ECB's roadmap of climate change-related actions', *EU Law Live*, weekend edition no. 67, 2–6.

22

Sustainability and Fit and Proper Testing in the Boards of Banks, Insurers and Investment Companies

Iris Palm-Steyerberg

22.1 INTRODUCTION

We live in a world in transition. Sustainability, and especially climate change, urges us to fundamentally change our way of life. The financial sector, in particular, faces unprecedented challenges. Financial institutions are not, in themselves, high-emitting industries. The financial sector is, however, expected to play a key role in financing the transition to a more sustainable economy.[1] Financial institutions are important intermediaries between those who provide and those who need capital and are therefore well placed to channel private savings and investments towards sustainable activities. For now, the financial sector is to encourage sustainable investments mainly through transparency and disclosure requirements. EU regulation, like the Non-Financial Reporting Directive,[2] the Taxonomy Regulation[3] and the Sustainable Finance Disclosure Regulation,[4] increasingly forces financial institutions to consider the impact of their

---

[1] See EU Action Plan (March 8, 2018, COM(2018) 97 final); EU Green Deal (Communication from the Commission on the European Green Deal (COM/2019/640 final) and EU Sustainable Finance Strategy (EC, Strategy for Financing the Transition to a Sustainable Economy, COM (2021) 390 final). The European Commission also states in its explanatory memorandum to the proposal to amend the (revised) CRD IV, CRD VI, that in order to finance the transition to a sustainable economy bank financial intermediation will play a crucial role, see Proposal for a Directive of the European Parliament and of the Council amending Directive 2013/36/EU as regards supervisory powers, sanctions, third-country branches and environmental, social and governance risks, and amending Directive 2014/59/EU, 27 October 2021, COM (2021) 663 final 2021/0341 (COD).

[2] Directive 2014/95/EU of the European Parliament and of the Council of 22 October 2014 amending Directive 2013/34/EU as regards disclosure of non-financial and diversity information by certain large undertakings and groups (NFRD).

[3] Regulation (EU) 2020/852 of the European Parliament and of the Council of 18 June 2020 on the establishment of a framework to facilitate sustainable investment, and amending Regulation (EU) 2019/2088 (Taxonomy Regulation).

[4] Regulation (EU) 2019/2088 of the European Parliament and of the Council of 27 November 2019 on sustainability-related disclosures in the financial services sector (SFDR). The SFDR requires market participants and advisers to publicly disclose how they integrate sustainability risks into their advice and decisions about investment and insurance.

investments on sustainability factors and report on it.[5] The proposed Corporate Sustainability Due Diligence Directive[6] and the Corporate Sustainability Reporting Directive[7] go even further by creating a substantive corporate duty on companies and certain (large) financial institutions to prevent and end external harm resulting from adverse human rights and environmental impacts. This duty extends not only to the company's own operations and its subsidiaries, but also to the whole value chain. This includes companies with whom the financial institution has an established business relationship, providing financing, insurance or reinsurance.

At the same time, financial institutions face a whole new set of sustainability risks.[8] These risks, and especially risks from climate change and environmental degradation, may endanger the financial soundness, profitability and possibly even the viability of the institution. It is urgent that financial institutions become more resilient to these risks.[9] The European Central Bank (ECB) recently warned that while physical and transition risks have a material impact on most institutions, the management of these risks still show significant weaknesses.[10]

So financial institutions face huge challenges regarding sustainability, having to promote sustainable activities on the one hand and managing their own sustainability risks on the other (double materiality). Financial institutions, however, are mere abstract concepts, and as such they do not make sustainable decisions or engage in sustainable behaviour without direction from the individuals who manage these institutions. Members of management body, in particular, have a decisive influence on the course of the institution as they are responsible for all major decision-making processes. Since the active involvement of the financial sector is considered necessary for the success of the sustainability transition, an important responsibility rests on their shoulders. As put forward by Frank Elderson, a member of the Executive Board of the ECB and Vice-Chair of the Supervisory Board of the ECB:

---

[5] For an overview of disclosure requirements applicable to banks, see Loizzo and Schimperna 2022.

[6] Proposal for a Directive of the European Parliament and of the Council on Corporate Sustainability Due Diligence and amending Directive (EU) 2019/1937, Brussels, 23 February 2022, COM(2022), 71 final (CSDDD). The Council's negotiating position reduced the applicability of the CSDDD to financial institutions to a member state option, see Permanent Representatives Committee, *Proposal for a Directive of the European Parliament and of the Council on Corporate Sustainability Due Diligence and amending Directive (EU) 2019/1937 – General Approach*, 2022/0051 (COD), 6533/22, 30 November 2022. The CSDDD contains several exceptions for financial institutions.

[7] Directive (EU) 2022/2464 of the European Parliament and of the Council of 14 December 2022 amending Regulation (EU) No 537/2014, Directive 2004/109/EC, Directive 2006/43/EC and Directive 2013/34/EU, as regards corporate sustainability reporting (CSRD).

[8] 'Sustainability risk' means an environmental, social or governance event or condition that, if it occurs, could cause an actual or a potential material negative impact on the value of the investment (Art. 2 (22) SFDR).

[9] See, for example, European Commission 2021.

[10] ECB 2022a.

Management bodies play a key role in steering the strategic course of a bank and setting in on the path towards sustainable long-term objectives.[11]

It is up to the members of the management body to integrate both material sustainability impacts and sustainability risks in their decision-making processes. This may require a whole new set of qualifications, knowledge, skills, mindset and expertise.

In EU regulation, fit and proper testing is the designated (supervisory) tool to ensure that members of the management body are up to their task, not only at the time of appointment but throughout their directorship. Members of the management body should be fit, meaning that they should possess the appropriate knowledge, skills and expertise to adequately fulfill their function, and proper, meaning that they should be of good repute. The central question in this chapter is whether and to what extent sustainability can be integrated into fit and proper testing. This is a relevant question because if the answer is yes, fit and proper testing could, and perhaps should, be used as a (supervisory) tool to ensure the resilience of the financial sector to sustainability risks and to fulfill its central role in stimulating the transition to a sustainable economy.

To answer this central question, the chapter first analyses the impact of sustainability on the roles and responsibilities of boards and individual boardroom members in financial institutions, in particular in banks, insurers and investment companies. The chapter then discusses the fit and proper test. It is examined how sustainability translates into specific fit and proper requirements, such as knowledge, skills and expertise, conflicts of interest and good reputation and integrity. The distinction between the collective suitability and individual suitability is explored, including whether each individual member of the board should possess a certain, minimum level of expertise with regard to ESG. Reference is made to the supervisory practices in The Netherlands, as the Dutch supervisory authorities like the Dutch Central Bank are lead supervisors in integrating ESG into fit and proper assessments. The chapter concludes with some final remarks on legal certainty and the European level playing field.

22.2 SCOPE AND DEFINITIONS

Sustainability, in this chapter, is defined as encompassing all three ESG factors: environmental, social and governance aspects. The focus, however, is on environmental aspects and especially on climate change. This is not to say that social or governance aspects are not important. But in terms of significance and impact on the world economy and on financial institutions, environmental developments, and especially climate change, seem to be the most specific and prominent risks financial institutions are facing today. The terms 'sustainability' and 'ESG' will be used interchangeably.

---

[11] Elderson 2022.

The terms 'sustainability risks' and 'sustainability factors' are used as defined in the Sustainable Finance Disclosure Regulation (SFDR).[12] Sustainability risks refer to an environmental, social or governance event or condition that, if it occurs, could cause an actual or a potential material negative impact on the value of the investment. Sustainability factors refer to environmental, social and employee matters, respect for human rights, anti-corruption and anti-bribery matters.

This chapter focusses on three types of financial institutions: banks, investment firms and (re)insurance companies. The term 'institutions' is used to indicate all three types of institutions. (Re)insurance companies will, more briefly, be referred to as 'insurance companies' or 'insurers'.

The analysis and conclusions of this chapter may also apply to the members of the management body of other types of financial institutions, such as UCITS and AIF fund managers and pension funds, which also play an important role in realizing ESG goals and ambitions. The members of the management body in these institutions are subject to a similar fit and proper test.[13]

In EU banking and investment firm regulation, the term 'management body' is used to describe both the executive board and the supervisory board, or, in a one-tier board structure, both the executive and non-executive members of the board. Insurance-related regulation usually speaks of the administrative, management or supervisory body (AMSB). For consistency, the term 'members of the management body' or 'board' is used to refer to both members of the management body in banks and investment firms as well as to members of the AMSB in insurance companies.

In this chapter, the terms 'fit and proper' and 'suitability' are used as synonyms. It is noted that fit and proper tests do not only apply to members of the board but also to key function holders, like the holders of internal control functions. On the heads of Audit, Compliance, and especially Risk, rests the important task of integrating ESG-related aspects into their work and function. This chapter, however, focusses on the fit and proper test of members of the management body as it is ultimately their responsibility to ensure the proper functioning of all internal control functions and all key personnel.

22.3 ESG AND THE ROLES AND RESPONSIBILITIES OF THE MANAGEMENT BODY

According to EU financial legislation, the management body bears the ultimate and overall responsibility for the institution. The role of the management body in its management function (executive board) is to effectively manage and direct the institution. The role of the management body in its supervisory function (supervisory board or the non-executive members in the management body in a one-tier board

---

[12] Art. 2(22) and (24) SFDR.
[13] Palm-Steyerberg 2021, 217–233.

structure) is to oversee and challenge the management function and provide appropriate advice.[14]

Core responsibilities of the management body include: (i) responsibility for the overall business strategy; (ii) responsibility for the institution's risk strategy, including the risk appetite of the institution and the risk management framework; and (iii) responsibility for the internal governance arrangement and internal control framework.[15]

The roles and responsibilities of the management body in banks and investment firms are explained in detail in ESA Guidelines, in particular the EBA Guidelines on Internal Governance and the EBA and ESMA Guidelines on Suitability.[16] Following these guidelines, the management body's responsibilities also include the implementation of a risk culture and a corporate culture and values that foster responsible and ethical behaviour, including a code of conduct or similar instrument. With respect to insurance companies, the rules are less detailed. However, depending on the circumstances, similar roles and tasks of the AMSB may follow from the more generic requirement that the AMSB should effectively manage and oversee the undertaking in a professional manner.[17]

It follows from the roles and responsibilities described that the management body should take the lead and bears the overall responsibility in ensuring that sustainability risks, as well as the impact of the institution on sustainability factors, are adequately managed.

Most attention so far has been placed on the management of sustainability risks. The EU prudential framework has been amended, specifying that sustainability risks should be included in the risk framework in investment firms, banks and insurers. See the amended MiFID II Delegated Regulation,[18] the amended Solvency II Delegated Regulation, the amendments to the EBA Guidelines on

---

[14] EBA 2021a, EBA 2021b and EBA/ESMA 2021. For insurers, the different roles within the AMSB are not further explained or clarified in EU supervisory legislation. However, a similar differentiation between the roles and responsibilities of the management body in its management and supervisory function may follow from national law in EU Member States.

[15] For banks, this follows from Article 88(1) CRD IV as further specified by the EBA 2021a. For investment firms, these responsibilities are laid down in Article 9, 16 and 25 Directive 2014/65/EU of the European Parliament and of the Council of 15 May 2014 on markets in financial instruments and amending Directive 2002/92/EC and Directive 2011/61/EU (MiFID II), Article 26 and 28 IFD and the EBA 2021b, paras. 18, 22 and 25. For insurance companies, this follows (in slightly different wording) from Article 40 Solvency II, Article 258 (1) (c) Delegated Regulation (EU) 2015/35 and the EIOPA 2014, para. 1.50. See also EIOPA 2019a, para. 84.

[16] EBA and ESMA Guidelines on Suitability (EBA/ESMA 2021).

[17] See Article 258 (1) (c) Delegated Regulation (EU) 2015/35.

[18] Delegated Regulation (EU) 2021/1253 of 21 April 2021 amending Delegated Regulation (EU) 2017/565 as regards the integration of sustainability factors, risks and preferences into certain organizational requirements and operating conditions for investment firms, in particular Article 23(1). See also EBA 2021b, paras. 14 and 26, requiring that investment firms should take into account environmental, social and governance (ESG) risk factors within their risk management framework and the EBA/ESMA 2022, stating that ESG risk should also be part of the ICAAP/SREP process. See also Colaert 2021.

Internal Governance under CRD VI[19] and the EBA Guidelines for the SREP process and supervisory stress testing under CRD IV.[20] The proposed amendments of Solvency II[21] and CRD IV[22] also request insurance companies and banks to explicitly integrate sustainability risks into their risk management process. This means that the responsibilities of the management body with respect to risk management also include sustainability risks.[23]

EU regulation is less specific with regard to the impact of financial institutions on sustainability factors and the responsibility of the management body in this respect.[24] However, institutions that are obliged to disclose principal adverse impacts on sustainability factors in accordance with the SFDR, and large banks, insurers and listed companies that need to report on the institution's impact on environmental, social and employee matters in accordance with the NFRD[25] as well as provide information on how and to what extent the institution's activities are associated with economic activities that qualify as environmentally sustainable according to the Taxonomy Regulation,[26] should adapt their processes, systems and internal controls with respect to those disclosures.[27] This is, again, the responsibility of the management body. Since breaches of the rules regarding transparency and disclosure may lead to supervisory measures and reputational risks, the impact on sustainability factors should also be a part of the risk management system.

In addition, the amended Solvency II Delegated Regulation requires insurers to take into account the long-term impact of the investment strategy on sustainability factors. Where relevant, that strategy and those decisions shall reflect the sustainability preferences of its customers, taken into account in the product approval process referred to in Article 4 of Commission Delegated Regulation (EU) 2017/2358.[28] This may require the management body to integrate new perspectives into their investment policy.

---

[19] EBA 2021a. See in particular paras. 20 and 152. The guidelines apply from 31 December 2021.
[20] EBA 2022, para. 3 and para. 95(g).
[21] Proposal for a Directive of the European Parliament and or the Council amending Directive 2009/138/EC as regards proportionality, quality of supervision, reporting, long-term guarantee measures, macro-prudential tools, sustainability risks, group and cross-border supervision, Brussels, 22 September 2021, COM(2021) 581 final, 2021/0295 (COD), in particular Article 45a. Insurers classified as low-risk profile undertakings are exempted from scenario analyses.
[22] Proposal for a Directive of the European Parliament and of the Council amending Directive 2013/36/EU as regards supervisory powers, sanctions, third-country branches, and environmental, social and governance risks, and amending Directive 2014/59/EU, Brussels, 27 October 2021, COM(2021) 663 final 2021/0341 (COD), in particular Article 73, 74, 76 and 87a.
[23] See also ECB 2020, Expectation 3, ECB 2021, 41/42 and ECB 2022b.
[24] This may change in the future, in particular after adoption and implementation of the CRD VI proposal.
[25] Art.19a and 29a NFRD.
[26] Art. 8 Taxonomy Regulation.
[27] See also the amended Delegated Solvency II Regulation.
[28] Art. 275a (2) Delegated Solvency II Regulation. See also van den Hurk, Chapter 23 in this volume.

The CRD VI proposal contains even more far-reaching provisions, requiring banks, among other things, to align their business models with European sustainable economy objectives.[29] The management body will be required to develop specific plans to address risks arising from ESG factors, including those arising from transition and alignment with European sustainability goals, including, in particular, the European goal of achieving climate neutrality by 2050.[30] At the time of writing, the trilogues on the CRD VI proposal (and the CRR3 proposal, which includes a requirement for banks to report their exposure to ESG risks to competent authorities and to disclose their ESG risks) are ongoing.

So, on a more fundamental level the management body in insurers, banks, very large institutions or institutions active in high (emitting) impact sectors[31] may need to radically shift from a focus on shareholder value, or on adjusted shareholder value incorporating sustainability risks, to sustainable finance that integrates both financial values and social and environmental values or even puts social and environmental values first.[32] This requires a fundamental shift in thinking, and it is up to the management body to take the lead in this.

Against this backdrop, the following tasks can be identified as part of the core responsibilities of the management body.

22.3.1 *Identifying Relevant ESG-Related Risks and Performing an Impact Assessment*

First of all, the management body will have to set, approve and oversee effective processes to identify ESG risks that the institutions are or might be exposed to, as well as the impact of the institution on ESG factors. The materiality of those risks and impacts need to be assessed. For material climate-related risks, which usually cannot be determined (solely) on the basis of historical data, it may be necessary to run climate change scenarios and perform stress tests.[33] The selection and specification of the scenarios is the ultimate responsibility of the management body. The assessment of ESG-related risks should also be integrated in the ICAAP/

---

[29] See also Bierman 2019 and Van der Eerden 2022.

[30] See the amended – and made more stringent by the European Parliament – Arts. 87a and 76(2) CRD VI proposal. See also the proposals to amend Arts. 73, 74 and 76 (other paragraphs). The European Parliament recently made a number of amendments to the CRD VI proposal, including enhancements on ESG. See Report of the Committee on Economic and Monetary Affairs, February 10, 2023, A9-0029/2023.

[31] This CSDDD-proposal applies to (a) a company with more than 500 employees on average and a net worldwide turnover of more than EUR 150 million and (b) a company with more than 250 employees on average and a net worldwide turnover of more than EUR 40 million, provided that at least 50% of this net turnover was generated in high impact sectors like the manufacture of textile, agriculture, forestry, fisheries and the extraction of gas and coal. See Art. 3 of the proposed directive.

[32] See also Schoenmaker 2020, 463–469.

[33] See EIOPA 2022, ECB 2020 and the proposed amendments of Solvency II and CRD IV.

SREP and ORSA processes,[34] for which the management body bears the ultimate responsibility.

22.3.2 *Adapting the Institution's Business Model and Strategy, If Needed*

Depending on the outcome of the impact assessment, (substantial) changes in the business model, profile, goals and strategy may be required. Such adjustments are the role of the management body par excellence. The management body needs to identify existing gaps between the business model and strategy of the institution and the transition trends towards a sustainable economy, and ensure alignment between the two.[35]

22.3.3 *Ensure that Adequate Risk Mitigation Measures Are Put into Place*

In case of material ESG risks, the management body should ensure that those risks are adequately controlled and managed.[36] Risk mitigation strategies may include appropriate pricing of climate risks (e.g., higher premiums for insurance of property in areas vulnerable to flooding-risks), setting limits on exposure to carbon-intensive economics, holding more capital for (high) climate risk positions and limiting dividend payments to create financial buffers against future ESG-related risks. These are no easy decisions to make. The decision to stop offering insurance to policyholders in certain areas or significantly increase premiums, for example, will lead to reductions in affordability or availability of insurance cover. This may be an undesirable result from a socio-economic perspective and may have a negative reputational impact on the insurance sector. Also, shareholders may object to management decisions to increase capital buffers and/or limit dividend payments. It is the task of the management body to consider these different viewpoints, develop a view on them and take the necessary decisions.

Ensure the integration of ESG into existing internal policies and practices. Depending on the materiality of ESG risks and impacts, internal policies and practices like the policies for investment, credit, internal capital allocation and remuneration and the product approval process, will probably have to be adapted. The management body has a crucial role in making sure that these new policies and

---

[34] See EBA 2022 and EBA/ESMA 2022. See also the proposed new Art. 73 CRD VI.

[35] This follows from the core responsibilities of the management body, described in Section 22.1. See also, explicitly, the EBA 2021c, para. 204, ECB 2020, Expectation 3 and the proposed amendment of CRD IV. Article 76 (b) CRD IV (new) requires the management body to develop specific plans and quantifiable targets to monitor and address such existing gaps. The plans and targets should address the risks arising in the short, medium and long-term from the misalignment of the business model and strategy of the institutions, with the relevant Union policy objectives or broader transition trends towards a sustainable economy in relation to environmental, social and governance factors.

[36] This follows from the core responsibilities of the management body, described in Section 22.1. See also, explicitly, EIOPA 2022, 36.

practices are developed, adopted and implemented. EIOPA, for instance, underlines that the management body (AMSB) has a crucial role in realizing that sustainability risks are properly integrated in the investment decision process in insurance companies.[37] For banks, adapting existing credit policies may be a key task for the management body. Also, the remuneration policies may have to be adapted, to ensure that these policies are aligned with the institution's long-term interests, business strategy and objectives.[38]

Embed clear roles and responsibilities regarding ESG into the governance structures of the institution. It is the task of the management body to monitor and periodically assess the effectiveness of the institution's governance arrangements and to take appropriate steps to address any deficiencies.[39] This means, *inter alia*, that the management body is responsible for the integration of ESG risks and impacts in governance structures, establishing clear working procedures and responsibilities for business lines, internal control functions, the relevant committee(s) and the management body itself. Tasks and responsibilities related to ESG risks and impacts in the decision-making process should be clearly allocated and arrangements for the effective management of ESG risks and impacts should be put into place.[40]

Provide adequate internal control mechanisms, including the integration of ESG into internal control functions. The management body should manage and oversee the implementation of adequate internal control mechanisms, including the integration of ESG into internal control functions (Risk, Audit, Actuarial and Compliance functions). The management body should ensure that these control functions have a sufficient knowledge and understanding of sustainability-related issues, to ensure the proper functioning of these functions and to ensure compliance with new ESG-related legislation.[41] The measurement of sustainability risks is an evolving science and is still very challenging. Professional advisers and/or the recruitment of dedicated experts may well be needed.

Enhance knowledge and expertise regarding ESG by education and training of all relevant personnel, including the management body itself. Given the relative novelty of ESG risks and impacts, the management body should ensure that staff are adequately trained. This encompasses their own education.[42] Members of the management body should develop their experience and understanding with regard to ESG and, to this end, integrate ESG factors and ESG risks in the induction and training policies and programmes.

---

[37] EIOPA 2019a.
[38] See the amended Solvency II Delegated Regulation and the EBA 2021c.
[39] See Section 22.1.
[40] See, explicitly, EBA 2021c. For further reading on sustainable corporate governance, please see Pacces 2021.
[41] See, explicitly, EBA 2021c.
[42] See EBA 2021c, paras. 216 and 345, and EIOPA 2019a, paras. 90–91.

Foster an appropriate risk and compliance culture. For all the new policies and strategies to be effective, employees in all layers of the organization have to show commitment to the new rules, goals and ambitions, and good intentions must be put into practice. Little awareness in the organization of ESG-related risks and impacts, and/or an underestimation of these risks and impacts can lead to resistance against the making and following of new rules and policies. While there seems to be a growing awareness in financial institutions regarding the need to take account of sustainability risks, the need to consider the impact of the institution on sustainability factors does not seem to be widely accepted and may require a profound change in mindset and mentality within the management body and in all personnel. Also, even with respect to sustainability risks, too many institutions still follow a passive, wait-and-see approach.[43]

Depending on the materiality of the sustainability risks and impact on the institution, a substantial change in corporate culture, values and behaviour may be necessary. The management body should be at the head of this, taking appropriate measures to promote ESG awareness throughout the institution, including knowledge of the institutions' ESG strategic objectives and corporate values. Clear communication from the management body, the *tone from the top* and members of the management body giving the right example are also essential for the success of a (profound) shift in culture and focus.[44]

Periodically repeat ESG impact assessment and periodically review policies and compliance framework. The management body should periodically review the strategies and policies with regard to sustainability risks and impacts, and ensure that ESG risks are at all times adequately managed and mitigated.[45]

Ensure adequate reporting, disclosure and communications with supervisors. As mentioned before, stricter rules have been imposed on financial institutions regarding transparency and disclosure on ESG-related risks and ESG aspects, and more rules are in the making. Here lies an important role for the management body. The management body should manage and oversee the process of disclosure and ensure proper communications with external stakeholders and competent authorities.[46]

22.4 INTEGRATION OF ESG ASPECTS INTO THE FIT AND PROPER TEST

According to EU regulation, members of the management body in financial institutions have to be fit and proper (suitable). The purpose of the fit and proper test is to ensure that these persons, who have a decisive influence on the direction of

---

[43] ECB 2022a.
[44] For banks and investment firms, the role of the management board with regard to corporate culture is specified in EBA 2021a, Sections 9 and 10 and EBA 2021b. See also EBA 2021c, para. 216.
[45] See the proposed amendment of Article 76(1) CRD IV and ECB 2020, Expectation 3.
[46] See, for banks, Art. 88 1 (c) CRD IV and the 2021a, CRD IV, para. 27.

the company, will duly perform their duties in the interests of the financial sound-ness and integrity of the institution, the interests of clients and the safeguarding of the public trust in the financial system. While financial institutions are primarily responsible for making sure that the members of the management body are fit and proper, the suitability of these members is also assessed by supervisory authorities like the European Central Bank and national competent authorities like, in The Netherlands, the Dutch Central Bank.

Members of the management body in banks and investment companies must meet the following five fit and proper criteria:[47]

(1) *individual expertise/ individual fitness*; individual expertise means that each individual member of the management body has to possess the necessary qualifications, competency, skills and professional experience to perform the tasks assigned;

(2) *collective suitability/collective fitness*, meaning that all necessary experience, skills and expertise are present in the management body as a collective;

(3) *sufficient time commitment*, meaning that every member of the management body should possess sufficient time to adequately perform his or her function;

(4) *independence of mind and conflicts of interest*, meaning the ability to form one's own objective and independent judgement; conflicts of interest may prevent this ability, and should be mitigated; and

(5) *good repute/ properness*, meaning having a good reputation, taking into account criminal, financial, supervisory, tax and administrative law anteced-ents, as well as past personal and business conduct.

Members of the AMSB in insurance and reinsurance undertakings are bound to sim-ilar criteria.[48] The requirement to have sufficient time to fulfill one's duties and the criterium of independence of mind (criteria 3 and 4), are not explicitly mentioned in Solvency II or other insurer-related EU rules or guidelines. However, these require-ments can be considered to follow implicitly from the mandate of the AMSB to effec-tively manage and oversee the undertaking in a professional manner.

Insofar as EU regulators and supervisory authorities explicitly mention ESG aspects in relation to the fit and proper test, ESG is only connected to the first two criteria: individual expertise and collective suitability (the rules of fitness). In particular, the recently amended EBA and ESMA Guidelines on Suitability and the updated ECB Guide to fit and proper assessments specify that ESG aspects should be part of both the collective and individual suitability test of members of the management body in banks and investment firms. As for insurers, the rules of

---

[47] Art. 91 CRD IV, Art. 9 MiFID II and EBA/ESMA 2021. For investment firms, the requirement to have independence of mind is not explicitly laid down in MiFID II regulation but follows from the EBA/ESMA 2021, Chapters 9.1 and 9.2. and ECB 2021.

[48] Art. 42(1) Solvency II, Article 258(1)(c) and (d) and Art. 273(2), (3) and (4) Delegated Regulation (EU) 2015/35 and EIOPA 2014, para. 1.43.

fitness in the Solvency II Delegated Regulation do not explicitly refer to ESG topics. However, EIOPA considers that AMSB members are already required to possess the necessary qualifications, competency, skills and professional experience in the relevant areas of the business in order to effectively manage and oversee the undertaking in a professional manner. A further explicit reference to sustainability risks is therefore not deemed necessary.[49]

Sustainability risks and factors may, however, not only be relevant for the rules of fitness but for all five fit and proper criteria.[50]

22.5 INTEGRATING ESG INTO THE CRITERION OF COLLECTIVE SUITABILITY

The management body needs to collectively possess the necessary knowledge, skills and expertise to live up to the tasks and responsibilities described in Section 22.3.[51] 'Collective suitability' means that all areas of knowledge and expertise required for the institution's business activities should be covered by the board as a whole, or, in a two-tier board structure, in the board of directors as well as in the board of supervisors.

A suitability matrix can be used to provide an overview of the knowledge and experience present in the members of the collective. In this matrix, members of the management body are scored on knowledge and experience with regard to the different areas of expertise. Relevant areas of expertise are, for example, financial markets, business strategy and business model, system of governance, financial analysis and regulatory framework and requirements.[52] In The Netherlands, the Dutch Central Bank has added sustainability to the matrix. On EU level, the ECB has explicated that adequate knowledge of climate-related and environmental risks is an essential requirement to conclude that a board has a sufficient degree of collective suitability.[53]

Each (new) member of the management body will be assessed on his or her contribution, in terms of knowledge, skills and experience, to the collective suitability regarding ESG. However, tasks and responsibilities may be divided within the management body, as it cannot be expected that each individual member of the board is accomplished in all the necessary fields of expertise.[54] This means that it is possible to assign the primary responsibility for sustainability to a dedicated ESG

---

49 EIOPA 2019b, paras. 84–92 and EIOPA 2019a, paras. 88–92.

50 See also Palm-Steyerberg 2019, 7–10.

51 See specifically EBA/ESMA 2021, para. 70 and the proposed new Article 91(4) CRD IV requiring the management body to possess collective knowledge, skills and experience to be able to adequately understand the institution's activities, as well as the associated risks it is exposed to, in the short, medium and long term, taking into account the ESG factors.

52 See 1.43 EIOPA 2014 and EBA/ESMA 2021.

53 ECB 2021, 41/41.

54 See also Articles 68 and 70 EBA/ESMA 2021.

director (like a Chief Sustainable Risk Officer) and/or a Sustainability Committee composed of non-executive directors. This may be helpful, as expertise regarding ESG, including knowledge of relevant technological developments and climate-related regulations, can be bundled together in a committee and a dedicated director or committee can keep oversight on all sustainability developments within the institution. However, this does not remove the need to integrate sustainability into all relevant parts of the organization, nor does it relieve the other board members of their responsibilities.

The required collective knowledge, skills and experience will be assessed taking into account the principle of proportionality. Relevant factors are the materiality of the ESG risks the institution faces as well as if and to what extent the institution is bound to regulation and/or vulnerable to social pressure regarding its impact on ESG factors (by, for example, financing mainly carbon-intensive industries). The process of identifying relevant ESG-related risks and assessing the impact of those risk on the institution, should, however, be performed by all institutions.[55] The knowledge and expertise to perform such an impact assessment, or at least to adequately interpret the results of this assessment, should be present in the management body.

In addition, different requirements apply to members of the management body in its management (executive) function and members of the management body in its supervisory (non-executive) function. The management body in its management function should appropriately direct the institution, taking into account the relevant ESG risks and its ESG impacts. The management body in its supervisory function should adequately oversee and monitor management decision-making relating to ESG.[56] Thus, ESG is not the sole responsibility of the executive board. On the contrary, an adequate understanding of ESG, and in particular climate-related and environmental risks, by the management body in its supervisory function is deemed necessary for effective oversight.[57]

22.6 INTEGRATING ESG INTO THE CRITERION OF INDIVIDUAL EXPERTISE

Each member of the management body should possess sufficient knowledge, skills and experience to perform one's duties. This entails skills, knowledge and experience relating to ESG risks and the impact of the institution on ESG factors. The EBA/ESMA Guidelines on suitability state that assessing the theoretical and practical experience of the individual appointee relating to risk management is part of the fit and proper test, which should explicitly include environmental, governance and

---

[55] See, for example, EIOPA 2019a (Insurance and reinsurance undertakings, irrespective of their particular investment strategy and of their nature (life or non-life), are inevitably exposed to sustainability risks and they should, at least, assess the materiality of those risks).

[56] See, with respect to ESG risks, the EBA 2021c, 345

[57] See, for instance, ECB 2021, 41/42 and EBA 2021c, para. 206.

social risks and risk factors.[58] The ECB Fit and Proper Guide adds that ESG topics can also be discussed in ECB interviews performed as part of the fit and proper test. This interview should cover, *inter alia*, the appointee's views on the main risks and challenges faced by the credit institution and their proposed and current role in managing such issues, and the appointee's experience with and knowledge of climate-related and environmental risks.[59]

The Dutch Central Bank has started to integrate ESG into fit and proper assessments in 2021. This means that climate-related and environmental risks will feature more prominently in the assessment interviews. For example, a question may be asked about the candidate's knowledge in the area of climate-related and environmental risks, relevant legislation and its impact on the institution.

The Dutch Central Bank also published the following list of expectations for proposed board members in banks, insurance companies and pension funds with respect to climate-related and environmental risks:

(1) be able to define these risks;
(2) be aware of relevant laws and regulations and of reporting obligations;
(3) be able to identify, monitor and manage them;
(4) know who is responsible for managing them in the institution;
(5) understand their impact within the institution's specific context, and to be able to cite examples;
(6) be able to formulate a strategy and policies to tackle them;
(7) take responsibility for ensuring their adequate management;
(8) in the case of supervisory board members: to monitor their adequate management; and
(9) have sufficient relevant competencies, such as a helicopter view, leadership, autonomy, sensitivity to their environment, strategic guidance and sense of responsibility.[60]

The Dutch Central Bank not only focusses on knowledge but also, in line with the EBA and ESMA Guidelines on Suitability, on skills and competencies. Sustainability and the role of the financial sector in reorienting private capital to more sustainable investments requires a comprehensive shift in perspective in the financial sector. To bring about such a fundamental change process in the organization, it is not enough for the management body to possess the necessary knowledge and experience. Skills

---

[58] EBA/ESMA 2021, para. 63 (When assessing the knowledge, skills and experience of a member of the management body, consideration should be given to theoretical and practical experience relating to: [...] d. risk management (identifying, assessing, monitoring, controlling and mitigating the main types of risk of an institution including environmental, governance and social risks and risk factors).

[59] ECB 2021, para. 94 and p. 66.

[60] See www.dnb.nl under the heading 'Climate-related risks are now a part of fit and proper assessments'.

and competences, necessary to lead the change, may well be the most crucial elements for success.

Obviously, it is not an easy task to assess whether members of the management body possess competences like 'strategic guidance' or 'sense of responsibility'. Although some supervisors, like the Dutch Central Bank, use specialized behavioural experts and psychologists to conduct these assessments, it remains difficult to predict whether candidates will actually be able to put these skills into practice. Assessing these aspects remains largely a matter of professional judgement and a certain amount of subjectivity can hardly be avoided. Still, asking about these competences during the fit and proper interview can emphasize the importance of these skills and raise awareness.

The actual assessment and the specific experience, knowledge and skills that are needed will differ, taking into account – again – the principle of proportionality. The requirements will be tailored to the specific institution and the candidate's position. Different expertise may be required of the CEO, CRO, Chair and members of a Sustainability Committee. A director responsible for risk management is expected to have more and deeper knowledge, skills and expertise regarding ESG than a director with a more general portfolio. Also, the necessary expertise will differ depending on the role (executive or non-executive member of the management body).[61]

An interesting question is the relationship between individual expertise and collective suitability. Should each individual member of the management body possess a certain minimum expertise regarding ESG, even when sufficient if ESG expertise is already present in the management body as a collective?

Noticeably, the CRD VI proposal adds ESG only to the criterion of collective suitability (see the proposed changes of Art. 91 CRD) and not, explicitly, to the criterion of individual expertise. However, it follows from existing fit and proper rules and regulation that *all* members of the management body should have an up-to-date understanding of the business of the institution and its main risks. This includes an appropriate understanding of those areas for which an individual member is not directly responsible but is collectively accountable, together with the other members of the management body. Also, collective suitability cannot compensate for a lack of basic individual expertise (as was confirmed by a Dutch District Court).[62] Without such basic knowledge and understanding, an individual member of the management body is not supposed to be able to adequately fulfill his or her role to manage and oversee the financial institution at hand.

---

[61] For investment firms, applying the fit and proper test to non-executive board members is a Member State option. For (re)insurance companies it is required that non-executive members in a one-tier board structure are fit and proper. However, applying the fit and proper test to non-executive members in a two-tier board structure is a Member State option. See Arts. 1(43), 258(1)(d) and 273(3) Delegated Regulation 2015/35 and EIOPA 2014.

[62] District Court of Rotterdam, 22 July 2019, ECLI:NL:RBROT:2019:6755.

So, even if the financial institution has a highly skilled ESG expert on the board, this does not mean that other board members can stay completely off the subject. While it is not necessary that each and every member of the management body possesses in depth knowledge of ESG-related risks and impacts, *all* members of the management body may be expected to possess a basic understanding of the overall activity, financial and risk situation of the institution, including ESG risks and impacts.

22.7 INTEGRATING ESG INTO THE CRITERION OF SUFFICIENT TIME

Members of the management body in banks and investment firms are explicitly required to be able to devote sufficient time to perform one's function. This is explicated in CRD IV, the EBA/ESMA Guidelines on suitability and the ECB Guide on fit and proper assessments. It may be assumed that members of the AMSB in insurance companies must also meet this criterion, since having sufficient time can be considered an indispensable condition for being able to properly perform one's duties.

What exactly is meant by 'sufficient time' will vary from case to case. The greater the impact of ESG risks on the institution and the greater the challenges the company faces, the more time members of the management body will need to have available to lead the necessary changes. 'Sufficient time' also includes time spent on training and education. Given the speed with which ESG rules and regulations are created in the EU and the impact of these rules on financial institutions, board members will need to reserve sufficient time to regularly update their knowledge. The necessary time commitment is of course also dependent on the specific role and function of the appointee and his or her specific responsibilities regarding ESG risks.

The requirement of sufficient time commitment may, ultimately, have implications for any ancillary positions, which may need to be terminated.

22.8 INTEGRATING ESG INTO THE CRITERION OF INDEPENDENCE OF MIND AND CONFLICTS OF INTEREST

Independence of mind means the capacity to make one's own sound, objective and independent judgement and to act objectively, critically and independently.[63] Independence of mind is deemed necessary for all members of the management body, executive members and non-executive members alike. This quality may be of specific importance in financial institutions where awareness of climate-related risks may still be low. It may take courage and the ability to resist group pressure to keep

---

[63] See EBA/ESMA 2021, Arts. 80 and 82.

the ESG issues on the table and make sure that relevant risks are, indeed, adequately assessed and mitigated.

Supervisors also assess whether or not a member of the management body has conflicts of interest to an extent that would impede his or her ability to perform his or her duties independently and objectively. Many different situations can lead to actual or potential conflicts of interests. For example, the member's acceptance of another job or position at heavily polluting companies may damage the credibility of the financial institution and jeopardize its sustainability strategy. The same holds true for members of the management body with considerable economic interests in such industries.

Having a conflict of interest does not necessarily mean that the board member concerned is not suitable to fulfill his or her function. Mitigating measures, like not participating in deliberations and voting, should be considered. However, should ESG require fundamental changes in the institution, adequate mitigating measures may be hard to find.

22.9 INTEGRATING ESG INTO THE CRITERION OF GOOD REPUTE (PROPERNESS/INTEGRITY)

Finally, members of the management body in financial institutions have to be of good repute ('proper'). To establish good repute, or at least to establish that there is no reliable evidence to suggest the *absence* of good repute, financial supervisors examine criminal, financial, supervisory and administrative law antecedents as well as past personal and business conduct. The proportionality principle does not apply when assessing good repute. All members of the management body should fulfill the integrity requirements, in all types of institutions and independent of their function.[64]

When assessing good repute, breaches of financial regulation will be taken into account even when those breaches are committed by the financial institution and not by the board members in person. Obviously, the involvement and responsibilities of the specific board members regarding these breaches will be taken into careful consideration. However, as sustainability-related rules and regulations increase, the risk of non-compliance also increases. Should this lead to actual breaches of ESG-related regulation, and should it be concluded that these breaches were intentional or the result of deliberate recklessness of individual board members, supervisors may conclude to impropriety.

In the same way, *greenwashing*, or the adherence to sustainability Codes and Guidelines without the intention to actually live up to the responsibilities and commitments that come with it, may not only affect the financial institution itself but also the individual board members who are responsible and accountable for these malpractices. An appearance of impropriety may, at the least, be created.

---

[64] See EBA/ESMA 2021, Arts. 26, 73 and 78.

22.10 CONCLUSION

The central question posed in this chapter was if and to what extent ESG considerations could be translated into the fit and proper test. It follows from the analysis
carried out in this chapter that this is indeed possible. Members of the management
body have been given significant responsibility for managing the financial institution's exposure to sustainability risks and shaping the central role the financial sector has to play in channelling savings and investments towards sustainable activities.
These changing roles and responsibilities have implications also for the fit and proper
test. Based on the EU rules and regulations analysed in this chapter, it can be concluded that ESG affects all five elements of the fit and proper test, with a focus on
the requirements of collective suitability and individual expertise. This applies to
members of the management body of banks, investment firms and insurance companies alike.

This means that supervisory authorities can integrate ESG into their fit and
proper testing. The next question may be if it is advisable for them to do so. As
indicated, the integration of ESG aspects into fit and proper testing is standard
practice in The Netherlands since 2021. The International Association of Insurance
Supervisors (IAIS) has recognized this practice as an example of supervisory practices of climate-related risks in the insurance sector.[65] In my opinion, this example
is worth following. If we want the sustainability transition to actually succeed, the
active involvement of the financial sector is crucial. It is therefore of the greatest
importance that members of the management body in financial institutions possess
the right qualifications to properly perform their (mostly new) roles and responsibilities. Without the awareness, commitment and expertise in the management body
of financial institutions, the EU sustainability goals and ambitions can hardly be
realized. While the disastrous effects of climate change are already visible today,
many financial institutions are lagging behind and do not take sufficient action. To
effectively change this wait-and-see approach, fit and proper testing may be a powerful tool.

At the same time, supervisors should be aware of the complexity, novelty and
many uncertainties of ESG and the difficult considerations that the management
body faces in this respect. For example, the science to assess climate risk is still
developing. Also, there are no easy solutions to mitigate risks, once identified. For
example, stopping investing in fossil fuels may not be that easy as long as fossil
fuels are still needed for the economy. Pricing decisions, like higher credit costs
for loans to companies exposed to higher physical risks, risk limits, risk mitigation
strategies and holding additional internal capital, are even less straightforward, given
the potentially large impact of such decision-making on the institution itself and its
stakeholders. Supervisors should be aware of these difficulties. In all cases, a clear

---

[65] IAIS 2021.

two-way communication between the supervisor and the supervised entities is essential. Such communication helps to better understand the challenges faced by the institutions and find solutions to overcome them.

Besides using fit and proper testing in its role as gatekeeper to the financial sector, one of the most important functions of these tests may be to create awareness of ESG risks and impact among directors and financial institutions, and act as a driving and stimulating force to help ensure that financial institutions actually have their boards prepared for their tasks. Integrating ESG into fit and proper testing may, in this respect, be very effective.

Also, supervisors can be flexible when supervised entities want to appoint new members of the management body who have specific knowledge of ESG. It can be quite difficult for financial institutions to attract such candidates and even if an interested candidate is found, they are unlikely to have the required knowledge and experience in the financial sector. How can they pass the fit and proper test?

It is important for supervisors to be aware of this problem and not create unnecessary barriers. All board members, including ESG specialists, should possess a certain minimum knowledge and understanding of the institution where he or she will be appointed. Also, all other fit and proper elements should be fulfilled. But once these conditions are met, financial supervisors should not put too high a demand on specific financial, banking or insurance-related expertise. Both the Dutch Central Bank and the ECB follow this approach when assessing candidates who do not meet the regular threshold of individual financial/banking knowledge, skills and expertise.[66]

22.11 FINAL REMARKS: LEGAL CERTAINTY AND EQUALITY (LEVEL PLAYING FIELD)

As this chapter shows, the fit and proper test can include quite a lot of specific and detailed requirements for members of the management body relating to ESG risks and impacts. However, is it sufficiently clear to members of the management body that this is the case? And is this also sufficiently clear to national competent authorities in all EU Member States? Do they all integrate ESG aspects in the fit and proper test in the same way?

Fit and proper regulation largely consists of openly formulated standards, which are open to multiple interpretation. For banks and investment firms, these standards are set out in the CRD and MIFID Directives, which have been transposed into national law.[67] However, during this transposition process, national legislators may have interpreted and implemented the standards in very different ways. Moreover,

---

[66] See ECB 2021, 13.
[67] Notably, the proposal to amend CRD VI, which would introduce explicit reference to environmental, social and governance factors in the collective suitability test, concerns a directive and not a regulation.

the CRD and MiFID set only minimum requirements. Consequently, fit and proper legislation varies considerably from one Member State to another.[68]

It is true that detailed explanations on how the (open) standards should be understood and applied have been drawn up for both banks and investment firms, notably in the EBA/ESMA Guidelines on suitability and the ECB Guide on fit and proper assessments. Both documents explicitly state that ESG should be part of the suitability test. However, neither the Guidelines nor the Guide are legally binding instruments. The ESA Guidelines are issued at level 3 of the European legislative process. While national supervisors should make every effort to apply the guidelines in their supervisory practice, they can disapply (part of) the guidelines through the 'comply or explain' mechanism.[69] Thus, although the ESA Guidelines are intended to promote harmonization among national competent authorities, these authorities have relatively wide discretion to deviate from the Guidelines. Nor are national legislators obliged to transpose the guidelines into national law.

Previous studies, such as the EBA Peer Review[70] and the ECB,[71] show that the harmonizing effect of the EBA and ESMA guidelines on fit and proper rules is very limited. Fit and proper rules and supervisory practices still vary widely across Member States. So while the EBA/ESMA Guidelines on suitability and the ECB Guide to fit and proper assessments explicitly state that ESG aspects are part of the fit and proper test, it is questionable whether this also means that this is done in practice.

For insurers, the Solvency II Delegated Regulation specifies the fit and proper criteria set out in the Solvency II directive. EIOPA did not find it necessary to add an explicit reference to ESG in this regulation. Although EIOPA did state in its opinion and technical advice that ESG is part of the rules on fitness, these EIOPA opinions and advice have no legal status and cannot legally bind national competent authorities nor insurance companies themselves. Previous EIOPA peer reviews have shown that significant differences exist between fit and proper legislation in different Member States (just as is the case for banks).[72] It can therefore be doubted whether these statements by EIOPA are sufficient to achieve consistent integration of ESG in the fit and proper test for insurers in all Member States.

All in all, the fit and proper test in EU Member States is still largely national in character, partly driven by national customs, cultures and national corporate and labour law, and only very partially harmonized. It may be expected that national supervisory practices regarding the integration of ESG considerations into the fit and proper testing, varies accordingly.

---

[68] Palm-Steyerberg and Busch 2019, 191–192.
[69] Art. 16 ESA Regulations. Further, on the legal status of guidelines, see Van Rijn 2022.
[70] EBA 2015.
[71] ECB 2017 and ECB 2018.
[72] EIOPA 2019c and EIOPA 2018.

It would be advisable, in the interest of legal certainty and the European level playing field, to clarify in (delegated) regulation (Level 1 or 2 legislation) that ESG and in particular climate change is part of the fit and proper test, in the manner described in this chapter. Level 3 guidelines or other forms of soft law, such as ECB guidance, have proven too weak an instrument to accomplish harmonized fit and proper rules and practices in the EU. (Delegated) regulations, by contrast, have direct effect in Member States, without the transposition problems of directives. (Delegated) regulations should clarify that knowledge, skills and experience regarding ESG are included in both the collective and the individual suitability test. Also, these regulations should provide a detailed and clear overview of the (minimum) requirements with regard to the knowledge, skills and expertise of the individual members of the management body, and an explanation of how ESG may affect criteria like sufficient time, independence of mind and good repute.

Off course, it can be argued that this explicitness is unnecessary because the existing, openly formulated and principle-based legislation already gives room to integrate ESG into fit and proper testing. However, to avoid uncertainty among board members, appointees and financial institutions and to ensure a EU level playing field, it is recommended to lay down in EU regulation how exactly ESG considerations form part of the fit and proper test. By explicitly referring to sustainability in EU fit and proper legislation, the aim is to provide clarity and to promote that institutions take proper consideration of sustainability risks and impacts in the future.

REFERENCES

Bierman, B. (2019), 'Sustainable capital: Prudential supervision on climate risks for banks', in Beekhoven van den Boezem, F.-J., Jansen, C. and Schuijling, B. (eds.), *Sustainability and Financial Markets, Law of Business and Finance*, vol. 17, (Deventer: Wolters Kluwer), 129–160.

Colaert, V. (2021), 'Integrating sustainable finance into the MiFID II and IDD investor protection frameworks', in Busch, D., Ferrarini, G. and Grünewald, S. (eds.), *Sustainable Finance in Europe. Corporate Governance, Financial Stability and Financial Markets, EBI Studies in Banking and Capital Markets Law* (London: Palgrave Macmillan), 445–475.

EBA (European Banking Authority) (2015), *Report on the Peer Review of the Guidelines on the Assessment of the Suitability of Members of the Management Body and Key Function Holders*, EBA/GL/2012/06, 16 June, available at: https://bit.ly/4aWYKoI.

EBA (European Banking Authority) (2021a), 'Guidelines on Internal Governance under Directive (EU) 2013/36/EU (CRD IV)', EBA/GL/2021/05, 2 July, available at: https://bit.ly/3RjOArq.

EBA (European Banking Authority) (2021b), 'Guidelines on Internal Governance under Directive (EU) 2019/2034 (IFD)', EBA/GL/2021/17, 22 November, available at: https://bit.ly/4aTKw8b.

EBA (European Banking Authority) (2021c), *Report on Management and Supervision of ESG Risks for Credit Institutions and Investment Firms*, EBA/REP/2021/18, 23 June, available at: https://bit.ly/45geL86.

EBA (European Banking Authority) (2022), 'Guidelines on common procedures and methodologies for the supervisory review and evaluation process (SREP) and supervisory stress testing under Directive 2013/36/EU (CRD IV)', EBA/GL/2022/03, 18 March, available at: https://bit.ly/3x2HTmL.

EBA and ESMA (European Banking Authority/European Securities and Markets Authority) (2021), 'Guidelines on the assessment of the suitability of members of the management body and key function holders under Directive 2013/36/EU and Directive 2014/65/EU', ESMA35-36-2319 EBA/GL/2021/06, 2 July, available at: https://bit.ly/3XdhcpV.

EBA and ESMA (European Banking Authority/European Securities and Markets Authority) (2022), 'Guidelines on common procedures and methodologies for the supervisory review and evaluation process (SREP) under Directive (EU) 2019/2034 (IFD)', EBA/GL/2022/09 ESMA35-36-2621, 21 July, available at: https://bit.ly/45jaPn9.

ECB (European Central Bank) (2017), 'Opinion on amendments to the Union framework for capital requirements of credit institutions and investment firms' (CON/2017/46), 8 November, available at: https://bit.ly/3xb602A.

ECB (European Central Bank) (2018), 'Fit and proper for better governance', 14 February, available at: https://bit.ly/3Tkskhi.

ECB (European Central Bank) (2020), 'Guide on climate-related and environmental risks', November, available at: https://bit.ly/3Rnfm2e.

ECB (European Central Bank) (2021), 'Guide to fit and proper assessments', December, available at: https://bit.ly/3RfzMd9.

ECB (European Central Bank) (2022a), 'Walking the talk. Bank gearing up to manage risks from climate change and environmental degradation', Results of the 22 thematic review on climate-related and environmental risks, 2 November, available at: https://bit.ly/3VvNU4F.

ECB (European Central Bank) (2022b), 'Good practices for climate related and environmental risk management: Observations from the 2022 thematic review', November, available at: https://bit.ly/4ejmbM7.

EIOPA (2014), 'Guidelines on system of governance' (EIOPA-BoS-14/253), 1 January, available at: https://bit.ly/3VBzCP1.

EIOPA (2018), 'Peer review of key functions: Supervisory practices and application in assessing key functions', available at: https://bit.ly/45iafWI.

EIOPA (2019a), 'Technical Advice on the integration of sustainability risks and factors in Solvency II and the Insurance Distribution Directive' (EIOPA-BoS-19/172), 30 April, available at: https://bit.ly/3VAGRb5.

EIOPA (2019b), 'Opinion on Sustainability within Solvency II', EIOPA-BoS-19/241, 30 September, available at: https://bit.ly/3KAgsUf.

EIOPA (2019c), 'Results of the peer review on propriety of administrative, management or supervisory body members and qualifying shareholders', 25 January, available at: https://bit.ly/4aTzQ9K.

EIOPA (2022), 'Application guidance on running climate change materiality assessment and using climate change scenarios in the ORSA', EIOPA-BoS-22/329, 2 August, available at: https://bit.ly/3yY8m5C.

Elderson, F. (2022), speech, 'Sitting on Bank boards: Suitability and better governance', 11 June, available at: https://bit.ly/3yW2vh5.

European Commission (2021), 'Strategy for Financing the Transition to a Sustainable Economy', 6 July, available at: https://bit.ly/4cb3mbP.

International Association of Insurance Supervisors (IAIS) (2021), 'Application Paper on the Supervision of Climate-related Risks in the Insurance Sector', May, available at: https://bit.ly/3RgkAwI.

Loizzo, T. and Schimperna, F. (2022), 'ESG disclosure: Regulatory framework and challenges for Italian banks', Banca d'Italia Occasional Papers 2022/744.

Pacces, A. M. (2021), 'Sustainable corporate governance: The role of the law', in Busch, D., Ferrarini, G. and Grünewald, S. (eds.), *Sustainable Finance in Europe. Corporate Governance, Financial Stability and Financial Markets, EBI Studies in Banking and Capital Markets Law* (London: Palgrave Macmillan), 151–174.

Palm-Steyerberg, I. P. (2019), 'Climate change and fit and proper-testing in the Dutch financial sector', 13(1) *Law and Financial Markets Review*, 17–29.

Palm-Steyerberg, I. P. (2021), *Fit and Proper-Testing in the Financial Sector. A Study from the Perspective of Dutch and European Law, Series Company and Law Part 127* (Deventer: Wolters Kluwer).

Palm-Steyerberg, I. P. and Busch, D. (2019), 'Fit and proper requirements in EU financial regulation, towards more cross-sectoral harmonization', in Busch, D., Ferrarini, G. and van Solinge, G. (eds.), *Governance of Financial Institutions* (Oxford: Oxford University Press), 175–203.

Schoenmaker, D. (2020), 10 'A financial sector at the service of a sustainable economy', *Journal of Financial Law*, 463–469.

van der Eerden, F. (2022), 'Sustainability and banks', in van Loopik, M. and Palm-Steyerberg, I. P. (eds.), *The Twin Transition: Digital and Sustainable Finance,* (Deventer: Wolters Kluwer), 233–250.

van Rijn, M. (2022), *Judicial Protection for Banks under the Single Rulebook and the Single Supervisory Mechanism, Series Law of Business and Finance*, vol. 22. (Deventer: Wolters Kluwer).

23

Integration of Sustainability Risks and Sustainability Factors in Insurance Regulation

Arthur van den Hurk

23.1 INTRODUCTION

This chapter discusses the integration of sustainability risks and sustainability factors in EU insurance regulation.[1] An important element of the broader European Commission's initiative on sustainable development is to put sustainability considerations at the heart of the financial system. The intention is to support the European economy in becoming a greener, more resilient and circular system in line with the European Green Deal objectives. In its Action Plan 'Financing Sustainable Growth'[2] the European Commission announced its intention to clarify the integration of sustainability in so-called fiduciary duties in sectoral legislation. The objective of the European Commission is to direct financial and capital flows to green investment and to avoid stranded assets,[3] which could be facilitated if sustainability is more clearly integrated in such duties of financial undertakings.

23.2 SUSTAINABILITY RISKS AND SUSTAINABILITY FACTORS

When reference is made in this chapter to sustainability risks and to sustainability factors, the definitions correspond to the definitions used in the Solvency II Delegated Regulation, which in turn refer to the definitions in the SFDR. Consequently, 'sustainability risk' means an environmental, social or governance event or condition that, if it occurs, could cause an actual or a potential material negative impact on the value of the investment. 'Sustainability factors' means environmental, social and employee matters, respect for human rights, and anti-corruption and anti-bribery matters. Roughly, sustainability risks are risks that the insurance undertaking is exposed to (outside-in), sustainability factors relate to the impact the insurance undertaking, through its activities, might have (inside-out).

---

[1] This chapter was finalised on 1 September 2024. Developments after 1 September 2024 have not been taken into account.
[2] Communication of the Commission 2018.
[3] Communication of the Commission 2021.

23.3 BRIEF DESCRIPTION OF THE SOLVENCY II FRAMEWORK

23.3.1 *Quantitative Prudential Requirements Applicable to Insurance Undertakings*

Before focussing on the specific topic of sustainability, it is useful to provide a brief description of the relevant parts of the Solvency II framework, in particular of the quantitative requirements and parts of the qualitative requirements of the framework.

On an abstract level, the quantitative part of insurance prudential regulation, in accordance with Solvency II, consists of a number of building blocks: requirements regarding (1) technical provisions, (2) capital requirements and (3) the regulation of the assets of insurers, in particular investments, through the prudent person principle, within the overriding principle of freedom of investment.[4]

The main objective of insurance and reinsurance regulation and supervision is the adequate protection of policy holders and beneficiaries. The Solvency II Directive acknowledges, to a certain extent, other objectives (financial stability and fair and stable markets), but is clear that these objectives, while they should be taken into account, should not undermine the main objective.[5]

Insurance liabilities (technical provisions) are determined by calculating a best estimate of the liabilities (reflecting the present value of future liabilities), increased by a risk margin, reflecting the amount – in addition to the best estimate – that an insurer would expect to require in order to take over and meet the insurance obligations.[6] Technical provisions need to be fully covered by assets (e.g., investments). Asset regulation, in particular the application of the prudent person principle, is discussed in Section 23.5.3. While the investment requirements in the earlier Solvency I regime more clearly formed part of the quantitative requirements of the framework, this part of the Solvency II requirements is as much part of the quantitative requirements in Pillar I, as it is part of the qualitative requirements in Pillar 2.

In addition to the technical provisions, insurers are subject to additional buffer requirements (capital requirements), at two levels. The lower capital requirement is the Minimum Capital Requirement (MCR), which corresponds to a level of eligible own funds, below which policyholders and beneficiaries would be exposed to an unacceptable level of risk (while still meeting the level of the technical provisions) were insurers allowed to continue their operations.[7] The Solvency Capital Requirement (SCR) is the higher capital requirement. Insurers are expected to maintain a capital level of at least 100% of the SCR, and to prevent (regular)

---

[4] Article 133 of the Solvency II Directive, Directive (EC) 2009/138, OJ 2009, L 335, 17 December 2009.
[5] Recital 16, Solvency II Directive.
[6] Article 77(3) of the Solvency II Directive.
[7] Article 129(1)b of the Solvency II Directive.

breaches of the SCR. A breach of the SCR results in supervisory intervention, consisting of the preparation and execution of a recovery plan to recover to the level of the SCR.[8] The SCR is calculated on the basis of a Value at Risk (VaR) of 99.5% over a one-year time horizon. Both the MCR and SCR need to be covered by eligible own funds, divided into three tiers, depending on the quality of the own funds. Solvency II has adopted a total balance sheet approach: assets and liabilities are valued on a market-consistent basis and more comprehensive solvency requirements have been introduced, including for market risk, credit and operational risk.

In the context of the topic of this chapter, it is important to point out that the Solvency II framework intends to capture all material risks an insurance undertaking is exposed to, regardless of the nature of the risk. As pointed out above, the capital requirements are calculated over a one-year time horizon, which will not necessarily capture all risks the insurance undertakings is exposed to over a longer period of time, which is clearly a relevant notion with respect to sustainability risks. To embed and capture such longer-term risks in an appropriate manner in the Solvency II framework, an important role is attributed to the own risk and solvency assessment (ORSA).[9]

23.3.2 *Qualitative Requirements*

In addition to the quantitative requirements of Solvency II, great emphasis is placed in the Solvency II framework on the qualitative requirements, in particular on the system of governance. Important elements of the system of governance in accordance with Solvency II are the key functions, including the risk management and actuarial function, the risk management system, including the own risk and solvency assessment, and an important part, the prudent person principle, which complements the principle of freedom of investment, embedded in the Solvency II framework, with a duty to invest its assets in a prudent manner.

Aside from the element of group supervision, the three-pillar structure of Solvency II is complemented with supervisory reporting and public disclosure requirements, in particular through the Solvency and Financial Condition Report (SFCR) and Regular Supervisory Reporting (RSR).[10]

[8] Recovery measures may consist of various measures, of which amending the contractual obligations towards policyholders is usually not available. A breach of the MCR triggers a comparable intervention (requiring a short-term financing plan) with shorter timelines to recover to the level of the MCR.

[9] According to Van Hulle, the ORSA has become a key element of enterprise risk management in insurance and reinsurance undertakings. The ORSA was inspired by the internal capital adequacy assessment process (ICAAP) in the banking sector, and adapted to the Solvency II approach, which is more sophisticated as it includes a scenario-based analysis of risk. Van Hulle 2019, 431, in particular footnote 137. See also Van den Hurk and Joosen 2019, 129–159.

[10] The chapter does not address group supervision nor will it address in detail disclosure requirements.

23.4 FIDUCIARY DUTIES

In its Action Plan on Financing Sustainable Growth, the European Commission observes that several pieces of EU legislation, including Solvency II, require institutional investors and asset managers to act in the best interest of their end-investors/beneficiaries and labels this duty as 'fiduciary duty.' However, according to the European Commission, current rules to consider sustainability risks and factors in the investment decision process are neither sufficiently clear nor consistent across sectors.

It should be noted that the qualification of the duty described by the European Commission to act in the best interest of end-investors/beneficiaries as a 'fiduciary duty' is not necessarily evident for all types of financial undertakings or might at least lead to confusion. It goes beyond the scope of this chapter to discuss this in detail, but it may be questioned if the relationship of an insurance undertaking towards its policyholders/beneficiaries is correctly labelled as a fiduciary relationship, which suggests a separation between legal powers and economic interests and should be distinguished from a duty of care.[11] In any case, fundamental differences exist between different types of financial undertakings (e.g., insurance companies, pension funds, asset managers, banks) and their relationships with their clients and their capital structures, which may have different consequences as well for the manner in which sustainability risks and factors may need to be considered.

Such differences can be demonstrated, as an example, through the prudential rules that govern the investment of assets by pension funds and insurance companies in the IORP II Directive and Solvency II Directive respectively. The prudent person rule in the IORP II Directive and the prudent person principle in the Solvency II Directive have important similarities, but also relevant differences.[12] Both concepts evolve in the specific context of the two frameworks, as well as independent from the common law background from which they have been derived.[13]

Consistency across sectors should be considered in that context, namely taking into account the specific features of each type of financial undertaking.

As noted before, it is important to stress in this context that the main purpose of insurance regulation and supervision is the protection of policyholders and beneficiaries. Other objectives are financial stability and fair and stable markets. These objectives should also be taken into account, but should not undermine the main objective.[14]

---

[11] See Maatman 2020.

[12] In its 2023–2025 strategy and its revised single programming document, EIOPA indicates that it has planned to advise the European Commission on sustainability aspects of the fiduciary duties and stewardship rules of pension funds, considering long-term best interests of members and beneficiaries and the notion of double materiality in the 'prudent person rule': EIOPA 2022b.

[13] See in more detail: Van den Hurk 2024.

[14] Recital 25, Solvency II Directive.

23.5 INTEGRATION OF SUSTAINABILITY IN THE SOLVENCY II FRAMEWORK

23.5.1 *Amendments to the Solvency II Delegated Regulation*

As part of the EU Action Plan, the integration of sustainability risks and factors in EU insurance regulation is being addressed in the Solvency II Delegated Regulation. A number of amendments to the existing provisions have entered into effect as at 2 August 2022. Rather than creating new obligations for insurance undertakings, the amendments mainly specify already existing obligations to take into account sustainability risks, as risks an insurer could be exposed to, in specific parts of the Solvency II framework. Specifically, insurers are obliged to:

- reflect sustainability risks in their risk management, including in the Own Risk and Solvency Assessment;
- incorporate the identification and assessment of sustainability risks in the tasks of the risk management function, which is one of the key functions identified in the Solvency II framework;
- require the actuarial function to take into account sustainability risks in the assessment of uncertainty associated with estimates made in the calculation of technical provisions;
- ensure that the remuneration policy of the insurer provides information on how the insurer takes into account sustainability risks in the risk management system; and
- take into account sustainability risks in the application of the prudent person principle.

In addition, insurers shall take into account the potential long-term impact of their investment strategy and decisions on sustainability factors and, where relevant, that strategy and those decisions shall reflect the sustainability preferences of its customers, taken into account in the product approval process referred to in Article 4 of Commission Delegated Regulation (EU) 2017/2358. The reference to the long-term impact of the investment strategy and decisions on sustainability factors deserves some further elaboration. According to the technical advice, provided by EIOPA to the European Commission in the context of the amendments to the Solvency II Delegated Regulation, EIOPA considers it prudentially relevant to require insurance undertakings to take into account the impact of their investment on sustainability factors. EIOPA considers that the resilience of the real economy, and the stability of the financial system, fuelled by integrating sustainability considerations in the investment strategy and decisions, has the potential to impact on the risk-return characteristics of a portfolio, as other factors.[15] However, this does not mean,

---

[15]   EIOPA 2019a, paragraph 114, 23.

according to EIOPA, that insurance undertakings are required to make sustainable investments or to invest with impact, or to accept lower risk-adjusted returns.[16] EIOPA suggests that the consideration of sustainability factors can also be achieved through the adoption of a stewardship approach,[17] by exercising voting rights for equity holdings, but also by implementing or adapting investment strategies, for example for best-in-class investments or exclusions.[18]

The amendments to the Solvency II Delegated Regulation are limited to amendments to that specific regulation. The Solvency II Directive itself is not amended. Future changes to the Solvency II Directive are discussed in Sections 23.5.4 and 23.8.

23.5.2 *Reflection of Sustainability Risks in the ORSA*

In its Opinion to the European Commission on Sustainability in Solvency II, EIOPA acknowledges that the medium- to long-term impacts of climate change cannot be captured fully in the Solvency II capital requirements, which are designed to reflect the risks that undertakings are exposed to over a one-year time horizon. However, EIOPA does not consider that this time horizon should be changed, but rather that complementary tools such as scenario analysis and stress testing would be more appropriate to capture impacts of climate change. Scenario analysis will allow undertakings to consider the impact of sustainability risks beyond the one-year time horizon or where timing is unpredictable. Such analysis should be embedded in the undertakings' risk management system, its system of governance and in the ORSA. This should enable undertakings to identify and assess the climate change-related risks they would be exposed to in a forward-looking manner and inform business planning and strategy. Stress testing at national or European level could also contribute to identify risks over a longer-term horizon.[19]

The amendments to the Delegated Regulation include amendments to the provision on the calculation of the overall solvency needs of the insurance undertaking.[20] Article 269(1a) of the Solvency II Delegated Regulation provides that emerging risks

---

[16] EIOPA 2019a, paragraph 115, 23.
[17] Reference can also be made in the context to Article 3g of the Shareholders Rights Directive II (SRD II), which requires the disclosure of the engagement policy of (inter alia) institutional investors, including insurance companies. In the European Commission's Renewed Sustainable Finance Strategy of July 2021 (Communication of the Commission 2021, 15), the European Commission indicates that it will review relevant frameworks relating to investors' stewardship and engagement activities. In particular, the Commission will explore how the Shareholder Rights Directive II may better reflect EU sustainability goals and align with global best practices in stewardship guidelines.
[18] EIOPA 2019a, paragraph 115, 23.
[19] EIOPA 2019b, paragraphs 4.40–4.42.
[20] Article 260 of the Solvency II Delegated Regulation.

and sustainability risks,[21] identified by the risk management function, form part of the risks referred to in Article 269(1) point a of the Solvency II Delegated Regulation. This provision specifies the requirement in Article 45(1)a of the Solvency II Directive for insurance and reinsurance undertakings[22] to conduct an 'own risk and solvency assessment' (ORSA).

The ORSA is an assessment of the overall solvency needs of the insurance undertaking, taking into account its specific risk profile, approved risk tolerance limits and its business strategy. The Solvency II legislator has considered it important that insurance and reinsurance undertakings not only calculate their capital requirements in accordance with Solvency II requirements, but also regularly assess their own risk profile, independent from the assumptions according to which the capital requirements are being calculated and to identify any significant divergences between their own assessment and the capital requirements. The outcome of this regular process can lead to measures to be taken by the insurer, either from a capital perspective or a risk management perspective.

It is important to note that the ORSA does not serve to calculate or to recalculate the capital requirements of the insurance undertaking. If the outcome of the ORSA process leads to the conclusion that – for instance – the risk profile of the insurance undertaking deviates from the assumptions underlying the calculation of the capital requirements, the supervisory authorities can – temporarily – impose a capital add-on and require the insurance undertaking to, for example, change its risk profile or recalculate its capital requirements, possibly through the use of a full or partial internal model, should the standard calculation in the Solvency II Directive insufficiently capture the risks, embedded in the specific risk profile of the insurance undertaking.

In April 2021, EIOPA published an Opinion on the supervision of the use of climate change risk scenarios in ORSA. The Opinion sets out supervisory expectations on the integration of the use of climate change scenarios by insurance undertakings in their ORSA.[23] According to EIOPA, insurance and reinsurance undertakings will be impacted by climate change-related physical and transition risks. Therefore, EIOPA believes it is important to encourage a forward-looking management of these risks, also in the long term. EIOPA observes in its opinion that currently only a small minority of undertakings assess climate change risk using scenario analysis in the ORSA. Moreover, where undertakings perform a quantitative analysis of climate change risk, most assessments take a short-term perspective.

As follow-up on this Opinion, EIOPA published, on 2 August 2022, additional application guidance on climate change materiality assessments and climate change

---

[21] Notably, in the Solvency II Delegated Regulation, 'sustainability risks' are identified separately from 'emerging risks', suggesting that such risks cannot, or not entirely, be considered to be emerging risks, but are, in whole or in part, actual risks an undertaking can be confronted with.

[22] For readability purposes, I will refer only to insurance undertakings in the rest of this chapter.

[23] EIOPA 2021.

scenarios in the ORSA.[24] While the EIOPA Opinion sets out supervisory expectations on the use of climate change scenarios in the ORSA, the application guidance is positioned by EIOPA as optional guidance for insurance undertakings, and as an initial aid for undertakings to conduct climate change scenario analysis. Additionally, it should support in particular small and mid-sized insurance undertakings and enhance comparability of reported information. The application guidance is not intended to be a supervisory convergence tool.[25] The application guidance discusses various elements that should be considered by insurance undertakings: conducting a materiality assessment, running climate change scenarios on the basis of the materiality assessment (i.e., for material risks) and transforming climate change scenarios into climate change risks. In the amendments to the Solvency II Directive, agreed at European level on 23 December 2023, following the Solvency II 2020 review, an obligation to assess if the insurance or reinsurance undertaking is exposed to material climate change risks is included in the revised article 45(2) and newly included article 45a of the Solvency II Directive. See further paragraph 23.5.4 below.

23.5.3 *Prudent Person Principle*

23.5.3.1 Description of the Prudent Person Principle in Solvency II

In accordance with Article 132 (1) of the Solvency II Directive, Member States shall ensure that insurance and reinsurance undertakings invest all their assets in accordance with the prudent person principle. Through this provision, the prudent person principle in its current form took shape at European level in the insurance regulatory framework, in force as at 1 January 2016. Already under the EU insurance directives preceding Solvency II there was a requirement for insurers to invest the assets backing the technical provisions in a manner that (i) took account of the type of business carried on by the insurer, (ii) in such a way as to secure the safety, yield and marketability of its investments and (iii) in a diversified manner and adequately spread.[26] However, this requirement was complemented by (i) a list setting out the categories of assets in which insurers could invest and (ii) requirements with respect to diversification and matching.[27] The initial proposals for the third-generation EU insurance directives contained not only a list of categories of admissible assets, but also maximum percentages that insurers could invest in for each category. During the negotiations for the Solvency II Directive some Member States, including the Netherlands and the

---

[24] EIOPA 2022c.

[25] In the meaning of Article 29 of Regulation (EU) 1094/2010.

[26] See, for example, Article 20 of Council Directive 92/96/EEC of 10 November 1992 on the coordination of laws, regulations and administrative provisions relating to direct life assurance and amending Directives 79/267/EEC and 90/619/EEC (3rd life assurance Directive) (as in force at 31 December 2015).

[27] Article 24 of the 3rd Life Assurance Directive (as in force at 31 December 2015).

UK, argued instead to rely primarily on more generic investment principles (as listed above), which resulted in a compromise text in the directives that complemented these principles with relatively generically formulated investment categories and introduced maximum limits only for a few investment categories. This compromise text was sufficiently broad to allow for a prudent person approach at Member State level in those Member States that opted for such an approach. At the same time, the third generation of insurance directives had relaxed the existing requirements with respect to matching and localisation of the earlier generation's EU insurance directives.[28]

Solvency II has taken the Member State freedom to opt for a prudent person approach a significant step further, with the choice at European level for a principles-based approach, providing for freedom of investment,[29] subject to the application of the prudent person principle.

The accompanying documents to the Solvency II proposal provide some context to the choice for this revised approach.[30] An important difference between Solvency I and Solvency II is that investment risk was not covered in the calculation of required capital under Solvency I. Instead, the required capital calculation under Solvency II (the Solvency Capital Requirement or SCR) captures quantifiable risks including investment risk to a much greater extent. This raised the question whether investment rules regarding the admissibility of assets as well as the imposition of quantitative limits were still necessary, and if so, whether they should apply only to assets covering technical provisions or assets covering both technical provisions and the SCR.[31]

Insurance companies are required to maintain assets of sufficient quality to cover their overall financial requirements. All investments held by insurance companies should be managed in accordance with the prudent person principle.[32] As mentioned before, the prudent person principle is contained in Article 132 of the Solvency II Directive. With respect to the whole portfolio of assets, insurers shall only invest in assets and instruments whose risks it can properly identify, measure, monitor, manage, control and report, and appropriately take into account in the assessment of its overall solvency needs, performed as part of the ORSA. Article 135(1) of the

---

[28] With respect to localisation, the European Community was considered as one territory as a whole and with respect to matching, obligations denominated in the currency of a Member State could be matched with assets denominated in ECU.

[29] Article 133 of the Solvency II Directive.

[30] Commission staff working document 2007.

[31] According to the Impact assessment report (Commission staff working document 2007), the previously applicable investment rules contained a number of shortcomings: (1) the investment rules did not provide incentives for insurers to improve their risk management, (2) regulatory requirements and industry practices lacked alignment, contributing to unnecessary administrative burden for insurers and costs, in particular for insurers operating cross-border and resulting in uneven protection of policyholders, (3) the investment rules prevented insurers from optimising their risk-return profile and efficiently managing their investment portfolios, which in turn reduced profitability and increased policyholder premiums and (4) the rules resulted in a suboptimal allocation of capital in the economy as a whole (in particular affecting unlisted equity investment (e.g. venture capital and investment in start-ups).

[32] Recital 71, Directive 2009/138/EC.

Solvency II Directive provides that the European Commission may adopt delegated acts, specifying certain aspects of the prudent person principle:

- the identification, measurement, monitoring and managing of risks arising from investments;[33] and
- the identification, measurement, monitoring and managing of risks arising from derivatives, assets not admitted to regulated markets, excessive reliance on particular assets, issuers, groups of undertakings or on specific geographical areas and excessive accumulation of risks in the portfolio as a whole and excessive concentration of risks on the same issuer or group to which the issuer belongs.

Thus far, the European Commission has not adopted any delegated acts in accordance with Article 135(1), with the exception of the recent Delegated Regulation as regards the integration of sustainability risks in the governance of insurance and reinsurance undertakings[34] that became effective from 2 August 2022.[35]

The application of the prudent person principle varies to a certain extent, depending on the financial liabilities the relevant assets cover. As discussed below, basic requirements apply to the whole portfolio of assets, and specific requirements apply to the assets covering the technical provisions. Furthermore, certain additional requirements apply, in addition to the basic requirements, to the investment of all assets, in particular those assets covering the MCR andSCR. Many life insurance companies offer life insurance contracts where the investment risk is borne (in full or subject to certain guarantees) by the policyholder. For these types of contracts, the prudent person principle has a specific application. Specific rules apply as well to the use of derivatives[36] and certain other categories of assets.

A first observation is that, according to Article 132(1), the prudent person principle applies to *all* assets of the insurer. Under the earlier generations of EU insurance directives, investment rules were only imposed on the assets covering technical provisions. In fact, Article 31 of the Life Assurance Directive[37] explicitly stated that Member States were not allowed to prescribe any rules as to the choice of the assets, other than those covering the technical provisions.[38] In this way, a distinction was made between (i) assets covering the technical provisions, which were subject to asset eligibility criteria and quantitative limits and (ii) free assets, which were not subject to quantitative restrictions under Solvency I (which includes assets backing capital requirements as well as assets held in excess of required capital). This distinction has been abolished under Solvency II. However, due to the total balance sheet approach that is

---

[33] Article 135(1) sub a of the Solvency II Directive.
[34] Commission Delegated Regulation (EU) 2021/1256, dated 21 April, 2021.
[35] Article 2, Commission Delegated Regulation (EU) 2021/1256.
[36] For the purpose of efficient portfolio management, not for speculative purposes, see also EIOPA 2018b.
[37] Directive 2002/83/EC.
[38] Article 31(1) of Directive 2002/83/EC.

fundamental to the Solvency II framework, in addition to the liabilities, the asset side of the Solvency II balance sheet is also taken into account when calculating capital requirements, commensurate with the insurance undertakings' specific (market) risk profile.[39] The policy choice to extend the investment rules to other assets than those covering technical provisions is not discussed in detail in the Solvency II Directive's impact assessment.[40] However, it should be borne in mind that in the calculation of capital requirements, Solvency II requires insurers to take into account risks (such as market risk) that arise at both sides of the balance sheet, that is, both at the asset and the liability side. Therefore, exposure to more riskier and/or volatile assets is expected to result in higher capital requirements. Through the capital requirements/total balance sheet approach of Solvency II, insurers are already encouraged to a prudent investment approach, in any case to consider the additional capital charges incurred by investing in riskier assets. Consequently, the extension of investment requirements beyond the assets covering technical provisions might – in itself – not have been a major shift in Solvency II, or have been overshadowed by the fundamental shift in the calculation of capital requirements under the revised framework.

A second observation is that – within the prudent person principle – Article 132 (2) of the Solvency II Directive distinguishes between different types of liabilities. The generic requirements that apply to all assets are complemented by a requirement that – while still applicable to all assets – requires assets backing the MCR and the SCR to be invested in such a manner as to ensure the security, quality, liquidity and profitability of the (asset) portfolio as a whole. In addition, the localisation of such assets should be such as to ensure their availability. Article 132(2) does not distinguish between assets backing the SCR and the MCR, so it may be assumed that a similar level of prudence may be applied to both categories of assets.

Assets backing the technical provisions should be invested in a manner appropriate to the nature and duration of the insurance liabilities. Those assets need to be invested in the best interest of all policyholders and beneficiaries, taking into account any disclosed policy objective.[41] The words 'any disclosed policy objective' suggest that, while assets need to be invested in the best interest of all policyholders and beneficiaries, insurers are allowed to pursue additional objectives as well. Recital 25 of the Solvency II Directive provides some context in this respect:

> Supervisory authorities should be able to take account of the effects on risk and asset management of voluntary codes of conduct and transparency complied with by the relevant institutions dealing in unregulated or alternative investment instruments.[42]

At the same time, the room to take into account additional policy objectives, besides policyholder protection, is not unlimited. Recital 16 provides:

---

[39] Solvency II Directive Impact assessment report, paragraph 4.13.
[40] See, however, CEIOPS 2007, paragraph 4.2.
[41] Article 132(2) 3rd paragraph Solvency II Directive.
[42] Recital 25, Solvency II Directive.

The main objective of insurance and reinsurance regulation and supervision is the adequate protection of policy holders and beneficiaries. The term beneficiary is intended to cover any natural or legal person who is entitled to a right under an insurance contract. Financial stability and fair and stable markets are other objectives of insurance and reinsurance regulation and supervision which should also be taken into account but should not undermine the main objective.[43]

As mentioned, specific requirements apply to assets that are linked to life insurance contracts where the investment risk is borne by the policyholders, such as unit-linked insurance contracts. If insurance benefits are linked to the value of investment funds[44] or linked to a share index or other type of reference value, stricter rules with respect to the application of the prudent person principle apply: the assets must represent the technical provisions (i.e., the contractual obligations) as much as possible.[45] Clearly, these specific requirements for the application of the prudent person principle offer insurance undertakings limited discretion in their investments for these types of obligations. On the other hand, discretion for the insurance undertaking can be found in the design of the insurance product itself. An insurance undertaking has the liberty to develop insurance products that are linked to a specific asset portfolio, to a fund or to specific funds or to another type of reference value or index. Obviously, the insurance undertaking does need to take into account other regulatory requirements as well.[46]

In case the investment risk is borne by the policyholder, the Solvency II Directive does allow Member States to restrict the types of assets or reference values to which policy benefits may be linked.[47] In these circumstances, an exception is made possible to the principle of freedom of investment.

A third observation is that Article 132(2) suggests that the prudent person principle applies to the *portfolio* of assets.[48] The question may be raised if this means that all requirements with respect to the prudent person principle should be applied at portfolio level only or to some extent a more granular approach would be appropriate or necessary. Both the European Commission and EIOPA have so far refrained from

---

[43] Recital 16, Solvency II Directive.

[44] Such as in UCITS funds or internal funds held by the insurance undertakings.

[45] Article 132(3) of the Solvency II Directive.

[46] Also, EIOPA expects insurers to avoid as possible underlying of investment-based investment products, instruments for which ESMA has issued a ban or restriction. In 2018 EIOPA issued a statement in this respect aimed at policyholder exposures to contracts for differences and binary options: EIOPA 2018a. In the statement, EIOPA points at the product intervention powers that national competent authorities and, additionally, EIOPA have at their disposal, but the statement also has clear links to the application of the prudent person principle, in this case in respect of assets underlying PRIIPs.

[47] Article 133(3) of the Solvency II Directive. The restrictions may not be more stringent than those set out in Directive 85/611/EEC (UCITS Directive).

[48] Article 132(2) 3rd paragraph refers to 'the security, quality, liquidity and profitability of the portfolio as a whole'. This appears to be consistent with the application of the prudent person rule pursuant to the IORP Directive; see, for example, Maatman 2007.

608 *Arthur van den Hurk*

providing detailed guidance on the application of the prudent person principle.[49] However, in the explanatory notes in the final report on the EIOPA Guidelines on the System of Governance, EIOPA does clarify that the features of the prudent person principle of security, quality, liquidity and profitability apply to the portfolio as a whole and not to individual investments. According to EIOPA, this means that insurers may have individual investments in their investment portfolio that do not fulfill every feature, even if they will finally contribute to the security, quality, liquidity and profitability of the portfolio as a whole.[50]

Although neither the European Commission nor EIOPA has so far provided more guidance, it is interesting to mention a development in this respect in the UK. In May 2020 the Prudential Regulation Authority has issued a supervisory statement on the application of the prudent person principle under Solvency II. The PRA interprets the requirement in such a manner that in some cases, the rules or regulations apply at a portfolio level while in others the requirements are to be applied on more granular basis.[51] Accordingly, the level of granularity at which the expectations in this supervisory statement should be applied will depend in each case on (among other things) the scope of all relevant requirements to which the expectation refers or relates and the specific circumstances of each firm case by case, taking into account the principle of proportionality.[52]

A last observation or question that may be raised is to what extent the investment rules, including the prudent person principle also apply (in full) to assets held by insurers in excess of their financial liabilities (above the SCR). Article 132(1) of the Solvency II Directive suggests that the prudent person principle applies to all assets, regardless of the financial liabilities the assets are destined to cover. Also, Article 132(2), second paragraph, which applies to 'all assets, in particular those covering the MCR and SCR', suggests that the prudent person principle applies to all assets. On the other hand, recital 71 suggests that the intention of the investment rules is to regulate assets covering an insurers' financial liabilities, which could indicate only the assets covering technical provisions, MCR and SCR. A reasonable and logical position might be that the investment rules, including the prudent person principle, apply to all assets, regardless of the financial liabilities they intend to cover, but the application of the prudent person principle allows for investment in riskier assets, when the solvency ratio is higher. At the same time,

---

[49] The EIOPA Guidelines on the system of governance provide some high-level guidance, but in EIOPA 2015, paragraph 2.13, EIOPA acknowledges that it would be premature to provide extensive guidelines om the prudent person principle at that point in time. Accordingly, EIOPA has limited the guidelines to very basic minimum requirements, reminding undertakings that greater flexibility for investments is linked with firm responsibilities on the governance around the investment activities, and that the level of prudence required is not diminished under Solvency II.

[50] Final report, paragraph 2.142.

[51] As an example, the PRA refers to the use of derivatives, in which case an assessment at portfolio level only would be insufficient, PRA 2020.

[52] PRA 2020, 3.

it should be noted that the investment in riskier assets is likely to result in higher capital requirements as well.

Based on the description of the prudent person principle above, the question may be raised what the amendments to the prudent person principle in the Solvency II Delegated Regulation with respect to sustainability entail.

23.5.3.2 Taking into Account Sustainability Risks in the Prudent Person Principle

According to EIOPA, it has become clear, over the past years, that sustainability risks and in particular climate change risks will affect insurance and reinsurance undertakings. EIOPA finds that there is a lack of evidence that undertakings across Europe effectively and consistently consider sustainability risks in their investment strategy, which can, according to EIOPA, be explained by a lack of a clear taxonomy of sustainable ('green')/non-sustainable ('brown') investments, a lack of reliability and comparability on ESG information, a lack of experience and ESG skills among institutional investors and asset managers, or the impact on costs and risk-adjusted performance.[53] This seems to be addressed over time by the implementation of the EU Taxonomy Regulation, as well as more generally the evolution of sustainable finance that should allow insurance and reinsurance undertakings over time to assess these risks. EIOPA acknowledges that the prudent person principle already allows for sustainability risks to be taken into account, in analogy with other risks. However, EIOPA did recommend changes to the relevant Solvency II provision, as the principle as stated in the Solvency II Directive did not require explicitly undertakings to consider these risks.

In its technical advice, EIOPA indicated that it had considered including an additional requirement to the prudent person principle, requiring insurance and reinsurance undertakings to consider the sustainability of their investment portfolio, in addition to the assessment of the security, quality, liquidity and profitability of the investment portfolio. Instead, EIOPA has opted to include the requirement to consider sustainability risks when assessing their investment portfolio. Where sustainability risks materialise, they can affect the security and/or the quality and/or the liquidity and/or the profitability of the investment portfolio.

23.5.3.3 Taking into Account the Potential Long-Term Impact of the Investment Strategy on Sustainability Factors

The Solvency II Delegated Regulation not only requires undertakings to take into account sustainability risks, but additionally requires undertakings to assess

---

[53] EIOPA 2019a, paragraph 102–106.

the potential long-term impact of their investments on sustainability factors. This might give the impression that, through this requirement, insurance and reinsurance undertakings may be required to invest in sustainable investments. However, this is not necessarily the case. EIOPA indicates that it strongly believes that the transition towards a sustainable economy cannot be achieved by simply implementing a binary approach between sustainable investments and non-sustainable investment.[54] The European Commission has followed EIOPA's technical advice to include such a requirement in the Solvency II Delegated Regulation.[55] The wording in the Solvency II Delegated Regulation is more prescriptive than the requirement in the IORP II Directive, that reads as follows: 'within the prudent person rule, Member States shall allow IORPs to take into account the potential long-term impact of investment decisions on environmental, social, and governance factors'.[56] For insurance and reinsurance undertakings, EIOPA favours a compulsory requirement to support a European effort of (re)industry towards a resilient and inclusive economy. By addressing both sides of the investment, the impact of the investments and the impact on the investments, a sustainable investment cycle would be implemented.[57] EIOPA considers that this approach has the potential to impact on the risk-return characteristics of a portfolio, as other factors. According to EIOPA, as long-term investors with an overall balance sheet of around €8 trillion, insurers in the European Economic Area (EEA) can play a significant role in putting our economies on a more sustainable track. Against that backdrop, EIOPA has recently published a fact sheet, in which it provides the high-level results of an analysis, based on the EU Taxonomy of sustainable activities how much of EEA insurers' investments can be considered environmentally sustainable at present.[58] As detailed asset-level data is required for this analysis, EIOPA chose to focus on insurers' direct investments in corporate bonds and equities, which together account for around 29% of their total investments. The analysis shows that 2.6% of insurers' direct corporate bond and equity investments are aligned with the Taxonomy while another 15.5% are eligible. When excluding securities issued by financial firms, the share of Taxonomy-aligned investments rises to 5.7% with another 34.1% being eligible. It should be noted that this limited analysis is based on the currently available data from insurers, which only recently have commenced reporting Taxonomy-related eligibility information, for which they in turn are dependent on externally available data from the investee companies, which have often started to report such information only recently as well. No information is yet included on the alignment of the investments with the EU Taxonomy, which is not yet generally available.

---

[54] EIOPA 2019a, paragraph 110.
[55] See Section 23.5.1, which describes how EIOPA suggests such an approach can be shaped.
[56] Article 19(1)b of Directive (EU) 2016/2341.
[57] EIOPA 2019a, paragraph 113.
[58] EIOPA 2023c.

23.5.3.4 Taking into Account Sustainability Preferences

In addition to the requirement to take into account the long-term impact of the investment strategy on sustainability factors, insurance undertakings need to take into account sustainability preferences of its customers that are taken into account in the product approval process.[59] Through this requirement, a link is established between the amendments to the Insurance Distribution Directive, that integrate sustainability in the product oversight and approval process[60] and the prudent person principle. The purpose of these requirements is that undertakings in their risk management and investment strategy and decisions consequently implement the commitments made to policyholders and beneficiaries on ESG characteristics of a specific product.

23.5.4 *Amendments to the Solvency II Directive*

On 22 September 2021, the European Commission has published a legislative proposal to amend the Solvency II Directive. The 2009 Solvency II Directive itself contained several mandates for the European Commission to review key elements of the directive. In addition, beyond these mandates, the European Commission has reflected more broadly on the lessons learned since the entry into force of the Solvency II Directive. In this context, the European Commission has also assessed whether the insurance sector could contribute to the EU's political priorities, including the climate and environmental targets under the European Green Deal. On sustainability, the European Commission has considered an EIOPA Opinion published in September 2019 on Sustainability within Solvency II. This has resulted in the addition to the European Commission's legislative proposal an obligation to conduct long-term climate scenario analysis. The European Commission indicated that it may consider, at a later stage, extending this obligation to other environmental risks. In addition, the proposal contains a mandate to conduct further work to assess the suitability of the existing Solvency II capital requirements for green assets.[61]

On 17 June 2022, the Council adopted its general approach to the European Commission's proposal. With respect to the sustainability related proposals made by the European Commission, the Council was largely supportive, with the addition of some elements, in particular the inclusion of a mandate to EIOPA to review biodiversity loss risks.[62]

---

[59] Art. 275a paragraph 2 of the Solvency II Delegated Regulation.
[60] Commission Delegated Regulation (EU) 2021/1257, OJ L 227/18. These amendments are discussed in more detail in Och, Chapter 13 in this volume.
[61] European Commission 2021 (Solvency II 2020 Review Commission Proposal). Paragraph 91 introduces the new Article 304a with two mandates to EIOPA as regards sustainability risks. EIOPA is mandated to explore by 2023 a dedicated prudential treatment of exposures related to assets or activities associated substantially with environmental and/or social objectives and to review regularly the scope and the calibration of parameters of the standard formula pertaining to natural catastrophe risk.
[62] Council of the European Union 2022, Article 304a(3).

On 6 June 2022, the rapporteur of the European Parliament for the Solvency II proposal published its draft report. This draft report reflected a different viewpoint. According to the rapporteur, the current framework is sufficiently capable to deal with sustainable and social risks and is concerned that any amendment in this area might lead to viable and sustainable businesses becoming 'un-insurable' or 'un-investable' for no good reason. Furthermore, according to the rapporteur, based on the EIOPA Regulation, EIOPA already has the power to present a report in relation to ESG risks.[63] Accordingly, the draft report suggests that the proposals made by the European Commission, relating to sustainability, should be deleted.

As might have been expected, this position of the rapporteur did not remain undisputed. In addition to the proposals made by the rapporteur in its draft report, several members of the European Parliament have proposed additional amendments to be included in the European Parliaments' report, relating to sustainability, thereby proposing to re-insert the topic of sustainability to the European Parliament's report.

The final report of the rapporteur of the European Parliament was adopted on 27 July 2023. According to the European Parliament, insurers should 'explicitly' take into account environmental and social risks. For this, supervisory authorities should ensure that insurers develop the necessary tools to measure, manage and monitor these risks and develop specific plans and quantifiable targets to address them. As regards proportionality and reporting complexity by small and medium-sized insurers, the report envisages that they may limit their sustainability reporting to (i) a brief description of the business model and strategy, (ii) the policies in relation to sustainability matters, (iii) the adverse impact of the insurer on sustainability matters, and actions taken and (iv) the principal risks to the insurer related to sustainability matters and how the undertaking manages those risks.[64]

A political agreement on the Solvency II proposal was reached on 13 December 2023. A provisional text of the amending directive, reflecting the political agreement, was published on 24 January 2024.[65] The final text of the agreement includes an obligation for insurers to develop climate change transition plans for prudential purposes.[66] In addition, as part of the application of the prudent person principle, insurers and reinsurers shall also take into account the impact of sustainability risks on their investments, and the potential long-term impact of their investment decisions on sustainability factors when they decide on their investment strategy. Furthermore, additional text is included in the provisions on the risk-management system,[67] reflecting the different time horizons over which sustainability risks should be assessed.

---

[63] Explanatory statement to the draft report of Ferber 2022.

[64] European Parliament briefing on the proposal to amend the Solvency II Directive, available at: https://bit.ly/45zLpC1.

[65] https://bit.ly/3KBKerT. At the time of finalisation of this chapter, it is expected that the amending directive will be published in the Official Journal of the EU in December 2024. This means that the provisions will enter into effect in EU member states by the end of December 2026 or 1st of January 2027.

[66] Article 44(2b) Solvency II Directive (new).

[67] Article 44(2) last paragraph Solvency II Directive.

Meanwhile, EIOPA has initiated work, motivated by the proposed mandate in the Commission Proposal[68] in the form of, initially, a discussion paper on the prudential treatment of sustainability risks,[69] and more recently, a consultation paper.[70] In this latest paper, EIOPA proposes to focus its activities in this area on three aspects.

The first area of the analysis is dedicated to the potential link between prudential market risks in terms of equity, spread and property risk and transition risks. The second area of the analysis focuses on the potential link between non-life underwriting risks and climate-related risk prevention measures, since the prudential treatment of assets or activities as referred to in the mandate includes insurance undertakings' underwriting activities. The third area of the analysis is related to the potential link between social risks and prudential risks, including market and underwriting risks.

23.6 CLIMATE CHANGE SCENARIO ANALYSIS

As mentioned, the European Commission proposed to introduce, as part of the risk management obligations of insurers, an obligation to assess whether it has any material exposure to climate change risks and demonstrate the materiality of its exposure in the own risk and solvency assessment.[71] This obligation will be included in Article 45a of the Solvency II Directive. Where the insurance undertaking has material exposure to climate risk, it shall specify at least two long-term climate change scenarios, including the following:

- a long-term climate change scenario whereby the global temperature increase remains below 2 degrees Celsius; and
- a long-term climate change scenario whereby the global temperature increase is equal to or higher than 2 degrees Celsius.

Such scenario analyses should be repeated periodically, with intervals no longer than three years. The scenarios would be reviewed periodically, at least every three years, and updated where necessary.

Whether this amendment needed to be adopted in the Solvency II Directive, appears to a large extent rather academic. Climate change risk can have a material impact on insurers and given the potential impact, EIOPA already now expects that insurance undertakings integrate these risks in their ORSA.[72] Furthermore, the recent amendments to the Solvency II Delegated Regulation already include an obligation

---

[68]   Article 304a of the Solvency II 2020 Review European Commission 2021.
[69]   EIOPA 2022a.
[70]   EIOPA 2023c, EIOPA 2023d.
[71]   Reference can be made as well to the ongoing work at international level by the IAIS on the same topic, from both micro- and macroprudential perspectives. See in particular the IAIS Draft Application Paper on climate change scenario analysis in the insurance sector, November 2023: https://bit.ly/3Vy916t.
[72]   EIOPA 2021.

to take into account emerging risks and sustainability risks in the assessment of the overall solvency needs of the insurance undertaking. Moreover, EIOPA has recently published an extensive document, setting out application guidance on running a climate change materiality assessment and using climate change scenarios in the ORSA. In addition, some national competent authorities have also published expectations with respect to the assessment by insurers of sustainability risks in the ORSA.[73] The main challenge, as also highlighted by EIOPA, is to reconcile the very long-term dynamics of climate change with the operational ability to assess the impact of related risks based on the insurers' current business model and to reconcile the potential long-term impact of climate change risk on the insurance undertaking with the usual time horizon that is being used by insurance undertaking to conduct an ORSA, which is usually a period of 3 to 5 years. As indicated above, the overall solvency needs in accordance with the ORSA process are assessed by an insurance undertaking in accordance with a different, longer time horizon than the time horizon on which the capital requirements for the insurance undertaking are being calculated.

23.7 CLIMATE CHANGE TRANSITION PLANS

In the (near) future, many insurance undertakings may become (subject to) be subject to the Corporate Sustainability Due Diligence Directive (CSDDD)[74] with respect to the obligation to adopt a climate change transition plan either on a stand-alone or on a group basis.[75] The CSDDD contains an obligation to adopt a plan to ensure that the business model and strategy of the company are compatible with the transition to a sustainable economy and with limiting global warning to 1.5 degrees Celsius. This plan should identify, on the basis of the information available to the company, the extent to which climate change is a risk for, or an impact of, the company's operations. If climate change risk is identified as a principal risk, the company should include emission reduction objectives in its plan.

Leaving aside voluntary commitments that insurance undertakings may have made on the alignment with the Paris Agreement, this obligation resulting from

---

[73] For example, Dutch Central Bank 2021 and Dutch Central Bank 2019.

[74] Directive (EU) 2024/760, PbEU L Series, 5 July 2024.

[75] While financial sector undertakings are largely excluded from the application of the CSDDD with respect to the due diligence requirements, which will apply only to their own operations and upstream value chain, many insurance undertakings will be subject to the requirement to develop a climate change transition plan. The Council's COREPER Committee reached an agreement on a revised text of the CSDDD, which was approved by the European Parliament on 24 April 2024. A final approval at Council level, as well as the subsequent publication of the CSDDD is expected after the European Parliament elections. The CSDDD will start to apply to the largest undertakings in scope of the directive (more than 5,000 employees on average and a net worldwide turnover of EUR 1,500 million in the preceding financial year), three years after the entry into force. A staged application period (four to five years) is foreseen for smaller undertakings in scope of the CSDDD.

the CSDDD, seems to overlap significantly with the obligation to assess the impact of climate change through different scenarios in the ORSA. A difference between the Solvency II requirements and the CSDDD requirements is that the CSDDD describes a different, less severe scenario. Furthermore, the CSDDD provides that infringements of the obligations would be subject to sanctions under that framework.

It should be noted that, as indicated in Section 23.5.4, the Solvency II Directive will include a requirement to have a prudential transition plan. Such prudential transition plans seek to ensure that insurance and reinsurance undertakings develop and monitor the implementation of plans, have quantifiable targets and processes to monitor and address the financial risks arising in the short, medium and long term from sustainability factors, including those arising from the process of adjustment and transition trends towards the relevant member states and European Union regulatory objectives and legal acts in relation to sustainability factors, in particular those set out in the EU Climate Law.

23.8 POTENTIAL AMENDMENT OF SOLVENCY CAPITAL REQUIREMENTS TO TAKE INTO ACCOUNT SUSTAINABILITY RISK

The key focus of the amendments to the Solvency II framework in relation to sustainability has been on explicitly embedding sustainability risk in the risk management system and system of governance more generally, with a clear focus on the ORSA. In addition, the provisions on the prudent person principle have been amended to better reflect both sustainability risks and sustainability factors. So far, the capital requirements have not been reviewed.

According to the revised Solvency II Directive (according to the agreed compromise text),[76] EIOPA will be mandated to assess if a dedicated prudential treatment would be justified for exposures related to assets or activities substantially with environmental or social objectives or which are substantially with harm to these objectives.[77] EIOPA will, in consultation with the ESRB, have to assess what effect such a dedicated treatment would have on the protection of policyholders and the financial stability in the European Union. EIOPA should submit a report on its findings to the European Commission by 30 September 2024. EIOPA has already taken this work into account in its strategy and work programme for the coming years.[78]

---

[76] Council, provisional text: https://bit.ly/3KBKerT.

[77] Article 304a of the Solvency II Directive, in accordance with the revisions pursuant to the compromise text, agreed on 13 December 2023.

[78] See EIOPA 2022b, which includes the following actions:

- assess the prudential treatment under Solvency II of assets and activities associated substantially with environmental and social objectives or which are associated substantially with harm to such objectives (subject to the deadline in the final version of SII);
- initiate reassessment of the natural catastrophe risk standard formula capital charges (Q4 2024).

In addition, as mentioned in Section 23.5.4, EIOPA published on 29 November 2022, ahead of a formal mandate in the Solvency II Directive,[79] a discussion paper on the prudential treatment of sustainability risks.[80] In this paper, EIOPA proposes to focus its activities in this area on three areas:[81]

> Firstly, as a risk-based environmental objective for insurance undertakings' investment activities, EIOPA proposes to study the link between climate change-related transition risks and prudential risks, since data availability seems to be most advanced in this regard. Secondly, in terms of the underwriting activities of insurance undertakings, EIOPA proposes to focus on climate change adaptation in terms of climate-related risk prevention. As climate change is substantially raising physical risk exposures, climate change adaptation can be considered as a risk-based environmental objective of outstanding importance to increase the resilience of the society and economy against climate change. Finally, given the stage of the public debate on the appropriate definition of social objectives and social risks, EIOPA aims as regards social aspects to provide an initial analysis of the corresponding Pillar II and III requirements under Solvency II and to identify potential areas for further analysis, as well as to initiate discussions on the appropriate prudential consideration.[82]

In addition, EIOPA announced[83] further publications are to be expected, that are either directly or partly related to prudential treatment of sustainability risks, on the following themes:

- the macro-prudential impact of the protection gap;
- 'impact underwriting': whether adaptation measures can help in increasing the supply of insurance;
- the reassessment of the natural catastrophe risk capital charges; and
- an analysis of the drivers of demand for property insurance.

Accordingly, EIOPA has indeed recently undertaken further steps in these areas and has released various papers and reports on these themes. On 24 April 2023, EIOPA and the European Central Bank (ECB) released a joint discussion paper that deals with the question how to enhance the insurance of European households and companies against climate-related catastrophes. The paper sets out possible actions to increase the uptake and efficiency of catastrophe insurance while

---

[79] Motivated by the mandate in article 304a of the Solvency II Directive, pursuant to the compromise text of January 24, 2024

[80] EIOPA 2022a. EIOPA invited stakeholders to provide feedback on the discussion paper until 5 March 2023.

[81] EIOPA acknowledges that, while the prudential analysis should be risk-based and policy implications evidence-based, ESG data-gaps are a constraining factor for the scope of the prudential analysis, Chapter 1, paragraph 6 of the discussion paper.

[82] EIOPA 2022a, paragraph 7.

[83] At the occasion of the launch of the EIOPA dashboard, that depicts the insurance protection gap for natural catastrophes across Europe, EIOPA 2022d.

creating incentives to adapt to and reduce climate risks.[84] On 6 February 2023, EIOPA published a report, reflecting the outcome of a pilot exercise on impact underwriting that EIOPA conducted with 31 volunteering insurance undertakings from 14 European countries in 2022. It provides an overview of the main findings of the pilot exercise regarding current underwriting practices and challenges mentioned by the participating insurance undertakings.[85]

In addition, as referred to above, on 13 December 2023, EIOPA has published a consultation paper on the prudential treatment of sustainability risks. The consultation period ended on 22 March 2024. In the consultation paper, EIOPA focuses its analyses on the following three conceptual areas that are considered to be appropriate for a risk-based analysis. EIOPA describes these areas as follows:

> The first area of the analysis is dedicated to the potential link between prudential market risks in terms of equity, spread and property risk and transition risks. Although the availability of sustainability-related data is still a material challenge for prudential analyses, EIOPA considers the progress that has been made in this regard to be sufficient to provide meaningful evidence. EIOPA considers that transition risks can be already sufficiently reflected in Solvency II's requirements as regards risk management (Pillar II) and disclosure (Pillar III).
>
> The second area of the analysis focuses on the potential link between non-life underwriting risks and climate-related risk prevention measures, since the prudential treatment of assets or activities as referred to in the mandate includes insurance undertakings' underwriting activities. While a direct and risk-based link between the policyholders' level of greenhouse gas emissions and the respective insured losses remains uncertain (climate change mitigation), EIOPA focuses on the environmental objective of climate change adaptation on which a direct and risk-based link to insured losses is given. The expected growth in physical risk exposures and insured claims due to climate change will increase risk-based premium levels over time, potentially impairing the mid- to long-term affordability and availability of insurance products with coverage against climate-related hazards. In this regard, the environmental objective of climate change adaptation becomes increasingly important, and the insurance industry has a unique role to play by helping society and the economy become more climate resilient through developing innovative insurance products that could incentivize climate-related risk prevention, consistent with actuarial risk-based principles. EIOPA focuses its analysis on the solvency capital requirements, as risk management and disclosure requirements are considered to sufficiently reflect the effects of climate-related risk prevention in the non-life underwriting business.
>
> The third area of the analysis is related to the potential link between social risks and prudential risks, including market and underwriting risks. Social risks are a nascent topic from a prudential perspective, and EIOPA considers it to affect insurance undertakings conceptually in a similar manner as other sustainability

---

[84] EIOPA and ECB 2023.
[85] EIOPA 2023a.

risks. Starting with the identification of social risks and objectives, EIOPA discusses how social risks can translate into prudential risks on undertakings' balance sheets. In light of the Commission's mandate, EIOPA provides an initial analysis of the Pillar II and III requirements under Solvency II to identify potential areas for further work.[86]

Furthermore, in a related area, EIOPA observes and acknowledges that protecting nature's biodiversity and ecosystems has in recent years emerged as an important aspect in the fight against climate change. The failure to account for, mitigate and adapt to the consequences of nature loss can have economic implications that may put overall financial stability at risk. In a recent staff paper, EIOPA explores how nature-related risks can affect (re)insurers and examines ways in which the insurance sector can meaningfully contribute to the conservation and restoration of nature through investments and underwriting activity.[87] In the revised Solvency II Directive, an additional mandate is included in Article 304a for EIOPA to evaluate whether and to what extent insurance and reinsurance undertakings assess their material exposure to risks related to biodiversity loss as part of the ORSA.

23.9 FINAL REMARKS

As becomes clear from this chapter, the integration of sustainability considerations in the insurance regulatory framework of Solvency II is progressing with a steady pace, in parallel to the developments in sustainable finance regulation in other parts of the financial sector, as well as developments in sustainable finance regulation, not related specifically to the financial sector, such as the Corporate Sustainability Reporting Directive and the Corporate Sustainability Due Diligence Directive.

While the Solvency II framework generally seems to be capable of taking into account all relevant risks that insurance companies are exposed to, regardless of the nature of the risks, including sustainability risks, sustainability risks do merit specific attention. Insurance companies are, by the specific nature of the insurance business, familiar with assessment over longer periods of time and with the management of uncertainty. However, sustainability risk may materialise over different time periods than insurance companies take into account in their assessments of risks. Furthermore, different groups of policyholders may be exposed differently to those risks. In addition, it is not yet clear if and to what extent sustainability and sustainability risks justifies a different capital treatment. So far, there appears to be a broad consensus that capital requirements should remain based on an economic and risk-based assessment of risk.

In addition to the assessment of sustainability risk in the Solvency II framework, the question can be raised if and to what extent insurance companies can take into

---

[86] EIOPA 2023d.
[87] EIOPA 2023b.

account other considerations than the principal objective of the Solvency II framework, policyholder protection. There appears to be some room to take into account such other objectives, as long as the principal objective is not undermined. So far, the integration of sustainability in the Solvency II framework has taken place in the Solvency II Delegated Regulation and through the adoption of supervisory measures, such as opinions, Q&As and other types of guidance, on the basis of existing regulation by national supervisory authorities and by EIOPA With the amendments to the Solvency II Directive, on which an agreement has been reached in December 2023 and which are expected to be formally published in December 2024, further sustainability-related amendments will be included in the Solvency II Directive, with further detailed technical and implementing standards and guidelines still to be developed ahead of the application of the amendments (expected as of 2027).

The integration of sustainability considerations in the Solvency II framework has so far been focussed primarily on the risk management and the system of governance. In addition, changes have been made to the prudent person principle, which means to the regulation of assets, which has both quantitative (Pillar 1) and qualitative (Pillar 2) elements. This seems a logical approach, that reflects the nature of sustainability risks and sustainability considerations at this stage. More fundamental changes, such as dedicated capital treatment for 'green' or 'brown' assets and activities, integration of transition planning as well as stewardship considerations, might be valuable, but will require further analysis and debate, as this might mean in some cases a partial departure from the original objectives of the Solvency II framework. While there might be good reason to pursue such an approach, it is not entirely clear yet if this can be easily integrated in a prudential framework such as Solvency II.

REFERENCES

CEIOPS (Committee of Insurance and Occupational Pensions Regulators) (2007), 'Advice to the European Commission in the Framework of the Solvency II Project on Safety Measures (Limits on Assets)', March, CEIOPS-DOC-07-07, available at: www.mnb.hu/letoltes/szolvencia-consulpaper16-2.pdf.

Commission staff working document (2007), 'Accompanying document to the Proposal for a Directive of the European Parliament and of the Council concerning life assurance on the taking-up and pursuit of the business of Insurance and Reinsurance – Solvency II – Impact assessment report', COM(2007) 361 final, available at: https://bit.ly/3xkYBoB

Communication of the Commission to the European Parliament, the European Council, the European Central Bank, the European Economic and Social Committee and the Committee of the Regions (2018), 'Action Plan: Financing Sustainable Growth', COM (2018) 97 final, 8 March, available at: https://bit.ly/497N6GU.

Communication of the Commission to the European Parliament, the European Council, the European Central Bank, the European Economic and Social Committee and the Committee of the Regions (2021), 'Strategy for Financing the Transition to a Sustainable Economy', COM (2021) 390 final, 6 July, available at: https://bit.ly/3VxrT5y.

Council of the European Union (2022), 'General approach, proposal for a Directive of the European Parliament and of the Council, amending Directive 2009/138/EC as regards proportionality, quality of supervision, reporting, long-term guarantee measures, macro-prudential tools, sustainability risks, group and cross-border supervision', Confirmation of the final compromise text with a view to agreement, 2 June, 2021/0295 (COD), available at: https://bit.ly/4c8nrzu.

Dutch Central Bank (2019), 'Good practice on the treatment of climate-related risks in the ORSA', 4 November, available at: https://bit.ly/3VAdYf2.

Dutch Central Bank (2021), 'Q&A of the Dutch Central Bank on climate risks for insurers', 2 February, available at: https://bit.ly/4aUBzLU.

EIOPA (European Insurance and Occupational Pensions Authority) (2015), *Final Report on Public Consultation No. 14/017 on Guidelines on the System of Governance*, 28 January, EIOPA-BoS-14/253, available at: https://bit.ly/3x1H4Lo.

EIOPA (European Insurance and Occupational Pensions Authority) (2018a), 'Statement on consumer detriment resulting from policyholder exposure to contracts for differences and binary options', 1 June, EIOPA-18/215, available at: https://bit.ly/3Xgf15d.

EIOPA (European Insurance and Occupational Pensions Authority) (2018b), 'What are the requirements that shall be met by the transactions on derivatives to be considered as facilitating effective portfolio management by the undertaking? What are the types of transactions on derivatives that cannot be considered as facilitating effective portfolio management?', Q&A 1388, 23 July, available at: https://bit.ly/4bSmtYv.

EIOPA (European Insurance and Occupational Pensions Authority) (2019a), 'Technical Advice on the integration of sustainability risks and factors in the delegated acts under Solvency II and IDD', 30 April, EIOPA-BoS-19/172, available at: https://bit.ly/3yJx9di.

EIOPA (European Insurance and Occupational Pensions Authority) (2019b), 'Opinion to the European Commission on Sustainability in Solvency II', 30 September, EIOPA-BoS-19/241, available at: https://bit.ly/3KAgsUf.

EIOPA (European Insurance and Occupational Pensions Authority) (2021), 'Opinion on the supervision of the use of climate change risk scenarios in the ORSA', 19 April, EIOPA-BoS-21-127, available at: https://bit.ly/3yVdQoQ.

EIOPA (European Insurance and Occupational Pensions Authority) (2022a), 'Prudential treatment of sustainability risks', Discussion Paper, 29 November, EIOPA-BoS-22-527, available at: https://bit.ly/3XfQSeM.

EIOPA (2022b), 'Revised single programming document 2023-2025, including Annual Work Programme 2023', 29 September, EIOPA-BoS-22/460, available at:. www.eiopa.europa.eu/document/download/7ca47d26-eab3-48ac-b739-4053606e0661_en?filename=Revised%20single%20programming%20document%202023-2025%20Including%20Annual%20Work%20Programme%202023.pdf.

EIOPA (European Insurance and Occupational Pensions Authority) (2022c), 'Application guidance on running climate change materiality assessment and using climate change scenarios in the ORSA', 2 August, EIOPA-BoS-22/329, available at: https://bit.ly/3yY8m5C.

EIOPA (European Insurance and Occupational Pensions Authority) (2022d), 'Dashboard on insurance protection gap for natural catastrophes', 5 December, available at: https://bit.ly/4aoRM2l.

EIOPA (European Insurance and Occupational Pensions Authority) (2023a), *Impact Underwriting: Report on the Implementation of Climate-related Adaptation Measures in Non-life Underwriting Practices*, EIOPA-BoS-22-593, 6 February 2023, available at: https://bit.ly/3VfXSpA.

EIOPA (European Insurance and Occupational Pensions Authority) (2023b), 'Staff paper on nature-related risks and impacts for insurance', EIOPA-23/247, 29 March 2023, available at: https://bit.ly/3VtE2J7.

EIOPA (European Insurance and Occupational Pensions Authority) (2023c), 'Fact Sheet: Insurers' Green Investments', 1 March, available at: https://bit.ly/3Vz7kGt.

EIOPA (European Insurance and Occupational Pensions Authority) (2023d), 'Consultation paper, Prudential treatment of sustainability risks, 13 December 2023, EIOPA-BoS-23-460, available at: https://bit.ly/3VBbkG3.

EIOPA and ECB (European Insurance and Occupational Pensions Authority/European Central Bank) (2023), 'Staff paper on policy options to reduce the climate insurance protection gap', 26 April 2023, available at: https://bit.ly/3xeY8wv.

European Commission (2021), 'Proposal for a Directive of the European Parliament and of the Council amending Directive 2009/138/EC as regards proportionality, quality of supervision, reporting, long-term guarantee measures, macro-prudential tools, sustainability risks, group and cross-border supervision', Brussels, 22 September, COM (2021) 581 final, available at: https://bit.ly/3VxEGVG.

Ferber, M. (2022), 'Draft report of the European Parliament on the proposal for a directive of the European Parliament and the Council, amending Directive 2009/138/EC as regards proportionality, quality of supervision, reporting, long-term guarantee measures, macro-prudential tools, sustainability risks, group and cross-border supervision', Committee on Economic and Monetary Affairs, 6 June, 2021/0295 (COD), available at: https://bit.ly/3RjIpUe.

Maatman, R. H. (2007), Prudent-person regel en verantwoord beleggingsbeleid', 6 *Tijdschrift voor Ondernemingsbestuur*, 177–187.

Maatman, R. H. (2020), 'Pensioenfondsen en zorgplichten: uitdijen of indammen?', in Busch, D. et al. (eds.), *Zorgplicht in de financiële sector, Bundel ter gelegenheid van het tienjarig bestaan van het Instituut voor Financieel Recht, Serie Onderneming & Recht, deel 122* (Deventer: Wolters Kluwer), p. 141–169.

PRA (Prudential Regulatory Authority) (2020), 'Supervisory Statement, Solvency II: Prudent Person Principle', SS 1/20, May, available at: https://bit.ly/3VwZsoe.

Van den Hurk, A. J. A. D. and Joosen, E. P. M. (2019), 'A cross-sectoral analysis of micro-prudential regulation', in Colaert, V., Busch, D. and Incalza, T. (eds.), *European Financial Regulation, levelling the cross-sectoral playing field* (Oxford, London, New York, New Delhi, Chicago: Hart Publishers), p. 129–159.

Van den Hurk, A. J. A. D. (2024), 'Prudent person approaches and ESG', in van Meerten, H., Bennett, P. and van Zanden, J. (eds.), *EU Pensions Law* (Cheltenham: E. Elgar Publishing) (forthcoming).

Van Hulle, K. (2019), *Solvency II, Solvency Requirements for EU Insurers, Solvency II Is Good for You* (Cambridge, Antwerp, Chicago: Intersentia), p. 431.

24

Sustainability Enforcement through Multilevel Financial Tools

Tomasz Braun

24.1 MULTILEVEL ENFORCEMENT TOOLS: GENERAL REGULATORY TRENDS

There are various tools of multiple characters that can serve as means to ensure the introduction of environmentally friendly policies and behaviours by businesses and by public authorities. Their range spreads from various sorts of subsidies and grants, through CO_2 and renewable energy–related financial instruments, to environment-protecting covenants in financing agreements. They differ in terms of their character, reach and efficiency.[1] While not necessarily being perfect, they still contribute to the growing universal recognition of the need to take tangible policy and regulatory actions to protect the environment.[2]

The chapter generally analyses a number of useful pro-climate policies and regulatory trends that support environmental and social sustainability.[3] In doing so, it addresses three main topics: (1) multilevel governance analysed from the normative theory viewpoint, (2) impact of global corporates on societies and (3) the regulatory approach to environmental sustainability challenges. The analysis proposed in this chapter combines these three topics and illustrates interrelationships among them to argue that environmental sustainability – as a major contemporary challenge – requires novelty of the regulatory approach which can draw on both official sector regulatory practices and the private-sector practice of corporations and other business entities to provide a more informed view of the type of multilevel governance that is needed to address environmental and social sustainability challenges.

The chapter attempts to provide a structured overview of the current state of debate around multilevel governance and regulation of environmental sustainability.[4] The

---

[1] O'Farrell and Anderson 2010, 62.
[2] Millar et al. 2021, 798.
[3] Rishi 2022, 150.
[4] Partial results of this research were discussed within the presentation entitled: 'Multilevel governance tools within the EU pro-climate policies' during the Annual University Association for Contemporary European Studies (UACES) Conference, in Belfast (online) on 10 September 2020 and 'Sustainability

chapter addresses the universal concern that the painful process of environmental degradation requires both preventive and reparatory regulations. Regulations that most of all would be purposeful but also operational, actionable and impactful.

The chapter is intended to provide a reference for these who realise that contemporary governance instruments need to be introduced and enforced on multiple levels.[5] It is hoped that the opinions presented here serve as support for the search for efficiency improvement in regulatory tools and provide a voice in a discussion on normative legal theory.

The importance of and cross-generational acceptance for sustainability allow for the use of multiple tools to ensure accurate implementation and efficient enforcement of sustainable environmental policies. Societal acceptance for the novel policy implementation tools and the openness for direct dialogue with regulators derive from the awareness of the existential threat to the planet related to the anthropogenic roots of damage to the environment and the complexity of how to respond adequately to this threat. Environmental policies vary even among EU Member States, despite the fact that EU states are strongly unified in other spheres.[6] However, enforcement of environmental policies requires close and orchestrated co-operation globally. The inefficiency of inward-looking policies misses the opportunity for public engagement, given the fact that properly implemented multilevel enforcement of environmental policies could play an integrating and economically beneficial role, especially regarding the use of financial tools, which will be discussed in this chapter.

Even the most universally acclaimed ideas of sustainability are only beneficial insofar as they are translated into implementable laws. And even the best written laws are only as good insofar as they are effective in practice. It is for lawmakers and regulators to use multiple enforcement instruments at their disposal to ensure the laws and regulations are complied with. The task is not easy, as globally connected dependencies pose a challenge for regulators, who act largely at the national and regional levels. The number of actors being held accountable for (non)sustainable practices is growing, while those stakeholders who are holding them accountable are playing a greater role.[7] The harmful effects of unsustainability have impacted a large range of industries, activities, geographies and actors.

A wide acceptance of a pro-nature governance is a new global paradigm and an unprecedented opportunity at the same time. However, if truly considering universal establishment and then enforcement of sustainability policies, there are multiple challenges confronting policymakers. They begin with different understanding of

enforcement through multi-level financial tools' during the online webinar of the Jean Monnet Centre for Excellence on European Union Sustainable Finance and Law on 9–10 September 2021. Reassuring feedback was received that there was a need for more research on multilevel governance of environmental and sustainability as discussed in this chapter.

5 Vantagiatto 2020, 183.
6 Roelfsema et al. 2020, 2096.
7 Ganguly et al. 2018, 852.

basic notions and conclude with uneven implementation due to varying local interests or different degrees of enforcement of national regulations. Therefore, enforcement of sustainability policies continues to be an unresolved problem, not in the sense that it is a failure but in the sense that its success could be much greater. To achieve this, it is necessary to extend the scope of implementation and enforcement tools that have been already tested in other industries to the area of sustainability. Not using this extended choice of implementation tools is a missed opportunity.

The problem should be analysed from the three angles: first, multilevel governance regarded from the normative theory viewpoint; second, the impact of global corporates on societies and the potential of using them as agents in the process of sustainability enforcement; and third, the regulatory approach to environmental sustainability challenges. The proposed approach to this problem combines all three areas and illustrates interrelations among them. In fact, it proves that a major contemporary challenge, which the environmental sustainability is, requires novelty in the regulatory approach, which lawmakers and regulators can learn from the corporates and other organised societies' experience.[8] It also argues that the governance instruments that need to be introduced require an approach on multiple levels so that their efficient enforcement is assured. Both the efficient use of regulatory tools and the discussion of how normative legal theory can enhance this improvement are important topics to be addressed.

Much of the literature referring to the problem of global environmental policy governance addresses sustainability enforcement either from a purely political science angle or from the socio-economic one. Relatively fewer discussions refer to the current regulatory status of multilevel governance tools proposed within the environmental policies. At the same time, innovative and multilevelled approaches become a daily reality of regulators in other spheres. Whatever happens in environmental regulation now is going to have an impact on the future sustainability of societies. Though it is still difficult to measure this impact at present, it is nonetheless becoming an urgent issue.

From the policy-making perspective, the use of the multilevel regulatory instruments is a beginning of the journey. In the present decisive moment when there is growing acceptance of the necessity to introduce efficient measures to ensure sustainability implementation, an opportunity arises to provide a well-thought-out, efficient and just regulatory framework, one which will shape the approach towards the current environmental challenges for future generations. Within this process of rethinking the tools that have been used so far, the focus is put on the financial institutions and more generally on other global corporates as well. The overarching presumption is that if lessons learned from global corporate policies have proven to be efficient when tackling some earlier social challenges, then similar approaches involving corporations and especially financial institutions could be used to address the challenges caused by uncontrolled industrial development that degrade the environment. Therefore, the need for an efficient regulatory approach to address these complex challenges

---

[8] Barnes and Hoerber 2013, 7.

requires a hybrid regulatory approach involving official sector policymakers, regulators and private-sector companies and financial intermediaries. For example, a variety of approaches by corporations to compliance norm-making and implementation practices could serve as benchmarks to develop robust sustainability regulations.[9]

Multilevel legislative and regulatory governance tools range from discouragement to incentives – from consulting, engaging, encouraging and sandboxing to hard-regulating. Similarly, multilevel enforcement can and should be effectuated throughout a range of various measures, from audits and controls that result in recommendations backed by executable fines to more non-obvious and indirect measures that include the political and financial ones. Most of these measures have already been tested while regulating other areas, in particular those in which irregularities and wrongdoings have been socially unacceptable, like bribery and corruption.

24.2 BOTTOM-UP APPROACH TO SUSTAINABILITY POLICIES' IMPLEMENTATION

The weakness of top-down policies is that they are inward-looking, miss the opportunity of public engagement and eventually make the laws less effective than they could be if a more creative approach had been deployed. To ensure this efficiency it is crucial to engage various actors – organised civil society, businesses and financial institutions – in the implementation of sustainability regulations and, potentially, in their enforcement.

From the policy-making perspective, deployment of the multilevel enforcement model is at the beginning phase. Thus there is an opportunity to construct a well-thought-out, efficient and just regulatory framework for the future. Particular focus should be put on the instruments in the hands of the financial institutions and more generally on the power possessed by the global corporations, but also on other players such as the NGOs, which in many instances have proved more successful in achieving certain goals than the public authorities.[10]

The well-known earlier concepts of ubiquitous regulatory tools have become present in the current discussion again. The soft norms implemented by various stakeholders at different levels can lead to better enforcement results but require an openness from the policymakers and their readiness to accept an agile approach to the traditional concepts of the societal division of roles and responsibilities.[11] The task is not too complex, though, as it refers to well-recognised wider compliance concepts that corporations have previously applied successfully. The roles of corporate governance, internal conduct codes and risk policies have already introduced a normative environment for global corporations in addressing environmental and social challenges.[12]

---

[9] Heddeman-Robinson 2018, 42.
[10] Pereira et al. 2021, 1918.
[11] Knodt 2019, 181.
[12] Sheehy 2019, 80.

24.3 TOP-DOWN FINANCIAL MEASURES BY
MULTILAYERED REGULATORY POWERS

There are numerous stakeholders engaged in nature protection policy discussions: intergovernmental organisations, their member states and their markets; states and societies; international organisations and third countries; organised stakeholders, activists etc.[13] As a result of these discussions a number of the internationally adopted environmental policies have been conceptually conceived, politically consented and implemented at multiple levels,[14] for example, policies that focus on pro-climate agendas like reduction of emissions, renewable energy, waste management, deforestation and protection of waters.[15] Various political agencies spell out their environmental positions and strive to ensure their implementation. The United Nations and its agencies, the Council of Europe, the EU, the states and local authorities – on each level political acceptance turns into regulatory measures.[16] Still their efficiency remains uneven. In particular, present cross-border environmental policy discussions in the EU that are multi-vectoral and take place between numerous stakeholders, including, among others, the EU and Member States, States and markets, the EU and societies, the EU and third countries, organised stakeholders, activists etc.

Among a number of financial measures that ultimately can have regulatory power are public debt instruments. Aside from that, probably the most efficient financial innovations in the area of sustainable finance have been the development of green, sustainability and social bonds. In principle they are constructed similarly to other types of investment bond.[17] The difference is in the purpose of their use. They are issued to finance green, sustainability or socially beneficiary investments and cannot be used to raise capital for other conventional corporate projects.[18] For instance, they can only be used for financing or re-financing projects, assets or products that are in line with environmental or social purposes. They are unique in that the bond buyer has recourse to the balance sheet of the issuer if the bonds have not been used in accordance with their environmental or social purpose and at the same time is not exposed to the financial risks of the specific projects financed through labelled bond finances.[19]

The most important challenge that green and other sustainably labelled bonds respond to is the scarcity of access to long-term financing for investment in climate or generally environmental projects. The issuing of the sustainability bonds can be executed by both private and public financial institutions. However, public financial institutions, due to their wider responsibility mission, may sometimes

---

[13] Alexander 2022, 114.
[14] Hoerber 2012, 152.
[15] Fernandez 2021, 94.
[16] Hoerber et al. 2021, 51.
[17] Hill 2020, 27.
[18] See Chiu and Schiammo, Chapter 14 in this volume. Also Sachs et al. 2020, 7.
[19] Maltais and Nykwist 2020, 8.

be better placed to respond to this scarcity and to support the green sector. State-owned or state-missioned banks in countries, as well as such intergovernmental financial institutions as the Bank of Reconstruction and Development and the European Investment Bank, provide financing amounting to hundreds of billions of euros. They provide equity and finance investments for transition of economies by injecting liquidity and covering cost of risk guarantees for energy efficiency transformations, renewable energy investments and sustainable transport projects.[20]

Sustainably engaged financial institutions open dedicated credit or investment lines with specific products and projects for green-labelled financing. Additionally, they integrate sustainability considerations into conventional project financing. Many financial institutions use sustainability criteria, measurement, monitoring and auditing to evaluate some performance indicators such as greenhouse gas emission reductions.[21] In parallel to well-established approval concepts and procedures, they use more sophisticated methodologies referring to risk management. They differ depending on the specific industry sector and technology: from renewable energy production and storage to transport; from research and development to deployment and modernisation; from protection of waters and sewage systems to waste management and the circle economy.[22]

24.4 A NEED FOR UNIFICATION OF SUSTAINABILITY ENFORCEMENT MEASURES

Environmental challenges, by definition, are cross-border and global. The enforcement tools that address them need to be global as well. Moreover, they have to be efficient, hence they need to be smart and adjusted to the changing societal, economic, cultural and political reality.[23] In the complexity of today's interconnected dependencies this means they need to be multilevelled, as the environmental problems occur on various levels. Recent complications in the global situation caused by such issues as wars, droughts, floods, fires, energy deficits and social unrest, among others, have made this need even more apparent. This is a new and important task for regulators and lawmakers as well as for all other actors participating in the sustainability and environmental debate.

Involving all interested stakeholders prior to issuing regulations is the best lawmakers can do to assure participatory engagement.[24] This is not simply the right thing to do from the democratic dialogue perspective;[25] it can also help ensure that regulations are more fit for purpose and it increases the probability that these regulations will be better

---

[20] Sugiawan and Manag 2019, 9.
[21] Ziolo et al. 2021, 38.
[22] Taghizadeh-Hesary and Yoshino 2020, 788.
[23] Weiss and Kammel 2015, 14.
[24] Bellucci and Manetti 2018, 111.
[25] Fiorino 2018, 92.

complied with by their targets. It is therefore for lawmakers to select from a variety of instruments at their disposal to correctly adjust them to modern society expectations. This selection would first of all refer to the soft-law instruments which from the efficiency point of view have their own well-established position on the map of normative tools. Some would argue that this approach has been re-invented by lawmakers who observed that corporations had adhered to soft norms prior to launching new projects. Compliance has been increasingly used as a concept referring to the way the subjects of norms adhere to them.[26] It refers not only to huge business conglomerates in which it is being successfully introduced. However, the regulatory instruments which utilise indirect channels to make these norms more generally understood are still underused.

Introducing new regulatory approaches that involve implementing corporate policies merits a more informed debate. The importance of the pro-nature subject and the necessity for cross-generational acceptance for sustainability allows for the use of multiple tools and experience in implementing the environmental policies. However, one of the main lessons from the corporate experience is the observation that sustainability enforcement requires close and orchestrated co-operation of various actors globally. Uneven implementation and in particular weak enforcement mechanisms of environmental policies, even within such a legally unified organisation as the EU, poses significant challenges.[27] The EU laws and regulations refer equally to all subjects operating within its territory, but the level of implementation varies dramatically among the Member States.

It is a missed opportunity given the fact that properly implemented multilevel enforcement of sustainability programmes could promote EU integration and economic development. The particularly urgent problem of the use of financial enforcement tools in this process needs to be more thoroughly explored in practice.

24.5 INTERRELATIONS AMONG SUSTAINABILITY ENFORCEMENT TOOLS AND CORPORATE PRACTICES

There are well tested methods which measure, control, ensure and correct the prudent approach of businesses to selected matters. The use of fit and proper testing is one of them, and can be used for addressing environment-related risks within the process of sustainability policies' implementation.[28] Another example is the obligation to introduce a rigorous approach to sustainability measures and implementation indicators together with a accountability framework for those responsible for carrying out implementation.[29] Previously, financial institutions have successfully undertaken a monitoring role of their stability indicators. Similar mechanisms may refer to sustainability enforcement based on the principle that compliance with

---

[26] Rogers 2022, 75.
[27] Rossinioli et al. 2021, 32.
[28] See Palm-Steyerberg, Chapter 22 in this volume. Also Bastedas-Orteaga and Stewart 2019, 20.
[29] Waas et al. 2014, 5530.

environment protection norms has to be measured and controlled. Assurance of a rigorous approach to sustainability indicators could then be similar to the way it has been for financial stability. Additionally, this process, supported by the growing role of technology, results in an increased number of sustainable fintechs and technology-enhanced controls over the sustainability enforcement assured by the other financial institutions.[30] Another corporate practice that may contribute to sustainability enforcement is the reference to environment-friendly policies in prospectus regulations and the role of non-financial disclosures within corporate reports and other documents.[31] Consequently, the accountability for trustworthiness and delivery of environmental indicators is the condition under which the disclosed corporate reports can be useful sustainability enforcement tools.[32]

The lessons learned from corporate compliance management practices prove that the real threat to environmental policies is a tolerance for any sort of wrongdoing, fraud and misreporting.[33] Countering environmental wrongdoings is a key responsibility of all stakeholders engaged in this process. And, as in many other internal corporate compliance processes, this one should be properly structured, managed and monitored. There are many examples of wrongdoings and greenwashing practices that should not distract from the true picture. Also, other tools deriving from the wider compliance concept can be accordingly adjusted to the needs of sustainability enforcement.[34] The analysis of the role of corporate governance codes and various policy-related incentive instruments that they introduce is particularly useful.[35]

24.6 SUSTAINABILITY POLICIES: LESSONS FROM THE FINANCIAL SECTOR

Multilevel financial tools range from incentives to disincentives. Numerous – sometimes non-obvious and indirect – methods have been used: from consulting, to engaging; from encouraging and sandboxing to hard-regulating, auditing and project implementation monitoring. Most of these measures have already been tested while regulating other industries and social spheres. Multicentricity is a response to the inefficiency of very often inward-looking public policies. A crucial role should be played by organised civil society, businesses and financial institutions in assisting in the enforcement of sustainability goals. The research questions are not limited to analyses of the impact of existing financial tools but also refer to what else could be done to enhance them.

One of many innovative approaches to global environmental policy governance relates to the use of financial instruments that serve as the enforcement tools. They

---

[30] Machiavello and Siri 2022, 130.
[31] Gargantini and Di Noia 2020, 370.
[32] Lepore and Pisano 2022, 28.
[33] Ghoogossian 2015, 368.
[34] Baldwin and Cave 2021, 82.
[35] Gargantini 2019, 291.

vary from public money and fiscal incentives such as subsidies, grants and tax levies to CO_2 and renewable energy–related certificates as well as other tradable financial instruments. The efficient design of financial instruments requires the involvement of engaged partners, including businesses and financial institutions. Their role is instrumental in relating governance policies to corporate practices and then in promoting them widely among the addressees of these policies.

The same relates to prudential requirements imposed by the regulators on financial institutions, which can serve as a reference for sustainability enforcement. Introducing them has not happened immediately and has been a result of hard lessons learned throughout several repeated financial crises. It required a combination of public approval, lawmaker willingness and the capacity to endure economic costs that may inhibit the process. Introducing innovative yet efficient and safe financial instruments as tools to enhance enforcement of sustainability requires an engaged and informed environmental debate. The particular role in this debate play public actors that introduce sustainable finance governance tools.[36] The same applies to other market-related instruments that may support sustainability enforcement for those who seek investment from financial institutions.

The concept of engaging financial institutions in sustainability implementation is built on a principle of delegating the enforcement one level down from public institutions. It may be regarded as a *sui generis* subsidiarising of this process, or as privatisation of enforcement. It usually takes place with the use of formalising contractual obligations by introducing environment-protecting covenants in investment, trade or project finance agreements. The use of financial institutions as intermediaries within the process of sustainability regulations enforcement may expand also to the fit and proper testing of environment-related risk management performed by them. Again, the best method that can and increasingly has been implemented refers to the contractual mandates that the financial institutions have over businesses and the counterparties of agreements executed by them.

There are other financial instruments that have become efficient sustainability enforcement measures due to their globally tradable character. The EU Emissions Trading System (ETS) involves the use of green and renewable energy certificates.[37] They have been established as a result of public regulatory policies supporting the Clean Development Policy (CDM). On 14 July 2021, the European Commission adopted the legislative measures setting out the plan to attain a goal of climate neutrality.[38] These measures intend to achieve the 55% net reduction of greenhouse gas emissions by 2030.[39] The proposals change several EU regulations.[40] Among the changes are those that set out the ways in which the Commission intends to reach the EU climate targets

[36] Colgan et al. 2021, 588.
[37] See Annunziata, Chapter 25 in this volume.
[38] Eyl-Mazzega and Mathieu 2019, 25.
[39] Busch et al. 2021, 15.
[40] de Oliveira Neves 2022, 157.

under the European Green Deal, including the Emissions Trading System, the Effort Sharing Regulation and transport and land use legislations, among others.

The Paris Agreement established a new market mechanism to replace the CDM and Joint Implementation (JI) after 2020. Until 2020, subject to some restrictions, participants in the EU ETS could use international credits from CDM and Joint Implementation (JI) as part of their obligations under the EU ETS.[41] The role of technology in achieving environmental goals has already been indicated in the context of fintech and other innovative financial institutions.[42] However, they extend far beyond it and refer to the analytical capacities of financial institutions that use such new technologies as big data, machine learning, cloud computing, blockchain and artificial intelligence.

24.7 MULTILEVEL SUSTAINABILITY ENFORCEMENT TOOLS

The regulators should and can lead in implementing an innovative policy approach designed to enhance efficiency. The environmental problems are, by their nature, intricate and require carefully designed regulatory measures. The richness of measures reflected in multicentric and multilevel legislation at international, national and subnational levels refers to a variety of sectors and industries impacted by environmental challenges. All this creates a complex network of interrelated regulations. Some of them already exist, some are emerging.

There is a wide range of tools in the hands of law- and policymakers. And many of them are *per se* a challenge to limitations of a traditional approach to normative landscape. They require from them an open-minded view on the role of the sustainability regulation and sometimes the involvement of multiple actors on various levels. Some eminent examples of these tools can be pointed out while observing the EU initiatives. The EU began as a loose economic co-operation organisation that evolved into a Union which expanded its policy areas to include sustainability, climate change, ecological agriculture, forest protection, fishery quotas, environmental justice and energy solidarity.[43] To realise them the EU established specialised agencies and equipped them with enforcement tools. Several of them are actively implemented by the Committee of the Regions. This subsidiary body of the EU institutions established to support the implementation of its legislation at the local and regional level actively

---

[41] International credits refer to financial instruments that represent a tonne of CO_2 removed or reduced from the atmosphere as a result of an emissions reduction project. International credits are generated through two mechanisms set up under the Kyoto Protocol: Clean Development Mechanisms (CDM), allowing industrialised countries with a greenhouse gas reduction commitment to invest in projects that reduce emissions in developing countries as an alternative to more expensive emissions reductions in their own countries and the JI, allowing industrialised countries to meet part of their required cuts in greenhouse gas emissions by paying for projects that reduce emissions in other industrialised countries provides for the creation of Emission Reduction Units (ERUs), whereas this provides for the creation of Certified Emission Reductions (CERs).

[42] Macchiavello and Siri 2020, 6.

[43] Wenta et al. 2019, 109.

promotes the multilevel approaches. In line with these promotional undertakings, the Committee of the Regions adopted a Charter for Multilevel Governance in Europe calling public authorities of all levels to use and promote multilevel governance in their future policies.[44] The EU Cohesion Policy utilises almost a third of the total EU budget and supports sustainability initiatives that aim to increase stakeholder ownership in multilevel governance and partnership strengthening.[45]

The practice of financial institutions has become instrumental for sustainability enforcement as they are influenced by their investors and customers to undertake socially responsible lending and investment.[46] They have shifted from using narrowly defined environmental criteria to a broader range of factors, such as: achievement of zero net carbon emissions or percentage reductions in carbon emissions; commissioning and achieving sustainability accreditations by rating agencies; introducing policies that refer to monitoring of environmental, social and governance indicators; assessment of supply chains for human and employee rights abuses, slavery and poor labour standards; maintaining appropriate corporate codes of ethics; and participating in initiatives to improve local communities.

Sustainable law and its enforcement are multilevel and pluralistic. They are multilevel as no single institution can solely generate all the rules nowadays. They are pluralistic as the creation, implementation and enforcement of laws require the participation of stakeholders from all sectors of the society.[47] In this sense multicentricity and multilevel governance are ready-to-use tools that need to involve various stakeholders and to take into account the characteristics of the enforcing bodies and the country in which they are located. Their efficiency may be affected by the country's legal tradition and other variables, such as its size, ownership structure and the sector in which it operates.[48]

The well-known path is also to engage companies in the process of enforcement of sustainability policies. One of the most important recent developments in this direction is the current discussion on the implementation of sustainability policies through the enrolment of companies. This approach relies on the intuition that companies should be directed and controlled so that they become the enforcement vectors for sustainability policies. This overall agenda constitutes the concept of sustainable corporate governance.[49]

Although sustainability as a catch-all term refers to multiple areas, companies address sustainability issues more effectively when they combine missions and long-term plans by focussing on specific sustainability topics.[50] When such specific

---

[44] Och 2020.
[45] Dobravec 2021, 11.
[46] Siri and Zhu 2019, 4.
[47] Plater 2006.
[48] Fernandez-Feijoo et al. 2015.
[49] See Sjåfjell, Chapter 2 in this volume and Helleringer and Parajon Skinner, Chapter 4 in this volume. Also: World Economic Forum 2021.
[50] Lasalla et al. 2021, 428.

sustainability topics are in line with the company's priorities, they have a greater chance for efficient implementation. Once they define the selected sustainability topics that matter to them, companies therefore become efficient enforcement agents due to their coverage and reach. The question of the motivations of the companies to do so remains separate. Incentives in this regard usually come from the fact that sustainability concerns can be relevant to the business or because they pertain to areas in which the company is uniquely positioned, and this helps build a competitive advantage. Whichever commercial motivation backs the decision to take part in the sustainability agenda, the involvement of the commercial and growth-driven corporations is becoming increasingly important.[51]

Engaging various actors of the civil society, businesses and financial institutions is therefore crucial for setting the sustainability goals and also enforcing them. There are numerous examples of NGOs being more successful in achieving certain goals than public administration. Their involvement into the process towards sustainability may positively contribute to efficiency. Most of these measures have already been tested while regulating other industries and social spheres – multicentricity and multilevel governance are thus the ready-to-use tools. It is for law-making institutions to deploy all available instruments at their hands to ensure the efficiency of the proposed measures.

There are also examples of other tools tested in the corporate word that have proven to support enforcement efficiently. The most powerful among them are public funding and fiscal incentives, like subsidies, grants, tax levies and other similar mechanisms. Subsidies or other types of direct financial support can take many forms. They can be direct subsidies, provided to the industry as a whole or to selected recipients, for instance by lowering the price of a certain technology or supporting prices as a reward for good practice. Subsidies can also take the form of research and development programmes which promote innovative solutions. Even though direct subsidies can be effective, by definition they come at the expense of the taxpayers who finance them. A critical question therefore refers to the level of financial support to be provided by the state. On one hand, the amount of subsidies must encourage firms to switch to more sustainable technologies and, on the other hand, the stronger the support, the greater the cost for taxpayers. However, when subsidies are only apparently efficient, the burden of the financing rests on the shoulders of taxpayers and not the polluters, as in reality they actually reduce the negative externality.[52]

Fiscal policy direction is always a lawmaker's choice. The imposition of taxes as well as the grant of tax rebates and tax exemptions can directly impact the development of sustainable technologies. Similarly, carbon pricing has been a popular policy instrument, although it endangers the competitiveness of some economies.

---

[51] McKinsey 2021.
[52] Tanaka 2011, 6547.

Taxation to promote sustainability leads to limiting emissions, but on the other hand they may also be detrimental to competitiveness. Therefore, public authorities need to face a complex dilemma before proposing such measures. At the same time, the issue of fairness and equity along with efficiency emerges in every instance when introducing these measures.[53] Energy efficiency and renewable energy are essential measures to control CO_2 emissions. Fiscal policy and other CO_2 and renewable energy–related financial instruments are vital policy tools regarding energy generation, storage and consumption. However, while fiscal policies supporting these strategies have proven effective in reducing CO_2 emissions, they can also negatively impact economic growth.[54]

On the other side of the spectrum of sustainability enforcement measures are the environment-protecting covenants in financing agreements. The mechanism is straightforward. These covenants increase the costs of polluting the environment and incentivise borrowers to reduce pollution and adhere to environmental best practices. They trigger preventive actions to avoid environmental damages or take remedial actions when these damages occur. They allow lenders to require necessary information and audits to evaluate environmental risks. In case there are events qualifying as breach of environmental covenants, the lenders may have right to impose more costly loan terms or even cancel the loan. The borrowers may face criminal charges if they continue polluting after lenders uncover environmental violations. If the borrowers comply with environmental regulations, they avoid these consequences.[55] This is the main strength of environmental covenants as enforcement measures.

There is another, growingly important set of enforcement tools: the new technology-enhanced controls. Effective and forward-looking use of technology can become a tool that adapts to the changes taking place in society in ensuring sustainability within the production processes. Appropriate policies supporting environmental sustainability can leverage on the implementation of the new technologies that determine how inputs of raw materials, information and energy can be controlled. Then, during the deployment and production processes, these technologies can also ensure the quality of products. Finally, new technologies can support waste treatment and reduce emissions of greenhouse gases and contaminations of waters and soils. They can also help determine what can be fed back into the production processes, thus facilitating the use of by-products as resources. Also, the new technologies can support the regeneration of the ecosystem.[56]

Addressing sustainability challenges requires new technologies solutions that can help mitigating the adverse impacts of production. The sustainable technological change is also a societal, organisational, political and economic shift that recognises

---

[53] Sarker et al. 2020, 6.
[54] Akbar et al. 2021, 2605.
[55] See Schoutens et al., Chapter 27 in this volume. Also: Choy et al. 2022.
[56] Olah et al. 2020, 4674.

that many sectors, such as energy generation, water supply and waste re-use, need networks of actors. For example, a carbon-free technologies may require the establishment of new value chains. It may mean a long process that can alter society in several ways by changing consumer behaviour, distributional effects, infrastructure development and establishing new business models.[57]

None of the measures listed above can be truly efficient unless preceded by an informed debate engaging stakeholders prior to regulating. Good examples of that approach can be the enforcement of the Trade and Sustainable Development (TSD) chapters within the EU Free Trade Agreement, where there is a consensus on how to proceed to achieve the goals set by the document. This consensus relies on a list of practicable actions and recommendations categorised around such areas as: working together; enabling civil society (including the social partners such as NGOs) to play a greater role in implementation; delivering; and transparency and communication. All of them refer to the informed and participatory debate.

The substantial strengthening of sustainability-related measures and the facilitation of innovation proposed above can involve such areas as climate change, engagement of civil society and use of the resources to support the implementation of TSD chapters. More assertive enforcement can further improve on this picture. The European Commission together with interested stakeholders have been mandated to review the functioning and impact of the implementation of TSD chapters and will continue to engage to analyse the effectiveness of the implementation of the TSD chapters.[58]

24.8 SUSTAINABILITY ENFORCEMENT AND CORPORATE ETHICAL INTEGRITY: TAKEAWAYS

One of the greatest successes of compliance programmes implemented within the global businesses is assurance of engagement of all stakeholders. Multijurisdictional corporate superpowers together with public authorities have the potential to create a sustainable policies enforcement system. Additionally, environmental conduct requirements introduced in legislation at various levels can constitute criteria for the assessment of the extent to which the managements of the businesses are sustainably compliant. This strategy has been tested within the internal corporate policies, so there are good reasons to believe it can be an equally useful tool within the multilevel governance of the implementation of environmental policies.

Moreover, institutional investors have their role in assessing to what extent financing of environment-friendly products and technologies – and thus enforcing corporate sustainability – has been assured by corporations. They may use various criteria

---

[57] Soderholm 2020, 5.
[58] Prevost and Alexovicova 2019, 239.

and approaches to evaluate this element and are obliged to report it.[59] The control over compliance with the internal environmental conduct is certainly a novel measure of sustainability assurance.

Overall, various concepts and methods have been developed to improve both individual and collective decision making about actions that will affect the environment. However, what criteria would be appropriate for calling an environmental decision a good choice is still debated and will likely remain an open issue. Six parameters for evaluating environmental decisions are: human and environmental well-being, competence about facts and values, fairness in process and outcome, reliance on human strengths rather than weaknesses, the opportunity to learn and efficiency. Hopefully, an explicit discussion of the appropriate criteria for environmental decisions will lead to better conceptualisations, better tools and ultimately better decisions.[60]

Stakeholder engagement, as an important factor boosting efficiency, can be conceptualised in different ways. It can be seen as capturing knowledge, increasing ownership of the project, reducing conflict, encouraging innovation and facilitating spin-off partnerships. From an ethical perspective, it can be seen as fostering inclusive decision making, promoting equity, enhancing local decision and building social capital. The benefits of stakeholder engagement are vital for sustainability.[61] It can also be seen from the perspective of an opportunity for a social process where stakeholders mutually learn about their values on a common forum, reflect upon these values and strive to establish a common set of them. Dialogue is useful in increasing awareness, changing attitudes and affecting behaviours. There is a need for an approach that enhances ethical perspectives of sustainability where an open dialogue is an important part of the axiological assessment of the sustainability. An open dialogue approach to integrated sustainability assessment could provide an ideal means to enforce policies and laws.[62] Moreover, the continuing economic crisis and global consequences of regional conflicts have extended the debate on the importance of a corporate sustainability agenda for corporate social responsibility initiatives and practices and their ethical consequences.[63]

24.9 CONCLUSIONS

To be efficient, sustainability enforcement needs to enlist multilevel tools, including the financial ones. The use of multilevel enforcement tools, that is, those that engage various private and public stakeholders, is a general regulatory trend that has already been tested in various sectors. By engaging businesses and other social

[59] Cremasco and Boni 2022, 7.
[60] Dietz 2003, 33–39.
[61] Manetti 2011, 112.
[62] Narin Mathur et al. 2008, 601–609.
[63] Kartadjumena and Rodgers 2019, 1673.

organisations, it ensures a bottom-up approach to the implementation of sustainability policies.[64] On the other side, top-down financial measures used by multi-layered regulatory powers like lawmakers and public administration demonstrate that the legal system needs to be hybrid in nature, as it needs to continue deploying more traditional tools apart from soft powers.[65] Despite a subsidiarity left to countries that may select their own ways to assure sustainability implementation, there is a need for unification of sustainability enforcement measures as sustainability is a global problem and the risks it aims to tackle are entirely global. Particular benefits for the efficiency of sustainability enforcement programmes derive from the inter-relations of sustainability enforcement tools and corporate practices. Especially promising are the lessons on sustainability policies' implementation taken from the financial industry, which is crucial for facilitating investments on new technologies and for improving the existing ones. To be sure, the use of multilevel sustainability enforcement tools may evoke numerous ethical dilemmas.[66] However, even within this area, the corporate world and specifically the financial industry may rely on methodologies that support the enforcement of sustainability polices in an efficient manner.

REFERENCES

Akbar, M. W., Yuelan, P., Zia, Z. and Arshad, M. I. (2021), 'Role of fiscal policy in energy efficiency and CO_2 emission nexus: An investigation of Belt and Road Region', 2 *Journal of Public Affairs*, e2603.

Alexander, K. (2022), 'Global financial governance and banking regulation: Redesigning regulation to promote stakeholder interests', in Pauwellyn, J., Maggeti, M., Buthe, T. and Berman, A. (eds.), *Rethinking Participation in Global Governance: Challenges and Reforms in Financial and Health Institutions* (Oxford: Oxford University Press), 111–126.

Baldwin, R. and Cave, M. (2021), *Taming the Corporation: How to Regulate for Success* (Oxford: Oxford University Press).

Barnes, P. M. and Hoerber, T. C. (eds.) (2013), *Sustainable Development and Governance in Europe: The Evolution of the Discourse on Sustainability* (London: Routledge).

Bastedas-Orteaga, E. and Stewart, M. G. (2019), *Climate Adaptation Engineering: Risks and Economics for Infrastructure Decision-Making* (Oxford: Butterworth-Heinemann).

Bellucci, M. and Manetti, G. (2018), *Stakeholder Engagement and Sustainability Reporting* (London: Routledge).

Busch, D., Ferrarini, G. and Grünewald, S. (2021), *Sustainable Finance in Europe* (London: Palgrave Macmillan).

Choy, S., Jiang, S., Liao, S. and Wang, E. (2022), 'Public environmental enforcement and private lender monitoring: Evidence from environmental covenants', 10(1) *Rotman School of Management Working Paper*, 3860178.

Colgan, J., Green, J. and Hale, T. (2021), 'Asset revaluation and the existential politics of climate change', 75(2) *International Organization*, 586–610.

---

[64] Smith 2008, 361.
[65] Eicken et al. 2021, 473.
[66] Crane et al. 2019, 233.

Crane, A., Matten, D., Glozer, S. and Spence, L. J. (2019), *Business Ethics: Managing Corporate Citizenship and Sustainability in the Age of Globalization* (Oxford: Oxford University Press).

Cremasco, C. and Boni, L. (2022), 'Is the European Union (EU) Sustainable Finance Disclosure Regulation (SFDR) effective in shaping sustainability objectives? An analysis of investment funds' behaviour', 9 *Journal of Sustainable Finance & Investment*, 1–19.

de Oliveira Neves, R. (2022), 'The EU Taxonomy Regulation and its implications for companies', in Camara, P. and Morais, F. (eds.), *The Palgrave Handbook of ESG and Corporate Governance* (London: Palgrave Macmillan).

Dietz, T. (2003), 'What is a good decision? Criteria for environmental decision making', 10(1) *Human Ecology Review*, 33–39.

Dobravec, V., Matak, N., Sakulin, C. and Krajacic, G. (2021), 'Multilevel governance energy planning and policy: A view on local energy initiatives', 11(2) *Energy, Sustainability and Society*, 1–17.

Eicken, H., Danielsen, F., Sam, J.-M. et al. (2021), 'Connecting top-down and bottom-up approaches in environmental observing', 71(5) *BioScience*, 467–483.

Eyl-Mazzega, M. A and Mathieu, C. (2019), 'Strategic dimensions of the energy transition: Challenges and responses for France, Germany and the EU', Etudes de l'IFRI, available at: https://bit.ly/45hdo9l.

Fernandez-Feijoo, B., Romero, S. and Ruiz, S. (2015), *Multilevel Approach to Sustainability Report Assurance Decisions*, 14 December, available at: https://doi.org/10.1111/auar.12104.

Fernandez, R. (2021), 'Community Renewable Energy Projects: The Future of the Sustainable Energy Transition?', 56 *The International Spectator*, 87–104.

Fiorino, D. J. (2018), *Can Democracy Handle Climate Change* (Cambridge, UK: Polity).

Ganguly, G., Setzer, J. and Heyvaert, V. (2018), 'If at first you don't succeed: Suing corporations for climate change', 38(4) *Oxford Journal of Legal Studies*, 841–868.

Gargantini, M. (2019), 'Corporate governance, financial information and EU market abuse regulation', in Busch, D., Ferrarini, G. and van Solinge, G. (eds.), *Corporate Governance of Financial Institutions* (Oxford: Oxford University Press), p. 291.

Gargantini, M. and Di Noia, C. (2020), 'The approval of prospectus: Competent authorities, notification and sanctions', in Busch, D., Ferrarini, G. and Franx, J. P. (eds.), *Prospectus Regulation and Prospectus Liability* (Oxford: Oxford University Press), p. 370.

Ghoogossian, C. (2015), 'Evading the transparency tragedy: The legal enforcement of corporate sustainability reporting', 11(2) *Hastings Business Law School*, 361–384.

Heddeman-Robinson, M. (2018), *Enforcement of International Environmental Law: Challenges and Responses at the International Level* (London: Routledge).

Hill, J. (2020), *Environmental, Social, and Governance Investing: A Balanced Analysis of the Theory and Practice of a Sustainable Portfolio* (Amsterdam: Elsevier Science/Academic Press).

Hoerber, T. (2012), *The Origins of Energy and Environmental Policy in Europe: The Beginnings of a European Environmental Conscience* (London: Routledge).

Hoerber, T., Kurze, K. and Kuenzer, J. (2021), 'Towards ego-ecology? Populist environmental agendas and the sustainability transition in Europe', 56 *The International Spectator*, 1–15.

Kartadjumena, E. and Rodgers, W. (2019), 'Executive compensation, sustainability, climate, environmental concerns, and company financial performance: Evidence from Indonesian commercial banks', 11(6) *Sustainability*, 1673.

Knodt, M. (2019), 'Multilevel coordination in EU energy policy: A new type of "harder" soft governance?', in Behnke, N., Broschek, J. and Sonnicksen, J. (eds.), *Configurations, Dynamics, and Mechanisms of Multilevel Governance* (London: Palgrave Macmillan), 173–192.

Lasalla, C., Orero-Blat, M. and Ribeiro-Navarette, S. (2021), 'The financial performance of listed companies in pursuit of the Sustainable Development Goals (SDG)', 34(11) *Economic Research*, 427–449.

Lepore, L. and Pisano, S. (2022), *Environmental Disclosure. Critical Issues and New Trends* (London: Routledge).

Macchiavello, E. and Siri M. (2020), 'Sustainable finance and fintech: Can technology contribute to achieving environmental goals. A preliminary assessment of "Green FinTech"', European Banking Institute Working Papers 71.

Machiavello, E. and Siri, M. (2022), 'Sustainable finance and fintech: Can technology contribute to achieving environmental goals? A preliminary assessment of "green fintech" and "sustainable digital finance"', 19(1) *European Company and Financial Law Review*, 128–174.

Maltais, A. and Nykwist, B. (2020), 'Understanding the role of green bonds in advancing sustainability', 14(2) *Journal of Sustainable Finance and Investment*, 1–20.

Manetti, G. (2011), 'The quality of stakeholder engagement in sustainability reporting: Empirical evidence and critical points', 18(2) *Corporate Social Responsibility and Environmental Management*, 110–122.

McKinsey (2021), 'Sustainability, organizing for sustainability success: Where, and how, leaders can start', 10 August, available at: https://mck.co/3VFpV3i.

Millar, H., Bourgeois, E., Bernstein, S. and Hoffmann, M. (2021), 'Self-reinforcing and self-undermining feedbacks in subnational climate policy implementation', 30(5) *Environmental Politics*, 791–810.

Narin Mathur, V., Price, A. D. F. and Austin, S. (2008), 'Conceptualizing stakeholder engagement in the context of sustainability and its assessment', 16(6) *Construction Management and Economics*, 601–609.

O'Farrell, P. J. and Anderson, P. M. L. (2010), 'Sustainable multifunctional landscapes: A review to implementation', 2(1–2), *Current Opinion in Environmental Sustainability*, 59–65.

Och, M. (2020), 'Sustainable finance and the EU Taxonomy Regulation – Hype or hope?', 05 KU Leuven Working Papers.

Olah, J., Aburumman, N., Popp, J. et al. (2020), 'Impact of Industry 4.0 on environmental sustainability', 12(11) *Sustainability*, 4674.

Pereira, L., Asrar, G. R., Bhargava, R. et al. (2021), 'Grounding global environmental assessments through bottom-up futures based on local practices and perspectives', 16 *Sustainability Science*, 1907–1922.

Plater, Z. J. B. (2006), 'Law, media and environmental policy: A fundamental linkage in sustainable democratic governance', 33 *B.C. Environmental Law Review*, 511–521.

Prevost, D. and Alexovicova, I. (2019), 'Mind the compliance gap: Managing trustworthy partnerships for sustainable development in the European Union's free trade agreements', 6(3) *International Journal of Public Law and Policy*, 236–269.

Rishi, P. (2022), *Managing Climate Change and Sustainability through Behavioural Transformation. Sustainable Development Goals Series* (London: Palgrave Macmillan).

Roelfsema, M., van Soest, H. L., Harmsen, M. et al. (2020), 'Taking stock of national climate policies to evaluate implementation of the Paris Agreement', 11 *Natural Communication*, 2096.

Rogers, D. T. (2022), *Environmental Compliance Handbook: Sustainability and Future Environmental Regulations* (London: Routledge).

Rossinioli, F., Stacchezzini, R. and Lai, A. (2021), 'Financial analysts' reaction to voluntary integrated reporting: Cross-sectional variation in institutional enforcement contexts', 23(1) *Journal of Applied Accounting Research*, 29–54.

Sachs, J. D., Woo, T. W., Yoshino, N. and Taghizadeh-Hesary, F. (2020), 'Importance of green finance for achieving sustainable development', in Sachs, J. D., Woo, W. T., Yoshino, N. and Takhizadeh-Hezary, F. (eds.), *Handbook of Green Finance. Energy, Security and Sustainable Development, Goals and Energy Security* (Singapore: Springer), 3–12.

Sarker, T., Taghizadeh-Hesary, F., Mortha, A. and Saha, A. (2020), 'The role of fiscal incentives in promoting energy efficiency in the industrial sector: Case studies from Asia', (08) Asian Development Bank Institute Working Paper 1172.

Sheehy, B. (2019), 'TNC code of conduct or CSR? A regulatory systems perspective', in Rahim, M. M. (ed.), *Code of Conduct on Transnational Corporations. Challanges and Opportunities* (Cham: Springer), 45–62.

Siri, M. and Zhu, S. (2019) 'Will the EU Commission successfully integrate sustainability risks and factors in the Investor Protection Regime? A research agenda', 11(22) *Sustainability*, 6292.

Smith, J. L. (2008), 'A critical appreciation of the "bottom-up" approach to sustainable water management: Embracing complexity rather than desirability', 13(4) *Local Environment*, 353–366.

Soderholm, P. (2020), 'The Green Economy Transition: The challenges of technological change for sustainability', 3(6) *Sustainable Earth*, 1–11.

Sugiawan, Y. and Manag, S. (2019), 'Public acceptance of nuclear power plants in Indonesia: Portraying the role of a multilevel governance system', 26 *Energy Strategy Reviews*, 100427.

Taghizadeh-Hesary, F. and Yoshino, N. (2020), 'Sustainable solutions for green financing and investment in renewable energy projects', 14(4) *Energies*, 788.

Tanaka, K. (2011), 'Review of policies and measures for energy efficiency in industry sector', 39(10) *Energy Policy*, 6532–6550.

Vantagiatto, F. P. (2020), 'Regulatory relationships across levels of multilevel governance systems: From collaboration to competition', 33 *Governance* 173–189.

Waas, T., Hugé, J., Block, T. et al. (2014), 'Sustainability assessment and indicators: Tools in a decision-making strategy for sustainable development', 6 *Sustainability*, 5512–5534.

Weiss, F. and Kammel, A. J. (eds.) (2015), *The Changing Landscape of Global Financial Governance and the Role of Soft Law* (Leiden: Brill).

Wenta, J., McDonald, J. and McGee, J. S. (2019), 'Enhancing resilience and justice in climate adaptation laws', 8(1) *Transnational Environmental Law*, 89–118.

World Economic Forum (2021), 'The EU wants business to be sustainable. But it must empower companies to do that', 26 October, https://bit.ly/3KYlSZL.

Ziolo, M., Filipiak, B. Z. and Tundys, B. (2021), *Sustainability in Bank and Corporate Business Models*, (London: Palgrave Macmillan).

PART V

Financial Innovation and Sustainability

25

Can Financial Regulation Truly Support the Reduction of CO$_2$ Emissions?

The Complicated Puzzle of EU Emission Allowances

Filippo Annunziata

25.1 THE EU EMISSIONS TRADING SCHEME

The European emissions trading scheme ('ETS'), in place since 2003,[1] was introduced within the broader framework of the Kyoto Protocol and of the international agreements for the reduction of CO$_2$ emissions.[2] In operation since 2005, the scheme was revised and updated a number of times,[3] to address some of its weak points and also to reflect evolving market conditions. Similarly to what can be found in other comparable contexts globally, the EU ETS introduced a

---

[1] For a focus on economic and regulatory topics see, also for further references, Van Zeben 2014; Skjaerseth and Wettestad 2014; Wettestad and Jevnaker 2016.

[2] In September 2004, the European Commission launched a consultation on a global climate change regime for the future. A conference was held on 22 November and the comments and information included into the Commission's report for the Council, that is, the Communication 'Winning the battle against global climate change', adopted on 9 February 2005.

[3] The EU ETS was established and extended over four successive phases:
  – Phase I started in 2005 and ended in 2007 and is often referred to as 'the pilot phase', or the 'pre-Kyoto' period. This a pilot phase, introduced to test the system and to establish its infrastructure. Almost all EUAs were allocated for free. Reliable data on emissions were unavailable at the time, and emission caps were set on the basis of estimates.
  – Phase II started in 2008 and ended in 2012, coinciding with the first commitment period under the Kyoto Protocol. EU Member States (and the three EFTA states Iceland, Norway and Liechtenstein, which joined the EU ETS) had to meet concrete emission reduction targets. Free allocation covered roughly 10% of EUAs auctioned on the market. There was a surplus of credits, which, together with the 2008 crisis, led to very low carbon prices. In 2012 aviation emissions from flights within the EEA were brought in scope of the EU ETS.
  – Phase III started in 2013 and ended in 2020. The EU ETS Directive was revised and improved in several aspects. Even though a number of EUAs was still allocated for free, auctioning was set as the default mechanism. Some criteria were introduced in order to prevent transfer of production to other countries with less stringent constraints. The third phase started with a significant surplus of EUAs: as a consequence, auctioning of a considerable number of EUAs was delayed (so-called back-loading).

standardised system of electronic registers, which enables the recording, transfer, safekeeping and writing-off of rights on emission allowances. Since 2012, the national registers that were previously maintained at the level of each Member State have been superseded by the single European register.

The ETS is one of the largest schemes in operation for reducing GHG emissions, accounting for more than three quarters of international carbon trading worldwide, and serving as a model for similar solutions adopted by other countries in the world.

Emission trading schemes are market-based instruments for the trading and control of emissions. They have been used in conjunction with other publicly-based tools, such as caps on emissions set by public bodies, and tax measures, as the combination of these different elements appears to be more effective than the use of a single policy alone. In the words of the EU Commission:

> The economic rationale for using market-based instruments lies in their ability to correct market failures in a cost-effective way. Market failure refers to a situation in which markets are either entirely lacking (e.g. environmental assets having the nature of public goods) or do not sufficiently account for the 'true' or social cost of economic activity. Public intervention is then justified to correct these failures.[4]

In light of the prevailing academic debate, there appears to be a general consensus that emission allowances trading schemes may have positive effects on the indirect reduction of gas emissions.[5] For instance, they can contribute to the formation of a more objective price on carbon, supported by market price discovery mechanisms.[6] Nevertheless, and as anticipated, there also seems to be a consensus that emissions trading schemes do not typically result in the actual and direct reduction of greenhouse gas emissions. This statement was also supported by the EU Court of Justice. In *Société Arcelor Atlantique et Lorraine et al.*[7] the Court noted (paragraph 31):

> While the ultimate objective of the allowance trading scheme is the protection of the environment by means of a reduction of greenhouse gas emissions, the scheme does not of itself reduce those emissions but encourages and promotes the

---

– Phase IV started in 2021 and is expected to run until 2030. This phase is characterised by a cap aligned to the EU's target of reducing greenhouse gas emissions by 40% compared to 1990 levels.

Some further amendments to the ETS were ultimately announced (April 20 2023) by the Commission, and will need to be discussed in the next legislative process (https://bit.ly/3TQ798q).

4 European Commission 2007, point 2.1.
5 Tietenberg 2006.
6 For further information reference should be made to European Commission 2019a.
7 Case C-127/07, *Société Arcelor Atlantique et Lorraine and Others versus Premier ministre, Ministre de l'Écologie et du Développement durable, Ministre de l'Économie, des Finances et de l'Industrie*, Judgment of the Court of Justice of 16.12.2008, ECLI:EU:C:2008:728.

pursuit of the lowest cost of achieving a given amount of emissions reductions (…). The benefit for the environment depends on the stringency of the total quantity of allowances allocated, which represents the overall limit on emissions allowed by the scheme.

A reduction in emissions is therefore the consequence of a combination of different tools, particularly cap limits. If public bodies fix a declining cap on emissions, the trading scheme may offer a path for their reduction, to be exploited in the long term by business entities.

Another element frequently cited in favour of emissions trading schemes is their flexibility, as they can be designed in a variety of ways, thereby better accommodating diversified economic systems and environments. Furthermore, an ETS can be linked with other systems, increasing their capacity and enhancing their robustness and efficiency.[8]

Gradually, the EU legislator became increasingly aware of the need to improve the framework of secondary markets trading for EUAs, seeking to facilitate increased transparency, liquidity and integrity.[9] Most of these arguments, as we shall discuss in the following section, formed the basis of the decision to fully integrate EU Allowances ('EUAs') into the MiFID framework.

25.2 EU CAPITAL MARKETS LAW AND EMISSION ALLOWANCES

The growing debate on emissions allowances and their potential contribution to environmental policy has led to their progressive inclusion within the scope of European financial legislation. This process was actually articulated in two distinct phases:

- in phase I, the EU legislators opted to incorporate, into sectoral regulations on auctions and exchange of emission allowances, certain rules modelled upon capital markets and financial legislation, especially with the intention of limiting risks of market manipulation;
- in phase 2, following a strategy that actually prevailed over the first, emission allowances were directly incorporated into the scope of EU Capital Markets Law: initially, this involved MiFID I, followed by MiFID II and MAR.

The decision to directly include emission allowances within the scope of MiFID, was originally driven by the necessity to prevent fraudulent conducts on the relevant market. Article 12(1a) of the EU ETS Directive – as amended by the 2009

---

[8] The number of emissions trading systems around the world has been steadily growing. In addition to the EU ETS, national or sub-national systems are operating in Canada, China, Japan, New Zealand, South Korea, Switzerland and the United States. The European Commission is also a founding member of the International Carbon Action Partnership (ICAP), which brings together countries and regions with mandatory cap-and-trade systems.

[9] See on these aspects, European Commission 2019b.

Directive[10] – empowered the Commission with the task to 'examine whether the market for emissions allowances is sufficiently protected from insider dealing or market manipulation' and, if appropriate, 'bring forward proposals to ensure such protection'.

In this respect, the Commission noted[11] that:

> although the European carbon market has grown significantly both in size and sophistication during its first six years of operation, it remains a relatively young market. It is therefore important to ensure that such market can continue to expand and safely be relied upon to give an undistorted carbon price signal. It follows that the market needs to have an appropriate market oversight framework. Such framework needs to secure fair and efficient trading conditions for all market participants through transparency requirements as well as by preventing and sanctioning market misconduct, in particular insider dealing and market manipulation.[12]

Indeed, measures aimed at preventing market abuse in the EUAs auction market had already been implemented, as these were set out in Regulation (EU) No 1031/2010 of 12 November 2010 (the so-called 'Auction Regulation').[13]

In particular, in a regulatory framework based on the definition of financial instrument given by MiFID I – which did not include emission allowances except when they represented the underlying of derivative contracts – the Auction Regulation actually applied similar rules and safeguards to those established by the Market Abuse Directive of 2003 ('MAD') to the ETS, regardless of the qualification of emission allowances as financial instruments. To this end, a first regulatory microcosm on market abuse was established by the Auction Regulation, mirroring the provisions of the MAD, including its definitions, the identification of prohibited conducts, supervisory powers and sanctions. Those rules also extended to EUAs the definition of inside information, as well as the basic division between insider trading and market manipulation, as defined in the MAD.[14]

---

[10] Reference is made to Directive 2009/29/EC amending Directive 2003/87/EC so as to improve and extend the greenhouse gas emission allowance trading scheme of the Community. More recently, the EU ETS Directive was also amended by Directive (EU) 2023/959 of 10 May 2023.

[11] Reference is made to COM (2010) 796 final, named 'Towards an enhanced market oversight framework for the EU ETS', issued in Brussels on 21 December 2010, 2.

[12] The European Commission observed that, during 2009 and 2010, several incidents occurred in the European carbon market which illustrated the wider range of risks that needed to be dealt with. Although these incidents did not constitute market abuse in the sense of the Market Abuse Directive, they did support the need for stricter regulation of the European carbon market. These cases revolved around (i) frauds on value-added tax (VAT) detected in the carbon market in 2009–2010; (ii) phishing attacks from fraudsters trying to get unauthorised access to accounts of market participants; and (iii) the resale in the European carbon market by a Member State of emission units that had already been used for EU ETS compliance.

[13] "The Regulation was repealed and replaced by the Commission Delegated Regulation (EU) 2023/2830 of 17 October 2023".

[14] According to Art. 3(28) of the Regulation 'insider dealing' is 'the use of inside information as prohibited pursuant to Articles 2, 3 and 4 of Directive 2003/6/EC in relation to a financial instrument within the meaning of Article 1(3) of Directive 2003/6/EC referred to in Art. 9 of that Directive unless otherwise stated in this Regulation', thereby referring to MAD conducts. Under Art. 3(30) of the Auction Regulation, 'market manipulation' was also defined in a similar way, by referring to Art. 1(2) of Directive 2003/6/EC.

As anticipated, this was merely an initial action. Building extensively upon the definition of commodity derivatives originally introduced by the Investment Services Directive of 1993, MiFID I broadened the scope of derivatives that fell within its remit. The catalogue subsequently encompassed derivatives on emission allowances. The expansion of the Directive's scope, and consequently of the regulation of investment services and activities, to encompass a part of the secondary market for EUAs, was not, however, an easy exercise. The need clearly arose to keep some of the main lines of business of commodity producers and traders away from the grips of financial markets regulations. MiFID I thus introduced a number of complex exemptions for commodity derivatives trading by firms not otherwise engaged in financial activities, setting an intricate web of rules that still persist in MiFID II. Another challenging aspect pertains to the delineation of the border between commodity and financial derivatives, that in the context of MiFID may result in the inclusion or exclusion of a certain asset within the purview of investment services provisions.

Ultimately, the room that MiFID I left to the provisions of the Auction Regulation was quite significant. It could be argued that, prior to MiFID II, the lead in terms of addressing market efficiency and preventing market abuse in relation to emission allowances was effectively left to the Auction Regulation and its rules, which were modelled on those of the MAD of 2003. Most of the transactions on emission allowances would, in fact, have fallen outside the scope of MiFID I.

In 2014 the situation changed. MiFID II now directly classifies rights on emission allowances falling in the EU ETS regime – and not only derivatives on allowances – as financial instruments.[15] Consequently, the list of financial instruments, attached to the Directive under Annex I, has been amended to include item no. 12, regarding emission allowances within the purview of the EU ETS. It follows that if an emission allowance is referenced as the underlying of a derivative contract, to be qualified as 'financial' for MiFID purposes, the latter will fall within the scope of the regime governing investment services and activities, exactly as it was under MiFID I.[16]

The inclusion of emission rights in the scope of MiFID could not address the issue of qualifying them more precisely under general private law: however, this is a general shortcoming of MiFID (and, more recently, of the Regulation on crypto-assets, MiCA as well), and probably an unnecessary exercise due to the fact that investment services rules aim at regulating the markets of financial instruments, leaving it to national law to qualify/define their legal nature. As observed by the Court of Justice, this is actually not covered by EU law.[17]

---

[15] Annunziata 2021; Przybojewska and Pyka 2023.

[16] On these topics cf. Sciarrone Alibrandi and Grossule 2017, Chapter 16, 439 ff. Some preliminary remarks, before MiFID II came into force, can also be found in Annunziata 2013, 13 ff.

[17] Case C-321/15, *ArcelorMittal Rodange et Schifflange SA versus State of the Grand Duchy of Luxembourg*, Judgment of the Court of Justice of 08.03.2017, ECLI:EU:C:2017:179. The Court stated

In addition, from an empirical perspective, the unclear legal qualification of EUAs does not seem to be an obstacle to the development of secondary markets that prioritize the liquidity and transferability of EUAs.[18]

In the course of MiFID II deliberations, the decision to directly include EUAs within the Directive's scope was weighed against the alternative of developing, under EU law, a special regime for secondary trades involving allowances.[19] Ultimately, the decision was taken to extend MiFID to spot transactions in EUAs on the grounds that this solution might provide greater transparency and efficiency in the secondary market, thereby improving its liquidity and contributing to reduced transaction costs.[20]

As MiFID II began to take shape, it became evident that the previous approach – a complicated mixture of the Auction Regulation and MiFID I – was no longer sufficient. In its FAQ of 2014 the Commission noted that:

> Trading in allowance derivatives already falls under the scope of MiFID and Market Abuse Directive. By now bringing emission allowances under the same framework, the regulation on emission allowances trading (EUA), the spot market will be aligned with what is applicable to the EUA derivative markets. Together, MiFID and the rules on market abuse provide a comprehensive framework for trading in financial instruments and the integrity of the market. The extension to EUAs will introduce greater security for traders of EUAs but without interfering with the purpose of the market, which remains emissions reduction.

In the Commission's words, the issue of market abuse appears to be a consequence of the expected inclusion of emission allowances in the scope of MiFID II. However, it is our contention that the statement should, in fact, be reversed. Given the necessity to prevent manipulative practices on the markets of emission allowances, these would effectively need to be fully covered by MiFID II. Furthermore, since rules against market abuse apply to financial instruments as defined by MiFID II, two objectives are achieved simultaneously. The classification of emission allowances as financial instruments has also resulted in the application of MiFID II provisions on trading venues to trading platforms on which the allowances are exchanged via spot transactions.

---

that forcing "surrender of EUAs would not mean the expropriation of an asset which already formed an integral part of the operator's property, but simply the withdrawal of the act allocating the allowances, on account of the failure to comply with the conditions laid down in Directive 2003/87 "(point 38 of the judgment). In the literature, the prevailing opinion seems to uphold the qualification of EUAs as intangible property rights. See Holligan 2020, 982–989 and 1007; Wilhelmi 2016, 203. For further references, see also Bennet 2010; Colangelo 2012, 177–181; Gorzelak 2014; Low and Lin 2015; Yliheljo 2021.

[18] This is a general feature of MiFID: for instance, MiFID does not even define what is, from a private law perspective, a 'share', a 'bond', a 'transferable instrument', etc., leaving it to national legislation. See European Commission 2019b.

[19] European Commission 2011.

[20] Clausen and Sørensen 2012, 278 and 296–297.

25.3 THE MARKET ABUSE REGULATION AND EMISSION ALLOWANCES

The inclusion of emission allowances within the scope of EU capital markets legislation was also accelerated by Regulation (UE) No. 596 of 16 April 2014 (so-called 'MAR'), which replaced the previous Market Abuse Directive. Recital (37) of the MAR recalls the pre-existing specific market abuse rules included in the Auction Regulation and clarifies that 'as a consequence of the classification of emission allowances as financial instruments, this regulation should constitute a single rule book of market abuse measures applicable to the entirety of the primary and secondary markets in emission allowances'. Therefore, the MAR 'should also apply to behaviours or transactions, including bids, to the auctioning on an auction platform authorised as a regulated market of emission allowances or other auctioned products based thereon, including when auctioned products are not financial instruments, pursuant to Auction Regulation.'

As a consequence thereof, the concerns of a regulatory vacuum were no longer justified, since emission allowances were entirely brought into the warm embrace of EU capital markets legislation.

Considering the MAR regime, emission allowances exhibit peculiar features in at least two key aspects:

– emission allowances are also regulated in other areas of EU legislation, which address issues of transparency, market information and efficiency. Specific rules aimed at preventing abuses in emission allowances markets had already been introduced before MAR, with the aforementioned Auction Regulation. The combined effect of MiFID II and MAR indicated that such provisions were to be repealed. Nevertheless, emission allowances remain subject to their own sectoral rules, which require coordination with the MAR. This is a distinctive feature of emission allowances, as other financial instruments included in MiFID II or MAR are not subject to the same approach[21];
– the MAR must acknowledge the fact that inside information, for emission allowances, is subject to a specific set of rules, with an impact on the disclosure regime, or on topics such as insider trading or information-based market manipulation.

Concerning the first element (i.e. the inter-relationship between MAR and other sectoral legislation), the text of the Regulation provides numerous examples. A particularly noteworthy example is the notorious 'reasonable investor test'. According to Recital (14), the 'reasonable investor test' should, in general, take into account the *ex-ante* available set of information, and its 'anticipated impact', to be considered in light 'of the totality of the related issuer's activity, the

---

[21] On the functioning of MAR, particularly in relation to oversight and enforcement, in relation to EUAs, see the extreme valuable information available in ESMA 2022.

reliability of the source of information and any other market variables likely to affect the financial instruments, the related spot commodity contracts, or the auctioned products based on the emission allowances in the given circumstances'. However, for emission allowances, the test must be necessarily carried out also in the light of 'any other market variables', including – as Recital (14) clarifies – 'auctioned products based on emission allowances'. In a similar way, for emission allowances, the 'precise' nature of inside information needs to be assessed by looking at its 'potential effect on the prices of the financial instruments, the related spot commodity contracts, or the auctioned products based on the emission allowances' (MAR, Recital 18). In addition, 'for derivatives which are wholesale energy products, information required to be disclosed in accordance with Regulation (EU) No 1227/2011 of the European Parliament and of the Council should, in particular, be considered as inside information' (MAR, Recital 18).[22] This set of rules has an integrative effect on the basic notion of inside information, in the context of the MAR.

In Recitals (14) and (18), MAR, reference is made to 'auction products based on the emission allowances', thereby creating a link between the regulation of the auction markets for emission allowances, and that of secondary markets: an approach that derives from the one originally taken in the (now repealed) Auction Regulation. All of this seems to be the consequence of re-shaping of market abuse provisions for emission allowances, from the previous to the current regime.

Recital (21) MAR also sets out a specific, and quite elaborate, background for certain exemptions applicable to emission allowances, most of which are justified by the presence of preexisting sectoral legislation.[23] Again, in this context, the link

---

[22] Consistently with MAR, Art. 2 of REMIT Regulation – Regulation (EU) No 1227/2011 – establishes that 'inside information' means information of a precise nature which has not been made public, which relates, directly or indirectly, to one or more wholesale energy products and which, if it were made public, would be likely to significantly affect the prices of those wholesale energy products.

[23] MAR, Recital (21):

Pursuant to Directive 2003/87/EC of the European Parliament and of the Council, the Commission, Member States and other officially designated bodies are, inter alia, responsible for the technical issuance of emission allowances, their free allocation to eligible industry sectors and new entrants and more generally the development and implementation of the Union's climate policy framework which underpins the supply of emission allowances to compliance buyers of the Union's emissions trading scheme (EU ETS). In the exercise of those duties, those public bodies can, inter alia, have access to price-sensitive, non-public information and, pursuant to Directive 2003/87/EC, may need to perform certain market operations in relation to emission allowances. As a consequence of the classification of emission allowances as financial instruments as part of the review of Directive 2004/39/EC of the European Parliament and of the Council, those instruments will also fall within the scope of this Regulation. In order to preserve the ability of the Commission, Member States and other officially designated bodies to develop and implement the Union's climate policy, the activities of those public bodies, insofar as they are undertaken in the public interest and explicitly in pursuit of that policy and concerning emission allowances, should be exempt from the application of this Regulation. Such exemption should not have a negative impact on overall market transparency, as those

between general capital markets rules and sector-specific legislation becomes a distinctive feature. According to Article 6(3) MAR: 'This Regulation does not apply to the activity of a Member State, the Commission or any other officially designated body, or of any person acting on their behalf, which concerns emission allowances and which is undertaken in pursuit of the Union's climate policy in accordance with Directive 2003/87/EC.'

Clearly, therefore, there is a dual regulatory approach for emission allowances: on the one side, sectoral legislation, on the other, the standard, general market abuse regime, applicable to all financial instruments. However, considering the interplay between the two, after MAR, it is the latter that ultimately prevails. Recital (37)[24] already goes in this direction, which is then confirmed by Article 2(1), according to which:

> This Regulation also applies to behaviour or transactions, including bids, relating to the auctioning on an auction platform authorised as a regulated market of emission allowances or other auctioned products based thereon, including when auctioned products are not financial instruments, pursuant to Regulation (EU) No 1031/2010. Without prejudice to any specific provisions referring to bids submitted in the context of an auction, any requirements and prohibitions in this Regulation referring to orders to trade shall apply to such bids.

In this respect, emission allowances are truly unique in the context of MAR, as this is a topic where the Regulation actually 'spills over' and directly regulates matters originally addressed by sectoral legislation. Naturally, this also has significant consequences in terms of enforcement, sanctions and related provisions.

Another unique consequence arising from the inclusion of emission allowances in the MAR is that the key notion of 'inside information' for these products is clearly more linked to trades and position, rather than to information

---

public bodies have statutory obligations to operate in a way that ensures orderly, fair and non-discriminatory disclosure of, and access to, any new decisions, developments and data that have a price-sensitive nature. Furthermore, safeguards of fair and non-discriminatory disclosure of specific price-sensitive information held by public authorities exist under Directive 2003/87/EC and the implementing measures adopted pursuant thereto. At the same time, the exemption for public bodies acting in pursuit of the Union's climate policy should not extend to cases in which those public bodies engage in conduct or in transactions which are not in the pursuit of the Union's climate policy or when persons working for those bodies engage in conduct or in transactions on their own account.

[24] MAR, Recital (37):

Regulation (EU) No 1031/2010 provides for two parallel market abuse regimes applicable to the auctions of emission allowances. However, as a consequence of the classification of emission allowances as financial instruments, this Regulation should constitute a single rule book of market abuse measures applicable to the entirety of the primary and secondary markets in emission allowances. This Regulation should also apply to behaviour or transactions, including bids, relating to the auctioning on an auction platform authorised as a regulated market of emission allowances or other auctioned products based thereon, including when auctioned products are not financial instruments, pursuant to Regulation (EU) No 1031/2010.

affecting the issuer of a certain instrument. Rules on disclosure and treatment of inside information are therefore addressed to market participants, as defined by Article 3(20): 'emission allowance market participant' means any person who enters into transactions, including the placing of orders to trade, in emission allowances, auctioned products based thereon, or derivatives thereof and who does not benefit from an exemption pursuant to the second subparagraph of Article 17(2)'.[25]

The need to carve out emission allowances from the general approach of MAR in relation to inside information is also visible through the specific definition of 'inside information' provided by Article 7. Here, for emission allowances, there is no reference to an 'issuer' (in the general sense of MAR):

> (c) in relation to emission allowances or auctioned products based thereon, information of a precise nature, which has not been made public, relating, directly or indirectly, to one or more such instruments, and which, if it were made public, would be likely to have a significant effect on the prices of such instruments or on the prices of related derivative financial instruments.[26]

25.3.1 *Inside Information for Emission Allowances*

As with any other form of inside information, price sensitivity is naturally a prerequisite for inside information concerning emission allowances as well. Once again, emission allowances have their own peculiarities in the context of the MAR.

Recital (51) firstly states that:

> In order to avoid exposing the market to reporting that is not useful and to maintain cost-efficiency of the measure foreseen, it appears necessary to limit the regulatory impact of that requirement to only those EU ETS operators which, by virtue of their size and activity, can reasonably be expected to be able to have a significant effect on the price of emission allowances, of auctioned products based thereon, or of derivative financial instruments relating thereto and for bidding in the auctions pursuant to Regulation (EU) No 1031/2010.[27]

---

[25] Art. 8(4) consequently establishes that 'This Article applies to any person who possesses inside information as a result of: (a) being a member of the administrative, management or supervisory bodies of the issuer or emission allowance market participant [...]'.

[26] As a practical demonstration of the well-established attention to MAR precautions in relation to inside information, it is worth referring to the structure of the main allowances trading platforms, where regulatory reporting services are often provided with reference to MiFID II/MiFIR, REMIT Transaction Reporting, EMIR Trade Reporting and, inside information reporting. See, for instance, the section 'Regulatory Reporting Services' of the German auction platform (EEX DE) website, available at www.eex.com/en/markets/reporting-of-inside-information.

[27] It is, again, noteworthy that this passage 'links' the primary auction market to secondary markets, by setting out that price sensitivity needs to be assessed on both sides: again, an approach that is peculiar to that of emission allowances.

Setting a quantitative threshold of materiality for emission allowances is a unique rule, with no equivalent for other financial instruments falling within the scope of the MAR. This approach is, on the one side, the consequence of the lack of an 'issuer' of financial instruments on the market, and, on the other side, the inter-relationship with sectoral legislation.

According to Recital (52):

> Where emission allowance market participants already comply with equivalent inside information disclosure requirements, notably pursuant to Regulation (EU) No 1227/2011, the obligation to disclose inside information concerning emission allowances should not lead to the duplication of mandatory disclosures with substantially the same content. In the case of participants in the emission allowance market with aggregate emissions or rated thermal input at or below the threshold set, since the information about their physical operations is deemed to be non-material for the purposes of disclosure, it should also be deemed not to have a significant effect on the price of emission allowances, of auctioned products based thereon, or of the derivative financial instruments relating thereto. Such participants in the emission allowance market should nevertheless be covered by the prohibition of insider dealing in relation to any other information they have access to, and which is inside information.

All of the above is clearly reflected in the disclosure regime applicable to market participants of emission allowances. According to Article 17, MAR:

> An emission allowance market participant shall publicly, effectively and in a timely manner disclose inside information concerning emission allowances which it holds in respect of its business, including aviation activities as specified in Annex I to Directive 2003/87/EC or installations within the meaning of Article 3(e) of that Directive which the participant concerned, or its parent undertaking or related undertaking, owns or controls or for the operational matters of which the participant, or its parent undertaking or related undertaking, is responsible, in whole or in part. With regard to installations, such disclosure shall include information relevant to the capacity and utilisation of installations, including planned or unplanned unavailability of such installations. The first subparagraph shall not apply to a participant in the emission allowance market where the installations or aviation activities that it owns, controls or is responsible for, in the preceding year have had emissions not exceeding a minimum threshold of carbon dioxide equivalent and, where they carry out combustion activities, have had a rated thermal input not exceeding a minimum threshold.

Notwithstanding the specific definitions set out by MAR in relation to emission allowances, the identification of what effectively amounts to inside information in this respect is far from being an easy exercise. Useful hints were provided, amongst EU supervisors, by BaFin in Germany:

> The insertion <<in respect of its business>> in the first sentence of the first subparagraph of Article 17(2) clarifies that participants are only required to disclose inside information if they operate installations or aviation activities. Under

certain circumstances, however, these may also include (legally independent) trading units if they belong to a company with activities within the meaning of the Emissions Trading Directive 2003/87/EC establishing a scheme for greenhouse gas emission allowance trading.

On the contrary: 'Other market participants such as credit institutions or brokers are not subject to the requirements of Article 17(2) of the MAR.'[28]

However, these differences between emission allowances and other financial instruments in the context of MAR tend to disappear in relation to rules on market manipulation, especially transaction-based manipulation, or in relation to the prohibitions against insider trading. In these contexts, ultimately, emission allowances are treated (mostly) as financial instruments like all others, apart from the fact that market manipulation prohibitions apply to emission allowances and also to auctioned products based on the allowances. Similar remarks apply to the indicators of manipulative behaviour set out in Annex I of the Regulation.

25.4 REMIT AND EMISSION ALLOWANCES

Due to the interconnections between capital markets legislation and sectoral EU legislation on emission allowances, also the REMIT Regulation (Regulation (EU) No 1227/2011 of October 25 2011 on wholesale energy market integrity and transparency) voices similar concerns for energy products. There is clearly a link between wholesale markets on energy products and the MiFID-MAR regime: abusive conducts on the first may impact on the secondary market of emission allowances. Recital (14) REMIT provides examples of manipulative practices that are quite close to the ones that are captured by MAR, according to Recital (13) MAR:

> Manipulation on wholesale energy markets involves actions undertaken by persons that artificially cause prices to be at a level not justified by market forces of supply and demand, including actual availability of production, storage or transportation capacity, and demand. [...] Manipulation and its effects may occur across borders, between electricity and gas markets and across financial and commodity markets, including the emission allowances markets.

The REMIT Regulation, albeit not directly applicable to emissions trading, is inspired by principles employed in the context of capital markets regulation. As a matter of fact, contracts for emission allowances (as well as green certificates) are not wholesale energy products as they do not fulfil the requirements set out in Article 2(4) REMIT.[29] However, these contracts can have a significant price effect

---

[28]   Available at: https://bit.ly/3IRAzg8.
[29]   According to Art. 2(4) REMIT:

   'wholesale energy products' means the following contracts and derivatives, irrespective of where and how they are traded: (a) contracts for the supply of electricity or natural gas where delivery

on wholesale energy markets. According to Article 10 REMIT, therefore, information on emission allowances or derivatives relating to emission allowances – collected by trade repositories or competent authorities overseeing trading in emission allowances or derivatives thereof – must be provided to the Agency for the Cooperation of Energy Regulators (ACER) together with access to records of transactions in such allowances and derivatives.

There are other interconnections between MAR and REMIT that were already explored in ESMA's Discussion Paper on MiFID II/MiFIR of 22 May 2014 (ESMA/2014/548). More precisely:

(1) MAR applies to financial instruments; however, it also expressly extends the scope of market manipulation and insider trading prohibitions to spot commodity contracts where any transaction or order in them or any behaviour in relation to them is likely to have an effect on the price or value of a financial instrument.

(2) Market manipulation and insider trading prohibitions set out in MAR do not apply to 'wholesale energy products' as defined in Article 2(4) REMIT. REMIT, in its turn, establishes a regime applicable to wholesale energy products that includes spot and derivative contracts in electricity and gas. Therefore, while the REMIT obligation to publish inside information applies to both spot and derivative contracts in electricity and gas, the prohibitions of insider trading and market manipulation do not apply to financial instruments where MAR prevails, and financial regulators are the competent authorities.

In short, the interplay between REMIT and MAR-MiFID can be summarised as follows: wholesale energy products are exempted from the scope of MAR, except for the prohibitions of market manipulation and insider trading in electricity and gas derivatives, where REMIT declares MAR applicable. It must be said, however, that the boundaries between these two areas of EU legislation are quite complex.

25.5 EXEMPTIONS FOR EMISSION ALLOWANCES

The choices made in the context of MiFID II in relation to the treatment of emission allowances require a proper balancing between financial markets legislation and regulation of the industrial sector. Ultimately, financial law is not intended to regulate industry directly.

---

is in the Union; (b) derivatives relating to electricity or natural gas produced, traded or delivered in the Union; (c) contracts relating to the transportation of electricity or natural gas in the Union; (d) derivatives relating to the transportation of electricity or natural gas in the Union. Contracts for the supply and distribution of electricity or natural gas for the use of final customers are not wholesale energy products. However, contracts for the supply and distribution of electricity or natural gas to final customers with a consumption capacity greater than the threshold set out in the second paragraph of point (5) shall be treated as wholesale energy products.

The rules in MiFID II are therefore assisted by a number of exceptions. Considering derivatives in emission allowances, MiFID II (similarly to MiFID I) exempts from its scope trading in derivatives that: (i) is closely linked to the main line of a (broadly speaking) non-financial business and (ii) is not provided in the context of other investment services. It should be noted that these exemptions are the same that would apply to other kinds of commodities directives, having underlying assets other than emission allowances.

There are, however, some specific exemptions for emissions trading in MiFID II.

Article 1(1)(e) of MiFID II provides an exemption for the trading of emission allowances that: (i) falls in the scope of the reporting requirements set out by the EU ETS Directive and (ii) is carried out by dealing on own account, without providing services to clients. However, this exemption does not apply when algorithms or HFT techniques are employed.

The second case is the so-called ancillary exemption. According to Article 2(1)(j), the Directive shall not apply to 'persons: (i) dealing on own account, including market makers, in commodity derivatives or emission allowances or derivatives thereof, excluding persons who deal on own account when executing client orders; or (ii) providing investment services, other than dealing on own account, in commodity derivatives or emission allowances or derivatives thereof to the customers or suppliers of their main business'. However, the exemptions apply provided that: – for each of those cases individually and on an aggregate basis this is an ancillary activity to their main business, when considered on a group basis, and that main business is not the provision of investment services within the meaning of this Directive or banking activities under Directive 2013/36/EU, or acting as a market-maker in relation to commodity derivatives; – those persons do not apply a high-frequency algorithmic trading technique; and – those persons notify annually the relevant competent authority that they make use of this exemption and upon request report to the competent authority the basis on which they consider that their activity under points (i) and (ii) is ancillary to their main business.

Other exemptions, based on the character of activities undertaken while dealing in EUAs, increase the risk of regulatory fragmentation. For instance, an entity that issues EUAs can be exempted from MiFID when it deals in emissions for its own account, or provides services to customers on an ancillary basis. On a related plan, exemptions might be partial in relation to transactions carried out for the purpose of hedging risks of its parent company. Some activities may instead be entirely subject to MiFID, as for the case of services provided to customers or suppliers if they exceed the thresholds provided for the ancillary exemption. Recital (22) MiFID II seems to state that exemptions introduced by MiFID II apply cumulatively, and that combining exemptions should be allowed.[30] However, the

---

[30] See FCA 2022.

simultaneous application on a single entity/person of the exemptions specified for in Articles 2 and 3 MiFID II proved to be controversial.[31]

Another attempt to counterbalance MiFID II's far-reaching approach is the fact that Member States have the possibility to introduce optional, additional exemptions. Under Article 3(1):

> Member States may choose not to apply this Directive to any persons for which they are the home Member State, provided that the activities of those persons are authorised and regulated at national level and those persons: provide investment services exclusively in emission allowances and/or derivatives thereof for the sole purpose of hedging the commercial risks of their clients, where those clients are exclusively operators as defined in point (f) of Article 3 of Directive 2003/87/EC, and provided that those clients jointly hold 100% of the capital or voting rights of those persons, exercise joint control and are exempt under point (j) of Article 2(1) of this Directive if they carry out those investment services themselves.

This optional exemption, when introduced by EU Member States, is, however, only partial: Member States must, in fact, submit exempted persons to requirements that are at least analogous to the requirements under Article 3(2) MiFID II.

In conclusion, after MiFID II there are four different regimes for EUAs secondary markets: full application of the MiFID regime; full exemptions regulated by EU law; partial exemptions regulated by EU law; and national exemptions.

When trading emission allowances falls within the scope of MiFID II, these would be covered by rules on investment services and activities, including licensing; fit and proper requirements for the management body and qualifying shareholders; prudential rules; conduct of business rules, etc. In some cases, this might even support the decision of setting up an autonomous investment firm within the perimeter of an industrial group.

If MiFID II is applicable, the alternative is that trading on emission allowances is carried out through a third-party bank or investment firm.

25.6 THE IMPACT OF MIFID II

In examining the post-MiFID II landscape, a first remark is self-explanatory: trading in emission allowances now becomes an activity that might be fully regulated by capital markets legislation, unless it falls into one of the various exceptions. This is not the first time that financial regulation has expanded its scope into new, non-traditional areas or markets. MiFID II is clearly aimed at providing

---

[31] FCA 2022, Q46, for instance, considered this as not allowed. The criteria used to determine that an activity is 'ancillary' to the main business are set out in Arts. 2–3 of the Commission Delegated Regulation (EU) 2017/592, and combine three tests: the Overall Market Threshold Test, the Trading Test and the Capital Employment Test. The ultimate result of this approach turned out to be, to say the least, a bit puzzling. Directive (EU) 2021/338 of 16 February 2021, and the Commission Delegated Regulation (EU) 2021/1833 of 14 July 2021 therefore introduced some modifications to the ancillary test to make it more manageable.

more transparency and efficiency to secondary markets on emission allowances. However, the impact that this may ultimately have on the protection of the environment and on the ultimate goal of the entire system of emission trading legislation – that is, reducing the overall amount of CO_2 emissions – remains unclear.

Will the system effectively work? Will it effectively contribute to the reduction of emissions in the end? We believe that the issue should be raised. Transaction costs in emission allowances trading are increasing as a consequence of their inclusion into capital markets legislation, but it is unclear how these will be offset by the positive impacts of the new rules, not simply within the scope of capital markets, but more widely on the environment itself. For instance, the trade-off between these increased costs and the expected enhancement in market liquidity, arising, for instance, from compliance with MiFIR standards, is still unclear.

We believe that, for CO_2 emissions, capital markets law should not be considered as pursuing its own autonomous objectives: it should, instead, facilitate the ultimate goal of reducing emissions and safeguarding the environment. Most likely, this should be a feature common to the entire range of so-called 'ESG' regulation: the ultimate goal of that legislation is not to develop a new financial markets regime, but to directly contribute to the protection of the planet and the environment.

Sturdy statistical and analytical data will be needed in order to provide, in the next years, further clarification on this critical issue. However, due to the difficulties in measuring the real impact of emission allowances trading systems, it is likely that reliable data will not be available and conclusive for a long period of time. A significant challenge would consist of separating the effects of MiFID II from other measures adopted locally and/or at an international level, to support the reduction of emissions.

Notwithstanding the challenges above, some further aspects might be considered.

In light of the positive effects that may be derived from the inclusion of emission allowances for environmental protection, it can be posited that, following MiFID II and MiFIR, secondary markets should effectively become more transparent, efficient and secure. While empirical research and evidence are yet to be forthcoming this assumption can, at least for the moment, be accepted.

More transparency and efficiency should lead an increasing number of investors to consider emission allowances as a potential target for their asset allocation. This should support an increase in the volume of transactions, making the price formation mechanism more efficient for emission allowances. The market for emission allowances nowadays looks much more like a typical financial market, where different trading strategies are pursued by different actors.

The reduced risk of market abuse practices in secondary markets for emission allowances also increases transparency and the efficiency of the price-discovery mechanism for emission allowances and relative derivatives.

Since, as anticipated, these are benefits are also generally associated with traditional emissions trading programmes, if MiFID II reaches its objectives, it should have a positive impact on the reduction of CO_2 emissions, at least within the Union.

Setting lower emission caps over time might become easier for legislators, given that the relative targets would be more readily attainable thanks to the increased efficiency of secondary markets and trading activities on allowances.

25.7 A COMPLEX MARKET LANDSCAPE

The inclusion of EUAs into the full scope of MiFID resulted in a complex regulatory set-up.

MiFID II regime also supported the development of multiple trading venues for EUAs, either as regulated markets, multilateral trading facilities (MTFs) and/or trading facilities (OTFs), such as EEX (Germany), ICE Endex (Netherlands) and Nasdaq Oslo (Norway). This supports high levels of liquidity,[32] but market fragmentation may have negative impacts.[33]

As already mentioned, increases in the cost of trading should also be considered. Trading professionally in emission allowances became more expensive after MiFID II, and transaction costs – comparatively higher for smaller entities – might impact negatively on the liquidity of the market.[34]

Prudential requirements might also require important levels of capital allocation that could otherwise be diverted from direct investments in the industry. However, the impact of such measures on the system is, as yet, uncertain.

Considering the target of globally reducing greenhouse gas emissions, most authors agree that trading emissions does not directly contribute to such reduction. Environmental effectiveness of emission rights is in fact mostly the result of the reduction of EUAs available on the market.

However, the MiFID II regime might support a reduction of emissions below the cap, if prices of EUAs rise and trading possibilities are reduced. In fact, if prices of EUAs rise significantly, this may lead to emitters adopting measures for reducing emissions directly, rather than resorting to secondary markets in order to buy extra allowances.

A recent analysis shows that there has been a significant increase in the price of EUAs over time. However, this might be due to factors that are not directly linked to MiFID. For instance, in 2018 the price increased after the introduction of the Market Stability Reserve ('MSR').[35] More recently, prices have fluctuated because of geo-political factors, including the pandemic[36] and the war in Ukraine.[37]

---

[32] See ESMA 2022, 14.
[33] See, for example, Chang, Chen and Chevallier 2018.
[34] Ellerman et al. 2010, 259; Weber 2017, 369.
[35] See Perino and Willner 2017, who argue that the introduction of the MSR is expected to increase prices of EUAs in the short term but that, in the long term, the effect on prices will be irrelevant. See also Flachsland et al., 134–135.
[36] Oxera Consulting LLP 2022, 44–46.
[37] See ESMA 2022, 7:

> ESMA is acutely aware that the war in the Ukraine has a major impact apparently also on the carbon market. While EUA prices were declining by 30% in just a few days in late February

Also, the price of EU allowances has varied considerably over time: (i) in 2006, there was a fall in the demand, due to an over-allocation of installations; (ii) in 2008, the financial crisis drastically reduced demand on the carbon market; (iii) in 2013, the EU ETS showed a staggering surplus of about two billion allowances: as a consequence, prices in EUA dropped. The Commission's decision, taken in 2012, to postpone the auctioning of 900 million allowances from 2014–2015 to 2019–2020 (the so-called backload), was only partially successful and, in 2015, the MSR was established, with the backloaded allowances stacked as initial reserve.[38] Prices have risen considerably after that.

In its report, ESMA notes that the increase in EUA prices might be the result of an increased trading activity by emitters (either directly or through intermediaries), and not by speculative traders:[39] the percentage of trades that could be considered as speculative trade remains low.[40]

Therefore, at least until now, there does not seem to be a discernible correlation between MiFID II, surges in speculative trading on EUAs, and the increase in prices. This lends further support to the view that, as of today, there lacks sufficient evidence that including EUAs in the scope of capital markets legislation may directly impact on the reduction of emissions.[41]

25.8 SOME CONCLUSIONS

The reforms of the secondary markets in EUAs advanced by MiFID II exert detrimental impacts on the effectiveness of the EU ETS. Simultaneously, the costs of participation in the secondary trade in EUAs have increased for all categories of market participants, including emitters of greenhouse gases that trade in EUAs. On the other hand, neither the fragmentation of the legal regime for secondary trades in EUAs, nor the increased costs of that trade, seem to outweigh the benefits brought to traders by increased legal security provided for by MiFID II.

An increase in prices of EUAs, and, consequently, in energy prices, is probably provoked by factors other than MiFID II reforms. Volumes do increase, and this

and early March, natural gas prices reached all-time highs in Europe. There are a number of macro-economic and also technical factors which may explain these latest developments specifically in the carbon market which ESMA is referring to in this report. There are indications that the decline in the carbon price may be associated with concerns around possible gas supply disruptions or import bans leading to a reduced need for emission allowances, combined with general assumptions concerning an economic downswing and EU countries exiting fossil fuels at an earlier point in time but additional analysis may be required in the future.

[38] The MSR is a mechanism that adjusts the number of allowances to be auctioned to the market surplus (i.e., the difference between the cumulative amount of allowances available for compliance at the end of a given year, and the cumulative amount of allowances effectively used for compliance with the emissions up to that given year).

[39] ESMA 2022, 44 ff.

[40] ESMA 2021, 35.

[41] In a similar sense, Przybojewska and Pyka 2023.

can be explained as a MiFID II effect. In light of the available data, recognition of EUAs as financial instruments generated a strong incentive for greenhouse gas emitters and financial intermediaries acting on their behalf to participate in the trading of EUAs and, in this respect, a significant risk of increasing merely speculative trading did not materialise.

Ultimately, all of this must, sooner or later, come to grips with an excessively complex and fragmented legislative environment.

There are at least two, if not three, different sets of comprehensive EU rules that are potentially relevant for trading emission allowances, either on the spot, or on the derivatives market: the 'old' EU ETS, MiFID II-MAR, and, less important, REMIT.

Opting in and out of each of these systems is a complicated exercise. This creates a risk of negative externalities, and of reducing the positive outcomes that might be expected from the legislation. Capital markets legislation may be useful to support a more efficient functioning of emission allowances' markets, as long as it remains flexible, coherent, and clear enough. Can one say that this is effectively the case?

REFERENCES

Annunziata, F. (2013), 'Strumenti derivati, disciplina del mercato dei capitali ed economia reale: una frontiera mobile. Riflessioni a margine del progetto di revisione della MiFID', in Morera, U. and Bencini, R. (eds.), *I contratti 'derivati': dall'accordo alla lite* (Bologna: Il Mulino), 13.

Annunziata, F. (2021), 'Emission allowances as financial instruments', in Busch, D., Ferrarini, G. and Grünewald, S. (eds.), *Sustainable Finance in Europe: Corporate Governance* (Cham: Palgrave Macmillan), 477.

Bennet, L. (2010), 'Are tradable carbon emissions credits investments? Characterization and ramifications under international investment law', *New York University Law Review*, 85(5), 1597–1598.

Chang, K., Chen, R. and Chevallier, J. (2018), 'Market fragmentation, liquidity measures and improvement perspectives from China's emissions trading scheme pilots', *Energy Economics*, 75(C), 259–260.

Clausen, N. J. and Sørensen, K. E. (2012), 'Reforming the regulation of trading venues in the EU under the proposed MiFID II – Levelling the playing field and overcoming market fragmentation?', *European Company and Financial Law Review*, 9(3), 278.

Colangelo, M. (2012), *Creating Property Rights. Law and Regulation of Secondary Trading in the European Union* (Leiden: Martinus Nijhoff Publishers).

Ellerman, A. D., Convery, F. J. and De Perthuis, C. (2010), *Pricing Carbon: The European Union Emissions Trading Scheme* (Cambridge: Cambridge University Press).

ESMA (European Securities and Markets Authority) (2021), *Preliminary Report on Emission Allowances and Derivatives Thereof*, 15 November, ESMA 70-445-7, available at: https://tinyurl.com/4n82tsjr.

ESMA (European Securities and Markets Authority) (2022), *Final Report: Emission Allowances and Associated Derivatives*, 28 March, ESMA70-445-38, available at: https://tinyurl.com/3fwdcnvk.

European Commission (2007), 'Green paper on market-based instruments for environment and related policy purposes', March 28, COM(2007)140 final, available at: https://tinyurl.com/3w5782zk.

European Commission (2011), 'Commission Staff Working Paper. Impact assessment accompanying the document Proposal for a Directive of the European Parliament and of the Council on Markets in Financial Instruments and the Proposal for a Regulation of the European Parliament and of the Council on Markets in Financial Instruments', SEC(2011)1226 final, Brussels, 20 October, available at: https://tinyurl.com/35c294s9.

European Commission (2019a), *Report from the Commission to the European Parliament and the Council – Report on the Functioning of the European Carbon Market*, (COM/2019/557 final/2), available at: https://tinyurl.com/2ufdezvp.

European Commission (2019b), *Legal Nature of EU ETS Allowances*, Final report, Luxembourg, available at https://tinyurl.com/wubf7znn.

Financial Conduct Authority (FCA) (2022), 'FCA Handbook. The Perimeter Guidance Manual. Guidance on the scope of the UK provisions which implemented MiFID and CRD IV.Q46A', available at: www.handbook.fca.org.uk/handbook/PERG/13/?view=chapter.

Gorzelak, K. (2014), 'The legal nature of emission allowances following the creation of a Union Registry and adoption of MiFID II – are they transferable securities now?', *Capital Markets Law Journal*, 9(4), 373–387.

Holligan, B. (2020), 'Commodity or propriety? unauthorised transfer of intangible entitlements in the EU emissions trading system', *Modern Law Review*, 83(5), 980.

Low, K. F. K. and Lin, J. (2015), 'Carbon credits as EU like it: property, immunity, TragiCO$_2$medy?', *Journal of Environmental Law*, 27(3), 377–404.

Oxera Consulting LLP (2022), 'Carbon trading in the European Union. An economic assessment of market functioning in 2021', 15 February, available at: https://bit.ly/3TPmXYQ.

Perino, G. and Willner, M. (2017), 'EU-ETS phase IV: Allowance prices, design choices and the market stability reserve', *Climate Policy*, 17(7), 937.

Przybojewska, I. and Pyka, M. (2023), 'EU carbon emission allowances as environmental and financial instruments – Is it possible to kill two birds with one stone?', *Journal of Energy & Natural Resources Law*, 41(1), 1–26.

Sciarrone Alibrandi, A. and Grossule, E. (2017), 'Commodity derivatives', in Busch, D. and Ferrarini, G. (eds.), *Regulation of the EU Financial Markets. MiFID II and MiFIR* (Oxford: Oxford University Press), 439.

Skjaerseth, J. B. and Wettestad, J. (2014), *EU Emissions Trading: Initiation, Decision-Making and Implementation* (Surrey: Ashgate).

Tietenberg, T. H. (2006), *Emissions Trading. Principles and Practices: Resources for the Future*, 2nd ed. (Washington, DC: Routledge).

Van Zeben, J. (2014), *The Allocation of Regulatory Competence in the EU Emissions Trading Scheme* (Cambridge: Cambridge University Press).

Weber, R. H. (2017), 'Emission trading schemes: A Coasean answer to climate change?', in Mathis, K. and Huber, B. R. (eds.), *Environmental Law and Economics* (New York: Springer International Publishing), 369.

Wettestad, J. and Jevnaker, T. (2016), *Rescuing EU Emissions Trading: The Climate Policy Flagship* (London: Palgrave Macmillan).

Wilhelmi, R. (2016), 'Commodification and financialization in the energy sector: Emission allowances and electricity', in Godt, C. (ed.), *Regulatory Property Rights: The Transforming Notion of Property in Transnational Business Regulation* (Leiden: Brill/Nijhoff), 203.

Yliheljo, E. (2021), 'The variable nature of ownership of emission units in the intersection of climate law, property law, and the regulation of financial markets', *Climate Law*, 11(1), 45–75.

26

Climate Risk and Financial Markets

The Case of Green Derivatives

*Paolo Saguato** *

26.1 INTRODUCTION

The European financial markets have been placed on the path to a sustainable and green transition.[1] With the European Union ("EU") Green Deal, the European Commission ("EC" or "Commission") set the blueprint for a transformational change in the European economy. The EC embraced a new growth strategy built on a sustainable economic model that aims to make the EU the first carbon-neutral continent by 2050.[2] The EC calculated that this generational economic and industrial transition set by the EU Green Deal will require at least €1 trillion in initial public and private sustainable investments[3] and more than €260 billion in additional annual investments to achieve the 2050 climate and energy targets.[4] Significant private and public investments are necessary to meet the ambitious goals set by the Green Deal,[5] and this critical push for sustainable finance has influenced and incentivized the development of a new type of derivatives: "green derivatives."[6]

[*] Hope Damico, Tim Wieroniey, and Sam Katulich provided excellent research assistance. Kern Alexander, Filippo Annunziata, Nathan de Arriba-Sellier, Ilya Beylin, Matteo Gargantini, and Michele Siri provided helpful comments. I further thank participants at the EUSFiL International Research Working Group on Sustainable Finance Conference. Comments are welcomed at psaguato@gmu.edu.
[1] European Commission 2019a.
[2] The European Union's efforts to support a transition to a low-carbon, more resource-efficient and sustainable economy are aimed at achieving the climate and energy goals in line with the 2016 Paris Agreement and the 2030 UN Sustainable Development Goals ("UNSDGs"). Ibid.
[3] See European Commission 2019b.
[4] Ibid.
[5] The European Green Deal Investment Plan (EGDIP) – also referred to as Sustainable Europe Investment Plan (SEIP) – is the financial pillar of the European Green Deal that aims at mobilizing the public and private financial resources necessary to support the green transition. See European Commission 2019c.
[6] The market for derivatives linked to climate change, to green investments, and to sustainability goals is still developing and not yet mature, and therefore there is not yet a consolidated and uniformed terminology. This chapter uses the term "green derivatives" as a catch-all term to refer to those derivatives that, directly or indirectly, touch on climate-related risk.

This chapter analyzes how derivatives markets can contribute to support the green transition, enable private markets to raise capital towards sustainable goals, and help market participants manage the market and transition risk to a sustainable economy.

To support this generational sustainable capital raising, European policymakers have created a multilayered legislative and regulatory framework for sustainable finance in the EU.[7] A critical pillar of the EU effort to foster investments in sustainable projects is the EU Taxonomy for sustainable activities[8] – an EU-wide classification system for sustainable activities, intended to signal to companies and investors what economic activities are considered to be environmentally sustainable, and thus to channel private capital into sustainable projects and investments.[9] Within the broader Green Deal framework, the Taxonomy creates and supports a publicly endorsed market for financial products tied to sustainable economic activities and long-term European green objectives.[10] More specifically the Taxonomy Regulation plays a twofold role in the markets. First, it directly affects the demand and supply of sustainable capital. Providing set definitions of environmentally sustainable economic activities, the Taxonomy supports the demand for green investments, which guides companies to raise capital for climate-friendly projects. At the same time, the Taxonomy supports the supply of green capital: the Commission is empowered by the Regulation to screen economic activities and to identify the "environmentally sustainable" ones and, by doing so, investors and intermediaries can be guided in directing capital to green investments. Second, the Taxonomy will affect, indirectly, the demand and supply – i.e., the market – of derivative contracts linked to sustainable and green projects, investments, or goals. Derivatives, in fact, offer market participants the tools to manage the risks associated with sustainable investments by providing a hedge against climate-related risk.

Financial markets are thus central in supporting the European green transition. Yet, while a great deal of attention has been given to equity and debt markets and their role in allocating capital towards sustainable investments, derivatives markets have been largely left at the periphery of the policy and academic discussion.[11] Derivatives markets are a vital component of a dynamic financial system: they allow

---

[7] See European Commission 2021a.

[8] Regulation (EU) 2020/852 of the European Parliament and of the Council of 18 June 2020 on the establishment of a framework to facilitate sustainable investment and amending Regulation (EU) 2019/2088 (OJ L 198/13, 22.6.2020) (hereinafter, "Taxonomy Regulation").

[9] See Taxonomy Regulation, Art. 1.

[10] "Making available financial products which pursue environmentally sustainable objectives is an effective way of channeling private investments into sustainable activities. Requirements for marketing financial products or corporate bonds as environmentally sustainable investments […] aim to enhance investor confidence and awareness of the environmental impact of those financial products or corporate bonds, to create visibility and to address concerns about 'greenwashing'. […]" see Recital (11) Taxonomy Regulation.

[11] Three worthy exceptions are Lannoo and Thomadakis 2020; Baker 2022; Beylin 2023.

firms to manage and hedge risks, facilitating – among other things – long-term investment and capital raising.[12] Derivatives allow risk transfer between parties that assume different and opposite positions against future outcomes.[13] And in the current scenario of a green transition, the malleability of derivatives as risk management instruments might grant derivatives markets and their participants a central role in supporting greener and more resilient economies.

This chapter explores the role derivatives can play in the transition to a more sustainable economy and in achieving the goals set by the EU Green Deal. In doing so, this chapter begins with a primer on derivatives markets and their role and functions in the financial system. It then considers a few examples of "green derivatives," derivatives that address climate-related risk using different contractual structures. Commodity derivatives, disaster derivatives, ESG-linked swaps, and carbon emission futures (i.e., emission allowance derivatives) are just some examples of financial innovation in the green derivatives space. This chapter then offers an overview of the current public initiatives that envision a role of financial markets in the transition to a greener economy, with a specific focus on policy considerations regarding the role of derivatives markets. The EU Strategy for Financing the Transition to a Sustainable Economy in the EU,[14] and the Commodities Futures Trading Commission ("CFTC") Climate-Related Market Risk Report[15] and its recent Request for Information on Climate-Related Financial Risk in the US,[16] are the two public initiatives on the two sides of the Atlantic that, while completely different in their nature, offer useful preliminary insights on the role that derivatives markets might play in climate finance.[17] This chapter then concludes by providing a few early critical considerations on the private-public synergies and opportunities that might result from the growth and expansion of sustainable derivatives markets and the possible risks that policymakers should consider in the evolution process of such markets.

Policymakers will face a delicate challenge if or when they decide to engage with the growing green derivatives markets. On one hand, some commentators have been evoking the events of the 2008 financial crisis and warning about green derivatives as purely risky speculative bets to be restrained.[18] On the other, derivatives markets have been innovating, complying with the existing regulatory framework, and providing market participants with financial instruments that respond to market demand.[19] The challenging role of policymakers will be to support the growth of

---

[12]   See Culp 2004.
[13]   Ibid.
[14]   See note 6.
[15]   CFTC 2020.
[16]   CFTC 2022a.
[17]   See Giglio et al. 2021, reviewing the finance literature on the interaction between climate change and financial markets.
[18]   See Steele 2020.
[19]   See Lannoo and Thomadakis 2020.

accountable, resilient, and efficient markets for green derivatives, while, at the same time, to avoid setting up implicit public back-stop guarantees, which would result in excessive risk taking, moral hazard, and distorted incentives in the markets.

26.2 A PRIMER ON DERIVATIVES MARKETS: ECONOMIC AND MARKET STRUCTURE

Derivatives are financial instruments that "derive" their value from that of an underlying asset, index, or specified future event.[20] Because of their flexible structure, they can reference diverse classes of underlying values. Some common but not exhaustive examples of reference values are fluctuation of commodities, equities, and bond prices, interest rate, currency exchange rate, and credit rating, financial indexes, and, recently, in the case of green derivatives, even ESG metrics/indexes and sustainability goals.[21] Parties in a derivative contract agree to exchange money or other types of assets in the future if certain conditions are met or if certain events occur.

26.2.1 *Structure and Functions of Derivatives*

One of the most common types of derivatives is a swap.[22] In a swap, the two parties of a contract commit to periodically exchange payments over a specified period of time: generally one party pays a fixed payoff, while the other commits to variable payoffs that fluctuate depending on the movements of the underlying value. The underlying value of swaps can vary greatly. Two practical examples of an interest rate swap ("IRS") and of a credit default swap ("CDS") offer a useful tool to illustrate the legal structure and economic functions of a swap and will help analyze how green derivatives are designed. In an IRS, one party agrees to make – i.e., "swap" – a periodic payment at a fixed interest rate to its contractual counterparty, who in turn agrees to pay a "floating" rate – typically based on a financial benchmark. Historically, that benchmark has been the London Interbank Offered Rate (LIBOR), but after the scandal surrounding how this rate was set, the industry is now transitioning to the Euro Short-Term Rate (€STR), or to the Secured Overnight

---

[20] For a general discussion of the legal and economic structure of derivatives, see Tondel (2009).

[21] See Section 26.3.

[22] There are four main types of derivatives: forwards, futures, options, and swaps. Forwards are bespoke contracts traded over-the-counter where two parties agree on reciprocal obligations: one party agree to buy or sell and the other agree to sell or buy a specific quantity and quality of an underlying asset at a set price and at given date. A future has the same legal structure of a forward, but futures are standardized contracts traded on an organized exchange; like a forward, two parties agree to buy or sell an asset in the future at pre-set price. An option contract gives the holder a *right* to buy or sell a specific quantity of an underlying asset at a set price and at a future date; the contractual counterparty to the holder of the right to buy or sell – i.e. the option writer – has an *obligation* to buy an asset, and the other party to sell it, at a specified price and time. Options can be traded over-the-counter or an organized exchange. See Awrey 2019, 504–505; Schwarcz 2020, 551–552.

Financing Rate (SOFR). When the periodic date payments are due, the parties calculate their payments based on the net difference of the interest rates applied to the "notional amount" of the contract. Put differently, if at the payment date the floating interest rate is higher than the fixed rate, then the party that agreed to swap the floating for the fixed rate pays the net difference between the two rates. And vice versa, if the fixed rate is higher than the floating rate, then the party that agreed to swap the fixed for the floating rate pays the net difference of the two. The contractual dynamics in a CDS are slightly different. In a CDS, the underlying value is not an interest rate, but rather the credit risk (i.e., risk of default) of an entity or an asset; and one party, the protection "buyer," agrees to make periodic payments to the protection "seller," who, in turn, agrees to pay a set amount to the "buyer" if a defined credit event occurs like default, bankruptcy, credit rating downgrades, etc.

Generally speaking, derivatives have developed as contractual mechanisms to manage financial risks, like market and credit risk. Risk transfer is an embedded critical feature of derivatives.[23] Their quintessential economic function is to allow parties to exchange the risk of an underlying asset. The protection buyers generally hedge an exposure to a specific market or credit risk, while the protection sellers are in the market for gaining exposure to a specific risk. When there is a party who seeks to reduce or shift its risk on a specific asset, there is often another party, with different market expectations, who is interested in taking on that risk to make a profit – generally referred to as a speculator or market maker.[24]

In addition to their critical function as a risk management mechanism, derivatives support the markets via their price insurance and price discovery functions. For instance, if a corn farmer enters into a water future,[25] she can lock in today the price at which she will buy water a year from now. By doing so, the farmer is able to (1) hedge against expected (and unexpected) price fluctuations in water resources, which is the typical risk management result; (2) lock in the future price of factors of production or supplies, which will allow the farmer to plan for long-term investments for its business; and (3) contribute to creation of accurate and reliable future prices of corn.

With regard to derivatives markets structure, derivatives can be either traded over-the-counter ("OTC") or on a trading facility or exchange. OTC derivatives are bespoke contracts, negotiated and executed bilaterally by a derivative dealer and its customer in a marketplace with very limited pre-trade transparency but subject to some post-trade reporting obligations.[26] Their "bespokeness" allows OTC derivatives

---

[23] Greenspan 2005.
[24] Parties can enter into a derivative because they have an open exposure on a specific asset, rate, or index and they want to reduce the risk and the impact of future fluctuations in its value. However, parties can also enter into a derivative without either owning the underlying assets or without an actual exposure to an index or rate. In this instance, the derivative is often referred to as a "naked" derivative, and the derivative allows to create synthetic exposures on the underlying assets.
[25] Stafford 2020.
[26] Ferrarini and Saguato 2015.

to be modeled on the specific financial needs and risks that a party intends to transfer, and to incorporate the specific features intended by the parties.[27] This makes them effective risk management tools that promptly respond to the demands of the contractual parties.[28] Standardized derivatives, on the other hand, are generally traded on a trading venue, like a multilateral trading facility or an organized trading facility[29] that provides market participants access to more liquid markets, with pre- and post-trade transparency. The benefits of liquidity, standardization, and transparency come at the costs of the specific tailoring of the contracts to set contractual circumstances. OTC and exchange-traded derivatives are complementary sources of risk transfer tools and allow market participants the ultimate decision on what financial product better fits the participant's needs.

26.2.2 *How Can Derivatives Support Sustainability Goals?*

As discussed in the previous section, derivatives serve the primary function of managing market and credit risk.[30] When thinking about climate change, risk manifests primarily in two types, physical risk and transition risk.[31] Physical risk reflects the "uncertain economic costs and financial losses from tangible climate-related adverse trends and more severe extreme events"[32] on property, infrastructures, and business supply chain. On the other hand, transition risk "stems from the uncertain pace and scope of the economic transformation required to produce fewer carbon emissions,"[33] and might manifest in the depreciation of assets – i.e., stranded assets – in sectors that rely on high carbon emissions. Both physical and transition risk do not create new forms of financial risk, but they might exacerbate market and credit risk for market participants. A severe drought, for instance, can destroy crop cultivation (physical risk) and then manifest in a sudden spike and high volatility in the price of corn futures (market risk). Similarly, the adoption by the government of a severe carbon-tax (transition risk) might directly impose massive costs on the coal, gas, and oil industry, undermining their business and their creditworthiness (credit risk) and indirectly, it might increase the costs of energy for the industrial sector, resulting in major losses for energy-intensive businesses (market risk). Similarly, wildfires or the rise of sea levels might force some firms to relocate (physical risk), with a potential substantial impact on their financial resilience (credit risk).

[27] Ibid.
[28] See Culp 2004.
[29] Markets in Financial Instruments Directive (MiFID) II Definition, Article 4(1)(21). In the United States, futures are traded on a designated contract market and standardized swaps on swap execution facilities.
[30] See So 2021.
[31] Alvarez et al. 2020; Landry et al. 2019.
[32] Rudebusch 2021, 2.
[33] Ibid.

Within the framework of the EU sustainable finance initiative related to the EU Green Deal and within the broader market trend to a more sustainable economy, derivatives can provide two primary risk mitigation functions. First, derivatives can provide a hedging tool against the market risk of sustainable investing, thus reducing the cost of capital for either investors or borrowers, with the ultimate goal of encouraging sustainable investments. The peculiarity of green derivatives is the interesting mutual public and private benefits the "green lender" and "green borrower" can derive from the transaction. In practice, for instance, this would look like a "green loan" issued by a bank, which also includes as part of the transaction an interest rate swap with ESG triggers. On one side, the borrower initially commits to a green investment and seeks green financing. On the other, the bank lender agrees to finance the borrower's green project and to build into the transaction contractual commitment mechanisms to set ESG objectives by agreeing, for instance, to adjust interest rates more favorably to the borrower if the ESG objectives incorporated in the swap are met. The borrower benefits from the deal because it can obtain a cheaper cost of funding if it meets the ESG objectives, and the lender may benefit by signaling to the markets and regulators its commitment to green financing, or even potentially, by obtaining some regulatory benefits in the future (if, for instance, ESG-linked capital requirements are introduced). In general, the overall outcome of the transaction and its financial incentive mechanisms might also result in a social benefit that manifests in the eventual successful achievement of the ESG targets by the borrower. Both lender and buyer, by engaging in this ESG financial transactions – both green lending and green hedging – might signal to regulators their compliance to the sustainable finance commitment embraced by the EU, and to (private and public) investors their commitment to sustainable financing.

Derivatives can also allow market participants to more directly hedge against financial risks related to a green or ESG transition. A bank exposed via lending to the oil industry, for instance, might want to protect against its exposure to a borrower whose financial results are sensitive to transition risk. The bank can enter into an ESG-related interest rate swap, which would essentially function as a commitment device by requiring the industrial counterparty to pay an increased amount if it misses a pre-agreed ESG target. Or, alternatively, or even in conjunction, the bank can structure a swap with a derivatives dealer, which would entitle the protection buyer – i.e., the bank – to receive a payment from the protection seller – i.e., the derivative dealer – if the reference entity – i.e., the oil firm – misses ESG compliance benchmarking. Ultimately, if the bank is still concerned about the very creditworthiness of its counterparty in light of growing transition costs, then it can protect itself by using an additional, and more traditional, credit default swap, where a derivatives dealers agree to pay the bank if, for instance, the reference entity – i.e., the oil firm – incurs credit downgrading or even defaults on its obligations because of the effect of transition risk.

As discussed later in this chapter, derivatives allow market participants to create bespoke contracts that address a multitude of ESG factors. The existing landscape of green derivatives is quite diverse and split between more traditional commodity futures and other types of futures, which are standardized derivatives traded on exchanges,[34] and a novel set of swaps, like ESG-linked or sustainability-linked swaps, that have largely developed as bilateral bespoke solutions in the OTC markets.[35] While this chapter recognizes the importance that commodity derivatives play in the transition to a more sustainable economy and acknowledges the already existing practices to incorporate climate-related considerations in pricing commodities futures, it does not dive into these mature markets where market participants have set robust institutional arrangements and are subject to comprehensive supervision and regulation by public authorities.[36]

Section 26.3 looks at how markets have incorporated ESG considerations into OTC derivative contracts and provides an overview of different types of green derivatives.

26.3 CURRENT PRIVATE INITIATIVES IN THE GREEN DERIVATIVES MARKETS

As previously discussed, the transition to a sustainable economy requires massive investments, and derivatives markets can play a central role in supporting this process. This section provides example contracts of green derivatives to show how markets have created products that are crafted to manage different forms of risk in climate finance.[37] Sustainability-linked swaps, emissions allowances derivatives,[38] renewable energy and renewable fuels derivatives, and catastrophe/weather derivatives are all examples of financial innovation in climate and sustainable finance.[39]

Since 2019, markets have experimented with new forms of sustainability-linked swaps. Building on the traditional contractual structures of an interest rate swap (IRS) or of a foreign exchange (FX) derivative – like a cross-currency swap – derivatives

---

[34] A fast-growing market segment for exchange-traded products are ESG index-linked derivatives, equity index futures, and options tied to ESFG benchmarks. These derivatives track equity indices with companies weighted and evaluated on different ESG standards, such as the E-mini S&P 500 ESG Future, the Euronext Eurozone ESG Large 80 Index Futures, and the MSCI Emerging Markets ESG Leaders NTR Index Future. See ISDA 2021a, 8.

[35] See Futures Industry Association 2020; ISDA 2021a; ISDA 2021b; ISDA 2021c; ISDA 2022a; Lovells 2021.

[36] For an academic discussion on physical and financial commodities markets, see Engel 2019, 310; Sciarrone Alibrandi and Grossule 2017, 439.

[37] ISDA 2021a (offering a comprehensive overview of ESG-related derivatives products); So 2021 (describing different categories of ESG derivatives); Baker 2022, 740–756 (discussing six main categories of ESG derivatives); Beylin 2023, 20–26 (analyzing some ESG-linked swaps).

[38] ISDA 2021d.

[39] So 2021; Lannoo and Thomadakis 2020.

dealers have been able to include an ESG pricing component that, generally speaking, operates as a financial incentive for market participants to improve ESG performance. A recent study by the International Swaps and Derivatives Association ("ISDA") highlights 11 notable transactions in the green derivatives space. All of these sustainability-linked derivatives are bilateral and bespoke contracts conducted over-the-counter by a derivatives dealer with a client. What is particularly interesting is that the vast majority of the players in these OTC green derivatives are European entities – both derivatives dealers and the customers/end-users – a sign perhaps of the sustainability-oriented direction that the EU has embraced. In the next paragraphs, this chapter provides a descriptive account of some of these green derivatives.[40]

The first green derivative, or as defined by the parties, a "sustainability improvement derivative," was created in August 2019 between ING, the largest Dutch global bank, and SBM Offshore, a global supplier of floating production solutions to the offshore energy industry.[41] SBM Offshore operates traditional oil and gas projects but also invests in renewable energy projects such as offshore wind farms and wave energy convertor systems.[42] The contract was designed to hedge the interest rate risk of SBM Offshore's $1 billion five-year floating-rate credit facility and was structured as a fixed-for-floating interest rate swap. On top of the traditional IRS, the parties included the ESG component. SBM Offshore could obtain a discount of 5–10 basis points on its fixed rate or had to pay a penalty in a similar amount if SBM did not meet its target ESG score. ING reserved the authority to set target ESG scores for SBM at the beginning of every year for the duration of the contract. The parties assigned a third party, Sustainalytics, an independent provider of ESG research and ratings, the right to score SBM's ESG performance.[43] This new form of sustainability-linked IRS shows how derivatives dealers have included ESG targets as incentive mechanism for clients to meet sustainability objectives. And clients, as in the case of the IRS, would benefit from achieving the set ESG goals by obtaining a cheaper cost of capital.

In September 2019, a major French bank, Société Générale, executed with its client, Enel, an Italian power and gas company, a different form of green derivative, a sustainable-development-goal-linked cross-currency swap.[44] In its commitment to the UNSDGs, Enel issued a €1.5 billion bond, whose coupon would be adjusted depending on Enel's ability to take its installed renewable electricity generation capacity from 45.9% (as of June 30, 2019) to 55% by December 2021.[45] If Enel did not achieve the stated renewable energy target, then the interest on the bond

---

[40] See also Beylin 2023 (using the same dataset to describe ESG-linked swaps).
[41] ING 2020.
[42] SBM Offshore: www.sbmoffshore.com/creating-value/new-energies.
[43] ISDA 2021a, 3.
[44] Société Générale 2019.
[45] Ibid.

would have risen by 25bp, from 2.65% to 2.9%.[46] Tied to this "green bond," Société Générale and Enel executed a foreign exchange cross-currency swap that enabled Enel to hedge its exposure against the euro/dollar exchange rate and interest rate risk. Enel, in fact, had its bond repayments denominated in US dollars, but Enel's major source of repayments is euro-denominated.[47] The parties linked the swap pay-offs to the same commitment mechanism to sustainability performance set in the green bond. The interest rate premium or discount on the bond by 25bp was linked to the company's ability to increase its installed renewable electricity generation capacity and carried over to the linked cross-currency swap, which would have been rebooked if the bond's coupon had changed.[48]

In October 2020, Enel entered into a similar sustainability-linked cross-currency swap connected with the issuance of £500 million of sustainability-linked bonds, however, this time the derivative dealer was JP Morgan Chase.[49] Like the previous contract with Société Générale, the interest rate on the bonds was tied to Enel's ability to reach at least 60% renewable generation within its total installed capacity by December 31, 2022.[50] In this case, however, the achievement of the environmental target was certified by an auditor's specific assurance report and not by Enel itself, and the interest rate would have increased if the target had not been achieved. What is particularly interesting in this case is the structure of the cross-currency swap, where each party committed to ESG goals and agreed to pay higher interest to each other if either side did not keep up to its ESG targets.[51] On one side, Enel committed to increase its renewable generation; on the other, JP Morgan pledged to help arrange $200 billion of funding for climate change actions and the UNSDGs, which include activities such as underwriting green bonds.[52]

Like Enel, Siemens Gamesa, a supplier of wind power solutions, had been quite active in the green derivatives markets and its commitment to the UNSDGs.[53] In October 2019, the month after Enel entered into the sustainable-development-goal-linked cross-currency swap with Société Générale, Siemens Gamesa arranged a green foreign exchange swap with BNP Paribas to hedge the foreign exchange exposure of selling offshore wind turbines in Taiwan[54] and to contribute to the UNSDGs

---

[46] Ibid.
[47] ISDA 2021a, 4.
[48] Ibid.
[49] Balasta 2020,
[50] Hirtenstein 2020.
[51] ISDA 2021a, 6.
[52] Recently, Enel issued a multi-tranche $4 billion sustainability-linked bonds tied with a "Sustainability-Linked Cross Currency Swaps" with a panel of banks, to be hedged against the euro-dollar exchange rate and interest rate risk. Also in this swap, the commitment to achieve a specific Sustainability Performance Target was mutual and resulted in a discount or penalty in the cost of the transaction based on the ability of Enel or the syndicate of bank to meet their ESG targets; Enel 2020.
[53] Siemens Gamesa 2019.
[54] ISDA 2021a, 5.

targets related to climate action and affordable and clean energy. The peculiarity of this contract, which distinguishes it from the FX contract concluded by Enel, is the sustainability-linked characteristics. If Siemens Gamesa reached its sustainability targets, then BNP Paribas would reinvest any premium into reforestation projects, but if Siemens Gamesa missed its annual minimum ESG score, Siemens Gamesa would pay a sustainability premium to BNP Paribas, which would reinvest in reforestation projects.[55]

Finally, in March 2020, HSBC and Siemens Gamesa executed a fixed-for-floating ESG-linked IRS. The swap allowed Siemens Gamesa to exchange a floating rate on a €250 million tranche of a €2.5 billion sustainability-linked loan into fixed rate.[56] What is peculiar about this contract is the operation of the ESG commitment device. In the other discussed green derivatives, meeting or missing the ESG targets would have resulted respectively in a discount or penalty in the interest rate applied to the underlying transaction. But in this case, the fixed rate of the swap remained stable, and changes in Siemens Gamesa's ESG rating would require charitable donations. If Siemens Gamesa's ESG rating improved and it met its rating, then HSBC would donate annually to projects of non-profit organizations. If Siemens Gamesa's ESG rating declined, then the company would donate.[57]

The collection of green derivatives gathered by ISDA is a sign of the dynamics of the OTC ESG-related derivatives markets. There are a few considerations that can be drawn from this overview. First, the majority of the parties in these contracts are European, and this should be no surprise to the reader. European policymakers have fully embraced the transition to a sustainable economy. These market developments can be viewed as the first effect of the adoption of the EU Green Deal and the decision of market participants to position themselves in a sustainable economy path in anticipation of a full roll-out of the Taxonomy and other regulations and directives in the EU sustainable finance plans. Second, OTC green derivatives are highly customizable; firms have been able to tailor with their derivative dealer the sustainability-linked characteristic of their contract to better fit their ESG targets, goals, and commitments. Some parties contracted for adjustments of interest rates if set ESG standards are met, others required payoff to third parties or projects engaged in sustainability goals. Finally, some contracts rely on self-assessment of ESG goals or specific operational outcomes as triggered for the sustainability-linked payoff, other contracts rely on third-party ESG rating and assessments.[58]

In parallel with the ESG-linked swaps, derivatives markets have created other classes of green derivatives that, directly or indirectly, are going to play a role in

---

[55] The premium is calculated using a metric assigned by third-party sustainable finance specialists RobecoSAM.

[56] Siemens Gamesa 2020.

[57] ISDA 2021a, 3.

[58] Beylin 2023, 784–792 (offering an insightful analysis on ESG quantitative performance targets and the rise of social accounting).

supporting sustainable and climate finance.[59] Emissions allowances derivatives allow companies subject to carbon cap-and-trade programs to use derivatives based on carbon allowances and offsets to meet their obligations and manage their risks in a cost-effective way.[60] Renewable energy and renewable fuel derivatives allow market participants to hedge against the risks associated with fluctuations in renewable energy production and encourage more capital to be directed to sustainable investments. Catastrophe and weather derivatives protect companies against losses from different forms of natural disasters while weather derivatives mitigate risks associated with unexpected weather patterns. Finally, ESG-related exchange-traded derivatives, built on equity index futures and options contracts tied to ESG benchmarks, can help managers to hedge their ESG investments.

26.4 CURRENT PUBLIC INITIATIVES: EU TAXONOMY REGULATION AND CFTC CLIMATE-RELATED MARKET RISK SUBCOMMITTEE REPORT

As shown in the previous section, markets have already moved in the direction of incorporating climate-related risks and factors into derivative contracts. This section focuses on the public initiatives surrounding green derivatives. As experienced in the EU and US, a transition to a greener economy, and even more to a net-zero carbon economy, will unlikely succeed unless legislative measures are used to provide incentives to market participants to embrace these principles and to adopt more sustainable business models. The next subsections offer an overview of the ongoing public initiatives in the EU and US that touch on green derivatives.

26.4.1 *The EU Green New Deal: The EU Taxonomy Regulation, MiFID II/MiFIR, and the Role of ESMA*

The EU's economy and regulatory landscape have been shifting towards a sustainability paradigm. The EU Green Deal and all the policy initiatives that flow from it, coupled with a sizable public spending campaign, are aiming at helping the EU reach its goal of net-zero carbon emissions by 2050.[61] To achieve this generational goal, the EU has been adopting a number of strategic reforms aimed at supporting the formation of "sustainable capital." In the EC Action Plan, the EC outlines ten reforms in three different areas for financing sustainable growth. The three areas are: (1) reorienting capital flows towards sustainable investments, in order to achieve sustainable and inclusive growth; (2) mainstreaming sustainability into risk management; and (3) fostering transparency and long-termism in financial and economic

---

[59] ISDA 2021a (presenting different types of derivatives that play a role in sustainable finance); Baker 2022 (exploring the role of the derivative ecosystem in promoting ESG objectives).
[60] Annunziata, Chapter 25 in this volume; ISDA 2021d; ESMA 2022.
[61] European Commission 2021a.

activities.[62] The purpose of these reforms is to work towards a sustainable financial system within the EU and provide the legislative measures to help reach such purpose. In this direction, the EC has built the EU sustainable finance framework on three pillars: (1) a classification system of sustainable activities – "taxonomy;" (2) a disclosure regime for the social and environmental impact of the activities of both non-financial and financial institutions; and (3) a set of investment tools – benchmarks, standards, labels – that can support market participants to align their investment strategies with the EU's climate and environmental goals.[63]

Among these new statutory measures is the Taxonomy Regulation,[64] which creates a classification framework of sustainable economic activities and plays a central role in supporting the reorientation of capital towards sustainable investments.[65] The purpose of EU Taxonomy is to create security for investors, protect from greenwashing, help entities become climate-friendly, and help shift investments where they are needed the most.[66] Under the Taxonomy Regulation, the EC published the first EU Taxonomy Climate Delegated Act on June 4, 2021.[67] This first delegated act is directed at supporting sustainable investments by making it clearer – through technical screening criteria – which economic activities most contribute to meeting the EU's environmental objectives of climate change mitigation and climate change adaptation, and do not cause harm to any of the other relevant environmental objectives set the Green Deal. The second major delegated Act,[68] which was published

---

[62] Ibid.

[63] See European Commission 2021a, 2.

[64] Taxonomy Regulation.

[65] For a commentary of the Taxonomy Regulation see White & Case 2020; Hauman et al. 2020; Wockener and Hauman 2019.

[66] The taxonomy is a "list of economic activities with performance criteria to assess the activities' contribution toward six environmental objectives…." The six objectives include: (1) climate change mitigation; (2) climate change adaptation; (3) sustainable use and protection of water and marine resources; (4) transition to a circular economy, water prevention and recycling; (5) pollution prevention and control; and (6) protection of healthy ecosystems. In addition to meeting these six environmental objectives (first requirement), there are three other requirements (totaling to four overall requirements). The second requirement is that the activity must not do any harm to the other environmental objectives, and the third requirement is that the activity must comply with minimum social and governance safeguards. The activity, fourthly, must comply with certain technical screening criteria ("TSC").

[67] Commission Delegated Regulation (EU) 2021/2139 of June 4, 2021 supplemented Regulation (EU) 2020/852 by establishing the technical screening criteria for determining the conditions under which an economic activity qualifies as contributing substantially to climate change mitigation or climate change adaptation and for determining whether that economic activity causes no significant harm to any of the other environmental objectives.

[68] The Commission also adopted the Commission Delegated Regulation (EU) 2021/2178 specifying the content, methodology, and presentation of the information must be disclosed by both non-financial and financial undertakings that are required to report about the eligibility and alignment of their activities with the EU Taxonomy (the "Taxonomy Disclosures Delegated Act") on July 6, 2021. And on March 9, 2022, the Commission adopted Commission Delegated Regulation (EU) 2022/1214 amending the Taxonomy Climate Delegated Act and the Taxonomy Disclosures Delegated Act. These amendments included certain activities in the EU Taxonomy on energy generation from nuclear energy and from natural gas and set out specific disclosure requirements for those activities.

by the Commission in November 2023,[69] sets the technical screening criteria to identify the economic activities that address the remaining four objectives of the EU
Taxonomy (i.e., the sustainable use and protection of water and marine resource; the
transition to a circular economy; pollution prevention and control; and the protection and restoration of biodiversity and ecosystems). In general, financial instruments
like derivatives are neutral for the purposes of the Taxonomy Regulation (i.e., they
are not automatically considered "green" investments), yet their underlying reference might or might not be neutral. While the Taxonomy does not address green
derivatives, it directly affects the markets of the underlying assets of derivative contracts and the future decisions of market participants over capital allocations. Thus,
it plays a central role in potentially directing and influencing the expansion of green
derivatives markets.

No ad hoc measures on green derivatives have been either adopted or appear
in the pipeline of EU lawmakers or regulators. Derivatives are mentioned in a few
ESG-related regulatory initiatives, mostly to make sure their use supports, or at
least is compatible with, the mandatory or declared ESG purpose of other financial products. Within the framework of the Regulation on sustainability-related disclosures in the financial services,[70] the EC requires financial market participants
that make available financial products promoting environmental or social characteristics, or that have sustainable investment as their objective, to disclose (and
explain) how the use of derivatives is compatible with such goals and support ESG
factors.[71] In a similar direction, to support transparency in the market and reduce
asymmetries of information for investors, the proposal for an EU Ecolabel for retail
financial products defines how managers of collective investment schemes can use
derivatives in their investment strategies and obtain the label of an environmentally
friendly product.[72]

---

[69] Commission Delegated Regulation (EU) 2023/2486 supplemented Regulation (EU) 2020/852 of the
European Parliament and of the Council by establishing the technical screening criteria for determining the conditions under which an economic activity qualifies as contributing substantially to the
sustainable use and protection of water and marine resources, to the transition to a circular economy,
to pollution prevention and control, or to the protection and restoration of biodiversity and ecosystems
and for determining whether that economic activity causes no significant harm to any of the other
environmental objectives and amending Delegated Regulation (EU) 2021/2178 as regards specific
public disclosures for those economic activities.

[70] Regulation (EU) 2019/2088 of the European Parliament and of the Council of 27 November 2019 on
sustainability-related disclosures in the financial services sector.

[71] See Arts. 51 and 59 Commission Delegated Regulation (EU) 2022/1288 of 6 April 2022 supplementing
Regulation (EU) 2019/2088 of the European Parliament and of the Council with regard to regulatory
technical standards specifying the details of the content and presentation of the information in relation to the principle of "do no significant harm", specifying the content, methodologies and presentation of information in relation to sustainability indicators and adverse sustainability impacts, and the
content and presentation of the information in relation to the promotion of environmental or social
characteristics and sustainable investment objectives in pre-contractual documents, on websites and
in periodic reports.

[72] European Commission 2021b, 22–24; 28–31;

Interesting developments in the derivatives markets policies are coming from the emission allowances and carbon markets[73] where the European Securities Market Authority ("ESMA") has recently published a report analyzing the role of derivative contracts in the secondary market trading in emission allowances and putting forward policy recommendations to enhance transparency in these markets.[74] Finally, the European Central Bank and the European Systemic Risk Board in a report on climate-related risk and financial stability acknowledged the role financial instruments can play in mitigating climate-related risk, by redistributing risks to sectors or entities that are either better equipped – or more simply are willing – to deal with them or withstand the associated losses.[75]

26.4.2 *The CFTC's "Managing Climate Risk in the US Financial System" Report and Beyond*

Differently from the EU, where the EC and the EU Parliament have embarked on major legislative and regulatory reforms to transition to a greener and more sustainable economy, in the US, structural green reforms are unlikely to occur in the near future. Nevertheless, a few interesting initiatives by regulatory agencies have analyzed the effects of climate-related financial risk on different segments of the financial system and explored and offered policy approaches or solutions to strengthen the accountability of markets to climate risk.

26.4.2.1 The Commodity Futures Trading Commission's Initiatives

The Commodity Futures Trading Commission (CFTC), the US regulatory agency for derivatives markets, has taken three major initiatives regarding climate finance. In September 2020, the Commission's Climate-Related Market Risk Subcommittee of the Market Risk Advisory Committee (MRAC) released a report entitled "Managing Climate Risk in the US Financial System" (Climate Report). In March 2021, the agency established a Climate Risk Unit ("CRU") to focus on the derivative markets' role in addressing climate-related risk and transitioning to low-carbon economy.[76] Finally, in June 2022, the CFTC solicited public comments on climate-related financial risk to better inform its understanding and oversight of climate-related financial risk as pertinent to the derivatives markets and underlying commodities markets.[77]

---

[73] See Annunziata, Chapter 25 in this volume.
[74] ESMA 2022.
[75] ECB/ESRB 2021, 39–41.
[76] CFTC 2021a.
[77] CFTC 2022b.

The 2020 Climate Report, adopted unanimously by the Climate-Related Market Risk Subcommittee,[78] represents the first systematic analysis of the emerging risks that climate change poses to the US financial system and offers policymakers 53 recommendations to mitigate these risks.[79] The Climate Report urges US financial regulators to recognize that climate change poses serious emerging risks to the US financial system,[80] and recommends that they measure, understand, and address these risks decisively.[81] The report discusses how regulators and markets should position to address climate-related financial risk and support the financing of a net-zero transition.[82] In doing so, the report identifies derivatives markets as part of the solution to the risk posed by climate change and elaborates on the role and functions derivatives can perform. Within their risk mitigation function, for instance, "commodity derivatives exchanges could address climate and sustainability issues by incorporating sustainability elements into existing contracts and by developing new derivative contracts to hedge climate-related risks." The report further identifies new products, which "may include weather, ESG, and renewable generation and electricity derivatives."[83]

Focusing on the strategies and mechanisms to catalyze structural changes and private capital to a net-zero transition, the Climate Report points at derivatives as financial instruments aimed at reducing exposure to climate-rated risks. Commodities

---

[78] "[The June 2019] meeting laid the groundwork for the Commission's approval of the establishment of the Climate-Related Market Risk Subcommittee, which drew applicants and ultimately members from financial markets, the banking and insurance sectors, as well as the agricultural and energy markets, data and intelligence service providers, the environmental and sustainability public policy sector, and academic disciplines focused on climate change, adaption, public policy, and finance." CFTC 2020.

    The general public comments about the Report's adoption were positive. With a focus on the current chapter, the Futures Industry Association, in its response letter, outlined their efforts to consider and address climate-related risks and their belief that derivates markets are a powerful catalyst for change and have an integral in supporting the climate-related goals; Futures Industry Association 2022.

[79] CFTC 2020.

[80] The report identifies physical and transition risks, including the risk of stranded capital, as the major manifestation of climate-related risk; see ibid., 19. In addition, the report claims that climate-related risk presents a complex set of financial risk that can manifest as systemic shocks and liquidity disruptions. Ibid., 27–30.

[81] See CFTC 2020, ii. The report outlines that "financial markets will only be able to channel resources efficiently to activities that reduce greenhouse gas emissions if an economy-wide price on carbon is in place at a level that reflects the true social cost of those emissions." Ibid. In the absence of such a price, financial markets will operate sub optimally, and carbon will flow in the wrong direction. Ibid. This is also the first recommendation given by the report and the report considers it "the single most important step to manage climate risk and drive the appropriate allocation of capital. Ibid., vi.

[82] Ibid.

[83] Ibid. The Report also acknowledges that the development of new derivatives will require that the relevant climate-related data is transparent, reliable, and trusted by market participants. See CFTC 2020, 107. "Credible data is the foundation of any financial product's sustainability credentials. It can be attained from emerging public source and proprietary data providers, as well as from corporate disclosure and reporting. The goal is consistent and comparable information. A lack of available climate risk data is hindering the development of sustainable investment products, including derivatives based on ESG or sustainable assets." Ibid.

derivatives, for instance, might be restructured to incorporate sustainability and climate-related elements; in doing so, agricultural suppliers might be required to supply "greener" commodities with specified environmental traits.[84] In addition to the role that derivatives exchanges have been playing in responding to investors' demand for greener "hedges," the report acknowledges the growing innovation that is occurring in the OTC derivatives markets, where derivatives dealers have incorporated sustainability performance target as incentive mechanisms for improving environmental performance or to shift specific climate-related risks or exposures.[85]

Despite being the product of a purely advisory subcommittee, the Climate Report lists numerous cross-cutting agency recommendations,[86] and, in particular, calls the CFTC to action on a few pressing issues. In addition to recommending the CFTC review of the ramifications of climate-related risk in the markets,[87] the report recommends that the CFTC, in order to catalyze climate finance market development, "survey market participants about their use of climate-related derivatives, the adequacy of product availability and market infrastructure, and the availability of data to incorporate climate impacts into existing and new instruments…[and to] coordinate with other regulators to support the development of a robust ecosystem of climate-related risk management products."[88]

Since the Climate Report was published, the CFTC announced the formation of the CRU, comprised of staff from all across the agency, which supports the agency by focusing on the role of "derivatives in understanding, pricing, and addressing climate-related risk and transitioning to a low-carbon economy."[89] In addition, the CRU "is intended to accelerate early CFTC engagement in support of industry-led and market-driven processes in the climate – and the larger ESG – space."[90]

In 2021, after the publication of the report and the creation of the CRU, the CFTC Energy and Environmental Markets Advisory Committee (EEMAC) held

---

[84] See ibid., 112. The Report describes the modifications by the Commodity Exchange (COMEX), a designated contract market that operated under the CFTC supervision, of the contractual terms of all COMEX physically delivered gold futures exchanged on its market to ensure compliance with the Responsible Sourcing program for precious metals set by the London Bullion Market Association (LMBA). Ibid.

[85] Ibid., 112–114.

[86] Recommendation 4.1, for instance, recommends relevant regulatory agencies should incorporate climate-related risks into their mandates and develop a strategy for integrating these risks; ibid., 50; Recommendation 7.5 recommends the SEC to review and update the guidance on climate disclosure; ibid., 100; and, ultimately, Recommendation 4.2 requires FSOC to (1) incorporate climate-related financial risks into the existing oversight function, (2) encourage the sharing of best practices across agencies, (3) task the Office of Financial Research with developing a long-term research program on climate-related risks to the financial system – including spillover risk and interconnectivity; ibid., 49–50.

[87] See Recommendation 4.11 and 4.16, CFTC 2020, 51–53; Recommendation 7.7, Ibid., 101.

[88] See Recommendations 8.5, ibid., 117.

[89] CFTC 2021b, 1.

[90] CFTC 2021b.

two public meetings to discuss different aspects of climate finance. In its June 3 meeting, the EEMAC discussed how derivatives markets can facilitate the transition to a low-carbon economy, including the status of carbon reduction through cap-and-trade and other carbon trading market mechanisms.[91] In its September 1 meeting, the Advisory Committee discussed a proposal to form an EEMAC sub-committee, which would provide a report to the EEMAC on guiding principles for the design of the derivatives and underlying cash markets for environmental products, such as carbon allowances and offsets that are used to address greenhouse gas emissions.[92] Finally, in June 2022, the CFTC released a request for information on climate-related financial risk to better inform its understanding and oversight of climate-related financial risk as pertinent to the derivatives market and underlying commodities market.[93] Particularly interesting for the purpose of this chapter is the request for information concerning product innovation.[94] The Commission is interested in understanding how derivatives products are currently used to manage financial risk;[95] how innovation in climate risk–related technology can shape derivative products innovation;[96] and how novel climate-related derivatives are affected by and manage risk.[97] The information collected by the CFTC will provide critical insights on how markets are positioning with respect to green derivatives.[98]

[91] CFTC 2021c, f.

[92] CFTC 2021d, f.

[93] CFTC 2022b.

[94] CFTC 2022a, 34859–34860

[95] Ibid., "What derivatives products are currently used to manage climate related financial risk, facilitate price discovery for climate-related financial risk, and/or allocate capital to climate benefiting projects? Please explain how these products are used, negotiated, and traded. What, if any, conditions, including market practices and/or regulatory requirements, may constrain or promote their expanded use or development to address climate-related financial risk? Are there ways in which Commission regulations or guidance could better address particular considerations relating to the listing of these types of products for trading?" Ibid.

[96] Ibid., "Are there any potential innovations in climate-risk-related technology that could shape derivatives product innovation or are otherwise likely to impact the derivatives markets overseen by the Commission?" Ibid.

[97] CFTC 2022a, Question 21. "Are the pricing and terms of climate-related derivatives products affected by or related to the pricing and terms of other products? Are climate related derivatives products effective hedges for a portion of the risks related to transactions in commodities other than the commodities underlying the derivative products? Are there any climate-risk factors that will specifically affect derivatives products and their respective underlying commodities that should be addressed within the Commission's regulations, guidance, or oversight of these markets?"

[98] See Saguato 2024, (offering a political economy account of the public responses to the CFTC request for information). A preliminary take on the 82 responses submitted to the agency shows that 13 respondents provided information on product innovation in climate-risk-related technology. As discussed in Section 26.4.2.1, innovation is happening in parallel both in OTC bilateral markets and contracts, as shown by ISDA 2021a – and in established commodities derivatives exchanges with the creation of more standardized contracts – as discussed in the comments by the major US and EU derivatives exchanges.

26.4.2.2 The Financial Stability Oversight Council's Report

On October 21, 2021, the Financial Stability Oversight Council (FSOC) issued its Report on Climate-Related Financial Risk.[99] The report provides a comprehensive set of 30 specific recommendations to US financial regulators, which address climate-related risk and promote resilience of the financial system to those risks.[100] These recommendations cover four broad categories: (1) building capacity and expanding efforts to address climate-related financial risk;[101] (2) filling climate-related data and methodological gaps;[102] (3) enhancing public climate-related disclosures;[103] and (4) assessing and mitigating climate-related risks to financial stability.[104]

With a focus on derivatives markets, the FSOC report restates the function of the newly established CFTC's Climate Risk Unit as a cross-disciplinary unit focused on investigating the role of derivatives in understanding, pricing, and addressing climate-related risk in the financial system and the transition to a net-zero economy, and also outlines the engagement of the CFTC and the EEMAC on climate-related financial risk issues. The CFTC report on climate-related risk and the public meetings on carbon markets explores the role of carbon markets in the transition to a net-zero economy. The linkages between primary, secondary, and derivative carbon markets, are evidence of the CFTC engagement activities on this critical climate-related issues.[105]

26.5 THE FUTURE AHEAD

Derivatives markets can play a major role in helping the European Green Deal achieve its goal of a low-carbon economy and more broadly can support sustainable and climate finance.[106] The green industrial plan embraced by the European institutions relies on massive public and private investments. European policymakers have committed to create a regulatory framework that incentivizes private capital formation for sustainable economic activities and channels private capital towards green investing. Derivatives markets can operate on multiple fronts to support such transition. They can reduce the cost of funding sustainable investments because of their risk transfer function; they can contribute to more efficient green capital markets by supporting price discovery and transparency for the underlying instruments; and they can support long-term investments by protecting users from fluctuations in prices of commodities and capital.

---

[99] See FSOC 2021.
[100] Ibid.
[101] Ibid., 5.
[102] Ibid., 6.
[103] Ibid., 7.
[104] Ibid., 8.
[105] FSOC 2021, 36.
[106] ISDA 2020.

Efficient and effective derivative markets, however, are not immune from abuses. The events of the 2008 financial crisis and the dynamics of the derivatives markets, where CDSs transformed from hedging tools and became financial weapons of mass destruction, as famously labeled by Warren Buffett, have been mentioned by a few commentators as a warning against sustainable derivatives. These warnings might have a true foundation in the market and political dynamics that supported the boom of CDSs back in 2008, but they do not completely take into account the effect of the post-financial crisis structural reforms of the OTC derivatives markets, and they do not fully internalize and assess whether markets and market participants will operate in the same way, despite the existence of a completely reformed regulatory environment.

In 2008, financial markets experienced an asset bubble in the real estate sector, fueled by large capital investments supported by homeownership public policies. Large amounts of public and private money were invested, and derivatives flourished as risk management tools and as speculative instruments. When the bubble burst and the "music stopped," the financial markets collapsed. The value of the underlying assets to the many derivatives plummeted, and dealers that transacted in these products faced serious financial distress. Structural reforms in the EU and in the US intervened to address some of the vulnerabilities in the derivatives markets and created a financial system that is more prepared to address future potential systemic shocks.

The Green Deal envisions substantial public and private spending in sustainable economic activities that would result in the creation of new classes of green assets. Both the supply of green assets and the demand for green assets will be influenced and driven by the political determination of the EU rather than being organically produced by market forces. These market dynamics might set the foundations for possible regulatory-fueled asset bubbles that might even contribute to the misalignment of incentives of market participants. A growing demand for green investments would result in new risks that market participants will try to hedge against. Derivatives markets can support this risk transfer objective, but some commentators see green derivatives as a potential accelerator of such a bubble. However, the derivatives markets nowadays are substantially different from the pre-2008 financial crisis ones.[107] The Dodd–Frank Act in the US and EMIR and MiFID II/MiFIR in the EU have created a strong regulatory framework for exchange-traded and centrally cleared derivatives and have imposed stringent margin requirements for non-centrally cleared swaps. The post-2008 derivatives markets are more transparent and more collateralized than before. But this regulatory framework might impose excessive regulatory and compliance costs to derivatives market which would undermine market incentives and hamper financial innovation in the green derivatives. Thus, regulators must strike a balance in robust regulation to protect investors and markets without dampening the incentives to participate in the markets and to innovate.[108]

---

[107] Beylin 2020.
[108] Beylin 2023.

Policymakers should allow green derivatives markets to grow organically. They should support markets and the development of market-based institutional arrangements for green markets. Creating new markets is a costly and delicate process, as the experience of the Chicago and European Climate Exchanges shows.[109] Right now, bespoke OTC green derivatives are the predominant structures in the market, but as soon as green assets and sustainability benchmark standardization become the norm,[110] then exchange-traded green derivatives might start to develop more strongly, providing a valuable and reliable support to a green transition.[111]

REFERENCES

Alvarez, N., Cocco, A. and Patel, K. (2020), 'A new framework for assessing climate change risk in financial markets', Chicago Fed Letter, Essay on Issues, available at: www.chicagofed.org/publications/chicago-fed-letter/2020/448.

Awrey, D. (2019), 'Split derivatives: Inside the world's most misunderstood contract', *Yale Journal on Regulation*, 36(2), 495.

Baker, C. (2022), 'Derivatives and ESG', *American Business Law Journal*, 59(4), 725.

Balasta, S. (2020), 'Enel issues £500 million of sustainability-linked bond', available at: https://bit.ly/3Pyy31Q.

Beylin, I. (2020) 'Designing regulation for mobile financial markets', *UC Irvine Law Review*, 10, 497, available at: https://scholarship.law.uci.edu/ucilr/vol10/iss2/5.

Beylin, I. (2023), 'ESG-linked swaps and the next chapter of regulatory innovation', *Review of Banking and Financial Law*, 42, 755, available at: https://bit.ly/4ctlDSG.

CFTC (Commodity Futures Trading Commission) (2020), *Managing Climate Risk in the U.S. Financial System*, Report of the Climate-Related Market Risk Subcommittee, Market Risk Advisory Committee of the U.S. Commodity Futures Trading Commission, available at: https://tinyurl.com/4p4etb35.

CFTC (Commodity Futures Trading Commission) (2021a), 'Acting Chairman Behnam establishes new climate risk unit', available at: www.cftc.gov/PressRoom/PressReleases/8368-21.

CFTC (Commodity Futures Trading Commission) (2021b), 'Acting Chairman Behnam establishes new Climate Risk Unit Interdivisional Group will focus on derivatives markets' role in addressing climate-related risk and transitioning to low-carbon economy', Press Release, 83698-21, March 17, 2021, available at: www.cftc.gov/PressRoom/PressReleases/8368-21.

CFTC (Commodity Futures Trading Commission) (2021c), 'Transcript: Energy Markets Advisory Committee Meeting on June 3, 2021', available at: https://bit.ly/3x9eK96.

CFTC (Commodity Futures Trading Commission) (2021d), 'Transcript: Energy Markets Advisory Committee Meeting on September 15, 2021', available at: https://bit.ly/43xPW6X.

CFTC (Commodity Futures Trading Commission) (2022a), 'Notice, Request for Information on Climate Related Financial Risk', available at: https://bit.ly/4cu5Wur (accessed February 18, 2023).

CFTC (Commodity Futures Trading Commission) (2022b), 'CFTC Releases Request for Information on Climate-Related Financial Risk', available at: www.cftc.gov/PressRoom/PressReleases/8541-22.

---

[109] Sandor 2012.
[110] Ritchie and Ainger 2021.
[111] ISDA 2020; Lannoo and Thomadakis 2020, 17; Kennedy and Zahabi 2021.

Culp, C. L. (2004), *Risk Transfer: Derivatives in Theory and Practice* (Hoboken, NJ: Wiley Finance).

ECB/ESRB (European Central Bank/European Systemic Risk Board) (2021), 'Project team on climate risk monitoring, climate-related risk and financial stability', July 2021, available at: https://bit.ly/4cnzslT.

Enel (2020), 'Enel successfully launches new multi-tranche 4 billion U.S. dollar sustainability-linked bonds', available at: https://bit.ly/4cHUmwf.

Engel, J. (2019), 'The politics of commodity derivatives reform in the EU and in the USA', in Avgouleas, E. and Donald, D. (eds.), *The Political Economy of Financial Regulation* (Cambridge, UK: Cambridge University Press), 310–344.

ESMA (European Securities and Markets Authority) (2022), 'Emission allowances and associated derivatives', available at: https://bit.ly/4crdQox.

European Commission (2019a), 'Communication from the Commission to the European Parliament, the European Council, the Council, the European Economic and Social Committee and the Committee of the Regions – The European Green Deal', COM(2019) 640 final, December 12, available at: https://tinyurl.com/5n7s54kr.

European Commission (2019b), 'A European Green Deal', available at: https://bit.ly/43wb4dC (accessed January 10, 2023).

European Commission (2019c), 'The European Green Deal Investment Plan and Just Transition Mechanism Explained', available at: www.eea.europa.eu/policy-documents/com-2019-640-final (accessed 26 February 2023).

European Commission (2021a), 'Communication from the Commission to the European Parliament, the Council, The European Economic and Social Committee and the Committee of the Regions, Strategy for Financing the Transition to a Sustainable Economy,' COM(2021) 390 final, July 6, 2021, available at: https://tinyurl.com/3s849txw.

European Commission (2021b), 'Development of EU Ecolabel criteria for Retail Financial Products', available at https://susproc.jrc.ec.europa.eu/product-bureau/product-groups/432/documents (accessed 26 February 2023).

Ferrarini, G. and Saguato, P. (2015), 'Regulating financial market infrastructure', in Moloney, N., Ferran, E., and Payne, J. (eds.), *The Oxford Handbook of Financial Regulation* (Oxford: Oxford University Press), 568–595.

Financial Stability Oversight Council (FSOC) (2021), 'The Financial Stability Oversight Council's response to climate-related financial risk', available at: https://bit.ly/3PBhrXo.

Futures Industry Association (2020), 'How derivatives markets are helping the world fight climate change', available at: www.fia.org/sites/default/files/2020.

Futures Industry Association (2022), 'Comment for Federal Advisory Committees and Subcommittees', 85 FR 21840, available at: https://bit.ly/3PBl13P.

Giglio, S., Kelly, B. and Stroebel, J. (2021), 'Climate finance', *Annual Review of Financial Economics*, 13, 15–36, available at: https://bit.ly/3PBhtPo.

Greenspan, A. (2005), "Transfer and financial stability" (May 5), available at www.federalreserve.gov/boarddocs/speeches/2005/20050505.

Hauman, M., O'Leary, L. and Wockener, K. (2020), 'EU Sustainable Finance Consultation – Ensuring the grass is greener on the other side', available at: https://bit.ly/43ynzoT.

Hirtenstein, A. (2020), 'JPMorgan currency deal highlights finance's green shift', Wall Street Journal, October 26, available at: https://on.wsj.com/43zyLSu.

ING (2020), 'Introducing the world's first sustainability improvement derivative', available at: https://bit.ly/3TyM8NY.

ISDA (International Swap and Derivatives Association) (2020), 'Derivatives in sustainable finance: Enabling the green transition', available at: www.isda.org/a/KOmTE/Derivatives-in-Sustainable-Finance.pdf.

ISDA (International Swap and Derivatives Association) (2021a), 'Overview of ESG-related derivatives products and transactions', available at: https://bit.ly/3TuDoZk.

ISDA (International Swap and Derivatives Association) (2021b), 'Regulatory considerations for sustainability-linked derivatives', available at: https://bit.ly/3Pvi12g.

ISDA (International Swap and Derivatives Association) (2021c), 'Sustainability-linked derivatives KPI guidelines', available at: https://bit.ly/3PwewPC.

ISDA (International Swap and Derivatives Association) (2021d), 'Role of derivatives in carbon markets', available at: https://bit.ly/3PAxkxn.

ISDA (International Swap and Derivatives Association) (2022a), 'Sustainability-linked derivatives: Where to begin', available at: https://bit.ly/43upivC.

Kennedy, A. and Zahabi, E. (2021), 'European green bonds and sustainability-linked derivatives – A brief update', available at: https://bit.ly/3TyOj3Y.

Landry, E., Schlosser, C. A., Chen, Y.-H. H., Reilly, J. and Sokolov, A. (2019), *MIT Scenarios for Assessing Climate-Related Financial Risk*, MIT Joint Program on the Science and Policy of Global Change. Report No. 339.

Lannoo, K. and Thomadakis, A. (2020), 'Derivatives in sustainable finance', CEPS-ECMI Study, Centre for European Policy Studies.

Lovells, H. (2021), 'ESG derivatives: New tools unlocking sustainable capital', available at: https://bit.ly/3TvFKqL.

Ritchie, G. and Ainger, J. (2021), 'Exotic world of ESG derivatives triggers warning from regulator', available at: https://bloom.bg/3TnFo6U.

Rudebusch, G. (2021), 'Climate change is a source of financial risk', *Federal Reserve Bank of San Francisco*, 70, 1.

Saguato, P. (2024), 'Green Bets?' (on file with author).

Sandor, R. (2012), *Good Derivatives – A Story of Financial and Environmental Innovation* (Hoboken, NJ: Wiley).

Schwarcz, S. (2020), 'Regulating derivatives: A fundamental rethinking', *Duke Law Journal*, 70(3), 546–606, available at: https://scholarship.law.duke.edu/dlj/vol70/iss3/2/.

Sciarrone Alibrandi, A. and Grossule, E. (2017), 'Commodities derivatives', in Busch, D. and Ferrarini, G. (eds.), *Regulation of the EU Financial Markets – MiFID II and MiFIR* (Oxford: Oxford University Press), 439–467.

Siemens Gamesa (2019), 'Siemens Gamesa pioneers the green foreign exchange hedging market', available at: https://bit.ly/3TpPRxk.

Siemens Gamesa (2020), 'Siemens Gamesa in ESG-linked interest rate swap', *Economic Times: Energyworld.com*, March 12, available at: https://bit.ly/3vwHBDF.

So, E. (2021), 'ESG derivatives', available at: www.whitecase.com/insight-our-thinking/esg-derivatives.

Société Générale (2019), 'Enel electrifies sustainability market with inaugural green-linked bond and swap', available at: https://bit.ly/3vA3Dp4.

Stafford, P. (2020), 'US regulator welcomes water futures as tool to manage climate risk', available at: www.ft.com/content/0368fd8b-67d5-4fc2-94ba-a06e180b7a65.

Steele, G. (2020), 'Confronting the 'climate Lehman moment': The case for macroprudential climate regulation', *Cornell Journal of Law and Public Policy*, 30, 109–157, available at: https://papers.ssrn.com/sol3/papers.cfm?abstract_id=3542840.

Tondel, L. (2009), 'Introduction to derivatives', in Aicher R.D. (ed.), *Derivatives: Legal Practice and Strategies* (Boston, MA: Aspen), § 1.01.

White & Case (2020), 'The EU Taxonomy: The answer to the question "what is green"?', August 20, available at: https://bit.ly/3IQCvoR.

Wockener, K. and Hauman, M. (2019), 'EU Sustainable Finance Regulation', available at: https://bit.ly/3Tylh4R.

27

The Skin-in-the-Game Bond

A Novel Sustainable Capital Instrument

Katrien Antonio, Jan De Spiegeleer, Wim Schoutens and Eva Verschueren

27.1 INTRODUCTION

Topics related to sustainable investing have risen more rapidly than ever on the public and scientific agenda. According to the European Commission's action plan for financing sustainable growth, sustainable investing refers to the process of taking due account of environmental (E), but also social (S) and corporate governance (G) considerations in investment decision-making.[1] Banks and asset management firms, as well as large institutional investors such as (re)insurers and pension funds, have a key role to play when reorienting finance towards such investments. Lessons learned from the 2008 financial crisis are driving forces in this transition. Skin-in-the-game, transparency, regulation and proper risk management tools are crucial, since the lack of these paved the way to the last crisis.

Within the toolkit of state-of-the-art sustainable investments, green, social and sustainability bonds play a pioneering role. A green bond is a debt instrument issued to exclusively finance projects or business activities with environmental benefits, while social bonds expand the scope of green bonds to projects with positive social outcomes. The hybrid of green and social bonds, sustainability bonds, finance projects with both social and environmental objectives.[2] The ever-growing popularity of these sustainable products raises awareness about key challenges that can undermine the evolution of the bonds as credible market products.[3] There is an emerging need to standardize the sustainable debt market,[4] despite the existence of several non-binding frameworks such as the Principles of the International Capital Markets Association,[5] the certification standard of the Climate Bonds Initiative[6] and the Green Bond Standard of

---

[1] European Commission 2018.
[2] Park 2019.
[3] Climate Bonds Initiative 2022.
[4] See, for example, Deschryver and de Mariz 2020 and Tuhkanen and Vulturius 2020.
[5] ICMA 2021.
[6] Climate Bonds Initiative 2021.

the EU Technical Expert Group.[7] The absence of universally accepted principles about what constitutes 'green' and no obligations to report on the use of allocated proceeds after issuance lead to so-called 'greenwashing'. Greenwashing refers to the deceptive promotion of the perception that an organization's products, aims or policies are environmentally friendly.[8] Moreover, due to the lack of a punishment if the bond's issuer fails to deliver the promised results, the issuer has no skin in the game, and moral hazard is created. Moral hazard is generally described as the situation in which an actor is inclined to take certain actions when consequences of the act are not all borne by the risk-taker himself but are also paid for by society or other third parties.

History demonstrates the severe consequences of moral hazard. As an example, at the end of April 2010, the Deepwater Horizon oil rig operated by BP killed 11 workers and sent millions of barrels of oil into the Gulf of Mexico.[9] A clear case of moral hazard was created in the years leading up to the oil spill; the 1990 US Oil Pollution Act capped a firm's liability for economic damages from oil spills at 75 million USD, while drilling in the deepest parts of the Gulf led to billion-dollar rewards. With ultimately more than 28 billion USD in damage claims and clean-up costs, the excess losses borne by US taxpayers were massive.[10]

The limited liability principle in today's economy thus constitutes a powerful source of moral hazard.[11] Once a firm is allowed to exist as a limited liability entity, it accesses the option to put excess losses back to the economy for free. Most of the time, these excess losses are quite moderate. However, so-called tail events may occur with very low probability, while having severe impact. That impact should not be underestimated, as the Deepwater Horizon example illustrates. Another tail event that shares a lot of similarities with the oil spill crisis, and is of particular interest to us, is the 2008 financial crisis. Due to conflict of interests and excessive risk-taking, we almost witnessed a breakdown of our financial system in 2008.[12] During and after the crisis, a tremendous amount of taxpayers' money was spent or put at risk to keep (too big to fail) financial institutions alive.

In the wake of the 2008 financial crisis, regulators tried to wipe out excessive risk-taking and moral hazard risk in the banking sector. In order to avoid further bail-outs financed with taxpayers' money, the Basel Committee proposed the Basel III framework to enforce higher capital levels and additional loss-absorbing buffers.[13] In the new banking regulations, contingent convertible (CoCo) bonds play an important role as high-yield instruments with loss-absorbing capacity.[14]

---

[7] EU TEG 2020.
[8] Doran and Tanner 2019.
[9] Friedman and Friedman 2014.
[10] Wood 2016.
[11] Djelic and Bothello 2013.
[12] Crotty 2009.
[13] Basel Committee on Banking Supervision 2010.
[14] De Spiegeleer et al. 2014.

A CoCo bond converts into shares or suffers a write-down of the face value upon the appearance of a trigger event, often characterized by a low value of the bank's CET1 ratio. This low CET1 ratio indicates a distressed situation for the financial institution, a tail event.

This contribution transfers the concept of a CoCo bond into a new capital instrument, focussed on delivering upon E, S and G commitments: a skin-in-the-game bond.[15] This instrument goes beyond the traditional green, social or sustainability bonds by embedding a financial penalty that connects sustainability promises with actual performance. If the issuer hits a preset trigger condition, investors miss out on a coupon payment or even forgo the complete face value of the bond. The issuer is obliged to direct the withheld part of this face value into a government-controlled fund. As such, the issuing company is not exempt from payment and society may be compensated for the damage caused. The skin-in-the-game bond is built on the principle that both parties, issuer and investor, should have skin in the game and suffer if sustainability promises are not delivered. Moreover, transparency is enhanced; in order to monitor the trigger, the issuer is forced to publish reliable information on its sustainability-related commitments.

On the one hand, the skin-in-the-game bond compares to what is called a sustainability-linked bond (SLB), of which the first was launched in September 2019 by the Italian energy company Enel.[16] The structural characteristics of this type of bond are adjusted depending on the achievement of predefined sustainable objectives. For most issued SLBs, failing to reach the sustainability performance targets (SPTs), measured through predefined key performance indicators (KPIs), results in a coupon step-up by a number of basis points (bps).[17] That way, the issuer creates an incentive to reach its sustainability goals. However, investing in these types of SLBs means speculating on *not* meeting sustainable targets, and a problematic revised incentive for the investor is created. Truly green investors should not be willing to earn money to the detriment of any sustainable objective. Our proposed skin-in-the-game bond therefore focusses on aligning a company's incentives with a true sustainable investor's interests.

On the other hand, with the involvement of the third party, the external fund, the skin-in-the-game bond shares some characteristics with catastrophe (cat) bonds or insurance-linked securities in general. The distinguishing feature of a cat bond is that the principal is used to cover the costs of a related catastrophe, when it occurs.[18] While some of these bonds are not necessarily related to E, S or G commitments of a company (hurricanes, earthquakes, etc.), others are, for example cat bonds for offshore oil spill liability. Catastrophe bonds are usually

---

[15] De Spiegeleer and Schoutens 2019.
[16] Enel 2021.
[17] ICMA 2020.
[18] Burnecki et al. 2011.

sold by (re)insurance companies and governments, who use them to mitigate their exposure to risk. In contrast, the skin-in-the-game bond aims for a wider applicability, by being open to issuance by companies in any sector. Also, that way, costs are not only covered by investor's money, via the principal, but are also partially paid for by the company who causes the costs, via the coupons. A catastrophe bond serves as a (re)insurance product, a risk transfer solution, whereas the skin-in-the-game bond has the primary purpose of enforcing skin-in-the-game and by that avoiding a catastrophe.

This paper is organized as follows. Section 27.2 investigates the design of several skin-in-the-game bonds, with a focus on versions with a continuous or counting benchmark. Section 27.3 outlines a custom-made valuation model inspired by the credit derivatives model for CoCo bonds.[19] Sections 27.4 and 27.5 focus on two illustrative examples; the ESG and nuclear skin-in-the-game bonds. Section 27.6 concludes.

27.2 THE DESIGN OF A SKIN-IN-THE-GAME BOND

The design of the skin-in-the-game bond finds inspiration in the construction of contingent convertible bonds, established in the aftermath of the 2008 financial crisis. While the CoCo bond is mainly created for the banking sector, the skin-in-the-game bond can be tailored to the specific characteristics of a company in any sector.

27.2.1 *The CoCo Bond*

Contingent convertible bonds are hybrid securities issued by financial institutions as a direct result of the more stringent capital requirements set out in the Basel III accord.[20] The standard corporate bond serves as a base for the instrument; investors receive a stream of fixed coupon payments together with a redemption of the notional investment at maturity. However, if a bank enters into a life-threatening situation due to unexpected losses, a so-called tail event, and its capital level consequently falls below a low threshold, investors will witness a complete or partial loss of their investment. This constitutes the loss-absorbing capacity of a CoCo bond; investors automatically bear part of the losses of the financial institution in distressed situations. As such, the institution can remain in a stable financial situation and the cost of a government bail-out is reduced.

The CoCo bond is a non-standardized instrument. Dependent on the type of the bond, the trigger event will cause a (full or partial) write-down of the bond's face value or a conversion of the bond into shares. The bottom line in any of these

---

[19] De Spiegeleer and Schoutens 2012.
[20] Basel Committee on Banking Supervision 2010.

situations is similar: the conversion or write-down is not voluntary, and investors will suffer an important loss if the trigger event occurs. As a consequence, the proposed yield on the investment has to be high enough in order to get investors to underwrite the additional risk. Moreover, the yield level of the bond acts as an indicator for the healthiness of the issuing institution. The more risk the institution takes, the higher the yield the market will charge. This way, the CoCo bond's mechanism reduces moral hazard; it provides an incentive for the issuer to control risks, since excessive risk-taking will immediately lead to a higher cost of capital.

The trigger mechanism of a CoCo bond can be activated in different ways. First, the healthiness of a bank's balance sheet is measured using an accounting or capital ratio. The ratio most often used in practice is the Common Equity Tier 1 (CET1) ratio. A life-threatening situation for the institution is then defined by the ratio falling below a preset trigger level. Second, a regulatory trigger allows for the national regulator of the bank to decide on the financial situation of the institution. This way, the CoCo bond can be triggered at any point in time if forced by the regulator, to prevent the bank's insolvency.

CoCo bonds thus offer investors a higher yield in return for loss-absorbing capacity. The instrument's mechanism enforces skin-in-the-game for both issuer and investor; it is in the best interest of the two parties to stabilize the financial health of the institution. The issuer lowers its cost of capital, while the investor will not lose out on (part of) the investment.[21]

27.2.2 *The Skin-in-the-Game Bond*

While the focus of CoCo bonds is on the financial health of banks, awareness grows globally about the achievements and intentions of companies in any sector regarding environmental, social and corporate governance topics. Therefore, we see potential in financial instruments with an embedded financial penalty for all parties involved, linked to at least one E-, S- or G-related commitment. The general aim of the product is to enforce skin-in-the-game, which fights moral hazard risk. When the instrument is issued by companies active in areas exposed to severe tail risk, the product may reduce the exposure of taxpayers, and in general society as a whole, to potential losses.

27.2.2.1 General Structure

The skin-in-the-game bond functions as a standard corporate bond when no trigger is hit; a fixed coupon is paid at regular points in time (e.g., annually) to the investor and the notional value is redeemed at maturity. However, when the trigger mechanism of the bond is activated, the investor will suffer a loss on his investment, the

---

[21] For a more extensive discussion on contingent convertibles see, for example, De Spiegeleer et al. 2014 and De Spiegeleer et al. 2018.

size of which depends on the characteristics of the bond. Upon this trigger event, the skin-in-the-game bond differs from the CoCo bond in the direct involvement of a third party: a (national) regulator or government controlling a fund. The regulatory fund is then used to collect the withheld part of the face value. This way, the bond's design creates an additional incentive for the issuer to deliver sustainability promises; the issuer is not exempt from payment, whereas this is the case for a CoCo bond's issuer. Like the CoCo bond, the skin-in-the-game bond is a non-standardized instrument where the benchmark, trigger type and trigger penalty can be tailored to the issuance. In what follows, we discuss these different components.

Benchmark and trigger type. For the skin-in-the-game bond to be a sustainable capital instrument, the benchmark must be related to sustainability in at least one of its pillars, being the environment, society or corporate governance. Once a decision is made on the benchmark, a trigger level is fixed. This level is chosen in such a way that the benchmark breaching the trigger level indicates a situation of high (tail) risk, with consequences harmful to the environment or society.

Inspired by the selection criteria of KPIs for sustainability-linked bonds,[22] an ideal benchmark is, in general, unambiguous, objective, easy to measure and monitor, relevant and ambitious. Unambiguity is needed as a trigger event has concrete, and often severe, financial consequences for all parties involved. In order to avoid conflict of interest, it must be possible to assess the value of the benchmark in an objective manner. An easy to measure and monitor benchmark will allow the bond to trigger timely and conduces effective risk assessment. Also, the benchmark should be relevant and related to the issuer's core business. Lastly, the trigger level may not be fixed such that a favourable benchmark value is too easy to achieve, which gives a false perception about a company's performance.

We distinguish between two types of benchmarks, both clarified with an example in Sections 27.4 and 27.5.

A first, so-called continuous benchmark is based on the quantification of a relevant parameter or rating, which, in principle, can be monitored continuously, for example, the greenhouse gas (GHG) emission or ESG rating of a company. A GHG skin-in-the-game bond triggers when a company fails to meet a preset (low) target level of GHG emission, whereas an ESG skin-in-the-game bond triggers when a company's ESG score falls below the trigger level (see Section 27.4).

A second benchmark is based on the occurrence of a number of events of interest in relation to the total exposure, as modelled by a counting process, that is, a so-called counting benchmark. Examples are the number of nuclear incidents occurring within a nuclear power plant with respect to the total net capacity of the plant (see Section 27.5) or the number of burn-outs within a company with respect to the total number of employees. Both skin-in-the-game bonds trigger when the event rate is too high, namely above a fixed trigger level.

---

[22] ICMA 2020.

Trigger penalty. Inspired by the trigger penalties of a CoCo bond, the activation of a skin-in-the-game bond's trigger clause will affect the payout of future coupons and in some cases also the redemption of the notional. For a continuous benchmark, we envisage the following trigger penalties, analogous to the different types of CoCo bonds.[23]

Permanent coupon loss	All future coupons are cancelled upon a trigger event. The trigger event is a non-cumulative coupon cancellation clause; once a coupon is not paid out, it is impossible to recuperate this cash flow in a later stage. Regardless of whether a trigger event occurs, the notional amount is paid to the investor at maturity.
Temporary coupon loss	Coupons are not paid out as long as the trigger clause is activated. Once the trigger condition is no longer met, coupons are paid out as planned to the investor. In any situation, the notional amount is redeemed at maturity.
Coupon withholding	As long as the trigger condition is met, coupons are withheld. Once the trigger is no longer activated at a payment date, withheld coupons, together with the normal coupon, are paid out. If the trigger condition still holds on the maturity date, only the notional is redeemed.
Full write-down	Once the trigger clause is activated, all outstanding coupons as well as the redemption of the notional are cancelled.

As an illustration, the evolution of a continuous benchmark and the payout structures of corresponding skin-in-the-game bonds with a maturity of five years, annual coupon payments and a varying trigger penalty are shown in Figure 27.1(a–e).

In case of a counting benchmark, we go one step further by not only taking into account the yearly number of events, but also the cumulative number of events, over the full duration of the bond. We therefore envisage the following generic skin-in-the-game bond structure, illustrated in Figure 27.2.

Assume that the yearly number of arrivals of an event of interest, in relation to a particular exposure, can be modelled by a counting process. The event of interest is specified in such a way that the higher the number of arrivals, the stronger the negative effect on at least one of the E, S or G pillars. Consider the skin-in-the-game bond with as underlying benchmark the number of arrivals of the event. The payout of the skin-in-the-game bond will depend on the evolution of the benchmark and two types of triggers, with a tailored trigger penalty.

The first trigger concerns the yearly number of events. This trigger is set at a level t_y, such that a penalty is imposed if the total number of events in a year exceeds t_y. The penalty can be determined by the issuer, ranging from a temporary coupon cancellation to a full write-down.

[23] De Spiegeleer et al. 2014.

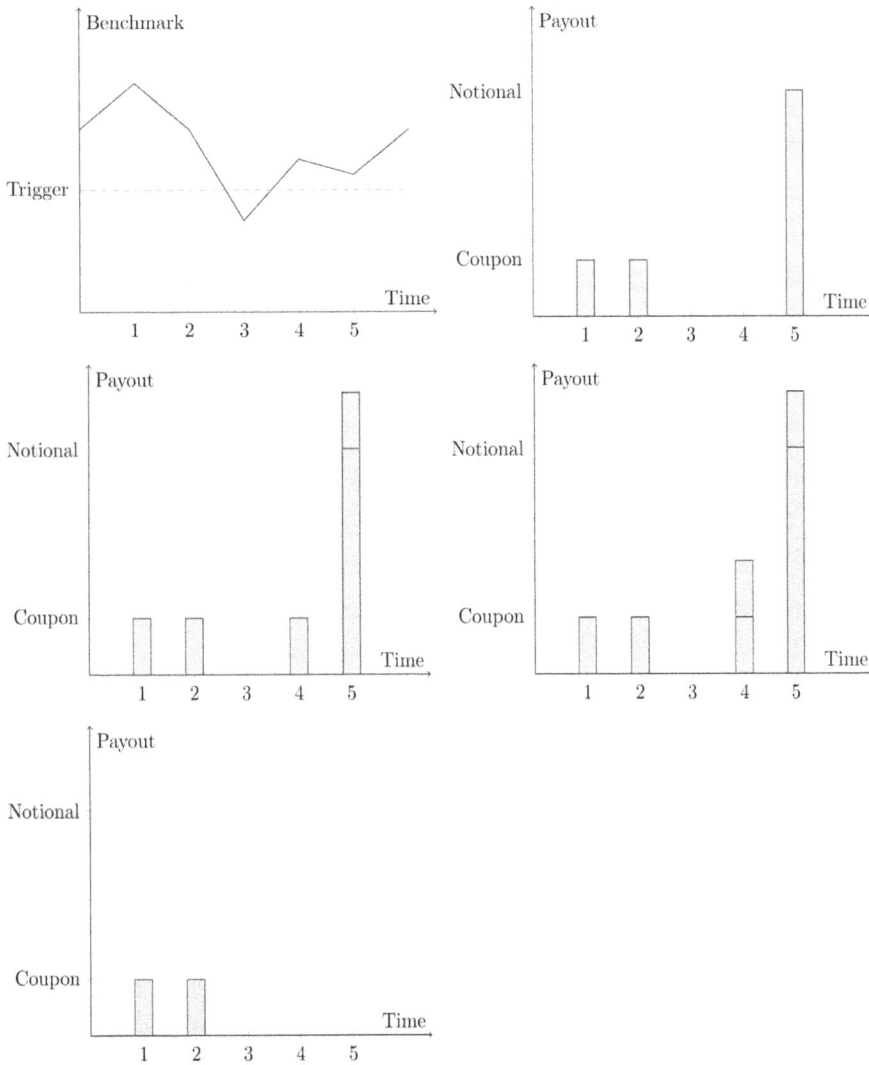

FIGURE 27.1 The evolution of a continuous benchmark over time is sketched in (a). The trigger level is only breached at the third payment date. The payout structure of a 5-year skin-in-the-game bond with annual coupon payment and as underlying the benchmark (a) is pictured in combination with: (b) a permanent coupon loss penalty, (c) a temporary coupon loss penalty, (d) a coupon withholding penalty or (e) a full write-down penalty

The second trigger concerns the cumulative number of events over the past duration of the bond. This trigger is a full write-down trigger and is set at level $t_c \cdot t$, for $t = 2, \dots, T$. All future coupons and the notional redemption are wiped out when the cumulative number of events up to time t exceeds $t_c \cdot t$. This way, an excessive

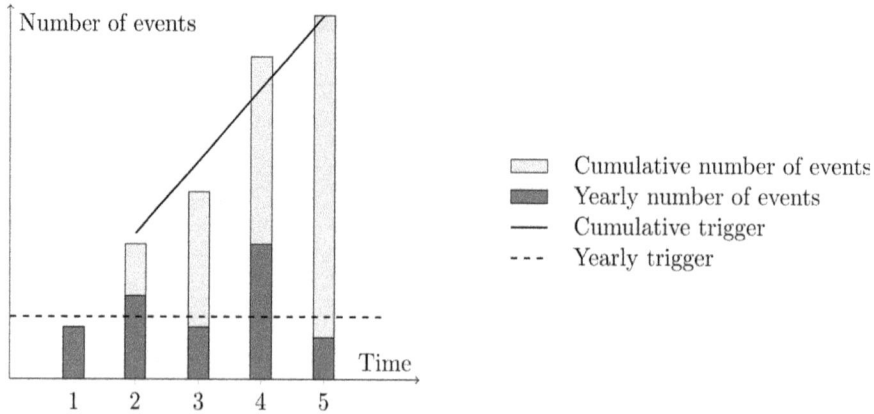

FIGURE 27.2 An illustration of the generic structure of a 5-year skin-in-the-game bond with a counting benchmark. The yearly trigger clause is activated at years 2 and 4. The cumulative trigger clause is activated at year 4

number of yearly triggers is punished. Note that t_c can be fixed at $t_c = \infty$, in case one does not want a cumulative trigger.

27.2.2.2 Impact of an Issuance on All Parties Involved

There are three major parties involved in the issuance of a skin-in-the-game bond: the issuer, the investor and the regulator. We shed light on the impact of the issuance of a skin-in-the-game bond on each of the three parties.

Issuer. Similar to a CoCo bond's issuer, the issuer of a skin-in-the-game bond has a clear market-driven incentive to optimize and stabilize the level of the benchmark underlying the bond. The issuer is said to have skin in the game. Excessive risk-taking and mismanagement regarding the benchmark will hit the issuing company where it hurts; its cost of capital goes up as investors will require a higher yield. Together with the cost of capital, a company's reputational risk will increase. Unlike the issuer of a CoCo bond, the skin-in-the-game bond's issuer is obliged to pay out all future cash flows of the bond, either to the investor or to the external fund.

Moreover, the issuance of a skin-in-the-game bond enhances transparency; in order to measure and monitor the benchmark, the issuer must be open on all measures taken and is forced to publish reliable information on its commitments. Intransparency will automatically translate into more uncertainty for investors and, again, the market will charge higher yields.

Investor. Not only the issuer, but also the investor has skin in the game. Where investors in SLBs speculate on *not* meeting sustainable targets, investors in skin-in-the-game bonds speculate on meeting the E-, S- and/or G-related goals. In return for this skin-in-the-game, investors cash in an above risk-free coupon on their invested amount.

Regulator. The third party involved in the issuance of a skin-in-the-game bond is the regulator or national government. This third party is essential for enforcing skin-in-the-game on the issuer side. Moreover, in case of a trigger event, with possibly large losses for society or damage to the environment, there are immediate funds available to mitigate these losses and (partially) cover the costs. The fund can be used to prevent a government bail-out with taxpayer's money; risks are shifted from taxpayers to private investors. Further, the cash is immediately available and not subject to a potentially lengthy procedure as it is often the case when an insured files a claim with his insurer.

27.3 THE VALUATION OF A SKIN-IN-THE-GAME BOND

Inspired by the credit derivatives pricing approach for CoCos,[24] we propose a valuation model for the skin-in-the-game bond. Compared to a standard corporate bond, which is subject to the issuer's bankruptcy risk, the trigger characteristic of the skin-in-the-game bond increases the probability for the investor to suffer a loss on the invested amount. To compensate for the embedded trigger risk, the skin-in-the-game bond offers a higher yield than vanilla corporate debt issued by the same company. The yield offered to the investor on a standard corporate bond consists of the risk-free rate r and a credit spread c_s. This credit spread reflects the default risk of the bond; it is the extra yield investor's request for the bankruptcy risk of the issuing company.[25] For fixed income investors, the skin-in-the-game bond's pricing problem then boils down to determining the extra yield needed on top of the risk-free rate r and the credit spread c_s in order to accept the risk of facing a loss upon a trigger event.

Standard corporate bond. In absence of any embedded trigger risk, let the random variable C_t be the cash flow at time t of a standard corporate bond with maturity T, notional N and yearly coupon payments at coupon rate c. In case of no default event, $C_t = c \cdot N$, for $t \in \{1,...,T-1\}$ and $C_T = (1+c) \cdot N$. However, due to the default probability of the issuing firm, future values of these random variables are unknown. The expected value of future cash flows, $\mathbb{E}_{\mathbb{Q}}[C_t]$, for $t \in \{1,...,T\}$, under a pricing probability measure $\mathbb{Q}$, is therefore used for pricing purposes.

At first issuance, the bond trades at par, which means that the risk-neutral price P of the bond, given as the discounted expected payout under the pricing measure $\mathbb{Q}$, equals the nominal value N. For a bond subject to a risk-free rate r, one determines the additional yield c_s, needed in order to get investors to underwrite the default risk, by computing the coupon rate $c = r + c_s$, such that

$$P = \sum_{t=1}^{T} \frac{\mathbb{E}_{\mathbb{Q}}[C_t]}{(1+r)^t} := N, \tag{27.1}$$

and the bond trades at par.

---

[24] De Spiegeleer and Schoutens 2012.
[25] Duffie and Singleton 2003.

Skin-in-the-game bond. The skin-in-the-game bond bears an additional trigger risk and investors therefore require an extra yield, called the trigger spread t_g. The trigger spread can be seen as the yield difference between a skin-in-the-game bond (with trigger risk) and a standard corporate bond (without trigger risk), with the same characteristics.

Under the assumption that both r and c_s are known, one's interest is in calculating the trigger spread t_g. Therefore, let the random variable C_t be the cash flow at time t, for $t \in \{1,\ldots,T\}$, of the skin-in-the-game bond. In absence of any trigger event, the value of the cash flow at time t is identical to that of a standard corporate bond. However, on the occurrence of a trigger event, the future value of these cash flows depends on the trigger penalty, fixed in the terms of the bond. At issuance, the future value of C_t, for $t \in \{1,\ldots,T\}$, is thus unknown, due to the trigger probability, and the expected value $\mathbb{E}_{\mathbb{Q}}[C_t]$ is used for pricing purposes. In order to incorporate the default probability of the firm, the expected cash flows of a skin-in-the-game bond are subject to a discount rate $r + c_s$. One then determines the additional yield t_g, needed in order to get investors to underwrite the trigger risk, by computing the coupon rate $c = r + c_s + t_g$, such that

$$P = \sum_{t=1}^{T} \frac{\mathbb{E}_{\mathbb{Q}}[C_t]}{\left(1+r+c_s\right)^t} := N, \qquad (27.2)$$

and the bond trades at par.

If both the risk-free rate r and the credit spread c_s are known, the only non-trivial value, needed to calculate the coupon rate and corresponding trigger level using Equation 27.2, is an estimate of the trigger probability at different points in time. To see this, consider a skin-in-the-game bond with a temporary coupon loss penalty. The probability that a cash flow is paid out at time t is equal to the probability that the trigger clause of the bond is *not* activated at that time. Suppose PT_t is equal to the trigger probability at time $t \neq T$, it then holds that

$$\mathbb{E}_{\mathbb{Q}}[C_t] = PT_t \cdot 0 + \left(1 - PT_t\right)\cdot c \cdot N = \left(1 - PT_t\right)\cdot c \cdot N. \qquad (27.3)$$

If we replace $\mathbb{E}_{\mathbb{Q}}[C_t]$, for each $t \in \{1,\ldots,T\}$, with an expression in function of the known trigger probability PT_t, we can solve Equation 27.2 for t_g.

Building a map from $\mathbb{P}$ to $\mathbb{Q}$. Calculating trigger probabilities is by far the most challenging task in pricing a skin-in-the-game bond. Moreover, Equation 27.2 requires these probabilities to be calculated under a pricing probability measure $\mathbb{Q}$. In practice, information on measure $\mathbb{Q}$ is often derived from market data such as option prices or spreads of credit default swaps.[26] Any probabilities derived from historical information will result in probabilities under a real-world

---

[26] See, for example, Figlewski 2018 and Hull et al. 2005.

probability measure $\mathbb{P}$, which is not used for pricing purposes. As the skin-in-the-game bond is not a traded instrument, we will not be able to calculate trigger probabilities under measure $\mathbb{Q}$ and so we are forced to make a rather strong assumption when mapping $\mathbb{P}$ to $\mathbb{Q}$.

A somewhat similar problem is studied in the credit scoring literature, namely the default risk of a company and the relationship between actual $PD^{\mathbb{P}}$ and pricing $PD^{\mathbb{Q}}$ default probabilities. There exists no unanimity on the exact form of this relationship, but one agrees in general that risk-neutral default probabilities are higher than actual default probabilities and that the actual default probability as a function of the pricing probability is increasing and convex.[27] We use a continuous and convex map that allows moving from one probability measure to another:[28]

$$ PD^{\mathbb{P}} = \exp\left[\left(PD^{\mathbb{Q}} \right)^{1.39} \right] - 1. \tag{27.4} $$

The default of a firm results in a loss for investors in debt security that is issued by that firm. Similarly, the trigger of a skin-in-the-game bond results in a loss for the investors of the skin-in-the-game bond. Motivated by our need to have a closed-form relation, the similarity between default and trigger probabilities, and the effect of a default and trigger event, we find it reasonable to assume that the market will apply a same relationship as proposed in Equation 27.4 to trigger probabilities of skin-in-the-game bonds. In what follows, we will therefore use the relation in Equation 27.4 to transform trigger probabilities under measure $\mathbb{P}$ to trigger probabilities under measure $\mathbb{Q}$. In the next sections, we elaborate on two different methodologies to calculate these probabilities, through the use of two illustrative examples.

27.4 THE ESG SKIN-IN-THE-GAME BOND

Many (inter)national companies are nowadays being rated on their ESG performance by various third-party providers, ranging from well-established, global data providers (e.g., MSCI, Bloomberg and Thomas Reuters) to niche ESG specialists (e.g., Sustainalytics, Vigeo Eiris and TruValue Labs).[29] Investors increasingly rely on ESG ratings as the basis of an investor engagement with the company.[30] The issuance of a skin-in-the-game bond linked to the ESG performance of the company provides the issuer with incentives to reach and maintain a favourable ESG rating, in order to, among other things, be attractive to new investors.

An extensive stream of research sheds light on the differences across the ratings published by the ESG rating providers.[31] A varying rating methodology, a different

---

[27] See, for example, Hull et al. 2005, Berg 2010 and Heynderickx et al. 2016.
[28] Cariboni et al. 2011.
[29] Kumar and Weiner 2019.
[30] Huber and Comstock 2017.
[31] See, for example, Berg et al. 2020, and Dorfleitner et al. 2015.

scope and coverage and the existence of discrete as well as continuous ratings hamper a comparison between the different rating agencies. Without a global ESG rating system, the discussion in this section of a skin-in-the-game bond with an ESG rating benchmark should merely be seen as an illustrative example of a skin-in-the-game bond with a tailored pricing technique.

ESG skin-in-the-game bonds use the ESG rating of a company, provided by a particular rating agency, as the benchmark underlying the trigger mechanism of the bond.[32] The bond triggers when the ESG rating of the company drops below a preset low level. This level must be determined according to the industry or sector in which the company operates. A hit of the trigger level then indicates that the issuer fails to deliver the E, S and/or G commitments realized by companies operating in a similar business. Besides the trigger level, the trigger penalty, maturity, frequency of coupon payments and notional of the bond need to be fixed.

27.4.1 ESG Data

We use a European ESG rating data set provided by Sustainalytics for the period January 2017 to September 2019.[33] Sustainalytics determines company-specific raw scores on 163 ESG-related indicators across the E (59), S (61) and G (43) pillars of sustainability. The individual scores range from 0 to 100, with a higher score indicating a better performance in managing the specific ESG issue. Using a proprietary weighting scheme, adapted to the specific characteristics of an industry, Sustainalytics aggregates raw indicator scores into an overall ESG rating for each of the $K = 3294$ European companies included in the data set:

$$\text{ESG}_k = \sum_{i=1}^{163} \text{raw score}_i \cdot \text{weight}_i, \qquad (27.5)$$

for company $k = 1,\ldots,K$.

The majority of a company's raw scores are subject to annual revisions, which occur in line with the release of the company's annual report. A minority of indicators, related to controversial events such as employee or business ethics incidents, are continuously monitored by an in-house team of analysts and adjusted in response to ESG-related news, for example, from news articles.

The Sustainalytics data set is a monthly snapshot of all indicator scores for each firm. All firm's scores are released on the same date, typically occurring within the first week of the month. Due to the continuous adjustment of some indicators, the dates within the data set do not necessarily coincide with the moment on which scores were really updated by the in-house team of Sustainalytics. As a result, the exact company-specific score on all indicators is only known at a finite

---

[32]   De Spiegeleer and Schoutens 2019.
[33]   More information can be found at www.sustainalytics.com/esg-data/.

series of data points, one for each month, and information in between dates is not available. Given these characteristics, we say that the available panel data on ESG indicator scores consists of intermittently observed, continuous-time processes.[34] In what follows, we will not work with the available time series of individual scores on the 163 indicators, but only with the time series of aggregated ESG ratings as calculated using Equation 27.5, on a monthly basis.

The companies in the data set are subdivided into two categories (public or private) according to the company type and grouped into 11 sectors, according to the Global Industry Classification Standard (GICS).[35]

27.4.2 A Valuation Framework

The trigger probability of an ESG skin-in-the-game bond is determined by the probability that the issuing firm's ESG rating drops to or below the trigger level. The similarities between ESG ratings and credit ratings are striking and the literature on credit ratings is therefore of great use to model the evolution of a company's ESG rating. To apply the tailored methodology, it is convenient to transform the raw ratings of Sustainalytics into ESG rating categories, as shown in Table 27.1. On the basis of this transformation lies the distribution of companies within each MSCI rating category.[36] First, the companies in the available Sustainalytics data set are ranked according to their ESG rating at the beginning of 2017. Next, the MSCI data percentiles are applied to the ranked data set, which results in a subdivision of the companies into seven categories. The given raw rating thresholds for the different categories are finally obtained from the ratings of all companies within a category.

Inspired by the literature on credit ratings, we model a company's movements, in continuous-time, between a finite set of ESG rating categories, using a first-order Markov multi-state model.[37] Suppose a company is in state $R(t)$ at time t, where $R(t)$ takes values in the state space $S = \{C, CCC, B, BB, BBB, A, AAA\}$.

TABLE 27.1 *Raw rating thresholds and data percentiles for Sustainalytics'*
ESG rating categories

Rating category	C	CCC	B	BB	BBB	A	AAA
Raw rating	0–48	48–54	54–61	61–69	69–74	74–79	79–100
Data percentile	0–10	10–25	25–45	45–65	65–80	80–90	90–100

[34] Wooldridge 2009.
[35] S&P Global Market Intelligence 2018.
[36] Dahl and Larsen 2014. MSCI uses rating categories to indicate a company's ESG performance. More information can be found at www.msci.com/our-solutions/esg-investing/esg-ratings.
[37] See, for example, Kalbfleisch and Lawless 1985.

Let $P(s,t)$ be the $|S| \times |S|$ transition probability matrix with probabilities $p_{ij}(s,t)$ to transition from one ESG state i to another state j over a predefined time horizon $t - s$:

$$p_{ij}(s,t) = P(R(t) = j \mid R(s) = i). \tag{27.6}$$

Under the first-order Markov assumption, the future rating state only depends on the current state and not on the full history of states. The transition intensities $q_{ij}(t)$ represent the instantaneous risk of moving from state i to state $j \neq i$, at time t:

$$q_{ij}(t) = \lim_{\delta t \to 0} \frac{p_{ij}(t,\, t+\delta t)}{\delta t} \quad \text{and} \quad q_{ii}(t) = -\sum_{j \neq i} q_{ij}(t), \tag{27.7}$$

for $i \neq j$, and $i = 1, \ldots, |S|$.

We additionally assume a time-homogeneous model, in which $q_{ij}(t) = q_{ij}$ and Q is the transition intensity matrix. This results in a time-invariant transition probability matrix $P(t) = P(s, s+t) = P(0,t)$. We know that[38]

$$P(t) = \exp(Qt) = \sum_{k=0}^{\infty} \frac{Q^k t^k}{k!}. \tag{27.8}$$

The essential building block in the estimation of the trigger probability of an ESG skin-in-the-game bond is the rating transition probability matrix $P(t)$. As an example, if the trigger level is set at a BB rating, the probability that the bond triggers within the first year then equals the probability that the issuer's rating drops to either BB, B, CCC or C within that year.

We apply an estimation method[39] that provides us with a maximum likelihood estimate of the transition matrix P, when exact transition times and class occupancy in between observation times are unknown. To this intent, let k index the K individual firms in the available ESG data set. The data of firm k consists of a series of time points and corresponding ESG categories: $\{(t_{k0}, R_{t_{k0}}), (t_{k1}, R_{t_{k1}}), \ldots, (t_{kn_k}, R_{t_{kn_k}})\}$. Note that the possible observation times $\{t_0, \ldots, t_n\}$ are fixed within the data set, but not all firms are evaluated over the entire period from t_0 (January 2017) to t_n (September 2019).

Consider the pair of consecutively observed ESG states $R_{t_{kj}}$ and $R_{t_{kj+1}}$ of firm k. The contribution to the likelihood L_k of observing the rating history of firm k, from this pair, is the probability to be in state $R_{t_{kj+1}}$ at time t_{kj+1}, given that the firm was in state $R_{t_{kj}}$ at time t_{kj}, which is exactly

$$p_{R_{t_{kj}} R_{t_{kj+1}}}(t_{kj},\, t_{kj+1}) = p_{R_{t_{kj}} R_{t_{kj+1}}}(t_{kj+1} - t_{kj}), \tag{27.9}$$

under the assumption of time-homogeneity. The first-order Markov assumption then results in the likelihood L_k of firm k:

---

[38] Cox and Miller 1965.
[39] See, for example, Kalbfleisch and Lawless 1985 and Jackson 2011.

$$L_k = \prod_{j=0}^{n_k-1} p_{R_{t_{kj}} R_{t_{kj+1}}} \left(t_{kj+1} - t_{kj} \right). \tag{27.10}$$

Under the assumption of independent rating paths for the different firms in the data set, the full likelihood L is the product over all terms L_k:

$$L = \prod_{k=1}^{K} \prod_{j=0}^{n_k-1} p_{R_{t_{kj}} R_{t_{kj+1}}} \left(t_{kj+1} - t_{kj} \right) = \prod_{l=0}^{n-1} \prod_{i,j \in S} \left[p_{ij} \left(t_{l+1} - t_l \right) \right]^{n_{ijl}}, \tag{27.11}$$

where n_{ijl} is the number of firms in state i at time t_l and j at time t_{l+1}. Moreover, $L = L(Q)$; the likelihood depends on the transition intensity matrix Q via Equation 27.8.

We fit a time-homogeneous, first-order Markov multi-state model under the likelihood in Equation 27.11.[40] The optimization is done using a Fisher scoring method. Additionally, we model the effect of a vector z_k of time-independent explanatory variables (company type and sector) on the transition intensities of firm k, using proportional intensities

$$q_{ij}(z_k) = \exp\left(\beta_{ij}^{(0)} + \beta_{ij}^{\mathrm{T}} z_k \right), \tag{27.12}$$

for $i \neq j$. A skin-in-the-game bond will be issued by a specific company, so by including these covariates, we are able to model a company's benchmark on the most granular level available.

The impact of each covariate varies across the different transitions from state i to state j. The likelihood in Equation 27.11 is then maximized over the coefficients $\beta_{ij}^{(0)}$ and β_{ij}^{T}. A likelihood ratio test shows that the model with both company type and sector as covariates performs significantly better than the model without or with only one of the covariates.

27.4.3 *The Trigger Spread*

By means of example, we calculate the trigger spread of an ESG skin-in-the-game bond with characteristics as summarized in Table 27.2. The risk-free rate r and credit spread c_s are fixed at a chosen level. We assume that the issuing company's rating is only assessed at the time a coupon has to be paid. This means that a drop of the issuing company's ESG rating to or below the trigger level will not trigger the bond, if the rating recovers before the next coupon date. Due to the permanent coupon loss penalty, at each year, we also need to take into account the possibility that the bond already triggered in the years before.

Since coupons are paid annually, we use the one-year transition matrix to assess the trigger probability of the ESG skin-in-the-game bond. Using the methodology as described in Section 27.4.2, the one-year transition matrix for a public firm in

---

[40] We use the implementation of Jackson 2011.

TABLE 27.2 *ESG skin-in-the-game bond characteristics*

Characteristics	Bond-specific values
Issuer	public firm in communication services sector
Risk-free rate r	0.010
Credit spread c_s	0.025
Issue date	1 January 2020
Maturity date	1 January 2025
Notional N	100
Coupon rate	c
Coupon frequency	annual
Initial rating	A
Trigger level	BB
Trigger penalty	permanent coupon loss

TABLE 27.3 *One-year transition matrix P, under $\mathbb{P}$, for a public firm in the communication services sector*

	C	CCC	B	BB	BBB	A	AAA
C	0.53213	0.18029	0.22725	0.05577	0.00409	0.00042	0.00005
CCC	0.12705	0.47922	0.30573	0.08110	0.00618	0.00065	0.00007
B	0.06587	0.10967	0.51331	0.27567	0.03119	0.00379	0.00050
BB	0.00884	0.02761	0.12200	0.67539	0.14099	0.02163	0.00355
BBB	0.00089	0.00364	0.01845	0.19021	0.62482	0.13169	0.03031
A	0.00009	0.00048	0.00263	0.03941	0.25367	0.58823	0.11549
AAA	0.00002	0.00012	0.00064	0.01078	0.08476	0.19875	0.70492

the communication services sector is calculated on the available data set. As this data set consists of historical ESG scores, the matrix in Table 27.3 contains transition probabilities under the real-world probability measure $\mathbb{P}$.

The probability that the ESG skin-in-the-game bond is triggered at the first coupon date equals the probability that the firm's rating, at issuance equal to A, is equal to either BB, B, CCC or C, at time 1. Using the transition probabilities in Table 27.3, we find that the first year's trigger probability, under the $\mathbb{P}$-measure, $PT_1^{\mathbb{P}}$, is equal to

$$PT_1^{\mathbb{P}} = 0.03941 + 0.00263 + 0.00048 + 0.00009 = 0.04261.$$

There are two scenarios that cause this particular ESG skin-in-the-game bond to be triggered at the second coupon date. First, if the bond was triggered at the first coupon date, time 1, it will still be triggered at the second date, since the trigger penalty is a permanent coupon loss. Second, given that the bond was not triggered at time 1, the bond will trigger when the firm's rating is equal to either BB, B, CCC or C, at time 2. Combining both scenarios, we find that the second year's trigger probability, $PT_2^{\mathbb{P}}$, under the $\mathbb{P}$-measure is equal to

TABLE 27.4 *Trigger probabilities under both the $\mathbb{P}$ and $\mathbb{Q}$ probability measures for an ESG skin-in-the-game bond with characteristics as given in Table 27.2*

	Year 1	Year 2	Year 3	Year 4	Year 5
$PT^{\mathbb{P}}$	0.04261	0.12309	0.20974	0.29175	0.36613
$PT^{\mathbb{Q}}$	0.10174	0.21241	0.30324	0.37521	0.43258

$$PT_2^{\mathbb{P}} = 0.04261 + 0.08048 = 0.12309.$$

A similar procedure can be used to calculate the $\mathbb{P}$-measure trigger probabilities at later time points, which are presented in Table 27.4.

The transition matrix in Table 27.3 provides valuable information on the dynamics of the ESG profile of a given firm, and results in trigger probabilities under the real-world probability measure $\mathbb{P}$. For pricing purposes, we now transform these $\mathbb{P}$-measure trigger probabilities to $\mathbb{Q}$-measure trigger probabilities, using the transformation as described in Equation 27.4. The results are again summarized in Table 27.4.

Given the characteristics of the skin-in-the-game bond in Table 27.2, we can calculate the trigger spread using the formulas in Equation 27.2 and Equation 27.3 and the trigger probabilities in Table 27.4. The trigger spread is determined as the additional yield t_s, needed in order to get investors to underwrite the trigger risk, by computing the coupon rate $c = r + c_s + t_s$ such that

$$P = \sum_{t=1}^{T} \frac{\mathbb{E}_{\mathbb{Q}}[C_t]}{(1+r+c_s)^t},$$
$$= \frac{0.89826cN}{1.035} + \frac{0.78759cN}{1.035^2} + \frac{0.69676cN}{1.035^3} + \frac{0.62479cN}{1.035^4} + \frac{0.56742cN+N}{1.035^5}, \quad (27.13)$$
$$= N = 100.$$

This results in a value of $c = 0.048567$, such that the trigger spread equals $t_s = 0.013567$, or approximately 136 basis points (bps).

We repeat the valuation exercise on multiple ESG skin-in-the-game bonds, with a varying issuer's initial rating, trigger level and trigger penalty. The resulting trigger spreads of this exercise are summarized in Table 27.5. These trigger spreads are illustrative spreads for a possible format of a skin-in-the-game bond. We clearly observe that, dependent on the issuer's initial rating, trigger level and trigger penalty, the bond's trigger spread varies from almost negligible to a significant percentage, especially in the case of a full write-down penalty. Moreover, the larger the distance between the initial rating and the trigger level, the smaller the trigger spread.

TABLE 27.5 t_s *in bps for a 5-year ESG skin-in-the-game bond with annual coupon payment, varying trigger penalties and trigger level (column). The issuer has initial rating (row)*

	Permanent coupon loss						Temporary coupon loss					
	C	CCC	B	BB	BBB	A	C	CCC	B	BB	BBB	A
CCC	173						100					
B	107	223					66	144				
BB	40	90	228				28	66	171			
BBB	15	35	84	300			12	27	69	251		
A	6	16	39	136	424		6	13	34	121	358	
AAA	4	8	21	75	222	459	3	7	18	68	197	414

	Coupon withholding						Full write-down					
CCC	99						1319					
B	66	144					857	1669				
BB	29	66	171				396	797	1763			
BBB	12	28	69	251			184	375	806	2279		
A	6	13	34	121	359		93	198	446	1255	3163	
AAA	3	7	19	68	197	414	53	118	273	796	1920	3448

27.5 THE NUCLEAR SKIN-IN-THE-GAME BOND

A nuclear power plant is a highly complex system, exposed to a set of diverse risk factors: mechanical breakdowns, human errors, tsunamis and many more. Consequently, there is always a (very small) probability of a nuclear disaster,[41] which can lead to a massive amount of losses in human lives, damage to the environment and infrastructure and a declining economic activity in the contaminated area. The losses in case of a nuclear tail event are huge and potentially way beyond the loss-absorbing capacity of the firm that owns the nuclear facility and/or the (re)insurer who covers (up to a certain limit) the damage caused.[42]

The severity of a nuclear and radiological event is rated on the International Nuclear Event Scale (INES), developed by the International Atomic Energy Agency (IAEA) in 1990.[43] It divides nuclear events with safety significance into two categories and seven levels. Events rated INES level 4 to 7 are classified as accidents. These accidents result in a release of radioactive material into the environment and in the radiation exposure of workers and the public. As an example, Chernobyl (Ukraine, 1986) and Fukushima (Japan, 2011) are, so far in history, the only INES 7 events. Events rated level 1 to 3 are called incidents and may have no

---

[41] Hofert and Wüthrich 2012.
[42] Nariai 2016.
[43] IAEA 2013.

actual consequences for society, but they indicate that the measures put in place to prevent incidents and accidents did not function as intended.

Skin-in-the-game bonds can clearly play a beneficial role in the nuclear industry. Reactor-specific risks are revealed through a higher coupon charged by the market. Moreover, lax plant management is penalized by an increased cost of capital and so further investments in safety and risk controlling are incentivized. We define the number of INES events of a certain level as the benchmark underlying a nuclear skin-in-the-game bond. Within this example we thus discuss the valuation of a skin-in-the-game bond with a specific counting benchmark.

27.5.1 *Nuclear Event Data*

The data used in this example consists of INES-rated nuclear events that took place between 2000 and 2018 in European nuclear power plants. The data is assembled on the basis of country reports published under the Convention on Nuclear Safety (CNS).[44] For the covered period, a total of 1938 INES 1 events are included in the data set as being reported on European territory. In contrast, the data only contains 29 events of level 2, 1 event of level 3 and none of level 4 or higher. Since the occurrence of a nuclear event rated INES 3 or higher is very exceptional, we will, later on, model categories 3 to 7 as a single INES category, denoted as INES 3+.

In addition to the number of INES events, we take into account the yearly net capacity in TWh electric energy as produced by the country's nuclear power plants.[45] That way, we account for the fact that the more electric energy a country produces, the higher the likelihood on the occurrence of an INES event. The net capacity of a country thus indicates the exposure to potential events. In what follows, the number of INES events will always be put in perspective to the net capacity.

27.5.2 *A Valuation Framework*

Based on the available INES data, we value three nuclear skin-in-the-game bonds with characteristics as summarized in Table 27.6. In all cases, the issuer is an average European nuclear power plant site with a fixed and constant yearly production of 10 TWh electric energy. Bonds 1, 2 and 3 are respectively built on the number of INES 1, 2 and 3+ events as the benchmark. As the consequences of a nuclear event get worse with increasing INES rating, the severity of the bonds' benchmarks increases significantly. It is then appropriate to also increase the severity of the penalty.

---

[44] The reports can be downloaded from www.iaea.org/topics/nuclear-safety-conventions/convention-nuclear-safety/documents.
[45] Ritchie 2020.

TABLE 27.6 *Nuclear skin-in-the-game bond characteristics*

Characteristics	Bond-specific values		
Issuer	European NPP with a yearly production of 10 TWh electric energy		
Risk-free rate r	0.010		
Credit spread c_g	0.025		
Issue date	1 January 2020		
Maturity date	1 January 2025		
Notional N	100		
Coupon rate	c		
Coupon frequency	annual		

		Bond 1	Bond 2	Bond 3
t_y	Level	3 INES 1 events	1 INES 2 event	1 INES 3+ event
	Penalty	temporary coupon loss	temporary coupon loss	full write-down
t_c	Level	4 INES 1 events	1 INES 2 event	∞
	Penalty	full write-down	full write-down	\

The valuation framework for the nuclear skin-in-the-game bond is based on the assumption that a Poisson process $\{N^{(i)}(t) \mid t \in (0,\infty)\}$ counts the number of INES level $i \in \{1,2,3+\}$ events that occur at a fixed intensity $\lambda^{(i)}$ per unit of time and unit of TWh electric energy.[46] For the scope of this illustrative example, it is sufficient to model the number of INES 1, INES 2 and INES 3+ events separately and independently. Using the Poisson process, the yearly trigger probability of a nuclear skin-in-the-game bond is modelled as the probability of occurrence of at least the number of INES i events within one year that triggers the bond, as fixed in the terms of the bond.

To this intent, define $M_t^{(i)} = N^{(i)}(t) - N^{(i)}(t-1)$, the number of INES i events that occur in year t, independently for different t and ω_t, the total net capacity in TWh electric energy produced in year t. Under the formal definition of a Poisson process,

$$M_t^{(i)} \sim Poisson\left(\lambda^{(i)}\omega_t\right), \tag{27.14}$$

for $t \in \{2000, 2001, \ldots\}$. We estimate $\lambda^{(i)}$ using the maximum likelihood estimator (MLE). The MLE of $\lambda^{(i)}$, estimated at time t, is denoted as $\hat{\lambda}_t^{(i)}$ and is equal to the sample mean of the yearly number of INES i events, per unit of TWh electric energy produced, yet available at the beginning of year t. This means for instance that $\hat{\lambda}_{2019}^{(i)}$ is based on the set of observations from 2000 up to the year 2018: $\left\{\frac{M_{2000}^{(i)}}{\omega_{2000}}, \ldots, \frac{M_{2018}^{(i)}}{\omega_{2018}}\right\}$, and is given by

$$\hat{\lambda}_{2019}^{(i)} = \frac{1}{2019 - 2000}\sum_{t=2000}^{2019-1}\frac{M_t^{(i)}}{\omega_t}. \tag{27.15}$$

[46] Hofert and Wüthrich 2012.

TABLE 27.7 *Maximum likelihood estimate for the intensity $\hat{\lambda}^{(i)}$ as used in Equation 27.14*

	INES 1	INES 2	INES 3+
$\hat{\lambda}^{(i)}$	0.11	0.0017	0.00006

We use $\hat{\lambda}^{(i)}_{2019}$ as the fixed rate in Equation 27.14 in the remainder of this valuation exercise and denote it with $\hat{\lambda}^{(i)}$. The values for different i are summarized in Table 27.7.

27.5.3 *The Trigger Spread*

We calculate the trigger spread of the nuclear skin-in-the-game bonds with characteristics as summarized in Table 27.6. Using the intensity $\hat{\lambda}^{(1)}$ from Table 27.7 and a fixed production of $\omega = 10$ TWh, the corresponding estimate for the expected number of yearly INES 1 events, in the years 2020 to 2025, is $\hat{\lambda}^{(1)}\omega = 1.1$, with a standard deviation equal to $\sqrt{\hat{\lambda}^{(1)}\omega} = 1.05$. The trigger of Bond 1 is set equal to three or more INES 1 events. That is, the bond triggers if the yearly number of INES 1 events of the plant is approximately more than 2 standard deviations away from the expected number of events. For Bond 2 and 3, the occurrence of an INES ≥ 2 event is so exceptional, that these bonds already trigger at the occurrence of a single event.

Bond 1. The bond's yearly trigger level is set at 3 INES 1 events, with a temporary coupon loss penalty upon a trigger event. The probability at year $t = 1,\dots,5$ that a coupon is withheld due to the yearly trigger then equals

$$P\left[M_t^{(i)} \geq 3\right] = \sum_{k=3}^{\infty} \frac{\exp\left(-\hat{\lambda}^{(1)}\omega\right)\left(\hat{\lambda}^{(1)}\omega\right)^k}{k!} = \sum_{k=3}^{\infty} \frac{\exp(-1.1)(1.1)^k}{k!} = 0.09958. \quad (27.16)$$

This is also the real trigger probability at time 1, $PT_1^{\mathbb{P}}$. Additionally, the bond triggers when the cumulative number of events exceeds $4 \cdot t$ INES 1 events, for $t = 2,\dots,5$. As an example, at time $t = 2$ we have that

$$P\left[N^{(1)}(t) - N^{(0)} \geq 4t\right] = P\left[M_1^{(1)} + M_2^{(1)} \geq 8\right] = \sum_{k=8}^{\infty} \frac{\exp\left(-\hat{\lambda}^{(1)}\omega t\right)\left(\hat{\lambda}^{(1)}\omega t\right)^k}{k!},$$
$$= \sum_{k=8}^{\infty} \frac{\exp(-2.2)(2.2)^k}{k!} = 0.00198. \quad (27.17)$$

Since the yearly and cumulative trigger are not mutually exclusive, we have a final trigger probability at year 2 equal to

$$PT_2^{\mathbb{P}} = P\Big[M_1^{(1)} \geq 3 \text{ or } M_1^{(1)} + M_2^{(1)} \geq 8 \Big],$$
$$= P\Big[M_1^{(1)} \geq 3 \Big] + P\Big[M_1^{(1)} + M_2^{(1)} \geq 8 \Big] - P\Big[M_1^{(1)} + M_2^{(1)} \geq 8, \, M_2^{(1)} \geq 3 \Big], \quad (27.18)$$
$$= 0.09958 + 0.00198 - 0.00172 = 0.09984.$$

The trigger probabilities at later years can be found in Table 27.8. Note that at year 5, we need to distinguish between the situation where the coupon is not paid due to a yearly trigger, but the notional is paid and the situation where the bond is wiped out completely.

In order to calculate the trigger spread, we transform the trigger probabilities under the measure $\mathbb{P}$ to trigger probabilities under the pricing measure $\mathbb{Q}$, using again Equation 27.4. Equation 27.2 and Equation 27.3 then ultimately result in a trigger spread equal to 106 bps.

Bond 2. We use the same procedure as in the case of Bond 1, to calculate the trigger probabilities of Bond 2. The results are summarized in Table 27.8. Bond 2 has a trigger spread equal to 29 bps.

Bond 3. The third bond is immediately withdrawn upon a trigger event: the occurrence of an INES 3+ event. For the first year, the trigger probability is equal to

$$PT_1^{\mathbb{P}} = P\Big[M_1^{3+} \geq 1 \Big] = \sum_{k=1}^{\infty} \frac{\exp(-0.0006)(0.0006)^k}{k!} = 0.00060. \quad (27.19)$$

For the second year, we have to take into account the possibility that the bond already triggered in the first year. We then have, using the independent increment property of a Poisson process,

$$PT_2^{\mathbb{P}} = P\Big[M_1^{(3+)} \geq 1 \text{ or } M_2^{(3+)} \geq 1 \Big],$$
$$= P\Big[M_1^{(3+)} \geq 1 \Big] + P\Big[M_2^{(3+)} \geq 1 \Big] - P\Big[M_1^{(3+)} \geq 1 \Big] \cdot P\Big[M_2^{(3+)} \geq 1 \Big] \quad (27.20)$$
$$= 0.00120.$$

A similar reasoning is used for the trigger probability at years 3, 4 and 5, as given in Table 27.8. The trigger spread of Bond 3 amounts 32 bps.

From Table 27.8, we observe on the one hand that the trigger spread of Bond 1 is three times higher than the trigger spreads of Bond 2 and 3. Though the trigger penalty of Bond 2 is more severe, the significantly higher probability on an INES 1 event, compared to INES ≥ 2 events, results in a higher trigger spread. On the other hand, the trigger spread of Bond 2 is comparable to that of Bond 3. Even though the probability on an INES 2 event is higher than the probability on an INES 3+ event, the stringent penalty of Bond 3, that is, the immediate write-down of the bond on the occurrence of an INES 3+ event, balances the risk in both products.

All calculations in this example start from an average European power plant. We therefore consider the calculated spreads as indicative for the market average. In reality, all issuers of nuclear skin-in-the-game bonds will have different

TABLE 27.8 *Trigger probabilities under both the $\mathbb{P}$ and $\mathbb{Q}$ probability measures and trigger spreads (in bps) for the nuclear skin-in-the-game bonds with characteristics as given in Table 27.6*

		Year 1	Year 2	Year 3	Year 4	Year 5		
						cN	N	t_s
Bond 1	$PT^{\mathbb{P}}$	0.09958	0.09984	0.10119	0.10135	0.10138	0.00202	106
	$PT^{\mathbb{Q}}$	0.18379	0.18412	0.18582	0.18602	0.18605	0.01150	
Bond 2	$PT^{\mathbb{P}}$	0.01686	0.01700	0.01738	0.01741	0.01742	0.00057	29
	$PT^{\mathbb{Q}}$	0.05268	0.05300	0.05384	0.05392	0.05393	0.00463	
Bond 3	$PT^{\mathbb{P}}$	0.00060	0.00120	0.00180	0.00240	0.00300	0.00300	32
	$PT^{\mathbb{Q}}$	0.00481	0.00791	0.01059	0.01302	0.01528	0.01528	

spreads, calculated in the same way, but based on the issuer specific history of INES events and electric energy produced. The market mechanism will ultimately point out the less safe power plants by charging a higher coupon rate than the market average we calculated.

27.6 CONCLUSION

To conclude, we argue for the implementation of a sustainable debt instrument with an embedded financial penalty related to E, S and/or G commitments. The skin-in-the-game bond provides clear incentives for the issuer to reduce excessive risk-taking, maintain a favourable benchmark value and to enhance transparency. It also provides a mechanism for investors to gain above risk-free returns in compensation for clearly upfront specified risks. The involvement of a third-party fund makes sure that collateral is available, in case of a major disaster, to reduce negative externality and make investments for recovery possible.

In general, the issuance of a skin-in-the-game bond should result in aligned incentives for both the issuer and investor. The skin-in-the-game bond improves on the currently existing green, social, sustainability and sustainability-linked bonds, by enforcing skin-in-the-game, which fights moral hazard risk. Moreover, the skin-in-the-game bond uses the market mechanism as a means to achieve an objective view on the underlying risks; financial markets will charge higher coupons if it is likely that promises turn out differently than promoted.

REFERENCES

Basel Committee on Banking Supervision (2010), *Basel III: A Global Regulatory Framework for More Resilient Banks and Banking Systems*, Technical Report June, Banks for International Settlement, available at: www.bis.org/publ/bcbs189.htm.

Berg, T. (2010), 'From actual to risk-neutral default probabilities: Merton and beyond', *Journal of Credit Risk*, 6(1), 55–86.

Berg, F., Koelbel, J. F., and Rigobon, R. (2020), 'Aggregate Confusion: The Divergence of ESG Ratings', MIT Sloan School Working Paper 5822–19.

Burnecki, K., Kukla, G., and Taylor, D. (2011), 'Pricing of catastrophe bonds', in Cizek, P., Hardle, W. K., and Weron, R. (eds.), *Statistical Tools for Finance and Insurance* (Berlin: Springer), 371–391.

Cariboni, J., Maccaferri, S., and Schoutens, W. (2011), 'Applying Credit Risk Techniques to Design an Effective Deposit Guarantee Schemes' Funds', in *Actuarial and Financial Mathematics Conference: Interplay between Finance and Insurance*, Royal Flemish Academy of Belgium for Science and Arts (KVAB), 107–112.

Climate Bonds Initiative (2021), 'Climate Bonds Standard and Certification Scheme', available at: www.climatebonds.net/standard.

Climate Bonds Initiative (2022), 'Sustainable debt: Global state of the market 2021', available at: https://bit.ly/4cuLQAf.

Cox, D. and Miller, H. (1965), *The Theory of Stochastic Process*, 1st ed. (London: Chapman & Hall).

Crotty, J. (2009), 'Structural causes of the global financial crisis: A critical assessment of the new financial architecture', *Cambridge Journal of Economics*, 33(4), 563–580.

Dahl, H. and Larsen, S. (2014), *ESG: A New Equity Factor*, Technical report, May, Nykredit Asset Management holds, available at: https://tinyurl.com/39vxj6mz.

De Spiegeleer, J. and Schoutens, W. (2012), 'Pricing contingent convertibles: A derivatives approach', *Journal of Derivatives*, 20(2), 27–36.

De Spiegeleer, J. and Schoutens, W. (2019), 'Sustainable Capital Instruments and Their Role in Prudential Policy: Reverse Green Bonds', Working paper, available at: https://papers.ssrn.com/sol3/papers.cfm?abstract_id=3415184.

De Spiegeleer, J., Schoutens, W., and Van Hulle, C. (2014), *The Handbook of Hybrid Securities: Convertible Bonds, CoCo Bonds, and Bail-In*, 1st ed. (Chichester: Wiley Finance).

De Spiegeleer, J., Marquet, I., and Schoutens, W. (2018), *The Risk Management of Contingent Convertible (CoCo) Bonds*, 1st ed. (Berlin: Springer International Publishing).

Deschryver, P. and de Mariz, F. (2020), 'What future for the Green Bond market? How can policymakers, companies and investors unlock the potential of the green bond market?' *Journal of Risk and Financial Management*, 13(61), 1–26.

Djelic, M.-L. and Bothello, J. (2013), 'Limited liability and its moral hazard implications: the systemic inscription of instability in contemporary capitalism', *Theory and Society*, 42, 589–615.

Doran, M. and Tanner, J. (2019), 'Critical challenges facing the green bond market', *International Financial Law Review*, October/November, 22–25.

Dorfleitner, G., Halbritter, G., and Nguyen, M. (2015), 'Measuring the level and risk of corporate responsibility: An empirical comparison of different ESG rating approaches', *Journal of Asset Management*, 16(7), 450–466.

Duffie, D. and Singleton, K. J. (2003), *Credit Risk: Pricing, Measurement, and Management*, 1st ed. (Princeton, NJ: Princeton University Press).

Enel (2021), 'Sustainability-linked bonds', available at: https://bit.ly/3TONnKb.

EU TEG (2020), *Taxonomy: Final Report of the Technical Expert Group on Sustainable Finance*. Technical Report. Brussels: European Commission.

European Commission (2018), 'Action Plan: Financing Sustainable Growth', COM(2018) 97, available at: https://bit.ly/497N6GU.

Figlewski, S. (2018), 'Risk-neutral densities: A review', *Annual Review of Financial Economics*, 10, 329–359.

Friedman, H. H. and Friedman, L. W. (2014), 'Lessons from the twin mega-crises: The financial meltdown and the BP oil spill', *Journal of Business Systems, Governance and Ethics*, 5(4), 34–45.

Heynderickx, W., Cariboni, J., Schoutens, W., and Smits, B. (2016), 'The relationship between risk-neutral and actual default probabilities: The credit risk premium' *Applied Economics*, 48(42), 4066–4081.

Hofert, M. and Wüthrich, M. V. (2012), 'Statistical review of nuclear power accidents', *Asia-Pacific Journal of Risk and Insurance*, 7(1), 1–19.

Huber, B. M. and Comstock, M. (2017), 'ESG Reports and Ratings: What They Are, Why They Matter', available at: https://bit.ly/4cuLSYT.

Hull, J., Predescu, M., and White, A. (2005), 'Bond prices, default probabilities and risk premiums', *Journal of Credit Risk*, 1(2), 53–60.

IAEA (International Atomic Energy Authority) (2013), *INES: The International Nuclear and Radiological Event Scale User's Manual*, available at: https://bit.ly/3TviRUu.

ICMA (2020), 'Sustainability-linked bond principles?', available at: https://bit.ly/3vs4VCM.

ICMA (2021), 'The principles, guidelines and handbooks', available at: https://bit.ly/3TOhSA5.

Jackson, C. H. (2011), 'Multi-state models for panel data: The msm package for R', *Journal of Statistical Software*, 38(8), 1–29.

Kalbfleisch, J. and Lawless, J. (1985), 'The analysis of panel data under a Markov assumption', *Journal of the American Statistical Association*, 80(392), 863–871.

Kumar, R. and Weiner, A. (2019), *The ESG Data Challenge*, Technical Report, March, State Street Global Advisors, available at: https://tinyurl.com/yvy8hy9y.

Nariai, H. (2016), 'Five years after the Fukushima Daiichi accident: Nuclear safety improvements and lessons learnt', *Journal of the Atomic Energy Society of Japan*, 58(8), 479–483.

Park, S. K. (2019), 'Green bonds and beyond', in Sjafjell, B. and Bruner, C. M. (eds.), *The Cambridge Handbook of Corporate Law, Corporate Governance and Sustainability* (Cambridge, UK: Cambridge University Press), 596–610.

Ritchie, H. (2020), 'Nuclear energy', available at: https://ourworldindata.org/nuclear-energy.

S&P Global Market Intelligence (2018), 'GICS: Global Industry Classification Standard? available at: https://bit.ly/49fniIF.

Tuhkanen, H. and Vulturius, G. (2020), 'Are green bonds funding the transition? Investigating the link between companies' climate targets and green debt financing', *Journal of Sustainable Finance & Investment*, 12(4), 1–23.

Wood, R. W. (2016), 'In BP's final $20 billion Gulf settlement, U.S. taxpayers subsidize $15.3 billion', *Forbes*, April, available at: https://tinyurl.com/mttw3kks.

Wooldridge, J. M. (2009), 'Econometrics: Panel data methods', in Meyers, R. A. (ed.), *Encyclopedia of Complexity and Systems Science* (New York: Springer).

28

Financial Innovation in the Process
of Financial Inclusion

Iwa Kuchciak

28.1 INTRODUCTION

The study of financial inclusion starts in the early 1990s, but the past two decades
have seen a rapid increase in interest in financial inclusion, both from policymakers
and from researchers. The global financial inclusion agenda emerged in the wake
of the 2008 Global Financial Crisis and has become a prominent feature of global
economic governance. There is a large body of academic literature about financial inclusion and financial exclusion in both applied and theoretical works. The
access of households to financial services is a long-standing topic in policy debates
in emerging markets and advanced economies.

As noted by the World Bank,[1] "financial inclusion means that individuals and
businesses have access to useful and affordable financial products and services that
meet their needs – transactions, payments, savings, credit, and insurance – delivered
responsibly and sustainably". Development theory provides important clues about
the impact of financial inclusion on economic development and individuals result
in macro and microeconomic benefits that can be derived from greater financial
inclusion.

The rapid adoption of digital technology in finance offers a large potential to
increase financial inclusion, namely, access to and usage of financial services by a
wide section of the population. There is also a growing body of empirical literature
that documents the potential development benefits of financial inclusion, especially
from the use of digital financial services, including mobile money services, payment cards, and other financial technology applications. As a result of digitalization,
the term "digital financial inclusion" was introduced and defined broadly as digital
access to and use of financial services by Salampasis and Mention.[2]

However, despite the existing well of consolidated knowledge, research gaps in
this field present an opportunity for further analysis. One area that provides such

[1] World Bank 2018a.
[2] Salampasis and Mention 2017.

opportunity results from the fact that existing literature primarily focuses on financial inclusion facilitated by financial institutions such as banks, that is, traditional financial inclusion. Taking into consideration that banks and nonbanks have begun to offer digital financial services for financially excluded and underserved populations to improve access channels for those already served by banks and other financial institutions, this chapter will summarize the existing literature considering innovative digital financial services. This work aims to make a far-reaching and meaningful contribution by taking a social and economic point of view to reflect on the challenges, problems, and opportunities arising from the processes of digitalization of financial services.

The chapter is organized as follows. First, financial exclusion will be characterized and discussed in contrast with financial inclusion. Next, the chapter will discuss he links between the digitization process in the financial sector and financial inclusion. It will then analyze the current situation in the financial market shaped by the COVID-19 pandemic. Finally, the role and functions of financial education in reducing the level of financial exclusion will be defined.

28.2 FINANCIAL INCLUSION, EXCLUSION, AND DIGITAL FINANCIAL INCLUSION

Financial inclusion and financial exclusion are binary terms. In the literature, the term "financial exclusion", just like its symmetric companion "financial inclusion", has a broad range of definitions, only some of which are made explicit.

The role of branch closure in the processes of financial exclusion have been the subject of academic work since at least the early 1990s. The term financial exclusion began to be used in the early 1990s, reflecting concern regarding bank branch closures because of the traditional way of using banking services via branches. One of the most often cited definitions explains "financial exclusion" as a process that prevents some sections such as economically weaker and underserved social groups, individuals, or areas from accessing the formal financial system which includes financial institutions like banks.[3]

Subsequently, financial inclusion has come to describe useful and affordable financial products and services that meet the needs of individuals and businesses. Being able to have access to a transaction account is the first step toward broader financial inclusion.[4] Financial inclusion is defined by the G20 Global Partnership for Financial Inclusion[5] as "effective and quality access to and usage of – at a cost affordable to the customers and sustainable for the providers – financial services provided by formal institutions." Financial inclusion may also be defined as the use

---

[3] Leyshon and Thrift 1995.
[4] World Bank 2022.
[5] GPFI 2016.

of formal financial services at an affordable cost to the vast section of disadvantaged and low-income groups.[6]

The broad consensus in the literature is that financial inclusion is a multifaceted concept, encompassing various dimensions, including access to and use of financial services as well as other aspects such as usefulness, quality, and awareness of financial services and products. The literature also sometimes emphasizes affordability and consumer protection in addition to financial access and usage for all.[7]

In recent years, there has also been a growing body of research relating to difficulties faced by some sections of societies in gaining access to modern payment instruments and other banking services, consumer credit, and insurance. Subsequently, financial exclusion has come to describe the inability, difficulty, or reluctance to access mainstream financial services, which can result in social exclusion, poverty, and inequality.[8]

Critically, non-users of financial services can be differentiated between those that are involuntarily excluded and those that are voluntarily self-excluded.[9] The problem of involuntary financial exclusion requires intervention to address market failures such as asymmetric information, unaffordable costs of financial services, lack of competition in the markets, or insufficient infrastructure. Most people vulnerable to financial exclusion indicate, as key barriers that they face, legal or financial requirements for accessing services and lack of required skills or means.[10] These failures make it difficult for certain population groups to use formal financial services. Typically, these groups are economically weaker, underserved, underprivileged, or gather those who have traditionally been more vulnerable, such as women, young people, or people who live in rural areas.[11] Voluntary self-exclusion can be attributed to a perceived lack of need for financial services.[12] The reason for self-exclusion may be a reaction to negative experiences. The lack of need often results from a lack of awareness of the benefits and convenience of using banking products.

Recent years have brought a development of electronic tools and an increase in their popularity, resulting among others in the introduction of digital finance. Digital finance challenges existing financial service providers, such as established banks or insurance providers, due to new competition by Fintech companies (technological innovation in the financial sector) and, in parallel, offers new opportunities for the incumbents to reach their younger and more technology-savvy clientele.[13]

---

[6]   Dev 2006.
[7]   Espinosa-Vega et al. 2020.
[8]   Kabeer 2000.
[9]   Fernández-Olit et al. 2020.
[10] Beck et al. 2008.
[11] Koku 2015.
[12] Cámara et al. 2015.
[13] Gomber et al. 2017.

The goal of financial services made available via digital platforms is to contribute, among the others, to poverty reduction and to contribute to the financial inclusion objectives of developing economies. Digital finance can lead to greater financial inclusion, expansion of financial services to areas previously not served, and the expansion of basic services offered by mobile phones.

Digital financial inclusion refers broadly to the use of digital financial services to advance financial inclusion. These services include digital payments, digital lending/credit, marketplace lending, mobile money, and mobile banking.[14] Following OECD,[15] digital financial inclusion involves "the deployment of digital means to reach financially excluded and underserved populations with a range of formal financial services suited to their needs, delivered responsibly at a cost affordable to customers and sustainable for providers".

According to the World Bank,[16] digital financial inclusion involves the deployment of cost-saving digital means to reach currently financially excluded and underserved populations with a range of formal financial services suited to their needs that are responsibly delivered at a cost affordable to customers and sustainable for providers. Digital payment technologies improve the ability to target cash assistance to households, particularly to the unbanked, women, and to the informal sector.[17] The process of digital financial inclusion begins with the assumption that the excluded and/or underserved population has some sort of formal bank account as an entry point for financial inclusion and needs digital access to enable them to carry out basic financial transactions remotely.[18] Digital finance is increasing financial inclusion by complementing or substituting traditional finance.[19]

Consequently, measures of financial inclusion quantify the ease of access to financial services based on detailed data concerning specific channels of financial inclusion. Data on financial inclusion reveals various gaps: for example, between rich and poor countries, between partial and universal inclusion (particularly understood as the possession of selected banking products or a wide range of them), as well as between the observed levels of access and usage, on the one hand, and the structural benchmarks taking into account demographic, social, economic characteristics for a given country at a specific time, on the other hand.[20]

An overview of the most prominent studies carried out at the international level from a supply side and demand side is presented in Table 28.1.

---

[14] Sahay at al. 2020.
[15] OECD 2020a.
[16] World Bank 2015.
[17] Agur et al. 2020.
[18] Ozili 2018.
[19] Tok and Heng 2022, 6.
[20] Barajas at al. 2020.

TABLE 28.1 *Selected international data sources on financial inclusion*

Type of survey	Content	Finding(s)
	Demand side	
Special Eurobarometer 373: Retail financial services This Eurobarometer survey examines public opinion in the area of retail financial services (bank accounts, mortgage credit, consumer credit, stocks/bonds/shares, investment funds, insurance, and payments). The survey covered 26 856 EU citizens in all 27 EU Member States.	Data included in the survey: – Type of financial products: current bank account, credit card, personal loan, mortgage, life insurance, shares or bonds, investment fund, other insurance products – Length of ownership of financial product – Socio-demographic data: gender, age, education, occupation	While 84% of respondents have a current bank account, ownership of other types of a financial products is much less common and one in ten EU citizens (10%) possess none of the financial products covered in the survey. People in the EU15 countries are more likely to own most types of the financial product than their counterparts in the NMS12 countries. Over half (56%) of the people who do not have a current bank account say they do not have one because they do not need or want one.
The OECD International Network on Financial Education (INFE) The questionnaire was first piloted in 2010 as part of the first OECD international financial literacy and financial inclusion measurement exercise. In 2015/16 around 40 countries and economies participated in an international survey of adult financial literacy competencies; using data collected using this toolkit. Results were published for the first set of 30 countries and then a complementary report was released focusing on the G20.	The OECD/INFE questionnaire collects relevant information about: financial literacy and financial inclusion within a country compares levels of financial literacy and financial inclusion across countries. Questions cover: – planning and managing finances – choosing and using financial products, – financial knowledge, – a range of attitudes and behaviors that impact financial literacy and financial well-being. The toolkit updated in 2018 incorporated a core questionnaire designed to capture information about financial behavior, attitudes, and knowledge, in order to asse the level of financial literacy and financial inclusion as well as optional questions designed to provide more depth on topics such as financial goal setting and experiencing financial scams.	The last available results indicate that on average, payment products were held by the majority of people in G20 countries (66%) and were typically the most common form of financial product held. However, in some countries, (notably Brazil, China, India, Indonesia, and South Africa) savings products were more widespread than payment products, and on average across G20 countries, a similar proportion held such a product (63%). It is possible that some of these savings products were being used to provide basic banking facilities. Credit products were held by half of the respondents (51%) on average in G20 countries. This varies from over four out of five respondents in the US (87%), Australia (86%), Canada (85%), and guest country Norway (81%) holding some form of credit product to 23% in India. Insurance use varied widely across countries, with just over half of respondents (52%) on average holding such a product.

Global Findex Database 2011/2014/2017
The indicators in the Global Financial Inclusion (Global Findex) Database are drawn from survey data covering more than 150,000 people in almost 150 economies representing more than 97% of the world's population.

The Global Findex database provides more than 200 indicators. Data included in the survey:
- account ownership,
- payments
- saving
- credit
- financial resilience – the socio-demographic data (gender, age, education, residence).

Since 2014 two categories of bank account holders have been distinguished: holders of a bank account with a financial institution and users of mobile services.

The 2017 edition includes updated indicators on access to and use of formal and informal financial services. And it adds new data on the use of financial technology (Fintech), including the use of mobile phones and the internet to conduct financial transactions.

The Global Findex database shows that 515 million adults worldwide opened an account at a financial institution or through a mobile money provider between 2014 and 2017. This means that 69% of adults now have an account, up from 62% in 2014 and 51% in 2011. In high-income economies 94% of adults have an account; in developing economies 63% do.

Globally, about 1.7 billion adults remain unbanked – without an account at a financial institution or through a mobile money provider.

Poorer people and women are overrepresented among the unbanked.

In high-income economies, more than three-quarters of savers (55% of all adults) save money by using an account at a financial institution.

About half of adults worldwide reported borrowing money in the past year. A higher share did so in high-income economies, where most borrowers rely on formal credit, extended by a financial institution or through a credit card.

Supply side

IMF's Financial Access Survey (FAS)
Survey launched in 2009 supply-side dataset on access to and use of basic financial services by individuals and firms compiled by central banks and other regulators. The dataset covers 189 countries.

FAS contains country time series and indicators tracking the availability and use of financial products such as:
- deposit accounts,
- loans,
- insurance policies,
- affordability and quality of financial services and products.

The FAS collects data on two types of digital financial services: mobile money, and mobile and internet banking.

In general, access to and use of traditional financial services, as measured by the FAS indicators, has deepened over time in low- and middle-income economies. The use of digital financial services grew during the past year, helping undisrupted access to financial services. Data for SMEs and women show mixed outcomes for these vulnerable groups.

(continued)

TABLE 28.1 (continued)

Type of survey	Content	Finding(s)
	The data is disaggregated by the type of financial service provider (e.g. commercial banks, credit unions, and microfinance institutions) and the type of financial service (e.g. deposits, loans, and insurance). The FAS started collecting data on mobile money in 2014 and gender-disaggregated data in 2017.	The fifth and latest iteration, GPSS 2018, shows generalized progress in most areas. In particular, in global terms, more payments are being made with instruments other than cash, reflecting a safer, more efficient and more inclusive provision of payment and settlement services. More specifically, the number of cashless transactions per capita per year rose to 88.31 in 2017, which represents a 25% increase over the indicator observed in the previous iteration in 2015.
The World Bank's Global Payment Systems Survey (GPSS) In April 2007, the World Bank launched the first Global Payment Systems Survey among national central banks. GPSS has assisted authorities and policymakers worldwide in making meaningful cross-country comparisons and assessing progress in national payments system development (as a critical enabler of financial inclusion) and has facilitated the dissemination of best practices.	The GPSS is the only global survey that combines quantitative and qualitative measures of payment system development and covers all aspects of national payment systems: – infrastructure – the legal environment – regulatory environment – technological and business model innovations – international remittances, – oversight framework. The fifth iteration of GPSS in 2018 integrated the module on "accounts and access points" in the main body of the survey and also added a section on Fintech and payment services, the latter focusing on the underlying innovations that enable enhanced access to and usage of transaction accounts. In the 2018 iteration, the first two classifications are maintained through sections by the level of per capita income and by geographical region.	As for concepts associated with enhancing financial access and inclusion, more than three-quarters of economies indicated the presence of regulations allowing agent-based models (79%), nonbank direct provision of payment services, and holding of customer funds for payments (77%), as well as provisions regulating individuals' access to accounts (76%). The regulation for basic payment accounts includes consumer protection clauses such as dispute resolution and disclosures in around 84% of reporting jurisdictions, and there is not much difference across the country groups. Basic payment accounts are protected by deposit insurance or a similar mechanism in 58% of the reporting jurisdictions and in 66% of the reporting high-income economies. Fifty-five percent of the reporting jurisdictions mandate financial literacy responsibilities for providers.

Source: Based on Demirgüç-Kunt and Klapper 2012; Demirgüç-Kunt et al. 2015, 2017; Kempson 2009; OECD 2018; OECD 2017.

From the perspective of usage, supply-side data provide information on the value and volume of transactions as well as data on the activity of accounts and the number of transactions via certain channels.

Demand-side data are collected from current and potential users of financial services, and this data is particularly valuable for measuring uptake and usage of financial services, and for assessing the distribution of financial services across key consumer segments (for example, women, rural residents) and the relationship between financial behaviors and other factors (for example, poverty, employment, and so forth).

Financial inclusion varies significantly depending on individual characteristics such as gender, education level, age, and rural or urban residence. Generally, in both high-income and developing economies men are more likely to have a bank account. In all regions, adults living in cities are significantly more likely than those living in rural areas to have a formal account (meaning an account at a formal financial institution). In developing economies adults with a tertiary or higher education are on average more than twice as likely to have an account as those with primary education or less. This type of data help identify common barriers to access and reasons for financial exclusion.

Due to the different values of information, which come from the supply-side and demand-side, it is valuable to combine both sources. The next challenge in the exercise of measuring financial inclusion is to take into consideration that financial inclusion is more than mere access to accounts and, therefore, financial inclusion measures should include the availability of a broader range of services than bank accounts.

28.3 IMPORTANCE OF FINANCIAL INCLUSION

Financial inclusion has received increasing attention from both researchers and policymakers in the past two decades as a potential source of benefits to the economy. Financial inclusion can be thought of as an aspect of financial development, and therefore potentially is associated with many of the benefits that are derived from this process. A large literature has emerged, in particular, to examine the effects of microfinance at the micro and macro level. The literature review pointed to the three main areas of research, as further analyzed below (Figure 28.1).

Early theoretical literature identifies that access to financial services by individuals can alter their production and employment choices and thereby can reduce poverty.[21] The first studies, from the 90s, evidence that financial exclusion can endanger economic growth due to the poor supply of financial infrastructure.[22]

---

[21] Aghion and Bolton 1997; Banerjee and Newman 1993.
[22] Gurley and Shaw 1955; Goldsmith 1969; Diamond and Dybvig 1983; Greenwood and Jovanovic 1990; Angadi 2003.

Micro (individual) level   **Macro level**

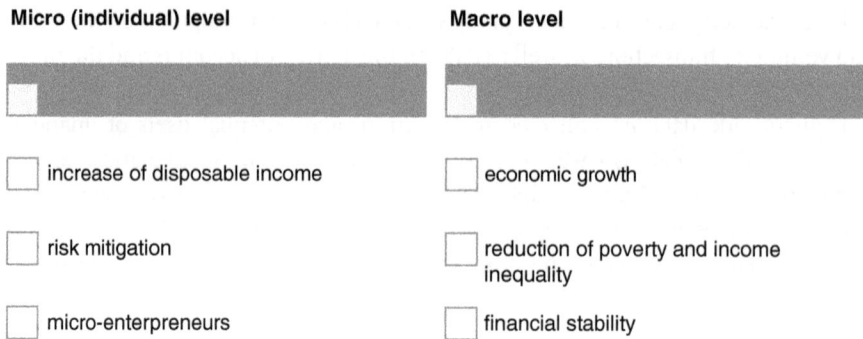

□ increase of disposable income   □ economic growth

□ risk mitigation   □ reduction of poverty and income
                                       inequality

□ micro-enterpreneurs   □ financial stability

FIGURE 28.1 Financial inclusion effects
Source: Own elaboration, based on Klapper and Lusardi 2020

More recent studies deliver emerging evidence that the welfare benefits of financial inclusion are particularly maximized in households. In most countries, savings,
borrowing, and investment decisions have a direct effect on income. Household
income is generally accepted in the literature as a sustainable tool for improving
household livelihood. It is believed that access to various financial services can
help individuals and households to build savings, smooth out their consumption,
make investments, and equip them to meet emergencies, which generally can
help overcome financial constraints.[23] Demirgüç-Kunt et al.[24] discuss the benefit of
financial inclusion in the reduction of poverty and inequality. Čihák and Sahay[25]
find that higher financial inclusion in payments is associated with a reduction in
inequality, particularly for those at the low end of the income distribution and when
female financial inclusion is high. Moreover, there is increasing evidence that savings provide a buffer against shocks.[26] In times of difficulty, financially included
individuals can easily avail themselves of their networks to obtain short-term support. Consequently, household consumption would fall less in the face of difficulties than it would for financially excluded individuals.[27] Therefore, improving and
expanding the accessibility of financial services can facilitate empowering people to
develop long-term consumption and investment.[28]

Symmetrically, unfair distribution of economic opportunities through external
distribution channels can lead to significant income inequality and harm individual well-being.[29] Households, communities, and firms, in contrast, are judged to be

[23] Raza et al. 2019.
[24] Demirgüç-Kunt et al. 2022.
[25] Čihák and Sahay 2020.
[26] Karlan et al. 2014.
[27] Ahmad et al. 2020.
[28] Mahmood et al. 2022; Claessens and Perotti 2007.
[29] Atkinson, andBourguignon 2014.

effective managers of their own idiosyncratic risks at a micro-level, so long as they can access the necessary tools to do so. From the bank's perspective, poor households are often excluded from formal markets for credit, insurance, and savings products.[30] For example, one of the main obstacles to the inclusion of vulnerable groups is the limited opportunity offered by financial institutions. Sometimes borrowers are not creditworthy, and if they are creditworthy they may be refused a loan due to a lack of formalities.[31]

The literature has largely discussed inclusive finance concerns in rural and gender empowerment contexts.[32] Gender equality and women empowerment are essential to global progress and they can be enhanced by providing affordable financial services to women.[33] Empirical evidence links the financial inclusion of women to the economic uplifting of their households as a result of stronger economic empowerment.[34] Moreover, the Mahmood et al. study[35] presents sufficient evidence to conclude that the opportunity effect[36] and the growth effect[37] increase the disposable income of low-income households.

The literature results suggest that financial inclusion is positively linked with entrepreneurship and it can open up economic opportunities for entrepreneurs.[38] The importance of ensuring finance to firms is documented by Beck and Demirgüç-Kunt,[39] who assert that financial inclusion helps alleviate MSMEs' growth constraints and increases their access to external finance, thus leveling the playing field between firms of different sizes. Capital – be it human, social, or financial – is important to facilitate the development of business opportunities in competitive markets. Therefore, the decision to start a business and the type of business chosen will be a function of both the environment and the human, financial, and social capital available.[40] Various studies have highlighted that financial capital availability is crucial in fostering entrepreneurial activities.[41] The main finding from Fareed et al.'s[42] analysis shows that financial inclusion is positively linked with women's entrepreneurship, meaning that financial inclusion opens up economic opportunities for women entrepreneurs.

---

[30] Taylor 2016.
[31] Adegbite and Machethe 2020.
[32] Bhatia and Singh 2019; Lal 2018.
[33] Holloway et al. 2017.
[34] Sakyi-Nyarko et al. 2022.
[35] Mahmood et al. 2022.
[36] Opportunity effect is measured in terms of economic opportunity which is defined as the potential benefits an individual can take to thrive in a financial system (Demirgüç-Kunt and Levine 2008).
[37] Growth effect is a process of extending the size of the economy by providing a level playing field to every individual without any discrimination (Ngepah 2017).
[38] Ajide 2020.
[39] Beck and Demirgüç-Kunt 2006.
[40] Bradley et al. 2012.
[41] Bradley et al. 2012; Chen et al. 2017.
[42] Fareed et al. 2017.

Raza et al.'s[43] study evaluates the relationship between financial inclusion and economic development and found that there is a need for more actions to connect prompt economic growth and development through inclusive participation of all economic agents in the financial system. Most of the empirical studies confirm that financial inclusion has a positive impact on economic growth. According to Andrianaivo and Kpodar,[44] who investigated whether financial inclusion spurs growth in a panel of 44 African countries, and Kim et al.,[45] who took into consideration Organization of Islamic Cooperation (OIC) countries, financial inclusion plays a vital role in raising a strong and well-organized structure of the financial system, which enhances the growth rate of the economy. In line with Sethi and Acharya,[46] long-run sustainable growth can be achieved through focused expansion of banking infrastructures and services. The overall argument for most of these studies emphasizes the accessibility of financial services and product for the majority of society – such as adequate credit at a reasonable cost, especially for poor people, payment system, transfer and deposit services, the soundness of the financial institution, and its sustainability – as a key factor to the positive effect of financial inclusion on growth.[47]

In general, the literature shows that financial inclusion is an engine toward economic growth in several dimensions, with various methods used to assess this link. However, some studies looked at non-linear correlations between financial inclusion and growth. They suggested that financial inclusion is good for growth when it interacts with other channels including mobile penetration and gender dimension.[48] Allen et al.[49] find evidence of a U-shaped relationship between financial development and inequality, so that more financial development is associated with reductions in income inequality below a certain threshold.

There are different findings on the relationship between financial inclusion and financial stability. The positive influence includes diversification of bank assets, increased stability of the deposit base, and increased monetary policy transmission.[50] However, there are different findings on the relationship between financial inclusion and financial stability suggesting the negative influence includes a decrease in loan standards and bank reputation risk, especially under inadequate regulations. A negative influence of financial inclusion on economic growth was found by Khan.[51] Moreover, Dupas et al.[52] added that the increase in banking services did not cause

[43] Raza et al. 2019.
[44] Andrianaivo and Kpodar 2011.
[45] Kim et al. 2018.
[46] Sethi and Acharya 2018.
[47] Bakar and Sulong 2018.
[48] Bakar and Sulong 2018.
[49] Allen et al. 2016.
[50] Hassan et al. 2011; Neaime and Gaysse 2018; Ahamed and Mallick 2019.
[51] Khan 2011.
[52] Dupas et al. 2012.

an increase in financial stability because it was not followed by a decrease in borrowing costs for the lower middle class as well as an increase in service quality and increased trust. Financial inclusion achieved through rapid loan growth or fund intermediation that is not accompanied by proper regulation can negatively influence financial stability.[53]

28.4 LEGAL AND REGULATORY FRAMEWORK

28.4.1 *International Level*

As a background to further discussion of financial inclusion, its relationship with microfinance needs to be considered because much of today's financial inclusion activity is still microfinance, which involves small, short-term, high-interest loans extended to low-income people. Microfinance institutions (MFIs) focus their attention mainly on women, socially excluded individuals, the unemployed, and microenterprises.[54] In terms of institutional characteristics, the sector is primarily made up of nonbank MFIs (91%) operating in the market under various legal forms. Microfinance has been developing and evolving, and not just in the poorest regions of the world. Microfinance products are also necessary for industrial and developing countries, where commercial banks are not interested in performing small transactions (loans or deposits) for impoverished people. Digital financial solutions can leverage the business of MFIs and increase the range of their activity, also in financial inclusion.

Financial inclusion has become a topic on the global policy agenda since early 2000. In 2007, as part of a review of the single market, the European Commission published a Green Paper on future EU policy on retail financial services in the single market.[55] The Green Paper sought to strengthen and deepen the understanding of the problems faced by consumers and industry in the field of retail financial services and to establish the scope for and impediments to further initiatives in this area. Consequently, the European Commission stated its aim of enhancing customer welfare, improving services, helping individuals make sound financial choices, and promoting the single market itself by facilitating the cross-border financial activity.

Consistent with the G20 Development Framework for Strong and Balanced Growth, the G20 equally recognizes the importance of financial inclusion. Working with the Alliance for Financial Inclusion (AFI),[56] the Consultative Group to Assist

---

[53] Mehrotra and Yetman 2015.
[54] Pluskota 2020.
[55] Commission of the European Communities 2007.
[56] AFI is committed to supporting its members in fully achieving their commitments to contributing towards more inclusive development and poverty alleviation. Launched at the 2011 Global Policy Forum (GPF) in Mexico's Riviera Maya, the Maya Declaration is a global initiative for responsible and sustainable financial inclusion that aims to reduce poverty and ensure financial stability for the benefit of all. It is a statement of common principles regarding the development of financial inclusion policy.

the Poor (CGAP),[57] and the International Finance Corporation (IFC),[58] the G20 launched in 2010 a Global Partnership for Financial Inclusion[59] to provide a systematic coordination and implementation structure for the Financial Inclusion Action Plan (FIAP). The first step towards improving access to a full range of financial services for unserved and underserved individuals and micro, small, and medium enterprises was to develop the G20 Principles for Innovative Financial Inclusion.

Those principles aim to help an enabling regulatory environment for innovative financial inclusion. They are designed to adapt to different country contexts. In the 2014 G20 FIAP, the GPFI expanded the scope of the Action Plan to the problem of financial inclusion's measurement, supporting the women's economic empowerment agenda from the financial inclusion point of view and responsible use of financial services through financial education and financial consumer protection. In the 2017 G20 FIAP identified new drivers of financial inclusion, as well as opportunities and challenges brought by digitalization. Moreover, the Financial Inclusion Action Plan aligned the GPFI work with the 2030 Agenda for Sustainable Development, as financial inclusion is a key enabler for several of the SDGs.[60]

In 2015, the Member States of the United Nations adopted the 2030 Agenda for Sustainable Development, where financial inclusion featured as a target in eight of the seventeen goals.[61]

The 2020 G20 FIAP, a revision of the earlier 2010 and 2014 editions and 2017 editions, came at a time of crisis, as the COVID-19 pandemic represented an extraordinary global challenge that had a profound impact on the global economy, including challenges for individuals and businesses, especially those related to financial inclusion.[62] The focus of the GPFI's efforts under the 2020 G20 FIAP was to enhance the financial inclusion of vulnerable and underserved groups through leveraging digital financial innovation while at the same time addressing new digital risks with financial education and financial consumer protection.

At the 2015 World Bank Group-IMF Spring Meetings, the World Bank Group, and public and private sector partners adopted measurable commitments to achieve Universal Financial Access by 2020[63] and help promote financial inclusion. The

---

[57] The Consultative Group to Assist the Poorest (CGAP) was set up at the World Bank as a three-year initiative (1995–1998) to increase the quality and quantity of sustainable microfinance institutions (MFIs) serving the poor.

[58] IFC, a member of the World Bank Group, advances economic development and improves the lives of people by encouraging the growth of the private sector in developing countries.

[59] GPFI, available at: www.gpfi.org/about-gpfi.

[60] GFPI 2017.

[61] This includes: SDG1, on eradicating poverty; SDG 2 on ending hunger, achieving food security, and promoting sustainable agriculture; SDG 3 on profiting health and well-being; SDG 5 on achieving gender equality and economic empowerment of women; SDG 8 on promoting economic growth and jobs; SDG 9 on supporting industry, innovation, and infrastructure; and SDG 10 on reducing inequality, SDG 17 on reduction the financing gap and ensure more sustainable the investment.

[62] G20 2020.

[63] UFA 2020.

UFA 2020 initiative focuses on 25 priority countries where almost 70% of all financially excluded people live.[64] The UFA goal envisioned that, by 2020, adults globally would have been able to have access to a transaction account or electronic instrument to store money and send and receive payments. Financial access is the first step toward broader financial inclusion, where individuals and firms can safely use a range of appropriate financial services, including savings, payments, credit, and insurance.

Financial sector policymakers and global standard-setting bodies (SSBs) increasingly pursue all four core policy objectives (financial inclusion, financial stability, financial integrity, and financial consumer protection), with encouragement from global bodies beyond the G20 and GPFI, such as the United Nations and the International Monetary Fund. Achieving sustainable development, particularly fighting against poverty, reducing inequality, and tackling climate change, requires a long-term perspective, with governments, the private sector, and civil society working together to tackle global challenges. Strengthened collective action based on integrated frameworks should not only respond to financing challenges, but also to changing global landscape.[65]

28.4.2 *National Financial Strategies*

Is worth stressing that regulatory compliance with statutes such as the Revised Payment Services Directive[66] has accelerated competition, and bringing payment systems out of the monopoly of the banks implies that the whole sector will be transformed.[67] One of the biggest challenges to achieving full financial inclusion for hundreds of millions of excluded people has always been how to reach, for example, rural populations with affordable financial services and products. New technologies involving Fintechs and Gigatechs have changed this, lowering the cost of service delivery. Fintech and Gigatech as innovating and experimenting institutions with new products, delivery channels, and analytics are redefining how banking fits in the daily life of consumers.[68]

The main direct impacts of EU regulation are increased capital requirements and new positions in compliance, data protection, and IT departments. The European Commission has adopted the AML/CFT RULES as robust legislation to fight money

---

[64] Bangladesh, Brazil, China, Colombia, Cote d'Ivoire, DRC, Egypt, Ethiopia, India, Indonesia, Kenya, Mexico, Morocco, Mozambique, Myanmar, Nigeria, Pakistan, Peru, Philippines, Rwanda, South Africa, Vietnam, Tanzania, Turkey, and Zambia.

[65] United Nations 2019.

[66] PSD2; 2015/2366 of the European Parliament and of the Council of 25 November 2015 on payment services in the internal market, amending Directives 2002/65/EC, 2009/110/EC and 2013/36/EU and Regulation (EU) No 1093/2010, and repealing Directive 2007/64/EC, OJ L 337, 23.12.2015, 35–127.

[67] Premchand and Choudhry 2018.

[68] Kuchciak and Warwas 2021.

laundering and financing of terrorists. This new legal framework has resulted in the increased importance of Know-Your-Customer (KYC), and the workforce responsible for performing KYC.[69] Knowledge of a customer is crucial to providing effective and efficient financial services. The inability of financial institutions to properly verify prospective clients will lead to financial exclusion. Innovations in KYC processes and requirements entail advances that makes it easier to identify and verify customers and citizens, thereby facilitating access to and use of financial services.

28.4.3 *Public and Private Sector Commitment*

As more and more governments are considering increased access to financial services in terms of broad financial inclusion, rather than more narrowly in microfinance, strategies are increasingly being framed as national inclusive finance strategies (NFIS). A NFIS can provide an effective instrument to chart a clear and coordinated path toward improving financial inclusion. Financial inclusion strategies can be defined as road maps of actions, agreed upon and defined at the national or subnational level, that stakeholders follow to achieve financial inclusion objectives.[70] An NFIS enables stakeholders to jointly define financial inclusion objectives, identify obstacles and opportunities relevant to the achievement of those objectives, and outline a prioritized set of actions to pursue in a coordinated manner.[71]

National financial inclusion strategies take into consideration the country's context, especially the macroeconomic as well as the socio-political situation. A NFIS is consistent with national macroeconomic and developmental goals and aligned with other national strategies such as national poverty reduction strategies or financial literacy strategies. Financial inclusion strategies look at the access and usage of financial services that make up the demand side of the picture as well as the capacity of providers and potential opportunities and barriers in the market that contribute to the supply side. An important feature of NFIS is their realism based on the level of support, technical and financial, required to implement the plan developed.[72]

The process of developing a national strategy should involve government or donors, ideally with active engagement of the private sector and civil society more broadly. On behalf of the government, the Central Bank or Ministry of Finance is the most common lead in the development of national strategies. The lead stakeholder manages the entire NFIS development process and acts as the NFIS champion. The second group of stakeholders actively involved in NFIS are the drafting

---

[69] Directive 2018/843 of the European Parliament and of the Council of 30 May 2018 amending Directive (EU) 2015/849 on the prevention of the use of the financial system for the purposes of money laundering or terrorist financing, and amending Directives 2009/138/EC and 2013/36/EU, OJ L 156, 19.6.2018, 43–74.

[70] Pearce and Ortega 2012.

[71] Sakariya 2013.

[72] Porter 2011.

stakeholders. These stakeholders typically include institutions involved in financial sector policy making and regulation, for example, sector financial authorities, The Financial Conduct Authority, the Ministry of Finance, the Ministry of Planning, as well as the Ministry of Microfinance, if one exists. Finally, the third group (the so-called "consultation stakeholders") encompasses those who will not play an active drafting role but will be consulted regularly and asked to provide feedback at key intervals during the drafting process. Mostly this group includes the private sector (for example, industry groups or leaders of major financial service providers), nongovernmental organizations, international organizations, and other public sector stakeholders. More inclusive strategies also involve consultation with Ministries of Telecommunication, Agriculture, Education, Social Welfare, and National Statistic Agencies. In some countries, parliamentarians are engaged in the process.[73]

28.5 MOBILE TECHNOLOGY AND FINANCIAL SERVICES IN DEVELOPING COUNTRIES AND DEVELOPED COUNTRIES

The rapid development of mobile technology has contributed, above all, to an increase in the volume of e-commerce, in which electronic money was widely used in developed countries. Together with technological development, digitalization has become an unavoidable requirement in the banking sector. The most significant drivers of change for the banking sector are connected with technology. Most authors conclude that digitalization is the most powerful driver of changes in the banking sector.[74]

The adoption of mobile telephony to provide financial services brings large benefits for the individual. Mbithi and Weil[75] proved that M-PESA (the mobile phone-based money transfer service) enhanced individual outcomes, understood as faster time, lower cost, and lower risk. Jack and Suri's[76] findings showed that M-PESA users were able to fully absorb large negative income shocks (such as severe illness, job loss, livestock death, and harvest or business failure) without any reduction in household consumption. Demombynes and Thegeya[77] found that those with registered M-PESA accounts were 32% more likely to have some savings than their peers who were not using those services. Widespread mobile money adoption is boosting financial inclusion, reducing transaction costs, and facilitating successful consumption smoothing and risk sharing among users.

Across the globe, there is a move toward faster, cashless payment systems, which can lower costs and provide more secure transactions than cash.[78] Digital

---

[73] World Bank 2018b.
[74] Beck et al. 2016; Puschmann 2017.
[75] Mbithi and Weil 2011.
[76] Jack and Suri 2014.
[77] Demombynes and Thegeya 2012.
[78] Mester 2020.

transformation in the banking sector covers the alternative distribution channels through which banks reach their customers – such as ATMs, Internet branches, and mobile branches. Banks are able to reach their customers on alternative platforms thanks to applications developed by these branches.[79]

The digitization of the banking sector is proceeding very smoothly because digital banks can help by providing broader access to core services and capital and finally result in higher financial inclusion. The technological advancement is evidenced by the results of the study Digital Banking Maturity,[80] the biggest global digital banking study, providing a comprehensive assessment of retail banks' digital channels and furthering discussion about future developments. The latest results from 2020 pointed out digital champions among banks, set key digital trends, and identified best practices for offering a wide range of functionalities relevant to customers and a compelling user experience. Many banks and credit unions developed new digital functionality, with organizations rethinking their back-office operations, their investment in technology, and their commitment to innovation. The pandemic created a sense of urgency within the banking industry as branches were closed and customers were forced to use digital channels to transact and engage with their financial institutions.

On the one hand digitalization of finance creates a large scope of opportunities for the banking sector but on the other Fintech and Gigatech represents a disruptive competitive force that will have a major role in shaping the structure of the financial industry. The entry of nonbanks into the financial services industry significantly increases competition and efficiency in the market but also adds fragility to the financial system.[81]

28.6 COVID-19 PANDEMIC AS AN ACCELERATOR TO DIGITAL ACCESS TO FINANCIAL SERVICES

Although digitalization in the financial sector started much earlier than the outbreak of the pandemic, COVID-19 the role of an accelerator of innovative solutions in access to financial services. The COVID-19 pandemic has affected not only the health of citizens but also the political, economic, and social situation on the national, European, and global level.[82] Virtually all spheres of professional, social, and personal life have changed, which has affected the mental and physical condition of society to varying degrees, as well as the level of functioning of all areas of the economy, including the habits and behavior of consumers.[83]

---

[79] Kaur et al. 2020.
[80] Deloitte 2020. Digital Banking Maturity (DBM) from 2020 covered 318 banks from 39 countries. DBM analyses digital retail banking in three channels, based on an outside-in 'mystery shopper' assessment of digital functionalities, customer needs research, and UX evaluation.
[81] Sy et al. 2019.
[82] Liu et al. 2020.
[83] Nurhayati et al. 2021.

COVID-19 has been classified as the most dangerous pandemic since 1918, making estimating medium- and long-term effects extremely difficult.[84] Looking from a financial perspective, undoubtedly the COVID-19 epidemic in 2019–2020 has become one of the most active catalysts in the entire history of the emergence of remote banking. Around the world, societies have experienced lockdowns, with citizens being asked to respect social distancing and stay at home. The banking system, as a dynamically changing and sensitive area, faced numerous challenges that required an immediate response.[85]

An important group of challenges faced by the financial sector in light of the COVID-19 pandemic is the increase in interest in electronic banking channels and changes in payment behavior. The financial sector faced the difficult task of understanding new behaviors and meeting consumer demands with the right products and convenient services, as well as adapting business services to social changes related to the pandemic situation.[86] The popularization of electronic solutions resulted from the imposed restrictions on the number of customers admitted to branches and reduced working hours and even temporary closure of branches and appreciation of the fact that electronic banking provides a variety of services and facilities that can be used remotely at any time and in any place, without the need for personal contact, which was important when taking action to limit the spread of COVID-19.

Shortly after the outbreak of the pandemic, there was a lot of information about the possible relationship between handling physical money and COVID-19 infections.[87] In response to these publications, several central banks have communicated that the risk of using banknotes and coins is low and that a sufficient supply of banknotes is guaranteed.[88] Despite these messages, research on the transmission of the virus through physical money has shown that a significant portion of the population has reduced the transactional use of cash in response to the pandemic and at the same time increased the demand for cash.[89] This phenomenon has become known as the "paradox of banknotes", indicating that the increased demand for cash is the result of its use to store value.[90]

For consumers who are convinced that cash handling is associated with a higher risk of infection, there is a visible preference for non-cash transactions both in current transactions and after the end of the pandemic.[91] According to Capgemini,[92] by 2025, instant payments and e-money payments will account for more than 25%

---

[84] Jordà et al. 2020.

[85] Kolodiziev et al. 2022.

[86] Mathew et al. 2022.

[87] Auer et al. 2020.

[88] The Bank of England, the Bundesbank, the Bank of Canada, and the South African Reserve Bank have been involved in this initiative.

[89] Chen et al. 2020.

[90] Zamora-Pérez 2021.

[91] Wisniewski et al. 2021.

[92] Capgemini 2021.

of the global non-cash transaction, up from 14.5% in 2020. The 2021 round of the Financial Access Survey (FAS) data confirms this development. The FAS[93] collects data on two types of digital financial services: mobile money, and mobile and internet banking. Of these, mobile money is more prevalent in low- and middle-income economies, and mobile and internet banking in developed economies.

The number of mobile and internet banking transactions grew significantly for upper middle-income economies in 2020, while mobile money strongly supports undisrupted financial transactions during the pandemic, especially in developing economies. First of all, mobile money has high levels of market penetration in many low- and middle-income economies. Moreover, transactions can be carried out with minimal physical contact. Finally, mobile money has high levels of usage among the unbanked and underbanked, making it a key mode of using financial services for the most vulnerable parts of the population.[94]

The increased interest in online transactions is also the result of the development of the e-commerce market. It was triggered by the transfer of sales from closed stationary stores in shopping malls, the growing number of parcel machines, or the growing popularity of deferred payment services. E-commerce and m-commerce are now mainstream and prime shopping for customers, making digital solutions the preferred method.[95] During the COVID-19 lockdowns, digital financial services enabled governments to provide quick and secure financial support to people and businesses, as demonstrated in Namibia, Peru, Zambia, and Uganda in research provided by Khera et al.[96]

The COVID-19 pandemic has also affected the financial resilience of consumers. This is largely the result of downtime in the functioning of some enterprises and even their closure, lack of availability or difficulties in stationary access to public administration, temporary closure of schools, kindergartens, and quarantines resulting in the need to reconcile remote work with childcare and sometimes also the risk of dismissal from work due to incomplete performance of duties. Loss of financial stability results in loss of income and problems with settling accounts and timely fulfillment of credit obligations.

According to the OECD,[97] consumers are more likely to build financial resilience when they trust the financial services sector, receive clear messages about their financial products, have access to tailor-made financial services, and are confident that they have been treated fairly and transparently. Access to high-quality information, advice, and guidance also plays an important role in helping people with lower levels of financial literacy improve their financial capacity and work

---

93 IMF 2021.
94 Bazarbash et al. 2020.
95 Capgemini 2022.
96 Khera et al. 2020.
97 OECD 2021.

towards their financial resilience. Financially resilient consumers are less exposed to difficulties in the event of a downturn and are more likely to be able to rebuild their well-being more quickly when the situation starts to improve.

Therefore, it can be concluded that the issue of building financial resilience, which the COVID-19 pandemic highlighted as crucial, includes the issue of financial education, as well as strengthening cybersecurity in response to the increased digitization of financial services.

28.7 PROMOTING DIGITAL AND FINANCIAL LITERACY

The importance of financial literacy has equally emerged during the outbreak of the COVID-19 pandemic. The pandemic has influenced a dynamic increase in the scale and scope of the use of electronic banking, including by people without sufficient financial knowledge.

Financial literacy is defined by the OECD[98] as a combination of financial awareness, knowledge, skills, attitudes, and behaviors necessary to make sound financial decisions and ultimately achieve individual financial well-being. In other words, financial literacy means people's ability to process economic information and make informed decisions about financial planning, wealth accumulation, pensions, and debt.[99]

In light of these definitions, financial literacy goes beyond having information and knowledge about the characteristics and risks associated with financial products, because it includes financial attitudes and behavior, and it de facto affects consumer protection in the financial market. The ability to understand the risks and characteristics of financial products and services has become a key skill for today's consumers, who make financial decisions daily.

The relationship between financial education and inclusion is often taken up in the literature. Usually, scholars point out the relationship between a low level of financial knowledge and staying in the group of financially excluded people and, as a consequence, they recommend raising the level of inclusion using financial education.[100]

The pandemic has resulted in a decrease in cash turnover for electronic payments and an increase in the use of remote channels in communication with banks, which has made it crucial to ensure cybersecurity and educate consumers in this area. On the other hand, the financial uncertainty triggered by the pandemic has negatively affected the financial resilience and well-being of households. In this context, it has become necessary to strengthen consumer protection in the financial services market also through education.[101]

---

[98] OECD 2020b.
[99] Lusardi and Mitchell 2014.
[100] Hajaj 2002; Kempson 2006; Lusardi and Mitchell 2014; Maciejasz-Świątkiewicz 2013; Polasik et al. 2018; Penczar 2014; Kuchciak and Wiktorowicz 2021.
[101] OECD 2020b.

Promoting financial literacy is an obvious and commonsense response to the increased complexity of the financial world. The OECD[102] recognized that financial literacy policies are broadly aimed at promoting the development of healthy, open, and competitive financial markets and supporting financial stability, and that financial literacy policies are a necessary complement to approaches aimed at reinforcing financial inclusion and consumer protection within appropriate regulatory and supervisory frameworks, to enhance financial resilience and well-being.

There is a range of instruments used to improve financial literacy but there are some problems in assessing the effects of financial literacy. According to many authors, only well-designed financial education tailored to a specific audience has the potential to increase financial knowledge and skills.[103]

Strengthening consumer protection through financial literacy requires financial education. According to the OECD,[104] financial education can be defined as "the process by which financial consumers/investors improve their understanding of financial products, concepts and risks and, through information, instruction and/or objective advice, develop the skills and confidence to become more aware of financial risks and opportunities, to make informed choices, to know where to go for help, and to take other effective actions to improve their financial well-being." The primary goal of financial education is therefore not only to provide the necessary knowledge to consumers, but also to shape their ability to navigate the financial market and to promote appropriate behavior in the financial services market, understood in the context of the risk incurred and, consequently, security in the financial services market.

Due to the wide range of financial issues, financial education can be conducted in the form of formal and non-formal programs, and educational content can be provided through traditional as well as modern distribution channels. Financial education programs in each country should focus on high-priority issues, which, depending on national circumstances, may cover aspects of financial planning with varying degrees of intensity, such as accumulating savings, investing, securing retirement, debt management, or buying insurance coverage.

The OECD work on national strategies for financial education was launched in 2009 as an integral part of its project on financial education. In 2012, OECD/INFE prepared High-level Principles on the Evaluation of Financial Education Programs, which defined a set of principles and actions for effective evaluation and monitoring of financial literacy and education programs. In 2022, the OECD published a report that summarized the results of monitoring and evaluation of

---

[102] OECD 2020b.
[103] Lusardi and Mitchell 2009; Fornero and Monticone 2011; Van Rooij et al. 2011; Klapper and Lusardi 2020.
[104] OECD 2005.

national strategies for financial literacy[105] of 29 countries and economies. This report stressed that the key challenge reported by jurisdictions has been to translate goals and objectives into measurable key performance indicators (KPIs). This obstacle creates some difficulty in pinning down the direct impact of financial literacy activities.

In general, the recent work of Kaiser et al.[106] shows clear evidence of the positive effects of financial education on financial behaviors (and knowledge). However, their research contradicts that of Fernandes et al.,[107] who suggest that financial education decays over time and that even large interventions with many hours of instruction have negligible effects on behavior 20 months or more from the time of intervention. Kaiser et al.[108] found the estimated effect of financial education to be at least three times as large as the effect documented in Fernandes et al.,[109] and, accounting for differences in programs, effects to be more than five times as large as the effects reported in Fernandes et al.[110] Moreover, they do not find clear evidence of a dramatic decay of the effects of financial education over time.

The latest research conducted in the area of financial literacy is embedded in a three-dimensional model that takes into account financial skills, financial behavior, and perception of the level of financial knowledge.[111] The relationship between the perception of own financial knowledge and real knowledge of finance is also emphasized.[112] Such an understanding of financial literacy leads to the conclusion that enduring financial literacy requires not only having financial knowledge and skills but also requires providing access to appropriate banking products so that they can be used in practice.

---

[105] National Strategy for financial literacy is defined as "a sustained, coordinated approach to financial literacy which:

- recognizes the importance of financial literacy – through legislation where appropriate – and agrees its scope at the national level, taking into account identified national needs and gaps;
- is coherent with other strategies fostering economic and social prosperity such as those focusing on financial inclusion and financial consumer protection;
- involves cooperation with relevant stakeholders as well as the identification of a national leader or coordinating body/council;
- includes the establishment of a roadmap to support the achievement of specific and predetermined objectives within a set period of time;
- provides guidance to be applied by individual programmers implemented under the national strategy in order to efficiently and appropriately contribute to the overall strategy; and
- incorporates monitoring and evaluation to assess the progress of the strategy and propose improvements accordingly."

[106] Kaiser et al. 2022.
[107] Fernandes et al. 2014.
[108] Kaiser et al. 2022.
[109] Fernandes et al. 2014.
[110] Ibid.
[111] Xiao et al. 2014.
[112] Allgood and Walstad 2016.

28.8 SUMMARY

One of the key areas which drives a country's economy is financial services. There is a large body of academic literature about financial inclusion and financial exclusion in both applied and theoretical works. The paper has analyzed causes, sizes, and consequences of both phenomena, and has formulated conclusions and recommendations regarding enhancing financial inclusion. An optimal level of financial inclusion would be obtained when policies succeed in extending financial services to a broad segment of the population and have done so in an efficient and sustainable manner.

Existing approaches to financial inclusion are complex. This paper surveyed not only the traditional perspective of financial inclusion and exclusion but also the role of new technologies, providing innovative solutions in increasing access to finance and COVID-19 and its influence on financial inclusion. The multidimensional approach is displayed in Figure 28.2.

Digital financial inclusion determines the possibility of access to financial services for the general public based on digital channels tailored to the needs and under leap-and-price conditions. Small firms and households can directly benefit from digital solutions such as mobile money services, online banking, and other financial technology innovations.[113]

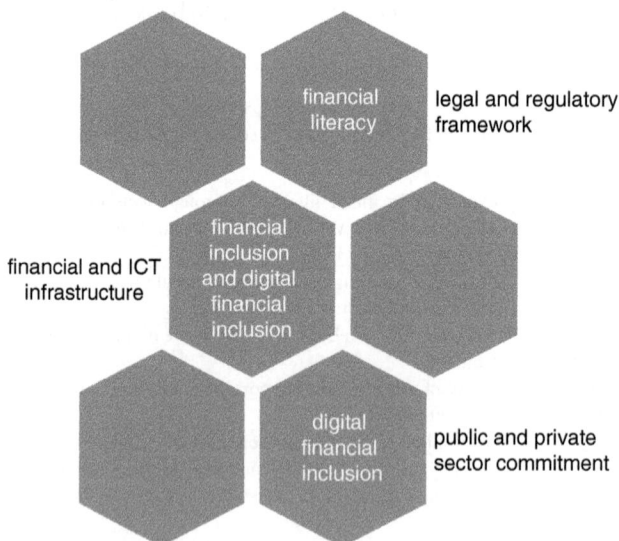

FIGURE 28.2 Multidimensional approach to financial inclusion
Source: Own elaboration based on World Bank 2016

[113] Naumenkova et al. 2019.

Financial inclusion and digital financial inclusion have been affected by regulatory issues that fall within the remit of different regulatory authorities, which requires effective communication and cooperation between them, but also education directed towards consumers.

REFERENCES

Accenture (2022), 'Top 10 trends for 2022', available at: https://accntu.re/3vujo2r (accessed on 5 August 2022).

Adegbite, O. O. and Machethe, C. L. (2020), 'Bridging the financial inclusion gender gap in smallholder agriculture in Nigeria: An untapped potential for sustainable development', *World Development*, 127, 104755, available at: https://doi.org/10.1016/j.worlddev.2019.104755.

Aghion, P. and Bolton, P. (1997), 'A theory of trickle-down growth and development', *Review of Economic Studies*, 64, 151–172.

Agur, I., Peria, M. S., and Rochon, C. (2020), 'Digital Financial Services and the Pandemic: Opportunities and Risks for Emerging and Developing Economies,' IMF Special Series on COVID-19, available at: https://bit.ly/3PAAzVf (accessed on 15 August 2022).

Ahamed, M. M. and Mallick, S. K. (2019), 'Is financial inclusion good for bank stability? International evidence', *Journal of Economic Behavior & Organization*, 157, 403–427, available at: https://doi.org/10.1016/j.jebo.2017.07.027.

Ahmad, A. H., Green, C. J., and Jiang, F. (2020), 'Mobile money, financial inclusion, and development: A review with reference to African experience', *Journal of Economic Surveys*, 34(4), 753–792.

Ajide, F. M. (2020), 'Can financial inclusion reduce the presence of corruption? Evidence from selected countries in Africa', *International Journal of Social Economics*, 47(11), 1345–1362.

Aker, J., Boumnijel, R., McClelland, A., and Tierney, N. (2013), 'How Do Electronic Transfers Compare? Evidence from a Mobile Money Cash Transfer Experiment in Niger', Tufts University Working Paper.

Allen, F., Demirgüç-Kunt, A., Klapper, L., and Martinez Peria, M. S. (2016), 'The foundations of financial inclusion: Understanding ownership and use of formal accounts', *Journal of Financial Intermediation*, 27, 1–30.

Allgood, S. and Walstad, W. (2016), 'The effects of perceived and actual financial literacy on financial behaviors', *Economic Inquiry*, 54(1), 675–697.

Andrianaivo, M. and Kpodar, K. (2011), ICT, 'Financial inclusion, and growth: Evidence from African countries', *Review of Economic and institution*, International Monetary Fund, Washington, WP11/73, Available at: www.imf.org/external/pubs/ft/wp/2011/wp1173.pdf (accessed on 12 October 2022).

Angadi, V. B. (2003), 'Financial infrastructure and economic development: Theory, evidence and experience', *RBI Occasional Papers*, 24(1), 191–223.

Auer, R., Cornelli, G., and Frost, J. (2020), 'COVID-19, cash, and the future of payments, Bank for International Settlements (BIS)', *BIS Bulletin*, 3, available at: www.bis.org/publ/bisbull03.pdf (accessed on 13 October 2022).

Atkinson, A. B. and Bourguignon, F. (2014), *Handbook of income distribution*, Vols. 2A & 2B (Amsterdam: Elsevier Science Publishing Co Inc.).

Babatz, G. (2013), 'Sustained Effort, Saving Billions: Lessons from the Mexican Government's Shift to Electronic Payments', Better Than Cash Alliance Evidence Paper: Mexico Study, available at: https://bit.ly/3TTRHbq (accessed on 6 August 2022).

Bakar, H. O. and Sulong, Z. (2018), 'The role of financial inclusion on economic growth: Theoretical and empirical literature review analysis', *Journal of Business & Financial Affairs*, 7(4), available at: https://doi:10.4172/2167-0234.1000356.

Banerjee, A. V. and Newman, A. F. (1993), 'Occupational choice and the process of development', *Journal of Political Economy*, 101(2), 274–298.

Barajas, A., Beck, T., Belhaj, M., and Naceur, S. B. (2020), 'Financial inclusion: What have we learned so far? What do we have to learn', WP/20/157, IMF Working Paper, available at: https://bit.ly/4a50m0b (accessed on 16 August 2022).

Bazarbash, M., Villanova, C., Chhabra, H. et al. (2020), 'Mobile money in the COVID-19 pandemic', IMF Special Series on COVID-19, available at: www.imf.org/en/Publications/SPROLLs/covid19-special-notes.

Beck, T. and Demirguc-Kunt, A. (2006), 'Small and medium size enterprises: Access to finance as a growth constraint', *Journal of Banking and Finance*, 30(11), 2931–2943.

Beck, T., Chen, T., Chen, L., and Song, F. (2016), 'Financial innovation: The bright and the dark sides', *Journal of Banking and Finance*, 72, 28–51, available at: https://doi.org/10.1016/j.jbankfin.2016.06.012.

Beck, T., Demirgüç-Kunt, A., and Martinez Peria, M. S. (2008), 'Banking services for everyone? barriers to bank access and use around the world', *The World Bank Economic Review*, 22(3), 397–430, available at: https://doi.org/10.1093/wber/lhn020.

Bhatia, S. and Singh, S. (2019), 'Empowering women through financial inclusion: A study of urban slum', *Vikalpa: The Journal for Decision Makers*, 44(4), 182–197.

Bradley, S. W., McMullen, J. S., Artz, K., and Simiyu, E. M. (2012), 'Capital is not enough: Innovation in developing economies', *Journal of Management Studies*, 49(4), 684–717.

Capgemini (2021), 'World Payments Report 2021: Embracing the Payments 4.X Era', available at: https://bit.ly/4avzM07 (accessed on 2 October 2022).

Capgemini (2022), 'Payment top trends 2022', available at: https://bit.ly/3Vx25He (accessed on 26 June 2022).

Chen, J., Chang, A. Y., and Bruton, G. D. (2017), 'Microfinance: Where are we today and where should the research go in the future?', *International Small Business Journal*, 35(7), 793–802.

Chen, H., Engert, W., Huynh, K. P. et al. (2020), 'Cash and COVID-19: The impact of the pandemic on the demand for and use of cash', Bank of Canada No 2020–6, Discussion Papers, available at: https://bit.ly/4ateP6o (accessed on 14 June 2022).

Claessens, S. and Perotti, E. (2007), 'Finance and inequality: Channels and evidence', *Journal of Comparative Economics*, 35(4), 748–773.

Clamara, N., Peña, X., and Tuesta, D., (2015), 'Factors that matter for financial inclusion: Evidence from Peru', *Aestimatio, The Ieb International Journal of Finance*, 9, 8–29.

Commission of the European Communities (1999), 'Communication from the Commission – Implementing the framework for financial markets: Action Plan', Brussels, 11.05.1999 COM(1999) 232 final, available at: https://bit.ly/4arNWz9 (accessed on 4 July 2022).

Commission of the European Communities (2007), 'Green Paper on Retail Financial Services in the Single Market', Brussels, 30.04.2007 COM(2007) 226 final, available at: https://bit.ly/3VyxzwK (accessed on 13 July 2022).

Čihák, M. and Sahay, R. (2020), 'Finance and Inequality', IMF Staff Discussion Notes 2020/001, International Monetary Fund, available at: https://bit.ly/494YzHa (accessed on 26 June 2022).

Deloitte (2020), 'Digital banking maturity', available at: https://bit.ly/4cnxUYS (accessed on 17 June 2022).

Demirgüç-Kunt, A. and Klapper, L. (2012), 'Measuring Financial Inclusion: The Global Findex Database', World Bank Policy Research Working Paper 6025.

Demirgüç-Kunt, A. and Levine, R. (2008), 'Finance and economic opportunity', (Washington, DC: World Bank), available at: https://bit.ly/49fvk4q (accessed on 03 January 2023).

Demirgüç-Kunt, A. and Singer, D. (2017), 'Financial Inclusion and Inclusive Growth: A Review of Recent Empirical Evidence', April 25. World Bank Policy Research Working Paper No. 8040, available at https://ssrn.com/abstract=2958542.

Demirgüç-Kunt, A., Klapper, L., Singer, D., and Van Oudheusden, P. (2015), 'The Global Findex Database 2014: Measuring Financial Inclusion around the World', Policy Research Working Paper 7255.

Demirgüç-Kunt, A., Klapper, L., and Singer, D. (2017), 'Financial Inclusion and Inclusive Growth: A Review of Recent Empirical Evidence', Policy Research Working Paper; No. 8040 (Washington, DC: World Bank), available at: https://openknowledge.worldbank.org/handle/10986/26479 (accessed on 16 June 2022).

Demirgüç-Kunt, A., Klapper, L., Singer, D., and Ansar, S. (2022), *The Global Findex Database 2021: Financial Inclusion, Digital Payments, and Resilience in the Age of COVID-19* (Washington, DC: World Bank).

Demombynes, G. and Thegeya, A. (2012), 'Public Kenya's Mobile Revolution and the Promise of Mobile Savings', Policy Research Working Paper 5988 (Washington, DC: World Bank).

Dev, M. (2006), 'Financial inclusion: Issues and challenges', *Economic and Political Weekly* 41(41), 4310–4313.

Diamond, D. W. and Dybvig, P. H. (1983), 'Bank runs, deposit insurance, and liquidity', *Journal of Political Economy*, 91(3), 401–419.

Dupas, P., Green, S., Keats, A., and Robinson, J. (2012), 'Challenges in banking the rural poor: Evidence from Kenya's Western Province', NBER Working Paper No. 17851 (Cambridge, MA: National Bureau of Economic Research), available at: www.nber.org/papers/w17851 (accessed on 10 June 2022).

Espinosa-Vega, M. A., Shirono, K., Villanova, H. C. et al. (2020), 'IMF Measuring Financial Access: 10 Years of the IMF Financial Access Survey', available at: https://bit.ly/3vrNFNS (accessed on 12 July 2022).

Fareed, F., Gabriel, M., Lenain, P., and Reynaud, J. (2017), 'Financial Inclusion and Women Entrepreneurship: Evidence from Mexico', OECD Economics Department Working Papers, No. 1411 (Paris: OECD Publishing), available at: https://bit.ly/3IPBSMz (accessed on 3 June 2022).

Fernandes, D., Lynch, J. G., and Netemeyer, R. G. (2014), 'Financial literacy, financial education and downstream financial behaviors', *Management Science*, 60(8), 1861–1883.

Fernández-Olit, B., Martín, M., Maria, J., and Poras Gonzales, E. (2020), 'Systematized literature review on financial inclusion and exclusion in developed countries', *International Journal of Bank Marketing*, 38(3), 600–626, available at: https://doi.org/10.1108/IJBM-06-2019-0203.

Fornero, E. and Monticone, C. (2011), 'Financial literacy and pension plan participation in Italy', *Journal of Pension Economics & Finance*, 10(4), 547–564.

G20 (2010), 'Principles for innovative financial inclusion', available at: www.g20.utoronto.ca/2010/to-principles.html (accessed on 14 June 2022).

G20 (2017), 'Financial Inclusion Action Plan', available at: https://bit.ly/3vsFktk (accessed on 29 June 2022).

G20 (2020), 'Financial Inclusion Action Plan October 2020', available at: www.gpfi.org/sites/gpfi/files/sites/default/files/G20%202020%20Financial%20Inclusion%20Action%20Plan.pdf (accessed on 27 June 2022).

GPFI (Global Partnership for Financial Inclusion) (2016), 'Global Standard-Setting Bodies Financial Inclusion: The Evolving Landscape', available at: https://bit.ly/3IUJM7j (accessed on 3 August 2022).

GPFI (Global Partnership for Financial Inclusion) (2017), 'Financial Inclusion Action Plan July 2017', available at: https://tinyurl.com/2s4jktnh.

GPFI (2022), available at: www.gpfi.org/about-gpfi (accessed on 15 June 2022).

Goldsmith, R. W. (1969), *Financial Structure and Development* (New Haven, CT: Yale University Press).

Gomber, P., Koch, J. A., and Siering, M. (2017), 'Digital finance and FinTech: Current research and future research directions', *Journal of Business Economics*, 87(5/2), 537–580.

Greenwood, J. and Jovanovic, B. (1990), 'Financial development, growth, and the distribution of income', *Journal of Political Economy*, 98(5), 1076–1107.

Gurley, J. G. and Shaw, E. S. (1955), 'Financial aspects of economic development', *The American Economic Review*, 45(4), 515–538.

Hajaj, K. (2002), 'Illiteracy, financial services and social exclusion', Opinion Papers, available at: https://files.eric.ed.gov/fulltext/ED473576.pdf (accessed on 26 May 2022).

Hassan, M. K., Sanchez, B., and Yu, J. S. (2011), 'Financial development and economic growth: New evidence from panel data', *The Quarterly Review of Economics and Finance*, 51(1), 88–104, available at: https://doi.org/10.1016/j.qref.2010.09.001.

Holloway, K., Niazi, Z., and Rouse, R. (2017), 'Women's Economic Empowerment through Financial Inclusion: A Review of Existing Evidence and Remaining Knowledge Gaps', New Haven: Innovations for Poverty Action, available at: https://bit.ly/4apDAji (accessed on 29 May 2022).

IMF (2021), 'Financial Access Survey 2021, Trends and Developments', available at: https://bit.ly/3x82wO7 (accessed on 28 June 2022).

Jack, W. and Suri, T. (2011), 'Mobile Money: The Economics of M-PESA', NBER Working Paper 16721, National Bureau of Economic Research, Cambridge, MA.

Jack, W. and Suri, T. (2014), 'Risk sharing and transactions costs: Evidence from Kenya's mobile money revolution', *The American Economic Review*, 104(1), 183–223.

Jordà, Ò., Singh, S. R., and Taylor, A. M. (2020), 'Longer-Run Economic Consequences of Pandemics', Covid Economics: Vetted and Real-Time Papers, 1 (April 3), 1–15.

Kabeer, N. (2000), 'Social exclusion, poverty and discrimination: Towards an analytical framework', *IDS Bulletin*, 31(4), 83–97.

Kaiser, K., Lusardi, A., Menkhoff, L., and Urban C. (2022), 'Financial education affects financial knowledge and downstream behaviors', *Journal of Financial Economics*, 145(2:A), 255–272, available at: https://doi.org/10.1016/j.jfineco.2021.09.022.

Karlan, D., Ratan, A. L., and Zinman, J. (2014), 'Savings by and for the poor: A research review and agenda', *Review of Income and Wealth*, 60(1), 36–78, available at: https://ssrn.com/abstract=2391550.

Kaur, N., Sahdev, S.L., Sharma, M., and Siddiqui, L. (2020), 'Banking 4.0: The influence of artificial intelligence on the banking industry & How AI is changing the face of modern day banks', *International Journal of Management*, 11(6), 577–585.

Kempson, E. (2006), 'Policy level response to financial exclusion in developed economies: Lessons for developing countries', Access to Finance: Building Inclusive Financial Systems (Washington, DC: World Bank).

Kempson, E. (2009), 'Framework for the Development of Financial Literacy Baseline Surveys: A First International Comparative Analysis', OECD Working Papers on Finance, Insurance and Private Pensions, 1, OECD Publishing, available at: https://doi:10.1787/5kmddpz7m9zq-en.

Khan, H. R. (2011), 'Financial Inclusion and Financial Stability: Are They Two Sides of the Same Coin', The Indian Bankers Association and Indian Overseas Bank, India, available at: www.bis.org/review/r111229f.pdf (accessed on 7 October 2022).

Khan, A. and Malaika, M. (2021), 'Central Bank Risk Management, Fintech, and Cybersecurity', IMF, WP/ 21/105, available at: https://bit.ly/4awLS9 (accessed on 6 October 2022).

Khera, P., von Allmen, U. E., Ogawa, S., and Sahay, R. (2020), 'Digital Financial Inclusion in the Times of COVID-19', IMF Blog, available at: https://bit.ly/3Pxn2hp (accessed on 1 October 2022).

Kim, D.-W., Yu, J.-S., and Hassan, M. K. (2018), 'Financial inclusion and economic growth in OIC countries', *Research in International Business and Finance*, 43(C), 1–14, available at: https://doi.org/10.1016/j.ribaf.2017.07.178.

Klapper, L. and Lusardi, A. (2020), 'Financial literacy and financial resilience: Evidence from around the world', *Financial Management, Financial Management Association International*, 49(3), 589–614.

Koku, P. S. (2015), 'Financial exclusion of the poor: A literature review', *International Journal of Bank Marketing*, (33), 654–668.

Kolodiziev, O., Shcherbak, V., Vzhytynska, K., Chernovol, O., and Lozynska, O. (2022), 'Clustering of banks by the level of digitalization in the context of the COVID-19 pandemic', *Banks and Bank Systems*, 17(1), 80–93.

Kuchciak, I. (2020), *Wykluczenie bankowe w Polsce w aspekcie ekonomicznym i społecznym*, (Łódź: Wydawnictwo Uniwersytetu Łódzkiego).

Kuchciak, I. and Warwas, I. (2021), 'Designing a roadmap for human resource management in the banking 4.0', *Journal of Risk and Financial Management*, 14(12), available at: https://doi.org/10.3390/jrfm14120615.

Kuchciak, I. and Wiktorowicz, J. (2021), 'Empowering financial education by banks – social media as a modern channel', *Journal of Risk and Financial Management*, 14(3), 118, available at: https://doi.org/10.3390/jrfm14030118.

Lal, T. (2018), 'Impact of financial inclusion on poverty alleviation through cooperative banks', *International Journal of Social Economics*, 45(5), 808–828.

Leyshon, A. and Thrift, N. (1995), 'Geographies of financial exclusion: Financial abandonment in Britain and the US', *Transactions of the Institute of British Geographers*, New series, 20(3), 312–341.

Liu, H., Manzoor, A., Wang, C., Zhang, L., and Manzoor, Z. (2020), 'The COVID-19 outbreak and affected countries stock markets response,' *International Journal of Environmental Research and Public Health*, 17(8), 2800, available at: https://doi.org/10.3390/ijerph17082800.

Lusardi, A. and Mitchell, O. S. (2007), 'Baby boomer retirement security: The roles of planning, financial literacy, and housing wealth', *Journal of Monetary Economic*, 54, 205–224.

Lusardi, A. and Mitchell, O. S. (2009), 'How ordinary consumers make complex economic decisions: financial literacy and retirement readiness', NBER Working Paper 15350.

Lusardi, A. and Mitchell, O. S. (2014), 'The economic importance of financial literacy: Theory and evidence', *Journal of Economic Literature*, 52(1), 5–44.

Maciejasz-Świątkiewicz, M. (2013), *Wykluczenie finansowe i narzędzia* (Opole: Uniwersytet Opolski).

Mahmood, S., Shuhui, W., Aslam, S., and Ahmed, T. (2022), 'The financial inclusion development and its impacts on disposable income', *SAGE Open*, 12(2), available at: https://doi.org/10.1177/21582440221093.

Mathew, S. M., Sunil, S., and Shanimon, S. (2022), 'A Study on the Impact of COVID-19 Pandemic in the Adoption of Tech-Driven Banking in India,' available at: https://osf.io/preprints/socarxiv/ugsj2/ (accessed on 5 August 2022).

Mbithi, I. and Weil, D. N. (2011), 'Mobile Banking: The Impact of M-pesa in Kenya', Working Paper Series, 17129, NBER, Massachusetts, available at: www.nber.org/system/files/working_papers/w17129/w17129.pdf (accessed on 10 May 2022).

Mehrotra, A. N. and Yetman, J. (2015), 'Financial inclusion-issues for central banks', *BIS Quarterly Review*, available at: www.bis.org/publ/qtrpdf/r_qt1503h.pdf (accessed on 11 May2022).

Mekinjić, B. (2019), 'The impact of Industry 4.0 on the transformation of the banking sector', *Journal of Contemporary Economics*, 1, available at: https://doi.org/10.7251/JOCE1901006M.

Mester, L. J. (2020), 'Fintech, Bigtech, and Financial Inclusion', Speech 89015, Federal Reserve Bank of Cleveland, available at: https://bit.ly/49d45Yh (accessed on 7 May 2022).

Naumenkova, S., Mishchenko, S., and Dorofeiev, D. (2019), 'Digital financial inclusion: Evidence from Ukraine', *Investment Management and Financial Innovations*, 16(3), 194–205.

Neaime, S. and Gaysse, I. (2018), 'Financial inclusion and stability in MENA: Evidence from poverty and inequality', *Finance Research Letters*, 24, 230–237, available at: https://doi.org/10.1016/j.frl.2017.09.007.

Ngepah, N. (2017), 'A review of theories and evidence of inclusive growth: An economic perspective for Africa', *Current Opinion in Environmental Sustainability*, 24, 52–57.

Nurhayati, I., Endri, E., Aminda, R. S., and Muniroh, L. (2021), 'Impact of COVID-19 on performance evaluation large market capitalization stocks and open innovation', *Journal of Open Innovation: Technology, Market, and Complexity*, 7(1), 56, available at: https://doi.org/10.3390/joitmc7010056.

OECD (2005), 'Recommendation on Principles and Good Practices for Financial Education and Awareness: Recommendation of the Council', available at: www.oecd.org/finance/financial-education/35108560.pdf.

OECD (2017), *G20/OECD INFE Report on Adult Financial Literacy in G20 Countries*, available at: https://bit.ly/3TP7ic5 (accessed on 12 October 2022).

OECD (2018), 'OECD/INFE Toolkit for Measuring Financial Literacy and Financial Inclusion', available at: https://bit.ly/4auR9hE (accessed on 5 August 2022).

OECD (2020a), 'Recommendation of the OECD Council on Financial Literacy', available at: https://bit.ly/3TPrwlT (accessed on 15 August 2022).

OECD (2020b), 'Advancing the Digital Financial Inclusion of Youth', available at: https://bit.ly/3TPRhCx (accessed on 20 August 2022).

OECD (2020c), 'Supporting the financial resilience of citizens throughout the COVID-19 crisis', available at: https://bit.ly/3xbJIop (accessed on 15 October 2022).

OECD (2021), 'Financial consumer protection and financial literacy in Asia in response to COVID-19', available at: https://bit.ly/3TQuN4u (accessed on 15 July 2022).

Ozili, P. K. (2018), 'Impact of digital finance on financial inclusion and stability', *Borsa Istanbul Review*, 18(4), 329–340, available at: https://doi.org/10.1016/j.bir.2017.12.003 (accessed on 26 October 2022).

Pearce, D. and Ortega, C. (2012), 'Financial inclusion strategies: Reference framework', World Bank Group, available at: https://bit.ly/3TRPJbw (accessed on 6 July 2022).

Penczar, M. (2014), 'Analiza skutków wykluczenia finansowego z punktu widzenia gospodarki, społeczeństwa i sektora finansowego', in M. Penczar, *Rola edukacji finansowej w ograniczaniu wykluczenia finansowego*, red., Instytut Badań nad Gospodarką Rynkową.

Pluskota, P. (2020), 'The use of microfinance to mitigate financial exclusion', *Argumenta Oeconomica Cracoviensia*, 2(23), 105–123.

Polasik, M., Huterska, A., and Meler, A. (2018), 'Wpływ edukacji formalnej na włączenie finansowe w zakresie usług płatniczych', *e-mentor* 1(73), 30–40.

Porter, B. (2011), 'National Strategies: Where Do They Get Us? A Roadmap for Financial Inclusion', Global Microcredit Summit, Commissioned Workshop Paper, 14–17 November 2011, Valladolid, Spain, available at: https://bit.ly/4cvBEYf (accessed on 16 July 2022).

Pranggono, B. and Arabo, A. (2021), 'COVID-19 pandemic cybersecurity issues', *Internet Technology Letter*, 4(2), available at: https://doi.org/10.1002/itl2.247.

Premchand, A. and Choudhry, A. (2018), 'Open Banking & APIs for Transformation in Banking', International Conference on Communication, Computing and Internet of Things (IC3IoT), 25–29, available at: https://doi:10.1109/IC3IoT.2018.8668107.

Puschmann, T. (2017), 'Fintech', *Business & Information Systems Engineering*, 59, 69–76, available at: https://doi.org/10.1007/s12599-017-0464-6.

Raza, M. S., Tang, J., Rubab, S., and Wen, X. (2019), 'Determining the nexus between financial inclusion and economic development in Pakistan', *Journal of Money Laundering Control*, 22(2), 195–209.

Sahay, R., von Allmen, U. E., Lahreche, A. et al. (2020), 'The Promise of Fintech: Financial Inclusion in the Post-Covid-19 Era', MCM Paper No. 20/09, (Washington, DC: International Monetary Fund), available at: https://bit.ly/3Vx2R76 (accessed on 26 June 2022).

Sakariya, S. (2013), 'Evaluation of financial inclusion strategy components: Reflections from India', *Journal of International Management Studies*, 13(1), 83–92.

Sakyi-Nyarko, C., Ahmad Hassan, A., and Green, C. J. (2022), 'The gender-differential effect of financial inclusion on household financial resilience', *The Journal of Development Studies*, 58(4), 692–712.

Salampasis, D. and Mention, A. L. (2017), 'FinTech: Harnessing innovation for financial inclusion', in Kuo Chuen, D. L., and Deng, R. (eds.), *Handbook of Blockchain, Digital Finance, and Inclusion* (Amsterdam: Elsevier Science Publishing Co Inc.), 451–461.

Sethi, D. and Acharya, D. (2018), 'Financial inclusion and economic growth linkage: Some cross country evidence', *Journal of Financial Economic Policy*, 10(3), 369–385, available at: https://doi.org/10.1108/JFEP-11-2016-0073.

Sy, A. N., Maino, R., Massara, A., Perez-Saiz, H., and Sharma, P. (2019), 'Fintech in Sub-Saharan African Countries: A Game Changer?', IMF Departmental Paper No. 19/04, International Monetary Fund, Washington, DC, available at: https://bit.ly/4crXHiH (accessed on 6 August 2022).

Taylor, M. (2016), 'Risky ventures: Financial inclusion, risk management and the uncertain rise of index-based insurance, research in political economy', in S. Soederberg (ed.), *Risking Capitalism*, 31 (Bingley: Emerald Publishing), 237–266.

Tok, Y. W. and Heng, D. (2022), 'Fintech: Financial Inclusion or Exclusion?', IMF Working Paper, WP/22/80, available at: https://bit.ly/4cxnjK (accessed on 14 June 2022).

UFA (2020), 'UFA2020 Overview: Universal Financial Access by 2020', available at: https://bit.ly/4a92CTZ (accessed on 1 July 022).

United Nations (2019), *Inter-agency Task Force on Financing for Development, Financing for Sustainable Development Report 2019*, New York: United Nations, available at: https://developmentfinance.un.org/fsdr2019 (accessed on 3 July 2022).

Van Rooij, M. C. J., Lusardi, A., and Alessie, R. J. M. (2011), 'Financial literacy and retirement planning in the Netherlands', *Journal of Economic Psychology*, 32, 593–608.

Wisniewski, T. P., Polasik, M., Kotkowski, R., and Moro, A. (2021), 'Switching from cash to cashless payments during the COVID-19 pandemic and beyond', NBP Working Paper No. 337.

World Bank (2015), 'Digital financial inclusion', available at: https://bit.ly/3PBuIz9 (accessed on 7 August 2022).

World Bank (2016), 'Payment aspects of financial inclusion', Committee on Payments and Market Infrastructures World Bank Group, available at: https://bit.ly/3PABu89 (accessed on 9 August 2022).

World Bank (2018a), 'Financial Inclusion Overview' (Washington, DC: World Bank), available at: www.worldbank.org/en/topic/financialinclusion/overview#1.

World Bank (2018b), 'Developing and Operationalizing a National Financial Inclusion Strategy: Toolkit' (Washington, DC: World Bank), available at: https://openknowledge .worldbank.org/handle/10986/29953 (accessed on 5 October 2022).

World Bank (2022), 'Digital financial inclusion' (Washington, DC: World Bank), available at: https://bit.ly/3PBuIz9 (accessed on 25 August 2022).

Xiao, J. J., Chen, C., and Chen, F. (2014), 'Consumer financial capability and financial satisfaction', *Social Indicators Research*, 118(1), 415–432, https://doi.org/10.1007/s11205-013-0414-8.

Zamora-Pérez, A. (2021), 'The paradox of banknotes: Understanding the demand for cash beyond transactional use', *Economic Bulletin Articles*, European Central Bank, 2, available at: https://bit.ly/3vgNrcx (accessed on 10 August 2022).

29

Sustainable Finance and Fintech

A *Focus on Capital Raising*

Eugenia Macchiavello[1]

29.1 GREEN FINTECH AND SUSTAINABLE DIGITAL FINANCE AS A NEW FIELD OF STUDY: OPPORTUNITIES AND RISKS IN MATCHING DIGITAL FINANCE AND SUSTAINABLE FINANCE, WITH A SPECIAL FOCUS ON CAPITAL RAISING

Both the 'Financing Sustainable Growth' Action Plan[2] and the 'Fintech' Action plan[3] were adopted by the Commission on 8 March 2018, in connection with the broader Capital Markets Action Plan.[4] Nonetheless, the two policy areas have been developing separately for years despite the critical relevance attributed to both digital finance and sustainable finance in the EU policy agenda. Only recently, the EU has showed increased interest in exploring and taking advantage of the opportunities that technology, and digital finance in particular, can offer to promote sustainable development and the synergies between the two.[5]

Well before 2018, international organisations had developed programmes and studies to enlist digital finance as well in promoting sustainable development and filling the existing funding gap and market failures in sustainable finance.[6] For instance, in September 2016 the United Nation Environmental Programme (UNEP) and the technology company ANT Financial services founded the Sustainable Digital Finance Alliance (SDFA) 'to leverage digital technologies & innovations to enhance financing for sustainable development'.[7] In November 2018 the Task Force

---

[1] This chapter represents a continuation and more in-depth analysis of the research conducted for the following background paper: Macchiavello and Siri 2022.
[2] European Commission 2018a.
[3] European Commission 2018b.
[4] European Commission 2015 and subsequent updates.
[5] See, for instance: Von de Leyen 2019; HLFCMU 2020, 6.
[6] ADB 2018 (referring in particular to the potential of mobile payment and peer-to-peer transfer networks, branchless banking, big data and AI in substituting credit bureaus); AFI 2018; UNSGSA, FinTech Working Group and CCAF 2019, 10ff; G20 2018; SDFA 2018; Zadek and Kharas 2018; UNEP 2016; UNTFDFSDG 2019, 28; UNTFDFSDG 2020; Dikau et al. 2022.
[7] See www.sustainabledigitalfinance.org/about-sdfa.

on Digital Financing of the Sustainable Development Goals was established by
the UN Secretary-General as part of the broader Roadmap for Financing the 2030
Agenda for Sustainable Development (2019–2021). The main mandate of the Task
Force is to 'recommend and catalyse ways to harness digitalisation in accelerating
financing of the SDGs'.[8] Moreover, the G20 Sustainable Finance Working Group,
created in 2016, received in 2018, under the Argentinian presidency, the mandate to
explore 'the potential applications of digital technologies to sustainable finance'.[9]

Also, public initiatives at the national level in the area of sustainable finance are
flourishing and encourage Fintech solutions for the green transition, such as the UK
Green Fintech challenge,[10] the Swiss Green Fintech Network[11] and the G20-Banca
d'Italia Techsprint.[12]

The academic literature has also showed a particular interest in 'green Fintech'
and 'Sustainable digital finance'. These two expressions are not often defined, or
not officially anyway. We might refer by 'green Fintech' or 'environmentally sustainable digital finance' to the use of technological innovations in the area of financial services (Fintech)[13] to support environmentally sustainable finance, facilitating
the channelling of funds to environmentally sustainable businesses or at least solving shortcomings evidenced in the sustainable finance sector, such as the lack of
high-quality sustainability data.[14] With the expression 'sustainable digital finance'
or 'sustainable Fintech', the reference is to the Sustainable Development Goals
going beyond the environment, therefore including economic and social sustainability.[15] A part of the literature has focussed on the opportunities offered by Fintech

---

[8] UNTFDFSDG 2020, 1.

[9] G20 2018; Zadek and Kharas 2018, 8ff. About international initiatives in this area, see Dell'Erba 2021, 67ff.

[10] See www.fca.org.uk/firms/innovation/green-fintech-challenge.

[11] See https://bit.ly/3VySorD.

[12] See https://bit.ly/3vo4glN.

[13] Fintech is commonly defined as 'technology-enabled innovation in financial services that could
     result in new business models, applications, processes or products with an associated material
     effect on the provision of financial services': FSB 2017, 7. More recently, the term 'digital finance'
     appears to be prevailing and it is 'used to describe the impact of new technologies on the financial
     services industry. It includes a variety of products, applications, processes and business models
     that have transformed the traditional way of providing banking and financial services': European
     Commission 2022b.

[14] See for a first analysis from a legal point of view, Macchiavello and Siri 2022.

[15] One of the first definitions of sustainable digital finance was provided by the ADB (Merrill et al.
     2018, 9): 'Sustainable Digital Finance refers to financing, as well as related institutional and mar-
     ket arrangements, that leverage technological ecosystems – including mobile payments platforms,
     crowd-funding, peer-to-peer lending, finance-related big data, artificial intelligence, machine learn-
     ing, blockchain, digital tokens, and the internet of things – to contribute to the attainment of strong,
     sustainable, balanced and inclusive growth, by directly and indirectly supporting the targets set in the
     Sustainable Development Goals'. The World Economic Forum defines Sustainable Digital Finance
     through two separate definitions of its components: 'Digital finance refers to the integration of big
     data, artificial intelligence (AI), mobile platforms, blockchain and the Internet of things (IoT) in the
     provision of financial services. Sustainable finance refers to financial services integrating environmen-
     tal, social and governance (ESG) criteria into the business or investment decisions. When combined,

to expand financial access and social/financial inclusion, therefore on the social dimension of the phenomenon.[16] Nonetheless, the urgency of solving several environmental issues (first of all climate change), the recent energy crisis and the EU choice to start focussing within its sustainable growth policies on environmental issues have moved the attention to the 'green' sector.[17]

The use of technology in the sustainable finance sector is perceived as beneficial for its potential to convey financial resources at lower cost, overcoming some typical obstacles to sustainable businesses as well as extensive, accurate and relevant data at a low price and at a fast pace, thus reducing investors' research and monitoring costs and improving the pricing of environmental risks and opportunities. In fact, the areas attracting the greatest attention in this intersection between digital finance and sustainable finance are: crowdfunding, Distributed Ledger Technology (DLT)–based offerings and other technologies to foster the financing of sustainable businesses; use of big data, artificial intelligence, machine learning, cloud computing, blockchain and the Internet of Things (IoT) to improve companies' reporting and sustainability assessment, pricing as well as investment process; Regtech and Suptech to facilitate compliance with sustainable finance regulation and relative supervision; and mobile payments, Open banking APIs, robo-advice and other Fintechs able to make financial services more accessible.[18]

Nonetheless, sustainable digital finance obviously also presents several risks, which are relevant from a financial regulation point of view (in terms of stability, client protection, etc.) and also from a sustainability perspective.

---

sustainable digital finance can take advantage of emerging technologies to analyse data, power investment decisions and grow jobs in sectors supporting a transition to a low-carbon economy' (see https://bit.ly/4ctsvzD. SDFA 2018, 12, specifies: 'While there is yet to be a common definition, [...] sustainable digital finance may be understood as an intended application of digital finance towards financing as well as supporting the related institutional and market arrangements that contribute to the achievement of sustainable development.'

[16] For instance in the legal area: Macchiavello 2018 (including, in particular, a chapter about financial regulation, Fintech and financial inclusion and one of the first peer-to-peer lending platforms with social orientation: Kiva); Arner et al. 2018; Chiu and Greene 2018 (advancing proposals to scale up the marketisation of sustainable and social finance, by building on insights derived from ICO markets); Chiu and Greene 2019, 139 (proposing the use of dual-class tokens to advance sustainable investing); Arner et al. 2020; Lin and Tjio 2020, 1; Alexander and Karametaxas 2021; Arner et al. 2022. See also, in the finance area, Fullwiler 2017, 21.

[17] See Macchiavello and Siri 2022 (preceded by the same authors' 2020 EBI Working paper); Dell'Erba 2021, 61–81; only more recently, Zetzsche and Anker-Sørensen 2022a. From an economic perspective: Dorfleitner and Braun 2019; Puschmann et al. 2020, 10691; Nassiry 2019; Herberger and Dötsch 2021; Al Hammadi and Nobanee 2019; Chueca Vergara and Ferruz Agudo 2021; Moro Visconti et al. 2020; Chen and Volz 2022; Nasir et al. 2021; Puschmann and Leifer 2020; Zhang-Zhang et al. 2020.

[18] See Macchiavello and Siri 2022; Arner et al. 2020; G20 2018, 10; UNEP 2018, 4; SDFA 2018, 6ff; Dikau et al. 2022. See also the work of Financial Centers for Sustainability (FC4S) in collaboration with Stockholm Green Digital Finance ('Sustainable Finance and Fintech in Europe'), with the rich database accessible at the following link: https://bit.ly/3xb1NM2.

In particular, starting from the latter perspective, technologies present a high level of energy consumption, especially in the case of DLT systems working with a Proof of Work method and data centres, thereby reducing the potential advantages for the environment.[19] Also, the production of the necessary hardware and software involves the use of a considerable amount of energy (mostly non-renewable) and the (environmentally risky) extraction of raw materials (e.g. lithium), while the disposal of the same is similarly complex and problematic.[20] While right now this might represent a serious obstacle to the deployment of existing major blockchain technologies in the green investment sector, there are also positive signals for the future. In fact, several blockchains have been moving to alternative and less energy-consuming forms of consensus method (e.g. Proof-of-Stake for Ethereum, and see also Federated Byzantine Agreement) or structures (again, permissioned, private or federated blockchains), which should also reduce both the time lapse between transaction validations and operational risk. Moreover, improving the energy efficiency of technologies is among the current priorities in EU policy[21] and the fast evolution of technology should contribute to reaching the goal.

Furthermore, green Fintech might have a negative sustainability impact from the social perspective. For instance, it might reduce the number of jobs for certain categories of workers (e.g. low-skilled ones)[22] or lead to the financial exclusion of certain categories of clients (e.g. the elderly) as a consequence of their lack of experience and skills, and limited access to the technologies necessary for using financial services, and the related reduction in the number of financial institution branches.

Other and related issues refer to the more traditional goals of financial regulation. In fact, the widespread adoption of digital finance and certain technologies creates new stability risks. Furthermore, relevant client protection issues might arise; for instance, digital finance creates new opportunities for frauds and cyber-security and data protection threats. Moreover, financial exclusion or clients' discrimination might also result from performing creditworthiness analyses, insurance underwriting or other evaluations (including sustainability ones) based on opaque algorithms that are 'discriminatory' by design (e.g. incorporating common biases towards certain ethnic minorities or gender-based) or by effect (excluding the ones having the riskiest characteristics).[23] Consequently, each sustainable digital finance (actual or potential) application should be carefully examined for its benefits, risks and legal implications.

---

[19] Fuessler 2018, 83–84; Neves and Prata 2018, 36ff; OECD 2020, 16.
[20] The current environmental footprint of the ICT sector seems to account for more than 2% of all global emissions: European Commission 2020a, 2. See also SDFA 2018, 47; Vinuesa et al. 2020.
[21] See European Commission 2020a, 10.
[22] SDFA 2018, 46–47; Vinuesa et al. 2020, 3.
[23] UNTFDFSDG 2019, 28.

The objective of this chapter is therefore to conduct such an assessment by starting to focus on capital raising within sustainable digital finance applications; in fact, exploring new opportunities for financing sustainable businesses represents a particularly urgent topic, given the pandemic's impact, the recent energy crisis and consequent credit crunch, as well as the worsening climate change problems.

Sustainable SMEs, in particular, might find it difficult to access financing because of the time- and resource-consuming ESG process, entailing the involvement of experts, dedicated personnel, ESG rating, etc. Moreover, renewable energy ventures or similar innovative green projects require substantial initial investments, not easily accessible to young companies without a significant track record or collateral. Technology therefore represents an opportunity to reduce costs and make sustainable finance more accessible to SMEs. On the other hand, technology itself remains so far hardly accessible to SMEs in several countries.

In the next sections, instruments developed in the area of Fintech/digital finance for capital raising will be analysed and discussed for their application in the area of sustainable finance, with particular regard to SMEs.[24]

29.2 'GREEN CROWDFUNDING'

29.2.1 *Crowdfunding and Sustainable Businesses: Opportunities, Characteristics and Examples*

29.2.1.1 Sustainability of Crowdfunding

Crowdfunding allows individuals or enterprises to receive many small sums from other users (the 'crowd') in the form of donations (donation-based crowdfunding), various forms of non-financial rewards (e.g. credits at the end of a movie/ documentary, right to private/pre-sales, etc.: reward-based crowdfunding),[25] loans (lending-based crowdfunding – LBC – or marketplace lending) or equity investments (equity-based crowdfunding – EBC) and/or, more generally, other forms of investments (investment-based crowdfunding – IBC – or marketplace investing; for

---

[24] Lending, even when provided by traditional banks and lenders, might fall within the digital sustainable finance category when deploying technologies to provide sustainable finance services more efficiently (e.g. better pricing and risk weighting): for instance, Rabobank monitors the sustainability indicators of companies requesting financing, consequently adjusting their cost of capital; ING Real Estate Finance offers loans at a lower price to its real-estate borrowers which adopt energy improvement measures for their buildings (see G20 2018, 68; SDFA 2018, 22). Nonetheless, this chapter will only focus on Fintech solutions narrowly considered (by start-ups and new entrants, not by incumbents) to limit its research scope and, consequently, its length.

[25] For references on donation-based crowdfunding and for an analysis of the legal issues and regulatory trends in Europe, see Macchiavello and Valenti 2022.

example, profit-sharing investment contracts), through an online platform facilitating the operation.[26]

The main advantage of crowdfunding consists in allowing the transfer of resources at lower costs and in short time thanks to the use of technology and the elimination of the long chain of traditional financial intermediaries (such as underwriters and banks). In particular, equity crowdfunding is expected to allow start-up and seed firms to meet their financing needs right after the 'family, friends and fools' stage and opening the door to future venture capital funds and private equity funds' financing rounds, while lending-based crowdfunding allows micro and young SMEs to fill a short-term funding and debt securities financing gap, reducing their dependence on banks' loans or other expensive financing (overdraft, credit cards, etc.).[27] At the same time, crowdfunding seems to offer investors the opportunity of diversification and investment in an alternative segment (therefore, more resilient).[28]

We generally use the term 'Green crowdfunding' to identify crowdfunding aimed at financing projects combating climate change or mitigating its effects in line with the objectives of the Paris Accord, as well as reaching other positive environmental goals in the area of land use, material flow and energy use.[29] The majority of these green projects presented on crowdfunding platforms pertain to solar energy, then wind mills and, to a lesser extent, biomass plants and hybrid plants (i.e. combining two or more different technologies).[30]

Green crowdfunding represents a sub-category of the more general 'sustainable crowdfunding', which refers to crowdfunding supporting sustainable development (as identified through the 17 UN Sustainable Development Goals) and therefore encompassing, in addition to the environmental dimension, also the economic (adequate level of income and GDP growth) and social (e.g. social justice and social inclusion, including adequate education, health, equality, etc.) ones.[31] This topic has attracted growing attention in literature.[32]

As mentioned in Section 29.1, the funding gap is more serious for innovative sustainable ventures because of the risk of becoming quickly obsolete and the complexity of projects from a technical point of view. For instance, renewable energy

[26] Also for further references, please refer to: Macchiavello 2015; Macchiavello 2018; Macchiavello 2021a; Macchiavello 2021c; Ferrarini and Macchiavello 2017; Ferrarini and Macchiavello 2018.

[27] See European Commission 2018c, 6, 13ff; Pierrakis and Collins 2013, 5–6; Jagtiani and Lemieux 2018, 43; De Roure et al. 2019. See also Macchiavello 2021b.

[28] For an overview of the benefits of crowdfunding and literature, please see Macchiavello 2021b, 29ff; Macchiavello 2022b, 6ff.

[29] See Maehle et al. 2020, 393–422, 397.

[30] In the respective following percentages: 56.7%, 21.0%, 5.2%: Adhami et al. 2017, 12 (covering 423 crowdfunding campaigns in the renewable energy sector, published on 27 European crowdfunding portals specialised in 'green' projects from 2011 to 2017).

[31] See again Maehle et al. 2020, 396. Lehner focusses on crowdfunding for social ventures, i.e. 'all kind of ventures that have a social or environmental mission as primary goal, which aim to be financially and legally independent and strive to become self-sustainable by means of the market': Lehner 2017, 140.

[32] See the bibliometric analysis in Martínez-Climent et al. 2019.

ventures are risky also for venture capitalists because of their capital-intensive nature, long development process and unproven technologies that might meanwhile be unexpectedly overcome, coupled with high regulatory risks deriving from changing public policies in the area of energy production.[33] The complexity of the science behind renewable energy makes the projects difficult to understand, especially for retail investors, who might fear that the double bottom line entails less profit and in any case feel less engaged with climate change problems because of its spatial and geographical distance. All this entails a higher level of information asymmetry and is therefore an issue in terms of perceived legitimacy and risk[34] to which crowdfunding can respond through community involvement, increased public support, local awareness and legitimacy of green projects.[35]

Given its ability to expand the access to funding of individuals and enterprises otherwise not served by traditional finance, crowdfunding might be regarded as socially sustainable per se, promoting financial inclusion. Furthermore, crowdfunding seems to facilitate the creation of a community around projects, attracting investors interested not necessarily or not only in receiving a financial return but also in satisfying their desire to freely choose where to invest[36] and to contribute to a project they believe in.[37]

Nonetheless, the concrete financial inclusion effect of crowdfunding is highly debated: for instance, some studies regard equity crowdfunding as conducive to a more democratic distribution of funding, compared to IPOs, across minorities, geographies and genders[38] but this view is not unanimous in literature.[39] Lending-based crowdfunding tends to provide financing to the financially excluded or banks' underserved clients,[40] but variations exist among countries.[41]

---

[33] Chiang 2015, 674. See also Alonso et al. 2017, 18–20 (about technical and administrative barriers to prosumers and small projects in the renewable energy area, negatively affecting investors' trust and interest in investing).

[34] On the obstacles to get funding for eco-innovation companies, see OECD 2011; OECD 2012. As regards obstacles to sustainable entrepreneurship and relevant literature: Maehle et al. 2020, 404; Lehner 2017, 140ff.

[35] See Cumming et al. 2017, 292–303 (on cleantech, e.g. green energy, renewable energy, recycling, wind power, solar power, biomass, hydro-electric, photovoltaic, geothermic, biofuel, green transport, gray water and electric motors); Adhami et al. 2017, 3, 7ff; Lehner 2017, 143; Wehnert et al. 2019, 130 (crowdfunding can positively signal a product but only in case of simple products or longer explanations); Messeni Petruzzelli et al. 2019; see also Wehnert and Beckmann 2021, 2; Böckel et al. 2021, 437; Maehle et al. 2021, 2.

[36] Siemroth and Hornuf 2021.

[37] See Vismara 2016; Cumming et al. 2019.

[38] Schwartz 2020.

[39] See Cumming et al. 2019 (rejecting the hypothesis that equity crowdfunding increases female entrepreneurs' opportunities).

[40] E.g. Jagtiani and Lemieux 2018, 43; Jagtiani et al. 2019; De Roure et al. 2019 (in German consumer credit market, P2P lenders target riskier borrowers, with the risk-adjusted interest rates lower than those offered by banks).

[41] Unbanked or underbanked borrowers represent the majority of alternative finance platforms in certain European countries (Balkans, Eastern Europe, Commonwealth of Independent States region, Georgia, Ireland): see Ziegler et al. 2021, 87.

Therefore, it cannot be assumed that crowdfunding is socially sustainable per se: crowdfunding platforms should demonstrate their sustainability, based on the usual international standards (e.g. number of clients within typically excluded people like unbanked, women, etc.).

In any case, if platforms also target environmentally sustainable businesses, it can also qualify as promoting environmentally sustainable finance, channelling resources to environmentally sustainable enterprises and responding to investors' interest in sustainable finance.[42] The importance of building a community around projects in crowdfunding is attested by several case studies, where most investors belonged to the same local communities and were interested in supporting, for instance, solar energy for businesses and families in certain counties.[43]

29.2.1.2 Crowdfunding Investors and Preferences for Sustainable Investments

The literature has started studying the influence of sustainability issues on crowdfunding campaigns with mixed results, especially as regards reward-based crowdfunding: some studies attest that campaigns with a sustainability orientation are more likely to get funding,[44] while others report that sustainability issues do not affect the success of a crowdfunding campaign or even present a negative correlation.[45] Studies focussing on lending-based or equity crowdfunding similarly convey mixed results.[46] However, a study seems to partially reconcile these results, attesting that, in equity crowdfunding, while sustainability per se does not increase the chances of success of equity offerings, it does attract more investors within the category of 'restricted' investors (e.g. retail/unsophisticated), instead of professional

---

[42] Adhami et al. 2017.

[43] See the Saint-Varentais Wind Park (crowdfunding platform *Lumo*) where the first round of financing was reserved to the residents of the county where the wind farm was going to be installed and of which 81% of the business flow could be traced to coupons assigned during a local fair (local marketing): Harder 2018, 19. On the scientific side, Adhami et al. 2017, 4.

[44] Calic and Mosakowski 2016 (positive for moderate emphasis and negative for high emphasis on pro-sustainable orientation); Hörisch 2018; Hsieh et al. 2019.

[45] Hörisch 2015; Motylska-Kuzma 2018; Laurell et al. 2019; Testa et al. 2019. Others differentiate between moderate and high emphasis on sustainable orientation, recognising a positive effect on the reward-based crowdfunding campaign success only in the first case: Defazio et al. 2021 (attesting a positive relation between pro-sustainable orientation and crowdfunding success only for moderate emphasis on pro-sustainable orientation, while negative for high emphasis); von Selasinsky and Lutz 2021; Corsini and Frey 2021 (generic 'sustainability' claims can negatively affect a campaign). See also Roma et al. 2021.

[46] Evidencing a positive correlation: Allison et al. 2015; Vasileiadou et al. 2016; Bento et al. 2019; Adhami et al. 2017, 4, 29 (especially in case of benefits to local communities, quality of local public services, larger local pollution, incidence of green energy production). Instead, linking sustainability orientation to a lower level of investor support: Hossain and Oparaocha 2017 (since additional social or environmental aims might be perceived by investors as corresponding to higher risks and uncertainties, resulting less attractive); Xiang et al. 2019.

ones (which remain motivated mainly by a financial-return logic).[47] Such results are confirmed by another study, which evidences that a significant portion of retail investors are willing to accept a lower return as long as there is a sufficiently large environmental impact and, to a lesser degree, a positive social impact.[48] Moreover, crowd investors attaching a larger importance to positive environmental impact (in addition to investors with a belief that green projects are more profitable) make up a significantly larger share of investments in green projects, pledging larger amounts and investing in more campaigns.[49]

29.2.1.3 Examples of Green Crowdfunding Platforms

The European Commission has funded the project CrowdFundRES aimed at studying crowdfunding for renewable energy[50] projects and developing guidelines for investors, entrepreneurs and policy makers.[51]

In fact the market already offers several crowdfunding platforms specialised in facilitating impactful investments in sustainable initiatives,[52] and these and more platforms are expected to flourish because of the recent institutional attention to sustainable finance in Europe.[53] Other platforms are not specialised in sustainable investments but allow investors to select 'green' projects through filters or dedicated sections.[54] Also, there are aggregators to identify platforms or, more directly,

---

[47] Vismara 2019. On this topic, see also Messeni Petruzzelli et al. 2019 and the literature review by Wehnert and Beckmann 2021, 8. On different categories of investors in equity crowdfunding and relative motivations, see Feola et al. 2021.

[48] Siemroth and Hornuf 2021 (the motivation to invest in green projects appears to be more consistent with a desire to achieve environmental impact rather than with social preferences). See also Mansouri and Momtaz 2022 (observing, in token-based crowdfunding offerings, a valuation premium for ESG-oriented projects, with investors willing to accept some financial losses in case of a sustainability orientation).

[49] Hornuf et al. 2022 (sustainability-oriented investors care are proved to care about non-financial returns by reacting more negatively when experiencing a default in their portfolio, since this indicates that they suffer beyond the pure financial loss).

[50] According to Article 2(1) Directive (EU) 2018/2001 on the promotion of the use of energy from renewable sources [2018] L 328/82, 'renewable energy' means 'energy from renewable non-fossil sources, namely wind, solar (solar thermal and solar photovoltaic) and geothermal energy, ambient energy, tide, wave and other ocean energy, hydropower, biomass, landfill gas, sewage treatment plant gas, and biogas'.

[51] See www.crowdfundres.eu/ and Harder and van Maaren 2016, 7, 29–30. The types of clean energy covered are: photovoltaic (PV), wind, biomass, combined heat and power (CHP), LED lighting, thermal heating and others. See also UNTFDFSDG 2020, 30.

[52] See Adhami et al. 2017; Bonzanini et al. 2016; Dorfleitner and Braun 2019, 217; G20 2018, 34, 63; SDFA 2018, 31. About sustainable crowdfunding, see also Messeni Petruzzelli et al. 2019, 138.

[53] About the correlation between regulatory policies and growth of crowdfunding platforms specialised in sustainable businesses, see Messeni Petruzzelli et al. 2019. Partially *contra*: Butticè 2019 (the probability of launching a green crowdfunding campaign is lower in countries where institutions have a stronger sustainability orientation since already traditional financing means are available).

[54] See Adhami et al. 2017, 12.

projects focussing, for instance, on green energy.[55] The large majority of 'green' campaigns are debt-based.[56]

As examples, the platform *Abundance* allows crowd investors (retail and professional) to invest even in long-term, tradeable but unlisted corporate debentures (without collateral) of public limited companies for renewable energy projects generating and selling low-carbon electricity.[57] In the case of retail investors, it focusses on companies with a track record of successful development (not start-ups).[58] It has also set up a 'marketplace' (bulletin board) where users can advertise their buying and selling interests pertaining to financial instruments previously issued on the platform.[59]

In France, *Lendosphere*[60] and *Lumo*[61] facilitate, respectively, loans and debt securities from individuals to businesses in the renewable energy sector. In particular, *Lumo* offers to crowd investors the opportunity to co-invest with professional investors (e.g. banks) through project finance senior bonds of certain companies (SA and SAS), although project finance junior bonds, corporate junior or senior bonds might also be offered depending on the entrepreneur.[62] While *Lumo* leaves most of the due diligence process on projects to partners (professional investors), it conducts a social screening, focussing on creating a community around the projects and acceptance of the same by local authorities and residents.[63]

Oneplanetcrowd, based in the Netherlands, channels funds in the form of subordinated loans and convertible loans to companies which are both financially viable and sustainable from an environmental and social point of view. It uses indicators to measure the contribution to each company to at least one SDG and requires

[55] For instance, *Green map* allows to identify projects based on certain 'icons' (preset group around a keyword), for instance 'crowdfunding platforms for community energy projects' (see https://bit.ly/4cuVOSo). Similarly, *Startups wallet* allows registered users to search for different categories of projects through tags (including 'sustainability': https://bit.ly/4czoidB), then redirecting to the relative platform. *Citizenenergy* is a platform funded by the EU and provides information on sustainable energy opportunities from both crowdfunding platforms and cooperatives, to encourage cross-border investment in sustainable energy: https://citizenergy.eu/story. A list of platforms covered can be found here: https://citizenergy.eu/featured_platform. *Crowdspace* lists 43 crowdfunding platforms, of which 29 were classified as lending-based, 20 as equity-based (some platforms offering both types) and only 2 as mini-bonds: https://bit.ly/4arKbKe.

[56] Adhami et al. 2017., 13; Hörisch 2019.

[57] In total, 52% of projects focus on solar technology, 28% on wind technology, 4% on hydro technology and 16% on biomass technology: Maehle et al. 2021, 408.

[58] See www.abundanceinvestment.com/. See also Nigam et al. 2018; Harder and van Maaren 2016, 35ff.

[59] However, the transaction shall be concluded outside the platform to avoid the risk of classification of the bulletin board as MiFID trading venue (MTF in particular) and therefore the sanction for the lack of authorisation and regulation as such. See also Harder and van Maaren 2016, 8. On the compatibility of crowdfunding bulletin boards with MiFID II, see Macchiavello 2021c, 573; Hakvoort 2021; Gargantini 2022.

[60] See www.lendosphere.com/.

[61] See www.lumo-france.com/qui-sommes-nous.

[62] Harder and Van Maaren 2016, 29.

[63] Ibid., 7, 29–30.

companies to insert a 'inclusiveness clause' aimed at having, for instance, women as 30% of board members, with periodic updates.[64]

Bettervest, in Germany, provides funding through the crowd in the form of subordinated loans to enterprises operating in the area of renewable and energy efficient projects (e.g. improving energy efficiency or in the production of renewable energy). It requires post funding disclosure with monitoring of technical and financial implementation and co-financing from borrowers.[65] *Green Rocket* is a crowdfunding platform operating in Germany and Austria and facilitating investments in and loans to companies presenting projects with a positive impact on the environment or society (mainly in the environment, mobility, health and digitalisation sectors), selected through a property ESG process.[66]

In Italy, *Ecomill* channels online equity investments to projects characterised by low emissions, low environmental impact and local renovation (energy transition and sustainability).[67] Again in Italy, *Ener2crowd*, facilitates instead the provision of loans to projects focussing on energy efficiency, renewable energy and environmental sustainability.[68]

29.2.2 *Risks and Legal Challenges: The European Crowdfunding Service Providers Regulation and Sustainability*

29.2.2.1 Special Risks of Green Crowdfunding

As mentioned, investing in cleantech[69] and other green technologies can be particularly risky per se, starting with the higher sums involved and the risk of becoming obsolete.[70] Crowdfunding can exacerbate these risks unless special legal protections have been introduced, since in the absence of traditional safeguards (disclosure, conduct duties on financial intermediaries, etc.), crowd lenders and crowd investors are at higher risk of losing the entire capital invested through the platform

---

[64] The platform offers also reward-based crowdfunding outside Dutch borders (including Germany) but not in the segment of renewable energy. See Harder and van Maaren 2016, 12. See www.oneplanetcrowd.com/en. About its approach to sustainability and double bottom line: www.oneplanetcrowd.com/en/s/sustainability.

[65] Hörisch 2019; Harder and Van Maaren 2016, 19–21.

[66] See https://rockets.investments/investing/green. Since 2022, the platforms Green Rocket, Home Rocket and Lion Rocket have been unified under the same Rockets platform (although operating as three different sections).

[67] See www.ecomill.it/.

[68] See https://bit.ly/49apAZB.

[69] The term 'cleantech' is used to refer to 'the use of advanced materials, agriculture and forestry, air and environment, biofuels and biochemicals, biomass generation, conventional fuels, energy efficiency, energy storage, fuel cells and hydrogen, geothermal, hydro and marine power, nuclear, recycling and waste, smart grid, solar, transportation, water and waste water, and wind' (Piroschka Otte and Maehle 2022; see also Cumming et al. 2016, 86).

[70] See Lam et al. 2016; Buttice 2019; Dorfleitner and Braun 2019, 208.

for causes related to either the platform or the particular recipients. Moreover, they face agency and asymmetric information problems since the money at risk belongs only to investors, generally without guarantees from the platform.

Furthermore, promising projects that also meet sustainability criteria might be few in number, raising concentration risk, unless diversification methods exist across a relevant number of projects.

Investments in risky and innovative projects are particularly illiquid. Moreover, clean energy projects, if not already at an advanced stage, might require more than hoped by an investor to start generating revenues. Meanwhile, there are generally no secondary markets for such investments (in particular if they are capital investments).

The technicality of renewable energy and other green projects and of ESG assessments, coupled with low due diligence by platforms,[71] might lead to greenwashing and a lack of adequate information for investors.

In particular, with special reference to sustainability information, there is generally no sanction on entrepreneurs for not realising the promised social or environmental target, which might create an opportunity for greenwashing.[72] Studies attest that, while the measures advertised are commonly implemented, only a minority of crowdfunding campaigns disclose information on their actual contribution to sustainable development in the post funding phase and in any case most do not provide quantitative data (e.g. energy bills showing lower energy consumption). The reasons might lie in the difficulty and costs involved in measuring impact or even in the refusal to show that sustainability targets have not been reached. This is why the authors suggest imposing a duty to disclose these aspects, for instance specifying the improvement of SDGs, using simple quantitative data or at least qualitative data.[73]

Market mechanisms might counterbalance some of these risks: for instance, platforms often present to projects crowd investors that are co-financed by banks or their parent firms to save time and costs, taking advantage of partners' due diligence and to reduce the risks for crowd investors investing in projects at an advanced stage or with an established investor guaranteeing the operation.[74] In addition, they often refer to independent experts to assess the viability of the project and provide advice. Disclosure, even when not mandated, is perceived as particularly important by platforms to reduce asymmetric information and gain investors' trust.[75] Maintaining a

---

[71] Attesting a risk of low due diligence, especially in terms of sustainability: Alonso et al. 2017, 29; Hörisch 2019; Dorfleitner and Braun 2019, 218.

[72] In addition, some studies provide indications to entrepreneurs about the most successful frames in the project descriptions to obtain financing (promotion goal frame, humans-related impact frame, positive valence frame, and near future and now time frame (see Maehle et al. 2021).

[73] Hörisch 2019; Maehle et al. 2021, 406–07; Messeni Petruzzelli et al. 2019.

[74] For instance, Torreilles solar park (involving the German bank SaarLB) and Solease projects (scrutinised by the parent company Start Green Capital) on Oneplatcrowd platform or Thrive Renewable Energy bond on Abundance platform (all described in Harder 2018, 6ff.

[75] Cumming et al. 2017.

good performance, finally, ensures that investors return to that platform and that other investors are attracted, increasing positive network effects.

We cannot then ignore risks for recipients which include concealed high costs and over-indebtedness, unfavourable contractual terms and privacy issues.[76] Other general problems for the system, already mentioned in Section 29.1, relate to money-laundering, inadequate technical infrastructure and cyber-security.[77]

Member States have provided different responses to the crowdfunding phenom-enon, resulting in regulatory fragmentation and different levels of investor protec-tion.[78] Countries present also relevant differences in renewable energy policies, increasing the complexity for platforms and investors.[79]

29.2.2.2 A Focus on the ECSPR and Related Texts

Against this backdrop, we need to consider the recent adoption of the EU Regulation on European Crowdfunding Services Providers (ECSPs) for Business No. 1503/2020,[80] in addition to the EU Green Deal[81] and several legislative acts within the EU Sustainable Finance Plan.

The ECSPs regulation represents an interesting response to the problem of reg-ulatory fragmentation, creating a harmonised EU regime for both business-lending and investment-based crowdfunding, facilitating cross-border crowdfunding while protecting investors. In fact, crowdfunding platforms have been subject so far to dif-ferent national regimes: for instance, among the 'green' platforms mentioned above, *Abundance* is a MiFID-regulated firm authorised and supervised in the UK by the FCA; *Lumo* was authorised and supervised in France by the *AMF* as *conseiller en investissement partificipatif* (CIP) under the (now superseded) special crowdfund-ing regulation, *Oneplanetcrowd*, in the Netherlands, was allowed to intermediate in the provision of loans by consumers to entrepreneurs and organisations based on an individual dispensation from holding a licence as a 'broker in redeemable funds' under section 4:3 Wft (the Dutch Financial Supervision Act), and was also super-vised by the AFM (the Dutch Financial Markets Authority); the German *Bettervest*

---

[76] European Commission 2014. For further references, see Macchiavello 2018. See also Testa et al. 2020.

[77] See also Harder 2018. The EU has recently adopted a cross-sectoral regime on digital security: Regulation (EU) 2022/2554 of the European Parliament and of the Council on Digital Operational Resilience for the financial sector (DORA) and amending Regulations (EC) No 1060/2009, (EU) No 648/2012, (EU) No 600/2014, (EU) No 909/2014 and (EU) 2016/1011 [2022] OJ L 333/1 (covering also crowdfunding platforms: Art. 2(1), letter s)).

[78] Macchiavello 2018; Ferrarini and Macchiavello 2018.

[79] See Aschenbeck-Florange and Dlouhy 2015.

[80] Regulation (EU) 2020/1503 of the European Parliament and of the Council of 7 October 2020 on European crowdfunding service providers for business, and amending Regulation (EU) 2017/1129 and Directive (EU) 2019/1937, [2020] OJ L 347 1. See Macchiavello 2019; Macchiavello 2021c; Macchiavello 2022a.

[81] European Commission 2019a.

has operated as a commercial broker under §34f GewO and is not subject, therefore, to a MiFID II-derived regime; in Italy, *Ener2crowd* has operated, through the EU PSD2 passport, as an agent of the French payment service institution *Lemonway*, while *Ecomill* was authorised under the special Italian equity crowdfunding regime (now superseded) and supervised by the Italian financial markets authority (Consob).

The ECSPR has introduced a special licence for crowdfunding providers, subject to various types of organisational and conduct requirements. It reserves several investor protection instruments to non-sophisticated investors, a residual new category within the retail investor one, to identify investors without particular investment experience or wealth and therefore deserving more protection.[82] Therefore, the 'entry-knowledge' test (close but different from an appropriateness test), the 'loss-simulation' system, warnings triggered by investments above a certain threshold and the four-day reflection period do not apply to professional and sophisticated investors, thus leaving a more simplified regime in place in this case. This might appear appropriate in the green finance field, where high-net-worth individuals or institutional investors might be interested in investing through an online platform for diversifying risks but not if the price incorporates costs of protections that are useless for them.

Nonetheless, other ECSPR provisions might not work so well in an ESG context, in particular as regards renewable energy. For instance, the maximum cap on the offers in terms of total consideration might frustrate the expectations of certain companies in the renewable energy segment where high initial investments are required. In fact, crowdfunding offers under the ECSPR cannot be above €5 million in total consideration, where the total consideration is calculated with a 'catch-all' method. In fact, not only offers of transferable securities are to taken into account, but also 'admitted instruments for crowdfunding purposes' (i.e. transferable shares of private limited companies not considered transferable securities in a particular country but included in a special list) and loans conducted through crowdfunding platforms by the same project owner (Art. 1(2)(c)(i)).[83] Moreover, any other offer of transferable securities to the public by the same project owner through other means within 12 months, when exempted under the mandatory or 'small offer' exemption of Arts. 1(3) or 3(2) Prospectus regulation (Art. 1(2)(c)(ii) ECSPR) is also included. Therefore, this will impede some of the operations described above and certainly the availability of crowdfunding to green ventures requiring big initial investments. As an example, one of the lessons learnt with the EU CrowdFundRes project for platforms and project developers was to conduct several rounds for the same project

---

[82] The category of non-sophisticated investors has been proposed by the Council, while the original proposal did not even distinguish between professional or retail investors (see Macchiavello 2021c).

[83] The ECSPR does not specify whether the provision refers only to the offers by a project owner on a single platform or to all offers available on the market and, therefore, on any platforms presented by the same project owner. Nonetheless, the large and all-inclusive calculation method as well as rationale (see recital 16) should favour the latter option. See Macchiavello 2022c; Staikouras 2020, 1077.

and present on the platform more projects by the same developer in order to opti-mise the process and offset the expenses (in terms of time and financial resources) faced in running the first campaign through economies of scale: the €5 million cap and the related strict criteria might limit the viability of this option.[84]

Second, bulletin boards can be operated by platforms without obtaining a MiFID/MiFIR licence to manage a regulated trading venue under several condi-tions, including not presenting the typical features of MTF, therefore without being a multi-lateral matching system of demand and offer interest for the conclusion of a contract: therefore, crowd investors interested in selling and buying shares/loans previously subscribed through the same platform will have to conclude the con-tract elsewhere.[85] Such restrictions might significantly limit the level of liquidity of the market, disincentivising investments. Moreover, crowdfunding service providers (CSPs) cannot participate as co-investors to the offers on their platforms: this might impede the alignment of interests among the different parties involved,[86] further reducing the platform's due diligence, and use some models of co-venture previ-ously used.

Furthermore, the restrictions in the ECSPR to the use of SPVs clash with the public–private partnerships structure typically used in the 'green' sector[87] or created to overcome regulatory obstacles in some countries.[88] Some instruments typically used in crowdfunding cleantech ventures in certain countries for regulatory reasons are not covered by the ECSPR. For instance, subordinated loans, used in Germany for renewable energy projects,[89] fall outside the definition of loan covered by the ECSPR.

---

[84] See Harder 2018, 35.
[85] See Hakvoort 2021; Gargantini 2022.
[86] See Macchiavello and Sciarrone Alibrandi 2022; Macchiavello 2021c.
[87] Macchiavello 2021c; Macchiavello 2021b, 42.
[88] See the Torreilles solar park crowdfunded together through the platforms *Lumo* (France) and *Oneplanetcrowd* (the Netherlands) within the EU CrowdFundRes project. The project entailed building a solar power plant in the French village of Torreilles to be used by local farmers. The power company *Amarenco* had already developed the solar park with its own equity but created a partnership with *Lumo* to refinance part of the equity through a crowdfunding campaign (€1 mil-lion of the total €6 million). Therefore, French crowd investors directly bought bonds from the project entity Torreilles Solar Park (the company *Ferme PV6 SAS*) for a total of €680,000, while, for Dutch investors operating through *Oneplanetcrowd*, a SPV had to be created for regulatory rea-sons. Consequently, *Amarenco Crowd SAS* was set up as local entity (with *Lumo* on its board) to which Dutch crowd investors of *Oneplanetcrowd* provided a subordinated loan for €120,000. Then, *Amarenco Crowd SAS* bought bonds for the same amount from *Ferme PV6 SAS* (the same bonds as sold by *Ferme PV6* to French crowd investors through *Lumo*). These 3-year bonds/loans were subordinated to a project finance bank loan of €18 million and had an annual interest rate of 5%. In another case (*Atlantis Resources*, through the UK-based platform *Abundance*), an SPV was cre-ated to avoid preparing a Prospectus, instead required if the (listed) parent company had to be used since the same would have reached, including previous rounds of financing, the maximum €5 mil-lion in 12 months threshold for the exemption. See Harder 2018, 6ff. On SPV and the ECSPR, see Hooghiemstra 2022, 74–85.
[89] Alonso et al. 2017, 22.

Moreover, as mentioned, especially in the innovative green business ventures area, co-investing with business angels and funds can help reduce asymmetric information, but, at the same time, might leave retail investors with 'lemons' if certain conditions are not met, for example disclosure and equal terms. In particular, professional investors might be able to get first pick of the best projects and get preferential terms. The ECSPR does not contain particular provisions in this regard, leaving the corresponding risks unaddressed.

Finally, existing experiences involving tokens related to renewable energy or sustainable behaviours exchanged on a P2P platform might suffer from the difficult interaction between the ECSPR and the uncertain regime for hybrid or security tokens (MiFID II, Prospectus, etc. with possible future adaptations) and utility tokens (MiCAR) (see Section 29.3).

More generally, the ECSPR has so far omitted any reference to sustainability requirements,[90] therefore maintaining a distance from the recent evolution of EU financial regulation: as discussed throughout this book, almost all pillars of financial regulation (MiFID II, IDD, UCITS/AIFM, CRD IV/CRR, etc.)[91] and EU company law (Non-financial Reporting Directive – NFRD)[92] have been recently reviewed or are currently under review to integrate sustainability risks, factors and preferences into corporate reporting and financial intermediaries' organisational and conduct duties. The introduction of similar requirements in the ECSPR (e.g. in terms of disclosure about sustainability risk integration and methodology to select sustainable projects) would probably ensure a level playing field and respect the EU sustainability objectives, but the additional compliance costs involved might discourage proceeding in this direction in order not to overburden the sector and to avoid related negative effects in terms of SMEs' access to finance. In fact, there are grounds for facilitating 'green crowdfunding' platforms. Article 45(2)(s) ECSPR allows the Commission to propose, after the first years of ECSPR application, 'specific measures […] to promote sustainable and innovative crowdfunding projects as well as the use of Union funds'.

Finally, despite reaching a high level of harmonisation, the ECSPR leaves to Member States' discretion in important areas, which might still create obstacles to cross-border activity.[93]

---

[90] On the ECSPR and sustainability, please also refer to Macchiavello 2022b; Macchiavello 2022a, chapter 31; Macchiavello 2022d.

[91] On these reforms, see also, among others, Busch 2020; Busch et al. 2021; Colaert 2021; Zetzsche and Anker-Sørensen 2022b.

[92] Directive No 2014/95/EU […] of 22 October 2014 amending Directive 2013/34/EU as regards disclosure of non-financial and diversity information by certain large undertakings and groups OJ [2014] L 330/1. On 21 April 2021 the Commission advanced a proposal to revise the NFRD in line with the Sustainable Finance Action Plan. The Proposal was adopted in December 2022 as Directive (EU) 2022/2464 […] of 14 December 2022 amending Regulation (EU) No 537/2014, Directive 2004/109/EC, Directive 2006/43/EC and Directive 2013/34/EU, as regards corporate sustainability reporting, [2022] OJ L 322/15 (enlarging to all large companies and listed SMEs – except micro ones – proportionate reporting obligations).

[93] See again Macchiavello 2022d.

29.3 DLT-BASED FINANCE AND SUSTAINABILITY

29.3.1 *DLT-Based Finance Potential*

Other potentially interesting green Fintech applications in the area of capital raising come from the DLT ecosystem,[94] where the use of DLT has allowed the creation of an entire new world of 'decentralised finance' (DeFi).[95] In fact, such technology seems to entail higher efficiency, lower costs and improved transparency and resilience (to cyber-risk and manipulations) in finance.[96]

29.3.2 *Main Applications: Examples*

Through tokens offerings (in the form of Initial Coin Offerings – ICOs – or Initial Tokens Offerings – ITOs – and Security Tokens Offerings – STOs),[97] green businesses can obtain financing at lower costs thanks to the absence of intermediaries and automation of contractual relationships (payments and even reporting), potentially tapping global markets while improving transparency and efficiency.[98]

Nonetheless, the applications of blockchain and tokens in the area of green capital raising and markets are varied. The first experiments have involved the free attribution of a virtual currency as a reward for 'green' shifts in lifestyle:[99] this is the case of *Drop in the Ocean* in Switzerland[100] and *Eco Coin* in the Netherlands,[101] platforms bringing together individuals and businesses and rewarding responsible behaviours with a virtual currency which can be used for buying services or products from partner enterprises. *SolarCoin* presents a more articulated model, rewarding people having installed systems for the production of solar energy with coins (1 *SolarCoin*

---

[94] For definitions and explanations of such concepts see: ESMA 2017; Rauchs et al. 2018; European Commission 2019b.

[95] For an overview on DeFi (and references), please see FSB 2019; Baker and Werbach 2021; Macchiavello 2022e;.

[96] On the advantages of DeFi, among others: ESAs 2022, 33–34; Baker and Werbach 2021, 151ff.

[97] The term 'ICOs' now generally refers to the offering of utility tokens but might be also used in general terms for the offering of any kind of DLT-based tokens, as ITOs. STOs, instead, consist of offerings of security tokens, therefore classified as securities under national law. About the regulatory treatment of these offerings, among many, see OECD 2019; Hacker and Thomale 2018; Chiu 2018; Blandin et al. 2019; Annunziata 2020; Boreiko et al. 2019, 480; Zetzsche et al. 2019, 267.

[98] OECD 2020, 19, 24, 28. In particular, ICOs' costs reach about 3% of total funds raised, compared to 3–5% of total funds for an IPO (for offerings of about USD 1 million), to which additional fees of about 7% must be considered as compensation to underwriters. ICOs' cost, in fact, would only consist of the expenses for setting up the DLT infrastructure and developing the protocol (almost eliminated after the creation of the Ethereum-based ERC20 standard protocol), and in exchange fees (Chiu 2018, 6); nonetheless, such operations often involve hidden costs such as fees for technical and legal support and for other services (pricing indexes, rating, wallet providers) (OECD 2019, 20–22).

[99] See UNEP 2018, 26, 38, 42; Nassiry 2019, 324ff; Merrill et al. 2018, 32; Schletz et al. 2020; Livingston et al. 2018; World Energy Council 2017; Basden and Cottrell 2017; Ahl et al. 2019.

[100] See https://bit.ly/43OCkEx.

[101] See www.ecocoin.com/.

per 1 MWh of verified electricity production), which can be used at participating businesses or exchanged for fiat currency or traded in market exchanges.[102]

More complex systems operate within peer-to-peer (P2P) energy networks based on DLT combined with smart contracts and IoT technologies, allowing prosumers to buy green energy or sell it when in excess at lower and more transparent costs and also to become more aware of their needs and consumption levels.[103] For instance, *NRGcoin* (Belgium), although still at a project stage, aims at creating a blockchain-based green energy network, managed by an energy company, which will sell energy to prosumers only when auto-produced energy is insufficient to satisfy the local demand. Instead, prosumers will obtain and/or sell green energy matching local offer/demand paying in *NRGcoins*, based on smart contracts and the data about produced energy detected through smart meters. Holders of *NRGcoins* will also be able to exchange them for fiat on an open currency exchange market.[104] *WePower* in Lithuania is a blockchain-based green energy trading platform also helping developers of wind or solar energy projects raise capital, in addition to issuing debt securities reserved to professional investors (conducting the due diligence), by selling directly to consumers utility/hybrid tokens. Such tokens, in fact, represent the right to receive clean energy that producers commit to deliver in the future and can also be traded among consumers.[105] *SunContract* in Slovenia allows independent producers and prosumers to sell the green energy – produced within a network – on algorithm-based digital auction (without intermediaries) in exchange for tokens (SNC), convertible in fiat.[106]

Other experiences pertain to other forms of green markets, with bigger scale and scope: *Climatecoin* in Switzerland has created a market in carbon credits represented by tokens, which can be used to compensate for carbo emissions by buying from mitigation projects.[107] The Danish start-up *Agreena* tracks soil cultivation regenerative practices of European farmers and then mints, verifies and sells carbon certificates.[108] In these cases, therefore, virtuous businesses can use such platforms and exchanges to reward their activity through favourable financing. More generally, the DLT-based infrastructure is expected to improve transparency and

[102] See https://solarcoin.org/. See also Andoni et al. 2019, 159.
[103] See Dorfleitner and Braun 2019, 230.
[104] The *NRGCoin* project has been developed by the Artificial Intelligence Lab of the Vrije Universiteit Brussel. For more information: https://nrgcoin.org/about/ and https://nrgcoin.org/faq/; Mihaylov et al. 2016; Mihaylov et al. 2018. See also Thalhammer et al. 2022, 29. Other examples also in Nassiry 2019, 324ff.
[105] See OECD 2020, 29; Thalhammer et al. 2022, 30; Thaker et al. 2022, 292; Lee 2019; Andoni et al. 2019, 158. See also https://ses.jrc.ec.europa.eu/node/31977. The *dominia* previously attributed to *WePower* company (http://wepower.com and https://wepower.network/), as of 9 January 2023, are not working any more.
[106] See https://suncontract.org/. See Dorfleitner and Braun 2019, 230.
[107] *Climatecoin* has been recently acquired by *Climate Trade*, which also allows the investment in sustainable projects: https://climatetrade.com/. See also OECD 2020, 34.
[108] See https://agreena.com/ and https://bit.ly/4a9LHAI.

information asymmetry, tracking, verification, liquidity and interaction between different emissions trading systems (ETSs).[109]

In other cases, the DLT ecosystem, coupled with various forms of artificial intelligence and data, allows the issuance of DLT-based green bonds at lower costs[110] and in a more efficient way, easing the process for the issuance, disclosure and benchmarking in the green bonds market.[111] It also allows investors to receive data on green energy production (e.g. from the same plant, satellites, etc.) and therefore also to check the sustainability performance after the investment in real time, screening documents and maintaining data permanently and accessibly, responding to a frequently highlighted lack of transparency[112] and of data about sustainability performance in this market segment, as well as to the potentially excessive costs involved in the compliance with the recent EU Green Bond standard.[113] The Bank for International Settlements, in co-operation with the Hong Kong Monetary Authority, has developed two prototype platforms for the offering of DLT-based green bonds, accessible also to retail investors and allowing them to continuously track coupon payments, the use of funds and the positive environmental impact.[114]

29.3.3 *Main Risks and Regulatory Issues*

Many risks (of fraud, loss, greenwashing, etc.) of ICOs/ITOs for investors are similar to the ones listed in Section 29.2.2 for crowdfunding, and even higher since, in blockchain-based finance, there is not even a platform screening projects. Tokens are in any case extremely liquid compared to crowdfunded shares or loans.

As regards the use of the DLT and smart contracts, in addition to the environmental concerns (see Section 29.1), public blockchains, especially if based on the Proof of Work for the consensus, still need to prove the scalability and interoperability of the model, as well as the ability to ensure real instant-time operations.[115] Furthermore,

---

[109] OECD 2020, 34; Thalhammer et al. 2022, 28. Also the World Bank has been working on the creation of a global, DLT-based and distributed market of climate-related assets (e.g. emission allowances, credits, renewable energy certificates) able to accommodate data from multiple public or private sources and certify production and operational data against new standards and, therefore, to overcome the existing diversity in monitoring, reporting and verification methodologies and rules: see World Bank 2018; Macinante 2017; Jackson et al. 2018.

[110] HSBC Centre of Sustainable Finance and SDFA 2019, 17 estimate expenses for bond issuance almost 10 times lower with blockchain compared with the standard process (€ 692,000 versus € 6,449,000).

[111] See also, recently, European Commission 2020b, 23. Schletz et al. 2020, 10: the authors indicate Liquid Token Market (https://liquidtoken.net) and Hiveonline (www.hivenetwork.online) as examples of green security tokens offerings (STOs, with tokens representing securities).

[112] Fuessler 2018, 32.

[113] See Regulation (EU) 2023/2631 of the European Parliament and of the Council of 22 November 2023 on European Green Bonds and optional disclosures for bonds marketed as environmentally sustainable and for sustainability-linked bonds OJ [2023] L 2631/1. About digitalisation and green bond, see also Pavlidis 2021.

[114] About project *Genesis*: www.bis.org/press/p211104.htm.

[115] Athanassiou 2018, 162ff; Dorfleitner and Braun 2019, 221. See also Cojoianu et al. 2020.

its decentralised character creates a significant operational risk because of the diffi-culty in ensuring the functioning of the system where no one has exclusive and total control over the same (e.g. core developers need the consent of the 51% of miners to revert a fork or actually to maintain the system updated), many developers are voluntary workers, the governance of the blockchain is not clear (with unclear dis-tribution/concentration of power and responsibility within the same) and errors are immutable.[116] Nonetheless, the type of blockchain often deployed in the sustainable finance sector has been permissioned-based, therefore not presenting the risks men-tioned above but, on the other hand, having lower resilience because of the higher level of centralisation and the recourse to APIs and oracles.[117]

The use of data, algorithms and DLT in the issuance of investment products and assessment of companies would require an in-depth discussion of risks and regu-latory issues, which, already anticipated elsewhere,[118] would require an excessive expansion of this section and will be therefore dealt with in future contributions.

As regards, in particular, crypto-assets, an intense debate has developed around the legal classification and consequent regulatory treatment of them, again with sig-nificant differences in regulatory treatment among Member States and consequent different levels of investor protection and regulatory arbitrage effects.[119] The ESAs have recognised the possibility to treat tokens as e-money or financial instruments – applying the respective rules but highlighting the need to partially adapt the same, especially in case of decentralised/public systems – on a case-by-case basis depending on the particular characteristics of each token and on national interpretations. In the literature, while some authors distinguish between security tokens (sharing fea-tures with financial instruments, such as the right to a share of profits and the right to vote on certain issues, in addition to free transferability), utility tokens (which can be used to claim a service or product from the issuer) and currency tokens (which have a function closer to payment instruments being accepted by others),[120] some others believe that the classification as securities should be recognised for all kind of tokens because of their innate nature to circulate (if not explicitly excluded) on crypto-exchanges and the consequent expected return.[121] Such legal uncertainty is not beneficial for the development of experiences with sustainable finance tokens similar to the ones described above.[122]

---

[116] FSB 2019; ESMA 2016, 14ff; Walch 2015, 837; Zetzsche et al. 2018; ROFIEG 2019, 32.

[117] Rauchs et al. 2018.

[118] Macchiavello and Siri 2022.

[119] See Blandin et al. 2019; ESMA 2019.

[120] Showing different opinions and proposals: Hacker and Thomale 2018; Chiu 2018; Annunziata 2020.

[121] See for instance, Boreiko et al. 2019.

[122] The ESAs have solicited from the Commission the issuance of harmonising interpretations as regards the legal classification of tokens and the harmonised application of related EU law: ESMA 2020; EBA 2020. As requested by Art. 2(5) MiCAR to clarify the scope of application of such Regulation, ESMA issued in January 2024 a consultation on the draft Guidelines on conditions and criteria for the classi-fication of tokens as financial instrument: ESMA 2024.

29.3.4 *The EU Responses: DLT Pilot, MiCAR and Other EU Legislation: Implications for DLT-Based 'Green' Case Studies*

The Commission issued in September 2020, within the 'Digital Finance Package', a Proposal for a Regulation on Markets in Crypto-Assets (MiCAR),[123] which was eventually adopted in May 2023.[124] This Regulation sets forth a special regulatory regime for offerings of tokens with a payment function and a stabilisation mechanism ('e-money tokens' – EMT[125] – and 'asset-referenced tokens' – ART[126] – such as stablecoins) or, in any event, crypto-assets not already classified and regulated under EU law (with the exclusion therefore of financial instruments or deposits or funds),[127] such as utility tokens, 'only intended to provide access to a good or a service supplied by its issuer' (Art. 3(1)(9) MiCAR). The regime is stricter in the case of offerings and issuers of EMTs and ARTs, while the systemic relevance of issuers triggers additional requirements and EBA supervision. In particular, offerings of crypto-assets other than EMT/ART (e.g. utility tokens) will only require issuers or people seeking admission to trading for such crypto-asset to make available a white paper with certain information, and comply with some general conduct duties, unless certain exemptions apply (e.g. tokens assigned for free or for the DLT maintenance, used only within a limited network, to be used for products and services already existing – 'pure utility tokens' –, etc., and, at the same time, there is no intention to seek admission to trading of the crypto-asset).[128] Instead, offerings of EMT and ART will also require issuers to obtain an authorisation (as, respectively, at least bank/e-money institutions or a new special licence) unless exemptions apply (e.g. offerings below €5 million; only to qualified investors) and, especially in case of ART, comply with organisational and prudential requirements (e.g. being a legal entity or having a legal form that similarly protects third parties; own funds, reserve

---

[123] See Proposal for a Regulation [...] on Markets in Crypto-assets, and amending Directive (EU) 2019/1937, COM/2020/593 final.

[124] The Proposal was adopted, with several amendments, as Regulation (EU) 2023/1114 of the European Parliament and of the Council of 31 May 2023 on markets in crypto-assets, and amending Regulations (EU) No 1093/2010 and (EU) No 1095/2010 and Directives 2013/36/EU and (EU) 2019/1937 [2023] OJ L 150/40.

[125] Art. 3(1), No. 7 MiCAR: '"e-money token" means a type of crypto-asset that purports to maintain a stable value by referencing the value of one official currency'.

[126] Art. 3(1), No. 6 MiCAR: '"asset-referenced token" means a type of crypto-asset that is not an electronic money token and that purports to maintain a stable value by referencing another value or right or a combination thereof, including one or more official currencies'.

[127] Article 3(1), No. 5 MiCAR: '"crypto-asset" means a digital representation of a value or of a right that is able to be transferred and stored electronically using distributed ledger technology or similar technology'.

[128] Recital 26 and Article 4(3)-(4) MiCAR. Instead, in case of private (directed only to qualified investors) or small offers (not above €1 million in consideration or directed to no more than 150 people), the issuers/offerors can only omit the preparation and publication of the white paper and notification to the authority of the marketing communications but are subject to the remaining rules of title II (Art. 4(2) MiCAR).

and orderly wind-down). Also, crypto-assets service providers, when dealing with any type of crypto-asset (even if issued in an exempted offering),[129] will be subject to authorisation for corresponding 'traditional financial services' or a new special one, with some requirements differentiated based on the type of service. The regime also includes a ban on insider dealing and market manipulations.

Instead, offerings of security tokens considered as financial instruments and related investment services are subject to existing laws (e.g. MiFID II, PR). However, the 'DLT pilot regime' (Regulation EU/2022/858)[130] has introduced a temporary sandbox for financial market infrastructures for secondary markets pertaining to simple illiquid security tokens (DLT-based equity shares, bonds or shares of collective investment vehicles issued by certain types of companies within certain thresholds). The regime extends to DLT markets and DLT depositaries the same requirements as, respectively, MTFs and CSDs, in addition to special requirements, such as clarity about the functioning and governance of the blockchain and market, adequate IT infrastructures and adequate measures for operational risk. However, it also leaves the option of requesting NCAs, with the ESMA issuing a non-binding opinion to grant exemptions from certain rules of such 'traditional' regimes (e.g. retail access, transaction reporting, finality requirements). Exemptions can be granted if the applicant demonstrates difficulties in applying such rules in their DLT context and subject to the identification of compensatory measures (with minimum requirements pertaining to cyber-risk, AML/CT, safeguarding clients' assets, record-keeping and redress procedures). After this pilot experience, the Commission might propose definitive adaptations of the traditional legal framework to DLT-based finance or extend the duration of the special framework with or without changes or even its elimination.

Such new regimes can affect also the green Fintech applications described in Section 29.3.2. Tokens assigned for free to reward sustainable behaviours and accepted as payment for services/goods might be regarded as utility tokens (only when issued by the same partner enterprises) or other crypto-assets with payment function, but their offerings can be considered exempted under the free-assignment or limited-network exemptions or since concerning already existing services/products (Art. 4(3), letters a), c), d) MiCAR).

Instead, tokens issued in P2P markets for the exchange of green energy and for the presale of green energy might be classified, depending on their specific features, either as utility tokens or as EMT (or even security tokens when the investment

---

[129] In case of cryptoassets issued in an exempted offering, the only crypto-asset services that can be provided without authorisation are the custody and administration services in relation to these exempted offerings. Nonetheless, this does not apply when the same cryptoassets are offered in a separate offering (not exempted) or are subsequently admitted to trading (Art. 4(5) MiCAR).

[130] Regulation (EU) 2022/858 of the European Parliament and of the Council of 30 May 2022 on a pilot regime for market infrastructures based on distributed ledger technology, and amending Regulations (EU) No 600/2014 and (EU) No 909/2014 and Directive 2014/65/EU [2022] OJ L 151/1.

function prevails), making the issuers and intermediaries involved subject to transparency obligations or even authorisation and other requirements. For example, SNC might be classified as utility tokens or crypto-asset with a payment function (other than EMT or ART) but their offerings exempted under, respectively, the 'pure utility tokens' exemption (used to buy already existing products/services) or the limited network exemption; instead, *WePower*'s energy tokens, which are issued and exchanged on the platform and assign a right to receive a certain amount of energy in the future, might qualify as utility tokens covered by MiCAR, giving access to a product not already existing and being tradeable, but might again be exempted under the limited-network exemption. However, all the highlighted exemptions do not operate if such crypto-assets are exchanged/traded on a crypto-exchange; as a consequence, their offerings, custody and administration would become subject to MiCAR. Moreover, as already mentioned, the exemptions pertain to the offering and certain limited services offered by third parties in connection with the same; therefore other crypto-services, such as crypto-markets or other intermediary services (placing, reception and transmission, etc.) remain subject in any case to MiCAR. Moving to another example, the different category of *WPR* tokens, representing the right of the holder to participate in the distribution of energy in the common pool (fed with 0.9% of every token issuance) and to a priority access to the auction sales,[131] might be even regarded by some as DLT financial instrument: for instance, a commodity derivative (if physically settled or traded on MTF), subject to MiFID II (since not included among DLT pilot–admitted instruments). On the other hand, *NRGcoins* can be exchanged on external crypto-exchanges and their value is linked to the energy price, with a speculation risk and similarities not only with utility tokens but also with commodity derivatives; however, they are automatically issued on a decentralised blockchain when green energy is produced, with no issuer identifiable. Offerings of tokens issued on a decentralised public blockchain seem to be excluded from MiCAR (recital 22) but not the services offered in relation to such tokens, while the DLT pilot also allows partially decentralised architecture and governance but covers only simple financial instruments.[132]

In conclusion, several use cases might fall within the scope of EU financial regulation. Nonetheless, such classifications might jeopardise the experimentation in this interesting field,[133] with reasons to exclude green hybrid utility tokens also from MiCAR, unless they are traded outside the network and instruments to speculate on the price of energy. Moreover, in consideration of their main utility functions, consumer protection measures should be improved, such as in terms of service continuity, warranty and consumers' initial (infrastructural) investment/expenses for joining the grid, unless other existing consumer sale/service law applies.

---

[131] See Lee 2019.

[132] See also Macchiavello 2022e, 1075–76, 1081–82.

[133] Supported also by the EU Digitalising the energy system action plan (European Commission 2022a, 10–11).

Finally, tokens incorporating emission allowances could be easily classified as DLT financial instruments subject to MiFID II (not covered by the DLT pilot).

In any case, it cannot be ignored that harmonisation and common conceptualisation about smart contracts and data recorded on the blockchain are still lacking. Therefore, relationships among participants to the above-mentioned energy grids are complicated by the lack of clarity about the legal validity, effects and interpretation of smart contracts and their interaction with off-grid contracts. Equally uncertain remains the distribution of liability among participants and contestability of data when distributed networks, IoT and algorithms are involved, as well as the compatibility of the DLT with GDPR.[134]

29.4 CONCLUSIONS

Sustainable digital finance presents great opportunities to channel funds to sustainable businesses in a more affordable and efficient way. Nonetheless, several risks and legal challenges need to be taken into account before supporting the widespread adoption of certain instruments in sustainable finance. Moreover, although grouped in the capital-raising sub-category, each of the described innovations presents different risks and legal issues, thus deserving a separate discussion.

This chapter represents a first attempt to analyse these instruments and facilitate their future implementation while balancing opportunities and risks and ensuring the correct application of the related legal framework.

REFERENCES

ADB (Asian Development Bank) (2018), 'Harnessing Technology for More Inclusive and Sustainable Finance in Asia and The Pacific', October, available at: http://dx.doi .org/10.22617/TCS189581-2.

Adhami, S., Giudici, G. and Anh, H. P. (2017), 'Crowdfunding for Green Projects in Europe: Success Factors and Effects on the Local Environmental Performance and Wellbeing', available at: https://bit.ly/3TudNjf.

AFI (Alliance for Financial Inclusion) (2018), 'FinTech for Financial Inclusion: A Framework for Digital Financial Transformation', September, available at: https://bit.ly/4avNuzN.

Ahl, A., Yarime, M., Tanaka, K. and Sagawa, D. (2019), 'Review of blockchain-based distributed energy: Implications for institutional development', 107 *Renewable and Sustainable Energy Reviews*, 200.

Al Hammadi, T. and Nobanee, H. (2019), 'FinTech and Sustainability: A Mini-Review', December 9, available at: https://ssrn.com/abstract=3500873.

Alexander, K. and Karametaxas, X. (2021), 'Digital transformation and financial inclusion', in I. H. Y. Chiu and G. Deipenbrock (eds.), *Routledge Handbook of Financial Technology and the Law* (London: Routledge), 273–290.

---

[134] Macchiavello and Siri 2022, 168ff. About the main legal issues surrounding p2p energy grids: Lee and Khan 2020; Chiu and Schneiders 2021, 287ff, 292. About the GDPR and blockchain: Fink 2019; Lyons et al. 2018.

Allison, T. H., Davis, B. C., Short, J. C. and Webb, J. W. (2015), 'Crowdfunding in a prosocial microlending environment: Examining the role of intrinsic versus extrinsic cues', 39(1) *Entrepreneurship Theory Pract*, 53–73.

Alonso, P., Caneva, S., Maidonis, T. et al. (2017), 'Policy recommendations on regulatory and market framework improvements for crowdfunding RES projects', CrowdFundRES, available at: https://bit.ly/3x2eBUL.

Andoni, M., Robu, V., Flynn, D. et al. (2019), 'Blockchain technology in the energy sector: A systematic review of challenges and opportunities', 100 *Renewable and Sustainable Energy Reviews*, 143–174.

Annunziata, F. (2020), 'Speak, if you can: What are you? An alternative approach to the qualification of tokens and initial coin offerings', 17(2) *European Company and Financial Law Review*, 129.

Arner, D. W., Buckley, R. P. and Zetzsche, D. A. (2018), 'Fintech for Financial Inclusion: A Framework for Digital Financial Transformation', UNSW Law Research Paper, September 4, available at: https://ssrn.com/abstract=3245287.

Arner, D. W. Buckley, R. P., Zetzsche, D. A. et al. (2020), 'Sustainability, FinTech and financial inclusion', 21 *European Business Organization Law Review*, 7.

Arner, D. W., Buckley, R., Charamba, K. et al. (2022), 'Governing FinTech 4.0: BigTech, platform finance and sustainable development', 27(1) *Fordham Journal of Corporate & Financial Law*, 1.

Aschenbeck-Florange, T. and Dlouhy, A. (2015), 'Review of Crowdfunding Regulation & Market Developments for RES project financing in the EU – "Unleashing the potential of Crowdfunding for Financing Renewable Energy Projects"', Osborne Clarke Germany, December, available at: https://bit.ly/3vqVD9V.

Athanassiou, P. L. (2018), *Digital Innovation in Financial Services: Legal Challenges and Regulatory Policy Issues* (Alphen aan den Rijn: Kluwer).

Baker, C. and Werbach, K. (2021), 'Blockchain in financial services', in J. Madir (ed.), *Fintech – Law and Regulation* (Cheltenham: Edward Elgar), 148–174.

Basden, J. and Cottrell, M. (2017), 'How utilities are using blockchain to modernize the grid', *Harvard Business Review*, 23 March, available at: https://bit.ly/4a8osXI.

Bento, N., Gianfrate, G. and Groppo, S. V. (2019), 'Do crowdfunding returns reward risk? Evidences from clean-tech projects', 141 *Technological Forecasting and Social Change*, 107.

Blandin, A., Cloots, A. S., Hussain, H. et al. (2019), 'Global Cryptoasset Regulatory Landscape Study', 16 April, available at: https://bit.ly/499NrZI.

Böckel, A., Hörisch, J. and Tenner, I. (2021), 'A systematic literature review of crowdfunding and sustainability: Highlighting what really matters', 71 *Management Review Quarterly*, 433.

Bonzanini, D., Giudici, G. and Patrucco, A. (2016), 'The crowdfunding of renewable energy projects', in V. Ramiah and G. Gregoriou (eds.), *Handbook of Environmental and Sustainable Finance* (London: Academic Press/Elsevier), 429–444.

Boreiko, D., Ferrarini, G. and Giudici, P. (2019), 'Blockchain startups and prospectus regulation', 20 *European Business Organization Law Review*, 665.

Busch, D. (2020), 'Sustainable finance disclosure in the EU financial sector', EBI Working Paper Series 70/2020, July 13, available at: https://ssrn.com/abstract=3650407.

Busch, D., Ferrarini, G. and Grünewald, S. (eds.) (2021), *Sustainable Finance in Europe. Corporate Governance, Financial Stability and Financial Markets* (Cham: Palgrave).

Butticè, V. (2019), 'Green oriented crowdfunding campaigns: Their characteristics and diffusion in different institutional settings', 141 *Technological Forecasting & Social Change*, 85–97.

Calic, G. and Mosakowski, E. (2016), 'Kicking off social entrepreneurship: How a sustainability orientation influences crowdfunding success', 53(5) *Journal of Management Studies*, 738.

Chen, Y. and Volz, U. (2022), 'Scaling up sustainable investment through blockchain-based project bonds', 40 *Development Policy Review*, 12582.

Chiang, A. (2015), 'How entrepreneurs can crowdfund renewable energy projects', 8(2)*Journal of Business, Entrepreneurship and the Law*, 659–697.

Chiu, I. H.-Y. (2018), 'Decoupling tokens from trading: Reaching beyond investment regulation for regulatory policy in initial coin offerings', *International Business Law Journal*, 265.

Chiu, I. H.-Y. and Greene, E. F. (2018), 'Can ICO markets offer insights into marketising sustainable or social finance? Proposals for a revolutionary regulatory framework', November 26, available at: https://ssrn.com/abstract=3290762.

Chiu, I. H.-Y. and Greene, E. F. (2019), 'The marriage of technology, markets and sustainable (and) social finance: Insights from ICO markets for a new regulatory framework', 20 *European Business Organization Law Review*, 139.

Chiu, I. H.-Y. and Schneiders, A. (2021), 'Blockchain technology-Enabled Business Arrangements, in R. M. Barker and I.-H. Chiu (eds.), *The Law and Governance of Decentralised Business Models* (London: Routledge), 271–306.

Chueca Vergara, C. and Ferruz Agudo, L. (2021), 'Fintech and sustainability: Do they affect each other?', 13 *Sustainability*, 7012.

Cojoianu, T., Hoepner, A. G. F., Georgiana, I. et al. (2020), 'Greenwatch-shing: Using AI to detect greenwashing', June 15, available at: https://ssrn.com/abstract=3627157.

Colaert, V. (2021), 'Integrating sustainable finance into the MiFID II and IDD investor protection frameworks', in D. Busch, G. Ferrarini and S. Grünewald (eds.), *Sustainable Finance in Europe. Corporate Governance, Financial Stability and Financial Markets* (Cham: Palgrave Macmillan), 445–475.

Corsini, F. and Frey, M. (2021), 'Exploring the development of environmentally sustainable products through reward-based crowdfunding', *Electronic Commerce Research*, September 2.

Cumming, D. J., Henriques, I. and Sadorsky, P. (2016), '"Cleantech" venture capital around the world', 44 *International Review of Financial Analysis*, 86.

Cumming, D. J., Leboeuf, G. and Schwienbacher, A. (2017), 'Crowdfunding cleantech', 65 *Energy Economics*, 292–303.

Cumming, D. J., Meoli, M. and Vismara, S. (2019), 'Investors' choice between cash and voting rights: Evidence from dual-class equity crowdfunding', 48(8) *Research Policy*, 103740.

De Roure, C., Pelizzon, L. and Thakor, A. V. (2019), 'P2P lenders versus banks: Creak skimming or bottom fishing?', SAFE Working Paper 206, available at: http://hdl.handle.net/10419/203316.

Defazio, D., Franzoni, C. and Rossi-Lamastra, C. (2021), 'How pro-social framing affects the success of crowdfunding projects: The role of emphasis and information crowdedness', 171 *Journal of Business Ethics*, 357–378.

Dell'Erba, M. (2021), 'Sustainable digital finance and the pursuit of environmental sustainability', in D. Busch, G. Ferrarini and S. Grünewald (eds.), *Sustainable Finance in Europe. Corporate Governance, Financial Stability and Financial Markets* (Cham: Palgrave Macmillan), 61–81.

Dikau, S., Haahr, M. and Volz, U. (2022), 'Enhancing digital sustainable finance: Digital solutions to mobilise capital, assess environmental risks and enhance financial inclusion', available at: https://bit.ly/4a5BJR1.

Dorfleitner G. and Braun, D. (2019), 'Fintech, digitalization and blockchain: Possible applications for green finance', in M. Migliorelli and P. Dessertine (eds.) *The Rise of Green Finance in Europe. Opportunities and Challenges for Issuers, Investors and Marketplaces* (Cham: Palgrave), 207–237.

EBA (European Banking Authority) (2020), 'Response to EC consultation on the digital finance strategy/action plan', 26 June, available at: https://bit.ly/4auKxj2.

ESAs (European Supervisory Authorities) (2022), 'Joint European Supervisory Authority Response to the European Commission's February 2021 Call for Advice on Digital Finance and Related Issues [...]', ESA 2022/01, 31 January.

ESMA (European Securities and Markets Authority) (2016), 'The Distributed Ledger Technology Applied to Securities Markets', Discussion Paper, ESMA/2016/773, 2 June.

ESMA (European Securities and Markets Authority) (2017), *The Distributed Ledger Technology Applied to Securities Markets – Report*, ESMA50-1121423017-285, 7 February.

ESMA (European Securities Markets Authority) (2019), 'Initial Coin Offerings and Crypto-Assets. Advice', ESMA50-157–1391, 9 January.

ESMA (European Securities and Markets Authority) (2020), 'Response to EC public consultation on a renewed sustainable finance strategy', ESMA30-22-821, 15 July.

ESMA (European Securities and Markets Authority) (2024), 'Consultation paper on the draft Guidelines on the conditions and criteria for the qualification of crypto-assets as financial instruments', ESMA75-453128700-52, 29 January.

European Commission (2014), 'Unleashing the potential of crowdfunding in the European Union', (Communication), COM (2014) 172 final 2.

European Commission (2015), 'Action Plan on Building a Capital Markets Union', COM, 468 final and subsequent updates.

European Commission (2018a), 'Action Plan: Financing Sustainable Growth', COM (2018) 97 final.

European Commission (2018b), 'FinTech action plan: For a more competitive and innovative European financial sector', COM (2018) 109 final.

European Commission (2018c), 'Impact Assessment Accompanying the Document Proposal for a Regulation [...] on European Crowdfunding Service Providers (ECSP) for Business', 8 March, SWD/2018/056 final.

European Commission (2019a), 'The European Green Deal', (Communication), COM (2019) 640 final.

European Commission (2019b), 'Consultation Document on an EU framework for markets in crypto-assets', December, available at: https://bit.ly/4a9LYne.

European Commission (2020a), 'Digital Finance Strategy for the EU', COM (2020) 591 final.

European Commission (2020b), 'Consultation on the renewed sustainable finance strategy', 8 April, available at: https://bit.ly/3PB44qc.

European Commission (2022a), '*Digitalising the Energy System – EU Action Plan*' (*Communication*), COM(2022) 552 final.

European Commission (2022b), 'What is digital finance?', available at: https://finance.ec.europa.eu/digital-finance/overview-digital-finance_en [last access 10.04.2024]

Feola, R. Vesci, M., Marinato, E. et al. (2021), 'Segmenting "digital investors": Evidence from the Italian equity crowdfunding market', 56 *Small Business Economics*, 1235.

Ferrarini, G. and Macchiavello, E. (2017), 'Investment-based crowdfunding: Is MiFID II enough?', in D. Busch and G. Ferrarini (eds.), *Regulation of EU Financial Markets: MiFID II* (Oxford: Oxford University Press), 659–692.

Ferrarini, G. and Macchiavello, E. (2018), 'FinTech and alternative finance in the CMU: The regulation of marketplace investing', in D. Busch and G. Ferrarini (eds.), *Capital Markets Union in Europe* (Oxford: Oxford University Press), 208–233.

Fink, M. (2019), 'Blockchain and the general data protection regulation. Can distributed ledgers be squared with European data protection law?', available at: https://bit.ly/3PDlvq6.

FSB (Financial Stability Board) (2017), 'Financial stability implications from FinTech. Supervisory and regulatory issues that merit authorities' attention', 27 June, available at: www.fsb.org/wp-content/uploads/R270617.pdf.

FSB (Financial Stability Board) (2019), *Decentralised Financial Technologies. Report on Financial Stability, Regulatory and Governance Implications*, 6 June, available at: www .fsb.org/wp-content/uploads/P060619.pdf.

Fuessler, J. (ed.) (2018), 'Navigating Blockchain and Climate Action: An Overview', available at: https://bit.ly/3x6UBjX.

Fullwiler, S. T. (2017), 'Sustainable finance: Building a more general theory of finance', in O. M. Lehner (ed.), *Routledge Handbook of Social and Sustainable Finance* (London: Routledge), 21.

G20 (2018), *Sustainable Finance Synthesis Report*, available at: https://bit.ly/4ar1VVP.

Gargantini, M. (2022), 'Secondary markets for crowdfunding: Bulletin boards (Art 25)', in E. Macchiavello (ed.), *Regulation on European Crowdfunding Service Providers for Business: A Commentary* (Cheltenham: Edward Elgar), 350–366.

Hacker, P. and Thomale, C. (2018), 'Crypto-securities regulation: ICOs, token sales and cryptocurrencies under EU financial law', 15 *European Company and Financial Law Review*, 645.

Hakvoort, A. (2021), 'Secondary trading of crowdfunding investments', in P. Ortolani and M. Louisse (eds.), *The EU Crowdfunding Regulation* (Oxford: Oxford University Press), 267–286.

Harder, K. (2018), 'Practical experience with applications of the guidelines', available at: https://bit.ly/4a7SUS2.

Harder, K. and van Maaren, R. (2016), *Report on the Practical Experience of RES Project Financing Using Crowdfunding*, WP 2.4., available at: https://bit.ly/43wdDw8.

Herberger, T. A. and Dötsch, J. J. (eds.) (2021), *Digitalization, Digital Transformation and Sustainability in the Global Economy. Risks and Opportunities* (Cham: Springer).

HLFCMU (High Level Forum on the Capital Markets Union) (2020), *A New Vision for Europe's Capital Markets – Final Report*, June, available at: https://bit.ly/43AczaK.

Hooghiemstra, S. N. (2022), 'The provision of crowdfunding services under the ECSPR (Art 3)', in E. Macchiavello (ed.), *Regulation on European Crowdfunding Service Providers for Business: A Commentary* (Cheltenham: Edward Elgar), 68–85.

Hörisch, J. (2015), 'Crowdfunding for environmental ventures: An empirical analysis of the influence of environmental orientation on the success of crowdfunding initiatives', 107 *Journal of Cleaner Production*, 636.

Hörisch, J. (2018), '"Think big" or "small is beautiful"? An empirical analysis of characteristics and determinants of success of sustainable crowdfunding projects', 10(1) *International Journal of Entrepreneurial Venturing*, 111.

Hörisch, J. (2019), 'Take the money and run? Implementation and disclosure of environmentally-oriented crowdfunding projects', 223 *Journal of Cleaner Production*, 127.

Hornuf, L., Stenzhorn, E. and Vintis, T. (2022), 'Are sustainability-oriented investors different? Evidence from equity crowdfunding', 47 *The Journal of Technology Transfer*, 1662.

Hossain, M. and Oparaocha, G. O. (2017), 'Crowdfunding: Motives, definitions, typology and ethical challenges', 7(2) *Entrepreneurship Research Journal*, 253.

HSBC Centre of Sustainable Finance and the Sustainable Digital Finance Alliance (SDFA) (2019), 'Blockchain: Gateway for sustainability linked bonds. Widening access to finance block by block', available at: https://bit.ly/3xb2lvY.

Hsieh, H.-C., Hsieh, Y.-C. and Vu, T. H. (2019), 'How social movements influence crowdfunding success', 53 *Pacific-Basin Finance Journal*, 308.

Jackson, A., Lloyd, A., Macinante, J. et al. (2018), 'Networked carbon markets: Permissionless innovation with distributed ledgers?', Edinburgh School of Law Research Paper No. 7/2018, 9 March, available at: https://papers.ssrn.com/sol3/papers.cfm?abstract_id=2997099.

Jagtiani J. and Lemieux, C. (2018), 'Do fintech lenders penetrate areas that are underserved by traditional banks?', 100 *Journal of Economics and Business*, 43.

Jagtiani, J., Lambie-Hanson, L. and Lambie-Hanson, T. (2019), 'Fintech lending and mortgage credit access', Federal Reserve Bank of Philadelphia Working Paper No. 19–47, November, available at: https://bit.ly/43zputx.

Lam, P., Law, A. and Law, A. (2016), 'Crowdfunding for renewable and sustainable energy projects: An exploratory case study approach', 60 *Renewable and Sustainable Energy Reviews*, 11.

Laurell, C., Sandström C. and Suseno, Y. (2019), 'Assessing the interplay between crowdfunding and sustainability in social media', 141 *Technological Forecasting & Social Change*, 117.

Lee, I. (2019), 'What is WePower? The green energy trading platform', 24 July, available at: https://blokt.com/guides/what-is-wepower.

Lee, J. and Khan, V. M. (2020), 'Blockchain and smart contract for peer-to-peer energy trading platform: Legal obstacles and regulatory solutions', 19 *UIC Review of Intellectual Property Law*, 285.

Lehner, O. M. (2017), 'Crowdfunding social ventures: A model and research agenda', in O. M. Lehner (ed.), *Routledge Handbook of Social and Sustainable Finance* (London: Routledge), 728.

Lin, L. and Tjio, H. (2020), 'Alternative investments, sustainability in the digital age', 21 *European Business Organization Law Review*, 1.

Livingston, D., Sivaram, V., Freeman, M. et al. (2018), 'Applying blockchain technology to electric power systems', Council on Foreign Relations Discussion Paper, July, available at: https://bit.ly/43wuTBC.

Lyons, T., Courcelas L. and Timsit, K. (2018), 'Blockchain and the GDPR', available at: https://bit.ly/4cyLfgY.

Macchiavello, E. (2015), 'Peer-to-peer lending and the "democratization" of credit markets: Another financial innovation puzzling regulators', 21(3) *Columbia Journal of European Law*, 521.

Macchiavello, E. (2017), 'Financial-return crowdfunding and regulatory approaches in the shadow banking, fintech and collaborative finance era', 14(4) *European Company and Financial Law Review*, 662.

Macchiavello, E. (2018), *Microfinance and Financial Inclusion: The Challenge of Regulating Alternative Forms of Finance* (London: Routledge).

Macchiavello, E. (2019), 'What to expect when you are expecting a European crowdfunding regulation: The current "Bermuda Triangle" and future scenarios for marketplace lending and investing in Europe', August 20, EBI Working Paper Series No. 55, available at: https://ssrn.com/abstract=3493688.

Macchiavello, E. (2021a), 'Disintermediation in fund-raising: Marketplace investing platforms and EU financial regulation', in I.-H. Y. Chiu and G. Deipenbrock (eds.), *Routledge Handbook on Financial Technology and the Law* (London: Routledge), 291–306.

Macchiavello, E. (2021b), 'The crowdfunding regulation in the context of the capital markets union', in P. Otolani and M. Louisse (eds.), *The EU Crowdfunding Regulation* (Oxford: Oxford University Press), 25–46.

Macchiavello, E. (2021c), 'The European Crowdfunding Service Providers Regulation and the future of marketplace lending and investing in Europe: The "crowdfunding nature's dilemma"', 32(3) *European Business Law Review*, 557.

Macchiavello, E. (ed.) (2022a), *Regulation on European Crowdfunding Service Providers for Business: A Commentary* (Cheltenham: Edward Elgar).

Macchiavello, E. (2022b), 'Introduction to the crowdfunding regulation', in E. Macchiavello (ed.), *Regulation on European Crowdfunding Service Providers for Business: A Commentary* (Cheltenham: Edward Elgar), 2–14.

Macchiavello, E. (2022c), 'The scope of the ECSPR: The difficult compromise between harmonization, client protection and level-playing field (Articles 1 & 2 (& 46, 48–49, 51))', in E. Macchiavello (ed.), *Regulation on European Crowdfunding Service Providers for Business: A Commentary* (Cheltenham: Edward Elgar), 44–67.

Macchiavello, E. (2022d), 'The challenges awaiting the European Crowdfunding Services Providers Regulation: Ready for launch?', 2 *Nordic Journal of Commercial Law*, 91.

Macchiavello, E. (2022e), 'Digital platforms, capital raising and EU capital markets law: Different shades of decentralisation', 33(7) *European Business Law Review*, 1057–1082.

Macchiavello, E. and Sciarrone Alibrandi, A. (2022), 'Marketplace lending as a new means of raising capital in the internal market: True disintermediation or reintermediation?', in E. Avgouleas and H. Marjosola (eds.), *Digital Finance in Europe: Law, Regulation, and Governance, European Company and Financial Law Review*, Special Vol. 5 (Berlin: De Gruyter), 37–85.

Macchiavello, E. and Siri, M. (2022), 'Sustainable finance and fintech: Can technology contribute to achieving environmental goals? A preliminary assessment of "Green FinTech"', 19(1), *European Company and Financial Law Review*, 128–174 (pre-published on SSRN as EBI Working Paper 71/2020).

Macchiavello, E. and Valenti, C. (2022), 'Beyond the ECSPR and financial-return: The regulation of donation and reward-based crowdfunding in the EU', in E. Macchiavello (ed.), *Regulation on European Crowdfunding Service Providers for Business: A Commentary* (Cheltenham: Edward Elgar), 619–645.

Macinante, J. D. (2017), 'A conceptual model for networking of carbon markets on distributed ledger technology architecture', 3 *Carbon & Climate Law Review*, 243.

Maehle, N., Otte, P. P., Huijben, B. et al. (2021), 'Crowdfunding for climate change: Exploring the use of climate frames by environmental entrepreneurs', 314 *Journal of Cleaner Production*, 128040.

Maehle, N., Otte, P. P. and Drozdova, N. (2020), 'Crowdfunding sustainability' in R. Shneor, L. Zhao and B. T. Flåten (eds.), *Advances in Crowdfunding* (Cham: Palgrave Macmillan), 393–422.

Mansouri, S. and Momtaz, P. P. (2022), 'Financing sustainable entrepreneurship: ESG measurement, valuation, and performance', 37(6) *Journal of Business Venturing*, 106258.

Martínez-Climent, C., Costa-Climent, R. and Oghazi, P. (2019), 'Sustainable financing through crowdfunding', 11(3) *Sustainability*, 934.

Merrill, R. K., Schillebeeckx, S. J. D. and Blakstad, S. (2018), 'Sustainable digital finance in Asia: Creating environmental impact through bank transformation', available at: https://bit.ly/3TS86fh.

Messeni Petruzzelli, A., Natalicchio, A., Panniello, U. et al. (2019), 'Understanding the crowdfunding phenomenon and its implications for sustainability', 141 *Elsevier Technological Forecasting & Social Change*, 138.

Mihaylov, M., Razo-Zapata I. and Nowé A. (2018), 'NRGcoin – A blockchain-based reward mechanism for both production and consumption of renewable energy', in A. Marke (ed.), *Transforming Climate Finance and Green Investment with Blockchains* (London: Elsevier), 111–131.

Mihaylov, M., Razo-Zapata, I., Rădulescu, R. and Nowé, A. (2016), 'Boosting the renewable energy economy with NRGcoin', available at: https://bit.ly/4cyLrgc.

Moro Visconti, R., Cruz Rambaud, S. and López Pascual, J. (2020), 'Sustainability in FinTechs: An explanation through business model scalability and market valuation', 12 *Sustainability*, 10316.

Motylska-Kuzma, A. (2018), 'Crowdfunding and sustainable development', 10(12) *Sustainability*, 46502018.

Nasir, A., Shaukat, K., Iqbal Khan, K. et al. (2021), 'Trends and directions of financial technology (Fintech) in society and environment: A bibliometric study', 11 *Applied Sciences*, 10353.

Nassiry, D. (2019), 'The role of fintech in unlocking green finance: Policy insights for developing countries', in J. D. Sachs et al. (eds.), *Handbook of Green Finance. Energy Security and Sustainable Development* (Singapore: Springer), 315.

Neves, L. and Prata, G. (2018), 'Blockchain contributions for the climate finance: introducing a debate', FGV International Intelligence Unit, available at: https://bit.ly/4atPqZW.

Nigam, N., Mbarek, S. and Benetti, C. (2018), 'Crowdfunding to finance eco-innovation: Case studies from leading renewable energy platforms', 2(26) *Journal of Innovation Economics & Management*, 195.

OECD (Organisation for Economic Co-operation and Development) (2011), 'Fostering innovation for green growth', OECD Green Growth Studies, available at: www.oecd.org/sti/inno/fosteringinnovationforgreengrowth.htm.

OECD (Organisation for Economic Co-operation and Development) (2012), 'The future of eco-innovation: The role of business models in green transformation', Background paper, available at: www.oecd.org/innovation/inno/49537036.pdf.

OECD (Organisation for Economic Co-operation and Development) (2019), 'Initial Coin Offerings (ICOs) for SME Financing', available at: https://bit.ly/43yftg8.

OECD (Organisation for Economic Co-operation and Development) (2020), 'Blockchain Technologies as a Digital Enabler for Sustainable Infrastructure – Case Study', OECD Environment Policy Paper, available at: https://bit.ly/3TybnAb.

Pavlidis, G. (2021), 'The digital transformation of the global green bonds market: New-fashioned international standards for a new generation of financial instruments', in J. Lee and A. Derbellay (eds.), *Data Governance in AI, FinTech and LegalTech* (Cheltenam: Edward Elgar), 263–278.

Pierrakis, Y. and Collins, L. (2013), 'Crowdfunding: A new innovative model of providing funding to projects and businesses', available at: https://papers.ssrn.com/sol3/papers.cfm?abstract_id = 2395226.

Piroschka Otte, P. and Maehle, N. (2022), 'The combined effect of success factors in crowd-funding of cleantech projects', 366 *Journal of Cleaner Production*, 132921.

Puschmann, T. and Leifer, L. (2020), 'Sustainable digital finance: The role of FinTech, InsurTech & Blockchain for shaping the world for the better', available at: https://bit.ly/49cxOAL.

Puschmann, T., Homann, C. H. and Khmarskyi, V. (2020), 'How Green FinTech can alleviate the impact of climate change – The case of Switzerland', 12 *Sustainability*, 10691.

Rauchs, M., Glidden, A., Gordon, B. et al. (2018), 'Distributed ledger technology systems: A conceptual framework', August, available at: https://bit.ly/43Fyhdp.

ROFIEG (Regulatory Obstacles to Financial Innovation Expert Group) (2019), 30 *Recommendations on Regulation, Innovation and Finance*, Final Report, December, available at: https://bit.ly/3PxZau3.

Roma, P., Vasi, M., Perrone, G. et al. (2021), 'Environmental sustainability orientation, reward-based crowdfunding, and venture capital: The mediating role of crowdfunding performance for new technology ventures', *IEEE Transactions on Engineering Management*, available at: https://bit.ly/3xkTWva.

Schletz, M., Nassiry, D. and Lee M.-K. (2020), 'Blockchain and tokenized securities: The potential for green finance', ADBI Working Paper 1079/2020, February, available at: https://bit.ly/3xb37P0.

Schwartz, A. (2020), 'Crowdfunding issuers in the United States', 61 *Journal of Law & Policy*, 155.

SDFA (Sustainable Digital Finance Alliance) (2018), 'Digital technologies for mobilizing sustainable finance applications of digital technologies to sustainable finance', available at: https://bit.ly/4avNSOL.

Siemroth, C. and Hornuf, L. (2021), 'Do retail investors value environmental impact? A lab-in-the-field experiment with crowdfunders', 9197 CESifo Working Paper, available at: https://ssrn.com/abstract=3892621.

Staikouras, P. (2020), 'The European Union proposal for a regulation on cross-border crowdfunding services: A solemn or pie-crust promise?', 31(6) *European Business Law Review*, 1047.

Testa, S., Nielsen, K. R., Bogers, M. et al. (2019), 'The role of crowdfunding in moving towards a sustainable society', 141 *Technological Forecasting and Social Change*, 66–73.

Testa, S., Roma, P., Vasi, M. et al. (2020), 'Crowdfunding as a tool to support sustainability-oriented initiatives: Preliminary insights into the role of product/service attributes', 29(2) *Business Strategy and the Environment*, 530.

Thaker, M. A. B. M. T., Khaliq, A. B., Thaker, H. B. M. T. et al. (2022), 'The potential role of fintech and digital currency for Islamic green financing: Toward an integrated model', in F. Taghizadeh-Hesary and S. Hyun (eds.), *Green Digital Finance and Sustainable Development Goals* (Singapore: Springer), 287–308.

Thalhammer, F., Schöttle, O., Janetschek, M. et al. (2022), 'Blockchain use cases against climate destruction: Cloud computing and data science', 3(2) *Cloud Computing and Data Science*, 39.

UNEP (United Nations Environment Programme) (2016), 'Fintech and sustainable development: Assessing the implications', available at: https://bit.ly/3TTvavj.

UNEP Inquiry (2018), 'Green digital finance: Mapping current practice and potential in Switzerland and beyond', Discussion Paper, available at: https://bit.ly/3TO1Oya.

UNSGSA (United Nations Secretary-General's Special Advocate for Inclusive Finance for Development), FinTech Working Group and CCAF (2019), 'Early lessons on regulatory innovations to enable inclusive FinTech: Innovation offices, regulatory sandboxes, and RegTech', available at: https://bit.ly/3vthmOC.

UNTFDFSDG (United Nations Secretary-General's Task Force on Digital Financing of the Sustainable Development Goals) (2019), 'Harnessing the digitalization of finance for the sustainable development goals', White Paper, June, available at: https://bit.ly/3TRvFGc.

UNTFDFSDG (United Nations Secretary-General's Task Force on Digital Financing of the Sustainable Development Goals) (2020), *People's Money: Harnessing Digitalization to Finance a Sustainable Future*, Final Report, August, available at: https://bit.ly/3PDjE4q.

Vasileiadou, E., Huijben, J. C. C. M. and Raven, R. P. J. M. (2016), 'Three is a crowd? Exploring the potential of crowdfunding for renewable energy in the Netherlands', 128 *Journal of Cleaner Production*, 142–155.

Vinuesa, R., Azizpour H., Leite, I. et al. (2020), 'The role of artificial intelligence in achieving the sustainable development goals', 11(233) *Nature Communications* 1.

Vismara, S. (2016), 'Equity retention and social network theory in equity crowdfunding', 46(4) *Small Business Economics*, 579.

Vismara, S. (2019), 'Sustainability in equity crowdfunding', 141 *Technological Forecasting & Social Change*, 98–106.

Von de Leyen, U. (2019), 'A Union that strives for more. My agenda for Europe – Political guidelines for the Next European Commission 2019–2024', available at: https://bit .ly/3TxM2Gn.

von Selasinsky, C. and Lutz, E. (2021), 'The effects of pro-social and pro-environmental orientation on crowdfunding performance', 13 *Sustainability*, 6064.

Walch, A. (2015), 'The bitcoin blockchain as financial market infrastructure: A consideration of operational risk', 18 *Legislation and Public Policy*, 837.

Wehnert, P. and Beckmann, M. (2021), 'Crowdfunding for a sustainable future: A systematic literature review', *IEEE Transactions on Engineering Management*, 1–16.

Wehnert, P., Baccarella, C. V. and Beckmann, M. (2019), 'In crowdfunding we trust? Investigating crowdfunding success as a signal for enhancing trust in sustainable product features', 141 *Technological Forecasting & Social Change*, 128.

World Bank (2018), *Blockchain and Emerging Digital Technologies for Enhancing Post-2020 Climate Markets* (Washington: World Bank).

World Energy Council (2017), 'The developing role of blockchain', available at: https://bit .ly/3TQsvlO.

Xiang, D., Zhang, L., Tao, Q. et al. (2019), 'Informational or emotional appeals in crowdfunding message strategy: An empirical investigation of backers' support decisions', 47(4) *Journal of the Academy of Marketing Science*, 1046.

Zadek, S. and Kharas, H. (2018), '2030 Agenda for Sustainable Development. Aligning financial system architecture and innovation with sustainable development', available at: https:// bit.ly/3TQrCJX.

Zetzsche, D. A. and Anker-Sørensen, L. (2022a), 'Building blocks of a green fintech system – Towards an regulatory antidote to greenwashing', July 14, available at: https://ssrn.com/ abstract=4163002.

Zetzsche, D. A. and Anker-Sørensen, L. (2022b), 'Regulating sustainable finance in the dark', 23 *European Business Organization Law Review*, 47.

Zetzsche, D. A., Buckley, R. and Arner, D. W. (2018), 'The distributed liability of distributed ledgers: Legal risks of blockchain', 4 *University of Illinois Law Review*, 1361.

Zetzsche, D. A., Buckley, R. P., Arner, D. W. et al. (2019), 'The ICO gold rush: It's a scam, it's a bubble, it's a super challenge for regulators', 63(2) *Harvard International Law Journal*, 267.

Zhang-Zhang, Y., Rohlfer, S. and Rajasekera, J. (2020), 'An eco-systematic view of cross-sector fintech: The case of Alibaba and Tencent', 12(21) *Sustainability*, 8907.

Ziegler, T., Shneor, R. and Wenzlaff, K. (eds.) (2021), *The 2nd Global Alternative Finance Market Benchmarking Report*, available at: https://bit.ly/3TPHsVn.

Index

For EU product safety concerns, contact us at Calle de José Abascal, 56–1°, 28003 Madrid, Spain or eugpsr@cambridge.org.

www.ingramcontent.com/pod-product-compliance
Ingram Content Group UK Ltd.
Pitfield, Milton Keynes, MK11 3LW, UK
UKHW032035180525
458693UK00010B/157

9 781009 483940